Fodor's 94
Europe

Fodor's Travel Publications, Inc.
New York • Toronto • London • Sydney • Auckland

Fodor's Europe

Editors: Christopher Billy, Andrew Collins
Contributors: Katrine Osa Aaby, Robert Andrews, Barbara Angelillo, Nikola Antonov, Victor Aquilina, Mark Baker, Marianne Bell, Toula Bogdanos, Richard Bruner, Brian Coleman, Roderick Conway-Morris, Nancy Coons, Nigel Fisher, George Hamilton, Emma Harris, Simon Hewitt, Alannah Hopkin, Michael Kallenbach, Elizabeth Konstantinova, Graham Lees, Virginia Marsh, Scott McNeely, Kristin Moehlmann, Richard Moore, Denise Nolty, Brian Owens, Kristen Perrault, Karina Porcelli, Mark Potok, Marcy Pritchard, Linda K. Schmidt, Kate Sekules, Alexandra Siegel, Eric Sjogren, Erszébet Szeip, Enrique Tessieri, Robert Tilley, Meltem Turkoz, Anne Yates.
Creative Director: Fabrizio La Rocca
Cartographer: David Lindroth
Illustrator: Karl Tanner
Cover Photograph: Jean-Marie Truchet/TSW

Design: Vignelli Associates

Special Sales

Fodor's Travel Publications are available at special discounts for bulk purchases for sales promotions or premiums. Special editions, including personalized covers, excerpts of existing guides, and corporate imprints, can be created in large quantities for special needs. For more information, contact your local bookseller or write to Special Markets, Fodor's Travel Publications, 201 East 50th Street, New York, NY 10022. Inquiries from Canada should be directed to your local Canadian bookseller or sent to Random House of Canada, Ltd., Marketing Department, 1265 Aerowood Drive, Mississauga, Ontario L4W 1B9. Inquiries from the United Kingdom should be sent to Fodor's Travel Publications, 20 Vauxhall Bridge Road, London, England SW1V 2SA.

MANUFACTURED IN THE UNITED STATES OF AMERICA
10 9 8 7 6 5 4 3 2 1

Contents

Maps

Maps

Maps

Foreword

While every care has been taken to assure the accuracy of the information in this guide, the passage of time will always bring change, and consequently, the publisher cannot accept responsibility for errors that may occur.

All prices and opening times quoted here are based on information supplied to us at press time. Hours and admission fees may change, however, and the prudent traveler will avoid inconvenience by calling ahead.

Fodor's wants to hear about your travel experiences, both pleasant and unpleasant. When a hotel or restaurant fails to live up to its billing, let us know and we will investigate the complaint and revise our entries where the facts warrant it.

Send your letters to the editor of Fodor's Travel Publications, 201 E. 50th Street, New York, NY 10022.

Highlights'94 and Fodor's Choice

Highlights '94

As a result of the landmark general agreement on economic unity, all trade barriers between the member states of the European Community (or Common Market) will have been removed by the end of 1993, turning much of Europe into one huge tariff-free market, the largest economic grouping in the world. Switzerland, Austria, Sweden, and Finland have applied to join the organization, and presumably a star for each will soon appear in the circle of stars on the blue field of the EC flag. At press time (spring 1993), Norway had been admitted and Turkey, Cyprus, and Malta, all of which have applied (and were initially turned down for membership), should join the EC by the year 2000. Several Eastern European countries are sure to follow.

Starting in 1993, citizens of EC-member countries no longer needed to show a passport when crossing borders, except into Britain. For travelers from non-EC countries entering EC countries, however, it will be business as usual, with passport checks required at each border.

The collapse of communism in Eastern Europe has had the most tragic consequences in Yugoslavia. Heralded as the most open and "western" communist country under President Josip Broz-Tito, this Balkan state has descended into a brutal war that at press time has left at least 15,000 people dead and forced 2 million to flee their homes.

At press time, U.S. State Department advisories were in effect for all republics except for Slovenia. For the forseeable future travel is likely to be extremely hazardous in this once-beautiful region.

Austria With tourism among the top industries, care is being taken to preserve the country's main attractions from overexploitation. Parking in the center of Vienna is now restricted, and tour buses are limited to specific routes. All of this means that visitors should be prepared to walk—the best way to see Austria anyway. A major new Japanese-run hotel will open on the Ring in Vienna in 1993.

Belgium The 50th anniversary of the liberation of Belgium during World War II will be celebrated in some sixty cities and villages between June and December, 1994. The most important event will be in Bastogne in the Ardennes, scene of heavy fighting during the Battle of the Bulge. Some 400 American veterans are expected on June 10, while the 10th Armored Division returns to the battlefield on August 15 and the 101st Airborne on September 23. It is hoped that President Clinton will attend the solemn commemoration of the siege of Bastogne on December 16.

On a lighter note, the President has also been invited to help celebrate the 100th anniversary of the death of Adolphe Sax, inventor of the saxophone, in the picturesque city of Dinant (Sax's birthplace).

A new terminal and international concourse will open at the Brussels National Airport, increasing the number of check-in counters to 200 from 98 and doubling the airport's capacity to 18 million passengers. Further expansion will increase the capacity to 25 million by 1996.

The main railway station in Brussels, the Gare du Midi, has been razed to make way for a new one designed to accommodate high-speed TGV trains. The first of these trains will inaugurate the Channel Tunnel service between Brussels and London (tentatively scheduled to start in July 1994). TGV links with Paris, Amsterdam, and Cologne are due for completion by 1996.

Bulgaria Tourism in Bulgaria increased threefold in 1992–1993, despite the country's crumbling economy. In the next few years, Bulgaria's tourist industry will undergo a process of total privatization. International hotel chains are showing special interest in the resort areas now attracting tourists who once frequented resorts in Yugoslavia. The first hotels to go private are Hotel Sofia and Hotel Bulgaria in Sofia, and Hotel Trimontzium in Plovdiv.

During this transition period, many hotels and restaurants will be temporarily closed for reconstruction and modernization by their new owners. As a result, facilities not up to Western standards are expected to improve and acquire more individual character. At the same time, hundreds of new hotels, hostels, and taverns are mushrooming throughout the country.

The Czech Republic Like all of Eastern Europe, the Czech Republic is changing rapidly (Slovakia, the eastern republic of the old *Czecho-Slovakia*, officially became an independent country in January 1993). Rail, bus, and air links to Prague from Western Europe are increasing. Several new luxury hotels opened in 1993, including the Hotel Praha, the former Communist Party lodgings taken over by the Hyatt chain. Old buildings such as a seminary in Litomysl and a spa sanatorium in Karlovy Vary are being converted into hotels. In 1994, Prague's Charles Bridge will be closed for much of the year for repairs.

Finland Finland's announcement to seek EC membership is considered by some leading Finnish academicians to be the most important decision this country has made since it declared independence from Russia on December 6, 1917. More significant for travelers was the country's decision to revalue its currency in 1993, part of an effort to lift the nation out of it worst-ever recession in this century. As a result of the revaluation of the Finnmark in May 1993, Finland was transformed from one of the most expensive European countries to a veritable bargain-basement for tourists.

France Don't be surprised to find people at work in the **Jardin des Tuileries in Paris:** A project for restoring these elegant gardens to their original glory was adopted in 1992 and may continue into 1994.

Thanks to the 1992 Winter Olympics, rail and road access to the northern French Alps has been thoroughly upgraded. Line 1 of the Paris Metro has been extended from Ponte de Neuilly to La Défence, where it joins the RER express-metro network. Another novelty for travelers in the capital is an automated, driverless metro linking Antony RER station to Orly Airport.

Germany GermanRail continues to expand its high-speed InterCity Express (ICE) operations. A new ICE line opened in 1992 linking Hamburg and Munich via Würzburg and Nürnberg, and in 1993 an ICE line connected Hamburg with Frankfurt and Basel. New ICE service is planned for the Hannover–Berlin route, with completion expected by 1997.

The German public continues to vigorously debate the role of the car in atmospheric pollution and damage to the country's beloved conifer forests. In 1993 gasoline-driven cars in the Bavarian alpine resorts of Berchtesgaden and Oberstdorf in the Allgau were banned; only electrically powered vehicles will be permitted.

Fans of Gothic architecture may be disappointed if they attempt to view the inside of Munich's 15th-century cathedral in late 1993 or early 1994. The church is undergoing a complete restoration. The work will be completed in early 1994, ready for celebrations marking the 500th anniversary of the church's consecration.

Great Britain The start of rail service between France and Britain via the **Channel Tunnel** has been pushed to late 1994.

Greece Despite the ongoing crisis in former Yugoslavia, Greek tourism officials remain optimistic, and bookings are up for 1994. Travel to Greece is easier than ever, with Delta's added direct flights from New York to Athens, and new catamarans that make the Patras-Italy trip in half the usual time.

The National Tourist Organization of Greece has plans for a new sea park, as well as three new golf courses in Halkidiki. Crete, and Kaifos in the Peloponnese. Naxos, one of the Cyclades, has opened an international airport that now handles charter flights coming from Northern Europe. In addition, Olympic Airlines may reinstate its inter-island flights from Thessaloniki to the eastern Aegean islands of Chios, Lebos, and Samos. The Greek Railway network has asked for 900 billion drachmes from the government to bring its trains upto par with the rest of Europe, especially the Piraeus-Athens-Thessaloniki route. In Athens, the new airport tax means work on the new Spata international airport should speed up, and in the city center, construction is underway to extend the metro, scheduled for completion in 1997. Despite Greece's high inflation, the strong dollar means Greece remains one of Europe's most affordable countries.

Holland   The Netherlands has named 1994 **Mondrian Year** and will be honoring the De Stijl painter with major exhibitions of the artist's work. Also in 1994, the National Museum H. W. Mesdag in The Hague reopens after an extensive two-year renovation program.

Hungary   Malev, the Hungarian national airline, began its own direct service from Newark International Airport to Budapest in summer 1993.

Major chain hotels in Budapest are expanding, and hotels under state control are going private and sprucing up. Small pensions are also popping up in green-belt areas. At the top end of the market, the Kempinski Grand Hotel Corvinus opened in late 1992. This five-star establishment has set a new standard of luxury in the downtown area. Outside the capital, a new chain of castle hotels is taking shape, some attached to thermal spas. For gourmets, the golden age of gastronomy was reborn in Budapest with the reopening of Gundel's Restaurant, the legendary eatery that fell on hard times after nationalization.

Travelers will find Hungary a bargain compared to western Europe, but rock-bottom prices are a thing of the past. At press time inflation was holding steady at 25%.

Iceland   One of the high points of the 1994 calendar in Iceland is the 13th Reykjavík Arts Festival. Held in the first half of June every other year since 1968, the festival strives to offer something for everyone, from the best of classical musicians to the weirdest avant-garde therater to an astounding variety of visual arts exhibitions. On the fringes of the festival, unexpected happenings are the norm—in the streets, cafés, schools, churches, everywhere.

Iceland has been going through a major environmental awakening. People are realizing that it's not enough to be on an island in the middle of the ocean—atmospheric and marine pollution can still occur. The increase in tourism and the fact that visitors tend to travel in the highlands, where the environment is very sensitive, has led to serious discussion about limiting access to the most vulnerable areas.

Ireland   Ireland used to rely on its unspoiled countryside and friendly, hospitable people to attract visitors. In the last four years, encouraged by the government, over IR £500 million has been invested in tourism, and the number of visitors is projected to double from 2 million to 4 million by 1994. Travelers can expect upgraded accommodations at all levels (most hotels and many bed-and-breakfasts now offer rooms with private bath, TV, and direct-dial phone), a wider choice of restaurants, better-organized cultural tourism, and greatly improved sporting facilities. Twenty-four new golf courses have been built, and as many again are in the making. Water sports, walking routes, fishing, cycling, and equestrian holidays have also been successfully developed.

Italy The Leonardo da Vinci airport in Fiumicino is undergoing an extensive modernization and expansion program that will continue into 1994. Similar expansion is under way at Milan's Malpensa airport.

One of Italy's most famous monuments, the Tower of Pisa, will remain closed while engineers try to reinforce it to keep it from toppling. Restoration of Leonardo da Vinci's *Last Supper* in Milan is about to be completed. In Florence, the gorgeously frescoed chapel in Palazzo Medici Riccardi has been restored; meanwhile Florentines are dismayed at how traffic on adjacent streets is damaging the Ponte Vecchio, which may still be undergoing reinforcement in 1994.

Malta The number of tourists here topped one million in 1992—the figure originally targeted for 1994. New hotels are popping up across the island, and the flagship of the hotel industry, Hotel Pheonicia, reopened last year after extensive refurbishment. Malta is also fast establishing itself as one of the top cruise destinations in the Mediterranean.

Norway The most important event affecting tourism in Norway is the **1994 Winter Olympics,** taking place February 12–27 in Lillehammer, about 2½ hours from Oslo. All in all, 114 events will be held at the Lillehammer site; ice-hockey matches are divided between Lillehammer and Gjøvik, and speed-skating races will be held at Hamar. Approximately 150,000 tickets will be allocated for sales abroad. Questions regarding tickets to the Winter Olympics should be addressed to The Lillehammer Olympic Information Center (LOI, Elvegata 19, N-2600 Lillehammer, Norway, tel. 62/71900, fax 62/71950). For more information about accommodations in the area, contact Troll Park A/S (Box 445, N-2601 Lillehammer, Norway, tel. 61 26 92 00, fax 62 26 92 50).

Poland The new Warsaw air terminal was opened and fully operational in summer 1993. This has greatly improved the speed and comfort of arrival at Poland's capital. Getting about within Poland is also becoming easier. New car-rental firms are popping up, and gasoline is now readily available.

The range of accommodations continues to broaden. At the top end of the scale, the luxurious **Hotel Bristol in Warsaw,** dating from 1901, was reopened by Trust House Forte in December 1992 after a ten-year renovation; there are also many new small private hotels and pensions countrywide.

Portugal The Portuguese telephone system is being upgraded. The result is that local telephone numbers will continue to change in a rolling program throughout 1994.

New road construction continues to ease access between major towns and cities in Portugal. In the north, the Oporto–Vila Real–Bragança N15 highway is now complete; EN125, the trans-Algarve highway, has been widened and greatly improved, and construction on the expressway from Vila Real de Santo António, the easternmost town of the Algarve, to Sagres in the west, is well under way.

An influx of funds from the European Community has resulted in improved tourism-related infrastructures and in the construction of a number of new hotels.

Romania Having established a democratic system, Romania is now trying to build a market economy. Peasants are being given back their land, and small private enterprises are being encouraged, leading to a increasing variety in the shops and markets. A number of hotels are expected to be sold by the state to international commercial buyers.

At press time the future is still unclear for Bucharest's Palace of the People, the enormous neoclassical structure for which Ceauşescu flattened homes, churches, and synagogues, but which is still unfinished. It vies with Versailles as Continental Europe's largest single building, but is too costly for the Bucharest municipality to run.

Spain Visitors to Spain will be rewarded with the legacy of the 1992 **International Exposition in Seville and the Summer Olympic Games in Barcelona,** including dramatic improvements in the nation's transportation infrastructure, new sports and performing arts venues, and refurbished monuments and city neighborhoods.

Barcelona possesses several new sports venues built to host the Olympic Games. They are scattered across the city, but you'll find several concentrated on Montjuic hill overlooking the port. Among the new luxury establishments that opened to take advantage of the Olympics were the five-star Barcelona Hilton and Gran Hotel Habana.

Two new museums have opened in Madrid: the **Palacio Villahermosa,** displaying the remarkable Thyssen-Bornemisza art collection; and the **Museo de la Ciudad,** focusing on the development of Madrid. Check with the tourist office for details. The old Teatro Real is slated to re-open in 1994 as the Teatro de la Opera, a splendid new opera house—but work has dragged on for seven years, and the opening date is still uncertain at press time.

Sweden Construction of the 18-kilometer bridge over the Öresund, the sound separating Sweden and Denmark, began in 1993 and will take years to complete. This rail-and-road bridge will create the first physical link between Sweden and the Continent, an appropriate symbol for a country that plans to become a member of the European Community by 1995. Although the Swedish government has promised to put the question to referendum, it can be expected that the Swedish travel inudstry will seek to bring hotel, restaurant, and travel costs in line with those of Continental Europe.

Switzerland Visitors to Lugano in the Ticino may be disappointed to find the doors locked on the Villa Favorita, the home of the famous and coveted art collection of the Baron von Thyssen-Bornemisza. Renovations have been under way while the much-publicized battle rages over its treasures; although the government of Spain won temporary custody of at least a portion of the inventory, many prized works remain in Lugano.

Turkey Two new luxury hotels opened in late 1992. The first is the spectacular **Çiragan Palace,** a 19th-century Ottoman palace that will be the city's most expensive hotel. The setting is exceptional, right on the Bosphorous and adjacent to lush Yildiz Park. The other property is the Conrad Istanbul, a big, showy place with extensive facilities and gardens, all overlooking the Bosphorous.

Fodor's Choice

No two people will agree on what makes a perfect vacation, but it's fun and can be helpful to know what others think. In compiling this list, we've included choices from each of the countries covered in the book, and we hope that you'll have a chance to experience some of them yourself. For more detailed information about each entry, refer to the appropriate chapters within this guidebook.

Sights to Remember

Bulgaria The panorama from the ramparts of Veliko Târnovo

Denmark Kronborg Castle overlooking the Baltic

Finland Olavinlinna Castle, Savonlinna

France Mont St-Michel at high tide

Germany Neuschwanstein Castle, Bavaria

Great Britain Tower Bridge and the Tower of London in floodlights

Greece Sunset over the Caldera on the island of Santorini

Holland Amsterdam canals by night

Hungary Parliament building at night, Budapest

Iceland Ice floes drifting on the Jökulsárlon lagoon (Skaftafell)

Ireland Dusk over the lakes of Killarney

Italy The Grand Canal in Venice at dawn

Malta The Grand Harbor in Valletta

Norway The midnight sun at the North Cape

Spain The perched white villages of Andalusia

Switzerland The Matterhorn from Gornergrat, Zermatt

Turkey Istanbul skyline at sunset from Camliça Hill

Hotels

Austria Imperial, Vienna (*Very Expensive*)

Finland Hotel Strand Inter-Continental, Helsinki (*Very Expensive*)

France The Ritz, Paris (*Very Expensive*)

Any Logis et Auberges (Country Hotels and Inns) de France hotel (*Inexpensive*)

Germany The Grand, Berlin (*Very Expensive*)

Great Britain The Halkin, London (*Very Expensive*)

Greece	Any of the "paradosiakoi oikismoi" (traditional homes)
Holland	Amstel Inter-Continental, Amsterdam (*Very Expensive*)
Hungary	Gellért, Budapest (*Expensive*)
Ireland	Park, Kenmare (*Very Expensive*)
Italy	Hassler-Villa Medici, Rome (*Very Expensive*)
Portugal	Buçaco Hotel, Buçaco (*Expensive*)
Switzerland	Monte Rosa, Zermatt (*Expensive*)
Turkey	Çirağan Palace, Istanbul (*Very Expensive*)

Restaurants

Austria	Landhaus Bacher, Mautern (*Very Expensive*)
Belgium	Comme Chez Soi, Brussels (*Very Expensive*)
Denmark	Ida Davidsen, Copenhagen (*Moderate*)
Finland	Palace Gourmet, Helsinki (*Very Expensive*)
Great Britain	Bibendum, London (*Very Expensive*)
Greece	Bajazzo, Athens (*Very Expensive*)
Holland	Excelsior, Amsterdam (*Very Expensive*)
Hungary	Gundel's, Budapest (*Very Expensive*)
Iceland	Perlan, Reykjavík (*Expensive*)
Ireland	Arbutus Lodge, Cork (*Expensive*)
Italy	El Toulà, Rome (*Very Expensive*)
Norway	Theatercafeen, Oslo (*Expensive*)
Portugal	Alcântara, Lisbon (*Moderate*)
Spain	Eldorado Petit, Barcelona (*Very Expensive*)
Sweden	Den Gyldene Freden, Stockholm (*Expensive*)
Switzerland	Bierhalle Kropf, Zürich (*Inexpensive*)

Monuments

The Czech Republic	Starý Židovsky Hřbitov (Old Jewish Cemetery), Prague
Finland	The Sibelius Monument, Helsinki
Great Britain	Scott Monument, Edinburgh
Ireland	The Rock of Cashel
Luxembourg	The Devil's Altar, Diekirch
Poland	The Solidarity Monument, Gdańsk
Romania	Palace of the People, Bucharest

Museums and Galleries

Austria	Kunsthistorisches Museum, Vienna
Bulgaria	National History Museum, Sofia
Finland	The Finnish National Gallery, Helsinki
France	Fondation Maeght, St-Paul-de-Vence
Great Britain	The British Museum, London
Greece	The N.J. Goulandris Museum of Cycladic Art, Athens
Holland	Rijksmuseum Vincent Van Gogh, Amsterdam
Hungary	Museum of Fine Arts, Budapest
Spain	Prado Museum, Madrid
Sweden	Wasa Museum, Stockholm
Switzerland	Musée International de la Croix-Rouge, Geneva
Turkey	Topkapi Palace and Harem, Istanbul

Festivals

Cyprus	Kataclysmos Festival
Denmark	The Copenhagen Jazz Festival
Finland	Kuhmo Chamber Music Festival, Kuhmo
Germany	Oktoberfest, Munich
Great Britain	Edinburgh International Festival
Hungary	Spring Festival, Budapest
Iceland	Reykjavík Arts Festival
Ireland	St. Patrick's Day Parade, Dublin
Italy	Venice Carnival
Norway	Bergen International Music Festival
Portugal	Santos Populares (Popular Saints) Festival, Lisbon
Sweden	Stockholm Water Festival

Churches, Temples, and Mosques

Austria	Karlskirche, Vienna
The Czech Republic	St. Vitus Cathedral, Prague
Finland	The Cathedral (Senate Square), Helsinki
France	Chartres Cathedral
Germany	Asamkirche, Munich
Great Britain	St. Paul's Cathedral, London
Hungary	The Central Synagogue, Budapest

Malta	St. John's Co-Cathedral, Valletta
Portugal	Jerónimos Monastery, Belém, Lisbon
Spain	The 10th-century Mezquita (Mosque), Córdoba

Classical Sights

Bulgaria	Roman amphitheater, Plovdiv
Cyprus	Curium
Great Britain	The Roman baths, Bath
Greece	Delphi
Italy	Herculaneum and the temples of Paestum
Turkey	Ruins of Ephesus

Parks and Gardens

Austria	Hellbrunn, Salzburg
Finland	Talvipuutarha, Helsinki
France	Monet's "Water Lily" garden, Giverny
Great Britain	Regent's Park and Queen Mary's Garden, London
Holland	Palace Het Loo, Apeldoorn
Ireland	Japanese Gardens, Tully, County Kildare
Poland	Łazienki Park, Warsaw
Sweden	Linné Gardens, Uppsala

For Children

Denmark	Legoland, Billund
Finland	Santa Claus's Workshop, Arctic Circle, near Rovaniemi
France	Le Jardin d'Acclimatation, Paris
	Ride to the top of the Eiffel Tower, Paris
Germany	Tierpark Hellabrun Zoo, Munich
Great Britain	The Planetarium, London
Holland	Musical Clock Museum, Utrecht
Italy	Exploring Castel Sant'Angelo, Rome
Norway	Cardamon Town, Kristiansand
Portugal	The beaches of the Algrave
Spain	Snowflake, the albino gorilla, Barcelona zoo

Shopping

Austria	Glass from the manufacturers at Neunagelberg
Belgium	Handmade Nihoul or Wittamer chocolates from Brussels
Finland	Iittala glass and Marimekko clothes
Great Britain	Cashmere sweaters from Edinburgh
Greece	Natural sponges from Athens
Holland	Tulip bulbs, Schiphol Airport
Iceland	Handmade woolen goods from Reykjavík
Ireland	Hand knits from Dublin, Cork, and Galway
Luxembourg	Villeroy & Boch porcelain
Portugal	Hand-embroidered carpets from Arraiolos
Romania	Art and craftwork from Transylvania
Spain	Pottery from Seville and Talavera de la Reina, outside Madrid
Turkey	Hand-woven carpets from Bodrum

Europe

World Time Zones

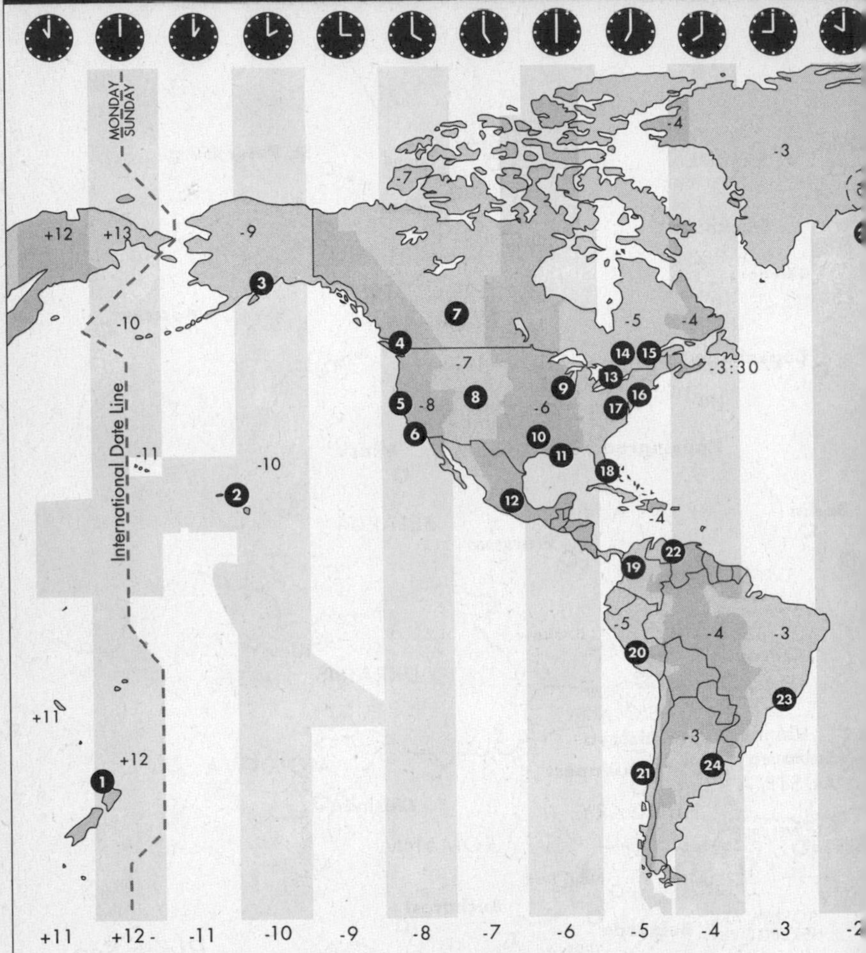

MONDAY
SUNDAY

International Date Line

+12   +13   -9

-10

3   -4   -3

-11   7

-10   4   7   -5   -4

2   -8   8   -6   9   14 15   -3:30
5   13
6   10   11   17 16
12   18   -4

+11   19   22
20   -5   -4   -3

23

+12   21   24   -4   -3

+11   +12 -   -11   -10   -9   -8   -7   -6   -5   -4   -3   -2

Numbers below vertical bands relate each zone to Greenwich Mean Time (0 hrs.).
Local times frequently differ from these general indications,
as indicated by light-face numbers on map.

Algiers, **29**	Berlin, **34**	Delhi, **48**	Istanbul, **40**
Anchorage, **3**	Bogotá, **19**	Denver, **8**	Jerusalem, **42**
Athens, **41**	Budapest, **37**	Djakarta, **53**	Johannesburg, **44**
Auckland, **1**	Buenos Aires, **24**	Dublin, **26**	Lima, **20**
Baghdad, **46**	Caracas, **22**	Edmonton, **7**	Lisbon, **28**
Bangkok, **50**	Chicago, **9**	Hong Kong, **56**	London (Greenwich), **27**
Beijing, **54**	Copenhagen, **33**	Honolulu, **2**	Los Angeles, **6**
	Dallas, **10**		Madrid, **38**
			Manila, **57**

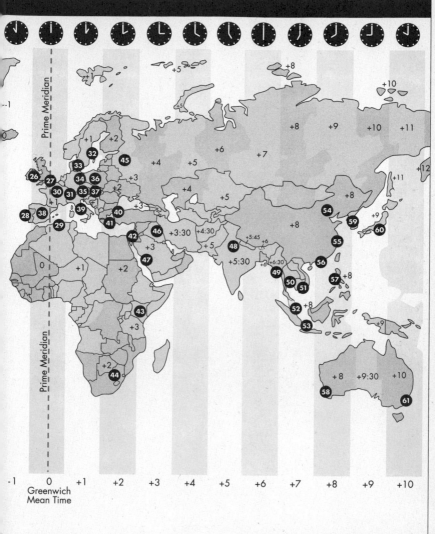

+8
+10
Prime Meridian
+1 +2
+8 +9 +10 +11
+5
+3
+4 +5 +6 +7
+12
+11
+4 +5
+3
+2
+8
+2
+3:30 +4:30
+8
+9
+3
+5:45 +6
+5
+5:30 +6:30
+8
0
+1
+2
+3
Prime Meridian
+2
+3
+2
+8 +9:30 +10

-1   0   +1   +2   +3   +4   +5   +6   +7   +8   +9   +10
Greenwich
Mean Time

Mecca, **47**	Ottawa, **14**	San Francisco, **5**	Toronto, **13**
Mexico City, **12**	Paris, **30**	Santiago, **21**	Vancouver, **4**
Miami, **18**	Perth, **58**	Seoul, **59**	Vienna, **35**
Montréal, **15**	Reykjavík, **25**	Shanghai, **55**	Warsaw, **36**
Moscow, **45**	Rio de Janeiro, **23**	Singapore, **52**	Washington, D.C., **17**
Nairobi, **43**	Rome, **39**	Stockholm, **32**	Yangon, **49**
New Orleans, **11**	Saigon (Ho Chi Minh	Sydney, **61**	Zürich, **31**
New York City, **16**	City), **51**	Tokyo, **60**	

1 Essential Information

Before You Go

Government Tourist Offices

Austria Austrian National Tourist Office. **In the United States:** 500 Fifth Ave., 20th Floor, New York, NY 10110, tel. 212/944–6880; 500 N. Michigan Ave., Suite 1950, Chicago, IL 60611, tel. 312/644–5556; 11601 Wilshire Blvd., Suite 2480, Los Angeles, CA 90025, tel. 213/477–3332; 1300 Post Oak Blvd., Suite 960, Houston, TX 77056, tel. 713/850–9999.
In Canada: 1010 Sherbrooke St. W, Suite 1410, Montreal, Quebec H3A 2R7, tel. 514/849–3709; 200 Granville St., Suite 1380, Vancouver, British Columbia V6C 1S4, tel. 604/683–5808; 2 Bloor St. E, Suite 3330, Toronto, Ontario M4W 1A8, tel. 416/967–3381.
In the United Kingdom: 30 St. George St., London W1R OAL, tel. 071/629–0461.

Belgium Belgian National Tourist Office. **In North America:** 745 Fifth Ave., Suite 714, New York, NY 10151, tel. 212/758–8130.
In The United Kingdom: Premier House, 2 Gayton Rd., Harrow, Middlesex HA1 2XU, tel. 081/861–3300.

Bulgaria Bulgarian National Tourist Office. **In North America:** Balkan Holidays (authorized agent), 161 E. 86th St., New York, NY 10028, tel. 212/573–5530.
In the United Kingdom: 18 Princes St., London W1R 7RE, tel. 071/499–6988.

Cyprus Cyprus Tourist Office. **In North America:** 13 E. 40th St., New York, NY 10016, tel. 212/213–9100.
In the United Kingdom: 213 Regent St., London W1R 8DA, tel. 071/734–9822; **North Cyprus Tourist Office,** 28 Cockspur St., London SW1Y 5BN, tel. 071/930–5069.

The Czech Republic and Slovakia Czech and Slovak Travel Bureau and Tourist Office (Čedok). **In North America:** 10 E. 40th St., New York, NY 10016, tel. 212/689–9720.
In the United Kingdom: 17–18 Old Bond St., London W1X 4RB, tel. 071/629–6058.

Denmark Danish Tourist Board. **In the United States:** 655 Third Ave., New York, NY 10017, tel. 212/949–2333.
In Canada: Box 115, Station N, Toronto, Ontario M8V 3S4, tel. 416/823–9620.
In the United Kingdom: Sceptre House, 169–173 Regent St., London W1R 8PY, tel. 071/734–2637.

Finland Finnish Tourist Board. **In the United States:** 655 Third Ave., New York, NY 10017, tel. 212/949–2333.
In Canada: 1200 Bay St., Suite 604, Toronto, Ontario M5R 2A5, tel. 416/964–9159.
In the United Kingdom: 66–68 Haymarket, London, SW1Y 4RF, tel. 071/839–4048.

France French Government Tourist Office. **In the United States:** 610 Fifth Ave., New York, NY 10020, tel. 212/315–0888 or 212/757–1125; 645 N. Michigan Ave., Chicago, IL 60611, tel. 312/337–6301; 2305 Cedar Springs Rd., Dallas, TX 75201, tel. 214/720–4010; 9454 Wilshire Blvd., Beverly Hills, CA 90212, tel. 213/271–6665.
In Canada: 1981 McGill College Ave., Suite 490, Montreal,

Quebec H3A 2W9, tel. 514/288–4264; 1 Dundas St. W, Suite 2405, Box 8, Toronto, Ontario M5G 1Z3, tel. 416/593–4717.
In the United Kingdom: 178 Piccadilly, London W1V OAL, tel. 071/491–7622.

Germany **German National Tourist Office. In the United States:** 122 E. 42nd St., New York, NY 10168, tel. 212/661–7200; 444 S. Flower St., Suite 2230, Los Angeles, CA 90071, tel. 213/688–7332.
In Canada: 175 Bloor St. E, Suite 604, Toronto, Ontario M4W 3R8, tel. 416/968–1570.
In the United Kingdom: Nightingale House, 65 Curzon St., London W1Y 7PE, tel. 071/495–3990.

Gibraltar **Gibraltar Government Tourist Office. In the United Kingdom:** Arundel Great Court, 179 The Strand, London WC2R 1EH, tel. 071/836–0777.

Great Britain **British Tourist Authority. In the United States:** 40 W. 57th St., New York, NY 10019, tel. 212/581–4700; 625 N. Michigan Ave., Suite 1510, Chicago, IL 60611, tel. 312/787–0490; World Trade Center, 350 S. Figueroa St., Suite 450, Los Angeles, CA 90071, tel. 213/628–3525; 2305 Cedar Springs Rd., Suite 210, Dallas, TX 75201, tel. 214/720–4040.
In Canada: 94 Cumberland St., Suite 600, Toronto, Ontario M5R 3N3, tel. 416/925–6326.
In the United Kingdom: Thames Tower, Black's Rd., Hammersmith, London W6 9EL, tel. 081/846–9000.

Greece **Greek National Tourist Organization. In the United States:** 645 Fifth Ave., New York, NY 10022, tel. 212/421–5777; 611 W. 6th St., Suite 2198, Los Angeles, CA 90017, tel. 213/626–6696; 168 N. Michigan Ave., Chicago, IL 60601, tel. 312/782–1084.
In Canada: 1233 Rue de la Montagne, Montreal, Quebec H3G 1Z2, tel. 514/871–1535; 1300 Bay St., Toronto, Ontario M5R 3K8, tel. 416/968–2220.
In the United Kingdom: 4 Conduit St., London W1R 0DJ, tel. 071/734–5997.

Hungary **Hungarian Travel Bureau (IBUSZ). In North America:** 1 Parker Plaza, Suite 1104, Fort Lee, NJ 07024, tel. 201/592–8585.
In the United Kingdom: Danube Travel Ltd. (authorized agent), 6 Conduit St., London W1R 9TG, tel. 071/493–0263.

Iceland **Iceland Tourist Board. In North America:** 655 Third Ave., New York, NY 10017, tel. 212/949–2333.
In the United Kingdom: 172 Tottenham Court Rd., 3rd floor, London W1P 9LG, tel. 071/388–5346.

Ireland **Irish Tourist Board. In the United States:** 757 Third Ave., New York, NY 10017, tel. 212/418–0800 or 800/223–6470.
In Canada: 160 Bloor St. E, Suite 934, Toronto, Ontario M4W 1B9, tel. 416/929–2777.
In the United Kingdom: Ireland House, 150 New Bond St., London W1Y OAQ, tel. 071/493–3201.

Italy **Italian Government Travel Office (ENIT). In the United States:** 630 Fifth Ave., Suite 1565, New York, NY 10111, tel. 212/245–4822; 500 N. Michigan Ave., Suite 1046, Chicago, IL 60611, tel. 312/644–0990; 360 Post St., Suite 801, San Francisco, CA 94108, tel. 415/392–6206.
In Canada: 1 Place Ville Marie, Suite 1914, Montreal, Quebec H3B 3M9, tel. 514/866–7667.
In the United Kingdom: 1 Princes St., London W1R 8AY, tel. 071/408–1254.

Luxembourg Luxembourg Tourist Information Office. **In North America:** 801 Second Ave., New York, NY 10017, tel. 212/370–9850.
In the United Kingdom: 122–124 Regent St., London W1R 5FE, tel. 071/434–2800.

Malta Malta National Tourist Office. **In North America:** Maltese Consulate, 249 E. 35th St., New York, NY 10016, tel. 212/725–2345.
In the United Kingdom: Mappin House, Suite 300, 4 Winsley St., London W1N 7AR, tel. 071/323–0506.

Monaco Monaco Government Tourist and Convention Bureau. **In North America:** 845 Third Ave., New York, NY 10022, tel. 212/759–5227.
In the United Kingdom: 3–18 Chelsea Garden Market, Chelsea Harbour, London SW10 0XE, tel. 071/352–2103.

Netherlands Netherlands Board of Tourism. **In the United States:** 355 Lexington Ave., New York, NY 10017, tel. 212/370–7367; 225 N. Michigan Ave., Suite 326, Chicago, IL 60601, tel. 312/819–0300; 90 New Montgomery St., Suite 305, San Francisco, CA 94105, tel. 415/543–6772.
In Canada: 25 Adelaide St. E, Suite 710, Toronto, Ontario M5C 1Y2, tel. 416/363–1577.
In the United Kingdom: 25–28 Buckingham Gate, London SW1E 6LD, tel. 071/630–0451.

Norway Norwegian Tourist Board. **In North America:** 655 Third Ave., New York, NY 10017, tel. 212/949–2333.
In the United Kingdom: Charles House, 5–11 Lower Regent St., London SW1Y 4LR, tel. 071/839–6255.

Poland Polish National Tourist Office (Orbis). **In North America:** 500 Fifth Ave., New York, NY 10110, tel. 212/867–5011; 333 N. Michigan Ave., Chicago, IL 60601, tel. 312/236–9013.
In the United Kingdom: 82 Mortimer St., London W1N 7DE, tel. 071/580–8028.

Portugal Portuguese National Tourist Office. **In the United States:** 590 Fifth Ave., New York, NY 10036, tel. 212/354–4403.
In Canada: 2180 Yonge St., Toronto, Ontario M4S 2B9, tel. 416/250–7575.
In the United Kingdom: 22–25A Sackville St., London W1X 1DE, tel. 071/494–1441.

Romania Romanian National Tourist Office. **In North America:** 573 Third Ave., New York, NY 10016, tel. 212/697–6971.
In the United Kingdom: 17 Nottingham Pl., London W1M 3RD, tel. 071/224–3692.

Slovakia *See* The Czech Republic and Slovakia, *above.*

Spain Spanish National Tourist Office. **In the United States:** 665 Fifth Ave., New York, NY 10022, tel. 212/759–8822; 845 N. Michigan Ave., Chicago, IL 60611, tel. 312/642–1992; San Vicente Plaza Bldg., 8383 Wilshire Blvd., Suite 960, Beverly Hills, CA 90211, tel. 213/658–7188.
In Canada: 102 Bloor St. W, Suite 1400, Toronto, Ontario M5S 1M8, tel. 416/961–3131.
In the United Kingdom: 57–58 St. James's St., London SW1A 1LD, tel. 071/499–0901.

Sweden Swedish Tourist Board. **In North America:** 655 Third Ave., New York, NY 10017, tel. 212/949–2333.

In the United Kingdom: 29–31 Oxford St., 5th floor, London W1R 1RE, tel. 071/437–5816.

Switzerland **Swiss National Tourist Office. In the United States:** 608 Fifth Ave., New York, NY 10020, tel. 212/757–5944; 260 Stockton St., San Francisco, CA 94108, tel. 415/362–2260.
In Canada: 154 University Ave., Suite 610, Toronto, Ontario M5H 3Y9, tel. 416/971–9734.
In the United Kingdom: Swiss Centre, 1 New Coventry St., London W1V 8EE, tel. 071/734–1921.

Turkey **Turkish Tourist Office. In North America:** 821 UN Plaza, New York, NY 10017, tel. 212/687–2194.
In the United Kingdom: 170–173 Piccadilly, 1st floor, London W1V 9DD, tel. 071/734–8681.

The Department of State's **Citizens Emergency Center** issues Consular Information Sheets, which cover crime, security, and health risks as well as embassy locations, entry requirements, currency regulations, and other routine matters. For the latest information, stop in at any passport office, consulate, or embassy; call the interactive hotline (tel. 202/647–5225); or, with your PC's modem, tap into the Bureau of Consular Affairs' computer bulletin board (tel. 202/647–9225).

Tours and Packages

Should you buy your travel arrangements to Europe packaged or do it yourself? There are advantages either way. Buying packaged arrangements saves you money, particularly if you can find a program that includes exactly the features you want. You also get a pretty good idea of what your trip will cost from the outset. You have two options: fully escorted tours and independent packages.

Escorted tours mean having limited free time and traveling with strangers, and if you prefer to get an overview of many places rather than an in-depth experience in just one. Escorted tours are most often via motorcoach, with a tour director in charge. Your baggage is handled, your time rigorously scheduled, and most meals planned. Escorted tours are therefore the most hassle-free way to see Europe, as well as generally the least expensive. Independent packages allow plenty of flexibility. They generally include airline travel and hotels, with certain options available, such as sightseeing, car rental, and excursions. Or they can be complex programs that include, in addition, travel by rail or cruise ship, special events, and entertainment. Independent packages are usually more expensive than escorted tours, but your time is your own.

While you can book directly through tour operators, you will pay no more to go through a travel agent, who will be able to tell you about tours and packages from a number of operators. Whatever program you ultimately choose, be sure to find out exactly what is included: taxes, tips, transfers, meals, baggage handling, ground transportation, entertainment, excursions, sports or recreation (and rental equipment if necessary). Ask about the level of hotel used, its location, the size of its rooms, the kind of beds, and its amenities, such as pool, room service, or programs for children, if they're important to you. Find out the operator's cancellation penalties. Nearly everyone charges them, and the only way to avoid them is to buy trip-cancellation insurance (*see* Trip Insurance, *below*). Also ask about the single supplement, a surcharge assessed to solo travelers. Some operators do not make you pay it if you agree to be matched up with a roommate of the same sex, even if one is not found by departure time. Remember that a program that has features you won't use may not be the most cost-wise choice. In some countries, and particularly on budget programs, don't assume you will have a private bathroom. Ask!

Fully Escorted Tours Escorted tours are usually sold in three categories: deluxe, first-class, and tourist or budget class. The most important differences are the price and the level of accommodations. Some operators specialize in one category, while others offer a range. Among the larger companies who have been in business for some time, consider **Abercrombie & Kent** (1520 Kensington Rd., Oak Brook, IL 60521, tel. 800/323–7308), **Maupintour** (Box 807, Lawrence, KS 66044, tel. 800/255–4266), and **Tauck Tours** (11 Wilton Rd., Westport, CT 06881, tel. 800/468–2825) in the deluxe category; **American Express Vacations** (300 Pinnacle Way, Norcross, GA 30093, tel. 800/241–1700), **Caravan** (401 N. Michigan Ave., Suite 3325, Chicago, IL 60611, tel. 800/227–2826), **Globus-Gateway** (95-25 Queens Blvd., Rego Park, NY 11374, tel. 800/221–0090), **Olson-Travelworld** (Box 10066, Manhattan Beach, CA 90226, tel. 800/421–5785, or from CA, 800/421–2255), and **Trafalgar Tours** (21 E. 26th St., New York, NY 10010, tel. 800/854–0103) in the first-class category; and, in the budget category, **Cosmos**, a sister company of Globus-Gateway, at the same address, and the "Cost Savers" from **Trafalgar Tours.**

Most itineraries are jam-packed with sightseeing, so you see a lot in a short amount of time (usually one place per day). To judge just how fast-paced the tour is, review the itinerary carefully. If you are in a different hotel each night, you will be getting up early each day to head out, travel to your next destination, do some sightseeing, have dinner, and go to bed, then you'll start all over again. If you want some free time, make sure it's mentioned in the tour brochure; if you want to be escorted to every meal, confirm that any tour you consider does that. Also, when comparing programs, be sure to find out if the motorcoach is air-conditioned and has a restroom on board. Make your selection based on price and stops on the itinerary.

Independent Packages Just about every airline that flies to Europe offers packages including round-trip airfare and hotels (plus breakfast in many cases). Contact **American Airlines Fly AAway Vacations** (tel. 800/321–2121), **Continental Airlines' Grand Destinations** (tel. 800/634–5555), **Delta Dream Vacations** (tel. 800/872–7786), **United Airlines' Vacation Planning Center** (tel. 800/328–6877). Others offering independent programs include **American Express** and **Abercrombie & Kent** (*see above*). **CIE Tours** (108 Ridgedale Ave., Box 2355, Morristown, NJ 07962-2355, tel. 800/243–8687) offers fly/drive packages to Great Britain and Ireland only. **DER Tours** (11933 Wilshire Blvd., Los Angeles, CA 90025, tel. 800/782–2424) has an innovative voucher program; you travel either via rental car or rail, and select your travel dates and hotels as you go, paying with vouchers. While most vouchers are for tourist-class hotels, some first-class properties are available as well.

Special-interest Travel Special-interest programs may be fully escorted or independent. Some require a certain amount of expertise, but most are for the average traveler with an interest and are usually hosted by experts in the subject matter. When the program is escorted, it enjoys the advantages and disadvantages of all escorted programs; because your fellow travelers are apt to be passionate or knowledgeable about the subject, they can prove as enjoyable a part of your travel experience as the destination itself. The price range is wide, but the cost is usually higher—sometimes a lot higher—than for ordinary escorted tours and packages because of the expert guiding and special activities.

Adventure If trekking through the Pyrenees in Spain, France, and Andorra or a breathtaking (in more ways than one) Alpine pass in Switzerland is your idea of fun, investigate **Mountain Travel/Sobek** (1089 Angels Camp, CA 95222, tel. 209/736–4524). Various cycling, skiing, backpacking, hiking, and walking tours are also available.

In the United Kingdom, **Top Deck Travel** (131–135 Earl's Court Rd., London SW5 9RH, tel. 071/244–8641) offers tours to Europe, with activities including flotilla sailing, a variety of water sports, and rafting.

Art and Architecture **Esplanade Tours** (581 Boylston St., Boston, MA 02116, tel. 800/426-5492) are accompanied by expert guides; the Rhine River cruises emphasize art and architecture as well.

In the United Kingdom, contact **Prospect Music & Art Tours Ltd.** (454–458 Chiswick High Rd., London W4 5TT, tel. 081/995–2151) and **Swan Hellenic Art Treasures Tours** (77 New Oxford St., London WC1A 1PP, tel. 071/831–1616).

Ballooning **Buddy Bombard Balloon Adventures** (6727 Curran St., McLean, VA 22101 tel. 800/862-8537) cover Austria, the Czech Republic, France, Italy, Switzerland, and Turkey, with days aloft and fine food and accommodations on the ground. **Abercrombie & Kent** (*see above*) also offers ballooning tours.

In the United Kingdom, **Air 2 Air** (Vauxhall House, Coronation Rd., Bristol BS3 1RN, tel. 0272/633333), a clearinghouse for balloon activities in Britain, has information about what's happening on the Continent.

Biking The nonprofit **Bicycle Adventure Club** (3904 Groton St., San Diego, CA 92110, tel. 800/775-2453) keeps costs low on the 30 tours it runs each year by using inexpensive hotels and volunteer leaders. Destinations include England, France, Spain, and Russia.

Health and Fitness **DER Tours** (11933 Wilshire Blvd., Los Angeles, CA 90025, tel. 213/479–4411 or 800/937–1234) offers a menu of Europe's most heralded spa resorts. Some maintain surprisingly sophisticated medical facilities; others are simply beautiful and healthy places to relax.

In the United Kingdom, **Moswin Tours Ltd.** (21 Church St., Oadby, Leicester LE2 5DB, tel. 0533/714982), has among its programs visits to health farms in Germany.

Music **Dailey-Thorp Travel** (330 W. 58th St., New York, NY 10019, tel. 212/307–1555; book through travel agents), specializing in classical music and opera programs throughout Europe, provides expert tour guides and tickets to events to which the general public would not have easy access. **Smolka Tours/All Around Travel** (Box 1108, Ridgefield, CT 06877, tel. 800/722–0057 or 203/431–9612 from CT) includes other performing arts as well as opera and music, and custom designs tours for art and history buffs.

In the United Kingdom, **Brompton Travel Ltd.** (64–66 Richmond Rd., Kingston-upon-Thames, Surrey KT2 5EH, tel. 081/549–3334) will arrange tickets and book your flights and accommodations for musical events in Europe and offers several opera tours. **Prospect Music & Art Tours** (*see* Art/Architecture Tours, *above*) has tours to many of the famous annual festivals, Savonlinna, Prague, Bregenz, and Munich among them.

Natural History   **Questers Worldwide Nature Tours** (257 Park Ave. S, New York, NY 10010, tel. 800/468–8668) explores the wild side of Europe in the company of expert guides.

In the United Kingdom, **Ramblers Holidays Ltd.** (Box 43, Welwyn Garden City, Herts. AL8 6PQ, tel. 0707/331133) arranges walking tours within Europe with walk leaders to point out natural features of interest.

Rail   **Abercrombie & Kent** (*see above*) has the market on Europe's luxury trains, including the transcontinental Venice Simplon-Orient-Express and the Andalusian Express, the luxury train of Spain. Both trains are made up of vintage rail carriages from the 1920s. A&K's less costly "Great Rail Journeys of Great Britain and Europe" offers travel by regularly scheduled trains with stays in first-class and deluxe hotels, accompanied by a traveling bellboy so you don't have to lug your bags from train to hotel every morning and night.

Singles and   **Trafalgar Tours** (*see above*) has a "Club 21" program of escorted
Young Couples   bus tours through Europe and Great Britain for those ages 21 to 35.

Sports   **Golf International** (275 Madison Ave., New York, NY 10016, tel. 212/986–9176 or 800/833–1389) has golf packages to the United Kingdom, Ireland, and France. **Keith Prowse & Co.** (234 W. 44th St., Suite 100, New York, NY 10036, tel. 800/669–7469) specializes in sporting events on the Continent and in Britain, including the British Open, tennis competitions such as Wimbledon (though Wimbledon itself is not offered every year), concerts, and events such as the Chelsea Flower Show. They will sell individual tickets as well as entire packages. **Lindenmeyer Travel Ltd.** (19 E. 37th St., Suite 4R, New York, NY 10016, tel. 800/248–2807) specializes in ski packages to the Alps; summer programs are also available. **Travel Concepts** (62 Commonwealth Ave., Suite 3, Boston, MA 02116, tel. 617/266–8450) packages such prestigious sporting events as the British Open golf tournament, the Henley Royal Regatta, and similar events on the Continent—but can also enroll you in polo school in England or in the SAS Bjorn Borg tennis clinic in Stockholm.

In the United Kingdom, **Algarve Select** (Emerson House, Heyes La., Alderley Edge, Cheshire SK9 7LF, tel. 0625/585196) has tennis and golf vacations in Portugal. If you prefer to watch rather than participate, **Page & Moy Ltd.** (136–140 London Rd., Leicester LE2 1EN, tel. 0533/552521) arranges vacations to see the international motor racing competitions in Europe.

Wine and Food   **Travel Concepts** (*see above*) also specializes in gourmet food and wine tours, with departures to England, France, Germany, Ireland, Italy, Scandinavia, and Switzerland, and deluxe or first-class accommodations.

In the United Kingdom, **Alternative Travel Group Ltd.,** (69–71 Banbury Rd., Oxford OX2 6PE, tel. 0865/310344) has wine-tasting tours of Germany, along the Rhine, and France in the region of Alsace, as well as of other countries. They also stage orchid, truffle, and mushroom hunts to Italy, France, and Portugal.

Climate

For the average daily maximum and minimum temperatures of the major European cities, *see* When to Go in each country chapter. For current weather conditions for cities abroad, plus the local time and helpful travel tips, call the **Weather Channel Connection** (tel. 900/WEATHER; 95¢ per minute) from a touch-tone phone.

What to Pack

Clothing What you pack depends more on the season than on any particular dress code. In general, northern and central Europe have cold, snowy winters, and the Mediterranean countries have mild winters, though parts of southern Europe can be bitterly cold, too. In the Mediterranean resorts you may need a warm jacket for mornings and evenings, even in summer. The mountains usually are warm on summer days, but the weather, especially in the Alps, is unpredictable, and the nights are generally cool. The Pyrenees don't have much snow except in the higher elevations, but they have extremely damp, foggy weather and rain year-round.

For European cities, pack as you would for an American city; formal outfits for first-class restaurants and nightclubs, casual clothes elsewhere. Jeans are as popular in Europe as they are in the rest of the world and are perfectly acceptable for sightseeing and informal dining. Sturdy walking shoes are appropriate for the cobblestone streets and gravel paths that fill many of the parks and surround some of the historic buildings. For visits to churches and cathedrals, especially in southern Europe, avoid shorts and immodest outfits. Italians are especially strict, insisting that women cover their shoulders and arms (a shawl will do). Women, however, no longer have to cover their heads in Roman Catholic churches.

To discourage purse snatchers and pickpockets, take a handbag with long straps that you can sling across your body, bandolier-style, and with a zippered compartment for money and other valuables.

Miscellaneous Bring an extra pair of eyeglasses or contact lenses. If you stay in budget hotels, take your own soap: Many do not provide soap, and those that do often give guests only one tiny bar per room. If you have a health problem that may require you to purchase a prescription drug, pack enough to last the duration of the trip, or have your doctor write a prescription using the drug's generic name, since brand names vary from country to country. And don't forget to pack a list of the addresses of offices that supply refunds for lost or stolen traveler's checks.

Electricity The electrical current in most of Europe is 220 volts, 50 cycles alternating current (AC); the United States runs on 110-volt, 60-cycle AC current. Unlike wall outlets in the United States, which accept plugs with two flat prongs, outlets in Europe accept plugs of varying styles, often with two or three round prongs.

Adapters, To plug in U.S.-made appliances abroad, you'll need an adapter
Converters, plug. To reduce the voltage entering the appliance from 220 to
Transformers 110 volts, you'll also need a converter, unless it is a dual-voltage appliance, made for travel. There are converters for high-wattage appliances (such as hair dryers), low-wattage items (such as electric toothbrushes and razors), and combination models. Hotels sometimes have outlets marked "For Shavers Only" near the sink; these are 110-volt outlets for low-wattage appliances; don't use them for a high-wattage appliance. If you're traveling with a laptop computer, especially an older one, you may need a transformer—a type of converter used with electronic-circuitry products. Newer laptop computers are autosensing, operating equally well on 110 and 220 volts (so you need only the appropriate adapter plug). When in doubt, consult your appliance's owner's manual or the manufacturer. Or get a copy of the free brochure "Foreign Electricity is No Deep Dark Secret," published by adapter-converter manufacturer Franzus (Murtha Industrial Park, Box 142, Beacon Falls, CT 06403, tel. 203/723–6664; send a stamped, self-addressed envelope when ordering).

Luggage Free baggage allowances on an airline depend on the airline,
Regulations the route, and the class of your ticket. In general, on domestic flights and on international flights between the United States and foreign destinations, you are entitled to check two bags—neither exceeding 62 inches, or 158 centimeters (length + width + height), or weighing more than 70 pounds (32 kilograms). A third piece may be brought aboard as a carryon; its total dimensions are generally limited to less than 45 inches (114 centimeters), so it will fit easily under the seat in front of you or in the overhead compartment. There are variations, so ask in advance. The single rule, a Federal Aviation Administration safety regulation that pertains to carry-on baggage on U.S. airlines, requires only that carryons be properly stowed and allows the airline to limit allowances and tailor them to different aircraft and operational conditions. Charges for excess, oversize, or overweight pieces vary, so inquire before you pack.

If you are flying between two foreign destinations, note that baggage allowances may be determined not by the piece method but by the weight method, which generally allows 88 pounds (40 kilograms) of luggage in first class, 66 pounds (30 kilograms) in business class, and 44 pounds (20 kilograms) in economy. If your flight between two cities abroad *connects* with your transatlantic or transpacific flight, the piece method still applies.

Safeguarding Before leaving home, itemize your bags' contents and their
Your Luggage worth; this list will help you estimate the extent of your loss if your bags go astray. To minimize that risk, tag them inside and out with your name, address, and phone number. (If you use your home address, cover it so that potential thieves can't see it.) At check-in, make sure that the tag attached by baggage handlers bears the correct three-letter code for your destination. If your bags do not arrive with you, or if you detect damage, do not leave the airport until you've filed a written report with the airline.

Taking Money Abroad

Traveler's Checks Although you will want plenty of cash when visiting small cities or rural areas, traveler's checks are usually preferable. The most widely recognized are **American Express, Barclay's, Thomas Cook,** and those issued by major commercial banks such as **Citibank** and **Bank of America.** American Express also issues *Traveler's Cheques for Two,* which can be signed and used by you or your traveling companion. Some checks are free; usually the issuing company or the bank at which you make your purchase charges 1% of the checks' face value as a fee. Be sure to buy a few checks in small denominations to cash toward the end of your trip, when you don't want to be left with more foreign currency than you can spend. Always record the numbers of checks as you spend them, and keep this list separate from the checks.

Currency Exchange Banks and bank-operated exchange booths at airports and railroad stations are usually the best places to change money. Hotels, stores, and privately run exchange firms typically offer less favorable rates.

Before your trip, pay attention to how the dollar is doing. If the dollar is losing strength, try to pay as many travel bills as possible in advance, especially the big ones. If it is getting stronger, pay for costly items overseas, and use your credit card whenever possible—you'll come out ahead, whether the exchange rate at which your purchase is calculated is the one in effect the day the vendor's bank abroad processes the charge, or the one prevailing on the day the charge company's service center processes it at home.

To avoid lines at airport currency-exchange booths, arrive in a foreign country with a small amount of the local currency already in your pocket—a so-called tip pack. **Thomas Cook Currency Services** (630 5th Ave., New York, NY 10111, tel. 212/757–6915) supplies foreign currency by mail.

Getting Money from Home

Cash Machines Automated-teller machines (ATMs) are proliferating; many are tied to international networks such as **Cirrus** and **Plus.** You can use your bank card at ATMs away from home to withdraw money from an account and get cash advances on a credit-card account (providing your card has been programmed with a personal identification number, or PIN). Check in advance on limits on withdrawals and cash advances within specified periods. Ask whether your bank-card or credit-card PIN number will need to be reprogrammed for use in the area you'll be visiting—a possibility if the number has more than four digits. If you know your PIN number as a word, learn the numerical equivalent before you leave, since some ATM keypads show no letters, only numbers. Remember that on cash advances you are charged interest from day you get the money from ATMs as well as from tellers. And note that, although transaction fees for ATM withdrawals abroad will probably be higher than fees for withdrawals at home, Cirrus and Plus exchange rates tend to be good.

Be sure to plan ahead: Obtain ATM locations and the names of affiliated cash-machine networks before departure. For specific foreign Cirrus locations, call 800/4–CIRRUS; for foreign Plus locations, consult the Plus directory at your local bank.

American Express Cardholder Services

The company's **Express Cash** system lets you withdraw cash and/or traveler's checks from a worldwide network of 57,000 American Express dispensers and participating bank ATMs. You must *enroll first* (call 800/CASH–NOW for a form and allow two weeks for processing). Withdrawals are charged not to your card but to a designated bank account. You can withdraw up to $1,000 per seven-day period on the basic card, more if your card is gold or platinum. There is a 2% fee (minimum $2.50, maximum $10) for each cash transaction, and a 1% fee for traveler's checks (except for the platinum card), which are available only from American Express dispensers.

At AmEx offices abroad, cardholders can also cash personal checks for up to $1,000 in any 21-day period; of this $200 can be in cash, more if available, with the balance paid in traveler's checks, for which all but platinum cardholders pay a 1% fee. Higher limits apply to the gold and platinum cards.

Wiring Money

You don't have to be a cardholder to send or receive an **American Express MoneyGram** for up to $10,000. To send one, go to an American Express MoneyGram agent, pay up to $1,000 with a credit card and anything over that in cash, and phone a transaction reference number to your intended recipient, who needs only present identification and the reference number to the nearest MoneyGram agent to pick up the cash. There are MoneyGram agents in more than 60 countries (call 800/543–4080 for locations). Fees range from 5% to 10%, depending on the amount and how you pay. You can't use American Express, which is really a convenience card—only Discover, MasterCard, and Visa credit cards.

You can also use **Western Union**. To wire money, take either cash or a check to the nearest office. (Or you can call and use a credit card.) Fees are roughly 5%–10%. Money sent from the United States or Canada will be available for pick up at agent locations in Europe within minutes. (Note that once the money is in the system it can be picked up at *any* location. You don't have to miss your train waiting for it to arrive in City A, because if there's an agent in City B, where you're headed, you can pick it up there, too.) There are approximately 20,000 agents worldwide (call 800/325–6000 for locations).

Passports and Visas

If your passport is lost or stolen abroad, report it immediately to the nearest embassy or consulate and to the local police. If you can provide the consular officer with the information contained in the passport, they will usually be able to issue you a new passport. For this reason, it is a good idea to keep a copy of the data page of your passport in a separate place, or to leave the passport number, date, and place of issuance with a relative or friend at home.

U.S. Citizens

All U.S. citizens, even infants, need a valid passport to enter the countries covered in this guide. You can pick up new and renewal application forms at any of the 13 U.S. Passport Agency offices and at some post offices and courthouses. Although passports are usually mailed within two weeks of your application's receipt, it's best to allow three weeks for delivery in low season, five weeks or more from April through summer. Call the Department of State Office of Passport Services' information line (1425 K St. NW, Washington, DC 20522, tel. 202/647–0518) for fees, documentation requirements, and other details.

Canadian Citizens Canadian citizens need a valid passport to enter the countries covered in this guide. Application forms are available at 23 regional passport offices as well as post offices and travel agencies. Whether applying for a first or subsequent passport, you must apply in person. Children under 16 may be included on a parent's passport but must have their own passport to travel alone. Passports are valid for five years and are usually mailed within two weeks of an application's receipt. For fees, documentation requirements, and other information in English or French, call the passport office (tel. 514/283–2152).

U.K. Citizens Citizens of the United Kingdom often need a valid passport for travel within Europe. Applications for new and renewal passports are available from main post offices as well as at the six passport offices, located in Belfast, Glasgow, Liverpool, London, Newport, and Peterborough. You may apply in person at all passport offices, or by mail to all except the London office. Children under 16 may travel on a parent's passport when accompanying them. All passports are valid for 10 years. Allow a month for processing.

A British Visitor's Passport is valid for holidays and some business trips of up to three months to Andorra, Austria, Belgium, Denmark, Finland, France, Germany, Gibraltar, Greece, Iceland, Italy, Liechtenstein, Luxembourg, Malta, Monaco, Netherlands, Norway, Portugal, Spain, Sweden, Switzerland, and Turkey. It can include both partners of a married couple. Valid for one year, it will be issued on the same day that you apply. You must apply in person at a main post office.

Customs and Duties

On Arrival Arrival formalities vary from country to country and are detailed in each chapter. In addition to specific duty-free allowances, most countries allow travelers also to bring in cameras and a reasonable amount of film and electronic equipment; most do not allow fresh meats, plants, weapons, and narcotics.

On Departure If you are traveling with a foreign-made camera or other equipment, carry the original receipt or register it with U.S. Customs before leaving home (Form 4457) to avoid paying duty on your return.

Returning Home
U.S. Customs Provided you've been out of the country for at least 48 hours and haven't already used the exemption, or any part of it, in the past 30 days, you may bring home $400 worth of foreign goods duty-free. So can each member of your family, regardless of age; and your exemptions may be pooled, so one of you can bring in more if another brings in less. A flat 10% duty applies to the next $1,000 of goods; above $1,400, the rate varies with the merchandise. (If the 48-hour or 30-day limits apply, your duty-free allowance drops to $25, which may not be pooled.) Please note that these are the *general* rules, applicable to most countries.

Travelers 21 or older may bring back 1 liter of alcohol duty-free, provided the beverage laws of the state through which they reenter the United States allow it. In addition, 100 non-

Cuban cigars and 200 cigarettes are allowed, regardless of your age. Antiques and works of art more than 100 years old are duty-free.

Gifts valued at less than $50 may be mailed duty-free to state-side friends and relatives, with a limit of one package per day per addressee (do not send alcohol or tobacco products, nor perfume valued at more than $5). These gifts do not count as part of your exemption, unless you bring them home with you. Mark the package "Unsolicited Gift" and include the nature of the gift and its retail value.

For a copy of "Know Before You Go," a free brochure detailing what you may and may not bring back to the United States, rates of duty, and other pointers, contact the **U.S. Customs Service** (Box 7407, Washington, DC 20044, tel. 202/927–6724).

Canadian Customs   Once per calendar year, when you've been out of Canada for at least seven days, you may bring in $300 worth of goods duty-free. If you've been away less than seven days but more than 48 hours, the duty-free exemption drops to $100 but can be claimed any number of times (as can a $20 duty-free exemption for absences of 24 hours or more). You cannot combine the yearly and 48-hour exemptions, use the $300 exemption only partially (to save the balance for a later trip), or pool exemptions with family members. Goods claimed under the $300 exemption may follow you by mail; those claimed under the lesser exemptions must accompany you on your return.

Alcohol and tobacco products may be included in the yearly and 48-hour exemptions but not in the 24-hour exemption. If you meet the age requirements of the province through which you reenter Canada, you may bring in, duty-free, 1.14 liters (40 imperial ounces) of wine or liquor *or* two dozen 12-ounce cans or bottles of beer or ale. If you are 16 or older, you may bring in, duty-free, 200 cigarettes, 50 cigars or cigarillos, and 400 tobacco sticks or 400 grams of manufactured tobacco. Alcohol and tobacco must accompany you on your return.

Gifts may be mailed to friends in Canada duty-free. These do not count as part of your exemption. Each gift may be worth up to $60—label the package "Unsolicited Gift—Value under $60." There are no limits on the number of gifts that may be sent per day or per addressee, but you can't mail alcohol or tobacco.

For more information, including details of duties on items that exceed your duty-free limit, ask the Revenue Canada Customs and Excise Department (Connaught Bldg., MacKenzie Ave., Ottawa, Ontario, K1A OL5, tel. 613/957–0275) for a copy of the free brochure "I Declare/Je Déclare."

U.K. Customs   British residents, *see* Customs and Duties in the Great Britain chapter.

Traveling with Cameras, Camcorders, and Laptops

About Film and Cameras   If your camera is new or if you haven't used it for a while, shoot and develop a few rolls of film before leaving home. Pack some lens tissue and an extra battery for your built-in light meter, and invest in an inexpensive skylight filter, to both protect your lens and provide some definition in hazy shots. Store film in a cool, dry place—never in the car's glove compartment or on the shelf under the rear window.

Film above ISO 400 is more sensitive to damage from airport security X-rays than others; very high speed film, ISO 1,000 and above, is exceedingly vulnerable. To protect your film, don't put it in checked luggage; carry it with you in a plastic bag and ask for a hand inspection. Such requests are honored at American airports and up to the inspector abroad. Don't depend on a lead-lined bag to protect film in checked luggage— the airline may very well turn up the dosage of radiation to see what you've got in there. Airport metal detectors do not harm film, although you'll set off the alarm if you walk through one with a roll in your pocket. Call the Kodak Information Center (tel. 800/242–2424) for details.

About Camcorders   Before your trip, put new or long-unused camcorders through their paces, and practice panning and zooming. Invest in a skylight filter to protect the lens, and check the lithium battery that lights up the LCD (liquid crystal display) modes. As for the rechargeable nickel-cadmium batteries that are the camera's power source, take along an extra pair, so while you're using your camcorder you'll have one battery ready and another recharging. Most newer camcorders are equipped with the battery (which generally slides or clicks onto the camera body) and, to recharge it, with what's known as a universal or worldwide AC adapter charger (or multivoltage converter) that can be used whether the voltage is 110 or 220. All that's needed is the appropriate plug.

About Videotape   Unlike still-camera film, videotape is not damaged by X-rays. However, it may well be harmed by the magnetic field of a walk-through metal detector. Airport security personnel may want you to turn the camcorder on to prove that that's what it is, so make sure the battery is charged when you get to the airport. Note that although the United States, Canada, Japan, Korea, Taiwan, and other countries operate on the National Television System Committee video standard (NTSC), some countries in Europe use PAL or SECAM technologies. So you will not be able to view your tapes through the local TV set or view movies bought there in your home VCR. Blank tapes bought in Europe can be used for NTSC camcorder taping, however—although you'll probably find they cost more in Europe and wish you'd brought an adequate supply along.

About Laptops   Security X-rays do not harm hard-disk or floppy-disk storage. Most airlines allow you to use your laptop aloft but request that you turn it off during takeoff and landing so as not to interfere with navigation equipment. Make sure the battery is charged when you arrive at the airport, because you may be asked to turn on the computer at security checkpoints to prove that it is what it appears to be. If you're a heavy computer user, consider traveling with a backup battery. For international travel, register your laptop with U.S. Customs as you leave the country, providing it's manufactured abroad (U.S.-origin items cannot be registered at U.S. Customs); when you do so, you'll get a certificate, good for as long as you own the item, containing your name and address, a description of the laptop, and its serial number, that will quash any questions that may arise on your return. If your laptop is U.S.-made, call the consulate of the country you'll be visiting to find out whether it should be registered with customs in that country upon arrival. Some travelers do this as a matter of course and ask customs officers to sign a document that specifies the total configuration of the system, computer and peripherals, and its value. In addition, before leaving home, find out about repair facilities at your destination, and don't forget any transformer or adapter plug you may need (*see* Electricity in What to Pack, *above*).

Staying Healthy

There are no serious health risks associated with travel in Europe, and no inoculations are required. However, the Centers for Disease Control (CDC) in Atlanta advises that international travelers swim only in chlorinated swimming pools if there is any question about contamination of local beaches and freshwater lakes. The CDC also cautions that most of southern Europe is in the "intermediate" range for risk of contracting traveler's diarrhea. Part of this may be due to an increased consumption of olive oil and wine, which can have a laxative effect on stomachs used to a different diet. The American Medical Association recommends Pepto-Bismol for minor cases of traveler's diarrhea.

Finding a Doctor The **International Association for Medical Assistance to Travellers** (IAMAT, 417 Center St., Lewiston, NY 14092, tel. 716/754–4883; 40 Regal Rd., Guelph, Ontario N1K 1B5; 57 Voirets, 1212 Grand-Lancy, Geneva, Switzerland) publishes a worldwide directory of English-speaking physicians whose qualifications meet IAMAT standards and who have agreed to treat members for a set fee. Membership is free.

Assistance Companies Pretrip medical referrals, emergency evacuation or repatriation, 24-hour telephone hot lines for medical consultation, dispatch of medical personnel, relay of medical records, up-front cash for emergencies, and other personal and legal assistance are among the services provided by several membership organizations specializing in medical assistance to travelers. Among them are **International SOS Assistance** (Box 11568, Philadelphia, PA 19116, tel. 215/244–1500 or 800/523–8930; Box 466, Pl. Bonaventure, Montréal, Québec. H5A 1C1, tel. 514/874–7674 or 800/363–0263), **Near Services** (450 Prairie Ave., Suite 101, Calumet City, IL 60409, tel. 708/868–6700 or 800/654–6700), and **Travel Assistance International** (1133 15th St. NW, Suite 400, Washington, DC 20005, tel. 202/331–1609 or 800/821–2828), part of Europ Assistance Worldwide Services, Inc. Because these companies will also sell you death-and-dismemberment, trip-cancellation, and other insurance coverage, there is some overlap with the travel-insurance policies discussed below, which may include the services of an assistance company among the insurance options or reimburse travelers for such services without providing them.

Insurance

For U.S. Residents Most tour operators, travel agents, and insurance agents sell specialized health-and-accident, flight, trip-cancellation, and luggage insurance as well as comprehensive policies with some or all of these features. But before you make any purchase, review your existing health and homeowner policies to find out whether they cover expenses incurred while travelling.

Health-and-Accident Insurance Supplemental health-and-accident insurance for travelers is usually a part of comprehensive policies. Specific policy provisions vary, but they tend to address three general areas, beginning with reimbursement for medical expenses caused by illness or an accident during a trip. Such policies may reimburse anywhere from $1,000 to $150,000 worth of medical expenses; dental benefits may also be included. A second common feature is the personal-accident, or death-and-dismemberment, provision, which pays a lump sum to your beneficiaries if your die or to you if you lose one or both limbs or your eyesight. This is similar to the flight insurance described below, although it is not necessarily limited to accidents involving airplanes or even other "common carriers" (buses, trains, and ships) and can be in effect 24 hours a day. The lump sum awarded can range from $15,000 to $500,000. A third area generally addressed by these policies is medical assistance (referrals, evacuation, or repatriation and other services). Some policies reimburse travelers for the cost of such services; others may automatically enroll you as a member of a particular medical-assistance company.

Flight Insurance This insurance, often bought as a last-minute impulse at the airport, pays a lump sum to a beneficiary when a plane crashes and the insured dies (and sometimes to a surviving passenger who loses eyesight or a limb); thus it supplements the airlines' own coverage as described in the limits-of-liability paragraphs on your ticket (up to $75,000 on international flights, $20,000 on domestic ones—and that is generally subject to litigation). Charging an airline ticket to a major credit card often automatically signs you up for flight insurance; in this case, the coverage may also embrace travel by bus, train, and ship.

Baggage Insurance In the event of loss, damage, or theft on international flights, airlines limit their liability to $20 per kilogram for checked baggage (roughly about $640 per 70-pound bag) and $400 per passenger for unchecked baggage. On domestic flights, the ceiling is $1,250 per passenger. Excess-valuation insurance can be bought directly from the airline at check-in but leaves your bags vulnerable on the ground.

Trip Insurance There are two sides to this coin. **Trip-cancellation-and-interruption insurance** protects you in the event you are unable to undertake or finish your trip. **Default** or **bankruptcy insurance** protects you against a supplier's failure to deliver. Consider the former if your airline ticket, cruise, or package tour does not allow changes or cancellations. The amount of coverage to buy should equal the cost of your trip should you, a traveling companion, or a family member get sick, forcing you to stay home, plus the nondiscounted one-way airline ticket you would need to buy if you had to return home early. Read the fine print carefully; pay attention to sections defining "family member" and "preexisting medical conditions." A characteristic quirk of default policies is that they often do not cover default by travel agencies or default by a tour operator, airline, or cruise line if you bought your tour and the coverage directly from the firm in question. To reduce your need for default insurance, give preference to tours packaged by members of the United States Tour Operators Association (USTOA), which maintains a fund to reimburse clients in the event of member defaults. Even better, pay for travel arrangements with a major credit card, so that you can refuse to pay the bill if services have not been rendered—and let the card company fight your battles.

Comprehensive Policies Companies supplying comprehensive policies with some or all of the above features include **Access America, Inc.**, underwritten by BCS Insurance Company (Box 11188, Richmond, VA 23230, tel. 800/284–8300); **Carefree Travel Insurance**, underwritten by The Hartford (Box 310, 120 Mineola Blvd., Mineola, NY 11501, tel. 516/294–0220 or 800/323–3149); **Tele-Trip** (Mutual of Omaha Plaza, Box 31762, Omaha, NE 68131, tel. 800/228–9792), a subsidiary of Mutual of Omaha; **The Travelers Companies** (1 Tower Sq., Hartford, CT 06183, tel. 203/277–0111 or 800/243–3174); **Travel Guard International**, underwritten by Transamerica Occidental Life Companies (1145 Clark St., Stevens Point, WI 54481, tel. 715/345–0505 or 800/782–5151); and **Wallach and Company, Inc.** (107 W. Federal St., Box 480, Middleburg, VA 22117, tel. 703/687–3166 or 800/237–6615), underwritten by Lloyds, London. These companies may also offer the above types of insurance separately.

U.K. Residents Most tour operators, travel agents, and insurance agents sell specialized policies covering accident, medical expenses, personal liability, trip cancellation, and loss or theft of personal property. Some policies include coverage for delayed departure and legal expenses, winter-sports, accidents, or motoring abroad. You can also purchase an annual travel-insurance policy valid for every trip you make during the year in which it's purchased (usually only trips of less than 90 days). Before you leave, make sure you will be covered if you have a preexisting medical condition or are pregnant; your insurers may not pay for routine or continuing treatment, or may require a note from your doctor certifying your fitness to travel.

For advice by phone or a free booklet, "Holiday Insurance," that sets out what to expect from a holiday-insurance policy and gives price guidelines, contact the **Association of British Insurers** (51 Gresham St., London EC2V 7HQ, tel. 071/600–3333; 30 Gordon St., Glasgow G1 3PU, tel. 041/226–3905; Scottish Provincial Bldg., Donegall Sq. W, Belfast BT1 6JE, tel. 0232/249176; call for other locations).

Trip Cancellation Consider purchasing trip-cancellation insurance if you are traveling on a promotional or discounted ticket that does not allow changes or cancellations. You are then covered if an emergency causes you to cancel or postpone your trip. Trip cancellation insurance is usually included in combination travel insurance packages available from most tour operators, travel agents, and insurance agents. Flight insurance, which covers passengers in the case of death or dismemberment, is often included in the price of a ticket when paid for with American Express, MasterCard, or other major credit cards.

Renting and Leasing Cars

Renting If you're traveling to more than one country, make sure your rental contract permits you to take the car across borders and that the insurance policy covers you in every country you visit.

Rental rates vary widely and depend on size and model and the number of days you use the car, and usually include unlimited free mileage and standard liability protection. Most major car-rental companies are represented in Europe, including **Avis** (tel. 800/331–1212, 800/879–2847 in Canada, 081/848–8765 in the United Kingdom); **Budget** (tel. 800/527–0700); **Hertz** (tel. 800/654–3131, 800/263-0600 in Canada, 081/679–1799 in the United Kingdom); **National** (tel. 800/227–7368, and 081/950–4080 in the United Kingdom). Unlimited-mileage rates vary, depending on where you rent the car and for how long, and usually do not include European value-added taxes (VAT), which also vary from country to country, ranging from zero in Switzerland to a whopping 18.6% in France.

Requirements Driver's licenses issued in the United States, Canada, and the United Kingdom are valid in Europe. Non-EC nationals must have Green Card insurance (*see* By Car in Getting Around Europe, *below*). An International Driver's Permit, available from the American or Canadian Automobile Association, is a good idea.

Extra Charges Picking up the car in one city or country and leaving it in another may entail drop-off charges or one-way service fees, which can be substantial. The cost of a collision or loss-damage waiver (*see below*) can be high, also. Automatic transmissions and air-conditioning are not universally available abroad; ask for them when you book if you want them, and check the cost before you commit yourself to the rental.

Cutting Costs If you know you will want a car for more than a day or two, you can save by planning ahead. Major international companies have programs that discount their standard rates by 15%–30% if you make the reservation before departure (anywhere from two to 14 days), rent for a minimum number of days (typically three or four), and prepay the rental. Ask about these advance-purchase schemes when you call for information. More economical rentals are those that come as part of fly/drive or other packages, even those as bare-bones as the rental plus an airline ticket (*see* Tours and Packages, *above*).

Renting from local companies can also be cost-wise. However, you'll have to weigh the convenience of renting a car from a major company with an airport office against the savings on a car from a budget company with offices in town.

Other sources of savings are the several companies that operate as wholesalers—companies that do not own their own fleets but rent in bulk from those that do and offer advantageous rates to their customers. Rentals through such companies must be arranged and paid for before you leave the United States. Among them are **Auto Europe** (Box 1097, Camden, ME 04843, tel. 207/236–8235 or 800/223–5555, 800/458–9503 in Canada), **Connex International** (23 N. Division St., Peekskill, NY 10566, tel. 914/739–0066, 800/333–3949, 800/843–5416 in Canada), **Europe by Car** (mailing address, 1 Rockefeller Plaza, New York, NY 10020; walk-in address, 14 W. 49th St, New York, NY 10020, tel. 212/581–3040 or 212/245–1713; 9000 Sunset Blvd., Los Angeles, CA 90069, tel. 213/252–9401 or 800/223–1516 in CA), **Foremost Euro-Car** (5430 Van Nuys Blvd., Suite 306, Van Nuys, CA 91401, tel. 818/786–1960 or 800/272–3299), and **Kemwel** (106 Calvert St., Harrison, NY 10528, tel. 914/835–5555 or 800/678–0678). You won't see these wholesalers' deals advertised; they're even better in summer, when business travel is down. Always ask whether the prices are guaranteed in U.S. dollars or foreign currency and if unlimited mileage is available. Find out about any required deposits, cancellation penalties, and drop-off charges, and confirm the cost of the CDW.

If you're flying into a major city and planning to spend some time there before using your car, you can also save money by arranging to pick it up on the day of your departure.

One last tip: Remember to fill the tank when you turn in the vehicle, to avoid being charged for refueling at what you'll swear is the most expensive pump in town.

Insurance and The standard rental contract includes liability coverage (for
Collision damage to public property, injury to pedestrians, etc.) and cov-
Damage Waiver erage for the car against fire, theft (not included in certain countries), and collision damage with a deductible—most commonly $2,000–$3,000, occasionally more. In the case of an accident, you are responsible for the deductible amount unless you've purchased the collision damage waiver (CDW), which costs an average $12 a day, although this varies depending on what you've rented, where, and from whom.

Because this adds up quickly, you may be inclined to say "no thanks"—and that's certainly your option, although the rental agent may not tell you so. Planning ahead will help you make the right decision. By all means, find out if your own insurance covers damage to a rental car while traveling (not simply a car to drive when yours is in for repairs). And check whether charging car rentals to any of your credit cards will get you a CDW at no charge. Note before you decline that deductibles are occasionally high enough that totaling a car would make you responsible for its full value.

In Spain and Greece, make sure you carry insurance that provides bail bond in case of an accident. When driving a rental car in Greece, beware of damaging the underside of the vehicle on Greek roads, which are among the worst in Europe. Normal collision-damage waivers, even from one of the major international chains, may not cover such damage, and you could face a crippling fine.

Leasing For trips of 21 days or more, you may save money by leasing a car. With the leasing arrangement, you are technically buying a car and then selling it back to the manufacturer after you've used it. You receive a factory-new car, tax-free, with international registration and extensive insurance coverage. Rates vary with the make and model of car and length of time used. Car-leasing programs are offered by Renault, Citroën, and Peugeot in France and by Volkswagen, Ford, Audi, and Opel, among others, in Belgium. Delivery can be arranged outside France and Brussels for an additional fee. Before you go, compare long-term rental rates with leasing rates. Remember to add taxes and insurance costs to the car rentals, something you don't have to worry about with leasing. Companies that offer leasing arrangements include Kemwel and Europe by Car (*see* Renting, *above*).

Rail Passes

An excellent value if you plan to rack up the miles, **EurailPasses** provide unlimited first-class rail travel during their period of validity in Austria, Belgium, Denmark, Finland, France, Germany, Greece, Hungary, the Irish Republic, Italy, Luxembourg, the Netherlands, Norway, Portugal, Spain, Sweden, and Switzerland (but not England, Scotland, Northern Ireland, and Wales). Standard **EurailPasses** are available for 15 days ($460), 21 days ($598), one month ($728), two months ($998), and three months ($1,260). **Eurail Saverpasses,** valid for 15 days, cost $390 per person; you must do all your traveling with at least one companion (two companions from April through September). **Eurail Youthpasses,** which cover second-class travel, cost $508 for one month and $698 for two; you must be under 26 on the first day you travel. Flexipasses allow you to travel for five, 10, or 15 days within any two-month period. You pay $298, $496, and $676 for the **Eurail Flexipass,** sold for first-class travel; and $220, $348, $474 for the **Eurail Youth Flexipass,** available to those under 26 on their first travel day, sold for second-class travel. Apply through your travel agent, or **Rail Europe** (226–230 Westchester Ave., White Plains, NY 10604, tel. 914/682–5172 or 800/848–7245).

Eurail also sells single-country passes for Austria, Czechoslovakia, Finland, France, Germany, Greece, Hungary, Poland, Portugal, Russia, Spain, and Switzerland, as well as multi-country passes that cover Britain and France jointly, all of Scandinavia, and the Benelux nations. Typically these are flexipasses, valid for a 5, 10, and 15, or other specified number of days, within a longer time period; rail-and-drive schemes are also available.

Don't make the mistake of assuming that your rail pass guarantees you seats on the trains you want to ride. Seat reservations are required on some trains, particularly high-speed trains, and are a good idea on trains that may be crowded. You will also need reservations for overnight sleeping accommodations. Rail Europe can help you determine if you need reservations and can make them for you (about $10 each, less if you purchase them in Europe at the time of travel).

Home Exchange and Villa Rentals

Apartment and Villa Rentals If you want a home base that's roomy enough for a family and comes with cooking facilities, a furnished rental may be the solution. It's generally cost-wise, too, although not always—some rentals are luxury properties (economical only when your party is large). Home-exchange directories do list rentals—often second homes owned by prospective house swappers— and there are services that can not only look for a house or apartment for you (even a castle if that's your fancy) but also handle the paperwork. Some send an illustrated catalogue and others send photographs of specific properties, sometimes at a charge; up-front registration fees may apply.

Among the companies are **At Home Abroad** (405 E. 56th St., Suite 6H, New York, NY 10022, tel. 212/421–9165); **Interhome Inc.** (124 Little Falls Rd., Fairfield, NJ 07004, tel. 201/882–6864); **Overseas Connection** (31 North Harbor Dr., Sag Harbor, NY 11963, tel. 516/725–9308); **Rent a Home International** (7200 34th Ave. NW, Seattle, WA 98117, tel. 206/789–9377 or 800/488–7368); **Vacation Home Rentals Worldwide** (235 Kensington Ave., Norwood, NJ 07648, tel. 201/767–9393 or 800/633–3284); **Villa Leisure** (Box 209, Westport, CT 06881, tel. 407/624–9000 or 800/526–4244); **Villas and Apartments Abroad** (420 Madison Ave., Suite 1105, New York, NY 10017, tel. 212/759–1025 or 800/433–3020); and **Villas International** (605 Market St., Suite

510, San Francisco, CA 94105, tel. 415/281–0910 or 800/221–2260). **Hideaways International** (15 Goldsmith St., Box 1270, Littleton, MA 01460, tel. 508/486–8955 or 800/843–4433). Membership ($79 yearly per person or family at the same address) includes two annual guides plus quarterly newsletters; rentals are arranged directly between members, not by the club staff.

Home Exchange This is obviously an inexpensive solution to the lodging problem, because house-swapping means living rent-free. You find a house, apartment, or other vacation property to exchange for your own by becoming a member of a home-exchange organization, which then sends you its annual directories listing available exchanges and includes your own listing in at least one of them. Arrangements for the actual exchange are made by the two parties to it, not by the organization. Principal clearinghouses include **Intervac U.S./International Home Exchange** (Box 590504, San Francisco, CA 94159, tel. 415/435–3497), the oldest, with thousands of homes for exchange in its three annual directories; membership is $62, or $72 if you want to receive the directories but remain unlisted. The **Vacation Exchange Club** (Box 650, Key West, FL 33041, tel. 800/638–3841), also with thousands of listings, publishes four annual directories plus updates; the $50 membership includes your listing in one book. **Loan-a-Home** (2 Park La., Apt. 6E, Mount Vernon, NY 10552, tel. 914/664–7640) specializes in long-term exchanges; there is no charge to list your home, but the directories cost $35 or $45 depending on the number you receive.

Student and Youth Travel

Travel Agencies The foremost U.S. student travel agency is **Council Travel**, a subsidiary of the nonprofit Council on International Educational Exchange. It specializes in low-cost travel arrangements, is the exclusive U.S. agent for several discount cards, and, with its sister CIEE subsidiary, **Council Charter,** is a source of airfare bargains. The Council Charter brochure and CIEE's twice-yearly *Student Travels* magazine, which details its programs, are available at the Council Travel office at CIEE headquarters (205 E. 42nd Street, New York, NY 10017, tel. 212/661–1450) and at 37 branches in college towns nationwide (free in person, $1 by mail). The **Educational Travel Center** (ETC, 438 N. Francis St., Madison, WI 53703, tel. 608/256–5551) also offers low-cost rail passes, domestic and international airline tickets (mostly for flights departing from Chicago), and other budget-wise travel arrangements. Other travel agencies catering to students include **Travel Management International** (TMI, 18 Prescott St., Suite 4, Cambridge, MA 02138, tel. 617/661–8187) and **Travel Cuts** (187 College St., Toronto, Ontario M5T 1P7, tel. 416/979–2406).

Discount Cards For discounts on transportation and on museum and attractions admissions, buy the **International Student Identity Card** (ISIC) if you're a bona fide student, or the **International Youth Card** (IYC) if you're under 26. In the United States the ISIC and IYC cards cost $15 each and include basic travel accident and sickness coverage. Apply to **CIEE** (*see* address *above*, tel. 212/661–1414; the application is in *Student Travels*). In Canada the cards are available for $15 each from **Travel Cuts** (*see above*). In the United Kingdom they cost £5 and £4 respectively at student unions and student travel companies, including

Council Travel's London office (28A Poland St., London W1V 3DB, tel. 071/437–7767).

Hosteling An **International Youth Hostel Federation** (IYHF) membership card is the key to more than 5,300 hostel locations in 59 countries; the sex-segregated, dormitory-style sleeping quarters, including some for families, go for $7–$20 a night per person. Membership is available in the United States through **American Youth Hostels** (AYH, 733 15th St. NW, Washington, DC 20005, tel. 202/783–6161), the American link in the worldwide chain, and costs $25 for adults 18–54, $10 for those under 18, $15 for those 55 and over, and $35 for families. Volume 1 of the two-volume *Guide to Budget Accommodation* lists hostels in Europe and the Mediterranean ($13.95, including postage). IYHF membership is available in Canada through the **Canadian Hostelling Association** (CHA, 1600 James Naismith Dr., Suite 608, Gloucester, Ontario K1B 5N4, tel. 613/748–5638) for $26.75, and in the United Kingdom through the **Youth Hostel Association of England and Wales** (Trevelyan House, 8 St. Stephen's Hill, St. Albans, Herts. AL1 2DY, tel. 0727/55215) for £9.

Rail Passes Special rail passes are available for those under 26. (*See* Rail Passes, *above*.)

Traveling with Children

Publications *Family Travel Times,* published 10 times a year by Travel With
Newsletter Your Children (TWYCH, 45 W. 18th St., 7th Floor Tower, New York, NY 10011, tel. 212/206–0688; annual subscription $55), covers destinations, types of vacations, and modes of travel.

Books *Great Vacations with Your Kids,* by Dorothy Jordan and Marjorie Cohen ($13; Penguin USA, 120 Woodbine St., Bergenfield, NJ 07621, tel. 800/253–6476) and *Traveling with Children—And Enjoying It,* by Arlene K. Butler ($11.95 plus $3 shipping per book; Globe Pequot Press, Box 833, Old Saybrook, CT 06475, tel. 800/243–0495, or 800/962–0973 in CT), both help plan your trip with children, from toddlers to teens. *Innocents Abroad: Traveling with Kids in Europe,* by Valerie Wolf Deutsch and Laura Sutherland ($15.95 or $4.95 paperback, Penguin USA, *see above*), covers child- and teen-friendly activities, food, and transportation.

Tour Operators **GrandTravel** (6900 Wisconsin Ave., Suite 706, Chevy Chase, MD 20815, tel. 301/986–0790 or 800/247–7651) offers international and domestic tours for grandparents traveling with their grandchildren. The catalogue, as charmingly written and illustrated as a children's book, positively invites armchair traveling with lap-sitters aboard. **Families Welcome!** (21 W. Colony Pl., Suite 140, Durham, NC 27705, tel. 919/489–2555 or 800/326–0724) packages and sells family tours to Europe. **Rascals in Paradise** (650 5th St., Suite 505, San Francisco, CA 94107, tel. 415/978–9800, or 800/872–7225) specializes in programs for families.

Getting There On international flights, the fare for infants under 2 not occupy-
Airfares ing a seat is generally 10% of the accompanying adult's fare; children ages 2–11 usually pay half to two-thirds of the adult fare. On domestic flights, children under 2 not occupying a seat travel free, and older children currently travel on the "lowest applicable" adult fare.

Baggage In general, infants paying 10% of the adult fare are allowed one carry-on bag, not to exceed 70 pounds or 45 inches (length + width + height). The adult baggage allowance applies for children paying half or more of the adult fare. Check with the airline for particulars, especially regarding flights between two foreign destinations, where allowances for infants may be less generous than those above.

Safety Seats The FAA recommends the use of safety seats aloft and details approved models in the free leaflet **"Child/Infant Safety Seats Recommended for Use in Aircraft"** (available from the Federal Aviation Administration, APA-200, 800 Independence Ave. SW, Washington, DC 20591, tel. 202/267-3479). Airline policy varies. U.S. carriers must allow FAA-approved models, but because these seats are strapped into a regular passenger seat, they may require that parents buy a ticket even for an infant under 2 who would otherwise ride free. Foreign carriers may not allow infant seats, may charge the child's rather than the infant's fare for their use, or may require you to hold your baby during takeoff and landing, thus defeating the seat's purpose.

Facilities Aloft Airlines do provide other facilities and services for children, such as children's meals and freestanding bassinets (to those sitting in seats on the bulkhead, where there's enough legroom to accommodate them). Make your request when reserving. The annual February/March issue of **Family Travel Times** gives details of the children's services of dozens of airlines ($10; *see above*). "Kids and Teens in Flight" (free from the U.S. Department of Transportation, tel. 202/366-2220) offers tips for children flying alone.

Lodging **Novotel** hotels (tel. 800/221-4542) permit up to two children to stay free in their parents' room. Many Novotel properties have playgrounds. **Sofitel** hotels (tel. 800/221-4542) offer a free second room for children during July and August and over the Christmas holiday. **Happy Family Swiss Hotels,** 22 properties in Switzerland, offer outstanding programs for children at reduced prices; contact the Swiss National Tourist Office (608 Fifth Ave., New York, NY 10019, tel. 212/757-5944) for a brochure. Many of **Germany's castle hotels** (represented by Europa Hotels and Tours, tel. 800/523-9570 or 206/485-6985, and by DER Tours, tel. 800/937-1234 or 213/479-4411) are on parklike grounds. **Italy's CIGA hotels** (reservations, tel. 800/221-2340) welcome families as well.

Club Med (40 W. 57th St., New York, NY 10019, tel. 800/258-2633) has "Baby Clubs" (from age four months), "Mini Clubs" (for ages four to six or eight, depending on the resort), and "Kids Clubs" (for ages eight and up during school holidays) at many of its resort villages in France, Italy, Switzerland, and Spain.

Baby-sitting Services For child-care agencies with English-speaking personnel, ask your hotel concierge, or call the American embassy or consulate. Some local tourist offices also maintain updated lists of local baby-sitters.

Hints for Travelers with Disabilities

Organizations Several organizations provide travel information for people with disabilities, usually for a membership fee, and some publish newsletters and bulletins. Among them are the Information Center for Individuals with Disabilities (Fort Point Pl., 27–43 Wormwood St., Boston, MA 02210, tel. 617/727–5540 or 800/462–5015 in MA between 11 and 4, or leave message; TDD/ TTY tel. 617/345–9743); Mobility International USA (Box 3551, Eugene, OR 97403, voice and TDD tel. 503/343–1284), the U.S. branch of an international organization based in Britain (*see below*) and present in 30 countries; MossRehab Hospital Travel Information Service (1200 W. Tabor Rd., Philadelphia, PA 19141, tel. 215/456–9603, TDD tel. 215/456–9602); the Society for the Advancement of Travel for the Handicapped (SATH, 347 5th Ave., Suite 610, New York, NY 10016, tel. 212/ 447–7284, fax 212/725–8253); the Travel Industry and Disabled Exchange (TIDE, 5435 Donna Ave., Tarzana, CA 91356, tel. 818/368–5648); and Travelin' Talk (Box 3534, Clarksville, TN 37043, tel. 615/552–6670).

In the United Main information sources include the **Royal Association for Dis-**
Kingdom **ability and Rehabilitation** (RADAR, 25 Mortimer St., London W1N 8AB, tel. 071/637–5400), which publishes travel information for the disabled in Britain, and **Mobility International** (228 Borough High St., London SE1 1JX, tel. 071/403–5688), the headquarters of an international membership organization that serves as a clearinghouse of travel information for people with disabilities.

Travel Agencies **Directions Unlimited** (720 N. Bedford Rd., Bedford Hills, NY
and Tour Operators 10507, tel. 914/241–1700), a travel agency, has expertise in tours and cruises for the disabled. **Evergreen Travel Service** (4114 198th St. SW, Suite 13, Lynnwood, WA 98036, tel. 206/ 776–1184 or 800/435–2288) operates Wings on Wheels Tours for those in wheelchairs, White Cane Tours for the blind, and tours for the deaf and makes group and independent arrangements for travelers with any disability. **Flying Wheels Travel** (143 W. Bridge St., Box 382, Owatonna, MN 55060, tel. 800/535–6790 or 800/722–9351 in MN), a tour operator and travel agency, arranges international tours, cruises, and independent travel itineraries for people with mobility disabilities. **Nautilus,** at the same address as TIDE (*see above*), packages tours for the disabled internationally.

Publications In addition to the fact sheets, newsletters, and books mentioned above are several free publications available from the Consumer Information Center (Pueblo, CO 81009): "New Horizons for the Air Traveler with a Disability," a U.S. Department of Transportation booklet describing changes resulting from the 1986 Air Carrier Access Act and those still to come from the 1990 Americans with Disabilities Act (include Department 608Y in the address), and the Airport Operators Council's *Access Travel: Airports* (Dept. 5804), which describes facilities and services for the disabled at more than 500 airports worldwide.

Twin Peaks Press (Box 129, Vancouver, WA 98666, tel. 206/ 694–2462 or 800/637–2256) publishes the *Directory of Travel Agencies for the Disabled* ($19.95), listing more than 370 agencies worldwide; *Travel for the Disabled* ($19.95), listing some 500 access guides and accessible places worldwide; the *Directory of Accessible Van Rentals* ($9.95) for campers and RV travelers worldwide; and *Wheelchair Vagabond* ($14.95), a collection of personal travel tips. Add $2 per book for shipping.

Hints for Older Travelers

Organizations   The **American Association of Retired Persons** (AARP, 601 E St. NW, Washington, DC 20049, tel. 202/434–2277) provides independent travelers the Purchase Privilege Program, which offers discounts on hotels, car rentals, and sightseeing, and arranges group tours, cruises, and apartment living through AARP Travel Experience from American Express (400 Pinnacle Way, Suite 450, Norcross, GA 30071, tel. 800/927–0111); these can be booked through travel agents, except for the cruises, which must be booked directly (tel. 800/745–4567). AARP membership is open to those 50 and over; annual dues are $8 per person or couple.

Two other membership organizations offer discounts on lodgings, car rentals, and other travel products, along with such nontravel perks as magazines and newsletters. The **National Council of Senior Citizens** (1331 F St. NW, Washington, DC 20004, tel. 202/347–8800) is a nonprofit advocacy group with some 5,000 local clubs across the United States; membership costs $12 per person or couple annually. **Mature Outlook** (6001 N. Clark St., Chicago, IL 60660, tel. 800/336–6330), a Sears Roebuck & Co. subsidiary with 800,000 members, charges $9.95 for an annual membership.

Note: When using any senior-citizen identification card for reduced hotel rates, mention it when booking, not when checking out. At restaurants, show your card before you're seated; discounts may be limited to certain menus, days, or hours. If you are renting a car, ask about promotional rates that might improve on your senior-citizen discount.

Educational Travel   **Elderhostel** (75 Federal St., 3rd floor, Boston, MA 02110, tel. 617/426–7788) is a nonprofit organization that has inexpensive study programs for people 60 and older. Programs take place at more than 1,800 educational institutions in the United States, Canada, and 45 countries overseas, and courses cover everything from marine science to Greek myths and cowboy poetry. Participants generally attend lectures in the morning and spend the afternoon sightseeing or on field trips; they live in dorms on the host campuses. Fees for two- to three-week international trips—including room, board, and transportation from the United States—range from $1,800 to $4,500.

Interhostel (University of New Hampshire, 6 Garrison Ave., Durham, NH 03824, tel. 800/733–9753) caters to a slightly younger clientele—that is, 50 and over—and runs programs overseas in some 25 countries. But the idea is similar: Lectures and field trips mix with sightseeing, and participants stay in dormitories at cooperating educational institutions or in modest hotels. Programs are usually two weeks in length and cost $1,500–$2,100, not including airfare from the United States.

Tour Operators   **Saga International Holidays** (222 Berkeley St., Boston, MA 02116, tel. 800/343–0273), which specializes in group travel for people over 60, offers a selection of variously priced tours and cruises covering five continents. If you want to take your grandchildren, look into **GrandTravel** (*see* Traveling with Children, *above*).

Arriving and Departing

Because the air routes between North America and Europe are among the world's most heavily traveled, the passenger can choose from many airlines and fares. But fares change with stunning rapidity, so consult your travel agent on which bargains are currently available.

From North America by Plane

Flights are either nonstop, direct, or connecting. A **nonstop** flight requires no change of plane and makes no stops. A **direct** flight stops at least once and can involve a change of plane, although the flight number remains the same; if the first leg is late, the second waits. This is not the case with a **connecting** flight, which involves a different plane and a different flight number.

Airlines The U.S. airlines that serve the major cities in Europe are **TWA** (tel. 800/892–4141); **United** (tel. 800/538–2929); **Continental** (tel. 800/231–0856); **American Airlines** (tel. 800/433–7300); **Northwest** (tel. 800/447–4747); and **Delta** (tel. 800/241–4141).

Many European national airlines fly directly from the United States to their home countries. The biggest advantage in arriving on a home airline is that the landing privileges are often better, as are the facilities provided at main airports. Here are the U.S. telephone numbers of those airlines that have representation in the United States; most of the numbers are toll-free.

Austria: Austrian Airlines (tel. 800/843–0002)
Belgium: Sabena Belgian World Airlines (tel. 800/950–1000)
Cyprus: Cyprus Airways (tel. 212/714–2190)
The Czech Republic and Slovakia: Czechoslovak Airlines (CSA, tel. 212/682–5833)
Denmark: Scandinavian Airlines (SAS, tel. 800/221–2350)
Finland: Finnair (tel. 800/950–5000)
France: Air France (tel. 800/237–2747)
Germany: Lufthansa (tel. 800/645–3880)
Great Britain: British Airways (tel. 800/247–9297); Virgin Atlantic (tel. 800/862–8621)
Greece: Olympic Airways (tel. 212/838–3600)
Holland: KLM Royal Dutch Airlines (tel. 800/777–5553)
Hungary: Malév Hungarian Airlines (tel. 212/757–6446)
Iceland: Icelandair (tel. 800/223–5500)
Ireland: Aer Lingus (800/223–6537)
Italy: Alitalia (tel. 800/223–5730)
Malta: Air Malta (tel. 415/362–2929)
Norway: Scandinavian Airlines (SAS, tel. 800/221–2350)
Poland: LOT Polish Airlines (tel. 212/869–1074)
Portugal: TAP Air Portugal (tel. 800/221–7370)
Romania: Tarom Romanian Airlines (tel. 212/687–6013)
Spain: Iberia Airlines (tel. 800/772–4642)
Sweden: Scandinavian Airlines (tel. 800/221–2350)
Switzerland: Swissair (tel. 800/221–4750)
Turkey: THY Turkish Airlines (tel. 212/986–5050)

Cutting Flight Costs The Sunday travel section of most newspapers is a good source of deals. When booking, particularly through an unfamiliar company, call the Better Business Bureau to find out whether any complaints have been registered against the company, pay with a credit card if you can, and consider trip-cancellation and default insurance (*see* Insurance, *above*).

Promotional Airfares All the less expensive fares, called promotional or discount fares, are round-trip and involve restrictions. The exact nature of the restrictions depends on the airline, the route, and the season and on whether travel is domestic or international, but you must usually buy the ticket—commonly called an APEX (advance purchase excursion) when it's for international travel—in advance (7, 14, or 21 days are usual). You must also respect certain minimum- and maximum-stay requirements (for instance, over a Saturday night or at least seven and no more than 30, 45, or 90 days), and you must be willing to pay penalties for changes. Airlines generally allow some changes for a fee. But the cheaper the fare, the more likely the ticket is nonrefundable; it would take a death in the family for the airline to give you any of your money back if you had to cancel. The cheapest fares are also subject to availability; because only a certain percentage of the plane's total seats will be sold at that price, they may go quickly.

Consolidators Consolidators or bulk-fare operators—also known as bucket shops—buy blocks of seats on scheduled flights that airlines anticipate they won't be able to sell. They pay wholesale prices, add a markup, and resell the seats to travel agents or directly to the public at prices that still undercut the airline's promotional or discount fares. You pay more than on a charter but ordinarily less than for an APEX ticket, and, even when there is not much of a price difference, the ticket usually comes without the advance-purchase restriction. Moreover, although tickets are marked nonrefundable so you can't turn them in to the airline for a full-fare refund, some consolidators sometimes give you your money back. Carefully read the fine print detailing penalties for changes and cancellations. If you doubt the reliability of a company, call the airline once you've made your booking and confirm that you do, indeed, have a reservation on the flight.

The biggest U.S. consolidator, C.L. Thomson Express, sells only to travel agents. Well-established consolidators selling to the public include **UniTravel** (Box 12485, St. Louis, MO 63132, tel. 314/569–0900 or 800/325–2222); **Council Charter** (205 E. 42nd St., New York, NY 10017, tel. 212/661–0311 or 800/800–8222), a division of the Council on International Educational Exchange and a longtime charter operator now functioning more as a consolidator; and **Travac** (989 6th Ave., New York, NY 10018, tel. 212/563–3303 or 800/872–8800), also a former charterer.

Charter Flights Charters usually have the lowest fares and the most restrictions. Departures are limited and seldom on time, and you can lose all or most of your money if you cancel. (Generally, the closer to departure you cancel, the more you lose, although sometimes you will be charged only a small fee if you supply a substitute passenger.) The charterer, on the other hand, may legally cancel the flight for any reason up to 10 days before departure; within 10 days of departure, the flight may be canceled only if it becomes physically impossible to operate it. The charterer may also revise the itinerary or increase the price after you have bought the ticket, but if the new arrangement constitutes a "major change," you have the right to a refund.

Before buying a charter ticket, read the fine print for the company's refund policy and details on major changes. Money for charter flights is usually paid into a bank escrow account, the name of which should be on the contract. If you don't pay by credit card, make your check payable to the escrow account (unless you're dealing with a travel agent, in which case, his or her check should be payable to the escrow account). The Department of Transportation's Consumer Affairs Office (I–25, Washington, DC 20590, tel. 202/366–2220) can answer questions on charters and send you its "Plane Talk: Public Charter Flights" information sheet.

Charter operators may offer flights alone or with ground arrangements that constitute a charter package. Well-established charter operators include **Council Charter** (205 E. 42nd St., New York, NY 10017, tel. 212/661–0311 or 800/800–8222), now largely a consolidator, despite its name, and **Travel Charter** (1120 E. Long Lake Rd., Troy, MI 48098, tel. 313/528–3570 or 800/521–5267), with Midwestern departures. **DER Tours** (Box 1606, Des Plains, IL 60017, tel. 800/782–2424), a charterer and consolidator, sells through travel agents.

Discount Travel Clubs Travel clubs offer their members unsold space on airplanes, cruise ships, and package tours at nearly the last minute and at well below the original cost. Suppliers thus receive some revenue for their "leftovers," and members get a bargain. Membership generally includes a regular bulletin or access to a toll-free telephone hot line giving details of available trips departing anywhere from three or four days to several months in the future. Packages tend to be more common than flights alone, so if airfares are your only interest, read the literature before joining. Reductions on hotels are also available. Clubs include **Discount Travel International** (114 Forrest Ave., Suite 203, Narberth, PA 19072, tel. 215/668–7184; $45 annually, single or family), **Moment's Notice** (425 Madison Ave., New York, NY 10017, tel. 212/486–0503; $45 annually, single or family), **Travelers Advantage** (CUC Travel Service, 49 Music Sq. W, Nashville, TN 37203, tel. 800/548–1116; $49 annually, single or family), and **Worldwide Discount Travel Club** (1674 Meridian Ave., Miami Beach, FL 33139, tel. 305/534–2082; $50 annually for family, $40 single).

Enjoying the Flight Fly at night if you're able to sleep on a plane. Because the air aloft is dry, drink plenty of beverages while on board; remember that drinking alcohol contributes to jet lag, as do heavy meals. Sleepers usually prefer window seats to curl up against; restless passengers ask to be on the aisle. Bulkhead seats, in the front row of each cabin, have more legroom, but since there's no seat ahead, trays attach awkwardly to the arms of your seat, and you must stow all possessions overhead. Bulkhead seats are usually reserved for the disabled, the elderly, and people traveling with babies.

Smoking Since February 1990, smoking has been banned on all domestic flights of less than six hours duration; the ban also applies to domestic segments of international flights aboard U.S. and foreign carriers. On U.S. carriers flying to Europe and other destinations abroad, a seat in a no-smoking section must be provided for every passenger who requests one, and the section must be enlarged to accommodate such passengers if necessary as long as they have complied with the airline's deadline for check-in and seat assignment. If smoking bothers you, request a seat far from the smoking section.

Foreign airlines are exempt from these rules but do provide no-smoking sections, and some nations, including Canada as of July 1, 1993, have gone as far as to ban smoking on all domestic flights; other countries may ban smoking on flights of less than a specified duration. The International Civil Aviation Organization has set July 1, 1996, as the date to ban smoking aboard airlines worldwide, but the body has no power to enforce its decisions.

From North America by Ship

Cunard Line (555 Fifth Ave., New York, NY 10017, tel. 800/221–4770 or 212/880–7545) operates four ships that make transatlantic crossings: The *Queen Elizabeth 2* is the only ocean liner that makes regular transatlantic crossings; the others—the *Sea Goddess I* and *II* and the *Vistafjord*—make repositioning crossings twice a year, as one cruise season ends in Europe and another begins in North America. The *QE2* sails from April through December between Baltimore, Boston, and New York City and Southampton, England. The *Sea Goddess I* and *II* sail between Madeira, Portugal, and St. Thomas in the U.S. Virgin Islands, for their repositioning crossings. The *Vistafjord* sails between Marseilles, France, and Fort Lauderdale, Florida, on its repositioning crossings. Cunard Line offers fly-cruise packages and pre- and post-land packages.

Royal Viking Line (750 Battery St., San Francisco, CA 94111, tel. 800/634–8000) has three ships that cruise out of European ports. Two of the ships make repositioning crossings between Fort Lauderdale and Lisbon, Portugal. Fly/cruise packages are available.

American Star Lines (660 Madison Ave., New York, NY 10021, tel. 800/356–7677 and, in New York, 212/644–7900) makes transatlantic crossings in spring and fall between Greece and Barbados (in the British West Indies). The crossings are regular cruises, with ports of call in Portugal, Italy, Turkey, and the Greek islands. Summer cruises are from Piraeus (Athens), to the Greek islands, and Turkey. Fly/cruise packages are available.

Check the travel pages of your Sunday newspaper for other cruise ships that sail to Europe.

From the United Kingdom by Plane

Air travel from Britain to continental Europe has undergone a quiet revolution during the past few years. Thanks in part to the ever-growing demand for inexpensive charter flights, in part to the British government's determination to break down the cozy system of intergovernmental fare setting, and above all to a stronger sense of a shared European identity, more and more Britons regard flying as an everyday means of transportation rather than as an occasional luxury. The result, as expected, is more flights, greater choice, and lower fares.

But it isn't all good news. For one thing, not all European governments share Britain's enthusiasm for more competitive fares. Of long-term concern is the evident incapacity of European air networks to cope with an explosion in passenger numbers. And, at least at peak periods, more people traveling means more congestion and more delays.

It's not just those in the cheaper seats who suffer, either. Scheduled flights are just as likely to be delayed as charter flights, though they are, it's true, mostly spared the major delays that can afflict the summertime charter flights. Nonetheless, Europe's more militant air-traffic controllers have never been slow to grasp that the most effective way to draw attention to increased work loads and, in many cases, antiquated air-traffic control systems is to go on strike when maximum disruption is guaranteed—in other words, at the busiest times. Shots of beleaguered tourists gamely bedding down for another night at the airport have become a commonplace on Britain's TV screens. France, Spain, and Greece currently head the list of countries with the most strike-happy air controllers.

None of which is intended to suggest that flying from Britain to the Continent is something that can be recommended only to those who don't mind not sleeping for three days. And not least, of course, because everyone agrees that Europe's prosperity depends more than ever on good communications, with air travel well up there in the forefront.

A unified European air-traffic control system in place of the current nationally operated systems may still be only a gleam in the eye of Utopian-minded Europhiles, but a new generation of air-traffic control systems is, at last, being installed in many countries. Once in place, they should improve dramatically the capacity of today's overworked machines. Likewise, in the certain knowledge that routine delays will eventually kill the goose that lays the golden egg, airlines, tour operators, and charter companies have exerted increasing pressure on governments to ensure that strikes become the exception, not the rule.

Scheduled Airlines If flying from a convenient airport, avoiding night flights at awkward hours, and relative reliability are more important to you than just finding the cheapest flight, scheduled flights are a better option than charters. London, with its two main airports—Heathrow and Gatwick—and three subsidiary airports—Luton, Stansted, and London City—is Europe's biggest air hub. Frequent scheduled services connect it with virtually every major European city and resort. British Airways (BA) is the largest single operator, but all other leading international European airlines have flights to and from their own countries. There is never less than one flight a day to all the European capitals; in most cases, many more.

The recent collapse of several smaller British airlines has made BA more dominant. The constantly changing situation, however, has meant that the smaller British airports have, if anything, become busier. Competition from up-and-coming airlines such as British Midland, determined to grab customers from BA, has increased the options available to travelers. These smaller airlines have pioneered routes to European capitals from regional British airports. Manchester, for instance, has become a busy northern hub for several carriers, with shuttle flights to London and several flights a day to Amsterdam and other European points. Other major European airlines also have flights from several regional British airports. Air France, for example, has daily flights from Edinburgh to Paris. Similarly, SAS has a daily flight from Edinburgh to Copenhagen. (Both Glasgow and Edinburgh are linked to London by frequent shuttle flights.)

Most airlines' weekday schedules cater principally to business flyers, who want to fly at clearly defined peak times (generally weekdays, first thing in the morning and late afternoon/early evening). As a result, lower fares are available outside these peak times. Look for better fares on midday flights, and check into weekend fares. Some are less than half the regular economy fares, though note that nearly all require that you spend at least one Saturday night at your destination. As a basic rule of thumb, remember that the cheaper a fare is, the more likely it is to carry restrictions. Always make sure you find out what these are before you buy your ticket.

The busiest routes also tend to be the cheapest. There are ever-more competitive fares between London and Paris and London and Frankfurt. Likewise, fares between London and Brussels are also lower than the European average, mile for mile. Fares between London and Amsterdam can be a bargain, the cheapest in Europe. What's more, there are excellent onward connections from Amsterdam to other European cities.

Finally, remember, too, that few European flights are longer than four hours; the majority, in fact, rarely top two hours. Such short journeys make flying business-class or first-class, where it exists, an unnecessary luxury for most travelers. It's also worth bearing in mind that on most European airlines business class is open to anyone with a full-fare economy (coach class) ticket.

Charter Airlines Charter airlines offer much cheaper fares to Europe than do the scheduled carriers, but the rules that bind them are more restrictive. While the British government turns a blind eye to sales of seat-only charter tickets, some European governments still require proof that you have bought an inclusive package vacation rather than just a flight. Most of the seat-only agencies will therefore give you a voucher stating that you have accommodations at a certain hotel. This is to comply with the rules—it won't necessarily get you a bed, even if you can find the hotel in question!

Greece specifically has expressed its determination to stamp out seat-only traffic by threatening passengers using such tickets with fines or deportation under international rules on charter sales. Its implementation of this rule has, though, been patchy so far.

Charter flights are by far the cheapest form of air transportation to main vacation destinations—particularly in the Mediterranean—and some of the charter fares available to last-minute buyers compare favorably even with bus or rail fares. Moreover, to destinations such as Spain, Greece, Turkey, and Italy, charter flights can give significant savings over scheduled fares. These are countries whose governments have vigorously resisted the introduction of cheaper scheduled fares and that remain zealously protective of their national airlines.

The main drawback of traveling by charter is rigid timetabling. Your return flight will be 7, 14, or 21 days from your departure date. The cheapest flights leave at inconvenient times—mainly in the early hours of the morning—and, in London, from airports a long way from the city center, such as Luton. The other major disadvantage is that charter flights are much more prone to delay than are scheduled flights. Delays of up to two days have been known, though these are admittedly exceptional. But on most flights it nonetheless makes sense to expect some delay, even if it's only an hour or so.

Arrival airports are often resorts rather than capital or major cities. In Spain, most charters fly to the Mediterranean coast rather than to Madrid or Seville; in Portugal, most flights arrive in the Algarve resort area rather than Lisbon. In Greece, this system can be an advantage rather than a drawback—many flights go to the islands rather than to Athens, so if your destination is, for example, Mykonos or Crete, you can fly there direct by charter without having to transfer to a domestic flight or ferry at Athens.

Charters bought at the last minute can be extremely cheap—check in travel agents' windows or in the classified sections of the London *Evening Standard* for cheap late-booking deals. Some of these may be so inexpensive that you may consider discarding the round-trip half of the ticket and traveling onward in Europe from your arrival point, rather than coming back to London.

From the United Kingdom by Car

Nearly all ferries from Britain to the Continent take cars, as does the long-awaited Channel Tunnel. Which route you take will be determined by your eventual destination and how much driving you want to do. The shortest routes are the fastest and the most popular: from Dover, Ramsgate, or Folkestone to Calais, Boulogne, and Ostend. These are the most convenient routes for much of France and Belgium, as well as central and southern Germany, Austria, Switzerland, Italy, and southeast Europe. If you're heading to western France or to Spain and Portugal, then Dieppe, Le Havre, Caen, Cherbourg, and St. Malo are better routes. Similarly, though the cost is much higher (though equally, the driving is greatly reduced) you should consider putting your car on the train in France or taking the ferry to Santander in northern Spain. The best routes to Holland and north Germany are from Dover and Felixstowe to Zeebrugge; from Sheerness to Vlissingen; and from Harwich to the Hook of Holland and Hamburg. If you're heading for Scandinavia, there are sailings from Harwich and Newcastle to Esbjerg in Denmark, Gothenburg in Sweden, and Stavangar and Bergen in Norway. There are regular sailings to Dublin from Holyhead and to Rosslare from Fishguard and Pembroke in Wales.

Unless you're traveling in the dead of winter, and sometimes even then, it's essential to book well in advance (*see* By Ferry/Ship, *below*, for addresses). Rates vary according to the length of your vehicle, the time of day and season you make the crossing. Morning and evening crossings in the summer months are most expensive, and national holidays should be avoided where possible.

Both the **Automobile Association** (Fanum House, Box 31, Basingstoke, Hants. RG21 2BH; tel. 0256/492998) and the **Roy-**

al **Automobile Club** (RAC House, Box 100, South Croydon CR2 6XW, tel. 0800/550–550) operate on-the-spot breakdown and repair services across Europe. Replacement cars can be provided in case of accidents. Both companies will also transport cars and passengers back to Britain in case of serious breakdowns. The AA's **5-Star Cover** costs £20.50 for 1 day, £26.50 for 5 days, £41.50 for 15 days, or £56.50 for 25 days, with extra charges of £1.50 per day up to 25 days and an extra £7 a week after that. Nonmembers are charged an extra £3; membership costs £36. (tel. 0800/800–555 for credit card sales). The RAC's **Eurocover** costs £29.95 for 4 days, £35.95 for 9 days, £49.95 for 16 days, £50.95 for 23 days, or £55.95 for 31 days. Nonmembers pay a £5 surcharge; basic membership costs £67. (tel. 0800/550–055 for credit card sales.)

For advice on whether to bring your own car or to buy or rent one on your trip, *see* Renting and Leasing Cars in Before You Go, *above*.

From the United Kingdom by Ferry/Ship

Ferry routes for passengers and vehicles link the North Sea, English Channel, and Irish Sea ports with almost all of Britain's maritime neighbors.

To France and Belgium By far the fastest and, for most visitors, the most convenient routes are those across the English Channel to France and Belgium. The principal routes are Dover–Calais (operated by **P&O European Ferries, Sealink,** and **Hoverspeed**); Dover–Boulogne (operated by P&O European Ferries and Hoverspeed); Dover–Ostend (operated by P&O European Ferries); Folkestone–Boulogne (operated by Sealink); and Ramsgate–Dunkirk (operated by **Sally Line**). Crossing times vary from 75 minutes for the Dover–Calais sailings to four hours for the Dover–Ostend sailings, depending on sea conditions. Make reservations well in advance for peak periods (Easter, July, and August).

The passengers-only Dover–Ostend Jetfoil (book through P&O European Ferries) is a good bet if you're traveling by train. It makes the crossing in only 100 minutes. But note that it is both more expensive than the regular ferries and much more liable to cancellation in bad weather.

There is a wide choice of other sailings to France: Newhaven–Dieppe (operated by Sealink); Portsmouth–Le Havre or Cherbourg (operated by P&O European Ferries); Southampton–Cherbourg (operated by Sealink); Portsmouth–Caen (operated by **Brittany Ferries**); Portsmouth–St. Malo (operated by Brittany Ferries); Poole–Cherbourg (operated by Brittany Ferries, summer only); and Plymouth–Roscoff (operated by Brittany Ferries). Journey times are longer (ranging from four hours for the Newhaven–Dieppe route to nine hours for the Portsmouth–St. Malo route) and fares higher, but you can avoid a great deal of unnecessary driving across northern France. Again, make reservations well in advance for peak periods.

To Spain and Portugal Brittany Ferries, which runs the St. Malo service, also sails from Plymouth or Portsmouth to Santander in northern Spain. The crossings take 24 and 28 hours respectively and the line's cruise ferries offer economy and luxury cabins, as well as entertainment facilities that include a cinema and restaurants. If you are traveling by car and plan to tour Spain, this route offers you the option of looping back through France and returning to Britain without retracing your tracks. Onward travel into Spain without a car, however, will be time-consuming and is really an option only for those with plenty of time to spare.

To Holland, North Germany, and Scandinavia   There are excellent ferry routes linking British east coast ports with Europe's North Sea coast. Crossings are longer than English Channel routes, and most North Sea ferry lines have adopted the ferry-cruise concept, with cabins with various degrees of comfort and on-board facilities that can include duty-free shopping, bars, restaurants, discos, and casinos.

For Holland and north central Germany, the best routes are Sheerness–Vlissingen (operated by **Olau Line**) and Harwich–Hook of Holland (operated by Sealink). If you're based farther north in England, the Hull–Rotterdam route (operated by **North Sea Ferries**) is also good. North Germany is best served by the Harwich–Hamburg route (operated by **Scandinavian Seaways**), the only direct ferry link with Germany. Services to Scandinavia include Harwich–Esbjerg, Denmark, and Newcastle–Esbjerg (both operated by Scandinavian Seaways); Harwich–Gothenburg, Sweden, and Newcastle–Gothenburg (also operated by Scandinavian Seaways); Newcastle–Stavanger and Bergen, Norway (operated by **Color Line**).

To Ireland   The principal ferry routes to Ireland are Holyhead–Dublin (operated by **B&I**); Holyhead–Dun Laoghaire (operated by Sealink); and Fishguard/Pembroke–Rosslare (operated by Sealink); and Pembroke–Rosslare (operated by B&I). There's a service between Swansea and Cork (operated by **Swansea Cork Ferries**) that runs from March through September. For Northern Ireland, take the Stranraer–Belfast ferry (operated by P&O European Ferries).

Useful Addresses   For information on the services mentioned above, contact:

B&I Line UK Ltd. (150 New Bond St., London W1Y 0AQ, tel. 071/491–8682).
Brittany Ferries (Millbay Docks, Plymouth PL1 3EW, tel. 0752/221321).
Color Line (Tyne Commission Quay, Albert Edward Dock, North Shields NE29 6EA, tel. 091/296–1313).
Hoverspeed (Maybrook House, Queens Gardens, Dover, Kent CT17 9UQ, tel. 0304/240202).
North Sea Ferries (King George Dock, Hedon Rd., Hull HU9 5QA, tel. 0482/795141).
Olau Line (Ferry Terminal, Sheerness, Kent ME12 1SN, tel. 0795/666666).
P&O European Ferries (Channel House, Channel View Rd., Dover, Kent CT17 9TJ, tel. 0303/223000).
Sally Line (Argyle Centre, York St., Ramsgate CT11 9PL, tel. 0843/595522).
Scandinavian Seaways (Scandinavia House, Parkeston Quay, Harwich, Essex CO12 4QG, tel. 0255/240240).
Sealink (Charter House, Park St., Ashford, Kent TN24 8EX, tel. 0223/647047).
Swansea Cork Ferries (Kings Dock, Swansea SA1 8RU, tel. 0792/456116).

From the United Kingdom by Train

Air travel may offer the fastest point-to-point service, car travel the greatest freedom, and bus transportation the lowest fares, but there is still an unparalleled air of romance about setting off for Europe by train from one of the historic London stations.

Boat trains timed to meet ferries at Channel ports leave London from Victoria, Waterloo, Paddington, and Charing Cross stations and connect with onward trains at the main French and Belgian ports. Calais and Boulogne have the best quick connections for Paris (total journey time about six to seven hours using the cross-Channel Hovercraft); the Dover–Ostend Jetfoil service is the fastest rail connection to Brussels (about 5½ hours, station to station), with good rail connections to Germany, northern France, and Poland.

Boat trains connecting with ferries from Harwich to the Dutch and Danish North Sea ports leave from London/Liverpool Street; there are good rail connections from the Dutch ports to Amsterdam and onward to Germany and Belgium and south to France.

For the Republic of Ireland, trains connecting with the ferry services across the Irish Sea leave from London/Paddington.

One-way and round-trip city-to-city tickets, including rail and ferry fares, can be booked in the United States through **BritRail,** either directly or through your travel agent. If you are traveling on one of the European rail passes bookable in the United States or in Britain, you may be entitled to free or discounted ferry crossings (*see* Rail Passes, *above*).

If all international rail journeys have a certain glamour, none has the cachet of the *Venice Simplon–Orient Express.* It's a reconditioned vintage train that, twice weekly from February through November, makes the 32-hour run between London/Victoria and Venice. Style and class abound. Prices are high. A peak-season one-way fare is £880; round-trip, £1,275. You can make reservations in Britain from **VSOE** (Sea Containers House, 20 Upper Ground, London SE1 9PF, tel. 071/620–0003). **Crystal Holidays** (Crystal House, Arlington Rd., Surbiton, Surrey KT6 6BW, tel. 081/390–8513) does short trips in Britain on the Orient Express from £145 (to Leeds Castle), including two lavish meals. In the United States, contact **Orient Express** (Suite 2841, One World Trade Center, New York, NY 10048, tel. 800/223–1588).

The Channel Tunnel Uncertainty has plagued the Channel Tunnel ever since its inception, and at presstime (spring 1993) very little definite information was available. Though there have been delays in construction, officials predict that train service will begin sometime in 1994. Fares have not yet been set.

The tunnel runs from Cheriton (near Folkestone), on England's south coast, to Coquelles (near Calais) in France. It is 31 miles (50 km) long, and consists of two large tunnels for trains, one in each direction, linked by a smaller service tunnel running between them. Cars will be loaded on to a half-mile-long train called Le Shuttle. Special single-story shuttles will carry trucks and buses. The crossing will take about 35 minutes. The tentative schedule has shuttles departing at about 15-minute intervals during the day, hourly during the night, 365 days a year. Eventually regular passenger trains will run direct from London to Paris and Brussels. These trains will run from a special depot in Waterloo, London, with a pickup stop at Ashford, Kent, to the Gare du Nord in Paris, and the Midi Station in Brussels. You will be able to make the entire trip without leaving your seat. Until this service is in operation, travelers without cars can use the tunnel by taking a seat on a bus carried by Le Shuttle. Britain has not yet created any special tracks, so the trip from London to the tunnel will be on normal trains. France has a high speed track ready from the Channel to Paris.

Useful Addresses For information about rail travel to Europe from London, contact **InterCity Europe,** the international wing of **BritRail,** at London/Victoria station (tel. 071/834–2345); bookings can be made by phone using American Express, Diners Club, MasterCard, and Visa (tel. 071/828–0892).

From the United Kingdom by Bus

Freeways (motorways) in the United Kingdom link London with the English Channel ferry ports and make bus travel—connecting with fast ferry, Jetfoil, or Hovercraft crossings—only a little slower than rail travel on the shorter routes into Europe.

Bus travel to cities such as Paris, Brussels, Amsterdam, Rotterdam, and Bruges is by fast and comfortable modern buses with reclining seats, air-conditioning, video entertainment, and airplane-style refreshment carts. There are frequent departures from central London pickup points. Fares by bus are a good deal less than the equivalent rail fare.

Euroways/Eurolines—an international consortium of bus operators—offers a range of day and night services linking London with Amsterdam, Paris, Antwerp, Brussels, and other points en route. Night services to Paris take about 10¼ hours; overnight journey time to Amsterdam is a little more than 13 hours.

Faster **Citysprint** daytime crossings use the Dover–Ostend Jetfoil service en route to Amsterdam, reducing journey time to a little more than eight hours. The fast Hoverspeed crossing to France cuts the day trip time to Paris to just under seven hours. There are also one-day round-trips to Antwerp and Brussels and "Eurobreakaway" holiday packages with accommodations for two or three nights in Paris, Amsterdam, and Brussels.

National Express uses Sealink ferries to the Republic of Ireland. A connecting bus service in Ireland is operated by **Bus Eireann.** Sailings are from Fishguard to Rosslare—a 3½-hour crossing. The onward service goes via Waterford and Cork to Killarney and Tralee.

There are summer buses to the Spanish vacation resorts, aimed mainly at British families on a tight vacation budget. Winter coaches that run to Europe's less pricey ski destinations, notably Andorra and some Italian resorts, can also be inexpensive.

The situation in Yugoslavia at press time means that the road route to Greece through that country is not an option.

Both Euroways/Eurolines and Hoverspeed City Sprint services can be booked in person at **National Express** offices at Victoria Coach Station (52 Grosvenor Gardens, London SW1W OAU, opposite Victoria Rail Station, tel. 071/730–0202), at any National Express agent throughout Britain, and at **Eurolines** (23 Crawley Rd., Luton LU1 1HX, tel. 0582/404–404511).

Getting Around Europe

By Car

Touring Europe by car has tremendous advantages over other ways of seeing the Continent. You can go where you want, when you want, traveling at your own pace, free of the petty restrictions of timetables. But there are pitfalls, too. For the American driver, used to a uniform system of signs and traffic rules from coast to coast, and accustomed to being able to ask directions in English, Europe can be a bewildering experience. On the excellent freeways of northern and central Europe, it's possible to drive through three or four countries in less time than it would take to cross one of the larger of the U.S. states—which means that in one day you may have to cope with perhaps four different languages and four sets of traffic rules!

Road Conditions In general, the richer European countries—France, Germany, Holland, Denmark, the Benelux countries, the United Kingdom, and Italy—all have excellent national highway systems. In Spain, freeway building is proceeding rapidly, and roads are much better than they were even 10 years ago.

By contrast, Greece has just two stretches of freeway-type road—the Odos Ethnikos, or National Road, between Athens and Thessaloníki, and the main road between Athens and Patras.

The Irish Republic's nearest equivalent to freeways are its National Primary Routes, but the low speed limit of 55 mph (88 kph) reflects the fact that their general size and standard falls below the usual European freeway network. Of the Western European countries, Portugal still lags furthest behind in freeway building, but the factor that holds it back—it is the poorest country in Western Europe—also means that far fewer people own cars, so its relatively poor roads are also less crowded.

In Scandinavia, the roads vary according to how far north they are. The harsh winters crack road surfaces in the far north of Norway, Sweden, and Finland. Minor roads have bumps and dips. Otherwise Scandinavia's main roads are well surfaced and refreshingly traffic-free.

Traffic Conditions On the freeway, U.S. drivers may find the pace of European traffic alarming. Speed limits in most countries are set much higher than those in the United States. Even on British motorways, where the upper limit is a very conservative 112 kph (70 mph), it is not uncommon to be passed by vehicles traveling 24–32 kph (15–20 mph) faster than that. On German *autobahns*, French *autoroutes*, or Italian *autostrade*, cars in the fast lane are often moving at 100 mph (113 kph). Much of the time traffic is heavier than is common on U.S. freeways outside major city rush hours.

Consequently, most tourists will find it more rewarding to avoid the freeways and use the alternative main routes. On these roads, where traffic moves more slowly, driving at a more leisurely pace is possible, and stopping en route is easier. This can also save money; many European freeways (such as those of France, Spain, Italy, and Greece) are toll roads, and a day's drive on them can be expensive. If you break down on any of the European highways, you can expect to pay a hefty fee for towing unless you have prudently joined one of the motorist plans offered by one of the many national associations such as the AA or RAC in Britain (*see* From the United Kingdom by Car in Getting to Europe, *above*).

As in many states in the United States, traffic officers in most European countries (with a few exceptions, such as the United Kingdom) are empowered to fine you on the spot for traffic violations. The language barrier will not make your case any easier. In Eastern Europe, police and frontier officials will pay much closer attention to your papers than they do in the West, but roads are emptier and foreign drivers are still a novelty. The language barrier may be greater, but the novelty value has been known to lead to foreigners being let off with a warning when local drivers might be fined for minor offenses.

Road Signs   In some European countries—Bulgaria and Greece, for example—the language barrier is compounded by an alphabet barrier. Main road signs in Greece, for example, are written in the Greek alphabet. The only solution is to carry a good map.

Rules of the Road   In the United Kingdom, the Republic of Ireland, Cyprus, and Gibraltar, cars drive on the left. In other European countries, traffic is on the right. Beware the transition when coming off ferries from Britain or Ireland to the Continent (and vice versa)!

Rush Hours   During peak vacation periods, main routes can be jammed with holiday traffic. In the United Kingdom, try to avoid driving during any of the long bank-holiday (public holiday) weekends, when motorways, particularly in the south, can be totally clogged with traffic. In France and Italy, where huge numbers of people still take a fixed one-month vacation in August, avoid driving during *le départ*, the first weekend in August, when vast numbers of drivers head south; or *le retour*, when they head back.

Frontiers   You may be surprised at the relatively casual approach many European countries have toward border controls for drivers. At many frontiers, you may simply be waved through; it is quite possible, for example, to drive from Amsterdam to Germany, via Belgium and France, without once being stopped for customs or immigration formalities. There are, however, spot checks at all borders, and at some—particularly those checkpoints used by heavy commercial truck traffic—there can be long delays at peak times. Ask tourist offices or motoring associations for latest advice on ways to avoid these tie-ups. If you are driving a rented car, the rental company will have provided you with all the necessary papers; if the vehicle is your own, you will need proof of ownership, certificate of roadworthiness (known in the United Kingdom as a Ministry of Transport, or MOT, road vehicle certificate), up-to-date vehicle tax, and a Green Card proof of insurance, available from your insurance company (fees vary depending on destination and length of stay).

By Train

European railway systems vary from the sublime to the ridiculous in terms of comfort and convenience. France, Germany, and the United Kingdom lead the field in developing high-speed trains, although the latter has fallen behind the other two. The **French National Railroads'** (SNCF's) Train à Grande Vitesse (TGV), for example, takes just 4½ hours to cover the 871 km (540 miles) from Paris to Marseille on the Mediterranean.

Rail Europe (230 Westchester Ave., White Plains, NY 10604, tel. 800/848–7245); has a catalog that outlines train, rental-car, and hotel programs in 23 European countries.

BritRail operates high-speed InterCity trains—with a top speed of 202 kph (125 mph)—on its main intercity routes in England and Scotland. Normal fares apply on the BritRail high-speed services, but there is a supplementary fare for travel on French TGV services.

The German rail system **Deutsche Bundesbahn** (DB, known in the United States as GermanRail) last year wrested the world rail speed record from the French, and its high-speed InterCity trains make rail travel the best public transportation option within Germany.

Swiss trains are not the fastest in Europe, but they are the most punctual and reliable, making onward travel connections remarkably stress-free.

International trains link most European capital cities, including those of Eastern Europe; service is offered several times daily. Generally, customs and immigration formalities are completed on the train by officials who board when it crosses the frontier.

Most European systems operate a two-tier class system. First class costs substantially more; its only outstanding advantage is that it is likely to be less crowded on busier routes. Train journeys in Europe tend to be shorter than in the United States—trains are much faster and distances much shorter—so first-class rail travel is usually a luxury rather than a necessity. Some of the poorer European countries retain a third class, but avoid it unless you are on a rock-bottom budget.

A number of European airlines and railways operate fast train connections to their hub airports, and these can sometimes be booked through the airline's computer reservation service. The *Lufthansa Express* connects Frankfurt and Köln/Bonn airports and is a splendid two-hour scenic journey along the Rhine valley.

Trains in Sweden and Norway offer supreme comfort, but greater distances and the more rugged terrain make for longer journey times; if you are on a tight schedule, you may prefer to take internal flights.

In Italy, there are some excellent rail services between major cities—but be sure that the train you book *is* a main intercity service, not one that stops at every minor station. Off the major lines, Italian rail services are slower and less frequent.

Trains are generally to be avoided in Spain and Portugal as point-to-point transportation—though there are some attractive scenic routes and special tourist trains. In Greece and Turkey anyone but the most fanatical rail traveler will find the more modern, more comfortable buses, with their more frequent service, preferable to the slow, unreliable, crowded, and dirty trains.

Rail travel is vital in Eastern Europe, and services within and between them are better and more comfortable than you might expect. Though usually much slower than the more modern Western European trains, service is frequent and reliable.

Scenic Routes While the high-speed expresses are an ideal and comfortable way of getting from one place to another, travelers who delight in train travel for its own sake will find plenty to please them in Europe's smaller rail lines.

In Norway and Sweden, almost any train journey offers a superb view of some of Europe's most grandiose scenery. The trains of Switzerland, Austria, the Czech Republic, and Slovakia are also a comfortable way to view impressive mountain vistas.

In Switzerland, the *Glacier Express* running between the Alpine resorts of Zermatt, St. Moritz, and Davos is a regular train that has been taken over almost entirely by tourists attracted by the dramatic scenic route. It makes one round-trip a day in winter, and three in summer; reservations are essential.

In Portugal, there are some charming journeys to be made on small local trains. For instance, the rail line north from Oporto to Viana do Castelo and the Spanish border passes through picturesque small towns and crosses over two remarkable river bridges built by Gustav Eiffel, designer of Paris's famed landmark. Branch lines from the same route run through some of Europe's prettiest and least-developed rural countryside.

In many countries, there are special tourist trains, a number of them using historic rolling stock or original steam engines. The *Venice Simplon-Orient Express* uses the original sleeping and dining cars and coaches of Europe's most romantic train (*see* From the United Kingdom by Train in Arriving and Departing, *above*). In Scotland, the *Royal Scot* travels the spectacular glens of the Highlands with antique cars from the heyday of rail travel.

In Spain, a tourist special runs in summer through the pretty north coast country of Cantabria and Asturias, leaving from Santander. From Seville, the luxurious *Andalus Express* uses four vintage cars built in the 1920s and operates five-day rail cruises via Cordoba and Granada to Málaga. The train features its own bar, with live music and dancing, restaurant cars, and a video and game room.

Almost all European countries offer discount rail passes. Many are available in the country (*see* country chapters). Others, for single countries and continent-wide, are available before you leave (*see* Rail Passes, *above*). In addition, travelers under 26 who have resided in Europe for at least six months qualify for the **Inter Rail Card,** an unbeatable value at £180. It gives unlimited rail travel in 24 countries, plus half-price travel within the United Kingdom and discounts of up to 50% on some ferry services to and from the United Kingdom. There are 15-day and one-month cards that allow for unlimited travel in 24 countries for £180, and £260, respectively. All cards are available from rail stations.

Useful Addresses Additional information on rail services and special fares is available from the addresses below or from national tourist offices.

In the United States **Belgian National Railroads** (745 Fifth Ave., New York, NY *and Canada* 10151, tel. 212/758–8130).

BritRail Travel International Inc. (630 Third Ave., New York, NY 10017, tel. 212/575–2667; 94 Cumberland St., Toronto, Ontario M5R 1A3; 409 Granville St., Vancouver, BC V6C 1T2).

French National Railroads (610 Fifth Ave., New York, NY 10020, tel. 212/582–2110; 9465 Wilshire Blvd., Beverly Hills, CA 90212; 11 E. Adams St., Chicago, IL 60603; 2121 Ponce de Leon Blvd., Coral Gables, FL 33114; 360 Post St., Union Sq., San Francisco, CA 94108; 1500 Stanley St., Montreal, Quebec H3A 1Re; 409 Granville St., Vancouver, BC V6C 1T2).

GermanRail (122 E. 42nd St., Suite 1904, New York, NY 10168, tel. 212/922–1616; 625 Statler Office Bldg., Boston, MA 02116, 617/542–0577; 95–97 W. Higgins Rd., Suite 505, Rosemont, IL 60018; 112 S. Ervay St., Dallas, TX 75201; 11933 Wilshire Blvd., Los Angeles, CA 90025; 442 Post St., 6th floor, San Francisco, CA 94102; 8000 E. Girard Ave., Suite 518S, Denver, CO 80231; 2400 Peachtree Rd. NE, Lenox Towers, Suite 1299, Atlanta, GA 30326, tel. 404/266–9555; Bay St., Toronto, Ontario M5R 2C3).

Italian State Railways (666 Fifth Ave., New York, NY 10103, tel. 212/397–2667).

In the United **Austrian Federal Railways** (30 St. George St., London WR1 *Kingdom* 0AL, tel. 071/629–0461).

Belgian National Railways (Premier House, 10 Greycoat Pl., London SW1P 1SB, tel. 071/233–8866).

French Railways (French Railways House, 179 Piccadilly, London, W1V OBA, tel. 071/493–9731).

German Federal Railways (Suite 18, Hudsons Pl., Victoria Station, London SW1X 1JL, tel. 071/233–6558).

Italian State Railways (CIT, Marco Polo House, 3–5 Lansdowne Rd., Croydon, Surrey CR9 1LL, tel. 081/686–0677).

Netherlands Railways (Egginton House, 25–28 Buckingham Gate, London SW1E 6LD, tel. 071/630–1735).

Norwegian State Railways Travel Bureau (21–24 Cockspur St., London SW1Y 5DA, tel. 071/930–6666).

Swiss Federal Railways (Swiss Centre, 1 New Coventry St., London W1V 8EE, tel. 071/734–4577).

For information about rail networks in other European countries, contact their tourist boards in London.

By Plane

Licenses to operate on a given international or internal route are issued by governments, and international route licenses are in most cases still issued on the basis of bilateral agreements between the two countries in question. This means that bus stop–style services, like those so common in the United States, do not yet exist in Europe, though they may begin to appear in the near future. So-called fifth freedom licenses, which grant airlines the right to land and pick up passengers at intermediary points on a given route, are jealously guarded by governments and consequently are hard to come by. This makes touring Europe entirely by air a costly process, and the best bet, if you plan to visit a number of European countries, is to combine air travel with other transportation options.

Hub Airports As in the United States, airlines are developing hub and spoke-style services within Europe. The idea is that you take a transatlantic flight to an airline's hub, then continue on its intra-European services to other European cities. Thus, **SAS** is actively developing Copenhagen as a Scandinavian hub; the Dutch airline **KLM** is doing the same at Amsterdam's Schiphol; **British Airways** at London's Heathrow and Gatwick; and **Lufthansa** at Frankfurt. If you plan to fly to other European cities, one of these hubs is your obvious choice.

Domestic Services Most Western European countries have good internal services linking the capital city with major business and industrial centers and with more remote communities. In Germany, France, and Spain, regional flights tend to connect major business cities rather than areas of touristic interest—though in Spain there is a considerable overlap between the two.

In such countries as Sweden, Norway, Greece, and to some extent the United Kingdom, however, air services are a vital link between remote island and mountain communities and are often subsidized by the central government. In Greece, for example, you can fly very inexpensively between Athens and the islands—though not *between* islands.

Before booking an internal flight, consider the alternatives. Flights from London to Edinburgh take about one hour—airport to airport—while the competing BritRail InterCity train takes 4½ hours. But if you add in the hour needed to get from central London to the airport, the need to check in as much as one hour before departure, the inevitable flight delays, the time spent waiting for luggage on arrival, and the transfer time back into town from Edinburgh Airport—you'll find you may not have saved any more than an hour in travel time for a considerably higher fare. When looking into air travel as an option, remember that distances between European cities can be deceptively short to an eye accustomed to U.S. routings.

Formalities For scheduled flights, you will be asked to check in at least one hour before departure; for charter flights, generally two hours. These are guidelines; if you are traveling with just hand luggage, it is possible to check in as late as 30 minutes before takeoff.

You may be pleasantly surprised by the Green Channel/Red Channel customs systems in operation at most western European airports and at other international frontier posts. Basically, this is an honor system: If you have nothing to declare, you walk through the Green Channel, where there are only random spot luggage checks. If in doubt, go through the Red Channel.

Eastern Europe Eastern European countries need hard Western currency so badly that they try not to set airfares intolerably high. Most routes are served by Western as well as local carriers, and anyone with an eye to comfort and safety will prefer the former.

By Bus

If you have opted for land rather than air travel, the choice between rail and bus is a major decision. In countries such as Britain, France, Germany, and Holland, bus travel was, until recently, something of a poor man's option—slow, uncomfortable, but cheap. Today, though, fast modern buses travel on excellent highways and offer standards of service and comfort comparable to those on trains—but still at generally lower fares. Between major cities and over long distances, trains are almost always faster; buses will take you to places that trains often do not reach.

In several southern European countries—including Portugal, Greece, much of Spain, and Turkey—the bus has supplanted the train as the main means of public transportation, and is often quicker and more comfortable, with more frequent service, than the antiquated national rolling stock. In these countries choose the bus over the rail unless there is a particular scenic rail route or a special tourist train you want to use—but be prepared to discover that the bus is more expensive. Competition among lines is keen, so compare services such as air-conditioning or reclining seats before you buy.

Information   Information on bus transportation in most countries is available from national or regional tourist offices. For reservations on major bus lines, contact your travel agent at home. For smaller bus companies on regional routes, you may have to go to a local travel agency or to the bus line office.

Note that travel agencies may be affiliated with a certain line and won't always tell you about alternative services—you may have to do some legwork to be sure of getting the best service.

By Ferry/Ship

Bounded by the sea on three sides and crossed by a number of major rivers, Europe offers an abundance of choices for anyone who loves water travel. Contact the appropriate national tourist office for more information.

The Baltic   In the north, ferries ply daily between most of the major Baltic ports in Western Europe, as well as between Finnish ports and those of Russia. Baltic crossings are not for those in a hurry—several of them last overnight—and shipping lines operate luxury cruise-ferry vessels with all kinds of entertainment facilities and duty-free shopping.

Major lines include **Silja,** which operates between Finland and Sweden/Germany (book through Scandinavian Seaways); **Viking Line,** which operates between Finland and Sweden (book through Scantours); **Color Line,** which operates between Sweden and Norway; **Stena Line,** which operates between Norway and Sweden (book through Sealink); and **TT-Line,** which operates between Sweden and Germany (book through Olau Lines).

Local ferries ply the Norwegian fjords and are an excellent way of seeing the country, whether you are traveling by car or on public transportation; a fjord trip in midsummer, the time of the Midnight Sun in northern Norway, should not be missed.

Main international Baltic ports are Copenhagen, Gothenburg, Malmö, Stockholm, Helsinki, Kristiansand, and Oslo—also Travemunde in Germany.

Useful Addresses **Viking Line** (Scantours, 8 Spring Gardens, Trafalgar Sq., London SW1A 2BG, tel. 071/839–2927).

For other Baltic ferry lines mentioned here, *see* From the United Kingdom by Ferry/Ship, *above*.

Scotland Ferry services are important, too, in the Scottish Western Isles, where the **Caledonian Macbrayne Ltd.** (Head Office, The Ferry Terminal, Gourock, Renfrewshire PA19 1QP, Scotland; tel. 0475/33755) has enjoyed a virtual monopoly for many years on its services linking the islands to the mainland port of Oban. The northern Scottish islands of the Orkney and Shetland groups are served by sea from Scrabster on the north coast of mainland Scotland—near John O'Groats.

Greece Many island communities have formed cooperative companies to operate services linking their island with others and with Piraeus, the port of Athens. While all Baltic ferries offer high standards of comfort, even luxury, Mediterranean ferry lines observe widely different standards. On Greek ships, for example, you can travel in a first- or second-class cabin or, for a much lower fare, rough it in deck class. The same is true for the international ferries plying between the Italian ports of Bari and Brindisi and the Greek ports of Corfu, Igoumenitsa, and Patras. The age of Greek ferry boats varies widely, too. Some are of pre–World War II vintage, while others—like the *Naxos*, which sails between Piraeus and Crete—are modern vessels.

Flying Dolphin Lines operates fast hydrofoil service from Piraeus to points popular with Athenian vacationers, including the Saronic Gulf islands and resorts on the eastern Peloponnese.

River Travel Major river systems crisscross Europe. Among the many attractive river trips available are a number of luxury cruises on the Rhine and Danube rivers. Contact national tourist offices for details.

The Danube passes through European countries in Western and Eastern Europe, and international cruises are possible. There is also an international hydrofoil service that operates several times a day on the Danube between Budapest in Hungary and Bratislava in Czechoslovakia. For details of Rhine trips, contact **KD German Rhine Line** (170 Hamilton Ave., White Plains, NY 10601, tel. 914/948–3600; 28 South St., Epsom, Surrey KT18 7PF, tel. 0372/742033).

Though a great deal less spectacular than either the Rhine or the Danube, the smaller rivers of Belgium, Holland, France, and other Western European countries can also provide a relaxed and fascinating vacation.

By Bicycle

Bicycling in Europe can be sheer pleasure or unadulterated torment—depending on when you go, where you go, and what you try to do.

If you're planning a European bike trip, you are probably experienced enough not to need advice on equipment and clothing. But it needs to be said that some European countries are far more user-friendly than others toward bicyclists. In countries like Holland, Denmark, Germany, and Belgium, bikes are very much part of the landscape—mainly because the landscape tends to be uniformly flat. City streets and many main roads in these countries have special bike lanes set aside, and car drivers are used to coping with large numbers of bicycle riders.

Cycling is a major sport in Italy, Spain, and Portugal, as well as in France, and there are regular "Tour" road races. Cyclists also get a good deal in the Eastern Bloc countries, where for economic reasons, the bicycle is still an everyday form of transportation.

Northern Scandinavia and Iceland, plus the Alpine countries Austria and Switzerland, with their steep terrain, are destinations only for the serious cyclist. The Scandinavian countries have plenty of excellent-value campsites. Ireland has emptier roads and a gentler landscape than Sweden or Norway and is a pleasant country to bicycle in, though the temptation to sample just one more Guinness at each wayside pub can be a hazard in itself.

Of the wealthier European countries, Britain has the most shameful record when it comes to providing facilities for bicyclists or considering their interests. Riding in London traffic is a stomach-churning experience requiring nerves of steel. Except in remoter areas—such as the north of Scotland—main roads are overcrowded and often dangerous to cyclists.

Bicycle Transport Transporting your bicycle from the United Kingdom to Europe holds no big problems—some ferry lines transport bicycles free, others charge a nominal fee. Shop around. Surprisingly, you can transport your bicycle by air as checked baggage—you won't have to pay extra so long as you are within the 44-pound total baggage allowance.

Most European rail lines will transport bicycles free of charge or for a nominal fee, though you may have to book ahead. Check with the main booking office. One of the joys of biking in Europe is being able to bike one way and return by train or to board a train with your bike when you need to cover long distances or simply when you need to take a rest. SNCF (French Railways) has converted wagons on four of its Motorail services from Boulogne to carry bicycles. Transporting your bike by bus is also possible.

Renting Bicycles Bicycles can be rented by the day or week in most European capitals and are most readily available in cities like Amsterdam and Copenhagen, where cycling is part of the way of life. Local tourist boards are the best source of information on reliable rental agencies with safe bicycles to rent; remember to check on local traffic rules and make sure your insurance covers you in case of an accident. **GermanRail (DB)** rents bicycles at selected stations in summer.

2 Andorra

The coprincipality of Andorra is a country that defies comparison: a tiny, 175-square-mile mountain enclave in the Pyrenees between France and Spain characterized by an odd and anachronistic political system. To trace its origins one must go back to the 12th century, when the French count of Foix ceded the valley of Andorra to the Spanish bishop of Urgell. Centuries of conflict between France and Spain failed to break the bishop's hold. And so, even today, Andorra enjoys dual protection as a coprincipality, ruled democratically but under the watchful eye of the French government (as descendants of the counts of Foix) and the present-day bishop of Urgell. This ancient condition has various modern advantages. Andorra is a low-tax, duty-free haven; a popular holiday center, especially for winter sports; and a unique little country, the only one in the world where Catalan—the language of Barcelona and the Roussillon (in southeastern France)—is the official tongue.

Andorra la Vella, the capital, is now a much-developed tourist center—one vast duty-free shop—but the medieval buildings have been retained and restored. Outside the town, Romanesque churches, bridges, and shrines dot the landscape, and the mountain setting is superb.

Essential Information

Before You Go

When to Go   Winter months bring a huge influx of ski buffs, though any time of year suits those with an eye on Andorra's tax- and duty-free shopping status. Andorra is a paradise for lovers of the outdoors. In winter there is reliable snowfall from December to early April, and efficient ski resorts at Soldeu, Arinsal, Pas de la Casa, and La Massana. In summer, hikers will find magnificent trails on the Grande Randonnée (GR) network and a score of shorter but still demanding routes. Botanists and birdwatchers should arrive by early April, in time for the bird migrations up from Africa and the first flush of spring flowers on the slopes and in the valleys. Be warned that even in summer the nighttime temperatures can drop to freezing.

Climate   The following are the average daily maximum and minimum temperatures for Andorra.

Jan.	43F	6C	May	62F	17C	Sept.	71F	22C
	30	− 1		43	6		49	10
Feb.	45F	7C	June	73F	23C	Oct.	60F	16C
	30	− 1		39	4		42	6
Mar.	54F	12C	July	79F	26C	Nov.	51F	10C
	35	2		54	12		35	2
Apr.	58F	14C	Aug.	76F	24C	Dec.	42F	6C
	39	4		53	12		31	− 1

Currency   The Spanish peseta is the major Andorran currency, but French francs are equally acceptable, and all prices are quoted in both currencies in Andorra. For exchange rates and coinage information, *see* Currency in Chapter 10, France, and Chapter 26, Spain.

What It Will Cost   Andorra's prices are refreshingly easy on the wallet. At press
Sample Prices   time, some sample costs were as follows: Coca-Cola, 90 ptas.;

Andorra

FRANCE

N

Pic de Siguer

Pic de Serrera

Pic de l'Estanyó

El Serrat

Valira del Norte

Coma Pedrosa

Sant Joan
de Caselles

Soldeu

Arinsal   La Cortinada

Canillo

Valira del Orient

N2

Erts

Ordino

■ Sanctuary of
Meritxell

Port de'Envalira

Pal   La Massana

■ Sant Roma
de les Bons

Alt del Griu

Pas de la
Casa

R. d'Arinsae

CG3

Encamp

Pont de
St. Antoni

■ Sant Miguel
d'Engolasters

R. de Aós

Andorra
la Vella ★   Les Escaldes

Pic de Pessons

Santa Coloma

Ramio

R. Madriu

Valira River

CG-1

Certers

Sant Julià
de Loria

SPAIN

Juberri

0   10 miles

0   15 km

cup of coffee, 60 ptas.; ham sandwich, 250 ptas.; glass of beer,
100 ptas.; one-mile taxi ride, 150 ptas.

Customs   Andorra is unusually lax in the matter of customs, duties,
visas, and the like. Non-Europeans can get in with only a passport. Europeans need only an identity card, but as visitors are
usually just waved in, the card is almost an irrelevance. (On the
way *out* of the country, however, be prepared for mega–traffic
jams: The French and Spanish customs officers take their jobs
far more seriously than do their Andorran counterparts.)

Language   Catalan is the official language of Andorra, a tongue shared
with the Catalan people who inhabit the area that includes the
Pyrenees from Barcelona in Spain to Perpignan in France.
French, Spanish, and, increasingly, English are also widely
spoken.

Getting Around

By Car   The maintenance of Andorran roads varies. The one main artery from France into Spain via Andorra la Vella is excellent
and copes with the heaviest traffic, as does the spur north toward the ski resorts at La Massana and Ordino. Elsewhere,
roads are narrow, winding, and best suited to four-wheel-drive
vehicles or, higher up, mules. During the winter, snow tires or
chains are essential.

By Bus   Minibuses connect the towns and villages, and fares are low;
100 ptas. will take you 5 kilometers (3 miles). Details on fares

and services are available at hotels and from tourist offices (*Sindicat d'Iniciativa*).

On Foot Mountainous Andorra is a mecca for hikers, hill-walkers, and backpackers. The mountains are high and the terrain is wild, so a degree of care and experience is advisable. There are two long-distance trails: the GR7, which runs from Portello Blanca on the French frontier to Escaldes on the road to Spain, and the GR75, also called the Ordino Route, a magnificent, high-mountain trail that stretches across the central range. Get details on local treks and walks from tourist offices.

Staying in Andorra

Telephones For the operator or local directory assistance, dial 11. It is not necessary to use Andorra's local area code, 628, when placing a call inside the country.

Mail You can buy Andorran stamps with French francs or Spanish pesetas, though the postal service within the country is free. The Spanish post office in Andorra la Vella is at Joan Maragall; the French post office is at 1 rue Pere d'Urg.

Opening and Closing Times **Banks** are open weekdays 9–1 and 3–5, and Saturday 9–noon. They are closed Sunday.

Churches. Andorra is predominantly Catholic. Most chapels and churches are kept locked around the clock, with the key being left at the closest house. Check with the tourist office for additional details.

Shops open daily 9–8, though some are closed between 1 and 3.

National Holidays January 1; April 4 (Easter Monday); May 1; May 23 (Pentecost Monday); June 23 (St. John); September 8 (La Verge de Meritxell); November 1 (All Saints' Day); December 25.

Local Holidays At Canillo: third Saturday in July and following Sunday and Monday; at Les Escaldes: July 25–27; at Sant Julià de Lòria: last Sunday in July and following Monday and Tuesday; at Andorra la Vella: first Saturday, Sunday, Monday in August; at Encamp and La Massana: August 15–17; at Ordino: September 16, 17.

Dining Andorra is no gastronomic paradise, but there are good restaurants serving French, Spanish, or Catalan cuisine and plenty of restaurants where the visitor will eat well at no great cost. Local dishes worth trying include *truites de casseroles* (a type of omelet with whole trout and mushrooms); *trixat*, a typical peasant dish of potatoes and cabbage; and such local delicacies as jugged *izard* (hare stew); local cheeses, such as *formatge de tup;* and *rostes amb mel* (ham baked with honey). Although most restaurants offer fixed-price menus, a number of more expensive establishments offer only à la carte.

Mealtimes True to their Spanish heritage, Andorrans eat late: Dinners don't usually get under way until 8:30 at least, and lunch is a substantial meal often followed by an afternoon siesta.

Dress Jacket and tie are recommended for restaurants in the top-price categories. Casual dress is acceptable elsewhere.

Ratings The following ratings are for a three-course meal for one person, excluding wine. Best bets are indicated by a star ★.

Category	Cost
Very Expensive	over 5,000 ptas
Expensive	2,500–5,000 ptas
Moderate	1,000–2,500 ptas
Inexpensive	under 1,000 ptas

Lodging The number of Andorran hotels continues to increase, and standards are improving. The architecture is usually functional, but the service is friendly and the facilities are excellent.

Most hotels are open year-round. Reservations are necessary during July and August. Hotel rates often include at least two meals.

Ratings As a general guide, the following price ratings apply for two people in a double room. Best bets are indicated by a star ★.

Category	Cost
Very Expensive	9,000–12,000 ptas
Expensive	6,000–9,000 ptas
Moderate	4,000–6,000 ptas
Inexpensive	2,500–4,000 ptas

Tipping Restaurants and cafés almost always tack on a 10%–15% service charge; if they don't, it's customary to leave a similar amount.

Arriving and Departing

By Plane The nearest international airports are at Barcelona (200 kilometers, 125 miles), Perpignan (136 kilometers, 85 miles), and Toulouse-Blagnac (180 kilometers, 112 miles).

By Train From Barcelona, take the train to Puigcerdá, then the bus to Seo de Urgel and Andorra la Vella; from Madrid, take the train to Lleida and then a bus to Seo de Urgel and Andorra la Vella; from Toulouse, take the train to Ax-les-Thermes or Tour de Carol (on the route to Perpignan), then the bus to Seo de Urgel and Andorra la Vella. Alternatively, take the train from Toulouse to L'Hospitalet (the bus meets the morning train from Toulouse).

By Bus A bus service runs twice daily from Barcelona (Ronda Universidad 4). During the summer there are direct buses from Perpignan and Toulouse to Andorra. The ride from Barcelona, Perpignan, or Toulouse to Andorra la Vella takes from 3½ to 4 hours.

By Car There are only two possible routes—the CG-1, which links Andorra with Spain, or the CG-2, which crosses the French border at the Pas de la Casa. (A third route, CG-3, runs due north from Andorra la Vella and dead-ends a few miles short of the combined French and Spanish borders.)

Important Addresses and Numbers

Tourist Information
Andorra La Vella. Sindicat d'Iniciativa (National Tourist Office, C/. Dr. Vilanova, tel. 628/20214. Open Mon.–Sat. 10–1 and 3–7, Sun. and holidays 10–1).

Barcelona (C/. Mariano Cubí, 159, tel. 93/200–0655, 93/200–0787).

Canillo (Unió Pro-Turisme, Caseta Pro-Turisme, tel. 628/51002).

Encamp (Unió Pro-Foment i Turisme, Plaça Consell General, tel. 628/31405).

Escaldes-Engordany (Unío Pro-Turisme, Plaça dels Co-Prínceps, tel. 628/20963).

La Massana (Unió Pro-Turisme, Plaça del Quart, tel. 628/35693).

Ordino (Oficina de Turisme, Cruïlla d'Ordino, tel. 628/36963).

Pas de la Casa (Unió Pro-Turisme, C./ Bernat III, tel. 628/55292).

St. Julia (Unió Pro Turisme, tel. 628/41352).

Consulates
U.S. (Via Layetana, Barcelona, tel. 93/319–9550). **Canadian** (Nunez de Balboa 35, Madrid, tel. 91/225–9119). **U.K.** (Apartado de Correos 12111, Barcelona, tel. 93/322–2151).

Emergencies
Doctor (tel. 628/21905). **Police** (tel. 628/21222). **Ambulance and Fire** (tel. 628/20020).

Travel Agency
American Express: in the Relax travel agency (Roc dels Escolls 12, Andorra la Vella, tel. 628/22044).

Guided Tours
Tours of the capital and the surrounding countryside are offered by several firms; check with the tourist office for details or call **Excursion Nadal** (tel. 628/21138) or **Solineu Excursion** (tel. 628/23653).

Exploring Andorra

Exploring Andorra takes time. The roads are narrow and steep, the views compel frequent stops, and every village is worth exploring. If possible, do as much sightseeing on foot as time permits.

Overlooking Andorra la Vella's main square is the stone bulk of the **Casa de la Vall** (House of the Valleys), a 16th-century medieval building that today acts as the seat of the Andorran government. A charmingly rustic spot, the Casa contains many religious frescoes of note, some of which were carefully transported here from village churches high up in the Pyrenees. The kitchen is particularly interesting, with a splendid array of ancient copper pots and other culinary implements. *Vall St. Admission free. Open weekdays 9–10 and 3–4, Sat. 9–10.*

The spa town of **Les Escaldes** is about a 15-minute walk from Andorra la Vella. The Romanesque church of **Sant Miguel d'Engolasters** lies on a ridge northeast of the capital and can be reached on foot—allow half a day for the round-trip—or by taxi up a mountain road. The views are well worth the climb. Just beyond Encamp, 6 kilometers (4 miles) northeast, is the 11th-century church of **Sant Romá de les Bons,** situated in a particularly picturesque spot of medieval buildings and mountain scenery.

Midway between Encamp and Canillo on the CG-2 is the **Sanctuary of Meritxell**, the focal point of the country's prodigious religious fervor. The Blessed Virgin of Meritxell is the principality's patron saint, though, oddly enough for such a religious country, this patronage wasn't declared until the late 19th century. The original sanctuary was destroyed by fire in 1972; the new gray stone building looks remarkably like a factory, but the mountain setting is superb. *Admission free. Open weekdays 10–1 and 3:30–6:30, Sat. 10–1.*

Another 3 kilometers (2 miles) farther, just before reaching the town of Canillo, you will see an old six-armed stone cross (actually five-armed, as one has broken off). A mile or so beyond is the Romanesque church of **Sant Joan des Caselles,** whose ancient walls have mellowed with age. The bell tower is stunning, three stories of weathered stone punctuated by rows of arched windows. Inside, the main building is a good example of a reredos (a wall or screen positioned behind an altar). It dates from 1525 and depicts the life of St. John the Apostle.

Retrace your way back to Andorra la Vella, and this time take the CG-3 due north out of the capital. After just a few miles you'll come to an ancient stone bridge, the **Pont de St. Antoni,** which spans a narrow river. Three kilometers (2 miles) farther is the picturesque mountain town of **La Massana;** take some time to stroll along its quaintly rustic streets. Another 5 kilometers (3 miles) farther is the tiny village of **Ordino.** Its medieval church is exceptionally pretty; to see it properly, go at night between 7 and 8, when mass is celebrated.

In **La Cortinada,** a mile or so farther, is the **Can Pal,** another fine example of medieval Andorran architecture. This time the building is a privately owned manor house (strictly no admittance), with a pretty dovecote attached. Note the turret perched high up on the far side.

Backtrack once more to Andorra la Vella, then take the CG-1 south. Within a few miles you'll come to the church of **Santa Coloma,** in the village bearing the same name; parts of the church date from the 10th century, and there are splendid Romanesque frescoes on the interior walls.

Shopping

Visitors to Andorra often list the shopping as one of the main attractions, but not all the goods displayed are actually at bargain prices. The French and Spanish come here to buy cigarettes, liquor, household items, and foodstuffs, but find electrical goods and cameras no cheaper than they are at home. Good buys are consumable items: perfume, cigarettes, whiskey, and gin. For cameras, tape recorders, and other imported items, compare prices and models carefully. The main shopping center is Andorra la Vella, but there are shops in all the new developments and in the towns close to the frontiers, at Pas de la Casa and Sant Julia de Loria.

Dining and Lodging

For details and price category definitions, *see* Dining and Lodging in Staying in Andorra.

Andorra la Vella
Dining

Chez Jaques. The varied menu features both classical and nouvelle French dishes, though other international cuisines are handled with flair. With good food and a cozy ambience, it's very popular with the locals. *Av. Tarragona, tel. 628/20325. Reservations accepted. AE, DC, MC, V. Closed July and Aug. Expensive.*

La Truita. A lively atmosphere enhances the local specialty, fresh mountain trout. La Truita offers simple Andorran cuisine, good service, and a small terrace for dining al fresco in good weather. *7 Avenida Meritxell 58, tel. 628/20773. Reservations accepted. AE, DC, MC, V. Expensive.*

★ **Versailles.** A tiny and authentic French bistro with only a handful of tables, Versailles is always packed. Leave room for pastries after the magret of duck! *Cap del Carrer 1, tel. 628/21331. Reservations advised. DC, MC, V. Closed Wed. and Thurs. lunch. Moderate.*

Niça. This is a simple local restaurant specializing in mountain trout. The atmosphere is unremarkable, but the trout is deliciously fresh. *Cap del Carrer 2, tel. 628/20825. No reservations. No credit cards. Inexpensive.*

Lodging

★ **Andorra Palace.** The large and modern Palace is widely considered one of the capital's best hotels. The rooms are spacious and the furnishing smartly contemporary. The outdoor terrace is a pleasant spot in which to relax and watch the bustle below. *Carrer Prat de la Creu, tel. 628/21072, fax 628/28245. 140 rooms with bath. Facilities: restaurant, parking, bar, sauna, fitness center, pool. AE, DC, MC, V. Very Expensive.*

Andorra Park. The Park ranks with the Palace as one of Andorra la Vella's two top hotels. It's a grand building away from the city's congestion of traffic and pedestrians. The American Bar is a popular watering hole for local society. There's a pretty garden, as well as a terrace and the deluxe guest rooms have private balconies. *Roureda de Guillemo, tel. 628/20979, fax 628/20983. 40 rooms with bath. Facilities: restaurant, tennis courts, croquet, parking, bar, pool. AE, DC, MC, V. Very Expensive.*

President. This modern hotel is clean and tidy and offers good value rather than charm. The restaurant commands a particularly dramatic mountain view. *40 av. Santa Coloma, tel. 628/22922, fax 628/61414. 88 rooms with bath. Facilities: bar, restaurant, sauna, pool. DC, MC, V. Very Expensive.*

Hotel Eden Roc. This small hotel has all the amenities of larger hotels and offers an exceptional dining room and attentive personal service. *Av. Dr. Mitjavlia 1, tel. 628/21000, fax 628/60319. 56 rooms with bath. Facilities: restaurant, bar, terrace. AE, V. Expensive.*

Florida. This cheerful hotel offers good value at relatively inexpensive rates. There's no restaurant, but there are several nearby. *Carrer La Llacuna 15, tel. 628/20105, fax 628/61975. 52 rooms, 32 with bath. Facilities: bar, lounge. DC, MC, V. Moderate.*

Encamp
Lodging

Belvedere. An expatriate English couple runs this friendly little inn, which is set amid some amazing mountain scenery. The exceptionally clean rooms tend toward the small side. *Carrer*

Ballàvista, tel. 628/31263. 10 rooms, 1 with bath. Facilities: restaurant, bar, garden, terrace. No credit cards. Closed mid-Oct.–mid-Dec. Moderate.

Les Escaldes
Dining
★

1900. The 1900 is a small, beautifully decorated restaurant that serves the best food in the principality, with a mixture of French, Spanish, and Andorran cuisines. It's expensive for Andorra, but Chef Alain Despretz's inventive cuisine is often worth it. *11 Carrer de la Unio, tel. 628/26716. Reservations advised. AE, DC, MC, V. Closed Mon. and July. Expensive.*

Lodging
★

Roc Blanc. Sleek, modern, and luxurious trappings—and a wealth of facilities to pamper the body, from mud baths to acupuncture—are what the Roc Blanc is all about. The rooms are large, and the hotel's restaurant, El Pi, is consistently good. *Plaça Co-Princeps 5, tel. 628/21486, fax 628/60244. 240 rooms with bath. Facilities: restaurant, piano bar, 2 pools, sauna, tennis courts, health club, thermal baths, hairdresser, terrace. AE, DC, MC, V. Very Expensive.*

Pas de la Casa
Dining

Le Grizzly. This is a popular French restaurant for lunch or dinner, especially during the ski season. The food is simple but well prepared, and it offers good value, with a choice of four fixed-price menus, from 800 to 1,300 ptas. Try the *entrecote roquefort* (steak) and the thick Provençal soups. *Calle Principal, tel. 628/55227. Reservations advised. AE, V. Inexpensive–Moderate.*

Sant Julia de Loria
Lodging
★

Pol. Gracefully modern surroundings and friendly staff are just two reasons why this hotel is so popular. Its disco is a popular nightspot. *Av. Verge de Canolich 52, tel. 628/41122, fax 628/41852. 80 rooms with bath. Facilities: restaurant, bar, garden, terrace. AE, MC, V. Moderate.*

3 Austria

What Austria lacks in size, it more than makes up for in diversity. Its Alps and mountain lakes in the central and southern provinces rival those of neighboring Switzerland; the vast Vienna Woods remind some of the Black Forest; the steppes of the province of Burgenland blend with those across the border in Hungary; and the vineyards along the Danube rival those of the Rhine and Mosel river valleys. In addition, nowhere else is there a Vienna or a Salzburg—or such pastry shops!

Austria has become considerably more expensive in recent years. But there are still bargains to be found, and discovering them can be one of the diversions of a vacation in Austria.

The country is highly accessible. There are virtually no outposts that are not served by public transport of one form or another. The rail network is well maintained, and trains are fast, comfortable, and punctual. Highways are superb and well marked. Public transportation in the cities, although not cheap, is safe, clean, and convenient. In short, the visitor to Austria spends more time having fun than coping with the logistics of getting from A to B.

The Austrians are for the most part friendly and welcoming. They are an outdoor people, given to heading off to the ski slopes, the mountains, the lakes, and the woods at a moment's notice. At the same time, they can be as melancholy as some of the songs of their wine taverns would suggest. Communication is seldom a problem, since most Austrians speak another language besides their native German, and English is the usual choice.

What you'll discover in conversation with Austrians is that they are more for evolution than revolution, so change is gradual, and old values tend to be maintained. Graceful dancers do execute the tricky "left waltz" on balmy summer evenings in Vienna, and at any time you may find an entire town celebrating some event, complete with brass band in lederhosen.

Essential Information

Before You Go

When to Go Austria has two main tourist seasons. The summer season starts at Easter and runs to about mid-October. The most pleasant months weather-wise are May, June, September, and October. June through August are the peak tourist months, and aside from a few overly humid days when you may wish for the wider use of air-conditioning, even Vienna is pleasant; the city literally moves outdoors in summer. The winter cultural season starts in October and runs into June; the winter sports season gets under way in December and lasts until the end of April, although you can ski in selected areas well into June and on some of the highest glaciers year-round. Some events—the Salzburg Festival is a prime example—make a substantial difference in hotel and other costs. Nevertheless, bargains are available in the (almost nonexistent) off-season.

Climate Summer can be warm; winter, bitterly cold. The southern region is usually several degrees warmer in summer, several degrees colder in winter. Winters north of the Alps can be

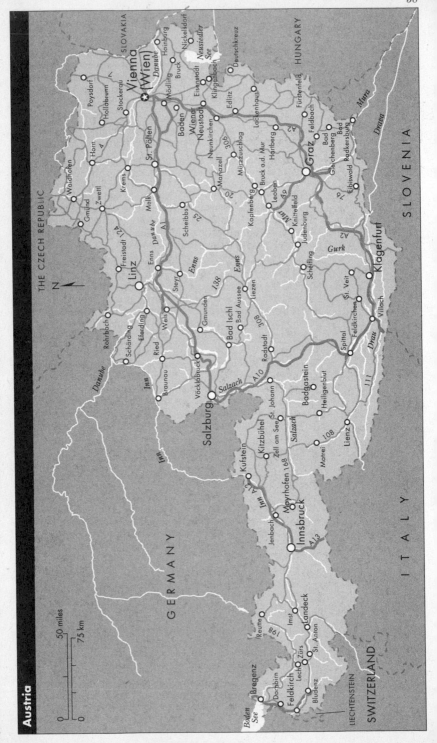

Austria

THE CZECH REPUBLIC

SLOVAKIA

HUNGARY

GERMANY

SLOVENIA

ITALY

SWITZERLAND

LIECHTENSTEIN

Vienna (Wien)

Poysdorf
Hollabrunn
Stockerau
Mistelbach
Hainburg
Nickelsdorf
Neusiedler See
Deutschkreuz
Waldhofen
Horn
Zwettl
Krems
Mödling
Baden
Eisenstadt
Klingenbach
Edlitz
Lockenhaus
Fürstenfeld
Feldbach
Bad Radkersburg
Gmünd
Freistadt
Melk
St. Pölten
Wiener Neustadt
Neunkirchen
Mariazell
Mürzzuschlag
Bruck a.d. Mur
Hartberg
Graz
Bad Gleichenberg
Eibiswald
Linz
Enns
Scheibbs
Kapfenberg
Leoben
Judenburg
Knittelfeld
Scheifling
St. Veit
Klagenfurt
Rohrbach
Schärding
Efferding
Ried
Wels
Steyr
Gmunden
Bad Ischl
Bad Aussee
Liezen
Radstadt
Gurk
Feldkirchen
Spittal
Villach
Braunau
Vöcklabruck
Salzburg
Kufstein
Kitzbühel
Zell am See
St. Johann
Badgastein
Heiligenblut
Lienz
Matrei
Jenbach
Mayrhofen
Innsbruck
Reutte
Imst
Landeck
St. Anton
Bregenz
Dornbirn
Feldkirch
Lech
Zürs
Bludenz

Danube
Inn
Enns
Salzach
Mur
Drau
Gurk
Mura
Drava
Boden See

50 miles
75 km

N

A1
A2
A9
A10
A13
A14
306
20
75
138
308
168
108
861
111

overcast and dreary, whereas the south basks in winter sunshine.

The following are the average daily maximum and minimum temperatures for Vienna.

Jan.	34F	1C	May	67F	19C	Sept.	68F	20C
	25	-4		50	10		53	11
Feb.	38F	3C	June	73F	23C	Oct.	56F	14C
	28	-3		56	14		44	7
Mar.	47F	8C	July	76F	25C	Nov.	45F	7C
	30	-1		60	15		37	3
Apr.	58F	15C	Aug.	75F	24C	Dec.	37F	3C
	43	6		59	15		30	-1

Currency The unit of currency is the Austrian schilling (AS), divided into 100 groschen. There are AS 20, 50, 100, 500, 1,000, and 5,000 bills; AS 1, 5, 10, and 20 coins; and 1-, 2-, 10-, and 50- groschen coins. The 1- and 2-groschen coins are scarce, and the AS20 coins are unpopular—though useful for some cigarette machines. The 500- and 100-schilling notes look perilously similar; confusing the two can be an expensive mistake.

At press time (spring 1993), there were about AS11.5 to the dollar and about AS17 to the pound sterling.

Credit cards are widely used throughout Austria, although not all establishments take all cards. American Express has money machines in Vienna at Parkring 10 (actually in Liebenberggasse, off Parkring) and at the airport.

Cash traveler's checks at a bank, post office, or American Express office to get the best rate. All charge a small commission; some smaller banks or "change" offices may give a poorer rate *and* charge a higher fee. All change offices at airports and the main train stations in major cities cash traveler's checks. Bank-operated change offices in Vienna with extended hours are located on Stephansplatz and in the Opernpassage. The Bank Austria machines on Stephansplatz and on Kärntnerstrasse 51 (to the right of the opera) and at the Raiffeisenbank on Kohlmarkt (at Michaelerplatz) change bills in other currencies into schillings, but rates are poor and a hefty commission is automatically deducted.

You may bring in any amount of foreign currency or schillings and take out any amount with you.

What It Will Cost Austria is not inexpensive, but since inflation is negligible, costs remain fairly stable. Vienna and Salzburg are the most expensive cities, along with such fashionable resorts as Kitzbühel, Seefeld, Badgastein, Bad Hofgastein, Velden, Zell am See, Pörtschach, Lech, and Zürs. Many smaller towns offer virtually identical facilities at half the price.

Drinks in bars and clubs are considerably higher than in cafés or restaurants. Austrian prices include service and tax.

Sample Prices Cup of coffee, AS25; half-liter of draft beer, AS27–AS35; glass of wine, AS35; Coca-Cola, AS25; open sandwich, AS25; theater ticket, AS200; concert ticket, AS250; opera ticket, AS600 and up; one-mile taxi ride, AS32.

Customs on Arrival Austria's duty-free allowances are as follows: 200 cigarettes or 100 cigars or 250 grams of tobacco, 2 liters of wine and 1 liter of spirits, 1 bottle of toilet water (about 300-milliliter size), 50 milliliters of perfume for those aged 18 and over arriving from other European countries. These limits may be liberalized or eliminated under the terms of the European Economic Area agreement. Visitors arriving from the United States, Canada, or other non-European points may bring in twice the above amounts.

Language German is the official national language. In larger cities and most resort areas, you will have no problem finding those who speak English; hotel and restaurant staff, in particular, speak English reasonably well. Most younger Austrians speak at least passable English, even if fluency is relatively rare.

Getting Around

By Car
Road Conditions The highway system is excellent, and all roads are well maintained and well marked. Secondary mountain roads may be narrow and winding, but traffic is generally light. Check the condition of mountain roads in winter before starting out: Many mountain passes are closed, though tunnels are kept open.

Rules of the Road Drive on the right. Seat belts are compulsory in front. Speed limits are as posted; otherwise, 130 kph (80 mph) on expressways, 100 kph (62 mph) on other main roads, 50 kph (31 mph) in built-up areas. Some city center areas have speed limits of 30 kph (19 mph). The right-of-way is for those coming from the right (especially in traffic circles) unless otherwise marked. A warning triangle—standard equipment in rental cars—must be set up in case of breakdown.

Parking Observe signs; tow-away in cities is expensive. Overnight parking in winter is forbidden on city streets with streetcar lines.

Gasoline Prices—AS9–AS10 per liter—are fairly consistent throughout the country. Only unleaded (*bleifrei*)—regular and premium—is sold in Austria.

Breakdowns Emergency road service is available from **ARBÖ** (tel. 123 nationwide) or **ÖAMTC** (tel. 120). Special phones are located along autobahns and major highways.

By Train Trains in Austria are fast and efficient, and most lines have now been electrified. Hourly express trains run on the key Vienna–Salzburg route. All principal trains have first- and second-class cars, as well as smoking and nonsmoking areas. Overnight trains have sleeping compartments, and most trains have dining cars. If you're traveling at peak times, a reserved seat—available for a small additional fee—is always a good idea.

Fares If you're visiting other European countries, a **Eurail Pass** (*see* Getting Around Europe, in Chapter 1, for details), valid throughout most of Europe, is the best deal. Austria has only two discount tickets. A **Bundesnetzkarte** offers unlimited travel for a month and costs AS5,400 for first class and AS3,600 for second class. The alternative is a **Rabbit** card, which is good for unlimited travel on any four days within a 10-day period. The cost is AS1,700 for first class and AS1,130 for second class unless you're under 27, in which case it costs AS1,050 for first class, AS700 for second class. Full details are available from travel agents or from the Austrian National Tourist Office.

By Plane Domestic service is expensive. **Austrian Airlines** flies between Vienna and Linz, Salzburg, Graz, and Klagenfurt. **Tyrolean Airlines** has service from Vienna to Innsbruck. **Rheintalflug** flies between Vienna and Altenhausen, just over the border in Switzerland, with bus connections to Feldkirch, Bregenz, and Bludenz in Vorarlberg.

By Bus Service is available to virtually every community accessible by highway. Winter buses have ski racks. Vienna's central bus terminal (Wien-Mitte/Landstrasse Hauptstrasse, opposite the Hilton) is the arrival/departure point for international bus routes; in most other cities the bus station is adjacent to the train station.

By Boat Boats ply the Danube from Passau in Germany all the way to Vienna and from Vienna to Bratislava (Slovakia), Budapest (Hungary), and the Black Sea. Only East European boats run beyond Budapest. Overnight boats have cabins; all have dining. The most scenic stretches in Austria are from Passau to Linz and through the Wachau Valley (Melk, Krems). From Vienna, there are day trips you can take upstream to the Wachau and downstream to Bratislava and Budapest. There are also special moonlight dancing and jazz excursions. Make reservations from **DDSG** (the Danube Steamship Company) in Vienna (tel. 0222/217100) or travel agents.

By Bicycle Bicycles can be rented at many train stations and returned to any of them. Most trains and some postal buses will take bikes as baggage. Bikes can be taken on the Vienna subway (year-round, Sun. all day; Oct.–Apr., Sat. after 2 PM; May–Sept., weekdays 9–3 and after 6:30, Sat. after 9 AM). Marked cycling routes parallel most of the Danube.

Staying in Austria

Telephones
Local Calls Pay telephones take AS 1, 5, 10, and 20 coins. A three-minute local call costs AS1. Emergency calls are free. Instructions are in English in most booths. Add AS1 when time is up to continue the connection. If you will be phoning frequently, get a phone "credit card" at a post office. This works in all *Wertkartentelefon* phones; the cost of the call will be deducted from the card automatically. Cards cost AS95 for AS100 worth of phoning, AS48 for calls totaling AS50.

Phone numbers throughout Austria are being changed. A sharp tone indicates no connection or that the number has been changed.

International Calls It costs more to telephone *from* Austria than it does to telephone *to* Austria. Calls from post offices are least expensive. Hotels time all calls and charge a "per unit" fee according to their own tariff, which can add AS100 or more to your bill. To avoid this charge, call overseas and ask to be called back. To make a collect call—you can't do this from pay phones—dial the operator and ask for an *R* (pronounced "err")-*Gespräch*.

International Information Dial 08 or 1614. Most operators speak English; if yours doesn't, you'll be passed to one who does.

Mail
Postal Rates Airmail letters to the United States and Canada cost AS11.50 minimum; postcards cost AS8.50. Airmail letters to the United Kingdom cost AS7; postcards cost AS6. An aerogram costs AS12.

Receiving Mail   American Express offices in Vienna, Linz, Salzburg, and Innsbruck will hold mail at no charge for those carrying an American Express credit card or American Express traveler's checks.

VAT Refunds   Value-added tax (VAT) at 20% is charged on all sales and is automatically included in prices. If you purchase goods worth AS1,000 or more, you can claim the tax back as you leave or once you've reached home. Ask shops where you buy the goods to fill out and give you the necessary papers. Get them stamped at the airport or border by customs officials (who may ask to see the goods). You can get an immediate refund of the VAT at the airport or at main border points, less a service charge, or you can return the papers by mail to the shop(s), which will then deal with the details. The VAT refund can be credited to your credit-card account or paid by check.

Opening and Closing Times   **Banks** are open weekdays 8–noon or 12:30 and 1:30–3 or 4. Hours vary from one city to another. Principal offices in cities stay open during lunch.

Museums. Opening days and times vary considerably from one city to another and depend on the season, the size of the museum, budgetary constraints, and assorted other factors. Your hotel or the local tourist office will have current details.

Shops are open weekdays from 8 or 9 until 6 and Saturday until noon or 1 only, except the first Saturday of every month, when they stay open until 5. Some shops in larger cities are open on Thursday evenings until 8 PM. Many smaller shops close for one or two hours at midday.

National Holidays   January 1; January 6 (Epiphany); April 3, 4 (Easter); May 1 (May Day); May 12 (Ascension); May 22, 23 (Pentecost); June 2 (Corpus Christi); August 15 (Assumption); October 26 (National Day); November 1 (All Saints' Day); December 8 (Immaculate Conception); December 25, 26.

Dining   Take your choice of sidewalk *Wurstl* (frankfurter) stands, *Imbissstube* (quick-lunch stops), cafés, Heuriger wine restaurants, self-service restaurants, modest *Gasthäuser* neighborhood establishments with local specialties, and full-fledged restaurants in every price category. Most establishments post their menus outside. Shops that sell coffee beans (such as Eduscho) also offer coffee by the cup at prices that are considerably lower than those in a café. Many Anker bakery shops also offer tasty *Schmankerl* (snacks) and coffee. Butcher shops (*Fleischer* or *Fleischhauer*) may also offer soup and a main course at noon. A growing number of shops and snack bars offer pizza by the slice.

Mealtimes   Austrians often eat up to five meals a day: a very early Continental breakfast of rolls and coffee; a slightly more substantial breakfast *(Gabelfrühstück)* with eggs or cold meat, possibly even a small goulash, at mid-morning (understood to be 9, sharp); a main meal at noon; afternoon coffee *(Jause)* with cake at teatime; and, unless dining out, a light supper to end the day.

Dress   A jacket and tie are generally advised for restaurants in the top price categories. Otherwise casual dress is acceptable, although in Vienna formal dress (jacket and tie) is preferred in some moderate restaurants at dinner. When in doubt, it's best to dress up.

Ratings Prices are per person and include soup and a main course, usually with salad, and a small beer or glass of wine. Meals in the top-price categories will include a dessert or cheese and coffee. Prices include taxes and service (but leaving an additional 4%–5% is customary). Best bets are indicated by a star ★.

Category	Major City	Other Areas
Very Expensive	over AS800	over AS600
Expensive	AS500–AS800	AS400–AS600
Moderate	AS200–AS500	AS170–AS400
Inexpensive	under AS200	under AS170

Lodging Austrian hotels and pensions are officially classified using from one to five stars. These grades broadly coincide with our own four-way rating system. No matter what the category, standards for service and cleanliness are high. All hotels in the upper three categories have either a bath or shower in the room; even the most inexpensive accommodations provide hot and cold water. Accommodations include castles and palaces, conventional hotels, country inns *(Gasthof)*, motels (considerably less frequent), and the more modest pensions.

Ratings All prices quoted here are for two people in a double room. Though exact figures vary, a single room generally costs more than 50% of the price of a comparable double room. Breakfast—which can be anything from a simple roll and coffee to a full and sumptuous buffet—is usually included in the room rate. In the top five-star hotels, however, it is extra (and expensive). Best bets are indicated by a star ★.

Category	Major City	Other Areas
Very Expensive	over AS2,300	over AS1,800
Expensive	AS1,250–AS2,300	AS1,000–AS1,800
Moderate	AS850–AS1,250	AS700–AS1,000
Inexpensive	under AS850	under AS700

Tipping Railroad porters get AS10 per bag. Hotel porters or bellhops get AS5–AS10 per bag. Doormen get AS10 for hailing a cab and assisting. Room service gets AS10 for snacks and AS20 for full meals. Maids get no tip unless your stay is a week or more, or special service is rendered. In restaurants, 10% service is included. Add anything from AS5 to AS50, depending on the restaurant and the size of the bill.

Vienna

Arriving and Departing

By Plane All flights use Schwechat Airport, about 16 kilometers (10 miles) southwest of Vienna (tel. 0222/71110–2231).

Between the Airport and Downtown Buses leave from the airport for the city air terminal (tel. 0222/5800–35404) by the Hilton on Wien-Mitte-Landstrasse Hauptstrasse every half hour from 5 to 8:30 AM and every 20 minutes from 8:50 AM to 7:30 PM, then every half hour to 11:30 PM. Buses also run every hour from the airport to the Westbahnhof (west train station) and the Südbahnhof (south train station). Be sure you get on the right bus! The one-way fare for all buses is AS60. A taxi from the airport to downtown Vienna costs about AS330–AS350; agree on the price in advance. Cabs (legally) do not meter the drive, as fares are more or less fixed (legally again) at about double the meter fare. A seat in a limousine costs less; book at the airport. **Mazur** (tel. 0222/711-10-6422 or 711-10-6491) offers cheaper pickup and delivery service by arrangement. If you are driving from the airport, follow signs to "Zentrum."

By Train Vienna has four train stations. The principal station, Westbahnhof, is for trains to and from Linz, Salzburg, and Innsbruck. Trains from Germany and France arrive here, too. The Südbahnhof is for trains to and from Graz, Klagenfurt, Villach, and Italy. Franz-Josefs-Bahnhof is for trains to and from Prague, Berlin, and Warsaw. Go to Wien-Mitte (Landstrasse) for local trains to and from the north of the city. Budapest trains use the Westbahnhof and Südbahnhof, and Bratislava trains use Wien-Mitte and Südbahnhof, so check.

By Bus If you arrive by bus, it will probably be at the central bus terminal, Wien-Mitte, opposite the city air terminal (and the Hilton).

By Boat All Danube riverboats dock at the DDSG terminal on Mexikoplatz. There's an awkward connection with the U-1 subway from here. Some boats also make a stop slightly upstream at Heiligenstadt, Nussdorf, from which there is an easier connection to the U-4 subway line.

By Car Main access routes are the expressways to the west and south (Westautobahn, Südautobahn). Routes to the downtown area are marked "Zentrum."

Getting Around

Vienna is fairly easy to explore on foot; as a matter of fact, much of the heart of the city—the area within the Ring—is largely a pedestrian zone. The Ring itself was once the city ramparts, torn down just over a century ago to create today's broad, tree-lined boulevard.

Public transportation is comfortable, convenient, and frequent, though not cheap. Tickets for bus, subway, and streetcar are available in most stations. Tickets in multiples of five are sold at cigarette shops, known as Tabak-Trafik, or at the window marked "Vorverkauf" at central stations such as Karlsplatz or Stephansplatz. A block of five tickets costs AS75, a single ticket AS20. If you plan to use public transportation frequently, get a **24-hour ticket** (AS45), a **three-day tourist ticket** (AS115), or an **eight-day ticket** (AS235). Maps and information are available at Stephansplatz, Karlsplatz, and Praterstern U-Bahn stations.

By Bus or Streetcar Inner-city buses are numbered 1A through 3A and operate weekdays to about 7:40 PM, Saturday until 2 PM. Reduced fares (buy a **Kurzstreckenkarte**; it gives four trips for AS30) are available for these routes as well as designated shorter stretches (roughly two to four stops) on all other bus or streetcar lines. Streetcars and buses are numbered or lettered according to route, and they run until about midnight. Night buses marked N follow special routes every hour on Saturdays and nights before holidays; the fare is AS25. The central terminal point is Schwedenplatz. The Nos. 1 and 2 streetcar lines run the circular route around the Ring, clockwise and counterclockwise, respectively.

By Subway Subway lines (U-Bahn; stations are marked with a huge blue "U") are designated U-1, U-2, U-3, U-4, and U-6 and are clearly marked and color-coded. Additional services are provided by a fast suburban train, the S-Bahn, indicated by a stylized blue "S" symbol. Both are tied into the general city fare system.

By Taxi Cabs can be flagged on the street if the "Frei" (free) sign is illuminated. Alternatively, dial 60160, 31300, or 40100 to call for one. All rides are metered. The basic fare is AS22, but expect to pay AS60 for an average city ride. There are additional charges for luggage and a night and Sunday surcharge of AS10.

Important Addresses and Numbers

Tourist Information City Tourist Office (Kärntnerstr. 38, behind the opera, tel. 0222/513–8892). Open daily 9–7.

Embassies U.S. (Gartenbaupromenade [Marriott Bldg., Parking 12a], tel. 0222/31339). **Canadian** (Dr. Karl Lueger-Ring 10, tel. 0222/533–3691). **U.K.** (Jauresg. 12, tel. 0222/713–1575).

Emergencies Police (tel. 133), **Ambulance** (tel. 144), **Doctor:** ask your hotel, or in an emergency, phone your embassy or consulate (*see* above). **Pharmacies:** open weekdays 8–6, Saturday 8–noon.

English-Language Bookstores Big Ben Bookshop (Porzellang. 24, tel. 0222/319–6412), **British Bookshop** (Weihburgg. 8, tel. 0222/512–1945), **English Book Shop** (Plankeng. 7, tel. 0222/512–3701–11), **Shakespeare & Co.** (Sterng. 2, tel. 0222/535–5053).

Travel Agencies American Express (Kärntnerstr. 21–23, tel. 0222/51540), **Austrian Travel Agency** (Opernring 3–5, tel. 0222/588628), **Wagons-Lits** (Kärntner Ring 2, tel. 0222/501600).

Guided Tours

Orientation Tours Vienna Sightseeing Tours (tel. 0222/712–4683) offers a short highlights tour or a lengthier one to the Vienna Woods, Mayerling, and other areas surrounding Vienna. Tours start in front of or beside the opera house. **Cityrama** (tel. 0222/534130) provides city tours with hotel pickup; tours assemble opposite the InterContinental Hotel.

Special-Interest Tours Tours are available to the Spanish Riding School, the Vienna Boys Choir, operettas and concerts, the wine suburb of Grinzing, nightclubs, and Vienna by night. Check with the city tourist office or your hotel for details.

Walking Tours *Vienna from A to Z* (in English) is available at most bookstores; it explains the numbered plaques attached to all major buildings in Vienna. *Vienna: Downtown Walking Tours* by Henriette Mandl outlines suggested routes and provides information on sights.

Excursions Day bus trips are organized to the Danube Valley, the Hungarian border, the Alps south of Vienna, Salzburg, and Budapest; get information from the city tourist office.

Exploring Vienna

Vienna has been described as an "old dowager of a town," not a bad description for this onetime center of empire. It's not just the aristocratic and courtly atmosphere, with monumental doorways and stately facades of former palaces at every turn. Nor is it just that Vienna has a higher proportion of middle-aged and older citizens than any other city in Europe, with a concomitant sense of stability, quiet, and respectability. Rather, it's these factors, combined with a love of music; a discreet weakness for rich food (especially cakes); an adherence to old-fashioned and formal forms of address; a high, if unadventurous, regard for the arts; and a gentle mourning for lost glories, that produce a stiff but elegant, slightly other-worldly, sense of dignity.

The Heart of Vienna Most main sights are in the inner zone, the oldest part of the city, encircled by the **Ring**, once the city walls and today a broad boulevard. Carry a ready supply of AS10 coins; many places of interest have coin-operated tape machines that provide English commentaries. As you wander around, train yourself to look upward; some of the most memorable architectural treasures are on upper stories and roof lines.

Numbers in the margin correspond to points of interest on the Vienna map.

Vienna's role as imperial city is preserved in the complex of buildings that make up the former royal palace. Start your tour at Albertinaplatz, behind the opera house. Head down Augustinerstrasse. To the right is the "Memorial to Victims of Fascism," disputed in part because the sculptor was once an admitted Communist. On your left is the **Albertina,** home to the world's largest collection of drawings, sketches, engravings, and etchings. There are works here by Dürer—these are perhaps the highlight of the collection—Rembrandt, Michelangelo, Corregio, and many others. The holdings are so vast that only a limited number can be shown at one time. Some original works are so delicate that they can be shown only in facsimile. *Augustinerstr. 1, tel. 0222/534830. Admission: AS45 adults, AS20 children. Open Mon., Tues., Thurs. 10–4; Wed. 10–6; Fri. 10–2; weekends 10–1; closed Sun. in July and Aug.*

Beethoven was a regular visitor at the Palais Lobkowitz across the street on Lobkowitzplatz. The renovated palace now houses the **Theater Museum**. Exhibits cover the history of theater in Vienna and the rest of Austria. A children's museum in the basement is reached by a slide! *Lobkowitzpl. 2, tel. 0222/512–8800. Admission: AS40 adults, AS20 children. Open Tues.–Sun. 10–5.*

Go back to Augustinerstrasse to the 14th-century **Augustinerkirche,** a favorite on Sundays, when the 11 AM mass is sung in Latin. The Habsburg rulers' hearts are preserved in a chamber here. Nearby is the **Nationalbibliothek** (the National Library), with its stunning Baroque great hall. Don't overlook the fascinating collection of globes on the third floor. *Josefsplatz 1, tel. 0222/534–10–397. Admission: AS15. Open May–Oct., Mon. and Wed.–Sat. 10–4, Tues. 10–6, Sun. and holidays 10–1; Nov.–Apr., Mon.–Sat. 11–noon. Globe museum: tel. 534–10–297. Admission: AS10. Open Mon.–Wed., Fri. 11–12, Thurs. 2–3.*

Josefsplatz is where much of *The Third Man* was filmed, specifically in and around the Palais Pallavicini across the street. The

⑤ entrance to the **Spanische Reitschule,** the Spanish Riding School, is here, too, though the famed white horses are actually stabled on the other side of the square. For tickets, write the Spanische Reitschule (Hofburg, A-1010 Vienna) or Austrian Tourist Office (Friedrichstr. 7, A-1010 Vienna) *at least* three months in advance. There are performances on Sunday at 10:45 AM from March through June, and from September through October. Evening performances are occasionally given on Wednesdays at 7 PM. Tickets for the few short performances on Saturday mornings at 9 AM are available only from ticket offices and travel agencies. You can watch the 10 AM–noon training sessions Tuesday to Saturday during much of the performance season; tickets are available only at the door (Josefsplatz, Gate 2; AS70 adults, AS20 children).

From here you're only a few steps from Michaelerplatz, the circu-

⑥ lar square that marks the entrance to the **Hofburg,** the royal palace. On one side of the square, opposite the entrance, on the corner of Herrengasse and Kohlmarkt, is the **Loos building** (1911), designed by Adolf Loos. Step inside to see the remarkable restoration of the foyer. Outside, it's no more than a simple brick-and-glass structure, but architectural historians point to it as one of the earliest "modern" buildings in Europe—a building where function determines style. In striking contrast is the Baroque **Michaelertor,** opposite, the principal entrance to the Hofburg.

Time Out Some insist that no visit to Vienna is complete without a visit to **Demel,** on the left just down the Kohlmarkt. The pastries and lunch are expensive even by Viennese standards, but new management has brought back quality and service to match the elegant tradition. *Tel: 0222/533–5516. Reservations advised at mealtimes. AE, D, MC, V.*

Head under the domed entrance of the Michaelertor to visit the

⑦ **imperial apartments** of Emperor Franz Josef and Empress Elisabeth. Among the exhibits is the exercise equipment used by the beautiful empress. Here, too, is the dress she was wearing when she was stabbed to death by a demented Italian anarchist on the shores of Lake Geneva in 1898; the dagger marks are visible. *Michaelerplatz 1, tel. 0222/587–5554–515. Admission: AS25 adults, AS10 children. Open Mon.–Sat. 8:30–noon, 12:30–4; Sun. and holidays 8:30–12:30.*

⑧ Be sure to see the **Schatzkammer,** the imperial treasury, home of the magnificent crown jewels. *Hofburg, Schweizerhof, tel. 0222/521–77–365. Admission: AS60 adults, AS30 children. Open Wed.–Mon. 10–6.*

⑨ The **Hofburgkapelle,** the court chapel, is where the Vienna Boys Choir sings mass at 9:15 AM on Sunday mid-September through June. You'll need tickets to attend; they are available at the chapel from 5 PM Friday (queue up by 4:30 and expect long lines) or by writing to Hofmusikkapelle, Hofburg, Schweizerhof, A-1010 Vienna. The city tourist office can sometimes help with ticket applications.

Head south to Heldenplatz, the vast open square punctuated with oversized equestrain statues of Prince Eugene and Archduke

⑩ Karl, in front of the **Neue Hofburg Museums.** The ponderously

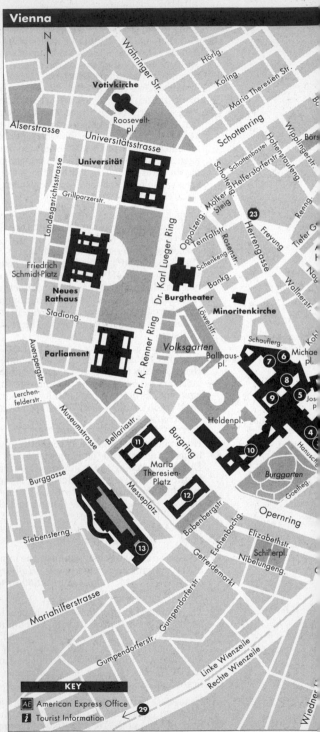

Vienna

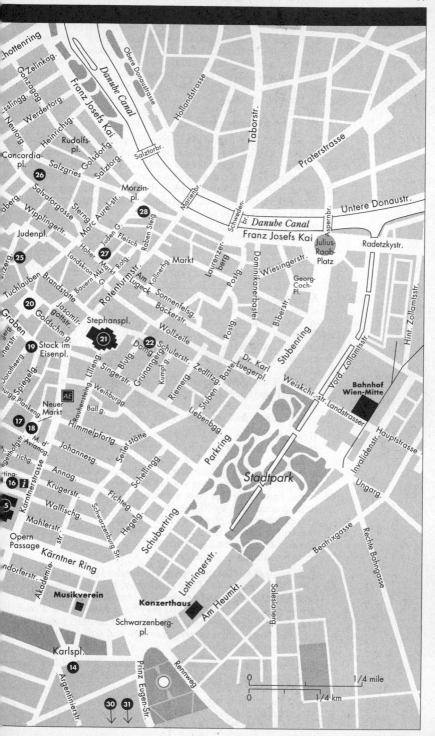

ornate 19th-century edifice—Hitler announced the annexation of Austria from the balcony in 1938—now houses a series of museums. Highlights are the Waffensammlung (the weapons collection), the collections of musical instruments, the ethnographic museum, and the exciting Ephesus museum, with finds from the excavations at that ancient site. The musical instruments collection has been undergoing refurbishing for years; by the end of 1993, it should be open again. *Neue Hofburg, Heldenplatz 1, tel. 0222/521770. Admission: AS45 adults, AS20 children. Open Wed.–Mon. 10–6.*

Walk west again under the unmonumental Hero's Monument archway and across the Ring, the broad boulevard encircling ⑪ the inner city, to the museum complex. The **Naturhistorisches Museum** (Natural History Museum) is on your right, the ⑫ **Kunsthistorisches Museum** (Art History Museum) is on your left. The latter is one of the great art museums of the world; this is not a place to miss. The collections focus on old-master painting, notably Brueghel, Cranach, Titian, Canaletto, Rubens, and Velazquez. But there are important Egyptian, Greek, Etruscan, and Roman exhibits, too. *Burgring 5, tel. 0222/521770. Admission: AS60 adults, AS30 children. Open Tues.–Sun. 10–6, limited galleries also Tues. and Fri. 10–9.*

Time Out Across the Messeplatz stretches Messepalast, the former court stables that now serve as a fair and exhibit space. Inside is one of Vienna's better-kept secrets, the **Glacis-Beisl** restaurant. Wine and the local specialties in the garden under the vine-clad arbors have to be experienced. *Tel. 0222/ 961658. Reservations advised. No credit cards. Closed Jan.–Feb., Sun., and hols.*

At the Mariahilferstrasse end of the Messepalast complex is ⑬ the small and fascinating **Tabak Museum,** the Tobacco Museum. *Mariahilferstr. 2, tel. 0222/526–1716. Admission: AS20 adults, AS10 children. Open Tues.–Fri. 10–5, weekends 10–2.*

Head east down the Getreidemarkt, with the Kunsthistorisches Museum on your left. Looming up ahead with the gilt cauliflower dome is the Sezession and beyond it a huge yellow and blue container. Both are art museums with changing exhibits. Beyond them, over Karlsplatz, is the heroic facade and ⑭ dome, flanked by vast twin columns, of the **Karlskirche.** It was built around 1715 by Fischer von Erlach. The oval interior is surprisingly small, given the monumental facade: One expects something more on the scale of St. Peter's in Rome. The ceiling has airy frescoes, and stiff shafts of gilt radiate like sunbeams from the altar.

Take the pedestrian underpass back under the Ring to Opernplatz. This is the site of the **Staatsoper,** one of the best opera ⑮ houses in the world and a focus of Viennese social life. Tickets are expensive and rare, so you may have to settle for a backstage tour. The tour schedule for the day is usually posted outside the doors on the Operngasse side and will depend on the activities going on inside.

Head up Kärntnerstrasse, Vienna's main thoroughfare, now a busy pedestrian mall. On your left is the creamy facade of ⑯ the **Sacher Hotel.** Take a look inside at the plush red-and-gilt decor, a fin de siècle masterpiece. The hotel is also the home of the original Sachertorte—the ultimate chocolate cake. Back on Kärntnerstrasse, around the corner from the Sacher, is the city tourist office. Leading off Kärntnerstrasse, to the left, is the little street of Marco d'Aviano-Gasse. Follow it to (17) **Kapuzinerkirche,** in whose crypt, called the **Kaisergruft** or the imperial vault, the serried ranks of long-dead Habsburgs lie. The oldest tomb is that of Ferdinand II; it dates from 1633. The most recent tomb is that of Empress Zita, widow of Austria's last kaiser, dating from 1989. *Neuer Markt 1, tel. 0222/512-6853–12. Admission free. Open daily 9:30–4.*

(18) In the center of the square is the ornate 18th-century **Donner Brunnen,** the Providence Fountain. The figures represent main rivers that flow into the Danube; Empress Maria Teresa thought the figures were obscene and wanted them removed or properly clothed.

Time Out   Coffee or tea and what are said, even by the French and Belgians, to be the best pastries in the world are available at the **Konditorei Oberlaa.** *Neuer Markt 16. Open weekdays 9–7, Sat. 9–6, Sun. and holidays 10–6.*

Continue north through Seilergasse to reach pedestrians-only (19) Graben. The **Pestsäule,** or Plague Column, shoots up from the middle of the street, looking like a geyser of whipped cream touched with gold. It commemorates the Black Death of 1697. A small turning to the right, just past the column, leads to the (20) Baroque **Peterskirche.** The little church, the work of Johann Lukas von Hildebrandt, finished in about 1730, has what is probably the most theatrical interior in the city. The pulpit is especially fine, with a highly ornate canopy, but florid and swirling decoration is everywhere. Many of the decorative elements are based on a tent form, a motif suggested by the Turkish forces that camped outside the city walls during the great siege of Vienna at the end of the 17th century.

Walk down Goldschmiedgasse to Stephansplatz, site of the (21) **Stephansdom** (St. Stephen's Cathedral). Its towering Gothic spires and gaudy 19th-century tiled roof are still the dominant feature of the Vienna skyline. The oldest part of the building is the 13th-century entrance, the soaring **Riesentor,** or Giant Doorway. Inside, the church is mysteriously dark, filled with an array of monuments, tombs, sculptures, paintings, and pulpits. Despite extensive wartime damage—and numerous Baroque additions—the building radiates an authentically medieval atmosphere. Climb up the 345 steps of **Alte Steffl,** Old Steven, the south tower, for a stupendous view over the city. An elevator goes up the north tower to **Die Pummerin,** the Boomer, a 22-ton bell first cast in 1711 from cannons captured from the Turks. Take a 30-minute tour of the crypt to see the entrails of the Habsburgs, carefully preserved in copper jars.

On a narrow street east of the cathedral is the house where Mo-(22) zart lived from 1784 to 1787. Today it's the **Mozart Erinnerungsräume,** the Mozart Museum. It was here that the composer wrote *The Marriage of Figaro* (thus the nickname Figaro House) and here, some say, that he spent the happiest years of his life. *Domgasse 5, tel. 0222/513–6294. Admission: AS15 adults, AS5 children. Open Tues.–Sun. 9–12:15 and 1–4:30.*

Other Corners   Walk back down the Graben and the narrow Naglergasse and **of Vienna**   turn left into the Freyung. On your left is the **Palais Ferstl,** now a stylish shopping arcade. At the back is the skillfully restored

Café Central, once headquarters for Vienna's leading literary
㉓ figures. Cross the Freyung to the dominant **Schottenkirche.**
The monks who were brought to found it were actually Irish,
not Scottish. Turn back through the Freyung to **Am Hof,** a remarkable square with the city's Baroque central fire station,
possibly the world's most ornate. Cross the square to the
㉔ **Kirche am Hof.** The interior is curiously reminiscent of many
Dutch churches.

Time Out For a typical meal or just a beer or coffee, stop at **Gustlbauer.**
The restaurant is a regular stop for the Fiaker coachmen, who
leave their livery and passengers briefly for a quick Schnapps.
The waiter will help you decipher the handwritten menu. *Am
Hof, Drahtgasse 2, tel. 0222/533–5889. Open weekdays 10–
midnight, Sat. 10–3.*

Continue to Judenplatz and turn right into Parisergasse to the
㉕ **Uhrenmuseum** (Clock Museum), located in a lovely Renaissance
house. *Schulhof 2, tel. 0222/533–2265. Admission: AS15
adults, AS5 children. Open Tues.–Sun. 9–4:30.*

Turn down the Kurrentgasse and, via Fütterergasse, cross the
Wipplingerstrasse into Stoss im Himmel (literally, a "thrust to
㉖ heaven"). To your left down Salvatorgasse is **Maria am
Gestade,** originally a church for fishermen on the nearby canal.
Note the ornate "folded hands" spire. Return along Wip-
㉗ plingerstrasse, across Marc Aurel-Strasse, to **Hoher Markt,**
with a central monument celebrating the betrothal of Mary and
Joseph. *Hoher Markt 3, tel. 0222/535–5606. Admission: AS15
adults, AS5 children; free on Fri. morning. Open Tues.–Sun.
9–12:15 and 1–4:30.*

On the north side of Hoher Markt is the amusing **Anker-Uhr,** a
clock that tells time by figures moving across a scale. The figures are identified on a plaque at the lower left of the clock; it's
well worth passing by at noon to catch the show. Go through
㉘ Judengasse to the **Ruprechtskirche** (St. Rupert's). The oldest
church in Vienna, dating from the 11th century, is small, damp,
dark, and, unfortunately, usually closed, though you can peek
through a window.

Vienna Environs It's a 15-minute ride from the city center on subway line U-4
㉙ (stop either at Schönbrunn or Hietzing) to **Schönbrunn Palace,**
the magnificent Baroque residence built between 1696 and
1713 for the Habsburgs. Here Kaiser Franz Josef I was born
and died. His "office" (kept as he left it in 1916) is a touching
reminder of his spartan life; other rooms, however, reflect the
elegance of the monarchy. The ornate public rooms are still
used for state receptions. A guided tour covers 45 of the palace's 1,441 rooms; among the curiosities are the Chinese room
and the gym fitted out for Empress Elisabeth, where she exer-
cised daily to keep her figure. *Schönbrunner Schlosstr., tel.
0222/81113–238. Admission: AS80 adults, AS30 children.
Guided tours only. Open Nov.–Mar., daily 9–4:30; Apr.–
June, and Oct., daily 8:30–5, July–Sept., daily 8:30–5:30.*

Once on the grounds, don't overlook the **Tiergarten** (Zoo). It's
Europe's oldest menagerie and, when established in 1752, was
intended to amuse and educate the court. It contains an extensive assortment of animals, some of them in their original Baroque enclosures. *Tel. 0222/877–1236. Admission: AS50
adults, AS20 children. Open Nov.–Jan., daily 9–4:30; Feb.,*

*Oct., daily 9–5; Mar., daily 9–5:30; Apr., daily 9–6; May–
Sept., daily 9–6:30.*

Follow the pathways up to the **Gloriette,** that Baroque ornament on the rise behind Schönbrunn, and enjoy superb views of
the city. Originally this was to have been the site of the palace,
but projected construction costs were considered too high. *Admission: AS20 adults, AS10 children. Open May–Sept., daily
8–6; Oct., daily 8–5.*

The **Wagenburg** (Carriage Museum), near the entrance to the
palace grounds, holds some splendid examples of early transportation, from children's sleighs to funeral carriages of the
emperors. *Tel. 0222/877–3244. Admission: AS30 adults, children free. Open Nov.–Mar., Tues.–Sun. 10–4; Apr.–Oct.,
Tues.–Sun. 10–6.*

㉚ Take the D streetcar toward the Südbahnhof to reach **Schloss
Belvedere** (Belvedere Palace), a Baroque complex often compared to Versailles. It was commissioned by Prince Eugene of
Savoy and built by Johann Lukas von Hildebrandt in 1721–22.
The palace is made up of two separate buildings, one at the foot
and the other at the top of a hill. The lower tract was first built
as residential quarters; the upper buildings were reserved for
entertaining. The gardens in between are among the best examples of natural Baroque ornamentation found anywhere.
The buildings have contemporary significance: The State Treaty that gave Austria its independence in 1955 was signed in the
great upper hall. The composer Anton Bruckner lived in an
apartment to the north of the upper building until his death in
1896. Both sections now house outstanding art museums: the
gallery of 19th- and 20th-century art in the Upper Belvedere
(Klimt, Kokoschka, Schiele, Waldmüller, Markart) and the Baroque museum (including medieval Austrian art) in the Lower
Belvedere. *Prinz-Eugen-Str. 27, tel. 0222/784158. Admission:
AS60 adults, AS30 children. Open Tues.–Sun. 10–5.*

㉛ Continue across the Gürtel from the Upper Belvedere southward to the **20th Century Museum,** containing a small but extremely tasteful modern art collection. *Schweizer Garten, tel.
0222/782550. Admission: AS30 adults, AS15 children. Open
Thurs.–Tues. 10–6.*

You can reach a small corner of the **Vienna Woods** by streetcar
and bus: Take a streetcar or the subway U-2 to Schottentor/
University and, from there, the No. 38 streetcar (Grinzing) to
the end of the line. Grinzing itself is out of a picture book; alas,
much of the wine offered in the taverns is less enchanting. (For
better wine and ambience, try the area around Pfarrplatz and
Probusgasse in Hohe Warte—streetcar 37, bus 39A—or the
suburb of Nussdorf—streetcar D.) To get into the woods,
change in Grinzing to the No. 38A bus. This will take you to
Kahlenberg, which provides a superb view over the Danube
and the city. You can take the bus or hike to Leopoldsberg, the
promontory over the Danube from which Turkish invading
forces were repulsed during the 16th and 17th centuries.

Off the Beaten Track

Vienna's **Bermuda Triangle** (around Judengasse/Seitenstet-
tengasse) is jammed with everything from good bistros to jazz
clubs. Also check the tourist office's museum list carefully:

There's something for everyone, ranging from Sigmund Freud's apartment to the Funeral and Burial Museum. The **Hundertwasserhaus** (Kegelgasse/Löwengasse; streetcar N), an astonishing apartment complex designed by artist Friedenreich Hundertwasser, with turrets, towers, odd windows, and uneven floors, will be of interest to those who do not think that architectural form has to follow function.

Children will enjoy the charming **Doll and Toy Museum,** next door to the Clock Museum (*see* Exploring Vienna, *above*). It's filled with trains, dollhouses, and troops of teddy bears. *Schulhof 4, tel. 0222/535–6860. Admission: AS60 adults, AS30 children. Open Tues.–Sun. 10–6.*

Shopping

Antiques The best (and most expensive) shops are in the inner city, many in and around **Dorotheergasse,** but there are good finds in some of the outer districts, particularly among the back streets in the **Josefstadt** (eighth) district.

Boutiques Name brands are found along the **Kohlmarkt** and **Graben** and their respective side streets, and the side streets off the **Kärntnerstrasse.**

Folk Costumes A good selection at reasonable prices is offered by the **NÖ Heimatwerk** (Herrengasse 6); also try **Trachten Tostmann** (Schottengasse 3a) or **Loden-Plankl** (Michaelerplatz 6).

Shopping Districts Tourists gravitate to the **Kärntnerstrasse,** but the Viennese do most of their shopping on the **Mariahilferstrasse.**

Food and Flea Markets The **Naschmarkt** (between Rechte and Linke Wienzeile; weekdays 6 AM–mid-afternoon, Sat. 6–1) is a sensational open-food market, offering specialties from around the world. The **Flohmarkt** (flea market) operates year-round beyond the Naschmarkt (subway U-4 to Kettenbrückengasse) and is equally fascinating (Sat. 8–4). An **Arts & Crafts Market** with better offerings operates on Saturday (2–6 or 2–7) and Sunday (10–6) alongside the Danube Canal near the Salztorbrücke.

Dining

In contrast to many cities, the leading Viennese hotels are in competition for the country's best cooks and therefore offer some of the city's best dining. Even the chain hotels have joined in the effort to see which can win over the leading chefs. The results are rewarding; you may not even have to leave your hotel to enjoy outstanding food and service. For details and price-category definitions, *see* Dining in Staying in Austria, *above*.

Very Expensive ★ **Korso.** You'll find outstanding food and atmosphere at this gourmet temple of "New Vienna Cuisine." Chef Reinhard Gerer produces exquisite variations on Austrian standards such as pork and beef by borrowing accents from Asian cuisine. *Mahlerstr. 2, tel. 0222/5151–6546. Reservations advised. AE, DC, MC, V. Closed Sat. lunch.*

★ **Rotisserie Prinz Eugen.** "New Vienna Cuisine"—the Austrian version of nouvelle cuisine—is combined successfully with more usual dishes at the Hilton's Rotisserie Prinz Eugen, which has managed to sustain its initial reputation for outstanding decor, service, and food. There is piano accompaniment in the evening. *Hilton Hotel, Am Stadtpark, tel. 0222/*

71700–355. Reservations advised. AE, DC, MC, V. Sat. and Sun. dinner only.

Steirer Eck. One food editor declared in 1992 that the Steirer Eck is Austria's best restaurant, but the judgment is not unanimous. Some of the standard dishes are more successful than the forays into the "New Vienna Cuisine." No one denies the elegance of the ambience, however. *Rasumofskygasse 2, tel. 0222/713–3168. Reservations advised. AE, V. Closed weekends and holidays.*

Zu den Drei Husaren. This is one of Vienna's enduring monuments to tradition, complete with candlelight and live piano music (except on Sundays). Casual visitors (as opposed to the "regulars") may have to settle for more atmosphere than service, however, but the food—mainly Viennese standards such as variations on rump steak—is of exceptional quality. The hors d'oeuvre trolleys are intentionally enticing and can easily double the lunch or dinner bill. *Weihburggasse 4, tel. 0222/512–1092. Reservations required. AE, DC, MC, V. Closed mid-July–mid-Aug.*

Expensive **Demel.** One of Vienna's most famous pastry shops offers magnificent snacks of delicate meats, fish, and vegetables, as well as the expected cakes and other goodies. The stuffed mushrooms and vegetable-cheese combinations are especially tempting—as is the hot chocolate. *Kohlmarkt 14, tel. 0222/533–5516. Reservations advised at lunchtime. AE, DC, MC, V. Closed after 6 PM.*

König von Ungarn. Dark wood paneling and framed prints create a comfortable, clublike atmosphere in these historic rooms (Mozart once lived upstairs). The *Tafelspitz* (boiled beef) here is particularly good. *Schulerstr. 10 (in the Hotel König von Ungarn), tel. 512–5319. Reservations essential at lunch, otherwise advised. MC. Closed Sat.*

★ **Vier Jahreszeiten.** This restaurant effortlessly manages to achieve that delicate balance between food and atmosphere. The service is attentive without being overbearing. The lunch buffet offers both excellent food and value. Evening dining includes grill specialties and live piano music. *Hotel Intercontinental, Johannesgasse 28, tel. 0222/711–22143. Reservations advised. AE, DC, MC, V. Closed Sat. lunch and Sun. dinner.*

Moderate **Bastei-Beisl.** A comfortable, wood-paneled restaurant offering good traditional Viennese fare. Outdoor tables are particularly pleasant on summer evenings. *Stubenbastei 10, tel. 0222/512–4319. Reservations usually not necessary. AE, DC, MC. Closed Sun.*

Bei Max. The decor is somewhat bland, but the tasty Carinthian specialties—*Kasnudeln* and *Fleischnudeln* (a kind of cheese- and meat-filled ravioli) in particular—keep this friendly restaurant packed. *Landhausgasse 2/Herrengasse, tel. 0222/533–7359. Reservations advised. No credit cards. Closed Sat., Sun., last week July, first 3 weeks Aug.*

★ **Gigerl.** It's hard to believe you're right in the middle of the city at this imaginative and charming wine restaurant that serves hot and cold buffets. The rooms are small and cozy but may get smoky and noisy when the place is full—which it usually is. The food is typical of wine gardens on the fringes of the city: roast meats, casserole dishes, cold cuts, salads. The wines are excellent. The surrounding narrow alleys and ancient buildings add to the charm of the outdoor tables in summer. *Rauhen-*

steingasse 3, tel. 0222/513–4431. Reservations advised. AE, DC, MC, V.

Kaiserwalzer. The rooms in this once-private house radiate the elegance of the old empire. Austrian specialties are prominent; the beet soup, roast chicken, and paprika sauces are all splendid. *Esterházygasse 9, tel. 0222/587–0494. Reservations advised. AE, DC, MC, V. Dinner only; closed Sun.*

Melker Stiftskeller. This is one of the city's half-dozen genuine wine taverns, or kellers; the food selection is limited but good, featuring pig's knuckle. House wines from the Wachau are excellent. *Schottengasse 3, tel. 0222/533–5530. Reservations usually not necessary. MC. Evenings only; closed Sun.*

★ **Ofenloch.** This place is always packed, which speaks well not only of the excellent specialties from some Viennese grandmother's cookbook but also of the atmosphere. Waitresses are dressed in appropriate period costumes, and the furnishings add to the color. At times the rooms may be too smoky and noisy for some tastes. If you like garlic, try *Vanillerostbraten*, a rump steak with as much garlic as you request. *Kurrentgasse 8, tel. 0222/533–8844. Reservations required. AE, DC, MC, V.*

Stadtbeisl. Good standard Austrian fare is served at this popular eatery, which is comfortable without being pretentious. The service gets uneven as the place fills up, but if you are seated outside in summer, you probably won't mind. *Naglergasse 21, tel. 0222/533–3507. Reservations advised. No credit cards.*

Zu den drei Hacken. This is one of the few genuine Viennese *Gasthäuser* in the city center; like the place itself, the fare is solid if not elegant. Legend has it that Schubert dined here; the ambience probably hasn't changed much since then. There are tables outside in summer, although the extra seating capacity strains both the kitchen and the service. *Singerstr. 8, tel. 0222/512–5895. No reservations. AE, DC, V. Closed Sat. dinner and Sun.*

Zu ebener Erde und erster Stock. Ask for a table upstairs in this exquisite, tiny, utterly original Biedermeier house, which serves good, standard Austrian fare; the downstairs space is really more for snacks. *Burggasse 13, tel. 0222/936254. Reservations advised. AE. Closed Sat. lunch, Sun., Mon., and late July–late Aug.*

Inexpensive **Figlmüller.** Known for its schnitzel, Figlmüller is always
★ packed. Guests share the benches, the long tables, and the experience. Food choices are limited, but nobody seems to mind. Only wine is offered to drink, but it is good. The small "garden" is now enclosed and is just as popular as the tables inside. *Wollzeile 5 (passageway), tel. 0222/512–6177. No reservations. No credit cards. Closed Sat. dinner and Sun.*

Ilona-Stüberl. Head to Ilona-Stüberl for a cozy Hungarian atmosphere—without the gypsy music. Be prepared to douse the fire if you ask for a dish with hot peppers! The tables outside in summer are pleasant but somewhat public. *Bräunerstr. 2, tel. 0222/533–9029. Reservations advised. AE, DC, MC, V. Closed Sun.*

Lodging

Vienna's inner city is the best base for visitors because it's so close to most of the major sights, restaurants, and shops. This accessibility translates, of course, into higher prices. For details and price-category definitions, *see* Lodging in Staying in Austria.

Very Expensive **Bristol.** Opposite the opera house, the Bristol is classic Vien-
★ nese, preferred by many for the service as well as the location.
The bar is comfortable, though not overly private; the restaurants associated with the hotel are outstanding, especially
Korso. Back and upper guest rooms are quieter. *Kärntner
Ring 1, tel. 0222/515160, fax 0222/515–16550. 152 rooms with
bath. Facilities: restaurants, bar. AE, DC, MC, V.*

★ **Imperial.** This former palace represents elegant old Vienna at
its best, with such features as heated towel racks in some
rooms. The location could hardly be better, although being on
the Ring sometimes makes the front and lower rooms a bit
noisy. The bar is intimate and pleasant. Lunch in the café is
both reasonable and good; the hotel restaurant has an excellent
reputation, though at press time a new chef had taken over in
the kitchen. *Kärntner Ring 16, tel. 0222/501100, fax 0222/501–
10410. 151 rooms with bath or shower. Facilities: beauty parlor, conference rooms. AE, DC, MC, V.*

★ **InterContinental.** Vienna's modern InterContinental has the
reputation of being one of the chain's very best. The rooms are
spacious; the main restaurant, exceptional. But whereas the
hotel succeeds in acquiring some Viennese charm, the bar fails
hopelessly, as does the Brasserie. Rooms in front overlooking
the park are quieter, particularly in winter when the ice-skating rink at the back is in operation. *Johannesgasse 28, tel. 0222/
711220, fax 0222/713–4489. 500 rooms with bath. Facilities:
sauna, health club, laundry, dry cleaning service, barber,
hair stylist, complimentary limousine, parking. AE, DC,
MC, V.*

Marriott. The only Viennese aspect here is the service; all else
is global modern. The atrium lobby, while pleasant, is anything
but intimate. The restaurants are satisfactory if not quite up to
the level of other top hotels, and Sunday brunch at the Marriott
has become immensely popular (book at least a week in advance). *Parkring 12A, tel. 0222/515180, fax 0222/515–186736.
304 rooms with bath. Facilities: sauna, health club, pool,
shops, garage. AE, DC, MC, V.*

Palais Schwarzenberg. The rooms are incorporated into a quiet
wing of a Baroque palace, a 10-minute walk from the opera. The
restaurant enjoys an excellent reputation; the view out over the
formal gardens is glorious. *Schwarzenbergplatz 9, tel. 0222/
784515, fax 0222/784714. 38 rooms with bath. Facilities: bar.
AE, DC, MC, V.*

Sacher. The hotel's reputation has varied considerably during
recent years, but it remains one of the legendary addresses in
Europe, with its opulent decor highlighted by original oil
paintings, sculptures, and objets d'art. The Blue and Red bars
are intimate and favored by nonguests as well, as is the café,
particularly in summer when tables are set up outside. Guest
rooms are spacious and elegantly appointed. *Philharmonik-
erstr. 4, tel. 0222/514560, fax 0222/514–57810. 117 rooms with
bath or shower. Facilities: coffee shop, bars. AE, DC, MC, V.*

Expensive **Altstadt.** You're one streetcar stop or a short walk from the
main museums in this newly renovated old-Vienna residential
building. Each of the spacious rooms is decorated individually,
though the predominant scheme involves fine wood period furniture set against light and blue-gray walls. The upper rooms
have views out over the city roofline. *Kirchengasse 41, tel.*

0222/526–33990, fax 0222/423–4901. 25 rooms with bath or shower. Facilities: bar. AE, DC, MC, V.

★ **Astoria.** Though the Astoria is one of Vienna's traditional old hotels, the rooms have been modernized considerably. The paneled lobby, however, has been preserved and retains an unmistakable Old World patina. The location is central, but because of the street musicians and the late-night crowds in the pedestrian zone, rooms overlooking the Kärntnerstrasse tend to be noisy in summer. *Kärntnerstr. 32–34, tel. 0222/515770, fax 0222/515–7782. 108 rooms with bath or shower. Facilities: restaurant. AE, DC, MC, V.*

Capricorno. This establishment overlooks the Danube Canal in a fairly central location. Although its facade is modern and somewhat short on charm, the hotel nonetheless represents good value. *Schwedenplatz 3–4, tel. 0222/533–3104, fax 0222/533–76714. 46 rooms with bath or shower. Facilities: garage. AE, DC, MC, V.*

Europa. The location—midway between the opera house and the cathedral—is ideal, but the rooms on the Kärntnerstrasse side are noisy in summer; ask for a room overlooking Neuer Markt. The building is postwar modern and lacks the charm of older hotels, but the staff is friendly and helpful. The café is popular, particularly in summer when tables are put outdoors. *Neuer Markt 3, tel. 0222/515940, fax 0222/513–8138. 102 rooms with bath. Facilities: restaurant, coffee shop, bar. AE, DC, MC, V.*

König von Ungarn. This utterly charming, centrally located hotel is tucked away in the shadow of the cathedral. The historic facade belies the modern efficiency of the interior, from the atrium lobby to the guest rooms themselves. The restaurant (just next door in a house that Mozart once lived in) is excellent, though not inexpensive, and is always packed at noon. *Schulerstr. 10, tel. 0222/515840, fax 0222/515848. 32 rooms with bath or shower. Facilities: restaurant, bar. DC, MC, V.*

Mailberger Hof. This is a favorite of opera stars, conductors, and those who want a central but quiet location. Some rooms have limited kitchenette facilities. The arcaded courtyard is very pretty. *Annagasse 7, tel. 0222/512–0641, fax 0222/512–064110. 80 rooms with bath or shower. AE, DC, MC, V.*

Moderate **Austria.** This older hotel is on a quiet side street in a historic
★ area. It is popular with tourists. *Wolfengasse 3/Fleischmarkt, tel. 0222/51523, fax 0222/512–4343. 51 rooms, 40 with bath or shower. Facilities: bar. AE, DC, MC, V.*

★ **Kärntnerhof.** Though tucked away in a tiny, quiet side street, Kärntnerhof is nevertheless centrally located. It's known for its particularly friendly staff. The rooms are functionally decorated but clean and serviceable. *Grashofgasse 4, tel. 0222/512–1923, fax 0222/513–222833. 45 rooms, 34 with bath or shower. AE, DC, MC, V.*

Pension Christina. This quiet pension, just steps from Schwedenplatz and the Danube Canal, offers mainly smallish modern rooms, warmly decorated with attractive dark-wood furniture set off against beige walls. Room 524 is particularly spacious and inviting. *Hafnersteig 7, tel. 0222/533–2961, fax 0222/533–296111. 32 rooms with bath or shower. MC.*

★ **Pension Zipser.** This 1904 house, with an ornate facade and gilt-trimmed coat of arms, has become a favorite with regular visitors to Vienna. It is slightly less central than some others on our list, but very comfortable. *Lange Gasse 49, tel. 0222/420828* *or 408–5266, fax 0222/408–526613. 46 rooms with bath or shower. Facilities: bar. AE, DC, MC, V.*

★ **Post.** Taking its name from the city's main post office, opposite, this is an older but updated hotel that offers a fine location, a friendly staff, and a good café. *Fleischmarkt 24, tel. 0222/515830, fax 0222/515–83808. 107 rooms, 77 with bath or shower. AE, DC, MC, V.*

Schweizerhof. This is more of a pension than a hotel, but the location is excellent and the smallish rooms are certainly adequate. *Bauernmarkt 22, tel. 0222/533–1931, fax 0222/533–0214. 55 rooms with bath or shower. AE, DC, MC, V.*

Wandl. The house is old and some of the rooms are small, but the Wandl's location and reasonable prices compensate for most of its deficiencies. *Petersplatz 9, tel. 0222/534550, fax 0222/534–5577. 134 rooms with bath or shower. No credit cards.*

The Arts

Theater and Opera Check the monthly program published by the city; posters also show opera and theater schedules. The **Staatsoper,** one of world's great opera houses will be under renovation in fall, 1994, and its repertory will be performed on other stages. The season startup may also be later than the usual September 1. Tickets for the Staatsoper, Volksoper, and the Burg and Akademie theaters are available at the central ticket office to the left rear of the Staatsoper (**Bundestheaterkassen,** Hanuschgasse 3, tel. 0222/514440, fax 0222/514–442969; open weekdays 9–5, weekends 9–1). Tickets go on advance sale a week before performances. Unsold tickets can be obtained at the evening box office. Plan to be there at least one hour before the performance; students can buy remaining tickets at lower prices, so they are usually out in force. Tickets can be ordered six days in advance from anywhere in the world by phone (tel. 0222/513–1513; AE, DC, MC, V). Theater is offered in English at **Vienna English Theater** (Josefsgasse 12, tel. 0222/402–1260) and **International Theater** (Porzellangasse 8, tel. 0222/316272).

Music Most classical concerts are in either the **Konzerthaus** (Lothringerstr. 20, tel. 0222/712–1211, fax 0222/713–1709) or **Musikverein** (Dumbastr. 3, tel. 0222/505–8190, fax 0222/505–9409). Tickets can be bought at the box offices (AE, DC, MC, V). Pop concerts are scheduled from time to time at the **Austria Center** (Am Hubertusdamm 6, tel. 0222/236–9150; U-1 subway to Vienna International Center stop). Tickets to various musical events are available via **Vienna Ticket Service** (tel. 0222/587–9843, fax 0222/587–9844).

Film Films are shown in English at **Burg Kino** (Opernring 19, tel. 0222/587–8406), **City** (Tuchlauben 13, tel. 0222/533–5232), **de France** (Schottenring 5, tel. 0222/345236), **Top Kino** (Rahlgasse 1, tel. 0222/587–5557), and **Film Museum** (Augustinerstr. 1, tel. 0222/533–7054). To find English-language movies, look for "OF" (Originalfassung) or "OmU" (original with subtitles) in the newspaper listings.

Nightlife

Cabarets Most cabarets are expensive and unmemorable. Two of the best are **Casanova** (Dorotheergasse 6, tel. 0222/512–9845), which emphasizes striptease, and **Moulin Rouge** (Walfischgasse 11, tel. 0222/512–2130).

Discos **Atrium** (Schwarzenbergpl. 10, tel. 0222/505–3594) is open Thursday through Sunday and draws a lively younger crowd. **Queen Anne** (Johannesgasse 12, tel. 0222/512 0203) is central, popular, and always packed. The **U-4** (Schönbrunnerstr. 222, tel. 0222/858307) ranks high among the young set. Live bands, dancing, and snacks are offered at **Chattanooga** (Graben 29, tel. 0222/533–5000).

Nightclubs A casual '50s atmosphere pervades the popular **Café Volksgarten** (Burgring 1, tel. 0222/533–0518), situated in the city park of the same name; tables are set outdoors in summer. The more formal **Eden Bar** (Liliengasse 2, tel. 0222/512–7450) is considered one of Vienna's classiest night spots; don't expect to be let in unless you're dressed to kill.

Wine Taverns For a traditional Viennese night out, head to one of the city's atmospheric wine taverns, some of which date as far back as the 12th century. You can often have full meals at these taverns, but the emphasis is mainly on drinking. **Melker Stiftskeller** (*see* Dining, *above*) is one of the friendliest and most typical. Other well-known ones: **Antiquitäten-Keller** (Magdalenenstr. 32, tel. 0222/566–9533; closed Aug.), which has a backdrop of classical music; **Augustinerkeller** (Augustinerstr. 1, tel. 0222/533–1026), open at lunchtime as well as during the evenings, in the same building as the Albertina collection; **Esterhazykeller** (Haarhof 1, tel. 0222/533–3482), a particularly mazelike network of rooms; **Piaristenkeller** (Piaristengasse 45, tel. 0222/429152), somewhat touristy, with zither music; and **Zwölf-Apostelkeller** (Sonnenfelsgasse 3, tel. 0222/512–6777), near St. Stephen's Cathedral.

The Danube Valley

The Danube Valley stretches about 88 kilometers (55 miles) west of Vienna, and many visitors enjoy it as part of an excursion from the country's capital. What this region offers is magnificent countryside, some of Austria's best food and wines, and comfortable, in some cases elegant, accommodations. Above the river are the ruins of ancient castles. The abbeys at Melk and Göttweig, with their magnificent libraries, dominate their settings. Vineyards sweep down to the river, which is lined with fruit trees that burst into blossom every spring. People here live close to the land, and at certain times of year vintners open their homes to sell their own wines and produce. Roadside stands offer flowers, fruits, vegetables, and wines. And this is an area of legend: The Danube shares with the Rhine the story of the mythical Niebelungen, defenders of Siegfried, hero of German myth.

Getting Around

By Car If you're pressed for time, take the Autobahn to St. Pölten, turn north onto Route S-33, and follow the signs to Melk. For a more scenic route, leave Vienna along the south shore of the Danube via Klosterneuburg and Greifenstein, taking Routes 14, 19, 43, and 33. Cross the Danube at Melk, then return to Vienna along the north bank of the river (Route 3).

By Train Depart from the Westbahnhof for Melk, then take the bus along the north bank of the Danube to Dürnstein and Krems. Side bus trips can be made from Krems to Göttweig.

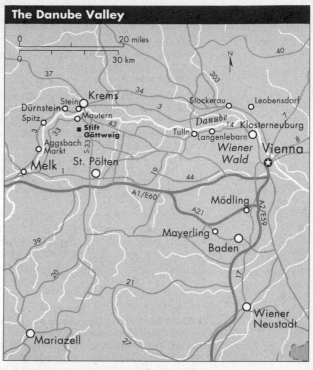

The Danube Valley

By Boat Travel upstream, with stops at Krems, Dürnstein, Melk, and points between. Return to Vienna by boat or by train from Melk (combination tickets available).

Guided Tours

Vienna travel agencies offer tours of the Wachau, as the Danube Valley is known. These range from one-day outings to longer excursions. For details, contact the **Lower Austria Tourist Office** (Heidenschuss 2, tel. 0222/533–3114, fax 0222/535–0319).

Tourist Information

Dürnstein (Parkplatz Ost, tel. 02711/219).
Klosterneuburg (Niedermarkt, Postfach 6, tel. 02243/2038, fax 02243/86773).
Krems (Undstr. 6, tel. 02732/82676, fax 02732/70011—also covers **Stein an der Donau**).
Melk (Linzerstr. 3–5, tel. 02752/2307, fax 02752/230727).
Tulln (Albrechtsg. 32, tel. 02272/5836).

Exploring the Danube Valley

North of Vienna lies **Klosterneuburg**, whose huge **abbey** dominates the market town. The abbey's extensive vineyards offer excellent wines; the abbey itself is a major agricultural landowner in the region. *Guided tours every half hour (winter*

*schedule may vary) Mon.–Sat. 9–11 and 1:30–5, Sun. 11 and
1:30–5.*

If you are driving, you have the choice of either following the
riverbank or heading up over the village of St. Andrae and
down to the river plain again. At **Tulln**, the **town hall** dominates
the town square.

You will see **Stift Göttweig** long before you reach it. This impressive, 11th-century Benedictine abbey affords sensational
views of the Danube Valley; walk around the grounds and view
the impressive chapel. *Rte. 303, on the south bank of the Danube, opposite Krems.*

Time Out Have lunch at the **Stiftskeller.** If the weather is clear, sit out on
the open terrace and enjoy the magnificent views of the Dan-
ube in the distance. The local wines are excellent. *Open Apr.–
Oct., daily.*

Farther along the valley is the abbey of **Melk,** holding a commanding position over the Danube. The library is rich in art as
well as books; the ceiling frescoes are particularly memorable.
*Tel. 02752/2312. Admission: AS45 adults, AS20 children. Ad-
mission (with guided tour): AS55 adults, AS30 children. Open
April–Sept., daily 9–5; Oct., daily 9–4; Nov.–Mar., daily 11
and 2 (by tour only).*

Cross to the north of the river and head back downstream. The
beautiful medieval town of **Dürnstein** is known for having kept
Richard the Lionhearted imprisoned in its now-ruined castle
for 13 months. The town is also known for its fine hotels, restaurants, and wines. Virtually next door is **Stein,** with its former
Imperial Toll House. Stein and Krems sit at the center of
Austria's foremost wine-growing region.

The road back to Vienna now wanders away from the Danube,
crossing through some attractive woodlands. When you reach
Leobensdorf, you'll spot **Burg Kreuzenstein,** perched to the left
upon a nearby hilltop. The castle includes a small museum of
armor. *Tours daily 9–4, according to demand.*

Dining and Lodging

For details and price-category definitions, *see* Dining and
Lodging in Staying in Austria.

Dürnstein **Schlosshotel.** This early Baroque castle has been luxuriously
Lodging converted. Try for a room overlooking the Danube. Eat in the
★ celebrated restaurant, and don't miss out on the house wines.
*Dürnstein 2, tel. 02711/212, fax 02711/351. 37 rooms with bath
or shower. Facilities: sauna, pool. Closed Nov.–Mar. AE, DC,
MC, V. Very Expensive.*

Krems **Alte Post.** A 16th-century house with an arcaded courtyard, the
Lodging Alte Post is conveniently positioned right in the center of town.
In good weather the courtyard is used for dining. *Obere
Landstr. 32, tel. 02732/82276. 20 rooms, most with bath. No
credit cards. Inexpensive.*

Langenlebarn **Zum Roten Wolf.** This outstanding, elegant country restaurant
Dining serves traditional local foods and superb wines. *Bahnstr. 58,
★ tel. 02272/2567. Reservations advised. Closed Mon. and Tues.
AE, DC, MC, V. Expensive.*

Mautern **Landhaus Bacher.** The Landhaus Bacher is one of Austria's
Dining best restaurants, elegant but entirely lacking in pretension.
★ Dining in the garden during the summer adds to the experi-
ence. *Südtirolerplatz 208, tel. 02732/829–370, fax 02732/74337.
Reservations required. Jacket and tie advised. Closed Nov.–
Apr., Mon., Tues., May–Oct. and late Jan.–late Feb., Mon.
and Tues. lunch. DC, V. Very Expensive.*

Salzburg

Arriving and Departing

By Plane For information, phone Salzburg airport, tel. 0662/852091.

Between the Airport Buses leave for the Salzburg train station at Südtirolerplatz ev-
and Downtown ery 15 minutes during the day, every half hour at night. Journey time is 18 minutes. Taxi fare runs about AS150–AS170.

By Train Salzburg's main train station is at Südtirolerplatz. Train information, tel. 0662/1717; telephone ticket orders and seat reservations, tel. 0662/1700.

By Bus The central bus terminal (information: tel. 0662/167) is in front
of the train station, although during construction of the underground garage in front of the rail station bus stops may be
moved to various points around the square.

By Car Salzburg has several autobahn exits; study the map and decide
which one is best for you. Parking is available in the cavernous
garages under the Mönchsberg, and in other garages around
the city; look for the large blue "P" signs.

Getting Around

By Bus and Service is frequent and reliable; route maps are available from
Trolleybus the tourist office or your hotel. Save money by buying a Salz-
burg-1 (24-hour) or Salzburg-3 (72-hour) ticket that is good on
all trolley and bus lines, on the funicular up to the fortress, on
the Mönchsberg lift, and on the rail line north to Bergheim;
half-price tickets for children 6–15. Local transportation information, tel. 0662/205–5131.

By Taxi At festival time, taxis are too scarce to hail on the street, so order through your hotel porter or phone 0662/8111.

By Fiaker Fiakers, or horsedrawn cabs, are available at the railroad station and at Residenzplatz (tel. 0662/844772).

By Car Don't even think of it! The old part of the city is a pedestrian
zone. Cars are totally forbidden in the entire Old City on weekends. Many other parts of the city have restricted parking (indicated by a blue pavement stripe), either reserved for
residents with permits, or for a restricted period. Get parking
tickets from coin-operated dispensers on street corners; instructions are also in English.

Guided Tours

Guided bus tours of the city and its environs are given by **Salzburg Sightseeing Tours** (Mirabellplatz 2, tel. 0662/881615) and
Salzburg Panorama Tours (Mirabellplatz/St. Andrä Church,

tel. 0662/874029). Both can organize chauffeur-driven tours for up to eight people. Your hotel will have details.

Tourist Information

Salzburg's official tourist office, **Stadtverkehrsbüro,** has an **information center** at Mozartplatz 5, tel. 0662/847568, and at the main train station, tel. 0662/871712. The main office is at Auerspergstrasse 7, tel. 0662/889870.

Exploring Salzburg

Numbers in the margin correspond to points of interest on the Salzburg map.

Salzburg is best known as the birthplace of Wolfgang Amadeus Mozart and receives its greatest number of visitors during the annual Music Festival in July and August. Dominated by a fortress on one side and a minimountain (Kapuzinerberg) on the other, this Baroque city is best explored on foot. Many areas are pedestrian precincts. Some of the most interesting boutiques and shops are found in the dozens of alleys and passageways that link streets and squares. And take an umbrella: Salzburg is noted for sudden, brief downpours that start as abruptly as they stop.

The Salzach River separates the old and new towns; for the best perspective on the old, climb the **Kapuziner** hill (pathways from the Linzerstrasse or Steingasse). Once back down at river level, walk up through Markartplatz to the **Landestheater,** where operas and operettas are staged during the winter months; the larger houses used during the festival are closed most of the year. Wander through the Baroque **Mirabell** gardens in back of the theater and enjoy a dramatic view of the Old City, with the castle in the background. If you are pressed for time, you can pass up the **Baroque Museum.** *Admission: AS30 adults, AS15 children. Open Tues.–Sat. 9–noon and 2–5, Sun. 9–noon.*

However, be sure to look inside **Schloss Mirabell.** It houses public offices, including that of the city's registrar; many couples come here for the experience of being married in such a sumptuous setting. The foyer and staircase, decorated with cherubs, are good examples of Baroque excess. *Mirabellplatz, tel. 0662/8072–2258. Open Mon.–Thurs. 8–4, Fri. 8–1.*

Head left down Schwarzstrasse, back toward the center of the city. On your left is the famed **Mozarteum,** a music academy (Schwarzstr. 26, tel. 0662/874492) whose courtyard encloses the summerhouse in which Mozart wrote his opera *The Magic Flute.* Cross over the Markartsteg footbridge to the Old City side of the Salzach river. Turn right and walk a short distance up the Kai to the **Carolino Augusteum Museum.** This is the city museum, whose collections include art, archaeology, and musical instruments. *Museumsplatz 1, tel. 0662/843145. Admission: AS40 adults, AS15 children; combined ticket with toy museum in Bürgerspital (see below), cathedral excavations, and Folklore Museum: AS60 adults, AS20 children. Open Tues. 9–8, Wed.–Sun. 9–5.*

Time Out From the Carolinum, as the museum is called, turn the corner into Gstättengasse. On your right is the Mönchsberg elevator, which will take you to the top of the promontory. Once here,

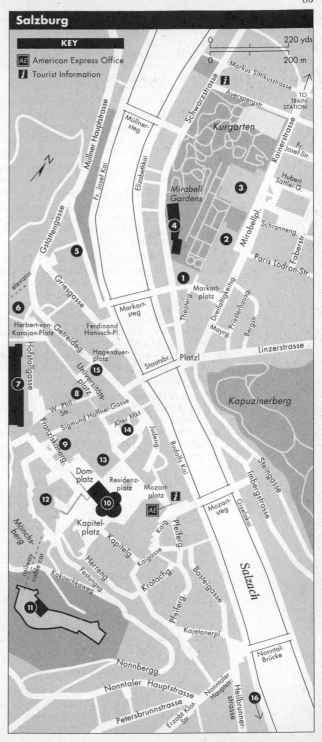

Salzburg

KEY

AE American Express Office

i Tourist Information

0   220 yds

0   200 m

TO
TRAIN
STATION

follow the signs and path south to **Burgerwehr-Einkehr** (Am Mönchsberg 19c, tel. 0662/841729); it offers superb views of the city, with the fortress in the background. It's a delightful hike over the ridge to the fortress from here (making the trip in reverse, however, will save you an uphill climb). *No credit cards. Closed mid-Oct.–May.*

⑥ Returning to city level, follow the Gstättengasse to the **Bürgerspital**, which houses a toy and musical instruments museum within its Renaissance arcades. *Bürgerspitalplatz 2, tel. 0662/847560. Admission: AS30 adults, AS10 children; combined ticket with Carolino Augusteum. Open Tues.–Sun. 9–5.*

⑦ Ahead is Herbert-von-Karajan-Platz, whose central **Pferdeschwemme** (Horse Fountain) is its most notable feature. Built into the side of the mountain itself is the **Festspielhaus**, a huge complex where Salzburg's annual festival, the Festspiel, is held. *Hofstallgasse 1, tel. 0662/80450. Admission: AS30. Guided tours (not during rehearsals) weekdays at 2. No tours in July and Aug.*

⑧ From the Festspielhaus, turn left into the Wiener-Philharmoniker-Strasse. The **Kollegienkirche** (Collegiate Church) on the left is the work of Fischer von Erlach and is one of the best examples of Baroque architecture anywhere; be sure to look inside. Cut under the covered passageway and turn right into Sigmund-Haffner Gasse. At the corner on the left stands the

⑨ 13th-century **Franziskanerkirche** (Franciscan Church), an eclectic mix of architectural styles, with Romanesque and Gothic

⑩ accents. Nearby, at Domplatz, is the Salzburg **Dom** (cathedral), a magnificently proportioned building; note the great bronze doors as you enter.

To reach the fortress on the hill above, walk under the arcade to the right side of the church and up the narrow Festungsgasse at the back end of Kapitalplatz. From here, you can either follow the footpath up the hill or take a five-minute ride on the Festungsbahn, the inclined railway cable car. On a sunny day, a far more pleasurable—and strenuous!—route is to hike up the Festungsgasse, turning frequently to enjoy the changing panorama of the city below.

Time Out **Stieglkeller** offers a wide choice of good Austrian fare, served outdoors in summer. The local beer is superb. Try the *Salzburger Nockerln*, a heavenly meringue dessert. Stop here during the day; evenings feature a *Sound of Music* dinner theater. *Festungsgasse 10, tel. 0662/842681. Closed Oct.–Apr.*

⑪ Once you've reached the **Festung Hohensalzburg** itself, you can wander around on your own (admission: AS20 adults, AS10 children) or take a tour (AS25 adults, AS10 children). The views from the 12th-century fortress are magnificent in all directions. The main attraction is **St. George's Chapel**, built in 1501. A year later, in 1502, the Festung acquired the 200-pipe barrel organ, which plays daily in summer at 7 AM, 11 AM, and 6 PM. *Mönchsberg, tel. 0662/8042–2133. Open June–Sept., daily 8–7; Oct.–May, daily 8–6. Guided tour schedule varies.*

⑫ Back down in the city, follow the wall to **Stiftskirche St. Peter** (St. Peter's Abbey). The cemetery lends an added air of mystery to the monk's caves cut into the cliff. The catacombs attached to the church can be visited by guided tour. *Just off*

Kapitalplatz, tel. 0662/844–5780. Admission: AS12 adults, AS8 children. Tours May–Sept., daily 10–5, Oct.–Apr., daily 11–noon and 1:30–3:30.

Head around the cathedral to the spacious Residenzplatz, a **①** vast and elegant square. The **Residenz** itself includes prince-arch-bishop's living quarters and representative rooms. *Residenzplatz 1, tel. 0662/8042–2690. Admission: AS40 adults, children free. Tours Sept.–June, weekdays at 10–noon, 2, and 3; July–Aug., daily every 20 mins. from 10 to 4:40.*

The **Residenzgalerie,** in the same building complex, has an outstanding collection of 16th- to 19th-century European art. *Residenzplatz 1, tel. 0662/8042–2270. Admission: AS40 adults, children free. Combined ticket with state rooms: AS60. Open daily 10–5. Closed on Wed. Nov.–Apr.*

⑭ From the lower end of Residenzplatz, cut across into the **Alter Markt,** which still serves as an open market. Salzburg's narrowest house is squeezed into the north side of the square. Turn left into Getreidegasse, a tiny street packed with boutiques and fascinating shops. At the head of the tiny Rathausplatz is **⑮** **Mozart's birthplace,** now a museum. *Getreidegasse 9, tel. 0662/844313. Admission: AS50 adults, AS10 children. Open daily 9–6; during festival, daily 9–7.*

Wander along Getreidegasse, with its ornate wrought-iron shop signs and the Mönchsberg standing sentinel at the far end. Don't neglect the warren of interconnecting side alleys: These include a number of fine shops and often open onto impressive inner courtyards that, in summer, are guaranteed to be filled with flowers.

⑯ One popular excursion from Salzburg is to **Schloss Hellbrunn,** about 5 kilometers (3 miles) outside the city. Take bus line 55. The castle was built during the 17th century, and its rooms have some fine trompe l'oeil decorations. The castle's full name is Lustschloss Hellbrunn—Hellbrunn Pleasure Castle. It was designed for the relaxation of Salzburg's prince-bishops and includes the **Wasserspiele,** or fountains, conceived by someone with an impish sense of humor. Expect to get sprinkled as water shoots up from unlikely spots, such as the center of the table at which you're seated. The Baroque fountains are also fascinating. Both the castle and the fountain gardens can be included on a tour. *Tel. 0662/820372. Admission: AS48 adults, AS24 children. Tours Apr. and Oct., daily 9–4:30; May–Sept., daily 9–5. Evening tours July–Aug. at 6, 7, 8, 9, and 10 PM.*

The Hellbrunn complex houses the **Tiergarten** (zoo), which is outstanding because of the way in which the animals have been housed in natural surroundings. *Tel. 0662/820176. Admission: AS45 adults, AS20 children. Open Oct.–Mar., daily 8:30–4; Apr.–Sept., daily 8:30–6.* You can also visit the small **folklore museum.** *Admission: AS20 adults, AS10 children. Open Easter–Oct., daily 9–5.*

Dining

Some of the city's best restaurants are in the leading hotels. This is a tourist town, and popular restaurants are always crowded, so make reservations well ahead, particularly during festival time. For details and price-category definitions, *see* Dining in Staying in Austria, *above.*

Expensive **Goldener Hirsch.** Outstanding creative cuisine is served in a chic atmosphere. The service can be slow, but the grilled hare is well worth any wait. *Getreidegasse 37, tel. 0662/848511. Reservations required. AE, DC, MC, V.*

Mirabell. Although it's housed in a chain hotel (the Sheraton), some will argue that the Mirabell is the city's top restaurant. The menu mixes international dishes with adventurous versions of such local specialties as Wiener schnitzel and *Wildschwein* (wild boar). *Auerspergstr. 4, tel. 0662/889990. Reservations advised. AE, DC, MC, V.*

★ **Zum Eulenspiegel.** The intimate rooms of an Old City house contribute to the charm of this city restaurant. *Hagenauerplatz 2, tel. 0662/843180. Reservations advised. MC, V. Closed Sun. except during festival, and early Jan.–mid-Mar.*

Moderate **Alt Salzburg.** After an attempt to reach for the stars, this atmospheric restaurant has settled back to offer good local fare in its elegant red-and-white rooms. Try the traditional *Tafelspitz* (Austrian pot roast). *Bürgerspitalgasse 2, tel. 0662/841476. Reservations advised. AE, DC, MC, V. Closed Sun.*

★ **Zum Mohren.** Arched ceilings in the lower rooms add atmosphere to this historic house. Duck and venison are specialties. *Judengasse 9, tel. 0662/842387. Reservations advised. No credit cards. Closed Sun. and holidays.*

Inexpensive **Mundenhamer.** Local favorites such as roast pork taste particularly good in this stylized rustic setting. The goulash soup is splendid, as are the steak sandwiches and vegetarian specialties. *Rainerstr. 2, tel. 0662/875693. Reservations advised. AE, DC, MC, V. Closed Sun. and holidays.*

Sternbräu. If you're not looking for anything too fancy, try the hearty sausages and roasted meats at this vast complex, which has a pleasant garden in summer. *Griesgasse 23, tel. 0662/842140. No credit cards.*

★ **Wilder Mann.** The atmosphere may be too smoky for some (choose the outside courtyard in summer), but the beamed ceiling and antlers are genuine, as are the food and value. Try the *Tellerfleisch* (boiled beef) or game in season. *Getreidegasse 20/ Griesgasse 17 (passageway), tel. 0662/841787. Reservations advised. No credit cards. Closed Sun.*

Lodging

Reservations are always advisable and are essential at festival time (both Easter and summer). For details and price-category definitions, *see* Lodging in Staying in Austria, *above.*

Very Expensive **Bristol.** The attractive Belle Epoque facade of the Bristol will prepare you for the comfortable rooms and period furnishings inside. It is one of Austria's classic hotels. *Markartplatz 3, tel. 0662/873557, fax 0662/873557–6. 76 rooms with bath or shower. Facilities: restaurant, bar, garage. AE, DC, MC, V. Closed Jan.–Mar.*

★ **Goldener Hirsch.** This old-timer—800 years old and an inn since 1564—is conveniently set right in the heart of the Old City. Arched corridors, vaulted stairs, rustic furniture, and antiques provide a medieval atmosphere; the essential modern appliances stay ingeniously hidden. The restaurant (*see* Dining, *above*) is excellent. *Getreidegasse 35–37, tel. 0662/848511, fax 0662/843349. 75 rooms with bath. Facilities: restaurant, garage. AE, DC, MC, V.*

Österreichischer Hof. Salzburg's grande dame occupies a lovely riverside location, and the favored rooms give views of the fortress and the Old City. All four restaurants are excellent, but reservations are essential. *Schwarzstr. 5–7, tel. 0662/88977, fax 0662/88977–14. 120 rooms, 118 with bath or shower. Facilities: 4 restaurants, garage. AE, DC, MC, V.*

Schloss Mönchstein. With its sensational location overlooking the city, this is a top, if expensive, hotel. The restaurant is one of the best in the city. *Mönchsberg 26, tel. 0662/848555, fax 0662/848559. 17 rooms with bath. Facilities: restaurant, garage, tennis. AE, DC, MC, V.*

Sheraton. A Sheraton is a Sheraton, but this one has one of Salzburg's best restaurants. The location, beside the Mirabell Gardens, is a plus. *Auerspergstr. 4, tel. 0662/889990, fax 0662/881776. 165 rooms with bath. Facilities: restaurant, garage, indoor pools, laundry, health spa adjacent. AE, DC, MC, V.*

Expensive **Bayrischer Hof.** Not as close to the downtown area as visitors may want, but only two blocks from the train station. The modern rooms are very comfortable—which may explain why they're almost always full. *Kaiserschützenstr. 1, tel. 0662/469700, fax 0662/46970–75. 60 rooms with bath or shower. Facilities: 3 restaurants, garage. AE, DC, MC, V.*

★ **Elefant.** This charming old inn in the heart of the Old City has been totally modernized without losing the carpets, country furniture, or resultant atmosphere. *Sigmund-Haffner-Gasse 4, tel. 0662/843397, fax 0662/840109–28. 36 rooms with bath or shower. Facilities: restaurant, garage. AE, DC, MC, V.*

Gablerbräu. A country inn transported to town, the Gablerbräu is cheerful and friendly and an obvious favorite with repeat visitors. *Linzergasse 9, tel. 0662/88965, fax 0662/88965–55. 51 rooms with bath or shower. Facilities: restaurant. AE, DC, MC, V.*

Moderate **Markus Sittikus.** This hotel is reasonably priced and more than reasonably comfortable. The train station is within walking distance unless you're loaded with luggage. *Markus-Sittikus-Str. 20, tel. 0662/871–1210, fax 0662/871121–58. 41 rooms with bath or shower. AE, DC, MC, V.*

The Arts

Festivals Tickets for the festival performances are almost impossible to get once you are in Salzburg. Write or fax ahead to **Salzburger Festspiele,** Postfach 140, A-5010 Salzburg, fax 0662/891114.

Opera, Music, Theater and opera are presented in the **Festspielhaus** (*see* Ex-
and Art ploring, *above*), opera and operetta at the **Landestheater** (Schwarzstr. 22, tel. 0662/871–5120), and concerts at the **Mozarteum** (Schwarzstr. 26, tel. 0662/873154). Chamber music—in costume—is performed in **Schloss Mirabell.** Special art exhibits in the **Carolino Augusteum** (*see* Exploring, *above*) are often outstanding.

Innsbruck

Arriving and Departing

By Plane The airport is 3 kilometers (2 miles) to the west of the city. For flight information, phone 0512/22220.

Between the Airport Buses (Line F) to the city center (Maria-Theresien-Str.) run
and Downtown every 20 minutes and take about 20 minutes. Get your ticket
from the bus driver; it costs AS18. Taxis should take no more
than 10–15 minutes into town, and the fare is about AS120–
AS150.

By Train All trains stop at the city's main station at Südtiroler-Platz.
Train connections are available to Munich, Vienna, Rome, and
Zurich. For train information, phone 0512/1717. Ticket reser-
vations, tel. 0512/1700.

By Bus The terminal is to the right of the main train station.

By Car Exit from the east–west autobahn or from the Brenner autobahn running south to Italy. Much of the downtown area is
paid-parking only; get parking vouchers at tobacco shops, coin-
operated dispensers, or the city tourist office at Burggraben 3.

Getting Around

By Bus and Most bus and streetcar routes begin or end at Südtiroler-Platz,
Streetcar site of the main train station. The bus is the most convenient
way to reach the five major ski areas outside the city. Many hotels offer free transportation with direct hotel pickup; for those
staying in the Old City, the buses leave from in front of the
Landestheater.

By Taxi Taxis are not much faster than walking, particularly along the
one-way streets and in the Old City. To order a radio cab, phone
0512/5311 or 0512/45500.

Guided Tours

Sightseeing Tours Bus tours lasting 1½ hours cover the city's highlights and leave
from the hotel information office at the railroad station
(Südtiroler-Platz) daily at noon and at 12:10 from the Hypo-
bank, across from the Tiroler Landesreisebüro on Bozner-
Platz. During the summer, additional buses are scheduled at 10
and 2. Your hotel or one of the tourist offices will have tickets
and details.

Tourist Information

The city's two main tourist offices are at Burggraben 3 (tel.
0512/5356, fax 0512/598507—Innsbruck) and Wilhelm-Greil-
Strasse 17 (tel. 0512/532–0170, fax 0512/532–0175—Tirol).

American Express (Brixnerstr. 3, tel. 0512/582491, fax 0512/
573385).
Wagon-Lits Travel (Brixnerstr. 2, tel. 0512/520790, fax 0512/
520–7985).

Exploring Innsbruck

*Numbers in the margin correspond to points of interest on the
Innsbruck map.*

Squeezed by the mountains and sharing the valley with the Inn
River, Innsbruck is compact and very easy to explore on foot.
The ancient city—it received its municipal charter in 1239—no
doubt owes much of its fame and charm to its unique situation.
To the north, the steep, sheer sides of the Alps rise like a shim-
mering blue-and-white wall from the edge of the city, an awe-

inspiring backdrop to the mellowed green domes and red roofs of the picturesque Baroque town.

Modern-day Innsbruck retains close associations with three historical figures: Emperor Maximilian I and Empress Maria Theresa, both of whom are responsible for much of the city's architecture, and Andreas Hofer, a Tirolean patriot. You will find repeated references to these personalities as you tour the city. A good starting point is the **Goldenes Dachl** (the Golden Roof), which made the ancient mansion whose balcony it covers famous. (It's actually made of copper tiles guilded with 14 kg [31 lbs.] of gold.) The building now houses an **Olympic Museum,** which features videotapes of the Innsbruck winter Olympics. *Herzog Friedrich-Str. 15, tel. 0512/536–0575. Admission: AS22 adults, children free. Open daily 9:30–5:30. Closed on Mon. Nov.–Feb.*

2 A walk up the Hofgasse brings you to the **Hofburg,** the Rococo imperial palace, with its ornate reception hall decorated with portraits of Maria Theresa's ancestors. *Rennweg 1, tel. 0512/ 587186. Admission: AS30 adults, AS5 children. Open mid-May–mid-Oct., daily 9–5; mid-Oct.–mid-May, Mon.–Sat. 9–5.*

3 Close by is the **Hofkirche,** the Imperial Church, built as a mausoleum for Maximilian. The emperor is surrounded by 24 marble reliefs portraying his accomplishments, as well as 28 oversize statues of his ancestors, including the legendary King Arthur. Andreas Hofer is also buried here. Don't miss the silver chapel with its ornate altar. The **Tiroler Volkskunstmuseum** (Tirolean Folk Art Museum) is housed in the Hofkirche, too, and shows costumes, rustic furniture, and farmhouse rooms decorated in styles ranging from Gothic to Rococo. *Universitätsstr. 2, tel. 0512/584302. Admission: AS20 adults, children free (Hofkirche), AS40 adults, AS15 children (Volkskunstmuseum); combined ticket: AS50 adults. Hofkirche open Sept.–June, daily 9–5; July–Aug. daily 9–5:30. Volkskunstmuseum open Sept.–June, Mon.–Sat. 9–5, Sun. 9–noon; July–Aug., Mon.–Sat. 9–5:30, Sun. 9–noon.*

4 Follow Museumstrasse to the **Ferdinandeum,** which houses Austria's largest collection of Gothic art, as well as paintings from the 19th and 20th centuries. *Museumstr. 15, tel. 0512/ 594–8971. Admission: AS50 adults, AS20 children. Open May–Sept., daily 10–5, Thurs. eve. 7–9; Oct.–Apr., Tues.– Sat. 10–noon and 2–5, Sun. and holidays 10–1.*

Time Out Relax over coffee, excellent pastries, and a newspaper in just about any language you want under the crystal chandeliers at **Café Central,** in the Hotel Central, just off Wilhelm Greil-Str. *Gilmstr. 5, tel. 0512/5920. AE, DC, MC, V.*

5 Cut back down Wilhelm Greil-Strasse to the **Triumphpforte** (Triumphal Arch), built in 1765, and walk up Maria Theresien-
6 Strasse past the **Annasäule** (Anna Column) for a classic "postcard" view of Innsbruck with the Alps in the background.

Off the Beaten Track

Just 3 kilometers (2 miles) southeast of the city and easily reached by either bus or streetcar is **Schloss Ambras,** one of Austria's finest and best-preserved castles. Originally dating

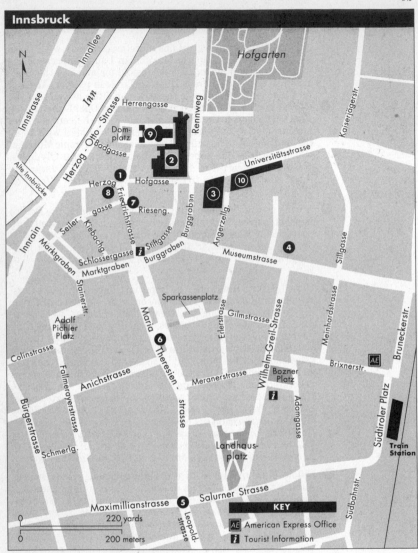

Innsbruck

Major Attractions
Annasäule, **6**
Ferdinandeum, **4**
Goldenes Dachl, **1**
Hofburg, **2**
Hofkirche, **3**
Triumphpforte, **5**

Other Attractions
Dom zu St. Jakob, **9**
Helblinghaus, **8**
Stadtturm, **7**
Tiroler Volkskunst-
museum, **10**

from the 11th century, it was later rebuilt as a residence for the archduke Ferdinand of Tirol (from 1564 to 1582), so most of what you now see is in German Renaissance style. The collection includes numerous pictures (including the only known portrait of Count Dracula), weapons, armor, objets d'art, and furniture. *In the village of Ambras (streetcar line 3 or bus K), tel. 0512/48446. Admission: AS30 adults, AS10 children. Open Apr.–Oct., Wed.–Mon. 10–5.*

In the mountains high above the city is the unique **Alpine Zoo,** with alpine animals and birds in their native environment and even an aquarium. And, of course, there's a restaurant at the top. You can either hike up or take the Hungerberg funicular, then the cable car. A combination funicular-cable entry card is available at the Hungerberg ticket office. *Weiherburggasse 37, tel. 0512/292923. Admission: AS56 adults, AS28 children. Open summer 9–6; winter 9–dusk.*

Dining

For details and price-category definitions, *see* Dining in Staying in Austria.

Expensive **Europa-Stüberl.** Regional specialties and the resplendent setting are two reasons why the Hotel Europa's restaurant is highly regarded by locals and visitors. *Brixnerstr. 6, tel. 0512/593–1648. Reservations advised. AE, DC, MC, V.*

Schwarzer Adler. This place drips with atmosphere, its massive-beamed rooms a perfect backdrop for typical Austrian dishes like *Knödeln* (dumplings) and *Tafelspitz* (boiled beef). *Kaiserjägerstr. 2, tel. 0512/587109. Reservations advised. AE, DC, MC, V.*

★ **Tiroler Stuben.** The rustic pine setting in the Alpotel is just right for garlic soup and house specialties such as *Bauernschöpsenes*, a delicious lamb plate. *Innrain 13, tel. 0512/577931. Reservations required. AE, DC, MC, V. Closed Sat. lunch, Sun., and holidays.*

Moderate **Goethestube.** The wine tavern of the city's oldest inn, the Goldener Adler (*see* Lodging, *below*), is one of Innsbruck's best. It was here that Goethe (who lent his name to the tavern) sipped quantities of red South Tirolean wine during his stays in 1786 and 1790. *Herzog Friedrich-Str. 6, tel. 0512/586334. Reservations not necessary. AE, DC, MC, V.*

★ **Hirschenstuben.** Old-fashioned hospitality and dark-wood trimmings are found in force at this charming local favorite. *Kiebachgasse 5, tel. 0512/582979. Reservations advised. AE, DC, MC, V. Closed Sun.*

★ **Ottoburg.** A rabbit warren of rooms, in a 13th-century building, the Ottoburg is exactly right for an intimate, cozy lunch or dinner. It's packed with Austriana and is 100% genuine. Go for the trout if it's available. *Herzog Friedrich-Str. 1, tel. 0512/574652. Reservations advised. AE, DC, MC, V.*

Stieglbräu. Lovers of good beer will be delighted to find this popular rustic spot, which, in addition to its thirst-quenching brews, provides good, solid Austrian fare. Portions are huge, the garden exceptionally pleasant. *Wilhelm-Greil-Str. 25, 0512/584338. No credit cards.*

Inexpensive **Gasthaus Steden.** The substantial portions and unassuming (if occasionally smoky) atmosphere attract visiting business people as well as many local regulars to this thoroughly genuine

Gasthaus. The roast pork is particularly tasty and the daily specials are a bargain. *Anichstr. 15, tel. 0512/580890. No reservations. No credit cards. Closed Sun.*

Weinhaus Happ. Some of the smaller rooms upstairs in this historic house may be a bit smoky, and service falters if groups arrive, but local specialties such as game in season are excellent. *Herzog Friedrich-Str. 14, tel. 0512/582980. Reservations advised. AE, DC, MC, V. Closed Sun.*

Lodging

For details and price-category definitions, *see* Lodging in Staying in Austria.

Very Expensive **Europa.** The Europa is a postwar building blessed with a considerable amount of charm. Some rooms have period furnishings; others are 20th-century modern. *Südtiroler Platz 2, tel. 0512/5931, fax 0512/587800. 132 rooms with bath. Facilities: restaurant, bar, beauty salon, sauna, solarium, garage. AE, DC, MC, V.*

★ **Goldener Adler.** The Golden Eagle has been an inn since 1390, and over the centuries it has welcomed nearly every king, emperor, duke, or poet who passed through the city. The facade looks suitably ancient, and inside, passages and stairs twist romantically and rooms crop up when least expected. The several restaurants offer well-prepared seasonal and local dishes. *Herzog Friedrich-Str. 6, tel. 0512/586334, fax 0512/584409. 40 rooms with bath or shower. Facilities: restaurants, bar, coffee shop. AE, DC, MC, V.*

Scandic Crown. Innsbruck's newest major hotel belongs to the leading Scandinavian chain. The rooms are modern plush; the facilities, including sauna, are extensive. The buffet lunch is good value and abundant. The train station is nearby. *Salurnerstr. 15, tel. 0512/59350, fax 0512/593-5220. 191 rooms with bath. Facilities: restaurants, bar, health club, pool, sauna, garage. AE, DC, MC, V.*

Schwarzer Adler. Rooms are individual, warm, and inviting in this traditional Romantik Hotel. It's an easy stroll to the Old City. *Kaiserjägerstr. 2, tel. 0512/587109, fax 0512/561697. 27 rooms. Facilities: 2 restaurants, bar, garage. AE, DC, MC, V.*

Expensive **Alpotel.** Abundant space, comfort, and modern style are the keys in this new hotel on the edge of the Old City. The staff is particularly helpful. Many rooms have balconies with splendid views. The Tiroler Stuben restaurant (*see* Dining, *above*) is outstanding. *Innrain 13 (Ursulinenpassage), tel. 0512/577931, fax 0512/577931-15. 75 rooms with bath. Facilities: restaurant, sauna, solarium, bar, café, garage, transportation to ski areas. AE, DC, MC, V.*

Moderate **Weisses Kreuz.** Occupying an honored position just steps away
★ from the famous Goldenes Dachl (*see* Exploring, *above*), Weisses Kreuz is itself a lovely old historic building. *Herzog Friedrich-Str. 31, tel. 0512/594790, fax 0512/59479-90. 39 rooms, 28 with bath or shower. Facilities: restaurant. AE, V.*

Inexpensive **Binder.** A short streetcar trip (Line 3) from the center of town shouldn't be too high a price to pay for less costly comfort at this small, friendly hotel. *Dr.-Glatz-Str. 20, tel. 0512/42236, fax 0512/42236-99. 32 rooms, most with bath or shower. AE, DC, MC, V.*

Weisses Lamm. You're across the river in this quaint older but comfortable house and still just minutes from the Old City on foot. *Mariahilfstr. 12, tel. 0512/283156. 37 rooms, some with bath or shower. MC, V.*

The Arts

Most hotels have a monthly calendar of events (in English). Tickets to most events are available at the main tourist office, Burggraben 3 (tel. 0512/5356, fax 0512/535643). Opera, operetta, musicals, and concerts take place at the **Tiroler Landestheater** (Rennweg 2, tel. 0512/520744) and **Kongresshaus.**

4 Belgium

Belgium covers a strip of land just under 320 kilometers (200 miles) long and 160 kilometers (100 miles) wide bordering the North Sea between France and Holland. With more than 10 million people, Belgium is the second most densely populated country in the world. Both Parisians and Amsterdammers tend to think of Belgium as a substandard version of "pure" French or Dutch culture. However, Belgium has a distinctive culture, or rather, two: Flemish and Walloon. The Flemish, who speak Dutch (Flemish), inhabit the northern half of the country and account for 56% of the population. The French-speaking Walloons live in the other half. The capital, Brussels, is officially designated a dual-language area.

Belgium is the world's most heavily industrialized country, with only 5% of the working population engaged in agriculture (though they still manage to produce 165 different cheeses and any number of fine sausages). Besides being natural entrepreneurs, the Belgians also work very hard—partly to make up for what has so long been denied them. In the course of history, the Belgians have been ruled by the Romans, French, Spanish, Austrians, Dutch, English, and Germans. Many of Europe's greatest battles have been fought on Belgian soil—from the Hundred Years' War to Waterloo to the long-slogging encounters of World War I. During World War II, this territory witnessed both the initial blitzkrieg of Nazi Panzer units and Hitler's final desperate counterattack against the advancing Allies in the Ardennes—an offensive that has gone down in history as the Battle of the Bulge.

The south of the country is a wild wooded area, with mountains rising to more than 620 meters (2,000 feet). In the Dutch-speaking north, on the other hand, the land is flat and heavily cultivated, much as it is in neighboring Holland. Here stand the medieval Flemish cities of Ghent and Brugge, with their celebrated carillons and canals—not to mention the 68 kilometers (42 miles) of sandy beaches that make up the country's northern coastline. Due north of Brussels lies Antwerp, the country's dynamic seaport. This city, where the painter Rubens lived, is now the world's leading diamond-cutting center.

Brussels stands in the very center of the country. A booming, expanding, and often expensive city, it is now the capital of Europe. Here the European Community (EC) has its headquarters. The city boasts more ambassadors than any other in the world—approximately 160. Partly as a result of this concentration of power and partly because of the Belgians' celebrated love of good food, Brussels has become one of the most renowned gastronomic cities in the world.

As befits a bourgeois culture, the Belgians are great believers in the quality of life. In practice, this means that meals, parks, cars, and houses are large. Homes are highly individualistic and comfortable; trendy designer bars are cozy as well as chic. Except on the road, Belgians are generous and have time for old-fashioned courtesy.

But Belgians are not just creatures of the senses. A robust culture is celebrated in paintings by Bruegel and Rubens, Magritte, and Delvaux; by exciting Gothic, Renaissance, and Art Nouveau architecture; and by the best jazz in Europe. Belgium is no self-publicist, but quietly and confidently waits to be discovered.

Belgium

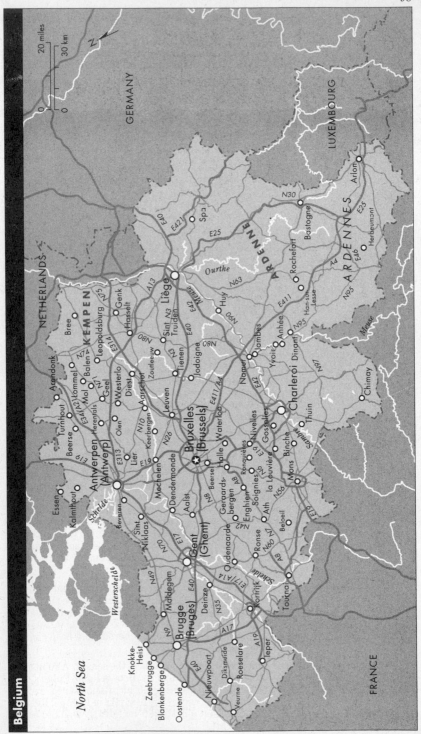

Essential Information

Before You Go

When to Go   The tourist season runs from early May to late September and peaks in July and August, when the weather is best. In recent years, however, off-season travel has become increasingly popular. In the coastal resorts, some hotels and restaurants remain open all year.

Climate   Temperatures range from around 65 F in May to an average 73 F in July and August. In winter, temperatures drop to an average of about 40 to 45 F. Snow is unusual except in the mountains of the Ardennes, where cross-country skiing is a popular sport in February and March.

The following are the average daily maximum and minimum temperatures for Brussels.

Jan.	40F	4C	May	65F	18C	Sept.	69F	21C
	30	−1		46	8		51	11
Feb.	44F	7C	June	72F	22C	Oct.	60F	15C
	32	0		52	11		45	7
Mar.	51F	11C	July	73F	23C	Nov.	48F	9C
	36	2		54	12		38	3
Apr.	58F	14C	Aug.	72F	22C	Dec.	42F	6C
	41	5		54	12		32	0

Currency   The unit of currency in Belgium is the franc. There are bills of 100, 500, 1,000, 5,000, and 10,000 francs in addition to coins of 1, 5, 20, and 50 francs. Do not confuse the new 50-franc coin and the old 5-franc coin. At press time (spring 1993), the exchange rate was about BF33 to the dollar and BF60 to the pound sterling.

Traveler's checks and credit cards are the safest and simplest ways to carry money. American Express, Bank of America, Barclays, Eurocheques, and Thomas Cook traveler's checks are all honored in Belgium. All major credit cards are widely accepted, too.

What It Will Cost   Brussels has dropped to 16th place on the list of Europe's most expensive cities, partially because prices have remained fairly stable here in the last few years. You can find deluxe hotels and restaurants as expensive as those in Paris or London, but there is also a wide selection of reasonably priced establishments. Substantially discounted weekend and summer rates are available at the leading Brussels hotels. The sales tax on most items ranges from 6% to 33% on luxury items, including jewelry, furs, and a wide selection of electronic goods. Many shops advertise goods "for export"; they provide documents you can use to reclaim the sales tax or value-added tax (VAT) when you leave the country (*see* Shopping in Staying in Belgium, *below*). A proper invoice (*facture*) will suffice, if it has been stamped by customs as you depart. If you're making substantial purchases, ask the shop to provide the export papers.

Sample Prices   A cup of coffee in a café will cost BF45–BF60; a glass of beer, BF35–BF85; and a glass of wine, about BF100. Train travel averages BF6 per mile, the average bus/metro/tram ride costs

BF45, theater tickets cost about BF500, and movie tickets about BF250.

Customs on Arrival Since the Europeau Community's 1992 agreement on a unified European market, the limits of what visitors from EC countries may bring in have become generous to the point of being meaningless. For example, travelers from EC nations may now bring in 120 bottles of wine, 10 liters of alcohol, and 800 cigarettes. Visitors from non-EC countries can bring in 200 cigarettes or 50 cigars or 250 grams of tobacco, 2 liters of still wine and 1 liter of spirits or 2 liters of aperitif wine, and 50 grams of perfume. Other goods from non-EC countries may not exceed BF2,000 in value. There are no restrictions on the import or export of currency.

Language Language is a sensitive subject that has led to the collapse of at least two governments. There are three national languages in Belgium: French, spoken primarily in the south of the country (Wallonia); Flemish, spoken in the north; and German, spoken in a small area in the east. Brussels is bilingual, with both French and Flemish officially recognized, though French predominates. Many people speak English in Brussels and in the north (Flanders). If your French is good but your Flemish nonexistent, it is politic to speak English to Flemings, especially in Antwerp or Flanders. In Wallonia you may have to muster whatever French you possess, but in tourist centers you will be able to find people with at least basic English.

Getting Around

By Car
Road Conditions Belgium has an excellent system of expressways, and the main roads are generally very good. Road numbers for main roads have the prefix N; expressways, the prefix A or E.

Rules of the Road Drive on the right and pass on the left (passing on the right is forbidden). Seat belts are compulsory in both front and rear seats. Each car must have a warning triangle to be used in the event of a breakdown or accident. At intersections, particularly in cities, traffic on the right has priority. Adhere strictly to this rule because there are few stop or yield signs. In Brussels, the system of tunnels and ring roads is generally effective. Cars within a traffic circle have priority over cars entering it. Buses and streetcars have priority over cars. Maximum speed limits are 120 kph (70 mph) on highways, 90 kph (55 mph) on major roads, and 50 kph (30 mph) in cities.

Road Signs Road signs are written in the language of the region, so you need to know that Antwerpen (Flemish) is Anvers (French) and Antwerp to us; likewise, Brugge and Brussel (Flemish) are Bruges and Bruxelles (French); Gent (Flemish) is Gand (French) and Ghent (English). Even more confusing, Liège and Luik are the same place, as are Louvain and Leuven and Namur and Namen. Even more difficult is Mons (French) and its Flemish equivalent, Bergen, or Tournai (French), which becomes Doornik in Flemish!

Parking Most cities have metered on-street parking (parking meters take 5- or 20-franc coins) and parking lots.

By Train Fast and frequent trains connect all main towns and cities. If you intend to travel frequently, buy a **Benelux Tourrail Ticket,** which allows unlimited travel throughout Belgium, Luxembourg, and the Netherlands for any five days during a 17-day period. If you are over 26, the cost of the five-day pass is BF4,620 first-class and BF3,080 second-class. For those under 26, the pass costs BF2,990 first-class and BF1,990 second-class. The **Belgian Tourrail Ticket** allows unlimited travel for five days in a 17-day period at a cost of BF2,700 first-class and BF1,800 second-class; for those under 26, BF2,030 first-class and BF1,350 second-class. Young people from 12 to 26 can purchase a **Go Pass** for BF990, valid for eight one-way trips in a six-month period on the Belgian rail network. All of the above are available at any Belgian train station.

Special weekend round-trip tickets are valid from Friday noon to Monday noon: A 40% reduction is available on the first traveler's ticket and a 60% reduction on companions' tickets. During the tourist season there are similar weekday fares to the seaside and the Ardennes.

By Bus Intercity bus service is almost nonexistent. Details of services are available at train stations and tourist offices.

By Bicycle You can rent a bicycle from Belgian railways at 48 stations throughout the country; train travelers get reduced rates. Bicycling is especially popular in the flat northern and coastal areas. Bicycle lanes are provided in many Flemish cities, but bicycling in Brussels is madness.

Staying in Belgium

Telephones
Local Calls Pay phones work with 5- and 20-franc coins or with Telecards, available in a number of denominations starting from BF200. The Telecards can be purchased at any post office and at many newsstands. Most phone booths that accept Telecards have a list indicating where these cards are sold. An average local call costs BF10 or BF20.

International Calls The least expensive method is to buy a high-denomination Telecard and make a direct call from a phone booth. A five-minute phone call to the United States at a peak time will cost about BF750 by this method. International calls can also be made at most hotels, but nearly all have a service charge that may double the cost. Operator-assisted international calls can also be made at most post offices.

Mail
Postal Rates Airmail letters to the United States cost BF32 for the first 5 grams and BF4 more for each additional 5 grams; postcards cost BF32. Airmail letters to the United Kingdom are BF15 for the first 20 grams.

Receiving Mail You can have mail forwarded directly to your hotel. If you're uncertain where you'll be staying, have mail sent in care of **American Express** (1 pl. Louise, B-1000 Brussels). Cardholders are spared the $2-per-letter charge.

Shopping
Sales-Tax Refunds When you buy goods for export, you can ask most shops to fill out special forms covering VAT or sales tax. An itemized invoice showing the amount of VAT will also do. When you leave Belgium, you must declare the goods at customs and have the customs officers stamp the documents. Once you're back home, you simply send the stamped forms back to the shop and your sales tax will be refunded. This facility is available in most boutiques and large stores and covers most purchases of more than BF2,000. There's another option as well: In shops displaying a "Europe Tax-Free" sign you will be given a check for slightly

less than the amount of TVA you have paid; this check can then be redeemed at the airport. It's up to you to decide whether the convenience is worth the slight charge.

Opening and Closing Times   **Banks** are open weekdays from 9 to 4; some close for an hour at lunch. Exchange facilities are usually open on weekends, but you'll get a better rate during the week.

Museums are generally open from 10 to 5 six days a week. Closing day is Monday in Brussels and Antwerp, Tuesday in Brugge. Check individual listings.

Shops are open weekdays and Saturdays from 10 to 6 and generally stay open later on Friday.

National Holidays   January 1; April 4 (Easter Monday); May 1 (May Day); May 12 (Ascension); May 23 (Pentecost Monday); July 21 (National Holiday); August 15 (Assumption); November 1 (All Saints' Day); November 11 (Armistice); December 25.

Dining   Nearly all Belgians take eating seriously and are discerning about fresh produce and innovative recipes. They are prepared to spend a considerable amount on a celebratory meal, and you will almost always find families sharing a meal even in the most expensive restaurants. At the top end of the scale, the *menus de dégustation* offer a chance to sample a large selection of the chef's finest dishes. Fixed-price menus are available in virtually all restaurants and often represent very considerable savings. Menus and prices are always posted outside. Belgian specialties include *lapin à la bière* (rabbit in beer), *faisan à la brabançonne* (pheasant with chicory), *waterzooi* (a rich chicken or fish hotpot), and *carbonnades* (chunky stews). A Belgian peculiarity is that dogs are allowed into most restaurants.

Local specialties include truly marvelous asparagus from Mechelen, at their best in May, *salade Liègoise*, a hot salad with beans and bacon (Liège); wild strawberries and freshwater fish from the Meuse River (Namur); different permutations of sprouts, chicory, and pheasant (Brussels); and shrimps, oysters, and mussels (Flanders).

Belgian snacks are equally appetizing. The waffle *(gaufre/wafel)* has achieved world fame, but *couques* (sweet buns), *speculoos* (spicy gingerbread biscuits), and *pain d'amandes* (nutty after-dinner biscuits) are less well known. For lunch, cold cuts, rich pâtés, and *jambon d'Ardenne* (Ardenne ham) are popular, often accompanied by goat's cheese and rye or wholemeal bread.

Mealtimes   Most hotels serve breakfast until 10. Belgians usually eat lunch between 1 and 3, some making it quite a long, lavish meal. However, the main meal of the day is dinner, which most Belgians eat between 7 and 10; peak dining time is about 8.

Dress   Belgians tend to be fairly formal and dress conservatively when dining out in the evenings. Generally speaking, the more prestigious the restaurant, the more formal the dress. Younger Belgians favor stylish, casual dress in most restaurants.

Ratings   Prices are per person and include a first course, main course, dessert, tip, and sales tax, but no wine. Best bets are indicated by a star ★.

Category	All Areas
Very Expensive	over BF3,000
Expensive	BF2,000–BF3,000
Moderate	BF1,000–BF2,000
Inexpensive	under BF1,000

Lodging You can trust Belgian hotels, almost without exception, to be clean and of a high standard. The more modern hotels in city centers can be very expensive, but there are smaller, well-appointed hotels, offering lodging at excellent rates. However, within the major cities, the moderate and inexpensive hotels are relatively disappointing in terms of charm and even value for the money, though not in terms of comfort and location. The family-run establishments in out-of-the-way spots, such as the Ardennes, can be surprisingly inexpensive, especially if you are visiting them out of season.

Pensions Pensions offer a double room with bath or shower and full board from BF2,500 to BF3,500 in Brussels and from BF2,000 to BF3,000 elsewhere. These terms are often available for a minimum stay of three days.

Youth Hostels For information about youth hostels, contact **Fédération Belge des Auberges de la Jeunesse** (tel. 02/215–31–00). In the United States: **American Youth Hostels, Inc.,** Box 37613, Washington, DC 20013. In the United Kingdom: **Camping and Caravan Club Ltd.,** 11 Lower Grosvenor Pl., London SW1, or **Youth Hostels Association International Travel Bureau,** 14 Southampton St., London WC2.

Camping Belgium is well supplied with camping and caravan sites. For details, contact the **Royal Camping and Caravaning Club of Belgium** (rue Madeleine 31, B-1000 Brussels, tel. 02/513-12-87).

Ratings Hotel prices are inclusive and are usually listed in each room. All prices are for two people in a double room. Best bets are indicated by a star ★.

Category	All Areas
Very Expensive	BF8,500–BF12,000
Expensive	BF6,000–BF8,500
Moderate	BF4,000–BF6,000
Inexpensive	under BF4,000

Tipping Tipping has been losing its hold in Belgium over the past few years because a service charge is almost always figured into the bill. For example, a tip of 16% is included in all restaurant and café bills. The tip is also included in taxi fares. If you want to give more, round the amount up to the nearest BF50 or BF100. Porters in railway stations ask a fixed per-suitcase price, BF30 in the day and BF35 at night. For moderately priced hotels, BF50 should be an adequate tip for bellhops and doormen; in the very expensive hotels, though, BF100 is usually more appropriate. At the movies, tip the usher BF20, whether or not he or she shows you to your seat. In theaters, tip about BF50 for programs. In restaurants, cafés, movie theaters, theaters, train stations, and other public places, you should tip the wash-room attendant BF10.

Brussels

Arriving and Departing

By Plane All international flights arrive at Brussels's Zaventem Airport, about a 30-minute drive or a 16-minute train trip from the city center. **Sabena, American, Delta, TWA,** and **United** all fly into Brussels from the United States. **Sabena, British Airways,** and newcomer **British Midland,** often cheaper and just as good, dominate the short-haul London (Heathrow)–Brussels route. **Air UK** flies to Brussels from London (Stansted), and **British Airways** from London (Gatwick). Several regional centers in the United Kingdom also have direct flights to Brussels.

Between the Airport There is regular train service from the airport to the Gare du
and Downtown Nord (North Station) and the Gare Centrale (Central Station), which leaves every 20 minutes. The trip takes 16 minutes and costs BF220 (first-class round-trip) and BF140 (second-class round-trip); you can buy a ticket on the train for a BF30 surcharge. The first train from the airport runs at 6:00 AM and the last one leaves at 11:46 PM. A taxi to the city center takes about half an hour and costs about BF1,000. You can save up to 25% on Autolux airport taxi fares by buying a voucher for the return trip at the same time. Beware free-lance taxi drivers who offer their services in the arrival hall.

By Train and From London, the train service connects with the Dover-
Boat/Jetfoil Oostende ferry or jetfoil services. From Oostende, the train takes you to Brussels. The whole journey by jetfoil takes just under five hours, but is longer by boat. For reservations and times, contact **British Rail International** in London (tel. 071/834–2345). A one-way London–Brussels ticket costs £44, excluding the £6–£9 (depending on the season) jetfoil supplement.

There are three main stations in Brussels: the Gare du Nord, Gare Centrale, and Gare du Midi (South Station). There is also a Gare du Quartier Léopold on the east side of the city. The Gare Centrale is most convenient for the downtown area, but is served mostly by commuter trains. For train information, telephone 02/219–26–40 or inquire at any station.

By Bus and From London, the Hoverspeed City Sprint bus connects with
Hovercraft/Ferry the Dover–Calais Hovercraft, and the bus then takes you on to Brussels. The journey takes 6½ hours; a one-way ticket costs £29. For reservations and times, contact **Hoverspeed** (tel. 081/554–7061). Overnight services by **National Express–Euro-lines** (tel. 071/730–0202) take the ferry and also cost £29 one way.

By Car Follow signs marked "Brussel Centrum" or "Bruxelles Centre." Many of the approaches are via an outer ring road, a belt-way surrounding the city, marked "ring." Exits for the city center are clearly marked. The same is true of the small ring within the city itself.

Getting Around

By Métro, Tram, and Bus The métro, trams (streetcars), and buses run as part of the same system. All three are clean and efficient, and a single ticket costs BF45. The best buy is a 10-trip ticket, which costs BF275, or a 24-hour card costing BF180. You need to stamp your ticket in the appropriate machine on the bus or tram; in the métro, your card is stamped as you pass through the automatic barrier. You can purchase these tickets in any métro station or at newsstands. Single tickets can be purchased on the bus.

Detailed maps of the Brussels public transportation network are available in most métro stations and at the Brussels tourist office in the Grand' Place (tel. 02/513–89–40). You get a map free with the new **Tourist Passport** (also available at the tourist office), which for BF200 allows you a 24-hour transport card and BF500 worth of museum admissions.

By Taxi Taxis are expensive, but tips are included in the fare. To call a cab, phone (or have the restaurant or hotel call) **Taxis Verts** (tel. 02/349–49–49) or **Taxis Oranges** (tel. 02/513–62–00) or catch one at a cabstand. The price per kilometer is BF35, but airport taxis charge higher rates.

Important Addresses and Numbers

Tourist Information The main tourist office for **Brussels** is in the Hôtel de Ville on the Grand' Place (tel. 02/513–89–40), open daily 9–6 during the main tourist season (Sun. off-season 10–2; Dec.–Feb., closed Sun.) The main tourist office for the rest of **Belgium** is near the Grand' Place (rue Marché-aux-Herbes 61, tel. 02/504–03–90) and has the same opening hours. There is a tourist office at **Waterloo** (chaussée de Bruxelles 149, tel. 02/354–99–10); it is open April–November 15, daily 9:30–6:30 and November 16–March, daily 10:30–5.

Embassies **U.S.** (blvd. du Régent 27, B–1000 Brussels, tel. 02/513–38–30). **Canadian** (av. de Tervuren 2, B–1000 Brussels, tel. 02/735–60–40). **U.K.** (rue d'Arlon 85, B–1040 Brussels, tel. 02/287–62–11).

Emergencies **Police** (tel. 101); **Accident** (tel. 100); **Ambulance** (tel. 02/649–11–22); **Doctor** (tel. 02/648–80–00 and 02/479–18–18); **Dentist** (tel. 02/426–10–26); **Pharmacy:** To find out which one is open on a particular night or on weekends, call 02/479–18–18.

English-Language Bookstores **House of Paperbacks** (chaussée de Waterloo 813, Uccle, tel. 02/343–11–22) is open Tuesday–Saturday 10–6. **W. H. Smith** (blvd. Adolphe Max 71–75, tel. 02/219–27–08) is open Monday–Saturday 9–6. **Librairie de Rome** (av. Louise 50b, tel. 02/511–79–37) is open Monday–Saturday 8 AM–10 PM, Sunday 9–6; the bookshop sells U.S. and U.K. newspapers, periodicals, and paperbacks.

Travel Agencies **American Express** (pl. Louise 2, B–1000 Brussels, tel. 02/512–17–40). **Wagons-Lits** (rue Ravenstein 22, tel. 02/512–98–78, and other locations).

Guided Tours

Orientation Tours **De Boeck Sightseeing** (tel. 02/513–77–44) operates city tours (BF700) with multilingual cassette commentary. Passengers are picked up at major hotels and at the tourist office in the town hall. More original are the tours run by **Chatterbus,** rue des Thuyas 12. For reservations, call 02/673–18–35 weekdays after 7 PM and weekends. Tours include a minibus tour of the main sites (BF600) and a walking tour that includes a visit to a bistro (BF250). Tours are operated early June–September.

Special-Interest Bus Tours **ARAU** organizes thematic city bus tours (in English), including "Brussels 1900: Art Nouveau" and "Brussels 1930: Art Déco." Tours begin in front of the post office and Bourse (stock exchange), rue Henri Maus; call 02/513–47–61 for times and bookings. The cost is around BF500 for a half-day tour.

Regional Tours **De Boeck Sightseeing Tours** (rue de la Colline 8, Grand' Place, tel. 02/513–77–44) visits Antwerp, the Ardennes, Brugge, Ghent, Ieper, and Waterloo.

Exploring Brussels

Brussels is a city of individualists. Walk along almost any street, and you will be surprised at how different each house is from its neighbor, often embellished in *Art Nouveau* style, in contrast with impersonal office blocks. Stop in the Grand' Place during a *son-et-lumière* (sound-and-light) show and your mood softens, or watch from a cozy bar, its tables stacked high with pancakes or covered with bottles of Duvel beer. Brussels is an odd mixture of the provincial and the international. Underneath the bureaucratic surface, the city is a subtle meeting of the Walloon and Flemish cultures. As the heart of the ancient Duchy of Brabant, Brussels retains its old sense of identity and civic pride. A stone's throw from the steel-and-glass towers, there are cobbled streets, canals where old barges still discharge their freight, and forgotten spots where the city's eventful and romantic past is plainly visible through its 20th-century veneer.

Numbers in the margin correspond to points of interest on the Brussels map.

The Grand' Place Begin in the **Grand' Place,** one of the most ornate market
❶ squares in Europe. There is a daily flower market and a colorful Sunday-morning bird market. On summer nights, the entire square is flooded with music and colored light. The Grand' Place also comes alive during local pageants, such as the *Mayboom;* the *Ommegang,* a splendid historical pageant (early July); and the biennial *Tapis de Fleurs,* when the entire square is covered by a carpet of flowers (mid-August, 1994).

The bombardment of the city by Louis XIV's troops left only
❷ the **Hôtel de Ville** (town hall) intact. Civic-minded citizens started rebuilding the Grand' Place immediately, but the highlight of the square remains the Gothic town hall. The central tower, combining boldness and light, is topped by a statue of St-Michel, the patron saint of Brussels. Among the magnificent rooms are the Salle Gothique, with its beautiful paneling; the Salle Maximilienne, with its superb tapestries; and the Council Chamber, with a ceiling fresco of the *Assembly of the Gods* painted by Victor Janssens in the early 15th century. *Admission: BF75. Open Tues.–Fri. 9:30–12:15 and 1:45–5 (in winter until 4), Sun. 10–12 and 2–4.*

❸ Opposite the town hall is the **Maison du Roi** (King's House)— though no king ever lived there—a 16th-century palace housing the **City Museum.** The collection includes important ceramics and silverware—Brussels is famous for both—church sculpture, and statues removed from the facade of the town hall, as well as an extravagant collection of costumes for Manneken Pis (*see* Exploring Brussels, *below*). *Grand' Place, tel. 02/511–27–42. Admission: BF80. Open weekdays 10–12:30 and 1:30–5, weekends 10–1.*

Time Out **La Rose Blanche** (Grand' Place 11, tel. 02/511–2754) is situated in a renovated three-story town house beside the town hall. Inside, brightly painted ceilings have been restored, but the minstrel's gallery, the creaking stairs, and the Chimay beer are original enough. Try a *fondue au parmesan* (cheese in batter) with a strong Chimay or a light *bière blanche.* A sweeter combination is coffee and a *dame blanche* (vanilla ice cream coated with hot chocolate sauce) or a *mousse au chocolat* (chocolate mousse). This is also the spot from which to view a son et lumière display on a summer's evening.

❹ Southwest of the town hall, on the corner of the rue de l'Etuve and rue du Chêne, stands the famous **Manneken Pis,** a fountain with a small bronze statue of a chubby little boy urinating. Made by Jerome Duquesnoy in 1619, the statue is known as "Brussels's Oldest Citizen" and is often dressed in costumes that are kept in the City Museum. The present Manneken is a copy; the original was kidnapped by 18th-century French and English invaders (soldiers, not tourists!).

Leaving the Manneken, cross the Grand' Place in the direction of the Marché-aux-Herbes. Opposite the tourist office (rue Marché-aux-Herbes 61), take the Petite rue des Bouchers, the main restaurant street in the heart of the tourist maelstrom. In Brussels fashion, each restaurant advertises its wares by means of large signs and carts packed with a selection of game and seafood. As a general rule, however, remember that the more lavish the display, the poorer the cuisine. From here, ex-
❺ plore the network of galleries called **Galeries St-Hubert,** which includes the Galerie de la Reine, Galerie du Roi, and Galerie des Princes, all built in 1847. Written on the central galleries is the motto "Omnibus Omnia" (Everything for Everyone), which is not altogether appropriate, given the designer prices.

Head south along the rue Marché-aux-Herbes and the rue Mad-
❻ eleine until you come to the **equestrian statue of King Albert.** To the left of the statue is the Central Station and to the right, the
❼ **Bibliothèque Nationale** (National Library). Walk through the formal gardens next to the National Library and look back at the ornate clock, with moving figures, over the lower archway. Try to hear—and see—it at noon, when it strikes the hour.

Place Royale If you continue walking through the gardens, you will arrive at the **place Royale,** the site of the Coudenberg palace, where the sovereigns once lived. Here you have a superb view over the
❽ lower town. On the northwest corner of the square is the **Musée d'Art Moderne** (Museum of Modern Art), housed in an exciting feat of modern architecture. On entry, a vertiginous descent into the depths reveals a sudden well of natural light. The paintings are displayed with the light and space they deserve. Although there are a few paintings by Matisse, Gauguin, Degas, and Dali, the surprise lies in the quality of Belgian modern art. See Magritte's luminous fantasies, James Ensor's

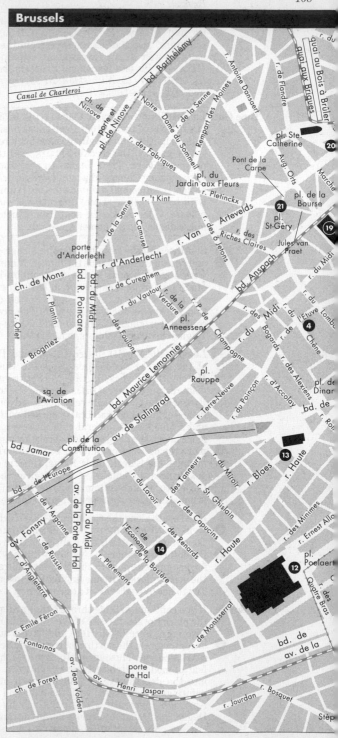

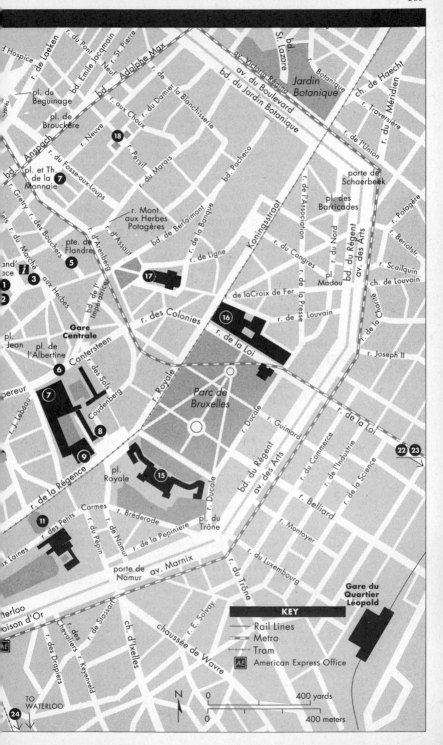

t Hospice
r. de Laeken
r. du Pont
bd. Emile Jacqmain
Neuf
r. St. Pierre
Adolphe Max
St. Lazare
av. Victoria Régina
av. du Boulevard
bd. du Jardin Botanique
Botanique
ch. de Haecht
Jardin Botanique

pl. du Beguinage
bd.
r. aux Choux
r. du Damier
la Blanchisserie
r. Traversière
r. de l'Union
r. du Méridien

Anspach
pl. de Brouckère
r. Neuve
r. du Fosse-aux-Loups
r. Persil
du Marais
r. Pacheco
porte de Schaerbeek

18

pl. et Th. de la Monnaie **7**
r. Grétry
r. des Bouchers
r. Mont. aux Herbes Potagères
Koningsstraat
r. de l'Association
bd. de Berlaimont
bd. de la Banque
pl. des Barricades
r. Potagère
r. Berlolstr.

pte. de Flandre
r. d'Arenberg
r. d'Assaut
r. de Ligne
r. du Nord
r. du Congres
pl. Madou
bd. du Régent
av. des Arts
r. Scailquin
ch. de Louvain

s r. du Marché
and'
ace **i**
5
aux Herbes
r. de l'Impératrice
17
r. de laCroix de Fer
r. de la Presse
r. Louvain
r. de la Charité

1
3
2
r. des Colonies
16
r. de la Loi
r. Joseph II

pl. Jean
Gare Centrale
pl. de l'Albertine
Cantersteen
r. des Sols

6
r. Royale
Parc de Bruxelles
r. Ducale
r. Guimard
r. de la Loi

pereur
r. J. Lebeau
7
Coudenberg
22 23

8
9
r. de la Régence
pl. Royale
15
bd. du Régent
av. des Arts
r. du Commerce
r. de l'Industrie
r. de la Science

Carmes
r. Bréderode
r. Ducale
r. Belliard

11
r. des Petits
r. du Pepin
r. de Namur
r. de la Pepinière
pl. du Trône
r. Montoyer

ux Laines
porte de Namur
av. Marnix
r. du Trône
r. du Luxembourg
Gare du Quartier Léopold

terloo
oison d'Or
r. des Chevaliers
r. de Stassart
r. E. Solvay
chaussée de Wavre

AE
r. des Draplers
r. des Keyenveld
ch. d'Ixelles

N

TO WATERLOO
24

KEY	
—	Rail Lines
⊟	Metro
⊞	Tram
AE	American Express Office

0   400 yards
0   400 meters

masks and still lifes, and Spilliaert's coastal scenes. Do not miss Permeke's deeply brooding *Fiancés* or Delvaux's Surrealist works. *Pl. Royale 1, tel. 02/513–96–30. Admission free. Open Tues.–Sun. 10–1 and 2–5.*

9 Next door is the **Musée Royale d'Art Ancien** (Royal Museum of Ancient Art). Here the collection is of Flemish and Dutch paintings, ranging from magnificent 15th- and 16th-century works—Cranach, Matsys, and Bruegel the Elder, among them—to Rubens (several fine canvases), Van Dyck, and David. Do not miss Bruegel's dramatic *La Chute d'Icare (The Fall of Icarus)* or Hieronymous Bosch's *Le Dernier Jugement (The Last Judgment)*, a malevolent portrait of humanity. *Rue de la Régence 10, tel. 02/513–96–30. Admission free. Open Tues.–Sun. 10–1 and 2–5.*

If you decide to divide your exploration of Brussels into two walks, this is a good place to break. You can pick up again at the same spot on the neoclassical place Royale. The Rue de la Régence runs from this square toward the Palais de Justice.
10 The Sablon lies along this street, on the right. The **Grand Sablon,** the city's most sophisticated square, is alive with cafés, restaurants, and antiques shops. Here, also, is the tempting Wittamer, the city's finest pastry shop. Toward the end of the square is the **church of Notre Dame du Sablon,** built in flamboyant Gothic style. Although much of the original workmanship was lost in restoration, it remains one of the city's best-loved churches. At night, the brilliant church windows illuminate the Grand Sablon and the Petit Sablon behind.

11 A small garden square, the **Petit Sablon** is surrounded by 48 statues representing Brussels's medieval guilds. Each craftsman carries an object that reveals his trade: The furniture maker holds a chair, for instance; the wine merchant, a goblet.

On the Petit Sablon is the **Musée Instrumental** (Museum of Musical Instruments). A huge collection of over 1,000 musical instruments is on display. Half of them are unique, and a few go back to the Bronze Age. The guide can often be persuaded to play one of the pianos. *Petit Sablon 17, tel. 02/511–35–95. Admission free. Open Tues., Thurs., and Sat. 2:30–4:30, Wed. 4–6, Sun. 10:30–12:30.*

Immediately behind the Petit Sablon is the **Palais d'Egmont,** at different times the residence of Christina of Sweden, Louis XV, and Voltaire. It is now used by the Belgian Ministry of Foreign Affairs for official meetings. If security allows, you can enter the Jardin d'Egmont, another small park, on this side. Come out of the entrance on rue du Grand Cerf and turn left toward the boulevard de Waterloo, a wide street full of bars and designer shops.

Time Out Among the bars on your right, **Le Nemrod** is the most typical. In summer, there is a sidewalk café. The interior is decorated like a Belgian hunting lodge, with lifelike deer and other stuffed animal heads on the walls. At the first chill, the Nemrod's fireplace is surrounded by drinkers of Gueuze and Kriek beers.

Palais de Justice to At the end of the rue de la Régence is the **Palais de Justice,** con-
the Black Tower structed during the reign of the empire-builder, Leopold II.
12 Often described as the ugliest building in Europe, the palais is

designed to impress upon you the majesty of justice. It's located on the site of the former Gallows Hill.

⑬ Down a rather steep hill from the Palais de Justice is the working-class **Marolles** district, where the artist Pieter Bruegel died in 1569. His imposing marble tomb is in **Notre Dame de la Chapelle,** his local church on rue Haute. From the church, head back to the Sablon via the cobbled rue Rollebeek. If you would rather see more of the authentic Marolles district, ignore the cluster of chic restaurants and designer shops on rue Rollebeek. Instead, from place de la Chapelle, take rue Blaes to the **⑭** flea market in **place du Jeu de Balle** (*see* Shopping, *below*). On the way, you will pass a number of rough Belgian bars and North African food shops. Until this century, bourgeois Belgians considered this labyrinth of small alleys a haven for thieves and political refugees. Although the Marolles continues to welcome immigrants and outsiders, it has lost its danger but kept its slightly raffish character.

⑮ Return via the Sablon to the place Royale. Directly ahead of you is the **Parc de Bruxelles** (Brussels Park) with the **Palais Royal** (Royal Palace) at the end closer to you (open for visits from July 22 to early September). You can walk through the park to **⑯** the **Palais de la Nation** (Palace of the Nation) at the opposite end, where the two houses of the Belgian Parliament meet. When Parliament is not sitting, you can visit the building. *Guided tours weekdays 10–noon and 2–5 (Sat. until 4).*

Surrounding the park are elegant turn-of-the-century houses. The prime minister's office is next to the Parliament building. A walk downhill (rue des Colonies) toward the downtown area **⑰** and a short right-hand detour bring you to the **Cathédrale St-Michel.** The cathedral's chief treasure is the beautiful stained-glass windows designed by Bernard van Orley, an early 16th-century painter at the royal court. In summer the great west window is floodlit from inside to reveal its glories. In the crypt, you can see the remnants of the original 12th-century church.

Time Out Situated between the cathedral and the galleries is **La Mort Subite** (Sudden Death) (rue Montagne-aux-Herbes-Potagères 7, tel. 02/513–13–18). Little known to outsiders, it is the city's most genuine beer hall. Locals sit on long benches and select drinks from the best beer list in Brussels. Choose a foamy *bière blanche* (white lager beer), a strong *trappiste* (brewed by monks), a *framboise* (made with raspberries), or a heady *kriek* (a cherry beer). Each has its own special glass. To accompany the beer, try the traditional *fromage 1900*, a pot of creamy white cheese, and crusty bread.

⑱ Continue downhill to the **place des Martyrs,** a dignified square over a mass grave for local patriots who died in the 1830 battle to expel the Dutch. This dilapidated square, where renovation is finally beginning, is at odds with the rue Neuve, the busy shopping street that runs along one side. Cross the rue Neuve and continue on to the boulevard Adolphe-Max. Turn left and **⑲** then right, in front of the imposing **Bourse** (stock exchange), to place Ste-Catherine.

⑳ The 12th-century **Tour Noir** (Black Tower) here is part of the city's first fortifications. Under the square runs the river Senne, channeled underground in the last century when the pollution of the canal basins and the stench from the open sewers became too great. As a result of its watery past, place Ste-Catherine and the old fish market (quai aux Briques) that extends north from it still have the city's best seafood restaurants. If you have enough energy, take the rue de la Vierge Noire to **place St-Géry,** the next square south. This whole area is undergoing extensive renovation.

Parc du Cinquantenaire and Bois de la Cambre To see the **European Community Headquarters** at the Rond Point Schuman, take the metro (Line 1) from the center. The vast 13-story cruciform building, now undergoing restoration to remove asbestos ceilings and partitions, houses the European Commission. The council offices are located nearby. The new European Parliament building is a couple of blocks away.

The **Cinquantenaire** is a huge, decorative archway, built in 1905 in a pleasant park. The buildings on either side of the archway house the **Royal Museums of Art and History.** Displays include Greek, Roman, and Egyptian artifacts and toys. *Parc du Cinquantenaire 10, tel. 02/741–72–11. Admission free. Open weekdays 9:30–12:30 and 1:30–4:45, weekends 10–4:45.*

The new **Autoworld Museum,** also in the Cinquantenaire, has one of the world's most handsome collections of vintage cars. *Parc du Cinquantenaire 11, tel. 02/736–41–65. Admission: BF150. Open daily 10–6 (Nov.–Mar. until 5).*

South of the Palais de Justice is the **Bois de la Cambre,** a popular, rambling park on the edge of town. Take tram No. 94 from Sablon or place Stéphanie for a pleasant 10-minute ride along avenue Louise. Just before the bois is the former **Abbaye de la Cambre,** a 14th-century church with cloisters, an 18th-century courtyard, and a terraced park. The Bois de la Cambre is a good place for a family outing, with a lake, boat trips, pony rides, and an outdoor roller-skating rink.

Waterloo No history buff can visit Brussels without making the pilgrimage to the site of the **Battle of Waterloo,** where Napoleon was finally defeated on June 18, 1815. It is easily reached from the city and lies 19 kilometers (12 miles) to the south of the Forêt de Soignes; take a bus from place Rouppe or a train from Gare Centrale to Waterloo station. In July and August, a red tourist train (tel. 02/354–78–06) runs from Waterloo station to all the main sights. (Visitors' Center, tel. 02/385–19–12; open Apr.–Oct. 9:30–6:30; Nov.–Mar. 10:30–4).

Wellington's headquarters, now a museum, presents the complex battle through illuminated 3-D maps, scale models, and military memorabilia, including the general's personal belongings. *Admission: BF60. Open Apr.–mid-Nov., Tues.–Sun. 9:30–6:30; mid-Nov.–Mar., Tues.–Sun. 10:30–5.*

Beside it is the pyramid-shape **Lion Monument,** erected by the Dutch. After climbing 226 steps, you'll find one of the bleakest views in the country before you. With a little imagination, you can quickly conjure up the desolation of the battlefield scene.

Time Out For a satisfying lunch of authentic Belgian cuisine, try the **Bivouac de l'Empereur,** an attractive 1720s farmhouse close to the Lion Monument. *Route de Lion 315, tel. 02/384–67–40. AE, DC, MC, V. Moderate.*

Musée du Caillou (Napoleon's Headquarters) is worth visiting to understand the French perspective of the battle. Tours of the site are led by multilingual guides. *Admission: BF60. Open Wed.–Mon. 9–5.*

Once every five years (next in 1995) the Battle of Waterloo is reenacted by a thousand local citizens, who dress as French, Prussian, and English soldiers and realistically shoot one another with old muskets. Unlike the real battle, which ended in over 40,000 deaths, this one ends in a large buffet, a son-et-lumière show, and a fireworks display.

Off the Beaten Track

Traditional methods are still used to make Gueuze and Lambic beer at the **Brasserie Cantillon** (Cantillon Brewery and Beer Museum). You may have questions about the strange fruit beers, *kriek* (cherry) and *framboise* (raspberry). Your visit includes a guided tour and a beer. *Rue Gheude 56, tel. 02/520–28–91 or 02/521–49–28. Admission: BF60. Open daily. Tours offered mid-Oct.–Apr., Sat. only at 11, 2, and 3:30; weekdays by request.*

The Maison d'Erasme is a beautifully restored 15th-century house where Erasmus, the great humanist, lived in 1521. Every detail of this atmospheric house is authentic, with period furniture, paintings by Holbein, Dürer, and Hieronymous Bosch and early editions of Erasmus's works, including *In Praise of Folly. Rue du Chapitre 31, tel. 02/521–13–83. Admission: BF20. Open Wed.–Thurs. and Sat.–Mon., 10–noon and 2–5.*

The new **Musée de la Bande Dessinée** celebrates the comic strip, emphasizing such famous Belgian graphic artists as Hergé, Tintin's creator. Hergé apparently invented the *ligne claire*, a simple, bold style of drawing. The display is housed in Victor Horta's splendid Art Nouveau building, once a department store. Horta's juggling of steel, glass, and light has created an exciting backdrop. *Rue des Sables 20, tel. 02/219–19–80. Tram Nos. 92, 93, 101. Admission: BF150. Open Tues.–Sun. 10–6.*

The **Musée Horta** (Horta Museum) was once the home of the Belgian master of Art Nouveau, Victor Horta. From the attic to the cellar, every detail of the house displays the exuberant curves of Art Nouveau style. Horta, who designed the house for himself, wanted to put nature back into daily life. Here his floral motifs, organic style, and refined curves of iron and stone succeed magnificently. *Rue Américain 25, tel. 02/537–16–92. Admission: BF150. Open Tues.–Sun. 2–5:30. Tram No. 92 or bus No. 60.*

Shopping

Gift Ideas

Crystal The Val-St-Lambert mark is the only guarantee of hand-blown, hand-carved lead crystal tableware. You can buy it in many stores, including **Art and Selection** (Marché-aux-Herbes 83) and **Buss,** across the street at No. 84, near the Grand' Place. For cut-price porcelain and china, try the **Vaisselle au Kilo** (rue Bodenbroek 8, near the Sablon district), which is also open on Sunday.

Chocolate For "everyday" chocolate, try the Côte d'Or variety, available in any chocolate shop or larger store. For the delicious pralines—rich chocolates filled with every fruit, liqueur, or nut imaginable—try the brands made by Godiva, Neuhaus, or Leonidas, available at shops scattered throughout the city. Godiva is the best known, Neuhaus the best-tasting, and Leonidas the best value for money. Exclusive handmade pralines can be bought at **Wittamer** (Grand Sablon 16) and **Nihoul** (Ave. Louise 300).

Lace   To avoid disappointment, ask the store assistant outright whether the lace is handmade Belgian or made in the Far East. As preparation, visit the **Lace Museum** (rue de la Violette 6, near the Grand' Place). **La Maison F. Rubbrecht,** on the Grand' Place, sells authentic, handmade Belgian lace. For a large choice of old and modern lace, try **Manufacture Belge de Dentelles** (Galerie de la Reine 6–8).

Shopping Districts   For boutiques and stores, the main districts are in the **ville basse** (low town), the **Galeries St-Hubert** (luxury goods or gift items), **rue Neuve** (inexpensive clothes), and **City 2** and the **Anspach Center** (large covered shopping complexes). In City 2, **FNAC** is a cherished French institution: As well as being an outlet for books, records, cameras, and stereo equipment at the best prices in town, it is also a trendy cultural and exhibition center.

You'll find designer names and department stores (such as **Sarmalux**) in the **ville haute** (high town). **Avenue Louise** is its center, complete with covered galleries; **Galerie Louise;** and **Galerie de la Toison d'Or,** the appropriately named street of the Golden Fleece! To offset prices, many of these stores operate sales-tax refunds (*see* Shopping in Staying in Belgium, *above*). The **place du Grand Sablon** is an equally expensive but more charming shopping district. This is the center for antiques, small art galleries, and designer shops. You'll also find **Wittamer** (12–13 Grand Sablon), Belgium's finest *patisserie* (pastry shop). Around the Sablon and its neighboring streets, **rue des Minimes** and **rue Lebeau,** it is possible to buy anything from Persian carpets and African primitives to 18th-century paintings and Art Nouveau.

Markets   On Saturdays (9–5) and Sundays (9–1), the Sablon square is transformed into an **antiques market.** In early December it runs a traditional **European Christmas Market** with crafts from many countries. The **flower market** on the Grand' Place (Tues.–Sun. 8–4) is a colorful diversion. **Midi Market** is far more exotic (by Gare du Midi train station). On Sunday morning (5 AM–1 PM) the whole area becomes a colorful *souk* (bazaar) as the city's large North African community gathers to buy and sell exotic foods and household goods. The **Vieux Marché** (Old Market) in place du Jeu de Balle is a rough flea market worth visiting for the authentic atmosphere of the working-class Marolles district. The market is open daily 7–2. To make real finds, get there as early in the morning as you can.

Dining

Apart from hearty Belgian cuisine, Brussels is proud of its foreign restaurants: Chefs from at least 50 countries work in the city, and many Asian restaurants provide a tasty and inexpensive alternative to European fare. The local *cuisine bruxelloise* is, in the more expensive restaurants, an imaginative variant of French cuisine. The ambience tends to be formal, dignified, and old-fashioned in the more exclusive restaurants and cozy or jovial in the simpler brasseries or bistros. Servings are plentiful everywhere. Most places offer fixed-price menus, which, especially at lunch, can reduce the bill by half. Less expensive restaurants also feature a *plat du jour* (daily special) at a reasonable price.

For details and price-category definitions, *see* Dining in Staying in Belgium.

Very Expensive
★ **Comme Chez Soi.** Pierre Wynants, the perfectionist owner-chef, has decorated the restaurant in Art Nouveau style. Every detail is authentic, from the stained-glass panels to the carved mahogany woodwork and the artistic menus. The inventive French cuisine, excellent wine list, and attentive service complement the warm decor. The specialties include fillets of sole with a white wine mousseline and shrimps, saddle of young rabbit with lemon and basil, venison, and pheasant. This is one of the world's top restaurants and well deserves its three Michelin stars. You need to make reservations at least a couple of months ahead. *Pl. Rouppe, tel. 02/512–29–21, fax 02/511–80–52. Reservations required. AE, DC. Closed Sun., Mon., July, and Christmas to New Year's.*

Les Délices de la Mer. Michel Beyls, one of the most talented chefs of his generation, has moved around a lot throughout his career. Brussels gourmets hope he will stay for a while at this address, a splendid villa in suburban Uccle. Beyls is the kind of magician who can turn a poached egg on a mousse of wild mushrooms into a memorable culinary experience. Seafood has pride of place on the menu. Try the quickly sauteed sea scallops in a light curry sauce, or turbot baked in a salt crust. *Chaussée de Waterloo 1020, tel. 02/375–54–67. Reservations required. AE, DC, MC, V. Closed Sat. lunch and Sun.*

Maison du Cygne. With decor to match its classical cuisine, this restaurant is set in a grand 17th-century guild hall on the Grand' Place. The formal dining room upstairs features paneled walls hung with Old Masters, and flawless service. Typical French-Belgian dishes include *lotte aux blancs de poireaux*, a monkfish-and-leeks specialty. *Rue Charles Buyls 2, tel. 02/511–82–44. Reservations required. AE, DC, MC, V. Closed Sat. lunch, Sun.*

Expensive
Castello Banfi. This up-market Italian restaurant is often packed with regulars, who seem to enjoy the ambience as much as the great food. The green-and-rose interior is decorated with oval mirrors and large flower arrangements. Try the superb carpaccio with celeriac and parmesan; other recommendations include black pasta with lobster, crayfish lasagna, and roast quail. The location just off the Grand Sablon is also a big plus. *Rue Bodenbroek 12, tel. 02/512–87–94. Reservations advised. AE, DC, MC, V. Closed Sun. eve., Mon. and second half of Aug.*

★ **La Porte des Indes.** The city's finest Indian restaurant brings an exotic touch to the bustling avenue Louise business district. Gracious staff, dressed in traditional Indian attire, create a warm, sensitive atmosphere. The plant-filled lobby, wood carvings, soft music, and soothing blue-and-white decor provide a restful backdrop. The cuisine is surprisingly versatile, from a mild pilaf to a spicy *vindaloo* (chili-flavored curry). Exotic fruits complete the meal. If in doubt, ask for a "brass tray," which provides a chance to sample a range of specialties. *Av.*

Louise 455, tel. 02/647–86–51. Reservations advised. AE, DC, MC, V. Closed Sun.

Ogenblik. This is a true bistro, with green-shaded lamps over marble-topped tables, sawdust on the floor, ample servings, and a great ambience. The long and imaginative menu changes frequently, but generally includes such specialties as *mille-feuille* of lobster and salmon and saddle or leg of lamb with fresh, young vegetables. *Galerie des Princes 1, tel. 02/511–61–51. No reservations after 8 PM. AE, DC, MC, V. Closed Sun.*

Moderate **Aux Armes de Bruxelles.** This restaurant is one of the few to escape the "tourist trap" label in this hectic little street. Inside, a lively atmosphere fills three rooms: The most popular section overlooks the street theater outside, but locals prefer the cozy rotunda. Service is fast and friendly, and portions are large. Specialties include *waterzooi de volaille* (a rich chicken stew) and *moules au vin blanc* (mussels in white wine). Order the *crêpe suzette* if you want to see your table engulfed by brandy flames! *Rue des Bouchers 13, tel. 02/511–55–98. Reservations advised. AE, DC, MC, V. Closed Mon. and June.*

La Manufacture. Here's the latest trendy brasserie where the city's beautiful young people like to gather. It is housed in a cleverly transformed workshop, with tables of polished stone, brick walls, and friendly servers dressed in long leather aprons. You may find the address, in a run-down part of the city center, a bit of a drawback. The cooking is stylish, with items like goat cheese salad or sautéed red mullet fillets, accompanied by great crusty bread. *Rue Notre-Dame du Sommeil 12, tel. 02/502–25–25. Reservations advised. AE, DC, MC, V.*

★ **La Quincaillerie.** The name means "the hardware store"—and the character has been retained, with tables perched on the balcony and a zinc oyster bar downstairs. The three-course *menu du patron* is a bargain. Excellent game dishes are nicely presented by a staff who, like the clientele, is young and pleasant. *Rue du Page 45, tel. 02/538–25–53. Reservations advised. AE, DC, MC, V.*

Inexpensive **Chez Leon.** This 100-year-old restaurant continues to do land-office business and has over the years expanded into a row of eight old houses. Heaping plates of mussels and other Belgian specialties, like eels in a green sauce, are served nonstop from noon to midnight all year round. *Rue des Bouchers 18, tel. 02/511–14–15. No reservations. AE, DC, MC, V.*

★ **Falstaff.** Some things never change, and Falstaff is one of them. This huge tavern, with an interior that is pure Art Nouveau, fills up for lunch and keeps going until 5 AM, with an ever-changing crowd from students to pensioners. Cheerful waitresses punch in your orders for onion soup, filet mignon, salads, and other straightforward dishes on electronic order pads. Falstaff II at No. 25 has the same food but not the ambience. *Rue Henri Maus 19, tel. 02/511–87–89. Reservations advised. AE, DC, MC, V.*

La Grande Porte. An old warren of interconnecting rooms provides a rustic setting for hearty and often rambunctious eating. Dressed in old bibs, the jovial waiters make no concessions to fashion or style; the genuine friendliness attracts Bruxellois from all backgrounds. Part of the appeal lies in the copious portions. The specialties include *carbonade à la flamande* (beef and onions stewed in beer); *ballekes à la marollienne* (spicy meatballs); steaks served with rice and/or french fries; and *salade folle* (mixed green salad with cold cuts), a meal in itself.

Rue Notre-Seigneur 9, tel. 02/539–21–32. Reservations advised. DC. Closed July.

Lodging

The *Hotel Guide*, published every year by Tourist Information Brussels (TIB), provides the most reliable and up-to-date information on prices and services. In general, finding accommodations is not difficult. There has been a boom in hotel construction lately, adding several more hotels in all price categories. However, as a center of business and of the EC, Brussels has many more choices in the Very Expensive and Expensive ranges. Hotels in categories below these are often comfortable but rather short on charm. Substantial weekend and summer rebates are available in many hotels; be sure to check when you book. The main hotel districts are in the ville basse and around the avenue Louise shopping area. Avoid the cheap hotel districts near Gare du Midi and Gare du Nord train stations. Hotels can be booked at the tourist office on the Grand' Place (tel. 02/513–89–40), and a deposit is required (deductible from the final hotel bill).

For details and price-category definitions, *see* Lodging in Staying in Belgium.

Very Expensive **Conrad.** A luxury hotel opened in 1993, the Conrad sees itself as a successor to the tradition of grand hotels and takes pride in its classic furniture and decor. Part of the facade fronting the elegant Avenue Louise has been retained, and there's a new shopping arcade. Business travelers can arrange to have PCs and fax machines brought to their rooms. *Avenue Louise 71, tel. 02/542–42–42, fax 02/542–43–42. 269 rooms. Facilities: 2 restaurants, bar, conference facilities, parking. AE, DC, MC, V.*

Hilton International. The 27-story Hilton was one of the first highrises in Brussels back in the '60s and remains a distinctive landmark. It is continuously being refurbished floor by floor. Corner rooms are the most desirable. The top-floor restaurant, Plein Ciel (lunch only), has a terrific view over the city. The second-floor Maison du Boeuf is an outstanding restaurant and the ground-floor Cafe d'Egmont highly popular. Centrally located, it is next to the main luxury shopping area and overlooks the quiet Parc d'Egmont. *Blvd. de Waterloo 38, tel. 02/513–88–77, fax 02/504–21–11. 450 rooms with bath. Facilities: health club, sauna, 2 restaurants, coffee shop, bar, solarium. AE, DC, MC, V.*

★ **SAS Royal Hotel.** This 1990 hotel, a few minutes' walk through the Galerie de la Reine from Grand' Place, was built for business travelers. The rooms are decorated in different styles: Scandinavian, Oriental, Italian, and Art Deco. A portion of the city wall from 1134, discovered during the construction, forms part of the Atrium. A business service center and fully equipped conference rooms cater to businesspeople's needs. The Sea Grill has become one of the city's top seafood restaurants. Rooms for nonsmokers and for the disabled are available. Travelers aged 65 or older qualify for special weekend and summer rates. *Rue du Fossé-aux-Loups 47, tel. 02/219–28–28, fax 02/219–62–62. 281 rooms with bath. Facilities: 2 restaurants, valet parking, fitness center, in-room checkout, airline check-in, Atrium coffee shop, bar. AE, DC, MC, V.*

Expensive **Amigo.** This world-famous, family-owned hotel, located off the
★ Grand' Place, was built in the 1950s, but it has the charm of an
older age. No one would guess that it was built on the site of the
city prison. Each room is individually decorated, often in silk,
velvet, and brocades. A recent refurbishing has smartened up
bedrooms and public rooms. The bar is very pleasant, though
the restaurant is not memorable. Room rates vary considerably, with the less expensive options being on lower floors. *Rue
d'Amigo 1, tel. 02/511–59–10, fax 02/513–52–77. 183 rooms
with bath. Facilities: restaurant, bar, parking. AE, DC, MC,
V.*

Cadettt. This 1991 addition to the Swiss Mövenpick chain does
spell its name with three *t*'s. The large, bright rooms have
blond wood furniture, modem phone jacks, and Lay-Z-Boy
chairs. The atrium bar and restaurant serves copious Swiss
breakfasts and a limited selection of Mövenpick specialties.
The Caveau wine bar offers wine tasting and light snacks. *Rue
Paul Spaak 15, tel. 02/645–61–11, fax 02/646–63–11. 128
rooms with bath. Facilities: restaurant, bars, café, sauna, fitness room, nonsmoking rooms, parking. AE, DC, MC, V.*

Metropole. A major restoration has returned the Metropole to
its Art Nouveau glory. The lobby sets the tone, with its high
coffered ceiling, chandeliers, marble, and oriental carpets. The
theme extends seamlessly to the bar with its potted palms and
deep leather sofas, to the gourmet restaurant and to the café,
which opens onto a heated terrace on the Place Brouckère. The
guest rooms, decorated in various pastel shades, are discreetly
modern. *Place de Brouckère 31, tel. 02/217–23–00, fax 02/218–
02–20. 410 rooms. Facilities: restaurant, bar, café, conference
rooms, airport courtesy bus. AE, DC, MC, V.*

Moderate **Arenberg.** Recently renovated, this hotel enjoys a central location near the central station. The pleasant restaurant offers
lunch for under BF500 and can cater to special dietary requirements. Weekend rates are available. *Rue d'Assaut 15, tel. 02/
511–07–70, fax 02/514–19–76. 156 rooms with bath. Facilities:
restaurant, coffee shop, bar, secretarial service, garden. AE,
DC, MC, V.*

Clubhouse. Formerly the Alfa Louise, this hotel recently had a
major facelift that transformed everything except the size of
the pastel guest rooms. The large lobby, opening on a small
garden, serves as a breakfast room and self-service bar; on chilly days there's usually a fire blazing in the open fireplace. On a
quiet side street off Avenue Louise. *Rue Blanche 4, tel. 02/537–
92–10, fax 02/537–00–18. 81 rooms. Facilities: bar, conference
room, garage. AE, DC, MC, V.*

★ **Manos Stéphanie.** The Louis XV furniture, marble lobby, and
plentiful antiques set a standard of elegance rarely encountered in a hotel in this price category. Even the corridors are
decorated with paintings and mirrors. This 1992 hotel occupies
a converted townhouse, and most rooms have good-sized sitting areas. Avenue Louise is just a few minutes' walk away.
*Chaussée de Charleroi 28, tel. 02/539–02–50, fax 02/537–57–
29. 55 rooms. Facilities: restaurant, bar, parking. AE, DC,
MC, V.*

Inexpensive **Arlequin.** Smack in the middle of the Ilôt Sacré restaurant area,
this hotel is reached by an arcade from the pedestrian Petite
Rue des Bouchers, or from the slightly seedy Rue de la
Fourche. Rooms are furnished with essentials only, but are
light and airy in shades of gray. Try to get a corner room (end-

ing with 02), the higher up the better. *Rue de la Fourche 17–19, tel. 02/514–16–15, fax 02/514–22–02. 60 rooms with bath or shower. Facilities: bar, breakfast room. AE, DC, MC, V.*

Gerfaut. In this 1991 hotel, the light beige rooms are of reasonable size. Three- and four-bedded rooms are available at modest supplements. Buffet breakfast is included in the price. The location may not be the greatest, but public transport is available. *Chaussée de Mons 115–117, tel. 02/522–19–22, fax 02/523–89–91. 48 rooms with bath or shower. Facilities: bar, parking. AE, DC, MC, V.*

Orion. This residential hotel opened in 1990 in the old fish market, which has become a lively restaurant district. The reception area is always staffed, but you make your own bed. Linen is changed weekly. Rooms are decorated in a cheerful, crisp red-and-white modern scheme. There are fully equipped kitchenettes in the studio rooms and two-room apartments and a quiet interior courtyard. *Quai au Bois-à-Brûler 51, tel. 02/221–14–11, fax 02/221–15–99. 169 rooms with bath. Facilities: parking. AE, DC, MC, V.*

The Arts

The best way to find out what's going on is to buy a copy of the English-language weekly magazine *The Bulletin*. It's published every Thursday and sold at newsstands for BF75.

Music Major classical music concerts are generally held at the **Palais des Beaux-Arts** (rue Ravenstein 23, tel. 02/507–82–00). Alternatively, there are many free Sunday morning concerts at various churches, including the Cathédrale St-Michel and the Petite Église des Minimes (rue des Minimes 62). Major rock and pop concerts are given at Forest National (av. du Globe 36, tel. 02/347–03–55).

Opera and Dance The national opera company, Compagnie Royale Belge de l'Opera, is based at the **Théâtre Royal de la Monnaie** (pl. de la Monnaie, tel. 02/218–12–02). The Monnaie is an attractive opera house, and its productions are of international quality. Tickets cost from BF500 to BF2,000 and are very hard to come by. Touring dance and opera companies often play at the **Cirque Royal** (rue de l'Enseignement 81, tel. 02/218–20–15).

Theater At Brussels's 30 theaters, actors perform in French, Flemish, and occasionally in English. The loveliest theater is the newly restored **Théâtre du Résidence Palace** (rue de la Loi 155, tel. 02/231–03–05). Avant-garde theater is performed at the enterprising **Théâtre Varia** (rue du Sceptre 78, tel. 02/640–82–58) and **Théâtre 140** (ave E. Plasky 140, tel. 02/733–97–08). Puppet theater is a Belgian experience not to be missed. In Brussels, visit the intimate **Théâtre Toone VII** (impasse Schuddeveld, Petite rue des Bouchers 21, tel. 02/511–71–37). In this atmospheric medieval house, satirical plays are performed in a Bruxellois dialect.

Film Movies are mainly shown in their original language, so many are in English. **The Acropole** (Galeries de la Toison d'Or, tel. 02/511–43–28), the new **UCG** complex (pl. de Brouckère, tel. 02/218–06–07), and the multiscreen **Kinepolis** (av. du Centenaire 1, tel. 02/478–04–50) feature comfortable armchairs and first-run movies. For unusual movies or screen classics, visit the **Musée du Cinéma** (Cinema Museum) (rue Baron Horta 9, tel.

02/513–41–55). Five movies are shown daily, at only BF50 each.

Nightlife

Nightclubs These are not always distinguishable from striptease shows and lack the Parisian look, verve, and high kicks. **Show Point** (pl. Stéphanie 14, tel. 02/511–53–64) does its best.

Disco **Griffin's** (rue Duquesnoy 5, tel. 02/511–42–15) at the Royal Windsor Hotel appeals to young adults and business travelers. **Le Mirano** (Chaussée de Louvain 38, tel. 02/218–57–72) attracts a self-styled jet set (Sat. only), while **Le Garage** (rue Duquesnoy 16, tel. 02/512–66–22) draws a younger crowd. The current favorite among the BCBG *(bon chic, bon genre)* is the **Jeux d'Hiver** in the Bois de la Cambre (Thurs. and Sat.), which is a members-only club; you'll be admitted if you look the part. In all of the above, the action does not start much before midnight.

Bars The diversity is greater here than in many other European capitals. These are just a few of the best: **La Fleur en Papier Doré** (rue des Aléxiens 53, tel. 02/511–16–59) is a quiet bar that attracts an artistic audience to drink local beer and look at the ancient walls covered with surreal paintings and old etchings. **Cirio** (rue de la Bourse 18, tel. 02/512–13–95) is a pleasantly quiet bar with nice decor. **Rick's Café** (av. Louise 344, tel. 02/647–75–30) is as popular with homesick Americans as it is with the British expatriate community. It serves fairly expensive American and Tex/Mex food. **De Ultieme Hallucinatie** (rue Royale 316, tel. 02/217–06–14) is another popular Art Nouveau bar and restaurant that serves imaginative cocktails, a full range of beers, and a short but appealing menu. **Henry J. Bean's** (rue du Montagne-aux-Herbes-Potagères 40, tel. 02/219–28–28) is a 1950s style bar and grill much frequented by the younger set.

Jazz Brussels lays claim to being Europe's jazz capital. Buy the monthly *Jazz Streets* magazine to find out details. Among the best venues are **Travers** (rue Traversière 11, tel. 02/218–40–86), **Preservation Hall** (rue de Londres 3 bis, tel. 02/511–03–04), and the **Bierodrome** (pl. Fernand Cocq 21, tel. 02/512–04–56), a smoky rough-and-ready club in Ixelles, a lively part of the city.

Antwerp

Arriving and Departing

By Plane Antwerp International Airport lies just 3 kilometers (2 miles) southeast of the city. For flight information, call 03/218–12–11. Antwerp is served by a small number of flights from neighboring countries. Most passengers arrive via Brussels National Airport, which is linked with Antwerp by hourly bus service (50 minutes one way).

Between the Airport and Downtown Buses bound for Antwerp's central station leave about every 20 minutes; travel time is around 15 minutes. Taxis are readily available as well.

By Train Express trains run between Antwerp and Brussels; the trip takes 35 minutes. Antwerp Central Station is at Koningin Astridplein 27 (tel. 03/233–39–15). Four trains leave every hour from Antwerp's central stations.

By Car Several major highways converge on Antwerp's inner-city ring expressway. It's a 10-lane racetrack, so be sure you maneuver into the correct lane well before you exit. Antwerp is an easy 45-kilometer (28-mile) drive from Brussels on E19.

Getting Around

By Streetcar In the downtown area, the streetcar (or tram) is the best, and most common, means of transportation. Some lines have been rebuilt underground (look for signs marked "M"); the most useful line runs between the central station (métro stop Diamant) and the Groenplaats (for the cathedral). For detailed maps of the transportation system, stop at the tourist office.

Guided Tours

Orientation tours by minibus (50 minutes) depart from the Grote Markt daily at 2, 3, and 4 (mid-Nov. to mid-Mar., weekends only). Tickets (BF330 adults, BF200 children) are sold on the bus. The tourist office operates a **Guide's Exchange** and, with a week's notice, is able to meet most requirements for city guides. Guides charge BF500 an hour, with a minimum of two hours.

Tourist Information

The tourist office is near the cathedral (Grote Markt 15, tel. 03/232–01–03). It is open Monday–Saturday 9–6, Sunday 9–5. Ask for their booklet on walks, which includes the famous "Rubens Walk." Various other popular walks are signposted throughout the city.

Exploring Antwerp

Antwerp, lying on the Scheldt River 50 kilometers (31 miles) north of Brussels, is the world's fifth-largest port and the main city of Belgium's Flemish region. Its name, according to legend, is derived from *handwerpen*, or "hand throwing." It seems a Roman soldier once cut off the hand of a malevolent giant and flung it into the river; his feat is commemorated by a statue on the Grote Markt. In the 16th century, Emperor Charles V made Antwerp the world's most important trading center, and a golden age followed, during which Rubens and other painters made their city an equally important center of the arts. Enterprising craftsmen began practicing diamond-cutting at about this time, and the city is still a world leader in the diamond trade. Much of the glory that was Antwerp has been preserved, and Antwerp's year as Cultural Capital of Europe 1993 resulted in a much-improved cultural infrastructure.

Numbers in the margin correspond to points of interest on the Antwerp map.

❶ Antwerp's **Centraalstation** is a good place to start exploring the city. This elegant neo-Baroque building, restored to its former glory, is surrounded by cafés and cinemas. To the east of the

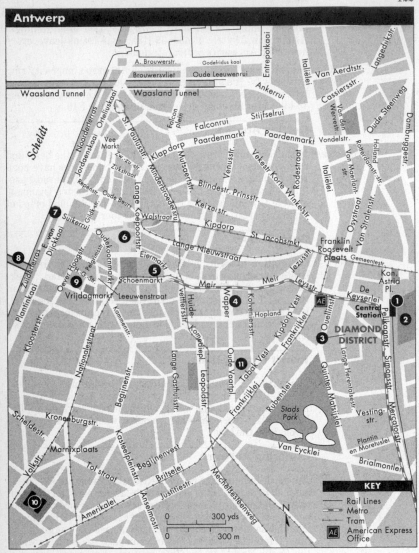

Antwerp

(Map labels, reading roughly top to bottom and left to right)

Waasland Tunnel

A. Brouwerstr.
Brouwersvliet
Godefridus kaai
Oude Leeuwenrui
Entrepotkaai
Italiëlei
Van Aerdtstr.
Langedijkstr.

Waasland Tunnel

Ankerrui
Cassierssstr.
Oude Steenweg
Dambruggestr.

Scheldt

Noorderterras
St. Paulusstr.
Orteliuskaai
Vee Markt
Falcon plein
Falconrui
Stijfselrui
Van den Wervestr.
Van Maerlantstr.
Vondelstr.
Holland str.
Rotterdamstr.

Jordaenskaai
Zw.zusstr.
Klapdorp
Mutsaertstr.
Paardenmarkt
Paardenmarkt
Italiëlei

Repenstr.
Oude Beurs
Zirkstraat
Lange Koepoortstr.
Minderbroedersr.
Venusstr.
Blindestr. Prinsstr.
Vekestr. Korte Winkelstr.
Rodestraat
Van Maerlant str.
Oude Steenweg

E. van Dijckkaai
Suikerrui
Gildk.str.
Wolstraat
Keizerstr.
Kipdorp
St. Jacobsmkt
Ossystraat
Van Stralenstr.

7

6

8

Zuiderterras
Oever Hoogstr.
H.G.G. str.
Pelgrimsstr.
Oude Koornmarkt
Eiermarkt
Lange Nieuwstraat
Jezusstr.
Franklin Roosevelt plaats
Gemeentestr.
Kon. Astrid Pl.

9

5

Plantinkaai
Vrijdagmarkt
Schoenmarkt
Leeuwenstraat
Meir
Meir
Leysstr.
De Keyserlei
1

Nationalestraat
Kammenstr.
Wapper
Kolveniersstr.
Kipdorp Vest
AE
Central Station

Kloosterstr.
Begijnenstr.
Huidevettersstr.
Hopland
Frankriklei
DIAMOND DISTRICT

2

4

Lange Gasthuisstr.
Komedieplein
Leopoldstr.
Oude Vaartpl.
11
Tabak Vest
Quinten Matsijslei
Lange Herentalsestr.

3

Kronenburgstr.
Kasteelpleinstr.
Frankriklei
Stads Park
Vestingstr.

Scheldestr.
Marnixplaats
Begijnenvest
Britselei
Van Eycklei
Plantin en Moretuslei

Volkstr.
Tot straat
Amerikalei
Justitiestr.
Anselmostr.
Mechelsesteenweg
Brialmontlei

10

N

0   300 yds
0   300 m

KEY

— Rail Lines
⇥ Metro
… Tram
[AE] American Express Office

2 station is **Antwerp Zoo,** one of the world's most reputable. The huge, well-designed complex also includes a winter garden, a planetarium, a good restaurant, and two natural-history museums. *Koningin Astridplein 26, tel. 03/231–16–40. Admission: BF370 adults, BF225 children. Open July–Aug., daily 8:30–6:30; Sept.–Feb., daily 9–5; Mar.–June, daily 8:30–6.*

Near the central station, along the Pelikaanstraat and the streets running off it, lies the **Diamond Quarter.** You can visit the diamond exhibition and see cutters at work at the **3** **Provinciaal Diamantmuseum** (Diamond Museum). *Lange Herentalsestraat 31–33. Admission free. Open daily 10–5. Cutting and polishing demonstrations Sat. 2–5.*

The broad De Keyserlei leads west from the central station to the main shopping area, the **Meir.** South of the Meir, on **4** Wapper, is **Rubenshuis** (Rubens House). The artist lived here from 1610 until his death in 1640. It's an atmospheric place, very much a patrician's home of the period, enriched with paintings by Rubens and his contemporaries. *Wapper 9. Admission: BF75. Open Tues.–Sun. 10–5.*

5 One of Europe's earliest skyscrapers, the 24-story **Torengebouw,** stands at the western end of the Meir. Pass to the left of this building, down the Schoenmarkt, and into the wide **6** Groenplaats, with its statue of Rubens. The towering **OnzeLieve-Vrouwekathedraal** (Our Lady of Sorrows Cathedral), whose restoration has just been completed, stands at the opposite end of the square. Built in Gothic style, it has seven naves and 125 pillars and is the largest church in Belgium. It also has three masterpieces by Rubens. *Admission: BF50. Open weekdays 10–6, Sat. 10–3, Sun. 1–4.*

The **Grote Markt,** flanked by the 16th-century city hall and surrounded by old guild houses, is just a few steps north of the cathedral. The area north of the square, with its narrow streets, churches, and old merchants' houses, is the heart of old Antwerp.

Returning to the cathedral, walk the short distance west along the Suikerrui to the river. To your right is the fortresslike **Steen,** the oldest building in Antwerp. Dating from the 12th **7** century, the Steen now houses the **Nationaal Scheepvaartmuseum** (Maritime Museum), which has many beautiful models of ships, especially of the East India clippers. *Steenplein 1, tel. 03/232–08–50. Admission: BF75. Open Tues.–Sun. 10–5.*

From the terraces around the Steen, you can see the main port installations. For a close look, a 2½-hour **boat excursion** around the port leaves from Quay 13 on weekdays and from Steen Landing stage on Sunday. *Cost: BF375 adults, BF240 children. Information from n.v. Flandria, Steenplein 1, tel. 03/231–31–00.*

Walking along the river south of the Steen, you come to a foot **8** tunnel, the **St. Annatunnel,** leading to the left bank of the river (the entrance is close to the Plantin-Moretus Museum, *see below*). From the riverside park, you get the best view of the city's great spires and wharves.

Return through the tunnel and walk east until you come to the **9** **Plantin-Moretus Museum,** a famous printing works founded in the 16th century. The building is a fine example of Renaissance architecture and is magnificently furnished. Among its treasures are many first editions, engravings, and a copy of Gutenberg's Bible, the *Biblia Regia. Vrijdagmarkt 22. Admission: BF75. Open Tues.–Sun. 10–5.*

From the Plantin, walk through the Vrijdagmarkt, where there is a **furniture and secondhand market** every Wednesday and Friday morning. Continue up the Oude Koornmarkt to the Groenplaats and catch a tram to the **Koninklijk Museum voor Schone Kunsten** (Royal Museum of Fine Arts). It lies in the southern part of the city and houses more than 1,500 paintings by old masters, including a magnificent array of works by Rubens, Van Dyck, Hals, and Bruegel. The second floor houses one of the best collections of the Flemish school anywhere in the world. The first floor is given over to more modern paintings. *Leopold de Waelplaats 1–9. Admission free. Open Tues.– Sun. 10–5.*

On Sunday morning you can see the famous **vogelmarkt,** or bird market, a few blocks south of Rubenshuis on the Oude Vaartplaats. You'll find everything from birds and domestic pets to plants, clothes, and food.

Time Out More than 350 kinds of Belgian beer and 150 foreign brews are available in **Café Kulminator**—including the lethal EKU-28, claimed by Kulminator to be "the strongest beer on Earth." The beers are best accompanied by the excellent cheeses. *Vleminckveld 32, tel. 03/232–45–38. No credit cards. Closed Sun. Inexpensive.*

Dining

Local specialties include herring and eel dishes and *witloof* (endives) cooked in a variety of ways. As for drink, there are 20 local beers; a city gin called *jenever;* and a strong liqueur, *Elixir d'Anvers.*

For details and price-category definitions, *see* Dining in Staying in Belgium.

Very Expensive **La Pérouse.** Seafood is an Antwerp specialty, and here you can sample it in style on a moored ship. It's small, so you *must* reserve ahead. *Steenplein, tel. 03/231–31–51. Reservations required. AE, DC, MC, V. Closed Sun., Mon., and May–mid-Sept.*

Expensive **De Kerselaar.** This is a favorite among Antwerp gourmets, both for its refined food—duck's liver with honey vinegar, "capuccino" of langoustines, red mullet with thyme—and for its unsnobbish ambience. This attractive spot is located in one of the pedestrian streets near the cathedral. *Grote Pieter Potstraat 22, tel. 03/233–59–69. Reservations recommended. AE, DC, MC, V. Closed Sat. lunch, Sun., Mon. lunch, and 3 weeks in Aug.*

★ **De Matelote.** At a tiny restaurant in a small house down a narrow street, the gifted chef concocts inventive dishes such as grilled asparagus with fresh morels and a poached egg, or langoustines in a light curry sauce. For dessert, try the outstanding *crème brulée. Haarstraat 9, tel. 03/231–32–07. Reservations advised. AE, DC, MC, V. Closed Mon. and Sat. lunch, Sun., 3 weeks in July.*

Moderate
★
Rooden-Hoed. Seafood is featured in this traditional cozy restaurant, reputed to be Antwerp's oldest. Specialties include eels and mussels, in season. Try the *paling in 't groen* (eel in green sauce). The restaurant recommends its dry, white wines from Alsace. *Oude Koornmarkt 25, tel. 03/233-28-44. Reservations advised. AE, MC. Closed Wed. and Thurs.*

Sir Anthony Van Dijck. The owner/chef has abandoned his two-star rating, cut prices in half, increased the number of tables, and introduced simpler, brasserie-type dishes based on less expensive products. The antiques-filled interior is still the same, and so is the setting in the charming Vlaaykensgang alley. *Oude Koornmarkt 16, tel. 03/231-61-70. AE, DC, MC, V. Closed Sun. and most of Aug.*

Inexpensive
★
In de Schaduw van de Kathedraal. As the name states, this budget restaurant, serving traditional food, lies "in the shadow of the cathedral." Try the seafood dishes, especially mussels in season. There is a terrace for outside dining. *Handschoenmarkt 17, tel. 03/232-40-14. Reservations accepted. AE, DC, MC, V. Closed Tues.*

Lodging

All hotels are modern, so expect comfort, rather than period charm. For details and price-category definitions, *see* Lodging in Staying in Belgium.

Very Expensive
Hilton. The newest contender among luxury hotels in Antwerp opened in mid 1993, and with just five floors, it is architecturally well integrated in Groenplaats, next to the cathedral. The lower floors are occupied by boutiques and shops. *Groenplaats, tel. 03/204-12-12, fax 03/204-12-13. 211 rooms. Facilities: 2 restaurants, bar, sauna, fitness center, parking. AE, DC, MC, V.*

Expensive
★
Alfa De Keyser. This well-maintained deluxe hotel is handily situated only 100 meters from the central station and near the diamond center. It has a restaurant that prides itself on its adaptation of local ingredients to nouvelle cuisine. *De Keyserlei 66, tel. 03/234-01-35, fax 03/232-39-70. 117 rooms with bath. Facilities: airport express bus that stops opposite the hotel, restaurant, café, bar, nightclub, parking, videos available. AE, DC, MC, V.*

Pullman Park Hotel. This ultramodern glass-and-marble hotel has been designed to reflect the diamond symbol of Antwerp. Set in a park near the De Singel cultural center, it offers large guest rooms. *Desguinlei 94, tel. 03/216-48-00, fax 03/216-47-12. 215 rooms with bath. Facilities: sauna, fitness center, disco, 3 restaurants. AE, DC, MC, V.*

Moderate
Alfa Theater. This plush, centrally located hotel is part of the reliable Alfa chain. The restaurant offers an appealing blend of nouvelle-cuisine presentation and Belgian portions. Try the lobster mousse. *Arenbergstr. 30, tel. 03/232-39-70, fax 03/233-88-58. 83 rooms with bath. Facilities: bar, restaurant, conference facilities. AE, DC, MC.*

Inexpensive
Arcade. This is a modern, impersonal hotel designed along the lines of a university campus. Its location, overlooking the weekend marketplace, makes it ideal for visiting the old district. *Meistr. 39 (Theaterplein), tel. 03/231-88-30, fax 03/234-29-*

21. 150 rooms with shower. Facilities: bar, access for the disabled, conference facilities. MC, V.
Waldorf. This pleasant, modern hotel is located near the diamond center. The smallish rooms are attractively decorated in gray and brown. *Belgielei 36, tel. 03/230-99-50, fax 03/230-78-70. 100 rooms with bath. Facilities: restaurant, bar. AE, DC, MC, V.*

Brugge

Arriving and Departing

By Train Trains run hourly at 28 and 59 minutes past the hour from Brussels (Gare du Midi) to Brugge. The London–Brussels service stops here as well. The train station is south of the canal that surrounds the downtown area; for information, tel. 050/38-23-82. Travel time from Brussels is 53 minutes.

By Car Brugge lies 97 kilometers (61 miles) northwest of Brussels. The most direct route between the two cities is the A10/E40.

Getting Around

By Horse-Drawn Cab An expensive means of seeing the sights is provided by the horse-drawn cabs that congregate in the Burg square, March–November, daily 10-6. A 35-minute trip will cost BF700, and the cabs take up to four people.

Guided Tours

Boat Trips Boat trips along the city canals are run by several companies and depart from five separate landings. Boats ply the waters March–November, 10-6. There is no definite departure schedule; boats leave when enough people have gathered, but you'll never have to wait more than 15 minutes or so. The following are just two of the companies in operation: **P.C.B. Stael** (tel. 050/33-21-71) and **Coudenys** (tel. 050/33-51-03). During the summer months, special evening cruises can be arranged.

Orientation Tours Fifty-minute minibus trips of the city center leave every hour on the hour from the Market Square in front of the Belfry. Tours are given in seven languages (individual headphones). Cost: BF330 (children 200). For further information and a full list of companies, check with the tourist office.

Tourist Information

The **Brugge Tourist Office** (Burg 11, tel. 050/44-86-86).

Exploring Brugge

Brugge (also known by its French name, Bruges) is an exquisitely preserved medieval town. It was Brugge's good fortune to be linked with the sea by a navigable waterway, and the city became a leading member of the Hanseatic League in the 13th century. Europe's first stock exchange was established here. Brugge was ignored for centuries after the Zwin River silted up in the 15th century, and the port became a romantic Flemish backwater. This past misfortune is its present glory. Little has changed in this city of interlaced canals, overhung with humpbacked bridges and weeping willows. The **Burg,** an intimate medieval square, is the inspiring setting for summer classical concerts.

Numbers in the margin correspond to points of interest on the Brugge map.

❶ ❷ The best place to start a walking tour is the **Markt** (Market Square). From the top of the **Belfort** (Belfry) there's a panoramic view of the town. The belfry has a carillon notable even in Belgium, where they are a matter of civic pride. On summer evenings, the Markt is brightly lit. *The Belfort. Admission: BF80. Open Apr.–Sept., daily 10–5:15. Oct.–Mar., 10–11:45 and 1:30–4:15. Carillon concerts Oct.–mid-June, Sun., Wed., and Sat. 2:15–3; mid-June–Sept., Mon., Wed., and Sat. 9–10 PM, Sun. 2:15–3.*

❸ On the eastern side of the Markt stands the **Provinciaal Hof,** the neo-Gothic provincial government building. Walk east from the Markt along Breidelstraat, to the Burg, a square at the center **❹** of ancient Brugge. On the left is the **Landshuis** (Provost's House), built in 1665. Across the square is a row of magnificent **❺** buildings—the **Stadhuis** (town hall), dating from the 14th cen- **❻** tury, its wonderfully ornate facade covered with statues; **Oude Griffie,** the former Recorder's House dating from the 1530s, and also ornamented with impressive windows; and the **❼** **Heilig-Bloed Basiliek** (the Basilica of the Holy Blood), a 12th-century Romanesque chapel built to enshrine the vial containing Christ's blood. Here, too, is a **Heilig-Bloed Museum** (Museum of the Holy Blood), with many treasures associated with the cult. The Procession of the Holy Blood on Ascension Day (May 12 in 1994) is a major pageant that combines religious and historical elements. *Stadhuis—Admission: BF40. Open daily 9:30–noon and 2–6. Heilig-Bloed Basiliek—Worship of the Blood, Fri. 8:30–11:45 and 3–4. Free guided visits daily 2–5. Museum—Admission: BF20. Open daily 9:30–noon and 2–6.*

❽ Walk through a passage between the town hall and the Oude Griffie and you'll come to the **Dijver,** the city canal. Canal boat trips leave from here. *Boats leave on demand. Average trip 30 minutes. Cost: BF130.*

❾ Walking south along the Dijver, you'll soon reach a group of museums. The **Groeninge Museum,** on the Dijver Canal, has a very rich, wide-ranging collection of Flemish masterpieces, with works by Van Eyck, Memling, Bosch, and Bruegel, among many others, plus some contemporary works. *Dijver 12. Admission: BF100. Open Apr.–Sept., daily 9:30–6; Oct.–Mar., Wed.–Mon. 9:30–noon and 2–5.*

❿ The **Gruuthuse Museum,** in the 15th century a palace of the aristocratic Gruuthuse family, contains archaeological exhibitions and a display of lace from all over Belgium. *Dijver 17. Admission: BF100; combined ticket for BF250 covers the Groeninge, Gruuthuse, and Memling museums (see below). Open Apr.–Sept., daily 9:30–noon and 2–6; Oct.–Mar., Wed.–Mon. 9:30–noon and 2–5.*

⓫ Here, too, is the **Memling Museum,** dedicated to the work of one of Brugge's most famous sons, the painter Hans Memling (1430–90), and housed in the former Sint Jans Hospital (Hospital of St. John), where the artist was nursed back to health af-

Brugge

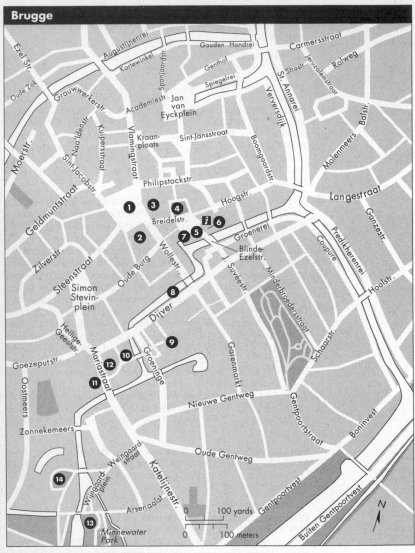

Begijnhof, **14**

Belfort, **2**

Dijver, **8**

Groeninge
Museum, **9**

Gruuthuse
Museum, **10**

Heilig Bloed
Basiliek, **7**

Landshuis, **4**

Markt, **1**

Memling Museum, **11**

Minnewater, **13**

Onze-Lieve-
Vrouwekerk, **12**

Oude Griffie, **6**

Provinciaal Hof, **3**

Stadhuis, **5**

ter being wounded in France. *Mariastraat 38. Admission: BF100. Open Apr.–Sept., daily 9:30–noon and 2–6; Oct.– Mar., Thur.–Tues. 9:30–noon and 2–5.*

⑫ Next to the Memling Museum is the **Onze-Lieve-Vrouwekerk** (Church of Our Lady), with, at 116 meters (375 feet), the highest tower in Belgium, a notable collection of paintings and carvings—especially a *Madonna* by Michelangelo—and some splendidly colorful tombs. *Mausoleums—Admission: BF30. Open weekdays 10–11:30 and 2:30–5, Sun. 2:30–5. No visits during services.*

⑬ Continue south to the enchanting **Minnewater** (Lake of Love) Park. From the Minnewater visit the adjoining 16th-century lockkeeper's house, usually surrounded by contented white swans, the symbol of the city.

⑭ Beside Minnewater, a picturesque bridge leads to the **Begijnhof,** the former almshouses and the most serene spot in Brugge. Founded in 1245 by the countess of Constantinople, the Begijnhof was originally a home for widows of fallen Crusaders. These women took partial vows and lived a devout life while serving the community. Although the last Béguines left in 1930, a Benedictine community has replaced them. The Begijnhof has kept its cloistered charm. Notice the harmonious pattern made by the gabled white houses, the expanse of green lawn, and the crooked trees that stretch diagonally across your view.

Time Out Overlooking the lake is a fairy-tale tower without a princess, but with a perfect setting in which to enjoy a drink or light lunch. The romantic **Kasteel** is divided into two sections, for formal and casual dining. Try a tasty ham or mushroom omelet with crusty bread or a witloof specialty. If you are dining outside, the swans may try to join in. *Tel. 50/33–42–54. DC, V. Inexpensive–Moderate.*

Explore the medieval ramparts near the Kasteel or retrace your steps to the Markt. Savor the side streets, the gabled houses, the lace shops, and the churches along the quay.

Dining

For details and price-category definitions, *see* Dining in Staying in Belgium.

Very Expensive **Vasquez.** In this marvelous 17th-century Spanish house, a talented young chef concocts superb dishes flavored with wild herbs. The monkfish tournedos with five spices is a specialty. *Zilverstraat 38, tel. 050/34–08–45. Reservations advised. AE, DC, MC, V. Closed Wed., Thurs. lunch, second half of July.*

Expensive **De Witte Poorte.** The fish here, fresh from the North Sea, is in a
★ class by itself; so is the game in season. Family run, and housed in an old, vaulted warehouse, the de Witte Poorte is *the* place for a meal you'll remember. *Jan Van Eyckplein 6, tel. 050/33–08–83. Reservations advised. AE, DC, V.*

Moderate **Oud Brugge.** Many of the city's restaurants are found in atmospheric ancient buildings, and this is one of them. Tasty local dishes are served under yet more vaulted ceilings. *Kuiperstraat 33, tel. 050/33–54–02. Reservations advised. No credit cards.*

Inexpensive **Gistelhof.** The Gistelhof serves hearty fish stews and other local dishes in historic Flemish surroundings. *West Gistelhof 23, tel. 050/33–62–90. Reservations accepted. AE, DC, MC, V.*

Lodging

In proportion to its size, Bruges has a large number of hotels; in fact, many more than Antwerp. Prices are relatively high, but so are the standards. For details and price-category definitions, *see* Lodging in Staying in Belgium.

Very Expensive **Die Swaene.** The Swan, sitting right in the center of town, is a
★ real find. The 15th-century building, lovingly restored by the Hessels-Dutoit husband-and-wife team, has many original features preserved. The courtyard has been converted into a pleasant garden. *Steenhouwersdijk 1, tel. 050/34–27–98, fax 050/33–66–74. 26 rooms with bath and shower. Facilities: bar, restaurant. AE, DC, MC, V.*

Expensive **Holiday Inn Crowne Plaza.** This hotel has been successfully integrated into the heart of the city. The rooms are modern and agreeable. In the basement conference area you can see remnants of a former cathedral. *Burg 10, tel. 050/34–58–34, fax 050/34–56–15. 96 rooms and suites with bath. Facilities: restaurant, bar, fitness center, sauna, solarium, swimming pool. AE, DC, MC, V.*

Moderate **Oud Huis Amsterdam.** Two 16th-century townhouses have been combined to create this hotel overlooking the canal near Jan Van Eyckplein. The rooms, all different, are large and modern. Free transfer in the evening by horse-drawn coach to the romantic restaurant 't Bourgoensche Cruyce. *Spiegelrei 3, tel. 050/34–18–10, fax 050/33–88–91. 19 rooms with bath. AE, DC, MC, V.*

Inexpensive **De Pauw.** At this spotless, family-run hotel, the quaintly furnished rooms have names rather than numbers, and breakfast comes with six different kinds of bread. *St. Gilliskerkhof 8, tel. 050/33–71–18. 8 rooms, 6 with bath. AE, DC, MC, V.*
Ter Brughe. If it's atmosphere and period charm you want, you won't be disappointed by this delightful canalside hotel, a 15th-century survival, with friendly service and a cozy atmosphere. There's no restaurant. *Oost-Gistelhof 2, tel. 050/34–03–24, fax 050/33–88–73. 24 rooms with bath. DC, MC, V. Closed Jan.–Feb.*

5 Bulgaria

Bulgaria, a land of mountains and seascapes, of austerity and rustic beauty, lies in the eastern half of the Balkan peninsula. From the end of World War II until recently, it was the closest ally of the former Soviet Union and presented a rather mysterious image to the Western world. This era ended in 1989 with the overthrow of Communist party head Todor Zhivkov. Since then, Bulgaria has gradually opened itself to the West as it struggles along the path toward democracy and a free-market economy.

Endowed with long Black Sea beaches, the rugged Balkan range in its interior, and fertile Danube plains, Bulgaria has much to offer the tourist year-round. Its tourist industry is quite well developed and is being restructured to shield visitors better from shortages of goods and services and the other legacies of rigid central planning.

The Black Sea coast along the country's eastern border is particularly attractive, with secluded coves and old fishing villages, as well as wide stretches of shallow beaches that have been developed into self-contained resorts. The interior landscape offers great scenic beauty, and the traveler who enters it will find a tranquil world of forested ridges, spectacular valleys, and rural communities where folklore is a colorful part of village life.

Founded in 681, Bulgaria was a crossroads of civilization even before that date. Archaeological finds in Varna, on the Black Sea coast, give proof of civilization from as early as 4600 BC. Bulgaria was part of the Byzantine Empire from AD 1018 to 1185 and was occupied by the Turks from 1396 until 1878. The combined influences are reflected in Bulgarian architecture, which has a truly Eastern feel. Five hundred years of Muslim occupation and nearly half a century of Communist rule did not wipe out Christianity, and there are many lovely, icon-filled churches to see. The 120 monasteries, with their icons and many frescoes, provide a chronicle of the development of Bulgarian cultural and national identity, and several merit special stops on any tourist's itinerary.

The capital, Sofia, is picturesquely situated in a valley near Mount Vitosha. There is much of cultural interest here, and the city has good hotels and restaurants serving traditional and international cuisine. Other main towns are Veliko Tǎrnovo, the capital from the 12th to the 14th century and well worth a visit for the old, characteristic architecture; Plovdiv, southeast of Sofia, which has a particularly interesting old quarter; and Varna, the site of one of Europe's first cultural settlements and the most important port in Bulgaria.

Essential Information

Before You Go

When to Go   The ski season lasts from mid-December through March, while the Black Sea coast season runs from May to October, reaching its crowded peak in July and August. Fruit trees blossom in April and May; in May and early June the blossoms are gathered in the Valley of Roses (you have to be up early to watch the harvest); the fruit is picked in September, and in October the fall colors are at their best.

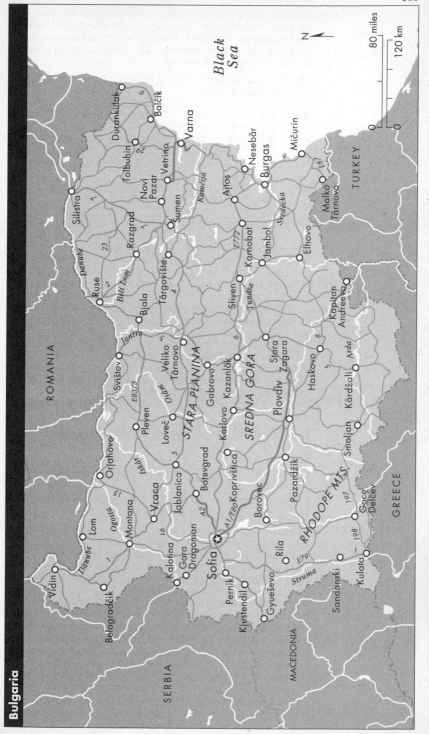

Bulgaria

ROMANIA

SERBIA

MACEDONIA

GREECE

TURKEY

Black Sea

Sofia

Vidin
Belogradčik
Lom
Montana
Vraca
Orjahovo
Kalotina
Gara Dragoman
Pernik
Kjustendil
Gyueševo
Rila
Borovec
Pazandžik
Plovdiv
Boroved
Pleven
Loveč
Botevgrad
Jablanica
Koprivštica
Veliko Tărnovo
Svištov
Bjala
Ruse
Silistra
Razgrad
Novi Pazar
Tolbuhin
Durankulak
Balčik
Varna
Vetrino
Šumen
Târgovište
Sliven
Kazanlăk
Katlovo
Gabrovo
Stara Zagora
Karnobat
Jambol
Elhovo
Nesebăr
Burgas
Ajtos
Mičurin
Malko Tărnovo
Kapitan Andreevo
Haskovo
Kărdžali
Smoljan
Goce Delčev
Kulata
Sandanski

STARA PLANINA
SREDNA GORA
RHODOPE MTS.

Danube
Iantra
Osăm
Iskăr
Ogosta
Danube
Beli Lom
Kamčija
Sredečka
Tundža
Struma
Arda

A1/E80
A2
E79
E83/3
E772
E87

Kjustendil

N

80 miles
120 km

Climate Summers are warm, winters are crisp and cold. The coastal areas enjoy considerable sunshine, though March and April are the wettest months inland. Even when the temperature climbs, the Black Sea breezes and the cooler mountain air prevent the heat from being overpowering.

The following are the average daily maximum and minimum temperatures for Sofia.

Jan.	35F	2C	May	69F	21C	Sept.	70F	22C
	25	– 4		50	10		52	11
Feb.	39F	4C	June	76F	24C	Oct.	63F	17C
	27	– 3		56	14		46	8
Mar.	50F	10C	July	81F	27C	Nov.	48F	9C
	33	1		60	16		37	3
Apr.	60F	16C	Aug.	79F	26C	Dec.	38F	4C
	42	5		59	15		28	– 2

Currency The unit of currency in Bulgaria is the lev (plural leva), divided into 100 stotinki. There are bills of 1, 2, 5, 10, 20, 50, 100, and 200 leva; coins of 1, 2, and 5 leva; and coins of 1, 2, 5, 10, 20, and 50 stotinki. At press time (spring 1993), as part of efforts at economic reform, hard-currency payments for goods and services are no longer permitted. The only legal tender for commercial transactions and tourist services in Bulgaria is the lev. These services include air, train, and long-distance bus travel; all accommodations, from camping to hotels; and car rentals and Balkantourist package tours. You may import any amount of foreign currency, including traveler's checks, and exchange it at branches of the Bulgarian State Bank, commercial banks, Balkantourist hotels, airports, border posts, and other exchange offices, which quote their daily selling and buying rates. The rate quoted by the Bulgarian State Bank at press time is 25.5 leva to the U.S. dollar, 38.7 leva to the pound sterling.

It is forbidden either to import or to export Bulgarian currency. Unspent leva must be exchanged at frontier posts on departure before you go through passport control. You will need to present your official exchange slips to prove that the currency was legally purchased.

The major international credit cards are accepted in the larger stores, hotels, and restaurants.

What It Will Cost Prices in Bulgaria have been low for years, but this is changing as the government tries to revive the economy and open it up to the West. If you choose the more moderate hotels, accommodations won't be very expensive. It is possible to cut costs even more by staying in a private hotel or private room in a Bulgarian house or apartment—also arranged by Balkantourist or other tourism companies—or by camping. The favorable cash exchange rate, linked to foreign-currency fluctuations, makes such expenses as taxi and public transport fares, museum and theater admission, and meals in most restaurants seem comparatively low by international standards. A little hard currency, exchanged at this rate, goes a long way. Shopping for imported and domestic wares in the duty-free shops also helps to keep travel expenses down. The following price list, correct as of spring 1993, can therefore be used only as a rough guide.

Sample Prices   Trip on a tram, trolley, or bus, 1 lev–5 leva; theater ticket, 4 leva–15 leva; coffee in a moderate restaurant, 5 leva–12 leva; bottle of wine in a moderate restaurant, 40 leva–100 leva.

Museums   Museum admission is very inexpensive, ranging from 1 lev to 10 leva (less than 40¢).

Visas   All visitors need a valid passport. Those traveling in groups of six or more do not require visas, and many package tours are exempt from the visa requirement. Americans do not need visas when traveling as tourists. Other tourists, traveling independently, should inquire about visa requirements at a Bulgarian embassy or consulate before entering the country, since fees may be higher for visas obtained at the border.

Customs on Arrival   You may import duty-free into Bulgaria 250 grams of tobacco products, plus 1 liter of hard liquor and 2 liters of wine. Items intended for personal use during your stay are also duty-free. Travelers are advised to declare items of greater value—cameras, tape recorders, etc.—so there will be no problems with Bulgarian customs officials on departure.

Language   The official language, Bulgarian, is written in Cyrillic and is very close to Old Church Slavonic, the root of all Slavic languages. English is spoken in major hotels and restaurants, but is unlikely to be heard elsewhere. It is essential to remember that in Bulgaria, a nod of the head means "no" and a shake of the head means "yes."

Getting Around

By Car   Main roads are generally well engineered, although some *Road Conditions* routes are poor and narrow for the volume of traffic they have to carry. A large-scale expressway construction program has begun to link the main towns. Completed stretches run from Kalotina—on the Serbian border—to Sofia and from Sofia to Plovdiv. Highway tolls of some $20 total are paid at the border; be prepared for delays during the summer season at border points (open 24 hours) while documents are checked and stamped.

Rules of the Road   Drive on the right, as in the United States. The speed limits are 50 or 60 kph (31 or 36 mph) in built-up areas, 80 kph (50 mph) elsewhere, except on highways, where it is 120 kph (70 mph). The limits for a car towing a trailer are 50 kph (31 mph), 70 kph (44 mph), and 100 kph (62 mph), respectively. You must obtain a Green Card or Blue Card from your car insurance company, as recognized international proof that your car is covered by International Civil Liability (third-party) Insurance. You may be required to show one of these cards at the border. Balkantourist recommends that you also take out collision, or Casco, insurance. You are required to carry a first-aid kit, fire extinguisher, and breakdown triangle in the vehicle, and you must not sound the horn in towns. Front seat belts must be worn. The drinking-driving laws are extremely strict—you are expressly forbidden to drive after consuming any alcohol at all.

Parking   Park only in clearly marked parking places. If you are in doubt, check with the hotel or restaurant.

Gasoline   Stations are regularly spaced on main roads but may be few and far between off the beaten track. All are marked on Balkantourist's free motoring map. As of press time, service stations sell unlimited quantities of fuel, supplies permitting, for leva (in spring 1993, 38¢ per liter, or $1.52 per gallon, for regular leaded). For motorist information contact the automobile club **Shipka,** located at 6 Sveta Sofia Street, Sofia (tel. 2/87–88–01).

Breakdowns In case of breakdown, telephone 146. The **S.B.A.** (Bulgarian Automobile Touring Association) trucks carry essential spares, but it's wise to carry your own spare-parts kit. Fiat, Ford, Volkswagen, Peugeot, and Mercedes all have car-service operations in Bulgaria offering prompt repairs by skilled technicians.

Car Rental The **Balkantourist/Hertz Rent-a-Car** organization has offices in most of the major hotels and at Sofia Airport (tel. 2/72–01–57). Its main headquarters in Sofia are at 1 Vitosha Boulevard (tel. 2/83–34–87). Rental cars and fly/drive arrangements can be prebooked through Balkantourist agents abroad. These agents can also provide you with a driver for a small extra charge. **Avis** (tel. 2/79–14–77) and **Europe Car** (tel. 2/72–01–57) also have offices in Sofia.

By Train Buy tickets in advance at a ticket office—there is one in each of the major centers—and avoid long lines at the station. Trains are very busy; seat reservations are obligatory on expresses. All medium- and long-distance trains have first- and second-class carriages and limited buffet services; overnight trains between Sofia and Black Sea resorts have first- and second-class sleeping cars and second-class couchettes. From Sofia there are six main routes—to Varna and Burgas on the Black Sea coast, to Plovdiv and on to the Turkish border, to Dragoman and the Serbian border, to Kulata and the Greek border, and to Ruse on the Romanian border. The main line is powered by electricity. Plans to electrify the rest are under way.

By Plane **Balkanair** (Balkan Bulgarian Airlines) has regular services to Varna and Burgas, the biggest ports of the Black Sea. Book through Balkantourist offices; this can take time, however, and overbooking is not unusual. Group travel and air-taxi services are available through privately run Hemus Air and Air Via. Business flights to other destinations in the country are also arranged by Hemus Air.

By Bus The routes of the crowded buses are mainly planned to link towns and districts not connected by rail. Within the cities a regular system of trams and trolley buses operates for a single fare of 1 lev–5 leva. Ticket booths, at most tram stops, sell single or season tickets; you can also pay the driver. The tourist information offices have full details of routes and times.

By Boat Modern luxury vessels cruise the Danube from Passau in Austria to Ruse. Hydrofoils link main communities along the Bulgarian stretches of the Danube and the Black Sea, and there are coastal excursions from some Black Sea resorts. A ferry from Vidin to Calafat links Bulgaria with Romania.

Staying in Bulgaria

Telephones Calls can be made from hotels or from public telephones in the post office in each major town or resort. Elsewhere, there is a new system of international telephones—modern, direct-dial phones with no coin slots—that operate only with special cards paid for in leva. Directions for buying the cards are given, often in English, on the phones.

Mail Letters and postcards to the United States cost 10 leva, 7 leva to the United Kingdom.

Opening and Closing Times Banks are open weekdays 9–3.

Museums are usually open 8–6:30 but are often closed on Monday or Tuesday.

Shops are open Monday–Saturday 9 AM–7 PM. Many shops are open on Sunday, and most grocery stores are open round-the-clock.

National Holidays January 1 (New Year's); March 3 (Independence Day); April 10 and 11 (Easter Sunday and Monday); May 1 (Labor Day); May 24 (Bulgarian Culture Day); December 24, 25, 26 (Christmas).

Dining There is a choice of hotel restaurants with their international menus, Balkantourist restaurants, or the inexpensive restaurants and cafeterias run privately and by cooperatives. The best bets are the small folk-style restaurants that serve national dishes and local specialties. The word *picnic* in a restaurant name means that the tables are outdoors. Standards have improved, but food is still rarely served piping hot, and visitors should be prepared for loud background music.

Specialties Balkan cooking revolves around lamb and pork, sheep cheese, potatoes, peppers, eggplant, tomatoes, onions, carrots, and spices. Fresh fruit, vegetables, and salads are particularly good in season, and so are the soups. Bulgaria invented yogurt (*kiselo mleko*), with its promise of good health and longevity, and there are excellent cold yogurt soups (*tarator*) during the summer. Rich cream cakes and syrupy *baklava* are served to round out a meal.

Bulgarian wines are good, usually full-bodied, dry, and inexpensive. The national drink is *rakia*—plum or grape brandy *slivova* or *grosdova*—but vodka is popular, too. Coffee is strong and is often drunk along with a cold beverage, such as cola or a lemon drink. Tea is taken with lemon instead of milk.

Dress In Sofia, formal dress (jacket and tie) is customary at Expensive and Very Expensive restaurants. Casual dress is appropriate elsewhere.

Ratings Prices are per person and include a first course, main course, dessert, and tip, but no alcohol. Best bets are indicated by a star ★.

Category	All Areas
Very Expensive	over 180 leva
Expensive	100 leva–180 leva
Moderate	40 leva–100 leva
Inexpensive	20 leva–40 leva

Credit Cards Increasingly, even restaurants in the Moderate category are accepting credit cards, although the list of cards accepted may not always be correctly posted. Before you place an order, check to see whether you can pay with your card.

Lodging   There is a wide choice of accommodations, ranging from hotels—most of them dating from the '60s and '70s—to apartment rentals, rooms in private homes, hostels, and campsites. Although hotels are improving, they still tend to suffer from temperamental wiring and erratic plumbing, and it is a good idea to pack a universal drain plug, as plugs are often missing in hotel bathrooms. In moderate and inexpensive hotels, bathrooms often look unusual. Don't be surprised if strangely placed plumbing turns the entire bathroom into a shower. Due to power cuts in the winter, flashlights and other battery-powered utilities are strongly recommended.

Hotels   Until recently, most hotels used by Western visitors were owned by Balkantourist and Interhotels. At press time (spring 1993), many of the government-owned or -operated hotels listed below were on the verge of privatization. The conversion is expected to take up to five years. Hotels may be closed for renovation for extended periods or may be permanently shut down. Visitors are strongly urged to call ahead to hotels to get the latest information. Some hotels were always privately run or run by municipal authorities or organizations catering to specific groups (Sipka for motorists, Orbita for young people, Pirin for hikers). Most have restaurants and bars; the large, modern ones have swimming pools, shops, and other facilities. Some coastal resorts have complexes where different categories of hotels are grouped, each with its own facilities.

Rented Accommodations   Rented accommodations are a growth industry, with planned, modern complexes as well as picturesque cottages. Cooking facilities tend to be meager, and meal vouchers are included in the deal. An English-speaking manager is generally on hand.

Private Accommodations   Staying in private homes, arranged by Balkantourist, is becoming a popular alternative to hotels as a means not only of cutting costs but of offering increased contact with Bulgarians. There are one-, two-, and three-star private accommodations. Some offer a bed or bed and breakfast only; some provide full board. Three-star rooms are equipped with kitchenettes. Booking offices are located in most main tourist areas. In Sofia, contact **Balkantourist** at 27 Stambolijski Boulevard (tel. 2/88–52–56), or go to the private accommodations office at 37 Dondukov Boulevard.

Hostels   Hostels are basic, but clean and cheap. Contact **Orbita** (45a Stambolijski Boulevard, Sofia, tel. 2/87–95–52 or 2/80–15–03).

Campsites   There are more than 100 campsites, many near the Black Sea coast. They are graded one, two, or three stars, and the best of them offer hot and cold water, grocery stores, and restaurants. Balkantourist provides a location map.

Ratings   Prices are for two people in a double room with half-board (breakfast and a main meal). Best bets are indicated by a star ★. You can pay in either Western or local currency, but if you pay in leva, you must show your exchange slips to prove that the money was legally changed.

Category	Sofia	Other Areas
Very Expensive	over 5000 leva	over 2000 leva
Expensive	2000–5000 leva	1500–2000 leva

Moderate	1000–2000 leva	800–1500 leva
Inexpensive	500–1000 leva	200–800 leva

Tipping   To tip, round out your restaurant bill 3%–5%.

Sofia

Arriving and Departing

By Plane   All international flights arrive at Sofia airport. For information on international flights, tel. 2/79–80–35; domestic flights, tel. 2/72–24–14.

Between the Airport and Downtown   Bus No. 84 (nonstop) serves the airport. Fares for taxis taken from the airport taxi stand run about 50 leva–120 leva for the 9-kilometer (6-mile) ride into Sofia. Avoid the taxi touts; they tend to overcharge or to insist on payment in hard currency.

By Train   The central station is at the northern edge of the city. For information, tel. 2/3–11–11 or 2/59–71–87. The ticket offices in Sofia are in the underpass of the National Palace of Culture (1 Bulgaria Sq., tel. 2/59–71–87) or at the Rila International Travel Agency (5 Gurko St., tel. 2/87–07–77). There is a taxi stand at the station.

By Car   Heading to or from Serbia, the main routes are E80, going through the border checkpoint at Kalotina on the Niš-Sofia road, or E871 going through the checkpoint at Gyueshevo. Traveling from Greece, take E79, passing through the checkpoint at Kulata; from Turkey, take E80, passing through checkpoint Kapitan-Andreevo. Border crossings to Romania are at Vidin on E79 and at Ruse on E70 and E85.

Getting Around

By Bus   Buses, trolleys, and trams run fairly often. Buy a ticket from the ticket stand near the streetcar stop and punch it into the machine as you board. (Watch how the person in front of you does it.) For information, tel. 2/3–12–41.

By Taxi   Since private taxi drivers were given permission to operate in 1990, it has become easier to find cabs in Sofia. Hail them in the street or at a stand—or ask the hotel to call one. Daytime taxi rates (at press time) run 4 leva per kilometer, 6 leva per kilometer after 10 PM. There is a 2-leva surcharge for taxis ordered by phone. To order by phone, call 142 or 68–01–01. To tip, round out the fare 5%–10%.

By Rented Car   You can rent a car, with or without driver, through Balkantourist, at the airport, and at hotel reception desks.

On Foot   The main sites are centrally located, so the best way to see the city is on foot.

Important Addresses and Numbers

Since late 1990, a national commission has been working to rename cities, streets, and monuments throughout the country. Names given in the following sections were correct as of spring 1993 but are subject to change.

Tourist **Balkantourist Head Office** (tel. 2/4–33–31) is at 1 Vitosha Boul-
Information evard; the tourist and accommodations office (tel. 2/88–44–30)
is at 37 Dondukov Boulevard. It also has offices or desks in all
the main hotels.

Embassies **U.S.** (1 Stambolijski Blvd., tel. 2/88–48–01). **U.K.** (65 Levski
Blvd., tel. 2/88–53–61).

Emergencies **Police:** Sofia City Constabulary (tel. 166), **ambulance** (tel. 150),
Fire (tel. 160), **Doctor:** Clinic for Foreign Citizens (Mladost 1, 1
Eugeni Pavlovski St., tel. 2/7–53–61), **"Pirogov"** Emergency
Hospital (tel. 2/5–15–31), **pharmacies** (tel. 178 for information
about all-night pharmacies).

Guided Tours

Orientation Tours Guided tours of Sofia and environs are arranged by Balkantourist from either of the main Sofia offices or from Balkantourist desks at the major hotels. Among the possibilities are
three- to four-hour tours of the principal city sights by car or
minibus or a longer four- to five-hour tour that goes as far as
Mount Vitosha.

Excursions Balkantourist offers 23 types of special-interest tours of various lengths, using Sofia as the point of departure. There are
trips to the most beautiful monasteries, such as the Rila Monastery, 118 kilometers (74 miles) south of Sofia; to museum
towns, such as Nesebâr and Koprivshtitsa; to sports areas and
spas; to the Valley of Roses; and to other places of exceptional
scenic or cultural interest.

Evening Tours Balkantourist has a number of evening tours, from a night out
eating local food and watching folk dances to an evening at the
National Opera.

Exploring Sofia

Sofia is set on the high Sofia Plain, ringed by mountain ranges:
the Balkan range to the north; the Lyulin Mountains to the
west; part of the Sredna Gora Mountains to the southeast; and,
to the southwest, Mount Vitosha, the city's playground, which
rises to 2,325 meters (7,500 feet). The area has been inhabited
for about 7,000 years, but the visitor's first impression is of a
modern city with broad streets, light traffic, spacious parks,
and open-air cafés. As recently as the 1870s it was part of the
Turkish Empire, and one mosque still remains. Most of the
city, however, was planned after 1880. There are enough intriguing museums and high-quality musical performances to
merit a lengthy stay, but if time is short, you need only two
days to see the main sights and another day, at least, for Mount
Vitosha.

*Numbers in the margin correspond to points of interest on the
Sofia map.*

❶ **Ploshtad Sveta Nedelya** (St. Nedelya Square) is a good starting
point for an exploration of the main sights. The south side of the
❷ square is dominated by the 19th-century **Tzarkva Sveta Nedelya**
(St. Nedelya Church). Go behind it to find Vitosha Boulevard, a
lively pedestrian street with plenty of stores, cafés, and dairy
bars.

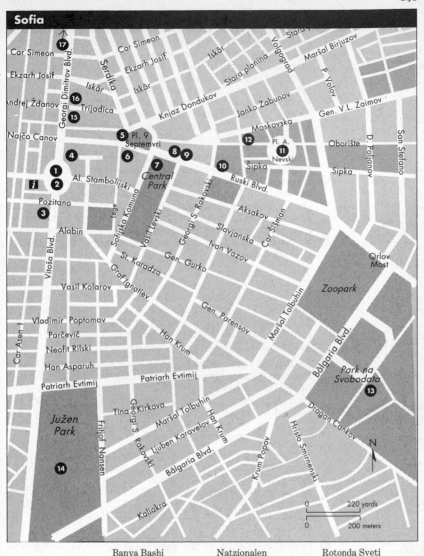

Sofia

Banya Bashi
Djamiya, **16**

Borisova Gradina, **13**

Hram-pametnik
Alexander Nevski, **11**

Mavsolei Georgi
Dimitrov, **7**

Nacionalen Dvoretz na
Kulturata **14**

Natzionalen
Archeologicheski
Musei, **6**

Natzionalen
Etnografski Musei, **8**

Natzionalen
Istoricheski Musei, **3**

Natzionalna
Hudozhestvena
Galeria, **9**

Partiyniyat Dom, **5**

Ploshtad Sveta
Nedelya, **1**

Rotonda Sveti
Georgi, **4**

Tsentralen
Universalen
Magazin, **15**

Tsentralni Hali, **17**

Tzarkva Sveta
Nedelya, **2**

Tzarkva Sveta
Sofia, **12**

Tzarkva Sveti
Nikolai, **10**

The first building along this boulevard, on the west side of the street, is the former Courts of Justice, now the **Natzionalen Istoricheski Musei** (National History Museum). Its vast collections, vividly illustrating the art history of Bulgaria, include priceless Thracian treasures, Roman mosaics, enameled jewelry from the First Bulgarian Kingdom, and glowing religious art that survived the years of Ottoman oppression. The courts are due to return to this location as soon as a new home is found for the National History Museum collection. *2 Vitosha Blvd., tel. 2/88–41–60. Open Tues.–Thurs. and weekends 10:30–6:30; Fri. 2–6:30.*

Return to the northeast side of St. Nedelya Square, and in the courtyard of the Sheraton Sofia Balkan Hotel you will see the **Rotonda Sveti Georgi** (Rotunda of St. George). Built in the 4th century as a Roman temple, it has served as a mosque and church, and recent restoration has revealed medieval frescoes. It is not open to the public. Head east to the vast and traffic-free Alexander Batenberg Square, which is dominated by the **Partiyniyat Dom** (the former headquarters of the Bulgarian Communist party).

Facing the square, but entered via Alexander Stambolijski Boulevard, is the former Great Mosque, which now houses the **Natzionalen Archeologicheski Musei** (National Archaeological Museum). The 15th-century building itself is as fascinating as its contents, which illustrate the culture of the different peoples who inhabited Bulgaria up to the 19th century. *Tel. 2/88–24–05. Open Tues.–Sun. 10–noon and 2–6.*

On the next block to the east is the former **Mavsolei Georgi Dimitrov** (Georgi Dimitrov Mausoleum), which until 1990 contained the embalmed body of the first general secretary of the Bulgarian Communist party, who died in Moscow in 1949 and was known as the "Father of the Nation." His remains have been moved to the Central Cemetery, and there is talk of converting the mausoleum into a museum, or destroying it.

Across from the mausoleum is the former palace of the Bulgarian Czar, which currently houses the **Natzionalen Etnografski Musei** (National Ethnographical Museum), with displays of costumes, handicrafts, and tools that illustrate the agricultural way of life of the country people until the 19th century. *Alexander Batenberg Sq., tel. 2/88–51–15. Open Wed.–Sun. 10–noon and 1:30–5:30.*

In the west wing of the same building is the **Natzionalna Hudozhestvena Galeria** (National Art Gallery). It houses a collection of the best works of Bulgarian artists, as well as a foreign art section that contains some graphics of famous artists. *6A Yanko Sakazov St., tel. 2/88–35–59. Open Wed.–Mon. 10:30–7.*

Nearby stands the ornate Russian **Tzarkva Sveti Nikolai** (Church of St. Nicholas), erected 1912–14.

From here you'll enter Tzar Osvoboditel Boulevard, with its monument to the Russians, topped by the equestrian statue of Russian Czar Alexander II. It stands in front of the National Assembly. Behind the National Assembly, just beyond Shipka Street, you'll be confronted by the neo-Byzantine structure with glittering onion domes whose image you may recognize from almost every piece of tourist literature, and which really

⓫ does dominate the city. This is the **Hram-pametnik Alexander Nevski** (Alexander Nevski Memorial Church), built by the Bulgarian people at the beginning of this century as a mark of gratitude to their Russian liberators. Inside are alabaster and onyx, Italian marble and Venetian mosaics, magnificent frescoes, and space for a congregation of 5,000. Attend a service to hear the superb choir, and, above all, don't miss the fine collection of icons in the **Crypt Museum**. *Admission: 30 stotinki. Open Wed.–Mon. 10:30–6:30.*

⓬ Cross the square to the west to pay your respects to the much older **Tzarkva Sveta Sofia** (Church of St. Sofia), which dates to the 6th century, though remains of even older churches have been found during excavations. Its age and simplicity are in stark contrast to its more glamorous neighbor.

⓭ Return to Tzar Osvoboditel Boulevard and continue east to the **Borisova Gradina** (Boris's Garden), with its lake and fountains, woods and lawns, huge sports stadium, and open-air theater. From the park take Dragan Tsankov west (back toward St. Nedelya Square) briefly, before going left on Patriarh Evtimij, toward Južen Park. The formal gardens and extensive woodlands here are to be extended as far as Mount Vitosha.

⓮ At the entrance to the park stands a large modern building, the **Natzionalen Dvoretz na Kulturata** (National Palace of Culture), with its complex of halls for conventions and cultural activities. Its underpass, on several levels, is equipped with a tourist information office, shops, restaurants, discos, and a bowling alley. *1 Bulgaria Sq., tel. 2/5–15–01. Admission: 5 leva. Open 10:30–6:30. Closed Tues.*

⓯ Back at St. Nedelya Square, follow Knyaginya Maria-Luiza Boulevard to the train station. The large building on the right is the recently refurbished **Tsentralen Universalen Magazin** (Central Department Store). *2 Knyaginya Maria-Luiza Blvd. Open Mon.–Sat. 8–8.*

⓰ Just beyond is a distinctive building, a legacy of Turkish domination, the **Banya Bashi Djamiya** (Banja Basi Mosque); it is closed to visitors. Nearby you will see the Public Mineral **⓱** Baths. Across the boulevard is the busy **Tsentralni Hali** (Central Market Hall), which is closed for renovations until the end of 1994.

Time Out Anyone doing the full tour is going to need at least one refreshment stop. There are several places to eat on the northern length of Vitosha Boulevard; three of the best cafés are **Magura, Medovina,** and **Kravay.** A café huddles near the 14th-century church of **Sveta Petka Samardzijska** (St. Petka of the Saddles) in the underpass leading to the Central Department Store. Or take a break in a café in the underpass at the National Palace of Culture or on St. Nedelya Square itself at the Complex Roubin.

Off the Beaten Track

The little medieval church of **Boyana,** about 10 kilometers (6 miles) south of the city center, is well worth a visit as is the small, elegant restaurant of the same name, next door. The church itself is closed for restoration, but a replica, complete with copies of the exquisite 13th-century frescoes, is open to visitors.

The **Dragalevci Monastery** stands in beechwoods above the nearby village of Dragalevci. The complex is currently a convent, but you can visit the 14th-century church with its outdoor frescoes. Shepherds can often be seen tending their flocks in the surrounding woods. From here take the chair lift to the delightful resort complex of **Aleko,** and another nearby chair lift to the top of Malak Rezen. There are well-marked walking and ski trails in the area. Both Boyana and Dragalevci can be reached by taking the No. 64 bus.

Shopping

Gifts and Souvenirs There are good selections of arts and crafts at the shop of the **Union of Bulgarian Artists** (6 Tzar Osvoboditel Blvd.) and at the **Bulgarian Folk Art Shop** (14 Vitosha Blvd.). You will find a range of souvenirs at **Sredec** (7 Lege St.), **Souvenir Store** (7 Stambolijski Blvd.), and **Prizma Store** (2 Tzar Osvoboditel Blvd). If you are interested in furs or leather, try **4 Slavjanska St., 7 Car Kalojan St., or 2 Tzar Osvoboditel Blvd.** For recordings of Bulgarian music, go to the **National Palace of Culture** (*see* Exploring Sofia, above).

Shopping Districts The latest shopping center is in the underpass below the modern **National Palace of Culture,** where stores sell fashions, leather goods, and all forms of handicrafts. The pedestrians-only area along **Vitosha Boulevard** features many new, privately owned shops. The colorful small shops along **Graf Ignatiev Street** also merit a visit.

Department Stores Sophia's biggest department store is the newly renovated **Central Department Store** (2 Knyaginya Maria-Luiza Boulevard).

Dining

Eating in Sofia can be enjoyable and even entertaining if the restaurant has a nightclub or folklore program. Be prepared to be patient and make an evening of it, as service can be slow at times. Or try a *mehana*, or tavern, where the atmosphere is informal and the service sometimes a bit quicker. For details and price-category definitions, *see* Dining in Staying in Bulgaria.

Very Expensive **Club Restaurant of the Hunting and Fishing Union.** Here you can choose from an excellent menu of game, fish, and fowl. *31– 33 Vitosha Blvd., tel. 2/87–94–65. Reservations essential. AE, DC, MC, V.*

Coop-35 Vitosha. Continental cuisine is served in a friendly, homey atmosphere that makes it a good choice for both business dinners and more intimate dining. *Dragalevci District, 1 Narcis St., tel. 2/67–11–84. No credit cards.*

Dionyssos Vip. This club and restaurant above the Central Department Store (Zum), opposite the Sheraton Hotel, provides a rich selection of international and Bulgarian cuisine spiced with a three-hour floor show. *2 Knyaginya Maria-Luiza Blvd., tel. 2/81–37–26. Reservations advised. AE, DC, V.*

Krim. This Russian restaurant serves the best beef Stroganoff in town. *2 Dobroudja St., tel. 2/87–01–31. Reservations advised. No credit cards.*

Expensive **Berlin.** German food is the specialty in this sophisticated restaurant in the Serdika Hotel. *2 Yanko Sakazov Blvd., tel. 2/44–12–58. Reservations accepted. AE, DC, MC, V.*

★ **Budapest.** This place enjoys a reputation as one of the best restaurants in Sofia for good food, wine, and live music. As the name suggests, Hungarian food takes center stage. *145 G.S. Rakovski St., tel. 2/87–37–50. Reservations accepted. AE, DC, MC, V.*

Havana. Cuban food is featured in this popular restaurant near the center of town. *27 Vitosha Blvd., tel. 2/80–05–44. Reservations accepted. AE, DC, MC, V.*

Moderate **Boyansko Hanche.** Local and national specialties are the main features in this restaurant and folklore center, 6 miles from downtown (take bus No. 63). *Near Bojanske church, tel. 2/56–30–16. No credit cards.*

Corea. This place is known for its Far Eastern ambience and Korean specialties. *24 Assen Zlatarov St., tel. 2/44–34–36. No credit cards.*

Ropotamo. With its central location and reasonable prices, Ropotamo is a good bet for visitors on a budget. *63 Trakia Blvd., tel. 2/72–22–10. AE, DC, MC, V.*

Rozhen. Conveniently located near the National Palace of Culture, this cozy, two-tier restaurant features traditional Bulgarian cuisine. *74 Vitosha Blvd., tel. 2/52–11–31. AE, DC, MC, V.*

Rubin. This eating complex in the center of Sofia has a snack bar and an elegant restaurant that serves Bulgarian and international food. A full meal can sometimes push the cost into the Expensive bracket. *4 St. Nedelya Sq., tel. 2/87–20–86. No credit cards.*

Vodeničarski Mehani. The English translation is "Miller's Tavern," which is appropriate, since it's made up of three old mills linked together. It is at the foot of Mount Vitosha and features a folklore show and a menu of Bulgarian specialties. Nightclub open till 4 AM. *Dragalevci District (bus No. 64), tel. 2/67–10–21. No credit cards.*

Inexpensive **Party Club.** This restaurant features international and Chinese cuisine. *3 Vasil Levski Blvd., tel. 2/81–50–44. Reservations accepted. No credit cards.*

Zheravna. Candlelight, stone walls, and wood tables set the scene for Zherzavna's country cuisine. *26 Levski Blvd., tel. 2/87–91–62. No credit cards.*

Zlatnite Mostove. This restaurant on Mount Vitosha has live music in the evenings. *Vitosha District, 19 km (12 mi) from the city center. No credit cards.*

Lodging

The following hotels maintain a high standard of cleanliness and are open year-round unless otherwise stated. If you arrive in Sofia without reservations, go to Interhotels Central Office (4 Sveta Sofia St.), Balkantourist (37 Dondukov Blvd.), Bureau of Tourist Information and Reservations (35 Eksarh Josif St.), the National Palace of Culture (1 Bulgaria Sq.), or the central rail station. For details and price-category definitions, *see* Lodging in Staying in Bulgaria.

Very Expensive **Novotel Europa.** This member of the French Novotel chain is near the train station and not far from the center of the city. *131 Knyaginya Maria-Luiza Blvd., tel. 2/3–12–61. 600 rooms with* *bath. Facilities: restaurant, cocktail bar, coffee shop, night-club, shops. AE, DC, MC, V.*

★ **Sheraton Sofia Hotel Balkan.** The former Grand Hotel Balkan has recently been done up to Sheraton standards. It is now a first-class hotel with a central location that is hard to match. It also has excellent restaurants. *1 St. Nedelya Sq., tel. 2/87–65–41. 188 rooms with bath. Facilities: 3 restaurants, fitness center, whirlpool, nightclub, bars. AE, DC, MC, V.*

★ **Vitosha.** There is a distinct Oriental flavor to this towering, trim Interhotel, which is not surprising, since it was designed by the Japanese. It is hard to match the range of services and activities available here. The Vitosha also has a superb Japanese restaurant. *100 James Boucher Blvd., tel. 2/6–24–51. 454 rooms with bath. Facilities: 3 restaurants, shopping and business center, tennis courts, sauna, fitness center, pool, night-club, casino. AE, DC, MC, V.*

Expensive **Grand Hotel Sofia.** This five-story, centrally located Interhotel conveys an atmosphere of relative intimacy, compared with some of its larger rivals in the capital. *1 Narodno Sobranie Sq., tel. 2/87–88–21. 172 rooms with bath or shower. Facilities: 3 restaurants, coffee shop, folk tavern, nightclub, cocktail bar, and shops. AE, DC, MC, V.*

Park Hotel Moskva. The pleasant park setting makes up for the fact that this hotel is not as centrally located as some other comparable hotels. The excellent Panorama restaurant is hidden away on the rooftop. *25 Nezabravka St., tel. 2/7–12–61. 390 rooms with bath. Facilities: 4 restaurants, coffee shop, cocktail bar, nightclub, shops. AE, DC, MC, V.*

Rodina. Sofia's highest building is not far from the city center and boasts the latest in modern facilities. *8 General Totleben Blvd., tel. 2/5–16–31. 536 rooms with bath. Facilities: 3 restaurants, coffee shop, cocktail bar, shops, summer and winter gardens, pool, gym, nightclub. AE, DC, MC, V.*

Moderate **Bulgaria.** Despite its central location, this small hotel is quiet and a bit old-fashioned. *4 Tzar Osvoboditel Blvd., tel. 2/87–19–77. 72 rooms, some with bath or shower. Facilities: restaurant, tavern, coffee shop, cocktail bar. AE, DC, MC, V.*

Deva-Spartak. This small new hotel is located behind the National Palace of Culture. It offers excellent sports facilities. *Valdo Georgiev St., tel. 2/66–12–61. Facilities: restaurant, indoor and outdoor swimming pools, Spartak sports complex, shop. AE, DC, MC, V.*

Hemus. This is a smaller place near the Vitosha Hotel. Guests can take advantage of the facilities of its larger neighbor while saving money for the casino or nightclub. *31 Cherni Vrah Blvd., tel. 2/6–39–51. 240 rooms, most with bath or shower. Facilities: restaurant, folk tavern, nightclub, shops. AE, DC, MC, V.*

Pliska-Cosmos. Part of the Balkan Airlines hotel chain, the Pliska-Cosmos, located at the entrance to Sofia, has been recently renovated. *87 Trakia Blvd., tel. 2/71–281. 200 rooms with shower. Facilities: restaurant, cocktail bar, shops. AE, DC, MC, V.*

Rila. A convenient, central downtown location makes it a low-cost alternative to the Sheraton. *6 Kaloyan St., tel. 2/88–18–61. 86 rooms with shower. Facilities: restaurant, folk tavern, art gallery. AE, DC, MC, V.*

Inexpensive   **Serdika.** The centrally located Serdika has an old Berlin-style
restaurant that serves German specialties. *2 Yanko Sakazov
Blvd., tel. 2/44–34–11. 140 rooms, most with bath or shower.
No credit cards.*

The Arts

The standard of music in Bulgaria is high, whether it takes the
form of opera, symphonic, or folk music, which has just broken
into the international scene with its close harmonies and colorful stage displays. Contact Balkantourist or the **Concert Office**
(2 Tzar Osvoboditel Blvd., tel. 2/87–15–88) for general information.

You don't need to understand Bulgarian to enjoy a performance
at the **Central Puppet Theater** (14 Gourko St., tel. 2/88–54–16)
or at the **National Folk Ensemble** (check with the tourist office
for details).

There are a number of fine art galleries: The art gallery of the
Sts. Cyril and Methodius International Foundation has a collection of Indian, African, Japanese, and Western European
paintings and sculptures (Alexander Nevski Sq., tel. 2/88–21–
81; open Wed.–Mon. 10:30–6). The art gallery of the **Union of
Bulgarian Artists** has exhibitions of contemporary Bulgarian
art (6 Shipka St., tel. 2/44–61–15; open daily 9–8).

The **Odeon, Serdika,** and **Vitosha cinemas** show recent foreign
films in their original languages with Bulgarian subtitles.

Nightlife

Nightclubs   The following hotel bars have floor shows and a lively atmosphere: **Bar Sofia** (Grand Hotel Sofia, 1 Narodno Sobranie Sq.,
tel. 2/87–88–21); **Bar Variety Ambassador** (Vitosha Hotel, 100
James Boucher Blvd., tel. 2/6–24–51); **Bar Variety** (Park Hotel
Moskva, 25 Nezabravka St., tel. 2/7–12–61); **Bar Fantasy**
(Sheraton Sofia Hotel Balkan, 1 St. Nedelya Sq., tel. 2/87–
65–41).

Discos   There is a disco, nightclub, and bowling alley at the **National
Palace of Culture** (1 Bulgaria Sq.). Other choices are **Orbylux,**
known as the classiest disco in town (76 James Boucher Blvd.,
tel. 2/66–89–97); **Angel** (centrally located at Narodno Sobranie
Sq.); and **Sky Club,** a big, two-tier disco (63 Hristo Botev Blvd.,
tel. 2/54–81–40).

Casino   Gamblers can try their luck at the casino in the **Vitosha Hotel,**
(100 James Boucher Blvd., tel. 2/62–41–51), or at the **Sheraton
Sofia Hotel** (1 St. Nedelya Sq., tel. 2/82–65–43).

The Black Sea
Golden Coast

Bulgaria's most popular resort area attracts visitors from all
over Europe. Its sunny, sandy beaches are backed by the easternmost slopes of the Balkan range and by the Strandja Mountains. Although the tourist centers tend to be huge state-built
complexes with a somewhat lean feel, they have modern amenities. Sunny Beach, the largest of the resorts, with more than

The Black Sea Golden Coast

Durankulak

Dobrich · Balčik · Shabla

Novi Pazar · Albena · Kavarna

Vetrino · Zlatni Pjasâci (Golden Sands)

Goljama · Sveti Konstantin

Varna

A2

Staro Orjahovo

Kamčija · Bjala

Kamčija · Obzor

Orizare · **Black Sea**

Ajtos · Slânčev Brjag (Sunny Beach)

Nesebâr

Pomorie

Burgas

Sredecka · Sozopol

Djuni

Primorsko

Mičurin

Ahtopol

TURKEY

0   40 miles
0   60 km

100 hotels, has plenty of children's amusements and play areas; baby-sitters are also available.

The historic port of Varna is a good center for exploration. It is a focal point of land and sea transportation and has museums, a variety of restaurants, and some nightlife. The fishing villages of Nesebâr and Sozopol are more attractive. Lodgings tend to be scarce in these villages, so private accommodations, arranged on the spot or by Balkantourist, are a good option. Whatever resort you choose, all offer facilities for water sports and some have instructors. Tennis and horseback riding are also available.

Getting Around

Buses make frequent runs up and down the coast and are inexpensive. Buy your ticket in advance from the kiosks near the bus stops. **Cars** and **bicycles** can be rented; bikes are particularly useful for getting around such sprawling resorts as Sunny Beach. A **hydrofoil** service links Varna, Nesebâr, Burgas, and Sozopol. A regular **boat** service travels the Varna–Sveti Konstantin (St. Konstantin)–Golden Sands–Albena–Balčik route.

Guided Tours

A wide range of excursions are arranged from all resorts. There are bus excursions to Sofia from Golden Sands, Sveti Konstantin, Albena, and Sunny Beach; a one-day bus and boat trip along the Danube from Golden Sands, Sveti Konstantin, and Albena; and a three-day bus tour of Bulgaria, including the Valley of Roses, departing from Golden Sands, Sveti Konstantin, and Albena. All tours are run by Balkantourist (*see* Tourist Information, *below*, or check with your hotel information desk).

Tourist Information

There is a Balkantourist office in most towns and resorts.

Albena (tel. 057/21–52 or 057/23–12).
Burgas (1 Gani-Ganev St., tel. 056/4–29–32).
Nesebâr (18 Yana Luskova St., tel. 055/41–38–17).
Sunny Beach (tel. 055/41–23–46 or 0554/23–12 or 23–15).
Sveti Konstantin and Golden Sands (tel. 052/6–56–27).
Varna (main office, 3 Moussala St., tel. 052/22–55–24; private accommodations office, 3 Kniaz Boris I Blvd.).

Exploring the Black Sea Golden Coast

Varna   **Varna,** Bulgaria's third-largest city, is easily reached by rail (about 7½ hours by express) or road from Sofia. If you plan to drive, allow time to see the Stone Forest (Pobiti Kammani) just off the Sofia–Varna road between Devnya and Varna. The unexpected groups of monumental sandstone tree trunks are thought to have been formed when the area was the bed of the Lutsian Sea. There is plenty to see in the port city of Varna. The ancient city, named Odessos by the Greeks, became a major Roman trading center and is now an important shipbuilding and industrial city. The main sights can be linked by a planned walk.

Begin with the **Museum of History and Art,** one of the great—if lesser known—museums of Europe. The splendid collection includes the world's oldest gold treasures from the Varna necropolis of the 4th millennium BC, as well as Thracian, Greek, and Roman treasures and richly painted icons. *41 Osmi Primorski Polk Blvd., tel. 52/23–70–57. Open Tues.–Sun. 10–5.*

Near the northeastern end of Osmi Primorski Polk Boulevard are numerous shops and cafés; the western end leads to Mitropolit Simeon Square and the monumental **cathedral** (1880–86), whose lavish murals are worth a look. Running north from the cathedral is Vladislav Varnenchik Street, with shops, movie theaters, and eateries. Opposite the cathedral, in the City Gardens, is the **Old Clock Tower,** built in 1880 by the Varna Guild Association. On the south side of the City Gardens, on Nezavisimost Square, stands the magnificent Baroque **Stoyan Bucharov National Theater.**

Leave the square to the east and walk past the Moussala Hotel. The **tourist information office** is at 3 Moussala Street (tel. 52/22–55–24). Nearby, on the corner of Kniaz Boris I Boulevard and Shipka Street, are the remains of the **Roman fortress wall** of Odessos. Kniaz Boris I Boulevard is another of Varna's shopping streets. At No. 44 you can buy handcrafted souvenirs from one of the outlets of the Union of Bulgarian Artists.

Walk south along Odessos Street to Han Krum Street. Here you'll find the Holy Virgin Church of 1602 and the substantial remains of the **Roman Thermae**—the public baths, dating from the 2nd to the 3rd century AD. Buy the excellent English guide-book here to get the most out of your visit.

Not far from the baths, moving west, is old Drăzki Street, recently restored and comfortingly lined with restaurants, taverns, and coffeehouses.

Head toward the sea and November 8 Street. The old prison building at No. 5 houses the **Archaeological Museum** (open Tues.–Sun. 10–5). Continue to Primorski Boulevard and follow it, with the sea on your right, to No. 2 for the **Naval Museum** (tel. 52/24–06; open daily 8–6:30), with its displays of the early days of navigation on the Black Sea and the Danube. The museum is at the edge of the extensive and luxuriant **Marine Gardens,** which command a wide view over the bay. In the gardens there are restaurants, an open-air theater, and the fascinating **Copernicus Astronomy Complex** (tel. 2/82–94; open weekdays 8–noon and 2–5) near the main entrance.

Sveti Konstantin Eight kilometers (5 miles) north along the coast from Varna is **Sveti Konstantin,** Bulgaria's oldest Black Sea resort. Small and intimate, it spreads through a wooded park near a series of sandy coves. Warm mineral springs were discovered here in 1947, and the five-star **Grand Hotel Varna,** the most luxurious on the coast, offers all kinds of hydrotherapy under medical supervision (*see* Lodging, *below*).

In contrast to the sedate atmosphere of Sveti Konstantin is lively **Zlatni Pjasâci** (Golden Sands), a mere 8 kilometers (5 miles) to the north, with its extensive leisure amenities, mineral-spring medical centers, and sports and entertainment facilities. Just over 4 kilometers (2 miles) inland from Golden Sands is **Aladja Rock Monastery,** one of Bulgaria's oldest, cut out of the cliff face and made accessible to visitors by sturdy iron stairways.

From Sveti Konstantin, if time permits, take a trip 16 kilometers (10 miles) north to **Balčik.** Part of Romania until just before World War II, it is now a relaxed haven for Bulgaria's writers, artists, and scientists. On its white cliffs are crescent-shaped tiers populated with houses, and by the Balčik Palace, the beautiful **Botanical Gardens** are dotted with curious buildings, including a small Byzantine-style church.

Albena, the newest Black Sea resort, is located between Balčik and Golden Sands. It is well known for its long, wide beach and clean sea. The most luxurious among its 35 hotels is the **Dobrudja,** with extensive hydrotherapy facilities.

Slânčev Brjag Another popular resort, this time 36 kilometers (22.5 miles) south of Varna, is **Slânčev Brjag** (Sunny Beach). It is enormous and especially suited to families because of its safe beaches, gentle tides, and facilities for children. During the summer there are kindergartens for young vacationers, children's concerts, and even a children's discotheque. Sunny Beach has a variety of beachside restaurants, kiosks, and playgrounds.

Nesebâr is 5 kilometers (3 miles) south of Sunny Beach and accessible by regular excursion buses. It would be hard to find a town that exudes a greater sense of age than this ancient settlement, founded by the Greeks 25 centuries ago on a rocky peninsula reached by a narrow causeway. Among its vine-covered houses are richly decorated medieval churches. Don't miss the frescoes and the dozens of small, private, cozy pubs all over Nesebâr.

Continue traveling south along the coast. The next place of any size is **Burgas,** Bulgaria's second main port on the Black Sea. Burgas is rather industrial, with several oil refineries, though it does have a pleasant **Maritime Park** with an extensive beach below.

For a more appealing stopover, continue for another 32 kilometers (20 miles) south to **Sozopol,** a fishing port with narrow cobbled streets leading down to the harbor. This was Apollonia, the oldest of the Greek colonies in Bulgaria. It is now a popular haunt for Bulgarian and, increasingly, foreign writers and artists who find private accommodations in the rustic Black Sea–style houses, so picturesque with their rough stone foundations and unpainted wood slats on the upper stories. It is also famous for the Apollonia Arts Festival, held each September.

Ten kilometers (6 miles) farther south is the vast, modern resort village of **Djuni,** where visitors can stay in up-to-date cottages, in the modern Monastery Compound, or in the Seaside Settlement. The wide range of amenities—cafés, folk restaurants, a sports center, shopping center, yacht club, and marina—make it another attractive vacation spot for families.

Dining and Lodging

For details and price-category definitions, *see* Dining and Lodging in Staying in Bulgaria. Gradually, even restaurants in the moderate category are beginning to accept credit cards. Check with a restaurant before ordering.

Albena
Dining

Bambuka (Bamboo Tree). This open-air restaurant serves international and Bulgarian cuisine and seafood. *Albena Resort, tel. 5772/24–04. Moderate. No credit cards.*

Lodging

Dobrudja Hotel. This is a big, comfortable hotel with a mineral-water health spa. *Albena Resort, tel. 5722/20–20. 272 rooms with bath. Facilities: restaurants, nightclub, coffee shops, cocktail bars, shops, indoor and outdoor swimming pools, fitness center, hydrotherapy. AE, DC, MC, V. Moderate.*

Burgas
Dining

Starata Gemia. The name of this restaurant translates as "old boat," appropriate for a beachfront restaurant featuring fish specialties. *39 Pârvi Maj St., tel. 56/45708. Moderate. No credit cards.*

Lodging

Bulgaria. The Bulgaria is a high-rise Interhotel in the center of town. It features its own nightclub with floor show and a restaurant set in a winter garden. *21 Pârvi Maj St., tel. 56/4–28–20. 200 rooms, most with bath or shower. AE, DC, MC, V. Moderate.*

Slânčev Brjag
Dining

Hanska Šatra. Situated in the coastal hills behind the sea, this combination restaurant and nightclub has been built to resemble the tents of the Bulgarian khans of old. It has entertainment well into the night. *4.8 km (3 mi) west of Slânčev Brjag, tel. 0554/2811. No credit cards. Moderate.*
Ribarska Hiza. This lively beachside restaurant specializes in fish and has music until 1 AM. *Northern end of Slânčev Brjag Resort, tel. 0554/2437. No credit cards. Inexpensive.*

Lodging **Burgas.** Large and comfortable, this hotel lies at the southern end of the resort. *Slânčev Brjag Resort, tel. 0554/23–58. 250 rooms with bath or shower. Facilities: restaurant, 2 pools, sports hall, coffee shop, cocktail bar. AE, DC, MC, V. Moderate.*

★ **Globus.** Considered by many to be the best in the resort, this hotel combines a central location with modern facilities. *Slânčev Brjag Resort, tel. 0554/22–45. 100 rooms with bath or shower. Facilities: indoor pool, restaurant, sports hall, coffee shop, cocktail bar. AE, DC, MC, V. Moderate.*

Kuban. Near the center of the resort, this large establishment is just a short stroll from the beach. *Slânčev Brjag Resort, tel. 0554/23–09. 216 rooms, most with bath or shower. Facilities: restaurants, coffee shops. AE, DC, MC, V. Moderate.*

Čajka. This hotel offers the best location at a low cost. *Slânčev Brjag Resort, tel. 0554/23–08. 36 rooms, some with bath or shower. No credit cards. Inexpensive.*

Sveti Konstantin **Bulgarska Svatba.** This folk-style restaurant with dancing is on
Dining the outskirts of the resort; charcoal-grilled meats are especially recommended. *Sveti Konstantin Resort, tel. 052/861283. No credit cards. Moderate.*

Manastirska Izba. Centrally located, this eatery is a modest but pleasant restaurant with a sunny terrace. *Sveti Konstantin Resort, tel. 056/6–11–77. No credit cards. Moderate.*

Lodging **Grand Hotel Varna.** This Swedish-built hotel has a reputation
★ for being the best hotel on the coast. It is set just 139 meters (150 yards) from the beach and offers a wide range of hydrotherapeutic treatments featuring the natural warm mineral springs. *Sveti Konstantin Resort, tel. 052/6–14–91. 325 rooms with bath or shower. Facilities: 3 restaurants, nightclub, 2 swimming pools, sports hall, tennis courts, bowling alley, coffee shops, cocktail bars, shops. AE, DC, MC, V. Expensive.*

Čajka. Čajka means "sea gull" in Bulgarian, and this hotel has a bird's-eye view of the entire resort from its perch above the northern end of the beach. *Sveti Konstantin Resort, tel. 052/861332. 130 rooms, most with bath or shower. No restaurant. No credit cards. Moderate.*

Varna **Starata Kušta.** This restaurant's name means "the old house."
Dining Part of a catering complex, along with several bars and restaurants, it provides national specialties in a pseudo old-time atmosphere. *14 Drăzki St., tel. 052/23–90–65. No credit cards. Moderate.*

Lodging **Černo More.** One of the best things about this modern Inter-
★ hotel is the panoramic view from the 22nd floor; another is the modern facilities. *33 Slivnitza Blvd., tel. 052/33–91 or 3–50–66. 230 rooms with bath or shower. Facilities: 3 restaurants, ground-floor café with terraces, nightclub, cocktail bar. AE, DC, MC, V. Expensive.*

Inland Bulgaria

Inland Bulgaria is not as well known to tourists as the capital and the coast, but an adventurous traveler, willing to put up with limited hotel facilities and unreliable transportation, will find plenty to photograph, paint, or simply savor. Wooded and mountainous, the interior is dotted with attractive "museum" villages (entire settlements listed for preservation because of

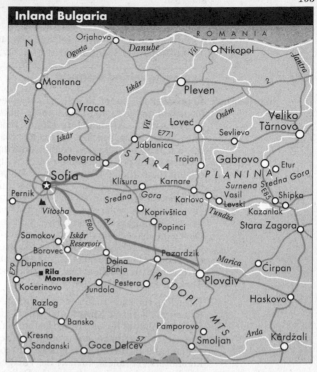

Inland Bulgaria

their historic cultural value) and ancient towns; the folk culture is a strong survivor from the past, not a tourist-inspired re-creation of it. The foothills of the Balkan Range, marked Stara Planina ("old mountains") on most maps, lie parallel with the lower Sredna Gora Mountains, with the verdant Valley of Roses between them. In the Balkan range is the ancient capital of Veliko Târnovo; south of the Sredna Gora stretches the fertile Thracian plain and Bulgaria's second-largest city, Plovdiv. Between Sofia and Plovdiv is the enchanting old town of Koprivshtitsa. To the south, in the Rila Mountains, is Borovec, first of the mountain resorts. A round-trip covering all these towns, with a side excursion to Rila Monastery, could be made in four or five days, although more time is recommended.

Getting Around

Rail and bus services cover all parts of inland Bulgaria, but the timetables are not easy to follow and there are frequent delays. The best bet is to rent a car. You may also prefer to hire a driver; Balkantourist can arrange this.

Guided Tours

Organized tours set out from Sofia, each covering different points of interest. Check with your Sofia hotel information desk or with Balkantourist for specific information.

Tourist Information

Plovdiv (34 Bulgaria Blvd., tel. 32/5–38–48).
Veliko Târnovo (1 Vasil Levski St., tel. 62/2–02–36).

Exploring Inland Bulgaria

Koprivshtitsa **Koprivshtitsa,** one of Bulgaria's showpiece villages, is set in mountain pastures and pine forests, about 930 meters (3,000 feet) up in the Sredna Gora range. It is 105 kilometers (65 miles) from Sofia, reached by a minor road south from the Sofia–Kazanlak expressway. Founded during the 14th century, it became a prosperous trading center with close ties to Venice during the National Revival period 400 years later. The architecture of this period, also called the Bulgarian Renaissance, features carved woodwork on broad verandas and overhanging eaves, brilliant colors, and courtyards with studded wooden gates. Throughout the centuries, artists, poets, and wealthy merchants have made their homes here, and many of the historic houses can be visited. The town has been well preserved and revered by the Bulgarians as a symbol of freedom since April 1876, when the rebellion that led, two years later, to the end of Turkish occupation ignited.

Return to the main road and turn right. After 15 kilometers (9 miles) you'll reach **Klisura** and the beginning of the **Rozova Dolina** (Valley of Roses). Here the famous Bulgarian rose water and attar, or essence, are produced. Each May and June, the whole valley is awash in fragrance and color. After another 17 kilometers (11 miles), turn at the village of Karnare; take the winding scenic road north over the Balkan range to the town of Trojan; and, a few miles away, you'll see the **Trojan Monastery,** built during the 1600s in the heart of the mountains. Trojan Monastery Church was painstakingly remodeled during the 19th century, and its icons, wood carvings, and frescoes are classic examples of National Revival art. Back at Trojan, continue north on the mountain road until it meets highway E771, where you turn right for Veliko Târnovo, 82 kilometers (50 miles) away.

Veliko Târnovo **Veliko Târnovo,** a town of panoramic vistas, rises up against steep mountain slopes through which the river Jantra runs its jagged course. During the 13th and 14th centuries, this was the capital of the Second Bulgarian Kingdom. Damaged by repeated Ottoman attack, and again by an earthquake in 1913, it has been reconstructed and is now a museum city of marvelous relics. The town warrants two or three days of exploration, but even in a short visit some sights should not be missed. Ideally, you should begin at a vantage point above the town in order to get an overview of its design and character. Next, seek out **Tszarevec** to the west (Carevec on some maps), protected by a river loop. This is where medieval czars and patriarchs had their palaces. The area is under restoration, and steep paths and stairways now provide opportunities to view the extensive ruins of the Patriarchite and the royal palace. In summer, there is a spectacular sound-and-light show, presented at night, which can be seen from the surrounding pubs.

The prominent feature to the south is **Baldwin's Tower,** the 13th-century prison of Baldwin of Flanders, onetime Latin emperor of Constantinople. Nearby are three important churches: the 13th-century **church of the Forty Martyrs,** with its Târnovo school frescoes and two inscribed columns, one dating to the 9th century; the **church of Saints Peter and Paul,** with vigorous murals both inside and out; and, across the river, reached by a bridge near the Forty Martyrs, the restored **church of Saint Dimitrius,** built on the spot where the Second Bulgarian Kingdom was launched in 1185.

Back toward the center of town, near the Yantra Hotel, is Samovodene Street, lined with restored crafts workshops—a fascinating place to linger in and a good place to find souvenirs, Turkish candy, or a charming café. On nearby Rakovski Street are a group of buildings of the National Revival period. One of the finest is **Hadji Nikoli,** a museum that was once an inn. *17 Georgi Sava Rakovski, tel. 62/2–17–10 for opening times.*

Moving east from Veliko Târnovo toward Varna on E771, you can go back farther in time by visiting the ruins of the two capitals of the First Bulgarian Kingdom in the vicinity of **Šumen** (spelled Shoumen in some English translations). The first ruins are the fortifications at **Pliska,** 23 kilometers (14 miles) southeast of Šumen, and date from 681. At **Veliki Preslav,** 21 kilometers (13 miles) southwest of Šumen, there are ruins from the second capital that date from 893 to 927. The 8th- to 9th-century **Madara Horseman,** a bas-relief of a rider slaying a lion, appears 18 kilometers (11 miles) east of town on a sheer cliff face.

If you leave Veliko Târnovo by E85 and head south toward **Plovdiv,** you can make three interesting stops en route. The first, near the industrial center of Gabrovo—interesting in itself for its House of Humor Museum—is the museum village of **Etur,** 8 kilometers (5 miles) to the southeast. Its mill is still powered by a stream, and local craftsmen continue to be trained in traditional skills. The second is the **Shipka Pass,** with its mighty monument on the peak to the 200,000 Russian soldiers and Bulgarian volunteers who died here in 1877, during the Russian-Turkish Wars. The third is **Kazanlak,** at the eastern end of the Valley of Roses, where you can trace the history of rose production, Bulgaria's oldest industry. Here, in early June, young rose pickers dress in traditional costumes for rose parades and other carnival processions. There is also a highly decorated replica of a Thracian tomb of the 3rd or 4th century BC, set near the original, which remains closed for its preservation.

Plovdiv From Kazanlak, take the road west through the **Valley of Roses** to either Vasil Levski or Karlovo, another Rose Festival town. Then turn south for **Plovdiv,** Bulgaria's second-largest city, one of the oldest cities in Europe and a major industrial center. The old town, on the hillier southern side of the Marica River, is worth a visit.

Begin at the **National Ethnographical Museum** in the House of Arghir Koyumdjioglu, an elegant example of National Revival style that made its first impact in Plovdiv. The museum is filled with artifacts from that important period. *2 Čomakov St. Open Tues.–Sun. 9–noon and 1:30–5.*

Below the medieval gateway of Hissar Kapiya are the attractive **Georgiadi House,** on Starina Street, and the steep, narrow **Strumna Street,** lined with workshops and boutiques, some reached through little courtyards. Follow Saborna Street westward to its junction with the pedestrians-only Kniaz Alexander I Street; here you'll find the remains of a **Roman stadium.** Nearby, the **Kapana District** has many restored and traditional shops and restaurants. Turn east off Kniaz Alexander I Street and walk to the fine hilltop **Roman Amphitheater,** sensitively renovated and frequently used for dramatic and musical performances. On the other side of the old town, toward the river, is the **National Archaeological Museum,** which holds a replica of the 4th-century BC Panagjuriste Gold Treasure, the original of which is in Sofia. *1 Suedinie Sq., Open Tues.–Sun. 9–12:30 and 2–5:30.*

Travel west along the E80 Sofia Road. At Dolna Banja, turn off to **Borovec,** about 1,333 meters (4,300 feet) up the northern slopes of the Rila Mountains. This is an excellent walking center and winter sports resort, well equipped with hotels, folk taverns, and ski schools. The winding mountain road leads back to Sofia, 70 kilometers (44 miles) from here, past Lake Iskar, the largest in the country.

On the way back to Sofia, you should consider a visit to the **Rila Monastery,** founded by Ivan of Rila during the 10th century. Cut across to E79, travel south to Kočerinovo, and then turn east to follow the steep forested valley past the village of Rila. The monastery has suffered so frequently from fire that most of it is now a grand National Revival reconstruction, although a rugged 14th-century tower has survived. The atmosphere in this mountain retreat, populated by many storks, is still heavy with a sense of the past—although part of the complex has been turned into a museum and some of the monks' cells are now guest rooms. The visitor can see 14 small chapels with frescoes from the 15th and 17th centuries, a lavishly carved altarpiece in the new Assumption church, the sarcophagus of Ivan of Rila, icons, and ancient manuscripts—a reminder that this was a stronghold of art and learning during the centuries of Ottoman rule. It is well worth the detour of 120 kilometers (75 miles)—or a special trip from Sofia.

Dining and Lodging

For details and price-category definitions, *see* Dining and Lodging in Staying in Bulgaria. In the moderate hotels and restaurants, check to see whether your credit card will be accepted.

Koprivshtitsa
Dining

Djedo Liben Inn. This attractive folk restaurant with cocktail bar and nightclub is built in the traditional style of the area—with half-timbered, high stone walls. The menu reflects similar attention to traditional detail. *Tel. 997184/21–09. Moderate. No credit cards.*
Barikadite. This small hotel is located on a hill 15 kilometers (9 miles) from Koprivshtitsa. *Tel. 997184/20–91. 20 rooms with shower. Facilities: restaurant, nightclub, cocktail bar. No credit cards. Inexpensive.*

Lodging

Koprivshtitsa. This good-value hotel is popular with Bulgarians themselves and is just over the river from the center of town. *Tel. 32/21–18. 30 rooms. No credit cards. Inexpensive.*

Plovdiv
Dining

Pldin. This is an attractive folk restaurant in the center of town. A video presentation in the lobby highlights the city's past. *3 Knyaz Tseretenov St., tel. 32/23–17–20. AE, DC, MC, V. Expensive.*
Alafrangite. This charming folk-style restaurant is located in a

restored 19th-century house with wood-carved ceilings and a vine-covered courtyard. *15 Nektariev St., tel. 32/22–98–09. No credit cards. Moderate.*

Filipopoli. This is an elegant folk-style restaurant with a menu combining traditional Bulgarian, Greek, and international cuisine (including seafood), served by candlelight with the accompaniment of a jazz piano. Try the rich salads and *chushka byurek. 56 Stamat Matanov St., tel. 32/22–52–96. Reservations accepted. No credit cards. Moderate.*

Rhetora. This coffee bar is in a beautifully restored old house near the Roman amphitheater in the old part of the city. *8A G. Samodoumov St., tel. 32/22–20–93. No credit cards. Moderate.*

Lodging   **Novotel Plovdiv.** The large, modern, and well-equipped Novotel is across the river from the main town, near the fairgrounds. *2 Zlatju Boyadjiev St., tel. 32/5–51–71. 322 rooms with bath. Facilities: restaurant, folk tavern, nightclub, cocktail bar, sports hall, swimming pools, shop. AE, DC, MC, V. Expensive.*

Trimontium. This centrally located Interhotel built in the 1950s is comfortable and ideal for exploring the old town. *2 Kapitan Raico St., tel. 32/2–55–61. 163 rooms with bath or shower. Facilities: restaurant, cocktail bar, folk tavern, shop. AE, DC, MC, V. Expensive.*

Marica. This is a large, modern hotel that offers a less expensive alternative to its neighbor, the Novotel. *5 Vazrazhdane St., tel. 32/55–27–35. 171 rooms with bath or shower. Facilities: restaurant, bar. No credit cards. Inexpensive.*

Veliko Târnovo
Dining

Boljarska Izba. In the center of the busy district just north of the river, this place is a folk tavern. *Dimiter Blagoev St., no telephone. No credit cards. Moderate.*

Lodging   **Veliko Târnovo.** Located right in the middle of the most historic part of the town, this modern Interhotel boasts some of the best facilities for this class of hotel. *2 Emile Popov St., tel. 62/3–05–71. 195 rooms with bath or shower. Facilities: 2 restaurants, cocktail bar, coffee shop, disco, sports hall, indoor pool, shops. AE, DC, MC, V. Expensive.*

Yantra. The Yantra has some of the best views in town, looking across the river to Tsaravec. *1 Velchova Zavera Sq., tel. 62/2–03–91. 60 rooms, most with shower. Facilities: restaurant, coffee shop, bar. No credit cards. Moderate.*

Etur. This moderate-size hotel, with an address near the more expensive Veliko Târnovo, makes it a good base for sightseeing within town. *I. Ivailo St., tel. 62/2–68–51. 80 rooms, most with shower. Facilities: restaurant, coffee shop, bar. No credit cards. Inexpensive.*

6 Cyprus

The Mediterranean island of Cyprus was at one time a center for the cult of Aphrodite, the Greek goddess who is said to have risen naked and perfect from the sea near what is now the beach resort of Paphos. Wooded and mountainous, with a 751-kilometer-long (466-mile-long) coastline, Cyprus lies just off the southern coast of Turkey. Oranges, olives, lemons, grapes, and cherries grow here, and fish are plentiful. The summers are hot and dry, the spring gentle. Snow covers the Troodos Mountains in winter, making it possible to ski in the morning and sunbathe on a beach in the afternoon.

Cyprus's strategic position in the eastern Mediterranean has made it subject to regular invasions by powerful countries. Greeks, Phoenicians, Assyrians, Egyptians, Persians, Romans, and Byzantines—all have ruled here. In the Middle Ages, the English King Richard I took Cyprus from the Byzantine Empire by force and gave it to Guy of Lusignan. Guy's descendants ruled the island until the late 15th century, when it was annexed by the Venetians.

The influence of diverse cultures especially adds to the island's appeal to tourists. Many fortifications built by the Crusaders and the Venetians still stand. The tomb of the Prophet Muhammad's aunt (Tekke of Hala Sultan), located on the shores of the great salt lake near Larnaca, is one of Islam's most important shrines. A piece of the true cross is said to exist in the Monastery of Stavrouni, and Paphos has the remains of a pillar where St. Paul was allegedly tied and beaten for preaching Christianity.

The upheavals are not over. The northern third of Cyprus is occupied almost entirely by the Turkish, who invaded the region in 1974, expelling the indigenous Greek Cypriot population. The settlement is recognized as the Turkish Republic of North Cyprus by only Turkey. The two sections are divided by the UN Green Line, or "Attila-Line," which cuts right through the capital city of Nicosia.

Talks aimed at uniting the communities into one bizonal federal state have been going on for years, lately under the auspices of the United Nations secretary-general. It is possible to visit the Turkish-occupied north of the island from the south on a day trip through the checkpoint in Nicosia, but visitors are requested by the Cypriot Administration to return to the south by 5 PM. It is not possible to visit the south from the north.

Tourism is more thoroughly developed in the south than in the north. The south has better facilities and more nightlife. The noticeable military presence in the north prevents touring much of the region.

Essential Information

Before You Go

When to Go The tourist season runs throughout the year, though prices tend to be lower from November through March. Spring and fall are best, usually warm enough for swimming but not uncomfortably hot.

Climate The rainy season is in January and February, and it often snows in the highest parts of the Troodos Mountains from January

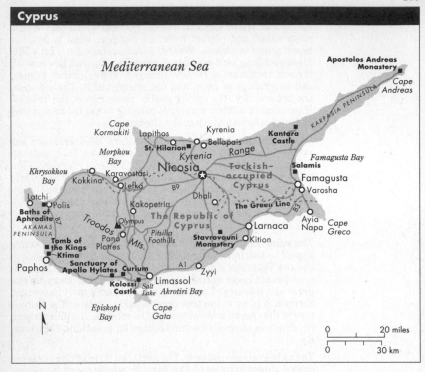

Mediterranean Sea

through March. January and February can be cold and wet; July and August are always very hot and dry.

The following are the average daily maximum and minimum temperatures for Nicosia.

Jan.	59F	15C	May	85F	29C	Sept.	92F	33C
	42	5		58	14		65	18
Feb.	61F	16C	June	92F	33C	Oct.	83F	28C
	42	5		65	18		58	14
Mar.	66F	19C	July	98F	37C	Nov.	72F	22C
	44	7		70	21		51	10
Apr.	75F	24C	Aug.	98F	37C	Dec.	63F	17C
	50	10		69	21		45	7

Visas   No visas are necessary for holders of valid passports from the United States, Canada, and the United Kingdom.

Customs on Arrival   Duty-free allowances are: 250 grams of tobacco, 1 liter of spirits, 750 ml of wine, 300 ml of perfume, and up to C£50 in other goods.

The export of antiques and historical artifacts, whether gathered on land or during undersea explorations, is strictly forbidden unless a license is obtained from the Ministry of Tourism in Nicosia.

Language   Greek is the main language, but English is widely spoken in hotels, *tavernas*, and other tourist haunts. Off the beaten track, sign language may have to do.

Credit Cards Major credit cards are widely accepted, especially in shops and hotels. Banks usually allow you to draw cash upon your credit card account, so payment is rarely a problem.

The Republic of Cyprus

Currency

The monetary unit in the Republic of Cyprus is the Cyprus pound (C£), which is divided into 100 cents. There are notes of C£20, C£10, C£5, C£1, and 50 Cyprus cents and coins of 50, 20, 10, 5, 2, and 1 Cyprus cents. At press time (spring 1993) there were C£0.47 to the U.S. dollar and C£0.72 to the pound sterling.

What It Will Cost

A cup of coffee or tea costs Cyprus 50¢–80¢; a glass of beer 75¢–C£1; a kebab around C£1–C£1.50; a bottle of local wine 60¢–C£2. Admission to museums and galleries costs 50¢–C£1.

Arriving and Departing

By Plane There are no direct flights from the United States. **Cyprus Airways** and **British Airways** fly direct from London, Birmingham, and Manchester to Larnaca and Paphos. **Cyprus Airways** also operates from Athens, Amsterdam, Brussels, Frankfurt, Munich, Paris, Vienna, and Zurich. **Alitalia** flies from Rome.

By Boat Passenger ships connect Cyprus with various Greek, Egyptian, Italian, and Middle Eastern ports.

Getting Around

By Car An international or national license is acceptable for driving in Cyprus. Drive on the left. Main roads between large towns are good. Minor roads can be unsurfaced, narrow, and winding. Gas costs 30¢–32¢ per liter and is available around the clock in larger towns. Cars may be rented from C£18 per day.

By Bus This is the cheapest form of transportation in urban areas; the fare is 25¢–30¢. Buses operate every half-hour and cover an extensive network. In Nicosia, buses run until 7:30 PM (winter 6:30 PM). In tourist areas during the summer, services extend until midnight.

Intercity bus fares range between C£1 and C£3. For information on the Nicosia–Limassol–Paphos route, tel. 02/464636; or on the Limassol–Larnaca–Ayia Napa route, tel. 05/351031.

By Service Taxi Shared taxis accommodate four to seven passengers and are a cheap, fast, and comfortable way of traveling between towns. Taxis operate between the main towns—Nicosia, Limassol, Larnaca, and Paphos. Tarrifs are from C£1 to C£3.50. Seats must be booked by phone, and passengers may embark/debark anywhere within the town boundaries. The taxis run every half-hour (Mon.–Sat. 5:45 AM–6:30 PM). Sunday service is less frequent and rides must be booked one day ahead. Contact the **Kypros Taxi Office** (tel. 02/464811).

By Private Taxi Private taxis operate 24 hours throughout the island. They are generally very cheap within towns but far more expensive than service taxis between towns. Telephone from your hotel or hail one in the street. Urban taxis have an initial charge of 55¢ and charge 21¢ per mile in the daytime, more at night. Ask the driver what it will cost before you depart, and don't be afraid to barter. In-town journeys range from C£1 to about C£3.

Staying in the Republic of Cyprus

Telephones Pay phones take 2¢, 10¢, and 20¢ coins. Some newer pay phones also take 5¢ coins, and others take telecards of C£2, C£5, and C£10, which can be purchased at post offices, souvenir shops, and kiosks. Local, national, and international calls can be made from these phones; cheaper rates apply from 8 PM to 7 AM. Hotels will add a small service charge for placing a call for you. For telephone inquiries service, dial 192 in all towns.

Mail At press time (spring 1993). a 20-gram letter to the United States costs 36¢, a postcard, 26¢. To Europe, a 20-gram letter costs 31¢, and a postcard 21¢. Post offices are open Mon.–Fri. 7:30 AM–2:30 PM. Stamps are also sold at hotels, newsstands, and kiosks.

Opening and Closing Times **Banks** are open Monday–Friday 8:15AM–12:30 PM. Some have afternoon tourist services and will cash traveler's checks weekdays 3–6 in winter, 4–7 in summer, and Saturday 8:30–noon.

Museum hours vary greatly. It pays to check ahead. Generally, museums are closed for lunch and on Sunday. Most ancient monuments are open from dawn to dusk.

Shops are open Monday–Saturday 8–1 and 4–7 PM (summer); 2–5:30 PM (winter). Shops are closed Wednesday and Saturday afternoons and on Sundays. In tourist areas shops generally maintain longer hours.

National Holidays January 1; January 6 (Epiphany); April 29–May 2 (Greek Easter); May 1 (May Day); June 20 (Pentecost Monday); August 15 (Assumption); October 1 (Cyprus Independence Day); October 28 (Greek National Day); December 25, 26.

Tipping A service charge of 10%, a 3% charge by the Cyprus Tourist organization, and a 5% VAT are usually added to all bills. If service has been especially good, add 5%.

Important Addresses and Numbers The main **tourist information office** is in Nicosia (19 Limassol Ave., tel. 02/315715). This is the head office; for personal and telephone inquiries, call the other Nicosia office at Laiki Yitonia (tel. 02/444264). There are local offices at all major resorts.

Embassies or High Commissions **U.S. Embassy** (Metochiou Ploutarchou, Engomi, Nicosia, tel. 02/476100). **British High Commission** (Alexander Pallis St., Nicosia, tel. 02/473131–7).

Emergencies **Ambulance, Fire Brigade,** and **Police** (tel. 199). **Doctor: Nicosia General Hospital** (tel. 02/451111); **Limassol Hospital** (tel. 05/330333); **Paphos Hospital** (tel. 06/240111). **Pharmacies** (tel. 192 for information about opening times in English). A list with additional opening details appears in the English-language *Cyprus Mail* and *Cyprus Weekly*.

Guided Tours Guided tours are often the best way to see Cyprus and learn about its rich history. Try **National Sightseeing Tours** (c/o Louis

Tourist Agency, 54–58 Evagoras Ave., Nicosia, tel. 05/363161)
for half-day and full-day trips—expect to pay C£7–C£12.
Night tours are quite popular, and typically include dinner at a
local taverna, folk dancing, and bouzouki music. (tel. 05/
326108) arranges coastal cruises that usually include lunch on
board or at a seaside restaurant.

Exploring the Republic of Cyprus

Nicosia, the capital, is twice divided. The picturesque Old City
is contained within 16th-century Venetian fortifications that
separate it from the wide tree-lined streets, large hotels, and
high rises of the modern section. The second division is political
and more noticeable. The so-called Green Line (set up by the
United Nations) divides the island between the internationally
recognized Republic of Cyprus and the Turkish-occupied region. It is possible, at press time (spring 1993), to arrange a day
trip from the Greek to the Turkish-occupied sector through the
official checkpoint in Nicosia (Ledra Palace), though it is essential to return by 5 PM. Visits in the other direction are not permitted.

Although several ancient monuments lie in the northern, Turkish-
occupied sector, there is plenty to see in the Greek sector. A good
starting point is **Laiki Yitonia** at the southern edge of the Old
City, an area of winding alleys and traditional architecture.
Tavernas, cafés, and crafts workshops line the shaded, cobbled
streets. Here you will encounter everyday Cypriot life. Just to
the west lies Ledra Street, where modern shops alternate with
yet more crafts shops. Head north of the tourist information
center in Laiki Yitonia (tel. 02/444264) to visit the tiny **Tripiotis
Church.** This Greek Orthodox church, with its ornately carved
golden iconostasis and silver-covered icons, dates from 1690.

Within the walls to the east of the Old City is a cluster of museums. Housed in a wing of the Archbishopric, built in 1960 in
neobyzantine style, the new **Archbishop Makarios III Cultural
Foundation** consists of the **Byzantine Art Museum,** with fine
displays of icons spanning 1,000 years, and the **Greek War of Independence Gallery,** with a collection of maps, paintings, and
mementoes of 1821. *Tel. 02/456781. Admission: C£1.05. Open
weekdays 9–1 and 2–5 (winter 2–5:30), Sat. 9–1.*

Next door, the **Museum of the National Struggle** has dramatic
displays of the Cypriot campaigns against the British during
the preindependence years 1955–59; exhibits include letters,
newspapers, photos, and even torn uniforms, together with
other memorabilia. *Tel. 02/302465. Admission: 25¢. Open
weekdays 7:30–1:30 (winter 7:30–2) and 3–5, Sat. 7:30–1:30.*

Close by is the **Cyprus Folk Art Museum** (housed in the old part
of the Bishopric, dating from the 14th century), which offers
demonstrations of ancient weaving techniques and displays of
ceramics, olive and wine presses, and Cypriot costumes and
embroideries. *Tel. 02/463205. Admission: 50¢. Open weekdays
8:30–4, Sat. 8:30–1.*

Don't miss **St. John's Cathedral** (Ayios Ioannis), built in 1662
within the courtyard of the Archbishopric. Look for the 18th-
century wall paintings, which illustrate Cypriot moments of religious significance, including a depiction of the tomb of St.
Barnabas. **Famagusta Gate** is just a short walk to the east. It

was the strongest and most elaborate of three gateways into the old city. Now a cultural center, it houses exhibitions, a lecture hall, and a theater. *Tel. 02/430877. Open weekdays 10–1 and 4–7, Sat. 10–1.*

To the west of the city, stands the **Cyprus Museum.** Located outside the city walls near the Paphos Gate, it has extensive archaeological displays ranging from Neolithic to Roman times. Exhibits are well arranged and labeled in English. This stop is essential to understanding the island's ancient sites. *Museum St., tel. 02/302189. Admission: C£1. Open Mon.–Sat. 9–5, Sun. 10–1.*

Across the street from the museum lies the neoclassical style **Municipal Theatre** (1960) and the lush **Municipal Gardens.**

Many visitors choose to stay in the seaside resorts. Both Larnaca and Paphos, each of which has its own airport, make excellent centers. **Larnaca,** 51 kilometers (32 miles) southeast of Nicosia, is famous as the burial place of Lazarus and for its flamboyant Whitsuntide celebration, *Cataklysmos.* It has fine beaches, palm trees, and a modern harbor and marina, the starting point for boat trips. The tourist office at Democratias Square (tel. 04/654322; open weekdays, hours vary), is right at the marina district, and just a short walk from **Larnaca Museum,** with its displays of treasures including outstanding sculptures and Bronze-Age seals from the island's archaeological sites. *Kimon and Kilkis Sts., tel. 046/630169. Admission: 50¢. Open weekdays 7:30–2:30, Thurs. 4–7 (winter 3–6).*

A short walk north from the museum, along Kyman Street, will bring you to the site of **Kition** (the old Larnaca of biblical times and one of the most important ancient city-kingdoms), where you can observe the excavations from specially constructed walkways. Architectural remains of ancient temples date to the 13th century BC. *Admission: 50¢. Open weekdays 7:30–2:30 and 3–5.*

Southward from the marina is the 17th-century **Turkish fort,** built in the 9th century by Emperor Leo VI, open the same hours as the museum. The fort contains finds from Hala Sultan Tekke and Kition. The view from the top is impressive. On the way to the ancient fort is the **Pierides Collection,** a private collection of over 3,000 pieces distinguished by amusing Bronze-Age terra-cotta figures and fine carvings from gravestones. *Paul Zenon Kitieus St. near Lord Byron St., tel. 04/622345. Admission: 50¢. Open Mon.–Sat. 9–1.*

Walk inland from the fort to the town center and to one of the island's more important churches, **Ayios Lazarus,** resplendent with icons. It has a fascinating crypt containing Lazarus's sarcophagus.

South of Larnaca on the airport road, is the 2½-square-mile **Salt Lake.** Water covers the lake in spring, but by July you can watch local villagers collecting its salt. In winter it's a refuge for migrating birds. On the lake's edge, a mosque stands in an oasis of palm trees guarding the **Hala Suktan Tekke**—burial place of the prophet Mohammed's aunt. This is Islam's third most important shrine.

Nearby, the **Panayia Angeloktistos Church,** in Kiti, is famous for its outstanding Byzantine wall mosaics, which date from the 6th and 7th centuries.

A decade ago, **Ayia Napa,** which is 30 kilometers (20 miles) from Larnaca, was a small coastal fishing village, anchored by a **16th-century monastery** and renowned for its white, sandy beaches and views of the brilliant sea. Today's emergence of tavernas, bars, restaurants, and fine hotels reflects the town's transformation into Cyprus's premier vacationland: Watersports fanatics and *bons vivants* now flock here from points north and west. The town maintains the flavor of its historic past, however, and from the monastery's 14th-century sycamore tree, you can still enjoy the panoramic view of the Mediterranean.

Paphos, 142 kilometers (89 miles) southwest of Nicosia, in the west of the island, combines superb sea-swimming with archaeological sites and a rich history. Paphos, the birthplace of Aphrodite—the Greek goddess of love and beauty—is a modern town center with numerous ancient sights, including a picturesque harbor, and a 13th-century fort. Begin at the tourist office on Gladstone Street (tel. 06/2322841; open weekdays, hours vary) in Upper Paphos.

The **Paphos District Museum** is famous for its pottery, jewelry, and statuettes from the Roman villas. *Grivas Dighenis Ave., Ktima, tel. 06/240215. Admission: 50¢. Open weekdays 7:30–2:30 and 4–6 (winter 7:30–2 and 3–5), weekends 10–1.*

Nearby are the charming **Ethnographical Museum** (1 Exo Vrysi, tel. 062/232010) and notable icons in the **Byzantine Museum** in the Archbishopric (062/232092).

Don't miss the elaborate mosaics in the **Roman Villa of Theseus,** in the **House of Dionysos**, and in the recently excavated **House of Aion,** all in New Paphos. The mosaics are considered by many to be among the finest in the Eastern Mediterranean and have been expertly preserved and restored. The town bus stops nearby. Also worth seeing are the **Tombs of the Kings,** an early necropolis dating from 300 BC. Natural caves have been extended and linked by passages, and though the coffin niches are empty, a powerful sense of mystery remains. *Admission: C£1 (mosaics) and 50¢ (Tombs of the Kings). Open daily 7:30–sunset (winter 7:30–5:30).*

Limassol, a commercial port and wine-making center on the south coast, 75 kilometers (47 miles) from Nicosia, is a bustling, cosmopolitan, coastal town popular with tourists. Luxury hotels, apartments, and guest houses stretch along 12 kilometers (7 miles) of sea-frontage. The nightlife is the liveliest on the island. In Central Limassol, the elegant modern shops of Makarios Avenue contrast with those of the old part of town, where you'll discover local handicrafts.

The tourist information office (Spyros Araouzos St., tel. 05/362756) is open Mon.–Sat., hours vary. A short walk takes you to **Limassol Fort,** near the old port. This 14th-century castle was built on the sight of an earlier Byzantine fortification. According to tradition, Richard the Lionhearted married his future queen of England here in 1191. The **Cyprus Medieval Museum** is housed here and displays a variety of medieval armor and relics. *Tel. 05/330132. Admission: 50¢. Open weekdays 7:30–5, Sat. 9:30–5, Sun. 10–1.*

For a glimpse of Cypriot folklore, visit the **Folk Art Museum** on St. Andrews Street. The collection includes national costumes and fine examples of the island's crafts and woven materials. *Tel. 05/362303. Admission: 30¢. Open Mon. and Wed.–Fri. 8:30–1:30 and 4–7 (winter 3–5:30); Tues. 8:30–1:30.*

For a nice side trip, try the **KEO Winery,** just west of the town, which welcomes visitors daily. *Tel. 05/362053. Admission free. Tours are given weekdays 10–6.*

The **Troodos Mountains,** north of Limassol, are popular in summer for the shade of their cedar and pine forests and the coolness of their lakes and mineral spas. Small, painted churches in the Troodos and **Pitsilia foothills** are rich examples of a rare indigenous art form. **Asinou Church** and **St. Nicholas of the Roof,** south of Kakopetria, are especially noteworthy. Nearby is the **Tall Trees Trout Farm,** a shady oasis serving delicious fresh fish meals. In winter, skiers take over. **Platres,** in the foothills of Mount Olympus, is the principal resort. Be sure to visit the **Kykko Monastery,** whose prized icon of the Virgin is reputed to have been painted by St. Luke. Though founded in the 12th century, the monastery buildings and lavish church were added in the 19th-century.

Off the Beaten Track

Stavrovouni Monastery stands on a mountain west of Larnaca. It was founded by St. Helena (mother of the Emperor Constantine) in AD 326, though the present buildings date from the 19th century. Ideally, it should be visited in a spirit of pilgrimage rather than sightseeing, out of respect for the monks, though the views of the island are splendid. Male visitors are allowed inside the monastery daily from sunrise to sunset, except between noon and 3 (noon and 1 in winter). The monks keep vows as strict as those of the Mount Athos monks in Greece and have decreed that female visitors will be admitted only on Sunday mornings.

Curium (Kourion), west of Limassol, has numerous Greek and Roman ruins. There is an **amphitheater,** where actors occasionally present classical and Shakespearean drama. Next to the theater is the **Villa of Eustolios,** a summer house that belonged to a wealthy Christian; its mosaic floors are still in good condition. A nearby **Roman stadium** has been partially rebuilt. Two miles farther along the main Paphos road is the **Sanctuary of Apollo Hylates** (of the woodlands), an impressive archaeological site. *Admission: C£1. Open daily 7:30–sunset (winter 7:30–5:30).*

Other places to visit include **Kolossi Castle,** a Crusader castle of the Knights of St. John, a 15-minute drive outside Limassol; and the fishing harbor of **Latchi** on the west coast, 32 kilometers (20 miles) north of Paphos. Nearby are the **Baths of Aphrodite,** where the goddess of love is said to have seduced swains. The wild and undeveloped Akamas Peninsula is being declared a national park and is perfect for a hike through fields of wildflowers or a swim off isolated beaches.

Dining

Most hotels have restaurants, but these tend to serve bland international-style food garnished with french fries. Visitors with a sense of adventure will want to dine in local restaurants or in one of the informal, family-run tavernas featuring live music. Meals start with a variety of *mezes* (snacks)—many with

Middle Eastern origin. Kebabs are popular, as are *dolmades*—stuffed grape leaves or cabbage leaves—stews, fresh fish, and various lamb dishes. End with fruit or honey pastries and Greek coffee. Moderate establishments display a menu; in inexpensive ones it is the custom to go into the kitchen and choose your meal. Food is cheap in Cyprus, and the quality is good.

Prices are for a three-course meal for one person, not including drinks or tip.

Category	All Areas
Expensive	C£8–C£12
Moderate	C£4–C£8
Inexpensive	under C£4

Larnaca **Miliges.** This sea-view restaurant is popular with tourists and locals. Near the old fort, Miliges has a village ambience. *Kleftico* (lamb and goat meat wrapped in bay leaves) cooked in traditional clay ovens and *Sheftalia* (minced-meat-and-herb rissole) are specialties. *42 Bia-Pasha, tel. 04/655867. No credit cards. Moderate.*

Monte Carlo. On the road to the airport, this spot has outdoor seating on a balcony extending over the sea. Service is efficient, and the dining area is clean. Particularly worthy Cypriot dishes are the meat meze and casseroles. *28 Piale Pashia, tel. 04/653815. AE, DC, MC, V. Moderate.*

Limassol **Ladas.** This pleasant seafood restaurant is in Old Harbor. All the fish here is fresh; try the tender and sweet fried calamari and grilled *soupies* (ink fish). *1 Sadi St., tel. 05/365760. Closed Sunday. AE, DC, MC, V. Moderate.*

Porta. This quaint restored warehouse is home to a varied menu of international and Cypriot dishes, such as *Foukoudha Barbecue* (grilled strips of steak) and trout baked in prawn and mushroom sauce. On many nights, you'll be entertained by folk dancers and guitarists. *17 Yenethliou Mitella, Old Castle, tel. 05/360339. MC, V. Moderate.*

Nicosia **Archondiko.** A lively meeting place for business or pleasure, tables are on the walking path of the restored Laiki Yitonia area, indoors in cooler weather. Cypriot cuisine includes savory *lountza* (smoked fillet of pork) and grilled *haloumi* (a salty local cheese). *27 Aristokyprou St., Laiki Yitonia, tel. 02/450080. AE, DC, MC, V. Moderate.*

Cellari. This romantic, candlelit inn is lent a festive touch by a pair of guitarists strumming mellow Greek and Cypriot favorites. The highlight of this traditional cuisine is *chiromeri* (smoked pork). *22 Korai St., tel. 02/448338. No credit cards. Moderate.*

Paphos **Panicos Corallo Restaurant.** Sheltered from the main road by grapevines, this traditional family-run restaurant is just outside Paphos on the northern coastal road toward Coral Bay. The veal is recommended, as is the swordfish, a house specialty. Meals are served with fresh vegetables, many of which are home-grown. *Peyia. Tel. 06/621052. No credit cards. Moderate.*

Naftikos Omilos (Nautical Club). This huge seaside eatery seats more than 180. Fresh fish and *kleftiko* (lamb baked in a clay pot) are your best bets. *St. Paul's Ave., Old Harbor, tel. 062/33745. DC, MC, V. Moderate.*

Lodging

All hotels listed below have private bath or shower, but check when making reservations. Most have at least partial air-conditioning. In resort areas, hotel/apartments are a convenient choice for groups or families—many have kitchens.

Prices are for two people sharing a double room and include breakfast.

Category	All Areas
Expensive	C£40–C£90
Moderate	C£30–C£40
Inexpensive	C£20–C£30

Ayia Napa **Nissi Beach.** This modern, fully air-conditioned, family-style hotel is set in magnificent gardens overlooking a sandy beach. Its rooms and bungalows were recently refurbished. *Box 10, Ayia Napa, tel. 03/721021, fax 03/721623. 270 rooms. AE, MC, DC, V. Facilities: pool, disco, restaurant. Expensive.*
Pernera Beach Sun Hotel. Those on a budget should enjoy this hotel with a view of the beach. All rooms are air-conditioned. *Pernera Beach, Box 38, tel. 03/831011, fax 03/831020. 92 rooms. AE, DC, MC, V. Moderate.*

Larnaca **Golden Bay.** Comfort is high on the list at this beach hotel to the east of the town center. All rooms have balconies and views of the sea. The extensive range of sports facilities makes it ideal for summer or winter vacations. *Larnaca-Dhekelia Rd., Box 741, tel. 046/23444, fax 046/23451. 194 rooms. AE, DC, MC, V. Facilities: 2 restaurants, pool, minigolf, tennis. Expensive.*
Pasithea. This apartment/hotel near Salt Lake is a short stroll from the sandy beach. The management is friendly, the apartments spacious. *4 Michael Angelou, Box 309, Larnaca, tel. 046/25740, fax 046/25848. AE, DC, MC, V. Moderate.*
Cactus Hotel. This recent addition to Larnaca's hotels is 20 minutes from the seafront, with all its tavernas. The hotel offers bed-and-breakfast only. *6–8 Shakespeare St., Box 188, tel. 046/27400, fax 046/26966. 56 rooms. AE, MC, V. Facilities: pool. Inexpensive.*

Limassol **Le Meridien.** This spacious, luxurious hotel is one of the newest on the seafront; it also has one of the most striking lobbies—pink marble and glass. You'll find all the amenities expected in a first-class hotel—health and beauty club, gym, steam baths—as well as the island's largest swimming pool. *Old Limassol/Nicosia Rd., Box 6560, tel. 05/327000, fax 05/329222. AE, DC, MC, V. 191 rooms and 57 villas. Facilities: 3 restaurants, pool, watersports. Expensive.*
Azur Beach. This fine apartment/hotel has two restaurants, a sandy beach, and helpful management. *Potamios Yermasoyias, Box 1318, tel. 05/322667, fax 05/321897. 24 apartments. DC, MC, V. Moderate.*
Continental. This family hotel is close to the castle and has a great sea view. *137 Spyros Araouzos Ave., Box 398, tel. 05/362530, fax 05/373030. 27 rooms. AE, DC, MC, V. Inexpensive.*

Nicosia **Cyprus Hilton.** This is among the island's best hotels, with standards you'd expect from a Hilton. It has its own pool, sports facilities, dancing, and more. *Archbishop Makarios Ave., Box 2023, tel. 02/377777, fax 02/377788. 230 rooms. AE, DC, MC, V. Facilities: pool, tennis, nightclub. Expensive.*

Averof. A family-style hotel in a quiet location. The Averof's comfortable rooms are a great value. *19 Averof St., Box 4225, tel. 02/463447, fax 02/463411. No credit cards. Moderate.*

Cleopatra Hotel. Visitors enjoy its convenient location, cordial service, and well-prepared food served at poolside. *8 Florina St., Box 1397, tel. 02/445254, fax 02/452618. 55 rooms. AE, DC, MC, V. Facilities: pool, restaurant. Moderate.*

Paphos **Paphos Beach.** There are many facilities at this recently renovated, hotel surrounded by attractive gardens. Accommodations are either in the main hotel or in spacious bungalows on the grounds. *Posidonos St., Box 136, tel. 06/233091, fax 06/242818. 190 rooms. AE, DC, MC, V. Facilities: pool, tennis. Expensive.*

Ficardos Hotel Apartments. Clean, spacious apartments are located in Lower Paphos, a five-minute walk from the old port. *Contact Iris Travel, 10 Gladstone Ave., Upper Paphos, tel. 062/237585, fax 062/233960. 8 apartments. DC, MC, V. Moderate.*

Turkish-occupied Cyprus

Currency

The monetary unit in Turkish-occupied Cyprus is the Turkish lira (TL). There are bills for 100,000, 50,000, 20,000, 10,000, 5,000, 1,000, 500, 100, 50, 20, and 10 TL, and coins for lesser sums. The Turkish lira is subject to considerable inflation, so most of the prices in this section are quoted in dollars.

What It Will Cost

Prices for food and accommodations tend to be lower than those in the Republic of Cyprus, but standards dip as well. Wine and spirits, on the other hand, are imported from Turkey, and drinks will be slightly more expensive.

Sample Prices A cup of coffee should cost less than a dollar, a glass of beer about $1.60. Wine is good and cheap at around $2.10 per bottle. Taxis are also a bargain—an 80-kilometer (50-mile) ride costs about $13. Admission to museums costs less than $1.

Arriving and Departing

Turkish Airlines, Cyprus Turkish Airlines, and **Noble Air** run all flights via mainland Turkey, usually with a change of plane at Istanbul. There are also direct flights from Izmir and Ankara to Ercan Airport near Nicosia. Ferries run from Mersin and Tasucu in Turkey to Famagusta and Kyrenia, respectively, but in both cases the journey is long and tiring. *It is not possible to enter Turkish-occupied Cyprus from the Republic except for a day trip from Nicosia.*

Getting Around

By Car   *See* Getting Around by Car in the Republic of Cyprus, *above.*

By Bus   Buses and the shared taxi *(dolmuş)* are the cheapest forms of transportation. Service is frequent on main routes.

Fares   A bus from Nicosia to Kyrenia costs about U.S. 40¢, and to Famagusta about 70¢. A seat in a dolmus for the same trips would cost about 90¢ and $1.70, respectively.

Exploring Turkish-occupied Cyprus

The main tourist information office is at Mehmet Akif Avenue, Nicosia (tel. 020/83051).

There are two important things to bear in mind in Turkish-occupied Cyprus. One is to obey the "no photographs" signs wherever they appear. The other is to note that Turkish names have now been given to all towns and villages. These new names appear on the signposts—not always with the Greek version alongside—so it helps to know that **Nicosia** is known as **Lefkoşa,** Kyrenia as **Girne,** and **Famagusta** as **Gazimagusa.** A useful map showing these and other Turkish names is available free from tourist offices.

The Turkish half of **Nicosia** is the capital of Turkish-occupied Cyprus. In addition to the Venetian walls already mentioned (*see* Exploring the Republic of Cyprus, *above*), it contains the **Selimiyre Mosque,** formerly the 13th-century Cathedral of St. Sophia and a fine example of Gothic architecture, to which a pair of minarets has now been added. Near the Girne Gate is the former **tekke** (sacred place) of the Mevlevi Dervishes, a Sufi order popularly known as Whirling Dervishes. The building now houses a museum of Turkish history and culture. *Open Mon.–Sat. 8–1, Sun. 10–1.*

A walk around the **Old City,** within the encircling walls, is rich with glimpses from the Byzantine, Lusignan, and Venetian past. There is a great deal of restoration and reconstruction work going on, especially in the parts of the city beyond the walls.

Of the coastal resorts, **Kyrenia,** with its yacht-filled harbor, is the most appealing. There are excellent beaches to the east and west of the town. **Kyrenia Castle,** overlooking the harbor, is Venetian, though on the site of a much older Byzantine defensive structure. It now houses the **Shipwreck Museum,** whose prize possession is the remains of a ship that sank around 300 BC. *Open Mon.–Sat. 8–1, Sun. 10–1.*

Famagusta, the chief port of Turkish-occupied Cyprus, has massive and well-preserved Venetian walls and the late 13th-century Gothic Cathedral of St. Nicholas, now **Lala Mustafa Pasha Mosque.** The **Old Town,** within the walls, is the most intriguing part to explore.

Off the Beaten Track

It is well worth making two short excursions from Kyrenia—to St. Hilarion and to Bellapais. The fantastic ruins of the **Castle of St. Hilarion** stand on a hilltop 11 kilometers (7 miles) to the southwest. It's a strenuous walk, so take a taxi; the views are breathtaking. The ruins of the former **Abbey of Bellapais,** built in the 12th century by the Lusignans, are just as impressive. They lie on a mountainside 6 kilometers (4 miles) to the northeast. The showpiece is the refectory, but there are also dormitories, storerooms, and a church with frescoes.

Salamis, north of Famagusta, is an ancient ruined city, perhaps the most dramatic archaeological site on the island. St. Barnabas and St. Paul arrived in Salamis and set up a church near here. The present ruins date largely from the 12th-century Lusignan rulers of Cyprus, who came from France and used this as their major port before Famagusta was developed by the mid–16th-century Turks. Salamis does contain relics of earlier civilizations, including Greek and Roman settlements. The city was frequently devastated by earthquakes, but the setting is beautiful, and some of the ruins are sufficiently overgrown to give the visitor a satisfying sense of discovery.

The Czech Republic

Just three years after the dramatic but peaceful revolution that overthrew a Communist regime that had been in power for 40 years, Czechoslovakia again made world headlines in 1993 when its two constituent republics, Czech and Slovak, officially parted ways to form independent countries.

To observers from abroad, the rush to split the republics following federal elections in 1992 came as something of a surprise. Formed from the ruins of the Austro-Hungarian empire at the end of World War I, *Czecho-Slovakia* had portrayed itself to the world as a modern-day success story: a union of two peoples that had managed to overcome divisive nationalism in the higher interest of stabilizing a potentially volatile region.

Popular perceptions were reinforced by a long list of achievements. During the difficult 1930s, the Czechoslovak republic was the model democracy in Central Europe. The 1968 Prague Spring, an intense period of cultural renewal when Communists spoke openly of creating a more humane socialism, was centered largely on Czech territory, but was led by a courageous Slovak, Alexander Dubček. In 1989 the Communists were brought down by students in both Prague and Bratislava who shared a similar faith in the power of democracy and freedom.

The forces of separation, however, proved in the end to be too powerful. For all its successes, Czechoslovakia was ultimately an artificial creation, masking important and longstanding cultural differences between two outwardly similar peoples. The Czech Republic, linking the old Austrian crown lands of Bohemia and Moravia, can look to a rich cultural history going back some 600–700 years when the Bohemian Kingdom was at the center of the Holy Roman Empire. Bohemia and Moravia played pivotal roles in the great religious and social conflicts of European history.

Slovakia, by contrast, languished for nearly a millennium as the agrarian half of the Hungarian empire. Although great strides were made in the years following World War II to bring Slovakia's schools and industries to the level of their cousins to the west, many Slovaks are still stung by the label of cultural inferiority. Given the state of the national ego, independence was probably inevitable.

Although officially separate as of January 1993, the two republics still present themselves to the visitor in many respects as one country. At press time, both countries had vowed to coordinate their monetary policies; visa and customs regulations remain identical, as well. Combining a visit to Prague with an excursion to Slovakia's breathtaking High Tatras is as easy at it ever was (*see* Chapter 25, Slovakia).

Most visitors to the Czech Republic head straight for the Gothic, Baroque, and Art Nouveau splendors of Prague. But don't pass up a chance to visit the famous spas of western Bohemia or the lovely towns and castles of southern Bohemia. The crumbling Renaissance river town of Český Krumlov stands out as a "must-see."

It should be noted that the country still bears the scars of 40 years of Communism, in the form of Kafkaesque bureaucracies and, outside Prague, dilapidation and pollution. Unlike much of the West, however, most cities have remained much as they

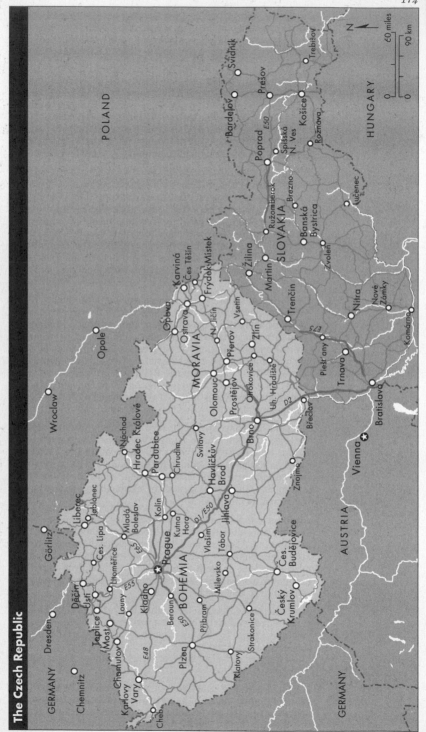

The Czech Republic

174

were, and streets are safe and have a refreshing lack of commercial hype. Tourist amenities certainly lack polish, and service can be frustratingly bad, but the beauty of the towns and the countryside and the rich heritage of art and architecture go a long way to compensate for these discomforts.

Essential Information

Before You Go

When to Go Organized sightseeing tours run from April or May through October. Some monuments, especially castles, either close entirely or open for shorter hours during the winter. Hotel rates drop during the off-season except during festivals. May, the month of fruit blossoms, is the time of the Prague Spring Music Festival. During the fall, when the forests are glorious, Brno, the cultural center of Moravia, hold its own music festival.

Climate The following are the average daily maximum and minimum temperatures for Prague.

Jan.	36F	2C	May	66F	19C	Sept.	68F	20C
	25	- 4		46	8		50	10
Feb.	37F	3C	June	72F	22C	Oct.	55F	13C
	27	- 3		52	11		41	5
Mar.	46F	8C	July	75F	24C	Nov.	46F	8C
	32	0		55	13		36	2
Apr.	58F	14C	Aug.	73F	23C	Dec.	37F	3C
	39	4		55	13		28	- 2

Currency The unit of currency in the Czech Republic is the crown, or koruna, written as Kč, and divided into 100 haléř. There are bills of 10, 20, 50, 100, 500, and 1,000 Kč and coins of 5, 10, 20, and 50 haléř and 1, 2, and 5 Kč. At press time (spring 1993), the koruna was trading at around 28.2 Kč to the dollar and 43.8 Kč to the pound.

Credit cards are widely accepted in establishments used by foreign tourists.

What It Will Cost Costs are highest in Prague and only slightly less in the Bohemian resorts and main spas, though even in these places you can now find very reasonable accommodations in private rooms. The least expensive area is southern Bohemia.

Sample Prices Cup of coffee, 10 Kč; beer (½ liter), 10½ Kč–15 Kč; Coca-Cola, 10 Kč–15 Kč; ham sandwich, 15 Kč; 1-mile taxi ride, 100 Kč.

Museums Admission to museums, galleries, and castles ranges from 5 Kč to 50 Kč.

Visas U.S. and British citizens do not need visas to enter the Czech Republic. Visa requirements have been temporarily reintroduced for Canadian citizens; check whether this is still the case with the consulate. Apply to the Consulate of the Czech Federal Republic, 50 Rideau Terrace, Ottawa, Ontario K1M 2A1, tel. 613/749–4442.

Customs Valuable items should be entered on your customs declaration.
On Arrival You can bring in 250 cigarettes (or their equivalent in tobacco), 2 liters of wine, 1 liter of spirits, ½ liter of eau de cologne, and gifts to the value of 1,000 Kč.

On Departure Crystal not purchased with hard currency may be subject to a tax of 100% of its retail price. To be on the safe side, hang on to all receipts. Only antiques bought at specially appointed shops may be exported.

Language English is spoken fairly widely among both the young and those associated with the tourist industry. You will come across English speakers elsewhere, though not frequently. German is widely understood throughout the country.

Getting Around

By Car Main roads are usually good, if sometimes narrow, and traffic is
Road Conditions light, especially away from main centers. An expressway links Prague, Brno, and Bratislava. Other highways are single-lane only.

Rules of the Road Drive on the right. Speed limits are 60 kph (37 mph) in built-up areas, 90 kph (55 mph) on open roads, and 110 kph (68 mph) on expressways. Seat belts are compulsory outside built-up areas; drinking and driving is strictly prohibited.

Parking Except for those belonging to hotel guests, all cars are banned in the center of Prague. In some areas of the capital you can pay to park for a limited period. If you're staying in a private room near Wenceslas Square, a good option is to look for a spot on one of the streets behind the National Museum, where parking is free and unlimited. Whenever you do, don't park in a no-parking area; your car is likely to be towed away. Elsewhere in the country there's little problem.

Gasoline At about $3 a gallon, gasoline is expensive. Service stations are usually located along main roads on the outskirts of towns and cities. Finding a station in Prague is notoriously difficult. Fill up on the freeway as you approach the city to avoid frustration. Lead-free gasoline, known as "Natural," is still only available at select stations, so tank up when you see it.

Breakdowns **Autotourist** (head office: Limuzská 12, Prague 10, tel. 02/ 773455) operates a patrol service on main highways. The emergency telephone number for motorists is 154; for ambulances, 155; for police (traffic accidents), 02/2366464.

By Train There is an extensive rail network throughout the country. As elsewhere in Eastern Europe, fares are relatively low and trains can be crowded. Also, you have to pay a supplement on all express trains. Most long-distance trains have dining cars; overnight trains between main centers have sleeping cars.

By Plane Remarkably good internal air service links Prague with eight other towns, including Brno, Bratislava, Poprad (for the High Tatras), Karlovy Vary, and Piešt'any. Prices are reasonable.

Make reservations at Čedok offices or directly at ČSA, Czecho-slovak Airlines (tel. 02/2146).

By Bus A wide-ranging bus network provides quicker service than trains at somewhat higher prices (though they are still very low by Western standards). Buses are always full, and, on long-distance routes especially, reservations are advisable.

Staying in the Czech Republic

Telephones
Local Calls
These cost 1 Kč from a pay phone. Lift the receiver, place the coin in the holder, dial, and insert the coin when your party picks up.

International Calls
You'll pay through the nose if you make calls from your hotel. There's automatic dialing to many countries, including North America and the United Kingdom. Special international pay booths in central Prague will take 5 Kč coins, but your best bet is to go to the main post office (Jindřišská 24, near Wenceslas Square). For international inquiries, dial 0132 for the United States, Canada, or the United Kingdom. ATT's USADirect number for the Czech Republic is 004200010.

Mail
Postal Rates
Airmail letters to the United States and Canada cost 11 Kč up to 10 grams, postcards 6 Kč. Airmail letters to the United Kingdom cost 8 Kč up to 20 grams, postcards 5 Kč.

Receiving Mail
Mail can be sent to Poste Restante at the main post office in Prague (Jindřišská 24, window 28) or to any other main post office. There's no charge. The American Express office on Wenceslas Square in Prague will hold letters addressed to cardholders or holders of American Express traveler's checks for up to one month free of charge.

Opening and Closing Times
Banks are open weekdays 8–3. **Museums** are usually open Tues.–Sun. 10–5. **Shops** are generally open weekdays 9–6 (9–8 on Thurs.); some close between noon and 2. Many are also open Sat. 9–noon (department stores, 9–4).

National Holidays
January 1; April 4 (Easter Monday); May 9 (Liberation Day); July 5; December 25, 26.

Dining
If you prepay your hotel through the **Czech Travel Bureau and Tourist Office (Čedok),** try to avoid being stuck with meal vouchers. With few Čedok-run hotels left, these are only a frustration. For meals not limited by vouchers, you can choose among restaurants, wine cellars *(vinárna),* the more down-to-earth beer taverns *(pivnice),* cafeterias, and a growing number of coffee shops and snack bars. Eating out is popular, and in summer you must reserve in advance. Most restaurants are remarkably reasonable, but privatization is beginning to push up prices in a few places.

Prague ham makes a favorite first course, as does soup, which is less expensive. The most typical main dish is roast pork (or duck or goose) with sauerkraut. Dumplings in various forms, generally with a rich gravy, accompany many dishes.

Mealtimes
Lunch is usually from 11:30 to 2 or 3; dinner from 6 to 9:30 or 10. Some places are open all day, and you might find it easier to find a table in off-hours.

Dress
A jacket and tie are recommended for Very Expensive and Expensive restaurants. Informal dress is appropriate elsewhere.

Ratings
Prices are reasonable by American standards, even in the more expensive restaurants. Czechs don't normally go in for three-course meals, and the following prices apply only if you're having a first course, main course, and dessert (excluding wine and tip). Best bets are indicated by a star ★.

Category	Other Areas	Prague
Very Expensive	over 400 Kč	over 800 Kč
Expensive	250 Kč–400 Kč	350 Kč–800 Kč
Moderate	100 Kč–250 Kč	200 Kč–350 Kč
Inexpensive	under 100 Kč	under 200 Kč

Lodging There's a choice of hotels, motels, private accommodations, and campsites. Many older properties are gradually being renovated, and the best have great character and style. There is still an acute shortage of hotel rooms during the peak season, so make reservations well in advance. Many private room agencies are now in operation, and as long as you arrive before 9 PM, you should be able to get a room. The standards of facilities and services hardly match those in the West, so don't be surprised by faulty plumbing or indifferent reception clerks.

Hotels These are officially graded with from one to five stars. Many hotels used by foreign visitors—Interhotels—belong to Čedok and are mainly in the three- to five-star categories. These will have all or some rooms with bath or shower. Čedok can also handle reservations for some non-Čedok hotels, such as those run by Balnea (the spa treatment organization); CKM (the Youth Travel Bureau); and municipal organizations, some of which are excellent.

Hotel bills can be paid in crowns, though some hotels still try to insist on hard currency.

Private Prague is full of travel agencies offering accommodation in pri-
Accommodations vate homes. These are invariably cheaper and often more comfortable than hotels, though you may have to sacrifice something in privacy. The best room-finding service is probably **AVE** in the main train station (open 7 AM–10:30 PM). Insist on a room in the center, however, or you may find yourself in a dreary, far-flung suburb. Another helpful agency is **Hello Ltd.** (Senovážné nám. 3, Prague 1, tel. 02/224283). Elsewhere, look for signs declaring "Room Free" or, more frequently, in German, "Zimmer Frei" or "Privatzimmer" along main roads. Čedok offices can also frequently help in locating private accommodation.

Camping Campsites are run by a number of organizations. A free map and list are available from Čedok.

Ratings Prices are for double rooms, generally not including breakfast. Prices at the lower end of the scale apply to low season. At certain periods, such as Easter or during festivals, there may be an increase of 15%–25%. Best bets are indicated by a star ★.

Category	Other Areas	Prague
Very Expensive	over $100	over $200
Expensive	$50–$100	$100–$200
Moderate	$15–$50	$50–$100
Inexpensive	under $15	under $50

Tipping Czechs are not usually blatant about the fact that tips are expected. Small sums of hard currency will certainly be most welcome. Otherwise, in Moderate or Inexpensive restaurants, add a few Kč; in more expensive ones, add 10%. For taxis, add 10 Kč. In the better hotels, doormen should get 5 Kč for each bag they carry to the check-in desk; bellhops get up to 10 Kč for taking them up to your rooms. In Moderate or Inexpensive hotels, you'll have to lug them yourself.

Prague

Arriving and Departing

By Plane All international flights arrive at Prague's Ruzyně Airport, about 20 kilometers (12 miles) from downtown. For arrival and departure times, tel. 02/367814 or 02/367760.

Between the Airport and Downtown Czechoslovak Air Lines (ČSA) provides bus services linking the airport with Town Terminal Vltava (Revoluční 25) and major hotels. Buses depart every 20 minutes during the day, every half hour evenings and on weekends. The trip into Prague costs 6 Kč and takes about 30 minutes. A special shuttle service serves main hotels and costs 50 Kč; buy the ticket before boarding. The cheapest way to get into Prague is by regular bus No. 119; the cost is 4 Kč, but you'll need to change to the subway at the Dejvícká station for the last leg of the trip. By taxi, expect to pay 300 Kč–400 Kč.

By Train The main station for international and domestic routes is Hlavni nádraží (tel. 02/2364441), Wilsonova, not far from Wenceslas Square. Some international trains arrive at and depart from Nádraží Holešovice, on the same metro line (C) as the main station.

By Bus The main bus station is Florenc (at Na Florenci, tel. 02/221445), not far from the train station. Take metro line C to Florenc station.

Getting Around

Public transportation is a bargain. Jizdenky (tickets) cost 4 Kč and can be bought at hotels, newsstands, and from dispensing machines in the metro stations. For the metro, punch the ticket in the station before getting on the escalators; for buses and trams, punch the ticket inside the vehicle. You can also buy one-day passes allowing unlimited use of the system for 30 Kč, two-day for 50 Kč, three-day for 65 Kč, and five-day for 100 Kč. The passes can be purchased at the main metro stations and at some newsstands.

By Subway Prague's three modern subway lines are easy to use and spotlessly clean. They provide the simplest and fastest means of transportation, and most new maps of Prague mark the routes.

By Tram/Bus You need to buy a new ticket every time you change vehicles. Express buses (marked with green badges) serve the suburbs and cost 4 Kč.

By Taxi Taxis (tel. 02/202951 or 02/2352611) are inexpensive and easily found in the center of town. Find them at taxi stands or hail them in the street. The basic charge is 6 Kč, increased by 8 Kč per kilometer. Be warned: Many drivers don't put on the meter. Either agree on a price beforehand (no more than 100 Kč within the city) or ask them to put on the meter. Some larger hotels have their own fleets, which are a little more expensive.

Important Addresses and Numbers

Tourist Information The main **Čedok** office (Na příkopě 18, tel. 02/2127111) is close to Wenceslas Square. Next door is the **Prague Information Service** (Na příkopě 20, tel. 02/544444). One of the best sources of information is the **American Hospitality Center,** just off Old Town Square (Malé náměstí 14, tel. 02/2367486 or 02/267770).

Embassies U.S. (Tržiště 15, Malá Strana, tel. 02/536641). **Canadian** (Mickiewiczova 6, Hradčany, tel. 02/3120251). **U.K.** (Thunovská 14, Malá Strana, tel. 02/533347).

Emergencies **Police** (tel. 158 or 2121); **Ambulance** (tel. 155); **Doctor: Fakultní poliklinika** (Karlovo náměstí 32, tel. 02/299381) or **Diplomatic Health Center for Foreigners** (Na homolce 724, Prague 5, weekdays tel. 02/5292–2146, evenings and weekends tel. 02/5292–1111); **24-Hour Pharmacy** (Na příkopě 7, near Wenceslas Sq., tel. 02/220081). Prague now has a **Lost Credit Card Hotline** (02/2366688).

English-Language Bookstores For the best selection of Penguin paperbacks and modern fiction, try **Bohemian Ventures** at the Charles University Philosophical Faculty (nám. Jana Palacha, near the Staroměstská metro station). **Video to Go** (Vitězné nám. 10, Prague 6, tel. 060/1209820) has a good selection of used and new paperbacks. For hiking maps and atlases, try **Melantrich** (Na příkopě 3, Prague 1, tel. 02/267166).

Guided Tours

Čedok arranges a variety of tours in and around Prague; they can either be arranged before you leave or booked in Prague.

Orientation Tours **Čedok** (tel. 02/2318255) offers a daily three-hour tour of the city, starting at 10 AM from the Čedok office at Bílkova 6 (tel. 02/2318255), opposite the Hotel Intercontinental. Contact any Čedok office for the current schedule and itinerary. From May to September, the organization also operates an afternoon tour, starting at 1:30. Both tours cost about 350 Kč.

Martin-Tour (tel. 02/527456) offers a similar but cheaper tour departing from náměstí Republiky daily at 9:30, 11:30, 1:30, and 3:30 (cost: about 270 Kč).

Special-Interest Tours The "U Fleku" brewery and beer-tasting tour departs on Friday mornings from Wenceslas Square 24 and lasts 1½ hours. For cultural tours, call Čedok *(see above)*. These include performances of folklore, Laterna Magika *(see* The Arts, *below)*, opera, and concerts. You can save money by buying tickets—if any are available—at box offices, but this will take time.

Excursions Čedok's one-day tours out of Prague cover principal historic and scenic sights and include lunch. The "Treasures of Bohemian Gothic" tour includes an excursion to the lovely medieval town of Kutná Hora; "Romantic Bohemian Paradise" features the bizarre sandstone and rock formations of northern Bohemia. Other tours include visits to famous spa towns and castles.

Personal Guides Contact Čedok *(see above)* to arrange a personal walking tour of the city. Times, prices, and itinerary are negotiable. Prices start at around 250 Kč per hour.

Exploring Prague

Prague is one of the most enchanting cities in Europe. Like Rome, Prague is built on seven hills, sprawling within the confines of a broad loop of the Vltava River. The riverside location, enhanced by a series of graceful bridges, makes a great setting for two of the city's most notable features: its extravagant, fairy-tale architecture and its memorable music. Mozart claimed that no one understood him better than the citizens of Prague, and he was only one of several great masters who lived or lingered here.

It was under Charles IV (Karel IV) during the 14th century that Prague briefly became the seat of the Holy Roman Empire—virtually the capital of Western Europe—and acquired its distinctive Gothic imprint. At times you'll need to look quite hard for this medieval inheritance; it's still here, though, under the overlays of graceful Renaissance and exuberant Baroque.

Prague escaped serious wartime damage, but it didn't escape neglect. Because of the long-term restoration program now under way, some part of the city is always under scaffolding. But what's completed—which is nearly all that's described in the following itineraries—is hard to find fault with as an example of sensitive and painstaking restoration.

Numbers in the margin correspond to points of interest on the Prague map.

The Nové Město and Staré Město

● ② **③** Václavské náměstí (Wenceslas Square) is the Times Square of Prague. Confusingly, it's not actually a square at all but a broad boulevard sloping down from the **Národní muzeum** (National Museum) and the equestrian **statue of St. Wenceslas.** The lower end is where all the action is. Na příkopě, once part of the moat surrounding the Old Town, is now an elegant pedestrian mall. Čedok's main office and Prague Information Service are

④ along here, on your way to the **Prašná brána** (Powder Tower), a 19th-century neo-Gothic replacement of the medieval original.

⑤ Turn into Celetná and you're on the old **Royal Route,** once followed by coronation processions past the foreboding Gothic

⑥ spires of the Týn Church through **Staroměstské náměstí** (Old

⑦ Town Square), down **Karlova,** across **Karlův most** (Charles Bridge), and up to the castle. Along this route, you can study every variety or combination of Romanesque, Gothic, Renaissance, and Baroque architecture. Two good examples are the town buildings at 12 Celetná and 8 Karlova. On Staroměstské náměstí, the crowds regularly gather below the famous **Clock Tower,** where, on the hour, the complex 16th-century mechanism activates a procession that includes the Twelve Apostles. Note the skeleton figure of Death that tolls the bell.

⑧ **Franz Kafka's birthplace** is just north of Staroměstské náměstí on U radnice. Following the 1989 revolution, Kafka's popularity has soared, and the works of this German Jewish writer are now widely available in Czech. A fascinating little museum has been set up in the house. *U radnice 5. Admission: 10 Kč. Open daily 10–6.*

⑨ In the **Starý židovský hřbitov** (Old Jewish Cemetery) in **Josefov** (Joseph's Town, the old Jewish quarter), ancient tombstones lean and jostle each other; below them, in a dozen layers, are 12,000 graves. As you stand by the tomb of the scholar Rabbi

Prague

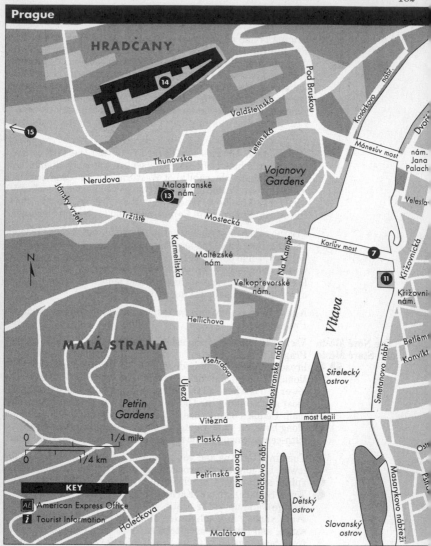

HRADČANY

Valdštejnská

Pod Bruskou

Kosárkovo nábř.

Dvoř

Mánesův most

nám.
Jana
Palach

Thunovska

Vojanovy
Gardens

Nerudova

Malostranské
nám.

Velesla

Jánský vršek

Tržiště

Mostecká

Karlův most

Křižovnická

Karmelitská

Maltézské
nám.

Na Kampě

Křižovní
nám.

Velkoprevorské
nám.

Vltava

Betlém

Hellichova

Konvikt

MALÁ STRANA

Všehrdova

Malostranské nábř.

Střelecký
ostrov

Smetanovo nábř.

Újezd

Petřín
Gardens

Vítězná

most Legii

Plaská

Ostr

Zborovská

Petřínská

Janáčkovo nábř.

Masarykovo nábřeži

Psin

Holečkova

Dětský
ostrov

Slovanský
ostrov

Malátova

N

0   1/4 mile
0   1/4 km

KEY

AE American Express Office

i Tourist Information

Betlémská kaple, **12**

Chram svatého
Mikuláše, **13**

Hradčany (Prague
Castle), **14**

Kafka's Birthplace, **8**

Karlův most, **7**

Loreto, **15**

Národní muzeum, **2**

Old Jewish
Cemetery, **9**

Prašná brána, **4**

Royal Route, **5**

Smetana Museum, **11**

Staroměstské
náměstí, **6**

State Jewish
Museum, **10**

Statue of
St.Wenceslas, **3**

Václavské náměstí, **1**

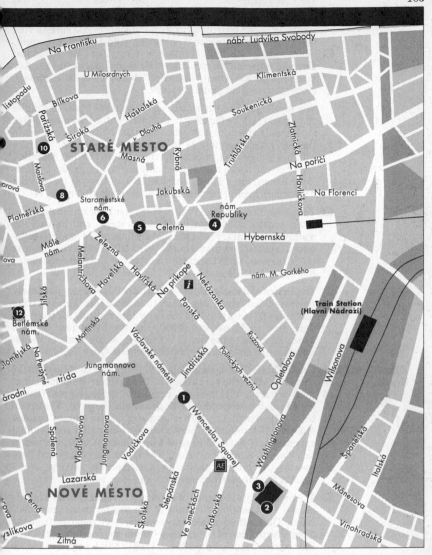

Low, who died in 1609, you may see, stuffed into the cracks, scraps of paper bearing prayers and requests. Be sure to visit the tiny Gothic **Staronová synagóga** (Old-New Synagogue), ⑩ which, along with the cemetery, forms part of the **Státní židovské múzeum** (State Jewish Museum). *Červená 101. Admission: 20 Kč. Open Sun.-Fri. 9-4:30 (9-5 in summer); closed Sat. and religious holidays.*

When you stand on Charles Bridge, you'll see views of Prague that would still be familiar to the 14th-century architect Peter Parler and to the sculptors who added the 30 Baroque statues in the early 18th century (a few have been replaced). They're worth a closer look, especially the 12th on the left (starting from the Old Town side of the bridge) (St. Luitgarde, by Matthias Braun, circa 1710), and the 14th on the left (in which a Turk guards suffering saints, by F. M. Brokoff, circa 1714).

⑪ The **museum** devoted to Prague composer **Bedřich Smetana,** located nearby at Novotného lávka, is small, and its exhibits mainly documentary. But it's a lovely quiet oasis in which to listen to tapes of Smetana's music—and admire the views across the Vltava and up to the castle. *Novotného lávka. Admission: 7 Kč. Open Wed.-Mon. 10-5.*

⑫ The **Betlémska kaple** (Bethlehem Chapel) has been completely reconstructed since Jan Hus thundered his humanitarian teachings from its pulpit in the early 15th century to congregations that could number 3,000. But the little door through which he came to the pulpit is original, as are some of the inscriptions on the wall. *Betlémské náměstí. Open daily 9-6.*

Malá Strana and Hradčany (Lesser Quarter and Castle) Cross Charles Bridge and follow Mostecká up to Malostranské náměstí. After the turbulence of the Counter-Reformation at the start of the 17th century, Prague witnessed a great flowering of what became known as Bohemian Baroque. The architects ⑬ (Dientzenhofer, father and son) of the **Chram svatého Mikuláše** (Church of St. Nicholas) were among its most skilled exponents. If you're in Prague when a concert is being given in this church, fight for a ticket. The lavish sculptures and frescoes of the interior make for a memorable setting. *Malostranské náměstí. Open daily 10-4 (9-6 in summer).*

⑭ The monumental complex of **Hradčany (Prague Castle)** has witnessed the changing fortunes of the city for more than 1,000 years. The scaffolding has only recently been removed from the latest restoration of the castle's **Chram svatého Víta** (St. Vitus Cathedral). It took from 1344 to 1929 to build, so you can trace the whole gamut of styles from Romanesque to Art Nouveau. This is the final resting place for numerous Bohemian kings. Charles IV lies in the crypt. Good King Wenceslas has his own chapel in the south transept, studded with semiprecious stones. Knightly tournaments often accompanied coronation ceremonies in the **Královský palác** (Royal Palace), next to the cathedral, hence the broad Riders' Staircase leading up to the grandiose **Vladislavský sál** (Vladislav Hall) of the Third Courtyard. Oldest of all the buildings, though much restored, is the Romanesque complex of **Bazilika svatého Jiří** (St. George's Church and Monastery). Behind a Baroque facade, it houses a superb collection of Bohemian art from medieval religious sculptures to decadent Baroque paintings. *Hradčanské náměstí. Admission to each museum building in the castle: 10 Kč. All are open Tues.-Sun. 10-5.*

Time Out At the small, pleasant snack bar of **U Ševce Matouše** (At the Cobblers) on Loretánské náměstí, you can get your shoes repaired while you have refreshments.

⑮ The Baroque church and shrine of **Loreto** is named for the Italian town to which the Virgin Mary's House in Nazareth was supposedly transported by angels to save it from the infidel. The crowning glory of its fabulous treasury is the glittering monstrance of the *Sun of Prague*, set with 6,222 diamonds. Arrive on the hour to hear the 27-bell carillon. *Loreta 12. Admission: 10 Kč. Open Tues.–Sun. 9–noon and 1–4:30.*

Off the Beaten Track

Cross the Vltava at the Hotel InterContinental (via the Čechův bridge) and climb the steps to the **Letenské sady** (Gardens on the Ramparts) for sweeping views of Prague.

Almost as old as the oldest parts of Prague Castle, the ruins of **Vyšehrad Castle** crown a rock bluff rising out of the Vltava, about 2 miles downstream from the Old Town. The quiet cemetery adjoining the **Church of Sts. Peter and Paul** is a place to pay homage to some of the nation's cultural giants, among them Bedřich Smetana and the playwright Karel Čapek.

Across the river, in Prague 5 district, Mozart stayed in the peaceful **Bertramka Villa**, and here completed his opera *Don Giovanni*. With luck, your trip will coincide with a concert here. If not, taped music will accompany your walk through the villa, restored to what it was in his day.

Although it's no longer possible to stroll around the grounds, you can still glimpse **Franz Kafka's grave** through the gates of the **Židovské hřbitovy** (New Jewish Cemetery) in Vinohrady, a rather depressing part of Prague. Take metro line A to Želivského, turn right at the main cemetery gate, and follow the wall for about 100 yards. Kafka's thin, white tombstone lies at the front of section 21.

Shopping

Specialty Shops Look for the name **Dilo** for objets d'art and prints; **ULUV** or **UVA** for folk art. At Na příkopě 12 you'll find excellent costume jewelry. **Moser** (Na příkopě 12) is the most famous for glass and porcelain. Shops specializing in Bohemian crystal, porcelain, ceramics, and antiques abound.

Shopping Districts Many of the main shops are in and around Wenceslas Square (Václavské náměstí) and Na příkopě, as well as along Celetná and Pařížská.

Department Stores Three central stores are **Bilá Labut'** (Na poříčí 23), **Krone** (Václavské nám. 21), and **Kotva** (nám. Republiky 8).

Dining

Eating out in Prague is a very popular pastime, so it's advisable to make reservations whenever possible, especially for dinner. For details and price-category definitions, *see* Dining in Staying in the Czech Republic, *above.*

Very Expensive **Parnas.** Freshly prepared nouvelle cuisine in an elegant, 1920s setting. Ask for a window seat for a stunning view of Prague castle. The beef Wellington is tender and flavorful, and the salmon dishes are sublime. There's also a good (short) wine list. *Smetanovo nábřeží 2, tel. 02/261250. Reservations advised. AE, DC, MC, V. Dinner only.*

U Malířů. This recently privatized old restaurant now serves exclusively French food and wines at the highest prices you'll see in the entire country. The specialty of the house is lobster, but the chef prepares a couple of elaborate set menus daily. *Maltézké náměstí 11, Malá Strana, tel. 02/531883. Reservations advised. AE, DC, MC, V. Closed Sun.*

★ **U Zlaté Hrušky.** Careful restoration has returned this restaurant to its original 18th-century style. It specializes in Moravian wines, which go down well with fillet steaks and goose liver. *Nový Svět 3, Castle area, tel. 02/531133. Reservations required. No credit cards. Dinner only.*

Expensive **Opera Grill.** Though called a grill, this is one of the most stylish
★ small restaurants in town, complete with antique Meissen candelabra and Czech specialties. *K. Světlé 35, Staré Město, tel. 02/265508. Reservations required. AE, DC, MC, V. Dinner only.*

U Labutí. Located in tastefully remodeled stables in the castle area, "At the Swans" has a stylish—if slightly rich and heavy—menu (haunch of venison, goose liver with ham and almonds), which includes some Expensive dishes. The place is rich in atmosphere, too. *Hradčanské náměstí 11, tel. 02/539476. Reservations required. AE, DC, MC, V. Dinner only.*

★ **U Mecenáše.** This wine restaurant manages to be both medieval and elegant despite the presence of an ancient gallows! Try to get a table in the back room. The chef specializes in thick, juicy steak, served with a variety of sauces. *Malostranské náměstí 10, Malá Strana, tel. 02/533881. Reservations required. AE, DC, MC, V. Dinner only.*

Moderate **Dům Slovenské Kultury.** You'll get good, hearty fare served in a relaxed, no-frills atmosphere at this "House of Slovak Culture," located behind Národní Třída in the New Town. The homemade sausage, accompanied by hearty Slovak wine, is excellent. The large *palačinky* (crêpes) for dessert are some of the best in Prague. *Purkyňova 4, tel. 02/291996. Reservations advised. AE.*

Myslivna. They took the antlers off the walls of this rustic restaurant a year or so after the Velvet Revolution, but the cooks still know their way around pheasant, boar, and quail. Try leg of venison in wine sauce with walnuts or wild boar, all prepared to please the eye and palette. *Jagellonská 21, Vinohrady, tel. 02/627029. Reservations advised. AE, DC, MC, V.*

Penguin's. A trendy crowd comes here for some of the best Czech cooking and freshest vegetables in town (and because they know they're getting excellent value for their money). The muted mauve and matte-black walls make a casually elegant setting. *Zborovská 5, tel. 02/545660. Reservations advised. No credit cards.*

U Lorety. Sightseers will find this an agreeable spot—peaceful except for the welcoming carillon from neighboring Loreto Church. The service here is discreet but attentive, the tables are private, and the food is consistently good. Venison and steak are specialties. *Loretánské náměstí 8, near the Castle, tel. 02/531395. Reservations advised. AE, DC, MC, V. Closed Mon. (and Tues. in winter).*

Inexpensive **Na Zvonařce.** This bright beer hall serves very good traditional fare at unbeatable prices. Sit on the terrace during the summer to escape the noisy crowd. Noteworthy dishes include fried chicken and English roast beef. Fruit dumplings for dessert are a rare treat. Service is slow. *Šafaříkova 1, tel. 02/6911311. Reservations advised. No credit cards.*

U Koleje. The friendly staff at this popular, laid-back pub suitable for the whole family serves good traditional pork and beef dishes and excellent beer. You may have to share a table. *Slavíkova 24, tel. 02/6274163. Reservations advised. No credit cards.*

U Zlatého Tygra. This impossibly crowded hangout is the last of a breed of authentic Czech *pivnice* (pubs). The smoke and stares preclude a long stay, but it's still worth dropping in for typical pub staples like ham and cheese plates or roast pork. The service is surly, but the beer is good. *Husova 17, tel. 02/265219. No reservations. No credit cards. Evenings only. Closed Sun.*

V Krakovské. This clean pub noted for its excellent traditional fare is the place to try Bohemian duck: it's cooked just right and offered at an excellent price. Wash it down with good dark beer from Domažlice in western Bohemia. *Krakovská 20, tel. 02/261537. Reservations advised. No credit cards.*

Lodging

Many of Prague's older hotels—some of which have great style—have recently been or are due to be renovated. If you haven't prebooked, go to Čedok when you arrive (*see* Tourist Information in Important Addresses and Numbers, *above*). For details and price-category definitions, *see* Lodging in Staying in Czechoslovakia. Interhotels belong to the Čedok network.

Very Expensive **Diplomat.** Completed in 1990 as part of a joint venture with an
★ Austrian company, the Diplomat succeeds in fusing elegance with "Western" efficiency. The effect is marred only by an unfortunate location, outside of the center on the road to the airport. *Evropská 15, tel. 02/3314111, fax 02/3314215. 387 rooms with bath. Facilities: sauna, nightclub. AE, DC, MC, V.*

★ **Palace Praha** (Interhotel). Beautifully renovated in art nouveau style, the newly reopened Palace is Prague's most elegant and luxurious hotel. Its central location just off Wenceslas Square makes this an excellent choice. *Panská 12, tel. 02/2359394, fax 02/2359373. 125 rooms with bath. Facilities: saunas, health club, nightclub. AE, DC, MC, V.*

U Páva. Recently remodeled suites in this svelte, neoclassical inn on a cobblestone street in Malá Strana afford unforgettable views of the Castle. The Old World staff is courteous, and the reception and public areas are elegant and discreet. *U lužického semináře 106, Prague 1, tel. 02/532251, fax 02/533379. 11 rooms with bath. AE, DC, MC, V.*

Expensive **Forum** (Interhotel). This modern 28-story high rise is near ancient Vyšehrad Castle, two subway stops south of the city center. Prices include half-board. *Kongresová ul., tel. 02/4190111, fax 02/420684. 531 rooms with bath. Facilities: saunas, pool, bowling alleys, miniature golf, gym, nightclub, roulette. AE, DC, MC, V.*

Jalta (Interhotel). The Jalta has a plum location on Wenceslas Square. Recently remodeled, it deserves at least four of the five stars awarded by Čedok. *Václavské náměstí 45, tel. 02/265541,* *fax 02/226390. 90 rooms with bath. Facilities: 2 nightclubs. AE, DC, MC, V.*

Paříž. Despite its overpriced rooms, this Art Nouveau gem near the center of the Old Town continues to be in high demand. The listless staff and mediocre restaurant detract only slightly from the grandness of the architecture. Request a room away from the street. *U Obecního domu 1, Prague 1, tel. 02/2360820, fax 02/2367448. 86 rooms with bath. AE, DC, MC, V.*

Moderate   **Atlantic.** Something of the 1970s hangs in the air of this well-run establishment, situated a stone's throw from the Powder Tower in central Prague. Dark, carpeted interiors and over-stuffed leather chairs set the subdued mood. The slickly appointed rooms, all with television sets and clean, modern bathrooms, date from a 1989 renovation. *Na poříčí 9, tel. 02/2318512, fax 02/2326077. 60 rooms with bath. Facilities: restaurant, bar. AE, DC, MC, V.*

Kampa. An early Baroque armory-turned-hotel, the Kampa is tucked away in a shady corner just south of Malá Strana. The rooms are clean, if spare, but the bucolic setting compensates for any discomforts. *Všehrdova 16, Prague 1, tel. 02/539045, fax 02/532815. 85 rooms with bath. Facilities: restaurant, café. AE, DC, MC, V.*

Meteor Plaza. Costly renovation and incorporation into the Best Western chain recently pushed this hotel from Inexpensive to the top end of Moderate. It may be worth a splurge, though: This elegant Baroque building is in a lovely setting just five minutes on foot from downtown. *Hybernská 6, tel. 02/2358517, fax 02/224715. 86 rooms with bath. Facilities: restaurant, business center, terrace. AE, DC, MC, V.*

The Arts

Prague's cultural life is one of its top attractions and its citizens like to dress up for it, but performances are usually booked far ahead. You can get a monthly program of events from the Prague Information Service, Čedok, or many hotels. The two English-language newspapers, *The Prague Post* and *Prognosis*, carry detailed entertainment listings. The main ticket agencies are **Bohemia Ticket International** (Karlova 8 and Na příkopě 16, tel. 02/228738) and **Čedok** (Bílkova 6, tel. 02/2318255); for concerts, try **Sluna** (in Alfa passageway, Václavské náměstí). It's much cheaper, however, to buy tickets at the box office.

Concerts   Performances are held in the **National Gallery** in Prague Castle; the **National Museum;** the **Gardens** below the castle (where music comes with a view); the **churches of St. Nicholas** in both the Old Town Square and in Malá Strana; and **St. James's Church** on Malá Stupartská (Staré Město), where the organ plays amid a flourish of Baroque statuary.

Year-round concert halls include the newly renovated **Rudolfinum** (home of the Czech Philharmonic Orchestra, Alšovo nábř. 12, Prague, tel. 02/2860111), **Smetana Hall** (Obecní dum, nám. Republiky 5, tel. 02/2322501), and **Palác Kultury** (Kvetna 65, tel. 02/4172791).

Opera and Ballet   Opera is of an especially high standard in Czechoslovakia. The main venues in the grand style of the 19th century are the beautifully restored **National Theater** (Národní třida 2, tel. 02/205364) and the **State Opera of Prague** (Wilsonova 4, tel. 02/

269746; formerly the Smetana Theater). The even older **Theater of Estates** (Ovocný trh 1, tel. 227281; formerly the Týl Theater) is occasionally used for opera performances.

Theater You won't need to know the language at **Divadlo na Zábradlí** (Theater on the Balustrade, Anenské nám. 3, tel. 02/2360449), home of the famous Black Theater mime group when it is (rather rarely) in Prague. **Laterna Magika** (Magic Lantern, Národní třída 40, tel. 02/206260) is a popular extravaganza combining live actors, mime, and sophisticated film techniques.

Puppet Shows These are brought to a high art form at the **Špejbl and Hurvínek Theater** (Římská 45).

Nightlife

Cabaret **The Alhambra** (Václavské náměstí 5, tel. 02/220467) has a three-part floor show. More moderately priced is **Variété Praha** (Vodičkova 30, tel. 02/2350861). You'll find plenty of fellow foreigners at both.

Discos and Clubs Discos catering to a young crowd (mostly 14–18-year-olds) line Wenceslas Square. The best bet is to stroll down the square and listen for the liveliest music. Excellent jazz can be heard nightly in Prague at several venues. Try **Reduta** (Národní třída 20, tel. 02/203825) or **Agharta** (Krakovská 5, tel. 02/224558). For live rock, check out the **Rock Cafe** (Národní třída 20, tel. 02/206656) or **Malostranská Beseda** (Malostranské nám. 21, tel. 02/539024).

Bohemian Spas and Castles

The Bohemian countryside is a restful world of gentle hills and thick woods. It is especially beautiful during fall foliage or in May, when the fruit trees that line the roads are in blossom. In such settings lie the two most famous of Czechoslovakia's scores of spas: Karlovy Vary and Mariánské Lázně. During the 19th and early 20th centuries, the royalty and aristocrats of Europe who came to ease their overindulged bodies (or indulge them even more!) knew these spas as Karlsbad and Marienbad.

To the south, the higher wooded hills of Šumava, bordering Germany, have their own folklore and give rise to the headwaters of the Vltava. You'll follow its tortuous course as you enter South Bohemia, which has probably spawned more castles than any other region of comparable size. The medieval towns of South Bohemia are exquisite, though be prepared to find them in various stages of repair or decay. In such towns was the Hussite reformist movement born during the early 15th century, sparking off a series of religious conflicts that eventually embroiled all of Europe.

Getting Around

There are bus or train connections to every corner of this region. The service is cheap, frequent, and reliable, though you may be frustrated by incomprehensible small print when trying to decipher timetables. The most convenient way to follow this entire itinerary is by car.

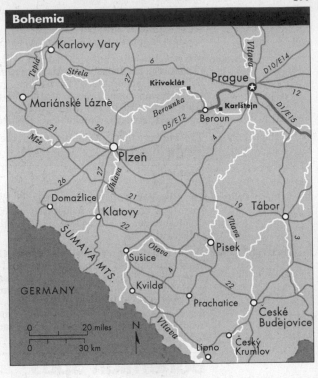

Bohemia

Karlovy Vary
Střela
Tepla
6
27
Křivoklát
Prague
Vltava
D10/E14
12
Mariánské Lázně
Berounka
Karlštejn
D5/E12
D1/E15
Beroun
21
20
Mže
4
Plzeň
27
Vltava
26
21
Domažlice
19
Tábor
Klatovy
22
Vltava
3
ŠUMAVA MTS
Otava
Pisek
Sušice
4
22
GERMANY
Kvilda
Prachatice
České
Budějovice

0   20 miles
0   30 km
N
Vltava
Lipno
Český
Krumlov

Guided Tours

Many of the attractions on this itinerary, and some additional
ones in Moravia, are covered by Čedok's escorted seven-day
"Short Tour of Czechoslovakia" out of Prague. Most of them
can also be visited during a series of day trips from the capital.

Tourist Information
České Budějovice (Hronznova 21, tel. 038/32381).
Český Krumlov (Svornosti náměstí, tel. 0337/2062).
Domažlice (Náměsti Míru 129, tel. 0189/2713).
Karlovy Vary (Tržiště 23, tel. 017/27798).
Mariánské Lázně (Odborářů 48, tel. 0165/2500).
Tábor (Tř. 9 května 1282, tel. 0361/144585).

Exploring Bohemian Spas and Castles

If you're traveling by car, the best—though not fastest—route
is to head south from Prague on Highway 4, then west along
minor roads up the Berounka Valley, taking in the castles of
Karlštejn and **Křivoklát**. The first is an admirable restoration of
the 14th-century castle built by Charles IV, but it isn't worth
the uphill slog unless the stunning Chapel of the Holy Rood is
reopened, its walls covered with 128 Gothic paintings and encrusted with 2,000 gems. Křivoklát's main attractions are its
glorious woodlands, a favorite royal hunting ground in times
past. *Both castles open May–Oct., Tues.–Sun. 9–6; closed the
day after public holidays.*

Karlovy Vary, or Karlsbad, was named after Charles IV, who,
while out hunting, was supposedly led to the main thermal

spring of Vřídlo by a fleeing deer. In due course, the spa drew not only many of the crowned heads and much of the blue blood of Europe but also leading musicians and writers. The same parks, promenades, and colonnades still border the little river Teplá, beneath wooded hills. For all its later buildings and proletarian patients, Karlovy Vary still has a great deal of elegance. The waters from the spa's 12 springs are uniformly foultasting. The thing to do is sip them from traditionally shaped cups while nibbling rich Karlovy Vary wafers (*oplatky*), then resort to the "13th spring," Karlovy Vary's tangy herbal liqueur called *Becherovka.*

Karlovy Vary and **Mariánské Lázně** have Czechoslovakia's two best golf courses. As a spa, Mariánské Lázně is younger and smaller, yet its more open setting gives it an air of greater spaciousness. It was much favored by Britain's Edward VII, though from all accounts, he didn't waste too much time on strict diets and rigorous treatments.

The spas of west Bohemia have long catered to foreign travelers. As you head south to the higher Šumava Mountains bordering Germany, you'll be following much less frequented trails. **Domažlice** is the heart of the region of the Chods, for centuries guardians of Bohemia's frontiers, a function that earned them a number of privileges. Their special folk culture is still very much alive, not least in their pottery and their contagious dances accompanied by local bagpipes (main festival in mid-August). It is a bustling if neglected little town with a lovely arcaded square, old fortifications, and a castle that houses the **Chod Museum** of local folk culture. *Open May–Oct., Tues.–Sun. 8–noon and 1–4:30.*

From Domažlice runs a tortuous but extremely pretty route, mainly along minor roads, through Sušice along the upper Otava River and over the hills to Prachatice and back to **Kvilda,** where the road joins the young Vltava River. Downstream, the Vltava has been trapped to form the great reservoir and recreational area of **Lipno.** You skirt part of it before turning northeast to Český Krumlov.

This entire part of South Bohemia has strong associations with such feudal families as the Rožmberks, who peppered the countryside with their castles and created lake-size "ponds" in which to breed highly prized carp, still the main feature of a Czech Christmas dinner. Once the main seat of the Rožmberks, **Ceský Krumlov** is a magical town dominated by a forbidding Renaissance castle, complete with romantic elevated walkways and delicate towers. The Vltava River snakes through the town, which is steeply stacked on either bank, with flights of steps linking various levels and twisting narrow lanes that converge on **Svornosti náměstí,** the main square of the Old Town. There are arcades, courtyards, and landscaped castle gardens with an 18th-century theater.

České Budějovice is on a much larger scale, and here your main stop should be the massive but handsome **Přemysla Ottokara II Square.** Previously named for the Hussite leader Žižka, the square's name was changed in 1991 to reflect historical reality—the town was firmly on the side of the Catholics. This is the home of the Czech version of Budweiser beer, known in Czech as Budvar, and well worth trying.

Farther north along Highway 3 is **Tábor,** the very cradle of the Hussite movement. Its twisting streets were designed to confuse the enemy. A labyrinth of tunnels and cellars below the town were used both as living quarters and as links with the outer defenses. Their story is told in the **Hussite Museum** just off Zižka Square. *Open Tues.–Sun. 9–5.*

Dining and Lodging

For details and price-category definitions, *see* Dining and Lodging in Staying in Czechoslovakia.

Český Krumlov   **Růže.** This former Renaissance monastery was lovingly restored in 1992, and now holds its own with other impressive sights in this enchanting town. Guest rooms are spacious and well-appointed; some are furnished in period style. *Horní ul. 153, tel. 0337/2245, fax 0337/3881. 110 rooms with bath. AE, DC, MC, V. Expensive.*

Krumlov. This 19th-century town house is a charming and very comfortable hotel, renovated in 1988. It's in the center of the old town. *Svornosti náměstí 14, tel. 0337/2255–8. 36 rooms, 13 with bath. AE, DC, MC, V. Moderate.*

Karlovy Vary   **Dvořak.** Opened in 1991, this Austrian-built hotel offers imaginative decor, friendly efficiency, and a superb array of facilities. *Nova louka 11, tel. 017/24145, fax 017/22819. 79 rooms with bath. Facilities: pool, fitness room, spa center. AE, DC, MC, V. Very Expensive.*

★ **Grand Hotel Pupp.** Founded in 1701, the Pupp still features a fine 18th-century hall, Slavností sál. It's one of the oldest surviving hotels in Europe, with a glittering list of guests, both past and present. *Mírové náměstí 2, tel. 017/22121–5. 358 rooms with bath. Facilities: saunas, tennis courts, golf, riding, 2 nightclubs, several restaurants and taverns. AE, DC, MC, V. Very Expensive.*

Atlantic. This hotel is right in the middle of town and is run by the nearby Hotel Central. The turn-of-the-century building was renovated recently, but it still bears its characteristic grotesque porcelain statues on the roof. *Divadelní náměstí, tel. 017/24715. 38 rooms, some with bath. AE, DC, MC, V. Moderate.*

Mariánské Lázně   **Golf.** Built in 1924 and renovated in 1982, this hotel is located a
★ bit out of town by the golf course. The decor is traditional and the restaurant serves good regional dishes, such as dumplings. *Zádub 55, tel. 0165/2651, fax 0165/2655. 26 rooms with bath. Facilities: pool, tennis, golf, riding. AE, DC, MC, V. Very Expensive.*

Palace Praha. Built in 1875 during the spa's heyday, this elegant building is conveniently situated just within the resort center. French foods are the specialty at one of the hotel's two restaurants. *Třída Odborářů 67, tel. 0165/2222. 35 rooms, 23 with bath. Facilities: nightclub. AE, DC, MC, V. Expensive.*

8 Denmark

Ebullience and a sense of humor have earned the Danes a reputation as "the Italians of Scandinavia." While one might expect a country comprising more than 400 islands to develop an island mentality, the Danes are famous for their friendliness and have even coined a term—*hyggelig*—for the feeling of well-being that comes from their own brand of cozy hospitality.

The stereotype of melancholic Scandinavia doesn't hold here: not in the café-studded streets of the larger cities, where musicians and fruit vendors hawk their wares to passersby; not in the tiny coastal towns, where the houses are the color of ice-cream flavors; not in the jam sessions that erupt in the Copenhagen jazz clubs, nor in the equally joyous "jam" sessions involved in the production of *smørrebrød* (the famous open-face Danish sandwich). Even the country's indoor/outdoor museums, where history is reconstructed through full-scale dwellings out in the open, indicate that Danes don't wish to keep life behind glass.

They even joke about their undeniably flat landscape. One of the country's highest hills—dwarfed by any self-respecting peak abroad—stands in Jutland, at 139.5 meters (450 feet). The Danes have dubbed it Himmkelbjerget, or Sky Mountain. This is a land of well-groomed agriculture, where every acre is rich in orchard and field. Nowhere are you far from water, as you drive on and off the ferries and bridges linking the three regions of Jutland, Fyn, and Zealand.

It is the sea surrounding the land that has helped shape Denmark's history. The Vikings were magnificent seafarers and had seen much of the world by the 8th century. Today the Danes remain expert navigators, using the 4,480 kilometers (2,800 miles) of coastline for sport—there are regattas around Zealand and Funen—as well as for fishing and trading.

Long one of the world's most liberal countries, Denmark has a highly developed social welfare system. The hefty taxes are the subject of grumbles and jokes, but Danes remain proud of their state-funded medical and educational systems. Evidence of the strong sense of community spirit is the uniquely Danish institution of the People's High School, or Folkehøjskole, where pupils live in and where the shared experience is deemed as important as the courses taken. In the summer, adults and even entire families attend these "schools for life," studying anything from weaving to the philosophy of Wittgenstein.

The country that gave the world Isak Dinesen, Hans Christian Andersen, and Søren Kierkegaard has a long-standing commitment to culture and the arts. In what other nation does the royal couple translate the writings of Simone de Beauvoir or the queen design postage stamps for Christmas? The Danish Ballet is world-renowned, while the provinces boast numerous theater groups and opera houses.

Perhaps Denmark's greatest charm is its manageable size—about half that of Maine. The ferry journey from Esbjerg, on the western coast of Jutland, to Copenhagen, on the eastern coast of Zealand, takes around five hours. From here you can make comfortable, unhurried expeditions by boat, car, bus, or train to cover what is one of the world's most civilized countries.

Denmark

North Sea

Skagerrak

TO GREENLAND

TO FAROE ISLANDS

Skagen

Hirtshals
Hjørring
Frederikshavn
Sæby

Brønderslev

SWEDEN

Læsø

Hanstholm

Thisted
Lim-fjord
Limfjord
Aalborg

Nykøbing

Skive

Lemvig
Struer
Holstebro

Viborg
Randers 16

Aalborg Bugt

Kattegat

Hadsund

Jylland

Silkeborg
Grenå

Ringkøbing
Herning
Skanderborg
Århus
Ebeltoft

15
Horsens
Samsø

Grindsted
E45
Vejle

Skjern
Billund
Holsted

Esbjerg
E20
Kolding
Fredericia
Middelfart

Fanø

Ribe
Vojens
Assens
Odense
Kerteminde

Rømø
Haderslev
Fyn
Nyborg

Skærbæk
Åbenrå
Fåborg

Tønder
8
Sønderborg
Als
Svendborg
Troense

Ærøskøbing
Ærø
Marstal

Langeland
Tranekær
Rudkøbing

Nakskov

Anholt

Tisvildeleje
Hornbæk
Helsingør
Hillerød

Nykøbing
Frederikssund

Kalundborg
Holbæk
Copenhagen

Storebælt
Jyderup
Roskilde
E47

Slagelse
E20
Sjælland
Amager

Ringsted
Køge
Køge Bugt

Korsør
Næstved
St. Heddinge

Karrebæksminde

Vordingborg
Stege
Møn

Nykøbing
Falster
TO BORNHOLM

Rødby
Maribo
Nysted

Lolland

E47

North Sea

Samsøbælt

Lillebælt

GERMANY

Ostsee

N

0   50 miles
0   75 km

SWEDEN

Baltic Sea

Bornholm

Rønne

Essential Information

Before You Go

When to Go Most travelers visit Denmark during the warmest months, July and August, but there are advantages to going in May, June, or September, when sights are less crowded and many establishments offer off-season discounts. However, few places in Denmark are ever unpleasantly crowded, and when the Danes make their annual exodus to the beaches, the cities have even more breathing space. Visitors may want to avoid the winter months, when the days are short and dark and when important attractions, Tivoli included, close for the season.

Climate The following are the average daily maximum and minimum temperatures for Copenhagen.

Jan.	36F	2C	May	61F	16C	Sept.	64F	18C
	28	-2		46	8		51	11
Feb.	36F	2C	June	67F	19C	Oct.	54F	12C
	28	-2		52	11		44	7
Mar.	41F	5C	July	71F	22C	Nov.	45F	7C
	31	-1		57	14		38	3
Apr.	51F	11C	Aug.	70F	21C	Dec.	40F	4C
	38	3		56	14		34	1

Currency The monetary unit in Denmark is the krone (kr. or DKK) which is divided into 100 øre. At press time (spring 1993), the krone stood at 6.19 kr. to the dollar and 9.33 kr. to the pound sterling. Most well-known credit cards are accepted in Denmark, though the American Express card is accepted less frequently than others. Traveler's checks can be changed in banks and in many hotels, restaurants, and shops.

What It Will Cost Denmark's economy is stable, and inflation remains reasonably low, without wild fluctuations in exchange rates. While Denmark is slightly cheaper than Norway and Sweden, the standard and the cost of living are nonetheless high, especially for such luxuries as alcohol. Prices are highest in Copenhagen while the least expensive areas are Fyn and Jutland.

Sample Prices Cup of coffee, 14–20 kr.; bottle of beer, 15–25 kr.; soda, 10–14 kr.; ham sandwich, 24 kr.; 1-mile taxi ride, 20 kr.

Customs on Arrival If you purchase goods in a country that is a member of the European Community (EC) and pay that country's value-added tax (VAT) on those goods: You may import duty-free 1½ liters of liquor or 3 liters of strong wine (under 22%), plus 5 liters of other wine; 300 cigarettes or 150 cigarillos or 75 cigars or 40 grams of tobacco. Other articles may be brought in up to a maximum of 2,800 kr.; you are also allowed 75 grams of perfume.

If you are entering Denmark from a non-EC country or if you have purchased your goods in an airport, on a ferryboat, or in another airport not taxed in the EC, you must pay Danish taxes on any amount of alcoholic beverages greater than 1 liter of liquor or 2 liters of strong wine, plus 2 liters of other wine. For tobacco, the limit is 200 cigarettes or 100 cigarillos or 50 cigars or 250 grams of tobacco. Other articles (including beer) are allowed up to a maximum of 350 kr.; you are also allowed 50 grams of perfume.

Language A wit once said that Danish was not so much a language as "a disease of the throat." It is a difficult tongue for foreigners, except those from Norway and Sweden, to understand, let alone speak. Danes are good linguists, however, and almost everyone, except elderly people in rural areas, speaks English well.

Getting Around

By Car
Road Conditions Roads here are good and largely traffic-free (except around Copenhagen); you can reach many islands by toll-free bridges.

Rules of the Road The driver needs a valid driver's license, and, if you're using your own car, it must have a certificate of registration and national plates. A triangular hazard-warning sign is compulsory in every car and is provided with a rented car. No matter where they are seated, all passengers traveling in cars must wear seat belts, and cars must have low-beam lights on at all times. Motorcyclists must always wear helmets and use low-beam headlights. All drivers must pay attention to cyclists, who drive on the outer right lane and have the right-of-way.

Drive on the right and give way to traffic from the left. A red-and-white triangular Yield sign, or a line of white triangles across the road, means you must yield to traffic on the road you are entering. Do not turn right on a red light. Speed limits are 50 kph (30 mph) in built-up areas; on highways, 100 kph (60 mph); and on other roads, 80 kph (50 mph). If you are towing a trailer, you must not exceed 70 kph (40 mph). Speeding and, especially, drinking and driving, are punished severely.

Parking "Parkering/Standsning Forbudt" means no parking and no stopping, though you are allowed a three-minute grace period to load and unload. In towns, automatic parking-ticket machines are used. Drop in coins, push the silver button, and a ticket will drop down with the expiration time. Display the ticket clearly on the dash. Parking for an hour is 6 kr.–15 kr. in Copenhagen, 7 kr. elsewhere.

Gasoline Gas costs around 5.90 kr. a liter.

Breakdowns Members of organizations affiliated with Alliance International de Tourisme (AIT) can get technical and legal assistance from the **Danish Motoring Organization** (FDM), (Firskovej 32, DK 2800 Lyngby, tel. 45/93–08–00). All highways have emergency phones, and you can even phone the car-rental company for help. If you cannot drive your car to a garage for repairs, the rescue corps, **Falck** (tel. 33/14–22–22), can help anywhere, night or day.

By Train and Bus Traveling by train or bus is easy because Danish State Railways (DSB) (tel. 33/14–17–01) and a few private companies cover the country with a dense network of train services, supplemented in remote areas by buses. Hourly intercity trains connect the main towns in Jutland and Fyn with Copenhagen and Zealand, using high-speed diesels, called IC–3s, on the most important stretches. All these trains make the one-hour ferry crossing of the Great Belt (Store Bælt), the waterway separating Funen and Zealand. You can reserve seats on intercity trains and Lyntog, and you *must* have a reservation if you plan to cross the Great Belt. Buy tickets at stations for trains, buses, and connecting ferry crossings. You can usually buy tickets on the bus itself. For most cross-country trips, children between four and 11 accompanied by an adult travel free, though they must have a seat reservation (30 kr.). Ask about discounts for senior citizens and groups.

Fares The **Nordpass** (Nordic Tourist Ticket) is a good buy for 21 days of unlimited travel by rail and on some sea routes in Denmark, Norway, Sweden, and Finland. The price for an adult traveling second-class is 1,830 kr., 1,380 kr. for young adults (12–26), and 915 kr. for children (4–11).

By Boat There is frequent service to Germany, Poland, Sweden, Norway, and the Faroe Islands (in the Atlantic Ocean, north of Scotland), as well as to Britain. Domestic ferries provide services between the three areas of Jutland, Funen, and Zealand and to the smaller islands, 100 of which are inhabited. Danish State Railways and several private shipping companies publish timetables in English, and you should reserve on domestic as well as overseas routes. Ask about off-season discounts.

By Bicycle Some say the Danes have the greatest number of bikes per capita in the world. Indeed, with its flat landscape and uncrowded roads, Denmark is a cycler's paradise. You can rent bikes at some train stations and many tourist offices, as well as from private firms. Contact the **Danish Cyclists' Association** (Dansk Cyklist Forbund) (Rømersgade 7, DK 1362 Copenhagen, tel. 33/32–31–21) for additional information. Danish tourist offices publish the pamphlet "Cycling Holiday in Denmark."

Staying in Denmark

Telephones Pay phones take 1-, 5-, and 10-kr. coins. You must use the area
Local Calls codes even when dialing a local number. Calling cards, which are sold at DSB stations, post offices, and some kiosks, cost 25, 50, or 100 kr., and are used at certain phones.

International Calls Dial 009, then the country code, the area code, and the number. Hotels add a hefty service charge, so use a pay phone.

Operators and To speak to an operator, most of whom speak English, dial 118;
Information for an international operator, dial 114.

Mail Surface and airmail letters, as well as aerograms, to the United
Postal Rates States cost 5 kr. for 20 grams; postcards also cost 5 kr. Letters and postcards to the United Kingdom and other EC countries cost 3.75 kr. Stamps are sold at post offices and some shops.

Receiving Mail If you do not know where you will be staying, have mail sent Poste Restante to any post office. American Express holds mail free of charge, but only for card- and/or traveler's check–holders. If no post office is specified, letters will be sent to the main post office in Copenhagen (Tietensgade 37).

Shopping Visitors from a non-EC country can save 20% by obtaining a re-
VAT Refunds fund of the value-added tax (VAT) at the more than 1,500 shops displaying Tax Free signs. If the shop sends your purchase directly to your home address, you pay only the sales price, exclusive of VAT. If you want to take the goods home yourself, pay the full price in the shop and get a VAT refund at the Danish duty-free shopping center at the Copenhagen airport. Get a copy of the *Tax-Free Shopping Guide* from the tourist office.

Opening and **Banks** in Copenhagen are open weekdays 9:30–3 and
Closing Times Thursdays until 6. Several *bureaux de change*, including the ones at Copenhagen's central station and airport, stay open until 10 PM. Outside Copenhagen, banking hours vary.

Museums are generally open 10–3 or 11–4 and closed Mondays. In winter, opening hours are shorter, some museums close for the season. Check the local papers or ask at tourist offices.

Shops are generally open weekdays 9–5:30; most stay open on Fridays until 7 or 8 and close on Saturdays at 1 or 2.

National Holidays January 1; April 1–3 (Easter); April 29 (Common Prayer); May 12 (Ascension); May 22 (Pentecost); June 5 (Constitution Day; shops close at noon); and December 24–26.

Dining Danes take their food seriously, and Danish food, however simple, is excellent, with an emphasis on fresh ingredients and careful presentation. Fish and meat are both of top quality in this farming and fishing country, and both are staple ingredients of the famous smørrebrød. Some smørrebrød are huge meals in themselves: Innocent snackers can find themselves faced with a dauntingly large (but nonetheless delicious) mound of fish or meat, slathered with pickle relish, all atop *rugbrød* (rye bread) and *franskbrød* (wheat bread). Another specialty is *wiener brød* (a Danish pastry), an original far superior to anything billing itself "Danish pastry" elsewhere.

All Scandinavian countries have versions of the cold table, but Danes claim that theirs, *det store kolde bord,* is the original and the best. It's a celebration meal; the setting of the long table is a work of art—often with paper sculpture and silver platters—and the food itself is a minor miracle of design and decoration.

In hotels and restaurants the cold table is served at lunch only, though you will find a more limited version at hotel breakfasts—a good bet for budget travelers because you can eat as much as you like.

Liquid refreshment is top-notch. Denmark boasts more than 50 varieties of beer made by as many breweries; the best-known come from Carlsberg and Tuborg. Those who like harder stuff should try *snaps*, the famous aquavit traditionally drunk with cold food. Do as the locals do, and knock it back after eating some herring. The Danes have a saying about the herring-snaps combo: "The fish should be swimming."

Mealtimes The Danes start work early, which means they generally eat lunch at noon. Evening meals are also eaten early, but visitors can be certain of being able to eat and drink until 10 or 11.

Dress The Danes are a fairly casual lot, and few restaurants require a jacket and tie. Even in the most chic establishments, the tone is elegantly casual.

Ratings Meal prices vary little between town and country. While approximate gradings are given below, remember that careful ordering can get you a Moderate meal at a Very Expensive restaurant. Prices are per person and include a first course, main course, and dessert, plus taxes and tip, but not wine. Best bets are indicated by a star ★.

Category	All Areas
Very Expensive	over 400 kr.
Expensive	200–400 kr.

Moderate	120–200 kr.
Inexpensive	under 120 kr.

Lodging Accommodations in Denmark range from the spare and comfortable to the resplendent. Even inexpensive hotels offer simple designs in good materials and good, firm beds. Many Danes prefer a shower to a bath, so if you particularly want a tub, ask for it, but be prepared to pay more. Except in the case of rentals, breakfast and taxes are usually included in prices, but check when making a reservation.

Hotels Luxury hotels in the city or countryside offer rooms of a high standard, and in a manor-house hotel you may find yourself sleeping in a four-poster bed. Less expensive accommodations, however, are uniformly clean and comfortable.

Inns A cheaper and charming alternative to hotels are the old stagecoach kro inns scattered throughout Denmark. You can save money by contacting **Kro Ferie** (Vejlevej 16, 8700 Horsens, tel. 75/64–87–00) to invest in a book of Inn Checks, valid at 66 inns. Each check costs 375 kr. per person or 535 kr. per couple and includes one overnight stay in a double room with bath, breakfast included. Family checks, for three (635 kr.) and four (705 kr.) are also available.

Farm Vacations These are perhaps the best way to see how the Danes live and work. You stay on a farm and share meals with the family; you can even get out and help with the chores. There's a minimum stay of three nights; bed-and-breakfast is 160 kr., while half board runs 230. (Full board can be arranged.) Children under 4 get 75% off; 4–11 get 50%. Contact the **Horsens Tourist Office** (Søndergade 26, DK 8700 Horsens, Jutland, tel. 75/62–38–22; fax 75/62–61–51) for details.

Youth Hostels The 100 youth hostels in Denmark are open to everyone regardless of age. If you have an International Youth Hostels Association card (obtainable before you leave home), the average rate is 60 kr. Without the card, there's a surcharge of 22 kr. For more information, contact **Danmarks Vandrehjem** (Vesterbrogade 39, DK–1620 V, tel. 31/31–36–12).

Rentals Many Danes rent out their summer homes, and a stay in one of these is another good way to see the countryside on your own terms. A simple house with room for four will cost from 1,000 kr. per week. Contact the Danish Tourist Board for details.

Camping Denmark has over 500 approved campsites, with a rating system of one, two, or three stars. You need an International Camping Carnet or Danish Camping Pass (available at any campsite and valid for one year). For more details on camping and discounts for groups and families, contact **Campingrådet** (Hesseløgade 10, tel. 39/27–88–44).

Ratings Prices are for two people in a double room and include service and taxes and usually breakfast. Best bets are indicated by a star ★.

Category	Copenhagen	Other Areas
Very Expensive	over 1,100 kr.	over 800 kr.
Expensive	800–1,100 kr.	600–800 kr.

Moderate	670–800 kr.	450–600 kr.
Inexpensive	under 670 kr.	under 450 kr.

Tipping The egalitarian Danes do not expect to be tipped. The exception is hotel porters, who get around 5 kr. per bag; you should also leave 1 or 2 kr. for the use of a public toilet, if there is an attendant.

Copenhagen

Arriving and Departing

By Plane The main airport for both international and domestic flights is Copenhagen Airport, 10 kilometers (6 miles) outside of town.

Between the Airport and Downtown There is frequent bus service to the city; the airport bus to the central station leaves every 15 minutes, and the trip takes about 25 minutes. You pay the 27 kr. fare on the bus. Public buses cost 18 kr. and run as often but take twice as long. Bus No. 32 or No. 32H takes you to Rådhus Pladsen, the city-hall square. A taxi ride takes 15 minutes and costs about 120 kr.

By Train Copenhagen's central station is the hub of the train networks. Express trains leave hourly, on the hour, from 6 AM to 10 PM for principal towns in Fyn and Jutland. Find out more from **DSB Information** at the central station (tel. 33/14–17–01). You can make reservations at the central station (tel. 33/14–88–00) and most other stations and through travel agents. In Copenhagen, for those with Inter-Rail cards there is an Inter-Rail Center (open July–mid-Sept., 7 AM–midnight) at the central station that offers rest but little else. Public shower facilities at the main train station are open 5:30 AM–midnight and cost 15 kr.

Getting Around

By Bus and Suburban Train The best bet for visitors is the **Copenhagen Card,** affording unlimited travel on buses and suburban trains (S-trains), admission to some 40 museums and sights around Zealand, and a reduction on the ferry crossing to Sweden. Buy the card, which costs about 120 kr. (one day), 200 kr. (two days), or 250 kr. (three days), at tourist offices, hotels, or from travel agents.

Buses and suburban trains operate on the same ticket system and divide Copenhagen and environs into three zones. Tickets are validated on the time system: On the basic ticket, which costs 9 kr. for an hour, you can travel anywhere in the zone in which you started. You can buy a packet of 10 basic tickets for 80 kr. Get zone information from the 24-hour information service: tel. 36/45–45–45 for buses, 33/14–17–01 for S-trains. Buses and S-trains run from 5 AM (6 AM on Sundays) to 12:30 AM.

By Car Copenhagen is a city for walkers, not drivers. The charm of its pedestrian streets is paid for by a complicated one-way road system and difficult parking. Leave your car in the garage: Attractions are relatively close together, and public transportation is excellent.

By Taxi Taxis are not cheap, but all are metered. The base charge is 12 kr., plus 8–10 kr. per kilometer. A cab is available when it displays the sign Fri (Free); it can be hailed or picked up at a taxi stand, or tel. 31/35–35–35.

By Bicycle   More than half the 5 million Danes are said to ride bikes, which are popular with visitors as well. Bike rental costs 30–50 kr. a day, with a deposit of 100–200 kr. Contact **Danwheel-Rent-a-Bike** (Colbjørnsensgade 3, tel. 31/21–22–27) or **Urania Cykler** (Gammel Kongevej 1, tel. 31/21–80–88).

Important Addresses and Numbers

Tourist   The main tourist information office is **Danmarks Turistråd**
Information   (Danish Tourist Board) (Bernstoffsgade 1, DK–1577 V, Copenhagen, tel. 33/11–13–25). Located on the Tivoli grounds, it is open May, weekdays 9–6, Sat. 9–2, Sun. 9–1; June–Sept., daily 9–6; Oct.–Apr., weekdays 9–5, Sat. 9–noon, closed Sun. There are also offices at Elsinore, Hillerød, Køge, Roskilde, Gilleleje, Hundersted, and Tisvildeleje. Youth information in Copenhagen is available at **Huset** (Rådhusstraede 13, tel. 33/15–65–18).

Embassies   **U.S.** (Dag Hammarskjöldsallé 24, tel. 31/42–31–44). **Canada** (Kristen Benikowsgade 1, tel. 33/12–22–99). **U.K.** (Kastelsvej 40, tel. 35/26–46–00).

Emergencies   **Police, Fire, Ambulance** (tel. 000). **Doctor** (tel. 33/12–00–41. Fees payable in cash only; night fees around 400–500 kr.). **Dentist: Dental Emergency Service,** Tandlægevagten, 14, Oslo Plads, near Østerport station (no telephone; emergencies only; cash only). **Pharmacies:** The following are open 24 hours in central Copenhagen: **Steno Apotek** (Vesterbrogade 6C, tel. 33/14–82–66); **Sønderbro Apotek** (Amagerbrogade 158 [Amager area], tel. 31/58–01–40); **Glostrup Apotek** (Hovedvegen 101 [Glostrup area], tel. 43/96–00–20).

English-Language   English-language publications can be found at the central-sta-
Bookstores   tion newsstand and in most bookstores around town. **Boghallen** (Rådhus Pladsen 37) has a particularly good selection.

Travel Agencies   **American Express** (Amagertorv 18, tel. 33/12–23–01). **Spies** (Nyropsgade 41, tel. 33/32–15–00) arranges charter flights and accommodations all over Europe.

Guided Tours

Orientation Tours   Tours are a good way to get acquainted with Copenhagen. From May to September you can sail on the Øre Sound on board the *Isefjord,* Denmark's oldest schooner. The four-hour tours include lunch or dinner and leave from Amaliehavn (tel. 33/15–17–29). The "Harbor and Canal Tour" (by boat; May–mid-Sept., daily every ½-hour 10–5) leaves from Gammel Strand and the east side of Kongens Nytorv, while the following bus tours, conducted by **Copenhagen Excursion** (tel. 31/54–06–06), leave from the Lur Blower Column in the Rådhus Pladsen: "City Tour" (mid-May–mid-Oct., daily at 10; June 15–Aug., daily at 10, 12, 4); "Grand Tour of Copenhagen" (Nov.–Mar., Sun.–Fri. and Sat. at 11, 1:30; Apr.–Oct., daily at 11, 1:30, 3); "Royal Tour of Copenhagen" (June–mid-Sept., Tues., Thurs., and Sat. at 10); "City and Harbor Tour" (combined bus and boat; May–mid-Sept., daily at 9:30, 1, 3). Tickets are available aboard the bus and boat or from travel agencies.

Special-Interest Tours The "Carlsberg Brewery Tour," which includes a look into the draft-horse stalls, meets at the Elephant Gate (Ny Carlsbervej 140) on weekdays at 11 and 2 or by arrangement for groups (tel. 33/27–13–14). Tuborg Breweries also provides tours (Strandvejen 54, bus No. 6 or No. 21) weekdays at 10, 12:30, and 2:30 or by arrangement for groups (tel. 33/27–22–12). The "Royal Copenhagen Porcelain" tour (Smallegade 45, tel. 31/86–48–48) is given on weekdays at 9, 10, and 11.

Walking Tours The tourist board supplies maps and brochures and can recommend a walking tour. The "Guided Stroll" walking tour has English-speaking guides daily in July and August and on weekends from April to October (tel. 31/51–25–90).

Regional Tours The Danish Tourist Board has full details of excursions outside the city, including visits to castles (such as Hamlet's castle), the Viking Ship Museum, and Sweden.

Personal Guides The tourist information center can recommend multilingual guides for individual needs, while travel agents have details on hiring a limousine and guide.

Exploring Copenhagen

When Denmark ruled Norway and Sweden in the 15th century, Copenhagen was the capital of all three countries. Today it is still the liveliest Scandinavian capital, with about 1 million inhabitants. It's a city meant for walking, the first in Europe to recognize the value of pedestrian streets in fostering community spirit. As you stroll through the cobbled streets and squares, you'll find that Copenhagen combines the excitement and variety of big-city life with a small-town atmosphere. If there's such a thing as a cozy metropolis, you'll find it here.

Nor are you ever far from water, be it sea or canal. The city itself is built upon two main islands, Slotsholmen and Christianshavn, connected by drawbridges. Walk down Nyhavn Canal, an area formerly haunted by a fairly salty crew of sailors. Now it's gentrified, and the 18th-century houses lining it are filled with chic restaurants. You should linger, too, in the five main pedestrian streets known collectively as "Strøget," with shops, restaurants, cafés, and street musicians and vendors. In summer Copenhagen moves outside, and the best views of city life are from the sidewalk cafés in the shady squares.

Rådhus Pladsen and Slotsholmen *Numbers in the margin correspond to points of interest on the Copenhagen map.*

The best place to start a stroll is the Rådhus Pladsen (City Hall Square), the hub of Copenhagen's commercial district. The mock-Renaissance building dominating it is the **Københavns Rådhus** (city hall), completed in 1905. A statue of Copenhagen's 12th-century founder, Bishop Absalon, sits atop the main entrance. Inside you can see the first World Clock, an astrological timepiece invented and built by Jens Olsen and put in motion in 1955. If you're feeling energetic, take a guided tour up the 350-foot tower for a panoramic view. *Rådhus Pladsen, tel. 33/66–25–82. Open weekdays 10–3. Tours in English: weekdays at 3, Sat. at 10. Tower tours: Mon.–Sat. at noon; additional tours June–Sept. at 10, noon, 2. Admission: tour 20 kr., tower 10 kr.*

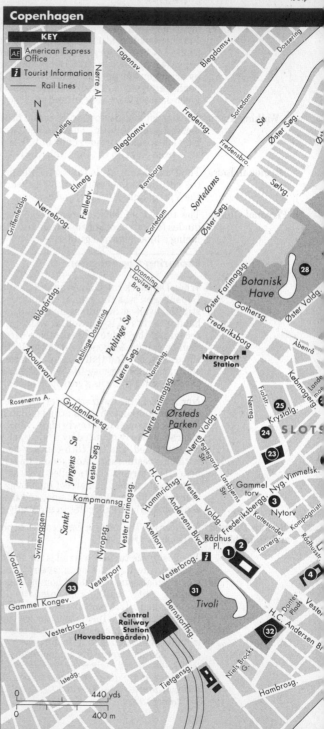

Copenhagen

KEY

AE American Express Office

i Tourist Information

— Rail Lines

2 On the right of Rådhus Pladsen is **LurblÆserne** (Lur Blower's Column), topped by two Vikings blowing an ancient trumpet called a *lur*. The artist took a good deal of artistic license—the lur dates from the Bronze Age, 1500 BC, while the Vikings lived a mere 1,000 years ago. The monument is a starting point for sightseeing tours of the city.

If you continue to the square's northeast corner and turn right, you will be in Frederiksberggade, the first of the five pedestri-
3 an streets that make up the **Strøget,** Copenhagen's shopping district. Walk past the cafés and trendy boutiques to the double square of **Gammel and Nytorv,** where, on April 16, golden ap-ples (really gilded metal balls) dance on the water jets in the fountain to celebrate the queen's birthday.

Turn down Rådhusstræde toward Frederiksholms Kanal, and continue to Nye Vestergade. Here you'll find the entrance to
4 the **Nationalmuseet** (National Museum), with extensive collec-tions that chronicle Danish cultural history to modern times and display Egyptian, Greek, and Roman antiquities. Viking enthusiasts will want to see the Runic stones in the Danish cul-tural history section. *Nye Vestergade 10, tel. 33/13–44–11. Ad-mission: 20 kr. adults, 15 kr. students and senior citizens, free for children under 16. Open Tues.–Sun. 10–5.*

Cross Frederiksholms Kanal to Castle Island, dominated by
5 the massive gray **Christiansborg Slot** (Christiansborg Castle). The complex, which contains the Folketinget (Parliament House) and the Royal Reception Chambers, is situated on the site of the city's first fortress, built by Bishop Absalon in 1167. While the castle that stands was being built at the turn of the century, the National Museum excavated the ruins beneath the site. *Christiansborg ruins, tel. 33/92–64–92. Admission: 12 kr. adults, 5 kr. children. Open May–Oct., daily 9:30–3:30; closed Nov.–Apr., Mon. and Sat. Folketinget, tel. 33/37–55–00. Admission free. Tours every hour on Sun., 10–4. Reception Rooms. Admission: 25 kr. adults, 10 kr. children. Open May–Oct., Tues.–Sun., English tours at 11, 1, and 3; Oct.–May, Tues.–Thurs., and Sun., English tours at 11 and 3.*

6 Just north of the castle, is **Thorvaldsens Museum.** The 19th-century Danish sculptor Bertel Thorvaldsen, buried at the cen-ter of the museum, was greatly influenced by the statues and reliefs of classical antiquity. In addition to his own works, there is a collection of paintings and drawings by other artists illus-trating the influence of Italy on Denmark's Golden Age artists. *Porthusgade 2, tel. 33/32–15–32. Admission free. Open Tues.–Sun. 10–5.*

7 Nearby, **Det Kongelige Bibliotek** (Royal Library) houses the country's largest collection of books, newspapers, and manu-scripts. Look for early records of the Viking journeys to Ameri-ca and Greenland and the statue of the philosopher Søren Kierkegaard in the garden. *Christians Brygge 8, tel. 33/93–01–11. Admission free. Open weekdays 9–7, Sat. 10–7.*

8 Close to the library is the **Teaterhistorisk Museet** (Theater His-tory Museum), in the Royal Court Theater of 1767. You can see extensive exhibits on theater and ballet history, then wander around the boxes, stage, and dressing rooms to see where it all happened. *Christianborg Ridebane 18, tel. 33/11–51–76. Ad-mission: 20 kr. adults, 10 kr. senior citizens and students, 5 kr. children. Open Wed. 2–4, Sun. noon–4.*

⑨ Across the street that bears its name is **Tøjhusmuseet** (Royal Armory), with impressive displays of uniforms, weapons, and armor in an arched hall 200 yards long. *Tøjhusgade 3, tel. 33/11–60–37. Admission: 20 kr. adults, 5 kr. children 6–17. Open Tues.–Sun. 10–4.*

⑩ A few steps from Tøjhuset is the old stock exchange, **Børsen,** believed to be the oldest still in use—although it functions only on special occasions. It was built by the 16th-century monarch King Christian IV, a scholar and warrior, and architect of much of the city. The king is said to have had a hand at twisting the tails of the four dragons that form the structure's distinctive green copper spire. With its steep roofs, tiny windows, and gables, the building is one of Copenhagen's treasures.

From Børsen, look east across the drawbridge (Knippelsbro) that connects Slotsholmen with Christianshavn, one of the old-**⑪** est parts of Copenhagen, to the green-and-gold spire of **Vor Frelsers Kirke** (Our Savior's Church). The Gothic structure was built in 1696. Local legend has it that the staircase encircling it was built curling the wrong way around, and that when its architect reached the top and saw what he had done, he jumped. Unfortunately, the delicate steeple is under repair (and scaffolding) until at least 1995. *Skt. Annægade, tel. 31/57–27–98. Admission free. Open Mar. 15–May, Mon.–Sat. 9–4:30, Sun. noon–3:30; June–Aug., Mon.–Sat. 9–4:30, Sun. noon–4:30; Sept.–Oct., Mon.–Sat. 9–3:30, Sun. noon–3:30. Nov.–Mar. 14, Mon.–Sat. 10–1:30, Sun. noon–1:30. Tower closed.*

Head back to Strøget, turning left along the Amagertov section. Toward the end and to the right (5 Niels Hemmingsens **⑫** Gad) is the 18th-century **Helligånds Kirken** (Church of the Holy Ghost). The choir contains a marble font by the sculptor Thorvaldsen.

In Østergade, the easternmost of the streets that make up **⑬** Strøget, you cannot miss the green spire of **Nikolaj Kirke** (Nikolaj Church). The building that currently stands was built in the 20th century; the previous structure, which dated to the 13th century, was destroyed by fire in 1728. Today the church's role is secular—it's an art gallery and an exhibition center.

Time Out   **Café Nikolaj,** inside the old Nikolaj Kirke, is a good place to stop for a Danish pastry or a light meal. *Open Mon.–Sat. noon–5. Inexpensive.*

While Strøget is famous as a shopping area, and elegant stores abound, it's also where Copenhagen comes to stroll. Outside the posh displays of the fur and porcelain shops, the sidewalks have the festive aura of a street fair.

Royal Palace Area   **Kongens Nytorv** (the King's New Market) is the square mark-**⑭** ing the end of Strøget. The **Kongelige Teater** (Danish Royal Theater), home of Danish opera and ballet as well as theater, sits on the south side. The Danish Royal Ballet remains one of the world's great companies, with a repertoire ranging from classical to modern. On the western side of the square you'll see the stately facade of the hotel D'Angleterre, the grande dame of Copenhagen hotels. When former president Ronald Reagan visited Denmark, he couldn't stay there for security reasons but asked for a tour of the place just the same.

The street leading southeast from Kongens Nytorv is **Nyhavn**. The recently gentrified canal was a longtime haunt of sailors. Now restaurants and boutiques outnumber the tattoo shops, but on hot summer nights the area still gets rowdy, with Scandinavians reveling amid a fleet of old-time sailing ships and well-preserved 18th-century buildings. Hans Christian Andersen lived at both nos. 18 and 20. Nearer the harbor are old shipping warehouses, including two—Nyhavn 71 and the Admiral—that have been converted into comfortable hotels.

Turn left at the end of Nyhavn to see the harbor front and then make an immediate left onto Sankt Annæ Plads. Take the third
⑮ right onto Amaliegade. Continue straight ahead for **Amalienborg,** the principal royal residence since 1784. When the royal family is in residence during the fall and winter, the Royal Guard and band march through the city at noon to change the palace guard. The palace interior is closed to the public.

Rest a moment on the palace's harbor side, amid the trees and
⑯ fountains of **Amaliehavn.** Across the square, it's just a step to
⑰ Bredgade and the **Marmorkirken** (Marble Church), a 19th-century Baroque church with a dome that looks several sizes too large for the building beneath it.

⑱ Bredgade is also home to the exotic onion domes of the **Russiske Ortodoks Kirke** (Russian Orthodox Church). Farther on is the
⑲ **Kundindustrimuseet** (Museum of Decorative Art), with a large selection of European and Oriental handicrafts, as well as ceramics, silver, and tapestries. *Bredgade 68, tel. 33/14–94–52. Admission: 30 kr. adults, 20 kr. students and senior citizens, children under 16 free. Permanent exhibition open Tues.–Sun. 1–4; special exhibitions open Tues.–Sat. 10–4, Sun. 1–4.*

A little farther, turn right onto Esplanaden and you'll come to
⑳ **Frihedsmuseet** (Liberty Museum), situated in Churchill Parken. It gives an evocative picture of the heroic Danish Resistance movement during World War II, which managed to save 7,000 Jews from the Nazis by hiding them in homes and hospitals, then smuggling them across to Sweden. *Esplanaden, tel. 33/13–77–14. Admission free. Open Sept. 16– April, Tues.–Sat. 11–3, Sun. 11–4; May–Sept. 15, Tues.–Sat. 10–4, Sun. 10–5.*

At the park's entrance stands the English church, St. Alban's,
㉑ and, in the center, the **Kastellet** (Citadel), with two rings of moats. This was the city's main fortress in the 18th century, but, in a grim reversal during World War II, the Germans used it as the headquarters of their occupation of Denmark. *Admission free. Open 6 AM to sunset.*

Continue on to the Langelinie, which on Sunday is thronged
㉒ with promenading Danes, and at last to **Den Lille Havrue** (The Little Mermaid), the 1913 statue commemorating Hans Christian Andersen's lovelorn creation, and the subject of hundreds of travel posters.

Around the Strøget From Langelinie, take the train or bus from Østerport station back to the center. Walk north from the Strøget on Nørregade
㉓ until you reach **Vor Frue Kirke** (The Church of Our Lady), Copenhagen's cathedral since 1924. The site itself has been a place of worship since the 13th century, when Bishop Absalon built a chapel here. The spare neoclassical facade is a 19th-century revamp, that repaired the damage incurred during

Nelson's famous bombing of the city in 1801. Inside you can see Thorvaldsen's marble sculptures of Christ and the Apostles. *Nørregade, Frue Plads, tel. 33/15-10-78. Open Mon.-Sat. 8-5, Sun. 9-4. Closed during mass.*

㉔ Head north up Fjolstraede until you come to the main **Københavns Universitet** (Cophenhagen University), built in the 19th century on the site of the medieval bishops' palace. Past the university, turn right onto Krystalgade. On the left is the **㉕** **Københavns Synaggoe** (Copenhagen Synagogue), designed by the famous contemporary architect Gustav Friedrich Hetsch. Hetsch drew on the Doric and Egyptian styles to create the arklike structure.

㉖ Just across Købmagergade is the **Runde tårn,** a round tower built as an observatory in 1642 by Christian IV. It is said that Peter the Great of Russia drove a horse and carriage up the 600 feet of the inner staircase. You'll have to walk, but the view is worth it. *Købmagergade, tel. 33/93-66-60. Admission: 12 kr. adults, 5 kr. children. Open Dec.-May and Sept.-Oct., Mon.-Sat. 10-5, Sun. noon-4; June-Aug. 10-8. Observatory and telescope open, with astronomer on hand to answer questions, mid-Oct.-mid-Mar., Tues.-Wed. 7-10.*

Turn right at Runde Tårn onto Landemærket, then left onto Åbenrå. If your appetite for museums is not yet sated, turn right out of Åbenrå until you reach Gothersgade, where anoth-**㉗** er right, onto Øster Voldgade, will bring you to **Rosenborg Slot.** This Renaissance castle—built by Renaissance man Christian IV—houses the Crown Jewels, as well as a collection of costumes and royal memorabilia. Don't miss Christian IV's pearl-studded saddle. *Øster Voldgade 4A, tel. 33/15-32-86. Admission: 35 kr. adults, 5 kr. children. Open Apr.-May, daily 11-3; June-Aug., daily 10-4; Sept.-Oct., daily 11-3; Nov.-Mar., Tues., Fri., and Sun. 11-3.*

The palace is surrounded by gardens, and just across Øster **㉘** Voldgade is **Botanisk Have,** Copenhagen's 25 acres of botanical gardens, with a rather spectacular Palm House containing tropical and subtropical plants. There's also an observatory and a geological museum. *Admission free. Open May-Aug., daily 8:30-6; Sept.-Apr., daily 8:30-4. Palm House open daily 10-3.*

㉙ Leave the gardens through the north exit to get to the **Statens Museum for Kunst** (National Art Gallery), where the collection ranges from modern Danish art to works by Rubens, Dürer, and the Impressionists. Particularly fine are the museum's 20 Matisses. *Sølvgade 48-50, tel. 33/91-21-26. Admission: 20 kr. adults, children under 16 free. Open Tues.-Sun. 10-4:30.*

Time Out   The subterranean **cafeteria** in the museum makes an excellent place to stop for lunch or coffee. Art posters deck the walls, and a cheerful staff serves hearty lunches. *Inexpensive.*

㉚ A nearby building houses **Den Hirschsprungske Samling** (the Hirschsprung Collection) of 19th-century Danish art. The cozy museum features works from the Golden Age, in particular those by a group of late-19th-century painters called the Skagen school. *Stockholmsgade 20, tel. 31/42-03-36. Admission: 20 kr. adults, 10 kr. students and senior citizens, children under 16 free. Open Wed.-Sat. 1-4, Sun. 11-4.*

From Stockholmsgade, turn right onto Sølvgade and then left onto Øster Søgade, just before the bridge. Continue along the canal (the street name will change from Øster Søgade to Nørre Søgade to Vester Søgade) until you reach the head of the harbor. Walk straight ahead and turn left onto Vesterbrogade.

㉛ On the right lies Copenhagen's best-known attraction, **Tivoli.** In the 1840s, the Danish architect Georg Carstensen persuaded King Christian VIII that an amusement park was the perfect opiate of the masses, preaching that "when people amuse themselves, they forget politics." In the comparatively short season, from May to September, about 4 million people come through the gates. Tivoli is more sophisticated than a mere funfair: It boasts a pantomime theater and open-air stage; elegant restaurants; and numerous classical, jazz, and rock concerts. On weekends there are elaborate fireworks displays and maneuvers by the Tivoli Guard, a youth version of the Queen's Royal Guard. Try to see Tivoli at least once by night, when the trees are illuminated along with the Chinese Pagoda and the main fountain. *Admission: 35 kr. adults, 20 kr. children. Open mid-Apr.–mid-Sept., daily 10 AM–midnight.*

㉜ At the southern end of the gardens, on Hans Christian Andersens Boulevard, is the **Ny Carlsberg Glyptotek** (New Carlsberg Picture Hall). This elaborate neoclassical building houses a collection of works by Gauguin and Degas and other Impressionists, as well as Egyptian, Greek, Roman, and French sculpture. *Dantes Plads 7, tel. 33/91–10–65. Admission: 15 kr. adults, children free; adults free on Wed. and Sun. Open Sept.–Apr., Tues.–Sat. noon–3, Sun. 10–4; May–Aug., Tues.–Sun. 10–4.*

㉝ Tucked between St. Jorgens Lake and the main arteries of Vesterbrogade and Gammel Kongevej is the new **Tycho Brahe Planetarium.** The modern cylindrical building is filled with astronomy exhibitions and an Omnimax Theater, which takes visitors on a visual journey up through space and down under the seas. *Gammel Kongevej 10, tel. 33/12–12–24. Admission: 65 kr. for exhibition and theater, 6–10 PM; exhibition only, 15 kr. Reservations advised for theater. (According to planetarium officials, the movie is not suitable for children under 7.) Open daily 10:30–9.*

Excursions from Copenhagen

Helsingør–
Kronborg Castle
Shakespeare immortalized the town and castle when he chose Kronborg Castle as the setting for *Hamlet*. Completed in 1585, the gabled and turreted structure is about 600 years younger than the fortress we imagine from the setting of Shakespeare's tragedy. Well worth seeing is the 200-foot-long dining hall, the luxurious chapel, and the royal chambers. The ramparts and 12-foot walls are a reminder of the castle's role as coastal bulwark—Sweden is only a few miles away. The town of Helsingør—about 29 miles north of Copenhagen—has a number of picturesque streets with 16th-century houses. There is frequent train service to Helsingør station. *Helsingør, tel. 49/21–30–78. Admission: 20 kr. adults, 10 kr. children. Open Easter and May–Sept., daily 10:30–5; Oct. and Apr., Tues.–Sat. 11–4; Nov.–Mar., Tues.–Sun. 11–3.*

Louisiana A world-class modern art collection is housed in a spectacular building on the "Danish Riviera," the North Zealand coast.

Even those who can't tell a Rauschenberg from a Rembrandt should make the 35-kilometer (22-mile) trip to see the setting: It's an elegant, rambling structure set in a large park with views of the sound, and, on a clear day, Sweden.

Louisiana is well worth the half-hour train ride from Copenhagen to Humlebæk. The museum is a 10-minute walk from the station. It's also accessible by the E4 highway and the more scenic coastal road, Strandvejen. *Gammel Strandvej 13, Humlebæk, tel. 42/19–07–19. Admission: 45 kr. adults, children free. Open Mon., Tues., Thurs., and Fri. 10–5, Wed. 10–10, weekends 10–6.*

Roskilde   History buffs should head 30 kilometers (19 miles) west of Copenhagen to the bustling market town of **Roskilde**. A key administrative center during Viking times, it remained one of the largest towns in northern Europe through the Middle Ages. Its population has dwindled, but the legacy of its 1,000-year history lives on in the spectacular cathedral. Built on the site of Denmark's first church, the **Domkirke** (cathedral) has been the burial place of Danish royalty since the 15th century. *Domkirkeplasden, Roskilde. Admission: 5 kr. adults, 2 kr. children. Open Apr.–Sept., weekdays 9–4:45, Oct.–Mar., weekdays 10–2:45; May–Aug., Sun. 12:30–4:45; Sept.–Apr., Sun. 12:30–3:45. For varying Sat. hrs, tel. 42/35–27–00.*

A 10-minute walk south and through the park takes you to the water and to the **Viking Ship Museum**. Inside are five Viking ships, discovered at the bottom of the Roskilde Fjord in 1962. Detailed placards in English chronicle Viking history. There are also English-language films on the excavation and reconstruction. *Strandengen, Roskilde, tel. 42/35–65–55. Admission: 28 kr. adults, 14 kr. children. Open Apr.–Oct., daily 9–5; Nov.–Mar., daily 10–4.*

Rungstedlund   About halfway between Copenhagen and Helsingør is **Rungstedlund,** the former manor of Karen Blixen. The author of *Out of Africa* and several accounts of aristocratic Danish life, Blixen wrote under the pen name Isak Dinesen. The manor, where she lived as a child and to which she returned in 1931, recently opened as a museum, and includes manuscripts, as well as photographs and memorabilia documenting her years in Africa and Denmark. A half-hour train ride from Copenhagen, the estate is a 10-minute walk from Rungsted station. *Rungsted Strandvej 111, Rungsted Kyst, tel. 42/57–10–57. Admission: 30 kr. adults, children free. Open May–Sept., daily 10–5; Oct.–Apr., Wed.–Fri. 1–4, Sat.–Sun. 11–4.*

Shopping

Gift Ideas   While Copenhagen is a mecca for shoppers in search of impeccable designs and top-notch quality, bargains are elusive. Several ideas for inexpensive gifts include simple table decorations—a porcelain candle holder or ashtray or the long-lasting candles, often handmade, for which Scandinavia is famous. Denmark also produces tasteful reproductions of Viking ornaments and jewelry, in bronze as well as silver and gold.

Specialty Shops   Synonymous with shopping are Strøget's pedestrian streets. For glass, try **Holmegaard** at Østergade. Just off the street is Pistolstræde, a typical old courtyard that's been lovingly restored and filled with intriguing boutiques. **Illums** and

Magasin offer department-store variety, and **Illums Bolighus** offers home furnishings in near-gallery surroundings. There are such specialists as **Royal Copenhagen Porcelain,** which has a small museum attached, as does **Georg Jensen,** one of Denmark's most famous silversmiths.

Off the eastern end of Strøget on Ny Østergade, the **Pewter Center** has a large pewterware collection, and on Fridjof Nansens Plads there's another pewter designer, **Royal Selangor,** founded in 1885. Back along Strøget, **Birger Christensen** will offer you a glass of sherry while you look at the furs, unless you decide to take your patronage to their competition, **A. C. Bang.** FONA is the place to buy Bang and Olufsen stereo systems, so renowned that they are in the permanent design collection of New York's Museum of Modern Art.

Dining

Food remains one of the great pleasures of a stay in Copenhagen, a city with over 2,000 restaurants. Traditional Danish fare spans all the price categories: You can order a light lunch of the traditional smørrebrød, snack from a *store kolde bord* (cold buffet), or dine out on lobster and Limfjord oysters. Those who are strapped for cash can enjoy fast food Danish style, in the form of *pølser* (hot dogs) sold from trucks on the street. Team any of this with some pastry from a bakery (look for them under the sign of the upside-down gold pretzel), and you've got yourself a meal on the go.

For details and price-category definitions, *see* Dining in Staying in Denmark.

Very Expensive **Kong Hans Kaelder.** Chef Daniel Letz's French-inspired cooking is superb, while the setting is subterranean and mysterious, with whitewashed arching ceilings, candles, and wooden carvings. *Vingårdsstræde 6, tel. 33/11–68–68. Reservations advised. AE, DC, MC, V. Dinner only. Closed Sun. and mid-July–mid-Aug.*

Pakhuskælderen. Cozily situated in the basement of the Nyhavn 71 hotel, with old Pomeranian beams along the ceilings, this is principally a grill house, serving fish as well as meat dishes, both French and Danish style. Look for store kolde bord at lunchtime. *Nyhavn 71, tel. 33/11–85–85. Reservations required. AE, DC, MC, V.*

★ **Skt. Gertrude's Kloster.** Chef Lars Torndahl prepares international cuisine in this 700-year-old cloister. You feast on fish and meat specialties by the light of 1,200 candles, among vaulted spiral stairways and ecclesiastical antiques. *Hauser Plads 32, tel. 33/14–66–30. Reservations required. AE, DC, MC, V. Dinner only.*

Expensive **Els.** When it opened in 1853, the intimate Els was the place to
★ be seen before the theater, and the painted muses on the walls still watch diners rush to make an eight o'clock curtain. The antique wooden columns and furniture complement Chef Kim Doee's nouvelle Danish/French menu. The menu changes daily and incorporates game, fish, and market-fresh produce. *Store Strandstæde 3, tel. 33/14–13–41. Reservations advised. AE, DC, MC, V. Closed Dec. 24–25 and 31, Jan. 1.*

La Brasserie. This is the place where Copenhagen's see-and-be-seen set goes to eat. Diners enjoy French-inspired food in charming bistro surroundings, under a giant illuminated clock suspended from the ceiling. *Hotel D'Angleterre, Kongens Nytorv 34, tel. 33/32–01–22. Reservations advised. AE, DC, MC, V. Closed Sun.*

L'Alsace. The paintings of Danish surrealist Wilhelm Freddie deck bright white walls at L'Alsace, and the food matches the understated elegance of the surroundings. Talented chef Franz Stockhammer's French repertoire includes a delicious rendition of quail, as well as some superb fresh-fruit tarts and cakes for dessert. Ask for a seat with a view of the old courtyard on Pistolstraede. *Ny Østergade 9, tel. 33/14–57–43. Reservations advised. AE, DC, MC, V. Closed Sun.*

Moderate   **Copenhagen Corner.** Diners get a great view of the Rådhus
★   Pladsen here, and terrific smørrebrød besides. Plants hang from the ceiling; waiters hustle platters of herring, steak, and other Danish/French dishes; and businessmen clink glasses. In summer you can eat outside. *Rådhus Pladsen, tel. 33/91–45–45. Reservations advised. AE, DC, MC, V. Closed Dec. 24.*

El Meson. Ceiling-hung pottery, knowledgeable waiters, and a top-notch menu make this Copenhagen's best Spanish restaurant. Choose carefully for a moderately priced meal, which might include beef spiced with spearmint, lamb with a honey sauce, or paella valenciano for two. *Hauser Plads 12 (behind library), tel. 33/11–91–31. Reservations advised. AE, DC, MC, V. Dinner only; closed Sun.*

Havfruen. A life-size wooden mermaid swings langorously from the ceiling in this snug fish restaurant in Nyhavn. Copenhagen natives love the maritime-bistro ambience and the French-inspired fish specialties. *Nyhavn 39, tel. 33/11–11–38. Reservations advised. DC, MC, V. Closed Sun.*

★   **Ida Davidsen.** A Copenhagen institution, this world-renowned lunch place has become synonymous with smørrebrød. A buffet displays heartbreakingly beautiful sandwiches, piled high with caviar, salmon, smoked duck, and other elegant ingredients. *Skt. Kongensgade 70, tel. 33/91–36–55. Reservations advised. DC, MC, V. Lunch only. Closed weekends and July.*

Peder Oxe. In an 18th-century square in the old center of town, the Peder Oxe is classically elegant, with whitewash walls, an open fireplace, and crisp damask tablecloths. It's usually crowded with diners from every walk of life. *Gråbrødertorv 11, tel. 33/11–00–77. Reservations accepted. DC, MC, V.*

Inexpensive   **Café Asbæk.** Attached to a modern art gallery, this little establishment makes creative use of fresh ingredients. The menu changes every day, while the art on the walls changes with every new exhibition. *Ny Adelgade 8, tel. 33/12–24–16. Reservations accepted. AE, DC, MC, V.*

Green's. A vegetarian buffet by day and a restaurant by night, Green's serves healthy food with much emphasis on grains, natural sweeteners, and fresh fruit and vegetables. It's frequented by chic bohemians who welcome the classical music and friendly service of the youthful staff. *Grønnegade 12–14, tel. 33/15–16–90. Reservations accepted. MC, V. Closed Sun.*

Krasnapolsky. It's near the university, and there's a brooding youth at every table. The food is light and inventive—market-fresh produce is used religiously. Not as healthy as the quiches and sandwiches, but equally delicious, are the cakes and tarts, made in-house. *Vestergade 10, tel. 33/32–88–00. Reservations accepted. No credit cards.*

Victor. This French-style corner café offers great people-watching and bistro fare. It's best during weekend lunches, when young and old gather for specialties like rib roast, homemade pâté, smoked salmon, and cheese platters. The menu changes—and becomes pricier—after 6. *Ny Østergade 8, tel. 33/13–36–13. Reservations advised. AE, DC, MC, V.*

Lodging

Copenhagen is well served by a wide range of hotels, and you can expect your accommodations to be clean, comfortable, and well run. Most Danish hotels include a substantial breakfast in the room rate, but this isn't always the case with foreign chains. In summer reservations are always recommended, but if you should arrive without one, try the booking service at the *kiosk* (Rooms Service booth) in the central station. This service will also locate rooms in private homes, with rates starting at about 140 kr. for a single. Young travelers should head for "Use It" (Huset) at Rådhusstræde 13 (tel. 33/15–65–18); after hours, they can check the bulletin board outside for suggestions.

For details and price-category definitions, *see* Lodging in Staying in Denmark.

Very Expensive **D'Angleterre.** Clint Eastwood and Bruce Springsteen stay
★ here, as do NATO generals and various heads of state. Built in 1755, the place has undergone several renovations, but it retains an Old World, old-money aura. The rooms are done in pinks and blues, with overstuffed chairs and antique escritoires and armoires. There's a liberal use of brass, mahogany, and marble in the bathrooms. *Kongens Nytorv 34, tel. 33/12–00–95, fax 33/12–11–18. 130 rooms with bath. Facilities: 2 restaurants, bar, barber, beauty salon. AE, DC, MC, V.*

Nyhavn 71. This cozy hotel started life in 1804 as a humble harbor warehouse, though its subsequent metamorphosis has won several design awards. Ask for a room overlooking the harbor—the quaint, porthole-style windows add to the charm. *Nyhavn 71, tel. 33/11–85–85, fax 33/93–15–85. 82 rooms with bath. Facilities: restaurant, bar. AE, DC, MC, V.*

SAS Scandinavia. A modern, cloud-scraping tower, the Scandinavia is the city's tallest building. It's set midway between the airport and downtown, facing the old city moats. The prevalent atmosphere is of efficiency and functionality, tempered with expensive plush. *Amager Blvd. 70, tel. 33/11–23–24, fax 31/57–01–93. 542 rooms with bath. Facilities: casino, sauna, pool, restaurant, bar, coffee shop. AE, DC, MC, V.*

Expensive **Neptun.** Renovated and expanded, the centrally situated Neptun has been in business for nearly 150 years and shows no signs of flagging. Guest rooms are decorated with blond wood and are usually reserved ahead by American visitors. *Skt. Annæ Plads 18, tel. 33/13–89–00, fax 33/14–12–50. 137 rooms, 10 apartments, all with bath. Facilities: restaurant, café, conference rooms. AE, DC, MC, V. Closed Dec. 24–Jan. 2.*

★ **Savoy.** Tucked behind clothing stores on a busy shopping street, the Savoy is a hidden treasure, an oasis of peace and fin-de-siècle charm. The recently renovated rooms are decorated in cool blues and light woods, with Scandinavian-designed furniture and marble bathrooms. *Vesterbrogade 34, tel. 31/31–40–73, fax 31/31–31–37. 65 rooms with bath. Facilities: restaurant. AE, DC, MC, V.*

Webers. Webers is a modern hotel housed in a century-old building. Decorators have made liberal use of pastel tones and understated prints. Light sleepers should try for a room at the back, preferably overlooking the courtyard and its fountain. *Vesterbrogade 11b, tel. 31/31–14–32, fax 31/31–14–41. 103 rooms with bath. Facilities: restaurant (breakfast only), lounge, bar, solarium. AE, DC, MC, V.*

Moderate **Ascot.** A charming old building in the city's downtown area, the Ascot features a classically columned entrance and an excellent breakfast buffet. The rooms have colorful geometric-patterned bedspreads and cozy bathrooms. Many have been recently remodeled; a few have kitchenettes. *Studiestræde 61, tel. 33/12–60–00, fax 33/14–60–40. 120 rooms, 16 apartments, all with bath. Facilities: conference rooms, restaurant (breakfast only), bar. AE, DC, MC, V.*

Cab-Inn Copenhagen. Copenhagen's answer to Japanese-style hotel minirooms is more cozy than futuristic, with shiplike "berths" brightly decorated in purple and blue. All offer standard hotel furnishings, including private shower and small wall-hung desks with chairs. *Danasvej 32, tel. 31/21–04–00, fax 31/21–74–09. 86 rooms with shower. Facilities: café, gym. (Also a 200-room location at Vodroffsvej 55, tel. 35/36–11–11, fax 35/36–11–14.) AE, DC, MC, V.*

Copenhagen Admiral. A converted 18th-century granary, the Admiral has a massive and imposing exterior. Inside, sturdy wooden beams harmonize with an ultramodern decor. A few duplex suites are in the Expensive category. *Toldbodgade 24–28, tel. 33/11–82–82, fax 33/32–55–42. 365 rooms with bath. Facilities: restaurant, bar, café, shop, sauna. AE, MC, V.*

Triton. Streamlined and modern, the Triton has a cosmopolitan clientele and a central location. The large rooms, in blond wood and warm tones, are equipped with every modern convenience, and many of the bathrooms have been recently updated. The buffet breakfast is exceptionally generous. *Helgolandsgade 7–11, tel. 31/31–32–66, fax 31/31–69–70. 123 rooms with bath. Facilities: restaurant (breakfast only), bar. AE, DC, MC, V.*

Inexpensive **Skovshoved.** A charming hotel about 8 kilometers (5 miles) from the center of town, the Skovshoved has as neighbors a few old fishing cottages beside the yacht harbor. Licensed since 1660, it has retained its Old World charm, though it is fully modernized. Individual rooms vary from spacious ones overlooking the sea to smaller rooms overlooking the courtyard. The restaurant provides gourmet dishes but ranks in the Expensive category. *Strandvejen 267, Charlottenlund, tel. 31/64–00–28, fax 31/64–06–72. 20 rooms with bath. Facilities: conference room. AE, DC, MC, V.*

Viking. A comfortable, century-old former mansion close to Amalienborg Castle, Nyhavn, and the Little Mermaid, the Viking is convenient to most sights and public transportation. The rooms are surprisingly spacious. *Bredgade 65, tel. 33/12–45–50, fax 33/12–46–18. 90 rooms, 19 with bath. Facilities: restaurant (breakfast only). AE, DC, MC, V.*

The Arts

Copenhagen This Week has good information on musical and theatrical events, as well as on special events and exhibitions. Concert and festival information is available from the **Dansk Musik Information Center (DMIC,** Vimmelskaftet 48, tel. 33/11–20–66). Copenhagen's main theater and concert season runs from September through May, and tickets can be obtained either directly from theaters and concert halls or from ticket agencies; ask your hotel concierge for advice.

Music   Tivoli Concert Hall (Vesterbrogade 3, tel. 33/15–10–12), home of the Zealand Symphony Orchestra, offers more than 150 concerts (many free of charge) each summer, featuring a host of Danish and foreign soloists, conductors, and orchestras.

Theater, Opera, and Ballet   The Royal Theater (Kongens Nytorv, tel. 33/14–10–02) regularly holds theater, ballet, and opera performances. For English-language theater, attend a performance at the Mermaid Theater (27 Skt. Peder Stræde, tel. 33/11–43–03).

Film   Copenhagen natives are avid movie buffs, and since the Danes rarely dub films or television imports, you can often see original American and British movies and TV shows.

Nightlife

Many of the city's restaurants, cafés, bars, and clubs stay open after midnight, some as late as 5 AM. Copenhagen is famous for jazz, but you'll find night spots catering to musical tastes ranging from bop to ballroom music. Younger tourists should make for the Minefield, the district around the Nikolaj Kirke, which has scores of trendy discos and dance spots, with admission only the price of a beer. Privé (Ny Østergade 14) and U-Matic (Vestergade 10) are particularly popular with the young set.

A few streets behind the railway station is Copenhagen's redlight district, where sex shops share space with grocers. While the area is fairly well lighted and lively, women may feel uncomfortable going there alone at night.

Nightclubs   Some of the most exclusive nightclubs are in the biggest hotels: Fellini's in the SAS Royal (Hammerichsgade 1, tel. 33/14–14–12).

Jazz   Copenhagen has a worldwide reputation for sophisticated jazz clubs. These are a few of the best: De Tre Musketerer (Nikolaj Plads 25); Jazzhus Slukefter (Tivoli); La Fontaine (Kompagnistræde 11); and Kridhuset (Nørregade 1).

Fyn and the Central Islands

It was Hans Christian Andersen, the region's most famous native, who dubbed Fyn (Funen) "The Garden of Denmark." Part orchard, part farmland, Fyn is sandwiched between Zealand and Jylland, and with its tidy, rolling landscape, seaside towns, manor houses, and castles, it is one of Denmark's loveliest islands. Its capital is 1,000-year-old Odense in the north, one of Denmark's best-known cities and the birthplace of Hans Christian Andersen. It has two museums detailing his life and works. In a country crowded with castles, Fyn has two of the best-preserved ones: the 12th-century castle Nyborg Slot, in the east, and the famed 16th-century Egeskov Slot, near Svendborg, in the south. From Svendborg it's easy to hop on a ferry and visit some of the smaller islands, such as Tåsinge, Langeland, and Ærø, whose main town, Ærøskøbing, with its twisting streets and half-timbered houses, seems caught in a time warp. The lo-

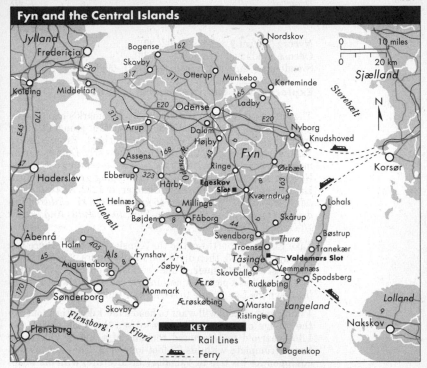

Fyn and the Central Islands

KEY
— Rail Lines
- - - Ferry

cal people speak with a slightly singsong accent, and claim it is the tongue spoken by angels on Sundays!

Getting Around

The best starting point is Nyborg on Fyn's east coast, just across the Store Bælt (Great Belt) from Korsør on Zealand. From Nyborg, the easiest way to travel is by car, though public transportation is good. (Get details of car rentals from local tourist offices.) Distances on Fyn and its islands are short, but there is much to see and you can easily spend two or three days here. The choice is to circle the islands from Nyborg or to base yourself in Odense or Svendborg and make excursions. Whichever you choose, you can use the itinerary given below.

Guided Tours

There are few organized tours of any area of Denmark outside Copenhagen. The Fyn town of Odense has a two-hour tour that operates Monday through Saturday during July and August. Expect to see anything and everything to do with native son Hans Christian Andersen.

There's also a day trip to Odense from Copenhagen every Sunday from mid-May to mid-September. Lasting about 11 hours, the trip includes stops at several picturesque villages and a lightning visit to Egeskov Slot. Departure is at 8:30 AM from Copenhagen's city-hall square.

Tourist Information

Nyborg (Torvet 9, tel. 65/31–02–80).
Odense (Rådhuset, tel. 66/12–75–20).
Svendborg (Centrumpladsen, tel. 62/21–09–80).

Exploring Fyn and the Central Islands

The 13th-century town of **Nyborg** was Denmark's capital during the Middle Ages, as well as an important stop on a major trading route between Zealand and Jutland. From 1200 to 1413, Nyborg housed the Danehof, the early Danish parliament. Nyborg's major landmark is its 12th-century castle, the **Nyborg Slot.** It was here that Erik Glipping granted the first Danish constitution, the Great Charter, in 1282. *Slotspladsen, tel. 65/31–02–07. Admission: 15 kr. adults, 8 kr. children under 16. Open Mar.–June, Tues.–Sun. 10–3; July–Aug., daily 10–5; Sept.–Oct., Tues.–Sun. 10–3.*

Take Route 160 northwest to the Avnslev junction, where you pick up Route 165, then drive the 15 kilometers (9 miles) along the coast to **Kerteminde,** Funen's most important fishing village, as well as a picturesque summer resort. It's worth strolling down the Langegade to see its half-timbered houses.

Viking enthusiasts will want to head a few kilometers south to the village of **Ladby.** Stop here to see the **Ladbyskibet,** the 1,100-year-old underground remains of a Viking chieftain's burial, complete with his 72-foot-long ship. The warrior was equipped for his trip to Valhalla (the afterlife) with his weapons, 4 hunting dogs, and 11 horses. *Vikingsvej 123, tel. 65/32–16–67. Admission: 15 kr. adults, 10 kr. students and senior citizens, children under 16 free. Open May–Sept., Tues.–Sun. 10–6; Oct.–Apr., Tues.–Sun. 10–3.*

Twenty kilometers (12 miles) southwest on Route 165 lies **Odense,** Denmark's third-largest city. Plan on spending at least one night here; in addition to its museums and pleasant pedestrian streets, Odense gives a good feel for a provincial capital.

If you can't take quaintness, don't go to the **H. C. Andersens Hus** (Hans Christian Andersen Museum). The surrounding area has been carefully preserved, with cobbled pedestrian streets and low houses with lace curtains. Inside, exhibits use photos, diaries, drawings, and letters to convey a sense of the man and the time in which he lived. Attached to the museum is an extensive library with Andersen's works in more than 100 languages, where you can listen to fairy tales on tape. *Hans Jensenstræde 37–45, tel. 66/13–13–72. Admission: 20 kr. adults, 10 kr. children under 14. Open Apr., May, daily 10–5; June–Aug., daily 9–6; Sept., Mar., daily 10–3.*

Nearby is the **Carl Nielsen Museum,** a modern structure with multimedia exhibits on Denmark's most famous composer (1865–1931) and his wife, the sculptress Anne Marie Carl-Nielsen. *Claus BergsGade 11, tel. 66/13–13–72, ext. 4671. Admission: 15 kr. adults, 5 kr. children. Open daily 10–4.*

Montegården, Odense's museum of cultural and urban history fills four houses built from the Renaissance to the 18th century, all grouped around a shady cobbled courtyard. The innovative exhibits inside feature dioramas, an extensive coin collection, clothed dummies, toys, and tableaux. *Overgade 48–50. Admission: 15 kr. adults, 5 kr. children. Open daily 10–4.*

Brandt's Passage, off Vestergade, is a heavily boutiqued walking street. At the end of it, in what was once a textile factory, is a four-story art gallery, the Brandts Klædefabrik, incorporating the **Museum for Photographic Art,** the **Graphic Museum,** and other spaces, with temporary exhibits for video art. It's well worth the short walk to see Funen's version of a Soho loft. *37–43 Brandts Passage, tel. 66/13–78–97. Admission: art museum, 25 kr. adults, 20 kr. children; photography museum, 20 kr. adults, 15 kr. children; graphics museum, 15 kr. adults, 10 kr. children; combined admission, 40 kr. adults, 30 kr. children. Open Tues.–Fri. 10–5, weekends 11–5.*

Don't neglect **Den Fynske Landsby** (Funen Village), 3 kilometers (2 miles) south; an enjoyable way of getting there is to travel down the Odense River by boat. The open-air museum-village is made up of 20 farm buildings, including workshops, a vicarage, a water mill, and a windmill. There's a theater, too, which in summer stages adaptations of Andersen's tales. *Sejerskovvej 20, tel. 66/13–13–72, ext. 4642. Admission: 20 kr. adults, 10 kr. children. Open Apr.–May and Sept.–mid-Oct., daily 10–4; June–Aug., daily 9–7:30; mid-Oct.–Mar., Sun. and holidays only, 10–3.*

Head 30 kilometers (18 miles) south on Route 43 to **Fåborg,** a lovely little town dating from the 12th century. Four times a day, it echoes with the dulcet chiming of the Klokketårnet's (Belfry's) carillon, the largest in Fyn. Dating from 1725, **Den Gamla Gård** (the Old Merchant's House) chronicles the cultural history of Funen. *Holkegade 1, tel. 62/61–33–38. Admission: 20 kr. adults, 3 kr. children under 14. Open May 15–Sept. 15, daily 10:30–4:30.*

Visit the **Fåborg Museum for Fynsk Malerkunst** (Art Gallery for Funen Artists), which has a good collection of paintings and sculpture—dating mainly from 1880 to 1920—by the Fyn Painters, whose works are full of the dusky light that so often illuminates Scandinavian painting. *Grønnegade 75, tel. 62/61–06–45. Admission: 20 kr. adults, 10 kr. senior citizens and students. Open Apr.–May and Sept.–Oct., daily 10–4; June–Aug., daily 10–5; Nov.–Mar., daily 11–3.*

From Fåborg, take the car ferry to Søby at the northern tip of Ærø Island, the "Jewel of the Archipelago," where roads wend through fertile fields and past thatched farmhouses. South from Søby on Route 16, 13 kilometers (8 miles), is the charming town of Ærøskøbing on the island's north coast. When you've spent an hour walking through its cobbled 17th- and 18th-century streets, you'll understand its great appeal.

From Ærøskøbing, the ferry takes just over an hour to reach Svendborg, Funen's southernmost town. It's also the gateway to the country's southern islands, so leave it for the moment and cross over the bridge onto the tiny island of **Tåsinge.**

Dating from around 1640, **Valdemars Slot,** now a sumptuously furnished home, is one of Denmark's oldest privately owned castles. Upstairs, the rooms are furnished to the smallest detail. Downstairs is the castle church, illuminated only by candlelight. There's a restaurant (*see* Dining and Lodging, *below*) situated beneath the church. The Tea Pavilion is now a café overlooking Lunkebugten Bay, with one of south Fyn's best stretches of beach. *Slotsalleen 100, Troense, tel. 62/22–61–06. Admission: 30 kr. adults, 10 kr. children. Open May–Oct., daily 10–5. Closed Nov.–May.*

Pretty **Troense** is one of Denmark's best-preserved villages. Once the home port for many sailing ships, both commercial and Viking, today the harbor is stuffed with pleasure yachts.

Tåsinge is connected with the island of **Langeland** by a causeway-bridge. The largest island in the southern archipelago, Langeland is rich in relics of the past, and the beaches are worth scouting out.

Head back now, passing through Tåsinge, to Fyn's **Svendborg.** Just north of town is **Egeskov Slot,** one of the best-preserved island castles in Europe. Egeskov means "Oak Forest," and an entire one was felled around 1540 to form the piles on which the rose-stone structure stands. The park contains noteworthy Renaissance, Baroque, English, and peasant gardens and an antique-car museum. Unfortunately, little of the castle is open to the public. *Egeskovgade 18, Kvaerndrup, tel. 62/27–10–16. Admission (to castle and museum): 85 kr. adults, 42.50 kr. children under 12. Castle open May 1–Sept. 30, daily 10–5. Museum open June 1–Aug. 31, daily 9–6; Sept. daily 10–5.*

Dining and Lodging

Fyn boasts a wide range of hotels and inns, many of which offer off-season (October through May) rates, as well as special weekend deals. The islands are also endowed with numerous campsites and youth hostels, all clean and attractively located. Some, like Odense's youth hostel, are set in old manor houses. For information, contact the local tourist office. For details and price-category definitions, *see* Dining and Lodging in Staying in Denmark.

Ærøskøbing
Lodging

Ærøhus. A half-timbered building with a steep red roof, the Ærøhus looks more like a barn than a hotel. Inside you'll find rustic simplicity in the simple wooden furniture and cheerful curtains and duvets. The garden's eight cottages have small terraces. *Vestergade 38 (Ærø), tel. 62/52–10–03, fax 62/52–21–23. 35 rooms, 14 with bath; 8 cottages. Facilities: restaurant, garden, terrace. Closed December 24–Jan. 20. Moderate.*

Fåborg
Dining and Lodging

Falsled Kro. This thatched establishment, a Danish roadside inn since the 15th century, is one of Denmark's finest. The rooms are furnished in a mixture of antiques and contemporary Danish designs; most have a sitting area and a fireplace. The superb restaurant specializes in game and seafood. Try the fresh mussels from the local bed, and order some wine from the exceptional selection. *Assensvej 513, Falsled, 13 km. (8 mi.) northwest of Fåborg on the Millinge–Assens highway, tel. 62/68–11–11, fax 62/68–11–62. 14 rooms with bath. AE, DC, MC. Closed Jan.–Feb. Very Expensive.*

Steensgård Herregårdspension. Set in a magnificent manor house dating from the early 1300s, this is the archetypal stately home hotel. The interior elegantly blends wood paneling, parquet floors, antiques, and porcelain stoves. The candle-lit restaurant is top-notch. Try the game if it's on the menu. *Steensgård 4 (Funen), in Millinge, 7 km. (4 mi.) northwest of Fåborg, tel. 62/61–94–90, fax 62/61–78–61. 15 rooms, 13 with* *bath. Facilities: tennis, horseback riding, restaurant. AE, DC, MC, V. Closed Jan. Expensive.*

Nyborg
Lodging

Nyborg Strand. A seaside location adds to the charm of this typical Danish hotel. It's clean, bright, and popular. *Østerøvej 2, tel. 65/31–31–31, fax 65/31–37–01. 250 rooms with bath. Facilities: pool, sauna, game room, restaurant, bar, garden. AE, DC, MC, V. Moderate.*

Odense
Dining

Restaurant Provence. A few minutes from the pedestrian mall, this cozy, blue-and-white dining room puts a Danish twist on Provençal cuisine. Specialties include venison with blackberry sauce, and duck breast cooked in sherry. *Pogstræde 31, tel. 66/12–12–96. Reservations advised. DC, MC, V. Moderate.*

Rudolf Mathis. You'll enjoy delectable seafood specialties and a splendid view of Kerteminde Harbor at this traditional Danish restaurant. *Dosseringen 13, Kerteminde, 13 km. (8 mi.) northeast of Odense on Rte. 165, tel. 65/32–32–33. Reservations accepted. No credit cards. Closed Mon. Moderate.*

Målet. A spirited local clientele frequents this sports club and restaurant filled with soccer memorabilia. Schnitzels are the specialty, prepared with mushrooms, paprika, or even Italian and Madagascar style. *Jernbanegade 17, tel. 66/17–82–41. No reservations. No credit cards. Inexpensive.*

Lodging

Reso Grand Hotel. They don't make spacious, gracious places like this anymore. Dating from 1897, the Grand offers spruced-up fin-de-siècle elegance. The decor is cool and green, and there are lovely marble bathrooms in the rooms, as well as a sweeping staircase and a spectacular Pompeiian red dining room. *Jernbanegade 18, tel. 66/11–71–71, fax 66/14–11–71. 137 rooms with bath. Facilities: sauna, solarium, restaurant, bar, parking. AE, DC, MC, V. Closed Christmas–New Year's Day. Very Expensive.*

Missionshotellet Ansgar. The rooms are a trifle boxlike but clean and comfortable nonetheless. This hotel offers solid lodgings (with satellite television) near the station. *Østre Stationsvej 32, tel. 66/11–96–93, fax 66/11–96–75. 44 rooms with bath. MC, V. Moderate.*

Svendborg
Dining

Sandig. At this austere white eatery, just near the harbor, the food is owner-chef-waiter-dishwasher Volkert Sandig's priority. His daily French-Danish menu includes inventive fish and beef specialties, such as cod served with mussel and garlic sauce. *Kullinggade 1b, tel. 62/22–92–11. Reservations advised. DC, MC, V. Closed Sun. and Dec. 24–Jan. 4. Moderate.*

Troense
Dining

Valdemars Slot. Situated in the ancient vaults beneath the church of Valdemar Castle, this restaurant provides a cool retreat and an excellent meal. Arched ceilings, tiled floors, and candlelight set the elegant tone. *Slotsalleen 100, Tåsinge, tel. 62/22–59–00. Reservations advised. MC. Closed Mon. Expensive.*

Jylland and the Lakes

The peninsula of Jylland (Jutland) is the only part of Denmark that is attached to the mainland of Europe; its southern boundary is the frontier with Germany. It's a region of carefully groomed pastures punctuated by stretches of rugged beauty. The windswept landscapes of *Babette's Feast*, the film version of Isak Dinesen's novel, are in northwest Jylland. One-tenth of

Jylland

0   40 miles

0   60 km

N

KEY

🚌 Ferry

the peninsula consists of moors and sand dunes; the remaining land is devoted to agriculture and forestry. To the east of the peninsula, facing Fyn, lie the well-wooded fjords, which run inland for miles. The region of rustic towns and stark countryside also boasts gracious castles, parklands, and the famed Legoland. Ribe, Denmark's oldest town, lies to the south, while to the east is Århus, Denmark's second-largest city, with its superb museums and new concert hall.

Getting Around

If you're following this itinerary directly after the tour around Fyn, head northwest from Odense through Middlefart and then on to Vejle. By train, either from Odense or Copenhagen, the starting point is Kolding, to the south of Vejle. While there are good train and bus services between all the main cities, this tour is best done by car. Delightful though they are, the offshore islands are suitable only for those with a lot of time, since many involve an overnight stay.

Guided Tours

Guided tours are scarce in these parts. However, you can stop by any tourist office for maps and suggestions for a walking tour. Århus also offers a "Round and About the City" tour, which leaves from the tourist office daily from mid-June to mid-Aug. at 10 AM.

Tourist Information

Aalborg (Østerå 8, tel. 98/12–60–22).
Århus (Rådhuset, tel. 86/12–16–00).
Billund (c/o Legoland A/S, tel. 75/33–19–26).
Herning (Bregade 2, tel. 97/12–44–22).
Kolding (Hellingkorsgade 18, tel. 75/53–21–00).
Randers (Erik Menveds Plads 1, tel. 86/42–44–77).
Ribe (Torvet 3–5, tel. 75/42–15–00).
Silkeborg (Godthåbsvej 4, tel. 86/82–19–11).
Vejle (Den Smidske Gård, Søndergade 14, tel. 75/82–19–55).
Viborg (Nytorv 9, tel. 86/61–16–66).

Exploring Jylland and the Lakes

If **Kolding** is your starting point, don't miss the well-preserved 13th-century **Koldinghus** castle, a royal residence during the Middle Ages. *Tel. 75/50–15–00. Admission: 25 kr. adults, children free. Open April–Sept., daily 10–5; Oct.–Mar., Mon.–Fri. noon–3, weekends 10–3.*

The Den Geografiske Have (Geographical Garden) has a rose garden with more than 120 varieties, as well as some 2,000 plants from all parts of the world, arranged geographically. *Admission: 30 kr. adults, children free. Open June and Aug., daily 9–7; July, daily 9–8; Sept.–May, daily 10–6.*

Vejle, about 20 kilometers (12 miles) to the north of Kolding, is beautifully positioned on the fjord; amid forest-clad hills, the town looks out toward the Kattegat, the strait that divides Jylland and Fyn. You can hear the time of day chiming on an old Dominican monastery clock; the clock remains, but the monastery has long since given way to the town's imposing 19th-century city hall.

Leaving Vejle, take the road 10 kilometers (6 miles) north through the Grejs Valley to **Jelling.** In Jelling you'll find two 10th-century burial mounds marking the seat of King Gorm the Old and his wife, Thyra. Between the mounds are the Jelling runic stones, one of which is known as "Denmark's Certificate of Baptism" because it shows the oldest known figure of Christ in Scandinavia. The inscription explains that the stone was erected by Gorm's son, King Harald Bluetooth, who brought Christianity to the Danes in AD 960.

Head north toward **Silkeborg,** set on the banks of the river Gudena in Jylland's lake district. The region stretches from Silkeborg in the west to Skanderborg in the east and contains some of Denmark's loveliest scenery, as well as one of the country's meager "mountains." The best way to explore the area is by water because the Gudena winds its way some 160 kilometers (100 miles) through lakes and wooded hillsides down to the sea. You can take one of the excursion boats or, better still, the world's last coal-paddle steamer, *Jjejlen,* which runs in the summer and is based at Silkeborg. Since 1861, it has paddled its way through narrow stretches of fjord, where the treetops meet overhead, to the foot of the Himmelbjerget at Lake Julso. From that point you can clamber up the narrow paths through the heather and trees to the top, where an 80-foot tower stands sentinel, placed there on Constitution Day in 1875 in memory of King Frederik VII.

Silkeborg's other attraction is housed in the **Silkeborg Kultur-historiske Museum** (Museum of Culture and History): the 2,200-year-old Tollund Man, one of the so-called bog people, whose corpse was preserved by natural ingredients in the soil and water. *Hovedgaardsvej 7, Tel. 86/82–14–99. Admission: 20 kr. adults, 5 kr. children. Open Apr. 15–Oct. 23, daily 10–5; Oct. 24–Apr. 14, Wed. and weekends noon–4.*

On the coast, lying directly east of Silkeborg, is **Århus,** Denmark's second-largest city. The town is at its liveliest during the 10-day Århus Festival in September, which brings together everything from classical concerts to jazz and folk music, clowning, theater, exhibitions, beer tents, and sports. The town's cathedral, the 15th-century **Domkirke,** is Denmark's longest church; it contains a beautifully executed three-paneled altarpiece. Look up at the whimsical sketches around the drains on the ceiling.

Nearby is the **Vor Frue Kirke,** formerly a Dominican abbey. Underneath the 13th-century structure is the eerie but interesting crypt church, rediscovered in 1955 and, dating from 1060, one of the oldest preserved stone churches in Scandinavia. The vaulted room houses a replica of an old Roman crucifix.

Not to be missed is the town's open-air museum, known as **Den Gamle By** (The Old Town). A sophisticated version of Disneyland, it features 65 half-timbered houses, a mill, and a mill-stream. The meticulously re-created period interiors range from the 15th to the early 20th century. *Viborgvej, tel. 86/12–31–88. Admission: 40 kr. adults, 12 kr. children. Open Jan.–Mar. and Nov., daily 11–3; Apr. and Oct., Mon.–Sat. 10–4; May and Sept., daily 10–5; June–Aug., daily 9–5; Dec., Mon.–Sat. 10–3, Sun. 10–4.*

Set in a 250-acre forest in a park south of Århus is the indoor/
outdoor **Moesgård Prehistoric Museum,** with exhibits on ethnography and archaeology, including the famed Grauballe
Man, an eerie, well-preserved corpse from 2,000 years ago.
Take the "Prehistoric Trail" through the forest, which leads
past Stone and Bronze Age displays to some reconstructed
houses from Viking times. *Ny Moesgård Allé 20, Højbjerg, tel.
86/27–24–33. Admission: 25 kr. adults, children under 15 free.
Open Jan.–Mar. and Sept. 16–Dec., Tues.–Sun. 10–4; Apr.–
Sept. 15, daily 10–5.*

Heading north 21 kilometers (15 miles), you'll come to the medieval town of **Randers,** where, in 1340, the Danish patriot Niels
Ebbesen killed the German oppressor, Count Gert the Bald of
Holstein, whose army was then occupying most of Jutland. To
the east of Randers is the Djursland Peninsula, a popular vacation area, with fine manor houses open to the public. If time is
of the essence, choose **Gammel Estrup,** a grand 17th-century
manor in the tiny village of **Auning;** it's full of rich period furnishings, including an alchemist's cellar. *Tel. 86/48–30–01. Admission: 20 kr. adults, 5 kr. children. Manor and farm open
May–Oct., daily 10–5; Nov.–Apr., (manor) Tues.–Sun. 11–3,
(farm) daily 10–5.*

Aalborg, 55 kilometers (35 miles) to the north, is set at the narrowest point of the Limfjord, the great waterway of northern
Jutland and the gateway between north and south. You'll find
charming combinations of new and old; twisting lanes filled
with medieval houses; and, nearby, broad modern boulevards.
Jomfru Ane Gade is a tiny cobbled street in the center of Aal-
borg, with a number of restaurants, inns, and sidewalk cafés.
Major sights include the magnificent **Jens Bangs Stenhus** (Jens
Bang's Stone House). A five-story building dating from 1642, it
has an atmospheric restaurant and an excellent wine cellar.
You'll also want to take in the Baroque cathedral, the **Budolfi
Kirke,** dedicated to the English saint Butolph, and the 15th-
century **Helligandsklosteret** (Monastery of the Holy Ghost).
One of Denmark's best-preserved monasteries, it is now a home
for the elderly.

If you have some time to spare, head north up to the tip of
Jylland, to **Skagen,** where the picturesque streets and the
luminous light have inspired painters and writers alike. The
19th-century Danish artist Holger Drachmann (1846–1908)
and his friends founded the Skagen school of painting; you can
see their efforts on display in the local **Skagens Museum.** *4
Brøndumsvej, tel. 98/44–64–44. Admission: 25 kr. adults,
children free. Open Apr. and Oct., Tues.–Sun. 11–4; May and
Sept., daily 10–5; June–Aug., daily 10–6; Nov.–Mar., Wed.–
Fri. 1–4, Sat. 11–4, Sun. 11–3.*

Heading south once more, you next come to **Viborg,** whose history goes back to the 8th century, when it was a trading post
and a place of pagan sacrifice. Later it became a center of
Christianity, with monasteries and an episcopal residence.
The 1,000-year-old **Haervejen,** the old military road that starts
near here, was once Denmark's most important connection
with the outside world. Legend has it that in the 11th century,
King Canute set out from Viborg to conquer England; he succeeded and ruled from 1016 to 1035.

Built in 1130, Viborg's **Domkirke,** the cathedral, was once the largest granite church in the world. Today the crypt is all that remains of the original building, restored and reopened in 1876. The early 20th-century biblical frescoes are by Danish painter Joakim Skovgaard.

There's terrific walking country 8 kilometers (5 miles) south of Viborg, beside **Hald Sø** (Hald Lake) and on the heatherclad **Dollerup Bakker** (Dollerup Hills). Next head southwest 45 kilometers (28 miles) to **Herning,** an old moorland town. There you'll find a remarkable circular house, with a 400-foot outer frieze by contemporary artist Carl-Henning Pedersen; it houses the **Carl-Henning Pedersen and Else Afelt's Museum,** set within a sculpture park. *Uldjydevej 3, tel. 97/22–10–79. Admission: 20 kr. adults, children free. Open Apr.–Oct., Tues.–Sun. 10–5, Nov.–Mar., Tues.–Sat. noon–5.*

About 100 kilometers (60 miles) to the south, but well worth the extra driving time, is **Ribe,** Denmark's oldest town, whose medieval town center is preserved by the Danish National Trust. From May to mid-September, a night watchman goes around the town telling of its ancient history and singing traditional songs. Visitors can accompany him nightly by gathering in the main square at 10 PM.

Before heading back to Vejle, stop off at **Billund** to see the country's most famous tourist attraction. **Legoland** is a park filled with scaled-down versions of cities, towns, and villages, as well as working harbors and airports, a Statue of Liberty, a statue of Sitting Bull, Mount Rushmore, a safari park, even a Wild West saloon—all constructed of millions of tiny plastic Lego bricks. There are also exhibits of toys from pre-Lego days, including Legoland's high point, Titania's Palace, a sumptuous dollhouse built in 1907 by Sir Neville Wilkinson for his daughter. *Billund, tel. 75/33–13–33. Admission: 95 kr. adults, 75 kr. children under 14. Open May–Sept. 15, daily 10–7.*

Dining and Lodging

For details and price-category definitions, *see* Dining and Lodging in Staying in Denmark.

Aalborg **Duus Vinkælder.** Occupying part of Jens Bang's house, and
Dining with 300 years of tradition behind it, Duus Vinkælder is one of
★ Aalborg's best-known restaurants. The wine cellar is phenomenal. *9 Østerå, tel. 98/12–50–56. Reservations required. No credit cards. Closed Sun. Moderate.*

Dining and Lodging **Phønix.** A centrally located hotel in a historic building, the Phønix is discreet, traditional, and exceptionally popular. The rooms are comfortable and spacious, the staff pleasant and helpful. One of the Phønix's restaurants, the Halling, serves excellent French and Danish cuisines. *Vesterbro 77, tel. 98/12–00–11, fax 98/16–31–66. 179 rooms with bath. Facilities: sauna, solarium, game room, 2 restaurants, bar, café. AE, DC, MC. Very Expensive.*
Scheelsminde. A pleasantly austere manor house built in 1808, the Scheelsminde was originally a farm. A traditional atmosphere prevails in the public rooms, while bedrooms are Danish modern. The restaurant has fine food and an extensive wine list. *Scheelsmindevej 35, tel. 98/18–32–33, fax 98/18–33–34. 70*

rooms with bath. Facilities: sauna, Jacuzzi, solarium, garden, restaurant. AE, DC, MC, V. Expensive.

Århus
Dining
★

De Fire Årstider. The Four Seasons, renowned as one of Scandinavia's finest restaurants, serves Danish and French nouvelle cuisines behind an unassuming facade on a busy shopping street. *Åboulevarden 47, tel. 86/19–96–96. Reservations required. AE, DC, MC, V. Closed Sun. Expensive.*

Kashmir. In his popular, casual eatery, owner Mirza Zaman serves spicy Pakistani and Indian specialties made from his grandmother's recipes. *Vesterbrogade 36, tel. 86/13–16–37. Reservations advised. MC. Dinner only. Inexpensive.*

Lodging

Royal. Open since 1838, Århus's grand hotel has recently been restored and rebuilt, with its period elegance left intact. Cool pastels abound, as does cheerful chintz. The bathrooms are marble; the service is excellent. *Store Torv 4, tel. 86/12–00–11, fax 86/76–04–04. 106 rooms with bath. Facilities: 5 cinemas, restaurant, nightclub, casino, sauna, solarium. AE, DC, MC, V. Very Expensive.*

Randers
Dining and Lodging

Randers. Anyone who loves pampering would do well to come here. The service is friendly and prompt, the decor is as plush as Denmark ever gets, and the Grill Room restaurant regularly produces memorable meals. *Torvegade 11, tel. 86/42–34–22, fax 86/40–15–86. 79 rooms with bath. Facilities: restaurant (reservations advised). AE, DC, MC, V. Closed Dec. 23–Jan. 1. Expensive.*

Ribe
Dining and Lodging

Dagmar. Occupying a building dating from 1581, the Dagmar is a cozy place, encapsulating all the charm of the 16th century, with stained-glass windows, frescoes, sloping floors, and carved chairs. The restaurant has a delightful central fireplace, and the food is first-class. Try the fillet of veal à la Dagmar. *Torvet 1, tel. 75/42–00–33, fax 75/42–36–52. 50 rooms with bath. Facilities: restaurant (reservations advised). AE, DC, MC, V. Expensive.*

Skagen
Dining and Lodging

Brøndums. With an attractive beachside location, the Brøndums is a friendly hotel, decorated throughout with paintings by 19th-century artists of the Skagen school. The restaurant has lots of fish specialties and outside dining in the summer. *Anchersvej 3, tel. 98/44–15–55, fax 98/45–15–20. 46 rooms with bath. Facilities: restaurant (reservations advised). AE, MC, V. Expensive.*

Vejle
Dining and Lodging

Munkebjerg. A remote location and marvelous views characterize this establishment, which dates from 1880. The original building has long since gone, but the nearby beech woods and fjord remain. Guest rooms are modern and light, with fresh colors and stripped-pine decor. The Munkebjerg has two fine restaurants specializing in French cuisine. *Munkebjergvej 125, tel. 75/72–35–00, fax 75/72–08–86. 148 rooms with bath. Facilities: 2 restaurants, café, fitness room, pool, sauna, solarium, game room, tennis, heliport, horseback riding, golf course, and biking, jogging, and walking trails. AE, DC, MC, V. Very Expensive.*

9 Finland

If you like majestic open spaces, fine architecture, and civilized living—and can afford the prices—Finland is for you. It is a land of lakes, 187,888 at the last count, and forests. It is a land where nature is so prized that even the design of city buildings reflects the soaring spaces of the countryside.

The music of Sibelius, Finland's most famous son, tells you what to expect from this Nordic landscape. Both can swing from the somber nocturne of midwinter darkness to the tremolo of sunlight slanting through pine and bone-white birch or from the crescendo of a sunset before it fades into the next day's dawn. Similarly, the Finnish people reflect the changing moods of their land and climate. They can get annoyed when described as "children of nature," but the description is apt. Their affinity with nature has produced some of the world's greatest designers and architects. Many American cities have buildings designed by Alvar Aalto and the Saarinens, Eliel and son Eero. In fact, Eliel and his family moved to the United States in 1923 and became American citizens—but it was to a lonely Finnish seashore that Saarinen had his ashes returned.

Until 1917, Finland (the Finns call it *Suomi)* was under the domination of its nearest neighbors, Sweden and Russia, who fought over it for centuries. After more than 600 years under Swedish rule and 100 under the czars, the country inevitably bears many traces of these two cultures, including a small (6%) but influential Swedish-speaking population and a scattering of Russian Orthodox churches.

But the Finns themselves are neither Scandinavian nor Slavic. All that is known of their origins is that they are descended from wandering groups of people who probably came from west of the Ural Mountains before the Christian era and settled on the swampy shores of the Gulf of Finland.

There is a tough, resilient quality in the Finns. No other people fought the Soviets to a standstill as the Finns did in the Winter War of 1939–40. This resilience, in part, stems from the turbulence of the country's past, but also comes from the people's strength and determination to work the land and survive the long winters. No wonder there is a poet-philosopher lurking in most Finns, one who sometimes drowns his melancholic, darker side in the bottle. For the Finn is in a state of constant confrontation—with the weather, the land, and most recently a huge eastern neighbor that is engulfed in political and economic turmoil. The Finn is stubborn, patriotic, and self-sufficient, yet he is not aggressively nationalistic. On the contrary, rather than being proud of past battles, the Finn is proud of finding ways to live in peace. His country's neutrality and his own personal freedom are what he tenaciously holds on to and will never easily relinquish.

The average Finn doesn't volunteer much information, but that's due to reserve, not indifference. Make the first approach and you may have a friend for life. Finns like their silent spaces, though, and won't appreciate back-slapping familiarity—least of all in the sauna, still regarded by many as a spiritual, as well as a cleansing, experience.

Finland

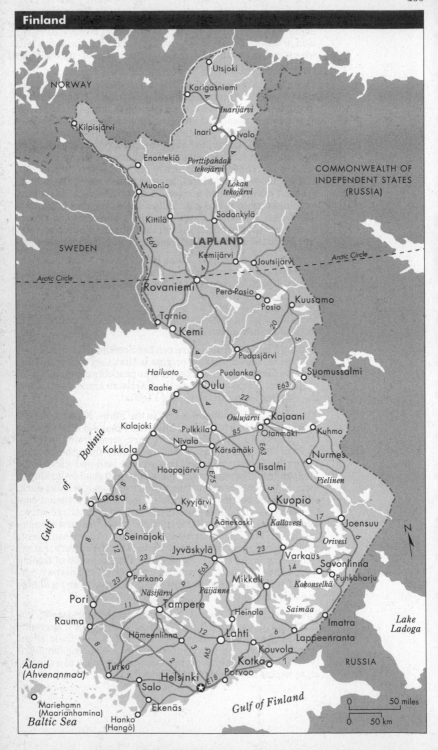

NORWAY

Utsjoki

Karigasniemi

Inarijärvi

Kilpisjärvi

Inari

Ivalo

Enontekiö

Porttipahdan tekojärvi

COMMONWEALTH OF INDEPENDENT STATES (RUSSIA)

Muonio

Lokan tekojärvi

SWEDEN

Kittilä

Sodankylä

E69

LAPLAND

Kemijärvi

Joutsijärvi

Arctic Circle

Arctic Circle

Rovaniemi

4

Perä-Posio

Kuusamo

Tornio

Posio

Kemi

20

5

4

Pudasjärvi

Hailuoto

Puolanka

Suomussalmi

Raahe

Oulu

E63

8

4

22

Oulujärvi

Kajaani

Kalajoki

Pulkkila

85

Otanmäki

Kuhmo

Nivala

E63

Kokkola

Kärsämäki

Nurmes

8

Haapajärvi

Iisalmi

Pielinen

Gulf

E75

5

Vaasa

16

Kyyjärvi

Kuopio

of

Kallavesi

17

Joensuu

12

Seinäjoki

Äänekoski

Orivesi

6

8

Bothnia

9

23

Jyväskylä

23

Varkaus

23

Parkano

E63

14

Savonlinna

Pori

Näsijärvi

9

Mikkeli

Kokonselkä

Punkaharju

11

Päijänne

Tampere

Saimaa

Rauma

Heinola

Imatra

Lake Ladoga

8

Hämeenlinna

12

Lahti

6

Lappeenranta

3

M5

Kouvola

1

RUSSIA

Turku

2

Kotka

Åland (Ahvenanmaa)

1

Salo

E18

Porvoo

Helsinki

Mariehamn (Maarianhamina)

Ekenäs

Gulf of Finland

Baltic Sea

Hanko (Hangö)

N

0   50 miles

0   50 km

Essential Information

Before You Go

When to Go   The tourist summer season runs from mid-June until mid-August, a magnificently sunny and generally dry time marked by unusually warm temperatures in recent years. Outside this period, many amenities and attractions either close or operate on much reduced schedules. But there are advantages to visiting Finland off-season, not the least being that you avoid the mosquitoes, which can be fearsome, especially in the north. Also, hotel rates, especially in vacation villages, may drop by up to 50%, and the fall colors (from early September in the far north, October in the south) are spectacular. January through March (through April in the north) is the main cross-country skiing season. Spring is brief but magical, as the snows melt, the ice breaks up, and nature explodes into life almost overnight.

Climate   Generally speaking, the spring and summer seasons begin a month earlier in the south of Finland than they do in the far north. You can expect warm (not hot) days in Helsinki from mid-May; in Lapland from mid-June. The midnight sun can be seen from May to July, depending on the region. In midwinter there is a corresponding period when the sun does not rise at all, but it is possible to see magnificent displays of the Northern Lights. Even in Helsinki, summer nights are brief and never really dark, whereas in midwinter daylight lasts only a few hours.

The following are average daily maximum and minimum temperatures for Helsinki.

Jan.	26F	– 3C	May	56F	13C	Sept.	56F	13C
	17	– 8		44	6		46	8
Feb.	26F	– 3C	June	66F	19C	Oct.	49F	9C
	17	– 8		51	10		39	4
Mar.	34F	1C	July	73F	23C	Nov.	39F	4C
	23	– 5		57	14		30	– 1
Apr.	44F	6C	Aug.	66F	19C	Dec.	32F	0C
	32	0		55	13		21	– 6

Currency   The unit of currency in Finland is the Finnmark (FIM), divided into 100 penniä. There are bills of FIM 20, 50, 100, 500, and 1,000. Coins are 10 and 50 penniä, and FIM 1, FIM 5, and FIM 10. At press time (spring 1993), the exchange rate was about FIM 5.15 to the dollar and FIM 7.83 to the pound sterling. Credit cards are widely accepted even in many taxicabs. Traveler's checks can be changed only in banks.

What It Will Cost   Prices are highest in Helsinki; otherwise they vary little throughout the country. Taxes are already included in hotel and restaurant charges, and there is no airport departure tax. However, the price of many goods includes an 18% sales tax, less on food (*see* Shopping in Staying in Finland, *below*).

Sample Prices   Cup of coffee, FIM 5; glass of beer, FIM 10–FIM 20; Coca-Cola, FIM 7; ham sandwich, FIM 15–FIM 20; 1-mile taxi ride, FIM 20.

Customs on Arrival Europeans age 16 and over entering Finland may bring in 200 cigarettes or 250 grams of other tobacco; visitors from outside Europe may bring in twice as much. All visitors aged 20 or over may also bring in 2 liters of beer, 1 liter of alcohol under 22% volume, and 1 liter over 22% volume; or 2 liters of beer and 2 liters of alcohol under 22%. Visitors aged 18 or over may import 2 liters of beer and 2 liters of alcohol under 22% volume. Goods up to a value of FIM 1,500 may be imported.

Language The official languages of Finland are Finnish and Swedish, though only a small minority (about 6%) speak Swedish. English is widely spoken among people in the travel industry and by many younger Finns, though they're often shy about using it. Nearly all tourist sites and attractions provide texts in English. In the north the Lapp people, called *Same*, have their own language.

Getting Around

By Car
Road Conditions Finland has no superhighways, but there is an expanding network of efficient major roads, some of which are multilane. In some areas, however, especially in the north, you can expect long stretches of dirt road. These roads are usually adequate to good, although during the spring thaw they become difficult to negotiate. Away from the larger towns, traffic is light, but take moose and reindeer warning signs seriously.

Rules of the Road Drive on the right. At intersections, cars coming from the right have priority. Speed limits (usually marked) are 50 kph (30 mph) in built-up areas and between 80 kph and 100 kph (50 mph and 62 mph) in the country and on main roads. Low-beam headlights must be used at all times outside city areas, seat belts are compulsory (on rear as well as front seats), and you must carry a warning triangle in case of breakdown.

Parking Parking is a problem only in some city centers. Major cities offer multistory garages; most towns have on-street meters. Illegally parked cars may be towed away.

Breakdowns and Accidents The **Automobile and Touring Club of Finland** (Autoliitto ry, Kansakoulukatu 10, 00100 Helsinki, tel. 90/ 694–0022; outside of Helsinki, tel. 9700/8080) operates a road-patrol service on main roads from 6 PM Friday to 10 PM Sunday. If you're involved in an accident, report it without delay to the **Finnish Motor Insurers' Bureau** (Bulevardi 28, Helsinki, tel. 90/680401) as well as to the police.

By Train Finland's extensive rail system reaches all main centers of the country and offers high standards of comfort and cleanliness. A special **Finnrail Pass** entitles you to unlimited travel for one, two, or three weeks; second-class prices are FIM 470 (one week), FIM 730 (two weeks), and FIM 920 (three weeks); first-class tickets are FIM 705 (one week), FIM 1,095 (two weeks), and FIM 1,380 (three weeks). Children pay half fare. These tickets can be purchased both inside and outside the country. In Finland, the Finnrail Pass is available from the Finnish State Railways (VR) (tel. 90/1010117). In the United States and Canada they can be purchased by calling **Rail Europe** (tel. 914/ 682–2999); in the United Kingdom, from **Finlandia Travel** (tel. 071/409–7334).

By Plane Finnair (tel. 90/818800) operates an elaborate network of flights linking 22 towns in Finland. For $300, a **Holiday Ticket**

guarantees you unlimited travel for 15 days; visitors aged 17–24 can get a **Youth Holiday Ticket** for $250. These tickets are available in most countries, and in Finland they can be purchased at major travel agencies.

By Bus   Bus travel plays a leading role in Finland, and the country's bus system provides the most extensive travel network of all; it can take you virtually anywhere. A **Coach Holiday Ticket,** available from bus stations and travel agencies, entitles you to 1,000 kilometers (625 miles) of bus travel for FIM 300 for two weeks.

By Boat   Helsinki and Turku have regular sea links with the Åland Islands in the Baltic Sea. From mid-June to mid-August you can cruise the labyrinthine lakes of the Finnish interior. Complete timetables are available from the Finnish Tourist Board.

By Bicycle   Planned bicycle routes are provided in many areas. The main advantages for the cyclist are the lack of steep hills and the absence of heavy traffic. Bikes can be rented in most youth hostels. The Finnish **Youth Hostel Association** (Yrjönkatu 38B, Helsinki, tel. 90/694–0377) offers accommodation packages of four, seven, or 14 days to tie in with visitors' cycling tours.

Staying in Finland

Telephones   Hotels charge a substantial fee for all calls. You can avoid this
Local Calls   fee by using the pay phones provided in most lobbies. Have some FIM 1 and FIM 5 coins ready. Note that the Finnish letters å, ä, and ö come at the end of the alphabet; this may be useful when looking up names in the telephone book.

International Calls   You can dial directly to Britain and the United States from anywhere in Finland. Calls to other countries can be made from a telegraph office; these are marked "Lennätin" or "Tele" and usually adjoin the post office. An operator will assign you a private booth and collect payment at the end of the call.

Operators and   For information about telephone charges, dial 92023; for num-
Information   ber inquiries, dial 118.

Mail   At press time (spring 1993), airmail rates to North America
Postal Rates   were FIM 3.40 for a letter of up to 20 grams. Letters to the United Kingdom cost FIM 2.90.

Receiving Mail   If you're uncertain about where you'll be staying, be sure that mail sent to you is marked "Poste Restante" and addressed to the Main Post Office, Mannerheimintie 11, 00100 Helsinki, or to major post offices in other towns. American Express offers a free clients' mail service and will hold mail for up to one month (*see* Important Addresses and Numbers in Helsinki, *below*). The Finland Travel Bureau also provides a free mail service for foreigners: Mail should be addressed to its Mail Department, Box 319, 00101 Helsinki, and collected from the office at Kaivokatu 10A.

Shopping   If you purchase goods worth more than FIM 100 in any of the
Sales Tax Refunds   many shops marked "tax-free for tourists," you can get a 10%–16% refund when you leave Finland. Show your passport and the store will give you a check for the appropriate amount that you can cash at most departure points.

Opening and   **Banks** are open weekdays 9:15–4:15.
Closing Times
Museums. Opening hours vary considerably, so check individual listings. Most close one day a week, usually Monday. Many

museums in the countryside are open only during the summer months.

Shops are generally open weekdays 9–6, Saturday 9–2. Department stores and supermarkets sometimes stay open until 8 from Monday through Friday.

Sightseeing. Schedules for most attractions vary widely outside the main tourist season. Check local tourist offices for opening days and hours.

National Holidays January 1; January 6 (Epiphany Day); April 1–4 (Easter); May 1 (May Day); May 12 (Ascension); May 22 (Pentecost); June 24 (Midsummer's Eve); June 25 (Midsummer's Day); November 1 (All Saints' Day); December 6 (Independence Day); December 25–26.

Dining You can choose among restaurants, taverns, coffeehouses, and snack bars. As in other parts of Scandinavia, the *voileipäpöytä* (cold table) is often a work of art as well as a feast. Special Finnish dishes include *poronkäristys* (reindeer casserole; superb in Lapland); salmon, herring, and various freshwater fish; and *lihapullia* (meatballs) with a tasty sauce. Crayfish parties are popular between the end of July and early September. For a delicious dessert, try cloudberries (related to blackberries) and other forest fruits.

Mealtimes The Finns eat early; lunch runs from 11 or noon to 1 or 2, dinner from 4 to 7 (a bit later in Helsinki).

Dress Except for the most elegant restaurants, where a jacket and tie are preferred, casual attire is acceptable for restaurants in all price categories; however, jeans are not allowed in some of the Expensive and Very Expensive establishments.

Ratings Prices are per person and include first course, main course, dessert, and service charge—but not wine. All restaurant checks include a service charge (*sisältää palvelupalkkion*). If you want to leave an additional tip—though it really isn't necessary—it's enough to round the figure off to the nearest FIM 5 or FIM 10. Best bets are indicated by a star ★.

Category	Helsinki	Other Areas
Very Expensive	over FIM 180	over FIM 150
Expensive	FIM 130–FIM 180	FIM 110–FIM 150
Moderate	FIM 80–FIM 130	FIM 65–FIM 110
Inexpensive	under FIM 80	under FIM 65

If you select the fixed-price menu, which usually covers two courses and coffee and is served at certain hours in many establishments, the cost of the meal can be as little as half these prices.

Lodging The range of accommodations available in Finland includes hotels, motels, boarding houses, private homes, rented chalets and cottages, farmhouses, youth hostels, and campsites. There is no official system of classification, but standards are generally high. If you haven't reserved a room in advance, you can make reservations at the **Hotel Booking Center** at the Railway Station (Rautatieasema, 00100 Helsinki, tel. 90/171133) or through a travel agency; the booking fee is FIM 10. There are added reductions of 40%–60% in Helsinki-area hotels from June 17 through August 14 when you buy a Helsinki Card. These cards are sold by the Hotel Booking Center and the Helsinki City Tourist Office (Pohjoisesplanadi 19, 00100 Helsinki, tel. 90/169–3757, or 90/174088).

Hotels Nearly all hotels in Finland are modern or will have been recently renovated; a few occupy fine old manor houses. Most have rooms with bath or shower. Prices generally include breakfast and often a morning sauna and swim. The **Finncheque** voucher system, operating in many hotels from June through August, offers good discounts. Only the first night can be reserved, but subsequent reservations can be made free from any Finncheque hotel. For additional information, inquire at the Hotel Booking Center or the Finnish Tourist Board (Eteläesplanadi 4, 00130 Helsinki, tel. 90/403011).

Summer Hotels University students' accommodations are turned into "summer hotels" from June through August; they offer modern facilities at slightly lower-than-average prices.

Boarding Houses and Private Homes These provide the least expensive accommodations and are found only outside Helsinki. Local tourist offices have lists.

Rentals The choice is huge, and the chalets and cottages are nearly always in delightful lakeside or seashore settings. For comfortable (not luxurious) accommodations, count on paying FIM 1,000–FIM 3,000 for a four-person weekly rental. A central reservations agency is **Lomarengas** (Malminkaari 23C, 00700 Helsinki, tel. 90/3516–1321, or Eteläesplanadi 4, 00130 Helsinki, tel. 90/170611).

Farmhouses These are located in attractive settings, usually near water. A central reservations agency is **Suomen 4H-liitto** (Abrahaminkatu 7, 00180 Helsinki, tel. 90/642233).

Youth Hostels These range from empty schools to small manor houses. There are no age restrictions, and prices range from FIM 45–FIM 150 per bed. The Finnish Tourist Board can provide a list of hostels.

Camping There are about 350 Finnish campsites, all classified into one of three grades. All offer showers and cooking facilities, and many include cottages for rent. A list is available from the Finnish Tourist Board.

Ratings Prices are for two people in a double room and include breakfast and service charge. Best bets are indicated by a star ★ .

Category	Helsinki	Other Areas
Very Expensive	over FIM 750	over FIM 650
Expensive	FIM 550–FIM 750	FIM 440–FIM 650
Moderate	FIM 350–FIM 550	FIM 270–FIM 440
Inexpensive	under FIM 350	under FIM 270

Tipping The Finns are less tip-conscious than other Europeans. (For restaurant tips, *see* Dining, *above*.) You can give taxi drivers a few small coins, but it's not essential. Train and airport porters have a fixed charge. It's not necessary to tip hotel doormen for carrying bags to the check-in counter, but give bellhops FIM 5–FIM 10 for carrying bags to your room. The obligatory checkroom fee of FIM 3–FIM 4 is usually clearly indicated; if not, give FIM 3–FIM 10, depending on the number in your party. FIM 5 is a standard tip for all minor services.

Helsinki

Arriving and Departing

By Plane All international flights arrive at Helsinki's Vantaa Airport, 20 kilometers (12 miles) north of the city. For arrival and departure information, call 9700–8100.

Between the Airport Finnair buses leave two to four times an hour for the city termi-
and Downtown nals, located at the Inter-Continental hotel (Töölönkatu 21, tel. 90/40551) and the main Railway Station. The trip takes about 30 minutes and costs FIM 20. A local bus service (No. 615), which takes about 40 minutes, goes to the train station and costs FIM 15. Expect to pay between FIM 100 and FIM 120 for a taxi into the city center. If you are driving, the way is well marked to Highway 137 (Tuusulantie) and Keskusta (downtown Helsinki).

By Train Helsinki's Railway Station is in the heart of the city. For train information, phone 90/101–0115.

By Bus The terminal for many local buses is the Railway Station square, Rautatientori. The main long-distance bus station is located off Mannerheimintie between Salomonkatu and Simonkatu. For information, phone 9600–4000.

By Sea The Silja Line terminal for ships arriving from Stockholm is at Olympialaituri, on the west side of the South Harbor. The Finnjet-Silja Line and Viking Lines terminal for ships arriving from Travemünde and Stockholm is at Katajanokka, on the east side of the South Harbor.

Getting Around

The center of Helsinki is compact and best explored on foot. If you want to use public transportation, your best buy is the **Helsinki Card,** which gives unlimited travel on city public transportation, as well as free entry to many museums, a free sightseeing tour, and a variety of other discounts. It's available for one, two, or three days (FIM 80, FIM 105, and FIM 125; about half-price for children). You can buy it at most hotels and at the Helsinki City Tourist Office.

By Subway Helsinki's only subway line runs from the western suburb of Ruoholahti to Mellunmäki, in the eastern suburbs. It runs from around 5:45 AM to 11:20 PM, and each ride costs FIM 9; you can transfer for free if you do so within an hour from the start of travel. Each trip costs FIM 7.50 if you buy a 10-trip ticket. Tickets are available from some kiosks and vending machines.

By Streetcar These run from 6 AM to 1:30 AM, depending on the line. They can be very handy, but be sure to get route advice because route maps are practically nonexistent. The fare is the same as for the subway. The 3T streetcar follows a figure-eight circuit around the city center and, during summer, provides commentary on an electric screenboard in several languages.

By Taxi Taxis are all marked "taksi." The meters start at FIM 12, with the fare rising on a kilometer basis. There is a surcharge after 6 PM and 10 PM, and on weekends. Car services have a minimum charge and should be ordered well in advance. A listing of all taxi companies appears in the white pages under "Taksi"—try to choose one that is located nearby, because they charge from point of dispatch. Many accept credit cards.

By Boat In summer there are regular boat services from the South Harbor market square to the islands of Suomenlinna and Korkeasaari.

Important Addresses and Numbers

Tourist Information The **Helsinki City Tourist Office** is near the South Harbor (Pohjoisesplanadi 19, tel. 90/169–3757); open September 16– May 15, Monday 8:30–4:30, Tuesday–Friday 8:30–4; May 16– September 15, weekdays 8:30–6, Saturday 8:30–1. The **Finnish Tourist Board's Tourist Information Office** (covering all Finland) is nearby at Eteläesplanadi 4, tel. 90/4030–1211 or 90/4030–1300; open June–August, weekdays 8:30–5, weekends 10–2; September–May, weekdays 8:30–4.

Embassies **U.S.** (Itäinen Puistotie 14, tel. 90/171931). **Canadian** (Pohjoisesplanadi 25B, tel. 90/171141). **U.K.** (Itäinen Puistotie 17, tel. 90/661293).

Emergencies **General** (tel. 112); **Police** (tel. 112); **Ambulance** (tel. 112); **Doctor** (tel. 10023); **Dentist** (tel. 90/736166); **Pharmacy: Yliopiston Apteekki,** Mannerheimintie 96, open 24 hours (tel. 90/415778).

English-Language Bookstores You'll find a good selection of books and newspapers in English at **Akateeminen Kirjakauppa** (Keskuskatu 1) and **Suomalainen Kirjakauppa** (Aleksanterinkatu 23).

Travel Agencies **American Express** (Area Travel Agency, Pohjoisesplanadi 2, 00170 Helsinki, tel. 90/18551, or Kanavaranta 9, 00160 Helsinki, tel. 90/1251600). **Thomas Cook** (Finland Travel Bureau, Kaivokatu 10A, Box 319, tel. 90/18261).

Guided Tours

Orientation Tours **Suomen Turistiauto** (tel. 90/588–5166) runs a "City Tour" (1½ hours; Jan.–Apr., Sun. 11 AM; May, Tues., Thur., and Sun. 11 AM; June–Aug., daily 11 AM and 1 PM; Sept., Tues., Thur., and Sun., 11 AM; Oct.–Dec. 20, Sun. 11 AM) that covers the main city-center sights. The tour starts from Asema aukio, across from the main post office, and you can buy tickets on the bus 15 minutes before departure. **Ageba Travel Agency** (tel. 90/669193) offers a similar tour (2 to 2½ hours), starting from the Olympic Harbor (Apr.–Oct., daily 9:30 AM and 11 AM; Nov.–Mar., Sat. and Sun. 11 AM). **Royal Line Rautakorpi** (tel. 90/652088 from June–Sept.; and 90/351–1885 year-round) operates "Helsinki by Sea" boat tours (1½ hours; May 15–June 9, daily 11 AM, 1 PM, and 3 PM; June 13–Aug. 16, daily on the hour 10 AM to 4 PM; June 22–Aug. 8, daily on the hour 10 AM to 5 PM) from the South Harbor market square in the summer. The same agency runs "Porvoo Old Town Cruises" (7 hours; June 13–Aug. 16, Tues., Thurs., Sat., and Sun. 10:20 AM; July 1–Aug. 2, daily except Mon. and Fri. 10:20 AM; Aug. 23–30, Sun. 10:20 AM).

Excursions **Uudenmaan Seuramatkat** (Uudenmaankatu 5–9, Hyvinkää, tel. 914/14700) offers eight- to ten-hour tours of historic homes

of Finnish artists. There is a nine-hour tour to Sibelius's home
in Ainola (minimum 10 persons). No-visa trips by sea to St. Petersburg, Russia, and Tallinn, Estonia, are offered by **Finnsov
Tours** (tel. 90/694–2011). **Atlas Cruising Center** offers visa-free
cruises to Tallinn (one-day), and St. Petersburg (three-days)
(tel. 9800/22584 or 90/651011).

Exploring Helsinki

Helsinki is a city of the sea. It was built on peninsulas that stab
into the Baltic, and streets and avenues curve around bays,
bridges arch over to nearby islands, and ferries reach out to islands farther offshore. Sweet-tasting salt air hovers over the
city, and the sounds from the vessels steaming into port reso-
nate off the city's buildings.

Like other European capitals, Helsinki has expanded its
boundaries and now absorbs about one-sixth of the Finnish
population, and the suburbs sprawl from one peninsula to another. Helsinki residents must know the peninsulas in order to
know their city. However, most of the city's sights, hotels, and
restaurants cluster on one peninsula, thus forming a compact
hub that is of special interest to the traveler.

Unlike most other European capitals, Helsinki is "new." About
400 years ago, King Gustav Vasa of Sweden decided to woo
trade from the Estonian city of Tallinn and thus challenge the
monopoly of the Hanseatic League. To do this, he commanded
the people of four Finnish towns to pack up their belongings
and relocate at the rapids on the river Vantaa. This new town
became Helsinki.

For three centuries, Helsinki had its ups and downs as a trading
town. Turku, to the west of Helsinki, remained the capital and
the center of the country's intellectual pursuits. Ironically, not
until Finland was thrust under the dominance of Russia did
Helsinki's fortunes improve. Czar Alexander I wanted Finland's political center closer to Russia and, in 1812, selected
Helsinki as the new capital. Shortly after the capital was
moved from Turku to Helsinki, Turku suffered a monstrous
fire. So great was the inferno that the university was also
moved to Helsinki. From then on Helsinki's future was secure.

Fire was indeed fortuitous for the future of Helsinki. Just before the czar's proclamation, a fire had swept through the town,
permitting the construction of new buildings suitable for a nation's capital. The German-born architect Carl Ludvig Engel
was commissioned to rebuild the city, and, as a result, Helsinki
has some of the purest neoclassical architecture in the world.
Add to this foundation the stunning outlines of the Jügend period (early 20th century) and the modern buildings designed by
talented Finnish architects, and you have a European capital
city that is as architecturally eye-catching as it is different from
its Scandinavian neighbors or the rest of Europe.

*Numbers in the margin correspond to points of interest on the
Helsinki map.*

❶ Across from the city tourist office and beside the South Harbor
is the **Kauppatori** (Market Square). Sometimes it seems that
half the city is here seeking the best buys for the day or simply
catching up on the gossip. All around are stalls selling everything from colorful, freshly cut flowers to ripe fruit, from vege-

tables trucked in from the hinterland to handicrafts made in small villages. Look at the fruit stalls—mountains of strawberries; raspberries; blueberries; and, if you're lucky, *lakka* (cloudberries), which grow largely above the Arctic Circle in the midnight sun. Closer to the dock are fresh fish, caught that morning in the Baltic Sea and still flopping. You can't miss the **statue of Havis Amanda** standing in the square. This beautiful lady is loved by all Finns, and every May Day eve she is embraced by students who wade through the protective moat to crown her with their white caps.

The market ends at 2 PM, and, in the summer, the fruit and vegetable stalls are replaced with arts-and-crafts stalls. This happens at 3:30 PM and lasts until about 8 PM.

Another heartbeat of Helsinki is across the street, on the other side of **Pohjoisesplanadi** (North Esplanade). The uniformed guards will prevent you from entering, but the building is the ➋ **Presidentinlinna** (President's Palace), and next to it are the city hall and various administrative offices. Across from the palace is the waterfront, where ferries and sightseeing boats set out into the bay. On a summer's day it is a sailor's vision: sails hoisted and taut to the wind, yacht clubs beckoning, and island waters to explore. The redbrick edifice perched above the east ➌ side of the market is the Orthodox **Uspenskin Kirkko** (Uspenski Cathedral).

Just behind the cathedral is the district of **Katajanokka.** Here the 19th-century brick warehouses are slowly being renovated to form a complex of boutiques, arts-and-crafts studios, and restaurants. You'll find innovative designs at these shops, and the restaurants tend to offer lighter fare, which can make this a tempting area to stop for lunch. While in Katajanokka, you might enjoy a visit to **Wanha Satama,** a small complex of cafés and food stores attached to an art gallery.

A one-minute stroll north of city hall will take you into ➍ **Senaatintori** (Senate Square), the heart of neoclassical Helsinki and one of the most graceful squares in Europe, dominated ➎ by the domed **Tuomiokirkko** (Lutheran Cathedral). The square is the work of Ludvig Engel. The harmony created with the Tuomiokirkko, the university, and the state council building places you amid one of the purest styles of European architecture. Senaatintori has a dignified, stately air, enlivened in summer by sun worshipers who gather on the wide steps leading up to Tuomiokirkko and throughout the year by the bustle around the **Kiseleff Bazaar** on the square's south side.

Back on the market, head southward along the western shore of the South Harbor on Eteläranta Street. You'll soon come to the ➏ old brick **Market Hall**—it's worth taking a look at the voluminous displays of meat, fish, and other gastronomic goodies (open weekdays 8–5, Saturday 8–2). A little farther on is the **Olympia Terminal,** where the huge ferries from Sweden, Estonia, and Poland berth. Beyond this is **Kaivopuisto,** the elegant parkland district much favored by Russian high society during the 19th century. It is now popular as a strolling ground for Helsinki's citizens and as a residential area for diplomats.

Time Out   Perched on the shore is the **Ursula café.** However welcome the refreshments may be, the view of the harbor with its waterborne traffic is all the reason you need to stop here.

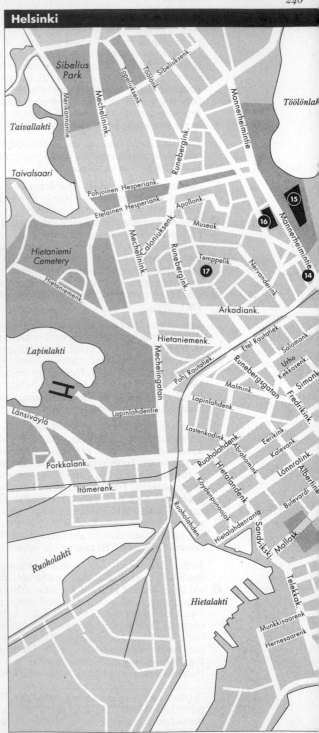

Helsinki

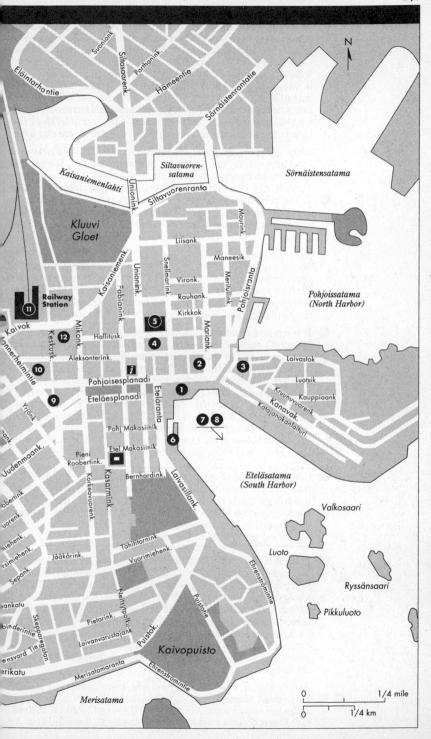

N

Suonionk.
Siltasaarenk.
Porthanink.
Hämeentie
Sörnäistenrantatie
Eläintarhantie
Kaisaniemenlahti
Unioninkatu
Siltavuoren-
satama
Siltavuorenranta
Sörnäistensatama
Kluuvi
Gloet
Maurink.
Liisank.
Maneesik.
Vironk.
Meritullink.
Rauhank.
Pohjoisranta
Kirkkok.
Kaisaniemenk.
Unioninkatu
Fabianink.
Snellmarink.
Pohjoissatama
(North Harbor)

Railway Station
(11)
Kaivok.
Keskusk.
(12)
Mikonk.
Hallitusk.
(5)
(4)
Mariank.
Mannerheimintie
Aleksanterink.
(10)
(2)
(3)
Laivastok.
i
Pohjoisesplanadi
Luotsik.
(9)
Eteläesplanadi
(1)
Kruununvuorenk.
Kauppiaank.
Yrjönk.
Eteläranta
Kanavak.
Kalajonokanlaituri
Pohj Makasiink.
(7)(8)
Uudenmaank.
Pieni
Roobertink.
Etel Makasiink.
(6)
Kasarmink.
Roobertink.
vuorenk.
Bernhardink.
Eteläsatama
(South Harbor)
niehenk.
rsimiehenk.
Korkeavuorenk.
Laivasillank.
Valkosaari
Sepank.
Jääkärink.
Tähtitornink.
Vuorimiehenk.
Luoto
ankatu
binderintie
Skepparegatan
ensvard Tie
Pietarink.
Neitsypolku
Ryssänsaari
erikatu
gatan
Laivanvarustajank.
Puistok.
Pikkuluoto
Puistotie
Ehrenströmintie
Merisatamaranta
Kaivopuisto
Ehrenströmintie

Merisatama

0   1/4 mile
0   1/4 km

You can avoid the long walk back by cutting across Kaivopuisto to Tehtaankatu and catching streetcar No. 3T to the market-place. From here, there's a frequent ferry service to **Suomen-linna.** *Suomenlinna* means "Finland's Castle," and for good reason. In 1748 the Finnish army helped build this fortress, which grew so over the years that today Suomenlinna is a series of interlinked islands. For a long time the impregnable fortress was referred to as the "Gibraltar of the North." While it has never been taken by assault, its occupants did surrender twice without a fight—once to the Russians in the war of 1808–19 and then to the British, who bombarded the fortress, causing fires.

Although still a fortress, Suomenlinna is today a collection of museums, parks, and gardens. In early summer it is engulfed in mauve and purple mists of lilacs, the trees introduced from Versailles by the Finnish architect Augustin Ehrensvärd. One of the museums you may care to visit is the **Pohjoismainen Taidekeskus** (Nordic Arts Center), which exhibits and pro-motes Scandinavian art. *Admission free. Open Tues.–Sun. 11–6.*

Back on the mainland, head west from the marketplace up Pohjoisesplanadi. To your left are the Esplanade gardens. On your right are the showrooms and boutiques of some of Finland's top fashion designers (*see* Shopping, *below*). The cir-cular **Svenska Teatern** (Swedish Theater) marks the junction of the Esplanade and Helsinki's main artery, Mannerheimintie.

If you take a right up Keskuskatu, you'll come to **Stockmann's,** Helsinki's most famous store, well worth a shopping stop. Next you'll come to the **railway station** and its square, the bustling commuting hub of the city. The station's huge red-granite fig-ures are by Emil Wikström, but the solid building they adorn was designed by Eliel Saarinen, one of the founders of the early 20th-century National Romantic style. The **Ateneumin Taidemuseo** (Finnish National Gallery) is on the south side of the square facing the **National Theater.** *Admission: FIM 10 adults, children free. Open year-round Tues. and Fri. 9–5, Wed. and Thurs. 9–9, weekends 11–5.*

Time Out **Café Socis,** in the Seurahuone Hotel opposite the Railway Sta-tion, provides a restful turn-of-the-century atmosphere for a fixed-price lunch or afternoon tea. **Ekberg's café** has gained a good reputation for its traditional confectionery line. Located at Bulevardi 9, it is a favorite of literary people and the various publishing companies in the vicinity.

In front of the main post office west of the station is the **statue of Marshal Mannerheim** gazing down Mannerheimintie, the major thoroughfare named in his honor. Perhaps no man in Finnish history is so revered as Marshal Baron Carl Gustaf Man-nerheim, the military and political leader who guided Finland through much of the turbulent 20th century. When he died in Switzerland on January 28, 1951, his body was flown back to his native land to lie in state in the cathedral. For three days, young war widows, children, and soldiers filed past his bier by the thousands.

About half a mile along, past the colonnaded red-granite **Parliament House,** stands **Finlandiatalo** (Finlandia Hall), one of the last creations of Alvar Aalto. If you can't make it to a con-cert there, take a guided tour. Finlandia Hall will be shut for interior renovations from 1994 to February 1995. Behind the hall lies the inland bay of Töölönlahti and, almost opposite, the ⑯ **Suomen Kansallismuseo** (National Museum), another example of National Romantic exotica in which Eliel Saarinen played a part. *Admission: FIM 10 adults, FIM 5 children. Open May–Sept., daily 11–4; Oct–Apr., Mon.–Sat. 11–3, Sun. 11–4; free admission on Tues. year-round 6–9 PM.*

Tucked away in a labyrinth of streets to the west is the strik-⑰ ingly modern **Temppeliaukion Kirkko** (Temple Square Church). Carved out of solid rock and topped with a copper dome, this landmark is a center for religious activities, church services, and concerts. From here it's only a short distance back to Mannerheimintie, where you can pick up any streetcar for the downtown area. *Lutherinkatu 3. Open June–Aug., weekdays 10–8, weekend hours vary; Sept.–May, Mon. 10–8, Tues. 10–12:45 and 2:15–8, Wed.–Fri. 10–6, weekend hours vary.*

Off the Beaten Track

Located in Espoo, Helsinki's next-door neighbor, is the garden city of **Tapiola,** one of Finland's architectural highlights. Designed by Alvar Aalto, the urban landscape of alternating high and low residential buildings, fountains, gardens, and swimming pools blends into the natural surroundings. What began as an experiment in communal, affordable housing has now lost its radical appeal, but Tapiola still holds interest for anyone interested in urban planning. Sightseeing tours are available from the Espoo City Tourist Office, tel. 90/460311.

Akseli Gallen Kallela (1865–1931) was one of Finland's greatest artists. His studio-home can be seen at Gallen-Kallelan tie 27, Tarvaspää. To get there, take tram No. 4 to Munkkiniemi, then it's a 1 ½-mile walk through the woods. *Admission: FIM 30 adults, FIM 10 children. Open mid-May–Aug., Mon.–Thurs. 10–8, Fri.–Sun. 10–5; Sept.–mid-May, Tues.–Sat. 10–4, Sun. 10–5.*

Shopping

Shopping Districts and Specialty Shops You should find everything you need on **Pohjoisesplanadi** (North Esplanade) and **Aleksanterinkatu,** in the **Forum Shopping Mall** at Mannerheimintie 20, or on the pedestrian mall **Iso Roobertinkatu.** You can make purchases until 10 PM, seven days a week, in the shops along the Tunneli underpass leading from the Railway Station.

Some of the shops in **Kiseleff Bazaar** and along Eteläesplanadi and Pohjoisesplanadi are open on Sundays from noon to 4 in summer. Along the latter you'll find some of Finland's top design houses: **Hackman Arabia** (Iittala and Nuutajärvi) ceramics and glass at No. 25; **Pentik** leather at No. 27C; **Aarikka** accessories, and wooden toys at No. 25–27 and Eteläesplanadi 8; **Marimekko** fashions at No. 31 and Eteläesplanadi 14; and **Artek** furniture and ceramics at Eteläesplanadi 18. Helsinki's three top jewelry boutiques are almost adjacent: **Galerie Björn Weckström,** Unioninkatu 30; **Kalevala Koru,** Unioninkatu 25; and **Kaunis Koru,** Kiseleff Bazaar.

Department Stores **Stockmann's,** a huge store that fills an entire block between Aleksanterinkatu, Mannerheimintie, and Keskuskatu, is your best bet if you want to find everything under one roof.

Markets The **Kauppatori market** beside the South Harbor (*see* Exploring Helsinki, *above*) is an absolute must. Also try to find time for the variety of goods at the **Hietalahti flea market,** located at the west end of Bulevardi on Hietalahti. (Open Mon.–Sat. 7 AM–2 PM.)

Dining

For details and price-category definitions, *see* Dining in Staying in Finland. Best bets are indicated by a star ★.

Very Expensive **Alexander Nevski.** Helsinki has gained a reputation for having
★ the best Russian-cuisine restaurants in Scandinavia. Situated right across from the Havis Amanda statue is Finland's most celebrated Russian restaurant, Alexander Nevski. The decor of the restaurant is dominated by hues of green and palm trees, in the Russian-French style of 19th-century St. Petersburg restaurants. Be sure to try the blinis and smoked sturgeon. *Pohjoisesplanadi 17, tel. 90/639610. Reservations advised. AE, DC, MC, V. Closed Sun., Christmas, and June 24–25.*

★ **Amadeus.** Situated in an old town house near the South Harbor, Amadeus specializes in game dishes, such as baked ptarmigan and reindeer fillets. *Sofiankatu 4, tel. 90/626676. Reservations advised. AE, DC, MC, V. Closed Sun., Christmas, June 24–25, and bank holidays.*

Galateia. Located on top of the Hotel Inter-Continental with a magnificent view of Töölö bay and the city is Helsinki's best seafood restaurant. *Mannerheimintie 46, tel. 90/405–5900 or 90/40551. Reservations advised. AE, DC, MC, V. Open weekday evenings only. Closed weekends, Christmas, and Easter.*

★ **Palace Gourmet.** One of Helsinki's top restaurants, Palace Gourmet offers elegant surroundings with a splendid view of South Harbor. Chef Markku Taimi has been with the restaurant for six years and specializes in French and Finnish fare. As an appetizer, try the grilled tartar of whitefish with scallops, followed by a tasty dish of mosaic of salmon and pike perch with white wine sauce. *Eteläranta 10, tel. 90/134561. Reservations advised. AE, DC, MC, V. Closed weekends, bank holidays, and July.*

Savoy. With its airy dining room overlooking the Esplanade park, the Savoy is a favorite for business lunches. The interior was designed by the architect Alvar Aalto in the functionalist style. The restaurant was Finnish statesman Marshal Baron Carl Gustaf Mannerheim's favorite, and he is rumored to have introduced the *Vorschmack* (minced lamb and anchovies) recipe to the restaurant. *Eteläesplanadi 14, tel. 90/176571. Reservations advised. AE, DC, MC, V. Closed Sun., Easter, June 24–25, and bank holidays.*

Expensive **Bellevue.** Established in 1917, Bellevue is one of Helsinki's
★ oldest restaurants. Despite its French name, the restaurant is Russian, both in decor and cuisine. Fillet à la Novgorod and chicken à la Kiev are the authentic articles here. *Rahapajankatu 3, tel. 90/179560. Reservations advised. AE, DC, MC, V. Closed June 24–25.*

Kosmos. Located only a short walking distance from Stockmann's is Kosmos, which serves good food at reasonable prices for Helsinki. The restaurant is a favorite among artists, writers, and journalists during the evenings, and it's popular among business people during lunchtime. One of Kosmos's specialties is sweetbread. *Kalevankatu 3, tel. 90/607603. Reserva-*

tions advised. AE, DC, MC, V. Closed weekends and national holidays.

Rivoli. Rivoli is divided into two restaurants that share the same menu. The seafood section is friendly and more low-key while the other section has a more sophisticated atmosphere and is decorated in elegant white and black tones. Rivoli specializes in Finnish and international dishes. *Albertinkatu 38, tel. 90/643455. Reservations advised. AE, DC, MC, V. Closed Christmas, Easter, and June 24–25.*

Svenska Klubben. The restaurant resembles an English stately home. You can enjoy an aperitif before having lunch or dinner at the lobby bar, which has a fireplace and big, comfortable armchairs. Svenska Klubben specializes in local fish, roe, game, and fowl dishes. *Maurinkatu 6, tel. 90/135–4706. Reservations advised. AE, DC, MC, V. Closed weekends, Christmas, June 20–Aug. 16, and bank holidays.*

Troikka. The Troikka takes you back to czarist times in decor, paintings, and music, and offers exceptionally good food and friendly service. Try the Siberian *pelmens* (small meat pasties). *Caloniuksenkatu 3, tel. 90/445229. Reservations advised. AE, DC, MC, V. Closed June–mid-Aug., weekends; mid-Aug.–May, Sun. and national holidays.*

Moderate **Kynsilaukka (Garlic).** Garlic is the pungent theme of this restaurant, where the rustic decor suits the menu. *Fredrikinkatu 22, tel. 90/651939. Reservations advised. AE, DC, MC, V.*

Omenapuu. This cozy family restaurant, set in the midst of a busy shopping district, features special dishes for weight watchers. *Keskuskatu 6, second floor, tel. 90/630205. Reservations advised for lunch. AE, DC, MC, V. Closed Christmas.*

Wellamo. The decor at this restaurant draws upon changing exhibitions by new artists. Try the lamb steak in garlic butter. *Vyökatu 9, tel. 90/663139. Reservations advised. AE, MC, V. Closed Mon., Christmas, and June 24–25.*

Inexpensive **China.** Located in the heart of Helsinki, China specializes in Cantonese fare. The Peking Duck is recommended. *Annankatu 25, tel. 90/640258. Reservations advised. AE, DC, MC, V. Closed Christmas, June 24–25.*

Perho Mechelin. This is the restaurant connected with Helsinki's catering school. During summer the emphasis is on Finnish food, particularly salmon and reindeer. *Mechelininkatu 7, tel. 90/493481. Reservations advised. AE, DC, MC, V. Closed Christmas, Easter, and June 24–25.*

Pizzeria Dennis. This pleasant spot serves the best pasta and pizza in town. *Fredrikinkatu 36, tel. 90/694–5271. Reservations advised. DC, MC, V. Closed Christmas, June 24–25.*

Lodging

For details and price-category definitions, *see* Lodging in Staying in Finland. Best bets are indicated by a star ★.

Very Expensive **Hesperia.** Enlarged and redecorated in 1986 and fully renovated in 1993, the Hesperia is modern in the best Finnish tradition and just a short stroll from the center of the city. *Mannerheimintie 50, 00260, tel. 90/43101, fax 90/431–0995. 376 rooms; 295 with bath and 81 with shower. Facilities: sauna, pool, golf simulator, nightclub, helicopter service. AE, DC, MC, V. Closed Christmas.*

★ **Inter-Continental.** This is the most popular hotel in the city—

with American visitors, at least. It's modern and close to
Finlandia Hall, although its rooms are on the small side. Res-
taurant noise may disturb guests staying on the top floor.
*Mannerheimintie 46–48, 00260, tel. 90/40551, fax 90/405–5255.
555 rooms with bath. Facilities: sauna, pool, disco. AE, DC,
MC, V.*

Palace. The Palace has a splendid location overlooking the
South Harbor—but make sure you ask for a room with a view;
these rooms are on the ninth floor. *Eteläranta 10, 00130, tel.
90/134561, fax 90/654786. 50 rooms with bath or shower. Facilities: 2 restaurants, sauna. AE, DC, MC, V. Sometimes closed
during Christmas.*

Ramada Presidentti. Located in the heart of Helsinki is the
Ramada Presidentti, one of the city's top luxury hotels. Apart
from its spacious rooms, the hotel also offers a wide range of
facilities. In 1991, Finland's first international casino was inaugurated at the hotel. The hotel's main restaurant, Four Seasons, serves tasty buffet meals. *Eteläinen Rautatiekatu 4,
00100, tel. 90/6911, fax 90/694–7886. 495 rooms with bath. Facilities: sauna, pool, nightclub, casino. AE, DC, MC, V.*

Rivoli Jardin. Rivoli Jardin is a central town house, with all
rooms overlooking a quiet courtyard. The rooms are rather
small but well equipped and attractively designed. Breakfast is
served in the winter garden, but there's no restaurant.
*Kasarmikatu 40, 00130, tel. 90/177880, fax 90/656988. 54
rooms with shower. Facilities: sauna. AE, DC, MC, V. Closed
Christmas.*

SAS Royal Hotel. This luxury hotel is centrally located and a 10-
minute walk from the Railway Station. The rooms are elegant
and decorated in one of three styles: Scandinavian (light
woods), Oriental (lots of bamboo), and Italian (strong colors).
The Johan Ludvig restaurant specializes in tasty dishes like
prime rib of beef. The hotel's other restaurant, Ströget, is
cheaper and serves Danish sandwiches. *Runeberginkatu 2,
00100, tel. 90/69580, fax 90/6958–7100. 260 rooms with bath.
Facilities: 2 restaurants, sauna. AE, DC, MC, V.*

★ **Strand Inter-Continental.** Centrally located, the hotel is adjacent to the Old City on the waterfront. The hotel's distinctive
use of stone, granite, and marble in the central lobby is accentuated by a soaring atrium and softened by a cozy fireplace.
There is a choice of restaurants—from Pamir's elegant gourmet dishes of seafood, steak, and game to the Atrium Plaza's
buffet restaurant for light meals. *John Stenbergin ranta 4,
00530, tel. 90/39351, fax 90/761362. 200 rooms with bath. Facilities: 2 restaurants, sauna, indoor pool, lounge-bar. AE, DC,
MC, V.*

Expensive **Rantasipi Airport Hotel.** Just 3.2 kilometers (2 miles) from the
airport, the Rantasipi was built in 1981 and expanded in 1986.
Although the rooms are rather small, they have forest views.
Airport shuttle service is provided. *Robert Huberintie 4,
01510, Vantaa, tel. 90/87051, fax 90/822846. 300 rooms with
shower. Facilities: sauna, pool, piano bar. AE, DC, MC, V.
Sometimes closed during Christmas.*

★ **Seurahuone.** This is a traditional town house from 1914, renovated in 1982, facing the Railway Station. The room decor
ranges from sleek modern to crystal chandeliers and brass bedsteads, so specify your preference. Streetside rooms get some
traffic noise. *Kaivokatu 12, 00100, tel. 90/170441, fax 90/*

664170. 118 rooms; 95 with bath, 23 with shower. Facilities: sauna, café. AE, DC, MC, V.

Moderate **Aurora.** About a mile from the city center, the Aurora is just opposite the Linnanmäki amusement park. Reasonable prices, cozy rooms, and good facilities have made this hotel a favorite with families. *Helsinginkatu 50, 00530, tel. 90/717400, fax 90/ 714240. 70 rooms with shower, 6 with bath. Facilities: restaurant, sauna, pool, squash courts, health spa, solarium. AE, DC, MC, V. Closed Dec. 23–Jan. 2.*

Hospiz. A property of the Helsinki YMCA, the Hospiz is located on a quiet, central street and is unpretentious but comfortable. *Vuorikatu 17B, 00100, tel. 90/173441, fax 90/626880. 160 rooms with bath or shower. Facilities: sauna, restaurant. AE, DC, MC, V.*

Marttahotelli. This hotel was fully renovated in 1990. The rooms are small but pleasantly decorated. It's only a 10-minute walk from the Railway Station. *Uudenmankatu 24, 00120, tel. 90/646211, fax 90/680–1266. 45 rooms with shower or bath. Facilities: sauna. AE, DC, MC, V. Closed Christmas and June 24–25.*

Merihotelli. Located on the seafront, the Merihotelli is a 10-minute walk from the center of town. The rooms are somewhat small but modern; those with a sea view get some traffic noise. *John Stenbergin ranta 6, 00530, tel. 90/708711, fax 90/760271. 87 rooms with shower. Facilities: sauna. AE, DC, MC, V.*

Inexpensive **Academica.** The Academica is a town house with simple but adequate rooms, 10 minutes' walk from the town center. *Hietaniemenkatu 14, 00100, tel. 90/1311–4265 or 90/402–0206, fax 90/441201. 217 rooms, most with shower. Facilities: sauna, pool, indoor tennis, disco. AE, MC, V. Closed Sept.–May.*

Skatta. Located in the elegant neighborhood of Katajanokka Island, and 2 kilometers (1¼ miles) from the Railway Station, is modest Skatta. Each room has a kitchenette. *Linnankatu 3, 00160, tel. 90/659233 or 90/669984, fax 90/631352. 24 rooms with shower. Facilities: sauna, gym. AE, DC, MC, V. Sometimes closed during Christmas.*

The Arts

For a list of events, pick up the free publication *Helsinki This Week*, available in hotels and tourist offices. For recorded program information in English, dial 058. A central reservations office for all events is **Lippupalvelu,** Mannerheimintie 5, tel. 9700–4700 or 90/664466 when calling from abroad. Call **Tiketti,** Yrjönkatu 29C, tel. 90/693–2255, when making reservations for small concerts and restaurants.

Theater Although all performances are in Finnish or Swedish, summertime productions in such bucolic settings as **Suomenlinna Island, Kekuspuisto Park, Mustikkamaa Island,** the **Rowing Stadium** (operettas), **Indoor Ice Rink** (rock concerts), and the **Savoy Theater** (ballet and music performances) make enjoyable entertainment. The splendid new **Opera House** opened in 1993 in a waterside park by **Töölönlahti** just a few hundred feet from Finlandia Hall.

Concerts The two main locations for musical events are **Finlandia Hall** (tel. 90/40241) and **Temppeliaukio Church** (*see* Exploring, *above*).

Festivals   Finland holds many festivals throughout the country, especially during the summer months. The **Helsinki Festival** is said to be the biggest in Scandinavia. For more than two weeks during August to September, the city is turned over to the arts. Scores of musical happenings and art exhibitions are organized throughout Helsinki. Each Helsinki Festival has a theme (in 1994 it's Great Britain). Contact Helsinki Festival, Unioninkatu 28, tel. 90/659688. For more information on festivals, call Finland Festivals, Mannerheimintie 40, B49, tel. 90/445763 or 90/445686.

Nightlife

Nightclubs   The most popular nightclub in town is the **Hesperia** (Hesperia, Kivelänkatu 2, tel. 90/43101). **Fizz** (Arctia Hotel Marski, Mannerheimintie 10, tel. 90/68061), **Fennia** (Mikonkatu 17, tel. 90/666355), **Café Adlon** (Fabianinkatu 14, tel. 90/664611), and **Kaivohuone** (Kaivohuone Kaivopuisto, tel. 90/177881) are also popular.

Discos   The liveliest and most popular are **Old Baker's** (Mannerheimintie 10, tel. 90/641579) and **Fanny & Alexander** (Pitkänsillanranta 3, tel. 90/701–4424). The most popular among young people is **KY Exit** (Pohjoinen Rautatiekatu 21, tel. 90/407238). If you are looking for tropical salsa music, try **La Havanna** (Erottajankatu 7, tel 90/680–2668).

The Lakelands

This is a region of lakes, forests, and islands in southeastern and central Finland. The light in these northern latitudes has a magical softness, and the vistas are constantly changing. For centuries the lakeland region was a buffer between the warring empires of Sweden and Russia. After visiting the people of the lakelands, you should have a basic understanding of the Finnish word *sisu* (guts), a quality that has kept Finns independent, fiercely guarding their neutrality.

Getting Around

Savonlinna is the best-placed town in the Lakelands and can make a convenient base from which to begin exploring. You can fly to the Savonlinna area from Helsinki in 40 minutes; a connecting bus takes you the remaining 16 kilometers (10 miles) into town. By train, the journey takes 5½ hours; by bus, 6 hours.

If you travel by car, you can do the lake trips as separate excursions. The alternative is to take advantage of the excellent network of air, rail, bus, and boat transportation. Take the boat from Savonlinna to Kuopio in 12 hours (**Roll Line**, tel. 971/262–6744). From Kuopio, take the 320-kilometer (200-mile) crosscountry bus ride via Jyväskylä to Tampere. Continue by boat to Hämeenlinna for a little over eight hours (**Finnish Silverline**, tel. 931/124803). The final leg by bus or train back to Helsinki takes about 1¼ hours.

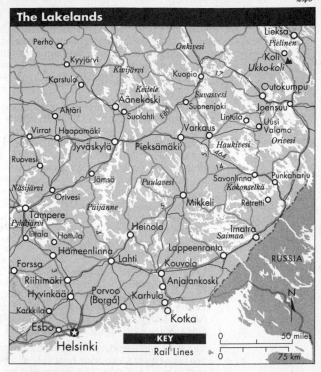

The Lakelands

Guided Tours

A program of **Friendly Finland Tours**, available through a number of travel agencies, offers escorted lakeland packages from two to 11 days, starting from Helsinki. Brochures are available from the **Finnish Tourist Board** (Eteläesplanadi 4, tel. 90/403011) and its overseas offices (*see* Government Tourist Offices in Chapter 1).

Tourist Information

Hämeenlinna (Sibeliuksenkatu 5A, 13100 Hämeenlinna, tel. 917/142388). Open June–Aug., weekdays 9–6, Sat. 9–2; Sept.–May, weekdays 9–5.

Kuopio (Haapaniemenkatu 17, 70110 Kuopio, tel. 971/182584). Open weekdays 8–5; June 11–Aug. 13, also Sat. 9–1.

Savonlinna (Puistokatu 1, 57100 Savonlinna, tel. 957/273492). Open June and Aug., daily 8–6; July, daily 8 AM–10 PM; Sept.–May, weekdays 9 AM–4 PM.

Tampere (Verkatehtaankatu 2, 33211 Tampere, tel. 931/126652). Open June–Aug., weekdays 8:30 AM–8 PM, Sat. 8:30–6, Sun. 11:30–6; Sept.–May, weekdays 8:30–5.

Exploring the Lakelands

Savonlinna The center of **Savonlinna** is a series of islands linked by bridges. First, stop at the tourist office for information; then cross the bridge east to the **open-air market** that flourishes alongside the main passenger quay. It's from here that you can catch the boat to Kuopio. In days when waterborne traffic was the major form of transportation, Savonlinna was the central hub of the passenger fleet serving Saimma, the largest lake system in Europe. Now the lake traffic is dominated by cruise and sightseeing boats.

A 10-minute stroll from the quay to the southeast brings you to Savonlinna's most famous sight, the castle of **Olavinlinna.** First built in 1475 to protect Finland's eastern border, the castle retains its medieval character and is one of Scandinavia's best-preserved historic monuments. Still surrounded by water that once formed part of its defensive strength, the fortress rises majestically out of the lake. The Savonlinna Opera Festival is held in the courtyard each July. The combination of music and setting is spellbinding. You will need to make reservations well in advance (tel. 957/514700 or 957/273492), both for tickets and for hotel rooms. *Castle admission: FIM 14 adults, FIM 7 children; includes a guided tour. Open June–Aug., daily 10–5; Sept.–May, daily 10–3.*

Close to the castle are the 19th-century steam schooners, *Mikko, Salama,* and *Savonlinna.* The *Salama* houses an excellent museum on the history of lake traffic, including the fascinating floating timber trains that are still a common sight on Saimaa today. *Admission: FIM 12 adults, FIM 6 children. Open June–Aug., daily 10–8; Sept.–May, Tues.–Sun. 11–5.*

The most popular excursion from Savonlinna is to **Retretti.** You can take either a two-hour boat ride or a 30-minute, 29-kilometer (18-mile) bus trip. The journey by bus takes you along the 8-kilometer (5-mile) ridge of **Punkaharju.** This amazing ridge of pine-covered rocks, which rises out of the water and separates the lakes on either side, predates the Ice Age. At times it narrows to only 25 feet, yet it still manages to accommodate a road and train tracks. *Admission: FIM 60 adults, FIM 55 senior citizens and students, FIM 25 children. Open July, daily 10–7; May 21–June and Aug., daily 10–6.*

Near Retretti is the **Punkaharju National Hotel.** The building started as a gamekeeper's lodge for Czar Nicholas I in 1845, but has been subsequently enlarged and restored; it is now a restful spot for a meal or an overnight visit.

Kuopio The 12-hour boat trip from Savonlinna to **Kuopio** is probably the best opportunity you'll get to feel the soul of the Finnish lakeland. Meals are available on board. The boat arrives at Kuopio passenger harbor, where you'll find a small evening market in action daily from 3 to 10. If you go by car, the best route is by Highways 14, 464, and 5, via Rantasalmi and Varkaus.

The Kuopio Tourist Office is located close to the **Tori** (marketplace). The Tori should be one of the places you visit first, for it is one of the most colorful outdoor markets in Finland. *Open May–Aug., Mon.–Sat. 7–3; Sept.–Apr., Mon.–Sat., 7–2.*

Only a 15-minute walk from the heart of Kuopio is another picturesque market square by the Kuopio passenger harbor. *Open May 15–Aug. 31, daily noon–10.*

The **Orthodox Church Museum** has one of the most interesting and unusual collections of its kind in the world. When Karelia was ceded to the Soviet Union after World War II, the religious art was taken out of the monasteries and brought to Kuopio. The collection is eclectic and, of its type, one of the rarest in the world. *Karjalankatu 1, Kuopio, tel. 971/261–8818. Open May–Aug., Tues.–Sun. 10–4; Sept.–Apr., weekdays noon–3, weekends noon–5.*

Visitors who are fascinated by the treasures in the museum will want to visit the Orthodox convent of Lintula and the **Monastery of Valamo.** The monastery is a center for Russian Orthodox religious and cultural life in Finland. The precious 18th-century icons and sacred objects are housed in the main church and in the icon conservation center. The Orthodox library is the most extensive in Finland and is open to visitors. Church services are held daily. There is a café-restaurant, and hotel and hostel accommodations are available at the monastery. It can be reached by car and bus routes from Kuopio, Joensuu, and Varkaus. *Uusi Valamo, tel. 972/61911 (972/61959 for hotel reservations). Admission free. Guided tours: FIM 20 adults, FIM 5 children. Open daily 10–6.*

The **convent of Lintula** can be reached by boat from Valamo, or you can visit both the convent and the monastery by boat on scenic day excursions from Kuopio that run from June 9 through August 9. Tickets, available from the tourist office, cost FIM 240 for adults and FIM 125 for children.

Puijo Tower is best visited at sunset, when the lakes shimmer with reflected light. The slender tower is located 3 kilometers (2 miles) northwest of Kuopio. It has two observation decks and a revolving restaurant on top where you can enjoy the marvelous views. *Open June 1–Aug. 15, daily 9 AM–10 PM; Aug. 16–May 31, daily 10–6.*

Tampere The 320-kilometer (200-mile) journey from Kuopio to **Tampere** will take four to five hours, whether you travel by car or bus. The train ride from Helsinki to Tampere takes about two hours. Almost every guide will inform you that Tampere, the country's third-largest city, is Finland's Pittsburgh. However, the resemblance begins and ends with the concentrated presence here of industry—the settings themselves have little in common.

From about the year 1000, this part of Finland was a base from which traders and hunters set out on their expeditions to northern Finland and even to Lapland. But it was not until 1779 that a Swedish king, Gustav III, actually founded the town of Tampere. One hundred and three years later, a Scotsman by the name of James Finlayson came to the infant city and established a factory for spinning cotton. This was perhaps the beginning of "big business" in Finland. The firm of Finlayson exists today and is still one of the country's large industrial enterprises.

An isthmus, little more than half a mile wide at its narrowest point, separates the lakes Näsijärvi and Pyhäjärvi, and at one spot the **Tammerkoski Rapids** provide an outlet for the waters of one to cascade through to the other. Called the "Mother of Tampere," these rapids provide a small part of the power on which the town's livelihood depends. Their natural beauty has been preserved in spite of the factories on either bank, and the well-designed public buildings of the city grouped around them enhance their general effect. Also in the heart of town is

Hämeensilta Bridge, with its four statues by the well-known Finnish sculptor Wäinö Aaltonen.

Close to the Hämeensilta bridge, near the high-rise Hotel Ilves, are some old factory buildings that have been restored as shops and boutiques. Nearby, at Verkatehtaankatu 2, is the city tourist office, where you can buy a 24-hour **Tourist Ticket** (FIM 25 adults, FIM 20 children) that allows unlimited travel on local city transportation.

Parts of the ridge of **Pyynikki** separating the two lakes form a natural park, including the Särkänniemi peninsula, about a 20-minute walk northwest of the city center. On the way there, visit one of Tampere's best small museums, **The Amuri Museum of Workers' Housing.** It consists of a block of old timber houses, with descriptions and illustrations of how the original tenants lived; it is so well done that you half expect them to return at any minute. *Makasiininkatu 12. Admission: FIM 10 adults, FIM 3 children. Open May 11–Sept. 19, Tues.–Sat. 9–5, Sun. 11–5.*

At Särkänniemi, a 15-minute walk from downtown Tampere, is Finland's tallest structure, the 168-meter (550-foot) **Näsinneula Observation Tower.** There is an observatory on top, as well as a revolving restaurant. The views are magnificent, commanding the lake, forest, and town. The contrast between the industrial maze of Tampere at your feet and the serenity of the lakes stretching out to meet the horizon is unforgettable. *Open May 1–Aug. 29, Mon.–Sun. 10–8; Aug. 30–Apr. 30, weekdays 10–4, weekends 10–5.*

The same building complex houses the first **planetarium** in Scandinavia and a well-planned **aquarium,** which includes a separate dolphinarium. Near this complex is another striking example of Finnish architecture, the **Sarah Hildén Art Museum,** where modern Finnish and international artists (including Miró, Leger, Picasso, and Chagall) are on display. *Joint admission: FIM 60 adults, FIM 30 children; Hildén Museum only: FIM 10 adults, FIM 3 children. Open June–Aug., daily 11–6; Sept.–May, Tues.–Sun. 11–6.*

On the east side of the town is the modern **Kaleva Church.** What may appear from the outside to be a grain elevator is, in fact, as seen from the interior, a soaring monument to space and light. *Open May–Aug., daily 10–6; Sept.–Apr., daily 11–1.*

Most buildings in Tampere, including the cathedral, are comparatively modern. However, though the cathedral was built only in 1907, it is worth a visit to see some of the best-known masterpieces of Finnish art, including Magnus Encknell's frescoes, *The Resurrection,* and a few works by Hugo Simberg, such as *Wounded Angel* and *Garden of Death.*

It was in Tampere that Lenin and Stalin first met, and this fateful occasion is commemorated with displays of photos and mementoes in the **Lenin Museum.** *Hämeenpuisto 28. Admission: FIM 10 adults, FIM 3 children. Open weekdays 9–5, weekends 11–4.*

One of the most popular excursions from Tampere is the **Poet's Way** boat tour along Lake Näsijärvi. The boat passes through the agricultural parish of Ruovesi, where J. L. Runeberg, Finland's national poet, used to live. Shortly before the boat docks at Virrat, you'll pass through the straights of Visuvesi, where many artists and writers spend their summers. *Finnish Silverline and Poet's Way, PL 87, Verkatehtaankatu 2, 33221 Tampere, tel. 931/124804. Round-trip fare: FIM 220.*

Hämeenlinna The Finnish Silverline's white motor ships leave Tampere for **Hämeenlinna** from the Laukontori terminal. If you're traveling by car, take Highway 3 and stop en route at the famous **Iittala Glassworks,** which offers guided tours and has a museum and shop. The magnificent glass is produced by top designers, and the "seconds" are bargains you won't find elsewhere. *Open Jan. 2–Apr., daily 10–6; May–Aug., daily 9–8; Sept.–Nov. 14, daily 10–6; Nov. 15–Dec. 23, weekdays 10–8, weekends 10–6.*

Hämeenlinna's secondary school has educated many famous Finns, among them composer Jean Sibelius (1865–1957). The only surviving timber house in the town center is the **birthplace of Sibelius,** a modest dwelling built in 1834. Here you can listen to tapes of his music and see the harmonium he played when he was a child. *Hallituskatu 11. Admission: FIM 10 adults, FIM 5 children; admission includes a free guided tour. Open May–Aug., daily 10–4; Sept.–Apr., Sun. noon–4.*

The much-altered medieval **Häme Castle,** on the lakeshore half a mile north of the town center, doesn't compare with Savonlinna's, but it has seen a lot of action in its time and has been used as a granary and a prison. *Admission: FIM 14 adults, FIM 7 children. Open May–Aug., daily 10–6; Sept.–Apr., daily 10–4.*

Hattula Church, 6 kilometers (3½ miles) to the north, is the most famous of Finland's medieval churches. The interior is a fresco gallery of biblical scenes whose vicious little devils and soulful saints are as clear and fresh as when they were first painted around 1510. There is a regular bus service from the town center. *Admission: FIM 10 adults, FIM 5 children. Open May 15–Aug. 15, daily 10–4.*

Rail and bus departures to Helsinki are frequent. If you're traveling by car, take Highway 3. As you pass by **Riihimäki,** you'll see signs to the **Finnish Glass Museum.** Follow them! It's an outstanding display of the history of glass from early Egyptian times to the present, beautifully arranged in an old glass factory. *Admission: FIM 10 adults, FIM 5 children. Open Apr.–Sept., daily 10–6.*

Dining and Lodging

For details and price-category definitions, *see* Dining and Lodging in Staying in Finland. Best bets are indicated by a star ★.

Hämeenlinna **Fransmanni.** Located at the Vaakunna Hotel and only a stone's
Dining throw from the railway station is Fransmanni, one of Hämeenlinna's favorite restaurants. There's a wide range of salads as well as fish and meat dishes. *Possentie 7, tel. 917/5831. Reservations advised. AE, DC, MC, V. Expensive.*
Piiparkakkutalo. Located in a renovated old timber building, Piiparkakkutalo has a restaurant upstairs, a pub downstairs. The menu offers fine Finnish fare. *Kirkkorinne 2, tel. 917/121606. Reservations advised. DC, MC, V. Expensive.*

Lodging **Rantasipi Aulanko.** One of Finland's top hotels sits on the lake-
★ shore in a beautifully landscaped park 6.4 kilometers (4 miles)
from town. *14999 Hämeenlinna, tel. 917/58801, fax 917/21922.
245 rooms with bath. Facilities: saunas, pool, tennis, golf, riding, boating, nightclub, tax-free shop. AE, DC, MC, V. Expensive–Very Expensive.*

Kuopio **Mustalammas.** Located near the passenger harbor, Musta-
Dining lammas has been attractively adapted from a beer cellar and
features steaks and basic fish dishes. *Satamakatu 4, tel. 971/
262–3494. Reservations advised. AE, DC, MC, V. Very Expensive.*
Sampo. Situated in the town center, Sampo specializes in
muikku (vendace), a kind of whitefish. Try the smoked variety.
The atmosphere is unpretentious and lively. *Kauppakatu 13,
tel. 971/261–4677. MC, V. Moderate.*

Lodging **Arctia.** Completed in 1987, the Arctia is the most modern and
best equipped of local hotels. It has all the advantages of a lakefront location and is close to the center of town. *Satamakatu 1,
70100 Kuopio, tel. 971/195111, fax 971/195170. 141 rooms with
bath or shower. Facilities: sauna, swimming pool, Jacuzzi, solarium, boat rental. AE, DC, MC, V. Expensive.*
Rauhalahti. About 4.8 kilometers (3 miles) from the town center, Rauhalahti is set near the lakeshore and has a number
of amenities catering to sportsmen and families. The hotel
has three restaurants, including the tavern-style Vanha
Apteekkari—a local favorite. *Katiskaniementie 8, 70700 Kuopio, tel. 971/311700, fax 971/311843. 106 rooms with bath or
shower, 15 apartments, and 5 inexpensive youth hotel rooms.
Facilities: 3 restaurants, saunas, swimming pool, solarium,
gymnasium, children's playroom, nightclub, tennis, horseback riding, squash, spa, boat rental. AE, DC, MC, V.
Moderate–Expensive.*
Hotelli Iso-Valkeinen. Located by the lakeshore and only 5 kilometers (2.5 miles) from the town center, this hotel has large,
quiet rooms. *Päiväranta, 70420 Kuopio, tel. 971/341444, fax
971/341344. 100 rooms with shower. Facilities: 4 restaurants,
nightclub, 2 saunas, swimming pool, mini-golf, tennis, swimming beach, fishing, boat rental. DC, MC, V. Moderate.*

Savonlinna **Rauhalinna.** This romantic turn-of-the-century timber villa
Dining was built by a general in the Imperial Russian Army. From
town it's 16 kilometers (10 miles) by road, 40 minutes by boat.
Both the food and atmosphere are old Russian, but some Finn-
ish specialties are also available. *Lehtiniemi, tel. 957/523119.
Reservations required during festival season. AE, DC, MC, V.
Closed Sept.–May. Expensive.*
Snellman. This small 1920s-style mansion is in the center of
town. Meals are served against a quiet background of classical
music. One of the specialties of the house is cold-salted salmon
and steak with morel sauce. *Olavinkatu 31, tel. 957/273104.
Reservations advised. AE, DC, MC, V. Expensive.*
Majakka. Centrally located, Majakka goes in for home cooking
and a family atmosphere. *Satamakatu 11, tel. 957/21456. Reservations required during festival season. AE, DC, V. Moderate.*
Paviljonki. Paviljonki is connected with the Savonlinna restaurant school. Located 1 kilometer (½ mile) west of the city
center, the restaurant serves homemade Finnish dishes.
Rjalahdenkatu 4, tel. 957/520960. V. Inexpensive.

Lodging **Casino Spa.** Built in the 1960s and renovated in 1986, the Casino Spa has a restful lakeside location on an island linked by a pedestrian bridge to the center of town. *Kylpylaitoksentie, Kasinosaari, 57130 Savonlinna, tel. 957/57500, fax 957/272524. 80 rooms with shower. Facilities: saunas, pool, marina, spa treatment. AE, DC, MC, V. Expensive.*

Savonlinnan Seurahuone. This old town house is located near the market and passenger harbor. A new extension opened in 1989. Some older rooms are small. *Kauppatori 4, 57130 Savonlinna, tel. 957/5731, fax 957/273918. 84 rooms with shower. Facilities: 2 restaurants, lobby bar, saunas, disco, nightclub. AE, DC, MC, V. Expensive (Very Expensive in July).*

Vuorilinna Summer Hotel. Guests at this modern hotel use the facilities, including the restaurant, of the nearby Casino Spa Hotel. *Kasinonsaari, 57130 Savonlinna, tel. 957/57500, fax 957/272524. 230 rooms, with shower for every 2 rooms. AE, DC, MC, V. Closed Sept.–May. Inexpensive (Moderate in July).*

Tampere **Tiilihovi.** Tiilihovi is a romantic cellar restaurant that special-
Dining izes in fish, meat, and game dishes. *Kauppakatu 10, tel. 931/121220. Reservations advised. AE, DC, MC, V. Expensive.*

Natalie. Russian in atmosphere, cuisine, and background music, Natalie is housed in the old Workers' Theater near the center of town. *Hallituskatu 19, tel. 931/232040. Reservations advised. AE, DC, MC, V. Moderate.*

Salud Bodega. Salud Bodega has a well-earned reputation for Spanish specialties, though it also features a few Finnish dishes. *Otavalankatu 10, tel. 931/235996. Reservations advised. DC, MC, V. Moderate.*

Silakka. Although its atmosphere is casual and unpretentious, Silakka has earned a great reputation for its Finnish fish specialties. *Hatanpään valtatie 1, tel. 931/149740. DC, MC, V. Moderate.*

Lodging **Cumulus Koskikatu.** Overlooking the tamed rapids of Tammerkoski, Cumulus Koskikatu is central and modern. The Finnair terminal is in the same building. *Koskikatu 5, 33100 Tampere, tel. 931/242–4111, fax 931/242–4399. 230 rooms with shower. Facilities: restaurant, wine bar, nightclub, saunas, pool. AE, DC, MC, V. Expensive (Moderate mid-June–early-Aug.).*

Ilves. This hotel soars above a newly gentrified area of old warehouses near the city center. It is favored by Americans. *Hatanpään valtatie 1, 33100 Tampere, tel. 931/121212, fax 931/132565. 336 rooms with bath or shower, special floor for nonsmokers. Facilities: 3 restaurants, nightclub, gymnasium, saunas, pool, Jacuzzi. AE, DC, MC, V. Expensive.*

Domus Summer Hotel. About 3 kilometers (2 miles) from the center of town in the Kaleva district, this hotel is a good value. *Pellervonkatu 9, 33540 Tampere, tel. 931/550000, fax 931/225409. 197 rooms, 85 with shower. Facilities: saunas, pool. MC, V. Closed Sept.–May. Inexpensive.*

Finnish Lapland

Lapland is often called Europe's last wilderness, a region of endless forests, fells, and great silences. So often the arrival of settlers has obliterated all that came before, but here man has walked gently and left the virgin solitude of this country almost unspoiled. Now easily accessible by plane, train, or bus, this

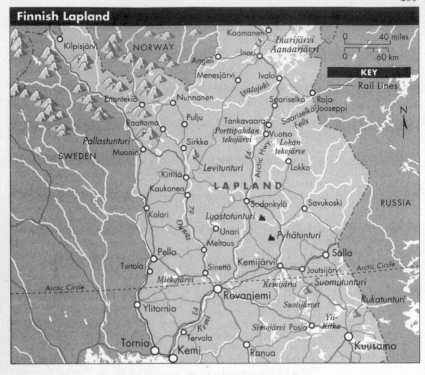

Finnish Lapland

Arctic outpost offers comfortable hotels and modern amenities, yet you won't have to go very far to find yourself in an almost primordial solitude.

The oldest traces of human habitation in Finland have been found in Lapland, and hoards of Danish, English, and even Arabian coins indicate the existence of trade activities many centuries ago. The origins of the Lapps themselves are lost in the mists of history. There are only about 4,500 pure Lapps still living here; the remainder of the province's population of 220,000 are Finns. Until the 1930s, Lapland was still largely unexploited, still a region where any trip was an expedition. Then the Canadian-owned Petsamo Nickel Company completed the great road that connects Rovaniemi with the Arctic Sea. Building activities increased along this route (later to be known as the Arctic Highway), the land was turned and sown, and a few hotels were built to cater to increasing numbers of visitors.

Summer has the blessing of daylight up to 24 hours long and often beautiful weather to go with it. In early fall the colors are so fabulous that the Finns have a special word for it: *ruskaa*. If you can take the intense but dry cold, winter is also a fascinating time in Lapland, not only for the Northern Lights but for such experiences as the reindeer roundups.

In December and January, reindeer owners round up their herds from all over Lapland province and corral them by the thousands. Sometimes dressed in colorful costumes, the Lapps (and also many Finns) lasso the reindeer in true Wild West fashion, recognizing their own animals by brand marks on the ears. The roundups are attended by many buyers, for reindeer meat is considered a delicacy and is exported to the south and abroad.

To get to some of the remoter roundups, you may have to travel by taxi plane, though other corrals are near the road, especially around Ivalo, Inari, and Enontekiö. Most Lapps and northern Finns get there on the motorized sledges that have almost entirely replaced the much more attractive (and silent) reindeer-drawn *pulkka* (a kind of boat-shaped sleigh on one runner). In southern Lapland especially, an increasing number of roundups occur in the fall. Finding out exactly when and where a roundup is taking place isn't easy, for much depends on the whims of the weather and the reindeer, so you must check locally. The information offices in Rovaniemi, however, will be able to give some guidance.

A few words should be said about the Lapps—a proud, sensitive, and intelligent people who prefer their own name for themselves, *Same* (pronounced Sah-me)—some of whom resent visitors who regard them as a tourist attraction put there for their benefit. Modern influences (and intermarriage) have regrettably changed many aspects of their traditional way of life; for example, the attractive costumes are less frequently seen, except on festive occasions. The young, especially, have been affected by the changes, and many of them are far more interested in becoming teachers, lawyers, or engineers than in breeding reindeer or hunting from their remote homesteads. Yet others have found profit from selling souvenirs to the tourists. But most prefer to go about their daily lives, minding their own business. The Lady Day Church Festival in Enontekiö in March is a particularly colorful event, attended by many Lapps in their most brilliant costumes and usually featuring reindeer racing or lassoing competitions.

The experienced traveler who would like to roam through the wilds for days on end without meeting a fellow human being can still do so without any problem at all. Be warned, however, that climatic conditions change rapidly and often unpredictably, especially on those lonely Arctic fells. Always seek local advice and let your hotel and friends know where you're heading and how long you intend to be away. An attractive alternative is provided by organized canoeing or hiking trips with nights in huts or tents in the wilderness.

Getting Around

Rovaniemi is the best base for traveling around the Arctic area. It connects with Helsinki and the south by road, rail, and air links; there is even a car-train from Helsinki. Within the area, driving is the best way to get around, although a regular bus service connects most centers. There are also daily flights from Rovaniemi to Ivalo.

Guided Tours

Friendly Finland Tours (tel. 90/18261) features an escorted five-day "North Cape Tour" out of Helsinki. You can get details from the Finnish Tourist Board's overseas offices (*see* Government Tourist Offices in Chapter 1) or at Eteläesplanadi 4, 00130 Helsinki, tel. 90/403011.

Tourist Information

Ivalo (Inari Lake Area) (Bus Station, Piiskuntie 5, 99800 Ivalo, tel. 9697/12521).

Rovaniemi (Aallonkatu 1, 96200, tel. 960/346270). Open June–August, daily 10–6; September–May, weekdays 8–6. For further information on the region, contact **Lapland Travel** (Maakuntakatu 10, tel. 960/346052).

Sodankylä (Sodänkylän Matkailu Oy) (Jäämerentie 9, 99600, tel. 9693/13474).

Exploring Lapland

Rovaniemi Your best launching point is the town of **Rovaniemi,** where the Ounas and Kemi rivers meet almost on the Arctic Circle. Rovaniemi is the so-called Gateway to Lapland and the administrative hub and communications center of the province.

If you're expecting an Arctic shanty town, you're in for a surprise. Rovaniemi was nearly razed by the retreating German army in 1944, so what you'll see today is a modern city strongly influenced by Alvar Aalto's architecture. The old way of life is preserved in museums. During the process of rebuilding, the population rose from 8,000 to around 33,000, so be prepared for a contemporary city on the edge of the wilderness, with various amenities and some incredible architecture—notably **Lappia Hall,** the concert and congress center that also houses the world's northernmost professional theater, designed by Aalto. Rovaniemi also has the best shops in the region.

After collecting information from the tourist office, find a window table in the restaurant of the nearby **Pohjanhovi Hotel,** and plan your itinerary while gazing out at the fast-flowing Kemi River.

You can get a good instant introduction to the region and its natural history at the **Museum of the Province of Lapland** at the **Arctic Research Center,** located 1 kilometer (½ mile) north of Lappia House. The collection also includes exhibits of Same culture. *Pohjoisranta 4, Rovaniemi, tel. 960/317840. Admission: FIM 30 adults, FIM 10 children. Open June 15–Aug., daily 10–6; Sept.–June 14, Tues.–Sun. 10–6.*

But you'll get more of a feel for the living past from the **Pöykkölä Museum,** located in 18th-century farm buildings 3 kilometers (2 miles) from the town center. *Admission: FIM 5 adults, FIM 2 children. Open June–Aug., Tues.–Sun. 1–4. Bus service available.*

Arctic Highway The Arctic Highway (Highway 4) is the main artery of central and northern Lapland; you'll follow it north for most of this tour. Eight kilometers (5 miles) north of Rovaniemi, right on the Arctic Circle, is **Santa Claus's Workshop,** where gifts can be bought in midsummer for shipping any time of year, with a special Santa Claus Land stamp. For most visitors, however, the main attraction is to mail postcards home from the special Arctic Circle post office. There's also a very good souvenir shopping complex and the impressive sight of the mountains of mail that pour in from children all over the world. Yes, all of it gets answered. *Admission free. Open June–Aug., daily 8–8; Sept.–*

mid-Feb., weekdays 9–5; mid-Feb.–Apr., weekdays 9–5, weekends 9–7.

After driving north for a couple of hours, you may want to take a short detour to the modern tourist center at **Luostotunturi** in the fell district of southern Lapland—you'll turn right onto a secondary road 16 kilometers (10 miles) south of Sodankylä and follow it 22 kilometers (14 miles) to the center.

Continue north, through the village of Vuotso, to **Tankavaara,** the most accessible and the best developed of several gold-panning areas. The **Gold Museum** tells the century-old story of Lapland's hardy fortune seekers. For a small fee (FIM 40 per hour), authentic prospectors will show you how to sift gold dust and tiny nuggets from the dirt of an ice-cold stream. You can keep what you find, but don't expect to be able to retire early. *Admission: FIM 20 adults, FIM 5 children. Open June 1–Aug. 16, daily 9–6; Aug. 17–Sept., daily 9–5; Oct.–May, hours vary, so check locally.*

Thirty kilometers (19 miles) north of Tankavaara is the holiday center of **Saariselkä,** which has a variety of accommodations and makes a sensible base from which to set off on a trip (alone or in a group) into the true wilderness; during the snowy months, there is some of the best cross-country and downhill skiing in Finland. There are marked trails through forests and over fells where nothing much has changed since the last Ice Age and where you can experience the timeless silence of the Arctic landscape. More than 2,500 square kilometers (965 square miles) of this magnificent area has been named the **Urho Kekkonen National Park.**

Northern Lapland Just south of the village of Ivalo, the highway passes the **Ivalo River** (Ivalojoki). Canoeing trips are organized on its fast waters down to Lake Inari, returning by bus. The village of **Ivalo** is the main center for northern Lapland. However, except for a first-class hotel, an airport, and many of the amenities of a modern community, it has little to offer the tourist in search of a wilderness experience.

The huge island-studded expanses of **Lake Inari** (Inarinjärvi), north of Ivalo, offer endless possibilities for wilderness exploration. It is a beautiful 40-kilometer (25-mile) drive northwest from Ivalo, along the lakeshore, to **Inari.** This is a good base for summer boat excursions. The **Sami Museum,** on the village outskirts, covers all facets of Lapp culture. *Admission: FIM 12 adults, FIM 5 children. Open June 1–Aug. 10, daily 8–10; Aug. 11–30, daily 8–8; Sept. 1–20, daily 9–3:30.*

In recent years, a growing number of small holiday villages have blossomed near Inari and to the north of it, usually with a small restaurant and shop attached. Amenities are simple, but the locations are often magnificent and bring you very close to the true pulse of Lapland. Usually there will be a boat at your disposal, fishing possibilities, and the experience of preparing your own sauna. From Kaamanen, north of Inari, a side road leads to **Sevettijärvi,** home of the Skolt Lapps, and eventually into Norway.

It is an attractive drive back south from Inari to **Menesjärvi** along a relatively new, secondary road that passes through a wilderness of forest and swamp. Take every opportunity to leave your car and do some walking; it's the only way to experience the vastness of these Arctic spaces. The hills get gentler and the ride less dramatic as you continue south to Levitunturi, the last of the gently sloping fells before you reach the banks of the Ounas River and return to Rovaniemi via Highway 79.

Dining and Lodging

For details and price-category definitions, *see* Dining and Lodging in Staying in Finland.

Inari
Lodging

Kultahovi. This recently renovated old inn is located on the wooded banks of a swiftly flowing river. *99870 Inari, tel. 9697/ 51221, fax 9697/51250. 29 rooms with shower. Facilities: restaurant, saunas. MC, V. Moderate.*

Ivalo
Lodging

Hotel Ivalo. Right on the riverside about a kilometer (½ mile) from the village center, Ivalo is modern and well equipped. One of its two restaurants serves Lapland specialties, including *poronkäristys*, a reindeer casserole. *Ivalontie 34, 99800 Ivalo, tel. 9697/21911, fax 9697/21905. 94 rooms with bath or shower. Facilities: 2 restaurants, saunas, pool, boating. AE, DC, MC, V. Moderate.*

Kultahippu. Located in the heart of Ivalo, next to the Ivalo River, Kultahippu claims to have the northernmost nightclub in Finland. The guest rooms are cozy. *Petsamontie 1, 99800 Ivalo, tel. 9697/21825, fax 9697/12510. 30 rooms (7 with saunas). Facilities: restaurant, nightclub, sauna, Jacuzzi, swimming beach. AE, DC, MC, V. Moderate.*

Levitunturi
Lodging

Levitunturi. Built in traditional log style at the foot of the fells, Levitunturi is a particularly well-equipped and modern tourist complex. *99130 Sirkka, tel. 9694/81301, fax 9694/81434. 121 rooms with shower. Special floor for nonsmokers. Facilities: saunas, pool, Jacuzzi, squash, gymnasium, tennis, boating, cross-country skiing, spa amenities. AE, DC, MC, V. Expensive.*

Luostotunturi
Lodging

Arctia Hotel Luosto. Situated amid the fells southeast of Sodankylä, this small-scale hotel is modern and comfortable. It is built in traditional timber style. *99600 Luostotunturi, tel. 9693/44400, fax 9693/44410. 54 cabins. Facilities: saunas, boating, cross-country skiing. AE, DC, MC, V. Moderate.*

Rovaniemi
Dining

Giovanni. Northern Finland may be the last place you'd expect to find a lively Italian restaurant. The emphasis is on pizzas, pastas, and grills. *Koskikatu 17, tel. 960/346406. No reservations. AE, DC, MC, V. Expensive.*

Ounasvaaran Pirtit. Ounasvaaran is one of Rovaniemi's favorite restaurants, specializing in traditional Finnish and Lapp food. Try the fried salmon with cream and morels. *Antinmukka 4, tel. 960/369056. Reservations advised. MC, V. Moderate.*

Lodging

Gasthof. Built in 1986, the Gasthof is a comfortable small hotel with a restaurant featuring Finnish specialties. *Koskikatu 41, 96100 Rovaniemi, tel. 960/23222, fax 960/23226. 44 rooms with shower. Special floor for nonsmokers. Facilities: restaurant, saunas, pool. AE, DC, MC, V. Expensive.*

Hotel Lapponia. Opened in 1992, Hotel Lapponia is one of the newest luxury hotels in Lapland. *Koskikatu 23, 96200 Rovaniemi, tel. 960/33661, fax 960/313770. 167 rooms with shower. Facilities: 5 restaurants, pub, café, saunas, Jacuzzi. AE, DC, MC, V. Expensive.*

Hotelli Pohjanhovi. With its pleasant location overlooking the Kemi River, this hotel is an old favorite with travelers to the north. It has been extended and modernized over the years. *Pohjanpuistikko 2, 96200 Rovaniemi, tel. 960/33711, fax 960/ 313997. 216 rooms with bath or shower. Special floor for nonsmokers. Some rooms in neighboring building. Facilities: saunas, pool, boating, disco. AE, DC, MC, V. Expensive.*

Vaakuna. Opened in January 1992, the Vaakuna is a recent addition to the high-class hotel scene in Rovaniemi. *Koskikatu 4, 96200 Rovaniemi, tel. 960/332211, fax 960/332–2199. 157 rooms (all doubles) with shower. Facilities: 2 restaurants, saunas, nightclub, pub, gymnasium. AE, DC, MC, V. Expensive.*

Oppipoika. This hotel belongs to the Hotel School of Rovaniemi. The rooms are spacious and comfortable, but the real reason to come here is the food: Chef Tapio Sointu has created the "Lappi à la Carte" program, featuring a variety of Lapland specialties. *Korkalonkatu 33, 96200 Rovaniemi, tel. 960/20321, fax 960/346969. 40 rooms with bath or shower. Facilities: restaurant, saunas, pool. AE, DC, MC, V. Moderate.*

Sky Hotel Ounasvaara. Located on a hilltop 3 kilometers (2 miles) from the center of town, Sky Hotel is the top choice for views and a tranquil atmosphere, but it's best if you have a car. *Hiihtokeskus, 96400 Rovaniemi, tel. 960/23371, fax 960/ 318789. 69 rooms (47 with saunas). Facilities: restaurant, saunas, cross-country skiing. AE, DC, MC, V. Moderate.*

Saariselkä **Riekonlinna.** The latest and best-equipped addition to this de-
Lodging veloping tourist complex on the fringes of the wilderness fells, Riekonlinna makes good use of its location. *99830 Saariselkä, tel. 9697/81601, fax 9697/81602. 124 rooms with shower. Facilities: saunas, tennis, boating, squash, cross-country skiing. AE, DC, MC, V. Very Expensive.*

Tankavaara **Wanhan Waskoolimiehen Kahvila.** Lapp specialties are fea-
Dining tured in this attractive café and restaurant; try the gold prospector's reindeer beefsteak with mashed potatoes. Accommodations are limited in the vicinity. *Tankavaara Gold Village, tel. 9693/46158. No reservations. DC, V. Moderate.*

10 France

The French are different. They don't have the Anglo-Saxon outlook you may find reassuring in, say, Germany or Scandinavia. They are a Mediterranean people—temperamental and spontaneous, closer to the Spanish and Italians than to northern Europeans. At the same time, they are heirs to the Cartesian tradition of logic ("I think, therefore I am"), as well as being inveterate theorizers. Their reluctance to take a shortcut to an obvious solution often frustrates English-speaking pragmatists.

One thing the French do well—probably because it's instinctive and they don't need to think about it—is live. The essence of French *savoir-vivre* is simplicity. Everyday things count: eating, drinking, talking, dressing, shopping. Get in the mood: Daily rituals are meant to be enjoyed. Food is the best example. The French don't like rushing their meals. They plan them in advance, painstakingly prepare them, look forward to them over an *apéritif*, admire the loving presentation of each dish, savor each mouthful. The pace is unhurried and the wine flows steadily.

French towns and villages are quietly attractive and historic. Chances are that the ornate *mairie* (town hall) has been there since the Revolution, and the church or cathedral since the Middle Ages. The main streets tend to be lined with sturdy trees planted before living memory. The 20th century is kept firmly at bay. Modern buildings—such as supermarkets—are banished to the outskirts or obliged to fit architecturally.

There is a bewildering variety of man-made marvels in France: Southern France is rich in Roman remains. Western France is dotted with Romanesque churches from the 10th and 11th centuries, with some of the best examples in Poitiers. Gothic architecture was born in the Ile de France around Paris: Such huge cathedrals as Notre-Dame rank among the world's finest. The Renaissance yielded the sumptuous Loire châteaux and the Palace of Fontainebleau, paving the way for the haughty Baroque of Versailles.

France boasts as much natural as man-made variety. You'll find ski slopes and towering peaks in the Alps or Pyrenees; beaches and cliffs in Brittany or along the Mediterranean; limitless horizons beyond the golden grain fields of the Beauce or the misty plains of the north; haunting evergreen forests stretching from the Ardennes down to the Midi (south); marsh and canals in the Marais Poitevin, the "Green Venice" of the west; lush, softly lit valleys along the Seine or Loire; steep-climbing terraces above the Rhône; and wherever you go, the swirl and sway of ripening vines.

Whatever you've heard, France is a welcoming country. Don't be misled by superficial coldness: They are a formal people who don't go out of their way to speak to strangers (except in anger). Above all, don't suppose that all Frenchmen are like Parisians—most are more approachable and friendly. A great many have foreign origins themselves. France has always attracted immigrants from less affluent areas: Italy, Spain, Portugal, Poland, and North Africa.

France considers itself to be, above all, a European power. It borders seven countries (Belgium, Luxembourg, Germany, Switzerland, Italy, Spain, Andorra) and looks across the Chan-

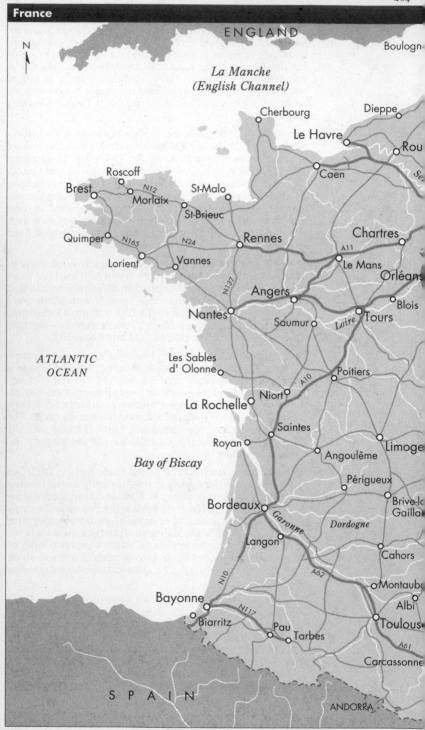

ENGLAND

*La Manche
(English Channel)*

Boulogn

Cherbourg

Dieppe

Le Havre

Rou

Roscoff

Brest

N12

Morlaix

St-Malo

Caen

Se

St-Brieuc

Quimper

N165

N24

Rennes

Chartres

A11

Lorient

Vannes

Le Mans

Orléans

N137

Angers

Blois

Nantes

Saumur

Loire

Tours

*ATLANTIC
OCEAN*

Les Sables
d' Olonne

Poitiers

Niort

A10

La Rochelle

Saintes

Royan

Limoge

Bay of Biscay

Angoulême

Périgueux

Brive-lo
Gailla

Bordeaux

Garonne

Dordogne

Langon

Cahors

N10

A62

Montaub

Bayonne

N117

Albi

Biarritz

Pau

Tarbes

Toulous

A61

Carcassonne

S P A I N

ANDORRA

BELGIUM

Lille

ais

A26

Arras
iens

Cambrai
St. Quentin

auvais

A1

LUXEMBOURG

Reims

A4

Paris

Châlons-sur-
Marne

Metz

Nancy

Strasbourg

GERMANY

Troyes

Sens

A31

Colmar

Auxerre

Mulhouse

A6

Belfort

Dijon

Besançon

urges

Nevers

Beaune

Saône

SWITZERLAND

Montluçon

Mâcon

Bourg-en-
Bresse

Clermont-
Ferrand

Lyon

Rhône

illac

A7

A43

Chambéry

Le Puy

Grenoble

dez

Rhône

Montélimar

ITALY

Millau

Avignon

Nîmes

A9

Montpellier

Aix-en-Provence

A8

Monte Carlo

Nice

Cannes

Narbonne

Marseille

erpignan

Toulon

Mediterranean Sea

Corsica

0   50 mi

0   75 km

Corsica

Calvi

Bastia

Corte

Ajaccio

N198

Bonifacio

nel at an eighth (Great Britain). France played a crucial role in the creation of the European Community (EC).

Still, deep down, most of the French are chauvinists who are proud of *La douce France*, worship Napoleon, and feel that the Liberty-Equality-Fraternity motto of the French Revolution confers moral superiority upon their country—as they showed during the patriotic celebrations in 1989 that marked the bicentennial of the Revolution.

Essential Information

Before You Go

When to Go June and September, free of the mid-summer crowds, are the best months to be in France. June offers the advantage of long daylight hours, while slightly cheaper prices, and frequent Indian summers (often lasting well into October) make September attractive. The second half of July and all of August are spoiled by inflated prices and huge crowds on the beaches. And July and August heat can be stifling in southern France. Paris, though pleasantly deserted, can be stuffy in August, too.

The ski season in the Alps and Pyrenees lasts from Christmas through Easter—steer clear of February (school vacation time) if you can. Anytime between March and November offers a good chance to soak up the sun on the Riviera. The weather in Paris and the Loire is unappealing before Easter. If you're dreaming of Paris in the springtime, May (not April) is your best bet.

Climate France's climate changes regionally. North of the Loire (including Paris), France has a northern European climate—cold winters, pleasant if unpredictable summers, and frequent rain. Southern France has a Mediterranean climate: mild winters, long, hot summers, and sunshine throughout the year. The more continental climate of eastern and central France is a mixture of these two extremes: Winters can be very cold and summers very hot. France's Atlantic coast has a temperate climate even south of the Loire, with the exception of the much warmer Biarritz.

The following are the average daily maximum and minimum temperatures for Paris and Marseille.

Paris	Jan.	43F	6C	May	68F	20C	Sept.	70F	21C
		34	1		49	10		53	12
	Feb.	45F	7C	June	73F	23C	Oct.	60F	16C
		34	1		55	13		46	8
	Mar.	54F	12C	July	76F	25C	Nov.	50F	10C
		39	4		58	14		40	5
	Apr.	60F	16C	Aug.	75F	24C	Dec.	44F	7C
		43	6		58	14		36	2

Marseille	Jan.	50F	10C	May	71F	22C	Sept.	77F	25C
		35	2		52	11		58	15
	Feb.	53F	12C	June	79F	26C	Oct.	68F	20C
		36	2		58	14		51	10
	Mar.	59F	15C	July	84F	29C	Nov.	58F	14C
		41	5		63	17		43	6
	Apr.	64F	18C	Aug.	83F	28C	Dec.	52F	11C
		46	8		63	17		37	3

Currency The unit of French currency is the franc, subdivided into 100 centimes. Bills are issued in denominations of 50, 100, and 500 francs (frs); coins are 5, 10, 20, and 50 centimes and 1, 2, 5, 10, and 20 francs. The small, copper-colored 5-, 10-, and 20-centime coins have considerable nuisance value, but can be used for tips in bars and cafés.

International credit cards and traveler's checks are widely accepted throughout France, except in rural areas. At press time (spring 1993), the dollar was worth 5.5 frs, the Canadian dollar was worth 4.70 frs, and the pound sterling was worth 8 frs.

What It Will Cost Hotel and restaurant prices compensate for travel expenses. Prices are highest in Paris, on the Riviera, and in the Alps during the ski season. But even in these areas, you can find pleasant accommodations and excellent food for surprisingly reasonable prices.

All taxes must be included in posted prices in France. The initials TTC *(toutes taxes comprises*—taxes included) are sometimes included on price lists but, strictly speaking, they are superfluous. Restaurant and hotel prices must *by law* include taxes and service charges: If they are tacked onto your bill as additional items, you should complain.

Sample Prices Prices vary greatly depending on the region, proximity to tourist sites, and—believe it or not—whether you're sitting down or standing up in a café! Here are a few samples: Cup of coffee, 4–9 frs; glass of beer, 9–12 frs; soft drink, 9–14 frs; ham sandwich, 12–15 frs; one-mile taxi ride, 22–27 frs.

Visas Citizens of the United States, Canada, and Britain do not require a visa to visit France.

Customs on Arrival Travelers from the United States and Canada may bring into France 400 cigarettes or 100 cigars or 100 grams of tobacco, 1 liter of liquor of 22% volume and 2 liters of wine, 0.50 liters of perfume and 0.25 liters of toilet water, and other goods to the value of 300 frs.

Adults traveling from the United Kingdom may bring into France 300 cigarettes or 150 cigarillos or 75 cigars or 400 grams of tobacco; 1.5 liters of liquor over 22% volume or 3 liters of liquor under 22% volume or 3 liters of fortified/sparkling wine, plus 4 liters of still wine; 0.9 liters of perfume and 0.375 liters of toilet water; plus other goods to the value of 2,400 frs.

Language The French study English for a minimum of four years at school, but few are fluent. English is widely understood in major tourist areas, and in most tourist hotels there should be at least one person who can converse with you. Be courteous, patient, and speak slowly: France has visitors from many countries and is not heavily dependent for income on English-speaking visitors. Even if your own French is rusty, try to master a few words: The French are more cooperative when they think you are at least making an effort to speak their language.

Getting Around

By Car
Road Conditions

France's roads are classified into five types, numbered and prefixed A, N, D, C, or V. Roads marked A *(Autoroutes)* are expressways. There are excellent links between Paris and most French cities, but poor ones between the provinces (the principal exceptions being A62 between Bordeaux and Toulouse and A9/A8 the length of the Mediterranean coast). It is often difficult to avoid Paris when crossing France—this need not cause too many problems if you steer clear of the rush hours (7–9:30 AM and 4:30–7:30 PM). A *péage* (toll) must be paid on most expressways: The rate varies but can be steep. The N *(Route Nationale)* roads—which are sometimes divided highways—and D *(Route Départementale)* roads are usually wide and fast, and driving along them can be a real pleasure. Don't be daunted by smaller (C and V) roads, either. The yellow regional Michelin maps—on sale throughout France—are an invaluable.

Rules of the Road

You may use your own driver's license in France but must be able to prove you have third-party insurance. Drive on the right. Be aware of the French tradition of yielding to drivers coming from the right. Seat belts are obligatory for all passengers, and children under 12 may not travel in the front seat. Speed limits are 130 kph (80 mph) on expressways, 110 kph (70 mph) on divided highways, 90 kph (55 mph) on other roads, 50 kph (30 mph) in towns. French drivers break these limits and police dish out hefty on-the-spot fines with equal abandon.

Parking

Parking is a nightmare in Paris and often difficult in other large towns. Meters and ticket machines (pay and display) are common: Make sure you have a supply of 1-fr coins. In smaller towns, parking may be permitted on one side of the street only—alternating every two weeks—so pay attention to signs.

Gasoline

Fuel is more expensive on expressways and in rural areas. Don't let your tank get too low—you can go for many kilometers in the country without passing a gas station—and keep an eye on pump prices as you go. These vary enormously; anything from 5.30 to 6.10 frs per liter.

Breakdowns

If your car breaks down on an expressway, go to the nearest roadside emergency telephone and call the breakdown service. If you have a breakdown anywhere else, find the nearest garage or contact the police (dial 17).

By Train

SNCF, the French national railroad, is generally recognized as Europe's best national train service: fast, punctual, comfortable, and comprehensive. The high-speed TGVs, with a top speed of 190 mph, are the best domestic trains, heading southeast from Paris to Lyon, the Riviera, and Switzerland; west to Nantes; and south–west to Bordeaux. Most TGV trains require passengers to pay a supplement—usually 20–40 frs, but a bit more during peak periods. Also, you need a seat reservation—easily obtained at the ticket window or from an automatic machine. Seat reservations are reassuring but seldom necessary on other French trains, except at holiday times.

You need to punch your train ticket in one of the orange machines you'll encounter alongside platforms. Slide your ticket in faceup and wait for a "clink" sound. (The small yellow tickets and automatic ticket barriers used for most suburban Paris trains are similar to those in the métro/RER.)

If you take an overnight train, you have a choice between *wag-ons-lits* (sleeping cars), which are expensive, and *couchettes* (bunks), which sleep six to a compartment (sheet and pillow provided) and are more affordable (around 80 frs). Ordinary compartment seats do not pull together to enable you to lie down. There are special summer night trains from Paris to Spain and the Riviera geared for a younger market, with discos and bars.

Fares Various reduced-fare passes are available from major train stations in France and from SNCF travel agents. If you are planning a lot of train travel, buy a special **France Vacances** card (around 1,400 frs for nine days). Families and couples are also eligible for big discounts. So are senior citizens (over 60) and young people (under 26), who qualify for different discount schemes (**Carte Vermeil** and **Carrissimo**). You can get 50% discounts in blue periods (most of the time) and 20% most of the rest of the time (white periods: noon Friday to noon Saturday; 3 PM Sunday to noon Monday). On major holidays (red periods) there are no reductions. Calendars are available at stations. The **Carte Kiwi** (395 frs) enables children and up to four accompanying adults to travel half-price.

By Plane Domestic flights from Paris, which are on **Air Inter,** leave from Orly. Contact your travel agent or Air Inter (tel. 45–46–90–00). Train service may be faster when you consider time spent to and from the airport.

By Bus Because of excellent train service, long-distance buses are rare and found mainly where train service is inadequate. Bus tours are organized by the **SNCF** and other tourist organizations, such as **Horizons Européens:** Ask for their brochures at any major travel agent, or contact France-Tourisme at 3 rue d'Alger, 75001 Paris, tel. 42–61–85–50.

By Boat France has Europe's busiest inland waterway system. Canal and river vacations are popular: Visitors can either take an organized cruise or rent a boat and plan their own leisurely route. Contact a travel agent for details or ask for a "Tourisme Fluvial" brochure in any French tourist office. Some of the most picturesque stretches are in Brittany, Burgundy, and the Midi. The Canal du Midi between Toulouse and Sète, constructed in the 17th century, is a historic marvel. Contact the French national tourist offices, **France-Anjou Navigation** (Quai National, 72300 Sablé-sur-Sarthe), or **Bourgogne Voies Navigables** (1 quai de la République, 89000 Auxerre).

By Bicycle There is no shortage of wide empty roads and flat or rolling countryside in France suitable for biking. The French are great cycling enthusiasts—witness the Tour de France. For around 40 frs a day bikes can be rented from 260 train stations; you need to show your passport and leave a deposit of about 500 frs (unless you have a Visa or MasterCard). Bikes may be sent as accompanied luggage from any station in France; some trains in rural areas don't even charge for this. Tourist offices supply details on the more than 200 local shops that rent bikes, or obtain the SNCF brochure "Guide du Train et du Vélo."

Staying in France

Telephones The French telephone system is modern and efficient. Phone
Local Calls booths are plentiful; they are nearly always available at post offices and cafés. A local call in France costs 73 centimes plus 12
centimes per minute; half-price rates apply between 9:30 PM
and 8 AM and between 1:30 PM Saturday and 8 AM Monday.

Pay phones take 1-, 2-, and 5-fr coins (1 fr minimum). Many
French pay phones are now operated by *télécartes* (phone cards),
sold in post offices and some shops (cost: 40 frs for 50 units; 96
frs for 120).

French phone numbers have eight digits; a code is required
only when calling the Paris region from the provinces (dial
16–1, then the number) and for calling the provinces from Paris
(dial 16, then the number).

International Calls Dial 19 and wait for the tone, then dial the country code, area
code, and number. Calls from your hotel room are very expen-
sive. Dial 12 for local operators.

Mail Airmail letters to the United States and Canada cost 4 frs for 20
Postal Rates grams. Letters to the United Kingdom cost 2.50 frs for up to 20
grams, as they do within France. Postcards cost 2.20 frs within
France and if sent to EC countries (2.30 frs for surface or 3.70
frs for airmail to North America). Stamps can be bought in post
offices and cafés sporting a red "Tabac" sign outside.

Receiving Mail If you're uncertain where you'll be staying, have mail sent to
American Express (if you're a cardmember), Thomas Cook, or
Poste Restante at most French post offices.

Shopping A number of shops, particularly large stores in cities and holi-
VAT Refunds day resorts, offer value-added tax (VAT) refunds to foreign
shoppers. You are entitled to an export discount of 13% or 23%,
depending on the item purchased, though this often applies
only if your purchases in the same store reach a minimum 2,800
frs (for residents of EC countries) or 1,200 frs (all others).

Bargaining Shop prices are clearly marked and bargaining is not a way of
life. Still, at outdoor markets, flea markets, and in antiques
stores, you can try your luck. If you're thinking of buying several items in these places, you have nothing to lose in cheerfully
suggesting to the proprietor, *"Vous me faites un prix?"* ("How
about a discount?").

Opening and **Banks** are open weekdays 9:30–4:30, but times vary. Most close
Closing Times for an hour to an hour and a half for lunch.

Museums are closed one day a week (usually Tuesday) and on
national holidays. Usual times are from 9:30 to 5 or 6. Many museums close for lunch (noon–2); on Sunday many are open afternoons only.

Shops in big towns are open from 9 or 9:30 to 6 or 7 without a
lunch break. Smaller shops often open earlier (8 AM) and close
later (8 PM), but take a lengthy lunch break (1–4). This siesta-
type schedule is more typical in the south of France. Corner
grocery stores frequently stay open until around 10 PM.

National Holidays January 1; April 4 (Easter Monday); May 1 (Labor Day); May 8
(VE Day); May 12 (Ascension); May 23 (Pentecost); July 14
(Bastille Day); August 15 (Assumption); November 1 (All
Saints' Day); November 11 (Armistice); December 25.

Dining Eating in France is serious business, at least for two of the three meals each day. For a light meal, try a *brasserie* (steak and french fries remain the classic), a picnic (a *baguette* loaf with ham, cheese, or pâté makes a perfect combination), or one of the fast-food places that have sprung up in urban areas over recent years.

French breakfasts are relatively modest—strong coffee, fruit juice if you insist, and croissants. International chain hotels are likely to offer American or English breakfasts, but in cafés you will probably be out of luck if this is what you want.

Mealtimes Dinner is the main meal and usually begins at 8. Lunch begins at 12:30 or 1.

Dress Jacket and tie are recommended for Very Expensive and Expensive restaurants, and at some of the more stylish Moderate restaurants as well. When in doubt, it's best to dress up. Otherwise casual dress is appropriate.

Precautions Tap water is perfectly safe, though not always very appetizing (least of all in Paris). Mineral water is a palatable alternative; there is a vast choice of *eau plate* (plain) as well as *eau gazeuse* (fizzy).

Ratings Prices are per person and include a first course, main course, and dessert plus taxes and service (which are always included in displayed prices), but not wine. Best bets are indicated by a star ★.

Category	All Areas
Very Expensive	over 400 frs
Expensive	250–400 frs
Moderate	150–250 frs
Inexpensive	under 150 frs

Lodging France has a wide range of accommodations, from rambling old village inns to stylishly converted châteaux. Prices must, by law, be posted at the hotel entrance and should include taxes and service. Prices are always by room, not per person. Breakfast is not always included, but you are usually expected to have it and often are charged for it whether you have it or not. In smaller rural hotels, you may be expected to have your evening meal at the hotel, too.

The quality of rooms, particularly in older properties, is uneven; if you don't like the room you're given, ask to see another. If you want a private bathroom, state your preference for *douche* (shower) or *baignoire (bath)*—the latter always costing more. Tourist offices in major train stations can reserve hotels for you, and so can tourist offices in most towns.

Hotels Hotels are officially classified from one-star to four-star-deluxe. France has—but is not dominated by—big hotel chains: Examples in the upper price bracket include Frantel, Holiday Inn, Novotel, and Sofitel. The Ibis and Climat de France chains are more moderately priced. Chain hotels, as a rule, lack atmosphere, with the following exceptions:

Logis de France. This is a group of small, inexpensive hotels that can be relied on for comfort, character, and regional cuisine. Look for its distinctive yellow and green sign. The Logis de France paperback guide is widely available in bookshops (cost: around 65 frs) or from Logis de France (83 av. d'Italie, 75013 Paris, tel. 45–84–83–84).

France-Accueil is another chain of friendly low-cost hotels. You can get a free booklet from France-Accueil (85 rue Dessous-des-Berges, 75013 Paris, tel. 45–83–04–22).

Relais et Châteaux. You can stay in style at any of the 150 members of this prestigious chain of converted châteaux and manor houses. Each hotel is distinctively furnished, provides top cuisine, and often stands in spacious grounds. A booklet listing members is available in bookshops or from Relais et Châteaux (9 av. Marceau, 75116 Paris, tel. 47–23–41–42).

Rentals *Gîtes Ruraux* offers families or small groups the opportunity for an economical stay in a furnished cottage, chalet, or apartment. These can be rented by the week or month. Contact either the **Fédération Nationale des Gîtes de France,** 35 ruc Godot-de-Mauroy, 75009 Paris, tel. 47–42–20–20 (indicate the region that interests you), or the French Government Tourist Office in New York or London (*see* Before You Go in Chapter 1, Essential Information).

Bed-and-Breakfasts These are known as *chambres d'hôte* and are increasingly popular in rural areas. Check local tourist offices for details.

Youth Hostels With inexpensive hotel accommodations in France so easy to find, you may want to think twice before staying in a youth hostel—especially as standards of French hostels don't quite approximate those in neighboring countries. Contact **Fédération Unie des Auberges de Jeunesse** (27 rue Pajol, 75018 Paris, tel. 46–07–00–01).

Villas The French Government Tourist Offices in London and New York publish extensive lists of agencies specializing in villa rentals. You can also write to **Rent-a-Villa Ltd.** (3 W. 51st St., New York, NY 10019) or, in France, **Interhome** (15 av. Jean-Aicard, 75011 Paris).

Camping French campsites have a good reputation for organization and amenities but are crowded in July and August. Many campsites welcome advance reservations, and if traveling in summer, it makes sense to book in advance. A guide to France's campsites is published by the **Fédération Française de Camping et de Caravaning,** 78 rue de Rivoli, 75004 Paris, tel. 42–72–84–08.

Ratings Prices are for double rooms and include all taxes. Best bets are indicated by a star ★.

Category	All Areas
Very Expensive	over 850 frs
Expensive	450–850 frs
Moderate	250–450 frs
Inexpensive	under 250 frs

Tipping The check in a bar or restaurant will include service, but it is customary to leave some small change unless you're dissatisfied. The amount varies, from 30 centimes for a beer to a few francs after a meal. Tip taxi drivers and hairdressers about 10%. Give ushers in theaters 1–2 frs. Cloakroom attendants will expect nothing if there is a sign saying *Pourboire interdit*—no tip; otherwise give them 5 frs. Washroom attendants usually get 5 frs—a sum that is often posted. Bellhops should get 10 frs per item.

If you stay in a moderately priced hotel for more than two or three days, it is customary to leave something for the chambermaid—perhaps 10 frs per day. Expect to tip 10 frs for room service—but nothing is expected if breakfast is routinely served in your room.

Service station attendants get nothing for giving you gas or oil, and 5 or 10 frs for checking tires. Train and airport porters get a fixed sum (6–10 frs) per bag. Museum guides should get 5–10 frs after a guided tour. It is standard practice to tip guides (and bus drivers) after an excursion.

Paris

Arriving and Departing

By Plane International flights arrive at either Charles de Gaulle Airport (Roissy), 24 kilometers (15 miles) northeast of Paris, or at Orly Airport, 16 kilometers (10 miles) south of the city.

Between the Airport and Downtown **From Charles de Gaulle:** Buses leave every 20 minutes from 5:40 AM to 11 PM. The fare is 48 frs and the trip takes 40 minutes (up to 1½ hours during rush hour). You arrive at the Arc de Triomphe or Porte Maillot, on the Right Bank by the Hotel Concorde-Lafayette. Alternatively, the **Roissybus,** operated by RATP, runs directly to and from rue Scribe at Paris Opera every 15 minutes and costs 30 frs.

From Orly: Buses leave every 12 minutes from 6 AM to 11 PM and arrive at the Air France terminal near Les Invalides on the Left Bank. The fare is 32 frs, and the trip takes between 30 and 60 minutes, depending on traffic. RATP also runs the **Orlybus** to and from Denfert-Rochereau and Orly every 15 minutes for 23 frs.

Both airports provide free bus shuttles to the nearest train stations, where you can take the RER service to Paris. The advantages of this are speed, price (33 frs to Paris from Charles de Gaulle in Roissy, 42 frs from Orly on the shuttle-train **Orlyval**), and the fact that the RER trains link up directly with the métro system. The disadvantage is having to lug your bags around. Taxi fares from airports to Paris range from 150 to 200 frs, with a 5 fr surcharge per bag.

By Train Paris has five international stations: Gare du Nord (for northern France, northern Europe, and England via Calais or Boulogne); Gare de l'Est (for Strasbourg, Luxembourg, Basle, and central Europe); Gare de Lyon (for Lyon, Marseille, the Riviera, Geneva, Italy); Gare d'Austerlitz (for the Loire Valley, southwest France, Spain); Gare St-Lazare (for Normandy, England via Dieppe). The Gare Montparnasse serves western France (mainly Nantes and Brittany) and is the terminus for the new TGV Atlantic service from Paris to Bordeaux. For train information, tel. 45–82–50–50. You can reserve tickets at any Paris station regardless of the destination. Go to the Grandes Lignes counter for travel within France or to the Billets Internationaux (international tickets) desk if you're heading out of France.

By Bus Long-distance bus journeys within France are uncommon, which may be why Paris has no central bus depot. The leading Paris-based bus company is **Eurolines Nord** (3 av. de la Porte de la Villette, 19e, tel. 40–38–93–93).

By Car The highway system fans out from Paris. You arrive from the north (England/Belgium) via A1; from Normandy via A13; from the east via A4; from Spain and the southwest via A10; from the Alps, the Riviera, and Italy via A7. Each of these expressways connects with the *Périphérique* (beltway). Note that exits here are named by "Porte" and are not numbered. The "Périphe" can be extremely fast—but it gets very busy and is best avoided between 8 and 10 AM and between 5 and 7:30 PM.

Getting Around

Paris is relatively small as capital cities go, and most of its prize monuments and museums are within walking distance of one another. A river cruise is a pleasant way to get an introductory overview. The most convenient form of public transportation is the métro; buses are a slower alternative, though they do allow you to see more of the city. Taxis are not expensive but not always easy to hail, either. Car travel within Paris is best avoided because parking is chronically difficult.

By Métro There are 13 métro lines crisscrossing Paris and the nearby suburbs, and you are seldom more than a five-minute walk from the nearest station. It is essential to know the name of the last station on the line you take, since this name appears on all signs within the system. A connection (you can make as many as you please on one ticket) is called a *correspondance*. At junction stations, illuminated orange signs, bearing the names of each line terminus, appear over the corridors leading to the various correspondances.

The métro runs from 5:30 AM to 1:15 AM. Some lines and stations in the seedier parts of Paris are a bit risky at night—in particular Line 2 (Porte-Dauphine–Nation) and the northern section of Line 13 from St-Lazare to St-Denis/Asnières. The long, bleak corridors at Jaurès and Stalingrad are a haven for pickpockets and purse snatchers. But the Paris métro is relatively safe, as long as you don't walk around with your wallet hanging out of your back pocket or travel alone (especially women) late at night.

The métro network connects at several points in Paris with RER trains that race across Paris from suburb to suburb: RER trains are a sort of supersonic métro and can be a great time-saver. All métro tickets and passes are valid for RER and bus travel within Paris. Métro tickets cost 6 frs each, though a *carnet* (10 tickets for 36.50 frs) is a far better value. If you're staying for a week or more, the best deal is the *coupon jaune* (weekly) or *carte orange* (monthly) ticket, sold according to zone. Zones 1 and 2 cover the entire métro network (cost: 57 frs per week or 201 frs per month). If you plan to take a suburban train to visit monuments in the Ile de France, you should consider a four-zone ticket (Versailles, St-Germain-en-Laye; 103 frs per week) or a six-zone ticket (Rambouillet, Fontainebleau; 131 frs per week). For these weekly or monthly tickets, you need to obtain a pass (available from train and major métro stations) and provide two passport-size photographs.

Alternatively there are two kinds of unlimited-travel tickets for the metro, bus, and RER: *Formule 1* for second-class travel and *Paris Visite* for first-class. The advantage is that unlike the *coupon jaune*, which is good from Monday morning to Sunday evening, the latter are valid starting any day of the week and give you discounts on a limited number of museums and tourist attractions. The price is 25, 60, 85, and 135 francs for Paris only; 80, 140, 185 and 225 francs for suburbs including Versailles, St-Germain-en-Laye, and Euro Disney.

Access to métro and RER platforms is through an automatic ticket barrier. Slide your ticket in flat and pick it up as it pops up farther along. Keep your ticket; you'll need it again to leave the RER system.

By Bus Most buses run from around 6 AM to 8:30 PM; some continue until midnight. Night buses operate from 1 AM to 6 AM between Châtelet and nearby suburbs. They can be stopped by hailing them at any point on their route. You can use your metro tickets on the buses, or you can buy a one-ride ticket on board. You need to show weekly/monthly/special tickets to the driver as you get on; if you have individual yellow tickets, you should state your destination and be prepared to punch one or more tickets in the red and gray machines on board the bus.

By Taxi There is no standard vehicle or color for Paris taxis, but all offer good value. Daytime rates (7 AM to 7 PM) within Paris are about 2.80 frs per kilometer, and nighttime rates are around 4.50 frs, plus a basic charge of 11 frs. Rates outside the city limits are about 40% higher. It is best to ask your hotel or restaurant to call for a taxi, since cruising cabs can be hard to find. There are numerous taxi stands, but you have to know where to look. Note that taxis seldom take more than three people at a time.

Important Addresses and Numbers

Tourist Information Paris Tourist Office (127 av. des Champs-Elysées, tel. 47–23–61–72). Open daily 9 AM–8 PM. (Closed Dec. 25, Jan 1.) Offices in major train stations are open daily 8–8.

Embassies U.S. (2 av. Gabriel, 75008 Paris, tel. 42–96–12–02). **Canada** (35 av. Montaigne, 75008 Paris, tel. 44–43–32–00). **U.K.** (35 rue du Faubourg St-Honoré, 75008 Paris, tel. 42–66–91–42).

Emergencies Police: dial 17 for emergencies. Automatic phone booths can be found at various main crossroads for use in police emergencies *(Police-Secours)* or medical help *(Services Medicaux)*; **Ambulance** (tel. 15 or 43–78–26–26); **Doctor** (tel. 47–07–77–77); **Hospitals: American Hospital** (63 blvd. Victor-Hugo, Neuilly, tel. 46–41–25–25); **British Hospital** (3 rue Barbes, Levallois-Perret, tel. 47–58–13–12); **Dentist** (tel. 43–37–51–00; open 24 hours). **Pharmacies: Dhéry** (Galerie des Champs, 84 av. des Champs-Elysées, tel. 45–62–02–41; open 24 hours); **Drugstore** (corner of blvd. St-Germain and rue de Rennes, 6e; open until 2 AM); **Pharmacie des Arts** (106 blvd. Montparnasse, 6e; open until midnight).

English-Language Bookstores W. H. Smith (248 rue de Rivoli); **Galignani** (224 rue de Rivoli); **Brentano's** (37 av. de l'Opéra); **Shakespeare & Co.** (rue de la Bûcherie).

Most newsstands in central Paris sell *Time, Newsweek,* and the *International Herald Tribune,* as well as the English dailies.

Paris Métro

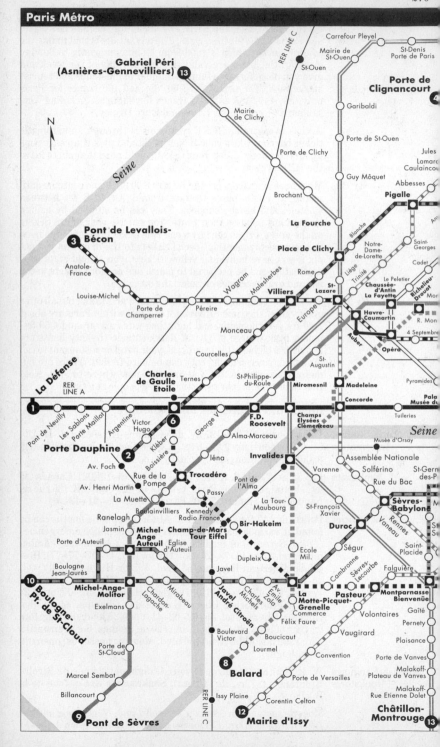

Gabriel Péri
(Asnières-Gennevilliers) 13

Carrefour Pleyel

Mairie de
St-Ouen

St-Denis
Porte de Paris

St-Ouen

Porte de
Clignancourt 4

Garibaldi

Mairie
de Clichy

Porte de St-Ouen

Jules
Lamar
Caulaincou

Porte de Clichy

Guy Môquet

Abbesses

Brochant

Pigalle

An

Pont de Levallois-
Bécon 3

La Fourche

Blanche

Saint-
Georges

Place de Clichy

Notre-
Dame-
de-Lorette

Anatole-
France

Rome

Liège

Cadet

Le Peletier

Louise-Michel

Wagram

Malesherbes

Villiers

St-
Lazare

Trinité

Chaussée-
d'Antin
La Fayette

Richelieu-
Drouot

Mor

Porte de
Champerret

Péreire

Europe

Havre-
Caumartin

R. Mon

Monceau

Auber

4 Septembre

Courcelles

St-
Augustin

Opéra

Pyramides

La Défense

RER
LINE A

Charles
de Gaulle
Etoile

Ternes

St-Philippe-
du-Roule

Miromesnil

Madeleine

Pala
Musée d

1

Pont de Neuilly

Les Sablons

Porte Maillot

Argentine

Victor
Hugo

6

George V

F.D.
Roosevelt

Concorde

Tuileries

Champs
Elysées
Clémenceau

Porte Dauphine 2

Kléber

Alma-Marceau

Seine

Av. Foch

Boissière

Iéna

Musée d'Orsay

Rue de la
Pompe

Trocadéro

Invalides

Assemblée Nationale

Av. Henri Martin

Passy

Pont de
l'Alma

Varenne

Solférino

St-Germ
des-P

La Muette

Boulainvilliers

La Tour-
Maubourg

Rue du Bac

Ranelagh

Kennedy
Radio France

Bir-Hakeim

St-François
Xavier

Duroc

Sèvres-
Babylone

Jasmin

Michel-
Ange
Auteuil

Champ-de-Mars
Tour Eiffel

Rennes

Porte d'Auteuil

Eglise
d'Auteuil

Ségur

Vaneau

Saint-
Placide

Boulogne
Jean-Jaurès

Dupleix

Ecole
Mil.

Cambronne

Sèvres-
Lecourbe

Falguière

10

Michel-Ange-
Molitor

Chardon-
Lagache

Mirabeau

Javel
André Citroën

Charles
Michels

Av.
Emile
Zola

La
Motte-Picquet-
Grenelle

Pasteur

Montparnasse
Bienvenüe

Boulogne-
Pt. de St-Cloud

Exelmans

Javel

Commerce

Volontaires

Gaîté

Félix Faure

Vaugirard

Pernety

Porte de
St-Cloud

Boulevard
Victor

Boucicaut

Plaisance

Marcel Sembat

Lourmel

Convention

Porte de Vanves

Billancourt

8

Balard

Porte de Versailles

Malakoff-
Plateau de Vanves

9 Pont de Sèvres

Issy Plaine

Corentin Celton

Malakoff-
Rue Etienne Dolet

RER LINE C

12

Mairie d'Issy

Châtillon-
Montrouge 13

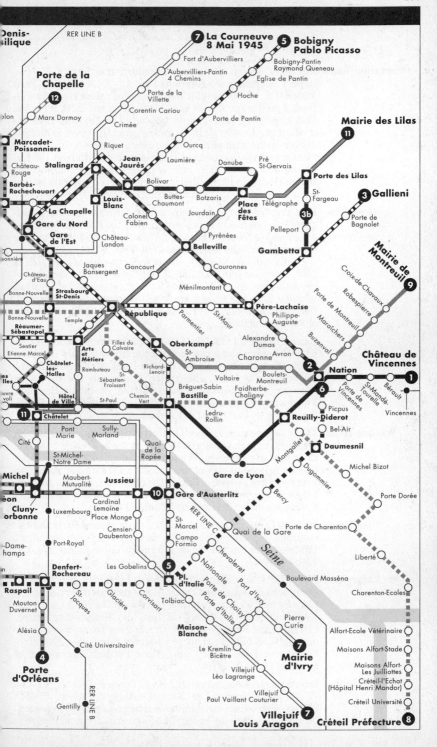

| Travel Agencies | **American Express** (11 rue Scribe 75009 Paris, tel. 47–77–70–00). **Wagons-Lits** (8 rue Auber, 75009 Paris, tel. 42–66–90–90). |

Guided Tours

| Orientation Tours | Bus tours of Paris offer a good introduction to the city. The two largest operators are **Cityrama** (tel. 42–60–30–14) and **Paris Vision** (tel. 42–60–31–25). Tours start from their respective offices, 4 pl. des Pyramides and 214 rue de Rivoli. Both are in the first *arrondissement* (ward), opposite the Tuileries Gardens (toward the Louvre end). Tours are generally given in double-decker buses with either a live guide or a tape-recorded commentary. They last two to three hours and cost about 150 frs. The same operators also offer a variety of other tours with a theme (Historic Paris, Modern Paris, Paris by Night) lasting from 2½ hours to all day and costing between 120 and 300 frs. |

| Boat Trips | Boat trips along the Seine are a must for first-time Paris visitors. The two most famous services are the **Bâteaux Mouches,** which leaves from the Pont de l'Alma, at the end of the avenue George V, and the **Vedettes du Pont-Neuf,** which sets off from the square du Vert Galant, on the western edge of the Ile de la Cité. Price per trip is around 35 frs. Boats depart in season every half-hour from 10:30 AM to 5 PM (slightly less frequently in winter). Evening cruises are available most of the year and, thanks to the boats' powerful floodlights, offer unexpected views of Paris's riverbanks. |
| | **Canauxrama** (tel. 42–39–15–00) organizes canal tours in flat-bottom barges along the picturesque but relatively unknown St-Martin and Ourcq Canals in East Paris. Departures from 5 bis quai de la Loire, 19e (métro Jaurès), or the Bassin de l'Arsenal, opposite 50 blvd. de la Bastille, 12e (métro Bastille). Times vary, so phone to check hours. Tours cost from 70 frs, depending on the time of day and length of trip. |

| Walking Tours | There are numerous special-interest tours concentrating on historical or architectural topics. Most are in French, however. Charges vary between 30 and 50 frs, depending on fees that may be needed to visit certain buildings. Tours last about two hours and are generally held in the afternoon. Details are published in the weekly magazines *Pariscope* and *L'Officiel des Spectacles* under the heading "Conférences." |

| Bike Tours | **Paris by Cycle** organizes daily bike tours around Paris and the environs (Versailles, Chantilly, and Fontainebleau) for about 180 frs, 95 frs for bike rental (99 rue de la Jonquiere, 17e, tel. 42–63–36–63). |

| Excursions | The **RATP** (Paris Transport Authority) organizes many guided excursions in and around Paris. Ask at its tourist service on the place de la Madeleine (north of place de la Concorde), or at the RATP office at St-Michel (53 quai des Grands-Augustins). **Cityrama** and **Paris Vision** *(see* Orientation Tours, *above)* organize half- or full-day trips to Chartres, Versailles, Fontainebleau, the Loire Valley, and Mont St-Michel at a cost of between 150 and 750 frs. |

| Personal Guides | **International Limousines** (182 blvd. Pereire, 17e, tel. 45–74–77–12) and **Executive Car** (5 rue d'Astorg, 8e, tel. 42–65–54–20) have limousines and minibuses that take up to seven passengers around Paris or to surrounding areas for a minimum of |

three hours. The cost starts from about 200 frs per hour. Phone for details and reservations.

Exploring Paris

Paris is a compact city. With the possible exception of the Bois de Boulogne and Montmartre, you can easily walk from one sight to the next. Paris is divided in two by the River Seine, with two islands (Ile de la Cité and Ile St-Louis) in the middle. The south—or Left—Bank has a more intimate, bohemian flavor than the haughtier Right Bank. The east–west axis from Châtelet to the Arc de Triomphe, via the rue de Rivoli and the Champs-Elysées, is the principal thoroughfare for sightseeing and shopping on the Right Bank.

A special **Carte Musées** pass, allowing access to Paris museums and monuments, can be obtained from museums or métro stations (price: one-day pass, 55 frs; three days, 110 frs; five days, 160 frs).

Though attractions are grouped into four logical touring areas, there are several "musts". If time is a problem, explore Notre-Dame and the Latin Quarter; head to place de la Concorde and enjoy the vista from the Champs-Elysées to the Louvre; then take a boat along the Seine for a waterside rendezvous with the Eiffel Tower. You could finish off with dinner in Montmartre and consider it a day well spent.

Numbers in the margin correspond to points of interest on the Paris map.

Notre-Dame and the Left Bank

❶

The most enduring symbol of Paris, and its historical and geographical heart, is **Notre-Dame Cathedral,** around the corner from Cité métro station. This is the logical place from which to start any tour of the city—especially as the tour starts on the Ile de la Cité, one of the two islands in the middle of the Seine, where Paris's first inhabitants settled around 250 BC. Notre-Dame has been a place of worship for more than 2,000 years; the present building is the fourth on this site. It was begun in 1163, making it one of the earliest Gothic cathedrals, although it was not finished until 1345. The facade seems perfectly proportioned until you notice that the north (left) tower is wider than the south. The interior is at its lightest and least cluttered in the early morning. Bay-by-bay cleaning is gradually revealing the original honey color of the stone. Window space is limited and filled with shimmering stained glass; the circular rose windows in the transept are particularly delicate. The 387-step climb up the towers is worth the effort for a perfect view of the famous gargoyles and the heart of Paris. *Cathedral admission free. Towers admission 30 frs adults, 16 frs children. Open daily 10–5. Treasury (religious and vestmental relics) open Mon.–Sat. 10–6, Sun. 2–6. Admission: 15 frs adults, 10 frs students, 5 frs children.*

The pretty garden to the right of the cathedral leads to a bridge that crosses to the city's second and smaller island, the **Ile St-Louis,** barely 600 meters (1,868 feet) long and an oasis of inner-city repose.

❷

The rue des Deux Ponts bisects the island. Head left over the Pont de la Tournelle. To your left is the **Tour d'Argent,** one of the city's most famous restaurants (*see* Dining, *below*).

Paris

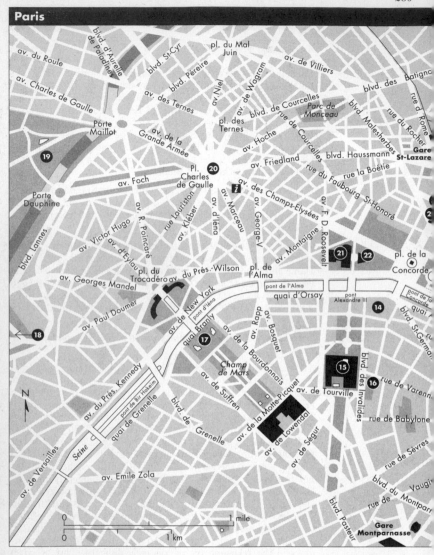

```
0                    1 mile
0              1 km
```

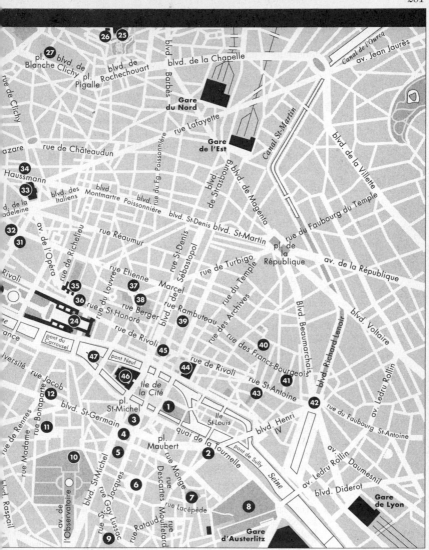

Continue along quai de la Tournelle past Notre-Dame, then turn left at rue St-Jacques. A hundred yards ahead, on the ❸ right, is the back end of the **Eglise St-Séverin,** an elegant and unusually wide 16th-century church. Note the spiraling column among the forest of pillars behind the altar.

Turn left out of the church, cross the bustling boulevard St-Germain, and take rue de Cluny to the left. This leads to the ❹ **Hôtel de Cluny.** Don't be misled by the name. This is a museum devoted to the late Middle Ages and Renaissance. Look for the *Lady with the Unicorn* tapestries and the beautifully displayed medieval statues. *6 pl. Paul-Painlevé. Admission: 17 frs adults, 9 frs students and children; 9 frs for all on Sun. Open Wed.–Mon. 9:30–5:15.*

❺ Head up rue de la Sorbonne to the **Sorbonne,** Paris's ancient university. Students here used to listen to lectures in Latin, which explains why the surrounding area is known as the Quartier Latin (Latin Quarter). The Sorbonne is the oldest university in Paris—indeed, one of the oldest in Europe—and has for centuries been one of France's principal institutions of higher learning.

Walking up rue Victor-Cousin and turning left into rue Cujas, ❻ you come to the **Panthéon.** Its huge dome and elegant colonnade are reminiscent of St. Paul's in London but date from a century later (1758–89). The Panthéon was intended to be a church, but during the Revolution it was swiftly earmarked as a secular hall of fame. Its crypt contains the remains of such national heroes as Voltaire, Rousseau, and Zola. The interior is empty and austere, with principal interest centering on Puvis de Chavanne's late 19th-century frescoes, relating the life of Geneviève, patron saint of Paris. *Admission: 25 frs adults, 14 frs senior citizens, 6 frs children. Open daily 10–5:30.*

Behind the Panthéon is **St-Etienne du Mont,** a church with two claims to fame: its ornate facade and its curly Renaissance rood-screen (1521–35) separating nave and chancel—the only one of its kind in Paris. Don't forget to check out the fine 17th-century glass in the cloister at the back of the church.

Take the adjoining rue Clovis, turn right into rue Descartes, then left at the lively place de la Contrescarpe down rue Rollin. ❼ Cross rue Monge to rue de Navarre. On the left is the **Arènes de Lutèce** (always open during daylight hours, admission free), a Gallo-Roman arena rediscovered only in 1869; it has since been landscaped and excavated to reveal parts of the original amphitheater, and counts as one of the least-known points of interest in Paris.

❽ Rue de Navarre and rue Lacépède lead to the **Jardin des Plantes** (Botanical Gardens), which have been on this site since the 17th century. The gardens have what is reputedly the oldest tree in Paris, a robinia planted in 1636 (allée Becquerel), plus a zoo, alpine garden, hothouses, aquarium, and maze. Natural science enthusiasts will be in their element at the various museums, devoted to insects (Musée Entomologique), fossils and prehistoric animals (Musée Paléontologique), and minerals (Musée Minéralogique). *Admission: 12–25 frs. Museums open Wed.–Mon. 9–11:45, 1–4:45.*

Head back up Rue Lacépède from the Jardin des Plantes. Turn left into rue Gracieuse, then right into rue Ortolan, which soon crosses the rue Mouffetard—site of a colorful market and many restaurants. Continue along rue du Pot-de-Fer and rue Rataud. At rue Claude-Bernard, turn right; then make your first left up rue St-Jacques.

❾ Set slightly back from the street is the **Val de Grâce,** a domed church designed by the great architect Jules Hardouin-Mansart and erected in 1645–67 (after the Sorbonne church but before the Invalides). Its two-tiered facade, with capitals and triangular pedestals, is directly inspired by the Counter-Reformation Jesuit architectural style found more often in Rome than in Paris. The Baroque style of the interior is epitomized by the huge twisted columns of the baldachin (ornamental canopy) over the altar.

From the crossroads by the Closerie des Lilas, there is an enticing view down the tree-lined avenue de l'Observatoire toward the **Palais du Luxembourg.** The palace was built by Queen Maria de' Medici at the beginning of the 17th century in answer to Florence's Pitti Palace. It now houses the French Senate and is not open to the public. In the surrounding gardens, mothers push their baby carriages along tree-lined paths among the majestic fountains and statues.

⓫ Head through the gardens to the left of the palace into rue de Vaugirard. Turn left, then right into rue Madame, which leads down to the enormous 17th-century church of **St-Sulpice.** Stand back and admire the impressive, though unfinished, 18th-century facade, with its unequal towers. The interior is overwhelmingly impersonal, but the wall paintings by Delacroix, in the first chapel on the right, are worth a visit.

⓬ Rue Bonaparte descends to boulevard St-Germain. You can hardly miss the sturdy pointed tower of **St-Germain-des-Prés,** the oldest church in Paris (begun around 1160, though the towers date to the 11th century). Note the colorful nave frescoes by the 19th-century artist Hippolyte Flandrin, a pupil of Ingres.

Time Out The spirit of writers Jean-Paul Sartre and Simone de Beauvoir still haunts the **Café de Flore** opposite the church, though this, and the neighboring **Les Deux Magots,** have more tourists than literary luminaries these days. Still, you can linger over a drink while watching what seems to be all of Paris walking by. *Blvd. St-Germain. No credit cards.*

Rue de l'Abbaye runs along behind St-Germain-des-Prés to place Fürstemberg, a charming little square where fiery Romantic artist Eugène Delacroix (1798–1863) had his studio. If you go there on a summer evening, you'll sometimes find young Frenchmen singing love songs to guitar accompaniment. Turn left into rue Jacob and continue along rue de l'Université. You are now in the heart of the Carré Rive Gauche, the Left Bank's district of art dealers and galleries.

⓭ About a quarter of a mile along rue de l'Université, turn down rue de Poitiers. Ahead is the sandstone bulk of the **Musée d'Orsay.** Follow it around to the left to reach the main entrance. The new Musée d'Orsay—opened in late 1986—is already one of Paris's star tourist attractions, thanks to its imaginatively housed collections of the arts (mainly French) spanning the period 1848–1914. Exhibits take up three floors, but the visitor's immediate impression is one of a single, vast hall. This is not surprising: The museum was originally built in 1900 as a train station. The combination of hall and glass roof with narrow, clanky passages and intimate lighting lends Orsay a human, pleasantly chaotic feel.

The chief artistic attraction, of course, is the Impressionist collection, transferred from the inadequate Jeu de Paume museum across the river. Other highlights include Art Nouveau furniture, a faithfully restored Belle Epoque restaurant (formerly part of the station hotel), and a model of the Opéra quarter beneath a glass floor. *1 rue Bellechasse, tel. 40–49–48–14. Admission: 31 frs, 16 frs students, senior citizens, children, and Sun. Open Tues., Wed., Fri., Sat. 10–5:30; Thurs. 10–9:30; Sun. 9–5:30.*

⓮ Farther along on rue de l'Université is the 18th-century **Palais Bourbon,** home of the French National Legislature (Assemblée Nationale). The colonnaded facade commissioned by Napoleon is a sparkling sight after a recent cleaning program (jeopardized at one stage by political squabbles as to whether cleaning should begin from the left or the right). There is a fine view across to place de la Concorde and the Madeleine.

Follow the Seine down to the exuberant **Pont Alexandre III.** The Grand and Petit Palais are to your right, across the river. To the
⓯ left, the silhouette of **L'Hôtel des Invalides** soars above expansive if hardly manicured lawns. The Invalides was founded by Louis XIV in 1674 to house wounded (or "invalid") war veterans. Although only a few old soldiers live here today, the military link remains in the form of the **Musée de l'Armée**—a vast collection of arms, armor, uniforms, banners, and pictures. The **Musée des Plans-Reliefs** contains a fascinating collection of scale models of French towns made by the military architect Vauban in the 17th century.

The museums are far from being the only reason for visiting the Invalides. It is an outstanding Baroque ensemble, designed by Bruand and Mansart, and its church possesses the city's most elegant dome as well as the tomb of Napoleon, whose remains are housed in a series of no less than six coffins within a tomb of red porphyry. A *son-et-lumière* performance in English is held in the main courtyard on evenings throughout the summer (admission: 35 frs). *Admission to museums and church: 32 frs adults, 20 frs children. Open daily 10–6 (10–5 in winter).*

⓰ Alongside is the **Musée Rodin.** Together with the Picasso Museum in the Marais, this is the most charming of Paris's individual museums, consisting of an old house (built 1728) with a pretty garden, both filled with the vigorous sculptures of Auguste Rodin (1840–1917). The garden also has hundreds of rosebushes, with dozens of different varieties. *77 rue de Varenne. Admission: 21 frs, 11 frs Sun. Open Tues.–Sun. 10–5.*

Take avenue de Tourville to avenue de La Motte-Picquet. Turn left, and in a few minutes you will come face-to-face with the
⓱ **Eiffel Tower.** It was built by Gustave Eiffel for the World Exhibition of 1889. Recent restorations haven't made the elevators any faster—long lines are inevitable—but decent shops and two good restaurants have been added. Consider coming in the evening, when every girder is lit in glorious detail. Such was Eiffel's engineering precision that even in the fiercest winds the tower never sways more than 11½ centimeters (4½ inches). Today, of course, it is the best-known Parisian landmark.

Standing beneath it, you may have trouble believing that it nearly became 7,000 tons of scrap-iron when its concession expired in 1909. Only its potential use as a radio antenna saved the day; it now bristles with a forest of radio and television transmitters. The view from 1,000 feet up will enable you to appreciate the city's layout and proportions. *Admission: on foot, 8 frs; elevator, 17–51 frs, depending on the level. Open July– Aug., daily 9 AM–midnight; Sept.–June, Sun.–Thurs. 9:30 AM– 11 PM, Fri., Sat. 10 AM–midnight.*

West Paris and the Louvre

Our second itinerary starts at the **Musée Marmottan.** To get there, take the métro to La Muette, then head down chaussée
❶⑧ de la Muette, through the small Ranelagh park to the corner of rue Boilly and avenue Raphaël. The museum is a sumptuous early 19th-century mansion, replete with many period furnishings, and probably is the most underestimated museum in Paris. It houses a magnificent collection of paintings by Claude Monet, along with other Impressionist works and some delicately illustrated medieval manuscripts. *2 rue Louis-Boilly. Admission: 25 frs adults, 10 frs children and senior citizens. Open Tues.–Sun. 10–5:30.*

Continue along rue Boilly and turn left on boulevard Suchet.
⑲ The next right takes you into the **Bois de Boulogne.** Class and style have been associated with "Le Bois" (The Woods) ever since it was landscaped into an upper-class playground by Haussmann in the 1850s. The attractions of this sprawling 891-hectare (2,200-acre) wood include cafés, restaurants, gardens, waterfalls, and lakes. Pass Auteuil racetrack on the left and then walk to the right of the two lakes. An inexpensive ferry crosses frequently to an idyllic island. Rowboats can be rented at the far end of the lake. Just past the boathouse, turn right on the route de Suresnes and follow it to Porte Dauphine, a large traffic circle.

Cross over to avenue Foch, with the unmistakable silhouette of the Arc de Triomphe in the distance. Notice the original Art Nouveau iron-and-glass entrance to Porte Dauphine métro station, on the left. Continue along avenue Foch, the widest and
⑳ grandest boulevard in Paris, to the **Arc de Triomphe.** This 51-meter (164-foot) arch was planned by Napoleon to celebrate his military successes. Yet when Empress Marie-Louise entered Paris in 1810, it was barely off the ground and an arch of painted canvas had to be strung up to save appearances. Napoleon had been dead for more than 20 years when the Arc de Triomphe was finally finished in 1836.

Place Charles de Gaulle, referred to by Parisians as **L'Etoile** (The Star), is one of Europe's most chaotic traffic circles. Short of a death-defying dash, your only way to get over to the Arc de Triomphe is to take the pedestrian underpass from either the Champs-Elysées (to your right as you arrive from avenue Foch) or avenue de la Grande Armée (to the left). France's Unknown Soldier is buried beneath the archway; the flame is rekindled every evening at 6:30.

From the top of the Arc you can see the "star" effect of Etoile's 12 radiating avenues and admire two special vistas: one, down the Champs-Elysées toward place de la Concorde and the Louvre, and the other, down avenue de la Grande Armée toward La Tête Défense, a severe modern arch surrounded by imposing glass and concrete towers. Halfway up the Arc there is a small museum devoted to its history. *Museum and platform. Admission: 31 frs adults, 17 frs senior citizens, 6 frs children. Open daily 10–5:30; 10–5 in winter.*

The Champs-Elysées is the site of colorful national ceremonies on July 14 and November 11; its trees are often decked out with French tricolors and foreign flags to mark visits from heads of state. It is also where the cosmopolitan pulse of Paris beats strongest. The gracefully sloping 2-kilometer (1¼-mile) boulevard was originally laid out in the 1660s by André Le Nôtre as a garden sweeping away from the Tuileries. There is not much sign of that as you stroll past the cafés, restaurants, airline offices, car showrooms, movie theaters, and chic arcades that occupy its upper half. Farther down, on the right, is the **Grand Palais,** which plays host to Paris's major art exhibitions. Its glass roof makes its interior remarkably bright. *Admission varies. Usually open 10:30–6:30.*

The Grand Palais also houses the **Palais de la Découverte,** with scientific and mechanical exhibits and a planetarium. Entrance is in the avenue Franklin-Roosevelt. *Admission: 22 frs adults, 11 frs students; additional 15 frs (10 frs students) for planetarium. Open Tues.–Sat. 9:30–6, Sun. 10–7.*

Directly opposite the main entrance to the Grand Palais is the **Petit Palais,** built at the same time (1900) and now home to an attractively presented collection of French paintings and furniture from the 18th and 19th centuries. *Admission: 12 frs adults, 6 frs students. Open Tues.–Sun. 10–5:40.*

Continue down to place de la Concorde, built around 1775 and scene of more than a thousand deaths at the guillotine, including those of Louis XVI and Marie-Antoinette. The obelisk, a gift from the viceroy of Egypt, was erected in 1833.

To the east of the place de la Concorde is the **Jardin des Tuileries:** formal gardens with trees, ponds, and statues. Standing guard on either side are the **Jeu de Paume** and the **Orangerie,** identical buildings erected in the mid-19th century. The Jeu de Paume, home of an Impressionist collection before its move to the Musee d' Orsay, has been completely transformed. Its spacious, austere, white-walled rooms now house temporary exhibits of contemporary art, usually at its most brazen. The Orangerie contains fine early 20th-century French works by Monet (including his *Water Lilies*), Renoir, Marie Laurencin, and others. *Admission to Jeu de Paume: 30 frs adults, 20 frs students. Open Tues. noon–9:30, Wed.–Fri. noon–7, weekends 10–7. Admission to Orangerie: 26 frs, 14 frs Sun. Open Wed.–Mon. 9:45–5:45.*

Pass through the Tuileries to the Arc du Carrousel, a rather small triumphal arch erected more quickly (1806–08) than its big brother at the far end of the Champs-Elysées. Towering before you is the **Louvre,** with its glass pyramids. The Louvre, originally a royal palace, is today the world's largest and most famous museum. I. M. Pei's pyramids are the highlight of a major modernization program begun in 1984 and scheduled for completion in 1996. The plans include the extension of the museum interior and cleaning of the facades, restoration of the Carrousel gardens between the Louvre and the Tuileries, and the construction of an underground garage and shopping arcade. In the course of construction, the medieval foundations of the palace were unearthed and are maintained and displayed as an integral part of the museum's collection.

The Louvre was begun as a fortress in 1200 (the earliest parts still standing date from the 1540s) and completed under Napoleon III in the 1860s. The Louvre used to be even larger; a wing facing the Tuileries Gardens was razed by rampaging revolutionaries during the bloody Paris Commune of 1871.

Whatever the aesthetic merits of Pei's new-look Louvre, the museum has emerged less cramped and more rationally organized. Yet its sheer variety can seem intimidating. The main tourist attraction is Leonardo da Vinci's *Mona Lisa* (known in French as *La Joconde),* painted in 1503. The latest research, based on Leonardo's supposed homosexuality, would have us believe that the subject was actually a man! The *Mona Lisa* may disappoint you; it's smaller than most imagine, it's kept behind glass, and it's invariably encircled by a mob of tourists.

Turn your attention instead to some of the less-crowded rooms and galleries nearby, where Leonardo's fellow Italians are strongly represented: Fra Angelico, Giotto, Mantegna, Raphael, Titian, and Veronese. El Greco, Murillo, and Velázquez lead the Spanish; Van Eyck, Rembrandt, Frans Hals, Brueghel, Holbein, and Rubens underline the achievements of northern European art. English paintings are highlighted by works of Lawrence, Reynolds, Gainsborough, and Turner. Highlights of French painting include works by Poussin, Fragonard, Chardin, Boucher, and Watteau—together with David's *Coronation of Napoleon,* Géricault's *Raft of the Medusa,* and Delacroix's *Liberty Guiding the People.*

Famous statues include the soaring *Victory of Samothrace,* the celebrated *Venus de Milo,* and the realistic Egyptian *Seated Scribe.* Be sure to inspect the Gobelins tapestries, the Crown Jewels (including the 186-carat Regent diamond), and the 9th-century bronze statuette of Emperor Charlemagne. *Admission 31 frs adults, 16 frs students and Sun., children under 18 free. Open Wed.–Mon. 9–6 (9–9:45 PM Mon. and Wed.).*

Montmartre If you start at the Anvers métro station and head up rue de Steinkerque, with its budget clothing shops, you will be greeted by the most familiar and spectacular view of the Sacré Coeur basilica atop the Butte Montmartre. The **Sacré-Coeur** ㉕ was built in a bizarre, mock-Byzantine style between 1876 and 1910. It is no favorite with aesthetes, yet it has become a major Paris landmark. It was built as an act of national penitence after the disastrous Franco-Prussian War of 1870—a Catholic show of strength at a time when conflict between Church and State was at its most bitter.

㉖ Around the corner is the **place du Tertre,** full of would-be painters and trendy, overpriced restaurants. The painters have been setting up their easels on the square for years; avoid being talked into having your portrait done.

Despite its eternal tourist appeal and ever-growing commercialization, Montmartre has not lost all its traditional bohemian color. Walk down rue Norvins and descend the bustling rue Lepic to place Blanche and one of the favorite haunts of Toulouse-Lautrec and other luminaries of the Belle Epoque—the ㉗ legendary **Moulin Rouge** cabaret.

Montmartre is some distance from the rest of the city's major attractions, so go left up boulevard de Clichy as far as **place Pigalle,** then take the métro to Madeleine.

Central Paris ㉘ The **Eglise de la Madeleine,** with its array of uncompromising columns, looks like a Greek temple. The only natural light inside comes from three shallow domes; the walls are richly but harmoniously decorated, with plenty of gold glinting through the dim interior. The church was designed in 1814 but not consecrated until 1842, after efforts to turn the site into a train station were defeated. The portico's majestic Corinthian colonnade supports a huge pediment with a sculptured frieze of the *Last Judgment.* From the top of the steps you can admire the vista down rue Royale across the Seine. Another vista leads up boulevard Malesherbes to the dome of **St-Augustin,** a mid-19th-century church notable for its innovative use of iron girders as structural support.

㉙ ㉚ Place de la Madeleine is in the heart of Paris's prime shopping district: Jewelers line rue Royale; **Fauchon's** and **Hédiard's,** behind the Madeleine, are high-class delicatessens. Alongside the Madeleine is a **ticket kiosk** selling tickets for same-day theater performances at greatly reduced prices (open Tues.–Sat. 12:30–8).

Continue down boulevard de la Madeleine and turn right into rue des Capucines. This nondescript street leads to rue de la ㉛ Paix. Immediately to the right is **place Vendôme.** This is one of the world's most opulent squares, a rhythmically proportioned example of 17th-century urban architecture that shines in all its golden-stoned splendor since being sandblasted several years ago. Other things shine here, too, in the windows of jewelry shops that are even more upscale (and discreet) than those ㉜ in rue Royale—fitting neighbors for the top-ranking **Ritz** hotel. The square's central column, topped by a statue of Napoleon, is made from the melted bronze of 1,200 cannons captured at the Battle of Austerlitz in 1805.

Time Out Rue de la Paix leads, logically enough, to the **Café de la Paix** on the corner of the place de l'Opéra. There are few grander cafés in Paris, and fewer places where you can perch with as good a tableau before you.

㉝ Dominating the northern side of the square is the imposing **Opéra,** the first great work of the architect Charles Garnier, who in 1860 won the contract to build the opera house. He used elements of neoclassical architecture—bas reliefs on facades and columns—in an exaggerated combination that borders on parody. The lavishly upholstered auditorium, with its delightful ceiling painted by Marc Chagall in 1964, seems small—but this is because the stage is the largest in the world, accommodating up to 450 players. *Admission: 28 frs adults, 15 frs students and children. Open daily 10–4:30.*

㉞ Behind the Opéra are **les grands magasins,** Paris's most venerable department stores. The nearer of the two, the **Galeries Lafayette,** is the more outstanding because of its elegant turn-of-the-century glass dome. But **Printemps,** farther along boulevard Haussmann to the left, is better organized and has an excellent view from its rooftop cafeteria.

Take the métro at Chaussée d'Antin, near the Galeries Lafayette, and travel three stops (direction Villejuif) as far as
③ **Palais-Royal.** This former royal palace, built in the 1630s, has a charming garden, bordered by arcades and boutiques, that many visitors overlook.

③ On the square in front of the Palais-Royal is the **Louvre des Antiquaires,** a chic shopping mall full of antiques dealers. It deserves a browse whether you intend to buy or not. Afterward, head east along rue St-Honoré and left into rue du Louvre. Skirt the circular **Bourse du Commerce** (Commercial Ex-
③ change) and head toward the imposing church of **St-Eustache,** (1532–1637), an invaluable testimony to the stylistic transition between Gothic and Classical architecture. It is also the "cathe-
③ dral" of **Les Halles**—the site of the central market of Paris until the much-loved glass-and-iron sheds were torn down in the late '60s. The area has since been transformed into a trendy—and already slightly seedy—shopping complex, Le Forum.

Head across the topiary garden and left down rue Berger. Pass the square des Innocents, with its Renaissance fountain, to boulevard de Sébastopol. Straight ahead lies the futuristic,
③ funnel-topped **Centre Pompidou** (Pompidou Center)—a must for lovers of modern art. The Pompidou Centre, also known as the Beaubourg, was built in the mid-1970s and named in honor of former French president Georges Pompidou (1911–74). This "cultural Disneyland" is always crowded, housing a **Museum of Modern Art,** a huge library, experimental music and industrial design sections, a children's museum, and a variety of activities and exhibitions. Musicians, magicians, fire-eaters, and other street performers fill the large forecourt near the entrance. *Admission free. Art museum: 28 frs. 50 frs for daily pass covering all sectors of the center. Open Mon., Wed.–Fri. noon–10; weekends 10–10. Guided tours in English 3:30 PM weekdays and 11 AM weekends during summer and Christmas season.*

Continue east to the **Marais,** one of the most historic quarters of Paris. The spacious affluence of its 17th-century mansions, many restored to former glory, contrasts with narrow winding streets full of shops and restaurants. Rue de Rambuteau leads from the Centre Pompidou into rue des Francs-Bourgeois. Turn left on rue Elzivir to rue Thorigny, where you will find
④ the Hôtel Salé and its **Musée Picasso.** This is a convincing experiment in modern museum layout, whether you like Picasso or not. Few of his major works are here, but many fine, little-known paintings, drawings, and engravings are on display. *5 rue Thorigny. Admission: 26 frs., free under 18 yrs. Open Wed.–Mon. 9:30–6.*

Double back down rue Elzivir and turn left along rue des
④ Francs-Bourgeois until you reach the **place des Vosges.** Built in 1605, this is the oldest square in Paris. The square's harmonious proportions, soft pink brick, and cloisterlike arcades give it an aura of calm. In the far corner is the **Maison de Victor Hugo,** containing souvenirs of the great poet's life and many of his surprisingly able paintings and ink drawings. *6 pl. des Vosges. Admission: 12 frs., 6.50 frs students and children. Open Tues.–Sun. 10–5:40.*

Rue Birague leads from the middle of the place des Vosges down to rue St-Antoine. About 250 yards along to the left is the

㊷ **place de la Bastille.** Unfortunately, there are no historic vestiges here; not even the soaring column, topped by the figure of Liberty, commemorates the famous storming of the Bastille in 1789 (the column stands in memory of Parisians killed in the uprisings of 1830 and 1848). Only the new **Opéra de la Bastille,** which opened in 1989, can be said to mark the bicentennial.

Retrace your steps down rue St-Antoine as far as the large Ba-
㊸ roque church of **Saint-Paul-Saint-Louis** (1627–41). Then con-
㊹ tinue down the rue de Rivoli to the **Hôtel de Ville.** This magnificent city hall was rebuilt in its original Renaissance style after being burned down in 1871, during the violent days of the Paris Commune. The vast square in front of its many-statued facade is laid out with fountains and bronze lamps.

Avenue de Victoria leads to place du Châtelet. On the right is
㊺ the **Tour St-Jacques.** This richly worked 52-meter (170-foot) stump is all that remains of a 16th-century church destroyed in 1802.

From Châtelet take the pont-au-Change over the Seine to the
㊻ Ile de la Cité and the **Palais de Justice** (law courts). Visit the turreted **Conciergerie,** a former prison with a superb vaulted 14th-century hall (Salles des Gens d'Armes) that often hosts temporary exhibitions. The **Tour de l'Horloge** (clock tower) near the entrance on the quai de l'Horloge has a clock that has been ticking off time since 1370. Around the corner in the boulevard du Palais, through the imposing law court gates, is the **Sainte-Chapelle,** built by St-Louis (Louis IX) in the 1240s to house the Crown of Thorns he had just bought from Emperor Baldwin of Constantinople. The building's lead-covered wood spire, rebuilt in 1854, rises 75 meters (246 feet). The somewhat garish lower chapel is less impressive than the upper one, whose walls consist of little else but dazzling 13th-century stained glass. *Conciergerie and Sainte-Chapelle. Admission: joint ticket 40 frs; single ticket 25 frs. Open daily 9:30–6:30; winter 10–5.*

From boulevard du Palais turn right on quai des Orfèvres. This
㊼ will take you past the quaint place Dauphine to the **square du Vert Galant** at the westernmost tip of the Ile de la Cité. Here, above a peaceful garden, you will find a statue of the Vert Galant: gallant adventurer Henry IV, king from 1589 to 1610.

Off the Beaten Track

Few tourists venture into east Paris, but there are several points of interest tucked away here. The largest is the **Bois de Vincennes,** a less touristy version of the Bois de Boulogne, with several cafés and lakes. Rowboats can be taken to the two islands in Lac Daumesnil or to the three in Lac des Minimes. There is also a zoo, cinder racetrack *(hippodrome),* and an extensive flower garden (Parc Floral, route de la Pyramide). The **Château de Vincennes** (av. de Paris) is an imposing, high-walled castle surrounded by a dry moat and dominated by a 53-meter (170-foot) keep. It contains a replica of the Sainte-Chapelle on Ile de la Cité and two elegant classical wings added in the mid-17th century. *Best métro access to the woods is at Porte Dorée; to the flower garden and castle (admission: 25 frs, 14 frs students and senior citizens, 6 frs under 7; open summer 10–6, winter 10–4), at Château de Vincennes.*

Cemeteries aren't every tourist's idea of the ultimate attraction, but **Père Lachaise** is the largest, most interesting, and most prestigious in Paris. It forms a veritable necropolis with cobbled avenues and tombs competing in pomposity and originality. Steep slopes and lush vegetation contribute to a powerful atmosphere; some people even bring a picnic lunch. Leading incumbents include Chopin, Molière, Proust, Oscar Wilde, Sarah Bernhardt, Jim Morrison, Yves Montand, and Edith Piaf. Get a map at the entrance and track them down. *Av. du Père-Lachaise, 20e; métro Gambetta. Open daily 8–6, winter 8–5*.

The **Canal St-Martin** starts life just south of the Place de la Bastille but really comes into its own during the 1.5-kilometer (1-mile) stretch north across the 10th arrondissement. It has an unexpected flavor of Amsterdam, thanks to its quiet banks, locks, and footbridges. *Closest métro stations: Jaurès to the north and Jacques-Bonsergent to the south.*

Hidden away in a grid of narrow streets not far from the Opéra is Paris's central auction house, the **Hôtel Drouot.** It is open six days a week (except at Christmas, Easter, and midsummer), and its 16 salesrooms make a fascinating place to browse, with absolutely no obligation to bid—though you may wish to do so! Everything from stamps and toy soldiers to Renoirs and 18th-century commodes is available. The mixture of fur-coated ladies with money to burn, penniless art lovers desperate to unearth an unidentified masterpiece, and scruffy dealers trying to look anonymous makes up Drouot's unusually rich social fabric. *Viewing takes place 11–noon and 2–6, with auctions starting at 2. Entrance at the corner of rue Rossini and rue Drouot, métro Richelieu-Drouot.*

Shopping

Gift Ideas Paris is the home of fashion and perfume. Old prints are sold in *bouquinistes* (stalls) along the Left Bank of the Seine. For state-of-the-art home decorations, the shop in the **Musée des Arts Décoratifs** in the Louvre (107 rue de Rivoli) is well worth visiting. Regional specialty foods, herbs, and pâtés can be found at **Fauchon** and **Hediard,** two upscale grocers at 26 and 21 place de la Madeleine, 8e.

Antiques Antiques dealers proliferate in the **Carré Rive Gauche** between St-Germain-des-Prés and the Musée d'Orsay. There are also several dealers around the Drouot auction house near Opéra (corner of rue Rossini and rue Drouot; métro: Richelieu-Drouot). The **Louvre des Antiquaires,** near the Palais-Royal (*see* Exploring, *above*), and the **Village Suisse,** near the Champ de Mars (78 av. de Suffren), are stylish shopping malls dominated by antiques.

Boutiques Only Milan can compete with Paris for the title of Capital of European Chic. The top shops are along both sides of the Champs-Elysées, along the avenue Montaigne and the rue du Faubourg St-Honoré, and at **Place des Victoires. St-Germain-des-Pres, rue de Grenelle,** and **rue de Rennes** on the left bank are centers for small specialty shops and boutiques. If you're on a tight budget, search for bargains along the shoddy streets around the foot of Montmartre (*see* Exploring, *above*), or near **Barbès-Rochechouart** métro station. The streets to the north of the Marais, close to **Arts-et-Métiers** métro, are historically linked to the cloth trade, and many shops offer garments at wholesale prices.

Department Stores   The most famous department stores in Paris are **Galeries Lafayette** and **Printemps,** on boulevard Haussmann. Others include **Au Bon Marché** near Sèvres-Babylone (métro on the Left Bank) and the **Samaritaine,** overlooking the Seine east of the Louvre (métro Pont-Neuf).

Food and Flea Markets   The sprawling **Marché aux Puces de St-Ouen,** just north of Paris, is one of Europe's largest flea markets. Best bargains are to be had early in the morning (open Sat.–Mon.; métro Porte de Clignancourt). There are smaller flea markets at the Porte de Vanves and Porte de Montreuil (weekends only).

Dining

Eating out in Paris should be a pleasure, and there is no reason why choosing a less expensive restaurant should spoil the fun. After all, Parisians themselves eat out frequently and cannot afford five-star dining every night, either. For details and price-category definitions, *see* Dining in Staying in France.

Left Bank
Very Expensive   **Jules Verne.** Distinctive all-black decor, stylish service, and a top chef—not to mention its location on the 400-foot second level of the Eiffel Tower—have made the Jules Verne one of the hardest dinner reservations to get in Paris. Chef Bariteau's colorful, flavorful cuisine (including asparagus and foie gras aspic, sole fillet with crab sauce, and veal medallions with bell pepper sauce) is most accessible at lunch, when a table is easier to snag and there is a good fixed-price menu. *Eiffel Tower, 7e, tel. 45–55–61–44. Reservations required at least 3 weeks in advance. Jacket and tie required. AE, DC, MC, V.*

★   **La Tour d'Argent.** Dining at this temple to haute cuisine is a theatrical and unique event—from apéritifs in the ground-floor bar to dinner in the top-floor dining room, with its breathtaking view of Notre Dame. In recent years owner Claude Terrail has hired a series of young chefs, and today's menu is a mix of Tour classics and contemporary creations, including *caneton* Tour d'Argent (pressed duck), and scallop salad with truffles. The wine list is one of the greatest in the world. *15 quai de la Tournelle, 5e, tel. 43–54–23–31. Reservations required at least 1 week in advance. Jacket and tie required at dinner, advised at lunch. AE, DC, MC, V. Closed Mon.*

Moderate   **Campagne et Provence.** This small establishment, on the quai across from Notre Dame, specializes in country cooking. Fresh, colorful Provençal-inspired cuisine includes vegetables stuffed with *brandade* (creamed salt cod), ratatouille omelet, and beer *daube* (stew) with olives. The list of reasonably priced regional wines helps keep the cost low—almost in the Inexpensive range. *25 quai de la Tournelle, 5e, tel. 43–54–05–17. Reservations advised. Dress: casual. MC, V. Closed Sat. lunch, Sun.*

Lipp. Politicians, entertainers, rubber-necking tourists, and everyone else vie for tables here, especially in the ground-floor dining room of this classic Left Bank brasserie. Food is classic brasserie-style, too: herring in cream, *choucroute garni* (sausages and cured pork served with sauerkraut), and *millefeuille* (puffed pastry). Attractive 1920s decor includes historic ceramics. *151 blvd. St-Germain, 6e, tel. 45–48–53–91. No res-*

ervations; expect lines. Jacket required. AE, DC, MC, V.
Closed mid-July–mid-Aug.

La Rotisserie d'En Face. A long rotisserie is part of the attractive country-elegant decor at this bistro created by renowned
chef Jacques Cagna. The cuisine includes good roast chicken
with mashed potatoes, grilled salmon with fresh spinach, and
chocolate éclairs. The menu is fixed-price only, and it's cheaper
at lunch. *2 rue Christine, 6e, tel. 43–26–40–98. MC, V. Closed
Sat. lunch, Sun.*

Inexpensive **Au Sauvignon.** This tiny wine bar has the usual limited menu of
tartines, or open-faced sandwiches, on the famous Poilâne loaf,
topped with good-quality charcuterie, cheese, or both. The colorful murals will amuse you, but it's even more fun to crowd-
watch from one of the tables set on the narrow sidewalk. *80 rue
des Saints Pères, 7e, tel. 45–48–04–69. No reservations. Dress:
casual. No credit cards. Closed Sat. dinner, Sun., Aug.,
Christmas week, and Easter.*

West Paris **Robuchon/Jamin.** Surely it's the most difficult reservation to
Very Expensive obtain in France. Chef-owner Joël Robuchon, though under 50,
★ has already attained cult status, and his influence on cooks
around the globe is great. Under his inspired vision, everything from cream of cauliflower with caviar to John Dory with
ginger, saddle of lamb in a salt crust to pig's head becomes a
visual and gustatory revelation. The pretty, pastel dining room
is secondary to the cuisine; the restaurant is due to move into
its own hôtel particulier in the future. *32 rue de Longchamp,
16e, tel. 47–27–12–27. Reservations required. Jacket and tie
required. MC, V. Closed weekends and July.*

Taillevent. Many say it's the best restaurant in Paris. Within
the wood-paneled main dining rooms of this mid-19th-century
mansion you will find exceptional, subtle service, a world-
renowned wine list, and the neoclassic cuisine of young chef
Philippe Legendre. Specials here include celery turnover with
morels and truffles, and lamb with cabbage. Pastry chef Gilles
Bajolle is one of the finest in Paris. Book months ahead. *15 rue
Lamennais, 8e, tel. 45–63–39–94. Reservations required.
Jacket and tie required. MC, V. Closed weekends and Aug.*

Moderate **La Fermette Marbeuf.** It's a favorite haunt of French TV and
movie stars, who like the spectacular Belle Epoque mosaics,
tiles, and stained glass (discovered by accident when the restaurant was being redecorated), and the solid, updated classic
cuisine. Try *gâteau* of chicken livers and sweetbreads, lamb
navarin (stew), and bitter chocolate fondant. The Fermette becomes animated late, around 9. Prices here are surprisingly
reasonable, considering the quality, surroundings, and neighborhood. *5 rue Marbeuf, 8e, tel. 47–20–63–53. Reservations
advised. Dress: casual but elegant. AE, DC, MC, V.*

Inexpensive. **Berry's.** This tiny annex next door to the more expensive Le
Grenadin, near the Parc Monceau, is a bargain. Talented chef-
owner Patrick Cirotte prepares dishes of his native Berry region and serves local wines, including fine Sancerres. Decor is
lean and modern; the atmosphere, young and upbeat. It's open
until 1 AM. *46 rue de Naples, 8e, tel. 40–75–01–56. Reservations advised. Dress: casual. AE, MC, V. Closed Sun.*

Right Bank **Le Grand Véfour.** This sumptuously decorated restaurant is
Very Expensive perhaps the most beautiful in Paris, and its 18th-century origins make it one of the oldest. Chef Guy Martin impresses with

his unique blend of sophisticated yet rustic dishes, including langoustines with calf's ear, rabbit with carrot and curry, and cabbage ravioli with truffle cream. Luminaries from Napoléon to Colette have frequented this intimate address under the arcades of the Palais Royal; you can request to be seated at their preferred table. *17 rue Beaujolais, 1er, tel. 42–96–56–27. Reservations required 1 week in advance. Jacket and tie required. AE, DC, MC, V. Closed Sat. lunch, Sun., and Aug.*

Expensive **Benoît.** Founded in 1912, Benoît retains the feel of a classic bis-
★ tro—frosted glass, lace curtains, polished brass, a warm welcome—despite its high prices. Try the beef tongue/*foie gras Lucullus,* marinated salmon, cassoulet, *boeuf à la mode* (beef braised in red wine), or game in season. Patrons debate the merits of the front or back room, but conviviality reigns in both. *20 rue St. Martin, 4e, tel. 42–72–25–76. Reservations required. Dress: casual but elegant. No credit cards. Closed weekends and Aug.*

Moderate **Le Petit Bourbon.** This charming restaurant offers two fixed-price menus; the less-expensive one qualifies for our Inexpensive category. Both menus feature first and main courses that transcend the ordinary, such as mushroom terrine with shellfish sauce, stuffed rabbit medallions, and chocolate soup. The intimate dining room has exposed stone walls, cream colors, and pretty paintings of the Midi region. *15 rue du Roule, 1er, tel. 40–26–08–93. Reservations advised. Dress: casual. MC, V. Closed Sun., Mon.*

Inexpensive **Chez Jenny.** Order the filling choucroute Jenny and a carafe of Alsation wine, then sit back and watch the bustle at this large, Alsatian brasserie. Waitresses in regional costume wend their way through many salons on two levels, serving hearty fare. Decor includes museum-quality marquetry and woodwork. Although the clientele is not the chic crowd found in other brasseries, everyone's having just as much fun. *39 blvd. du Temple, 3e, tel. 42–74–75–75. Reservations advised. Dress: casual. AE, DC, MC, V.*

Montmartre and **A. Beauvilliers.** Pickwickian owner Edouard Carlier is a born
East Paris party-giver, and his flower-filled restaurant is one of the most
Very Expensive festive in Paris. The three dining rooms are filled with his personal collection of paintings and valuable bibelots, and a tiny, vine-covered terrace makes for delightful summer dining. Chefs here come and go, but Mr. Carlier maintains quality, serving both original creations and reinterpreted classics. Recommended are the red mullet *en escabèche,* foie gras, lobster, sweetbread *tourte,* and *rognonnade* of veal. The mouth-puckering lemon tart is not to be missed. One drawback: Service can be distant if you are not known. *52 rue Lamarck, 18e, tel. 42–54–54–42. Reservations required. Jacket and tie required. AE, MC, V. Closed Sun., Mon. lunch, and Sept.*

Expensive **La Table d'Anvers.** One of the best restaurants near Montmar-
★ tre, La Table d'Anvers serves an interesting menu, with Italian and Provençal touches in dishes like gnocchi of langoustines and *girolles* (wild mushrooms), saddle of rabbit with polenta, and *croustillant* of asparagus with crab. Desserts are among the best in Paris; serious sweet tooths can indulge in an all-dessert menu, which includes a fish dish. *2 pl. d'Anvers, 9e, tel. 48–78–35–21. Reservations advised. Dress: casual but elegant. AE, MC, V. Closed Sat. lunch, Sun., and mid-Aug.*

Moderate **Chez Philippe/Pyrénées-Cévennes.** Old-timers refer to this comfortable bistro by its original name—Pyrénées-Cévennes—while others know it as Chez Philippe. The eclectic menu combines the cooking of Burgundy, central France—even Spain—in such dishes as snails in garlic butter, coq au vin, cassoulet, and paella. An attentive staff bustles amid cozy surroundings that include a beamed ceiling and polished copper. *106 rue de la Folie-Méricourt, 11e, tel. 43–57–33–78. Reservations advised. Dress: casual. MC, V. Closed weekends and Aug.*

Lodging

Paris is popular throughout the year, so make reservations early. For details and price-category definitions, *see* Lodging in Staying in France.

Left Bank and **L'Hotel.** The cream of French society has signed the guest book
Ile St-Louis of this classic Left Bank hotel. Oscar Wilde died in room 16 ("I
Very Expensive am dying beyond my means"). Music-hall star Mistinguette liked to stay here. The stunning marble-clad hall boasts an extraordinary eliptical staircase. Each room or suite—some pleasantly time-worn—is individually and tastefully decorated. The hotel has a fine restaurant, Le Belier, whose decor includes a fountain with a live tree. The bar, open until 1 AM, is popular with a well-heeled international crowd. *13 rue des Beaux-Arts, 6e, tel. 43–25–27–22, fax 43–25–64–81. 16 rooms with bath, 8 with shower, 3 suites. Facilities: restaurant, bar. English spoken. AE, DC, MC, V.*

Expensive **Deux-Iles.** This cleverly converted 17th-century mansion on the
★ residential Ile St-Louis has long won plaudits for charm and comfort. Flowers and plants are scattered around the stunning hall. The fabric-hung rooms, though small, have exposed beams and are fresh and airy. Ask for a room overlooking the little garden courtyard. There's no restaurant, but drinks are served in the cellar bar until 1 AM. The lounge is dominated by a fine chimneypiece and doubles as a second bar. *59 rue St-Louis-en-l'Ile, 4e, tel. 43–26–13–35, fax 43–29–60–25. 17 rooms, 8 with bath, 9 with shower. Facilities: bar (closed Sun.). English spoken. No credit cards.*

Hôtel d'Angleterre. Some claim the Hôtel d'Angleterre is the ultimate Left Bank hotel—a little small and shabby, but elegant and perfectly managed. The 18th-century building was originally the British ambassador's residence; later, Hemingway made it his Paris home. Room sizes and rates vary greatly, though all rooms are individually decorated. Some are imposingly formal, others are homey and plain. Ask for one overlooking the courtyard. *44 rue Jacob, 6e, tel. 42–60–34–72, fax 42–60–16–93. 26 rooms with bath, 3 suites. Facilities: bar, patio. English spoken. AE, DC, MC, V.*

Moderate **Grands Ecoles.** Recently upgraded from no stars to two, this delightful hotel in three small old buildings is set far off the street in a beautiful garden. There are parquet floors, antiques, and a piano in the breakfast area. Most rooms have beige carpets and flowery wallpaper. You won't find a quieter, more charming hotel for the price. There's a faithful American clientele, including some back-packers. The rooms with bathroom facilities on the well-lit landings are inexpensive. *75 rue du Cardinal Lemoine, 5e, tel. 43–26–79–23, fax 43–25–28–15.*

29 rooms with bath, 20 with shower, 9 with shared bath. English spoken. V.

★ **Marronniers.** There are few better places in Paris than the Marronniers for great value and atmosphere. Located on appealing rue Jacob, the hotel is reached through a small courtyard. All rooms are light and full of character. Those on the attic floor have sloping ceilings, uneven floors, and terrific views over the church of St-Germain-des-Prés. The vaulted cellars have been converted into two atmospheric lounges. Prices can creep into the expensive range. *21 rue Jacob, 6e, tel. 43-25-30-60, fax 40-46-83-56. 17 rooms with bath, 20 with shower. Facilities: bar. English spoken. No credit cards.*

West Paris
Very Expensive
★ **Le Bristol.** Luxury and discretion are the Bristol's trump cards. The understated facade on rue du Faubourg St-Honoré might mislead the unknowing, but the Bristol ranks among Paris's top four hotels. The air-conditioned and spaciously elegant rooms all have authentic Louis XV and Louis XVI furniture, and the management has filled public areas with old-master paintings, sculptures, sumptuous carpets, and tapestries. The marble bathrooms are simply magnificent. Nonguests can take tea in the vast garden or dine in the summer restaurant; later, you can listen to the pianist in the bar, open till 1 AM. There's an enclosed pool on the roof, complete with solarium and sauna for guests only. The service throughout is impeccable. *112 rue du Faubourg St-Honoré, 8e, tel. 42-66-91-45, fax 42-66-68-68. 155 rooms with bath, 45 suites. Facilities: restaurant, bar, pool, sauna, solarium, parking. English spoken. AE, DC, MC, V.*

★ **Crillon.** There can surely be no more sumptuous a luxury hotel than this regal mansion overlooking Place de la Concorde. The Crillon was founded in 1909 by the champagne family Taittinger (which still runs it) with the express intention of creating the best hotel in the city. They chose as their setting two adjoining town houses built by order of Louis XV. Renovations in the '80s added comfort—all rooms are air-conditioned—although not at the expense of the original imposing interior. Mirrors, marbles, tapestries, sculptures, great sprays of flowers, and glistening floors are found in all the public rooms. The expansive bedrooms have judicious mixtures of original and reproduction antiques. The bathrooms are, of course, marble. If you want to enjoy the amazing view over place de la Concorde to the National Assembly, you'll have to reserve one of the palatial suites. Of the three restaurants, the best is Les Ambassadeurs, housed in what was originally the Grand Salon and offering some of the best hotel food in the city. *10 pl. de la Concorde, 8e, tel. 42-65-24-24, fax 44-71-15-02. 117 rooms with bath, 46 suites. Facilities: 3 restaurants, bars, private reception rooms. English spoken. AE, DC, MC, V.*

George V. Some say the George V lacks the this-could-only-be-Paris atmosphere of other super-deluxe Parisian hotels; its style is more international. But there's no lack of authentic period furniture, or, indeed, of excellent, highly trained staff. Most rooms are impeccably decorated and imposing, although the penthouse suites are the only ones to enjoy a commanding view over the city. There are two restaurants; the better is Les Princes, where, in summer, you can eat on the leafy patio. *31 av. George V, 8e, tel. 47-23-54-00, fax 47-20-40-00. 298 rooms with bath, 53 suites. Facilities: 2 restaurants, bars, shopping mall, hairdresser. English spoken. AE, DC, MC, V.*

Expensive **Etoile-Pereire.** Pianist Ferrucio Pardi, owner and manager of
★ the Etoile-Pereire, has created a unique small hotel, set behind
a quiet, leafy courtyard in a chic residential district. All rooms
and duplexes are decorated in soothing pastels—pinks, grays,
and apricots—with Laura Ashley curtains and chair covers,
and prints on the walls. There's no restaurant, but a copious
breakfast is available—with 23 different jams and jellies. The
bar is always busy in the evening. For a lively, personally run
hotel, few places beat this likeable spot. *146 blvd. Pereire, 17e,
tel. 42–67–60–00, fax 42–67–02–90. 18 rooms with bath, 3 with
shower, 4 duplexes, 1 suite. Facilities: bar. English spoken.
AE, DC, MC, V.*

Moderate **Keppler.** Ideally located on the edge of the 8th and 16th Arron-
dissements near the Champs-Elysées, this small two-star hotel
in a 19th-century building bursts with amenities (room service,
small bar) at extremely reasonable prices. The spacious and
airy rooms are simply decorated with modern furnishings.
Some rooms with shower are inexpensive. *12 rue Keppler, 16e,
tel. 47–20–65–05, fax 47–23–02–29. 31 rooms with bath, 18
with shower. Facilities: bar. English spoken. AE, MC, V.*

Inexpensive **Argenson.** This friendly, family-run hotel provides what may
★ well be the best value in the swanky 8th Arrondissement. Top
sights are just a 10-minute walk away. Old furniture, molded
ceilings, and skillfull flower arrangements add to the charm.
Room-by-room renovation means new bathrooms in many. The
best rooms have full bath, but they are moderately priced; reserve well in advance for one of these. The small rooms with
shared baths are very inexpensive. *15 rue d'Argenson, 8e, tel.
42–65–16–87. 5 rooms with bath, 19 with shower, 3 with shared
bath. Some English spoken. DC, MC, V.*

Montmartre and **Grand Hotel Inter-Continental.** It's Paris's biggest luxury ho-
Central Paris tel, with endless hallways and a facade that seems as long as
Very Expensive the Louvre. And after four years of thorough restoration this
19th-century gem sparkles like new. The grand salon, with its
Art Deco dome, is a registered landmark. All rooms and suites
have been luxuriously redecorated in Art Nouveau style. The
famed Café de la Paix is one of the city's great rendezvous and
people-watching spots. *2 rue Scribe, 9e, tel. 40–07–32–32, fax
42–66–12–51. 470 rooms with bath, 23 suites. Facilities: 3 restaurants, 2 bars, secretarial services, travel agency, shops,
parking. English spoken. AE, DC, MC, V.*

Pavillon de la Reine. The best hotel in the Marais, it's set
around two flower-filled courtyards behind the historic
Queen's Pavilion on the 17th-century place des Vosges. Although this cozy mansion looks old, it was actually reconstructed from scratch in 1986 following original plans and using
period timbers, rough-hewn paving stones, Louis XIII fireplaces, and antiques. Ask for a duplex with French windows
over the first courtyard (there are no rooms overlooking the
place des Vosges). Breakfast is served in a vaulted cellar. *28 pl.
des Vosges, 3e, tel. 42–77–96–40, fax 42–77–63–06. 31 rooms
with bath, 24 suites. Facilities: parking. English spoken. AE,
DC, MC, V.*

★ **Ritz.** The Paris Ritz, on the stunning place Vendôme, is one of
the world's most renowned hotels, located on the most famous
and elegant square in the city. Millions of dollars have been lavished on the hotel by Egyptian-born owner Mohammed al-
Fayed (who also owns Harrods in London). The building is a

sumptuous 18th-century town house, a delightful combination of elegance and comfort. The vast, marble-clad bathrooms, some with turn-of-the-century fixtures, are renowned. The centerpiece of the health club here is a huge, delightful pool. The luxurious suites are named after just some of the guests who have stayed here—Coco Chanel, Marcel Proust, and Edward VII among them. L'Espadon is one of the finest hotel restaurants in the city. The Hemingway Bar, named for its erstwhile habitué, is a favorite upscale watering hole. *15 pl. Vendôme, 75001, tel. 42–60–38–30, fax 42–86–00–91. 142 rooms and 45 suites, all with bath. Facilities: 2 restaurants, 2 bars, indoor pool, health and sports complex with pool. AE, DC, MC, V.*

Expensive **Gaillon-Opéra.** The oak beams, stone walls, and marble tiles of
★ the Gaillon-Opéra single it out as one of the most charming hotels in the Opéra neighborhood. The plants throughout and a flower-filled patio also delight. There's a small bar but no restaurant. *9 rue Gaillon, 2e, tel. 47–42–47–74, fax 47–42–01–23. 26 rooms with bath, 1 suite. Facilities: bar. English spoken. AE, DC, MC, V.*

Moderate **Place des Vosges.** A loyal American clientele swears by the
★ small, historic place des Vosges, which is located on a charming street just off the exquisite square of the same name. Oak-beamed ceilings and rough-hewn stone in public areas and some of the guest rooms add to the atmosphere. Ask for the top-floor room, the hotel's largest, with a view of Marais rooftops. Some rooms, the size of walk-in closets, are inexpensive. There's a welcoming breakfast room. *12 rue de Birague, 4e, tel. 42–72–60–46, fax 42–72–02–64. 4 rooms with bath, 11 with shower. English spoken. AE, DC, V.*
Regyn's Montmartre. Despite small rooms (all recently renovated), this small, owner-run hotel on Montmartre's place des Abbesses is rapidly gaining an enviable reputation for simple, comfortable accommodations. A predominantly young clientele and a correspondingly relaxed atmosphere have made this an attractive choice for some. Try for one of the rooms on the upper floors, with great views over the city. *18 pl. des Abbesses, 18e, tel. 42–54–45–21, fax 42–54–45–21. 14 rooms with bath, 8 with shower. English spoken. MC, V.*

Inexpensive **Castex.** This family-run, two-star hotel in a 19th-century building is a real find. The decor is strictly functional, but the extremely friendly owners and rock-bottom prices mean the Castex is often fully booked months ahead. There's a large American clientele. The eight least expensive rooms, two per floor, share toilets on the immaculate, well-lit landings. There's no elevator, and the only TV is in the lobby. *5 rue Castex, 4e, tel. 42–72–31–52, fax 42–72–57–91. 4 rooms with bath, 23 with shower. English spoken. MC, V.*

The Arts

The monthly magazine *Paris Boulevard* (in English) and the weekly magazines *Pariscope, L'Officiel des Spectacles,* and *7 à Paris* give detailed entertainment listings. Buy tickets is at the place of performance. Otherwise, try hotels, travel agencies (try **Paris-Vision** at 214 rue de Rivoli), and special ticket counters (in the **FNAC** stores at 26 av. de Wagram, near the Arc de Triomphe and the Forum des Halles). Half-price tickets for same-day theater performances are available at the ticket stand at the west side of the Madeleine church.

Theater There is no Parisian equivalent to Broadway or the West End, although a number of theaters line the grand boulevards between Opéra and République. Shows are mostly in French; classical drama is at the distinguished **Comédie Française** (by Palais-Royal). A completely different charm is to be found in the tiny **Théâtre de la Huchette,** near St-Michel, where Ionesco's short modern plays make a deliberately ridiculous mess of the French language.

Concerts The principal venues for classical music are the **Salle Pleyel** (252 rue du Faubourg St-Honoré), near the Arc de Triomphe, the new **Opéra de la Bastille,** and the **Chatelet** theater (pl. Chatelet). You can also attend one of the many inexpensive organ or chamber music concerts in churches throughout the city.

Opera The **Opéra** itself is a splendid building, and its dance program has reached new heights. Getting a ticket for an opera or ballet performance is not easy, though, and requires either luck, much preplanning, or a well-connected hotel receptionist. The **Opéra Comique** (the French term for opera with spoken dialogue), close by in the rue Favart, is more accessible. The **Opéra de la Bastille** stages both traditional opera and symphony concerts.

Film There are hundreds of movie theaters in Paris and some of them, especially in principal tourist areas such as the Champs-Elysées and the boulevard des Italiens near the Opéra, run English films marked "V.O." *(version originale*—i.e., not dubbed). Admission is around 35–45 frs, with reduced rates on Wednesday. Movie fanatics should check out the **Centre Pompidou** and **Musée du Cinéma** at Trocadéro, where old and rare films are often screened.

Nightlife

Cabaret This is what Paris is supposed to be all about. Its nightclubs are household names—more so abroad than in France, it would seem, judging by the hefty percentage of foreigners present at most shows. Prices range from 200 frs (basic admission plus one drink) up to 650 frs (dinner included). For 350–450 frs, you can get a good seat plus half a bottle of champagne.

The **Crazy Horse** (12 av. George-V, tel. 47–23–32–32) is one of the field leaders in pretty women and dance routines: It features lots of humor and a lot less clothes. The **Moulin Rouge** (place Blanche, tel. 46–06–00–19) is an old favorite at the foot of Montmartre. Nearby is the **Folies-Bergère,** (32 rue Richer, tel. 42–46–77–11), not as it once was due to recent budget problems, but still renowned for its glitter and vocal numbers. The **Lido** (116 bis av. des Champs-Elysées, tel. 40–76–56–10) is all razzle-dazzle.

Bars and Nightclubs Upscale nightclubs are usually private, so unless you have a friend who is a member, forget it. A good bet, though, for drinking and dancing the night away, is the **Club 79** (79 av. des Champs-Elysées). Give the wildly popular **Niel's** (27 av. Ternes, 17e) or **Sheherazade** (93 rue de Liege, 9e) a try on weeknights only, or you run the risk of spending the evening waiting in line on the sidewalk. For a more leisurely experience in an atmosphere that is part bar and part gentlemen's club, try an old haunt of Hemingway, Fitzgerald, and Gertrude Stein: **Harry's Bar** (5 rue Danou), a cozy wood-paneled spot for Americans, journalists, and sportsmen.

Jazz Clubs The Latin Quarter is a good place to track down Paris jazz, and the doyen of clubs is the **Caveau de la Huchette** (5 rue de la Huchette), where you can hear Dixieland in a hectic, smoke-filled atmosphere. **Le Slow Club** (130 rue de Rivoli), another favorite, tries to resurrect the style of early Bourbon street, and nearly succeeds.

Rock Clubs **Le Sunset** (60 rue des Lombards) is a small, whitewashed cellar with first-rate live music and a clientele that's there to listen. **New Morning** (7 rue des Petites Ecuries) is a top spot for visiting American musicians and good French bands.

Discos **Club Zed** (2 rue des Anglais off blvd. St.-Germain), is the best place for rock and roll. The long-established **Balajo** (9 rue de Lappe, 11e) is crowded and lots of fun, with plenty of nostalgic '60s sounds on some nights. **Memphis** (3 impasse Bonne-Nouvelle) boasts some impressive lighting and video gadgetry.

Ile de France

The area surrounding Paris is called the Ile (island) de France, reflecting the role it has played over the centuries as the economic, political, and religious center of the country. For many visitors to Paris, it is the first taste of French provincial life, with its slower pace and fierce devotion to the soil. Although parts of the area are fighting a losing battle to resist the encroaching capital, you can still see the countryside that was the inspiration for the Impressionists and other 19th-century painters and is home to a wealth of architecture dating to the Middle Ages. The most famous buildings are Chartres—one of the most beautiful of French cathedrals—and Versailles, the monumental château of Louis XIV, the Sun King. Before the completion of Versailles, king and court resided in the delightful château of St-Germain-en-Laye, west of Paris. This is within easy day-trip range from Paris, as are the châteaux of Vaux-le-Vicomte, Rambouillet, and Fontainebleau, and the newest Disney venture, Euro Disney.

Getting Around

The region is reached easily from Paris by car and by regular suburban train services. But you might find it convenient to group some sights together: Versailles, Rambouillet, and Chartres are all on the Paris–Chartres train line; Fontainebleau, Barbizon, and Vaux-le-Vicomte are all within a few miles of each other.

By Train Three lines connect Paris with Versailles; on each, the trip takes about 30 minutes. Best for the château is RER C2 (Express métro line) to Versailles Rive Gauche station. Trains from Gare St-Lazare go to Versailles Rive Droite. Trains from Gare Montparnasse go to Versailles Chantiers and then on to Rambouillet and Chartres. Fontainebleau is served by 20 trains a day from Gare de Lyon; buses for Barbizon leave from in front of the main post office in Fontainebleau. The RER-A line will take you to Euro Disneyland (journey time: about 40 minutes).

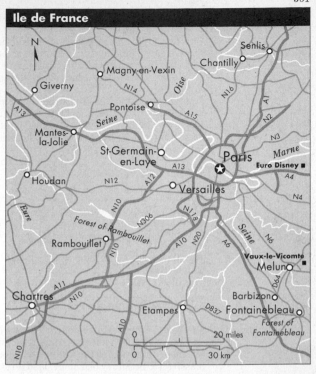

By Car Expressway A13, from the Porte d'Auteuil, followed by A12, will take you from Paris to Versailles. Alternatively, you can get to Chartres on A10 or N10 south from Porte d'Orleans. For Fontainebleau, take A6 from Porte d'Orleans or, for a more attractive route through the forest of Sénart and the northern part of the forest of Fontainebleau, take N6 from Porte de Charenton via Melun. Vaux-le-Vicomte is 6 kilometers (4 miles) northeast of Melun via N36 and D215. The 32-kilometer (20-mile) drive along the A4 expressway from Paris to Euro Disneyland takes about 30 minutes, longer in heavy traffic. Euro Disneyland is 4 kilometers (2½ miles) off the A4; follow the signs for the park.

Guided Tours

Two private companies, **Cityrama** and **Paris Vision,** organize regular half-day and full-day tours from Paris with English-speaking guides. Times and prices are identical. Cityrama tours depart from 4 place des Pyramides, 1er (tel. 42–60–30–14). Paris Vision leaves from 214 rue de Rivoli, 1er (tel. 42–60–31–25).

Versailles and the Les Trianons. Daily excursions starting at 9:30 include a complete tour of Paris in the morning followed by an afternoon at Versailles. Half-day excursions of Versailles leave mornings and afternoons daily (9:30 and 1:30, 250 frs) and include a guided tour of the château, Hall of Mirrors, and Queen's Suite. On Thursday only, a daylong excursion (420 frs) extends the tour to include an afternoon visit (starting 1:30) to the Trianons. Separate afternoon visits to the Trianons, again on Thursday, start at 1:30 (200 frs).

Chartres. Both companies organize half-day tours to Chartres on Tuesday, Thursday, and Saturday afternoons (departure at 1 PM, 250 frs), but if you're short of time or cash, you'd be better off taking the **Versailles–Chartres** day trips on Tuesday and Saturday (departure at 9:30, 430 frs).

Fontainebleau and Barbizon. Half-day trips (departure at 1:30, 245 frs) on Wednesday, Friday, and Sunday run to Fontainbleau and nearby Barbizon (which is otherwise difficult to reach), but can be linked to a Versailles tour leaving at 9:30 on the same days.

Tourist Information

Barbizon (41 rue Grande, tel. 60–66–41–87).
Chartres (Pl. de la Cathédrale, tel. 37–21–50–00).
Euro Disney (Euro Disney S.C.A., Central Reservations Office, Box 105 F77777, Marne-la-Vallée, Cedex 4 France, tel. 49–41–49–10).
Fontainebleau (31 pl. Napoléon-Bonaparte, tel. 64–22–25–68).
Rambouillet (8 pl. de la Libération, tel. 34–83–21–21).
Versailles (7 rue des Réservoirs, tel. 39–50–36–22).

Exploring the Ile de France

Versailles **Versailles** is the location of one of the world's grandest palaces and one of France's most popular attractions. Wide, tree-lined avenues, broader than the Champs-Elysées and bordered with massive 17th-century mansions, lead directly to the Sun King's château. From the imposing place d'Armes in front of the château, you enter the Cour des Ministres, a sprawling cobbled forecourt. Right in the middle, the statue of Louis XIV stands triumphant, surveying the town that he built from scratch to house those of the 20,000 noblemen, servants, and hangers-on who weren't lucky enough to get one of the 3,000 beds in the château.

The building of the château in its entirety took 50 years. Hills were flattened, marshes drained, forests transplanted, and water for the magnificent fountains was channeled from the Seine several miles away. Visit the **Grands Appartements,** the six salons that made up the royal living quarters, and the famous **Galerie des Glaces** (Hall of Mirrors). Both can be visited without a guide, but you can get a cassette in English. There are also guided tours of the **petits appartements,** where the royal family and friends lived in relative intimacy, and the miniature opera house—one of the first oval rooms in France, built on the *aile nord* (north wing) for Louis XV in 1770. *Grands Appartements and Galerie des Glaces. Admission: 31 frs adults, 16 frs students and seniors citizens. Open Tues.–Sun. 9–6, 9–5 in winter.*

The château's vast grounds are masterpieces of formal landscaping. At one end of the Petit Canal, which crosses the Grand Canal at right angles, is the **Grand Trianon,** a scaled-down pleasure palace built in the 1680s. The **Petit Trianon,** nearby, is a sumptuously furnished 18th-century mansion, commissioned by Louis XVI for Marie-Antoinette, who would flee here to avoid the stuffy atmosphere of the court. Nearby, she built the village, complete with dairy and mill, where she and her companions would dress as shepherdesses and lead a make-believe bucolic life. *Château grounds. Admission free. Open 8:30–dusk. Grand Trianon. Admission: 20 frs adults, 13 frs children and senior citizens. Open 9:45–noon and 2–5. Petit Trianon. Admission: 12 frs adults, 8 frs children and senior citizens. Open 2–5.*

Rambouillet Just a little more than 20 kilometers (12 miles) southwest of Versailles is the small town of **Rambouillet,** home of a château, adjoining park, and 13,770 hectares (34,000 acres) of forest. Since 1897, the château has been a summer residence of the French president; today, it is also used as a site for international summits. You can visit the château only when the president is not in residence—fortunately, he's not there often.

French kings have lived in the château since it was built in 1375. Highlights include the **Appartements d'Assemblée,** decorated with finely detailed wood paneling, and Napoleon's bathroom, with its Pompeii-inspired frescoes. The park stretches way behind the château. Beyond the **Jardin d'Eau** (Water Garden) lies the English-style garden and the **Laiterie de la Reine** (Marie-Antoinette's Dairy). This was another of her attempts to "get back to nature." *Château. Admission: 27 frs., 15 frs children and senior citizens. Open Apr.–Sept., Wed.–Mon. 10–noon and 2–6; Oct.–Mar. 10–noon and 2–5. Park. Admission free. Open sunrise–sunset. Marie-Antoinette's Dairy. Admission 13 frs. Open same hours as Château; closes at 4 in winter.*

Chartres From Rambouillet, N10 will take you straight to **Chartres.** Long before you arrive you will see its famous cathedral towering over the plain of the Beauce, France's granary. The attractive old town, steeped in religious history and dating to before the Roman conquest, is still laced with winding medieval streets.

Today's Gothic cathedral, **Notre-Dame de Chartres,** is the sixth Christian church to have been built on the site; despite a series of fires, it has remained virtually the same since the 12th century. The **Royal Portal** on the main facade, presenting "the life and triumph of the Savior," is one of the finest examples of Romanesque sculpture in the country. Inside, the 12th- and 13th-century rose windows come alive even in dull weather, thanks to the deep Chartres blue of the stained glass: Its formula remains a mystery to this day. *Cathedral tours available: Ask at the Maison des Clercs, 18 rue du Cloître Notre-Dame.*

Since the rest of the tour is on another side of Paris, it is probably easier to return to the capital to continue (*see* Getting Around in Ile de France, *above*).

Fontainebleau In the early 16th century, the flamboyant Francis I transformed the medieval hunting lodge of **Fontainebleau** into a magnificent Renaissance palace. His successor, Henry II, covered the palace with his initials, woven into the *D* for his mistress, Diane de Poitiers. When he died, his queen, Catherine de' Medici, carried out further alterations, later extended under Louis XIV. Napoleon preferred the relative intimacy of Fontainebleau to the grandeur of Versailles. Before he was exiled to Elba, he bade farewell to his Old Guard in the courtyard now known as the **Cour des Adieux** (Farewell Court). The emperor also harangued his troops from the **Horseshoe Staircase.** Ask the curator to let you see the **Cour Ovale** (Oval Court), the oldest and perhaps most interesting courtyard. It stands on the site of the original 12th-century fortified building, but only the keep remains today.

The **Grands Appartements** (royal suites and ballroom) are the main attractions of any visit to the château. The **Galerie de François I** is really a covered bridge (built 1528–30) looking out over the Cour de la Fontaine. The overall effect inside the Galerie—and throughout Fontainebleau—is one of classical harmony and proportion, combining to create a sense of Renaissance lightness and order. Francis I appreciated the Italian Renaissance, and the ballroom is decorated with frescoes by Primaticcio (1504–70) and his pupil, Niccolò dell'Abbate. If you're there on a weekday, you will also be able to join a guided tour of the Petits Appartements, used by Napoleon and Josephine. *Pl. du Gal-de-Gaulle, tel. 64–22–27–40. Admission: 30 frs, 19 frs under 25 and Sun., free under 18. Open 9:30–12:30 and 2–5. Closed Tues. and holidays.*

Barbizon The **Rochers des Demoiselles,** just south of the town, are good for an afternoon stroll. The **Gorges d'Apremont,** which offer the best views of the rocks, are near **Barbizon,** on the edge of the forest, 10 kilometers (6 miles) northwest of Fontainebleau. This delightful little village is scarcely more than a main street lined with restaurants and boutiques, but a group of landscape painters put it on the map in the mid-19th century. Théodore Rousseau and Jean-François Millet both had their studios here. Sculptor Henri Chapu's bronze medallion, sealed to one of the famous sandstone rocks in the forest nearby, pays homage to the two leaders of what became known as the Barbizon group.

Drop in at the **Ancienne Auberge du Père Ganne** (Père Ganne's Inn), where most of the landscape artists ate and drank, while in Barbizon. They painted on every available surface, and even now you can see some originals on the walls and in the buffet. Today, the back room is devoted to modern landscape artists. *Rue Grande, tel. 60–66–46–73. Admission free. Guided visits mid-Mar.–Oct., Wed.–Mon. 9:45–6; Nov.–mid-Mar., Fri. 2–6, weekends 10–6.*

Next to the church, in a barn that Rousseau used as a studio, you'll find the **Musée de l'Ecole de Barbizon** (Barbizon School Museum), containing documents of the village as it was in the 19th century as well as a few original works. *55 rue Grande, tel. 60–66–22–38. Admission: 15 frs adults, children free. Open Apr.–Sept., Mon. and Wed.–Fri. 10:30–12:30 and 2–6, weekends 10:30–6; Oct–Mar., Mon and Wed.–Fri. 10:30–12:30 and 2–5, weekends 10:30–5.*

From Barbizon, D64 offers a pleasant shortcut to Melun and then on to the château of **Vaux-le-Vicomte,** one of the greatest monuments of 17th-century French architecture. It was to have been Nicolas Fouquet's pride and joy, but turned out to be his downfall. This superintendent of France's finances under Louis XIV tended to use state resources for his own benefit—the château itself is damning evidence—and the Sun King eventually had him imprisoned for life. From the visitor's point of view, though, Fouquet's *folie de grandeur* is a treat. He had excellent taste (and a large budget) and chose the best-qualified team to build Vaux-le-Vicomte. Louis liked the results enough to reemploy them all when he built Versailles. Visit the kitchens, which have been preserved just as they were in the 17th century. The gardens (admission: 22 frs) are open all day.

Guided tours of château. Admission: 43 frs. Open Apr.–Oct.,
daily 10–6; Nov–Mar., daily 10–5. Candlelit visits. Admis-
sion: 50 frs. Open May–Sept., Sat. 8:30–11:30.

Getting There   Resort is on A4 motorway that runs from Paris to Strasbourg
By Car   (Exit 14—"Parc Euro Disneyland").

By Train   Express metro line (RER line A4) from Paris runs directly to
Marne-la-Vallee, a short walk from theme park entrance (travel time 40 minutes, 38 frs); as of June 1994 a new TGV line will
connect Euro Disney with Gare Montparnasse.

Euro Disney   Now you can get a dose of American pop culture in-between visits to the Louvre and the Left Bank. In April 1992 the **Euro Disney** complex opened in Marne-la-Vallée, just 32 kilometers (20
miles) east of Paris, much to the consternation of French cultural apologists. The complex is divided into several areas, including **Euro Disneyland,** the pay-as-you-enter theme park that
is the main reason for coming here. Occupying 136 acres, Euro
Disneyland is less than half a mile across and ringed by a railroad with whistling steam engines. Although smaller than its
U.S. counterparts, Euro Disneyland was built with great attention paid to the tiniest detail. Smack in the middle of the
park is the soaring Sleeping Beauty Castle, which is surrounded by a plaza from which you can enter the four "lands" of
Disney: **Frontierland, Adventureland, Fantasyland,** and **Discov-
eryland.** In addition, Main Street U.S.A. connects the castle to
Euro Disneyland's entrance, under the pointed pink domes of
the Disneyland Hotel. *Admission to Euro Disneyland: 225 frs
adults, 150 frs children under 12; 2-day Passport 425 frs
adults, 285 frs children; 3-day Passport 565 frs adults, 375 frs
children. Open Apr.–mid-June, weekdays 9–7, weekends 9–
midnight; mid-June–Aug., daily 9–midnight; Sept.–Oct.,
weekdays 9–7, weekends 9–9; Nov.–Mar., weekdays 10–5,
weekends 10–7.*

There are six hotels in the 4,800-acre Euro Disney complex, all
part of a section called the **Euro Disney Resort,** just outside the
theme park. The resort also comprises parking lots, a train station, and the Festival Disney entertainment center, with restaurants, a theater, dance clubs, shops, a post office, and a
tourist office. Cheaper accommodations—log cabins and campsites—are available at Camp Davy Crockett, but it is located
farther away from the theme park.

Dining and Lodging

For details and price-category definitions, *see* Dining and
Lodging in Staying in France.

Barbizon   **Le Relais.** The delicious specialties—particularly the beef and
Dining   the game (in season)—are served in large portions and there is
a good choice of fixed-price menus. The Relais is spacious, with
walls covered with paintings and hunting trophies, and there is
a big open fire. The owner is proud of the large terrace where
you can eat in the shade of lime and chestnut trees. *2 av.
Charles de Gaulle, tel. 60–66–40–28. Weekend reservations required. MC, V. Closed Tues., Wed., Aug. 20–Sept. 5, first half
Jan. Moderate.*

Lodging   **Auberge des Alouettes.** This delightful 19th-century inn is set on
8,000 square meters (2 acres) of grounds. The interior has been
redecorated in '30s style, but many rooms still have their origi-

nal oak beams. The restaurant, with a large open terrace, features nouvelle cuisine in sizable portions. *4 rue Antoine Barye, tel. 60-66-41-98. 22 rooms with bath or shower. Facilities: restaurant, tennis, parking. Reservations required for restaurant. AE, DC, MC, V. Moderate.*

Chartres
Dining

Vieille Maison. Located in a recently refitted 14th-century building only a stone's throw from the cathedral, Vieille Maison serves excellent nouvelle cuisine as well as more traditional dishes. Try the regional *menu beauceron* for the homemade foie gras and duck dishes or the mouth-watering *menu gourmand*, if the wallet allows. *5 rue au Lait, tel. 37-34-10-67. Reservations required. AE, DC, MC, V. Closed Sun. evening, Mon., and Jan. 1-15, July 15-31. Expensive.*

Buisson Ardent. Set in an attractive old oak-beamed building within sight of the cathedral's south portal, Buisson Ardent is a popular restaurant providing inexpensive fixed-price menus (especially good on weekdays) and a choice of imaginative à la carte dishes with delicious sauces. The wine list is comprehensive. *10 rue au Lait, tel. 37-34-04-66. Reservations advised. AE, DC, MC, V. Closed Sun. evenings. Moderate.*

Lodging

Grand Monarque. The most popular rooms in this 18th-century coaching inn are in a separate turn-of-the-century building overlooking a garden. Rooms have the level of comfort and consistency you would expect from a Best Western. The hotel also has an excellent reasonably priced restaurant. *22 pl. des Epars, tel. 37-21-00-72. 57 rooms, 52 with bath or shower. Facilities: restaurant. AE, DC, MC, V. Moderate.*

Euro Disney
Dining

Euro Disneyland is peppered with places to eat, ranging from snack bars and fast-food joints to full-service restaurants—all with a distinguishing theme. In addition, all Disney hotels have restaurants that are open to the public. But since these are outside the theme park, it is not recommended that you waste time traveling to them for lunch. Be aware that only the hotel restaurants serve alcoholic beverages; Disney's no-alcohol standard is maintained throughout the theme park. Eateries serve nonstop as long as the park is open. *AE, DC, MC, V accepted at sit-down restaurants; no credit cards at others. Reservations advised for sit-down restaurants. Counter-service restaurants: Inexpensive; sit-down restaurants: Moderate.*

Fontainebleau
Dining

Le Dauphin. Prices are reasonable in this homey, rustic restaurant located near the town hall and just five minutes from the château. Specialties include snails, confit of duck, and a variety of homemade desserts. *24 rue Grande, tel. 64-22-27-04. Reservations advised, especially on Sun. MC, V. Closed Tues. evening, Wed., Feb., and Sept. 1-8. Inexpensive.*

Lodging

Londres. The balconies of this tranquil, family-style hotel look out over the palace and the Cour des Adieux; the 19th-century facade is preserved by government order. Inside, the decor is dominated by the Louis XV–style furniture. *1 pl. Général de Gaulle, tel. 64-22-20-21. 22 rooms, most with bath or shower. Facilities: restaurant, tea room, bar, parking. AE, DC, MC, V. Closed Dec. 20–Jan. 31. Inexpensive–Moderate.*

Rambouillet
Dining

La Poste. Traditional, unpretentious cooking is the attraction of this former coaching inn, close to the château. Until 1988, it could seat only 36 people, but a new upstairs dining room has been opened, doubling the capacity. The service is good, as is

Burgundy and Lyon

For a region whose powerful medieval dukes held sway over large tracts of Western Europe and whose current image is closely allied to its expensive wine, Burgundy is a place of surprisingly rustic, quiet charm.

Despite the mighty Gothic cathedrals of Sens and Auxerre, Burgundy's leading religious monument is the Romanesque basilica at Vézelay. Once one of Christianity's most important pilgrimage centers, Vézelay is today a tiny village hidden in the folds of rolling, verdant hills. In its time, the abbey of Cluny farther south was equally important, but few of its buildings remain.

The heart of Burgundy consists of the dark, brooding Morvan Forest. Dijon is the region's only city and retains something of its medieval opulence. Its present reputation is essentially gastronomic, however; top-class restaurants abound, and local "industries" involve the production of mustard, *cassis* (blackcurrant liqueur), snails, and—of course—wine. The vineyards extending down toward the ancient town of Beaune are among the world's most distinguished and picturesque.

The vines continue to flourish as you head south along the Saône Valley, through the Mâconnais and Beaujolais, toward Lyon, one of France's most appealing cities. The combination of frenzied modernity and unhurried *joie de vivre* give Lyon a sense of balance. The only danger is a temptation to overindulge in its rich and robust cuisine.

Burgundy's winters are cold, its summers hot. The ideal times to come are late May, when the countryside is in flower, and September or October, for the wine harvest.

Getting Around

Burgundy is a region best visited by car. Its meandering country roads invite leisurely exploration. There are few big towns, and traveling around by train is unrewarding, especially since the infrequent cross-country trains steam along at the speed of a legendary Burgundy snail.

Guided Tours

The Dijon branch of the regional tourism office organizes a series of tours using Dijon as a base. These include wine tastings and historic tours of the famous religious centers. Write to Comité Régional de Tourisme (21 blvd. Brosses, 21000 Dijon).

Tourist Information

Auxerre (1 quai de la République, tel. 86–52–06–19).
Beaune (Rue de l'Hôtel-Dieu, tel. 80–22–24–51).
Dijon (29 pl. Darcy, tel. 80–43–42–12).
Lyon (Pl. Bellecoeur, tel. 78–42–25–75).
Sens (Pl. Jean-Jaurès, tel. 86–65–19–49).

Burgundy

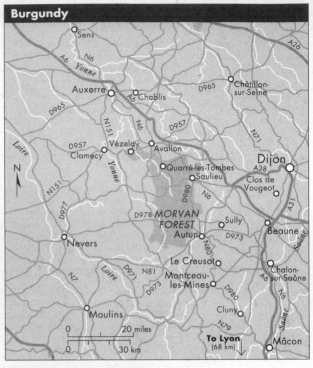

Sens
A6 N6 Yonne
A26
Auxerre
D965
Châtillon-sur-Seine
Chablis
A6
D965
N151
N6
D957
Loire
D957 Vézelay
Avallon
N71
Clamecy
Yonne
Quarré-les-Tombes
Saulieu
Dijon
A38
Clos de Vougeot
N151
D977
D980
N6
MORVAN FOREST
D978
Sully
A31
Nevers
Autun
D973
Beaune
N80
Saône
Le Creusot
N7
Loire
D971
N81
Chalon-sur-Saône
Montceau-les-Mines
D973
D980
A6
N6
Moulins
Cluny
Saône
0   20 miles
0   30 km
N79
To Lyon (68 km)
Mâcon
N

Exploring Burgundy and Lyon

It makes sense for **Sens** to be your first stop on the way down to
Burgundy, since it lies just 120 kilometers (75 miles) from Paris
on N6—a fast, pretty road that hugs the Yonne Valley south of
Fontainebleau. Sens is home to France's senior archbishop and
is dominated by the 12th-century **Cathédrale St-Etienne.** This
is one of the oldest cathedrals in France and has a foursquare
facade topped by towers and an incongruous little Renaissance
campanile. The vast, harmonious interior contains outstanding
stained glass of various periods.

The 13th-century **Palais Synodal** alongside, now a local museum, provides a first encounter with Burgundy's multicolored
tiled roofs; from its courtyard, there is a fine view of the cathedral's south transept, constructed in the fluid Flamboyant
Gothic style of the 16th century. *Rue des Déportés de la Résistance. Admission: 12 frs. Open Mar.–mid-Dec. daily 10–noon
and 2–5; mid-Dec.–Feb., Thurs.–Tues. 2–4:30.*

Auxerre N6 continues to **Auxerre,** a small, peaceful town with its own
Cathédrale St-Etienne, perched on a steepish hill overlooking
the Yonne. The muscular cathedral, built between the 13th and
16th centuries, has a powerful north tower similar to that at
Clamecy. The former **abbey of St-Germain** nearby contains an
underground church dating from the 9th century. *Rue Cochois.
Guided tour of crypt. Admission: 10 frs. Open Wed.–Mon. 10–
noon and 2–5.*

Chablis, famous for its dry white wine, makes an attractive excursion 16 kilometers (10 miles) to the east of Auxerre, along N65 and D965. Beware of village tourist shops selling local wines at unpalatable prices. The surrounding vineyards are dramatic: Their towering, steeply banked hills stand in marked contrast to the region's characteristic gentle slopes.

Clamecy From Auxerre, take N151 43 kilometers (27 miles) south along the Yonne to **Clamecy.** This sleepy town is not on many tourist itineraries, but its tumbling alleyways and untouched, ancient houses epitomize *la France profonde.* The many-shaped roofs of Clamecy, dominated by the majestic square tower of the **church of St-Martin,** are best viewed from the banks of the Yonne. The river played a crucial role in Clamecy's development: Trees from the nearby Morvan Forest were cut down and floated in huge convoys to Paris. The history of this curious form of transport *(flottage)*, now extinct, is detailed in the town **museum.** *Rue Bourgeoise. Admission: 6 frs. Open July–Sept., Wed.–Mon. 10–noon and 2–5; rest of the year by appointment.*

Vézelay lies 24 kilometers (15 miles) east of Clamecy, along D957. The **Basilica** is perched on a rocky crag, with commanding views of the surrounding countryside. It rose to fame in the 11th century as the resting place of the relics of St. Mary Magdalene and became a departure point for the great pilgrimages to Santiago de Compostela in northwest Spain. The church was rescued from decay by the 19th-century Gothic Revival architect Eugène-Emmanuel Viollet-le-Duc and counts as one of the foremost Romanesque buildings in existence. Its interior is long and airy, with superbly carved column capitals; the facade boasts an equally majestic tympanum.

Avallon is 13 kilometers (8 miles) farther along from Vézelay, via D957. Its site, on a promontory, is spectacular, and its old streets and ramparts make agreeable places to stroll. The imagination of medieval stone carvers ran riot at the portals of the venerable church of **St-Lazarus.**

The expressway passes close by Avallon and can whisk you along to Dijon, 96 kilometers (60 miles) away, in less than an hour. If you're in no rush, take the time to explore part of the huge **Morvan Regional Park;** the road twists and turns through lakes, hills, and forests. Take D10 south to **Quarré-les-Tombes**—so called because of the empty prehistoric stone tombs discovered locally and eerily arrayed in a ring around the church—before continuing southeast toward Saulieu. The **Rocher de la Pérouse,** 8 kilometers (5 miles) from Quarré-les-Tombes, is a mighty outcrop worth climbing for the view of the Cousin Valley. Continue to **Saulieu** via the N6, D264, and D977.

Saulieu's reputation belies its size (just 3,000 inhabitants). It is renowned for good food (Rabelais, that 16th-century authority, extolled its hospitality) and Christmas trees (a million are harvested each year). The **Basilica of St-Andoche** is almost as old as Vézelay's, though less imposing and much restored. The adjoining town **museum** (Admission: 7 frs. Open Wed.–Mon., 10–noon and 2–5) contains a room devoted to the sculptor of art deco animals, François Pompon.

Dijon N6 and then D977 link Saulieu to the Dijon-bound A38 expressway to the east. **Dijon** is capital of both Burgundy and gastronomy. Visit its restaurants and the **Palais des Ducs** (Ducal Palace), testimony to bygone splendor and the setting for one of

France's leading art museums (Admission: 12 frs. Open Wed.– Mon. 10–6). The tombs of Philip the Bold and John the Fearless head a rich collection of medieval objects and Renaissance furniture. Outstanding features of the city's old churches include the stained glass of **Notre-Dame,** the austere interior of the **cathedral of St-Bénigne,** and the chunky Renaissance facade of **St-Michel.** Don't miss the exuberant 15th-century gateway at the **Chartreuse de Champmol**—all that remains of a former charterhouse—or the adjoining **Puits de Moïse,** a "well" with six large, realistic medieval statues on a hexagonal base.

Beaune   A31 connects Dijon to **Beaune,** 40 kilometers (25 miles) to the south, but you may prefer a leisurely trip through the vineyards. Take D122, then N74 at Chambolle-Musigny; just to the south is the Renaissance **Château du Clos de Vougeot,** famous as the seat of Burgundy's elite company of wine tasters, the Confrérie des Chevaliers du Tastevin, who gather here in November at the start of the three-day festival Les Trois Glorieuses—which includes a wine auction at the Hospices de Beaune. *Château du Clos de Vougeot. Admission: 22 frs. Guided tours daily 9–11:30 and 2–5:30. Closed Dec. 24–Jan. 3.*

The **Hospices** (or Hôtel-Dieu) **de Beaune** owns some of the finest vineyards in the region yet was founded in 1443 as a hospital. Its medical history is retraced in a **museum** that also features Roger van der Weyden's medieval Flemish masterpiece *The Last Judgment,* plus a collection of tapestries, though a better series (late 15th century, relating the *Life of the Virgin*) hangs in Beaune's main church, the **Collégiale Notre-Dame**, which dates from 1120. *Hospices de Beaune. Admission: 27 frs adults, 14 frs children. Open Apr.–Nov., daily 9–6:30; Dec.– Mar., daily 9–11:30 and 2–5:30.*

The history of local wines can be explored at the **Musée du Vin de Bourgogne,** housed in a mansion built in the 15th and 16th centuries (Admission: 10 frs. Open Apr.–Oct., daily 9–noon and 1:30–6; Nov.–Mar., daily 10–noon and 2–5:30). The place to drink the stuff is in the candlelit cellars of the **Marché aux Vins** (wine market), on rue Nicolas Rolin, where you can taste as much as you please for 40 frs.

Autun   **Autun** is 48 kilometers (30 miles) west of Beaune along D973 but is worth a detour, if only for the Renaissance **château of Sully** on the way (Admission: 10 frs. Visits to grounds only, daily in summer, 10–noon and 2–5). The leading monument in Autun is the church of **St-Lazarus,** a curious Gothic cathedral redone in the Classical style by 18th-century clerics trying to follow fashion. The building actually dates back to the first half of the 12th century. Note the majestic picture by Ingres, the *Martyrdom of St-Symphorien,* in one of the side chapels. Across from the cathedral is the **Musée Rolin** (Admission: 10 frs. Open Wed.– Mon. 10–noon and 2–5; Sun. 2–5), with several fine paintings from the Middle Ages, although the town's importance dates back to Roman times, as you can detect at the **Porte St-André,** a well-preserved archway, and the **Théâtre Romain,** once the largest arena in Gaul.

Cluny   From Autun, head southeast along N80 and D980, via industrial Montceau-les-Mines, to **Cluny,** 80 kilometers (50 miles) away. The **Abbey** of Cluny, founded in the 10th century, was the largest church in Europe until St. Peter's was built in Rome in the 16th century. The ruins give an idea of its original grandeur. Note the **Clocher de l'Eau-Bénite** (a majestic bell tower) and the 13th-century **Farinier** (flour mill) with its fine chestnut roof and collection of statues. *Guided tours of ruins. Admission: 28 frs adults, 9 frs children. Open Easter–Oct., daily 9–noon and 2–5; Nov.–Easter, daily, late morning–early afternoon.*

A model of the original abbey can be seen in the **Musée Ochier,** the 15th-century abbot's palace. *Rue Conant. Admission: 8 frs. Open Wed.–Mon. 10–noon and 2–5. Closed Jan. 1–15.*

Cluny is a mere 28 kilometers (16 miles) northwest of **Mâcon,** a bustling town best known for its wine fair in May and for its stone bridge across the Saône; the low arches are a headache for large river barges. At Mâcon take N6 or A6 due south to Lyon, where the river Rhône runs parallel to the Saône before the two converge south of the city center.

Lyon   In recent years, **Lyon** has solidified its role as one of Europe's leading commercial centers, thanks to France's policy of decentralization and the TGV train that puts Paris at virtual commuter distance (two hours). Much of the city has an appropriate air of untroubled prosperity, and you will have plenty of choices when it comes to good eating.

The clifftop silhouette of **Notre-Dame de Fourvière** is the city's most striking symbol: an exotic mish-mash of styles with an interior that's pure decorative overkill. Climb the Fourvière heights for the view instead and then go to the nearby Roman remains. *Théâtres Romains. Admission free. Open Mar.–Oct., 8–noon and 2–5, Sat. 9–noon and 3–6, Sun. 3–6; Nov.–Feb., weekdays 8–noon and 2–5.*

The pick of Lyon's museums is the **Musée des Beaux-Arts** (open Wed.–Mon. 11–6). It houses sculpture, classical relics, and an extensive collection of Old Masters and Impressionists. Don't miss local artist Louis Janmot's 19th-century mystical cycle *The Poem of the Soul,* 18 canvases and 16 drawings that took nearly 50 years to complete. *20 pl. des Terreaux, tel. 78–28–81–11. Admission: 20 frs adults, 10 frs students, children free. Open Wed.–Sun. 10:30–6.*

Dining and Lodging

For details and price-category definitions, *see* Dining and Lodging in Staying in France.

Auxerre   **Jardin Gourmand.** As its name implies, the Jardin Gourmand
Dining   has a pretty garden where you can eat *en terrasse* during the summer. The interior, accented by light-colored oak, is equally congenial. The cuisine is innovative—try the ravioli and foie gras or the duck with black currants—and the service is discreet. *56 blvd. Vauban, tel. 86–51–53–52. Reservations advised. MC, V. Closed Mon. and Tues. lunch. Moderate.*

Lodging   **Normandie.** This picturesque creeper-covered construction is right in the town center, with its own garden but no restaurant. The rooms are well equipped and unpretentious. *41 blvd. Vauban, tel. 86–52–57–80, fax 86–51–54–33. 47 rooms, some with bath or shower. AE, DC, MC, V. Inexpensive.*

Avallon   **Moulin des Ruats.** The hotel is housed in an old flour mill just
Lodging   southwest of Avallon along D427. The rooms, many with their own balcony, are rustic. Most look onto the sparkling river

Cousin, and in the summer you can eat on the riverbank. Traditional dishes served in the wood-panelled restaurant make up the large menu; try the *coq au vin* (chicken) cooked in local Burgundy wine. This hotel is popular, so make sure to have a reservation in July or August. *Vallée du Cousin, tel. 86–34–07–14. 27 rooms, some with shower or bath. AE, DC, MC, V. Closed winter. Moderate.*

Beaune **L'Ecusson.** Despite its unprepossessing exterior, L'Ecusson is
Dining a comfortable, friendly, thick-carpeted restaurant, with four fixed-price menus offering outstanding value. For around 200 frs, you can have rabbit terrine with tarragon followed by leg of duck in oxtail sauce, then cheese, and dessert. *2 rue du Lieutenant-Dupuis, tel. 80–22–83–08. Reservations advised. AE, DC, MC, V. Closed Sun., mid-Feb.–mid-Mar. Moderate.*

Cluny **Bourgogne.** It is hard to find a better place to get into the med-
Dining and Lodging ieval mood of Cluny than this old-fashioned hotel, right next
★ door to the ruins of the famous abbey. There is a small garden and an atmospheric restaurant with sober pink decor and refined cuisine: foie gras, snails, and fish with ginger are specialties. *Pl. de l'Abbaye, tel. 85–59–00–58. 14 rooms with bath or shower. AE, DC, MC, V. Closed Wed. lunch, Mon., and mid-Nov.–mid-Feb. Moderate–Expensive.*

Dijon **Jean-Pierre Billoux.** M. Billoux's restaurant is reputedly the
Dining best of all in this most gastronomic of French cities. It is magnificently situated in a spacious, restored town house with garden, bar, and stone-vaulted restaurant. Service is charming. Specialties include steamed frogs' legs served with cress pancakes and guinea fowl with foie gras. *14 pl. Darcy, tel. 80–30–11–00. Reservations required. MC, V. Closed Sun. evening, Mon., part of Feb., and first half Aug. Expensive.*

Lodging **Chapeau Rouge.** This is a good choice if you want to be sure of getting a quiet, tasteful room in the center of town—it's close to Dijon cathedral. The Chapeau is even a better choice for its restaurant, renowned as a haven of regional cuisine. Snails, pigeon, and veal in mustard top the list of specialties. *5 rue Michelet, tel. 80–30–28–10. 29 rooms with bath or shower. Reservations required. AE, DC, MC, V. Moderate–Expensive.*

Lyon **Léon de Lyon.** A mixture of regional tradition (dumplings, hot
Dining sausages) and eye-opening innovation keep Léon de Lyon at the
★ forefront of Lyon's restaurant scene. It consists of two floors in an old house full of alcoves and wood panelling. The blue-aproned waiters melt into the old-fashioned decor, and such dishes as fillet of veal with celery or leg of lamb with fava beans will linger in your memory. *1 rue Pléney, tel. 78–28–11–33. Reservations required. MC, V. Closed Sun. dinner, Mon. lunch, and Aug. Expensive.*
A Ma Vigne. Here is a restaurant that's popular with tourists; it provides straightforward meals as a break from too much gourmet Lyonnais dining. French fries, *moules* (mussels), roast ham, and tripe lead the menu. Locals appreciate this, too, so get there early, especially at lunchtime. *23 rue Jean-Larrivé, tel. 78–60–46–31. Reservations not necessary. MC, V. Closed Sun., Aug. Moderate.*

Lodging **Royal.** The Royal is on the spacious and elegant place Bellecoeur in the very heart of Lyon. Beware of the huge range in room prices (460–820 frs); many rooms have been stylishly

renovated and some of the most expensive are positively luxurious. *20 pl. Bellecoeur, tel. 78–37–57–31. 90 rooms, most with
bath or shower. Facilities: parking. AE, DC, MC, V. Expensive.*

Sens
Lodging

Paris et Poste. This hotel makes a pleasant stopping point on the
way to Burgundy from Paris. The helpful service and sumptuous breakfasts (rare in France) confirm a sense of well-being
created by the robust evening meal (with fixed-price menus including duck, snails, and steak) served in the large, solemn restaurant, whose decor can be described as rustic Burgundian.
*97 rue de la République, tel. 86–65–17–43, fax 86–64–48–45.
25 rooms with bath or shower. AE, DC, MC, V. Moderate.*

Vézelay
Dining and Lodging
★

L'Espérance. In the small neighboring village of St-Père-sous-
Vézelay, L'Espérance is one of France's premier restaurants.
Chef Marc Meneau is renowned for the subtlety and originality
of his cuisine. Parisian gourmets think nothing of driving down
to Burgundy to eat here: Madame Meneau is a charming hostess, and the delightful setting—by a park and stream with
Vézelay's hill and basilica in the background—makes even a
long trip worth it. L'Espérance also has 34 luxurious guest
rooms (17 in a new annex) and four 1,800-franc suites. *St-Père-
sous-Vézelay, tel. 86–33–20–45, fax 86–33–26–15. Reservations required. Jacket and tie required. AE, DC, MC, V.
Closed Tues., Wed. lunch, and Jan. 1–Feb. 15. Very Expensive.*

Loire Valley

The Loire is the longest river in France, rising near Le Puy in
the east of the Massif Central and pursuing a broad northwest
curve on its 1,000-kilometer (620-mile) course to the Atlantic
Ocean near Nantes. The region traditionally referred to as the
Loire Valley—château country—is the 225-kilometer (140-
mile) stretch between Orléans, 113 kilometers (70 miles) south
of Paris and Angers, 96 kilometers (60 miles) from the Atlantic
coast. Thanks to its mild climate, soft light, and lush mea-
dowland, this area is known as the Garden of France. Its leading actor—the wide, meandering Loire—offers two distinct
faces: fast-flowing and spectacular in spring, sluggish and
sandy in summer.

To the north lies the vast grain plain of the Beauce; to the
southeast the marshy, forest-covered Sologne, renowned for
mushrooms, asparagus, and game. The star attractions along
the rocky banks of the Loire and its tributaries—the Rivers
Cher, Indre, Vienne, and Loir—are the famous châteaux:
stately houses, castles, or fairy-tale palaces. Renaissance elegance is often combined with fortresslike medieval mass. The
Loire Valley was fought over by France and England during
the Middle Ages. It took the example of Joan of Arc, the "Maid
of Orléans" (scene of her most rousing military successes), for
the French finally to expel the English.

The Loire Valley's golden age came under Francis I (1515–47),
France's flamboyant contemporary of England's Henry VIII.
He hired Renaissance craftsmen from Italy and hobnobbed
with the aging Leonardo da Vinci, his guest at Amboise. His
salamander emblem is to be seen in many châteaux, including
Chambord, the mightiest of them, begun in 1519.

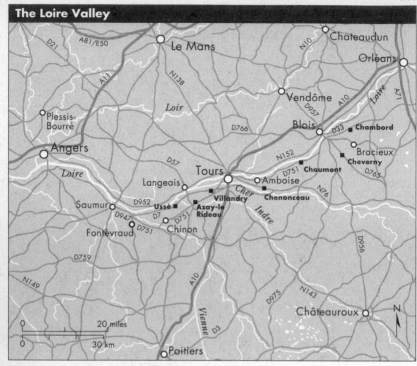

The Loire Valley

The best months to visit are June to October, though the weather can sometimes be hot and sticky in midsummer. Nature in the region is at its best in late spring and early fall, when there are fewer crowds. In peak season (especially August), it is essential to have your accommodations reserved.

Getting Around

The easiest way to visit the Loire châteaux is by car; N152 hugs the riverbank and offers excellent sightseeing possibilities. Trains run along the Loire Valley every two hours, supplemented by local bus services. A peaceful way to explore the region is to rent a bicycle at one of the SNCF train stations (some trains even transport bikes for free).

Guided Tours

Bus tours for the main châteaux leave daily in summer from Tours, Blois, Angers, Orléans, and Saumur: Ask at the relevant tourist office for latest times and prices. Most châteaux insist that visitors follow one of their own tours anyway, but try to get a booklet in English before joining the tour, as most are in French only.

Tourist Information

Angers (Pl. du Président Kennedy, tel. 41–87–72–50).
Blois (3 av. du Docteur Jean-Laigret, tel. 54–74–06–49).
Orléans (Pl. Albert-Ier, tel. 38–53–05–95).

Tours (rue B. Palissy, tel. 47–05–58–08).

Exploring the Loire Valley

Châteaudun Orléans, little more than an hour away by expressway (A10) or train, is the most obvious gateway to the Loire Valley if you're coming from Paris. Apart from its art museum and majestic Ste-Croix cathedral, however, Orléans has little going for it. Instead take the expressway from Paris to Chartres, then N10 to **Châteaudun,** whose colossal château stands resplendent on a steep promontory and houses graceful furniture and lavish tapestries. Its chapel contains 15 statues produced locally in the 15th century. *Admission: 27 frs. Open mid-Mar.–Sept. 9:30–11:45 and 2–6; Oct.–mid-Mar. 10–11:45 and 2–6.*

Continue along N10 to **Vendôme,** 40 kilometers (25 miles) to the southwest, where the Loir river (not to be confused with the larger and more famous *Loire* to the south) splits into many arms, lending the town a canal-like charm that harmonizes with its old streets and bridges. Architecture buffs will pinch themselves as they inspect the large but little-known main church, **Eglise de la Trinité,** an encyclopedia of different styles with brilliantly carved choir stalls and an exuberant west front—the work of Jean de Beauce, best known for his spire at Chartres Cathedral. Vendôme also has a ruined **castle** with ramparts and pleasant, uncrowded gardens. *Admission to castle: 8 frs. Open Mar.–June, Wed.–Mon. 10–noon and 2–6; July and Aug., daily 10–noon and 2–6.*

Blois **Blois** lies 32 kilometers (20 miles) southeast of Vendôme along D957. It is the most attractive of the major Loire towns, with its tumbling alleyways and its château. The **château** is a mixture of four different styles: Feudal (13th century); Gothic-Renaissance transition (circa 1500); Renaissance (circa 1520); and Classical (circa 1635). *Admission: 30 frs. Open May–Aug.; daily 9–6:30; Sept.–Apr., daily 9–noon and 2–5.*

Blois makes an ideal launching pad for a visit to the châteaux of Chambord and Cheverny. **Chambord** (begun 1519) is 20 kilometers (11 miles) east of Blois along D33, near Bracieux. It stands in splendid isolation in a vast forest and game park. There's another forest on the roof: 365 chimneys and turrets, representing architectural self-indulgence at its least squeamish. Grandeur or a mere 440-room folly? Judge for yourself, and don't miss the superb spiral staircase or the chance to saunter over the rooftop terrace. *Admission: 31 frs adults, 7 frs children. Open July–Aug., daily 9:30–6:30; Sept.–June, daily 9:30–11:45 and 2–sunset.*

About 20 kilometers (12 miles) south of Blois, along D751, stands the sturdy château of Chaumont, built between 1465 and 1510—well before Benjamin Franklin became a regular visitor. There is a magnificent Loire panorama from the terrace, and the stables—where thoroughbreds dined like royalty—show the importance attached to fine horses, for hunting or just prestige. *Admission: 25 frs adults, 13 frs students and senior citizens. Open Apr.–Sept., daily 9–12:30 and 2–4:30; Oct.–Mar., daily 9:30–12:30 and 2–3:30.*

Amboise Downstream (westward) another 16 kilometers (10 miles) lies the bustling town of **Amboise,** whose **château,** with charming grounds, a rich interior, and fine views over the river from the battlements, dates from 1500. It wasn't always so peaceful: In 1560, more than 1,000 Protestant "conspirators" were hanged from these battlements during the Wars of Religion. *Admission: 30 frs adults, 20 frs students, 10 frs children. Open July–Aug., daily 9–6:30; Sept.–June, daily 9–noon and 2–5.*

The nearby **Clos-Lucé,** a 15th-century brick manor house, was the last home of Leonardo da Vinci, who was invited to stay here by Francis I. Da Vinci died here in 1519, and his engineering genius is illustrated by models based on his plans and sketches. *Admission: 31 frs adults, 25 frs students and senior citizens. Same hours as château, but open till 6:30 in winter.*

The early 16th-century château of **Chenonceau,** 16 kilometers (10 miles) south of Amboise along D81 and then D40, straddles the tranquil river Cher like a bridge. It is surrounded by elegant gardens and a splendid avenue of plane trees. Inside, note the fine paintings, colossal fireplaces, and richly worked ceilings. A waxworks museum lurks in an outbuilding. *Admission: 35 frs adults, 25 frs children. Open mid-Feb.–mid-Mar., daily 9–sunset; mid-Nov.–mid-Feb., daily 9–4:30.*

Tours **Tours,** 25 kilometers (15 miles) farther on, is the unofficial capital of the Loire. It retains a certain charm despite its sprawling size (250,000 inhabitants) and extensive postwar reconstruction. Its attractive old quarter, Vieux Tours around place Plumereau, has been tastefully restored, while the **Cathedral of St-Gatien** (1239–1484) numbers among France's most impressive churches. The influence of local Renaissance sculptors and craftsmen is much in evidence on the ornate facade. The stained glass in the choir is particularly delicate; some of it dates from 1320.

The château of **Villandry,** 16 kilometers (10 miles) southwest of Tours along the river Cher, is known for its painstakingly relaid 16th-century gardens, with their long avenues of 1,500 manicured lime trees. The château interior, restored like the gardens in the mid-19th century, is equally beguiling. Note the painted and gilded ceiling from Toledo and the collection of Spanish pictures. *Admission: château and gardens, 37 frs; garden only, 24 frs. Open daily 9–6; gardens open 9–dusk.*

Langeais **Langeais** is just 14 kilometers (9 miles) west of Villandry: Keep on D7 to Lignières before turning right onto D57 and crossing the Loire. A massive **castle,** built in the 1460s and never altered, dominates this small town. Its apartments contain a superb collection of tapestries, chests, and beds. *Admission: 35 frs adults, 25 frs senior citizens, 17 frs students and children. Open Easter–Oct., daily 9–6:30; Nov.–Easter, Tues.–Sun. 9–noon and 2–5. Closed Mon.*

Azay-le-Rideau (1518–29), one of the prettiest of the Loire châteaux, lies on the river Indre 10 kilometers (6 miles) south of Langeais along D57. It has harmonious proportions and exquisite grounds, with a domesticated moat that is really a lake. This graceful ensemble compensates for the château's spartan interior, as does the charm of the surrounding village. *Admission: 26 frs adults, 17 frs senior citizens, 6 frs children. Open Apr.–Sept., daily 9:30–noon and 2–6; Oct.–Mar., daily 9:30–noon and 2–4:15.*

A short ride down the Indre Valley (on D17 and then D7) from Azay will help you judge whether **Ussé** really is, as the brochures claim, the fairy-tale setting that inspired *Sleeping Beauty*. Its bristling roofs and turrets, flowered terraces, and forest backcloth have undeniable romance. Don't forget the **chapel** in the park, built 1520–38 in purest Renaissance proportions. *Admission: 49 frs adults, 20 frs students. Open mid-Mar.–Nov., daily 9–noon and 2–6.*

Chinon **Chinon,** 13 kilometers (8 miles) from Ussé via D7 and D16, is an ancient town nestled by the river Vienne, with a rock-of-ages **castle** patrolling the horizon. This 12th-century fortress, with walls 370 meters (400 yards) long, is mainly in ruins, though small museums are installed in the Royal Chambers and sturdy Tour de l'Horloge (clock tower). There are excellent views from the ramparts over Chinon and the Vienne Valley. *Admission: 23 frs adults, 18 frs senior citizens, 16 frs children under 19. Open Nov.–mid-Mar., Thurs.–Tues. 9–noon and 2–5, closed Wed.; mid-Mar.–June and Sept., daily 9–6; July and Aug., daily 9–7; Oct., daily 9–5.*

From just south of Chinon, D751 heads off up the Vienne Valley toward **Fontevraud,** 21 kilometers (13 miles) away. This quiet village is dominated by its medieval **abbey,** where English kings Henry II and Richard the Lionhearted are buried. The church, cloisters, Renaissance chapter house, long-vaulted refectory, and octagonal kitchen are all still standing. The guided tours are in French, but you can get a brochure in English to keep track of where you are. *Admission: 25 frs. adults, 15 frs senior citizens, 7 frs children. Open June–mid-Sept., daily 9–noon and 2–6:30; Sept.–Apr., daily 9:30–12:30 and 2–5:30.*

Saumur, 16 kilometers (10 miles) west along the Loire from Fontevraud via D947, is a prosperous town famous for its riding school, wines, and château—a white 14th-century castle that towers above the river. The château contains two outstanding museums: the **Musée des Arts Décoratifs** (Decorative Arts Museum), featuring porcelain and enamels, and the **Musée du Cheval** (Equine Museum), with saddles, stirrups, skeletons, and Stubbs engravings. *Admission: 32 frs adults, 22 frs students and senior citizens. Open July–Sept., daily 9–6:30; Nov.–Mar., Wed.–Mon. 10–5.*

Angers **Angers** is a large, historic town on the river Maine just to the north of the Loire. D952 runs along the Loire Valley from Saumur, 45 kilometers (28 miles) away. The feudal **château** was built by St-Louis (1228–38) and has a dry moat, drawbridge, and 17 round towers along its half-mile-long walls. A modern, well-integrated gallery houses an exquisite tapestry collection, notable for the enormous *Tapestry of the Apocalypse*, woven in Paris around 1380. *Admission: 31 frs adults, 15 frs students and senior citizens, 6 frs children. Open July–Aug., daily 10–7; Sept.–June, daily 9:30–noon and 2–5:30.*

Dining and Lodging

For details and price-category definitions, *see* Dining and Lodging in Staying in France.

Angers **Le Toussaint.** An elegant bourgeois second-floor setting—
Dining gleaming mirrors and silverware—and the view across toward the castle provide the backdrop to some sturdy fish and meat

dishes. *7 pl. du Pdt-Kennedy, tel. 41–87–46–20. Reservations advised. AE, MC, V. Closed Sun. evenings, Mon., part of Feb. Moderate–Expensive.*

Dining and Lodging   **Hôtel d'Anjou.** An old friend of a hotel, this has spacious, well-modernized rooms and is handily situated by the Jardin du Mail, a pleasant park. Its restaurant, La Salamandre, prides itself on its classic cuisine (menus at 110 frs and 220 frs) served in a Renaissance-style dining room. *1 blvd. du Mal-Foch, 49100, tel. 41–88–24–82, fax 41–87–22–21. 53 rooms with bath or shower. Facilities: restaurant, parking. AE, DC, MC, V. Restaurant closed Sun. Moderate.*

Blois   **Bocca d'Or.** The old 14th-century stone vaults at this small res-
Dining   taurant, in the heart of Blois, provide a historical atmosphere that contrasts with its nouvelle cuisine, though both are refined. Fish, shellfish, and poultry figure prominently, and the wine list is comprehensive. Be sure to try the salman tartar and the coquilles of oysters. *15 rue Haute, tel. 54–78–04–74. Reservations advised. AE, MC, V. Closed Sun., Mon. lunch; first 2 weeks in Nov. and last 2 weeks in Feb. Moderate.*

Chambord   **Hôtel St-Michel.** Considering its location right across from the
Lodging   château, the St-Michel offers good value. Some of its rooms af-
★   ford splendid views of the château, its lawns, and the forest backdrop, as does the conveniently situated terrace, an ideal place for summer morning coffee before the tourist hordes arrive. *41250 Chambord, tel. 54–20–31–31. 38 rooms, some with bath or shower. Facilities: restaurant, tennis court, parking. MC, V. Closed Nov. 12–Dec. 19. Moderate.*

Saumur   **Le Prieuré.** Five miles northwest of Saumur via D751, Le
Lodging   Prieuré is a neo-Renaissance manor house perched high above the south bank of the Loire. It has its own restaurant overlooking the river, a heated swimming pool, and vast park. The rooms are large and luxuriously furnished, most with a view of the Loire. A reservation is advised, or you may find yourself in one of the less attractive houses in the park. *Chênehutte-les-Tuffeaux, 49400, Gennes, tel. 41–67–90–14, fax 41–67–92–24. 35 rooms with bath. Facilities: restaurant, pool. MC, V. Closed Jan., Feb. Expensive.*

Tours   **Jean Bardet.** Situated just north of the Loire in an early 19th-
Dining   century mansion, this restaurant overlooks a large garden and is decorated with colorful chairs and carpets. There is a superb wine list and each dish is a work of art and originality: Try the eel fricassée or lobster in wine spiced with lime and ginger. *57 rue Groison, 37000, tel. 47–41–41–11, fax 47–51–68–72. Reservations advised. AE, DC, MC, V. Closed Sun. evening off-season, Mon.; last week in Feb. and first 10 days in March. Very Expensive.*

Lodging   **Domaine de la Tortinière.** Ten kilometers (6 miles) due south of Tours along N10, this turreted building dates from the mid-19th century. It stands proudly on a hill amid vast fields and woodland. The bedrooms are individually decorated in styles ranging from conventionally old-fashioned to brash ultramodern. The airy restaurant looks out over the gardens. Salmon, pigeon, and rabbit with truffles are menu highlights. *10 rte de Ballan, 37250 Veigné, tel. 47–26–00–19. 14 rooms with bath. MC, V. Closed mid-Dec.–Feb. Restaurant closed Wed. lunch and Tues. in Nov., Dec., and Mar. Expensive.*

Vendôme
Lodging

Hôtel Vendôme. Near the banks of the Loir, Hôtel Vendôme makes a handy base for exploring the pedestrian streets of the old town. It is stylish and appropriately priced, with excellent, modernized rooms, though lacking a little in character. There is a trustworthy restaurant with quietly efficient English-speaking service. *15 Faubourg Chartrain, tel. 54–77–02–88. 35 rooms with bath or shower. Facilities: restaurant, parking. MC, V. Closed Christmas, New Year's Day, and weekends in winter. Restaurant closed Nov.–Mar. Moderate.*

The Riviera

Few places in the world have the same pull on the imagination as France's fabled Riviera, the Mediterranean coastline stretching from St-Tropez in the west to Menton on the Italian border. Cooled by the Mediterranean in the summer and warmed by it in winter, the climate is almost always pleasant. Avoid the area in July and August, however—unless you love crowds. To see the Riviera at its best, plan your trip in the spring or fall, particularly in May or September.

The Riviera is a land of contrasts. While the coastal resorts seem to live exclusively for the tourist trade and have often been ruined by high-rise blocks, the hinterlands remain relatively untarnished. The little villages perched high on the hills behind medieval ramparts seem to belong to another century. One of them, St-Paul-de-Vence, is the home of the Maeght Foundation, one of the world's leading museums of modern art.

Artists, attracted by the light, have played a considerable role in popular conceptions of the Riviera, and their presence is reflected in the number of modern art museums: the Musée Picasso at Antibes, the Musée Renoir and the Musée d'Art Moderne Mediterranéan at Cagnes-sur-Mer, and the Musée Jean Cocteau near the harbor at Menton. Wining and dining are special treats on the Riviera, especially if you are fond of garlic and olive oil. *Bouillabaisse*, a spicy fish stew, is the most popular regional specialty.

The tiny principality of Monaco, which lies between Nice and Menton, is included in this section despite the fact that it is a sovereign state. Although Monaco has its own army and police force, its language, food, and way of life are French. Its famous casino, the highly visible royal Grimaldi family, and the wealth of jetsetters, chic fashions, and opulent yachts all ensure that it maintains its reputation as a "golden ghetto."

Getting Around

By Car Expressway A8 is the only way to get around the Riviera quickly, but for the drama of mountains and sea, take one of the famous Corniche roads.

By Train The train line follows the coast from Marseille to the Italian border, providing excellent access to the seaside resorts, but you will have to take local buses (marked *Gare Routière*) or guided tours to visit Grasse and the perched villages.

The Riviera

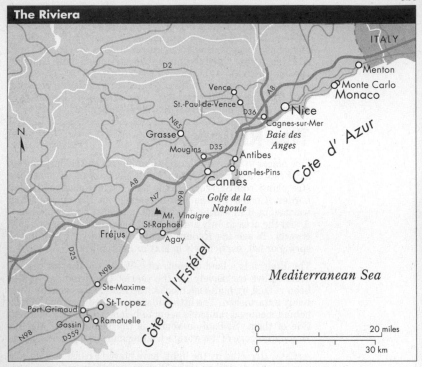

Guided Tours

SNCF, the French national railroad company, runs the greatest number of organized tours. For information, contact the Nice Tourist Office (*see* Tourist Information, *below*). Tours are most valuable to areas otherwise impossible to reach by public transportation: St-Paul-de-Vence, Upper Provence, and the spectacular Verdon Gorges.

Boats operate from Nice to Marseille; from St-Tropez to the charming Hyères Islands; and from Antibes, Cannes, and Juan-les-Pins to the Lérins Islands.

Tourist Information

Antibes (11 pl. du Général de Gaulle, tel. 93–33–95–64).
Cagnes-sur-Mer (6 blvd. du Mal-Juin, tel. 93–20–61–64).
Cannes (Palais des Congrès, La Croisette, tel. 93–39–24–53).
Fréjus (315 rue Jean-Jaurès, tel. 94–51–54–14).
Grasse (3 pl. Foux, tel. 93–36–03–56).
Menton (Palais de l'Europe, tel. 93–57–57–00).
Monaco (2a blvd. des Moulins, tel. 93–30–87–01).
Nice (Av. Thiers, tel. 93–87–07–07; 5 av. Gustave-V, tel. 93–87–60–60).
St-Paul-de-Vence (Maison Tour, rue Grande, tel. 93–32–86–95).
St-Tropez (Quai Jean-Jaurès, tel. 94–97–45–21).
Vence (Pl. du Grand Jardin, tel. 93–58–06–38).

Exploring the Riviera

St-Tropez **St-Tropez** was just another pretty fishing village until it was "discovered" in the 1950s by the "beautiful people," a fast set of film stars, starlets, and others who scorned bourgeois values while enjoying bourgeois bank balances. Today, its summer population swells from 6,000 to 60,000. In season, its top hotels, restaurants, nightclubs, and chic little shops are jammed. In the winter, it's hard to find a restaurant open. The best times to visit, therefore, are early summer or fall. May and June are perhaps the best months, when the town lets its hair down during two local festivals.

The **old port** is the liveliest part of town. You can kill time here at a café terrace, watching the rich and famous on their gleaming yachts. Between the old and new ports is the **Musée de l'Annonciade,** set in a cleverly converted chapel, which houses paintings by artists drawn to St-Tropez between 1890 and 1940—including Paul Signac, Matisse, Derain, and Van Dongen. *Quai Gabriel-Péri. Admission: 20 frs adults, 10 frs children. Open June–Sept., Wed.–Mon. 10–noon and 3–7; Oct.– May, Wed.–Mon. 10–noon and 2–6.*

Across the place de l'Hôtel de Ville lies the old town, where twisting, narrow streets, designed to break the impact of the terrible mistral (the cold, dry northerly wind common to this region), open onto tiny squares and fountains. A long climb up to the **citadel** is rewarded by a splendid view over the old town and across the gulf to **Ste-Maxime,** a quieter, more working-class family resort with a decent beach and reasonably priced hotels. St-Tropez is also a good base for visiting **Port Grimaud,** a pastiche of an Italian fishing village (take D558) and the nearby hilltop villages: the old Provençal town of **Ramatuelle** and the fortified village of **Gassin.**

The **Corniche des Issambres** (N98) runs along the coast from Ste-Maxime to **Fréjus,** a Roman town built by Caesar in 49 BC, standing on a rocky plateau between the Maures and Esterel hills. Two main roads link Fréjus and Cannes. Tortuous N7, originally a Roman road, skirts the northern flank of the rugged Esterel hills. Look for an intersection called the "carrefour du Testannier" and follow the signs to **Forêt Domaniale de l'Esterel** and **Mont Vinaigre** for a magnificent view over the hills.

Cannes In 1834, a chance event was to change the lifestyle of **Cannes** forever. Lord Brougham, Britain's lord chancellor, was en route to Nice when an outbreak of cholera forced the authorities to freeze all travel to prevent the disease from spreading. Trapped in Cannes, he fell in love with the place and built himself a house there as an annual refuge from the British winter. The English aristocracy, czars, kings, and princes soon caught on, and Cannes became a community for the international elite. Grand palace hotels were built to cater to them, and Cannes came to symbolize dignified luxury. Today, Cannes is also synonymous with the **International Film Festival.**

Cannes is for relaxing—strolling along the seafront on the **Croisette** and getting tanned on the beaches. Almost all the beaches are private, but that doesn't mean you can't use them, only that you must pay for the privilege. The Croisette offers splendid views of the **Napoule Bay.** Only a few steps inland is the old town, known as the **Suquet,** with its steep, cobbled streets and its 12th-century watchtower.

Grasse is perched in the hills behind Cannes. Take N85 or just follow your nose to the town that claims to be the perfume capital of the world. A good proportion of its 40,000 inhabitants work at distilling and extracting scent from the tons of roses, lavender, and jasmine produced here every year. The various perfumiers are only too happy to guide visitors around their fragrant establishments. Fragonard is the best known (20 blvd. Fragonard, tel. 93–36–44–65). The old town is attractive, with its narrow alleys and massive, somber **cathedral.** Three of the paintings inside the cathedral are by Rubens and one is by Fragonard, who lived here for many years.

Take N85 back down to the coast, but fork left at **Mougins,** an attractive fortified hilltop town, famous for one of France's best restaurants, Le Moulin de Mougins. D35 takes you to **Antibes** and **Juan-les-Pins,** originally two villages that now form one town on the west side of the **Baie des Anges** (Angels' Bay).

Antibes   **Antibes,** the older village, dates back to the 4th century BC, when it was a Greek trading port. Today, it is renowned throughout Europe for its industrial flower and plant production. Every morning, except Monday, the market on the Cours Masséna comes alive with the colors of roses, carnations, anemones, and tulips. The Grimaldis, the family that rules Monaco, built **Château Grimaldi** here in the 12th century on the remains of a Roman camp. Today, the château's main attraction is the **Musée Picasso**—a bounty of paintings, ceramics, and lithographs inspired by the sea and Greek mythology. *Pl. du Château, tel. 93–34–91–91. Admission: 25 frs adults, 12 frs students and senior citizens. Open Dec.–Oct., Wed.–Mon. 10–noon and 2–6.*

Nice   The 20-kilometer (13-mile) stretch of flat coast between Antibes and Nice lacks charm, but the hinterland makes up for it. With its population of 400,000, its own university, new congress hall, and nearby science park, Nice is the undisputed capital of the Riviera. Founded by the Greeks as Nikaia, it has lived through several civilizations and was attached to France only in 1860. It consequently boasts a profusion of Greek, Italian, British, and French styles. Tourism may not be the main business of Nice, but it is a deservedly popular center with much to offer. The double blessing of climate and geography puts its beaches within an hour-and-a-half's drive of the nearest ski resorts. There is an eclectic mixture of old and new architecture, an opera house, museums, flourishing markets, and regular concerts and festivals, including the Mardi Gras festival and the Battle of Flowers.

Numbers in the margin correspond to points of interest on the Nice map.

❶ The **place Masséna** is the logical starting point for an exploration of Nice. This fine square was built in 1815 to celebrate a local hero: one of Napoleon's most successful generals. The **❷** **Promenade des Anglais,** built by the English community here in **❸** 1824, is only a short stroll past the fountains and the **Jardin Albert I**er. It now carries heavy traffic but still forms a splendid strand between town and sea. The narrow streets in the old town are the prettiest part of Nice: Take the rue de l'Opéra to **❹ ❺** see **St-François-de-Paule** church (1750) and the **opera house.** At

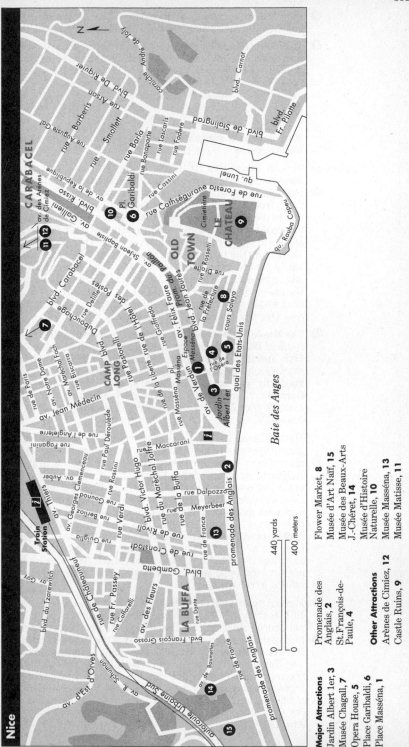

Nice

Major Attractions
Jardin Albert 1er, 3
Musée Chagall, 7
Opera House, 5
Place Garibaldi, 6
Place Masséna, 1

Promenade des
Anglais, 2
St.François-de-
Paule, 4

Other Attractions
Arènes de Cimiez, 12
Castle Ruins, 9

Flower Market, 8
Musée d'Art Naïf, 15
Musée des Beaux-Arts
J.-Chéret, 14
Musée d'Histoire
Naturelle, 10
Musée Masséna, 13
Musée Matisse, 11

6 the northern extremity of the old town lies the vast **place Garibaldi** —all yellow-ocher buildings and formal fountains.

7 The **Musée Chagall** is on the boulevard de Cimiez, near the Roman ruins. The museum was built in 1972 to house the Chagall collection, including the 17 huge canvases of *The Message of the Bible*, which took 13 years to complete. *Tel. 93–81–75–75. Admission: 26 frs adults, 17 frs students and senior citizens. Open July–Sept., Wed.–Mon. 10–7; Oct.–June, Wed.–Mon. 10–12:30 and 2–5:30.*

Numbers in the margin correspond to points of interest on the Monaco map.

Monaco Sixteen kilometers (10 miles) along the coast from Nice is **Monaco.** For more than a century Monaco's livelihood was cen-
1 tered in its splendid copper-roof **casino.** The oldest section dates from 1878 and was conceived by Charles Garnier, architect of the Paris opera house. It's as elaborately ornate as anyone could wish, bristling with turrets and gold filigree, and masses of interior frescoes and bas-reliefs. There are lovely sea views from the terrace, and the gardens out front are meticulously tended. The main activity is in the American Room, where beneath the gilt-edged ceiling busloads of tourists feed the one-armed bandits. *Pl. du Casino, tel. 93–50–69–31. Persons under 21 not admitted. Admission for American Room free. Open daily 10 AM–4 AM. Closed May 1.*

2 The **Musée National des Automates et Poupées d' Autrefois** (Museum of Dolls and Automatons) has a compelling collection of 18th- and 19th-century dolls and mechanical figures, the latter shamelessly showing off their complex inner workings. It's magically set in a 19-century seaside villa (designed by Garnier). *17 av. Princesse-Grace, tel. 93–30–91–26. Admission: 26 frs adults, 13 frs children. Open daily 10–12:15 and 2:30–6:30.*

Monaco Town, the principality's old quarter, has many vaulted passageways and exudes an almost tangible medieval feel. The
3 magnificent **Palais du Prince** (Prince's Palace), a grandiose Italianate structure with a Moorish tower, was largely rebuilt in the last century. Here, since 1297, the Grimaldi dynasty has lived and ruled. The spectacle of the **Changing of the Guard** occurs each morning at 11:55; inside, guided tours take visitors through the state apartments and a wing containing the **Palace Archives** and **Musée Napoléon** (Napoleonic Museum). *Pl. du Palais, tel. 93–25–18–31. Palace open July–Sept., daily 9:30–12:30 and 2–6:30. Admission: 34 frs. Musée Napoléon and Palace Archives open year-round, Tues.–Sun. Admission: 18 frs adults, 9 frs children.*

4 Monaco's **cathedral** (4 rue Colonel Bellando de Castro) is a late 19th-century neo-Romanesque confection in which Philadelphia-born Princess Grace lies in splendor along with past mem-
5 bers of the Grimaldi dynasty. Nearby is the **Musée Historial des Princes de Monaco** (Waxworks Museum), a Monégasque Madame Tussauds, with none-too-realistic wax figures stiffly portraying various episodes in the Grimaldi history. The waxworks may not convince, but the rue Basse is wonderfully atmospheric. *27 rue Basse, tel. 93–30–39–05. Admission: 22 frs. Open May–Sept., daily 9–8; Oct.–Dec., daily 10:30–5:30; Jan.–Apr., daily 9–6:30.*

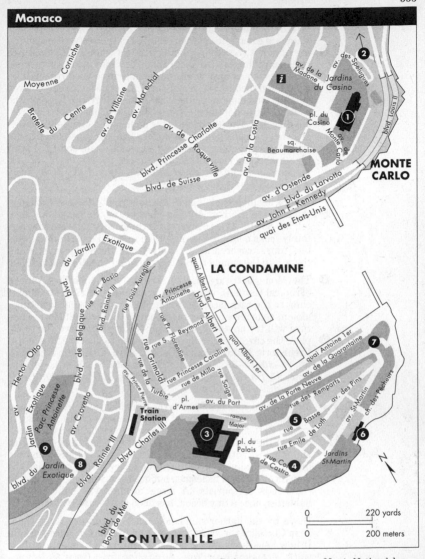

Casino, **1**
Cathedral, **4**
Fort Antoine Theater, **7**
Jardin Exotique, **8**
Musée Historial des Princes de Monaco, **5**

Musée National des Automates et Poupées d'Autrefois, **2**
Musée Océanographique, **6**
Museum of Prehistoric Anthropology, **9**
Palais du Prince, **3**

Next to the **St-Martin Gardens**—which contain an evocative bronze monument in memory of Prince Albert I (Prince Rainier's great-grandfather, the one in the sou'wester and flying oil skins, benignly guiding a ship's wheel)—is the **Musée Océanographique** (Oceanography Museum and Aquarium). This museum is also an internationally renowned research institute founded by the very Prince Albert who is remembered outside for being an eminent marine biologist in his day; the well-known underwater explorer Jacques Cousteau is the present director. The aquarium is the undisputed highlight, however, where a collection of the world's fish and crustacea live out their lives in public, some colorful, some drab, some the stuff nightmares are made of. *Av. St-Martin, tel. 93–30–15–14. Admission: 50 frs adults, 25 frs children. Open Sept.–June, daily 9:30–7; July and Aug., daily 9–9.*

Before heading back inland, take a stroll to the eastern tip of the rock, to the **Fort Antoine Theater** (av. de la Quarantaine, tel. 93–30–19–21), a converted 18th-century fortress that certainly looks a lot prettier now than it would have in more warlike times, covered as it is in ivy and flowering myrtle and thyme. In the summer, this is an open-air theater seating 350.

The Moneghetti area is the setting for the **Jardin Exotique** (Tropical Garden), where 600 varieties of cacti and succulents cling to the rock face, their improbable shapes and sometimes violent coloring a further testimony to the fact that Mother Nature will try anything once. Your ticket also allows you to explore the **caves,** next to the gardens, and to visit the **Museum of Prehistoric Anthropology,** adjacent. *Blvd. du Jardin Exotique, tel. 93–30–33–65. Admission: 30 frs adults, 20 frs senior citizens, 15 frs children. Open Oct.–May, daily 9–5:30; June–Sept., daily 9–7.*

Menton **Menton** also once belonged to the Grimaldis and, like Nice, was attached to France only in 1860. Because of its popularity among British visitors, the western side of the town was developed at the turn of the century to cater to the influx of the rich and famous, with spacious avenues, first-class hotels, and the inevitable casino. The eastern side of town long remained the domain of the local fishermen but has been developed to cater to the needs of tourists. A large marina was built and the **Sablettes,** once a tiny beach, has been artificially extended.

Down by the harbor stands a small 17th-century fort, where Jean Cocteau, the artist, writer, and filmmaker, once worked. It now houses the **Musée Jean Cocteau,** with a collection of his work. *111 quai Napoléon. Admission free. Open mid-June–mid-Sept., Wed.–Sun. 10–noon and 3–6; mid-Sept.–mid-June, 10–noon and 2–6.*

Dining and Lodging

For details and price-category definitions, *see* Dining and Lodging in Staying in France.

Antibes **Auberge Provençale.** The rooms and service are sunny, partly a
Lodging reflection of the manageable size of the hotel. Its popular restaurant serves lobster and shellfish as well as *boudin de rascasse,* a minced fish shaped into a sausage. *61 pl. Nationale, tel. 93–34–13–24. 6 rooms with bath. Restaurant reservations*

required. AE, DC, MC, V. Closed mid-Nov.–mid-Dec. Restaurant closed Mon., Tues. lunch. Moderate.

Cagnes
Lodging

Cagnard. This hotel is in an attractive 15th-century building in the old village. The restaurant—once the Grimaldi Château Guards Room—dates back to the early 14th century. The hotel has several suites in two houses in the garden and a third up the road. The view from them all—over the Cap d'Antibes—is memorable. *Rue du Pontis-Long, tel. 93–20–73–22. 19 rooms and suites with bath. AE, DC, MC, V. Restaurant closed Thurs. lunch and Nov.–mid-Dec. Expensive.*

Cannes
Dining

Mirabelle. For many, this is a favorite restaurant in the Suquet. The cuisine is inventive, the sauces light, and the desserts special. *24 rue St-Antoine, tel. 93–38–72–75. Reservations advised. MC, V. Closed Tues., Jan. 15–Feb. 15, and Nov. 15–30. Expensive.*

Lodging

Majestic. Unlike most luxury hotels lining the Croisette on the seafront, the Majestic has a discreet atmosphere. The rooms are spacious and traditional but refreshingly decorated in pastels. The restaurant also offers a reasonably priced evening meal in winter. *14 La Croisette, tel. 93–68–91–00. 283 rooms with bath. Facilities: private beach, swimming pool, air-conditioning, parking lot, tennis, golf, horseback riding. AE, DC, MC, V. Closed Nov. 11–Dec. 20. Very Expensive.*

Bristol. Despite its name—recalling that of one of Paris's leading palace-hotels—the Bristol offers an intimate, wallet-friendly contrast to the big names lurking nearby on La Croisette. Prices start at around 170 frs, but be prepared to go a bit higher if you fancy one of the 10 (quieter) rooms with a balcony at the back of the building. The beach, train station, and Palais des Festivals are all within a three-minute walk. *14 rue Hoche, tel. 93–39–10–66. 19 rooms, 15 with bath or shower. AE, MC, V. Closed Dec.–mid-Jan. Inexpensive.*

Grasse
Lodging

Panorama. The excellent views of the Massif d'Estérel and right across to Cannes are the vindication of this hotel's name. It is modern and well run and has ample parking. Most rooms have good views, but there is no restaurant. *2 pl. du Cours, tel. 93–36–80–80. 36 rooms with bath. MC, V. Moderate.*

Menton
Dining and Lodging

Chez Mireille-l'Ermitage. Best known for its restaurant, this elegant yet cozy hotel stands on the promenade du Soleil, overlooking the beach. Each room has its own style and all are different, although many have good views. The restaurant is a favorite for local specialties: *bourride* (fish soup) and bouillabaisse, salmon, and bass fillets. *30 av. Carnot, tel. 93–35–77–23. 21 rooms with bath or shower. AE, DC, MC, V. Hotel closed first half Dec., part of Jan.; restaurant closed Mon. evening, Tues., mid-Nov–mid-Apr. Moderate.*

Monaco
Dining
★

Louis XV. A strong contender for the best-in-Monaco award, Louis XV's opulent decor and chef Alain Ducasse's beautifully conceived dishes, such as ravioli with foie gras and truffles, contribute to the formal atmosphere. The wine cellar is exceptional. *Hôtel de Paris, pl. du Casino, tel. 93–50–80–80. Reservations required. AE, DC, MC, V. Very Expensive.*

Bec Rouge. This is where all the best Monégasques can be observed relishing their *gratin de langoustes* (lobster) at dinnertime, linen napkins billowing. Food is classic French, decor *le plus chic. 11 av. de Grande-Bretagne, tel. 93–30–74–91. Reser-*

vations required. AE, DC, MC, V. Closed Jan. and mid-June. Expensive.

Polpetta. This popular trattoria is close enough to the Italian border to pass for authentic. It's excellent value for the money, with delicious home cooking to boot. *2 rue Paradis, tel. 93–50–67–84. Reservations required in high season. MC, V. Closed Sat. lunch, Tues., Feb. 15–Mar. 15, Oct. 15–30. Moderate.*

Lodging
★
Hôtel de Paris. An exceptional establishment, where elegance, luxury, dignity, and Old World charm are the watchwords. Built in 1864, it still exudes the gold-plated splendor of an era when kings and grand dukes stayed here. *Pl. du Casino, tel. 93–50–80–80. 245 rooms with bath. Facilities: 2 restaurants, bar, pool, health club, shops, tennis court. AE, DC, MC, V. Very Expensive.*

Balmoral. Despite the name, there's nothing even vaguely Scottish about this somewhat old-fashioned hotel overlooking the harbor. Rooms are a reasonable size, if bland; many have balconies. *12 av. de la Costa, tel. 93–50–62–37. 75 rooms with bath or shower, half with air-conditioning. Facilities: restaurant. AE, DC, MC, V. Restaurant closed Nov. Moderate.*

France. The modest hotel France, near the train station, can't begin to compete with the opulence of some of the others listed here, but it's one of the cheapest around and worth a look if you are on a tight budget. *6 rue de La Turbie, tel. 93–30–24–64. 26 rooms, 18 with bath or shower. DC, MC, V. Inexpensive.*

Mougins
Dining and Lodging
Le Moulin de Mougins. Roger Vergé has created one of France's finest restaurants in a converted mill about 1½ miles from the village along D3. The cuisine ranges from apparently simple salads to rich, complicated sauces for lobster, salmon, or turbot. Considering that it is a gourmet favorite, the restaurant has a surprisingly informal atmosphere. There are five elegantly rustic guest rooms as well. *Quartier Notre-Dame-de-Vie, 424 Chemin du Moulin, tel. 93–75–78–24, fax 93–90–18–55. Reservations required. Jacket and tie required. AE, DC, MC, V. Closed Thurs. lunch and Mon., Feb.–Mar. Very Expensive.*

Nice
Dining
Ane-Rouge. Famous for generations as *the* place for Nice's best fish and seafood, this tiny, family-run restaurant is popular with locals, not least for the Vidalots, the pleasant couple who run it. *7 quai des Deux-Emmanuel, tel. 93–89–49–63. Reservations advised. MC, V. Closed weekends, mid-July–end of Aug. Expensive.*

Dining and Lodging
★
Negresco. Opened in 1912, the Negresco is officially listed as a historic monument and is a byword for Old World elegance. The public rooms have antique coffered ceilings and magnificent fireplaces. No two bedrooms are alike, but they all have antique furniture and paintings. Its main restaurant, Le Chantecler, is without doubt the best in Nice. *37 promenade des Anglais, tel. 93–88–00–58, fax 93–88–35–68. 130 rooms with bath. Facilities: 2 restaurants (reservations required). AE, DC, MC, V. Restaurants closed mid-Nov.–mid-Dec. Very Expensive.*

St-Tropez
Dining and Lodging
Byblos. This hotel is unique. Its luxury rooms and suites are built around tiled courtyards, fragrant with magnolia and orange trees, like a miniature Provençal village. Each room is different, with amusing touches and subtle lighting. Les Caves du Roy, one of its two nightclubs, and Le Chabichou, an independent restaurant within the complex, are considered among the best in town. Specialties include foie gras and lobster. Les

Arcades, the hotel's other restaurant, offers slightly more moderately priced meals. *Av. Paul Signac, tel. 94–97–00–04, fax 94–97–40–52. 59 rooms and 48 suites with bath. Facilities: 2 restaurants, 2 nightclubs, sauna, pool, hairdresser. AE, DC, MC, V. Closed winter. Very Expensive. Le Chabichou, tel. 94–54–80–00. Reservations required. AE, DC, MC, V. Closed Oct. 10–May 1. Very Expensive.*

11 Germany

A reunited Germany offers the traveler a unique experience. Today one country exists where previously there were two, and although the 40-year division was an artificial one, differences that developed during this period will take some years to even out. Travelers crossing from "west" to "east" Germany will soon notice the big gap in wealth between the two halves. In western Germany, a stable economy has resulted in cared-for cities, towns, and villages and in a manicured countryside. In eastern Germany, many cities and rural areas are scarred by a 19th-century approach to industrialization that had little or no concern for the environment. Still, the former Communist authorities did attempt to preserve and renovate some historic buildings.

Former West Germany was a founding member of the European Common Market, now the European Community (EC), and its government has always championed efforts to expand the "club." Apart from security checks, Germany abandoned bureaucratic border formalities with its EC neighbors (France, Holland, Belgium, Luxembourg, and Denmark) when all trade barriers within the EC were lifted at the beginning of 1993.

In many ways, Germany is already one country: the same language, the same currency, the same federal political structure. But some of the differences can be quirky. The united Germany is still a young country; the two sides came together again only on October 3, 1990.

Rapid reunification—critics said it was too hasty—has had a damaging effect on the German economy, which had previously been unaffected by the recession in other parts of the western world. The bid to quickly rejuvenate former East Germany and provide its 17 million inhabitants with better standards of living has so far proved elusive, while costing western German taxpayers thousands of millions of Deutschemarks. By the end of 1992, the effects of reunification had virtually stopped the great German economic locomotive, resulting in higher prices and the threat of higher taxes—and causing much grumbling in the west. The determined effort of the powerful German federal bank, the Bundesbank, to curb inflation at all costs, has been blamed by neighboring west European governments for slowing up their efforts to recover from the recession.

The problems of reunification, and the attendant social unrest in the east, also coincided with the massive influx of several hundred thousand "political" refugees as word spread far and wide that Germany had the most liberal asylum laws in the world, one of the central planks of a deliberately liberal post-Nazi constitution. The refugees—many of whom are believed to be economic rather than political—have added to the strains on the economy.

In the eastern part of the country Germans still earn only half of the salaries their fellow countrymen in the west make. But some basic costs of living are much lower, too. Apartment rents, for example, remain only a fraction of what Germans in the west pay, although rents and utility costs are rising. Eastern German shops are less numerous and elegant, but they are already filled with the sort of material goods that were unobtainable under the Communist regime. During the first six months after the fall of the Berlin Wall, the number of car owners in eastern Germany rose by 600,000.

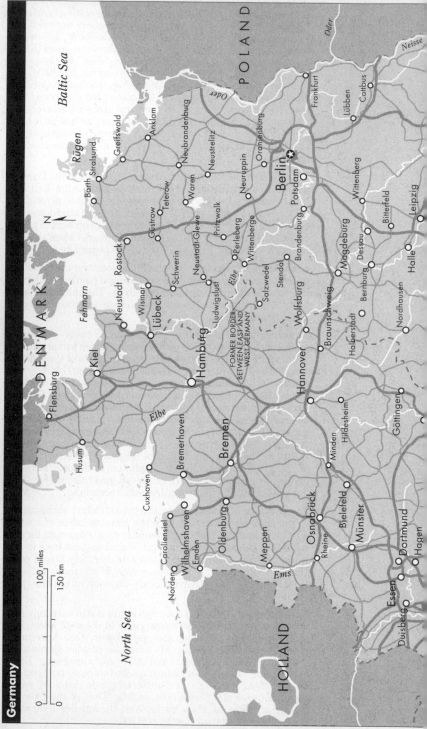

Germany

0 ___ 100 miles
0 ___ 150 km

North Sea

Baltic Sea

DENMARK

Flensburg

Husum

Cuxhaven

Kiel

Fehmarn

Neustadt

Wismar

Lübeck

Hamburg

Elbe

Rügen

Barth Stralsund

Greifswald

Anklam

Rostock

Güstrow

Teterow

Schwerin

Neustadt-Glewe

Ludwigslust

Pritzwalk

Neustrelitz

Waren

Neubrandenburg

Neuruppin

Oranienburg

Perleberg

Wittenberge

Salzwedel

Stendal

Brandenburg

Berlin

Potsdam

Wittenberg

FORMER BORDER BETWEEN EAST AND WEST GERMANY

Wolfsburg

Magdeburg

Dessau

Bernburg

Bitterfeld

Halle

Leipzig

Nordhausen

Braunschweig

Halberstadt

Hannover

Hildesheim

Minden

Göttingen

Bielefeld

Osnabrück

Rheine

Münster

Bremerhaven

Bremen

Oldenburg

Meppen

Ems

Wilhelmshaven

Emden

Caroliensiel

Norden

HOLLAND

Essen

Duisberg

Dortmund

Hagen

POLAND

Oder

Neisse

Frankfurt

Lübben

Cottbus

N

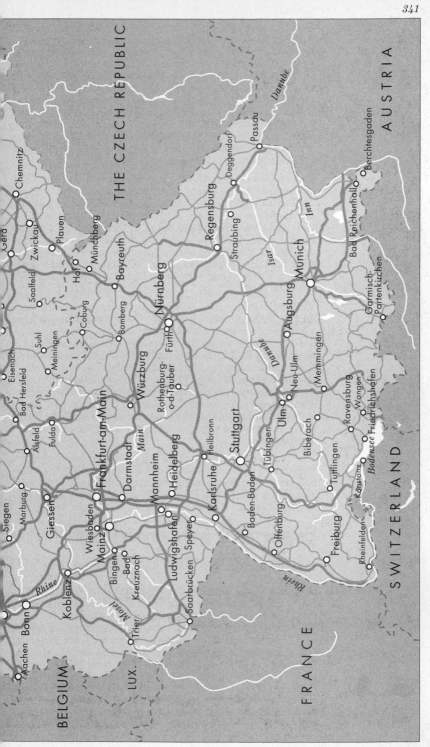

Germans tend to rise very early and are hammering away at the building site by 7 AM or seated at the office desk by 8 AM, but they take their leisure time just as seriously. Annual vacations of up to six weeks are the norm, and secular and religious festivals occupy another 12 days. Every town and village, and many city neighborhoods, manage at least one "Fest" a year, when the beer barrels are rolled out and sausages are thrown on the grill. The seasons have their own festivities: Carnivals (Fasching) herald the end of winter, countless beer gardens open up with the first warm rays of sunshine, fall is celebrated with the Munich Oktoberfest, and Advent brings Christkindlmarkt, colorful pre-Christmas markets held in town and city squares.

Eastern Germany's emergence from communism has not so much inspired a new sense of nationhood there as it has revived regional traditions and identities. The villages south of Leipzig and Dresden have more in common with their neighbors in northern Bavaria, from whom they were cut off for four decades, than with Berlin bureaucrats. Five old states—with their capitals in Dresden, Erfurt, Magdeburg, Potsdam, and Schwerin—have been re-created, making a total of 16 for all of reunited Germany. Each new state, with its own regional parliament, is certain to develop a cultural identity.

The great outdoors have always been an important escape hatch for the Germans, and *Lebensraum* (living space) is even more highly prized in the era of high technology and pressurized urban life. Germany does its best to meet the needs of its hard-working inhabitants. A Bavarian mountain inn, the glow of its lights reflected on the blanket of snow outside, may be only a short drive from Munich. The busy industrial city of Stuttgart lies at the gateway to the Black Forest (Schwarzwald), the popular region of spas, hiking trails, and its tempting cake. Berlin is surrounded by its own lakes and green parklands. The Green Party is a political expression of this feeling for the outdoors and nature.

The transportation system that links these various regions is a godsend to the visitor. German trains are fast, clean, and punctual, and a drive on a speed limit–free autobahn will give you an idea of just how fast all those BMW and Mercedes sports cars are meant to go.

Essential Information

Before You Go

When to Go The main tourist season in Germany runs from May to late October, when the weather is naturally at its best. In addition to many tourist events, this period has hundreds of folk festivals. The winter sports season in the Bavarian Alps runs from Christmas to mid-March. Prices everywhere are generally higher during the summer, so you may find considerable advantages in visiting out of season. Most resorts offer out-of-season (*Zwischensaison*) and "edge-of-season" (*Nebensaison*) rates, and tourist offices can provide lists of hotels offering special low-price inclusive weekly packages (*Pauschalangebote*). Similarly, many winter resorts offer lower rates for the periods immediately before and after the Christmas and New Year high season (*Weisse Wochen*, or "white weeks"). The other advantage of out-of-season travel is that there aren't as many crowds. The disadvantages of visiting out of season, especially in winter, are that the weather is often cold and gloomy and many tourist attractions, especially in rural areas, are closed. Ski resorts are an exception.

The major cities, especially Munich and Berlin, are active year-round. Avoid Leipzig around the first weeks in March and September; the trade fair commandeers all accommodations and prices soar.

Climate   Germany's climate is generally temperate. Winters vary from mild and damp to very cold and bright. Particularly chilly regions include the Baltic coast, the Alps, the Harz Mountains, and the Black and Bavarian forests. Summers are usually sunny and warm, though be prepared for a few cloudy and wet days. In Alpine regions, spring often comes late, with snow flurries well into April. Fall is sometimes spectacular in the south: warm and soothing. The only real exception to the above is the strikingly variable weather in southern Bavaria (Bayern) caused by the *Föhn*, a warm Alpine wind that brings sudden barometric changes and gives rise to clear but oppressive conditions in summer and, in winter, can cause snow to disappear overnight.

The following are the average daily maximum and minimum temperatures for Munich.

Jan.	35F	1C	May	64F	18C	Sept.	67F	20C
	23	– 5		45	7		48	9
Feb.	38F	3C	June	70F	21C	Oct.	56F	13C
	23	– 5		51	11		40	4
Mar.	48F	9C	July	74F	23C	Nov.	44F	7C
	30	– 1		55	13		33	0
Apr.	56F	14C	Aug.	73F	23C	Dec.	36F	2C
	38	3		54	12		26	– 3

Currency   The unit of currency in Germany is the Deutschemark, written as DM and generally referred to as the mark. It is divided into 100 pfennig. There are bills of 5 (rare), 10, 20, 50, 100, 200, 500, and 1,000 marks and coins of 1, 2, 5, 10, and 50 pf and 1, 2, and 5 marks. At press time (spring 1993), the mark stood at DM 1.64 to the dollar and DM 2.40 to the pound sterling.

The Deutschemark is legal tender throughout reunited Germany. The cost of living is still much lower in the former GDR (German Democratic Republic), where most people earn considerably less than their western colleagues doing the same jobs, and some of these lower costs benefit tourists—for example, on public transportation, in cafés and beer restaurants, and in simple accommodations such as country inns and private guest houses. But a growing number of places that cater specifically to visitors are now charging western rates.

Major credit cards are widely accepted in Germany, though not universally so. You can buy a seat on a Lufthansa flight with a credit card but not on a German train, for example. Most hotels, a significant number of restaurants, and all leading car-rental companies accept credit cards, however. A growing number of shops also honor them, but don't be surprised if you are offered a discount for cash.

What It Will Cost The early 1990s has seen inflation creeping up (at press time, the annual rate of inflation was more than 4%), primarily because of the cost of financing the rejuvenation and integration of former Communist East Germany. For example, a "reunification" tax has been levied on basic commodities such as gas, and telephone charges have risen. There were further modest increases in fares for most forms of public transportation.

The most expensive areas to visit are the major cities, notably Frankfurt, Hamburg, and Munich. Out-of-the-way rural regions, such as north and east Bavaria, the Saarland on the French border, and many parts of eastern Germany, offer the lowest prices.

Sample Prices Cup of coffee in a café, DM 3.50, in a stand-up snack bar DM 1.80; mug of beer in a beer hall, DM 3.50, a bottle of beer from a supermarket, DM 1.50; soft drink, DM 2; ham sandwich, DM 4; 2-mile taxi ride, DM 8.

Visas To enter the new Germany, only passports are required of visitors from the United States, Canada, and the United Kingdom, although U.S. citizens must obtain a visa if they plan to stay longer than three months. A passport is valid for travel throughout the country, and, of course, there are no limitations on movement in Berlin.

Customs From the beginning of 1993 and the start of a single, unrestricted market within the European Community (EC), there will no longer be any restrictions on importing items duty-free for citizens of the 12 member countries traveling among EC countries.

If you are entering Germany as a citizen of a country that does not belong to the EC, you may import duty-free: (1) 200 cigarettes or 50 cigars or 250 grams of tobacco; plus (2) 1 liter of spirits more than 22% proof or 2 liters of spirits less than 22% proof, and 2 liters of still wine; plus (3) 50 grams of perfume and ¼ liter of toilet water; plus (4) other goods to the value of DM 115.

Tobacco and alcohol allowances are for visitors aged 17 and over. Other items intended for personal use may be imported and exported freely. There are no restrictions on the import and export of German currency.

Language English has long been taught in high schools in the western part of Germany. Consequently, many people under age 40 speak some English, although the level of understanding varies considerably. Older people in rural areas are less familiar with the English language, but a substantial number have retained some basic words of communication from the immediate postwar years when American and British forces occupied the country. English is not as widely understood in eastern parts of the country, where before the collapse of communism Russian was the first foreign language taught in many schools. Still, young people exposed to American and British pop music are becoming increasingly familiar with basic English.

Germans who speak some English will take every opportunity to practice what they know, and they are delighted when someone makes an effort—no matter how elementary—to speak their language. For a visitor attempting to practice his or her German, the country's many dialects pose the biggest problem. Probably the most difficult to comprehend is Bavaria's, which is like another language—even books are written in "Bayerisch." Nonetheless, except for older people in remote, rural districts, virtually everyone can also speak Hoch Deutsch, the German equivalent of Oxford English. Hoch Deutsch is always used on TV and radio.

Getting Around

By Car
Road Conditions

The autobahn system in western Germany is of the highest standard. These roads are marked either A (on blue signs), meaning inter-German highways, or E (on green signs), meaning they form part of the Europe-wide *Europastrasse* network. All autobahns are toll-free. Local roads are called *Bundesstrassen* and are marked by their number on a yellow sign. All local roads are single lane and slower than autobahns.

The condition of the road system in eastern Germany has improved enormously. Many major roads have been repaired, and new autobahns are being added, most notably those linking Berlin with both western and eastern destinations.

Rules of the Road

Political reunification of the two Germanies did not bring a merging of road rules. Very high speeds on motorways continue in the west, while in the former territory of the GDR (the five states of Saxony, Saxony-Anhalt, Brandenburg, Thuringia, and Mecklenburg) a top limit of 100 kph (60 mph) remains in force. An absolute ban on alcohol and driving also remains in force in the east, but motorists in the west can still legally drive after drinking two small beers or wine. Despite eastern Germany's ban on alcohol, driving has become much more dangerous primarily because of a dramatic rise in traffic.

Motorway (autobahn) speeds of 160 kph (100 mph) in western Germany are common. The limit on Bundesstrassen is 100 kph (60 mph); in built-up areas it varies between 30 kph (18 mph) and 80 kph (50 mph). Limits are shown on the side of the road. The town limit in Germany is 50 kph (30 mph), with an 80 kph restriction on country roads other than motorways.

Parking

Daytime parking in cities is very difficult. If you can find one, use a parking lot or you'll risk having your car towed. Parking restrictions are not always clearly marked and can be hard to understand when they are. At night, parking-meter spaces are free.

Gasoline

Both leaded and unleaded gas and diesel are generally available all over Germany. At press time (spring 1993), the price of a liter of gas ranged from DM 1.40 to DM 1.70, depending on the grade. (To encourage the use of the more environmentally friendly unleaded gas, the government has made it cheaper.)

Breakdowns

The **ADAC,** the major German automobile organization, gives free help and advice to tourists, though you have to pay for any spare parts and labor you need. All autobahns have regularly spaced telephones with which you can call for help. The contact address for the ADAC is Am Westpark 8, 8000 Munich 70 (tel. 089/76760).

By Train

Despite reunification, the two publicly owned train networks of the former two Germanies were still operating independently at press time, but the merger is scheduled to take place during 1994. The western Deutsches Bundesbahn (DB) is developing a new high-speed service capable of traveling at 250 kph (156 mph), with half its 27,000 kilometers (16,800 miles) of track electrified. The smaller eastern sector, the Reichsbahn, still has one foot in the steam age, but a multimillion Deutschemark investment program will bring much-needed improvements in equipment, tracks, and service.

All major cities in western Germany are linked by fast Inter-City services with first- and second-class cars and some by the new super **InterCityExpress (ICE)** train service. New track is being laid for the ICE, and top speeds of up to 250 kph (155 mph) have already been achieved on the Hamburg–Frankfurt–Munich route. Fares are higher on ICE routes. Railroad links have been increased between western and eastern Germany, particularly to Berlin, but journeys on many eastern sections are slower than in the west because of older track and rolling stock. An 826-kilometer (512-mile) trip from Hamburg to Munich through the old West Germany takes 7 hours, while a 605-kilometer (375-mile) ride from Berlin to Munich takes 9½ hours. All long-distance routes have restaurant cars, and Intercity overnight trains have sleeper cars. Slower long-distance trains also operate between western cities (Inter-Regio), while E-trains provide shorter-distance services. A DM 6 surcharge (DM 10 on first class) is made regardless of distance on all InterCity journeys, but seat reservations are free. Bikes are not permitted on Intercity services.

New routes have opened up linking Hamburg, Frankfurt, and Munich with Berlin, Dresden, Erfurt, Leipzig, Magdeburg, and Rostock. The Reichsbahn runs train classifications similar to the DB. Many trains have first- and second-class cars, and longer-distance routes provide dining cars or buffet facilities. Since fewer people in the east have cars, trains are more heavily used and seat reservations are advisable for long journeys.

Fares   The DB offers a broad range of fares and inclusive tickets, from family rovers to a **Senior Citizen** card. But probably the best and most flexible deal for the foreign visitor is the German **Rail Pass**. It's available to all non-German residents and, most important, is valid for the entire country on both train networks. The Rail Pass can be bought for 5 days ($160), 10 days ($240), or 15 days ($300). These rates are for second-class travel, but first-class rates are also available. A German **Rail Twin Pass** gives a 10% discount on these rates when two people travel together. A German **Rail Youth Pass** (second class only) for travelers aged 12–26 costs $110, $145, and $180 for the same periods. The Rail Pass can be bought anywhere outside Germany, but the prices quoted here are available only in the United States. An added bonus permits you to "spend" your Rail Pass one day at a time over a period of a month, regardless of the length of your pass. The Rail Pass is also valid on all buses operated by the DB, as well as on tour routes along the Romantic and Castle roads served by Deutschen Touring, or DTG (contact DTG, Am Römerhof 17, 6000 Frankfurt, for reservations). It includes free rides on the Rhine and Mosel rivers, with cruises operated by the Köln-Düsseldorfer (KD) Line between Mainz and Cologne (Köln) and Koblenz and Cochem, as well as free admission to the Transportation Museum in Nürnberg (Lessingstrasse 6).

By Bus   Long-distance bus services in Germany are part of the Europewide Europabus network. Services are neither as frequent nor as comprehensive as those on the rail system, so make reservations. Be careful in selecting the service you travel on: All Europabus services have a bilingual hostess and offer small luxuries that you won't find on the more basic, though still comfortable, regular services. For details and reservations, contact **Deutsche Touring Gesellschaft** (Am Römerhof 17, 6000 Frankfurt/Main 90, tel. 069/79030). Reservations can also be made at any of the Deutsche Touring offices in Cologne, Hanover, Hamburg, Munich, Nuremberg (Nürnberg), and Wuppertal and at travel agents.

Rural bus services are operated by local municipalities and some private firms, as well as by Deutsche Bundesbahn (the west German railway) and the post office. Services are variable, however, even when there is no other means to reach your destination by public transportation.

By Plane Germany's national airline, **Lufthansa,** serves all major cities. **LTU International Airways** (in the United States, tel. 800/888–0200; in Germany, tel. 0211/410941) has connections between Düsseldorf and Munich and between Frankfurt and Munich (summer only). Regular fares are high, but you can save up to 40% with Flieg und Spar ("fly and save") specials; several restrictions apply, such as a DM 100 penalty for changing flights. Contact Lufthansa at Frankfurt International Airport (6000 Frankfurt 65, tel. 069/6961; in the United States at 750 Lexington Ave., New York, NY 10022, tel. 718/895–1277 or 800/645–3880; in Great Britain at 23–26 Piccadilly, London W1V 0EJ, tel. 071/355–4994 or 071/408–0442). A British Airways subsidiary, **Deutsche BA,** competes with Lufthansa on many domestic routes, including those between Berlin and Munich, Frankfurt, and Düsseldorf.

By Boat For a country with such a small coastline, Germany is a surprisingly nautical nation: You can cruise rivers and lakes throughout the country. The biggest fleet, and most of the biggest boats, too, belongs to the Cologne-based KD line, the Köln-Düsseldorf Rheinschiffahrt. It operates services on the Rivers Rhine, Moselle, and Main, ranging from luxurious five-day trips from Amsterdam or Rotterdam in Holland all the way down the Rhine to Basel in Switzerland, to short "riverboat shuffles" with jazz bands and freely flowing wine. For details, write **KD River Cruises of Europe** (Rhine Cruise Agency), 170 Hamilton Ave., White Plains, NY 10601) or **KD German Rhine Line** (Frankenwerft 15, 5000 Köln 1).

Services on the 160-kilometer (100-mile) stretch of the Danube (Donau) between the spectacular Kelheim gorge and Passau on the Austrian border are operated by **Donauschiffahrt Wurm & Köck** (Höllgasse 26, D-8390 Passau). The company has daily summer cruises on the Rivers Danube, Inn, and Ilz, which meet at Passau; some two-day cruises into Austria are also offered. Bodensee (Lake Constance), the largest lake in Germany, located at the meeting point of Germany, Austria, and Switzerland, has up to 40 ships crisscrossing it in summer. Write **Deutsche Bundesbahn,** Bodensee-Schiffsbetriebe, Hafenstrasse 6, D-7750 Konstanz. Bavaria's five largest lakes—Ammersee, Chiemsee, Königsee, Tegernsee, and Starnbergersee—have regular summer cruises and excursions. Details are available from local tourist offices.

KD has two new luxury cruise ships now plying the Elbe. Several different itineraries are being offered, ranging from five to eight days. All cruises stop at Dresden, and some include free bus transfers to Hamburg, Berlin, and Prague.

By Bicycle Bicycles can be rented at more than 280 train stations throughout Germany. The basic cost is DM 6 per day with a valid train ticket; otherwise it's DM 12. Two marks extra per day gets you a bike with gears. You can pick up a bike at one station and return it to another, provided the station is on the list of those renting bikes. There is a small charge for taking a bike on the train; Intercity and Intercity Express (ICE) trains do not carry bikes. Most cities also have bike-rental companies, usually priced about DM 15 per day or DM 80–DM 90 a week.

Staying in Germany

Telephones Telephone lines between western and eastern Germany are now much improved after an initial period of difficulty following reunification. All but the more remote eastern regions can be reached by direct dialing.

Since reunification, all phones in the east and west use the same coins: 10 pf, DM 1, and DM 5 for long-distance calls. A local call costs 30 pf and lasts six minutes. Card phones are rapidly replacing coin-operated phones: Cards cost DM 12 or DM 50 and can be purchased at the post office.

You'll also find public booths at the post office; if you have no change or need to make a lengthy overseas call: the counter clerk gets you a line, and you pay him or her afterward. If possible, avoid making international phone calls from your hotel room because the rates are double or more.

Mail Airmail letters to the United States and Canada cost DM 1.65; postcards cost 80 pf. Airmail letters to the United Kingdom cost DM 1; postcards cost 60 pf.

You can arrange to have mail sent to you in care of any German post office; have the envelope marked "Postlagernd." This service is free. Alternatively, have mail sent to any American Express office in Germany. There's no charge to cardholders, holders of American Express traveler's checks, or anyone who has booked a vacation with American Express. Otherwise, you pay DM 2 per collection (not per item).

Shopping German goods carry a 15% value-added tax (VAT). You can
VAT Refunds claim this back either as you leave the country or once you've returned home. When you make a purchase, ask the shopkeeper for a form known as an "Ausfuhr-Abnehmerbescheinigung"; he or she will help you fill it out. As you leave the country, give the form, plus the goods and receipts, to German customs. It will give you an official export certificate or stamp. In the unlikely event that there's a branch of the Deutsche Bank on the spot, you can take the stamped form to it, where you will receive the refund on the spot. Otherwise, send the form back to the shop, and it will send the refund.

Opening and **Banks.** Times vary from state to state and city to city, but
Closing Times banks are generally open weekdays from 8:30 or 9 to 3 or 4 (5 or 6 on Thursday). Some banks close from 12:30 to 1:30. Branches at airports and main train stations open as early as 6:30 AM and close as late as 10:30 PM. Many banks in eastern Germany have shorter hours but are slowly conforming to western times.

Museums are generally open Tuesday to Sunday 9–5. Some close for an hour or more at lunch, and some are open on Monday. Many stay open until 9 on Thursdays.

Shops are generally open weekdays from 8:30 or 9 until 6:30 PM and Saturdays until 1 or 2 PM. On the first Saturday of each month, many larger shops and department stores in Germany are open until 6. Some stores stay open until 8:30 PM on Thursdays.

National Holidays January 1; January 6 (Epiphany); April 1 (Good Friday); April 4 (Easter Monday); May 1; May 12 (Ascension); May 23 (Pentecost Monday); June 2 (Corpus Christi, south Germany only); October 3 (German Unity Day); November 1 (All Saints' Day); November 16 (Day of Prayer and Repentance); December 24–26.

Dining It's hard to generalize about German food beyond saying that standards are high and portions are large. In fact, the range of dining experiences is vast: everything from highly priced nouvelle cuisine to hamburgers. As a visitor, you should search out local restaurants if atmosphere and regional specialties are your priority. Beer restaurants in Bavaria, *Apfelwein* taverns in Frankfurt, and *Kneipen*—the pub on the corner cum local café—in Berlin nearly always offer best value and atmosphere. But throughout the country you'll find *Gaststätten* and/or *Gasthöfe*—local inns—where atmosphere and regional specialties are always available. Likewise, just about every town will have a *Ratskeller,* a cellar restaurant in the town hall, where exposed beams, huge fireplaces, sturdy tables, and immense portions are the rule.

In larger towns and cities throughout the country, Germans like to nibble at roadside or market snack stalls, called *Imbisse.* Hot sausages, spicy meatballs (*Fleischpflanzerl*), meatloaf topped with a fried egg (*Leberkäs*), in the south, and sauerkraut are the traditional favorites. But foods eaten on the hoof are creeping in, too: french fries, pizzas, gyros, and hamburgers. In eastern Germany, the old state-run self-service worker cafeterias may still be operating in some towns, but these are rapidly being replaced by commercial enterprises.

The most famous German specialty is sausage. Everyone has heard of frankfurters, but if you're in Munich, try *Weisswurst,* a delicate white sausage traditionally eaten only between midnight and noon. Nürnberg's sausage favorite is the *Nürnberger Bratwurst;* its fame is such that you'll find restaurants all over Germany serving it. Look for the "Bratwurststube" sign. Dumplings (*Knödeln*) can also be found throughout the country, though their natural home is probably Bavaria; farther north, potatoes often take their place.

The natural accompaniment to German food is either beer or wine. Munich is the beer capital of Germany, though there's no part of the country where you won't find the amber nectar. Say "Helles" or Export if you want light beer; "Dunkles" if you want dark beer. In Bavaria, try the sour but refreshing beer brewed from wheat, called *Weissbier.* Germany is a major wine-producing country, also, and much of it is of superlative quality. You will probably be happy with the house wine in most restaurants or with one of those earthenware pitchers of cold Moselle wine. If you want something more expensive, remember that all wines are graded in one of three basic categories:

Tafelwein (table wine); *Qualitätswein* (fine wines); and *Qualitätswein mit Prädikat* (top-quality wines).

Mealtimes Lunch is served from around 11:30 (especially in rural areas) to around 2; dinner is generally from 6 until 9:30 PM, or earlier in some quiet country areas. Big city hotels and popular restaurants serve later. Lunch tends to be the main meal, a fact reflected in the almost universal appearance of a lunchtime *Tageskarte*, or suggested menu; try it if you want maximum nourishment for minimum outlay. This doesn't mean that dinner is a rushed or skimpy affair, however; the Germans have too high a regard for food for any meal to be underrated. Breakfast, served anytime from 6:30 to 10, is often a substantial meal, with cold meats, cheeses, rolls, and fruit. Many city hotels offer Sunday "brunch," and the custom is rapidly catching on.

Dress Jacket and tie are recommended for restaurants in the Very Expensive and Expensive categories. Casual dress is appropriate elsewhere.

Ratings Prices are per person and include a first course, main course, dessert, and tip and tax. Best bets are indicated by a star ★.

The following chart gives price ranges for restaurants in the western part of Germany. Food prices in the territory of former East Germany are still somewhat unstable, although in the bigger cities many of the better quality restaurants are already starting to mimic "western" rates. Generally speaking, the prevailing price structure in the eastern part of the country, except for restaurants in the priciest hotels, falls into the Inexpensive to Expensive categories listed below. Bills in simple restaurants in country areas of the eastern region will, however, still come well below DM 35.

Category	Major Cities and Resorts	Other Areas
Very Expensive	over DM 100	over DM 90
Expensive	DM 75–DM 100	DM 55–DM 90
Moderate	DM 50–DM 75	DM 35–DM 55
Inexpensive	DM 25–DM 50	under DM 35

Lodging The standard of German hotels, from top-notch luxury spots (of which the country has more than its fair share) to the humblest pension, is generally excellent. Prices can be high, but not disproportionately so in comparison to other northern European countries. You can expect courteous service; clean and comfortable rooms; and, in rural areas especially, considerable old-German atmosphere.

In addition to hotels proper, the country also has numerous *Gasthöfe* or *Gasthäuser* (country inns); pensions or *Fremdenheime* (guest houses); and, at the lowest end of the scale, *Zimmer*, meaning, quite simply, rooms, normally in private houses. Look for the sign "Zimmer frei" or "zu vermieten," meaning "for rent." A red sign reading "besetzt" means there are no vacancies.

Lists of hotels are available from the German National Tourist Office (Beethovenstr. 69, 6000 Frankfurt/Main 1, tel. 069/75720), and from all regional and local tourist offices. Tourist offices will also make reservations for you—they charge a nominal fee—but may have difficulty doing so after 4 PM in peak season and on weekends. A reservations service is also operated by the German National Tourist Office (Allgemeine Deutsche Zimmer-reservierung, Cornelius-str. 34, 6000 Frankfurt/Main 1, tel. 069/740–767).

Most hotels have restaurants, but those describing themselves as *Garni* will provide breakfast only.

Tourist accommodations in eastern Germany are beginning to blossom under free enterprise after the straitjacket of state monopoly, although the choice and facilities are still far behind the western half of the country. The former state-owned Interhotel chain (34 hotels with several thousand rooms) has been dismantled, its components sold individually. Other hotel groups are keen to build new properties in the region or to convert old buildings with the potential for atmospheric lodgings. But for now, accommodations remain tight at the top- and middle-quality levels. It cannot be too greatly stressed: If you want to stay in good hotels in eastern Germany, book well in advance. Hotel rooms in the cities are under pressure year-round because of the comings and goings of businesspeople involved in rebuilding the east's economy. Traditional inn accommodations have run down during the past 40 years, and those that survive are rather antiquated—still, you may well come across the odd gem.

The real boom in lodgings has been at the inexpensive end of the market, where thousands of beds are now available for the adventurous traveler. For relatively few marks every village can now provide somewhere for the tourist to put his or her head and perhaps offer a simple but wholesome evening meal. Many guest houses have sprung up under the enterprising stewardship of housewives eager to supplement the family income. For a list of approved addresses, consult the local tourist office.

Romantik Hotels Among the most delightful places to stay and eat in Germany are the aptly named Romantik Hotels and Restaurants. All are in historic buildings—this is a precondition of membership— and are personally run by the owners. The emphasis generally is on solid comfort, good food, and style. A detailed listing of all Romantik Hotels is available in the United States from **Harm Meyer Romantik Hotels,** 14178 Woodinville-Duval Road, Box 1278, Woodinville, WA 98072, tel. 206/486–9394; for reservations only, tel. 800/826–0015.

Castle Hotels This is a similar hotel association, though you may find that some of the simpler establishments lack a little in the way of comfort and that furnishings can be basic. But most can be delightful, with antiques, imposing interiors, and out-of-the-way locations setting the tone. Prices are mostly moderate. Ask the German National Tourist Office or your travel agent for the "Castle Hotels in Germany" brochure. It details a series of good-value packages, most for stays of four to six nights.

Ringhotels This association groups 130 individually owned and managed hotels in the medium price range. Many are situated in the countryside or in pretty villages. Package deals of 2–3 days are available. Contact **Ringhotels,** Belfortstrasse 8, 8000 Munich 80, tel. 089/482720.

Rentals Apartments and hotel homes, most accommodating from two to eight guests, can be rented throughout Germany. Rates are low, with reductions for longer stays. Charges for gas and electricity, and sometimes water, are usually added to the bill. Local and regional tourist offices have lists of apartments in their areas; otherwise contact the **German National Tourist Office** (*see* Lodging in Staying in Germany, *above*).

Farm Vacations Taking an *Urlaub auf dem Bauernhof*, as the Germans put it, has increased dramatically in popularity over the past four or five years. Almost every regional tourist office has listings of farms by area offering bed and breakfast, apartments, or whole farmhouses to rent. Alternatively, write the **German Agricultural Association** (DLG), Zimmerweg 16, D-6000 Frankfurt/Main. It produces an annual listing of more than 1,500 farms, all of them inspected and graded, that offer accommodations. The brochure costs DM 7.50.

Camping There are 2,600 campsites in Germany, about 1,600 of which are listed by the **German Camping Club** (DCC), Mandlstrasse 28, D-8000, Munich 40. For details of camping facilities in eastern Germany, where facilities are neither common nor modern, contact **Camping und Caravanverband**, Postfach 105, 1080 Berlin. The German National Tourist Office also publishes a listing of sites. Most are open from May through October, with about 400 staying open year-round. They tend to become crowded during the summer, so it's always worthwhile to make reservations a day or two ahead. Prices range from DM 15 to DM 20 per night for two adults, a car, and trailer (less for tents).

Youth Hostels Germany's youth hostels—*Jugendherberge*—are probably the most efficient and up-to-date in Europe. There are 600 in all, many located in castles, adding a touch of romance to otherwise utilitarian accommodations. There's an age limit of 27 in Bavaria; elsewhere, there are no restrictions, though those under 20 take preference if space is limited. You'll need an International Youth Hostel card to stay in a German youth hostel; write **American Youth Hostels Association** (Box 37613, Washington, DC 20013) or **Canadian Hostelling Association** (333 River Rd., Ottawa, Ontario K1L 8H9). In Great Britain, contact the **Youth Hostels Association** (22 Southampton St., London WC2). The International Youth Hostel card can also be obtained from the **Deutsches Jugendherbergswerk** (Bismarckstr. 8, D-4930 Detmold, tel. 05231/74010), which provides a complete list of German hostels for DM 6.50.

Hostels must be reserved well in advance for midsummer, especially in eastern Germany. Bookings for hostels in the new German states (former East Germany) of Saxony, Thuringia, Saxony-Anhalt, Brandenburg, and Mecklenburg can be made directly through **Jugendtourist** (Alexanderplatz 5, 1026 Berlin).

Ratings Service charges and taxes are included in all quoted room rates. Similarly, breakfast is usually, but not always, included, so check before you book in. Rates are often surprisingly flexible in German hotels, varying considerably according to demand. Major hotels in cities often have lower rates on weekends or other periods when business is quiet. If you're lucky, you can find reductions of up to 60%. Likewise, rooms reserved after 10 PM will often carry a discount, on the basis that an occupied room at a reduced rate is better than an empty one. Although it's worthwhile to ask if your hotel will give you a reduction, don't count on finding rooms at lower rates late at night, especially in the summer. Prices are for two people in a double room. Best bets are indicated by a star ★.

The following chart is for hotels throughout Germany. Rooms in many of the bigger hotels of eastern Germany were priced similar to those in western Germany, even before reunification, and most of these hotels are now being bought by private chains. But smaller hotels in the east are often much cheaper—and shorter on facilities.

Category	Major Cities or Resorts	Other Areas
Very Expensive	over DM 300	over DM 180
Expensive	DM 200–DM 300	DM 120–DM 180
Moderate	DM 140–DM 200	DM 80–DM 120
Inexpensive	under DM 140	under DM 80

Tipping The Germans are as punctilious about tipping as they are about most facets of life in their well-regulated country. Overtipping is as frowned upon as not tipping at all, though the kind of abuse you risk in some countries for undertipping is virtually unknown here. Nonetheless, tips are expected, if not exactly demanded. Follow these simple rules and you won't go wrong.

In restaurants, service is usually included (under the heading *Bedienung*, at the bottom of the check), and it is customary to round out the check to the next mark or two, a practice also commonplace in cafés, beer halls, and bars. For taxi drivers, also round out to the next mark or two: for DM 11.20, make it DM 12; for DM 11.80, make it DM 13. Railway and airport porters (if you can find any) have their own scale of charges, but round out the requested amount to the next mark. Hotel porters get DM 1 per bag. Doormen are tipped the same amount for small services, such as calling a cab. Room service should be rewarded with at least DM 2 every time you use it. Maids should get about DM 1 per day. Double all these figures at luxury hotels. Service-station attendants get 50 pf or DM 1 for checking oil and tires or cleaning windshields.

Munich

Arriving and Departing

By Plane Munich's new Franz Josef Strauss (FJS) Airport, named after a former state premier, opened in May, 1992. It is 28 kilometers (17½ miles) northeast of the city center.

Between the Airport and Downtown The S8 suburban train line links FJS Airport with the city's main train station (Hauptbahnhof). Trains depart in both directions every 20 minutes from 3:55 AM to 12:55 AM daily. Intermediate stops are made at Ostbahnhof (good for hotels located east of the River Isar) and city center stations such as Marienplatz. The 38-minute trip costs DM 8 if you purchase a multi-use strip ticket (*see* Getting Around, *below*) and use 8 strips; otherwise an ordinary one-way ticket is DM 10 per person. A tip for families: Up to five people (maximum of two adults) can travel to or from the airport for only DM 16 by buying a Tageskarte (*see* Getting Around, *below*). This is particularly advantageous if you are arriving in Munich, because you can continue to use the Tageskarte in the city for the rest of the day. The only restriction is that you cannot use this special day ticket before 9 AM weekdays.

An express bus also links the airport and Hauptbahnhof, departing in both directions every 20 minutes. The trip takes about 40 minutes and costs DM 7. Bus service from the airport to the station runs from 6:25 AM to 12:25 AM; the bus runs from 3:10 AM to 9:30 PM in the opposite direction. A taxi will cost between DM 80 and DM 100. If you are driving from the airport into the city, follow the Munich autobahn signs to A92 and A9.

By Train All long-distance services arrive at and depart from the main train station, the Hauptbahnhof. Trains to and from destinations in the Bavarian Alps use the adjoining Starnbergerbahnhof. For information on train times, tel. 089/19419 or 592–991; English is spoken by most information office staff. For tickets and information, go to the station or to the ABR travel agency right by the station on Bahnhofplatz.

By Bus Munich has no central bus station. Long-distance buses arrive at and depart from the north side of the train station on Arnulfstrasse. A taxi stand is 20 yards away.

By Car From the north (Nürnberg, Frankfurt), leave the autobahn at the Schwabing exit and follow the "Stadtmitte" signs. The autobahn from Stuttgart and the west ends at Obermenzing; again, follow the "Stadtmitte" signs. The autobahns from Salzburg and the east, from Garmisch and the south, and from Lindau and the southwest all join up with the city beltway, the Mittlerer Ring. The city center is well posted.

Getting Around

Downtown Munich is only about one mile square, so it can easily be explored on foot. Other areas—Schwabing, Nymphenburg, the Olympic Park—are best reached on the efficient and comprehensive public transportation network. It incorporates buses, streetcars, subways (U-Bahn), and suburban trains (S-Bahn). Tickets are good for the entire network, and you can break your trip as many times as you like using just one ticket, provided you travel in one direction only and within a given time limit. If you plan to make only a few trips, buy strip tickets (Streifenkarten)—blue for adults, red for children. Adults get 10 strips for DM 10; children the same number for DM 8. For adults, short rides that span up to 4 stations cost 1 strip; trips spanning more than 4 stations cost 2 strips. Children pay 1 strip per ride. All tickets must be validated by time-punching them in the automatic machines at station entrances and on all buses and streetcars. The best buy is the Tageskarte: Up to two adults and three children can use this excellent-value ticket for unlimited journeys between 9 AM and the end of the day's service (about 2 AM). It costs DM 8 for the inner zone, which covers central Munich. A Tageskarte for the entire system, extending to the Starnbergersee and Ammersee lakes, costs DM 16. Holders of a Eurail Pass, a Youth Pass, an Inter-Rail Card, or a DB Tourist Card travel free on all S-Bahn trains.

By Taxi Munich's cream-colored taxis are numerous. Hail them in the street or call 089/21611 (there's an extra charge for the drive to the pickup point). Rates start at DM 2.90 and rise by DM 1.70 per kilometer (about DM 2.75 per mile). There are additional charges of 50 pf for each piece of luggage. Figure on paying DM 8 to DM 12 for a short trip within the city.

Important Addresses and Numbers

Tourist Information The address to write to for information in advance of your visit is **Fremdenverkehrsamt München,** Postfach, 8000 München 1. This address also deals with lodging questions and bookings. Two other offices provide on-the-spot advice: at the Hauptbahnhof (tel. 089/239–1256), daily between 8 AM and 10 PM, and at the corner of Rindermarkt and Pettenbeckstrasse, behind Marienplatz (tel. 089/239–1272), open weekdays between 9:30 AM and 6 PM.

Consulates **U.S. Consulate General** (Königinstrasse 5, tel. 089/28881). **British Consulate General** (Bürkleinstr. 10, tel. 089/211090). **Canadian Consulate** (Tal 29, tel. 089/222–661).

Emergencies **Police** (tel. 110). **Ambulance** and **emergency medical attention** (tel. 089/558661). **Dentist** (tel. 089/723–3093). **Pharmacies: Internationale Ludwigs-Apotheke,** Neuhauserstrasse 8, tel. 089/260–3021; **Europa-Apotheke,** Schützenstrasse 12 (near the Hauptbahnhof), tel. 089/595423. Open weekdays 8–5:30, Saturday 8–1. Outside these hours, call 089/594475.

English-Language Bookstores The **Anglia English Bookshop** (Schellingstrasse 3, tel. 089/283642) has the largest selection of English-language books in Munich. Also try the **Hugendubel** bookshops at Marienplatz and Karlsplatz. A library of English-language books is kept in **Amerika Haus** (Karolinenplatz 3, tel. 089/595369).

Travel Agencies **American Express** (Promenadeplatz 6, tel. 089/21990). **ABR,** the official Bavarian travel agency, has outlets all over Munich; tel. 089/12040 for information.

Guided Tours

Orientation Tours City bus tours are operated by **Münchner Stadt-Rundfahrten** (Arnulfstr. 8, tel. 089/120–4248). Tours run daily and take in the city center, the Olympic Park, and Nymphenburg. Departures are at 10 AM and 2:30 PM (and 11:30 AM in midsummer) from outside the Hertie department store across from the train station, and the cost is between DM 13 and DM 23 per person, depending on the duration of the tour.

Walking and Cycling Tours Under the auspices of the city council, students conduct walking tours of the historic center on Monday, Tuesday, and Thursday at 10 AM. The walks start from the Fischbrunnen (Fish Fountain) at Marienplatz and cost DM 6. Bike tours of the city, including bike rentals, are offered through **City Hopper Touren** (tel. 089/272–1131). They run Tuesday–Sunday starting at 10 AM. Tours on foot, by bicycle, and by streetcar are organized by **Radius Touristik** (Arnulfstr 3, north side of Hauptbahnhof, tel. 089/596113).

Excursions **PanoramaTours** (Arnulfstr. 8, next to Hauptbahnhof, tel. 089/591504) organizes bus trips to most leading tourist attractions outside the city, including the "Royal Castles Tour" (Schlösserfahrt) of "Mad" King Ludwig's dream palaces. This tour, which takes in Neuschwanstein, costs DM 65 per person. Reservations for these tours can also be made through all major hotels. All tours leave from outside the Hertie department store in front of the Hauptbahnhof.

Exploring Munich

Germans in other parts of the country sometimes refer to Munich as the nation's "secret capital." This sly compliment may reflect the importance of Munich—it's the number-one tourist destination in Germany, as well as the most attractive major German city—but there's nothing "secret" about the way Münchners make this brave claim. Indeed, the noise with which the people of Munich trumpet the attractions of their city could be dismissed as so much Bavarian bombast were it not for the fact that it is so enthusiastically endorsed by others. Flamboyant, easygoing Munich, city of beer and Baroque, is starkly different from the sometimes stiff Prussian influences to be found in Berlin, the gritty industrial drive of Hamburg, or the hard-headed commercial instincts of high-rise Frankfurt. This is a city to visit for its good-natured and relaxed charm—*Gemütlichkeit*, they call it here—and for its beer halls, its museums, its malls, its parks, and its palaces.

Munich is a crazy mix of high culture (witness its world-class opera house and art galleries) and wild abandon (witness the vulgar frivolity of the Oktoberfest). Its citizenry seems determined to perpetuate the lifestyle of 19th-century king Ludwig I, the Bavarian ruler who brought so much international prestige to his home city after declaring: "I want to make out of Munich a town which does such credit to Germany that nobody knows Germany unless he has seen Munich." He kept his promise with an architectural and artistic renaissance—before abdicating because of a wild romance with a Spanish dancing girl, Lola Montez.

The Historic Heart   *Numbers in the margin correspond to points of interest on the Munich map.*

❶ Begin your tour of Munich at the **Hauptbahnhof,** the main train station and an important orientation point. The city tourist office is here, too, ready with information and maps. Cross the street and you're at the start of a kilometer (½ mile) of pedestrian shopping malls, the first being Schützenstrasse. Facing you are **Hertie,** Munich's leading department store, and

❷ **Karlsplatz** square, known locally as *Stachus*. The huge, domed building on your left is the late-19th-century **Justizpalast** (Palace of Justice). It's one of Germany's finest examples of *Gründerzeit*, the 19th-century versions of Medieval and Renaissance architectural styles.

Head down into the pedestrian underpass—it's another extensive shopping area—to reach the other side and one of the

❸ original city gates, **Karlstor.** The city's two principal shopping streets—**Neuhauserstrasse** and **Kaufingerstrasse**—stretch away from it on the other side. Two of the city's major churches

❹ ❺ are here, too: the **Bürgersaal** and the **Michaelskirche.** The latter is one of the most magnificent Renaissance churches in Germany, a spacious and handsome structure decorated throughout in plain white stucco. It was built for the Jesuits in the late 16th century and is closely modeled on their church of the Gesù in Rome. The intention was to provide a large preaching space, hence the somewhat barnlike atmosphere. Ludwig II is buried here; his tomb is in the crypt. The large neoclassical tomb in the north transept is the resting place of Eugène de Beauharnais, Napoleon's stepson. The highly decorated Rococo interior of the Bürgersaal makes a startling contrast with the simplicity of the Michaelskirche.

6 A block past the Michaelskirche to your left is Munich's late-15th-century cathedral, the **Frauenkirche,** or Church of Our Lady. Towering above it are two onion-shaped domes, symbols of the city (perhaps because they resemble brimming beer mugs, cynics claim). They were added in 1525 after the body of the church had been completed. Step inside and you'll be amazed at the stark simplicity of the church. This is partly the result of the construction that followed the severe bombing in World War II. The crypt houses the tombs of numerous Wittelsbachs, the family that ruled Bavaria for seven centuries until forced to abdicate in 1918. The cathedral is due to reopen for Easter, 1994, after a two-year, $17 million renovation. The celebration will mark the 500th anniversary of the cathedral's consecration.

7 From the Frauenkirche, walk to the **Marienplatz** square, the heart of the city, surrounded by shops, restaurants, and cafés. It takes its name from the 300-year-old gilded statue of the Virgin in the center. When it was taken down to be cleaned in 1960, workmen found a small casket containing a splinter of wood said to have come from the cross of Christ. The square is domi-**8** nated by the 19th-century **Neues Rathaus,** the new town hall, built in the fussy, turreted style so loved by Ludwig II. The **9** **Altes Rathaus,** or old town hall, a medieval building of great charm, sits, as if forgotten, in a corner of the square. At 11 AM and 9 PM daily (plus May–October, 5 PM), the **Glockenspiel,** or chiming clock, in the central tower of the town hall, swings into action. Two tiers of dancing and jousting figures perform their ritual display. It can be worthwhile scheduling your day to catch the clock. Immediately after the war, an American soldier donated some paint to help restore the battered figures and was rewarded with a ride on one of the knight's horses, high above the cheering crowds.

Time Out Duck into the arcades at **Donisl** (Weinstr. 1), on your left as you face the town hall, for the first beer of your Munich visit. This is one of the most authentically Bavarian of the city's beer halls, where the beer flows freely all day—and all night long during the city's *Fasching* (carnival) celebration before Ash Wednesday. You can grab a bite to eat, too.

Heading south down Rosenstrasse to Sendlingerstrasse, you **10** come to the **Asamkirche** on your right. Some consider the Asamkirche a preposterously overdecorated jewel box; others consider it one of Europe's finest late-Baroque churches. One thing is certain: If you have any interest in church architecture, this is a place you shouldn't miss. It was built around 1730 by the Asam brothers—Cosmas Damian and Egid Quirin—next door to their home, the Asamhaus. They dedicated it to St. John Nepomuk, a 14th-century Bohemian monk who was drowned in the Danube. Pause before you go in to see the charming statue of angels carrying him to heaven from the rocky riverbank. Inside, there is a riot of decoration: frescoes, statuary, rich rosy marbles, billowing clouds of stucco, and

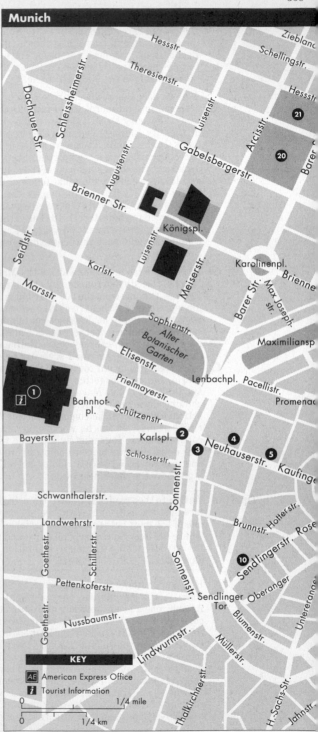

Munich

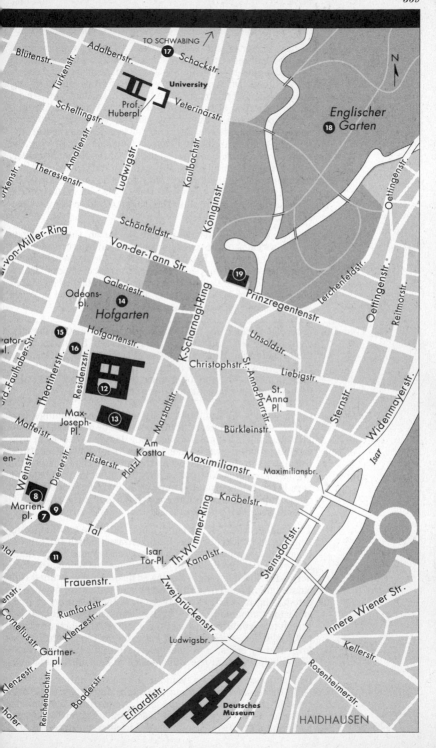

Blütenstr.
Türkenstr.
Adalbertstr.
TO SCHWABING
17 Schackstr.
Schellingstr.
University
Prof.-Huberpl.
Veterinärstr.
Amalienstr.
Theresienstr.
Ludwigstr.
Kaulbachstr.
Königinstr.
Englischer
18 Garten
N

Oettingenstr.

Schönfeldstr.
von-Miller-Ring
Von-der-Tann Str.
19 Prinzregentenstr.
Lerchenfeldstr.
Reitmorstr.
Oettingenstr.

Galeriestr.
Odeons-pl.
14
Hofgarten
K.-Scharnagl-Ring
Unsoldstr.

ator-l.
15 Hofgartenstr.
Christophstr.
St.-Anna-Pfarrstr.
Liebigstr.
Sternstr.
Widenmayerstr.
16
Residenzstr.
d.-Faulhaber-Str.
Theatinerstr.
12
St. Anna Pl.

Max-Joseph-Pl.
13
Marstallstr.
Bürkleinstr.
Isar

Maffeistr.
Dienerstr.
Am Kosttor
Maximilianstr.
Maximiliansbr.
en-
Weinstr.
Pfisterstr.
Platzl
8
Marien-pl.
9
7
Knöbelstr.
Tal
11
Isar Tor-Pl.
Th.-Wimmer-Ring
Kanalstr.
Steinsdorfstr.
Frauenstr.
Zweibrückenstr.
Innere Wiener Str.
enstr.
Rumfordstr.
Corneliusstr.
Klenzestr.
Gärtner-pl.
Ludwigsbr.
Kellerstr.
Klenzestr.
Reichenbachstr.
Baaderstr.
Erhardtstr.
Deutsches Museum
Rosenheimerstr.
HAIDHAUSEN
hofer

gilding everywhere. The decorative elements and the architecture merge to create a sense of seamless movement and color.

⑪ Go back to Marienplatz and turn right for the **Viktualienmarkt,** the food market. Open-air stalls sell cheese, wine, sausages, fruit, and flowers. Fortified with Bavarian sausage and sauer-
⑫ kraut, plunge into local history with a visit to the **Residenz,** home of the Wittelsbachs from the 16th century to their enforced abdication at the end of World War I. From Max-Joseph-Platz you'll enter the great palace, with its glittering Schatzkammer, or treasury, and glorious Rococo theater, designed by court architect François Cuvilliès. Also facing the
⑬ square is the stern neoclassical portico of the **Nationaltheater,** built at the beginning of the 19th century and twice destroyed. *Residenz and Schatzkammer, Max-Joseph-Platz 3. Admission to each: DM 3.50, children free. Open Tues.–Sun. 10–4:30 PM. Cuvilliès Theater admission: DM 2 adults, DM 1 children. Open Mon.–Sat. 2–5, Sun. 10–5.*

⑭ To the north of the Residenz is the **Hofgarten,** the palace gardens. Two sides of the gardens are bordered by sturdy arcades designed by Leo von Klenze, whose work for the Wittelsbachs in the 19th century helped transform the face of the city. Dominating the east side of the Hofgarten is the refurbished copper dome of Bavaria's former Army Museum, destroyed in World War II but now part of a new state chancellery.

Time Out Munich's oldest café, the **Annast,** is located on Odeonsplatz, right by the west entrance to the Hofgarten. Sit at one of the tables under the Hofgarten trees at the back of the café. The Hofgarten was a favorite haunt of Hitler, before and after he came to power—he and his cronies used to frequent the garden tables of another café farther down the street.

Odeonsplatz itself is dominated by two striking buildings. One
⑮ is the **Theatinerkirche,** built for the Theatine monks in the mid-17th century, though its handsome facade, with twin eye-catching domes, was added only in the following century. Despite its Italian influences, the interior, like that of the Michaelskirche, is austerely white. The other notable building
⑯ here is the **Feldherrnhalle,** built by Ludwig I and modeled on the Loggia dei Lanzi in Florence. Next to it is the site of Hitler's unsuccessful *putsch* of 1923, later a key Nazi shrine.

The Feldherrnhalle looks north along one of the most imposing boulevards in Europe, the **Ludwigstrasse,** which in turn becomes the **Leopoldstrasse.** Von Klenze was responsible for much of it, replacing the jumble of old buildings that originally stood here with the clean, high-windowed lines of his restrained Italianate buildings. The state library and the university are lo-
⑰ cated along it, while, halfway up it, is the **Siegestor,** or Arch of Victory, modeled on the Arch of Constantine in Rome. Beyond it is **Schwabing,** once a student and artist quarter but now much glossier, with a mix of bars, discos (*see* Nightlife, *below*), trendy cafés, and boutiques. Nightlife centers around Wedekindplatz, near the Münchener Freiheit subway station.

Back on Leopoldstrasse, wander down to the university, turn on to Professor-Huber-Platz (he was a Munich academic executed by the Nazis for his support of an anti-Hitler movement), and take Veterinärstrasse. It leads you to Munich's largest
⑱ park, the magnificent **Englischer Garten.** You can rent a bike

(tel. 089/397016) at the entrance to the park on summer week-ends (May–Oct). The cost is DM 5 per hour and DM 15 for the day.

The Englischer Garten, 4½ kilometers (3 miles) long and over a ½ kilometer (¼ mile) wide, was laid out by Count Rumford, a refugee from the American War of Independence. He was born in England, but it wasn't his English ancestry that determined the park's name as much as its open, informal nature, a style favored by 18th-century English aristocrats. You can rent boats, visit beer gardens—the most famous is at the foot of a Chinese Pagoda—ride your bike (or ski in winter), or simply stroll around. Ludwig II used to love to wander incognito along the serpentine paths. What would he say today, now that so much of the park has been taken over by Munich's nudists? This is no misprint. Late-20th-century Germans have embraced na-ture worship with almost pagan fervor, and large sections of the park have been designated nudist areas. The biggest is be-hind the **Haus der Kunst,** Munich's leading modern art gallery and a surviving example of Third Reich architecture. The building underwent major renovations in 1992. Part of the basement also houses one of the city's most exclusive discos, the PI. *Haus der Kunst, Prinzregentenstr. 1. Admission: DM 3.50 adults, 50 pf children; Sun. and holidays free. Open Tues.–Sun. 9–4:30, also Thurs. 7 PM–9 PM.*

You'll find more culture in Munich's two leading picture galler-ies, the Alte (meaning "old") and the Neue (meaning "new") Pinakothek. They are located on Barerstrasse, just to the west of the university. The **Alte Pinakothek** is not only the reposito-ry of some of the world's most celebrated Old Master paintings but an architectural treasure in its own right, though much scarred from wartime bomb damage. It was built by von Klenze at the beginning of the 19th century to house Ludwig I's collections. Early Renaissance works, especially by German painters, are the museum's strongest point, but there are some magnificently heroic works by Rubens, too, among much else of outstanding quality. *Barerstr. 27. Admission: DM 6, adults, 50 pf children; free Sun. and holidays. Combined ticket for Alte and Neue Pinakotheks: DM 10. Open Tues.–Sun. 9–4:30; also Tues. and Thurs. 7 PM–9 PM.*

The **Neue Pinakothek** was another of Ludwig I's projects, built to house his "modern" collections, meaning, of course, 19th-century works. The building was destroyed during World War II, and today's museum opened in 1981. The low, brick struc-ture—some have compared it with a Florentine palazzo—is an unparalleled environment in which to see one of the finest col-lections of 19th-century European paintings and sculpture in the world. *Barerstr. 29. Admission: DM 6 adults, 50 pf chil-dren; free Sun. and holidays. Combined ticket for Alte and Neue Pinakotheks: DM 10. Open Tues.–Sun. 9–4:30; also Tues. 7 PM–9 PM. Take the No. 18 streetcar from Karlsplatz for both the Alte and Neue Pinakothek.*

Suburban Attractions There are two trips you can take to attractions just out of the city center. One is to the **Olympic Park,** a 10-minute U-Bahn ride (U3); the other is to Nymphenburg, 6 kilometers (4 miles) northwest and reached by the U1 subway to Rotkreuzplatz, then the No. 12 streetcar.

Perhaps the most controversial buildings in Munich are the circus tent–shaped roofs of the **Olympic Park.** Built for the 1972 Olympics, the park, with its undulating, transparent tile roofs and modern housing blocks, represented a revolutionary marriage of technology and visual daring when first unveiled. Sports fans might like to join the crowds in the Olympic stadium when the local soccer team, Bayern Munich, has a home game. Call 089/30613577 for information and tickets. There's an amazing view of the stadium, the Olympic Park, and the city from the Olympic tower. An elevator speeds you to the top in seconds. *Admission: DM 5 adults; DM 2.50 children; combined tower and park tour (until 5 PM) DM 7 adults, DM 4 children. Open mid-Apr.–mid-Oct., daily 8 AM–midnight; mid-Oct.–mid-Apr., daily 9 AM–midnight.*

Schloss Nymphenburg was the summer palace of the Wittelsbachs. The oldest parts date from 1664, but construction continued for more than 100 years, the bulk of the work being undertaken in the reign of Max Emmanuel between 1680 and 1730. The gardens, a mixture of formal French *parterres* (trim, ankle-high hedges and gravel walks) and English parkland, were landscaped over the same period. The interiors are exceptional, especially the Banqueting Hall, a Rococo masterpiece in green and gold. Make a point of seeing the Schönheits Galerie, the **Gallery of Beauties.** It contains more than 100 portraits of women who had caught the eye of Ludwig I; duchesses rub shoulders with butchers' daughters. Among them is Lola Montez. Seek out the **Amalienburg,** or Hunting Lodge, on the grounds. It was built by Cuvilliès, architect of the Residenz Theater in Munich. That the lodge was designed for hunting of the indoor variety can easily be guessed by the sumptuous silver and blue stucco and the atmosphere of courtly high life. The palace also contains the **Marstallmuseum** (the Museum of Royal Carriages), containing a sleigh that belonged to Ludwig II, among the opulently decorated vehicles, and, on the floor above, the **Nymphenburger Porzellan,** with examples of the porcelain produced here between 1747 and the 1920s. *Schloss Nymphenburg. Admission: Combined ticket to all Nymphenburg attractions: DM 6. Combined ticket to Schloss, Gallery of Beauties, Amalienburg, and Marstallmuseum: DM 4.50. Botanic gardens: DM 1.50. Children under 15 free. Open Apr.–Sept., Tues.–Sun. 9–12:30 and 1:30–5; Oct.–Mar., Tues.–Sun. 10–12:30 and 1:30–4. Amalienburg and gardens open daily.*

Off the Beaten Track

Even though the Olympic Tower is higher, romantics say the best view of Munich and the Alps is from the top of the **Alte Peter** church tower (DM 2 adults, 50 pf children); it's just off Marienplatz. Check that a white disk is hanging on the wall outside the entrance: It means that visibility is good. There are 302 steps to climb to the top. For the most inexpensive sightseeing tour of the center, take a No. 19 streetcar from outside the train station at Bahnhofplatz and ride it to **Wienerplatz,** itself located in Haidhausen, one of Munich's most interesting areas. On a fine day, join the chess players at their open-air boards in Schwabing's **Münchener Freiheit** square. On a rainy day, pack your swimsuit and splash around in the Art Nouveau setting of the **Müllersches Volksbad** pool; it's located on the corner of the Ludwigsbrücke, one of the bridges over the Isar.

Shopping

Gift Ideas Munich is a city of beer, and beer mugs and coasters make an obvious gift to take home. There are many specialist shops in downtown Munich, but **Ludwig Mory,** located in the town hall on Marienplatz, is about the best. Munich is also the home of the famous Nymphenburg porcelain factory; its major outlet is on Odeonsplatz. You can also buy direct from the factory located on the half-moon–shaped road—Schlossrondell—in front of Nymphenburg Palace. *Tel. 089/172439. Salesroom open weekdays 8:30–noon and 12:30–5.*

Shopping Districts From Odeonsplatz you are poised to plunge into the heart of the huge pedestrian mall that runs through the center of town. The first street you come to, **Theatinerstrasse,** is also one of the most expensive. In fact, it has only one serious rival in the money-no-object stakes: **Maximilianstrasse,** the first street to your left as you head down Theatinerstrasse. Both are lined with elegant shops selling desirable German fashions and other high-priced goods from around the world. Leading off to the right of Theatinerstrasse is **Maffeistrasse,** where **Loden-Frey** has Bavaria's most complete collection of traditional wear, from green "loden" coats to Lederhosen. Maffeistrasse runs parallel to Munich's principal shopping streets: **Kaufingerstrasse** and **Neuhauserstrasse,** the one an extension of the other.

Department Stores All the city's major department stores—other than **Hertie** (*see* Exploring, *above*)—are along Maffeistrasse, Kaufingerstrasse, and Neuhauserstrasse. **Kaufhof** and **Karstadt-Oberpollinger** are probably the best. Both have large departments stocking Bavarian arts and crafts, as well as clothing, household goods, jewelry, and other accessories.

Antiques Antique hunters should make for **Blumenstrasse, Ottostrasse, Türkenstrasse,** and **Westenriederstrasse.** Also try the open-air Auer Dult fairs held on Mariahilplatz at the end of April, July, and October (streetcar No. 25).

Dining

Münchners love to eat just as much as they love their beer, and the range of food is as varied and rich as the local breweries' output. Some of Europe's best chefs are to be found here, purveyors of French nouvelle cuisine in some of the most noted—and pricey—restaurants in Germany. But these restaurants are mainly for the gourmet. For those in search of the local cuisine, the path leads to Munich's tried-and-true wood-paneled, flagstone beer restaurants and halls where the food is as sturdy as the large measure of beer that comes to your table almost automatically. Provided your pockets are deep enough, the choice is limitless—from a mountainous roast pork knuckle with dumplings to delicate slivers of salmon and truffle salad. The high-brow restaurants offer a low-key, library-quiet atmosphere, while many of the lower-brow establishments provide ear-splitting conviviality. Try the *Weisswurst* (white veal sausages with herbs), brought to your table in a tureen of boiling water to keep them fresh and hot. They are served with a sweet mustard and pretzels and are a breakfast or midmorning favorite. Equally good is *Leberkäs*, wedges of piping-hot meat loaf with a fried egg on top and pan-fried potatoes.

For details and price-category definitions, *see* Dining in Staying in Germany.

Very Expensive **Aubergine.** German gourmets swear by the upscale nouvelle
★ cuisine of Eckart Witzigmann, chef and owner of this sophisticated restaurant. The decor is a bit loud, incorporating aubergine, white, and silver into the color scheme. If you want a gastronomic experience on the grand scale, try the turbot in champagne or the breast of pigeon with artichoke and truffle salad. The equally exotic wine list includes an 1832 Lafite Rothschild. *Maximilianplatz 5, tel. 089/598171. Reservations required. DC, MC, V. Closed Sun., Mon., all public holidays, and first 3 weeks of Aug.*

Boettner's. This is the oldest of Munich's classy restaurants, in business since 1905. There's a time-honored and quiet quality to its gracious bar and dark, wood-paneled dining room. Fish dominates the menu; in season try *Waller*—a meaty river fish—in a spicy sauce. *Theatinerstr. 2, tel. 089/221210. Reservations required. AE, DC, MC, V. Closed Sat. for dinner, Sun., and holidays.*

Königshof. Located on the second floor of the postwar Königshof Hotel and overlooking the Karlstor at the northern entrance to the pedestrian-only center, the Königshof is without doubt Munich's most opulent restaurant. The neo-baroque style includes ceiling frescoes, subdued chandelier lighting, and heavy drapery. The kitchen offers nouvelle cuisine dishes—breast of goose with truffles, or veal in basil cream and mushroom sauce, for example. *Karlsplatz 25, tel. 089/551360. Reservations advised. AE, DC, MC, V.*

Sabitzer's. Further evidence of upscale Munich's love affair with nouvelle cuisine, though with Bavarian influences, is provided by the fabulous fare at Sabitzer's. Within its elegant gold-and-white 19th-century interior, you'll dine on such specialties as wolffish in sea urchin sauce or salmon lasagne. *Reitmorstr. 21, tel. 089/298584. Reservations required. AE, DC, MC, V. Closed Sun. and Aug.*

Expensive **Hunsinger.** It's worth the 6-kilometer (4-mile) ride out to the southern suburb of Harlaching, near the zoo, to test owner-chef Werner Hunsinger's French-dominated menu. Herb-flavored black noodles with mussels, ray-fish in champagne sauce, or rabbit in red wine are among the offerings in this dark wood-paneled, candlelit setting. *Braunstr. 6, tel. 089/642–2778. Reservations advised. DC, MC, V. Closed Mon. lunch, Sun.*

Käferschanke. Fresh fish, including lobster, crab, salmon, trout, and halibut, is imported daily. Try the grilled prawns in a sweet-sour sauce. The rustic decor, complemented by some fine antique pieces, is a delight. The restaurant is located in the classy Bogenhausen suburb, a 10-minute taxi ride from downtown. *Schumannstr. 1, tel. 089/41681. Reservations advised. AE, DC, MC. Closed Sun. and holidays.*

★ **Le Gourmet.** Imaginative combinations of French and Bavarian specialties have won this small bistro substantial praise from local critics. Try chef Otto Koch's soufflé of sole in lemongrass sauce, or filled marrowbones with *Rösti* (pan-fried potatoes). *Hartmannstr. 8, tel. 089/212–0958. Reservations advised. AE, DC, MC. Closed Sun., Mon., and first 10 days of Jan.*

★ **Preysing Keller.** Devotees of all that's best in modern German food—food that's light and sophisticated but with recognizably Teutonic touches—will love the Preysing Keller, a hotel/restaurant. It's in a 16th-century cellar, though this has been so overrestored that there's practically no sense of its age or original character. Never mind; it's the food, the extensive wine list, and the perfect service that make this place special. *Innere-Wiener-Str. 6, tel. 089/481015. Reservations required. No credit cards. Closed Sun., Christmas, and New Year's Day.*

Moderate **Augustiner Keller.** This 19th-century establishment, renovated from top to bottom in 1992, is the flagship beer restaurant of one of Munich's oldest breweries, Augustiner. The decor emphasizes wood—from the refurbished parquet floors to the wood barrels from which the beer is drawn. This is more the place to meet locals in a communal atmosphere of two baronial hall-like rooms, rather than a venue for a quiet meal for two. The menu changes daily and offers a full range of Bavarian specialties, but try to order *Tellerfleisch*—cold roast beef with lashings of horse radish, served on a big wood board. Follow that with *Dampfnudeln* (suet pudding served with custard) and you won't feel hungry again for 24 hours. *Arnulfstr. 52, tel. 089/594–393. Reservations not necessary. No credit cards.*

Grüne Gans. This small, chummy restaurant near Viktualienmarkt is popular with local entertainers, whose photographs clutter the walls. International fare with regional German influences dominates the menu, although there are a few Chinese dishes. Try the chervil cream soup, followed by calves' kidneys in tarragon sauce. *Am Einlass 5, tel. 089/266228. Reservations required. MC. Closed lunch and Sat.*

Weinhaus Neuner. Originally a seminary, this early 18th-century building houses Munich's oldest surviving wine hostelry, in the Neuner family since 1852. There is a timeless atmosphere in the high-ceilinged dining rooms lined with dark oak paneling. Look for the herb-filled pork fillets with noodles, and veal with Morchela mushroom sauce. *Herzogspitalstr. 8, tel. 089/260–3954. Reservations required. AE, DC, MC, V. Closed Sat. lunch, Sun., and holidays.*

Inexpensive **Alter Hackerhaus.** This upscale beer restaurant on one of
★ Munich's ritziest shopping streets is full of bric-a-brac and mementos that harken back to its origins as a medieval brewery and one-time home of the Hacker family, for whom one of the city's largest breweries is named. Beer has been brewed or served here since 1570. On a cold day, duck into one of the cozy little rooms and choose from the selection of hearty soups, then try a plate of *Käsespätzle* (egg noodles with melted cheese). In the heat of summer, try for a table in the tiny cool inner courtyard, probably the smallest beer garden in Munich. *Sendlingerstr. 75, tel. 089/260–5026. Reservations not necessary. No credit cards.*

Dürnbräu. A fountain plays outside this picturesque old Bavarian inn. Inside, the mood is crowded and noisy. Expect to share a table; your fellow diners will range from businessmen to students. The food is resolutely traditional. Try the cream of spinach soup and the boiled beef. *Dürnbräugasse 2, tel. 089/222195. Reservations advised. AE, DC, MC, V.*

Franziskaner. Vaulted archways, cavernous rooms interspersed with intimate dining areas, bold blue frescoes on the walls, and long wooden tables create a spick-and-span medieval atmosphere. Aside from the late-morning Weisswurst, look out for *Ochsenfleisch* (boiled ox meat) and dumplings. *Perusastr. 5, tel. 089/645548. No reservations. No credit cards.*

Haxnbauer. You can still order meat dishes here—*Bratwurstl* (roast sausages), *Schweinshaxe* (roast pork knuckle)—that have been cooked over an open charcoal fire. And, surprisingly for a Munich beer restaurant, the beer is from a north German brewery! The decor in the series of interlocking rooms is plain, with chunky, dark wood furniture. *Münzstr. 2, tel. 089/221922. Reservations advised. MC, V.*

Hofbräuhaus. The heavy stone vaults of the Hofbräuhaus contain the most famous of the city's beer restaurants. Crowds of singing, shouting, swaying beer drinkers fill the cavernous, smoky hall. Picking their way past the tables are hefty waitresses in traditional garb bearing frothing steins. The menu is strictly solid Bavarian. If you're not here solely to drink, try the more subdued upstairs restaurant, where the service is not so brusque and less beer gets spilled. It's located between Marienplatz and Maximillianstrasse. *Platzl 9, tel. 089/221676. No reservations. No credit cards.*

Hundskugel. This is Munich's oldest tavern, with a history stretching back to 1440. If *Spanferkel*—roast suckling pig—is on the menu, make a point of ordering it. This is simple Bavarian fare at its best. *Hotterstr. 18, tel. 089/264272. Reservations advised. No credit cards. Closed Sun.*

★ **Pfälzer Weinprobierstube.** A warren of stone-vaulted rooms of various sizes, wooden tables, glittering candles, dirndl-clad waitresses, and a vast range of wines add up to an experience as close to your picture of timeless Germany as you're likely to get. The food is reliable rather than spectacular. Local specialties predominate. *Residenzstr. 1, tel. 089/225628. No reservations. No credit cards.*

Zum Brez'n. A hostelry bedecked in the blue-and-white checked colors of the Bavarian flag. The eating and drinking are spread over three floors and cater to a broad clientele—from local business lunchers to hungry night owls emerging from Schwabing's bars looking for a bite at 2 AM. Brez'n offers a big all-day menu of traditional roasts, to be washed down with a choice of three draft beers. *Leopoldstrasse 72, tel. 089/390092. Reservations not necessary. No credit cards.*

Lodging

Make reservations well in advance and be prepared for higher-than-average rates. Though Munich has a vast number of hotels in all price ranges, most are full year-round. If you plan to visit during the "fashion weeks" (Mode Wochen) in March and September or during the Oktoberfest at the end of September, make reservations at least several months in advance. Munich's tourist offices will handle only written or personal requests for reservations assistance. Write to: Fremdenverkehrsamt, Postfach, 8000 Munich 1, fax 089/2391313. Your best bet for finding a room if you haven't reserved is the tourist office at the Hauptbahnhof, by the Bayerstasse entrance. The staff will charge a small fee.

Consider staying in a suburban hotel—where rates are often, but not always, lower—and taking the U-Bahn or S-Bahn into town. A 15-minute train ride is no obstacle to serious sightseeing. Check out the city tourist office "Key to Munich" packages. These include reduced-rate hotel reservations, sightseeing tours, theater visits, and low-cost travel on the U-and S-Bahn. Write to the tourist office (*see* Important Addresses and Numbers in Munich, *above*).

For details and price-category definitions, *see* Lodging in Staying in Germany.

Very Expensive **Bayerischer Hof.** This is one of Munich's most traditional luxury hotels. Public rooms are decorated with antiques, fine paintings, marble, and painted wood. Old-fashioned comfort and class abound in the older rooms; some of the newer rooms are rather functional. *Promenadeplatz 2–6, tel. 089/212–0900, fax 089/212–0906. 440 rooms with bath. Facilities: 3 restaurants, nightclub, rooftop pool, garage, sauna, masseur, hairdresser. AE, DC, MC, V.*

Rafael. A character-laden lodging in the heart of the old town (close to the Hofbräuhaus), the Rafael, which opened in 1989, retains many of the architectural features of its late-19th-century origins, including a sweeping staircase and stuccoed ceilings. Rooms are individually furnished and extravagantly decorated. The hotel restaurant, Mark's, is rapidly making a name for itself with its "new German" cuisine. *Neuturmstr. 1, tel. 089/290–980, fax 089/222–539. 67 rooms with bath. Facilities: restaurant, bar, indoor pool, sauna. AE, DC, MC, V.*

★ **Vier Jahreszeiten.** The Vier Jahreszeiten—it means the Four Seasons—has been playing host to the world's wealthy and titled for more than a century. It has an unbeatable location on Munich's premier shopping street and is only a few minutes' walk from the heart of the city. Elegance and luxury set the tone throughout; many rooms have handsome antique pieces. *Maximilianstr. 17, tel. 089/230390, fax 089/2303–9693. (Reservations in the U.S. from Kempinski International, tel. 800/426–3135). 341 rooms with bath, 25 apartments, presidential suite. Facilities: 3 restaurants, nightclub, rooftop pool, sauna, garage, car rental, Lufthansa check-in desk. AE, DC, MC, V.*

Expensive **Eden Hotel Wolff.** Chandeliers and dark wood paneling in the public rooms underline the old-fashioned elegance of this downtown favorite. It's directly across the street from the train station and the airport bus terminal. The rooms are comfortable, and most are spacious. Dine on excellent Bavarian specialties in the intimate Zirbelstube restaurant. *Arnulfstr. 4, tel. 089/551150, fax 089/5511–5555. 210 rooms with bath. Facilities: restaurant. AE, DC, MC, V.*

Intercity. Despite its proximity to the train station, double-glazing of all the windows ensures peace in this longtime downtown favorite. Try for one of the Bavarian-style rooms; others are plain. There's an excellent restaurant offering good-value Bavarian specialties. *Bahnhofplatz 2, tel. 089/558571, fax 089/545–56610. 208 rooms and 4 apartments with bath. Facilities: restaurant, bar, skittle alley. DC, MC, V.*

Platzl. This is a Bavarian-rustic–style but modern hotel in a building dating to 1573 and located in the heart of Munich's historic quarter—opposite the famous Hofbräuhaus beer hall. In fact, the Platzl is owned by an out-of-town brewery, Ayingerbräu. The rooms are smallish but comfortable. *Sparkassenstr. 10, tel. 089/237030, fax 089/2370–3800 (toll-free booking in the U.S., tel. 800/448–8355). 170 rooms with bath. Facilities: equipped for physically disabled guests, sauna, solarium, fitness rooms, rooftop terrace, restaurant, bar, underground garage. AE, MC, V.*

Regent. This hotel built in 1987 offers first-class facilities, including a notable gourmet restaurant with reasonable prices. It's located in a busy area near the Hauptbahnhof, but all the rooms are soundproof. *Seidlstr. 2, tel. 089/551590, fax 089/551–59154. 172 rooms with bath. Facilities: restaurant, nightclub, bar, sauna, solarium. AE.*

★ **Splendid.** Chandelier-hung public rooms, complete with antiques and Oriental rugs, give the small Splendid something of the atmosphere of a spaciously grand 19th-century hotel. The service is attentive and polished. Have breakfast in the small courtyard in summer. There's no restaurant, but the bar serves snacks as well as drinks. It's close to classy shops and the Isar River. *Maximilianstr. 54, tel. 089/296606, fax 089/291–3176. 37 rooms with bath and 1 suite. Facilities: bar. AE, MC, V.*

Torbräu. This atmospheric lodging, tucked away next to the city's 14th-century eastern gate, the *Isartor* (Tor means gate), is just a few minutes' walk from Marienplatz. Rooms are functional modern rather than luxurious. There's an Italian restaurant and a coffee shop that bakes its own cakes. *Tal 37, tel. 089/225–016, fax 089/225–019. 82 rooms with bath. Facilities: restaurant, coffee shop, bowling alley. AE, MC, V.*

Moderate **Arosa.** This plain, well-worn but friendly lodging in the old town is just a 5-minute walk to Marienplatz. If you're driving, make sure you reserve a spot in the hotel garage; parking in the area is difficult. Munich's oldest pub, the Hundskugel, is right down the street. *Hotterstr. 2, tel. 089/267087, fax 089/263–104. 77 rooms, some with bath. Facilities: restaurant, bar, garage. AE, DC, MC, V.*

Bauer. If the rustic Bavarian style of pinewood, blue-and-white check, and red geraniums appeals to you, you'll feel at home at the Bauer, a 20-minute ride east on the S-6 suburban train, or just a few miles by car along the A94 autobahn. The Bauer gives excellent value and facilities for the price. *Münchnerstr. 6, tel. 089/90980, fax 089/909–8414. 103 rooms with bath. Facilities: restaurant, terrace café, sauna, indoor pool. AE, DC, MC, V.*

Gästehaus am Englischer Garten. Despite the slightly basic rooms, you need to reserve well in advance to be sure of getting one in this converted, 200-year-old watermill. The hotel, complete with ivy-clad walls and shutter-framed windows, stands right on the edge of the Englischer Garten, no more than a five-minute walk from the bars and shops of Schwabing. Be sure to ask for a room in the main building; the modern annex down the road is cheaper but charmless. There's no restaurant, but in summer, breakfast is served on the terrace. *Liebergesellstr. 8, tel. 089/392034. 34 rooms, some with bath. No credit cards.*

★ **Königin Elizabeth.** Housed in a 19th-century neoclassical building, which was completely restored and opened for the first time as a hotel in 1989, the Elizabeth is modern and bright, with an emphasis on pink decor. The restaurant offers Hungarian specialties. The Elizabeth is a 15-minute streetcar ride northwest of the city center en route to Nymphenburg. *Leonrodstr. 79, tel. 089/126860, fax 089/126–86459. 80 rooms with bath. Facilities: bar, beer garden, sauna, solarium, and keep-fit equipment. AE, DC, MC, V.*

Villa Solln. Situated in the suburb of Solln, a 20-minute train ride on the S-7 line from Munich, this small hotel offers visitors some rural Bavarian comforts within the city's limits. Inside there's lots of pinewood and primary colors; outside are gardens. There is no restaurant, but guests can enjoy a buffet breakfast. *Wilhelm-Leibl-str. 16, tel. 089/792–091, fax 089/790–0428. 20 rooms with bath. Facilities: sauna, fitness room, terrace. MC.*

Inexpensive **Am Markt.** Although tucked away in a corner of the colorful Viktualienmarkt in the heart of the old town, this old-fashioned hotel has long ceased to be a secret. Its central location and slightly seedy charm make up for the lack of luxury. It's very popular, so book well in advance. Parking in the area is a problem. *Heiliggeistr. 6, tel. 089/225014. 28 rooms, some with bath. No credit cards.*

★ **Monopteros.** There are few better deals in Munich than this little hotel. It's located just south of the Englischer Garten, with a tram stop for the 10-minute ride to downtown right by the door. The rooms may be basic, but the excellent service, warm welcome, and great location more than compensate. There's no restaurant. *Oettingenstr. 35, tel. 089/292348. 11 rooms, 3 with shower. No credit cards.*

Pension Diana. It's difficult to get closer to central Munich for this price. The Diana, occupying one floor of an 18th-century building attached to a church, is a no-frills, family-run lodging offering a clean bed and breakfast. It's a stone's throw from many historic architectural attractions. *Altheimer Eck 15, tel. 089/260–3107. 11 rooms, none with bath. No credit cards.*

The Arts

Details of concerts and theater performances are available from the *Vorschau* or *Monatsprogramm* booklets obtainable at most hotel reception desks. Some hotels will make ticket reservations; otherwise use one of the ticket agencies in the city center: **Hieber Max,** Liebfrauenstr. 1 (tel. 089/226571) or the **Residenz Bücherstube,** Residenzstr. 1 (concert tickets only, tel. 089/220868). You can also book tickets at the two kiosks on the concourse below Marienplatz.

Concerts Munich's Philharmonic Orchestra entertains in Germany's biggest concert hall, the **Gasteig Cultural Center.** Tickets can be bought directly at the box office (the Gasteig center is on Rosenheimerstrasse, on a hill above the Ludwigsbrücke Bridge). The Bavarian Radio Orchestra performs Sunday concerts here. In summer, concerts are held at two Munich palaces, **Nymphenburg** and **Schleissheim,** and in the open-air interior courtyard of the **Residenz.**

Opera Munich's **Bavarian State Opera** company is world-famous, and tickets for major productions in its permanent home, the State Opera House, are difficult to obtain. Book far in advance for the annual opera festival held in July and August; contact the tourist office for the schedule of performances and ticket prices. The opera house box office (Maximilianstr. 11, tel. 089/221316) takes reservations one week in advance only. It's open weekdays 10:30–1 and 3:30–5:30, Saturday 10–12:30.

Dance The ballet company of the Bavarian State Opera performs at the **State Opera House.** Ballet productions are also staged at the attractive late-19th-century **Gärtnerplatz Theater** (tel. 089/201–6767).

Film Munich hosts an annual film festival each June. English-language films are shown regularly at the Europa film theater in the **Atlantik Palast** (Schwantalerstr. 2–6), **Cinema** (Nymphenburgerstr. 31), the **Film Museum** (St. Jakobs Platz), and the **Museum Lichtspiele** (Ludwigsbrücke).

Theater There are two state theater companies, one of which concentrates on the classics. More than 20 other theater companies (some of them performing in basements) are to be found throughout the city. An English-speaking company called the **Company** (tel. 089/343827) presents four productions a year.

Nightlife

Bars, Cabaret, Nightclubs Although it lacks the racy reputation of Hamburg, Munich has something for just about all tastes. For spicy striptease, explore the train station district (Schillerstrasse, for example) or the Hofbräuhaus neighborhood, perhaps along Maderbräustrasse.

Jazz The best jazz can be heard at the **Allotria** (Oscar-von-Miller Ring 3), the **Unterfahrt** (Kirchenstr. 96), and the **Podium** (Wagnerstr. 1). Or try **Jenny's Place in the Blue Note** (Moosacherstr. 24, tel. 089/351–0520), named for an English singer who settled in Munich.

Discos Disco bars abound in the side streets off Freilitzschstrasse surrounding Münchener Freiheit in Schwabing, especially on Occamstrasse. More upscale are **Nachtcafe** (Maximiliansplatz 5), open all night on weekends, and **P1** (adjoining the Haus der Kunst, Prinzregentenstr. 1). **Nachtwerk** (Landsbergerstr. 185) has everything from punk to avant garde, plus live bands.

For Singles Every Munich bar is singles territory. Three you might like to try are **Schumann's** (Maximilianstr. 36) anytime after the curtain comes down at the nearby opera house; **Alter Simpl** (Türkenstr. 57) but not before midnight; and **Harry's New York Bar** (Falkenturmstr. 9), which offers an escape from the German bar scene *and* serves genuine Irish Guinness. For the student, beards, and pipe scene, try **Bunte Vogel** in Schwabing (Herzogstr. 44), which also features an unusual collection of table lamps.

Frankfurt

Arriving and Departing

By Plane Frankfurt airport, the busiest in mainland Europe, is about 10 kilometers (6 miles) southwest of the city.

Between the Airport and Downtown There are several ways to get into town. Two suburban (S-Bahn) lines connect the airport and the center. The S-14 runs between the Hauptwache station and the airport, and the S-15 from the main train station, the Hauptbahnhof. The S-14 runs every 20 minutes and takes 15 minutes; the S-15 leaves every 10 minutes and takes 11 minutes. The trip costs DM 3.70 (DM 4.60 in rush hour, 6:30–8:30 AM and 4–6:30 PM. InterCity and InterCityExpress (ICE) trains also stop at Frankfurt airport train station on hourly direct runs to Cologne, Dortmund, Hamburg, and Munich. A No. 61 bus runs from the airport to the Südbahnhof station in Sachsenhausen, where there is access to the U-Bahn (subway) lines U-1 and U-3; the fare is DM 3.70 (DM 4.60 during rush hours). Taxi fare from the airport to downtown is about DM

35. By rented car, follow the signs to Frankfurt ("Stadtmitte") via the B-43 main road.

By Train Frankfurt's main train station, the Hauptbahnhof, and the airport station are directly linked with all parts of the country by fast Euro-City and InterCity services and by the high-speed InterCityExpress (ICE) trains. For train information, tel. 069/19419. For tickets and general information, go directly to the station or to the DER travel office at the Hauptbahnhof.

By Bus Long-distance buses connect Frankfurt with more than 200 European cities. Buses leave from the south side of the Hauptbahnhof. Tickets and information are available from **Deutsche Touring GmbH** (Am Römerhof 17, tel. 069/7903219).

By Car From the north, leave autobahn A5 at the Nordwestkreuz, join A66 and follow it to its end, in the Nordend district. From the east, A66 brings you into Enkheim, from where you follow the signs to the downtown area, the "Stadtmitte." From the west, leave autobahn A3 at the Frankfurt-south ("Frankfurt-Süd") exit and enter the city on B43/44. From the south, leave the autobahn at the Offenbach exit (the "Anschluss-stelle Offenbach") and enter the city on B459.

Getting Around

By Public Transportation A combination of subway and suburban train, streetcar, and bus services provides speedy transportation. Tickets cover travel on the complete network, which is divided into tariff zones. A single ticket for travel within the city costs DM 1.80 (DM 2.40 during rush hour). A multi-journey strip ticket costs DM 9. Each trip you make is paid for when you cancel a strip in the automatic machines found on buses, streetcars, and subways. A day ticket (for use during one calendar day) offers unlimited journeys in the inner zone for DM 5. Buy all tickets at newspaper kiosks or from blue automatic dispensing machines. For further information or assistance, call 069/269463.

By Taxi Taxi meters start at DM 3.60, and the fare is DM 1.80 per kilometer (about DM 2.90 per mile), or DM 2.35 on weekends. Count on paying DM 10 to DM 12 for a short city ride. Taxi drivers charge 50 pf for each piece of luggage carried. To order a taxi, call 069/250001 or 069/545011.

Important Addresses and Numbers

Tourist Information There are three city information offices. One is at the Hauptbahnhof, across from platform 23 (tel. 069/212–8849). It's open Monday–Saturday 8 AM–10 PM (November–March until 9 PM), Sunday and holidays 9:30 AM–8 PM. The other is in the town hall in the old town at Römerberg 27 (tel. 069/21238708). It's open weekdays 9AM–7PM, weekends and holidays 9:30AM–6PM. Both offices will help you find accommodations. A third information office (tel. 069/690–6211) is in the airport Arrival Hall B, daily 8 AM–9 PM. The DER Deutsches Reisebüro, Arrival Hall B6, can also help you find rooms. Open daily 8 AM–9 PM (tel. 069/693071). For information in advance of your trip, contact the **Verkehrsamt Frankfurt/Main** (Kaiserstrasse 52, 6000 Frankfurt, tel. 069/212–38800).

Consulates U.S. (Seismayerstrasse 21, tel. 069/75350). U.K. (Bockenheimer Landstrasse 42, tel. 069/170–0020).

Emergencies **Police** (tel. 110). **Doctor or Ambulance** (tel. 069/112). **Dentist** (tel. 069/660–7271). **Pharmacy Information** (tel. 069/11500).

English-Language **British Bookshop** (Börsenstrasse 17, tel. 069/280492). **Ameri-** Bookstores **can Book Center** (Jahnstrasse 36, tel. 069/552816).

Travel Agencies **American Express** (Kaiserstr. 8, tel. 069/210548). **DER Deutsches Reisebüro** (Emil-von-Behring Strasse 6, tel. 069/9588360).

Guided Tours

Orientation Tours From March through October, there are two daily bus tours of the city, including visits to Goethe's House and the Europa Tower for a view over Frankfurt; they depart at 10:15 AM and 2:15 PM from outside the tourist information office at the main train station, and at 10 AM and 2 PM from the Römer tourist office. The tour lasts about two and a half hours and costs DM 28 (children up to 16, half price). From November through February, there is only one daily tour, 10 AM from the Römer and 10:15 AM from the train station. These tours last about three and a half hours and cost DM 28 (children DM 14). On weekend afternoons, a gaily painted old streetcar, "The Ebbelwei Express," trundles around the city and Sachsenhausen, on the south side of the Main. The 40-minute ride—starting and ending at the Ostbahnhof train station, at Danzigerplatz in Frankfurt's Ostend district—includes a glass of apple cider (*Ebbelwei*) and a pretzel in the DM 3 fare. Further information and tickets can be obtained from the tourist offices (*see* Important Addresses and Numbers, *above*). Visitors who like to go at their own pace can buy a cassette in English for DM 12 from the tourist office at the Römer. The tape describes a one-hour walking tour. You can also rent a portable cassette player there.

Excursions Bus tours of the surrounding countryside, as far as the Rhine, are offered by **Noblesse Limousine Service** (tel. 06101/12055) in Bad Vilbel; the **Deutsche Touring GmbH** (Am Römerhof 17, tel. 069/7903219); and (on summer Sundays only) by the **Frankfurt tourist office**. One-day excursions are also offered by German Railways, the Deutsche Bundesbahn. These are described in a brochure, *"Der Schöne Tag,"* obtainable from the main train station and the DER tourist office. A "Casino-Express" bus service runs daily from Frankfurt (departing from Baselerplatz) to the casino at Bad Homburg in the Taunus Mountains. The DM 9.50 fare includes the entrance charge to the casino. The bus departs hourly, from 2:15 to 11:15 PM. Pleasure boats of the **Primus Line** cruise the Main and Rhine rivers from Frankfurt, sailing as far as the Lorelei and back in a day. For schedules and reservations, contact **Frankfurter Personenschiffahrt** (Mainkai 36, tel. 069/281884).

Exploring Frankfurt

Numbers in the margin correspond to points of interest on the Frankfurt map.

At first glance, Frankfurt-am-Main doesn't seem to have much to offer the tourist. Virtually flattened by bombs during the war, it now bristles with skyscrapers, the visible sign of the city's role as Germany's financial capital. Yet the inquisitive and discerning visitor will find many remnants of Frankfurt's illustrious past (besides being well placed for excursions to other historic cities, such as Heidelberg and Würzburg, and within easy reach of the Rhine).

Originally a Roman settlement, Frankfurt was later one of Charlemagne's two capitals (the other being Aachen). Still later, it was for centuries the site of the election and coronation of the emperors of that unwieldly entity, the Holy Roman Empire, which was the forerunner of a united Germany. It was also the birthplace of the poet and dramatist Goethe (1749–1832). The house in which he was born is one of many restored and reconstructed old buildings that inject a flavor of bygone days into the center of this busy modern city.

Although the true center of Frankfurt is its ancient **Römerberg Square,** where the election of Holy Roman emperors was traditionally proclaimed and celebrated, this tour of the city begins ➊ slightly to the north, at the **Hauptwache,** an 18th-century guardhouse that today serves a more peaceful purpose as a café. The lower ground floor houses Interpress, an information office that assists young visitors, including finding moderately priced accommodations. *Open weekdays 10–6, Sat. 10–1.*

➋ Head south along Kornmarkt, passing on the left the **Katerinenkirche** (Church of St. Catherine), the historic center of Frankfurt Protestantism, in whose 17th-century font Goethe was baptized. After crossing Berlinerstrasse, and still heading ➌ south, you'll pass the **Paulskirche** (Church of St. Paul). It was here that the first all-German parliament convened in 1848, and the church is therefore an important symbol of German unity and democracy. Continue down Buchgasse and within a few minutes you're on the north bank of the river **Main.** Turn left toward the great iron bridge known as the **Eiserner Steg** and at the **Rententurm,** one of the city's medieval gates, bear left ➍ again and you'll arrive at the spacious **Römerberg,** center of Frankfurt civic life over the centuries. In the center of the square stands the 16th-century **Fountain of Justitia** (Justice): At the coronation of Emperor Matthias in 1612, wine instead of water spouted from the stonework. The crush of people was so great, however, that the Germans have not repeated the trick since.

➎ Compared with many city halls, Frankfurt's **Römer** is a modest affair, with a gabled Gothic facade. It occupies most of one side of the square and is actually three patrician houses (the Alt-Limpurg, the Römer—from which it takes its name—and the Löwenstein). The mercantile-minded Frankfurt burghers used the complex not only for political and ceremonial purposes, but for trade fairs and commerce. The most important events to take place in the Römer, however, were the elections of the Holy Roman emperors. The **Kaisersaal** (Imperial Hall) was last used in 1792 to celebrate the election of Emperor Francis II, who was later forced to abdicate by arch-egomaniac Napoleon Bonaparte. (A 16-year-old Goethe smuggled himself into the banquet celebrating the coronation of Emperor Joseph II in 1765 by posing as a waiter.) Today, visitors can see the impressive full-length 19th-century portraits of the 52 emperors of the Holy Roman Empire that line the walls of the banqueting hall. *Admission: free. Open Mon.–Sat. 9–6, Sun. 10–4. Closed during official functions.*

Charlemagne's son, Ludwig the Pious, established a church on the present site of the Römerberg in AD 850. His church was

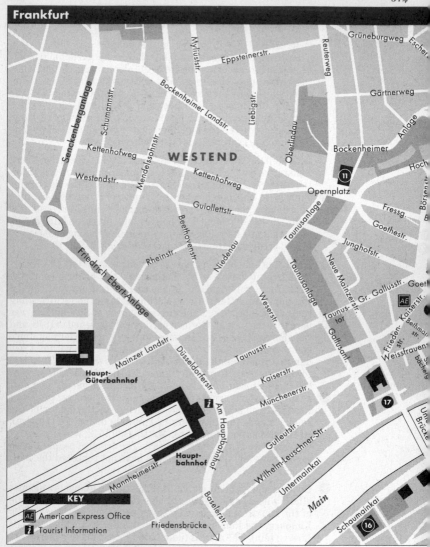

Frankfurt

(map labels)

Grüneburgweg — Escher
Reuterweg
Myliusstr.
Eppsteinerstr.
Bockenheimer Landstr.
Gärtnerweg
Schumannstr.
Liebigstr.
Kettenhofweg
Mendelssohnstr.
WESTEND
Oberlindau
Bockenheimer
Anlage
Senckenberganlage
Westendstr.
Kettenhofweg
11
Opernplatz
Hoch
Börsenstr.
Guiollettstr.
Fressg.
Taunusanlage
Goethestr.
Beethovenstr.
Niedenau
Junghofstr.
Rheinstr.
Taunusanlage
Neue Mainzer Str.
Gr. Gallusstr. — Goeth
Friedrich Ebert-Anlage
Weserstr.
Taunus-tor
AE
Frieden — Kaiserstr.
Beethmar-str.
Weissfrauen
bäckerg.
Mainzer Landstr.
Düsseldorferstr.
Taunusstr.
Kaiserstr.
Gallusanl.
Haupt-Güterbahnhof
i
Münchenerstr.
17
Am Hauptbahnhof
Haupt-bahnhof
Gutleutstr.
Umin-Brücke
Wilhelm-Leuschner-Str.
Mannheimerstr.
Untermainkai
Baselerstr.
Main

KEY

AE American Express Office

i Tourist Information

Friedensbrücke →

Schaumainkai
16

Alte Brücke, **14**
Alte Oper, **11**
Börse, **12**
Goethehaus und Goethemuseum, **10**
Hauptwache, **1**
Jewish Museum, **17**
Kaiserdom, **6**

Karmeliterkirche, **9**
Katerinenkirche, **2**
Kuhhirtenturm, **15**
Leonhardskirche, **8**
Museum of Modern Art, **13**
Nikolaikirche, **7**
Paulskirche, **3**
Römer, **5**
Römerberg, **4**
Städelsches Kunstinstitut und Städtische Galerie, **16**

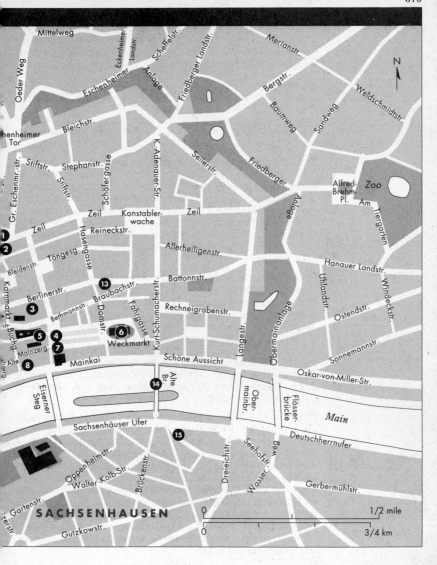

Mittelweg

Oeder Weg

Eckenheimer Landstr.

Scheffelstr.

Friedberger Landstr.

Merianstr.

Eschenheimer Landstr.

Anlage

Bergstr.

Weldschmidtstr.

Bleichstr.

Baumweg

Sandweg

henheimer Tor

Gr. Eschenm.-Str.

Stiftstr.

Stephanstr.

Schäfergasse

K.-Adenauer-Str.

Seilerstr.

Friedberger

Anlage

Alfred-Brehm-Pl.

Zoo

Am Tiergarten

Stiftstr.

Zeil

Konstabler-wache

Zeil

Zeil

Reineckstr.

Hasengasse

Bleidenstr.

Töngesg.

Allerheiligenstr.

Hanauer Landstr.

Kornmarkt

Buchg.

Berlinerstr.

Braubachstr.

Domstr.

Battonnstr.

Kurt-Schumacherstr.

Uhlandstr.

Ostendstr.

Windeckstr.

13

Bethmannstr.

Fahrgasse

Rechneigrabenstr.

3

5 **4**

6

7

Weckmarkt

Schöne Aussicht

Langestr.

Obermainanlage

Sonnemannstr.

8

Mainzerg.

Mainkai

Oskar-von-Miller-Str.

Alte

Eiserner Steg

14

Alte Br.

Obermainbr.

Flösser-brücke

Main

Sachsenhäuser Ufer

Deutschherrnufer

15

Oppenheimstr.

Brückenstr.

Dreieichstr.

Seehofstr.

Wasserweg

Gerbermühlstr.

Walter Kolb-Str.

SACHSENHAUSEN

Gartenstr.

Gutzkowstr.

0

0

1/2 mile

3/4 km

N

(6) replaced by a much grander Gothic structure, one used for imperial coronations; it became known as the **Kaiserdom,** the Imperial Cathedral. The cathedral suffered only superficial damage during World War II, and it still contains most of its original treasures, including a fine 15th-century altar.

(7) On the south side of the square stands the 13th-century **Nikolaikirche** (St. Nicholas's Church). It's worth trying to time your visit to the square to coincide with the chimes of the glockenspiel carillon, which ring out three times a day. *Carillon chimes daily at 9, noon, and 5. Nikolaikirche open Mon–Sat. 10–5.*

(8) From the Römerberg, stroll south toward the river, but turn right this time, past the riverside **Leonhardskirche** (St. Leonhard's Church), which has a fine 13th-century porch and a beautifully carved circa 1500 Bavarian altar, then into the nar-
(9) row Karmelitergasse to the **Karmeliterkirche** (Carmelite Church and Monastery). Within its quiet cloisters is the largest religious fresco north of the Alps, a 16th-century representation of the birth and death of Christ. *Admission free. Cloisters open weekdays 8–4.*

(10) From here, it's only a short way to the **Goethehaus und Goethemuseum** (Goethe's House and Museum). It was here that the poet was born in 1749, and though the house was destroyed by Allied bombing, it has been carefully restored and is furnished with pieces from Goethe's time, some belonging to his family. The adjoining museum contains a permanent collection of manuscripts, paintings, and memorabilia documenting the life and times of Germany's most outstanding poet. *Grosser Hirschgraben 23, tel. 069/282824. Admission: DM 3 adults, DM 2 children. Open Apr.–Sept., Mon.–Sat. 9–6, Sun. 10–1; Oct.–Mar., Mon.–Sat. 9–4, Sun. 10–1.*

From the Goethehaus, retrace your steps to the Hauptwache via Rossmarkt. From there, take a window-shopping stroll past the elegant boutiques of Goethestrasse, which ends at Opernplatz and Frankfurt's reconstructed opera house, the
(11) **Alte Oper.** Wealthy Frankfurt businessmen gave generously for the construction of the opera house during the 1870s (provided they were given priority for the best seats), and Kaiser Wilhelm I traveled from Berlin for the gala opening in 1880. Bombed in 1944, the opera house remained in ruins for many years while controversy raged over its reconstruction. The new building, in the classical proportions and style of the original, was finally opened in 1981.

If you have a camera, position yourself between the arches of the opera house entrance and frame a striking shot of the skyscrapers of Frankfurt's financial world, which rise in stark contrast before you. Cross busy Opernplatz, head down Grosse Bockenheimer Strasse (known locally as Fressgasse—literally "Food Street"—because of its abundance of gourmet shops and restaurants), turn left into Börsenstrasse, and you'll hit the center of the financial district. Just around the corner from
(12) Fressgasse is the Frankfurt **Börse,** Germany's leading stock exchange and financial powerhouse. It was founded by Frankfurt merchants in 1558 to establish some order in their often chaotic dealings. Today's dealings can also be quite hectic; see for yourself by slipping into the visitors' gallery. *Admission free. Gallery open weekdays 10 AM–1 PM.*

From the Börse, turn right into Schillerstrasse, and within two minutes you're back at the Hauptwache. Here begins Frankfurt's main shopping street, the **Zeil,** which claims the highest turnover per square yard of stores in all Germany. Resist if you can the temptations that shriek from the shop windows on both sides of this crowded pedestrian zone and head eastward to the nearby point where it is crossed by Hasengasse. Turn right into Hasengasse and you'll see the striking wedge form of Frankfurt's newest museum rising straight ahead of you. The
❸ **Museum of Modern Art** opened in June 1991 and contains an important collection of works by such artists as Siah Armajani, Joseph Beuys, Walter de Maria, and Andy Warhol. *Domstr. 10, tel. 069/21238819. Admission free. Open Tues.–Sun. 10–5, Wed. 10–8.*

Across the Main lies the district of **Sachsenhausen.** It's said that Charlemagne arrived here with a group of Saxon families during the 8th century and formed a settlement on the banks of the Main. It was an important bridgehead for the crusader Knights of the Teutonic Order and, in 1318, officially became
❹ part of Frankfurt. Cross to Sachsenhausen over the **Alte Brücke.** Along the bank to your left you'll see the 15th-century
❺ **Kuhhirtenturm,** the only remaining part of Sachsenhausen's original fortifications. The composer Paul Hindemith lived and worked in the tower from 1923 to 1927.

The district still has a medieval air, with narrow back alleys and quiet squares that have escaped the destructive tread of the city developer. Here you'll find Frankfurt's famous *Ebbelwei* taverns. Look for a green pine wreath over the entrance to tell passersby that a freshly pressed—and alcoholic—apple wine or cider is on tap. You can eat well in these little inns, too.

Time Out The main street in Sachsenhausen, **Neuer Wall,** is lined with atmospheric old taverns offering home-brewed apple wine and solid local fare. A favorite is Dauth-Schneider (Neuer Wall 7, closed Mon. in winter).

No fewer than seven top-ranking museums line the Sachsenhausen side of the Main, on **Schaumainkai** (locally known as the **Museumsufer** or Museum Bank). These range from exhibitions of art and architecture to the German Film Museum. The
❻ **Städelsches Kunstinstitut und Städtische Galerie** (Städel Art Institute and Municipal Gallery) has one of the most significant art collections in Germany, with fine examples of Flemish, German, and Italian Old Masters, plus a sprinkling of French Impressionists. *Schaumainkai 63. Admission: DM 6 adults, children free; free on Sun., after 4 PM on Wed., and public holidays. Open Tues.–Sun. 10–5, Wed. until 8.*

Across the river from this impressive lineup of museums is
❼ Frankfurt's **Jewish Museum** (cross the Untermain Bridge to reach it). The fine city mansion houses a permanent exhibit tracing the history of Frankfurt's Jewish community; its library is Germany's main registry for Jewish history. *Untermainkai 14–15, tel. 069/21235000. Admission free. Open Tues. and Thurs.–Sun. 10–5, Wed. 10–8.*

Dining

Several Frankfurt restaurants close for the school summer vacation break, a six-week period that falls between mid-June and mid-September. Always check to avoid disappointment.

For details and price-category definitions, *see* Dining in Staying in Germany.

Expensive
★ **Bistrot 77.** Mainly Alsatian specialties are served at this bright, light, and cheerful French restaurant in Sachsenhausen. *Ziegelhüttenweg 1–3, tel. 069/614040. Reservations accepted. AE, DC, MC, V. Closed Sat. lunch, Sun., and mid-June–mid-July.*

Humperdinck. The nouvelle dishes of chef Willi Tetz depend on what he finds in the market each morning; everything, from salads to soup, is of guaranteed freshness. Engelbert Humperdinck—the 19th-century composer (*Hänsel und Gretel*)—used to live and work in the Grüneburg house it occupies. *Grüneburgweg 95, tel. 069/722122. Reservations advised. AE, DC, MC, V. Closed Sat. lunch, Sun., and summer school vacation.*

Le Midi. When one Frankfurt restaurant critic gave up writing about food and took to preparing it instead, the result was this superior French restaurant, the scene of a monthly gathering of leading experts in the restaurant trade. *Liebigstr. 47, tel. 069/721438. Reservations advised. AE, DC, MC, V. Closed Sun. lunch and Sat.*

Weinhaus Brückenkeller. *Keller* is German for "cellar," and that's where the Brückenkeller is situated. The ancient vaulted interior (the restaurant has been in business since 1652) is set off by carefully selected antiques. The wine-list choice of 180 different labels is supported by an extraordinary stock of 85,000 bottles. Ask for a look at the wine cellar—and ask, too, for *Tafelspitz* (a version of pot roast) with *grüner* sauce. *Schützenstr. 6, tel. 069/284238. Reservations advised. AE, DC, MC, V. Dinner only. Closed Sun.*

Moderate
Börsenkeller. Solid Germanic food, with just a hint of French style, is served here to fortify the business community from the nearby stock exchange (*Börse* means "money market"). Steaks are a specialty. *Schillerstr. 11, tel. 069/281115. Reservations accepted. AE, DC, MC, V. Closed Sat. dinner and Sun.*

Casa Nova. The inviting exterior is fully matched by the cozy interior of this superior Italian restaurant, in an attractive Sachsenhausen house. Fish is prepared with imagination and skill, and if the pasta proves too plentiful, half-portions are willingly served. *Stresemannallee 38, tel. 069/632473. Weekend reservations required. MC. Closed Sat. and 2 weeks in Aug.*

Zur Müllerin. The *müllerin* (miller's wife) is Lieselotte Müller, who has been running this restaurant for 35 years. Her regulars are artists and actors from the nearby theaters; you'll find expressions of appreciation for the cooking skills of their beloved müllerin decorating the restaurant walls. *Weissfrauenstr. 18, tel. 069/285182. Reservations not necessary. No credit cards. Closed for lunch on Sat. and Sun.*

Inexpensive
Café GegenwART. The accent really is on art at this friendly, bustling café-restaurant. Art can be found both on the walls and in the cooking; exhibitions change as regularly as the menu. In summer, the tables spill out onto the sidewalk. Do try the freshly caught angler fish or tomato fondue if they are avail-

able. *Berger Str. 6, tel. 069/4970544. Reservations not necessary. MC.*

Knoblauch. Knoblauch is German for "garlic," and that's the staple of many of the imaginative dishes served in this fashionable Frankfurt haunt. The oysters in garlic sauce have made the place famous. The clientele is young and arty, drawn not only by the menu that changes daily but by the vernissages that take place regularly in the small art gallery on the premises. *Staufenstr. 39, tel. 069/722828. Reservations not necessary. MC.*

★ **Zum Gemalten Haus.** This is the real thing, a traditional wine tavern in the heart of Sachsenhausen. Its name means "At the Painted House," a reference to the frescoes that cover the place inside and out. In the summer and on fine spring and autumn days, the courtyard is the place to be (the inner rooms can get a bit crowded). But if you can't at first find a place at one of the bench-lined long tables, order an apple cider and hang around until someone leaves: It's worth the wait. *Schweizerstr. 67, tel. 069/614559. Reservations not necessary. No credit cards. Closed Mon. and Tues.*

Zum Schwarzen Stern. This is a colorful beer restaurant in the heart of the historic quarter. Schnitzel with mushrooms in cream sauce or roast hare in red wine are two examples of the solid and tasty local menu, washed down with good beer. It's a favorite haunt of newlyweds who come out of the Registry Office opposite. *Römerberg 6, tel. 069/281979. Reservations not necessary. No credit cards. Open daily but closed 3–6 PM.*

Lodging

For details and price-category definitions, *see* Lodging in Staying in Germany.

Very Expensive **Gravenbruch Kempinski.** This spacious, elegant hotel retains
★ the atmosphere of the manor house that once stood on its parkland site in leafy Neu Isenburg (a 15-minute drive south of Frankfurt). Some of its luxuriously appointed rooms and suites are arranged as duplex penthouse apartments. Make sure you get a room overlooking the lake. *6078 Neu Isenburg 2, tel. 06102/5050, fax 06102/505445. 317 rooms with bath. Facilities: restaurant, indoor and outdoor pools, tennis courts, health spa, hairdresser, Lufthansa check-in service, limo service to airport and city (both 15 minutes away). AE, DC, MC, V.*

Hessischer Hof. This former palace is still owned by a prince of Hesse, and fine antiques are deftly positioned in many guest rooms. A daily supply of fresh fruit delivered to all rooms is part of the outstanding service. One of the two bars, Jimmy's, numbers among Frankfurt's best, and the hotel restaurant is highly prized both for its gourmet cuisine and its refined ambience. *Friedrich-Ebert-Anlage 40, tel. 069/75400, fax 069/7540924. 120 rooms with bath. Facilities: restaurant, 2 bars, garage. AE, DC, MC, V.*

★ **Steigenberger Hotel Frankfurter Hof.** The Frankfurter Hof is one of the city's oldest established hotels, in the Victorian grand style. The German kaiser once slept here. *Am Kaiserplatz 17, tel. 069/21502, fax 069/215900. 359 rooms with bath. Facilities: 2 restaurants, café, 2 bars. AE, DC, MC, V.*

Expensive **An der Messe.** This place—the name means "at the fairgrounds"—is a small but stylish hotel with chicly appointed rooms. Comfort and attentive service push this venue into the quality class, despite the absence of a restaurant. *Westendstr. 104, tel. 069/747979, fax 069/748349. 46 rooms with bath. Facilities: garage. AE, DC, MC, V.*

Dorint Hotel. A palm-fringed, rooftop pool beckons after a day of touring downtown Frankfurt, which is a short walk across the river from this stylish member of the Dorint group. The hotel has all the comfort and facilities expected from this respected hotel chain. *Hahnstr. 9, tel. 069/663060, fax 069/66306600. 183 rooms with bath, 8 suites. Facilities: restaurant, 2 bars, indoor pool, sauna, parking. AE, DC, MC, V.*

Palmenhof. The city's west end houses this modernized turn-of-the-century hotel. In the basement is a cozy restaurant, the Bastei, which has an expensive nouvelle menu. *Bockenheimer Landstr. 89–91, tel. 069/753–0060, fax 069/75300666. 50 rooms with bath, plus 35 apartments. Facilities: restaurant, garage. AE, DC, MC, V.*

Moderate **Arcade.** This modern hotel is situated on the north bank of the Main river, just five minutes' walk from the train station. The rooms are furnished basically, though all have TV, and two are specially equipped for disabled guests. *Speicherstr. 3–5, tel. 069/273030, fax 069/237024. 200 rooms with bath. Facilities: restaurant, bar. AE, DC, MC, V.*

★ **Maingau.** This excellent-value hotel is in the city's Sachsenhausen district, within easy reach of the downtown area and just a stone's throw from the lively Altstadt quarter, with its cheery apple-cider taverns. The rooms are spartanly furnished, though clean and comfortable, and all have TV. *Schifferstr. 38–40, tel. 069/617001, fax 069/620790. 100 rooms with bath. Facilities: restaurant, garage. AE, MC.*

Neue Kräme. This small, friendly hotel is located on a quiet pedestrians-only street right in the downtown area. The rooms are basic, but all have TV and minibar. There's no restaurant, but drinks and snacks are available. *Neue Kräme 23, tel. 069/284046, fax 069/296288. 21 rooms with bath. AE, DC, MC, V.*

Inexpensive **Am Zoo.** This hotel provides modest but comfortable accommodations in Frankfurt's east end and, as the name suggests, is near the city's famous big zoo. *Alfred-Brehm-Platz 6, tel. 069/490771, fax 069/439868. 85 rooms with bath. Facilities: restaurant. AE, DC, MC, V. Closed Christmas.*

Hotel-Schiff *Peter Schlott.* Watch your step when returning to this unusual hotel after a night out in Frankfurt—it's a "hotel ship," moored on the River Main in the suburb of Höchst, a 15-minute train or tram ride from the city center. Guest cabins are predictably on the small side, but the marvelous river views more than compensate. *Mainberg, tel. 069/315480, fax 069/3004680. 19 rooms, about half with shower. Facilities: restaurant, parking. MC.*

Waldhotel "Hensel's Felsenkeller." Helmut Braun's traditional old hotel has the woods that ring Frankfurt as its backyard, yet the city center is just a 15-minute tram ride away (the nearest stop is a three-minute walk away from the hotel). Rooms are quite basic, but there are plans to modernize them to add more comfort. *Buchrainerstr. 95, tel. 069/652086, fax 069/658371. 14 rooms, 7 with bath. Facilities: restaurant, parking. MC.*

Hamburg

Arriving and Departing

By Plane Hamburg's international airport, Fuhlsbüttel, is 11 kilometers (7 miles) northwest of the city. Lufthansa flights connect Hamburg with all other major German cities and European capitals.

Between the Airport and Downtown A bus service between Hamburg's central bus station and the airport (stopping also at the hotels Atlantic and Plaza and the Schauspielhaus Theater) operates daily at 20-minute intervals between 5:15 AM and 9:30 PM. The first bus leaves the airport for the city at 6:30 AM. It takes about 25 minutes. One-way fare, including luggage, is DM 8. There is also an "Airport Express" bus, No. 110, which runs between the airport and the Ohlsdorf S-Bahn (suburban line) and U-Bahn (subway) station. The fare is DM 2.80. Taxi fare from the airport to the downtown area is about DM 25. By rented car, follow the signs to "Stadtmitte" (Downtown), which appear immediately outside the airport area.

By Train Hamburg is a terminus for mainline services to northern Germany; trains to Schleswig-Holstein and Scandinavia also stop here. There are two principal stations: the main train station (Hauptbahnhof) and Hamburg-Altona. Euro-City, Inter-City, and high-speed InterCityExpress services connect Hamburg with all German cities and the European rail network. For train information, tel. 040/19419.

By Bus Hamburg's bus station, the Zentral-Omnibus-Bahnhof, is in Adenauerallee, behind the Hauptbahnhof. For tickets and information, contact the **Deutsche Touring Gesellschaft** (Am Römerhof 17, 6000 Frankfurt/Main, tel. 069/79030).

By Car Hamburg has proportionately fewer cars than most other German cities and an urban road system that is the envy of many of them. Incoming autobahns end at one of Hamburg's three beltways, which then connect easily with the downtown area ("Stadtmitte").

Getting Around

By Public Transportation The comprehensive city and suburban transportation system includes a subway network (U-Bahn), which connects efficiently with S-Bahn (suburban) lines, and an exemplary bus service. Tickets cover travel by all three, as well as by harbor ferry. A ticket costs DM 2.10 (DM 3.20 for travel outside the inner city) and can be bought at the automatic machines found in all stations and most bus stops. A day's ticket permitting unlimited travel in the entire Hamburg urban area from 9 AM costs DM 6.50 for one adult and up to three children (DM 11.50 for a group of up to four adults and three children); a three-day ticket costs DM 19. The all-night buses (Nos. 600–640) tour the downtown area, leaving the Rathausmarkt and the Hauptbahnhof every hour. Information can be obtained from the **Hamburg Passenger Transport Board** (HHV), Steinstrasse 1, tel. 040/322911.

By Taxi Taxi meters start at DM 3.60, and the fare is DM 2.20 per kilometer (or about DM 3.16 per mile). To order a taxi, phone 040/441011, 040/686868, or 040/611061.

Important Addresses and Numbers

Tourist Information The principal Hamburg tourist office is at Bieberhaus, Hachmannplatz, next to the Hauptbahnhof. It's open weekdays 7:30–6, Saturday 8–3 (tel. 040/30051244). There's also a tourist information center inside the Hauptbahnhof itself (open daily 7 AM–11 PM, tel. 040/30051230) and in the arrivals hall of Hamburg Airport (open daily from 8 AM to 11 PM, tel. 040/30051240). Other tourist offices can be found in the Hanse-Viertel shopping arcade (tel. 040/30051220; open weekdays 10–6:30, Sat. 10–3, Sun. 11–3) and at the Landungsbrücken (tel. 040/30051200; open Mar.–Oct., daily 9–6; Nov.–Feb., daily 10–5). All centers will reserve hotel accommodations.

Consulates U.S. (Alsterufer 27, 1 (tel. 040/411710). U.K. (Harvestehuder Weg 8a, tel. 040/446071).

Emergencies Police (tel. 110). Doctor (tel. 040/228022). Dentist (tel. 11500). Ambulance (tel. 112). Pharmacy Information (tel. 040/228022).

English-Language Bookstores Try Frensche (Spitalerstr. 26e, tel. 040/327585) for a selection of English-language books.

Travel Agencies American Express (Rathausmarkt 5, tel. 040/33114).

Guided Tours

Orientation Tours Bus tours of the city, with an English-speaking guide, leave from Kirchenallee (across from the Hotel Europäischer Hof and in front of the Hauptbahnhof) at regular intervals (six times daily during the summer). The two-hour tour costs DM 22 for adults, DM 11 for children. A 2½-hour tour, taking in more of the city, starts at 10 and 2 daily from the same place. The fare is DM 28 for adults, DM 14 for children. A night tour of the city sets off from the Kirchenallee at 8 and returns shortly after midnight (Apr.–Oct., Tues.–Sat.; Nov.–Mar., Fri.–Sat.). The fare of DM 99 includes a drink at each stop.

Boat Tours Hamburg is a city dominated by water, and one of the best ways of getting a feel of the place is by taking one of the many boat trips offered. Tours of the harbor leave at regular intervals throughout the year from piers (Landungsbrucken) 1–7. The one-hour tour costs DM 14 (DM 7 for children). A special harbor tour with English-speaking guide leaves pier 1 at 11:15 daily from March 1 to October 30 (cost: DM 14 for adults, DM 7 for children). The Stortebeker line has a special party boat where you can wine, dine (a six-course banquet), and dance. The boat casts off at pier 6 every evening at 8. The all-inclusive cost of the cruise is DM 111, and reservations can be made by calling 040/22742375.

Cruises of the Binnenalster and Aussenalster leave from the Jungfernstieg every half hour between 10 and 6, April–October. The fare is DM 13 for adults, DM 7.50 for children. A tour including canals leaves three times daily (DM 19 and DM 9.50, respectively). For information, tel. 040/341141.

Excursions Bus tours of the surrounding countryside are offered by Jasper-Reisebüro (Colonnaden 72, tel. 040/343751).

Exploring Hamburg

The comparison that Germans like to draw between Hamburg and Venice is—like all such comparisons with the *Serenis-*

sima—somewhat exaggerated. Nevertheless, Hamburg is, like Venice, a city on water: the great river Elbe, which flows into the North Sea; the small river Alster, which has been dammed to form two lakes, the Binnenalster and Aussenalster; and many canals. Once a leading member of the Hanseatic League of cities, which dominated trade on the North Sea and the Baltic during the Middle Ages, Hamburg is still a major port, with 33 individual docks and 500 berths for oceangoing vessels.

Apart from its aquatic aspects, the most striking thing about Hamburg is its contradictions. Within the remaining traces of its old city walls, Hamburg combines the seamiest, steamiest streets of dockland Europe with the sleekest avenues to be found anywhere between Biarritz and Stockholm. During World War II and afterward, Hamburg was wrecked from without and within—by fire, then by Allied bombing raids, and finally by philistine town planners, who tore down some of the remaining old buildings to make way for modernistic glass-and-steel boxes. The result is a city that is, in parts, ugly, but still a fascinating mixture of old and new.

It is also a city in which escaping the urban bustle is relatively easy, since it contains more than 800 kilometers (500 miles) of riverside and country paths within its boundaries. The following itinerary includes a few detours, some by boat, which will enhance your enjoyment of Hamburg.

Numbers in the margin correspond to points of interest on the Hamburg map.

1 Hamburg's main train station, the **Hauptbahnhof,** is not only the start of the city tour but very much part of it. It's not often you are tempted to linger at a train station, but this is an exception. Originally built in 1906 and modernized since, it has a remarkable spaciousness and sweep, accentuated by a 148-meter-wide (160-yard-wide) glazed roof, the largest unsupported roof in Germany. Gather city travel guides and maps from the city tourist office here and ride one stop on the S-Bahn (suburban railroad) to the Dammtor station. Compare this Art Nouveau–style building with the one you've just left. You'll find splendid examples of Germany's version of Art Nouveau, the *Jugendstil*, throughout your tour of Hamburg.

The Dammtor station brings you out near Theodor-Heuss-Platz in **Wallringpark,** a stretch of parkland that runs for more than a kilometer alongside what was once the western defense **2** wall of the city. The first two sections of the park—the **Alter 3** **Botanischer Garten** (Old Botanical Garden) and the **Planten un Blomen**—have lots to attract the attention of gardeners and flower lovers. In summer, the evening sky over the Planten un Blomen lake is lighted up by the colored waters of its fountain, dancing what the locals romantically call a "water ballet."

The section of the park known as **Grosse Wallanlagen**—to the southwest—is interrupted abruptly by the northern edge of the **St. Pauli** district and its most famous—or infamous—thor-**4** oughfare, the **Reeperbahn** (*see* Nightlife, *below*). Unlike other business sections of Hamburg, this industrious quarter works around the clock; although it may seem quiet as you stroll down its tawdry length in broad daylight, any male tourist who stops at one of its bars will discover that many of the girls who work this strip are on a day shift.

Hamburg

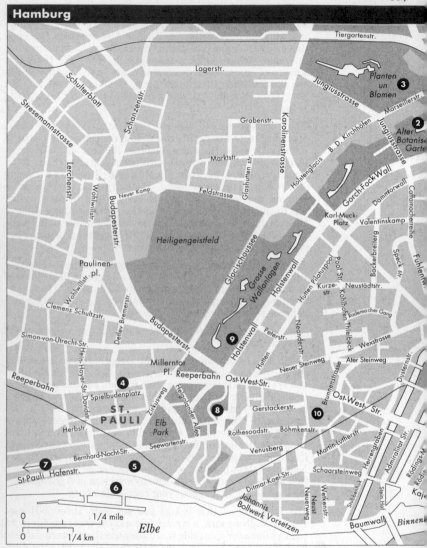

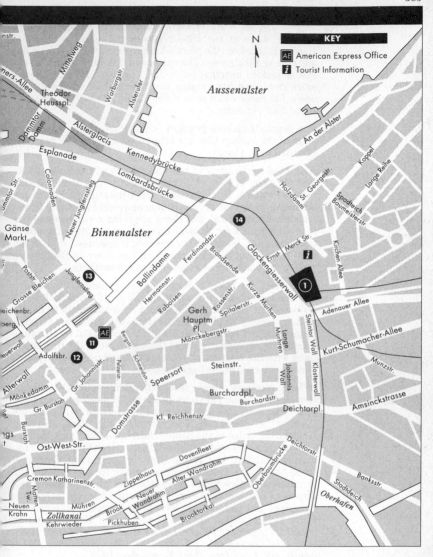

Aussenalster

Binnenalster

Zollkanal

Oberhafen

⑤ If it's a Sunday morning, join the late revelers and the early joggers and dog-walkers for breakfast at the **Fischmarkt** (fish market), down at the Elbe riverside between the St. Pauli Landungsbrücken (the piers where the excursion boats tie up) and Grosse Elbstrasse. The citizens of Hamburg like to breakfast on pickled herring, but if that's not to your taste, there's much more than fish for sale, and the nearby bars are already open. *The fish market is held every Sun., 5 AM–9:30 AM, starting at 7 AM in winter.*

⑥ The nearby **Landungsbrücken** is the start of the many boat trips of the harbor that are offered throughout the year (*see* Guided Tours, *above*).

Along the north bank of the Elbe is one of the finest walks Hamburg has to offer. The walk is a long one, about 13 kilometers (8 miles) from the St. Pauli Landungsbrücken to the **⑦** attractive waterside area of **Blankenese,** and that's only three-quarters of the route. But there are S-Bahn stations and bus stops along the way, to give you a speedy return to the downtown area. Do, however, try to reach Blankenese, even if you have to catch an S-Bahn train from downtown to Blankenese station and walk down to the riverbank from there.

Blankenese is another of Hamburg's surprises—a city suburb that has the character of a fishing village. If you've walked all the way from St. Pauli, you may not be able to face the 58 flights of stairs (nearly 5,000 individual steps) that crisscross through Blankenese between its heights and the river. But by all means attempt an exploratory prowl through some of the tiny lanes, lined with the retirement retreats of Hamburg's sea captains and the cottages of the fishermen who once toiled here.

A ferry connects Blankenese with Hamburg's St. Pauli, although the S-Bahn ride back to the city is much quicker. Back at St. Pauli, resume your tour at the riverside and head back toward the downtown area through Elb Park, crossing **⑧** Helgolander Allee to the **Bismarckdenkmal** (Bismarck Memorial)—an imposing statue of the Prussian "Iron Chancellor," the guiding spirit of the 19th-century unification of Germany. **⑨** Cross the square ahead of you and make for the **Museum für Hamburgische Geschichte** at Holstenwall 24. This fascinating display of Hamburg's history has a feature of great interest to American descendants of German immigrants, who can arrange to have called up from the microfilm files information about any ancestors who set out for the New World from Hamburg. *Holstenwall 24, tel. 040/35042360. Admission: DM 5 adults, DM 1 children. Open Tues.–Sun. 10–5.*

Cross Holstenwall to Peterstrasse, where you'll find a group of finely restored, 18th-century half-timbered houses. Turn right down Neanderstrasse and cross Ost-West-Strasse to Ham-**⑩** burg's principal Protestant church, the **Michaeliskirche** (St. Michael's Church), the finest Baroque church in northern Germany. Twice in its history, this well-loved 17th-century church has given the people of Hamburg protection—during the Thirty Years' War and again in World War II. From its 132-meter (440-foot) tower, there is a magnificent view of the city and the Elbe, and twice a day the watchman blows a trumpet solo from up there. *Cost for the elevator up to the tower: DM 3 adults, DM 1.50 children.*

From the Michaeliskirche, return to Ost-West-Strasse, turn right, then left down Brunnenstrasse to Wexstrasse. Follow Wexstrasse to Grosse Bleichen, cross the Bleichenbrücke and Adolphsbrücke (Bleichen and Adolph bridges), over two of Hamburg's canals (known as the Fleete), turn left into Alterwall, and you'll come to the **Rathausmarkt,** the town hall square. The designers of the square deliberately set out to create a northern version of the Piazza San Marco in Venice and, to a certain extent, succeeded. The 100-year-old **Rathaus** is built on 4,000 wooden piles sunk into the marshy ground beneath. It is the home not only of the city council but of the Hamburg state government, for Hamburg is one of Germany's federal, semiautonomous states. The sheer opulence of its interior is hard to beat. It has 647 rooms, 6 more than Buckingham Palace. Although visitors can tour only the state rooms, the tapestries, huge staircases, glittering chandeliers, coffered ceilings, and gilt-framed portraits convey forcefully the wealth of the city in the last century. *Marktplatz. Admission: DM 1. Guided tours in English Mon.–Thurs. every half hour 10:15–3:15, Fri.– Sun. hourly 10:15–1:15.*

If you've had enough sightseeing by this time, you've ended up at the right place, for an arcade at the western edge of the Rathausmarkt signals the start of Europe's largest undercover shopping area, nearly a kilometer of airy arcades, cool in summer and warm in winter, bursting with color and life. Three hundred shops, from cheap souvenir stores to expensive fashion boutiques, are crammed into this consumer-age labyrinth. There are expensive restaurants and cozy cafés, and one of the rare opportunities in Germany (or anywhere) to eat lobster and sip good wine at a fast-food outlet. It's easy to get lost here, but all the arcades lead at some point to the wide, seasidelike promenade, the **Jungfernstieg,** which borders Hamburg's two artificial lakes, the **Binnenalster** and the **Aussenalster.** Although called lakes, they are really dammed-up sections of the Alster River, which rises only 56 kilometers (35 miles) away in Schleswig Holstein. The river was originally dammed up at the beginning of the 13th century to form a millrace before it spilled into the Elbe. The original muddy dam wall is today the elegant Jungfernstieg promenade. From the Jungfernstieg, you can take a boat tour of the two Alster lakes and the canals beyond (*see* Guided Tours, *above*), passing some of Hamburg's most ostentatious homes, with their extensive grounds rolling down to the water's edge (the locals call it "Millionaires' Coast").

Hamburg has its share of millionaires, enriched by the city's thriving commerce and industry. But they, in turn, can claim to have enriched the artistic life of Hamburg. For example, it was a group of wealthy merchants who, in 1817, founded the Kunstverein, from which grew Hamburg's famous Kunsthalle collection. The **Kunsthalle** is well placed at the end of our Hamburg tour, next to the Hauptbahnhof, and its collection of paintings is one of Germany's finest. You'll find works by practically all the great northern European masters from the 14th to the 20th century, as well as by such painters as Goya, Tiepolo, and Canaletto. For many visitors, the highlight of the entire collection is the *Grabow Altarpiece*, painted in 1379 by an artist known only as Master Bertram; the central scene is the Crucifixion, but numerous side panels depict the story of man from Genesis to the Nativity. *1 Glockengiesserwall, tel. 040/*

24862612. Admission: DM 5 adults, DM 1 children. Open Tues.–Sun. 10–5.

Dining

For details and price-category definitions, *see* Dining in Staying in Germany.

Expensive **La Mer.** Located in the elegant Hotel Prem, on the southwest bank of the Aussenalster, La Mer offers a fine and varied menu. Try the marinated inoki mushrooms with imperial oysters and salmon roe or the spring venison with elderberry sauce. *An der Alster 9, tel. 040/241726. Reservations advised. AE, DC, MC, V. Closed Sat. and Sun. lunch.*

Landhaus Dill. Situated in a former coaching inn on the road to Blankenese (*see* Exploring, *above*), Landhaus Dill is an informal restaurant with an imaginative and varied menu. In summer, specialties include lobster salad, prepared at your table; in fall, wild duck with port wine sauce. *Elbchaussee 404, tel. 040/828443. Reservations advised. AE, DC, MC, V. Closed Mon.*

Landhaus Scherrer. A popular, country house-style restaurant located in the city's Altona district, Landhaus Scherrer specializes in fine regional cuisine and prides itself on its extensive wine list. It offers a separate bistro for lunches. *Elbchaussee 130, tel. 040/880–1325. Reservations required. AE, DC, MC. Closed Sun.*

L'Auberge Française. Generally regarded as Hamburg's most authentic French restaurant, L'Auberge Française specializes in traditional seafood dishes and fine wines. *Rutschbahn 34, tel. 040/410–2532. Reservations required. AE, DC, MC, V. Closed Sun.*

★ **Peter Lembcke.** This formal, traditional restaurant located just north of the train station offers the best of German cuisine. There's no better place to eat eel soup or *Labskaus* stew. Steaks are another specialty. *Holzdamm 49, tel. 040/243290. Reservations advised. AE, DC, MC, V. Closed Sun. and public holidays.*

Moderate **Ahrberg.** Located on the river in Blankenese, the Ahrberg has a
★ pleasant terrace for summer dining, and, for a warm retreat on cooler days, a cozy, wood-paneled dining room. The menu features a range of traditional German dishes and seafood specialties—often served together. Try the shrimp and potato soup and fresh carp in season. *Strandweg 33, tel. 040/860438. Reservations advised. AE, DC, MC. Closed Sun.*

Fischerhaus. Hamburg's famous fish market is right outside the door of this traditional old restaurant, which accounts for the variety and quality of fish dishes on its menu. Meat-eaters are also catered to, and the soups are legendary (the fish soup is understandably the pride of the house). *St. Pauli Fischmarkt 14, tel. 040/314053. AE, DC, MC, V.*

Noblesse. The Ramada Renaissance Hotel's stylish restaurant has won awards for the standard of its cuisine and service. The extensive menu is a combination of German traditional and nouvelle cuisine; the wine list embraces the best labels from Germany, France, and Italy. The buffet is a particularly good value. *Grosse Bleichen, tel. 040/349180. Reservations advised. Jacket and tie required. AE, DC, MC, V.*

Inexpensive **Atnali.** This is one of Hamburg's oldest and most popular Turkish restaurants. It is friendly and comfortable and offers a very reasonable and extensive menu. It stays open late—until 1 AM. *Rutschbahn 11, tel. 040/410–3810. Reservations advised. AE, DC, MC, V.*

Avocado. This popular, modern restaurant offers excellent value and an imaginative menu. Try the salmon in Chablis. *Kanalstr. 9, tel. 040/220–4599. Reservations required. No credit cards. Dinner only. Closed Sun., Mon.*

Lodging

For details and price-category definitions, *see* Lodging in Staying in Germany.

Very Expensive **Atlantic Hotel Kempinski Hamburg.** Since it first opened in 1909, the luxuriously appointed Atlantic, close by the Aussenalster and near the Hauptbahnhof, has been a focal point of the Hamburg social scene. The Atlantic Restaurant, stunning with its bird's-eye maple Empire-style decor and inlaid marble floor, serves haute cuisine, while the Atlantic Mühle serves traditional German fare in a rustic setting. *An der Alster 72, tel. 040/28880, fax 040/2803419. 256 rooms with bath. Facilities: 2 restaurants, bar, indoor pool, sauna, solarium, hairdresser, massage, Lufthansa check-in desk, garage. AE, DC, MC, V.*

Hamburg Marriott. The U.S. Marriott group chose downtown Hamburg as the site of its first hotel in Germany. It opened in 1988 amid the city's shopping arcades and smart restaurants. Among its many refinements are two floors reserved for nonsmokers. *ABC-Str. 52, Kleiner Gänsemarkt, tel. 040/35050, fax 040/35051723. 276 rooms with bath. Facilities: restaurant, pool, sauna, solarium, fitness center, sea grill, piano lounge, café. AE, DC, MC, V.*

★ **Vier Jahreszeiten.** This hotel, with its antique-style rooms, impeccable service, and excellent food, is rated among the world's best. It is continually being refurbished to maintain an impeccable standard, but you won't notice a blip in the hotel's smooth routine. Centrally located, it offers scenic views of the Binnenalster. *Neuer Jungfernstieg 9–14, tel. 040/34940, fax 040/3494602. 161 rooms and 10 suites, all with bath. Facilities: 2 restaurants, nightclub, pâtisserie, beauty salon. AE, DC, MC, V.*

Expensive **Aussen Alster.** Only seven minutes from the train station and a few steps from the Alster Lake, the Aussen Alster is a small, tranquil hotel occupying a gracious 19th-century house. The cool, modern decor is given warmth by a log-fed fireplace and friendly bar. *Schmilinskystr. 1, tel. 040/241557, fax 040/2803231. 27 rooms with bath. Facilities: restaurant, sauna, solarium. AE, DC, MC, V.*

Moderate–Expensive **Hotel Graf Moltke.** The sturdy old Graf Moltke, which rules majestically over central Steindamm street (a short walk from the main railway station), was completely renovated in 1991. Some rooms were enlarged and all were equipped with soundproofing. Special weekend deals are offered for families. *Steindamm 1, tel. 040/2801154, fax 040/2802562. 97 rooms with bath or shower. Facilities: restaurant, bar, boutiques. AE, DC, MC, V.*

Moderate **Baseler Hof.** Centrally located near the inner lake and the State Opera House, this hotel offers friendly and efficient service and neatly furnished rooms. There is no charge for children under 10 sharing a room with parents. *Esplanade 11, tel. 040/ 359060, fax 040/35906918. 160 rooms, most with bath. Facilities: restaurant, meeting rooms. AE, DC, MC, V.*

Steen's. This is a small, intimate hotel decorated in a light, airy Scandinavian style. It is conveniently located, close to the main train station. Guests enjoy breakfast in a pleasant garden. *Holzdamm 43, tel. 040/244642, fax 040/2803593. 11 rooms with shower. AE, MC.*

Wedina. Fully renovated and refurbished in 1992, the Wedina now offers a very high standard of accommodation in two attractive city mansions on a quiet street running down to the Alster. It has a bar, an outdoor pool in the attractive garden, and a sauna. *Gurlittstr. 23, tel. 040/243011, fax 040/2803894. 39 rooms with shower. AE, DC, MC, V. Closed Dec. 18–Jan. 1.*

Inexpensive **Alameda.** The Alameda offers guests good, basic accommodations. All rooms feature TV, radio, and minibar. *Colonnaden 45, tel. 040/344290. 18 rooms with shower. AE, DC, MC, V.*

Metro Merkur. Centrally located near Hamburg's main train station, the recently renovated Metro Merkur is a convenient, functional hotel. There is no restaurant, but the bar offers a selection of evening snacks and warm dishes. *Bremer Reihe 12– 14, tel. 040/247266. 100 rooms, most with bath. AE, DC, MC, V.*

Nightlife

Few visitors can resist taking a look at the **Reeperbahn,** if only by day. At night, however, from 10 onward, the place really shakes itself into life, and *everything* is for sale. Among the Reeperbahn's even rougher side streets, the most notorious is the Grosse Freiheit, which means "Great Freedom." A stroll through this small alley, where the attractions are on display behind plate glass, will either tempt you to stay or send you straight back to your hotel. Three of the leading clubs on the Grosse Freiheit are the **Colibri** (No. 34, tel. 040/313233), the **Safari** (No. 24, tel. 040/315400), and the **Nightlife-Club** (No. 32, tel. 040/3174996).

The Reeperbahn area is not just a red-light district, however. Side streets are rapidly filling up with a mixture of yuppie bars, restaurants, and theaters that complement the seamen's bars and sex shops. The **Hans-Albers-Platz** is a center of this revival, where the stylish bar La Paloma provides contrast to the Hans-Albers-Ecke, an old sailors' bar. The **Theater Schmidt** (Spielbudenplatz 24, tel. 040/314804) offers variety shows most evenings to a packed house.

A few tips for visiting the Reeperbahn: Avoid going alone; demand a price list whenever you drink (legally, it has to be on display), and pay as soon as you're served; if you have trouble, threaten to call the cops. If that doesn't work—call the cops.

The Rhine

None of Europe's many rivers is so redolent of history and legend as the Rhine. For the Romans, who established forts and colonies along its western banks, the Rhine was the frontier between civilization and the barbaric German tribes. Roman artifacts can be seen in museums throughout the region. The Romans also introduced viticulture—a legacy that survives in

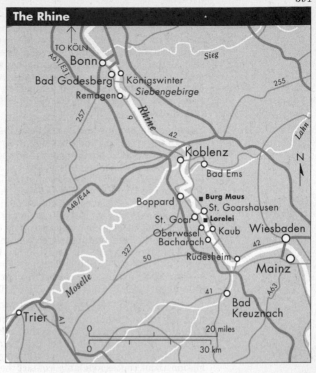

The Rhine

the countless vineyards along the riverbanks—and later, Christianity. Throughout the Middle Ages, the river's importance as a trade artery made it the focus of sharp, often violent, conflict between princes, noblemen, and archbishops. Many of the picturesque castles that crown its banks were the homes of robber barons who held up passing ships and barges and exacted heavy tolls to finance even grander fortifications.

For poets and composers, the Rhine—or *"Vater* (Father) *Rhein,"* as the Germans call it—has been an endless source of inspiration. As legend has it, the Lorelei, a treacherous, craggy rock, was home to a beautiful and bewitching maiden who lured sailors to a watery grave. Wagner based four of his epic operas on the lives of the medieval Nibelungs, said to have inhabited the rocky banks. To travel the Rhine by boat, especially in autumn, when the rising mists enshroud the castles high above, is to understand the place the river occupies in the German imagination.

The Rhine does not belong to Germany alone, but it is in Germany—especially the stretch between Mainz and Köln (Cologne) known as the Middle Rhine—that the riverside scenery is most spectacular. This is the "typical" Rhine: a land of steep and thickly wooded hills, terraced vineyards, tiny villages hugging the banks, and a succession of brooding castles.

Getting Around

By Train   One of the best ways to visit the Rhineland in very limited time is to take the scenic train journey from Mainz to Köln along the western banks of the river. The views are spectacular, and the entire trip takes less than two hours. Choose an InterCity (IC) train for its wide viewing windows. If you're traveling north toward Köln, make sure you get a window seat on the right-hand side. Better still, sit in the restaurant car where you can enjoy a meal or beverage while you watch the scenery unfold. Contact **German National Railways** in Frankfurt, Reisedienst, Friedrich-Ebert-Anlage 43, tel. 069/19419, or get details at any big train station travel office.

By Boat Passenger ships traveling up and down the Rhine and its tributaries offer a pleasant and relaxing way to see the region. **Köln-Düsseldorfer Steamship Company (KD)** operates a fleet of ships that travel daily between Düsseldorf and Frankfurt, from Easter to late October. They also offer cruises along the entire length of the Rhine. Passengers have a choice of buying an excursion ticket or a ticket to a single destination. For information about services, write to Frankenwerft 15,5000 Köln 1, or tel. 0221/20880. This company also offers trips up the Mosel as far as Trier. From March through November, **Hebel-Line** (tel. 06742/2420) offers a scenic cruise of the Lorelei Valley; night cruises feature music and dancing. For information about Neckar River excursions, contact **Neckar Personen Schiffahrt** in Stuttgart, tel. 0711/541073 or 0711/541074.

By Car If you prefer to drive, the Rhineland offers a comprehensive highway network that takes in some of the region's most spectacular scenery. Roads crisscross the entire province, from the historic vineyards of the Mosel Valley to the beautiful castle and wine-growing country of the Rhine's west bank. For information about routes available, contact the **German Automobile Club** (AVD), Lyonerstrasse 16, Frankfurt-am-Main 71, tel. 069/66060.

By Bicycle Tourist offices in all the larger towns will provide information and route maps. German Railways offers bikes for hire at numerous stations. For information, tel. 069/2651 or ask for the "Bikes for Rent" (*"Fahrrad am Bahnhof"*) brochure at any station.

Tourist Information

Bacharach (Fremdenverkehrsamt, Oberstrasse 1, tel. 06743/2968).
Boppard (Verkehrsamt, Karmeliterstrasse 2, tel. 06742/10319).
Koblenz (Fremden Verkehrsamt, Hauptbahnhof, tel. 0261/31304 and Fremdenverkehrsverband Rheinland-Pfalz, Löhrstrasse 103, tel. 0261/31079).
Köln (Verkehrsamt, Unter Fettenhennen 19, tel. 0221/221–3345).
Königswinter (Verkehrsamt, Drachenfelsstrasse 7, tel. 02223/889325).
Mainz (Verkehrsverein, Bahnhofstrasse 15, tel. 06131/286210).
Rüdesheim (Verkehrsamt, Rheinstrasse 16, tel. 06722/2962).

Guided Tours

In addition to a number of special-interest cruises, **KD** (Köln-Düsseldorfer) operates a series of guided excursions covering the towns along its routes (*see* Getting Around, *above*). The

British-run **European Yacht Cruises Ltd.** conducts a variety of Rhine cruises, some with optional shore excursions (tel. in London 081/462–8843). The tourist offices in Mainz, Köln, and Koblenz also offer tours (in English) of their respective cities.

Exploring the Rhine

Köln **Köln** (Cologne) is the largest city on the Rhine, marking the northernmost point of the river's scenic stretch before it becomes a truly industrial waterway through the Ruhr Valley. It's a very old city—first settled by the Romans in 38 BC—and today is a vibrant, zestful Rhineland center, with a very active cultural life and a business and commercial infrastructure that supports trade fairs year-round. It derives its name from the Latin Colonia Claudia Ara Agrippinensium, the title given to it by the Roman emperor Claudius in honor of his wife, Julia Agrippina, who was born there. The Franks and Merovingians followed the Romans before Charlemagne restored the city's fortunes in the 9th century, appointing its first archbishop and ensuring its ecclesiastical prominence for centuries.

By the Middle Ages, Köln was the largest city north of the Alps, and, as a member of the powerful Hanseatic League, it was more important commercially than either London or Paris. Ninety percent of the city was destroyed in World War II, and in the rush to rebuild it many mistakes were made. But although today's Köln lacks the aesthetic unity of many other rebuilt German cities, the heart of the Altstadt (Old Town), with its streets that follow the line of the medieval city walls, has great charm, and at night it throbs with life.

Towering over the old town is the extraordinary Gothic cathedral, the **Kölner Dom,** dedicated to Sts. Peter and Mary. It's comparable to the best French cathedrals; a visit to it may prove a highlight of your trip to Germany. What you'll see is one of the purest expressions of the Gothic spirit in Europe. Spend some time admiring the outside of the building (you can walk almost all the way around it). Notice that there are practically no major horizontal lines—all the accents of the building are vertical. It may come as a disappointment to learn that the cathedral, begun in 1248, was not completed until 1880. Console yourself with the knowledge that it was still built to original plans. At 157 meters (515 feet) high, the two west towers of the cathedral were by far the tallest structures in the world when they were finished (they are still the tallest in a church). The length of the building is 143 meters (470 feet); the width of the nave is 45 meters (147 feet); and the highest part of the interior is 42½ meters (140 feet).

The cathedral was built to house what were believed to be the relics of the Magi, the three kings or wise men who paid homage to the infant Jesus. Today the relics are kept just behind the altar, in the same enormous gold-and-silver **reliquary** in which they were originally displayed. The other great treasure of the cathedral is the **Gero Cross,** a monumental oak crucifixion dating from 975. Impressive for its simple grace, it's in the last chapel on the left as you face the altar.

Other highlights to admire are the stained-glass windows, some of which date from the 13th century; the 15th-century altar painting; and the early 14th-century high altar with its surrounding arcades of glistening white figures and its intricate choir screens. The choir stalls, carved from oak around 1310, are the largest in Germany, seating 104 people. There are more treasures to be seen in the **Dom Schatzkammer,** the cathedral treasury, including the silver shrine of Archbishop Engelbert, who was stabbed to death in 1225. *Admission: DM 3 adults, DM 1.50 children. Open Mon.–Sat. 9–5, Sun. 1–5.*

Outside again, you have the choice of either more culture or commerce. Köln's **shopping district** begins at nearby **Wallrafplatz.** Grouped around the cathedral is a collection of superb museums. If your priority is painting, try the ultramodern **Wallraf-Richartz-Museum** and **Museum Ludwig** complex. Together, they form the largest art collection in the Rhineland. The Wallraf-Richartz-Museum contains pictures spanning the years 1300 to 1900, with Dutch and Flemish schools particularly well represented (Rubens, who spent his youth in Köln, has a place of honor). The Museum Ludwig is devoted exclusively to 20th-century art; its Picasso collection is outstanding. *Bischofsgartenstr. 1. Admission: DM 8 adults, DM 4 children. Open Tues.–Thurs. 10–8, Fri.–Sun. 10–5.*

Opposite the cathedral is the **Römisch-Germanisches Museum,** built from 1970 to 1974 around the famous Dionysus mosaic that was uncovered at the site during the construction of an air-raid shelter in 1941. The huge mosaic, more than 91½ meters (100 yards) square, once covered the dining-room floor of a wealthy Roman trader's villa. Its millions of tiny earthenware and glass tiles depict some of the adventures of Dionysius, the Greek god of wine and, to the Romans, the object of a widespread and sinister religious cult. The pillared 1st-century tomb of Lucius Publicius, a prominent Roman officer, some stone Roman coffins, and a series of memorial tablets are among the museum's other exhibits. *Roncallipl. 4. Admission: DM 5 adults, DM 2.50 children. Open Tues.–Sun. 10–5.*

Now head south to the nearby **Alter Markt** and its **Altes Rathaus,** the oldest town hall in Germany (if you don't count the fact that the building was entirely rebuilt after the war). The square has a handsome assembly of buildings—the oldest dating from 1135—in a range of styles. There was a seat of local government here in Roman times, and directly below the current Rathaus are the remains of the Roman city governor's headquarters, the Praetorium. Go inside to see the 14th-century **Hansa Saal,** whose tall Gothic windows and barrel-vaulted wood ceiling are potent expressions of medieval civic pride. The figures of the prophets, standing on pedestals at one end, are all from the early 15th century. Ranging along the south wall are nine additional statues, the so-called *Nine Good Heroes,* carved in 1360. Charlemagne and King Arthur are among them. *Altes Rathaus, Alter Markt. Free guided tours (in German and English) Mon., Wed., Sat. 3 PM. Praetorium open Tues.–Sun. 10–5.*

Now head across Unter Käster toward the river and one of the most outstanding of Köln's 12 Romanesque churches, the **Gross St. Martin.** Its massive 13th-century tower, with distinctive corner turrets and an imposing central spire, is another landmark of Köln. Gross St. Martin is the parish church of Köln's colorful old city, the **Martinsviertel,** an attractive combination of reconstructed, high-gabled medieval buildings, winding alleys, and tastefully designed modern apartments and business quarters. Head here at night—the place comes to vibrant life at sunset.

To complete your daytime Köln tour, however, leave the Martinsviertel along Martinsstrasse and turn right into Gürzenichstrasse, passing the crenellated Gothic-style Gürzenich civic reception/concert hall. Take a left turn into Hohestrasse and another right turn into Cäcilienstrasse. At No. 29, you'll find the 12th-century St. Cäcilien church, and within its cool, well-lit interior one of the world's finest museums of medieval Christian art, the **Schnütgen Museum.** The museum is named after the cathedral capitular Alexander Schnütgen, who bequeathed his collection of religious art to the city in 1906. Enlarged considerably over the years, the collection was moved to St. Cäcilien in 1956. Although the main emphasis of the museum falls on early and medieval sacred art, the collection also covers the Renaissance and Baroque periods. *Cäcilienstr. 29, tel. 0221/2310. Admission: DM 5 adults, DM 2.50 children. Open Tues.–Sun. 10–5, every first Mon. in month 10–8. Guided tours on Sun. at 11.*

Around the corner, on Leonhard-Tietz-Strasse, is **St. Peter's Church,** where the painter Peter Paul Rubens was christened. There's a fine Rubens painting in the altar recess, joined recently by a modern triptych by the British painter Francis Bacon.

A few steps away is the expansive **Neumarkt** square, at whose western end is one of Köln's finest Romanesque basilicas, **St. Aposteln.** The Neumarkt was an early trading center; the church was built in the 11th century amid the hustle and bustle of a daily market. Today, its weighty east front, surmounted by two graceful hexagonal towers and the more traditional four-sided west steeple, dominates a very different scene, a green city park lined with elegant shops and offices.

South of Köln lies Germany's former capital, **Bonn,** preparing now to hand most of its legislative and administrative functions over to Berlin. **Bad Godesberg,** just south of Bonn, is the leafy community where many diplomats live and work, and across the river is **Königswinter,** site of one of the most visited castles on the Rhine. The ruins of **Drachenfels** crown the highest hill in the **Siebengebirge** (Seven Hills) area commanding a spectacular view of the river. The castle was built during the 12th century by the archbishop of Köln. Its name commemorates a dragon said to have lived in a nearby cave. As legend has it, the dragon was slain by Siegfried, the Niebelunglied hero.

Continuing south along the west bank, you come to the ancient, half-timbered town of **Remagen.** Originally a Roman village built near the source of a mineral spring, where the Ahr River meets the Rhine, Remagen was an important bridgehead during World War II. Here, American forces were able to capture the bridge and speed their advance into Germany. The Ahr Valley, lined with picturesque, terraced vineyards, produces some of Germany's finest red wines.

Koblenz   In the heart of the Middle Rhine region, at the confluence of the Rhine and Moselle rivers, lies the city of **Koblenz,** the area's cultural and administrative center and the meeting place of the two great wine-producing districts. It is also one of the most important traffic points along the Rhine. Here you are ideally placed to sample and compare the light, fruity Moselle wines and the headier Rhine varieties. The city's **Weindorf** area, just south of the **Pfaffendorfer Bridge,** has a wide selection of taverns, where you can try the wines in traditional Römer glasses, with their symbolic amber and green bowls.

The city of Koblenz began as a Roman camp—Confluentes— more than 2,000 years ago. The vaults beneath **St. Florin Church** contain an interesting assortment of Roman remains. A good place to begin your tour of Koblenz is the **Deutches Eck,** or "Corner of Germany," the tip of the sharp peninsula separating the Rhine and Moselle rivers. In the 12th century, the Knights of the Teutonic Order established their center here. The towering equestrian statue of Kaiser Wilhelm that once stood here was destroyed by Allied bombs during World War II; last year's plan to install a replica was met with controversy, because opponents feel that the statue is more a celebration of Prussian military might than of German unity. On summer evenings, concerts are held in the nearby **Blumenhof Garden.** Most of the city's historic churches are also within walking distance of the Deutsches Eck. The **Liebfrauenkirche** (Church of Our Lady), completed in the 13th century, incorporates Romanesque, late Gothic, and Baroque elements. **St. Florin,** a Romanesque church built around 1100, was remodeled in the Gothic style in the 14th century. Gothic windows and a vaulted ceiling were added in the 17th century. The city's most important church, **St. Kastor,** also combines Romanesque and Gothic elements and features some unusual altar tombs and rare Gothic wall paintings.

Although the city lost 85% of its buildings during wartime air raids, some of the old buildings survived and others have been built in complementary styles. Much of the **Old Town** of Koblenz is now a pedestrian district, and an attractive area for a leisurely stroll. Many of the ancient cellars beneath the houses have been rediscovered and now serve as wine bars and jazz clubs.

Koblenz also offers an assortment of castles and palaces. The former residence of the archbishop of Trier now houses the city administrative offices. The original 18th-century building was demolished during the war; today only the interior staircase remains. Across the river, on the Rhine's east bank, towers the city's most spectacular castle, the **Ehrenbreitstein.** The fortifications of this vast structure date to the 1100s, although the bulk of it was built much later, in the 16th and 17th centuries. To reach the fortress, take the cable car (*Sesselbahn*) or, if you're in shape, try walking up. The view alone is worth the trip. The fortress contains an interesting museum, the **Landesmuseum,** with exhibits tracing the industrial development of the Rhine Valley, including a reconstructed 19th-century tobacco factory and a pewter works. *Admission free. Open early March–mid-Nov., Tues.–Sun. 10–5:30, Wed. 10–9.*

Koblenz also has two noteworthy art galleries—one of which opened in 1993. The new **Ludwig Museum** contains outstanding contemporary works by Koblenz-born Peter Ludwig. The setting is spectacular—converted rooms of the historic Deutschherrenhaus on the Danziger Freiheit square. *Admission: DM 5 adults. Open Sun. 11–6; Wed., Fri., Sat. noon–7; Thurs. noon–9.*

The other gallery, the **Mittelrhein Museum,** features Rhenish art and artifacts from the Middle Ages to the present day. *15 Florinsmarkt. Admission free. Open Tues., Thurs.–Sun. 10–5:30; Wed. 10–9.*

Rhine Gorge Between the cities of Koblenz and Mainz, the Rhine flows through the 64-kilometer (40-mile) stretch known as the **Rhine Gorge.** It is here that the Rhine lives up to its legends and lore and where the river, in places, narrows to a width of 200 yards. Once it was full of treacherous whirlpools, sudden shallows, and stark rock outcroppings that menaced passing ships. Today, vineyards occupy every inch of available soil on the steep, terraced slopes. High above, ancient castles crown the rocky shelves.

South of Koblenz, at a wide, western bend in the river, lies the quiet old town of **Boppard,** once a bustling city of the Holy Roman Empire. Now the remains of its Roman fort and castle are used to house a museum of Roman artifacts and geological specimens. There are also several notable churches, including the **Carmelite Church,** with its fine Baroque altar, and the Romanesque Church of **St. Severus.** Boppard also offers a wonderful view across the Rhine to the ruined castles of **Liebenstein** and **Sterrenberg,** known as the "hostile brothers." As legend has it, the castles were built by two feuding brothers to protect their respective interests.

Continuing south from Boppard, you come to the little town of **St. Goar,** crowded against the steep gorge cliff and shadowed by the imposing ruin of **Rheinfels Castle.** A steep, narrow road takes you up to the castle—a fine spot for scenic river vistas. Rheinfels was built in the mid-13th century by Count Dieter von Katzenelnbogen (whose name means "cat's elbow"). The count's enormous success in collecting river tolls provoked the other river barons to join together and lay siege to his castle. What transpired is unclear, but through the years Rheinfels survived numerous sieges. It was finally destroyed by the French in 1797. During the 19th century, the ruins served as a source of inspiration for a host of Romantic poets and artists. It is now in the process of restoration, and a luxury hotel has been built on the site (*see* Dining and Lodging, *below*). *Admission: DM 4, children DM 2. Open Apr.–Oct., daily 9–5.*

On the east bank of the river, just across from the town of St. Goar, lies its sister village, **St. Goarshausen.** An hourly ferry service links the two. St. Goarshausen is dominated by **Burg Katz** (Cat Castle), a massive fortress built by a later Count von Katzenelnbogen. Tourists are not permitted inside, but the top of the cliff offers a lovely view of the famous Lorelei rock. About 3.2 kilometers (2 miles) north of St. Goarshausen is the **Burg Maus,** or Mouse Castle. Legend has it that an archbishop of Trier built the fortress to protect a strip of land he owned at the base of the cliff. The Count von Katzenelnbogen, annoyed at what he considered an intrusion into his territory, sent the archbishop a message explaining that his "Cat" (Burg Katz) was sufficient to protect the electoral "Mouse." Hence the nickname, Burg Maus.

Many tourists visit St. Goarshausen for its location—only a few kilometers from the legendary **Lorelei rock.** To get to Lorelei, follow the road marked with "Lorelei-Felsen" signs. Here the Rhine takes a sharp turn around a rocky, shrub-covered headland. This is the narrowest and shallowest part of the Middle Rhine, full of treacherous currents. According to legend, the beautiful maiden, Lore, sat on the rock here, combing her golden hair and singing a song so irresistible that passing sailors forgot the navigational hazards and were swept to their deaths.

Oberwesel, on the west bank, is a medieval wine town encircled by ancient walls and towers. Sixteen of the original 21 towers remain. Two churches deserve a visit: **St. Martin,** built in the 14th and 15th centuries, features a distinctive, brightly painted nave; the **Liebfrauen Kirche** (known as the "red church" because of its fiery facade) contains a magnificent choir screen, some fine sculpture, and an altarpiece depicting the magnanimous deeds of St. Nicholas.

One of the most photographed sites of the Middle Rhine region is the medieval village of **Kaub,** just south of Oberwesel on the east side of the river. Its unusual castles are well worth a visit. The **Pfalzgrafenstein,** situated on a tiny island in the middle of the Rhine, bristles with sharp-pointed towers and has the appearance of a small sailing ship. In the 14th century, the resident *Graf,* or count, was said to have strung chains across the Rhine in order to stop riverboats and collect his tolls. A special boat takes visitors to the island. *Admission: DM 1.50. Open Tues.–Sun. 9–noon and 2–5:30.*

On a hillside above Kaub hovers another small castle: **Burg Gutenfels.** Built in the 13th century, Gutenfels was renovated completely at the end of the 18th century and is now an exquisite hotel (*see* Dining and Lodging, *below*).

The picturesque little village of **Bacharach,** encircled by 15th-century walls, is the best-preserved town of the Middle Rhine. It takes its name from the Roman "Baccaracum," or "altar of Bacchus"—a great stone that stood here until it was dynamited by river engineers during the last century. As its name implies, Bacharach is also a wine-trade center.

Farther south, on the Rhine's east bank and at the center of the Rheingau region, lies another famous wine town. According to legend, **Rüdesheim's** first vines were planted by Charlemagne. More recent vintages can be enjoyed in the many taverns lining **Drosselgasse,** a narrow, colorful street in the heart of town. Rüdesheim is a tourist magnet—about the most popular destination on the Rhine—so if you plan to stay overnight, be sure to reserve well in advance. Besides its half-timbered houses, hidden courtyards, and medieval castles, Rüdesheim offers an interesting museum, **Rheingau und Weinmuseum,** devoted to the history of wine making and local lore. *Rheinstr. Admission: DM 3 adults, DM 1 children. Open Mar.–mid-Nov., daily 9–6.*

Mainz On the west side of the Rhine, at the mouth of the river Main, stands the city of **Mainz,** an old university town that's the capital of the Rhineland-Palatinate state. During Roman times, Mainz was a camp called Moguntiacum. Later it was the seat of the powerful archbishops of Mainz. But it is perhaps best known as the city in which, around 1450, printing pioneer Johannes Gutenberg established his first movable press. (He's such an important figure in Mainz that he has his own festival, Johannisnacht, celebrated in mid-June.) He is commemorated by a monument and square bearing his name and a museum containing his press and one of his Bibles. *Liebfrauenplatz 5.*

Admission free. Open Tues.–Sat. 10–6, Sun. and holidays 10–1. Closed Jan.

Today, Mainz is a bustling, modern city of nearly 200,000 inhabitants. Although it was heavily bombed during World War II, many of the buildings have been faithfully reconstructed, and the city retains much of its historic charm. On **Gutenbergplatz** in the **Old Town** stand two fine Baroque churches, **Seminary Church** and **St. Ignatius.** The Gothic church of **St. Stephen** features six windows by the French artist Marc Chagall. The city's **Dom** (cathedral) is one of the finest Romanesque churches in Germany. The Old Town also boasts the country's oldest Renaissance fountain—**the Marktbrunnen**—and the **Dativius-Victor-Bogen Arch,** dating to Roman times. The **Römisch-Germanisches Museum,** in the **Kurfürstliches Schloss,** contains a notable collection of archaeological finds. *Rheinstr. Admission free. Open Tues.–Sun. 10–6.*

Dining and Lodging

When it comes to cuisine, the Rhineland offers a number of regional specialties. Be sure to sample the wide variety of sausages available, the goose and duck dishes from the Ahr Valley, and Rhineland *Sauerbraten*—accepted by many as the most succulent of pot roasts. Hotels in the Rhineland range from simple little inns to magnificent castle hotels. Many smaller towns have only small hotels and guest houses, some of which close during the winter months. During the peak summer season and in early autumn—wine festival time—accommodations are scarce, so it is advisable to reserve well in advance.

For details and price-category definitions, *see* Dining and Lodging in Staying in Germany.

Bacharach **Hotel-Restaurant Steeger Weinstube.** Hearty three-course
Dining meals for under DM 20 are offered at this friendly, family-run tavern/restaurant located just off the Rhine tourist route. The menu changes daily, but Rhineland-style marinated beef, homemade potato dumplings, and in-season venison are often featured. *Blucherstr. 149, Bacharach-Steeg, tel. 06743/1240. Reservations not necessary. MC. Inexpensive.*

Lodging **Altkölnischer Hof.** This is a small but cozy rustic-style hotel. *Blücherstr. 2, tel. 06743/1339, fax 06743/2793. 18 rooms with bath. Facilities: restaurant, car park. AE, V. Closed Nov.– Easter. Moderate.*

Bonn **Halbedel's Gasthaus.** Rainer-Maria Halbedel's fine establish-
Dining ment in the Bad Godesberg diplomatic quarter is no ordinary German "Gasthof," but a restaurant of distinction. The decor is country-house style, with lead-paned windows and mahogany paneling and furniture. Herr Halbedel reigns supreme in the kitchen while his wife Irmgard runs the restaurant—a highly successful combination. *Rheinallee 47, tel. 0228/354253. Reservations advised. MC. Closed Mon. Expensive.*
Rhapsody. This restaurant in the Scandic Crown Hotel offers fish specialties in the Swedish style, courtesy of chef Joachim Lassner. *Berliner Freiheit 2, tel. 0228/72690. Reservations advised. AE, DC, MC, V. Closed Sun., holidays. Expensive.*

Lodging **Königshof.** The sleek, modern Königshof is a favorite hotel
★ among diplomatic visitors only partly for its convenient location near the Old Town and close to the Rhine. Patrons of the

fine terrace restaurant enjoy an excellent river view. There is also a well-stocked wine cellar. *Adenauerallee 9, tel. 0228/ 26010, fax 0228/2601529. 134 rooms with bath. Facilities: restaurant, bar, childcare service. AE, DC, MC, V. Expensive.*

Maritim. Opened in 1988, the Maritim is already an established part of the Bonn hotel scene. It's located across the river in Königswinter. *Rheinallee 3, 5330 Königswinter 1, tel. 02223/ 7070, fax 02223/707811. 250 rooms and suites with bath. Facilities: riverside terrace restaurant, pool, sauna, bar, cosmetic studio, hairdressing salon, beer and wine tavern. AE, DC, MC, V. Expensive.*

Rheinhotel Dreesen. The Rhine rolls by right outside this historic hotel, which recently underwent a complete renovation. Despite the modernization, a belle epoque atmosphere lingers in its stately public rooms, and on weekends an orchestra still strikes up for afternoon tea. *Rheinstr. 45–49, Bad Godesberg, tel. 0228/82020, fax 0228/8202153. 74 rooms, 4 apartments and suites. Facilities: restaurant, bar, café-terrace, parking. AE, DC, MC, V. Expensive.*

Boppard
Lodging

Bellevue Rheinhotel. This is one of the most majestic hotels of the Rhineland, an imposing turn-of-the-century building whose elegant white-and-yellow facade, under steep slate eaves, faces directly onto the river. *Rheinallee 41–42, tel. 06742/1020, fax 06742/102602. 95 rooms with bath. Facilities: restaurant, beer cellar, bar, indoor pool, sauna, Turkish bath, fitness center, tennis courts. AE, DC, MC, V. Expensive.*

Kaub
Lodging
★

Burg Gutenfels. The terrace of this luxurious castle hotel offers one of the finest views in the Rhine Valley. Guests can also enjoy wine from the hotel's own vineyard. Be sure to reserve well in advance. *Tel. 06774/220, fax 06774/1760. 12 rooms with bath. Facilities: restaurant, private chapel. AE, DC, MC. Very Expensive.*

Koblenz
Dining

Wacht am Rhein. The name of this attractive riverside restaurant, Watch on the Rhine, sums it up. In summer, take a table on the outside terrace and watch the river traffic roll by; in winter, choose a window table and dine with the Rhine outside and the atmospheric warmth of the fin de siècle fittings and furnishings inside. Fish is the basis of the extensive menu. *Adenauer-Ufer 6, tel. 0261/15313. Reservations not necessary. AE. Moderate.*

Weinhaus Hubertus. This restaurant, named for the patron saint of hunting, lives up to its sporting image. Its decor is 17th-century rustic, its specialty, fresh game in season. Guests enjoy generous portions and a congenial atmosphere. *Florinsmarkt 6, tel. 0261/31177. Reservations advised. No credit cards. Moderate.*

Lodging

Hohenstaufen. Hohenstaufen is located near the train station in a postwar building that was renovated in 1985. Facilities include a Chinese restaurant and garage. *Emil-Schuller-Str. 41– 43, tel. 0261/37081, fax 0261/32303. 50 rooms with bath or shower. AE, DC, MC, V. Expensive.*

Scandic Crown. This elegant, modern hotel stands directly on the Rhine river bank; most rooms have fine views of the river and Ehrenbreitstein fortress. A lovely garden and terrace also overlook the river. *Julius-Wegeler-Str. 2, tel. 0261/1360, fax 0261/1361199. 170 rooms with bath. Facilities: 2 restaurants, bar, sauna, whirlpool. AE, DC, MC, V. Expensive.*

Köln
Dining
★

Bado-La Poêle d'Or. At first glance, the heavy furnishings and hushed atmosphere of the Poêle d'Or make it seem like the last place you'd find light and sophisticated nouvelle cuisine in Germany. But for some years, those in the know have been claiming this as one of the finest dining establishments in Europe. Even such apparently simple dishes as onion soup have been winning plaudits. Order salmon with lemon-ginger sauce if you want to sample the full glory of the place. *Komödienstr. 50–52, tel. 0221/134100. Reservations required. AE, DC, MC, V. Closed Sun., Mon. for lunch. Expensive.*

Gaststätte Früh am Dom. For real down-home German food, there are few places to compare with this time-honored former brewery. Bold frescoes on the vaulted ceilings establish the mood. Such dishes as Hämchen provide an authentically Teutonic experience. The beer garden is delightful for summer dining, and a tavern room, the Glockenstube, has been added recently. *Am Hof 12–14, tel. 0221/2580394. Reservations advised. No credit cards. Moderate.*

★ **Weinhaus im Walfisch.** The black-and-white gabled facade of this 400-year-old restaurant signals that here, too, you'll come face-to-face with no-holds-barred traditional specialties in a time-honored atmosphere. Try *Himmel und Erde* (a mixture of potatoes, onions, and apples) and any of the wide range of wines. The restaurant is tucked away between the Heumarkt (Haymarket) and the river. *Salzgasse 13, tel. 0221/219575. Reservations advised. AE, DC, MC, V. Closed weekends and holidays. Moderate.*

Lodging
★

Dom-Hotel. The Dom is in a class of its own. Old-fashioned, formal, and gracious, with a stunning location right by the cathedral, it offers the sort of Old World elegance and discreetly efficient service few hotels aspire to these days. The antique-filled bedrooms are subdued in color, high-ceilinged, and spacious. The view of the cathedral is something to treasure; enjoy it from the glassed-in Atelier am Dom, where you can dine on anything from wild boar served with chanterelle ragout to tofu piccata with ratatouille and curried rice. *Domkloster 2A, tel. 0221/20240, fax 0221/2024444. 126 rooms with bath. Facilities: restaurant, terrace café, bar, parking. AE, DC, MC, V. Very Expensive.*

★ **Excelsior Hotel Ernst.** The Empire-style lobby in sumptuous royal blue, bright yellow, and gold is striking, and a similar boldly conceived grandeur extends to all the public rooms in this hotel founded in 1863, just down the street from the main train station and across from the cathedral. Old Master paintings (including a Van Dyke) are everywhere; you'll be served breakfast in a room hung with Gobelins tapestries. Guest rooms are appropriately more intimate in scale, with spectacular marble bathrooms and ultramodern fixtures. Looking like anything but a *Stube*, the lacquered-wood-paneled restaurant serves classic French cuisine imaginatively prepared. The wine cellar is renowned for its French Burgundies and Bordeaux. *Domplatz, tel. 0221/2701, fax 0221/135150. 160 rooms with bath. Facilities: restaurant, piano bar, hair salon, masseuse, fitness room. AE, DC, MC, V. Very Expensive.*

Weisser Schwan. An ordinary little hotel in the city center was transformed in 1992 into a luxurious establishment that owner Kurt Bohlscheid boasts is a Rhineland showplace. Each room is individually decorated, with fabric-covered walls, brass bedsteads, and fine Victorian antiques. An Italian restaurant is on the ground floor. *Thieboldsgasse 133–135, tel. 0221/217697, fax 0221/238516. 12 rooms with bath. AE, DC, MC, V. Expensive.*

★ **Alstadt.** Located close by the river in the old town, this is the place for charm and low rates. Each room is furnished differently, and the service is impeccable—both welcoming and efficient. There's no restaurant. *Salzgasse 7, tel. 0221/2577851, fax 0221/2577853. 28 rooms with bath. Facilities: sauna. AE, DC, MC, V. Closed Christmas. Moderate.*

Königswinter
Dining

Zum Alten Bräuhaus. Located in a pleasant, shady garden in the center of town, Zum Alten Bräuhaus features hearty German fare, served with a selection of local wines and beers. *Hauptstr. 454, tel. 02223/22528. Reservations advised. No credit cards. Moderate.*

Lodging

Günnewig Rheinhotel. A modern hotel situated right on the banks of the Rhine, Günnewig Rheinhotel offers pleasant river views. *Rheinallee 9, tel. 02223/24051, fax 0223/26694. 110 rooms with bath. Facilities: restaurant, bar, pool, sauna, solarium. AE, DC, MC, V. Expensive.*

Mainz
Dining
★

Drei Lilien. This beautifully appointed restaurant offers antique furnishings and excellent nouvelle cuisine. *Ballplatz 2, tel. 06131/225068. Reservations advised. AE, DC, MC, V. Closed Sun. Expensive.*

Rats und Zunftstuben Heilig Geist. Although the decor is predominantly modern, this popular restaurant also incorporates some Roman remains and offers a traditional atmosphere. The cuisine is hearty German fare. *Rentengasse 2, tel. 06131/225757. Reservations required. AE, DC, MC, V. Moderate.*

Lodging

Hilton International. This enormous, glossy hotel presents a number of attractive public rooms, including a rooftop restaurant and Roman wine cellar. The bedrooms are tastefully furnished. *Rheinstr. 68, tel. 06131/2450, fax 06131/245589. 435 rooms with bath. Facilities: pool, sauna, health club, conference center. AE, DC, MC, V. Very Expensive.*

Hotel-Restaurant Am Lerchenberg. The location isn't ideal—some 4 miles from the city center—but there's a bus stop right outside the door and open countryside only short steps away. Family-run, the hotel is friendly, comfortable, and peaceful. *Hindemithstr. 5, tel. 06131/73001, fax 06131/73004. 53 rooms with bath. Facilities: restaurant, sauna, solarium, fitness room. AE, DC, MC, V. Moderate–Expensive.*

Rüdesheim
Dining

Krone. The extensive restoration work carried out on the 450-year-old Krone Hotel included a complete renovation of its restaurant, which now ranks among the most outstanding in the region. Chef Hubert Pecher's terrines and pâtés draw regular customers from as far away as Frankfurt. His fish dishes are supreme, and the Rhine wines are the best. *Rheinuferstr. 10, Assmannshausen, tel. 06722/4030. Reservations advised. AE, DC, MC. Moderate–Expensive.*

Lodging

Central. This friendly, family-run hotel recently became a member of the Ring group and now offers all the comfort and facilities expected from that chain. It has a fine restaurant. *Kirchstr. 6, tel. 06722/2391, fax 06722/2807. 53 rooms with bath. AE, DC, MC, V. Moderate.*

Hotel und Weinhaus Felsenkeller. Located just around the corner from Drosselgasse, Hotel and Weinhaus Felsenkeller is a traditional 18th-century establishment offering modern comforts. *Oberstr. 39–41, tel. 06722/2094, fax 06722/47202. 60 rooms with shower. AE, MC, V. Inexpensive.*

St. Goar, **Roter Kopf.** This is a historic wine restaurant brimming with
St. Goarshausen rustic Rhineland atmosphere. *Burgstr. 5, St. Goarshausen,*
Dining *tel. 06771/2698. Reservations advised. No credit cards. Moderate.*

Lodging **Schlosshotel-Burg Rheinfels.** Situated high above St. Goar, on a hill commanding spectacular river views, the Schlosshotel-Burg Rheinfels rises from the ruins of the adjacent castle (*see* Exploring, *above*). *Schlossberg 47, tel. 06741/8020, fax 06741/7652. 59 rooms with shower. Facilities: restaurant, pool, sauna. AE, DC, MC, V. Expensive.*
Rhein Hotel Adler. Perched right on the edge of the Rhine, this is a turn-of-the-century, family-run establishment. Facilities include an attractive garden and terrace. *St. Goarshausen, Bahnhofstr. 6, tel. 06771/2613, fax 06741/1447. 73 rooms with bath. Facilities: restaurant, pool, solarium. AE, DC, MC, V. Moderate.*

The Black Forest

Only a century ago, the Black Forest (Schwarzwald) was one of the wildest stretches of countryside in Europe. It had earned its somber name because of the impenetrable stretches of dark forest that clothed the mountains and shielded small communities from the outside world. Today, it's a friendly, hospitable region, still extensively forested but with large, open valleys and stretches of verdant farmland. Among the trailblazing tourists of the adventurous 19th century was Mark Twain, who wrote enthusiastically about the natural beauty of the region. The deep hot springs first discovered by the Romans were rediscovered, and small forgotten villages became wealthy spas. Hikers treasured the lonely trails that cut through the forests and rolling uplands, skiers opened the world's first lift on the slopes of the region's highest mountain, and horseback riders cut bridle paths through the tangle of narrow river valleys.

The Black Forest is the southernmost German wine region and the custodian of some of the country's best traditional foods. (Black Forest smoked ham and Black Forest cake are worldfamous.) It retains its vibrant clock-making tradition, and local wood-carvers haven't yet died out. Best of all, though, it's still possible to stay overnight in a Black Forest farmhouse and eat a breakfast hearty enough to last the day, all for the price of an indifferent meal at a restaurant in, say, Munich or Frankfurt.

Getting Around

Today the Black Forest is easily accessible from all parts of the country. The Rhine Valley autobahn, the A5, runs the entire length of the Black Forest and connects at Karlsruhe with the rest of the German expressway network. Well-paved, single-lane highways traverse the region. A main north-south train line follows the Rhine Valley, carrying Euro-City and Intercity trains that call at hourly intervals at Freiburg and Baden-Baden, connecting those two centers directly with Frankfurt and many other German cities. Local lines connect most Black Forest towns, and two local east-west services, the Black Forest

The Black Forest

Karlsruhe

Pforzheim
Bad Liebenzell
Baden-Baden
Calw
Zavelstein Talmühle
Stuttgart
Kehl
Mummelsee
Baiersbronn
Nagold
Offenburg
Freudenstadt
Neckar
Zell
Alpirsbach
Lahr
Wolfach
Schiltach
Gutachtal Valley
Rottweil
Danube
Kaiserstuhl
Triberg
Freiburg
Furtwangen
Himmelreich
Titisee
Tuttlingen
Staufen
Schluchsee
Radolfzell
Zell
Friedrichshafen
Rheinfelden
Bodensee

FRANCE

N

SWITZERLAND

Railway and the Höllental Railway, are spectacular scenic runs. The nearest airports are at Stuttgart; Strasbourg, in the neighboring French Alsace; and the Swiss border city of Basel, just 64 kilometers (40 miles) from Freiburg.

Tourist Information

Baden-Baden (Augustaplatz 8, tel. 07221/275200).
Freiburg (Rotteckring 14, tel. 0761/368–900).
Freudenstadt (Promenadenplatz 1, tel. 07741/86420).
Pforzheim (Marktplatz 1, tel. 07231/302314).

Guided Tours

Guided bus tours of the Black Forest begin in both Freiburg and Baden-Baden. A choice of 25 day tours from Freiburg includes the French Alsace region, the Swiss Alps, and various attractions in the Black Forest. Prices range from DM 20 to DM 42 and include English-speaking guides. In Baden-Baden, tours are offered by the **Deutsches Reisebüro** (Sophienstr. 1b, tel. 07221/21050) and concentrate on the Black Forest.

Exploring the Black Forest

The regional tourist authority has worked out a series of scenic routes covering virtually every attraction the visitor is likely to want to see (obtainable from the **Fremdenverkehrsverband**, Bertoldstr. 45, 7800 Freiburg, tel. 0761/31317). Routes are basically intended for the motorist, but most points can be reached by train or bus. The following itinerary is accessible by all means of transportation and takes in parts of the Black Forest High Road, Low Road, Spa Road, Wine Road, and Clock Road.

The ancient Roman city of **Pforzheim** is the starting point here, accessible either from the Munich–Karlsruhe autobahn or by train from Karlsruhe, Frankfurt, or Stuttgart. Known even beyond Germany's borders as the Gold City because of its association with the jewelry trade, Pforzheim has the world's finest museum collection of jewelry in the **Reuchlinhaus,** spanning four centuries. (Jahnstr. 42; admission free; Tues.–Sun. 10–5). Pforzheim was almost completely destroyed by wartime bombing and is a fine example of reconstruction work: Visit the centrally located parish church of **St. Michael** to see how faithfully the experts stuck to the original mixture of sturdy Romanesque and later, finer Gothic styles. For a contrast, take a look at Pforzheim's **St. Matthew's Church,** a tentlike construction erected in 1953 when the designers of the similarly styled Olympic stadium in Munich were still at the drawing board.

On the way out of Pforzheim, toward B463, the Nagold Valley road, gardeners should make a detour to the **Alpine Garden** on the Tiefenbronn road. More than 100,000 varieties of plants, including the rarest Alpine flowers, are found here, and many are for sale. *Open Mar.–Oct., daily 8–7.*

Bad Liebenzell, our first stop on B463, is one of the oldest spas of the Black Forest, with the remains of 15th-century installations. Visitors are welcome to take the waters at the **Paracelsus baths** on the Nagold riverbank. *Tel. 07052/408250. Admission: DM 11.50 adults, DM 5 children for 2½ hours. Open Mon., Thurs. 8:30–5; Tues., Wed., Fri., Sat. 8:30–8; Sun. 8:30–7.*

Leave plenty of time to explore **Calw** (pronounced Calve), the next town on the road south. Its famous native son, the novelist and poet Hermann Hesse, called it the "most beautiful [town] of all I know." And Hesse, who died in Switzerland in 1962, had seen more than a few in his extensive travels. Pause on the town's 15th-century bridge over the rushing Nagold River—if you're lucky, you'll see a local tanner spreading hides over the river wall to dry, as his ancestors did for centuries past.

Back on the main road south, turn off at Talmühle for the **Neubulach silver mine.** Once the most productive workings of the Black Forest, the mine is now open to visitors. *Admission: DM 4 adults, DM 3 children (includes entry to mineral museum). Open Apr.–Oct., Mon.–Sat. 10–4, Sun. 9:30–5.*

Time Out In the town of **Nagold,** visit the 1697-built half-timbered **Alte Post** inn on Bahnhofstrasse 2. Kings and queens have taken refreshment here on journeys through the Black Forest. Enjoy the local beer and a plate of Black Forest smoked ham or a pot of strong coffee and a slice of delectable Black Forest cake.

From Nagold, the road travels on through lush farmland to **Freudenstadt,** another war-flattened German city that has been painstakingly restored. It was originally built during the early 17th century as a model city to house not only workers in nearby silver mines but refugees from religious persecution in what is now Austrian Carinthia. The streets are still laid out in the grid pattern decreed by the original planners, while the vast central square continues to wait for the palace that was intended to stand here. It was to have been built for the city's founder, Prince Frederick I of Württemberg, but he died before work could begin. Don't miss Freudenstadt's **Protestant parish church,** just off the square. It's L-shaped, a rare architectural liberty during the early 17th century, when this imposing church was built.

Quench your thirst at nearby **Alpirsbach,** where the unusually soft water gives the local beer an especially smooth quality. The brewery was once part of a monastic settlement whose pretty **Romanesque church** next to the brewhouse is well worth a visit. The brewery still produces a strong monastery beer *(Klosterbock)* and maintains the tradition of brewing a special Christmas beer.

South of Alpirsbach, stop at **Schiltach** to admire (and possibly giggle at) the frescoes on the 16th-century town hall that depict the history of this exceptionally pretty village. The devil figures prominently in the frescoes: He was blamed for burning Schiltach down on several occasions.

From here, take B294 to **Wolfach** to visit the last Black Forest factory where glass is blown by centuries-old techniques once common throughout the region. *Die Dorotheen-Glashütte, Glashüttenweg 4, tel. 07834/751. Admission: DM 4 adults, DM 3 children. Open weekdays 9–4:30, Sat. 9–2.*

The **Gutachtal Valley,** south of Wolfach, is famous for its traditional costumes, and if you're there at the right time (holidays and some Sundays), you'll see the married women sporting black pompoms on their hats to denote their matronly status (red pompoms are for the unmarried). At the head of the valley, at **Triberg,** are Germany's highest waterfalls, which reach a height of nearly 155 meters (500 feet). This is also cuckoo clock country. The **Clock Museum (Uhrenmuseum)** at Furtwangen is the largest in Germany. Its collection includes an astronomical timepiece weighing more than one ton. *Gerwigstr. 11, tel. 07723/656117. Admission: DM 4 adults, DM 2 children. Open Apr.–Oct., daily 9–5; Nov.–Mar., Mon.–Sat. 10–4.*

From Furtwangen, the road leads to the lakeland of the Black Forest. The two largest lakes, **Titisee** and **Schluchsee,** are beautifully set amid fir-clad mountains, but try to avoid them at the height of the summer holidays, when they are quite crowded. From here, it's a short run to Freiburg, capital of the Black Forest. The most direct route goes via the aptly named Höllental (Hell Valley). The first stop outside the narrow, gorgelike valley is called, appropriately enough, **Himmelreich,** meaning "Kingdom of Heaven." The village is said to have been given the name by railway engineers who were grateful finally to have run a line through Hell Valley. The Black Forest railway, more than 100 years old, still tackles the mountainous route, connecting Freiburg and the resort of Hinterzarten; details and tickets are available from the **Bundesbahn** (German Railways) in Freiburg (tel. 0761/19419).

Perched on the western slopes of the Black Forest, **Freiburg** was founded as a free market town in the 12th century. It was badly bombed in World War II. Towering over the rebuilt, medieval streets of the city is its most famous landmark, the cathedral, or **Münster.** The cathedral took three centuries to build and has one of the finest spires in the world. April through October, English-language walking tours of the old town include an explanation of the Münster's numerous architectural styles. Tours are led daily, except Tuesdays, at 10 AM and last two hours. *Admission: DM 6 adults, DM 3 children. (Contact tourist office;* see above.*)*

Try to visit Freiburg on a Friday, which is market day. The square in front of the cathedral then becomes a mass of color and movement, while a fitting backdrop is provided by **Kaufhaus,** the 16th-century market house.

Time Out Stroll up to the Oberlinden Square and stop in at **Zum Roten Bären** (The Red Bear), reputedly Germany's oldest inn; it has a documented history dating from 1091! Order a "Viertel" of the local wine and perhaps a plate of locally smoked ham—and if you like the atmosphere, why not stay the night?

Once you've braved Hell Valley to get to Freiburg, a visit to the nearby town where Dr. Faustus is reputed to have made his deal with the devil should hold no horrors. **Staufen,** which claims the inquisitive doctor as one of its early burgers, is some 19 kilometers (12 miles) south of Freiburg. Local records show there really was an alchemist named Faustus who blew himself up in his laboratory. According to legend, the devil dragged him off to hell from the **Gasthof zum Löwen** (Hauptstr. 47, tel. 07633/7078), an old inn in the village center. The inn has a tap room named for Faust, and there are comfortable guest rooms if you fancy staying the night.

From Staufen, turn northward to Baden-Baden along the **Wine Road,** skirting the French border to your left, through the southernmost vineyards of Germany, source of the prized Baden wine. Some of the best vineyards are situated on a volcanic outcrop known as the **Kaiserstuhl** (Emperor's Chair). Sample a glass of wine in the village of **Achkarren,** which has a fascinating **wine museum.** *Admission: DM 2 adults, DM 1 children. Open Apr.–Oct., weekdays 2–5, weekends 10:30–4.*

All the vineyards along the Wine Road offer tastings, so don't hesitate to drop in and try one or two. Leave the Wine Road at the town of Lahr and head inland, on B415, through the narrow Schuttertal valley to Zell, and from there to the Black Forest **High Road.** This is the land of fable and superstition, and if you're here during the mist-days of autumn, stop off at the mystery-shrouded **Mummelsee Lake,** immortalized by the poet Mörike in his ballad *The Spirits of the Mummelsee.* Legend has it that sprites and other spirits of the deep live in the cold waters of the small, round lake in its forest setting. It's true that no fish are found in the lake, but scientific sorts say this is a result of the high mineral content of the water.

From the Mummelsee, it's downhill all the way to fashionable **Baden-Baden,** idyllically set in a wooded valley of the northern Black Forest. The town sits on top of extensive underground hot springs that gave the city its name (*Bad,* German for "spa"). The Romans first exploited the springs, which were then rediscovered by wealthy 19th-century travelers. By the end of the 19th century, there was scarcely a crowned head of Europe who had not dipped into the healing waters of Baden-Baden. The town became the unofficial summer residence of numerous royal and titled families, and they left their imprint in the form of palatial houses that grace its tree-lined avenues.

One of the grand buildings of Baden-Baden's Belle Epoque is the pillared **Kurhaus,** home of Germany's first casino, which opened its doors to the world's gamblers in 1853. Entrance costs a modest DM 5, though visitors are required to sign a declaration that they enter with sufficient funds to settle subsequent debts! *Jacket and tie required. Passport necessary as proof of identity. Open Sun.–Fri. 2 PM–2 AM, Sat. 2 PM–3 AM. Daily tours (DM 3) from Apr.–Sept., daily 9:30–noon; Oct.– Mar., 10–noon.*

If jackets and ties are customary attire at the casino, no clothes at all are de rigueur at Baden-Baden's famous Roman baths, the **Friedrichsbad.** You "take the waters" here just as the Romans did nearly 2,000 years ago—nude. *Römerplatz 1, tel. 07221/275920. Admission: DM 28 for 3 hours (DM 38 with massage). Children under 16 not admitted. Open Mon.–Sat. 9 AM– 10 PM.*

The remains of the Roman baths that lie beneath the Friedrichsbad can be visited from April through October. *Admission: DM 2.*

Time Out Step into the warm elegance of the **Café König** in the nearby Lichtentalerstrasse pedestrian zone. Order a pot of coffee and a wedge of Black Forest cake and listen to the hum of contentment from the monied spa crowd who have made this quiet corner their haunt.

The attractions of the Friedrichsbad are rivaled by the neighboring **Caracalla baths,** renovated and enlarged in 1985. The huge, modern complex has five indoor pools, two outdoor ones, numerous whirlpools, a solarium, and what is described as a "sauna landscape"—you look out through windows at the countryside while steaming. *Römerplatz 11, tel. 07221/275940. Admission: DM 18 for 2 hours. Open daily 8 AM–10 PM.*

Dining and Lodging

For details and price-category definitions, *see* Dining and Lodging in Staying in Germany.

Bad Liebenzell **Thermen-Hotel.** This spacious spa hotel, on the edge of Bad
Lodging Liebenzell's spa park, is one of the region's most distinctive buildings: a flower-smothered, half-timbered mansion (and its more modern annex) where the Black Forest creeps to the very edge of the garden. Rooms are spacious and comfortable and most have pergola-like balconies. *Am Kurpark, tel. 07052/ 408300, fax 07052/408108. 23 rooms with bath or shower. Facilities: restaurant, garden café, terrace, fitness center, sauna, parking. MC. Moderate.*

Baden-Baden **Merkurius.** A log fire on cool days adds to the warm atmosphere
Dining of this country-style restaurant-cum-hotel in the district of
★ Varnhalt on the southern fringes of Baden-Baden. The menu offers classic and regional dishes with a light touch: goose-liver soufflé and wild hare with potato and vegetable topping. The adjoining hotel has four moderately priced rooms. *Klosterberg 2, tel. 07223/5474. Reservations required. AE, DC, MC. Closed Sat. lunch, Mon., and Tues. Very Expensive.*
Stahlbad. The Gallo-Germanic menu here is echoed by the restaurant's furnishings—19th-century French oils adorn the walls, while French and German china are reflected in the ma-

hogany gleam of antique tables and sideboards. An abundance of green velvet catches the tone of the parklike grounds of the stately house that accommodates this elegant restaurant. *Augustaplatz 2, tel. 07221/24569. Reservations advised. AE, DC, MC, V. Closed Sun. dinner and Mon. Expensive.*

Gasthaus zur Traube. Regional specialties, such as smoked bacon and homemade noodles, take pride of place in this cozy inn, south of the city center in the Neuweier district. If you like the food, you can also spend the night in one of the 18 neatly furnished rooms. *Mauerbergstr. 107, tel. 07223/57216. Reservations not essential. AE, DC, MC, V. Closed Wed. Moderate.*

Lodging **Brenner's Park Hotel.** This exceptional stately mansion is set in spacious private grounds. All rooms are luxuriously furnished and appointed—as they should be, since they cost up to DM 750 per day, with 20 apartments going for up to DM 2,000. *Schillerstr. 6, tel. 07221/9000, fax 07221/38772. 88 rooms with bath and balcony. Facilities: 2 restaurants, hairdresser, beauty salon, indoor pool, sauna, bridge room, bicycle hire. AE, DC, MC. Very Expensive.*

★ **Der Kleine Prinz.** Each room of this beautifully modernized 19th-century mansion is decorated in a different style, from romantic Art Nouveau to Manhattan modern (owner Norbert Rademacher was director of New York's Waldorf-Astoria for several years). Some rooms have whirlpool baths. The hotel's elegant restaurant offers "new German cuisine" with a French touch. *Lichtentalerstr. 36, tel. 07221/3464, fax 07221/38264. 39 rooms with bath. Facilities: restaurant. AE, DC, MC, V. Restaurant closed first 2 weeks of Jan. Expensive.*

Deutscher Kaiser-Etol. This centrally located old, established hotel, a few minutes' stroll from the Kurhaus, offers homey and individually styled rooms at comfortable prices in an otherwise expensive town. All the double rooms have balconies on a quiet street off one of the main thoroughfares. *Merkurstr. 9, tel. 07221/2700, fax 07221/270270. 44 rooms with bath. Facilities: restaurant (closed Sun. dinner), bar, wine and beer tavern, bicycle hire. AE, DC, MC, V. Moderate.*

Hotel am Markt. The Bogner family has run this historic, 250-year-old hotel for more than 30 years. It's friendly, popular, and right in the center of town. *Marktplatz 17–18, tel. 07221/22747. 28 rooms, 14 with bath or shower. Facilities: restaurant, terrace. AE, DC, MC, V. Inexpensive.*

Baiersbronn **Bareiss.** The mountain resort of Baiersbronn is blessed with
Dining two of Germany's leading restaurants. The most noted is the
★ Bareiss, in the Kurhotel Bareiss, with an elegantly appointed powder-blue dining room. Its menu of lightly prepared classic dishes attracts gastronomes from across the border in the French Alsace region. *Kurhotel Mitteltal, Gärtnerbuhlweg 14, tel. 07442/470. Reservations required. AE, DC, MC, V. Closed Mon., Tues., the 4 weeks directly after Whit Sun., and all Dec. Very Expensive.*

Traube Tonbach Schwarzwaldstube. French cuisine is the specialty here, where diners are settled at antique tables beneath a heavy ceiling of carved and polished beams. Try for a table by the large picture window overlooking the Tonbach valley. *Tonbachstr. 237, tel. 07442/665. Reservations required. AE, DC, MC, V. Closed Mon. and Tues. Very Expensive.*

Calw **Hotel Kloster Hirsau.** This country-house hotel on the wooded
Dining and Lodging outskirts of Calw stands on the site of a 900-year-old monas-

tery, whose Gothic cloisters are still largely intact. A small Renaissance palace, a Romanesque chapel, and some fine medieval half-timbered buildings are just a short walk away. The hotel prides itself on its award-winning restaurant, where owner-chef Joachim Ulrich's menu changes daily. The emphasis is on regional dishes enhanced with a light French touch: featured are Swabian farmhouse noodles along with truffle vinaigrette. *Wildbaderstr. 2, tel. 07051/56213, fax 07051/51795. 42 rooms with bath. Facilities: restaurant, bar, indoor pool, garden terrace, parking. MC, V. Expensive.*

Freiburg
Dining

Falkenstube. A 10-course "gourmet menu" is one of the many attractions of the oak-paneled Falkenstube restaurant in Freiburg's luxurious Colombi Hotel. The kitchen has a slight French accent, but there are also numerous regional dishes, plus such interesting fish specialties as turbot fillets in lentil sauce. *Colombi Hotel, Rotteckring 16, tel. 0761/31415. Reservations required. AE, DC, MC, V. Closed Sun. Expensive.*

Enoteca. Three dining possibilities are now offered by the refurbished and recently reopened Enoteca. Lunch is served in the crowded, friendly bistro, while dinner is a more leisurely affair in the adjacent restaurant, where subdued lighting glistens on honey-colored paneling. Late-night diners can get light meals at the Enoteca bar, which is open until 1:30 AM. Proprietor Manfred Schmitz is a respected local wine connoisseur as well as an accomplished chef, and he can be relied on to recommend just the right vintage to accompany such specialties as veal roulade with gorgonzola. *Schwabentorplatz, tel. 0761/30751. Restaurant reservations advised. AE, DC, MC, V. Closed Sun. Moderate–Expensive.*

Ratskeller. In the shadow of the cathedral, the popular Ratskeller has a typical Black Forest ambience (lots of wood paneling and beams), which is matched by a menu of mostly traditional dishes (roasts and rich sauces). *Münsterplatz 11, tel. 0761/37530. Reservations advised. AE, DC, MC, V. Closed Sun. dinner, Mon. Moderate.*

Zum Roten Bären. The Red Bear claims to be the oldest inn in Germany (it was first mentioned in official documents in 1091). It's the archetypal German history-book inn, with a traditional menu to match. Request Swabian *Spätzle* (a delicious variety of noodle) with everything. *Oberlinden 12, tel. 0761/36913. Reservations advised. AE, DC, MC, V. Moderate.*

Dining and Lodging

Markgrafler Hof. Even the French make a pilgrimage from Alsace to dine in Hans Leo Kempchen's restaurant in this traditional old hotel in Freiburg's quaint pedestrian zone. Kempchen rewards travelers with special gourmet menus and unbeatable two-day deals that include accommodations, a wine tasting, and a guided tour of the city. Call well in advance to reserve rooms—otherwise the French will have most likely beaten you to it. *Gerberau 22, tel. 0761/32540, fax 0761/37947. 29 rooms with bath or shower. Facilities: restaurant, parking. AE, DC, MC, V. Moderate.*

Lodging

Panorama Hotel Mercure. This modern hotel is situated high above Freiburg, although it's only a few minutes by car to the downtown area. It was recently taken over by the French Mercure group, who have maintained standards. All rooms have south-facing balconies, with fine views of the city and surrounding countryside. *Wintererstr. 89, tel. 0761/51030, fax 0761/5103300. 85 rooms with bath. Facilities: restaurant, in-*

door pool, sauna, solarium, tennis, ping-pong, bicycle hire. *AE, DC, MC, V. Very Expensive.*

★ **Romantik Hotel Stollen.** You'll need a car to reach this luxuriously decorated half-timbered country house located 9½ kilometers (6 miles) outside the town in Gutach im Elztal. The hotel is best reached from the Karlsruhe-Basel autobahn by taking the Freiburg north exit and following the Waldkirch road. The restaurant has won awards for its excellent concoctions. *7809 Gutach im Elztal, tel. 07685/207, fax 07685/1550. 10 rooms with bath and balcony. AE, DC, MC, V. Moderate–Expensive.*

Gasthaus und Pension Hirschen. This charming converted farmhouse has been in the possession of the Winterhalter family for four centuries, and today's Winterhalters take as much care in making their guests feel at home as did their ancestors. The pension is in the village of Wittnau, a 10-minute drive or 15-minute bus trip from Freiburg, but the disadvantages of its distance from the city are more than offset by its peaceful location amid open countryside, a walker's paradise. *Schönberg 11, 7801 Wittnau, tel. 0761/402137. 20 rooms, most with bath. Facilities: restaurant, bowling alley, parking. No credit cards. Moderate.*

Rappen Hotel. You'll sleep like a pampered farmhouse guest here, in brightly painted rustic beds, beneath soft feather quilts. It's as quiet as a country village, too: The Rappen is in the center of the traffic-free old city. In the countrified but comfortable restaurant, patrons have the choice of more than 200 regional wines. *Am Münsterplatz 13, tel. 0761/31353, fax 0751/382252. 13 rooms, most with bath. Facilities: bar-restaurant, terrace. AE, DC, MC, V. Moderate.*

Freudenstadt **Bären.** Fish is the Bären's strength (with local trout a special-
Dining ty), but simple, traditional Swabian dishes are also featured in this hotel restaurant (15 moderately priced rooms). If you want to eat as the locals do, try *Maultaschen,* a delicious meat-filled ravioli dish that Swabians swear by. *Langestr. 33, tel. 07441/2729. Reservations advised. AE, DC, MC, V. Closed Sun. dinner, Mon., and last 2 weeks in Jan. Moderate.*

Ratskeller. If it's cold outside, ask for a place near the Ratskeller's *Kachelofen,* a large, traditional, tiled heating stove. Swabian dishes and venison are prominent on the menu, but if the homemade trout roulade with crab sauce is featured, go for it. *Marktplatz 8, tel. 07441/2693. Reservations advised. MC, V. Closed Mon. Moderate.*

Lodging **Lutz Posthotel.** This is an old coaching inn in the heart of the town that has been managed by the same family since 1809. But there's nothing old-fashioned about the rooms, which are both modern and cozy. The restaurant offers Swabian delicacies. During the summer there's a coffee terrace. *Stuttgarterstr. 5, tel. 07441/2421, fax 07441/84533. 45 rooms with bath, some with balcony. Facilities: wine bar, library. AE, DC, MC, V. Moderate.*

Hinterzarten **Park Hotel Adler.** This hotel has been in the possession of the
Lodging Riesterer family for more than five centuries: Since 1446, when
★ an early ancestor gave 17 schillings for the original property, it has been developing into one of Germany's finest hotels. The hotel complex stands in nearly 10 acres of grounds ringed by the Black Forest. Among the seven rooms devoted to eating and drinking are a French restaurant and a paneled 17th-century dining room. An orchestra accompanies dinner and later moves

to the bar for dancing. *Adlerplatz 3, tel. 07652/1270, fax 07652/ 127717. 84 rooms with bath. Facilities: 2 restaurants, bar, pool, sauna, solarium, tennis (indoor and outdoor), horseback riding, bicycle hire, beauty salon, hairdresser, library, game rooms, child-care facilities. AE, DC, MC, V. Very Expensive.*

Nagold
Dining
Romantik Restaurant Alte Post. This centuries-old half-timbered inn has the kind of atmosphere lesser establishments believe can be built in with false beams. The menu ranges from Swabian traditional to pricey French, so stay with the local dishes (veal in a rich mushroom sauce or, in season, venison in the Baden-Baden style) and you won't be shocked by the bill. *Bahnhofstr. 2, tel. 07452/4221. Reservations required. AE, DC, MC, V. Closed Fri. lunch. Moderate.*

Lodging
Hotel Post Gästehaus. Run by the former proprietors of the adjacent Alte Post restaurant, this hotel is made up of an old coaching inn and modern additions. It offers a high degree of comfort—and homemade preserves for breakfast. *Bahnhofstr. 3, tel. 07452/4048, fax 07452/4040. 24 rooms with bath. Facilities: English-language cable TV. AE, DC, MC, V. Expensive.*

Pforzheim
Dining
Silberburg. This is a rustic restaurant offering classic and regional cooking at bargain prices. For best value, ask to see the *Tagesempfehlungen*—the chef's daily recommendations. *Dietlingerstr. 27, tel. 07231/41159. Reservations necessary. AE, DC, MC, V. Closed Mon., Tues. lunch, and 3 weeks in Aug. Inexpensive.*

Titisee
Lodging
Romantik Hotel Adler Post. This hotel is in the Neustadt district of Titisee, about 4½ kilometers (3 miles) from the lake. The solid old building has been in the possession of the Ketterer family for more than 140 years. The guest rooms are comfortably and traditionally furnished. The hotel's restaurant, the Rôtisserie zum Postillon, is noted for its regional cuisine. *Hauptstr. 16, tel. 07651/5066, fax 07651/3729. 32 rooms with bath. Facilities: pool, sauna, solarium, game room, library. AE, DC, MC, V. Moderate.*

Triberg
Lodging
Hotel Central Garni. From the sunny rooftop terrace of this hotel you have a sweeping view of the surrounding Black Forest, with Triberg's bustling market square directly below. The hotel occupies the upper floors of a new office building: Rooms are bright and airy, with selected Black Forest antiques giving them a homely feel. There's no restaurant, but the hotel's central location means you'll find plenty within a few minutes' walk. *Am Marktpl., tel. 07722/4360. Facilities: terrace, parking. MC. Moderate.*

Berlin

Berlin is now a united metropolis—again the largest in continental Europe—and only two small sections of the Wall have been left in place to remind visitors and residents alike of the hideous barrier that divided the city for nearly 30 years. Old habits die hard, however, and it will be a long time before Germans and even Berliners themselves can get accustomed to regarding Berlin as one entity with one identity. You'll still hear Berliners in the western, more prosperous half talking about "those Ossies over there" when referring to people in the still down-at-the-heels eastern part. All restrictions on travel within and beyond the city have, of course, disappeared, and the sense of newly won freedom hangs almost tangibly in the air. But there's still a strong feeling of passing from one world into another when crossing the scar that marks the line where the wall once stood. It's not just the very visible differences between the glitter of West Berlin and the relative shabbiness of the east. Somehow the historical heritage of a long-divided city permeates the place and penetrates the consciousness of every visitor. You'll almost certainly arrive in and depart from the western part of Berlin, but just as surely your steps will lead you into the east. On the way, ponder the miracle that made this easy access to a onetime fortress of communism possible.

Arriving and Departing

By Plane **Tegel Airport** is centrally located, only 7 kilometers (4 miles) from downtown. Airlines flying to Tegel include Delta, TWA, Air France, British Airways, Deutsche BA, Lufthansa, Euro-Berlin, and some charter specialists. Because of increased air traffic at Tegel following unification, the former military airfield at **Tempelhof** (even closer to downtown) is being used more and more. East Berlin's **Schönefeld** airport is about 24 kilometers (15 miles) outside the downtown area. For information on arrival and departure times at Tegel, call 030/41011; for Schönefeld, call 030/67870.

Between the The No. 109 bus runs every ten minutes between Tegel airport
Airports and and downtown. The journey takes 30 minutes and the fare is
Downtown DM 3.20. A taxi fare will cost about DM 25. If you've rented a car at the airport, follow signs for the "Stadtautobahn" highway.

A shuttle bus leaves Schönefeld airport every 10–15 minutes for the nearby S-Bahn train station. S-Bahn trains leave every 20 minutes for the Friedrichstrasse station. The trip takes about 30 minutes, and you can get off at whatever stop is nearest your hotel. The fare by bus or subway is DM 3.20 and covers travel throughout Berlin. Taxis are usually available at the stops from Ostbahnhof onward. You can also take a taxi from the airport; the fare to your hotel will be about DM 30–DM 35, and the trip will take about 40 minutes. By car, follow the signs for "Stadtzentrum Berlin."

By Train There are six major rail routes to Berlin from the western half of the country (from Hamburg, Hannover, Köln, Frankfurt, Munich, and Nürnberg), and the network is set to expand to make the rest of eastern Germany more accessible. Traveling time to and from Berlin is being progressively cut as the system in eastern Germany becomes modernized and streamlined to meet western standards. For the latest information on routes call **Deutsche Bundesbahn Info** (tel. 030/19419) or **Deutsche Reichsbahn** (tel. 030/311–02–111), or enquire at the local main train station if you are in western Germany, where you will also get details of reduced fare rates. Three people or more can often travel at discounted group rates. The West Berlin terminus for all lines is the main train station (Bahnhof Zoo).

International trains headed directly for East Berlin arrive at Friedrichstrasse or the Ostbahnhof. Train information: tel. 030/49541 for international trains, 030/49531 for domestic services.

By Bus Long-distance bus services link Berlin with numerous western German and other western European cities. For travel details, if you're in Berlin, call the main bus station (Messedam, tel. 030/301–8028), or if you're in western Germany, inquire at the local tourist office.

By Car The eight former "transit corridor" roads linking the western part of Germany with Berlin have now been incorporated into the country-wide autobahn network, but some are ill prepared for the vast increase of motor traffic between east and west that has followed unification. Be prepared for large traffic jams, particularly during weekends. At the time of writing, speed restrictions of 100 kph (60 mph) still apply on some autobahn sections, but on others they have now been raised to 120 kph (74 mph) or 130 kph (81 mph). You must carry your driver's license, car registration, and insurance documents. Seat belts must be worn at all times.

Getting Around

By Public Transportation Berlin is surprisingly large, and only the center can comfortably be explored on foot. Fortunately, the city is blessed with excellent public transportation, a combination of U-Bahn (subway) and S-Bahn (metropolitan train) lines, bus services, and even a ferry across the Wannsee lake. The eight U-Bahn lines alone have 116 stations. An all-night bus service (the buses are marked by the letter N next to their number) is also in operation. For DM 3.20 you can buy a ticket that covers travel on the entire system for 2 hours. A multiple ticket, valid for four trips, costs DM 11. Or, you can pay DM 12 for a 24-hour ticket that allows unlimited use (except on the Wannsee Lake ferries). Information can be obtained from the office of the city transport authority, the Berliner Verkehrsbetriebe (BVG) at Hardenbergplatz, in front of the Bahnhof Zoo, or by calling 030/752–7020.

Buses and streetcars in East Berlin are often crowded, and route maps, posted at each stop (marked H or HH), are not particularly clear to the uninitiated. The fare structure now covers both parts of Berlin, although cheap, subsidized tickets are still sold to East Berlin residents. Don't be tempted to buy one if you're traveling in East Berlin—the fine is quite heavy if unauthorized travelers are found in possession of tickets reserved for East Berliners. The fares in East Berlin are the same as those in the west.

By Taxi Taxi meters start at DM 3.60, and the fare is DM 1.79 (DM 1.99 after midnight). Taxi drivers charge 50 pf for each piece of heavy luggage carried. A drive along the Kurfürstendamm will cost about DM 15. Taxis can be ordered by telephone: Call 030/ 6902, 030/210–101, or 030/210–102; in East Berlin phone 030/ 6944.

Important Addresses and Numbers

Tourist Information The main tourist office, **Verkehrsamt Berlin,** is at the Europa Center (Budapesterstr., tel. 030/262–6031). It's open Mon.– Sat. 8 AM–10:30 PM, Sun. 9–9. There are other offices at the main hall of **Tegel airport** (tel. 030/4101–3145, open daily 8 AM–11 PM); the **Bahnhof Zoo** (the main train station, tel. 030/313–9063, open Mon.–Sat. 8 AM–11 PM). Accommodations can be reserved at all offices, which also issue a free English-language information brochure, "Berlin Turns On." Pretravel information on Berlin can be obtained by writing to the Verkehrsamt Berlin (Europa Center, D-1000 Berlin 30).

The main office of the tourist office in East Berlin is at Alexanderplatz 5 (tel. 030/242–4675, 242–4512). It's open weekdays 8–8, Saturday 9–6.

Consulates **U.S.** (Clayallee 170, tel. 030/832–4087). **Canada** (International Trade Center, Friedrich Str. 95, tel. 030/261–1161).

Emergencies **Police** (tel. 030/110). **Ambulance and emergency medical attention** (tel. 030/310031). **Dentist** (tel. 030/1141). **Pharmacies:** for emergency pharmaceutical assistance, call 030/247033.

English-Language **Marga Schoeller** (Knesebeckstr. 33, tel. 030/881–1112); **Buch-**
Bookstores **handlung Kiepert** (Hardenbergstr. 4–5, tel. 030/311–0090).

Guided Tours

By Bus English-language bus tours of West and East Berlin are offered by a number of operators, the chief of which are **Severin & Kühn** (Kurfürstendamm 216, Charlottenburg, tel. 030/883–1015); **Berliner Bären Stadtrundfahrt** (Rankestr. 35, corner of Kurfürstendamm, tel. 030/213–4077); **Reisebüro Berolina** (Meinekestr. 3, tel. 030/882–2091); and **Bus Verkehr Berlin** (**BVB,** Kurfürstendamm 225, tel. 030/885–9880). These four companies offer more or less identical tours in English, covering all the major sights in West and East Berlin, as well as day tours to Potsdam and Dresden. The Berlin tours cost DM 30–DM 45, those to Potsdam and the Sanssouci Palace, the favorite residence of Frederick the Great, DM 60–DM 70.

By Boat Berlin is a city of waterways, and boat trips can be made on the Spree River and on the canals that connect the city's network of big lakes. For details, contact the city tourist office at the Europa Center, Budapesterstrasse, tel. 030/262–6031.

Exploring Berlin

Visiting Berlin is a bittersweet experience, as so many of the triumphs and tragedies of the past are tied up with the bustling present. The result can be either dispiriting or exhilarating. And by European standards, Berlin isn't that old: Köln was more than 1,000 years old when Berlin was born from the fusion of two tiny settlements on islands in the Spree River. Although already a royal residence in the 15th century, Berlin really came into its own three centuries later, under the rule of King Friedrich II—Frederick the Great—whose liberal reforms and artistic patronage led the way as the city developed into a major cultural capital.

The events of the 20th century would have crushed the spirit of most other cities. Hitler destroyed the city's reputation for tolerance and plunged Berlin headlong into the war that led to the wholesale destruction of monuments and houses. And after World War II, Berlin was still to face the bitter division of the city and the construction of the infamous wall in 1961. But a storm of political events, beginning in 1989, brought the downfall of the Communist regime; the establishment of democracy in the east; and finally, in October 1990, the unification of Berlin and of all Germany. Now you can travel from one end of Berlin to the other and in and out of the long-isolated city as easily as you would in any other Western metropolis. You'll still notice the scars left by the infamous wall, however, and contrasts between the prosperous western half of the city and the run-down east are still very visible.

Numbers in the margin correspond to points of interest on the West Berlin map.

West Berlin The **Kurfürstendamm,** or Ku'damm as the Berliners call it, is one of Europe's busiest thoroughfares, throbbing with activity
❶ day and night. At its eastern end is the **Kaiser Wilhelm Gedächtniskirche** (Kaiser Wilhelm Memorial Church Tower). This landmark has come to symbolize not only West Berlin, but the futile destructiveness of war. The shell of the tower is all that remains of the church that was built at the end of the 19th century and dedicated to the memory of Kaiser Wilhelm. Inside is a historical exhibition of the devastation of World War II. *Admission free. Open Tues.–Sat. 10–6, Sun. 11–6.*

❷ Cross Budapesterstrasse to enter the **Zoologischer Garten,** Berlin's zoo. It has the world's largest variety of individual types of fauna along with a fascinating aquarium. *Admission: DM 8 adults, DM 4 children. Open daily from 9–7 PM or to dusk in winter.*

Double back to the Kurfürstendamm to catch bus No. 129 to Kemperplatz. Among the buildings that comprise the
❸ **Kulturforum** (Cultural Forum) on the large square is the **Philharmonie** (Philharmonic Hall), home of the famous Berlin Philharmonic orchestra, whose musical director is Claudio Abbado. You'll recognize it by its roof, which resembles a great wave. The main hall, built in 1963, reopened in the spring of 1992 after an ambitious renovation. *Matthäkirchstr. 1. Ticket office open weekdays 3:30–6 and weekends 11–2.*

Opposite is the **Kunstgewerbemuseum** (Museum of Decorative Arts), which displays arts and crafts of Europe from the Middle Ages to the present day. Among its treasures is the Welfenschatz (Guelph Treasure), a collection of 16th-century gold and silver plate from Nürnberg. *Tiergartenstr. 6, tel. 030/ 266–2911. Admission: DM 4 adults, DM 2 children. Open Tues.–Fri. 9–5, weekends 10–5.*

Leave the museum and walk south past the mid-19th-century church of St. Matthaeus to the **Neue Nationalgalerie** (New National Gallery), a modern glass-and-steel building designed by Mies van der Rohe and built in the mid-1960s. The gallery's collection consists of paintings, sculpture, and drawings from the 19th and 20th centuries, with an accent on works by the Impressionists. *Potsdamerstr. 50, tel. 030/266–2666. Admission: DM 4 adults, DM 2 children. Open Tues.–Fri. 9–5, weekends 10–5.*

The Kulturforum is adjacent to the 255-hectare (630-acre) **Tiergarten Park,** which has at last recovered from the war, when it was not only ripped apart by bombs and artillery, but was stripped of its woods by desperate, freezing Berliners in the bitter cold of 1945–46. In the northern section of the park is
❹ the **Englischer Garten** (English Garden), which borders the riverside **Bellevue Schloss,** a small palace built for Frederick the Great's brother: It is now the official Berlin residence of the German president.

The column in the center of a large traffic circle in the
⑤ Tiergarten is the **Siegessäule** (Victory Column), erected in 1873
to commemorate four Prussian military campaigns against the
French. The granite and sandstone monument originally stood
in front of the Reichstag (parliament), which was burned by
Hitler's men in 1933. Climb the 285 steps to its 65-meter (210-
foot) summit and you'll be rewarded with a fine view of both
West Berlin and East Berlin. *Admission: DM 1.50 adults, DM
1 children. Open Mon. 3–6, Tues.–Sun. 9–6.*

At the base of the Siegessäule, go east down the wide Strasse
des 17 Juni (June 17th Street), named in memory of the day, in
1953, when 50,000 East Germans staged an uprising that was
⑥ put down by force. On the left, you'll pass the **Soviet Victory
Memorial,** a semicircular colonnade topped with a statue of a
Russian soldier and flanked by what are said to be the first Soviet tanks to have fought their way into Berlin in 1945.

⑦ Ahead of you is **Brandenburger Tor** (Brandenburg Gate), built
in 1788 as a victory arch for triumphant Prussian armies. The
horse-drawn chariot atop the arch was reerected after the war.
The monumental gate was cut off from West Berlin by the Wall,
and it became a focal point of celebrations marking the unification of Berlin and of all Germany. It was here that German politicians formally sealed unification.

The wall that for so long isolated the Brandenburger Tor is no
more, but the history of the hideous frontier fortification can be
followed in the museum that arose at its most famous crossing
point. Checkpoint Charlie, as it was known, disappeared along
⑧ with the wall, but the **Checkpoint Charlie Museum** is still there.
You can walk to the museum by following Friedrichstrasse
south for about a mile, but it's easier to call a cab. *Friedrichstr.
44, tel. 030/251–4569. Admission DM 7.50 adults, DM 4 children. Open daily 9 AM–10 PM.*

Find the nearby Kochstrasse U-Bahn station and go two stops
south on the U-6 line to Mehringdamm. Head for Kreuzberg-
⑨ strasse. Just on the left is the 62-meter (200-foot) **Kreuzberg,** West Berlin's highest natural hill. (There are higher hills
made of the rubble gathered from the bombed-out ruins of the
city when reconstruction began in 1945.) On the sheltered
southern slopes of the Kreuzberg is a vineyard that produces
some of Germany's rarest wines: They are served only at official Berlin functions.

Bordering Kreuzberg to the west is the Schöneberg district,
where you'll find the seat of the city and state government of
⑩ Berlin, the **Rathaus Schöneberg,** the former West Berlin city
hall. (In 1991 the city administration moved back to the Rote
Rathaus in Berlin Mitte.) In the belfry of the Rathaus is a replica of the Liberty Bell, donated to Berliners in 1950 by the
United States and rung every day at noon. In a room at the base
of the tower are stored 17 million American signatures express-
ing solidarity with West Berlin, some, no doubt, inspired by
President Kennedy's famous "Ich bin ein Berliner" speech,
which he made here in 1963. *The tower is open to visitors Wed.
and Sun. only, 10–4.*

Time Out While at the Rathaus, go downstairs to the **Ratskeller
Schöneberg,** an inexpensive place to get a good, filling set-price
lunch. The atmosphere is busy and friendly.

West Berlin

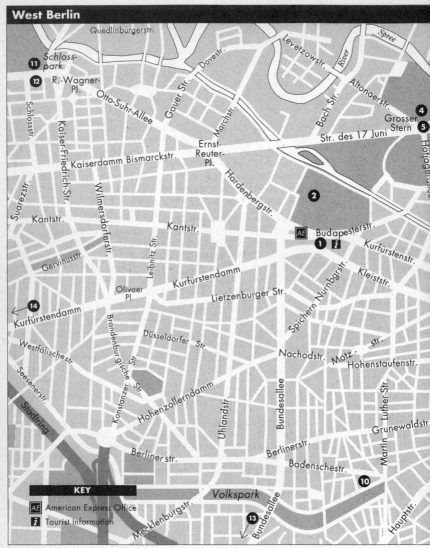

KEY

AE American Express Office

i Tourist Information

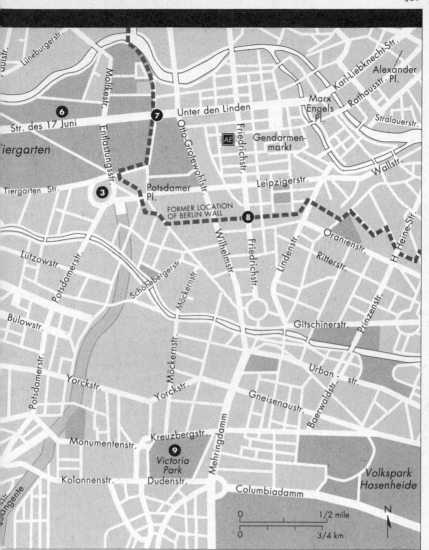

Lüneburgstr.

Moltkestr.

Str. des 17 Juni

6

iergarten

Entlastungsstr.

Tiergarten Str.

3

Unter den Linden

7

Otto-Grotewohlstr.

AE

Friedrichstr.

Gendarmen-markt

Karl-Liebknecht-Str.

Alexander Pl.

Marx Engels Pl.

Rathausstr.

Stralauerstr.

Wallstr.

Leipzigerstr.

Potsdamer Pl.

FORMER LOCATION
OF BERLIN WALL

8

Wilhelmstr.

Friedrichstr.

Lindenstr.

Ritterstr.

Oranienstr.

H. Heine-Str.

Lützowstr.

Potsdamerstr.

Schöneberger str.

Möckernstr.

Gitschinerstr.

Prinzenstr.

Bülowstr.

Yorckstr.

Yorckstr.

Möckernstr.

Gneisenaustr.

Urban - str.

Baerwaldstr.

Potsdamerstr.

Monumentenstr.

Kreuzbergstr.

9

Victoria
Park

Mehringdamm

Volkspark
Hasenheide

Kolonnenstr.

Dudenstr.

Columbiadamm

0   1/2 mile

0   3/4 km

N

Take the U-Bahn north one stop from Rathaus Schöneberg station and change to the U-7 line for eight stops, to Richard-Wagner-Platz station. From the station, walk left for about 465

⑪ meters (500 yards) to the handsome **Schloss Charlottenburg** (Charlottenburg Palace). Built at the end of the 17th century by King Frederick I for his wife, Queen Sophie Charlotte, the palace was progressively enlarged for later royal residents. Frederick the Great's suite of rooms can be visited; in one glass cupboard, you'll see the coronation crown he inherited from his father—stripped of jewels by the ascetic son, who gave the most valuable diamonds and pearls to his wife. *Luisenplatz. Admission: DM 4 adults, DM 2 children. Open Tues.–Fri. 9–5, weekends 10–5.*

⑫ Opposite the palace is the **Ägyptisches Museum** (Egyptian Museum), home of perhaps the world's best-known portrait sculpture, the beautiful Nefertiti. The 3,300-year-old Egyptian queen is the centerpiece of a fascinating collection of Egyptology that includes one of the finest preserved mummies outside Cairo. *Schlosstr. 70. Admission: DM 4 adults, DM 2 children. Open Mon.–Thurs. 9–5, weekends 10–5. Closed Fri.*

Take U-Bahn line U-7 back toward Schöneberg until Fehrbelliner Platz, where you change to line U-2 southwest for five stops to Dahlem-Dorf station. This is the stop for the magnificent **Dahlem museums,** chief of which is West Berlin's lead-

⑬ ing picture gallery, the **Gemäldegalerie.** The collection includes many works by the great European masters, with 26 Rembrandts and 14 by Rubens. Or is it 25 Rembrandts? *The Man in the Golden Hat,* until recently attributed to Rembrandt, has now been ascribed to one of the great Dutch master's pupils. Does it really matter? Maybe not to the public, which still sees it as a masterpiece, but it could affect the value of the painting by a million or two. *Arnimallee 23/27. Admission: DM 4 adults, DM 2 children. Open Tues.–Fri. 9–5, weekends 10–5.*

No visit to West Berlin is complete without an outing to the

⑭ city's outdoor playground, the **Grunewald** park. Bordering the Dahlem district to the west, the park is a vast green space, with meadows, woodlands, and lakes. There are a string of 60 lakes within Berlin's boundaries; some are kilometers long, others are no more than ponds. The total length of their shorelines—if stretched out in one long line—is 209½ kilometers (130 miles), longer than Germany's Baltic Coast. There's even space for nudist beaches on the banks of the Wannsee lake, while in winter a downhill ski run and even a ski jump operate on the modest slopes of the Teufelsberg hill.

East Berlin   The infamous Wall is now gone, but the spirit of division remains in a city that was physically split for 28 years. The stately buildings of the city's past are not as overwhelmed by new high-rise construction as in West Berlin, but East Berlin's postwar architectural blunders are just as monumental in their own way. These will be obvious—along with the sad shabbiness of years of neglect—as you explore the side streets together with the main thoroughfares.

Numbers in the margin correspond to points of interest on the East Berlin map.

For a sense of déjà vu, enter the eastern part of Berlin at

⑮ **Checkpoint Charlie,** the most famous crossing point between the two Berlins during the Cold War and the setting of numer-

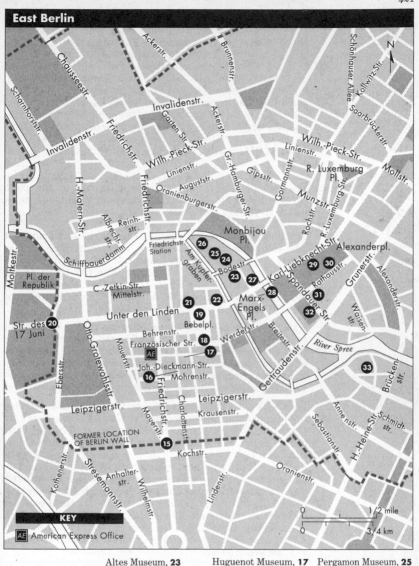

East Berlin

KEY

AE American Express Office

Altes Museum, **23**
Berliner Dom, **27**
Bodemuseum, **26**
Brandenburger Tor, **20**
Checkpoint Charlie, **15**
Deutsche
Staatsoper, **19**
Deutsches Historisches
Museum, **22**

Huguenot Museum, **17**
Humboldt
University, **21**
Marienkirche, **29**
Märkisches
Museum, **33**
Nationalgalerie, **24**
Nikolaikirche, **32**
Palast der
Republik, **28**

Pergamon Museum, **25**
Rathaus, **31**
Schauspielhaus, **16**
St. Hedwigs
Kathedrale, **18**
TV Tower, **30**

ous spy novels and films. At this point both ends of Friedrichstrasse—east and west—are lined with attractive new
shops and trendy restaurants. Turn right onto Mohren-
strasse and you'll arrive at **Gendarmenmarkt,** with its beauti-
❿ fully reconstructed **Schauspielhaus**—built in 1818, and now the
city's main concert hall—and the twin **German** (on the south,
undergoing restoration) and **French cathedrals.** In the latter,
⓱ you'll find the **Huguenot Museum,** which has some interesting
collections of the history and art of the French Protestant Hu-
guenots who took refuge in Germany after being expelled from
Catholic France in 1685. *Gendarmenmarkt. Admission: DM2
adults, DM1 children. Open Tues.–Thurs., Sat. noon–5; Sun.
1–5.*

Time Out The **Arkade Café** on the northwest corner of the plaza
(Französischer Str. 25) is perfect for a light snack; some excellent pastry; and a beer, coffee, or tea.

Continue east along the Französischer Strasse and turn left
into Hedwigskirchgasse to reach Bebelplatz. The peculiar
⓲ round shape of **St. Hedwigs Kathedrale** (St. Hedwig's Cathedral) calls to mind Rome's Pantheon. The tiny street named
Hinter der Katholischen Kirche (Behind the Catholic Church)
is a reminder that though Berlin was very much a Protestant
city, St. Hedwig's was built (about 1747) for Catholics.

Walk north across Bebelplatz to Unter den Linden, the elegant
central thoroughfare of Old Berlin. On your right is the
⓳ **Deutsche Staatsoper,** the great opera house of Berlin, now with
an entirely new interior. Just after Oberwallstrasse is the former crown prince's palace, the **Palais Unter den Linden,** now restored and used to house official government visitors.

Look back down the street to the western sector and you'll see
⓴ the monumental **Brandenburger Tor** (Brandenburg Gate), its
chariot-and-horses sculpture now turned to face the east.
Cross Unter den Linden and look into the courtyard of
㉑ **Humboldt University:** It was built as a palace for the brother of
Friedrich II of Prussia but became a university in 1810, and today is one of Germany's largest universities. Marx and Engels
were its two most famous students. Beyond the war memorial,
㉒ housed in a onetime arsenal (1695–1705) is the **Deutsches
Historisches Museum** (German Historical Museum), which
traces events from 1789 to the present. *Unter den Linden 2.
Admission: DM 4 adults, DM 2 children. Open Mon.–Thurs.
9–5, weekends 10–5.*

Turning left along the Spree canal (along Am Zeughaus and Am
Kupfergraben) will bring you to East Berlin's museum complex, at the northern end of what is known as **Museumsinsel**
(Museum Island). The first of the Big Four that you'll encoun-
㉓ ter is the **Altes Museum** (entrance on Lustgarten), an austere
neoclassical building just to the north of Marx-Engels-Platz.
The collections here include postwar art from some of Germany's most prominent artists and numerous etchings and draw-
㉔ ings from the Old Masters. Next comes the **Nationalgalerie,** on
Bodestrasse, which features 19th- and 20th-century painting
㉕ and sculpture. The **Pergamon Museum,** on Am Kupfergraben,
is one of Europe's greatest museums. Its name derives from
the museum's principal exhibit and the city's number-one attraction, the **Pergamon Altar,** a monumental Greek altar dating

from 180 BC that occupies an entire city block. Almost as impressive is the **Babylonian Processional Way.** The Pergamon Museum also houses vast Egyptian, early Christian, and Byzantine collections, plus a fine array of sculpture from the 12th to the 18th centuries. To the north is the **Bodemuseum** (also on Am Kupfergraben, but with its entrance on Monbijoubrücke), with an outstanding collection of early Christian, Byzantine, and Egyptian art, as well as exhibits of Italian Old Masters paintings. *Admission to each museum: DM 4 adults, DM 2 children. Museum complex open Mon.–Thurs. 9–5; weekends, holidays 10–5.*

From the museum complex, follow the Spree canal south to Unter den Linden and the vast and impressive **Berliner Dom** (Berlin cathedral). The hideous modern building in bronze mirrored glass opposite is the **Palast der Republik** (Palace of the Republic), a postwar monument to socialist progress that also housed restaurants, a theater, and a dance hall. Since 1991 the Palast has been closed down while the politicians argue about whether it should be torn down or used for other purposes. It formerly housed the Volkskammer, the East German People's Chamber (parliament).

Cross Spandauer Strasse diagonally for a closer look at the 13th-century **Marienkirche** (Church of St. Mary), especially noting its late-Gothic *Dance of Death* fresco. You are now at the lower end of Alexanderplatz. Just ahead is the massive **TV tower,** a Berlin landmark. A focal point for shopping is the **Kaufhof department store** (formerly the Centrum), alongside the Hotel Stadt Berlin, at the very top of the plaza.

The area adjacent to the so-called Rotes Rathaus (Red Rathaus)—itself somewhat of a marvel for its red-brick design and the frieze depicting scenes from the city's history—has been handsomely rebuilt. In the fall of 1991 the city administration and seat of the governing mayor were transferred from Schöneberg back to the Rotes Rathaus, renewing its prewar function. **Nikolaikirche** (on Spandauer Strasse), dating from about 1200, is Berlin's oldest building. It was heavily damaged in the war, but has been beautifully restored and is now a museum. The quarter surrounding the church is filled with delightful shops, cafés, and restaurants. Wander back down Muhlendamm into the area around the Breitestrasse—there are some lovely old buildings here—and on over to the **Fischerinsel** area. The throbbing heart of Old Berlin of 750 years ago, Fischerinsel retains a tangible medieval flavor.

Time Out The **Alt-Cöllner Schankstuben,** overlooking the Spree canal (Friedrichsgracht 50), is as charming and friendly a café as you'll find in East Berlin. On a sunny day, enjoy a glass of beer at an outdoor table.

Nearby is the **Märkisches Museum** (Museum of Cultural History), which has an amusing section devoted to automaphones—"self-playing" musical instruments, demonstrated Sundays 10–12 and Wednesdays 3–4. Live bears—the city's symbol—are in a pit next to the museum. *Am Köllnischen Park 5. Admission: DM 3 adults, DM 1 children. Open Wed.–Sun. 9–6.*

Shopping

Berlin is a city of alluring stores and boutiques. Despite the new capital's cosmopolitan gloss, prices are generally lower than in cities like Munich and Hamburg.

Fine **porcelain** is still produced at the former Royal Prussian Porcelain Factory, now called **Staaliche Porzellan Manufactur,** or KPM. This delicate, handmade, hand-painted china is sold at KPM's store at Kurfürstendamm 26A (tel. 030/881–1802), but it may be more fun to visit the factory salesroom at Wegelystrasse 1. It also sells seconds at reduced prices. If you long to have the Egyptian Queen Nefertiti on your mantlepiece at home, try the **Gipsformerei der Staatlichen Museen Preussicher Kulturbesitz** (Sophie-Charlotte-Str. 17, tel. 030/321–7011, open weekdays 9–4). It sells plaster casts of this and other treasures from the city's museums.

Shopping Districts The liveliest and most famous shopping area in West Berlin is the **Kurfürstendamm** and its side streets, especially between **Breitscheidplatz** and **Oliver Platz.** The **Europa Center** at Breitscheidplatz encompasses more than 100 stores, cafés, and restaurants—this is not a place to bargain-hunt, though! Running east from Breitscheidplatz is **Tauenzientstrasse,** another shopping street. At the end of it is Berlin's most celebrated department store, **KaDeWe.** Elegant malls include the **Gloria Galerie** (opposite the Wertheim department store on Ku'damm) and the **Uhland-Passage** (connecting Uhlandstrasse and Fasanenstrasse). In both, you'll find leading name stores as well as cafés and restaurants.

For trendier clothes, try the boutiques along **Bleibtreustrasse.** One of the more avant-garde fashion boutiques is **Durchbruch** (Schlutterstr. 54), around the corner. The name means "breakthrough," and the store lives up to its name by selling six different designers' outrageous styles. Less trendy and much less expensive is the mall, **Wilmersdorferstrasse,** where price-conscious Berliners do their shopping. It's packed on weekends.

East Berlin's chief shopping areas are along the Friedrichstrasse, Unter den Linden, and in the area around Alexanderplatz.

Department Stores The classiest department store in Berlin is **KaDeWe,** the Kaufhaus des Westens (Department Store of the West, as it's modestly known in English), at Wittenbergplatz. The biggest department store in Europe, the KaDeWe is a grand-scale emporium in modern guise. Be sure to check out the food department, which occupies the whole sixth floor. The other main department store downtown is **Wertheim** on the Ku'damm. Neither as big nor as attractive as the KaDeWe, Wertheim nonetheless offers a large selection of fine wares.

The main department store in East Berlin is **Kaufhof** (formerly Centrum), at the north end of Alexanderplatz. Under the old regime, you could find ridiculously cheap subsidized prices. Now it is filled with mainly Western-made products, superior, of course, but the prices are higher.

Antiques On Saturdays and Sundays from 10 to 5, the colorful and lively antiques and handicrafts fair on Strasse des 17 Juni swings into action. Don't expect to pick up any bargains—or to have the place to yourself. Not far from Wittenbergplatz is **Keithstrasse,**

a street given over to antiques stores. Eisenacherstrasse, Fuggerstrasse, Kalckreuthstrasse, Motzstrasse, and Nollendorfstrasse—all close to Nollendorfplatz—have many antiques stores of varying quality. Another good street for antiques is **Suarezstrasse**, between Kantstrasse and Bismarckstrasse.

In East Berlin, antiques are sold in the Metropol and Palast hotels in the Nikolai quarter and in the restored Husemannstrasse. Some private stores along the stretch of Friedichstrasse north of the Spree Bridge offer old books and prints.

Dining

Dining in Berlin can mean sophisticated nouvelle creations in upscale restaurants with linen tablecloths and hand-painted porcelain plates or hearty local specialties in atmospheric and inexpensive inns: The range is as vast as the city. Specialties include *Eisbein mit Sauerkraut,* knuckle of pork with pickled cabbage; *Rouladen,* rolled stuffed beef; *Spanferkel,* suckling pig; *Berliner Schüsselsülze,* potted meat in aspic; *Schlachtplatte,* mixed grill; *Hackepeter,* ground beef; and *Kartoffelpuffer,* fried potato cakes. *Bockwurst* is a chubby frankfurter that's served in a variety of ways and sold in restaurants and at Bockwurst stands all over the city. *Schlesisches Himmerlreich* is roast goose or pork served with potato dumplings in rich gravy. *Königsberger Klopse* consists of meatballs, herring, and capers—it tastes much better than it sounds.

East Germany's former ties to the Eastern Bloc persist in restaurants featuring the national cuisine of those other one-time socialist states, although such exotica as Japanese, Chinese, Indonesian, and French food is now appearing. Wines and spirits imported from those other countries can be quite good; try Hungarian, Yugoslav, and Bulgarian wines (the whites are lighter), and Polish and Russian vodkas.

For details and price-category definitions, *see* Dining in Staying in Germany.

West Berlin
Expensive
★

Bamberger Reiter. Considered by Berliners to be one of the city's best restaurants, Bamberger Reiter is the pride of its chef, Franz Raneburger. He relies heavily on fresh market produce for his *neue deutsche Küche* (new German cuisine), so the menu changes from day to day. Fresh flowers, too, abound in his attractive, oak-beamed restaurant. *Regensburgerstr. 7, tel. 030/218–4282. Reservations required. DC, V. Dinner only. Closed Sun., Mon., Jan. 1–15, and Aug. 1–20.*

Frühsammer's Restaurant an der Rehwiese. From your table you can watch chef Peter Frühsammer at work in his open kitchen. He's ready with advice on the daily menu: Salmon is always a treat here. The restaurant is located in the annex of a turn-of-the-century villa in the southern district of Zehlendorf (U-Bahn to Krumme Lanke and then bus No. 53 to Rehwiese). *Matterhornstr. 101, tel. 030/803–8032. Reservations required. MC, V. Dinner only. Closed Sun.*

Paris Bar. This top-class restaurant attracts a polyglot clientele of film stars, artists, entrepreneurs, and executives. The cuisine is high-powered, high-quality French. *Kantstr. 152, tel. 030/313–8052. Reservations advised. No credit cards. Closed Sun.*

Moderate **Alt-Nürnberg.** Step into the tavernlike interior and you could be in Bavaria: The waitresses even wear dirndls. The Bavarian colors of blue and white are everywhere, and such Bavarian culinary delights as *Schweinshaxe* (knuckle of pork) are well represented on the menu. If you prefer to eat in the Prussian style, the calves' liver *Berliner Art* is recommended. *Europa Center, tel. 030/261–4397. Reservations advised. AE, DC, MC, V.*

★ **Blockhaus Nikolskoe.** Prussian King Wilhelm III built this Russian-style wooden lodge for his daughter Charlotte, wife of Russia's Czar Nicholas I. It's located in the southwest of the city, on the eastern edge of Glienicke Park. In summer, you can eat on the open terrace overlooking the Havel River. In character with its history and appearance, the Blockhaus features game dishes. *Nikolskoer Weg, tel. 030/805–2914. Reservations advised. AE, DC, MC, V.*

Forsthaus Paulsborn. Game is the specialty in this former woodsman's home deep in the Grunewald Forest. You dine here as the forester did—from an oak table in a great dining room and under the baleful eye of hunting trophies on the wall. Apart from game, the menu extends to various German and international dishes. *Am Grunewaldsee, tel. 030/813–8010. Reservations advised on weekends. AE, DC, MC, V. Closed Mon., dinner in winter (Oct.–Mar.).*

Hecker's Deele. You could find yourself seated in one of the antique church pews that complete the oak-beamed interior of this restaurant that features Westphalian dishes. The *Westfälische Schlachtplatte* (a variety of meats) will set you up for a whole day's sightseeing—the Ku'damm is right outside. *Grolmannstr. 35, tel. 030/88901. No reservations. AE, DC, MC, V.*

Mundart Restaurant. Too many cooks don't spoil the broth (and certainly not the excellent fish soup) at this popular restaurant in the Kreuzberg district. Five chefs are at work in the spacious kitchen. Fortunately, they all agree on the day's specials, and you can follow their advice with impunity. *Muskauerstr. 33/34, tel. 030/612–2061. No reservations. No credit cards. Closed lunch, Mon., and Tues.*

Inexpensive **Alt-Berliner Weissbierstube.** A visit to the Berlin Museum (a permanent historical exhibition on Berlin) must include a stop at this pub-style restaurant in the museum building. There's a buffet packed with Berlin specialties, and a jazz band plays on Sunday morning after 10. *Berlin Museum, Lindenstr. 14, tel. 030/251–0121. Reservations advised, particularly evenings. No credit cards. Closed Mon.*

Thürnagel. Also located in the Kreuzberg district, Thürnagel is a vegetarian restaurant where it's not only healthy to eat but fun. The seitan in sherry sauce or the tempeh curry are good enough to convert a seasoned carnivore. *Gneisenaustr. 57, tel. 030/691–4800. Reservations advised. No credit cards. Dinner only.*

East Berlin **Ermeler-Haus.** The wine restaurant in a series of upstairs
Very Expensive rooms reflects the elegance of this restored patrician house, which dates from 1567 (it was moved to its present location in 1969, however). The atmosphere is subdued, the wines are imported, and the service matches the international specialties. There's dancing on Saturday evening. *Märkisches Ufer 12, tel. 030/279–4028. Reservations advised. No credit cards.*

Expensive **Schwalbennest.** This is a fairly new restaurant on the edge of the Nikolai quarter, overlooking the Marx-Engels-Forum. Both the food and service are variable, although on paper, at least, the choice is wide for both main dishes and wines. The grilled meats can be excellent, but note that no additional price is indicated on the menu for the flambéed dishes—ask about this, or you could be in for a surprise when the bill arrives! *Am Marstall, Rathausstr. at Marx-Engels-Forum, tel. 030/242–6919. Reservations required, even for lunch. No credit cards.*

Moderate **Ratskeller.** This is actually two restaurants in one—a wine and a beer cellar, both vast, atmospheric, and extremely popular. The menus are limited, but offer good, solid Berlin fare. The beer cellar is guaranteed to be packed at main dining hours, and attempts at reservations may be ignored (locals simply line up and wait). *Rathausstr. 15–18, in basement of the City Hall, tel. 030/242–3819. Reservations advised. No credit cards.*

Sofia. Bulgarian and Russian specialties are the basis of the imaginative menu offered at this popular, central restaurant, a few paces from Potsdamer Platz. The Bulgarian wines are particularly recommended. *Leipziger Strasse 46, tel. 030/229–1533 or 030/229–1831. Reservations advised. No credit cards.*

★ **Turmstuben.** Not for the infirm or those who are afraid of heights, the Turmstuben restaurant is tucked away below the cupola of the French Cathedral, the church that sits in classical splendor on one side of the beautiful Platz der Akademie. The restaurant, which runs a circular course around the base of the cupola, is approached by a long, winding staircase—fine for working up an appetite but certainly not recommended for the fainthearted. The reward at the top of the stairs is a table in one of Berlin's most original and attractive restaurants. The menu is as short as the stairway is long, but there's an impressive wine list. *Gendarmenmarkt, tel. 030/229–3969. Reservations strongly advised (the frustration of being turned away after that climb could spoil anyone's day). No credit cards.*

Zur Rippe. This famous eating place near Alexanderplatz serves wholesome food in an intimate setting with oak paneling and ceramic tiles. Specialties include the Märkische cheese platter and herring casserole. *Poststr. 17, tel. 030/217–3235. Reservations not necessary. No credit cards.*

Inexpensive **Alt-Cöllner Schankstuben.** A charming and genuine old Berlin house is the setting for this conglomerate of no fewer than four tiny restaurants, all of which provide exceptionally friendly service. *Friedrichsgracht 50, tel. 030/242–5972. No reservations. No credit cards.*

★ **Zur Letzten Instanz.** Established in 1525, this place combines the charming atmosphere of Old-World Berlin with a limited (but tasty) choice of dishes. Napoleon is said to have sat alongside the tiled stove in the front room. Mikhail Gorbachev enjoyed a beer here during a visit to Berlin in 1989. The emphasis here is on beer, both in the recipes and in the mug. Service can be erratic, though engagingly friendly. *Waisenstr. 14–16, tel. 030/242–5528. Reservations required for both lunch and dinner. No credit cards.*

Lodging

Berlin lost all its grand old luxury hotels in the bombing during World War II; though some were rebuilt, many of the best hotels today are modern. Although they lack little in service and comfort, you may find some short on atmosphere. For first-class or luxury accommodations, East Berlin is easily as good as West, because the East German government, eager for hard currency, built several elegant hotels—the Grand, Palast, Dom (now the Hilton International), and Metropol—which are up to the very best international standards and place in the very top price category. If you're seeking something more moderate, the better choice may be West Berlin, where there are large numbers of good-value pensions and small hotels, many of them in older buildings with some character. In East Berlin, however, the hostels run by the Evangelical Lutheran church offer outstanding value for your money.

In West Berlin, business conventions year-round and the influx of summer tourists mean that you should make reservations well in advance. If you arrive without reservations, consult the board at Tegel Airport that shows hotels with vacancies or go to the tourist office.

For details and price-category definitions, *see* Lodging in Staying in Germany.

West Berlin
Very Expensive

Bristol Hotel Kempinski. Located in the heart of the city, this grand hotel has the best of Berlin's shopping on its doorstep. English-style furnishings give the "Kempi" an added touch of class. All the rooms and suites are luxuriously decorated and equipped, with marble bathrooms, air-conditioning, and cable TV. Children under 12 stay for free if they share their parents' room. *Kurfürstendamm 27, tel. 030/884–340. 334 rooms with bath. Facilities: 3 restaurants, indoor pool, sauna, solarium, masseur, hairdresser, limousine service. AE, DC, MC, V.*

CC-City Castle Apartment Hotel. The CC (short for "Congress Center," which is nearby) is a fine fin de siècle Berlin mansion, commanding a corner on the Ku'damm (ask for one of the many quiet rooms at the back). *Kurfüstendamm 160, tel. 030/891–8005. 39 rooms with bath. Facilities: restaurant, bar. AE, DC, MC, V.*

★ **InterContinental Berlin.** The "Diplomaten Suite" is expensive, but it is in a class of its own: It's as large as a suburban house and furnished in the Oriental style. The other rooms and suites are not so exotically furnished but still show individuality and exquisite taste. The lobby is a quarter the size of a football field, opulently furnished, and just the place for afternoon tea and pastries. *Budapesterstr. 2, tel. 030/26020, fax 030/2602–80760. 600 rooms with bath. Facilities: 3 restaurants (including a rooftop garden), indoor pool, sauna, 24-hour room service, boutiques. AE, DC, MC, V.*

Expensive

Berlin Excelsior Hotel. Fixed rates that don't fluctuate with the seasons are offered by this modern, well-run establishment only five minutes from the Ku'damm. That means, however, that there are no special weekend offers (a usual feature of top German hotels). The comfortable rooms are furnished in dark teak, and the helpful front-office staff will arrange sightseeing tours and try to obtain hard-to-get theater and concert tickets. *Hardenbergerstr. 14, tel. 030/31993. 320 rooms with bath. Facilities: restaurant, garden terrace, winter garden. AE, DC, MC, V.*

★ **Palace.** The rooms here are comfortable and adequately furnished, but can't quite match the scale of the palatial lobby. Ask for a room on the Budapesterstrasse: The view is memorable. The Palace is part of Berlin's Europa Center, and guests have free use of the center's pool and sauna. *Europa Center, tel. 030/254970. 160 rooms with bath. Facilities: restaurant. AE, DC, MC, V.*

Schweizerhof Berlin. There's a rustic, Swiss look about most of the rooms in this centrally located hotel, but they have a high standard of comfort and facilities. Ask to be placed in the west wing, where the rooms are larger. The indoor pool is the largest of any Berlin hotel, and the hotel is opposite Tiergarten Park. *Budapesterstr. 21–31, tel. 030/26960. 430 rooms with bath. Facilities: restaurant, sauna, solarium, fitness room, hairdresser, beauty salon. AE, DC, MC, V.*

Moderate **Casino Hotel.** The owner of the Casino is Bavarian, so his restaurant serves south German specialties. The hotel itself is a former Prussian military barracks but bears little evidence of its former role: The rooms are large and comfortable and well equipped. The hotel is located in the Charlottenburg district. *Königin-Elisabeth-Str. 47a, tel. 030/303090. 24 rooms with bath. AE, DC, MC, V.*

★ **Ravenna.** This small, friendly hotel is located in the Steglitz district, close to the Botanical Garden and the Dahlen Museum. All the rooms are well equipped, but suite 111B is a bargain: It includes a large living room and kitchen for the rate of only DM 200. *Grunewaldstr. 8–9, tel. 030/792–8031. 45 rooms with bath or shower. AE, DC, MC, V.*

Riehmers Hofgarten. Located in the interesting Kreuzberg district, this hotel, in a late-19th-century building, is a short walk from the Kreuzberg hill and has fast connections to the center of town. The high-ceilinged rooms are elegantly furnished. *Yorckstr. 83, tel. 030/781011, fax 030/786–6059. 21 rooms with bath or shower. AE, DC, MC, V.*

Inexpensive **Econtel.** Families are well cared for at this hotel that's situated within walking distance of Charlottenburg Palace. Lone travelers also appreciate the touches in the single rooms, which come with a trouser press and hair dryer. *Sommeringstr. 24, tel. 030/346–810. 205 rooms with bath or shower. Facilities: snack bar. MC.*

East Berlin **Grand Hotel.** This is Berlin's most expensive hotel. There's
Very Expensive nothing of Eastern Europe here: Facilities range from the
★ plush atrium lobby, four restaurants, winter garden, beer stube, bars, and a concert café to a swimming pool, sauna, and squash courts. *Friedrichstr. 158–164, corner Behrenstr., tel. 030/23–270, fax 030/2327–3362. 336 rooms and suites with bath. Facilities: 4 restaurants, Bierstube, concert café, bar, shopping arcade, hairdresser, theater-ticket office, car and yacht rental. AE, DC, MC, V.*

Hilton International. The city's newest hotel (opened in 1990) the Hilton International is centrally located. The rooms feature heated tubs; house facilities are equally plush. *Gendarmenmarkt, tel. 030/23–820, fax 030/2382–4269. 366 rooms and suites, all with private bath. Facilities: 3 restaurants, pub, wine cellar, bar, discotheque, pool, sauna, health club, bowling, squash, hairdresser, garage, car rental. AE, DC, MC, V.*

★ **Metropol.** This is the businessperson's choice, not least for its excellent location opposite the International Trade Center. The best rooms are those in front, with a view toward the north. The main specialty restaurant (left of the lobby) is now one of the city's best and is full at noon (reservations advised); the other two restaurants are less memorable, except for their prices. The nightclub, in contrast, is excellent. *Friedrichstr. 150–153, tel. 030/203–070, fax 030/2030–7209. 336 rooms and apartments with bath. Facilities: 3 restaurants, nightclub, bars, pool, sauna, health club, shops; car, horse-drawn carriage, and yacht rental. AE, DC, MC, V.*

Radisson Plaza. This is another of Berlin's mega-facility hotels. Ask for a room overlooking the Spree River; those on Alexanderplatz can be noisy if you like your windows open. The shopping arcade includes an antiques gallery and the main central theater-ticket office. *Karl-Liebknecht-Str. 5, tel. 030/23–828, fax 030/2382–7590. 583 rooms and suites with bath. Facilities: 6 restaurants, 4 bars, beer stube, nightclub, pool, sauna, health club, car rental. AE, DC, MC, V.*

Expensive **Stadt Berlin.** With its 40 stories (it's the city's largest hotel), the Stadt Berlin, at the top end of Alexanderplatz, competes with the nearby TV tower for the title City Landmark. The roof dining room, Panorama, features not only good food and service but stunning views as well; reservations are essential. *Alexanderplatz, tel. 030/23–890, fax 030/2389–4305. 997 rooms and apartments with bath. Facilities: 4 restaurants, beer garden, 3 bars, sauna, shops. AE, DC, MC, V.*

★ **Unter den Linden.** The class may be missing, but the location on what was once Berlin's most elegant boulevard couldn't be better. The restaurant is drab. *Unter den Linden 14, corner Friedrichstr., tel. 030/220–0311. 300 rooms and apartments with bath. Facilities: restaurant, souvenir shop. AE, DC, MC, V.*

Moderate **Adria.** This hotel tends to be fully booked well in advance, attesting to its less expensive prices rather than to any particular charm. The rooms in back are quieter, if you have any choice. *Friedrichstr. 134, tel. 030/280–5105. 67 rooms, 10 with bath. Facilities: restaurant, dance/bar, hairdresser. No credit cards.*

Newa. The Newa—an older hotel just a 10-minute streetcar ride from downtown—is popular, but, as with the Adria, this is mainly due to the price. The rooms in front can be noisy. *Invalidenstr. 115, tel. 030/280–5173. 57 rooms, some with bath. No credit cards.*

Inexpensive **Hospiz am Bahnhof Friedrichstrasse.** For reasons of both price and convenience, this Lutheran hostel tends to be heavily booked months in advance. It appeals to families, so the public rooms are not always restful. *Albrechstr. 8, tel. 030/284–030. 110 rooms, some with bath. Facilities: restaurant. V, MC.*

Hospiz Auguststrasse. Another church-run hostel, this one has comfortable rooms and a particularly friendly staff. It's about a 10-minute streetcar ride to the downtown sights. Only breakfast is served. *Auguststr. 82, tel. 030/282–5321. 70 rooms, some with bath. No credit cards.*

The Arts

West Berlin Today's Berlin has a tough task in trying to live up to the reputation it gained from the film *Cabaret*, but if nightlife is a little toned down since the '20s, the arts still flourish. Apart from the many hotels that book seats, there are numerous ticket agencies, including **Europa-Center** (Tauentzienstrasse 9, tel. 030/261–7051); **Theaterkasse Centrum** (Meinekestrasse 25, tel. 030/882–7611); and at any of the Top Ticket branches (in all major stores, such as Hertie, Wertheim, and KaDeWe).

The Berlin Philharmonic, one of the world's leading orchestras, performs in the **Philharmonie** (Matthaikirchstrasse 1, tel. 030/254–880). It plays a major role in the annual festival months of August, September, and October. The **Deutsche Oper** (Opera House, Bismarckstrasse 35), by the U-Bahn stop of the same name, is the home of the opera and ballet companies. Tickets are hard to obtain, but call 030/341–0249 for information.

West Berlin is still Germany's drag-show capital, as you'll see if you go to **Chez Nous** (Marburgerstrasse 14). It's essential to book (tel. 030/213–1810). The girls are for real next door (No. 15) at the **Scotch Club 13.**

East Berlin The quality of opera and classical concerts in East Berlin is impressively high. Tickets are available at the separate box offices, either in advance or an hour before the performance. Tickets are also sold at the central tourist office of the Reisebüro (Alexanderplatz 5), at the ticket offices in the Radisson Plaza and Grand hotels, or from your hotel service desk. Check the monthly publication *Wohin in Berlin?*

Concerts **Schauspielhaus** (Gendarmenmarkt, tel. 030/2090–2122).

Opera and Ballet **Deutsche Staatsoper** (Unter den Linden 7, tel. 030/200–4762); **Komische Oper** (Behrenstrasse 55–57, tel. 030/229–2555); **Metropol Theater** (Friedrichstrasse 101, tel. 030/203–640).

Nightlife

West Berlin Nightlife in West Berlin is no halfhearted affair. It starts late (from 9 PM) and runs until breakfast. Almost 50 bars (*Kneipen*) have live music of one kind or another, and there are numerous small cabaret clubs and discos. The heart of this nocturnal scene is the Kurfürstendamm, but some of the best bar discos are to be found at Nollendorfplatz in Charlottenburg. Try the **Metropol** (Nollendorfplatz 5, tel. 030/216–2787).

Berlin is a major center for jazz in Europe. If you're visiting in the fall, call the tourist office for details of the annual international Jazz Fest. Throughout the year a variety of jazz groups appear at the **Eierschale** (Egg Shell, Podbielskiallee 50, tel. 030/832–7097; evenings after 8:30).

East Berlin The nightlife here is more modest than in West Berlin—but the prices are less extravagant, too. Music in the hotels is generally live; clubs have discos with DJs. For nightclubs with music and atmosphere, try one of the following: **Club Metropol** (in the Metropol Hotel); **Panorama Bar** (atop the Hotel Stadt Berlin); **Hafenbar** (Chauseestrasse 20); **Checkpoint Null** (Leipziger Strasse 55); **Jojo** (Wilhelm-Pieck-Strasse 216).

Saxony and Thuringia

Saxony and Thuringia—the very sound of those names conjures up images of kingdoms and forest legends, of cultural riches and booming industrial enterprises. The reality after 40 years of communism is markedly less glamorous. Isolated from the West for decades, these two regions in eastern Germany are today struggling to make the transition from state-planned economies to a free-market system. Slowly, progress is being made, thanks to massive injections of cash from the federal government and the arrival of foreign and western German inves-

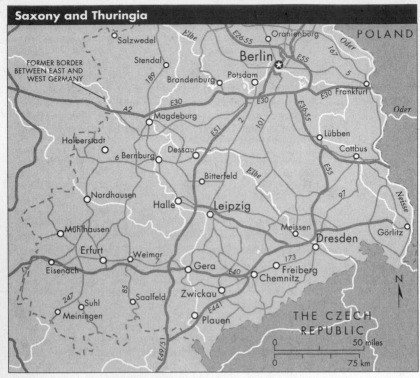

Saxony and Thuringia

tors. But many people have been made jobless in the process. In January 1992, the opening up of the "Stasi" secret police files revealed the full horror and extent of former East Germany's monitoring of its citizens' lives. Closely tied politically and economically to the former Soviet Union for 45 years, many eastern Germans remain uncomfortable with their newly won freedoms and uncertain about the future. In Saxony, though, people seem happy enough with their new "Freistaat Sachsen" title, something they share in common with the Free State of Bavaria.

Dresden was once the capital of the kingdom of Saxony, and no city could be prouder of its history. The sculpture of August the Strong atop his horse was back in his original place many years before East Berlin, remembering its Prussian past, removed the statue of Frederick the Great from its hiding place and put it back on show again on the Unter den Linden in the late 1970s.

Since German reunification, Saxony has thrown open its doors to visitors. Tourists are proudly conducted around the world-famous porcelain factory in Meissen. In Colditz, a small town southeast of Leipzig, foreigners are courteously shown the town's forbidding castle, which during World War II housed captured Allied officers. Leipzig may be renowned for its East-West trade fairs, but its true fame lies in its music and literary tradition, proudly upheld by the internationally famous Gewandhaus Orchestra and by its annual book fair.

Thuringia's fame, it is sometimes said, begins and ends with its vast green forests, an unfair assessment given its many other historical facets and the fact that for centuries it was the home of dozens of kingdoms. Back in the 14th century, Thuringia was known as the Rynestig or Rennsteig (literally, fast trail), when it attracted traders from the dark forested depths of the Thuringer Wald (Woods) to the prospering towns of Erfurt (today the state capital), Eisenach, and Weimar, then already 600 years old. It was in Weimar that the privy councillor and poet, Johann Wolfgang von Goethe, was inspired by the pristine beauties of the 168 kilometers (104 miles) of the Rennsteig in 1777 to write that "tranquility crowns all its peaks." Goethe enjoyed his time in Weimar—he stayed 57 years—as did his friend and contemporary Friedrich von Schiller, professor and poet, who taught history in Jena but preferred Weimar's cultured atmosphere in which to live with his family. The Hungarian composer Franz Liszt regularly spent the summer in Weimar, where he conducted the royal court's orchestra and championed the works of his friend and son-in-law, Richard Wagner, who was born in Leipzig. But it is Goethe who reigns supreme in Weimar. His face graces many a monument, and his sayings adorn the town's libraries.

The transportation and communications systems of the two halves of a country so long divided have yet to be completely integrated, and that will take time. The former East German tourism ministry and tourist boards are being taken over by German authorities, and the resultant bureaucratic problems are formidable. Former state-run hotels are passing into private ownership, and hundreds are being built to accommodate the surge of tourists and business travelers who followed the opening of the frontiers. As this process of price adjustment is still under way, it is difficult to accurately predict costs. Museums, for example, are still converting their old admission charges into the new Deutschemark currency. Existing businesses may close, or new ones open, without notice. Telephone exchanges in eastern Germany are also being expanded, and the numbers are being altered at a frustrating rate.

We have given addresses, telephone numbers, and other logistical details based on the best available information, but changes are taking place at a furious pace in everything from postal codes to street and even city names. We suggest that you contact the German National Tourist Office for the latest information, or phone ahead to confirm information locally.

Getting Around

By Car Some 1,600 kilometers (1,000 miles) of autobahn and 11,300 kilometers (7,000 miles) of secondary roads crisscross the five new federal states in the east. Resurfacing of some of the Communist-built highways has now resulted in the lifting of the previous strictly enforced 100 kph (62 mph) speed limits on some autobahns. The 100 kph limit does still apply in some cases, but there are stretches where the limit has now been raised to 120 kph (74 mph) or 130 kph (81 mph).

Gasoline is available at Minol or Intertank filling stations, although increasingly you find the familiar signs of gasoline brands you know. Remember that diesel fuel may not be available at all stations, and unleaded fuel is often sold only on expressways and in main towns. On back roads, filling stations are scarce, so be careful not to let fuel reserves get too low.

By Train   In Saxony and Thuringia, there are generally two types of trains: fast, shown as D in the timetables, and regular/local services indicated with an E. But the Euro-City and InterCity services of the German Federal Railways, the Deutsches Bundesbahn, are being progressively incorporated into the system in eastern Germany. The fast categories have varying supplementary fares; local trains do not. Most trains have first- and second-class cars, and many nowadays have either dining or buffet cars. It is advisable to make advance reservations at major stations or through travel agents, as trains are popular and they are often full.

Leipzig has an S-bahn city railway system. Tickets must be obtained in advance, at various prices according to the number of rides in a block. Get S-bahn tickets at the main railway station.

By Bus and   Within Saxony and Thuringia, most areas are accessible by
Streetcar   bus, but service is infrequent and serves chiefly to connect with rail lines. Check schedules carefully. In Dresden, Leipzig, and Weimar, public transport in the form of buses and streetcars is cheap and efficient.

By Taxi   Taxis in Dresden are inexpensive, but the city is small and walking is the best way to discover its hidden surprises. Leipzig has more cabs than any other eastern German city because of the number needed to cope with peak traffic at fair time. Weimar's chief attractions are within walking distance, but you may want to take a taxi from the main train station, which is somewhat removed from the city center.

By Boat   The **Weisse Flotte** (White Fleet) of inland boats, including paddle side-wheelers, ply the river Elbe, with their starting point at Dresden or at the beautiful forested border town of Bad Schandau, and on into Czechoslovakia. The **KD River Cruises of Europe** (in the U.S., tel. 914/948–3600 or 415/392–8817; in Köln, tel. 0221/208–8318) operates luxury cruises in both directions from May to October on the Elbe.

Tourist Information

Dresden (Box 201, Pragerstr. 10–11, tel. 0351/495–5025). A museum card good for one day and covering admission to all museums in the Staatlichen Kunstsammlungen, including the museums at the Albertinum and the Zwinger, is available at the participating institutions. The card costs DM 8 for adults, DM 4 for children.
Leipzig (Sachsenplatz 1, tel. 0341/79–590).
Weimar (Box 647, Marktstr. 4, tel. 03643/762–342).

Guided Tours

The tourist information office in **Leipzig** leads regularly scheduled bus and tram tours of the city. Although the guides ordinarily conduct the tours in German, they are happy to translate into English on request. Daily two-hour bus tours leave from the tourist office at Am Brühl at 1:30 PM (additional tours in summer at 10 AM); reservations are advised (tel. 0341/79–590). The cost is DM 12 adults, DM 6 children. A tram tour of the city center lasting one hour leaves from Am Brühl at 11 AM and 2 PM (DM 6 adults, DM 3 children). Walking tours conducted on demand from the tourist office last one, two, or three hours and cost DM 7.50 per hour.

Bus tours of the historic center of **Dresden** and Elbe River castles (DM 28 adults, DM 14 children) last about two hours. In winter there is one tour at 2 PM departing from the Augustusbrücke; in other seasons there is a 10:30 AM tour departing from Dr.-Kölz-Ring and a 3 PM tour leaving from the Augustusbrücke. Reservations can be made by the tourist information office. Walking tours in English (two-hour minimum) can be reserved at the tourist information office.

Two-hour walking tours of **Weimar** can be arranged in advance through the tourist information office (tel. 03643/762–342) for 1–20 people. The cost is DM 60 for adults; children are free.

Exploring Dresden

Dresden, superbly located on the banks of the river Elbe, suffered appalling damage during World War II but has been lovingly rebuilt. Italianate influences are everywhere, most pronounced in the glorious Rococo and Baroque buildings in pastel shades of yellow and green. Although many of Dresden's architectural and cultural treasures were destroyed during a fateful night of British bombing in 1945, some gems still remain.

The **Semper Opera House,** at Theaterplatz in the center of Dresden, is a mecca for music lovers. Named after its architect, Gottfried Semper, the hall has premiered Wagner's *The Flying Dutchman* and *Tannhäuser* (conducted by the composer) and nine operas of Richard Strauss. Dating from 1871–78 (the first building by Semper burned down in 1869), the opera house fell victim to the 1945 bombings, but fortunately Semper's architectural drawings had been preserved, so it was rebuilt on the same lines and reopened with much pomp in 1985. At concert intermissions, guests often mingle on the high-up balconies, which have breathtaking views of the city. Tickets are in great demand at the Semper (tel. 0351/484–20); try booking through your travel agent before you go or ask at your hotel. As a last resort, line up at the Abendkasse (Evening Box Office) half an hour before the performance begins.

From Theaterplatz, stroll down the Sophienstrasse to the largely 18th-century **Zwinger** palace complex, which remains one of the city's cultural wonders in the heart of the Altstadt. Completely enclosing a central courtyard of lawns and pools, the complex consists of six linked pavilions decorated with a riot of garlands, nymphs, and other Baroque ornamentation and sculpture, all created under the direction of Matthäus Daniel Pöppelmann. At press time (spring 1993), restoration work was still in progress on part of the palace.

As a result, the world-renowned **Sempergalerie collection** of Old Master paintings, among them works by Dürer, Holbein the Younger, Rembrandt, Vermeer, Raphael, Correggio, and Canaletto, has been on temporary display at the **Albertinum** (*see below*). But other treasures, including the Porzellansammlung (Porcelain Collection)—famous for its Meissen pieces—Zoological Museum, and salon displaying marvelous old scientific instruments (Mathematisch-Physikalischer Salon), remain on view at the palace. *Tel. 0351/484–0120. Porzellansammlung admission: DM 5 adults, DM 2.50 children. Open Sat.–Thurs. and weekends 9–5. Mathematisch-Physikalischer Salon admission: DM 3 adults, DM 1.50 chil-*

dren. Open Fri.–Wed. 9:30–5. Zoological Museum admission: DM 3 adults, DM 1.50 children. Open daily 9–5.

After leaving the Zwinger, head eastward along Ernst-Thälmann-Strasse and turn into the **Neumarkt** (New Market), which is, despite its name, the historic heart of old Dresden. The ruined shell on the right is all that remains of the mighty Baroque **Frauenkirche,** once Germany's greatest Protestant church, after the bombing raids of February 1945. Its jagged, precariously tilting walls had been left as a memorial, a poignant reminder of the evils of war. Reconstruction was scheduled to begin in 1993.

Behind the Frauenkirche looms Dresden's leading art museum, the **Albertinum.** This large, imperial-style building gets its name from Saxony's King Albert, who between 1884 and 1887 converted a royal arsenal into a convenient setting for the treasures he and his forebears had collected. It is on the upper story of the Albertinum that the Sempergalerie's priceless collection of Old Master paintings has been on view pending completion of restoration work at the Zwinger (*see above*).

Permanent exhibits at the Albertinum include the **Gemäldegalerie Neue Meister** (New Masters Gallery), displaying outstanding 19th- and 20th-century European pictures that include French Impressionist and Post-Impressionist works and Caspar David Friedrich's haunting *Das Kreuz im Gebirge.*

Despite the rich array of paintings, it is the **Grünes Gewölbe** (Green Vault) that invariably attracts most attention. Named after a green room in the palace of August the Strong, this part of the Albertinum (entered from Georg-Treu-Platz) contains an exquisite collection of unique objects d'art fashioned from gold, silver, ivory, amber, and other precious and semiprecious materials. Among them is the world's biggest "green" diamond, 41 carats in weight, and a dazzling group of tiny, gem-studded figures, some of which can be admired only through a magnifying glass. Somewhat larger and less delicate is the drinking bowl of Ivan the Terrible, perhaps the most sensational of the treasures to be found in this extraordinary museum. Next door is the **Skulpturensammlung** (Sculpture Collection), which includes ancient Egyptian and classical objects and Italian Mannerist works. *Tel. 0351/495–3056. Sempergalerie collection admission: DM 5 adults, DM 2.50 children. Open Fri.–Tues. 9–5, Wed. 9–6. Gemäldegalerie Alte Meister/Neue Meister admission: DM 5 adults, DM 2.50 children. Open Fri.–Tues. 9–5, Wed. 9–6. Grüne Gewölbe and Skulpturensammlung admission: DM 5 adults, DM 2.50 children. Open Fri.–Tues. 9–5, Wed. 9–6.*

The southern exit of the Albertinum, at Augustus-Strasse, brings you back to the Neumarkt and leads you to another former royal building now serving as a museum, the 16th-century **Johanneum,** once the royal stables. Instead of horses, the Johanneum now houses the **Vekehrsmuseum** (Transport Museum), a collection of historical vehicles, including vintage automobiles and engines. *Am Neumarkt, tel. 0351/495–3002. Admission: DM 4 adults, DM 2 children. Admission half-price on Fri. Open Tues.–Sun. 10–5.*

On the outside wall of the Johanneum is a prime example of Meissen porcelain art: a 102-meter-long (335-foot-long) painting on Meissen tiles of a royal procession. More than 100 members of the royal Saxon house of Wettin, half of them on horse-back, are depicted on the giant jigsaw made up of 25,000 porce-lain tiles, painted from 1904 to 1907.

Follow this unusual procession to the end and you arrive at the former royal palace, the **Herzogschloss,** where major restora-tion work will continue until the mid-1990s behind the fine Ren-aissance facade. Rooms now in use host historical exhibitions. *Sophienstr., tel. 0351/495–3110. Admission: DM 5 adults, DM 2.50 children. Open Mon., Tues., Fri.–Sun. 9–5, Thurs. 9–6.*

Standing next to the Herzogschloss is the **Katholische Hofkirche,** also known as the Cathedral of St. Trinitas, Saxony's largest church. The son of August the Strong, Fred-erick Augustus II (ruled 1733–63) brought architects and builders from Italy to construct this Catholic church, conse-crated in 1754, in a city that had been the first large center of Lutheranism. In the cathedral's crypt are the tombs of 49 Sax-on rulers and a precious vessel containing the heart of August the Strong.

Moving away from the treasures near the river, along the St. Petersburger Strasse, make a left into Lingnerplatz. The **Deutsches Hygiene-Museum** (German Health Museum) reflects Dresden's important role in the history of medicine. The most famous object is a glass model of a human, which caused a sen-sation when it was first displayed in 1930. *Lingnerplatz 1, tel. 0351/48460. Admission: DM 3 adults, DM 1.50 children. Open Tues.–Sun. 9–5.*

Two fine examples of Baroque architecture, both designed by Pöppelmann, general designer of the Zwinger palace, are with-in easy reach from Dresden. Take bus No. 85 from Schillerplatz to the chinoiserie-bedecked **Schloss Pillnitz** (tel. 0351/39325), once the summer residence of the Saxon court and situated in a huge park on the Elbe that embodies both Baroque and English landscape styles. The complex consists of two major palaces—the Wasserpalais (admission: DM 3 adults, DM 1.50 children; open Tues.–Sun. 9:30–5:30) and the Bergpalais (DM 3 adults, DM 1.50 children; open Wed.–Mon. 9:30–5:30)—both housing arts and crafts collections. Schloss Moritzburg, an imposing 17th-century hunting lodge once used by the Saxon royal fami-ly, was renovated and enlarged by Pöppelmann in the Baroque style and is now called the Jägerhof (Hunter's Court). Today it is home to the **Folk Art Museum,** where a decorative arts collec-tion, much of the building's original furniture, and a collection of hunting trophies is displayed. You can get there by taking the Grossenhein bus from the main train station in Dresden. *Kopckestr. 1, tel. 0351/570–817. Admission: DM 2 adults, DM 1 children. Open May–Oct., Tues.–Sun. 10–5; Nov.–Apr., shorter hours.*

Exploring Leipzig

With a population of about 560,000, Leipzig is the second-larg-est city (after Berlin) in the eastern half of Germany. Since the Middle Ages it has been an important market town and a center for printing, book publishing, and the fur industry. Nowadays, its twice-yearly fairs, staged in March and September, main-tain Leipzig's position as a commercial center. If commerce still plays a strong role, it is music and literature that most people associate with Leipzig. Johann Sebastian Bach (1685–1750) was organist and choir director at St. Thomas's church. The composer Richard Wagner was born in Leipzig in 1813. The Romantic writers Johann Wolfgang von Goethe (1749–1832) and Friedrich von Schiller (1759–1805) are also closely associated with the city and its immediate area. Trade and the arts are just two aspects of the city's fame. One of the greatest battles of the Napoleonic Wars—the Battle of the Nations—was fought here in 1813 and was instrumental in leading to the French general's defeat. Little remained of old Leipzig following the devastation of World War II, but reminders of its medieval and Renaissance character are still to be found in the city center.

Railroad buffs may want to start their tour of Leipzig at the **Hauptbahnhof,** the main train station. With its 26 platforms, majestic staircase, and great arched ceiling, it is Europe's biggest and is unique among German railway stations.

Cross the Platz der Republik to the pedestrian area, leading to Sachsenplatz and the **Markt,** the old market square. Here, in the rebuilt 12th-century marketplace, you will find the **Altes Rathaus,** the Renaissance town hall, now housing the municipal museum, where Leipzig's illustrious past is well documented. *Markt 1, tel. 0341–70921. Admission: DM 2 adults, DM 1 children. Open Tues–Fri. 10–6, weekends 10–4.*

On all sides of the Markt, small streets leading from the square attest to Leipzig's rich trading past. Tucked in among them are glass-roofed arcades of surprising beauty and elegance. At the **Apotheke** at Hainstrasse 9, you enter surroundings that haven't changed for 100 years or more, redolent of powders and perfumes, home cures and foreign spices. It's spectacularly Jugendstil, all stained glass and rich mahogany. Nearby, on Grimmaischestrasse, is Leipzig's finest arcade, the **Mädlerpassage.** Here, at No. 2, you'll find the **Auerbachs Keller** restaurant, built in 1530, and made famous in Goethe's tale of Faust (*see* Dining and Lodging, *below*).

Continuing west, Grimmaischestrasse becomes Thomasgasse, site of the **Thomaskirche,** where Johann Sebastian Bach worked for 27 years; he composed most of his cantatas for the church's boys' choir. Once the heart of a 13th-century monastery, rebuilt in the 15th century, the tall Gothic church now stands by itself, with only the names of adjacent streets recalling the cloisters that once surrounded it. The great composer's burial place, it is to this day the home of the Thomasknabenchor and a center of Bach tradition.

Time Out   In the Teehaus café opposite the church you can take your choice of more than a dozen exotic kinds of tea. The café is quite exotic, too, another splendid example of Leipzig Jugendstil.

Another church of more than historic interest is the **Nikolaikirche,** behind Grimmaischestrasse on Nikolaistrasse, where tens of thousands of East Germans demanding reform gathered in the months before the collapse of the Communist regime. *"Wir sind das Volk"* (We are the people) was their chant as they defied the government's efforts to silence them. The church, more impressive inside than outside, has an ornate 16th-century pulpit and an unusual diamond-pattern ceiling supported by classical pillars that are crowned with palm-treelike flourishes.

Looming above the Nikolaikirche in the city center is the 143-meter-high (470-foot-high) **Leipzig University tower,** dubbed the "Jagged Tooth" by students. Using the university skyscraper as a landmark, you come to **Augustus-Platz,** on which stands the modernistic **Opera House** and **Neues Gewandhaus** concert hall, both centers of Leipzig's musical life. By heading across the Ring and up the Grimmaisch Steinweg, you reach the **Grassimuseum** complex. It includes the **Museum of Arts and Crafts** (tel. 0341/21420; open Tues.–Thurs. 10–6, Wed. 2–10, Fri. 10–1, weekends 10–5), the **Geographical Museum** (open Tues.–Fri. 9:30–5:30, Sat. 10–4, Sun. 9–1), and the **Musical Instruments Museum** (enter from Taubchenweg 2; open Tues.–Fri. 9–5, Sat. 10–5, Sun. 10–1). *Johannesplatz 5–11. Admission to each museum: DM 3 adults, DM 1.50 children.*

Back on the Ring and heading clockwise (west), turn left into Harkorstrasse. You'll come to the city's most outstanding museum, the **Museum der Bildenden Kunste,** an art gallery of international stature that is especially strong in German and Dutch painting. *Georgi-Dimitroff-Platz 1, tel. 0341/313–102. Admission: DM 2 adults, DM 1 children; free Sun. Open Tues. and Thurs.–Sun. 9–5, Wed. 1:30–9:30.*

Still further out, reached by streetcar nos. 15, 20, 21, or 25, is the **Exhibition Pavilion** at Pragerstrasse 210. Its main feature is a vast diorama portraying the Battle of the Nations of 1813 (admission: DM 2 adults, DM 1 children; open Tues–Sun. 9–4). Nearby on Pragerstrasse is the massive **Völkerschlacht-denkmal** (open daily 9–4) a 91-meter-high (300-foot-high) granite and concrete memorial in a formal park; it, too, commemorates the battle. You must climb 500 steps to take in the view from the platform near the top. The Prussians did make one concession to Napoleon in designing the monument: A stone marks the spot where he stood during the battle.

Exploring Weimar

Weimar, wedged between Erfurt and Jena and southwest of Leipzig, sits prettily on the Ilm River between the Ettersberg and Vogtland hills, and has a place in German political and cultural history out of all proportion to its size (population 63,000). Its civic history, not long by German standards, began as late as 1410, but by the early 19th century Weimar had become one of Europe's most important cultural centers, where Goethe and Schiller were neighbors, Carl Maria von Weber wrote some of his best music, and Liszt was director of music, presenting the first performance of Wagner's *Lohengrin.* Walter Gropius founded his Staatliches Bauhaus design school in Weimar in 1919, and it was there in 1919–20 that the German National Assembly drew up the constitution of the Weimar Republic. After the collapse of the ill-fated Weimar government, a shadow was cast over the unsuspecting city when Hitler chose it as the site for the first national congress of his new Nazi Party, and later built—or forced prisoners to build for him—the notorious Buchenwald concentration camp on the outskirts of Weimar.

Weimar's greatness is bound up with the activity of the widowed Countess Anna Amalia, who in the late 18th century set about attracting cultural figures to enrich the glittering court her Saxon forebears had set up in the town. Goethe, who served the Countess as a councillor, advising on financial matters and town design, was one of them; Schiller was another. In front of the National Theater on **Theaterplatz** a statue of the famous pair, showing Goethe with a patronizing hand on the shoulder of the younger Schiller, commemorates them.

Adjacent to the National Theater is the Baroque **Wittums-palais,** once the home of Countess Anna Amalia. In the exquisite drawing room where her soirees were held, you find the original cherrywood table at which company sat. In the east wing is a small museum that is a fascinating memorial to her cultural gatherings. *Theaterpl. 9. Admission: DM 3 adults, DM 2 children. Open Mar.–Oct., Tues.–Sun. 9–noon and 1–5; Nov.–Feb., Tues.–Sun. 9–noon and 1–4.*

Goethe spent 57 years in Weimar, 47 years in the house that has since become a shrine for millions of visitors. **Goethehaus** is two blocks south of Theaterplatz on a street called Frauenplan. The museum it contains is testimony not only to the great man's literary might but also his interest in the sciences, particularly medicine, and his administrative skills (and frustrations) as Weimar's exchequer. Here you find the desk at which Goethe stood to write (he liked to work standing up), his own paintings (he was an accomplished watercolorist), and the modest bed on which he died. *Frauenplan 1, tel. 0621/64386. Admission: DM 5 adults, DM 3 children. Open Mar.–Oct., Tues.–Sun. 9–5; Nov.–Feb., Tues.–Sun. 9–4.*

On a tree-shaded square around the corner from Goethe's house is Schiller's green-shuttered home, **Schillerhaus,** in which he and his family spent a happy, all-too-brief three years (Schiller died there in 1805). The poet and playwright's study, dominated by the desk where he probably completed *William Tell,* is tucked up underneath the mansard roof. *Neugasse 2, tel. 0621/62041. Admission: DM 5 adults, DM 3 children. Open Mar.–Oct., Wed.–Mon. 9–5; Nov.–Feb., Wed.–Mon. 9–4.*

Another historic house worth visiting is found on the **Marktplatz,** the central town square. It was the home of the painter Lucas Cranach the Elder, who lived there during his last years, 1552–53. Its imposing facade, richly decorated, bears the coat of arms of the Cranach family. In its ground floor it now houses a private modern art gallery.

Around the corner and to the left is Weimar's 16th-century castle, the **Stadtschloss,** with its restored classical staircase, festival hall, and falcon gallery. The castle houses an impressive art collection, including several fine paintings by Cranach the Elder and many early 20th-century works by such artists as Böcklin, Liebermann, and Beckmann. *Burgplatz. Admission: DM 3 adults, DM 2 children. Open Mar.–Oct., Tues.–Sun. 10–6; Nov.–Feb., Tues.–Sun. 10–4.*

In Weimar's old, reconstructed town center stands the Late Gothic **Herderkirche,** with its large winged altarpiece started by Lucas Cranach the Elder and finished by his son in 1555. Nearby in Jakobstrasse you'll spot the Baroque facade of the **Kirms-Krackow** house.

A short walk south, past Goethehaus and across Wieland Platz, brings you to the cemetery, **Historischer Friedhof** (Historic Cemetery), where Goethe and Schiller are buried. Their tombs are in the classical-style chapel. The Goethe-Schiller vault can be visited daily (except Tuesday) 9–1 and 2–5; winter 9–1 and 2–4.

On the other side of the Ilm, amid meadowlike parkland, is Goethe's beloved **Gartenhaus** (Garden House), where he wrote much poetry and began his masterpiece *Iphigenie auf Tauris* (admission: DM 3 adults, DM 2 children; open daily 9–noon and 1–5, winter 9–noon, 1–4). Goethe is said to have felt very close to nature here, and you can soak up the same rural atmosphere today on footpaths along the peaceful little river, where time seems to have stood still. Just across the river from the Gartenhaus is a generous German tribute to another literary giant, William Shakespeare, a 1904 statue that depicts him jauntily at ease on a marble plinth, looking remarkably at home in his foreign surroundings.

Just south of the city (take the No. 1 bus from Goetheplatz) is the lovely 18th-century **Schloss Belvedere,** now housing a museum of Baroque art but once a hunting and pleasure castle. The formal gardens were in part laid out according to Goethe's concepts. *Tel. 0621/661831. Admission: DM 4 adults, DM 2 children. Open Mar.–Oct., Wed.–Sun. 10–6. Closed Nov.–Feb.*

North of Weimar, in the Ettersberg Hills, is a blighted patch of land that contrasts cruelly with the verdant countryside that so inspired Goethe: **Buchenwald,** where, from 1937 to 1945, 65,000 men, women, and children from 35 countries met their deaths through disease, starvation, and gruesome medical experiments. Each is commemorated today by a small stone placed on the outlines of the former barracks (no longer existing), and by a massive memorial tower. A free bus to Buchenwald leaves from Weimar's main train station. Also leaving from the station are bus tours of the camp organized by the Weimar tourist information office. The buses depart hourly from 9 to 4 daily; the cost is 50 pf for adults, 25 pf for children. *Campsite admission free. Open Tues.–Sun. 8:45–4:30.*

Dining and Lodging

Many of the best restaurants in Saxony and Thuringia are to be found in the larger hotels. You can expect hearty food in both regions. Roast beef, venison, and wild boar are often on Saxon menus, and in the Vogtland you'll find *Kaninchentopf* (rabbit stew). In Thuringia, regional specialties include *Thüringer Rehbraten* (roast venison); roast mutton served in a delicate cream sauce; tasty grilled Thuringian sausages; *Thüringer Sauerbraten mit Klössen* (roast corned beef with dumplings); *Börenschinken* (cured ham); and roast mutton shepherd-style, with beans and vegetables. The light Meissner Wein, wine from the Meissen region, is splendid.

The choice of hotels in Saxony and Thuringia remains limited, and although private householders may now rent rooms, these are also hard to come by, as the demand is far greater than the supply. Contact the local tourist information offices for names of bed-and-breakfasts. Note that during the Leipzig trade fairs, all hotels in the city increase their prices, sometimes significantly.

For details and price-category definitions, *see* Dining and Lodging in Staying in Germany.

Dresden
Dining

Kügelnhaus. A combination grill/coffee shop/restaurant/beer cellar, Kügelnhaus is extremely popular, so either get there early or reserve your table in advance. You'll find the usual hefty local dishes, but prepared with a deft touch. *Str. der Befreiung 13, tel. 0351/52791. Reservations advised. No credit cards. Moderate.*

Sekundogenitur. This famous complex consisting of a restaurant, now connected to the Dresdner Hof hotel complex (*see* Lodging, *below*), is situated right on the banks of the Elbe. There is outside dining when the weather permits. The Wiener schnitzel is excellent. *Brühlsche Terrasse, tel. 0351/495–1435. Reservations advised. No credit cards. Closed Mon. Moderate.*

Lodging

Dresdner Hof. The city's newest hotel fits snugly into a corner of the old city and is only a short distance away from the Zwinger palace, Albertinum, and other major sights. Housing a wine cellar, several bars, a bistro, and smart restaurants, it offers every possible comfort. The lobby is a stunning black-and-white evocation of Jugendstil. *An der Frauenkirche 5, tel. 0351/48410. 333 rooms with bath. Facilities: 7 restaurants, 2 bars, nightclub, 2 cafés, beer pub, wine cellar, indoor pool, sauna, fitness room, solarium, bowling alley, shops, garage. AE, DC, MC, V. Very Expensive.*

Hotel Bellevue. This modern hotel across the river from the Zwinger palace incorporates an old town house, now restored. The hotel views of the historic center are terrific, the rooms luxurious, and the service good. Its Cafe Pöppelmann is especially recommended for its atmosphere and hearty dishes. *Meissnerstr., tel. 0351/56–620. 328 rooms with bath. Facilities: 5 restaurants, wine cellar, café, beer pub, bar, nightclub, shops, sauna, solarium, jogging course. AE, DC, MC, V. Very Expensive.*

Newa. This modern monolith offers less charm than the Dresdner Hof or Bellevue, but is a good choice for comfort and is close to the main train station. The hotel is on the package-tour route and is often booked well in advance. *St.-Petersburger-Str. 34, tel. 0351/496–7112. 310 rooms with bath. Facilities: restaurant, nightclub, bar, sauna, shops. AE, DC, MC, V. Expensive.*

Astoria. A half mile away from the city center but close to the Dresden Zoo (take bus No. 72 from the main train station), the Astoria is a modern five-story hotel with a garden terrace. The staff is pleasant, but the decor hardly fancy—minimalist would describe it best. *Strehlener Platz 2, tel. 0351/471–5171. 82 rooms, most without bath. Facilities: restaurant, bar, shop. AE, DC, MC, V. Moderate.*

Leipzig
Dining
★

Auerbachs Keller. This historic restaurant (built in 1530) and nicely situated in the city center is immortalized in Goethe's *Faust*. The menu features regional dishes from Saxony, often with Faustian names. There is a good wine list. Both a visit and a reservation are musts. *Grimmaischestr. 2–4, tel. 0341/211–6034. Reservations required. Jacket and tie required. AE, DC, MC, V. Expensive.*

Sakura. Located in the Hotel Merkur (*see* Lodging, *below*), the Sakura offers good Japanese cuisine, perhaps out of respect for the Japanese firm that designed and built the hotel. *Gerberstr. 15 (in Hotel Merkur), tel. 0341/7990. Reservations required. Jacket advised. AE, DC, MC, V. Expensive.*

★ **Altes Kloster.** Game is featured in this fascinating restaurant, once part of a cloister. The Old World ambience enhances the excellent food. *Klostergasse 5, tel. 0341/282–252. Reservations advised. No credit cards. Moderate.*

Burgkeller. Romanian specialties are served here in the Doina Restaurant; the keller, at least, is authentic German. *Naschmarkt 1–3, tel. 0341/295–639. Reservations not necessary. No credit cards. Moderate.*

Kaffeebaum. Reputedly the country's oldest café (established 1694), Kaffeebaum has a limited menu, but the atmosphere of this Burgerhaus plus its regulars make a visit worthwhile. At press time (spring 1993) the restaurant was closed for renovation, and the opening date was not available. It is advisable to call ahead. *Fleischergasse 4, tel. 0341/200–452. Reservations advised. No credit cards. Moderate.*

★ **Paulaner.** This intimate restaurant is recommended for its quiet atmosphere and good regional cooking. *Klostergasse 3, tel. 0341/211–3115. Reservations advised. Dress: Informal. No credit cards. Moderate.*

Ratskeller. This large restaurant, which also has a *Jagdzimmer* (Hunting Room), prides itself on its good *Bürgliche* cooking. Specialties include the popular *Ratskeller Topf*, a savory stew with vegetables; homemade pasta; and *Schweineschnitzel* (pork cutlet). *Lotterstr. 1, tel. 0341/791–6201. Reservations advised. No credit cards. Closed Sun. dinner. Moderate.*

Lodging **Astoria.** This older, well-worn hotel is still preferred by many for its genteel ambience and central location next to the main rail station. Traffic in the area is considerable; ask for a room at the rear. *Platz der Republik 2, tel. 0341/72220, fax 0341/722–4747. 309 rooms with bath. Facilities: 2 restaurants, bar, café, nightclub, sauna, parking. AE, DC, MC, V. Very Expensive.*

Hotel Merkur. The city's newest and most luxurious accommodation is imposing for its high-rise profile as well as its Japanese restaurant and garden. It's close to the main rail station and is fully air-conditioned. *Gerberstr. 15, tel. 0341/7990, fax 0341/799–1229. 440 rooms with bath. Facilities: 4 restaurants, 2 bars, coffee bar, nightclub, indoor pool, sauna, solarium, bowling, jogging course, shops, garage. AE, DC, MC, V. Very Expensive.*

Hotel am Ring. This hotel is the logical choice for those who want to be close to the opera house and concert hall. The hotel is modern and efficiently run. Rooms at the rear of the hotel are quieter. *Palais Platz 5–6, tel. 0341/70520. 276 rooms with bath. Facilities: 2 restaurants, bar, nightclub, sauna, shops, parking. AE, DC, MC, V. Expensive.*

Hotel Stadt Leipzig. Considering its central location, this hotel is surprisingly quiet. Public rooms are attractive; dark wooden paneling in the Vignette restaurant sets the tone for a quiet meal. *Richard-Wagner-Str. 1–6, tel. 0341/21450, fax 0341/284–037. 340 rooms with a bath. Facilities: 3 restaurants, cafe, bar, nightclub, sauna, shops, car rental, parking. AE, DC, MC, V. Expensive.*

International. This charming older hotel is situated near the main rail station, within steps of the heart of Leipzig. Its spacious rooms offer old-fashioned comfort with modern facilities. The hotel's sidewalk café is popular. *Tröndlinring 8, tel. 0341/71880. 104 rooms, some with bath. Facilities: restaurant, beer pub, bar, shops, garage. AE, DC, MC, V. Moderate.*

Weimar **Weisser Schwan.** This historic restaurant in the center of town,
Dining right by Goethehaus, dates to 1500. It offers high-quality international cuisine and Thuringian specialties, particularly fish

and grilled meats. *Frauenstorstr. 23, tel. 03643/61715. Reservations essential. Jacket and tie advised. AE, DC, MC, V. Closed last Mon. of month. Expensive.*

Elephantenkeller. In the ancient cellar restaurant of the Elephant hotel (*see* Lodging, *below*), you'll dine on traditional Thuringian cuisine in surroundings that haven't changed much since Goethe's day. Try the *Weimarer Zwiebelmarkt* soup, an onion soup made with pork-knuckle stock. *Markt 19, tel. 03643/61471. Reservations advised. AE, DC, MC, V. Moderate.*

Ratskeller. This historic restaurant is located in the cellar of Stadthaus (City House), a Renaissance building dating back to the 17th century. The wholesome regional fare includes grilled sausages with sauerkraut and onions, and Thuringian onion soup. *Markt 10, tel. 0621/64142. Reservations not necessary. AE, DC, MC, V. Moderate.*

Felsenkeller. In this warm, rustic, country-style restaurant and drinking establishment in the Gasthaus Brauere, a variety of warm dishes is offered at prices between DM 5 and DM 30. The beer is brewed on the premises. *Humboldtstr. 37, tel. 03643/61941. Reservations not necessary. No credit cards. Inexpensive.*

Gastmahl des Meeres. Centrally located, this restaurant offers a wide range of fish dishes, as well as meat. It has fast service and friendly waiters but tends to get crowded between 1 and 2 PM, so it's best to arrive early for lunch. *Herder Platz 16, tel. 03643/4521. No reservations. No credit cards. Inexpensive.*

Lodging **Belvedere.** Opened in 1990, this luxurious hotel 1½ kilometers (1 mile) outside town is located across from a gorgeous wooded park. Rooms are, if anything, overly complete; you'll lack nothing, except proximity to Weimar's center. *Belvedere Allee, tel. 03643/2429. 300 rooms with bath. Facilities: 2 restaurants, café, beer pub, 3 bars, indoor pool, sauna, solarium, fitness room, garage. AE, DC, MC, V. Very Expensive.*

Elephant. This hotel, dating to 1696, is one of Germany's most famous; you'll follow the choice of Goethe, Schiller, Herder, Liszt—and Hitler—all of whom have been guests here. The rooms are comfortable and modern, thanks to recent renovations. A sense of the historic past is ever present. Book well in advance. *Am Markt 19, tel. 03643/61471. 116 rooms with bath. Facilities: 4 restaurants, bar, nightclub, sauna, garage. AE, DC, MC, V. Expensive.*

Russischerhof. This charming hotel built in 1805 was modernized and expanded in 1989. The pleasing rooms are attractively furnished, each equipped with bath, shower, TV, and radio. *Goethe Platz 2, tel. 03643/62331. 85 rooms with bath. Facilities: 2 restaurants, bar, beer cellar, garage. AE, DC, MC, V. Moderate.*

226–2442; 10 Victoria St., tel. 031/225–1721; 18 Union St., tel. 031/557–8451. MC. Closed Sun. Inexpensive.

Lodging **The Caledonian Hotel.** Popularly known as "the Caley," this hotel echoes the days of the traditional great railway hotel, though its neighbor station has long since closed. The imposing Victorian decor has been preserved in a total refurbishment. There are also two excellent restaurants (*see* Pompadour Room *above*). *Princes St., EH1 2AB, tel. 031/225–2433, fax 031/225–6622. 237 rooms with bath. Facilities: 2 restaurants, hairdresser, in-house movies. AE, DC, MC, V. Very Expensive.*

George Hotel. This extensively refurbished city-center hotel has elegant 18th-century features in the public rooms and up-to-date bedrooms. Though busy, the staff takes time to be helpful. *19 George St., EH2 2PB, tel. 031/225–1251, fax 031/226–5644. 195 rooms with bath. Facilities: restaurant. AE, DC, MC, V. Very Expensive.*

Scandic Crown. One of the latest hotels to open in Edinburgh, the Scandic Crown has been designed to blend in with the surrounding ancient buildings. The bedrooms are roomy and follow the color scheme of each floor. If what you want is modern ambience but proximity to the sights, this is the place. *80 High St., The Royal Mile, EH1 1TH, tel. 031/557–9797, fax 031/557–9789. 238 rooms with bath. AE, DC, MC, V. Very Expensive.*

Mount Royal Hotel. This modern hotel is ideally located for sightseeing and shopping. The front rooms have views of the castle. It has a friendly staff. *53 Princes St., EH2 2DG, tel. 031/225–7161. 160 rooms with bath. AE, DC, MC, V. Expensive.*

The Albany Hotel. Three fine 18th-century houses with many original features have been carefully converted into a comfortable city-center hotel. There's a good restaurant in the basement. *39 Albany St., EH1 3QY, tel. 031/556–0397, fax 031/557–6633. 20 rooms with bath. AE, DC, MC. Moderate.*

Brunswick Hotel. This bed-and-breakfast, close to the city center and near the Playhouse Theatre, is in a fine Georgian building that boasts easy parking. All rooms have tea/coffee making facilities and TVs; two of them have four posters. *7 Brunswick St., EH7 5JB, tel. and fax 031/556–1238. 10 rooms with shower. AE, MC, V. Moderate.*

Dorstan Private Hotel. A Victorian villa in a quiet area, the Dorstan has fully modernized rooms decorated in bright, country-cottage colors. *7 Priestfield Rd., EH16 5HJ, tel. 031/667–6721, fax 031/668–4644. 14 rooms, 9 with bath or shower. No credit cards. Inexpensive.*

13 Greece

You cannot travel far across the land in Greece without meeting the sea or far across the sea without meeting one of its roughly 2,000 islands. About the size of New York State, Greece has 15,019 kilometers (9,312 miles) of coastline, more than any other country of its size in the world. The sea is everywhere, not on three sides only but at every turn, reaching through the shoreline like a probing hand. The land itself is stunning, dotted with cypress groves, vineyards, and olive trees, carved into gentle bays or dramatic coves with startling white sand, rolling hills, and rugged mountain ranges that plunge straight into the sea. This natural beauty and the sharp, clear light of sun and sea, combined with plentiful archaeological treasures, make Greece one of the world's most inviting countries.

Poetry, music, architecture, politics, medicine, law—all had their Western birth here in Greece centuries ago, alongside the great heroes of mythology who still seem to haunt this sun-drenched land. Among the great mountains of mainland Greece are the cloud-capped peak of Mount Olympus, fabled home of the Greek gods, and Mount Parnassus, favorite haunt of the sun-god Apollo and the nine Muses, goddesses of poetry and science. The remains of the ancient past—the Acropolis and the Parthenon, the temples of Delphi, the Tombs of the Kings in Mycenae—and a later procession of Byzantine churches, Crusader castles and fortresses, and Turkish mosques are spread throughout the countryside.

Of the hundreds of islands and islets scattered across the Aegean Sea in the east and the Ionian Sea in the west, fewer than 250 are still inhabited. This world of the farmer and seafarer has largely been replaced by the world of the tourist. More than 8 million holiday makers visit Greece each year, almost as many as the entire native population; in fact, tourism has overtaken shipping as the most important element in the nation's economy. On some of the islands, the impact of the annual influx of visitors has meant the building of a new Greece, more or less in their image. But traditionalism survives: Now, pubs and bars stand next door to *ouzeri*, discos are as popular as *kafeneia*, and pizza and hamburger joints compete with *tavernes;* once-idyllic beaches have become overcrowded and noisy, and fishing harbors have become flotilla sailing centers. Prices rose steeply after Greece joined the European Community in 1981, and the simplicity and hardships of a peasant economy have largely disappeared from the islands' way of life.

Although mass tourism has taken over the main centers, it is still possible to strike out and find your own place among the smaller islands and the miles of beautiful mainland coastline. Except for some difficulty in finding accommodations (Greek families on vacation tend to fill the hotels in out-of-the-way places during high summer), this is the ideal way to see traditional Greece. Those who come only to worship the classical Greeks and gaze at their temples, seeing nothing but the glory that was, miss today's Greece. If you explore this fascinating country with open eyes, you'll enjoy it in all its forms: its slumbering cafés and buzzing tavernas; its elaborate religious rituals; its stark, bright beauty; and the generosity, curiosity, and kindness of its people.

Greece

Essential Information

Before You Go

When to Go Although the tourist season runs from May to October, the heat can be unpleasant in July and August, particularly in Athens. On the islands, a brisk northwesterly wind, the *meltemi*, can make life more comfortable. If you want to move about the country and avoid all the other tourists, the ideal months are May, June, and September. The winter months tend to be damp and cold virtually everywhere.

The following are the average daily maximum and minimum temperatures for Athens.

Jan.	55F	13C	May	77F	25C	Sept.	84F	29C
	44	6		61	16		67	19
Feb.	57F	14C	June	86F	30C	Oct.	75F	24C
	44	6		68	20		60	16
Mar.	60F	16C	July	92F	33C	Nov.	66F	19C
	46	8		73	23		53	12
Apr.	68F	20C	Aug.	92F	33C	Dec.	58F	15C
	52	11		73	23		47	8

Currency The Greek monetary unit is the drachma (dr.). Bank notes are in denominations of 50, 100, 500, 1,000, and 5,000 dr.; coins, 5, 10, 20, and 50. At press time (spring 1993), there were approximately 206 dr. to the U.S. dollar and 314 dr. to the pound sterling. Daily exchange rates are prominently displayed in banks. You'll get a better exchange rate at banks than from hotels or stores.

What It Will Cost Inflation in Greece is high—just under 18% a year—and fluctuations in currency make it impossible to do accurate budgeting long in advance, so keep an eye on the exchange rates before your vacation. On the whole, Greece offers good value compared with many other European countries. The values are especially good for modest hotels and restaurants, transportation, and entertainment.

There are few regional price differences for hotels and restaurants. A modest hotel in a small town will charge only slightly lower rates than a modest hotel in Athens, with the same range of amenities. The same is true of restaurants. The spread of tourism has made Rhodes, Corfu, and Crete as affordable as many other islands. Car rentals are expensive in Greece, but taxis are inexpensive even for long-distance runs.

Sample Prices At a central-city café, you can expect to pay about 300 dr. to 500 dr. for a cup of coffee or a bottle of beer, 200 dr. to 300 dr. for a soft drink, and around 300 dr. for a toasted cheese sandwich. These prices can, of course, vary considerably from one place to another. A 1½-kilometer (1-mile) taxi ride costs about 300 dr.

Customs on Arrival You may take in one carton of cigarettes or cigars or ¼ pound of smoking tobacco; 1 liter of alcohol, or 2 liters of wine; and gifts up to a total value of 10,000 dr. There's no duty on articles for personal use. Foreign bank notes in excess of $1,000 (about £560) must be declared for re-export. There are no restrictions on traveler's checks. Foreign visitors may take in an unlimited amount of Greek currency and export up to 40,000 dr. plus $1,400 ECU in foreign currencies. Larger amounts may be exported, depending on your export declaration on arrival.

Language English is widely spoken in hotels and elsewhere, especially by young people, and even in out-of-the-way places someone is always happy to lend a helping hand.

In this guide, names are given in the Roman alphabet according to the Greek pronunciation except when there is a familiar English form, such as "Athens."

Getting Around

By Car
Road Conditions Driving in Greek cities is not recommended unless you have iron nerves. For the ratio of collisions to the number of cars on the road, Greece has the worst accident rate in Europe. This is due, in part, it seems to extremely varied road conditions. Motorways tend to be good; tolls are between 400 dr. and 700 dr. and are charged according to distance. Many country roads are narrow but free of traffic. If you do decide to drive in Greece, keep your wits about you and expect the unexpected. Red traffic lights are frequently ignored, and it is not unusual to see motorists passing on hills and while rounding corners.

Rules of the Road Unless you are a citizen of an EC (European Community) country, you must have an International Driver's License. The **Automobile and Touring Club of Greece** (*see below*) issues them. Driving is on the right, and although the vehicle on the right has the right-of-way, as mentioned above, don't expect this or any other driving rule to be obeyed. The speed limit is 100 kph (62 mph) on the National Road, 80 kph (49 mph) outside built-up areas, and 50 kph (31 mph) in town. Seat belts are compulsory.

Parking In Greece's half-dozen large cities, parking spaces are hard to find. In Athens or Thessaloniki, you can pay to use one of the many temporary parking lots set up in vacant lots, but you're better off leaving your car in the hotel garage and walking or taking a cab. Elsewhere, however, parking is easy. There is free or cheap parking at most archaeological sites outside Athens.

Gasoline At press time gas cost about 185 dr.–205 dr. a liter (about 791 dr.–877 dr. a gallon). Gas pumps and service stations are everywhere, and lead-free gas is widely available. Be aware that many stations close at 7 PM.

Breakdowns **The Automobile and Touring Club of Greece** (ELPA, Athens Tower, Messoghion 2–4, Athens, tel. 01/779–1615 or fax 01/778–6642; in an emergency, tel. 104) assists tourists' breakdowns within town limits free of charge; otherwise, there is a charge.

By Bicycle Jeeps, dune buggies, pedal cycles, mopeds, and motorcycles can be rented on the islands. Use extreme caution. Crash helmets, although technically compulsory for motorcyclists, are not usually available, and injuries are common.

By Train Few tourists use the trains because they are slow and railway networks are limited. The main line runs north from Athens to Yugoslavia. It divides into three lines at Thessaloniki. The main line continues on to Yugoslavia, a second line goes east to the Turkish border and Istanbul, and a third line heads northeast to Bulgaria. The Peloponnese in the south is served by a narrow-gauge line dividing at Corinth into the Mycenae–Argos section and the Patra–Olympic–Kalamata section. For information, tel. 01/362–4402 or -3, -4, -5, -6.

By Plane **Olympic Airways** (Syngrou 96, Athens, tel. 01/961–6666) has service between Athens and several cities and islands. Thessaloniki is also linked to the main islands, and there are several interisland connections.

By Bus Travel by bus is inexpensive, usually comfortable, and relatively fast. The journey from Athens to Thessaloniki, for example, takes roughly the same amount of time as the slow train, though the express covers the distance 1¼ hours faster. In the Peloponnese, however, buses are much faster than trains. Bus information and timetables are available at tourist information offices throughout Greece. Make reservations at least one day before your planned trip. Railway-operated buses leave from the Peloponnisos railway station in Athens. All other buses leave from one of two bus stations: Liossiou 260—for central and eastern Greece and Evvia; Kifissou 100—for the Peloponnese and northwestern Greece.

By Boat There are frequent car ferries and hydrofoils from Piraeus, the port of Athens, to the central and southern Aegean islands and Crete. Nearby islands are also served by hydrofoils and ferries from Rafina, east of Athens. Ships to other islands sail from ports nearer to them. Connections from Athens/Piraeus to the main island groups are good, connections from main islands to smaller ones within a group less so, and services between islands of different groups or areas—such as Rhodes and Crete—are less frequent. Travel agents and shipping offices in Athens and Piraeus and in the main towns on the islands have details. Buy your tickets two or three days in advance, especially if you are traveling in summer or taking a car. Reserve your return journey or continuation soon after you arrive.

Timetables change very frequently, and boats may be delayed by weather conditions, so your itinerary should allow for some flexibility.

Staying in Greece

Telephones Most curbside kiosks have pay telephones for local calls only.
Local Calls You pay the man inside the booth 10 dr. per call after you've finished. At the international airport you can buy phone cards. So far these can be used only with airport phones.

International Calls The easiest way to make and pay for international and long-distance calls is to go to a Telecommunications Office (OTE), usually located in the center of towns and villages. There are several branches in Athens. There are also a few special telephone booths (distinguished by their orange band) for international and long-distance calls. Calls to the United States and Canada cost 1,112 dr. for a three-minute-minimum station-to-station connection and 1,482 dr. for a three-minute-minimum person-to-person connection, plus 471 dr. for each additional minute or part of a minute. Hotels tend to add a hefty service charge for long-distance calls. You can call the United States collect or use your calling card by dialing the **AT&T** operator (tel. 00/800–1311) or the **MCI** operator (tel. 00/800–1211).

Operators and There are English-speaking operators on the International Ex-
Information change. Ask your hotel reception desk or an employee at the

OTE for help in reaching one. It takes up to an hour for the operator to connect your call.

Mail
Postal Rates
Airmail letters or postcards for delivery within Europe cost 90 dr. for 20 grams and 180 dr. for 50 grams; outside Europe the cost is 120 dr. for 20 grams and 220 dr. for 50 grams.

Receiving Mail
Except for the main office on **Syntagma Square** (open Mon.–Sat. 8–8), most post offices are open weekdays 8–2. You can have your mail sent to Poste Restante, Aeolou 100, Athens 10200 (take your passport to pick up your mail), or to American Express, Ermou 2, Athens, 10225. For holders of American Express cards or traveler's checks, there is no charge for the service. Others pay 300 dr. for each pick-up.

Shopping
Value-Added Tax
Prices quoted in shops include the VAT. There are no VAT refunds.

Bargaining
Prices in large stores are fixed. Bargaining may take place in small owner-managed souvenir and handicrafts shops and in antiques shops. In flea markets, bargaining is expected.

Export Permits
Antiques and Byzantine icons require an export permit (not normally given if the piece is of any value), but beautiful replicas can be bought fairly cheaply, although even these require a certificate stating they are copies.

Opening and Closing Times
The government has freed opening hours for shops and businesses under its program to liberalize the economy. As a result, office and shopping hours can vary considerably and may also change according to the season. Check with your hotel for up-to-the-minute information on opening and closing times. Below is a rough guide:

Banks are open weekdays 8–2; closed weekends and public holidays.

Museums are open 8:30–3; some smaller ones close earlier. Generally, museums are closed on Monday, with shorter hours on Sunday and public holidays, during which admission is often free. During the summer, major museums may be open daily. Archaeological sites usually open at 8:30 and close at sunset during the summer, at 3 during the winter. Hours vary from one site to another and often change without notice; always check with tourist offices or travel agencies before visiting. *See* Exploring for hours, which were correct at press time (spring 1993) but may change by summer.

Shops are open Tuesday, Thursday, and Friday, 9–2 and 5:30–8; Monday, Wednesday, and Saturday, 9–2.

National Holidays
January 1; January 6 (Epiphany); March 14 (Clean Monday); March 25 (Independence); April 29 (Good Friday); May 1 (Easter Sunday); May 2 (Easter Monday); May 1 (Labor Day); June 19 (Pentecost); August 15 (Assumption); October 28 (Ochi Day); December 25–26.

Dining
Greek cuisine cannot be compared to that of France, and few visitors would come to Greece for its food alone. You'll certainly be able to find a delicious and inexpensive meal, but don't look in hotel restaurants, where the menus usually consist of bland, unimaginative international fare (although it's only here that you will find a reasonably priced fixed menu). The principal elements of Greek cuisine are such vegetables as eggplants, tomatoes, and olives, fresh and inventively combined with lots of

olive oil and such seasonings as lemon juice, garlic, basil, and oregano. While meat dishes are limited (veal, lamb, and chicken being the most common), fish is often the better, though more expensive choice, particularly on the coast. Your best bet is to look for tavernas and *estiatoria* (restaurants) and choose the one frequented by the most Greeks. The *estiatorio* serves oven-baked dishes called *magirefta*, precooked and left to stand, while tavernas offer similar fare plus grilled meats and fish. The decor of both types of establishment may range from simple to sophisticated, with prices to match.

Traditional fast-food in Greece consists of the *giro* (slices of grilled meat with tomato and onions in pita bread), *souvlaki* (shish kebab), and pastries filled with a variety of stuffings (spinach, cheese, or meat)—but hamburgers and pizzas can now be found even on the smaller islands.

Mealtimes Lunch in Greek restaurants is served from 12:30 until 3. Dinner begins at about 9 and is served until 1 in Athens and until midnight outside Athens.

Precautions Tap water is safe to drink everywhere, but it is often heavily chlorinated. Excellent bottled mineral water, such as *Loutraki*, is available.

Dress Throughout the Greek islands you can dress informally for dinner, even at Expensive restaurants; in Athens, you may want to wear a jacket and tie at some of the top-price restaurants.

Ratings Prices are per person and include a first course, main course, and dessert (generally fruit and cheese or a sticky pastry such as baklava). They do not include drinks or the 12%–15% service charge. Best bets are indicated by a star ★.

Category	Athens/ Thessaloniki	Other Areas
Very Expensive	over 10,000 dr.	over 7,000 dr.
Expensive	6,000 dr.– 10,000 dr.	5,000 dr.–7,000 dr.
Moderate	3,500 dr.–6,000 dr.	2,500 dr.–5,000 dr.
Inexpensive	under 3,500 dr.	under 2,500 dr.

Lodging Most accommodations are in standard hotels, sometimes called motels. There are a number of "village" complexes, especially at the beaches, and as part of some hotels. On islands and at beach resorts, large hotels are complemented by family-run pensions and guest houses—usually clean, bright, and recently built—and self-catering apartment and bungalow complexes. In a very few places, there are state-organized "traditional settlements"—fine old houses with guest accommodations.

Greek hotels are classified as Deluxe, A, B, C, etc. Within each category, which is set by the government, quality varies greatly, but prices usually don't. Still, you may come across an A-class hotel that charges less than a B-class, depending on facilities. In this guide, hotels are classified according to price: Very Expensive, Expensive, Moderate, and Inexpensive. All Very Expensive and Expensive hotels are assumed to have air-conditioning, so our listings in these categories mention it only when it is absent. If a Moderate or an Inexpensive hotel is air-conditioned, this is indicated. All have been built or completely renovated during the past 20 years, and all have private baths.

Prices quoted by hotels usually include service, local taxes, and VAT. At many hotels, breakfast is included. At certain times, though, you can negotiate the price, sometimes by eliminating breakfast. The official price should be posted on the back of the door or inside a closet. Seaside hotels, especially those in the Very Expensive and Expensive categories, frequently insist that guests take half-board (lunch or dinner included in the price).

Ratings Prices quoted are for a double room in high season, including taxes and service, but not breakfast. Rates are the same throughout the country for each category. Best bets are indicated by a star ★.

Category	All Areas
Very Expensive	over 35,000 dr.
Expensive	19,000 dr.–35,000 dr.
Moderate	12,000 dr.–19,000 dr.
Inexpensive	under 12,000 dr.

Tipping There are no absolute rules for tipping. In restaurants, cafés, and tavernas, in addition to the 15% service charge, you should leave a tip for the waiter of around 10% in the better restaurants and between 5% and 10% in cheaper tavernas. This should be left on the table for your waiter and not on the plate, where it will be taken by the head waiter. In hotels, tip porters 50 dr. or 100 dr. per bag for carrying your luggage—more in a top hotel. Taxi drivers don't expect tips, but Greeks usually give something, especially to round off the fare or if the driver has been especially helpful. Hairdressers usually get 10% or slightly more. In legitimate theaters, tip ushers 50 dr. if you are shown to your seat. In movie theaters, tip about the same if you receive a program from the usher. On cruises, cabin and dining-room stewards get about 400 dr. per day.

Athens

Arriving and Departing

By Plane Most visitors arrive by air at **Ellinikon** Airport, about 10 kilometers (6 mi) from the city center. All Olympic Airways flights, both international and domestic, use the Western terminal next to the ocean. All other flights arrive and depart from the Eastern terminal on the opposite side of the airport.

Between the Airport and Downtown A blue-and-yellow coach service connects the two air terminals, Syntagma Square, and Piraeus. The coaches run every 20 minutes from 6 AM until midnight (fare: 160 dr.) and every 90 minutes from midnight until 6 AM (fare: 200 dr.). A taxi to the center of Athens costs about 1,200 dr. (1,500 dr. midnight–5 AM).

By Train Athens has two railway stations, side by side, not far from Omonia Square. International trains from the north arrive at, and depart from, Stathmos Larissis, (tel. 01/524–0646, -7, -8).

Take bus No. 51 from the terminal to Omonia Square. Trains from the Peloponnese use the marvelously ornate and old-fashioned Stathmos Peloponnisos (tel. 01/513–1601) next door. To Omonia and Syntagma squares, take trolley No. 1 or bus No. 24.

By Bus Greek buses arrive at the Athens bus station (100 Kifissou, tel. 01/512–4910). International buses drop their passengers off on the street, usually in the Omonia or Syntagma Square areas or at Stathmos Larissis.

By Car Whether you approach Athens from the Peloponnese or from the north, you enter by the National Road and then follow signs for the center. Leaving Athens, routes to the National Road are well marked; signs usually name Lamia for the north and Corinth or Patras for the southwest.

By Ship Except for cruise ships, few passenger ships from other countries call at Piraeus, the port of Athens, 10 kilometers (6 miles) from Athens' center. If you do dock at Piraeus, you can take the metro right into Omonia Square. The trip takes 20 minutes and costs 100 dr. Alternatively, you can take a taxi, which may well take longer due to traffic and will cost a great deal more, around 1,000 dr.

Getting Around

Many of the sights you'll want to see, and most of the hotels, cafés, and restaurants, are within a fairly small central area. It's easy to walk everywhere.

By Metro An electric (partially underground) railway runs from Piraeus to Omonia Square and then on to Kifissia. It is not useful for getting around the central area. The standard fare is 75 dr. or 100 dr., depending on the distance. There are no special fares or day tickets for visitors, and there is, as yet, no public transport map.

By Bus The fare on blue buses and the roomier yellow trolley buses is 75 dr. Tickets should be purchased beforehand at one of the yellow kiosks, or from booths at one of the terminals. Validate your ticket by stamping it at the orange counter, or you may be fined 1,500 dr. Buses run from the center to all suburbs and suburban beaches until about midnight. For suburbs beyond central Kifissia, you have to change at Kifissia. Attica has an efficient bus network. Most buses, including those for Sounion, leave from the KTEL terminal, Platia Aigyptiou on Mavromateon, at the corner of Patission and Alexandras avenues.

By Taxi Taxis are plentiful except during rush hours and rainstorms. But drivers seem to lead a maverick life—those without occupants often refuse to pick up passengers, while those with occupants often stop to pick up more. Most drivers speak basic English and are familiar with the city center, though not necessarily with the suburbs. There is a 300 dr. minimum and a basic charge of 48 dr. per kilometer; this increases to 94 dr. between midnight and 5 AM. There is an additional 200 dr. charge for trips to and from the airport, and 100 dr. for trips to and from the port. There is also a 50 dr. charge per item for baggage. Some drivers overcharge foreigners, especially on trips from the airport or from Piraeus; insist that they turn on the meter as soon as you get in, and make sure they use the high tariff ("Tarifa 2") between only midnight and 5 AM.

Important Addresses and Numbers

Tourist Information There are **Greek National Tourist Offices** at Karageorgi Servias 2, in the bank, tel. 01/322–2545; at East Ellinikon Airport, tel. 01/961–2722; at Ermou 1, inside the General Bank building, tel. 01/325–2267; and at Piraeus, NTOG Building, Zea Marina, tel. 01/413–5716.

Embassies **U.S.** (Vasilissis Sofias 91, tel. 01/721–2951); **Canadian** (Gennadiou 4, tel. 01/723–9511); **U.K.** (Ploutarchou 1, tel. 01/723–6211).

Emergencies **Police:** Tourist Police (tel. 171); Traffic Police (tel. 01/523–0111); and City Police (tel. 100). **Fire** (tel. 199). **Ambulance** (tel. 166). **Doctors:** Top hotels usually have one on staff; any hotel will call one for you. You can also call your embassy. **Dentist:** Ask your hotel or embassy. **Pharmacies:** Most pharmacies in the central area have someone who speaks English and knows all the usual medical requirements. Try **Marinopoulos** (Kanari 23, tel. 01/361–3051). For information on late-night pharmacies, tel. 107.

English-Language Bookstores **Pantelides** (Amerikis 11, tel. 01/364–5161); **Eleftheroudakis** (Nikis 4, tel. 01/323–1051); **Compendium** (Nikis 28, upstairs, tel. 01/322–1248); **Reymondos** (Voukourestiou 18, tel. 01/354–8187, -8, -9).

Travel Agencies **American Express** (Ermou 2, tel. 01/324–4975); **Wagons-Lits Travel** (Stadiou 5, tel. 01/324–2281); **CHAT Tours** (Stadiou 4, tel. 01/322–2886); **Condor Travel** (Stadiou 47, off Omonia Sq., tel. 01/321–2453).

Guided Tours

Orientation Tours All tour operators offer a four-hour morning bus tour of Athens, including a guided tour of the Acropolis, for around 6,000 dr. Make reservations at your hotel or at a travel agency; besides those agents already mentioned, there are hundreds of others, many situated around Filellinon and Nikis streets off Syntagma Square.

Special-Interest Tours For those interested in folk dancing, there is a four-hour evening tour (May–September) for around 5,800 dr. that begins with a son et lumière (sound-and-light-show) at the Acropolis and then goes on to a performance of Greek folk dances in the open-air theater nearby. Another evening tour offers a dinner show at a taverna in the Plaka area, after the son et lumière, for around 8,400 dr. Any travel agency can arrange these tours—and the excursions below—for you, but go first to **CHAT Tours** (*see* Travel Agencies, *above*) for reliable and efficient service.

Excursions The choice is almost unlimited. A one-day tour to Delphi will cost up to 13,000 dr., with lunch included; a two-day tour to Corinth, Mycenae, Nauplio, and Epidaurus, around 23,000 dr., with meals and accommodations included. A full-day cruise from Piraeus, visiting three nearby islands—Aegina, Poros, and Ydra—costs around 9,000 dr., and a two-day cruise, including Mykonos and Delos, costs from 19,000 dr., including accommodations in standard-class hotels. A three-day classical tour to Delphi and the breathtaking Meteora monasteries costs from 56,000 dr.

Personal Guides Greek guides are some of the best in Europe, each having completed a two-year start at guide school. All the major tourist agencies can provide English-speaking guides for personally organized tours. Only hire one licensed by the National Tourist Organization.

Exploring Athens

Athens is essentially a village that outgrew itself, spreading out from the original settlement at the foot of the Acropolis. Back in 1834, when it became the capital of modern Greece, the city had a population of fewer than 10,000. Now it houses more than a third of the Greek population—around 4 million. A modern concrete city has engulfed the old village and now sprawls for 388 square kilometers (244 square miles), covering almost all the surrounding plain from the sea to the encircling mountains.

The city is very crowded, very dusty, and overwhelmingly hot during the summer. It also has an appalling air-pollution problem, caused mainly by traffic fumes; in an attempt to lessen the congestion, it is forbidden to drive private cars in central Athens on alternate workdays. Despite the smog, heat, and dust, Athens is an experience not to be missed. It has a tangible vibrancy that makes it one of the most exciting cities in Europe, and the sprawling cement has failed to overwhelm the few striking and astonishing reminders of ancient Athens.

The central area of modern Athens is small, stretching from the Acropolis to Mount Lycabettos, with its small white church on top. The layout is simple: Three parallel streets—Stadiou, Venizelou (a.k.a. Panepistimiou), and Akademias—link two main squares—Syntagma and Omonia. Try to wander off this beaten tourist track to catch some of the real flavor of living Athens. Seeing the Athenian butchers in the central market near Monastiraki sleeping on their cold, marble slabs during the heat of the afternoon siesta may give you more of a feel for the city than seeing hundreds of fallen pillars.

Numbers in the margin correspond to points of interest on the Athens map.

The Historic Heart At the center of modern Athens is **Syntagma (Constitution)**
❶ **Square.** It has several leading hotels, airline and travel offices, and numerous cafés. Along one side of the square stands the
❷ **Parliament Building,** completed in 1838 as the royal palace for the new monarchy. In front of the palace, you can watch the changing of the vividly costumed **Evzone guard** at the **Tomb of the Unknown Soldier.** Amalias Avenue, leading out of Syntagma, will take you to the **National Gardens,** a large oasis in the vast sprawl of this largely concrete city.

Time Out There are several breakfast/lunch spots around Syntagma Square. **Brazilian,** at Voukourestiou 1B, two blocks from the square, is ideal for a quick coffee and snack. Just down the street from the National Gardens, at Xenofontos 10, is **Diros,** efficiently serving good Greek food and steaks. **Jimmy's,** at Valaoritou 7 in a pedestrian zone, is also a popular place for a snack, with outside tables.

Across the street, at the far end of the National Gardens, you
❸ will see the columns of the once-huge **Temple of Olympian Zeus.**

This famous temple was begun in the 6th century BC, and, when it was finally completed 700 years later, it exceeded in magnitude all other temples in Greece. It was destroyed during the invasion of the Goths in the 4th century, and today only the towering sun-browned columns remain. *Vassilissis Olgas 1, tel. 01/922–6330. Admission: 400 dr. Open Tues.–Sun. 8:30–3.*

❹ To the right stands **Hadrian's Arch,** built at the same time as the temple by the Roman emperor. It consists of a Roman archway, with a Greek superstructure of Corinthian pilasters. Visiting heads of state are officially welcomed here.

About three-quarters of a kilometer (a half mile) east, down
❺ Leoforos Olgas Avenue, you'll come to the marble **Panathenaic Stadium** built for the first modern Olympic Games in 1896; it is a blindingly white, marble reconstruction of the ancient Roman stadium of Athens and can seat 80,000 spectators.

From Hadrian's Arch, take the avenue to the right, Dionysiou
❻ Areopagitou, a few blocks west to the **Theater of Dionysos,** built during the 6th century BC. Here the famous ancient dramas and comedies were originally performed in conjunction with bacchanalian feasts. *Tel. 01/322–4625. Admission: 400 dr. Open daily 8:30–2:30.*

A little higher up, on the right, you'll see the massive back wall
❼ of the much better preserved **Odeon of Herodes Atticus,** built by the Romans during the 2nd century AD. Here, on pine-scented summer evenings, the **Athens Festival** takes place. It includes opera, ballet, drama, and concerts (*see* The Arts, *below*). *Tel. 01/321–0219. It is not otherwise open to the public.*

❽ Beyond the theater, a steep, zigzag path leads to the **Acropolis.** After a 30-year building moratorium to commemorate the Persian wars, the Athenians built this complex during the 5th century BC to honor the goddess Athena, patron of the city. It is now undergoing conservation as part of an ambitious 20-year rescue plan launched with international support in 1983 by Greek architects. The first ruins you'll see are the **Propylaea,** the monumental gateway that led worshipers from the temporal world into the spiritual world of the sanctuary; now only the columns of Pentelic marble and a fragment of stone ceiling remain. Above, to the right, stands the graceful **Temple of Wingless Victory** (or Athena Nike), so called because the sculptor depicted the goddess of victory without her wings in order to prevent her from flying away. The elegant and architecturally complex **Erechtheion temple,** most sacred of the shrines of the Acropolis and later turned into a harem by the Turks, has now emerged from extensive repair work. Dull, heavy copies of the infinitely more beautiful Caryatids (draped maidens) now support the roof. The Acropolis Museum houses five of the six originals, their faces much damaged by acid rain. The sixth is in the British Museum in London.

❾ The **Parthenon** dominates the Acropolis and indeed the Athens skyline. Designed by Ictinus, with Phidias as master sculptor, it is the most architecturally sophisticated temple of that period. Even with hordes of tourists wandering around the ruins, you can still feel a sense of wonder. It was completed in 438 BC. The architectural decorations were originally picked out in vivid red and blue paint, and the roof was of marble tiles, but time and neglect have given the marble pillars their golden-white shine, and the beauty of the building is all the more stark and

Athens

striking. The British Museum houses the largest remaining part of the original 162-meter (523-foot) frieze (the Elgin Marbles). The building has 17 fluted columns along each side and 8 at the ends, and these lean slightly inward and bulge to cleverly counterbalance the natural optical distortion. The Parthenon has had a checkered history: It was made into a brothel by the Romans, a church by the Christians, and a mosque by the Turks. The Turks also stored gunpowder in the Propylaea, and when this was hit by a Venetian bombardment in 1687, a fire raged for two days and 28 columns were blown out, leaving the Parthenon in its present condition. *Tel. 01/321–0219. Admission: 1,500 dr., joint ticket to Acropolis and museum. Open weekdays 8–6:45 (8–4:30 in winter), weekends and holidays 8:30–2:30.*

⑩ The **Acropolis Museum,** just below the Parthenon, contains some superb sculptures from the Acropolis, including the Caryatids and a large collection of colored *kore* (statues of women dedicated by worshipers to the goddess Athena, patron of the ancient city). *Tel. 01/323–6665. Admission: 1,500 dr., joint ticket to the Acropolis. Open weekdays 11–5 (Mon. 11–2:30, Tues.–Fri. 8–4:30 in winter), weekends and holidays 8:30–2:30.*

On **Areopagus,** the rocky outcrop facing the Acropolis, St. Paul preached to the Athenians; the road leading down between it and the hill of Pnyx is called Agiou Pavlou (St. Paul). To the ⑪ right stands the **Agora,** which means "marketplace," the civic center and focal point of community life in ancient Athens. The sprawling confusion of stones, slabs, and foundations is domi- ⑫ nated by the best-preserved temple in Greece, the **Hephestaion** (often wrongly referred to as the Theseion), built during the 5th century BC. Nearby, the impressive Stoa of Attalus II, reconstructed by the American School of Classical Studies in Athens with the help of the Rockefeller Foundation, houses the ⑬ **Museum of the Agora Excavations.** *Tel. 01/321–0185. Admission: 800 dr. Open daily 8:30–7 (8:30–2:45 in winter).*

Next to the Agora you'll find the **Plaka,** almost all that's left of 19th-century Athens. During the 1950s and '60s, the area became garish with neon as nightclubs moved in and residents moved out. Renovation in recent years has restored the Plaka, and it is again lined with attractive red-tile-roofed houses and the vine-shaded courtyards of open-air tavernas and bars.

Below the Plaka, in Cathedral Square, stands a charming 12th- ⑭ century Byzantine church known as the "Old" or **"Little Cathedral,"** nestled below the vast structure of the 19th-century **Cathedral of Athens.** From here, a short walk up Mitropoleos will take you back to Syntagma.

Time Out Visit the **De Profundis Tea Room** in an old mansion at Hatzimichali 1. This quiet café serves delicious homemade pastries. **Kostis,** on the main square in Plaka at Kidathineon 18, is ideal for a Greek lunch—wild greens, roast chicken, *imam* (a spicy eggplant dish). It's the perfect place to people-watch, and you won't be overcharged for this prime location.

Downtown Athens If you walk along Venizelou Avenue (Panepistimiou) from the square, you will pass, on the right, three imposing buildings in ⑮ ⑯ Classical style: the **Academy,** the **Senate House of the University,** ⑰ ty, and the **National Library.** When you reach **Omonia Square,** a bedlam of touts and tourists, you are in the heart of downtown Athens.

⑱ Try to spare time to see the **National Archaeological Museum.** Despite being somewhat off the tourist route, a good 10-minute walk north of Omonia Square, it is well worth the detour. This is by far the most important museum in Athens. It houses one of the most exciting collections of antiquity in the world, including sensational archaeological finds made by Heinrich Schliemann at Mycenae, 16th-century BC frescoes from the Akrotiri ruins on Santorini, and the 6½-foot-tall bronze sculpture *Poseidon,* an original work of circa 470 BC, possibly by the sculptor Kalamis, which was found in the sea off Cape Artemision in 1928. *Patission 44 (28 Oktovriou Ave.), tel. 01/821–7717. Admission: 1,500 dr. Open Mon. 11–5, Tues.–Fri. 8–7 (8–5 in winter), weekends and holidays 8:30–3.*

Alternatively, from Syntagma you can take Vassilissis Sofias Avenue along the edge of the National Gardens to reach the ⑲ **Evzone Guards' barracks.** From here you have several options. If you continue farther along Vassilissis Sofias, it will eventually take you to the Hilton Hotel and the U.S. Embassy. Or, turn ⑳ right onto Herodes Atticus, which leads to the **Presidential Palace,** the former royal palace, now occupied by President Constantine Karamanlis.

㉑ Ahead two blocks on the left is the **Museum of Cycladic Art.** The collection spans 5,000 years, with nearly 100 exhibits of the Cycladic civilization (3,000–2,000 BC), including many of the slim marble figurines that so fascinated artists like Picasso and Modigliani. *Neofytou Douka 4, tel. 01/722–8321. Admission: 250 dr. Open Mon. and Wed.–Fri. 9–3 (10–4 in winter), Sat. 10–3.*

㉒ A little farther along Vassilissis Sofias is the **Byzantine Museum,** housed in an 1848 mansion that was built by an eccentric French aristocrat. It has a unique collection of icons and the very beautiful 14th-century Byzantine embroidery of the body of Christ in gold, silver, yellow, and green. Sculptural fragments provide an excellent introduction to Byzantine architecture. *Vassilissis Sofias 22, tel. 01/721–1027. Admission: 500 dr. Open Tues.–Sun. 8:30–3.*

Kolonaki, the chic shopping district and one of the most fashionable residential areas, occupies the lower slopes of **Mount** ㉓ **Lycabettos** and is only a 10-minute walk northeast of Syntagma; it's worth a stroll around if you enjoy window-shopping and people-watching. Three times the height of the Acropolis, Lycabettos can be reached by funicular railway from the top of Ploutarchou Street (the No. 23 bus from Kolonaki Square will drop you at the station; fare: 350 dr. round-trip). The view from the top—pollution permitting—is the finest in Athens. You can see all Athens, Attica, the harbor, and the islands of Aegina and Poros laid out before you.

Time Out Take a cappuccino break at one of the many trendy but friendly cafés, such as **Peros** or **Da Capo** on Kolonaki Square, or sip an ouzo with your *mezedes* (appetizers) atop Mount Lycabettos at **Dionyssos,** with its resplendent view of the city and the Acropolis.

Off the Beaten Track

Outside central Athens, on the slopes of Mount Ymitos (ancient Mount Hymettus), is one of the city's most evocative Byzantine remains, the **Kaisariani monastery.** Take a taxi or the No. 224 bus from the terminal on Akademias (across from Municipal Cultural Center) for 6 kilometers (4 miles) east of central Athens until you pass through the working-class suburb of Kaisariani. The monastery is an additional 30-minute walk up the lower slopes of Mount Ymitos. The well-restored 11th-century church, built on the site of a sanctuary of Aphrodite, has some beautiful frescoes dating from the 17th century. Outside there are plenty of shady places under the trees where you can sit and contemplate the view over Athens. If you feel particularly energetic, you can continue walking up Mount Ymitos— the roads wind through the forested slopes for 19 kilometers (12 miles)—and take your pick of the many picnic spots. *Tel. 01/ 723–6619. Admission 500 dr. Open Tues.–Sun. 8:30–3.*

Beyond the port of Piraeus, the little harbor of **Mikrolimano** is famed for its many seafood restaurants—22 at last count—but has lost favor with some Athenians because its pretty, crescent-shaped harbor suffers from pollution. The delightful atmosphere remains intact, however, and the harbor is crowded with the small yachts of its enthusiastic clientele. While it's not a particularly cheap place to eat, the freshness and quality of the fish and seafood at the Mikrolimano matches any elsewhere in Greece. If you don't like seafood, you'll still be enchanted by the terraces of lovely houses tucked up against the sloping hillsides, the elegant yachts, and the sturdy fishing craft. To get there from Athens, take the train from Omonia Square to Neo Faliron or a bus from Filellinon Street to the Neo Faliron train station; it's only five minutes' walk from there. Alternatively, a relatively expensive (1,800 dr.) taxi ride will take you 16 kilometers (10 miles) along the new coast road toward **Glyfada,** where the fish restaurants give you wonderful views of the Saronic Gulf.

Shopping

Gift Ideas Better tourist shops sell copies of traditional Greek jewelry, silver filigree, enamel, Skyrian pottery, onyx ashtrays and dishes, woven bags, attractive rugs (including *flokates*—shaggy wool rugs, often brightly colored), good leather items, and furs. Furs made from scraps are inexpensive. Some museums sell replicas of small items that are in their collections. The best handicrafts are sold in **National Welfare Organization shop** (Ypatias 6) near the cathedral. Other shops sell dried fruit, packaged pistachios, and canned olives. For books in English, go to **Pantelides** (Amerikis 11) or **Eleftheroudakis** (Nikis 4). Most large hotels also maintain English-language bookstores, although these have a fairly limited selection.

Antiques Many shops, especially on **Pandrossou Street,** sell small antiques and icons. Keep in mind, however, that there are many fakes around, and remember that you must have permission to export genuine objects from the Greek, Roman, or Byzantine periods.

Shopping Areas The central shopping area lies between Syntagma and Omonia. The **Syntagma** area has good jewelers, shoe shops, and handi-

crafts and souvenir shops, especially along **Voukourestiou.**
Stadiou Street is the best bet for men's clothing. Try **Ermou
Street** for shoes and the fascinating small streets that lead off it
for fabrics and housewares. Go to **Mitropoleos** for rugs and souvenirs. This is also the main furrier street, and most of the
moderately priced fur shops are here, including **Hydra, Voula
Mitsakou,** and **Samaras.** Ermou runs west to **Monastiraki,** a
crowded market area popular with Athenians. Below the cathedral, **Pandrossou** has antiques, sandals (an especially good
buy), and inexpensive souvenirs. **Kolonaki,** just beyond central
Athens, has the best shops for gifts. Here you'll find unique
jewelry by the famous **Ilias Lalounis** (Venizelou 6), with **La
Chrysoteque Zolotas** just down the street (Venizelou 10), and
designer boutiques, such as **Lanvin** (Anagnastopoulou 6) and
G. F. Ferre (Anagnastopoulou 4). For a broader selection, try
Bettina (Voukourestiou 4) for women's clothing and **Artisti
Italiani** (Kanari 5) for men's.

Department Stores The few that exist are neither large nor good. The best are **Min-
ion** (3 Septemvriou 10) and **Lambropoulos** (Aeolou 99–101).
Marinopoulos shops (Kanari 9, Kifissias 16, and elsewhere)
specialize in toiletries and inexpensive casual clothing.

Flea Market The flea market, based on **Pandrossou** and **Ifestou streets,** operates on Sunday mornings and sells almost anything: second-
hand clothes, daggers, cooking pots and pans, old books,
guitars, *bouzouki* (stringed instruments), old furniture and
carpets, and backgammon sets. Pontians—Greeks who lived in
the former Soviet Union—sell Russian caviar, vodka, and table
linen. However little it costs, you should haggle. Ifestou Street,
where the coppersmiths have their shops, is more interesting
on a weekday—and you can pick up copper wine jugs, candlesticks, cooking ware, etc., for next to nothing.

Dining

Be adventurous and go looking for the places that have at least
half a dozen tables occupied by Athenians—they're discerning
customers. Alternatively, if you would like a change of cuisine
and don't object to higher prices, pick up a copy of the monthly
English-language magazine, *The Athenian,* available at most
bookshops and central kiosks. It lists all kinds of ethnic restaurants—from French to Lebanese to Chinese—with relevant
addresses and telephone numbers. For details and price-
category definitions, *see* Dining in Staying in Greece.

Very Expensive **Bajazzo.** This elegant wood-paneled restaurant is housed in a
★ converted neoclassical mansion in fashionable Kolonaki. The
food is exquisitely presented, and specialties include duck in
mousseline sauce, salmon roulade, various game dishes—including pheasant, partridge, and red deer—and occasionally, a
Fisherman's Dream soup with clams, langoustines (crayfish),
moules (mussels), and ouzo. *Ploutarchou 35, tel. 01/729–1420.
Reservations advised. AE, DC, MC, V. No lunch.*
L'Abreuvoir. This restaurant, outstanding among the many average French restaurants, is ideal for a romantic candlelight
dinner. The classic French dishes are served in a shaded garden. Frequented by wealthy Athenians and resident expatriates seeking a break from Greek cuisine, it has an elegant,
dressed-up ambience. Specialties include spinach tart, steak
au poivre (with pepper), and *entrecôte* (steak) *Provençale.*

Xenokratous 51, tel. 01/722–9061. Reservations advised. AE, DC, MC, V.

Expensive **Aglamair.** The most civilized and expensive of the fish restaurants lining the picturesque Mikrolimano harbor, this is also one of the best in Athens. Practically on the water's edge, you can dine watching the lights shimmer across the bay. The decor is cheerful but sophisticated, with red tablecloths and green-and-black chairs. The menu includes lobster, shrimps, prawns, octopus, and squid. *Akti Koumoundourou 54–56, tel. 01/411–5511, -2, -3, -4, -5. Reservations advised. AE, DC, MC, V.*

Dionyssos. You may be able to get better food at better prices elsewhere in Athens, but the view of the Acropolis is unbeatable and the food is usually of a high standard. Try to go for dinner when there is a son-et-lumière performance on the Parthenon; the sight is unforgettable. The best view is from the terrace upstairs. House specialties include charcoal-grilled shrimps and veal mignonettes in oregano sauce. *Robertou Gali 43, tel. 01/923–3182. Reservations advised. AE, DC, MC, V.*

★ **Gerofinikas.** This cheerful and bustling restaurant, tucked away in a narrow alley off a street leading up to Kolonaki, has a loyal expense-account clientele. The two-tier dining room, has glass-fronted cases with inviting displays of seafood and Greek and Turkish specialties, such as *stifado lago* (a rabbit stew with onions and bay leaves). *Pindarou 10, tel. 01/362–2719. Reservations advised. AE, DC, MC, V.*

Symposio. After a show at the nearby Herodes Atticus, sit in the garden or the glass-enclosed dining room and enjoy some creative culinary combinations—crepes with caviar and smoked salmon, pasta with metsovone cheese, filets of St. Peter fish with oysters. Specials change weekly. *Erecthiou 46, tel. 01/922–5321. Reservations not necessary. AE, MC, V. No lunch.*

Moderate **Apotsos.** A famous ouzerie, close to Syntagma Square but hidden away down an arcade, this is an echoing barn of a place—truly Athenian in atmosphere. Politicians, journalists, and artists gather here at lunchtime. As well as ouzo, wine and beer are served, along with dishes of mezedes—though three or four of these will add up to a substantial meal. The walls are decorated with old advertisements; the tabletops are of well-worn marble. *Venizelou (Panepistimiou) 10 in the arcade, tel. 01/363–7046. Reservations not necessary. No credit cards. Lunch only Mon.–Sat. (11:30–5).*

Botsaris. Tucked away in a residential area, this bustling corner restaurant is a welcome alternative to the usual pricey seafood spots. Try grilled octopus, fish soup with large chunks of seafood and shrimp, or one of many fresh catches—red mullet, sea bream, grouper. Service is friendly and prompt. *Zisimopoulou 24, Paleo Faliron, tel. 01/941–3022. Reservations not necessary. AE, DC. No lunch Mon.–Sat.*

Ideal. This old Athenian restaurant, which opened in 1922, has been refurbished and still attracts Athenians of all ages, as well as students from the nearby university. It has an extensive menu featuring high-quality Greek and Continental dishes. *Venizelou (Panepistimiou) 46, tel. 01/361–4604 or 01/363–1000. Reservations not necessary. DC, MC, V. Closed Sun.*

★ **Kostoyannis.** If you're looking for authenticity, this is the place to go. One of the oldest and most popular tavernas in the area, located behind the Archaeological Museum, it has an impressively wide range of Greek dishes—including excellent shrimp salads, stuffed mussels, rabbit stifado, and sautéed brains. *Zaimi 37, tel. 01/821–2496. Reservations advised in summer. No credit cards. Dinner only. Closed Sun.*

Inexpensive **Eden.** This vegetarian restaurant, in a neoclassical Plaka house, serves vegetable pies and such hearty dishes as vegetable lasagna and spinach with cheese, rice, and carrots—a delightful experience for those who are tired of seeing lamb roasted on a spit at every corner. *Lyceou 12, tel. 01/324–8858. Reservations not necessary. AE, DC. Closed Tues.*

Karavitis. A neighborhood favorite, this taverna near the Olympic Stadium has outdoor garden seating and a winter dining room decorated with huge wine casks. The classic Greek cuisine is well prepared, including pungent *tzatziki* (yogurt-garlic dip), *bekri meze* (lamb chunks in a spicy red sauce), and *stamnaki* (beef baked in a clay pot). *Arktinou 35, tel. 01/721–5155. Reservations not necessary. No credit cards. No lunch.*

★ **O Platanos.** Set in a picturesque corner of the Plaka, this is one of the oldest tavernas in the area. It has a shady courtyard for outdoor dining. Don't miss the oven-baked potatoes, the roast lamb, and the exceptionally cheap but delicious barrel *retsina* (local wine). Although it's extremely friendly, not much English is spoken. *Diogenous 4, tel. 01/322–0666. Reservations not necessary. No credit cards. Closed Sun.*

Lodging

Since Athens is the starting point for so many travelers, its hotels are very full, and it's always advisable to reserve a room in advance. Which type of hotel you choose is really a matter of personal taste. Basically, the style of hotels in Athens can be divided into two neat brackets—traditional and modern—and these can be found both in the center of town, around Omonia and Syntagma Squares, near the U.S. Embassy, and farther out along the seacoast and near the airport. In the heat of summer, it might be preferable to go for the fresh, clean lines of a more modern-style hotel, leaving the older ones for winter visits. Hotels in the center of Athens can be so noisy that it's difficult to get a good night's sleep, while those out on the coast are more expensive, since you spend more money on taxis getting to and from town. For details and price-category definitions, *see* Lodging in Staying in Greece.

Very Expensive **Aphrodite Astir Palace.** Located in a coastal area 25 kilometers (16 miles) from Athens, this is actually a group of three hotels: Aphrodite; Arion, the least expensive; and Nafsika, the most exclusive and perhaps the most beautiful. The complex, on a pine-covered promontory, has its own beach, helicopter pad, and breathtaking views over Vouliagmeni Bay. This is Greece's most prestigious seaside hotel complex, and it is highly recommended. *Laimos Vouliagmeni, tel. 01/896–0211/0311, fax 01/896–2582. 570 rooms with bath. Facilities: 6 restaurants, 3 outdoor pools, 4 tennis courts, nightclub, snack bar. AE, DC, MC, V. Aphrodite and Nafsika open Apr.–Dec.*

Athenaeum Inter-Continental. Although outside the city center, the deluxe Inter-Continental is one of Athens' most modern hotels, a welcome reprieve for those who like their amenities. Rooms have a sitting area, TV, and marble bathrooms. Ask for one with an Acropolis view. An hourly shuttle delivers guests to and from Syntagma Square during the day. *Syngrou 89–93, tel. 01/906–3666, fax 01/924–3000. 133 rooms* *with bath. Facilities: 5 restaurants, pool, shops. AE, DC, MC, V.*

★ **Athens Hilton.** Set in a commanding position on a hill near the U.S. Embassy, the Hilton is about a 20-minute walk from Syntagma Square. All rooms and suites have fine views of either the Acropolis or Mt. Hymettos and soundproof windows; all have balconies. On summer evenings, there's a poolside barbecue and the Byzantine, open virtually all the time, has Sunday brunch for those who crave this distinctly non-Greek tradition. *Vassilissis Sofias 46, tel. 01/725–0201, fax 01/725–3110. 480 rooms with bath. Facilities: 2 restaurants, lounge, piano bar, outdoor pool with food and beverage service, shops. AE, DC, MC, V.*

★ **Grande Bretagne.** G.B., as it is known, is centrally located on Syntagma Square. An internationally famous landmark and the hub of Athenian social life, this distinguished hotel had a face-lift in 1992 and now recalls the days when Churchill was a guest. Ask for an inside room overlooking the courtyard to escape the noise of the traffic, or try one of several rooms with Acropolis views. The hotel houses the excellent G.B. Corner restaurant. *Syntagma Square, tel. 01/323–0251/9, fax 01/322–8034. 364 rooms with bath. Facilities: restaurant, rooftop garden. AE, DC, MC, V.*

Ledra Marriott. Between Athens center and the sea near the Inter-Continental, this is a popular chain hotel known for comfort and service well above the standard. Its cafés and restaurants are fashionable meeting places. The Marriott is renowned for its variety of dining options: You can sample Polynesian fare beside a cascading waterfall at Kona Kai, enjoy Japanese delights at Teppanyaki, graze at Zephyros's filling Sunday brunch, or try Tex-Mex or Asian cuisines, among others, during one of the hotel's theme nights. The rooftop swimming pool is spectacular. Shuttles run to and from Syntagma Square. *Syngrou 115, tel. 01/934–7711, fax 01/935–8603. 258 rooms with bath. Facilities: 4 restaurants, rooftop garden, outdoor pool, shops. AE, DC, MC, V.*

Expensive **Divani Palace Acropolis.** On a small street near the Acropolis and other ancient sites, this hotel seems to be gaining in popularity. It is also an ideal base from which to stroll and explore. The public areas are clean and attractive, and the upper-story bedrooms have excellent views. *Parthenonos 19, tel. 01/922–2945 or 01/922–9650, fax 01/921–4993. 269 rooms with bath. Facilities: restaurant, rooftop garden, outdoor pool. AE, DC, MC, V.*

Elektra Palace. At the edge of Plaka, this hotel offers cozy rooms done in warm hues—complete with TV, balconies, and minibar—for comparatively low prices. The staff is helpful, breakfast abundant, and best of all you can spend hours by the rooftop pool, sipping wine while gazing upon the Acropolis. *Nikodimou 18, tel. 01/324–1401, -2, -3, -4, -5, -6, -7, fax 01/324–1875. 106 rooms with bath. Facilities: restaurant, pool, roof garden. AE, DC, MC, V.*

★ **St. George Lycabettos Hotel.** Situated on the wooded slopes of Mount Lycabettos in upscale Kolonaki, this hotel has a splendid view. Getting there, however, involves a steep short walk or a ride up (remember, taxis are inexpensive). In 1992 plush new rooms and suites were added. The hotel has, as its trump card, Le Grand Balcon, a two-tiered rooftop restaurant with excellent food and a marvelous panoramic view. It also has terraces with snack tables, and a very attractive ground-floor bistro. *Kleomenous 2, tel. 01/729–0711/9, fax 01/724–1847. 162 rooms with bath. Facilities: 2 restaurants, bar, outdoor pool, roof garden. AE, DC, MC, V.*

Moderate **Ilissia Hotel.** This small hotel located near the Hilton, was taken over in 1992 by Best Western. Although the rooms are rather functional, it is within walking distance of many fine restaurants and night spots. *Mihalakopoulou 25, tel. 01/724–4051, fax 01/724–1847. 90 rooms with bath. Facilities: air-conditioning. AE, MC, V.*

Novotel Mirayia. Although not central, this hotel is just a 10-minute walk to the rail station and the national museum. One of the city's better values, it has an elegant lobby and soundproof rooms with sofas, minibars and TVs. The rooftop pool is beside an Italian restaurant. In summer you can watch the sun set behind the Acropolis. *M. Voda 4–8, tel. 01/862–7053, fax 01/883–7816. 195 rooms with bath. Facilities: 2 restaurants, boutique, bar, pool, air-conditioning. AE, DC, MC, V.*

Inexpensive **Acropolis View Hotel.** This hotel in a quiet neighborhood below
★ the Acropolis has agreeable rooms, most with Parthenon views. The staff is fit and friendly, and major sights lie a stone's throw away. *Webster 10, tel. 01/921–7303, -4, -5, fax 01/923–0705. 25 rooms with bath. Facilities: bar (summer), roof garden, air-conditioning. AE, DC, MC.*

Aphrodite Hotel. This is near Syntagma and perfectly comfortable. With all the facilities of other, more costly hotels, it offers excellent value for the money. Don't be put off by its cold-looking entrance. *Apollonos 21, tel. 01/323–4357, -8, -9, fax 01/322–5244. 84 rooms with bath. Facilities: bar, air-conditioning. AE, DC, MC, V.*

Attalos Hotel. The market area, where the Attalos is located, is full of life and color by day, but deserted at night. The hotel is pleasant and well run and has an exceptionally fine view of the Acropolis and Mount Lycabettos. Try to get a room on the 5th or 6th floor or in the rear, where the street noise is less. *Athinas 29, tel. 01/321–2801, -2, -3, fax 01/324–3124. 80 rooms with bath. Facilities: bar, roof garden. No credit cards.*

★ **Austria.** This small, unpretentious hotel is on Filopappou Hill, opposite the Acropolis, ideal as a base for wandering around the heart of ancient Athens. It has no restaurant and is at the top of the inexpensive category, but is well worth considering. *Mouson 7, tel. 01/923–5151, fax 01/902–5800. 37 rooms with bath. AE, DC, MC, V.*

The Arts

The **Athens Festival** runs from late June through September and includes concerts, recitals, opera, ballet, folk dancing, and drama. Performances are in various locations, including the open-air theater of Herodes Atticus at the foot of the Acropolis, nearby Philopappou Hill, and Mount Lycabettos. Tickets are available a few days before the performance from the festival box office in the arcade at Stadiou 4 (tel. 01/322–1459). Admission ranges from 1,500 dr. to 10,000 dr.

For those who are disappointed with the daytime view of the Acropolis, the **son-et-lumière** shows bring history to life. Performances are given nightly from April to October, in English, at 9:15 (the time is subject to change), and admission is 1,000 dr. The entrance is on Dionysiou Areopagitou, opposite the Acropolis, and from your seat on the top of Philopappou Hill, you watch the changing lighting of the monuments.

Cultural activity in the winter has improved enormously with the opening in 1991 of the **Megaron Athens Concert Hall** (tel. 01/ 728–2333), with two auditoriums equipped with state-of-the-art acoustics. Daily listings are published year-round in *The Athens News*, available in hotels and newsstands. The *Athenian* lists concerts, exhibitions, and showings of films in English.

Concerts Concerts are given September through June at the **Concert Hall** by Greek and world-class international orchestras. Information and tickets are available from the **Athens festival box office** (Stadiou 4, tel. 01/322–1459) or from the Concert Hall itself (Vassilissis Sofias and Kokkali, tel. 01/728–2333) opposite the U.S. embassy. Prices range from 1,000 dr. to 20,000 dr. Tickets can be charged in person with a credit card.

Opera The **Lyriki Skini Opera Company** has a winter season (Oct.– May) and a small—not very good—ballet season at the Olympia Theater (Akademias 59, tel. 01/361–2461). In summer they perform at the Herodes Atticus theater. The best seats cost about 4,000 dr.

Films Almost all cinemas now show foreign films, usually managing to show the latest Hollywood offerings within a month or two of their New York and London openings. *The Athens News* and *Greek News* list them in English. Downtown cinemas are the most comfortable. Try the **Embassy** in Kolonaki (Patriarchou Ioachim 5, tel. 01/722–0903) or the **Apollon** (tel. 01/323–6811) at Stadiou 19, just off Syntagma Square for new American films and, in summer, the outdoor **Cinema Thission** (Pavlou 7, tel. 01/ 342–0864 or 01/347–0980) for American and European classics, with a view of the Acropolis as a backdrop. Unless they have air-conditioning, most cinemas close June–September, giving way to wonderful outdoor cinemas such as the Thission or **Cine Paris** in Plaka (Kidathineon 22, tel. 01/322–2071), where the films change every few days, and you can order drinks from the bar during the screening.

Nightlife

Athens has an active nightlife, with hundreds of places offering some sort of entertainment, much of it distinctly Greek. One way to get a taste is to take an "Athens by Night" guided tour, which can be arranged for you by any good travel agent (*see* Important Addresses and numbers, *above*). If you want to go on your own, try a *bouzoukia*, or a taverna with a floor show. Tavernas with floor shows are concentrated in the Plaka area. It might help you to know that breaking plates by tossing them at the feet of the taverna's featured performers is a time-honored Greek tradition—you'll be provided some cheap, unglazed plates by the taverna, don't hurl the ones off which you've just eaten!

Be forewarned that you will have to pay for an overpriced, second-rate meal at most places. At the bouzoukia, there is usually a per-person minimum or a prix-fixe menu; a bottle of whiskey costs about 25,000 dr. The name, style, and quality of tavernas and bouzoukias change frequently. Ask your hotel for recommendations.

Tavernas **Palia Taverna Kritikou.** Here's a fun, although touristy, taverna where there's room for you to indulge in Greek dances to the amusement of the few Greek customers. *Mniskleous 24, tel. 01/322–2809. Reservations advised. AE, DC, V. Expensive.*

Stamatopoulou Palia Plakiotiki Taverna. Here in a converted 1822 Plaka house you'll find good food along with an acoustic band of three guitars, bouzouki, and accordion playing old Athenian songs. Greeks will often get up and dance, beckoning you to join them, so don't be shy. *Lyceou 26, tel. 01/322–8722. Reservations unnecessary. DC, V. Inexpensive.*

Bouzoukias **Diogenes Palace.** Currently the "in" place with Athenians who want to hear Greece's heartthrob, Lefteris Pantazes, croon; it's also the most expensive. *Leoforos Syngrou 255, tel. 01/942–4267. Reservations required. AE, DC, MC, V. Closed July–Aug. Very Expensive.*

Posidonio. Decadence reigns as diners dance the seductive *tsifteteli* with enthusiasm and order flower vendors to shower gardenias on their favorite singers. *Posidonios 18, tel. 01/894–1033. Reservations advised. No credit cards. Closed Sun. and June–Sept. Expensive.*

The Peloponnese

Suspended from the mainland of Greece like a large leaf, with the isthmus of Corinth as its stem, the ancient land of Pelops offers beautiful scenery—rocky coasts, sandy beaches, and mountains—and a fascinating variety of ruins: temples, theaters, mosques, churches, palaces, and medieval castles built by crusaders.

Legend and history meet in Mycenae, where Agamemnon, Elektra, and Orestes played out their grim family tragedy. This city dominated the entire area from the 18th to the 12th century BC, and may even have conquered Minoan Crete. According to Greek mythology, Paris, son of the king of Troy, abducted the beautiful Helen, wife of Menelaus, the king of Sparta. Agamemnon, the king of Mycenae, was Menelaus's brother. This led to the Trojan War in which Troy was defeated. The story of the war is told in Homer's *Iliad*. Following Heinrich Schliemann's discoveries of gold-filled graves and a royal palace during excavations in 1874, Mycenae has become a world-class archaeological site and, of all the sites in the Peloponnese, is most worthy of a visit.

Sparta, once a powerful city-state, is today, unfortunately, devoid of charm or character. Like Corinth, once the largest, richest, and most pleasure-loving city of ancient Greece, Sparta now appears sadly lifeless and unattractive. Neither of these modern townships seems to bear any relation to their original vibrancy; Corinth, in fact, was destroyed by earthquakes in 1858 and 1928, and each time experienced a more practical and banal reconstruction, the last of which left it 5 kilometers (3 miles) from its original site.

During the Middle Ages, the Peloponnese was conquered by leaders of the Fourth Crusade and ruled as a feudal state by French and Italian nobles. It formed the cornerstone of Latin (Christian) power in the eastern Mediterranean during the 13th and 14th centuries. In 1821, when the bishop of Patras

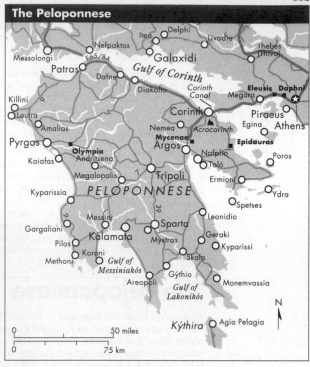

The Peloponnese

raised the standard of revolt against Turkish domination, the Peloponnese played a key role in the Greek War of Independence. Nafplio was, for a short time during the 1800s, the capital of Greece. Among the region's many fine contributions to humanity are the Olympic Games, founded in 776 BC in Olympia.

Getting Around

The best way to see all the important sights of the Peloponnese at your own pace is by car. If you take the car ferry from Italy to Patras, capital of the Peloponnese, or if you rent a car in Patras, you can tour the area on the way to Athens. Otherwise, your tour will begin in Athens. Take the route suggested in the itinerary below. You could encounter a shortage of hotel rooms in summer, especially at Nafplio, so plan in advance.

Guided Tours

CHAT Tours (4 Stadiou, Athens, tel. 01/322–2886) and **Wagons-Lits Travel** (Stadiou 5, Athens, tel. 01/324–2281) both organize tours in the Peloponnese. A four-day tour of the Peloponnese and Delphi, including the sites, a qualified guide, and accommodations at first-class hotels, costs around 75,000 dr. A two-day tour, again including accommodations, to Corinth, Mycenae, and Epidauros, will cost around 23,000 dr. A six-day grand tour of the Peloponnese, taking in all the main sites and with accommodations at the best available hotels, costs around 108,000 dr.

Tourist Information

In Patras, visit the **Greek National Tourist Office** (Iroon Polytechniou 10, Glyfada, tel. 061/653–358, -9) or the **American Express** representative at **Albatros Travel** (Othonos 48, tel. 061/220–993). The **Tourist Police** are at Patreos 53 (tel. 061/220–902). There are many tourist agencies along this street; Albatros can help you with all travel arrangements, including boat excursions to the Ionian islands, yacht hire, car hire, and rail bookings. The **Olympic Airlines** office is at Agios Andreou 16 (tel. 061/222–901). The **Automobile and Touring Club of Greece** (ELPA) has a branch office at Patroon Athinon 18 in Patras (tel. 061/425–411). In Olympia you'll find the **Tourist Office** in the town hall (tel. 0624/23–100). The **Tourist Police** are at Spiliopoulou 15 (tel. 0624/22–550).

Exploring the Peloponnese

Eleven kilometers (7 miles) northwest of Athens, after you have passed the last houses of the Athenian urban sprawl, you'll come to the 6th-century monastery of **Daphni**. It was sacked in 1205 by Frankish crusaders, who later installed Cistercian monks from Burgundy to rebuild it. The monastery has superb mosaics. *End of Iera Odos, tel. 01/581–1558. Admission: 500 dr. Open daily 8:30–3.*

Descending from Daphni to the sea, you face the narrow straits where the Persian fleet of Xerxes was defeated in 480 BC by Sparta. Shortly beyond are the ruins of **Eleusis**, site of antiquity's most important harvest celebrations, the Eleusinian Mysteries, where participants underwent rites commemorating the gift of corn cultivation given by Demeter, goddess of grain. Now the area is unattractive, surrounded by factories and their pollution, and there is almost nothing left of the ancient Eleusis but a few fallen pillars and overgrown pathways. Admission to the site includes entrance to a small museum. *Iera Odos 2, tel. 01/554–6019. Admission: 400 dr. Open Tues.–Sun. 8:30–3. Closed Mon.*

When you cross the **Corinth Canal**, about 84 kilometers (52 miles) from Athens, you will have entered the **Peloponnese**. Modern **Corinth** lies by the sea; the ancient Greek city stood higher up. An important ruin is the **Doric Temple of Apollo**, built during the 6th century BC and one of the few buildings that still stood when Julius Caesar decided to restore Corinth. In AD 51, St. Paul fulminated against the sacred prostitutes who served Aphrodite on the **Acrocorinth**, the peak behind the ancient city. A museum beside the ruins contains finds from the excavations. Be sure to see the fine display, next to the museum, of the evolution of Greek columnar architecture. *Tel. 0741/31–207. Admission: 1,000 dr. Open daily 9–3.*

Drive from the square of ancient Corinth (about 80 dr. by taxi) to the tourist pavilion below the **Fort of Acrocorinth**, then continue on foot for 10 minutes to explore the imposing Franco-Turkish fortifications. *Tel. 0741/31–207. Admission free. Open daily 8:30–sunset.*

Mycenae, 44 kilometers (28 miles) from Corinth, was the fabulous stronghold of the Achaean kings of the 13th century BC. Destroyed in 468 BC, it was forgotten until 1874 when German archaeologist Heinrich Schliemann, who discovered the ruins

of ancient Troy, uncovered the remains of this ancient fortress
city. Mycenae was the seat of the doomed House of Atreus—of
King Agamemnon and his wife, Clytemnestra, sister of Helen
of Troy, and of their tragic children, Orestes and Elektra.
When Schliemann uncovered six shaft graves (so named because the kings were buried standing up) of the royal circle, he
was certain that one was the tomb of Agamemnon. The gold
masks and diadems, daggers, jewelry, and other treasures
found in the graves are now in the Athens Archaeological Museum; the new local museum is dedicated to archaeological
studies. Along with the graves, you'll find the astounding bee-
hive tombs built into the hillsides outside the reconstructed
wall, the **Lion Gate,** dating to 1250 BC, and the castle ruins
crowning the bleak hill, all remnants of the first great civilization in continental Europe. The tombs, the acropolis, the palace, and the museum can all be explored for the cost of
admission. *Tel. 0751/76–585. Admission: 1,000 dr. Open weekdays 8–7 (8–5 in winter), weekends and holidays 8:30–3.*

Moving south, 11 kilometers (7 miles) from Mycenae, you'll
pass **Argos,** prominent during the 8th century BC, and the Cy-
clopean ramparts (huge, irregular stones) of **Tiryns.** One version of the legend has Tiryns as the birthplace of Hercules, but
the present remains, including the walls, date mostly from the
13th century BC when Tiryns was one of the most important
Mycenaean cities.

Farther on is **Nafplio,** a picturesque town below the Venetian
fortifications. Modern Greece's first king lived for a year or two
within the walls of the higher fortress when Nafplio was capital
of Greece. His courtiers had to climb 999 steps to reach him; you
can still climb the long staircase or drive up to the **fortress.** *Tel.
0752/28–036. Admission: 400 dr. Open weekdays 8–7 (8:30–
4:45 in winter), weekends and holidays 8:30–2:45.*

The **Venetian naval arsenal** on the town square houses a museum crowded with Mycenaean finds. *Tel. 0752/27–502. Admission: 400 dr. Open Tues.–Sun. 8:30–3.*

Epidauros, 24 kilometers (15 miles) east of Nafplio, was the
sanctuary of Asklepios, the Greek god of healing. You can visit
the foundations of the temples and ancient hospital. The most
important site is the ancient open-air theater, which seats
14,000. In summer, during the **Epidauros Festival,** ancient
Greek plays are staged here (*see* The Arts, *below*). The theater
merits a visit anytime of year. The acoustics are so good that
you can sit in the top row and hear a whisper onstage. *Tel. 0753/
22–009. Admission: 1,000 dr. Museum and theater open weekdays (except Mon. when museum opens at noon) 7:30–7
(7:30–5 in winter), weekends and holidays 8:30–7 (8:30–3 in
winter).*

From here you can return to Athens along the coast, a lovely
drive, or continue on to **Olympia** by way of the rugged mountains of Arcadia. The site of ancient Olympia lies a few kilometers from the sea, northwest of **Megalopolis,** where a huge
assembly hall was built to hold the Ten Thousand representa-
tives of the Arcadian League. The first Olympic Games were
held in Olympia in 776 BC and continued to be celebrated every
four years until AD 393, when the Roman emperor Theodosius
I, with his Christian sensibility, banned these "pagan rites."
Women were excluded from the games under penalty of death,

although no one was ever executed. They always held their own games a few weeks prior. Archaeologists are still uncovering statues and votive offerings among the pine trees surrounding **Olympic Stadium** and the imposing **ruins of the temples of Zeus and Hera** within the sacred precinct. *Stadium tel. 0624/22–517, museum tel. 0624/22–522. Admission: 1,000 dr. museum; 1,000 dr. stadium. Stadium open weekdays 7:30–7 (8–5 in winter), weekends 8:30–3. Museum open same hours except Mon. noon–7 (11–5 in winter).*

The **International Olympic Academy,** 6.4 kilometers (4 miles) east, houses the **Museum of the Olympic Games,** with its collection of commemorative postage stamps and mementos. *Tel. 0624/22–544. Admission: 500 dr. Open weekdays 8–3:30, weekends 9–3:30.*

Northeast of Olympia, 122 kilometers (76 miles) away, is **Patras,** the third-largest city in Greece, its main western port, and the hub of the business world in the Peloponnese. Walk up to the **Byzantine kastro,** built on the site of the ancient acropolis, to take a look at the fine view along the coast. The **Cathedral of St. Andrew's,** reputedly the largest in Greece and built on the site of the crucifixion of St. Andrew, is also worth exploring. Its treasure is the saint's silver-mounted skull, returned to Patras in 1964 after 500 years in St. Peter's, Rome. The cathedral is on the far west side of the harbor at the end of Ag. Andreou. Apart from the kastro and the cathedral, there is little of particular interest here. The city's prettiest features are its squares, surrounded by neoclassical-style buildings, and its arcaded streets.

The shortest route back to Athens follows the National Road along the southern shore of the Gulf of Corinth, an exceptionally beautiful drive. You could instead cross the entrance to the gulf and visit Delphi (*see* Exploring in Mainland Greece, *below*) on your way back to Athens.

Dining and Lodging

Many of the hotels in the Peloponnese have good dining rooms, so try these as well as the usual tavernas serving their traditional Greek cuisine and fresh seafood. For details and price-category definitions, *see* Dining and Lodging in Staying in Greece.

Nafplio **Savouras.** Fresh seafood is served in this unpretentious taverna
Dining overlooking the bay; it is generally regarded as one of the best fish restaurants in the area. Specialties are red mullet, pandora, and dorado. *Bouboulinas 79, tel. 0752/27–704. Reservations not necessary. No credit cards. Moderate.*

Lodging **Xenia Palace.** Compulsory half-board boosts the price, but Xenia Palace has an unbeatable location. It's the only hotel allowed to build within the citadel of Akronafplio. Rooms are spacious, the bougainvillea-framed pool overlooks the harbor, and in the lounge you can sip a pot of hot chocolate or coffee for 250 dr. (the best deal in town) while gazing upon the isle of Bourtzi. Check out the bizarre elevator to the hotel, tunneled out of the rock. *Akronapflio, tel. 0752/29–981, -2, -3, -4, -5, fax 0752/28–987. 103 rooms with bath, some suites and bungalows. Facilities: restaurant, bar, pool. Very Expensive.*

★ **Amalia.** The attractive hotel occupies a fine neoclassical building in large gardens 3 kilometers (2 miles) outside town, on the
sea, near ancient Tiryns. The public rooms are spacious and
comfortable, the service attentive, and the swimming pool very
inviting. With a beach nearby, this makes the ideal base for a
relaxing stay. *Tel. 0752/24–401, fax 0752/24–400. 173 rooms
with bath. Facilities: restaurant, outdoor pool, gardens. AE,
DC, MC, V. Expensive.*

Diosouri. Located above the old town, with a fine view across
the gulf of Nafplio, this family-run hotel is cool and quiet.
*Zigomala 7, tel. 0752/28–550, fax 0752/21–202. 50 rooms with
bath. No credit cards. Inexpensive.*

Olympia **Thraka.** This family-run taverna has a large variety of home-
Dining cooked Greek food including *arnaki giouvetsi* (lamb with bite-
size noodles), *kokkinisto* (beef in red sauce), and *stifado* (beef
stew with onions) made the old-fashioned way, with vinegar
and garlic. Desserts are from the family's nearby pastry shop.
Off-season, the cook (and family matriarch) will prepare meals
for you at home; just give her a call. *Main St., above church, tel.
0624/22–575; off-season, 0624/22–477. Reservations not necessary. AE, DC, MC. Closed Nov.–Mar. Moderate.*

Pete's Den. Owned by a Greek-German couple, this restaurant
mixes traditional Greek and German cuisines, with sensational
results. *Saganaki* (the name refers to the oval platter in which
it is baked) is served hot and bubbling with cheese and brandy,
and the toasted bread—complete with hot garlic butter—is a
delightful change from the usual heavy white bread. *Main St.,
tel. 0642/22–066. Reservations not necessary. No credit cards.
Inexpensive.*

Lodging **Amalia.** Pleasantly situated a little outside the village near the
★ museum, the Amalia is comfortable and well run. Unfortunately, the Greek- and European-style fare in the restaurant is
served with little panache, but the other facilities of the hotel
make up for this drawback. *Pirgos-Olympia Rd., tel. 0624/22–
190, -1, fax 0624/22–444. 147 rooms with bath. Facilities: restaurant, pool, roof garden. AE, DC, MC, V. Expensive.*

Altis. The Altis is reasonably priced and in a convenient location, opposite the old museum and near the archaeological site.
Blue-hued rooms have balconies and plenty of light, and the
garden is ideal for enjoying the restaurant's hearty *spesiota*
(perch baked with onion). *Platia Dimarchiou (town hall sq.),
tel. 0624/23–101, -2, fax 0624/22–525. 61 rooms with bath. Facilities: cafeteria-style restaurant, air-conditioning. AE, DC,
MC, V. Closed Nov.–Feb. Moderate.*

Hotel Europa. Run by the friendly Spiliopoulos family, this
Best Western hilltop hotel overlooks ancient Olympia, the Arcadian mountains, and the sea in the distance. Rooms have
large beds, flokati rugs, and marble bathrooms. Most face the
pool, but try to book one of the six that look onto the archaeological site. *Off rd. to ancient Olympia, tel. 0624/22–650 or 624/
22–700, fax 0624/23–166. 42 rooms with bath. Facilities: restaurant, bar, pool, air-conditioning. AE, MC, V. Moderate.*

Patras **Kalypso.** One of the newer and better restaurants, with garden
Dining seating, Kalypso offers fresh grilled red mullet and dorado,
mussels, and a lemon-fish soup, in addition to grilled meats and
the usual Greek *magirefta*. The wine list features several Patras vintages as well as barrel wine. Top it off with baked apple

with whipped cream. *Iroon Politechniou 74, tel. 061/432–944. Reservations not necessary. AE, DC, MC, V. Moderate.*

Trikoyia. Down by the port, the Trikoyia family cooks delicious food in its traditional taverna, where a typical menu showcases *kalofaga* (beef baked with ham) and fresh grilled fish. Enjoy the ocean view as you complete your meal with a piece of baklava. *Amalias 45, tel. 061/279–421. Reservations not necessary. AE, DC, MC, V. Inexpensive.*

Lodging **Astir.** Recently renovated, this large hotel enjoys an excellent location on the waterfront near the center of town. Spacious and pleasant, it looks out on the busy harbor and across to the mountains on the other side of the gulf. *Ag. Andreou 16, tel. 061/277–502, fax 061/271–644. 121 rooms with bath. Facilities: restaurant, roof garden, outdoor pool, conference rooms, sauna, air-conditioning. AE, DC, V. Expensive.*

★ **Porto Rio.** There's a large and varied selection of rooms and cottages with a wide range of prices at this hotel complex on the sea at Rion, about 10 kilometers (6 miles) from Patras. Rooms over the front have outstanding views across the narrow entrance to the Gulf of Corinth. *Tel. 061/992–212, fax 061/992–115. 267 rooms and cottages with bath. Facilities: 2 restaurants, outdoor pool, 4 tennis courts, children's playground. AE, DC, MC, V. Moderate.*

The Arts

The **Festival of Ancient Drama** in the theater at Epidauros takes place from mid-July to mid-September, weekends only, at 9 PM. Tickets can be bought either at the theater itself before performances or in advance from the festival box office at Stadiou 4, Athens, tel. 01/322–1459. Patras also stages a lively summer arts festival. Check with the Greek National Tourist Office (061/653–358, -9) for details.

Mainland Greece

The dramatic rocky heights of mainland Greece provide an appropriate setting for man's attempt to approach divinity. The ancient Greeks placed their gods on snowcapped Mount Olympus and chose the precipitous slopes of Parnassus, "the navel of the universe," as the site for Delphi, the most important religious center of the ancient Greek world. Many centuries later, pious Christians built a great monastery (Ossios Loukas) in a remote mountain valley. Others settled on the rocky mountain peninsula of Athos, the Holy Mountain. Later, devout men established themselves precariously on top of strange, towerlike rocks and, to be closer to God, built monasteries, such as those at Meteora. In fact, many of mainland Greece's most memorable sights are closely connected with religion—including the remarkable Byzantine churches of Thessaloniki. Of course, there are remains of palaces and cities, but these do not have the impact of the great religious centers.

In this land of lonely mountain villages, narrow defiles, and dark woods, bands of *klephts* (a cross between brigands and guerrillas) earned their place in folk history and song during the long centuries of Turkish rule. The women of Souli, one of the mountain strongholds of the klephts, threw themselves dancing and singing over a cliff rather than be captured by the

558

Mainland Greece

Turks. In these same mountains during the German occupation of Greece during World War II, guerrilla bands descended to the valleys and plains to assault the occupying army and drive it from their land.

Farmers have flourished since Greece joined the European Community, and few villages, even those tucked away in the hills, are still poor and isolated. Despite the arrival of video clubs and discos, the traditional way of life still survives. This is a beautiful area to explore. The mainland Greeks see fewer tourists and have more time for those they do see, hotels are unlikely to be full, and the sights—steep, wooded mountains, cypress trees like candles, narrow gorges, the soaring monasteries of Meteora—are beautiful.

Getting Around

This proposed itinerary begins in Athens. It can be done by public transportation, car, or guided tour. A one-day trip to Delphi is rushed; two days will give you more leisure time. Your best bet is a three-day trip that includes Delphi and Meteora. The five-day tour takes in more remote parts of western Greece, Epirus, and other main sights. A longer trip through the mainland should include Ossios Loukas. Thessaloniki is usually included only in lengthy guided tours of northern Greece. If you don't have a car, you can leave the Delphi–Meteora tour at Trikala, take the train to Thessaloniki, and return to Athens by plane or train. You can also take a guided tour of northern Greece and leave the group at Thessaloniki. In

September, during the Thessaloniki International Trade Fair, there are no hotel rooms to be had; make reservations well in advance.

Guided Tours

Travel agencies in Athens with tours of mainland Greece include **American Express** (Ermou 2 and in the Hilton Hotel), **Wagons-Lits Travel** (Stadiou 5), **CHAT Tours** (Stadiou 4), and **Key Tours** (Ermou 2). American Express also has a representative in Thessalonki at **Doucas Travel** (Eleftherios Venizelou 8, tel. 031/224–100 or 031/269–984, -5, -6). A one-day tour to Delphi, with lunch, costs around 13,000 dr. Other, lengthier tours cost considerably more. A six-day Macedonia tour, including Delphi, Meteora, Thessaloniki, Philippi, Kavala, Pella, and Vergina costs around 126,000 dr., with meals and accommodations.

Tourist Information

In **Delphi,** visit the New Delphi Tourist Office on Frederikis 44, open Mon.–Sat. 8:30–3 (tel. 0265/82–900); the Tourist Police is at Apollonos 40 (tel. 0265/82–220). At **Kalambaka,** the Tourist Police can be found at Hatzipetrou 10–11 (tel. 0432/22–813). In **Thessaloniki,** visit the Greek National Tourist Office (Mitropoleos 34 on Platia Aristotelous, tel. 031/222–935 or at the airport, tel. 031/421–170); here, the Tourist Police is at Egnatia 10 (tel. 031/251–316).

Exploring Mainland Greece

To get from Athens to Delphi, take the National Road toward Thessaloniki and turn off to **Thebes** (Thiva), the birthplace of the legendary Oedipus, who unwittingly fulfilled the prophesy of the Delphic Oracle by slaying his father and marrying his mother. Little now remains of the ancient city. At **Livadia,** 45 kilometers (28 miles) farther along the road, the ruins of a medieval fortress tower above the springs of Lethe (Oblivion) and Mnemosyne (Remembrance). Halfway between Livadia and Delphi is the crossroads where, according to mythology, Oedipus killed his father.

The road to the left leads to a serene upland valley and the **Monastery of Ossios Loukas,** a fine example of Byzantine architecture and decoration. Built during the 11th century to replace the earlier shrine of a local saint, it has some of the world's finest Byzantine mosaics. *Tel. 0267/22–797. Admission: 600 dr. Open daily 8–7 (8–5 in winter).*

Back on the road to Delphi, you'll climb a spur of Mount Parnassus to reach the village of **Arahova,** 32 kilometers (20 miles) from Livadia, known for its brightly colored woolen handicrafts, especially rugs. From Arahova, a short, spectacular drive down to Delphi will take you across the gorge of the Pleistos. You'll see a great cliff called the Phaedriades split by the **Castalian spring, which** gushes with cool, pure water. It was here that pilgrims to the Delphic Oracle came for purification.

The ancient Greeks believed that **Delphi** was the center of the universe because two eagles released by the gods at opposite

ends of Earth met here. For hundreds of years, the worship of
Apollo and the pronouncements of the Oracle here made Delphi
the most important religious center of ancient Greece. As you
walk up the Sacred Way to the **Temple of Apollo,** the **theater,**
and the **stadium,** you'll see Mount Parnassus above; silver-
green olive trees below; and, in the distance, the blue Gulf of
Itea. This is one of the most rugged and lonely sites in Greece,
and one of the most striking; if you can get to the site in the early morning or evening, avoiding the busloads of tourists, you
will feel the power and beauty of the place. You may even see an
eagle or two. First excavated in 1892, most of the ruins date
from the 5th to the 3rd century BC. *Tel. 0265/82–313. Admission: 1,000 dr. Open Tues.–Fri. 8–7 (7:30–5 in winter), Mon.
noon–7 (noon–5 in winter), weekends and holidays 8–3.*

Don't miss the famous bronze charioteer (early 5th century BC)
in the **Delphi Museum.** Other interesting and beautiful works of
art here include a statue of Antinoüs, Emperor Hadrian's lover;
pediments from the Temple of Apollo; the statues of Kleobis
and Viton who, according to legend, pulled their mother 80 kilometers (50 miles) by chariot to the Temple of Hera so she
could worship, then died from exhaustion; and the stone representing the navel of the earth. Don't miss the delicate ivory
statuettes and the bull made out of silver leaf; both are in an
air-conditioned inner gallery. *Tel. 0265/82–313. Admission:
1,000 dr. Open Tues.–Fri. 8–7 (7:30–5 in winter), Mon.
noon–7 (noon–5 in winter), weekends and holidays 8–3.*

From Delphi, the road descends in sharp bends past groves of
gnarled, ancient olive trees. Continue 17 kilometers (11 miles)
to Amphissa and over the Pournaraki (Bralos) Pass to the town
of **Lamia.** Follow the road to Karditsa and around the Thessali-
an plain to Trikala. You will then arrive at **Kalambaka** (139 kilometers, or 86 miles, from Lamia), the base for visits to the
monasteries of **Meteora,** which sit atop gigantic rocks above the
town. Monks and supplies once reached the top of the slopes by
ladders or baskets. Today steps are cut into the boulders, and
some of the monasteries can easily be reached by car now. Not
all of them are open to the public, however. Of the original 24
monasteries, only five are now inhabited. Female visitors
should wear skirts, not shorts or jeans.

The fortresslike **Aghios Varlaam** monastery is easy to reach and
has beautiful Byzantine frescoes. To get a better idea of what
living in these monasteries was like 300 years ago, climb the
steep rock steps to the **Great Meteoron,** the largest of the rocks.
Make sure that you allow time for the trek up if it's nearing closing hours. The monasteries are all closed during midday. The
hours vary from place to place, but they are generally open 9–1
and 3–6, although to complicate matters Varlaam is closed on
Friday and Great Meteoron on Tuesday. *Admission: 300 dr.
per monastery.*

Leaving Kalambaka for Thessaloniki, you'll find that the road
crosses the plain of Thessaly, one of Europe's hottest places
during the summer, and joins the National Road at Larissa.
Eventually you will see Mount Olympus, Greece's highest
mountain. The road runs for 154 kilometers (96 miles) through
the valley of Tempe and then on up the coast to **Thessaloniki**—
Greece's second-largest city, its second port after Piraeus, and
the capital of northern Greece. It is the cocapital of the country

as a whole; as a shopping center, it is possibly superior to Athens.

Although Thessaloniki still has some remains from the Roman period, the city is best known for its fine Byzantine churches. The city is compact enough for you to see the main sights on foot. Start at the 15th-century grayish **White Tower,** landmark and symbol of Thessaloniki, previously named "Tower of Blood," referring to its use as a prison. Now it temporarily houses a museum, with an exhibition on the history and art of Byzantine Thessaloniki, including pottery, mosaics, and ecclesiastical objects. *Pavlou Mela and Nikis, tel. 031/267–832. Admission: 500 dr. Open Mon. 10:30–5, Tues.–Fri. 8–7 (8–5 in winter), weekends 8:30–3.*

Then walk up Pavlou Mela toward Tsimiski, the elegant tree-lined shopping street, and cut across to the green-domed basilica-style church of **Aghia Sophia,** which dates from the 8th century and has beautifully preserved mosaics.

Walk to Egnatia, which partially traces the original Roman road leading from the Adriatic to the Bosphorous. Continue north along the **Roman Agora** (town center) to **Agios Dimitrios,** the principal church. Though it is only a replica of the original 7th-century church that burned down in 1917, it is adorned with many 8th-century mosaics that were in the original building. Follow Aghiou Dimitriou east to **Agios Georgios,** a rotunda built by Roman emperor Galerius as his tomb during the 4th century AD. His successor, Constantine the Great, the first Christian emperor, turned it into a church. Have a look at the superb 4th-century mosaics of flowers, birds, and fish.

Return to Egnatia and the **Arch of the Emperor Galerius,** built shortly prior to the rotunda to commemorate the Roman victories of Emperor Galerius over forces in Persia, Armenia, and Mesopotamia. A short walk downhill toward the sea wall will bring you to the **Archaeological Museum.** Among its many beautiful objects are a huge bronze vase and a delicate, gold myrtle wreath from Derveni, as well as gold artifacts from recent excavations of the royal tombs of Vergina, including a 10-kilogram gold casket standing on lions' feet that contains bones thought to be those of Philip II, father of Alexander the Great. *Platia Hanti, tel. 031/830–538. Admission: 1,000 dr. Open Mon. 10:30–7 (10:30–5 in winter), Tues.–Fri. 8–7 (8–5 in winter), weekends and holidays 8:30–3.*

Dining and Lodging

For details and price-category definitions, *see* Dining and Lodging in Staying in Greece.

Delphi **Iniochos.** Traditional Greek cuisine, with a smattering of
Dining French dishes, is what this excellent taverna offers. In winter, warm yourself at the fireplace while listening to nightly piano music; in summer, dine on the veranda overlooking Delphi. Especially good are the *kokkora krasato* (chicken stewed in wine), pork with celery, lamb on the spit, and lamb *kleftiko* (baked in a pastry shell with vegetables). *Frederikis 19, tel. 0265/82–480. Reservations not necessary. AE, DC, MC, V. Moderate.*

Lodging **Fedriades.** Named after Delphi's famous rocks, this 1992 hotel has a neoclassical exterior, which gives way to a light, airy lobby and rooms done in marble and wood with views of the Gulf of

Itea. *Main St., tel. 0265/82–919 or 0265/82–370, fax 0265/82–208. 24 rooms with bath. AE, DC, MC, V. Moderate.*

★ **Hotel Vouzas.** The hotel sits on the edge of a gorge and has wonderful views from every room. Renovated in 1991, with air-conditioning added, it fills up on weekends with visitors from Athens. *Vas. Pavlou and Frederikis 1, tel. 0265/82–232, fax 0265/82–033. 58 rooms with bath. Facilities: restaurant. AE, V. Moderate.*

Kastalia. Designed to fit in with the other village houses, the hotel has simple rooms with paintings of the area and views either over Mt. Parnassos or to the Corinthian gulf. The restaurant is quite good, serving Greek food with a twist; lamb *fricassee,* for example, has lettuce rather than the typical cabbage. Be sure to sample the local sweet cheese, *formaella. Main rd. in town center, tel. 0265/82–205, -6, fax 0265/82–208. 26 rooms with bath. Facilities: restaurant. AE, DC, MC, V. Moderate.*

Kalambaka **Gertzos.** A local favorite since it opened in 1925, Gertzos fea-
Dining tures the cooking of family matriarch Ketty Gertzos, who pre-
★ pares such succulent dishes as *tsoutsoukakia smirnaika* (spicy meat patties as they were made in Asia Minor), rabbit stew, and chicken in wine with green peppers and garlic. The wine list is heavily regional. *Ekonomou 4, on town hall sq., tel. 0432/22–316. Reservations not necessary. No credit cards. Closed Nov.–Mar. Inexpensive.*

Lodging **Motel Divani.** Below the Meteora is a hotel (in spite of its name)
★ that is more comfortable than you might expect to find so far off the beaten path. *Main rd. (Odos Trikalon) in town center, tel. 0432/22–583, fax 0432/23–638. 165 rooms with bath. Facilities: restaurant, snack bar, outdoor pool. AE, DC, MC, V. Moderate–Expensive.*

Hotel Edelweiss. Bright and clean, this hotel shines like a new pin. Its comfortable rooms look out over the swimming pool to the daunting Meteora rocks towering beyond. The hotel bar is a lively and crowded local meeting spot. *El Venizelou 3, tel. 0432/23–966, fax 0432/24–733. 50 rooms with bath. Facilities: restaurant, outdoor pool, snack bar, disco, TV, air-conditioning. MC, V. Inexpensive.*

Thessaloniki **Vita-Vita.** For a romantic evening made memorable by a flaw-
Dining less meal, try this trendy Salonica favorite, where there's a decidedly French influence. Don't miss the fresh mushrooms in parsley-and-fennel sauce or the crepes with raspberry sauce, before moving on to lamb with artichokes in an egg-lemon sauce, followed perhaps with Vita-Vita's famous profiteroles, made with a hard chocolate sauce. There's an extensive wine list—French, Greek, and California vintages—and nightly piano music sets the mood. *Tsimiski 46, tel. 031/287–443. Reservations advised. DC, MC. No lunch Mon.–Sat. Closed July–Aug. Expensive.*

Cyprus Corner. It is well worth making the trip outside town to this popular restaurant in the hilltop suburb of Panorama. Pink tablecloths, waiters in black tie, and a piano-and-sax duo lend an elegant and sophisticated air. A good variety of dishes—Continental and Greek cuisine—are served with style and flair, including a white *taramosalata* (much better than the usual bright-pink roe salad), wild pheasant and venison with red sauce, steak flambé, and for dessert a rum-laced tiramisu.

Komninon 16, Panorama, tel. 031/341–220. Reservations advised. MC, V. Moderate–Expensive.

Ta Nissia. This very bright, clean restaurant, with tiled floor and wooden tables, is excellent for fresh seafood, especially mussels. The *mezedes* (hors d'oeuvres) are particularly unusual and tasty. *Koromila 13, tel. 031/285–991. Reservations advised. DC. Dinner only. Moderate.*

Lodging **Makedonia Palace.** This large, stylish hotel is beautifully positioned at the edge of a bay in a new residential section on reclaimed land; however, it is several kilometers from the center of town. Generally, this is a comfortable, luxurious hotel with all the amenities, and, although it's considered the city's best, it is totally lacking in charm. Ask for rooms overlooking the bay, if you're willing to pay the extra 7,000 dr. *Megalou Alexandrou 2, tel. 031/837–521 or 031/837–529, fax 031/837–948. 288 rooms with bath. Facilities: 3 restaurants, 2 bars, conference hall, roof garden. AE, DC, MC, V. Expensive–Very Expensive.*

★ **Elektra Palace.** This recently renovated hotel is built in a neo-Byzantine style to match the other buildings on the square. It's conveniently located in the center of town, and it has a nonsmoking floor, rare in Greece. Rooms have refrigerators and TV. *Platia Aristotelous 5, tel. 031/232–221, -2, -3, -4, -5, -6, -7, -8, -9, -30, fax 031/235–947. 131 rooms with bath. Facilities: restaurant. AE, DC, MC, V. Expensive.*

Capsis. Two blocks from the rail station, this hotel is popular with Greek business travelers for its reasonable prices and downtown location. Rooms are simply furnished, but spacious "business" rooms, with TV and minibar, are available for an extra 5,000 dr. *Monastiriou 18, tel. 031/521–421, -2, -3, -4, -5, -6, -7, -8, -9, -10, fax 031/510–555. 428 rooms with bath. Facilities: restaurant, pool, roof garden, air-conditioning. AE, DC, MC, V. Moderate–Expensive.*

Panorama. If you don't mind taking a taxi to and from downtown, this is a delightful hotel tucked into the wealthy, foothill suburb of Panorama. Rooms are modern and quiet, and those in front have a sweeping vista of the city below. *Analipseos 26, tel. 031/341–123, 031/341–266, or 031/341–229. 50 rooms with bath. Facilities: restaurant, bar. AE, DC, V. Moderate–Expensive.*

The Greek Islands

The islands of the Aegean have colorful legends of their own—the Minotaur in Crete; the lost continent of Atlantis, which some believe was Santorini; and the Colossus of Rhodes, to name a few. Each island has its own personality. Mykonos has windmills, dazzling whitewashed buildings, hundreds of tiny churches and chapels on golden hillsides, and small fishing harbors. Visitors to volcanic Santorini sail into what was once a vast volcanic crater and anchor near the island's forbidding cliffs. Crete, with its jagged mountain peaks, olive orchards, and vineyards, contains the remains of the Minoan civilization. In Rhodes, a bustling modern town surrounds a walled town with a medieval castle.

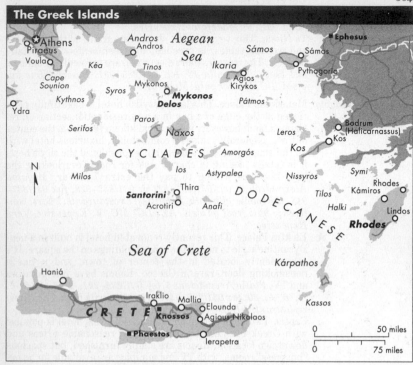

The Greek Islands

Aegean Sea

Sea of Crete

Athens · Piraeus · Voula · Kéa · Cape Sounion · Kythnos · Ydra · Serifos · Milos · Andros · Andros · Tinos · Syros · Mykonos · **Mykonos** · **Delos** · Paros · Náxos · Ios · **Santorini** · Thira · Acrotiri · Anafi · Sámos · Ikaria · Agios Kirykos · Pátmos · Amorgós · Astypalea · Sámos · Pythagorio · Ephesus · Leros · Kos · Kos · Bodrum (Halicarnassus) · Nissyros · Symi · Tilos · Kámiros · Rhodes · Halki · Lindos · **Rhodes** · Kárpathos · Kassos · Haniá · Iraklio · Mallia · Elounda · **Knossos** · Agious Nikolaos · **Phaestos** · Ierapetra

CYCLADES · DODECANESE · CRETE

N

0   50 miles
0   75 miles

Getting Around

The simplest way to visit the Aegean Islands is on a cruise, lasting from 1 to 10 days. Visitors should consider a three-day cruise to the four most popular islands—Mykonos, Rhodes, Crete, and Santorini. Car and passenger ferries sail to these main destinations from Piraeus, the port of Athens. There is also frequent air service from Athens, but most flights are fully booked year-round. It's vital to book well in advance and to confirm and reconfirm in order to be sure of your seat. (*See* Getting Around, By Boat, at the beginning of this chapter.)

Guided Tours

Aegean Cruises From April through October there are many cruises to the Greek Islands from Piraeus. Try any of the following, all based in Athens; **Chandris Cruises** (tel. 01/429–0300), **Cycladic Cruises** (tel. 01/822–9468), **Epirotiki** (tel. 01/452–6641), **Royal Cruise Lines** (tel. 01/428–2240), **Saronic Cruises** (tel. 01/323–4292) or **Sun Line** (tel. 01/452–3417). They all offer one- to seven-en-day cruises. Contact **Epirotiki Cruises** (in the United Kingdom, Westmoreland House, 127/131 Regent St., London W1R, tel. 071/734–0805).

Tourist Information

There are **Greek National Tourist Organization** offices on **Crete,** at Kriari 40, Hania (tel. 0821/26–426), and at Xanthoulidou 1, Iraklio (tel. 081/228–203); on **Mykonos,** at the harbor, near the departure point for Delos (tel. 0289/22–482 or 0289/22–716); on **Rhodes,** at Archbishop Makarios and Papagou 5, Rhodes (tel. 0241/23–655).

Exploring the Greek Islands

Cruise ships and car ferries to Mykonos leave from Piraeus or Rafina. As you sail to Mykonos, you will be able to see one of the great sights of Greece: the Temple of Poseidon looming on a hilltop at the edge of Cape Sounion, about two hours from the mainland.

Mykonos is the name of the island and also of its chief village—a colorful maze of narrow, paved streets lined with whitewashed houses, many with bright blue doors and shutters. Every morning, women scrub the sidewalks and streets in front of their homes, undaunted by the many donkeys that pass by each day. During the 1960s, the bohemian jet set discovered Mykonos, and most of the old houses along the waterfront are now restaurants, nightclubs, bars, and discos—both gay and straight, all blaring loud music until the early morning; a quiet café or taverna is hard to find. Mykonos is still a favorite anchorage with the international yacht set, as well as being *the* holiday destination for the young, lively, and liberated—finding yourself alone on any of its beaches is unlikely.

A half hour by boat from Mykonos and its 20th-century holiday pleasures is the ancient isle of **Delos,** the legendary sanctuary of Apollo. Its **Avenue of the Lions,** a remarkable group of five Naxian marble sculptures from the 7th century BC, is a must. Worth seeing, too, are some of the houses of the Roman period, with their fine floor mosaics. The best of these mosaics are in a museum, the **sanctuary of Dionysos.** *Tel. 0289/22–259. Admission (including fee to the site): 1,000 dr. Open Tues.–Sun. 10–3.*

The large island of **Rhodes,** 170 kilometers (106 miles) southeast of Mykonos, is 11.2 kilometers (7 miles) off the coast of Turkey. The northern end of the island is one of Greece's major vacation centers, and the town of Rhodes is full of the trappings of tourism, mainly evident in the pubs and bars that cater to the large Western European market. The island as a whole is not particularly beautiful—most of the pine and cedar woods that covered its hilly center were destroyed by fire in 1987 and 1988—but it has fine beaches and an excellent climate. The town of Rhodes has an attractive harbor with fortifications; the gigantic bronze statue of the Colossus of Rhodes is supposed to have straddled the entrance. The old walled city, near the harbor, was built by crusaders—the Knights of St. John— who ruled the island from 1309 until they were defeated by the Turks in 1522. Within its fine medieval walls, on the Street of the Knights, stands the **Knights' Hospital,** now the Archaeological Museum, housing two statues of Aphrodite. *Tel. 0241/21– 954. Admission: 600 dr. Open Tues.–Sun. 8:30–3.*

Another museum that deserves your attention is the restored and moated medieval **Palace of the Grand Master.** Destroyed in 1856 by a gunpowder explosion, the palace was renovated by the Italians as a summer retreat for Mussolini. It is especially noted for its splendid Roman and early Christian floor mosaics. *Tel. 0241/21–954. Admission: 800 dr. Open Tues.–Sun. 8:30– 3.*

To get the best overall view of the walled city, including the surviving Turkish buildings, go to one of the flower-filled parks that surround it. Try to see the son et lumière—English-language performances are held on Sunday evening.

Many attractive souvenir and handicrafts shops in the old town sell decorative Rhodian pottery, local embroidery, and relatively inexpensive jewelry.

From the town of Rhodes, drive about 60 kilometers (37 miles) down the east coast to the enchanting village of **Lindos.** Take a donkey from the village center and ride, or put on your comfortable shoes and walk up the steep hill to the ruins of the ancient **Acropolis of Lindos,** which is circled by a medieval castle. The sight of its beautiful colonnade with the sea far below is unforgettable. Look for little St. Paul's Harbor, far below the cliffs of the acropolis; seen from above, it appears to be a lake, as the tiny entrance from the sea is obscured by the rocks. *Tel. 0241/21–954. Admission: 800 dr. Open Tues.–Sun. 8:30–3.*

Rhodes is also a good base for visiting other islands of the Dodecanese—the 12 islands near the Turkish coast—with their mixture of Aegean and Turkish architecture.

Crete, situated in the south Aegean and Greece's largest island, was the center of Europe's earliest civilization, the Minoan, which flourished from about 2000 BC to 1200 BC. It was struck a mortal blow by a devastating volcanic eruption on the neighboring island of Santorini (Thera) in about 1450 BC.

The most important Minoan remains are to be seen in the **Archaeological Museum in Heraklion** in Iraklio, Crete's largest city. The museum houses many Minoan treasures, including some highly sophisticated frescoes and elegant ceramics depicting Minoan life. *Plateia Eleftherias, tel. 081/226–092. Admission: 1,000 dr. Open Mon. 11–5, Tues.–Sat. 8–7, Sun. and holidays 8–6.*

Not far from Iraklio is the partly reconstructed **Palace of Knossos,** which will also give you a feeling for the Minoan world. Note the simple throne room, which contains the oldest throne in Europe, and the bathrooms with their efficient plumbing. The palace was the setting for the legend of the Minotaur, a monstrous offspring of Queen Pasiphae and a bull confined to the Labyrinth under the palace. *Tel. 081/226–092. Admission: 1,000 dr. Hours vary.*

Crete belonged to Venice from 1210 to 1669, at which time it was conquered by the Turks. The island did not become part of Greece until early in this century. The **Venetian ramparts** that withstood a 24-year Turkish siege still surround Iraklio. In addition to archaeological treasures, Crete can boast beautiful mountain scenery and a large number of beach resorts along the north coast. One is **Mallia,** which contains the remains of another Minoan palace and has good sandy beaches. Two other beach resorts, **Ayios Nikolaos** and the nearby **Elounda,** are east of Iraklio. The south coast offers good, quieter beaches for those who want to get away from it all.

The best way to approach **Santorini** is to sail into its harbor, once the vast crater of its volcano, and dock beneath its black and red cliffs. In some parts, the cliffs rise nearly 310 meters (1,000 feet) above the sea. The play of light across them can produce strange color effects. The white houses and churches of the main town, Thira, cling to the rim in dazzling white contrast to the somber cliffs.

Most passenger ferries now use the new port, Athinios, where visitors are met by buses, taxis, and a gaggle of small-hotel owners hawking rooms. The bus ride into Thira takes about a half hour, and from there you can make connections to other towns on the island. Despite being packed with visitors in the summer, the tiny town is charming and has spectacular views. It has the usual souvenir and handicrafts shops and several reasonably priced jewelry shops. Be sure to try the local white wines. The volcanic soil produces a unique range of flavors from light and dry to rich and aromatic.

The island's volcano erupted during the 15th century BC, destroying its Minoan civilization. At **Akrotiri,** on the south end of Santorini, the remains of a Minoan city buried by lava are being excavated. The site, believed by some to be part of the legendary Atlantis, is open to the public. *Tel. 0286/81–366. Admission: 1,000 dr. Open Tues.–Fri. 8:30–3, weekends and holidays 9:30–2:30.*

At **Ancient Thira,** a clifftop on the east coast of the island, a well-preserved ancient town includes a theater and agora, houses, fortifications, and ancient tombs. *Tel. 0286/22–217. Admission free. Open Tues.–Sun. 8:30–3.*

For an enjoyable but slightly unnerving excursion, take the short boat trip to the island's still-active small offshore volcanoes called the **Kamenes** or Burnt Islands. You can descend into a small crater, hot and smelling of sulfur, and swim in the nearby water that has been warmed by the volcano.

Dining and Lodging

For details and price-category definitions, *see* Dining and Lodging in Staying in Greece.

Crete Iraklio has many moderately priced open-air restaurants in the
Dining central area around Platia Venizelou and Platia Daedelou. The island is known for its fine local wine, fresh seafood, and fresh local produce, which is available year-round.

Minos Taverna. This is one of the many outdoor restaurants near the Venetian fountain. Lamb, fresh seafood, and yogurt dishes make this one of the island's most popular restaurants. Service is prompt and attentive. *Daedelou 10, tel. 081/281–263. Reservations not necessary. No credit cards. Moderate.*

Taverna Faros. Located near the new port in Iraklio, this is an excellent, inexpensive choice for a Greek fish supper. The distinct fisherman's ambience is created by fishnet drapes, conch shells, and razor clams on the walls. *Tel. 081/423–233. Reservations not necessary. No credit cards. Inexpensive.*

Lodging **Elounda Beach.** Located 4.8 kilometers (3 miles) north of Ayios Nikolaos, this is probably the best seaside resort complex on Crete. It is spacious, attractive, and spotlessly maintained. It's set in beautiful grounds—the pool is cleverly landscaped among carob trees—and has a private beach. *Tel. 0841/41–412/3. 301 rooms with bath. Facilities: restaurants, outdoor pool, miniature golf, tennis courts, nightclub, cinema. AE. Closed Nov.–Mar. Very Expensive.*
Ikaros Village. This hotel complex, near Mallia on Crete's north

coast, was created by a German company and fits the image of a typical Greek village. It's on the beach, about 32 kilometers (20 miles) east of Iraklio, and near the ruins of a Minoan palace. *Malla Pediados, tel. 0897/31–267/9. 181 rooms with bath. Facilities: restaurant, outdoor pool, tennis courts, private beach. AE. Closed Nov.–Mar. Expensive.*

★ **Mediterranean.** This is another comfortable hotel in the center of Iraklio and 4.8 kilometers (3 miles) from the beach. It's priced at the top of its category. *Smyrnis 1, tel. 081/289–331. 55 rooms with bath. Facilities: restaurant, roof garden, partially air-conditioned. AE, MC, V. Moderate.*

Mykonos
Dining
Chez Cat'rine. A favorite with Greeks as well as foreigners, this is where you can enjoy simple but superbly cooked French dishes, plus a selection of mouth-watering Greek fare, in an informal, brightly furnished dining room. *In town, opposite St. Gerasimos's church, tel. 0289/22–169. Reservations necessary. AE, MC, V. Dinner only. Expensive.*

Lodging
★ **Cavo Tagoo.** Within walking distance of the center of town, this small, charming hotel sits above a beach. Built to blend in with the Mykonian architecture, it has an attractively designed saltwater pool in the garden and is well worth the high rates. *Tagoo Beach, tel. 0289/23–692/4. 24 rooms with bath. Facilities: restaurant, outdoor pool. AE, MC, V. Closed Nov.–Mar. Expensive.*

Kouneni Hotel. This is a comfortable family-run hotel in the town center, and it's quieter than most. It is set in a cool green garden, a rarity on Mykonos. Rooms are fairly large; the slightly shabby, but cozy lounge has a tiled floor. *Tria Pigadia, tel. 0289/22–301. 20 rooms with bath. No credit cards. Moderate.*

Rhodes
Dining
Casa Castelana. Set in a 15th-century Inn of the Knights, this restaurant has a wonderful medieval atmosphere indoors; outdoors, there's an elegant but comfortable garden area for dining. The food is unusual and delicious, featuring a combination of non-Greek dishes and Rhodian specialties—including *trahanas,* an island village soup, and *stifado,* a pot-au-feu-style lamb dish. *Aristotelous 35, tel. 0241/28–803. Reservations advised. AE, DC, V. Expensive.*

The Plaka Taverna. This restaurant on the first floor, overlooking the fountain in the square, offers one of the prettiest settings in the town. The specialty here is fresh seafood, grilled or fried to order; the red mullet is particularly tasty. *Ippocratous Sq., tel. 0241/22–477. Reservations not necessary. AE, DC. Expensive.*

Kavo d'Oro. You can't go wrong at this tiny restaurant, which is one of the best in the town of Rhodes and possibly on the entire island. *Sokratous 41, tel. 0241/36–181. Reservations not necessary. No credit cards. Inexpensive.*

Lodging
Grand Hotel Astir Palace. This beachfront establishment, on the edge of the town of Rhodes, houses one of Greece's three casinos, as well as two restaurants and cocktail bars, an English-style pub, and the Isabella nightclub. Although the beach is ordinary, the setting is a great asset. Some rooms with verandas face the gardens, lawns, and pools; others, slightly more expensive, face the sea with views of the coast of Turkey. *Vass. Konstantinou St., tel. 0241/26–284/9. 378 rooms with bath. Facilities: restaurants, 1 indoor and 2 outdoor pools, private beach, tennis courts, casino. AE, DC, MC, V. Very Expensive.*

Steps of Lindos. This hotel, 4.8 kilometers (3 miles) out of the village of Lindos, is built on a sloping hillside above a long, good beach. The steps—and there are lots of them—link the whitewashed buildings to the pool and beach. The service is friendly and efficient, and the food is plentiful, although variable. *Vlyha Lindos, tel. 0244/24–371/2. 156 rooms with bath. Facilities: restaurant, outdoor pool, tennis courts, beach. AE. Closed Nov.–Mar. Expensive.*

Spartalis Hotel. Many rooms in this simple but lively hotel near the city's port have balconies overlooking the bay. *Plastira 2, tel. 0241/24–371/2. 79 rooms with bath. AE, V. Moderate.*

Santorini   **Camille Stefani.** This is one of the island's best restaurants,
Dining   where you can enjoy seafood, Greek and Continental cuisine, and the local wines. A taste of the mellow Santorini Lava red wine, a product of the volcanic ash, is a must! *Main St., Thira, tel. 0286/22–265. Reservations advised. AE, MC, V. Moderate.*

Lodging   **Atlantis Hotel.** Located in the main village, this is the island's best hotel. It has a magnificent view. *Thira, tel. 0286/22–232. 22 rooms with bath. Facilities: restaurant. AE, MC, V. Closed Nov.–Mar. Expensive.*

Perivolas. This group of traditional houses has been carefully restored by the Greek National Tourist Organization. Located in Ia, they overlook the sea and the volcano and offer comfortable, self-catering accommodations in an authentic island setting. *Tel. 0286/364–1024. 12 houses, each with 2 rooms and bath. Facilities: kitchen. AE, MC, V. Closed Nov.–Mar. Expensive.*

14 Holland

If you come to the Netherlands expecting to find its residents shod in wooden shoes, you're years too late; if you're looking for windmills at every turn, you're looking in the wrong place. The bucolic images that brought tourism here in the decades after World War II have little to do with the Netherlands of the '90s. Sure, tulips grow in abundance in the bulb district of Noord and Zuid Holland provinces, but today's Netherlands is no backwater operation: This tiny nation has an economic strength and cultural wealth that far surpass its size and population. Sophisticated, modern Netherlands has more art treasures per square mile than any other country on earth, as well as a large number of ingenious, energetic people with a remarkable commitment to quality, style, and innovation.

The 41,040 square kilometers (15,785 square miles) of the Netherlands are just about half the number in the state of Maine, and its population of 15 million is slightly less than that of the state of Texas. Size is no measure of international clout, however. The Netherlands owns more property in the United States than Japan does, and is second only to Great Britain as an investor in the American economy. The Netherlands encourages internal accomplishments as well, particularly of a cultural nature. Within a 120-kilometer (75-mile) radius are ten major museums of art and several smaller ones that together contain the world's richest and most comprehensive collection of art masterpieces from the 15th to the 20th centuries, including the majority of paintings by Rembrandt and nearly every painting produced by Vincent van Gogh. In the same small area are a half dozen performance halls offering music, dance, and internationally known performing arts festivals.

The marriage of economic power and cultural wealth is nothing new to the Dutch; in the 17th century, for example, money raised through their colonial outposts overseas was used to buy or commission portraits and paintings by young artists such as Rembrandt, Hals, Vermeer, and van Ruisdael. But it was not only the arts that were encouraged: the Netherlands was home to the philosophers Descartes, Spinoza, and Comenius; the jurist Grotius; the naturalist van Leeuwenhoek, inventor of the microscope; and others like them who flourished in the country's enlightened tolerance. The Netherlands continues to subsidize its artists and performers, and it supports an educational system in which creativity in every field is respected, revered, and given room to express itself.

The Netherlands is the delta of Europe, located where the great Rhine and Maas rivers and their tributaries empty into the North Sea. Near the coast, it is a land of flat fields and interconnecting canals; in the center of the country it is surprisingly wooded, and in the far south are rolling hills. The country is too small for there to be vast natural areas, and it's too precariously close to sea level, even at its highest points, for there to be dramatic landscapes. Instead, the Netherlands is what the Dutch jokingly call a big green city. Amsterdam is the focal point of the nation; it also is the beginning and end point of a 50-kilometer (31-mile) circle of cities that includes The Hague (the Dutch seat of government and the world center of international justice), Rotterdam (the industrial center of the Netherlands and the world's largest port), and the historic cites of Haarlem, Leiden, Delft, and Utrecht. The northern and eastern provinces are rural and quiet; the southern provinces that

Holland

North Sea

Wadden Islands

Schiermonnikoog

Ameland

Terschelling

Vlieland

Texel

Waddenzee

Dokkum

Groningen

Delfzijl

Winschoten

Leeuwarden

Drachten

Assen

N34

Emmen

Harlingen

Bolsward

Sneek

A32

N371

A28/E232

Hoogeveen

N48

N36

Den Helder

IJsselmeer

A7/E22

Enkhuizen

A50

Meppel

N34

Zwolle

Almelo

N35

Hengelo

Alkmaar

Hoorn

Lelystad

A6

A28/E232

Deventer

A1/E30

Enschede

Purmerend

Zaanstad

Amsterdam

Apeldoorn

Winterswijk

Haarlem

A9

Bussum

Amersfoort

Arnhem

Doetinchem

Hilversum

A2

Rijn

Utrecht

A12

Lek

A12/E35

Rijn

Rhine

GERMANY

Leiden

A4/E14

Den Haag
(The Hague)

E30

Delft

Rotterdam

A27

A25

Tiel

Nijmegen

A50

Oss

A15/E31

Waal

Dordrecht

Maas

A59

's Hertogenbosch

Veghel

Haringvliet

Overflakkee

Grevelingen

Schouwen/
Duiveland

Tholen

Oosterschelde

A58

A16/E22

Steenbergen

Breda

Tilburg

A67/E34

Eindhoven

A2/E25

Weert

Roermond

Bergen op Zoom

Goes

Walcheren

Beveland

Middelburg

Westerschelde

Breskens

Terneuzen

Schelde

Antwerp

Sittard

Maastricht

Aachen

Vaals

Liège

KEY

--- Ferry

0   40 miles

0   60 km

N

BELGIUM

Brussels

hug the Belgian border are lightly industrialized and sophisticated. The great rivers that cut through the heart of the country provide both geographical and sociological borders. The area "above the great rivers," as the Dutch phrase it, is peopled by tough-minded and practical Calvinists; to the south are more ebullient Catholics. A tradition of tolerance pervades this densely populated land; aware that they cannot survive alone, the Dutch are bound by common traits of ingenuity, personal honesty, and a bold sense of humor.

Essential Information

Before You Go

When to Go The prime tourist season in Holland runs from April through October and peaks during school vacation periods (Easter, July, and August), when hotels may impose a 20% surcharge. Dutch bulb fields bloom from early April to the end of May—not surprisingly, the hotels tend to fill up then, too. June is the ideal time to catch the warm weather and miss the crowds, but every region of the Netherlands has its season. Delft is luminous after a winter storm, and fall in the Utrecht countryside can be as dramatic as in New England.

Climate Summers are generally warm, but beware of sudden showers and blustery coastal winds. Winters are chilly and wet but are not without clear days. After a cloudburst, notice the watery quality of light that inspired Vermeer and other great Dutch painters.

The following are the average daily maximum and minimum temperatures for Amsterdam.

Jan.	40F	4C	May	61F	16C	Sept.	65F	18C
	34	1		50	10		56	13
Feb.	41F	5C	June	65F	18C	Oct.	56F	13C
	34	1		56	13		49	9
Mar.	47F	8C	July	70F	21C	Nov.	47F	8C
	38	3		59	15		41	5
Apr.	52F	11C	Aug.	68F	20C	Dec.	41F	5C
	43	6		59	15		36	2

Currency The unit of currency in Holland is the *guilder*, written as NLG (for Netherlands guilder), Fl., or simply F. (from the centuries-old term for the coinage, *florin*). Each guilder is divided into 100 cents. Bills are in denominations of 1,000, 250, 100, 50, 25, and 10 guilders. Coins are 5, 2.5, and 1 guilder and 25, 10, and 5 cents. Be careful not to confuse the 2.5- and 1-guilder coins and the 5-guilder and 5-cent coins. Bills have a code of raised dots that can be identified by touch; this is for the blind.

At press time (spring 1993), the exchange rate for the guilder was Fl. 1.85 to the U.S. dollar and Fl. 2.70 to the pound sterling.

Most major credit cards are accepted in hotels, restaurants, and shops, but check first.

What It Will Cost Holland is a prosperous country with a high standard of living, so overall costs are similar to those in other northern European countries. Prices for hotels and other services in major cities are 10%–20% above those in rural areas. Amsterdam and The Hague are the most expensive. Hotel and restaurant service charges and the 18.6% value-added tax (VAT) are usually included in the prices quoted.

The cost of eating varies widely in Holland, from a snack in a bar or a modest restaurant offering a *dagschotel* (day special), or "tourist menu" at around Fl. 20 to the considerable expense of gourmet cuisine. A traditional Dutch breakfast is occasionally included in the overnight hotel price.

One cost advantage Holland has over other European countries is that because it is so small, traveling around is inexpensive—especially if you use the many price-saving transportation deals available. The **Leisure Card,** for example, is a comprehensive discount card that provides significant reductions on rail travel, car rentals, hotels, tours, entertainment, and shopping. Valid for a year, it costs Fl. 25 and is available from the Netherlands Board of Tourism (NBT) or main train stations and local information offices (VVV).

Sample Prices   Half-bottle of wine, Fl. 25; glass of beer, Fl. 3; cup of coffee, Fl. 2.50; ham and cheese sandwich, Fl. 5; 1-mile taxi ride, Fl. 5.

Museums   The **Museumkaart,** which can be purchased from some museums and all tourist offices, provides a year's free admission to about 350 museums. It costs Fl. 40, Fl. 25 if you're over 65, and Fl. 15 if you're under 18. A photo and passport are required for purchase. If your time is limited, you might want to check the list; not all museums participate.

Customs on Arrival   For travelers arriving from a country that is not a member of the European Community (EC) or those coming from an EC country who have bought goods in a duty-free shop, the allowances are (1) 200 cigarettes or 50 cigars or 100 cigarillos or 250 grams of tobacco, (2) 1 liter of alcohol more than 22% by volume or 2 liters of liqueur wine or 2 liters of sparkling wine, (3) 50 grams of perfume or 25 centiliters of toilet water, and (4) other goods to the value of Fl. 125.

Since Jan. 1, 1993, allowances for travelers within the EC member states have been effectively removed. Those that still exist are designed to prevent unlicensed business and are unlikely to pose a problem for the average tourist. For example, the Netherlands currently limits travelers to importing (1) 800 cigarettes or (2) 10 liters of alcohol more than 22% by volume, or 90 liters of wine, or 110 liters of beer.

All personal items are considered duty-free, provided you take them with you when you leave Holland. Tobacco and alcohol allowances are for those 17 and older. There are no restrictions on the import and export of Dutch currency.

Language   Dutch is a difficult language for foreigners, but luckily the Dutch are fine linguists, so almost everyone speaks at least some English, especially in larger cities and tourist centers.

Getting Around

By Car   Holland has one of the best road systems in Europe, and even
Road Conditions   the longest trips between cities take only a few hours. Multilane expressways (toll-free) link major cities, but the smaller roads and country lanes provide more varied views of Holland. In towns many of the streets are narrow, and you'll have to con-

tend with complex one-way systems and cycle lanes. Information about weather and road conditions can be obtained by calling 070/3313131.

Rules of the Road The speed limit on expressways is 120 kph (75 mph); on city streets and in residential areas it is 50 kph (30 mph) or less, according to the signs. Driving is on the right.

Parking Parking in the larger towns is difficult and expensive, with illegally parked cars quickly towed away or subject to a wheel clamp. Fines for recovery can reach Fl. 120. So consider parking on the outskirts of a town and using public transportation to get to the center.

Gasoline Gas, *benzine* in Dutch, costs around Fl. 1.73 per liter for regular; Fl. 1.85 for super.

Breakdowns Experienced, uniformed mechanics of the **Wegenwacht** patrol the highways in yellow cars 24 hours a day. Operated by ANWB (Royal Dutch Touring Club), they will help if you have car trouble. ANWB also maintains phone boxes along major roads on which to call for assistance. To use these services, you may be asked to take temporary membership in ANWB.

By Train Fast, frequent, and comfortable trains operate throughout the country. All trains have first- and second-class cars, and many intercity trains have buffet or dining-car services. Intercity trains run every 30 minutes and regular trains run to the smaller towns at least once an hour. Sometimes one train contains two separate sections that divide during the trip, so be sure you are in the correct section for your destination. Trains have specially designed entryways for wheelchairs.

Fares The best value in the Netherlands is the **Rail Pass,** a ticket for unlimited train travel; you can buy one for one or seven days, with no reductions for children. A second-class day pass costs Fl. 58; a seven-day pass costs Fl. 139. If you buy a Rail Pass, for a small additional charge (Fl. 6.50 per day; Fl. 25 per week) you can also get a **Link Rover,** which is good for unlimited travel on all public transportation. Another great deal is the **Eropueit,** a special day-pass that includes train travel, bus or metro fare, and admission to a museum. Rates vary according to the distance. The **Domino Holland** ticket is a good option for longer stays and the occasional side trip, permitting unlimited rail travel on any three-, five-, or 10-day period within a month. A first-class pass costs $151, a second-class pass $101. Your passport may be needed when you purchase these tickets.

If you are also traveling through Belgium and Luxembourg, the five-day **Benelux Tourrail** card is the best bet. It allows for unlimited travel and is valid for any five days within a period of 17 consecutive days. It costs about $185 first class or $124 second class and must be purchased prior to entering the Netherlands. **Dagtochtkaartjes** are special combined tickets covering train, boat, and bus trips. Using the Leisure Card (*see* What it Will Cost, *above*) is another option. Ask about these fares at railway information bureaus or local tourist offices. **The Netherlands Board of Tourism's** (NBT) offices abroad have information on train services, as do overseas offices of Netherlands Railways *(see* Before You Go in Chapter 1).

By Plane **KLM Royal Dutch Airlines,** under the banner of CityHopper, operates several domestic services connecting major cities. In this small country, however, you'd probably travel just as fast by car or train.

By Bus Holland has an excellent bus network between towns that are not connected by rail and also within towns. Bus excursions can be booked on the spot and at local VVV offices. In major cities, the best buy is a **strippenkaart** ticket (Fl. 9.75), which can be used for all bus, tram, and metro services. Each card has 15 strips, which are canceled either by the driver as you enter the buses or by the stamping machine at each door of the trams. More than one person can travel on a strippenkaart—it just gets used up more quickly. A strippenkaart with 45 strips is available for Fl. 28. You can buy it at train stations, post offices, and some VVV offices, or in Amsterdam at the GVB (national bus system) ticket office in the plaza in front of the central railway station. A two-day **dagkaart,** a travel-anywhere ticket, covers all urban bus/streetcar routes and costs Fl. 12.60; three days, Fl. 15.60.

By Bicycle Holland is a "cyclist-friendly" country with specially designated cycle paths, signs, and picnic areas. Bikes can usually be rented at train stations in most cities and towns, and Dutch trains are "cycle-friendly," too, with extra spacious entryways designed to accommodate bicycles. You will need an extra ticket for the bike, however. The basic cost is Fl. 14 round-trip to anywhere in the country; the price goes up to Fl. 22.50 during the busy summer months. Rental costs for bicycles are around Fl. 7 per day or from Fl. 22.50 per week, plus a deposit of Fl. 50–Fl. 200. Advice on rentals and routes is available from offices of The Netherlands Board of Tourism in North America or in Holland, or from local VVV offices; cycling packages can be booked at the larger offices.

Staying in Holland

Telephones
Local Calls The telephone system in Holland is excellent and reliable. All towns and cities have area codes that are to be used only when you are calling from outside the area. Pay phones take 25¢, Fl. 1, and Fl. 2.50 coins. Local calls cost 25¢ per minute. Increasingly, public phone booths are being converted to a credit-card payment system (for Dutch phone subscribers only), which may necessitate either a search for a coin phone or a long wait at the booth, or both.

International Calls Direct-dial international calls can be made from post offices, but not from a phone booth without a credit card issued by PTT, the Dutch telephone service. Lower rates are charged from 7 PM to 10 AM weekdays, and from 7 PM Friday to 10 AM Monday. The average cost per minute to the U.S. is Fl. 2.60 (Fl. 2.30 nights and weekends). Think twice about making international calls from your hotel room because high service charges may double or triple the cost over and above the already doubled or tripled rates that are charged for calls from Europe to North America.

Operators In Holland, dial 06/022911 to reach **ATT USA Direct;** tel. 06/0229122 to reach **MCI Call USA;** tel. 06/0229116 to reach **Bell Canada.** To telephone elsewhere internationally, call 06–0410 for an English-speaking operator; to call within Holland, dial the same number.

Mail *Postal Rates*	The Dutch post office is as efficient as the telephone network. Airmail letters to the United States cost Fl. 1.30 for the first 10 grams; postcards cost 75¢; aerograms cost Fl. 1. Airmail letters to the United Kingdom cost 75¢ for the first 20 grams; postcards cost 55¢; aerograms cost 65¢.
Receiving Mail	If you're uncertain where you'll be staying, have mail sent to Poste Restante, GPO, in major cities along your route, or, if you're an American Express customer, to American Express offices, where a small charge is made on collection.
Shopping *VAT Refunds*	Purchases of goods in one single store in one single day amounting to Fl. 300 or more qualify for a value-added tax (VAT) refund of 18.5%, which can be claimed at the airport or main border crossing when you leave Holland, or by mail. Ask the salesperson for a VAT refund form when you buy anything that may qualify.
Bargaining	The prices in most shops are fixed, but you can try to bargain for items in any of the open-air markets.
Opening and Closing Times	**Banks** are open weekdays from 9 to 4. You can also change money at GWK Border Exchange Offices at major railway stations and Schiphol Airport, which are open Monday–Saturday 8–8 and Sunday 10–4. GWK offices in major cities or at border checkpoints are open 24 hours. Many VVV offices exchange funds, too.
	Museums now close on Monday, but not all, so check with local VVV offices. In rural areas, some museums close or operate shorter hours during winter. Usual hours are 10–5.
	Shops are open weekdays and Saturdays from 8:30 or 9 to 5:30 or 6, but outside the cities, some close for lunch. Department stores and most shops, especially in shopping plazas (in The Hague and Amsterdam) do not open on Monday until 1 PM, and a few close one afternoon a week on whichever day they choose. Late-night shopping usually can be done until 9 PM on Thursday or Friday. Few shops are open Sunday.
National Holidays	January 1; April 3–4, (Easter); April 30 (Queen's Day; shops are open unless it falls on Sunday); May 5 (Liberation); May 12 (Ascension); May 22–23 (Pentecost); December 25–26.
Dining	Of the many earthly pleasures the Dutch indulge, eating probably heads the list. There is a wide variety of cuisines from traditional Dutch to Indonesian—the influence of the former Dutch colony.
	Breakfast is hearty and substantial—including several varieties of bread, butter, jam, ham, cheese, boiled eggs, juice, and steaming coffee or tea. Dutch specialties for later meals include *erwtensoep*, a rich, thick pea soup with pieces of tangy sausage or pigs' knuckles, and *hutspot*, a meat, carrot, and potato stew; both are usually served only during winter. *Haring* (herring) is particularly popular, especially the "new herring" caught between May and September and served in brine, garnished with onions. If Dutch food begins to pall, try an Indonesian restaurant, where the chief dish is *rijsttafel*, a meal made up of 20 or more small dishes, many of which are hot and spicy.
	The indigenous Dutch liquor is potent and warming *jenever* (gin), both "old" and "new." Dutch liqueurs and beers are also popular.

Eating places range from snack bars, fast-food outlets, and modest local cafés to gourmet restaurants of international repute. Of special note are the "brown cafés," traditional pubs of great character that normally offer snack-type meals.

Mealtimes The Dutch tend to eat dinner around 6 or 7 PM, especially in the country and smaller cities, so many restaurants close at about 10 PM and accept final orders at 9. In larger cities dining hours vary, and some restaurants stay open until midnight.

Dress Jacket and tie are suggested for restaurants in the Very Expensive and Expensive categories. The Dutch are tolerant, and almost any outfit is acceptable in most eateries.

Ratings Prices are per person including three courses (appetizer, main course, and dessert), service, and sales tax but not drinks. For budget travelers, many restaurants offer a tourist menu at an officially controlled price, currently Fl. 20. Best bets are indicated by a star ★.

Category	Amsterdam	Other Areas
Very Expensive	over Fl. 75	over Fl. 60
Expensive	Fl. 50–Fl. 75	Fl. 40–Fl. 60
Moderate	Fl. 35–Fl. 50	Fl. 30–Fl. 40
Inexpensive	under Fl. 35	under Fl. 30

Lodging Holland offers a wide range of accommodations, from the luxurious Dutch-owned international Golden Tulip hotel chain to traditional, small-town hotels and family-run guest houses. For young or adventurous travelers, the provinces abound with modest hostels, camping grounds, and rural bungalows. Travelers with modest budgets may prefer to stay in friendly bed-and-breakfast establishments; these are in short supply and must be booked well ahead at local VVV offices.

Hotels Dutch hotels are generally clean, if not spotless, no matter how modest their facilities, and service is normally courteous and efficient. There are many moderate and inexpensive hotels, most of which are relatively small. In the provinces the range of accommodations is more limited, but there are pleasant, inexpensive family-run hotels that are usually centrally located and offer a friendly atmosphere. Some have good—if modest—dining facilities. English is spoken or understood almost everywhere. Hotels usually quote room prices for double occupancy, and rates often include breakfast, service charges, and VAT.

To book hotels in advance, you can use the free **National Reservation Center** (Box 404, 2260 AK Leidschendam, tel. 070/3202500, fax 070/3202611). Alternatively, for a small fee, VVV offices can usually make reservations at short notice. Bookings must be made in person, however.

Ratings Prices are for two people sharing a double room. Best bets are indicated by a star ★.

Category	Amsterdam	Other Areas
Very Expensive	Fl. 400–Fl. 500	over Fl. 300
Expensive	Fl. 300–Fl. 400	Fl. 200–Fl. 300

| Moderate | Fl. 200–Fl. 300 | Fl. 150–Fl. 200 |
| Inexpensive | under Fl. 200 | under Fl. 150 |

Tipping Hotels and restaurants almost always include 15% service and VAT in their charges. Give a doorman 50¢ to Fl. 1 for calling a cab. Bellhops in first-class hotels should be tipped Fl. 1 for each bag they carry. The official minimum for porters in train stations is Fl. 2.50 a bag. Hat-check attendants expect at least 25¢, and washroom attendants get 50¢. Taxis in almost every town have a tip included in the meter charge, but you are expected to make up the fare to the nearest guilder nevertheless.

Amsterdam

Arriving and Departing

By Plane Most international flights arrive at Amsterdam's Schiphol Airport, one of Europe's finest. Immigration and customs formalities on arrival are relaxed, with no forms to be completed.

Between the Airport and Downtown The best transportation between the airport and the city center is the direct rail link to the central station, where you can get a taxi or tram to your hotel. The train runs every 10 to 15 minutes throughout the day and takes about half an hour. Second-class fare is Fl. 5.

Taxis from the airport to central hotels cost about Fl. 50.

By Train The city has excellent rail connections with the rest of Europe. Fast services link it to Paris, Brussels, Luxembourg, and Cologne. Centraal Station is conveniently located in the center of town.

Getting Around

By Bus, Tram, and Metro A zonal fare system is used. Tickets (starting at Fl. 2) are bought from automatic dispensers on the metro or from the drivers on trams and buses; or buy a money-saving **strippenkaart** (*see* Getting Around, By Bus, *above*). Even simpler is the two-day **dagkaart,** which covers all city routes for Fl. 12.60. These discount tickets can be obtained from the main GVB ticket office in front of Centraal Station, along with route maps of the public transportation system. Recently introduced water buses in the city center also have day cards. The **Canalbus,** which travels between the central station and the Rijksmuseum, is Fl. 12.50.

By Taxi Taxis are expensive: A short 3-mile ride costs around Fl. 15. Taxis are not usually hailed on the street but are picked up at stands near stations and other key points. Alternatively, you can dial 020/67777777. Water taxis (tel. 02/6222181) are even more expensive (about Fl. 2 per minute).

By Car Parking in Amsterdam has always been difficult, and, as of press time (spring 1993), city authorities have made it impossible by launching an experimental ban on cars in the city center. Even if the ban is eventually lifted, the city's concentric ring of canals, one-way systems, and lack of parking facilities will continue to plague drivers. It's best to put your car in one of the parking lots on the edge of the old center and abandon it for the rest of your stay.

By Bicycle Rental bikes are readily available for around Fl. 7 per day with a Fl. 50–Fl. 200 deposit. Bikes are an excellent and inexpensive way to explore the city. Several rental companies are close to the central station, or ask at VVVs for details. Lock your bike up at all times; thieves have been known to abscond with them in fewer than 30 seconds.

By Boat The **Museum Boat** (*see* Guided Tours, *below*), which makes seven stops near major museums, is Fl. 15 for adults, Fl. 13 for children.

On Foot Amsterdam is a small, congested city of narrow streets, which makes it ideal for exploring on foot. The VVV issues seven excellent guides that detail walking tours around the center. The best are "The Jordaan," a stroll through the lively canalside district, and "Jewish Amsterdam," a walk past the symbolic remains of Jewish housing and old synagogues.

Important Addresses and Numbers

Tourist Information There are two **VVV** offices: one across from the central station in the Old Dutch Coffee House and the other at Leidsestraat 106. The VVV reserves for accommodations, tours, and entertainment, but reservations must be made in person. *Open Easter–Sept., daily 9 AM–11 PM; Oct.–Easter, daily 9–5.*

Consulates U.S. (Museumsplein 19, tel. 020/6790321). **Canadian** (7 Sophialaan, The Hague, tel. 070/3614111). **U.K.** (Koningslaan 44, tel. 020/6764343).

Emergencies The general number for emergencies is 06–11, but note direct numbers. **Police** (tel. 020/6222222); **Ambulance** (tel. 020/5555555); **Doctor Academisch Medisch Centrum** (Meibergdreef 9, tel. 020/5669111). **Central Medical Service** (tel. 020/6642111) will give you names of pharmacists and dentists as well as doctors. **Dentist Practice AOC** (W.G. Plein 167, tel. 020/6161234) is also open on weekends. Also helpful in a crisis is the **Amsterdam Tourist Assistance Service** (Nieuwezijds Voorburgwal 118, tel. 02/6239314), open daily 10–10.

English-Language Bookstores **American Discount Book Center** (Kalverstraat 158, 020/6255537). **Athenaeum Boekhandel** (Spui 14, tel. 020/6233933). **English Bookshop** (Lauriergracht 71, tel. 020/6264230).

Travel Agencies **American Express** (Damrak 66, tel. 020/5207777, Van Baerlestraat 38, tel. 020/6714141); **Holland International** (Rokin 54, tel. 020/65512812); **Key Tours** (Wagon-Lits) (Dam 19, tel. 020/6247310); **De Vries & Co.** (Damrak 6, tel. 020/5550800); **Thomas Cook** (Bureau de Change, 31a Leidseplein, tel. 020/6267000).

Guided Tours

Boat Tours The most enjoyable way to get to know Amsterdam is by taking a boat trip along the canals. Several operators run trips, usually in glass-top boats. There are frequent departures from points opposite the central station, along the Damrak and along the Rokin and Stadhouderskade (near the Rijksmuseum). For a tour lasting about 1½ hours, costs range from Fl. 8 to Fl. 12, but the student guides expect a small tip for their multilingual commentary. On summer evenings, longer cruises include wine and cheese or a full buffet dinner. A few tours feature increasingly drunken stops for wine tastings in canalside bars. Costs range from Fl. 30 for wine and cheese tours to Fl. 135 for a candlelight dinner. Trips can be booked through the VVV.

Alternatively, you may want to rent a pedal-boat and make your own canal tour. At **Canal-Bike,** prices begin at Fl. 19 per hour; for details, tel. 020/6265574.

The **Museum Boat** (Stationsplein 8, tel. 02/6222181) combines a scenic view of the city with seven stops near 20 museums. Tickets, good for the entire day, are Fl. 15; a combination ticket for Fl. 25 includes free entrance to three museums.

Bus Tours Guided bus tours around the city are also available and provide an excellent introduction to Amsterdam. A combined bus-and-boat tour includes the inevitable trip to a diamond factory. Costing Fl. 25–Fl. 35, the comprehensive three-hour tour can be booked through **Lindbergh** (Damrak 26–27, tel. 020/6222766) or **Key Tours** (Dam 19, tel. 020/6247310).

Exploring Amsterdam

Amsterdam is a gem of a city for the tourist. Small and densely packed with fine buildings, many dating from the 17th century or earlier, it is easily explored on foot or by bike. The old heart of the city consists of canals, with narrow streets radiating out like the spokes of a wheel. The hub of this wheel and the most convenient point to begin sightseeing is the central station. Across the street, in the same building as the Old Dutch Coffee House, is a VVV tourist information office that offers helpful tourist advice.

Amsterdam's key points of interest can be covered within two or three days, with each walking itinerary taking in one or two of the important museums and galleries. The following exploration of the city center can be broken up into several sessions.

Around the Dam *Numbers in the margin correspond to points of interest on the Amsterdam map.*

❶ Start at the **Centraal Station** (Central Station). Designed by P. J.H. Cuijpers and built in 1885, it is a good example of Dutch architecture at its most flamboyant. The street directly in front of the station square is Prins Hendrikkade. To the left, a good
❷ vantage point for viewing the station, is **St. Nicolaaskerk** (Church of St. Nicholas), consecrated in 1888. Of interest are the baroque altar with its revolving tabernacle, the swinging pulpit that can be stowed out of sight, and the upstairs gallery.

Around the corner from St. Nicolaaskerk, facing the harbor, is
❸ the **Schrierstoren** (Weepers' Tower), where seafarers used to say good-bye to their women before setting off to sea. The tower was erected in 1487, and a tablet marks the point from which Henrik (aka Henry) Hudson set sail on the *Half Moon* on April 4, 1609, on a voyage that took him to what is now New York and the river that still bears his name. Today the Weeping Tower is used as a combined reception and exhibition center, which includes a maritime bookshop.

Three blocks to the southwest along the Oudezijds Voor-
❹ burgwal is the **Museum Amstelkring,** whose facade carries the inscription "Ons Lieve Heer Op Solder" ("Our Dear Lord in the Attic"). In 1578, Amsterdam embraced Protestantism and out-

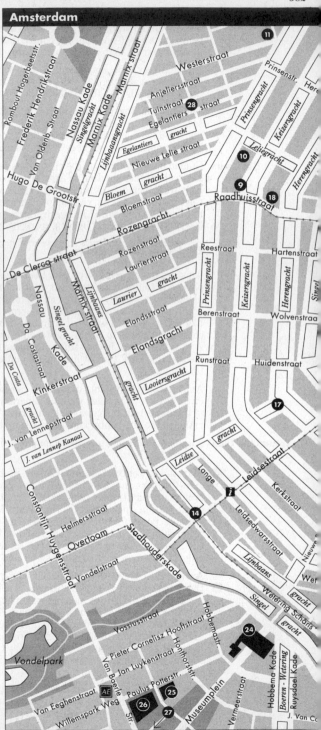

Amsterdam

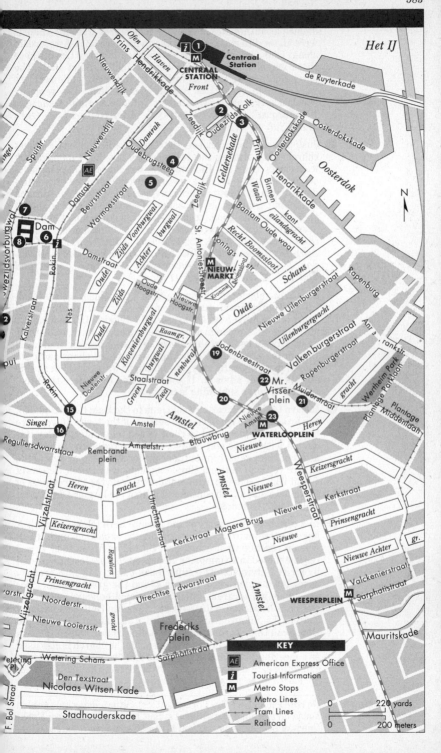

Het IJ

CENTRAAL STATION
Front
Centraal
Station

de Ruyterkade

Prins Hendrikkade

Ofen

Haven

Nieuwendijk

Damrak

Oudebrugsteeg

Nieuwendijk

Beursstraat

Warmoesstraat

Spuistr.

Damrak

Zeedijk

Oudezijds Kolk

Geldersekade

Zeedijk

Prins Hendrikkade

Oosterdokskade

Oosterdokskade

Oosterdok

Binnen

Waals

kant

eilandsgracht

Oude waal

Bantam

Recht Boomssloot

Rapenburg

N

AE

Dam

i

Damstraat

Zijds Voorburgwal

Achter

burgwal

Oude

Zijds

Nes

Oude
Hoogstr.

Nieuwe
Hoogstr.

St. Antoniesbreestr.

Konings
str.

Kromma

Boomssloot

NIEUW
MARKT

Oude

Schans

Nieuwe Uilenburgerstraat

Rapenburg

Uilenburgergracht

Valkenburgerstraat

Rapenburgerstraat

Anna rankstr.

Wertheim
Park

Plantage Parklaan

Plantage
Middenlaan

Kalverstraat

Kloveniersburgwal

Raamgr.

burgwal

nieuwbural

Groen

Zuid

Nieuwe
Doelenstr.

Staalstraat

Jodenbreestraat

Mr.
Visser-
plein

Muiderstraat

gracht

Heren

pui

Rokin

Amstel

Amstel

Blauwbrug

Nieuwe
Amstel

WATERLOOPLEIN

Singel

Reguliersdwarrstraat

Rembrandt
plein

Amstelstr.

Nieuwe

Nieuwe

Nieuwe

Keizersgracht

Kerkstraat

Prinsengracht

Vijzelstraat

Heren

gracht

Utrechtsestraat

Amstel

Weesperstraat

Nieuwe

Nieuwe Achter

gr.

Keizersgracht

Reguliers

Kerkstraat

Magere Brug

Prinsengracht

Nieuwe Looiersstr.

Noorderstr.

gracht

Utrechte

dwarstraat

Amstel

Valckenierstraat

Sarphatistraat

WEESPERPLEIN

Vijzelgracht

Frederiks
plein

Sarphatistraat

Mauritskade

etering
Pl.

Wetering Schans

Den Texstraat

Nicolaas Witsen Kade

Stadhouderskade

F. Bol Straat

lawed the church of Rome. So great was the tolerance of the municipal authorities, however, that secret Catholic chapels were allowed to exist; at one time there were 62 in Amsterdam alone. One such chapel was established in the attics of these three neighboring canalside houses, built around 1661. The lower floors were used as ordinary dwellings, while services were held in the attics regularly until 1888, the year St. Nicolaaskerk was consecrated for Catholic worship. *Oudezijds Voorburgwal 40, tel. 020/6246604. Admission: Fl. 4. Open Mon.–Sat. 10–5, Sun. 1–5.*

⑤ Just beyond, you can see the **Oude Kerk**, the city's oldest church. Built during the 14th century but badly damaged by iconoclasts after the Reformation, the church still retains its original bell tower and a few remarkable stained-glass windows. From the tower, there is a typical view of old Amsterdam stretching from St. Nicolaaskerk to medieval gables and, if your eyesight is good, to glimpses of negotiations between a prostitute and a prospective client immediately below! *Oudekerksplein 23, tel. 020/624–9183. Admission: Fl. 3. Open Apr.–Oct., Mon.–Sat. 11–5, Sun. 1:30–5; Nov.–Mar., Mon.–Sat. 1–3, Sun. 1:30–3. Tower open June–Sept., Mon. and Thurs. 2–5, Tues. and Wed. 11–2.*

This area, bordered by Amsterdam's two oldest canals (Oudezijds Voorburgwal and Oudezijds Achterburgwal), is the heart of the *rosse buurt*, the red-light district. In the windows at canal level, women in sheer lingerie slouch, stare, or do their nails. Drawn red curtains above suggest a brisker trade. Although the area can be shocking, with its sex shops and porn shows, it is generally safe, but midnight walks down dark side streets are not advised. If you do decide to explore the area, take care; purse snatching is common.

⑥ Return to the Damrak and continue to the **Dam** (Dam Square), the broadest square in the old section of the town. It was here that the fishermen used to come to sell their catch. Today it is circled with shops and people, and bisected with traffic; it is also a popular center for outdoor performers. At one side of the square you will notice a simple monument to Dutch victims of World War II. Eleven urns contain soil from the 11 provinces of Holland, while a 12th contains soil from the former Dutch East Indies, now Indonesia.

⑦ In a corner of the square is the **Nieuwe Kerk** (New Church). A huge Gothic church, it was gradually expanded until 1540, when it reached its present size. Gutted by fire in 1645, it was reconstructed in an imposing Renaissance style, as interpreted by strict Calvinists. The superb oak pulpit, the 14th-century nave, the stained-glass windows, and the great organ (1645) are all shown to great effect on national holidays, when the church is bedecked with flowers. As befits Holland's national church, the Nieuwe Kerk is the site of all inaugurations (as the Dutch call their coronations), including that of Queen Beatrix in 1980. But in democratic Dutch spirit, the church is also used as a meeting place and is the home of a lively café, temporary exhibitions, and concerts. *Tel. 020/6268168. Open daily 11–5, but closed often for special occasions.*

Time Out   **De Drie Fleschjes** (The Three Bottles). Situated in a bell-gabled house on a crooked, medieval street behind the Nieuwe Kerk, this is one of the most typical 17th-century *proeflokalen* (wine-

and spirit-tasting houses). The tone is set by the burnished wood interior, the candlelit bar, and the profusion of kegs and taps. Brokers are big buyers here when the markets close. Although the main emphasis is on drink, light snacks are also available. *Gravenstraat 18. Open Mon.–Sat. noon–8.*

⑧ Dominating Dam Square is the **Het Koninklijk Paleis te Amsterdam** (Royal Palace at Amsterdam), or **Dam Palace,** a vast, well-proportioned structure on Dam Square that was completed in 1655. It is built on 13,659 pilings sunk into the marshy soil. The great pedimental sculptures are an allegorical representation of Amsterdam surrounded by Neptune and mythological sea creatures. *Open Wed. noon–4; daily noon–4 during Easter, summer, and fall holidays.*

From behind the palace, Raadhuisstraat leads west across **⑨** three canals to the **Westermarkt** and the **Westerkerk** (West Church), built in 1631. The church's 85-meter (275-foot) tower is the highest in the city. It also features an outstanding carillon (set of bells). Rembrandt and his son Titus are buried in the church. On summer afternoons, you can climb to the top of the tower for a fine view over the city.

Opposite, at Westermarkt 6, is the house where René Descartes, the great 17th-century French philosopher ("Cogito, ergo sum"—"I think, therefore I am") lived in 1634. Another more famous house lies farther down Prinsengracht. This is the **⑩** **Anne Frankhuis** (Anne Frank House), immortalized by the poignant diary kept by the young Jewish girl from 1942 to 1944, when she and her family hid here from the German occupying forces. A small exhibition on the Holocaust can also be seen in the house. *Prinsengracht 263, tel. 020/6264533. Admission: Fl. 6. Open June–Aug., Mon.–Sat. 9–7, Sun. 10–7; Sept.–May, Mon.–Sat. 9–5, Sun. 10–5.*

Continuing across the Prinsengracht, you'll reach the **⑪** **Noorderkerk,** built in 1623. In the square in front of the church, the Noorderplein, a bird market, is held every Saturday.

South of the Dam Turn down Kalverstraat, a shopping street leading from the Royal Palace. You will notice a striking Renaissance gate (1581) that guards a series of tranquil inner courtyards. In medieval times, this area was an island devoted to piety. Today the bordering canals are filled in.

The medieval doorway just around the corner in St. Luciensteeg leads to the former Burgerweeshuis (City Orphanage), **⑫** once a nunnery but now the **Amsterdam Historisch Museum** (Museum of History). The museum traces the city's history from its origins as a fishing village through the 17th-century Golden Age of material and artistic wealth to the decline of the trading empire during the 18th century. The engrossing story unfolds through a display of old maps, documents, and paintings, often aided by a commentary in English. *Kalverstraat 92, tel. 020/5231822. Admission: Fl. 5. Open daily 11–5.*

A small passageway and courtyard link the museum with **⑬** the **Begijnhof,** an enchanting, enclosed square of almshouses founded in 1346. The *beguines* were women who chose to lead a form of convent life, often taking the vow of chastity. The last beguine died in 1974 and her house, No. 26, has been preserved as she left it. No. 34, dating from the 15th century, is the oldest and the only one to keep its wooden Gothic facade. *Tel. 020/ 6233565. Open weekdays 11–4.*

In the center of the square is a church given to Amsterdam's English and Scottish Presbyterians more than 300 years ago. On the church wall and also in the chancel are tributes to the Pilgrim Fathers who sailed from Delftshaven to New York in 1620. Opposite the church is another of the city's secret Catholic chapels, built in 1671.

Continuing along Kalverstraat, you soon come to Spui, a lively square in the heart of the university area. It was a center for student rallies in revolutionary 1968. Now it is a center for bookstores and bars, including the cozy "brown cafés."

Beyond is the Singel Canal and, following the tram tracks, Leidsestraat, an important shopping street that terminates in ⑭ the **Leidseplein,** a lively square that is one of the night-life centers of the city.

If you continue straight along Kalverstraat instead of turning ⑮ at Spui, you'll soon reach the **Muntplein,** with its **Munttoren** (Mint Tower, built in 1620), a graceful structure whose clock and bells still seem to mirror the Golden Age. Beginning at the ⑯ Muntplein is the floating **Flower Market** on the Singel Canal. *Open Mon.–Sat. 9:30–5.*

From the Singel, take Leidsestraat to the Herengracht, the city's most prestigious "Gentlemen's Canal." The stretch of ca- ⑰ nal from here to Huidenstraat is named The **Golden Bend** for its sumptuous patrician houses with double staircases and grand entrances. Seventeenth-century merchants moved here from the Amstel River to escape the disadvantageous byproducts of their wealth: the noisy warehouses, the unpleasant smells from the breweries, and the risk of fire in the sugar refineries. These houses display the full range of Amsterdam facades: from neck, bell, and step gables to grander Louis XIV–style houses with elaborate cornices and frescoed ceilings. In particular, look at Nos. 364–370, as well as No. 380, with its sculpted angels and Louis XIV facade; Nos. 390 and 392 display neck-shaped gables surmounted by statues of a couple in matching 17th-century garb. These houses are best seen from the east side of the canal. For more gables, turn down Wolvenstraat into the Keizersgracht, the Emperor's Canal. Walk northward toward Westerkerk and the Anne Frank Huis (*see above*).

Time Out   On the corner of Keizersgracht and Reestraat is the well-restored **Pulitzer Hotel** and restaurant complex. Inside, you can wander around quiet inner courtyards and a modern art gallery before sitting down in the **Café Pulitzer,** which overlooks the canal, for a well-deserved apple tart or pastry. *Keizersgracht 236. Open daily 11–4.*

⑱   Along Herengracht, parallel to the Westerkerk, is the **Nederlands Theater Instituut.** This theater museum is a dynamic find on such a genteel canal. Two frescoed Louis XIV–style merchants' houses form the backdrop for a history of the circus, opera, musicals, and drama. Miniature theaters and videos of stage productions are just two entertaining features. During the summer, the large garden is open for buffet lunches. *Herengracht 168. Admission: Fl. 5. Open Tues.–Sun. 11–5.*

Jewish Amsterdam Take the Museumboat or the metro from the central station to Waterlooplein and walk east to Jodenbreestraat. This is the heart of **Jodenbuurt,** the old Jewish district and an important area to all Amsterdammers. The original settlers here were wealthy Sephardic Jews from Spain and Portugal, later followed by poorer Ashkenazic refugees from Germany and Poland. At the turn of the century, this was a thriving community of Jewish diamond polishers, dyers, and merchants. During World War II, the corner of Jodenbreestraat marked the end of the *Joodse wijk* (Jewish neighborhood), by then an imposed ghetto. Although the character of the area was largely destroyed by highway construction in 1965, and more recently by construction of both the metro and the Town Hall–Muziektheater complex, neighboring Muiderstraat has retained much of the original atmosphere. Notice the gateways decorated with pelicans, symbolizing great love; according to legend, the pelican will feed her starving young with her own blood.

From 1639 to 1658, Rembrandt lived at Jodenbreestraat No. 4, now the **Museum Het Rembrandthuis** (Rembrandt's House). For more than 20 years, the ground floor was used by the artist as living quarters; the sunny upper floor was his studio. It is fascinating to visit, both as a record of life in 17th-century Amsterdam and as a sketch of Holland's most illustrious artist. It contains a superb collection of his etchings and engravings. From St. Antonies Sluis bridge, just by the house, there is a canal view that has barely changed since Rembrandt's time. *Jodenbreestraat 4–6, tel. 020/6249486. Admission: Fl. 4. Open Mon.–Sat. 10–5, Sun. 1–5.*

After visiting Rembrandt's House, walk back to the canal and go left to pass the Waterlooplein flea market. Ahead of you is the Amsterdam **Muziektheater/Stadhuis** (Music Theater/Town House) complex, which presents an intriguing combination of bureaucracy and art. Amsterdammers come to the Town Hall section of the building by day to obtain driving licenses, to pick up welfare payments, and to be married. They return by night to the rounded part of the building facing the river to see opera and ballet by Holland's well-known performing companies. Feel free to wander into Town Hall (there are some interesting sculptures and other displays to see). Opera and ballet fans can go on a tour of the Muziektheater, which takes you around the dressing rooms, dance studios, and even the wig department. *Amstel 3, tel. 020/5518100. Cost: Fl. 8.50. Guided tours every Wed. and Sat. at 4.*

Facing the Muziektheater is the 17th-century **Portuguese Israelitische Synagogue.** As one of Amsterdam's four neighboring synagogues, it was part of the largest Jewish religious complex in Europe. The austere interior is still intact, even if the building itself is marooned on a traffic island. *Admission: Fl 2.50. Open May–Oct., Sun.–Fri. 10–4; Nov.–Apr., Mon.–Thurs. 10–4, Fri. 10–2.*

Jonas Daniel Meijerplein is a square behind the Portuguese Synagogue. In the center is a statue of the **Dokwerker** (Dockworker), a profession that has played a significant part in the city's history. The statue commemorates the 1942 strike by which Amsterdam dockworkers expressed their solidarity with persecuted Jews. A memorial march is held every year on February 25.

㉓ On the other side of the square is the intriguing **Joods Historisch Museum** (Jewish History Museum), set in a complex of three ancient synagogues. These synagogues once served a population of 100,000 Jews, which shrank to less than 10,000 after 1945. The new museum, founded by American and Dutch Jews, displays religious treasures in a clear cultural and historical context. Since the synagogues lost most of their treasures in the war, their architecture and history are more compelling than the individual exhibits. *Jonas Daniël Meijerplein 2–4, tel. 020/6269945. Admission: Fl. 7. Open daily 11–5.*

Time Out **Cafeteria Kosher.** Situated within the oldest part of the museum, the cafeteria is built above the former kosher meat halls that later became ritual baths. It still looks like part of a clandestine Catholic church, the original model for the synagogue. Jewish delicacies include fish cakes, cheese tarts, bagels, and spicy cakes with gingerbread and almond cream filling. *Open daily 11–5.*

Instead of returning on foot, you can catch the Museum Boat from the Muziektheater to the central station or to a destination near your hotel. If you feel like a breath of fresh air, stroll along Nieuwe Herengracht, once known as the "Jewish Gentlemen's Canal." In Rembrandt's day, there were views of distant windjammers sailing into port, but today the canal is oddly deserted.

The Museum Quarter By crossing the bridge beyond the Leidseplein and walking a short distance to the left on Stadshouderskade, you'll find three of the most distinguished museums in Holland—the Rijksmuseum, the Stedelijk Museum, and the Rijksmuseum ㉔ Vincent van Gogh. Of the three, the **Rijksmuseum,** easily recognized by its towers, is the most important, so be sure to allow adequate time to explore it. It was founded in 1808, but the current, rather lavish, building dates from 1885. The museum contains significant collections of furniture, textiles, ceramics, sculpture, and prints, as well as Italian, Flemish, and Spanish paintings, many of which are of the highest quality. But the museum's fame rests on its unrivaled collection of 16th- and 17th-century Dutch masters. Of Rembrandt's masterpieces, make a point of seeing *The Nightwatch,* concealed during World War II in caves in Maastricht. The painting was misnamed because of its dull layers of varnish; in reality it depicts the Civil Guard in daylight. Also worth searching out are Jan Steen's family portraits, Frans Hals's drunken scenes, Van Ruysdael's romantic but menacing landscapes, and Vermeer's glimpses of everyday life bathed in his usual pale light. *Stadshouderskade 42, tel. 020/6732121. Admission: Fl. 6.50. Open Tues.–Sat. 10–5, Sun. 1–5.*

㉕ A few blocks beyond is the **Rijksmuseum Vincent van Gogh.** This museum contains the world's largest collection of the artist's works—200 paintings and 500 drawings—as well as works by some 50 other painters of the period. *Paulus Potterstraat 7, tel. 020/5705200. Admission: Fl. 10. Open Tues.–Sat. 10–5, Sun. 1–5; Easter–Sept. 21, additional hours Mon. 10–5.*

㉖ Next door is the **Stedelijk Museum** (Municipal Museum), with its austere neoclassical facade designed to counterbalance the Rijksmuseum's neo-Gothic turrets. The museum has a stimulating collection of modern art and ever-changing displays of contemporary art. Before viewing the works of Cézanne, Chagall, Kandinsky, and Mondrian, check the list of temporary exhibitions in Room 1. Museum policy is to trace the development of the artist rather than merely to show a few masterpieces. Don't forget the museum's restaurant overlooking a garden filled with modern sculptures. *Paulus Potterstraat 13, tel. 020/5732911. Admission: Fl. 7. Open daily 11–5.*

Diagonally opposite the Stedelijk Museum, at the end of the broad Museumplein, is the **Concertgebouw,** home of the country's foremost orchestra, the world-renowned Concertgebouworkest. Many visiting orchestras also perform here. The building has two auditoriums, the smaller of which is used for chamber music and recitals. A block or two in the opposite direction is **Vondelpark,** an elongated rectangle of paths, lakes, and pleasant shady trees. A monument honors the 17th-century epic poet Joost van den Vondel, for whom the park is named. From Wednesday to Sunday during the summer, free concerts and plays are performed in the park.

The Jordaan One old part of Amsterdam that is certainly worth exploring is the **Jordaan,** the area bordered by Herengracht, Lijnbaansgracht, Brouwersgracht, and Raadhuisstraat. The canals and side streets here are all named for flowers and plants. Indeed, at one time, when this was the French quarter of the city, the area was known as *le jardin* (the garden), a name that over the years has become Jordaan. The best time to explore this area is on a Sunday morning, when there are few cars and people about, or in the evening. This part of the town has attracted many artists and is something of a bohemian quarter, where rundown buildings are being renovated and converted into restaurants, antiques shops, boutiques, and galleries.

Time Out The Jordaan is the best part of Amsterdam for relaxing in a brown café, so named because of the rich wood furnishings and—some say—the centuries-old pipe-tobacco stains on the ceilings. You can while away a rainy afternoon chatting to friendly strangers over homemade meatballs or apple tarts. Spend an hour or three over a beer or coffee at either **'t Doktorje** (Rozenboomsteegweg 4) or **De Egelantier** (Egelantierstraat 72).

Off the Beaten Track

Another "see-worthy" district is the burgeoning **Maritime Quarter.** To reach it, walk from the central station along the Prins Hendrikkade and the Eastern Harbor, the hub of shipping activity during Holland's Golden Age. A growing permanent collection of restored vessels is moored at the **National Maritime Museum** (Scheepvaart Museum), a former naval complex at Kattenburgerplein 1. A short stroll farther down the Kattenburgergracht-Wittenburgergracht to the footbridge over the canal leads to the **Kromhout Museum** (Hoogte Kadijk 147). Many early steamships were built at this wharf, where models and motors are on display.

About three blocks from the central station, at **Haarlemmerstraat 75,** a plaque commemorates the occasion, in 1623, when the directors of the Dutch West India Company planned the founding of Nieuw Amsterdam on the southernmost tip of the island of Manhattan. In 1664, this colony was seized by the English and renamed New York.

An otherwise unremarkable building at **Singel 460** (near Herengracht) has special significance for Americans. In this building John Adams raised the first foreign loan ($2 million) for the United States from the banking house of Van Staphorst in 1782. Additional loans from this and other banks soon followed, for a total of $30 million—a gesture of Dutch confidence in the future of America.

Beer lovers—or anyone with an interest in the production of a world-class product—will want to take time to visit the **Heinekenontvangstgebouw,** formerly the Heineken Brewery. The guided weekday tours (year-round 9:30 and 11, additional summer tours at 1 and 2:30) take in a slide presentation, the old brewery stables, and, of course, include free beer at the end of the tour. *Van der Helstraat. Admission: Fl. 2. Children under 18 not admitted.*

Shopping

Serious shoppers should buy the VVV's four excellent shopping guides to markets, art and antiques shops, boutiques, and department stores (Fl. 10).

Gift Ideas   **Diamonds.** Since the 17th century, "Amsterdam cut" has been synonymous with perfection in the quality of diamonds. You can see this craftsmanship at any of the diamond-cutting houses. The cutters explain how the diamond's value depends on the four *c*'s—carat, cut, clarity, and color—before encouraging you to buy. There is a cluster of diamond houses on the Rokin. Alternatively, try **Van Moppes Diamonds.** *Albert Cuypstraat 2–6, tel. 020/6761242. Open daily 9–5.*

Porcelain. The Dutch have been producing Delft, Makkum, and other fine porcelain for centuries. **Focke and Meltzer** stores have been selling it since 1823. The objects vary from affordable, newly painted tiles to expensive Delft blue-and-white pitchers. One store is situated near the Rijksmuseum (P.C. Hooftstraat 65–67, tel. 020/6231944).

Shopping Districts   Amsterdam's chief shopping districts, which have largely been turned into pedestrianized areas, are the **Leidsestraat, Kalverstraat,** and **Nieuwendijk. Rokin,** somber and sedate, houses a cluster of boutiques and renowned antiques shops selling 18th- and 19th-century furniture, antique jewelry, Art Deco lamps, and statuettes. By contrast, some of the **Nieuwe Spiegelstraat**'s old curiosity shops sell a more inexpensive range. Haute couture and other fine goods are at home on P.C. Hooftstraat, Van Baerlestraat, and Beethovenstraat. For trendy small boutiques and unusual crafts shops, locals browse through the Jordaan. For A-to-Z shopping in a huge variety of stores, visit the new **Magna Plaza** shopping center, built inside the glorious old post office behind the Royal Palace. When leaving Holland, remember that Schiphol Airport is Europe's best tax-free shopping center.

Department Stores   **De Bijenkorf** (Dam Square), the city's number-one department store, is excellent for contemporary fashions and furnishings. Running a close second is **Vroom and Dreesman** (Kalverstraat 201), with well-stocked departments carrying all manner of goods. More sedate is **Maison de Bonneterie en Pander** (Rokin

140–142 and Beethovenstraat 32). The restaurants and cafés in these department stores are also worth trying.

Markets There is a lively open-air **flea market** on Waterlooplein around the Musiektheater (Mon.–Sat. 9:30–4). The **floating flower market** on the Singel is popular with locals and visitors alike (Open Mon.–Sat. 9:30–5). An unusual Saturday **bird market** is held in the Noordermarkt. Philatelists will not want to miss the **stamp market** at Nieuwezijds Voorburgwal (Wed. and Sat. 1–4). For antiques, especially silver and toys, visit the **Sunday Waterlooplein Market** during the summer. You can also try the **Antiekmarkt de Looier** (Elandsgracht 109. Open Sun.–Wed. 11–5, Thurs. 11–9). During the summer, art lovers can buy etchings, drawings, and watercolors at the Sunday **art markets** on Thorbeckeplein and the Spui.

Dining

Amsterdammers are less creatures of habit than are the Dutch in general. Even so, set menus and early dinners are preferred by these health-conscious citizens. For travelers on a diet or budget, the blue-and-white "Tourist Menu" sign guarantees an economical (Fl. 20) yet imaginative set menu created by the head chef. For traditionalists, the "Nederlands Dis" soup tureen sign is a promise of regional recipes and seasonal ingredients. "You can eat in any language" is the city's proud boast, so when Dutch restaurants are closed, Indonesian, Chinese, and Turkish restaurants are often open. Between meals, you can follow your nose to the nearest herring cart or drop into a cozy brown café for coffee and an apple tart. For details and price-category definitions, *see* Dining in Staying in Holland.

Very Expensive **Amstel Inter-Continental.** This world-class restaurant in a re-
★ cently renovated grand hotel is fit for royalty. There are three differently decorated rooms, two of which have canal views. The French cuisine, with an awe-inspiring "truffle menu" of dishes prepared with exotic (and expensive) ingredients, is nonpareil. Epicureans seeking the ultimate should inquire about the "Chef's table": With a group of six you can sit in the heart of the kitchen and watch chefs describe each of your courses as it is prepared. *Professor Tulpplein 1, tel. 020/622–6060. Reservations advised. AE, DC, MC, V.*

★ **Excelsior.** Hôtel de l'Europe's renowned restaurant offers a varied menu of French cuisine that is based on local ingredients; choose from an array of seafood dishes, including smoked eel. The service is discreet and impeccable. *Nieuwe Doelenstraat 2–4, tel. 020/6234836. Reservations required. AE, DC, MC, V. Closed Sat. lunch.*

Le Tout Court. This small, meticulously appointed restaurant features seasonal specialties (spring lamb, summer fruits, game during autumn and winter) personally prepared by owner-chef John Fagel, a member of Holland's first family of food. *Runstraat 13, tel. 020/6258637. Reservations advised. AE, DC, MC, V. No lunch weekends.*

Expensive **d'Vijff Vlieghen.** Take a trip back in time to a warren of 17th-
★ century charm. Formerly a wine-and-cheese hole-in-the-wall, this restaurant has of the seven dining rooms, each decorated in a different Renaissance style. The menu has a touch of nouvelle cuisine, more in presentation than in proportion; the game specialties are attractive and substantial. The vegetarian menu is a

delight. As befits an ex-tavern, the candlelight atmosphere is warm and relaxed. *Spuistraat 294, tel. 020/6248369. Reservations advised. AE, DC, MC, V. Dinner only.*

Edo. The Grand Hotel Krasnapolsky is home to a Dutch notion of Japanese cuisine. Artistic portions of raw fish and grilled meat are served against a background of polished pine and equally polished service. You'll marvel at the way Dutch seafood lends itself to sushi preparation. *Sashimi* (raw fish) is prepared before your eyes. The view of a serene Japanese garden completes the atmosphere. *Dam 9, tel. 020/5546096. Reservations required. AE, DC, MC, V.*

Les Quatre Canetons. Pleasantly informal, this canalside restaurant is popular with local businesspeople. It serves mainly nouvelle cuisine and freshwater trout, but also try the duckling breast and smoked ploeca, a traditional Dutch fish. *Prinsengracht 1111, tel. 020/6246307. Closed Sat. lunch and Sun. Reservations advised. AE, DC, MC, V.*

★ **'t Swarte Schaep.** The Black Sheep is named after a proverbial 17th-century sheep that once roamed the area. With its creaking boards and array of copper pots, the interior is reminiscent of a ship's cabin. The Dutch chef uses seasonal ingredients to create classical French dishes with regional flourishes and a touch of nouvelle cuisine. Dinner orders are accepted until 11 PM—unusually late even for Amsterdam. *Korte Leidsedwarsstraat 24, tel. 020/6223021. Reservations required. AE, DC, MC, V.*

Moderate–Expensive **Eerst Klas.** Amsterdam's best-kept secret is in the most obvious of places: the former first-class waiting lounge of the central train station. The classic, dark-wood paneling and soft interior lighting create the perfect hideaway from the city's hustle and bustle. The convenient location is also perfect for business lunches. French nouvelle cuisine includes a delicious marinated salmon. *Stationsplein 15, Spoer 2B, tel. 020/6250131. AE, DC, MC, V. Reservations advised.*

Moderate **De Orient.** Excellent Indonesian food is just minutes away from
★ major museums and the Concertgebouw. Complementing the rijsttafel are excellent *loempia* (egg rolls) and soups. Every Wednesday night there is a rijsttafel buffet. *Van Baerlestraat 21, tel. 020/6734958. Reservations required. AE, DC, MC, V.*

Luden. Located in the trendy Spui area and decorated simply yet elegantly, this is an excellent spot for dinner or just an after-dinner drink. The menu changes regularly, but retains a French flavor. Most dishes feature a suggested wine. *Spuistraat 304–308, tel. 020/6228979. Reservations advised. AE, DC, MC, V. No weekday lunch.*

Oesterbar. As its name suggests, the Oyster Bar specializes in seafood, some of which eyes you from the tank. The upstairs dining room is more formal than the downstairs bistro, but prices don't vary. Salmon, seawolf, and halibut are favorite seafood entrées; oysters are a good, if pricey, appetizer. *Leidseplein 10, tel. 020/6232988. Reservations advised. AE, DC, MC.*

Sea Palace. The Sea Palace is an appropriate establishment for a city built on canals—it's a huge, floating Chinese restaurant. The menu, which ranges from Cantonese to Indonesian, is of only modest quality, but the surroundings make up for it. A special children's menu is also available. *Oosterdokskade (near the central station), tel. 020/6264777. Reservations accepted. AE, DC, MC, V.*

Speciaal. Although set in the Jordaan area, this Indonesian restaurant is slightly off the beaten track. From the outside, the Speciaal looks very mundane, but inside, the soothing Indonesian prints, raffia work, and bamboo curtains create an intimate atmosphere. Along with the usual rijsttafel, chicken, fish, and egg dishes provide tasty variants on a sweet-and-sour theme. *Nieuwe Leliestraat 142, tel. 020/6249706. Reservations accepted. AE, MC, V.*

Inexpensive **Eettuin.** An "eating garden" in the heart of the arty Jordaan area, there's something here for everyone—from vegetarian dishes to spare ribs and the house special, pork. Unusual for Europe is the salad bar. *Tweede Tuindwarsstraat 10, tel. 020/6237706. Reservations advised. No credit cards. No lunch.*

Haesje Claes. Traditional Dutch food is served here in a traditional Dutch environment, with prices that are easy on the wallet; it sounds like a tourist's dream and, in ways, it is. There's a cozy feeling here and a relaxed simplicity. Menu choices can be as basic as traditional *stamppot* (mixed potatoes and sauerkraut) or as elaborate as filet of salmon with lobster sauce. There is a tourist menu. *Spuistraat 273–275, tel. 020/6249998. Reservations advised. AE, DC, MC, V. Closed Sun. lunch.*

Pancake Bakery. Here is a chance to try a traditionally Dutch way of keeping eating costs down. The name of the game is pancakes—for every course including dessert, for which the topping can be ice cream, fruit, or liqueur. The Pancake Bakery is not far from Anne Frankhuis. *Prinsengracht 191, tel. 020/6251333. No reservations. No credit cards.*

Lodging

Accommodations are tight from Easter to summer, so early booking is advised if you wish to secure a popular hotel. The other snag is parking. Since few hotels have parking lots, cars are best abandoned in a multistory parking ramp for the duration of your stay. Most tourists prefer to stay inside the concentric ring of canals. This area, the quiet museum quarter, is a convenient choice for the Rijksmuseum yet is near enough to the Vondelpark for light jogging. More atmospheric lodgings can be found in the historic canalside neighborhood with its gable-roof merchants' houses. For details and price-category definitions, *see* Lodging in Staying in Holland.

Very Expensive **Amstel Inter-Continental.** Amsterdam's grand dame opened in ★ 1867 and was completely renovated in late 1992. The result is spectacular. It is frequented by many of the nation's top businesspeople and visited at times by the royal family. *Professor Tulpplein 1, tel. 020/6226060, fax 020/6225808. 92 rooms with bath. AE, DC, MC, V.*

Amsterdam Hilton. This hotel is the site of John Lennon and Yoko Ono's famous bedroom strike, when the couple stayed in bed protesting for world peace; you can still stay in the room, now the honeymoon suite. One of the first international chain hotels to open in Amsterdam, the Hilton is still one of the most gracious. In the residential part of the city, it overlooks the attractive Noorder Amstelkanaal. All the rooms are luxuriously appointed. *Apollolaan 138, tel. 020/6780780. 271 rooms with bath. Facilities: casino. AE, DC, MC, V.*

Golden Tulip Barbizon Palace. The newest Golden Tulip Hotel in Amsterdam combines past and present with fantasy and flair. Sneak a peak at the adjoining conference center, which was built recently in the rúins of a 15th-century chapel. *Prins Hendrikkade 59–72, tel. 020/5564564. 268 rooms with bath; 5 suites, 5 apartments (monthly). AE, DC, MC, V.*

★ **Hôtel de l'Europe.** Owned by the Heineken brewers, the hotel hides its modern facilities behind a Renaissance-style facade. It has larger-than-average rooms, often decorated with old prints and Empire furniture. Apart from its world-renowned Excelsior restaurant, de l'Europe houses a sophisticated leisure complex and hotel swimming pool in Roman style. *Nieuwe Doelenstraat 2–4, tel. 020/6234836, fax 020/5242962. 100 rooms with bath. Facilities: restaurant, pool, leisure complex. AE, DC, MC, V.*

Ramada Renaissance. Situated in the old port area, the Sonesta incorporates a striking domed church and its own brown café. Lobby-lounge service (drinks and snacks) in comfortable artistic surroundings make this a favorite spot to meet. Contemporary pictures and sculpture are also scattered throughout the bars and bedrooms. *Kattengat 1, tel. 020/6212223. 432 rooms with bath. Facilities: restaurant, bar, health club, shopping complex. AE, DC, MC, V.*

Expensive **Ciga Pulitzer.** The Pulitzer succeeds in making living in the
★ past a positive pleasure. Recent renovations make this excellent hotel even better. This is one of Europe's most ambitious hotel restorations, using the shells of a row of 17th-century merchants' houses. Inside, the refined atmosphere is sustained by the modern art gallery, the lovingly restored brickwork, oak beams, and split-level rooms—no two are alike. The tranquil inner courtyards are equally adapted to contemplation and outdoor concerts. *Prinsengracht 315–331, tel. 020/5235235. 236 rooms with bath. Facilities: restaurant, bar. AE, DC, MC, V.*

Grand Hotel Krasnapolsky. This is one of the fine, Old World hotels in Amsterdam, dominated by its Winter Gardens restaurant recently restored to its original 1818 luster. The cosmopolitan atmosphere carries through all the rooms, with decor ranging from Victorian to Art Deco. Each room is well equipped, and there is a choice of restaurants. *Dam 9, tel. 020/ 5549111. 331 rooms with bath. Facilities: parking. AE, DC, MC, V.*

Moderate **Ambassade.** With its beautiful canalside location, its Louis
★ XV–style decoration, and its Oriental carpets, the Ambassade seems more like a stately home than a hotel. Service is attentive and room prices include breakfast. For other meals, the neighborhood has a good choice of restaurants for eating out. *Herengracht 341, tel. 020/6262333. 49 rooms with bath. AE, MC, V.*

Atlas Hotel. Renowned for its friendly atmosphere, this small hotel has moderate-size rooms decorated in Art Nouveau style. It's also very handy for Museumsplein, whose major museums are within easy walking distance. *Van Eeghenstraat 64, tel. 020/6766336. 22 rooms with bath. Facilities: bar, restaurant. AE, DC, MC, V.*

Het Canal House. The American owners of this canalside hotel also opt to put antiques rather than televisions in the rooms. Spacious rooms overlook the canal or the illuminated garden. A hearty Dutch breakfast comes with the room. *Keizergracht 148, tel. 020/6225182. 26 rooms with bath or shower. AE, DC, MC, V.*

RHO Hotel. Just off Dam Square, at the head of the street that is Amsterdam's equivalent of Off Broadway, this hotel is housed in a building once used by Holland's foremost gold company. The lobby, bar, and breakfast room occupy a chamber built originally as a theater in 1908. The rooms are cheerful, modern, and attractively furnished in contemporary style. *Nes 11–23, tel. 020/6207826. 153 rooms with bath. Facilities: parking. AE, MC, V.*

Inexpensive–Moderate **Hotel Toren.** The former home of Abraham Kuyper, founder of the Protestant University and a former prime minister of Holland, this delightful, huge canal house was converted to a hotel in 1968 but was recently rebuilt to return it to its original, 17th-century atmosphere. *Keizersgracht 164, tel. 020/6226352, fax 020/6269705. 43 rooms with bath. AE, DC, MC, V.*

Inexpensive **Agora.** Near the Singel flower market, this small hotel reflects
★ the cheerful bustle. The rooms are light and spacious, some decorated with vintage furniture; the best overlook the canal or the university. Recently refurbished, this 18th-century house has a considerate staff, and a relaxed neighborhood ensures the hotel's popularity. Book well in advance. *Singel 462, tel. 020/6272200. 14 rooms with bath or shower. AE, DC, MC, V.*

Amsterdam Classic Hotel. In a building that once was a distillery has been created an attractive, though somewhat stark, small Best Western hotel near Dam Square. The rooms are bright and spacious and furnished in light colors for an open, airy feeling. *Gravenstraat 14–16, tel. 020/6233716. 33 rooms with bath. AE, DC, MC, V.*

Hotel Seven Bridges. Named for the scene beyond its front steps, this small canal-house hotel offers clean, simple rooms with private bathrooms (also small but clean). The Rembrandtsplein is nearby. For a stunning view of the city, request one of the two large double rooms. *Reguliersgracht 31, tel. 020/6231329. 6 rooms with bath. No credit cards.*

The Arts

The arts flourish in tolerant and cosmopolitan Amsterdam. The best sources of information about performances are the monthly publications *City Life* (in English) and *Uit Krant* (in Dutch) and the biweekly *What's On in Amsterdam*, which can be obtained from the VVV office, where you can secure tickets for the more popular events. Tickets must be booked in person from Monday to Saturday, 10 to 4. You also can book at the **Amsterdam Uit Buro,** Stadsschouwburg, Leidseplein 26, tel. 020/62112111.

Classical Music Classical music is featured at the **Concertgebouw** (Concertgebouwplein 2–6), home of one of Europe's finest orchestras. A smaller auditorium in the same building is used for chamber music, recitals, and even jam sessions. While ticket prices for international orchestras are fairly high, most concerts are good value and the Wednesday lunchtime concerts are free. The box office is open from 9:30 to 7; you can make telephone bookings (020/6718345) from 10 to 3.

Opera and Ballet The Dutch national ballet and opera companies are housed in the new **Muziektheater** (tel. 020/625–5455) on Waterlooplein. Guest companies from foreign countries perform there during the three-week Holland Festival in June.

Theater **Stalhouderij Theater** (1e Bloemdwarsstraat 4, tel. 020/
6262282). An international cast performs a wide range of English-language plays in a former stable in the Jordaan. For experimental theater and colorful cabaret in Dutch, catch the
shows at **Felix Meritis House** (Keizersgracht 324, tel. 020/
6231311).

Film The largest concentration of movie theaters is around
Leidseplein and near Muntplein. Most foreign films are subti-
tled rather than dubbed, which makes Amsterdam a great
place to catch up on movies you missed at home. The **City 1–7**
theater near Leidseplein is the biggest (seven screens), but the
Art Deco–era **Tuschinski** on Reguliersbreestraat is the most
beautiful cinema house.

Nightlife

Amsterdam has a wide variety of discos, bars, and exotic
shows. The more respectable—and expensive—after-dark activities are in and around Leidseplein, Rembrandtsplein, and
Thorbeckeplein; fleshier productions are on Oudezijds
Achterburgwal. Names and locations change from year to year,
but most bars and clubs are open every night from 5 PM to 2 AM
or 5 AM. On weeknights, very few clubs charge admission, though
the more lively ones sometimes ask for a "club membership" fee of
Fl. 20 or more. Drink prices are for the most part not exorbitant.
It is wise to steer clear of the area behind the central station at
night.

Bars The **Bamboo Bar** (Lange Leidsedwarsstraat, tel. 020/6243993)
is informal, expensive, relaxing, and typically international. It
boasts good jazz and blues around the longest bar in Amsterdam.

Jazz Clubs Set in a converted warehouse, the **Bimhuis** is currently the
most fashionable jazz club. Ticket holders can sit in the adjoining BIMcafé and enjoy a magical view across Oude Schans to
the port (Oude Schans 73–77, tel. 020/6233373. Open Thurs.–
Sat. from 9 PM). If you long for good Dixieland jazz, go to **Joseph
Lam Jazz Club** (Van Diemenstraat 242, tel. 020/6228086); it's
only open on Saturdays.

Rock Clubs **Maloe Melo** (Lijnbaansgracht 160) caters to the slightly older-
than-teenage crowd.

Discos Mostly only hidden in cellars around the Leidseplein, the discos
fill up after midnight. **Roxy** (Singel 465, tel. 020/6200354) is the
Netherland's current hot spot. Also popular are **Escape**
(Rembrandtsplein 11–15, tel. 020/6223542) and **It** (Amstelstraat 24, tel. 020/6250111), generally straight Thurs., Sun.;
gay Fri.–Sat.). **Mazzo** (Rozengracht 114, tel. 020/267500) uses
dramatic lighting and slick videos to attract gay and straight
student poseurs, would-be musicians, and artists.

Casinos Blackjack, roulette, and slot machines have come lately—but
not lightly—to the thrifty Dutch. Now everyone wants to play.
The newest and most elegant venue, **Holland Casino** (Max
Euweplein 62, tel. 020/6201006), just off Leidseplein, opened in
1991. You'll need your passport to get in; the minimum age is
18.

Gay and Amsterdam has a vibrant gay and lesbian community, concen-
Lesbian Bars trated principally on Warmoestraat, Reguliersdwarsstraat,

Amstelstraat, and Kerkstraat near Leidseplein. The **Gay & Lesbian Switchboard** (tel. 020/6236565) can provide information on the city's nightlife.

Historic Holland

This circular itinerary can be followed either clockwise or counterclockwise, but whichever way you decide to follow it, you'll be sure to see some of Holland's most characteristic sights. There are the historic towns of Leiden and Utrecht and the major museums in Haarlem; in between these towns, you'll see some of Holland's windmill-dotted landscape and pass through centers of tulip growing and cheese production.

Getting Around

The most convenient way to cover the following itinerary is by rented car out of Amsterdam. If you want someone else to do the navigating, then all the towns listed below can be reached by bus or train. From Amsterdam there are, for example, three direct trains per hour to Haarlem, Leiden, and Utrecht. Check with the VVV office in Amsterdam for help in planning your trip, or inquire at the central station.

Guided Tours

Alternatively, these towns are covered, in various permutations, by organized bus tours out of Amsterdam. Brochures for tour operators are available from the VVV offices in Amsterdam, either from Stationplein 10, tel. 020/6266444, or from Leidsestraat 106.

The VVV in Utrecht organizes several excursions, including a boat trip along the canals and a sightseeing flight over the city. There are also day trips to country estates and castles, often enclosed by Dutch baroque gardens.

Tourist Information

Amersfoort (Stationsplein 9–11, tel. 033/635151).
Apeldoorn (Stationsplein 6, tel. 055/788421).
Gouda (Markt 27, tel. 01820/13666).
Haarlem (Stationsplein 1, tel. 023/319059).
Leiden (Stationsplein 210, tel. 071/146846).
Lisse (Grachtweg 53a, tel. 02521/14262).
Utrecht (Vredenburg 90, tel. 030/331544).
Zandvoort (Schoolplein 1, tel. 02507/17947).

Exploring Historic Holland

Amersfoort Traveling southeast from Amsterdam, 90 kilometers (56 miles) along highway A1, you will reach Apeldoorn, but if you have time, stop off at **Amersfoort** en route. Although today it is a major industrial town, Amersfoort still manages to retain much of its medieval character and charm. Starting at the **Koopelport,** the imposing water gate across the Eem, dating from 1400, walk down Kleine Spui. On the right is **St. Pieters-en-Bloklands Gasthuis,** a hospice founded in 1390. Close by is the **Museum Flehite,** with its unusual medieval collections that give a fasci-

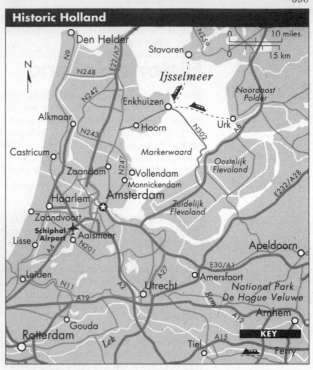

Historic Holland

Den Helder

Stavoren

Ijsselmeer

Noordoost
Polder

Enkhuizen

Alkmaar

Hoorn

Urk

Castricum

Markerwaard

Zaandam

Vollendam
Monnickendam

Amsterdam

*Oostelijk
Flevoland*

Haarlem

*Zuidelijk
Flevoland*

Zaandvoort

Schiphal
Airport   Aalsmeer

Apeldoorn

Lisse

Leiden

Utrecht

Amersfoort

*National Park
De Hoge Veluwe*

Arnhem

Gouda

Rotterdam

Tiel

KEY

Ferry

nating insight into the history of the town. *Westsingel 50. Admission: Fl. 2. Open Tues.–Fri. 10–5, weekends 2–5.*

Continuing along Breestraat, you'll come to the graceful, 102-meter- (330-foot-) high **Onze Lieve Vrouwetorn** (Tower of Our Lady). The musical chimes of this Gothic church can be heard every Friday between 10 and 11 AM. Turning left down Langstraat, past the Gothic **St. Joriskerk,** you will come to the **Kamperbinnenpoort,** the turreted land gate dating from the 15th century. Making your way left down Muurhuizen, you'll come to a short canal, the **Hovik,** which was once the old harbor.

Apeldoorn The main attraction at **Apeldoorn** is the **Rijksmuseum Paleis Het Loo.** This former royal palace was built during the late 17th century for Willem III and has been beautifully restored to illustrate the domestic surroundings enjoyed by the House of Orange for more than three centuries. The museum, which is housed in the stables, has a fascinating collection of royal memorabilia, including cars and carriages, furniture and photographs, silver and ceramics. The formal gardens and the surrounding parkland offer attractive walks. *Tel. 055/212244. Admission Fl. 7.50. Open Tues.–Sun. 10–5.*

From Apeldoorn, it is well worth the 5-kilometer (3-mile) drive on N304 to the **Kröller-Muller Museum.** Located in the woods in the middle of a national park, it displays one of the finest collections of modern art in the world. It possesses 278 works by Vincent van Gogh, as well as paintings, drawings, and sculptures by such masters as Seurat, Redon, Braque, Picasso, and Mondrian. The building, too, is part of the experience; it seems to bring the museum's wooded setting right into the galleries with you. The major sculptures are shown in the garden; don't miss them. *National Park De Hoge Veluwe, tel. 08382/1041. Admission: Fl. 6.50. Open Tues.–Sat. 10–5, Sun. 11–5 (Nov.– Apr. 1–5). Sculpture garden closes ½ hour earlier.*

Arnhem If you have children in tow, consider a visit to the **Nederlands Openlucht Museum** (Open Air Museum) in **Arnhem,** 15 kilometers (9¼ miles) from Apeldoorn on A90. In a 44-acre park, the curators have brought together original buildings and furnishings from all over the Netherlands to establish both a comprehensive display of Dutch rural architectural styles as well as a depiction of traditional ways of living. There are farmhouses and barns, workshops, and windmills—animals, too. *Schelmseweg 89, tel. 085/576111. Admission: Fl. 10. Open Apr.–Oct., weekdays 9–5, weekends 10–5.*

Utrecht West of Apeldoorn, 72 kilometers (44 miles), is the city of **Utrecht.** The high gabled houses of the Nieuwegracht, the canals with their water gates, the 13th-century wharves and storage cellars of the Oudegracht, and the superb churches and museums are just some of the key attractions, most of which are situated around the main cathedral square. The **Domkerk** is a late-Gothic cathedral containing a series of fine stained-glass windows. The Domtoren (bell tower) opposite the building was connected to the cathedral until a hurricane hit in 1674. The bell tower is the tallest in the country, and it has 456 steep steps that lead to a magnificent view. A guide is essential in the labyrinth of steps and passageways. *Domplein, tel. 030/310403. Admission free to cathedral; Fl. 1.50 to Domtoren. Open May– Sept., daily 10–5; Oct.–Apr., weekends 1–5.*

Not far from the cathedral is the merry **Rijksmuseum van Speelklok tot Pierement** (National Museum from Musical Clock to Street Organ), devoted solely to music machines—from music boxes to street organs and even musical chairs. During the guided tour, music students play some of the instruments. The museum is housed in Utrecht's oldest parish church. *Buurkerkhof 10, tel. 030/312789. Admission: Fl. 6. Open Tues.–Sat. 10–5, Sun. 1–5.*

Behind the museum is **Pieterskerk,** the country's oldest Romanesque church, built in 1048. The grandeur of the city's churches reflects the fact that Utrecht was Holland's religious center during the Middle Ages. Most churches are open during the summer and a church concert is held almost every day.

Walk south out of Domplein, down Lange Nieuwstraat. Halfway down is the **Rijksmuseum Het Catharijneconvent.** In addition to its collection of holy relics and vestments, this museum contains the country's largest display of religious art and history. *Nieuwegracht 63, tel. 030/317296. Admission: Fl. 3.50. Open Tues.–Fri. 10–5, weekends 11–5.*

There are more museums to be explored on Agnietenstraat, which crosses Lange Nieuwstraat. The **Centraal Museum** houses a rich collection of contemporary art and other city exhibits. Amid the clutter is an original Viking ship (discovered in 1930) and a 17th-century dollhouse complete with period furniture, porcelain, and miniature old masters. *Agnietenstraat 1, tel. 030/362362. Admission: Fl. 2.75. Open Tues.–Sat. 10–5, Sun. 1–5.*

An important part of the Central Museum's collection is a house that is located just a few blocks away; it is known as the **Rietveld Schröder House.** Designed in 1924 by the architect Gerrit Rietveld working with Truus Schröeder, this is considered to be the architectural pinnacle of the style known as De Stijl (The Style). The use of primary colors (red, yellow, blue) and black and white, and the definition of the interior space are unique and innovative even today. The experience of the house is, as one art historian phrased it, "like wandering into a Mondrian painting." The house was completely restored to its original condition in 1987. Allow 15 minutes to walk to the house; there is a guided tour through the rooms. *Prins Hendrikiaan 50, tel. 030/517926. Admission: Fl. 9. Open Tues.–Sun. 12:30–5.*

Gouda   West of Utrecht, 36 kilometers (22 miles) along the A12, you'll come to **Gouda,** famous for its cheese. Try to be there on a Thursday morning in July or August, when the cheese market, centered around the **Waag,** or Weigh House, is held. Brightly colored farm wagons are loaded high with orange cheeses. Take a good look at the **Stadhuis** (Town Hall); it's one of Holland's quaintest, with parts dating to 1449. (Admission: Fl. 1. Open weekdays 10–4.) After trying all five types of Gouda cheese, leave some space for syrup waffles, the city's other specialty.

By the side of the market square is **Sint Janskerk** (Church of St. John); what you see today was built during the 16th century. It has the longest nave in the country, and 70 glorious stained-glass windows, the oldest of which dates from 1555. Around the corner from the cathedral is the Catharina Gasthuis, now the **Stedelijk Museum Het Catharina Gasthuis,** the municipal museum that houses many unusual exhibits, including a fearsome medieval torture chamber and an equally horrific operating room. *Oosthaven 9, Achter de Kerk 14. Admission: Fl. 3. Open Mon.–Sat. 10–5, Sun. 1–5.*

Leiden   Heading north on N11, you'll come to the ancient city of **Leiden,** renowned for its spirit of religious and intellectual tolerance and known for its university and royal connections. Start at the **Lakenhal,** built in 1639 for the city's cloth merchants and now an art gallery, cloth, and antiques museum. Pride of place in the collection goes to the 16th- and 17th-century Dutch paintings, with works by Steen; Dou; Rembrandt; and, above all, Lucas van Leyden's *Last Judgment*—the first great Renaissance painting in what is now the Netherlands. Other rooms are devoted to furniture and to the history of Leiden's medieval guilds: the drapers, tailors, and brewers. *Oude Singel 32. Admission: Fl. 3. Open Tues.–Sat. 10–5, Sun. 1–5.*

Near the Lakenhal is the **Molenmuseum De Valk** (Windmill Museum), housed in an original windmill, built in 1747, which was worked by 10 generations of millers until 1964. The seven floors still contain the original workings, an old forge, washrooms, and living quarters. On summer Saturdays, the mill turns—but for pleasure, not business. *2e Binnenvesstgracht 1a. Admission: Fl. 3. Open Tues.–Sat. 10–5, Sun. 1–5.*

Crossing the canal and walking into narrow, bustling Breestraat, you'll come to the imposing **St. Pieterskerk,** with its memories of the Pilgrim Fathers who worshiped here and of their spiritual leader, John Robinson, who is buried here. A narrow street by the **Persijnhofje** almhouse, dating from 1683, takes you downhill, across the gracious Rapenburg Canal. In Leiden, as in most old Dutch towns, the aristocracy continues to live in the center. The tree-lined canal is crossed by triple-arched bridges and bordered by stately 18th-century houses, including the prince's current home.

Continuing on, you find the **Academie** (university) and the **Hortus Botanicus** gardens. The university was founded by William the Silent as a reward to Leiden for its victory against the Spanish in the 1573–74 siege. During the war, the dikes were opened and the countryside flooded so that the rescuing navy could sail right up to the city walls. Members of the royal family generally attend Leiden's university, a tradition maintained by the present crown prince. Founded in 1587, these botanical gardens are among the oldest in the world. The highlights are a faithful reconstruction of a 16th-century garden, the herb garden, the colorful orangery, and the ancient trees. *Rapenburg 73. Admission: Fl. 1.50. Open Apr.–Oct., weekdays 9–4:30, weekends 10:30–3; Nov.–Mar., weekdays 9–4:30, Sun. 10:30–3.*

Follow Keiserstraat out of Rapenburg and turn left into Boisotkade. On your left is the **Pilgrim Fathers Documentatie Centrum.** This tiny museum contains photocopies of documents and maps related to the Pilgrims during their stay in Leiden, before they went to Delftshaven on the first stage of their arduous voyage to the New World. *Vliet 45. Admission free. Open weekdays 9:30–4:30.*

Lisse/Aalsmeer   North from Leiden toward Haarlem, you can stop to visit (in spring only) the 70-acre **Keukenhof Gardens.** Set in a park intersected by canals and lakes, the world's largest flower show draws huge spring crowds to its regimental lines of tulips, hyacinths, and daffodils. (A lazier way of seeing the flowers is from the windows of the Leiden–Haarlem train.) *Admission: Fl. 13. Open Easter–late May, daily 8–7:30.*

During the rest of the year, or certainly as a complement to a spring visit to Keukenhof, you will want to see how flowers are marketed. Flowers are very big business to the Dutch, and the Netherlands is home to the world's largest complex of flower auction houses. The biggest of these auction facilities (it also is the single largest in the world) is the **Bloemenveiling** (Flower Auction) in the town of Aalsmeer near the national airport and not far from Amsterdam. In a building the size of three football fields, there are three separate auction rooms all functioning at the same time. Flowers, plants, greens, and even dried flowers are bought and sold in staggering quantities five days a week, year round. Get there early; it's all over by 10 AM. *Legmeerdijk 313, tel. 02977/34567. Open weekdays 7:30–11 AM. Closed weekends and holidays.*

Haarlem   With its secret inner courtyards and pointed gables, **Haarlem** can resemble a 17th-century canvas, even one painted by Frans Hals, the city's greatest painter. The area around the **Grote Markt,** the market square, provides an architectural stroll through the 17th and 18th centuries. Some of the facades are adorned with such homilies as "The body's sickness is a cure for the soul." Haarlem's religious faith can also be sensed in any of its 20 almshouses. The **Stadhuis** (Town Hall) was once a hunting lodge. Nearby is the **Vleeshal,** or meat market, which has an especially fine gabled front. This dates from the early 1600s and is now used as an art gallery and a museum of local history. *Lepelstraat. Admission free. Open Mon.–Sat. 10–5, Sun. 1–5.*

Across from the Vleeshal is the **Grote Kerk,** dedicated to St. Bavo. The church, built between 1400 and 1550, houses one of Europe's most famous organs. This massive instrument has 5,000 pipes, and both Mozart and Handel played on it. It is still used for concerts, and an annual organ festival is held here in July. Make your way down Damstraat, behind the Grote Kerk, and turn left at the **Waag** (Weigh House). On the left is the **Teylers Museum,** which claims to be the oldest museum in the country. It was founded by a wealthy merchant in 1778 as a museum of science and the arts; it now houses a fine collection of The Hague school of painting as well as a collection of drawings and sketches by Michelangelo, Raphael, and other non-Dutch masters. Since the canvases in this building are lit by natural light, try to see the museum on a sunny day. *Spaarne 16. Admission: Fl. 4. Open Tues.–Sat. 10–5, Sun. 1–5.*

Follow the Binnen Spaarn and turn right into Kampervest and then Gasthuisvest. On your right, in Groot Heiligland, you'll find the **Frans Hals Museum.** This museum, in what used to be a 17th-century hospice, contains a marvelous collection of the artist's work; his paintings of the guilds of Haarlem are particularly noteworthy. The museum also has works by Hals's contemporaries. *Groot Heiligland 62. Admission: Fl. 4.50. Open Mon.–Sat. 11–5, Sun. 1–5.*

Dining and Lodging

In towns such as Apeldoorn and Gouda, which have few good hotels, bed-and-breakfast accommodations, booked through the VVV office, make a more interesting choice. Rooms in Utrecht are often in short supply, so book in advance or immediately upon arrival. For details and price-category definitions, *see* Dining and Lodging in Staying in Holland.

Apeldoorn
Dining

De Echoput. Near to Het Loo, this delightful restaurant is a member of the Alliance Gastronomique Nederlandaise, a guarantee of an expensive meal of local and gourmet specialties. There is an attractive terrace, overlooking fountains and greenery, for summer dining. *Amersfoortseweg 86, tel. 057691248. Reservations required. AE, DC, MC, V. Closed Sat. lunch, Mon. Very Expensive.*

Lodging

Hotel de Keizerskroon. A perfect complement to the nearby royal palace is a stay at the Keizerskroon (the name means King's Crown). In style and amenities it is a business hotel; in comfort and cordiality it is a traveler's hotel; in setting—at the edge of the city on a quiet street leading toward the woods—it is a weekend getaway inn. *Koningstraat 7, tel. 055/217744. 101 rooms with bath. AE, DC, MC, V. Expensive.*

Gouda
Dining

D'Ouwe Stee. If the weather permits, dine on the waterside terrace; if not, the antique Dutch interior is just as charming. Though about 4 miles out of town, the trip is worth it for the fresh seafood; try the *maatjes haring* (raw herring). *'s-Gravenbroekseweg 80, Reeuwijk, tel. 01829/4008. Reservations advised. AE, DC, MC. Closed Tues. Expensive.*

Haarlem
Dining
★

Café de la Paix. A stained-glass ceiling and Tiffany-style lamps reflect a stunning art deco atmosphere. Rock lobster with truffles, fillet of ostrich in Calvados sauce, and similar dishes are served to the accompaniment of live musical entertainment (lunch and dinner). *Baan 7, tel. 023/19091. Reservations advised. AE, DC, MC, V. Expensive.*

Lodging **Golden Tulip Lion d'Or.** Situated just five minutes from the old city center and conveniently near the railway station, this comfortable but unprepossessing hotel offers all the luxuries associated with a Golden Tulip hotel. Special weekend deals include reduced room prices, gourmet evening meals, and free cocktails. *Kruisweg 34–36, tel. 023/321750. 38 rooms with bath. Facilities: restaurant, conference rooms. AE, DC, MC, V. Expensive.*

Leiden **Oudt Leiden Pannekoekenhuijsje.** This Old Dutch restaurant is
Dining in fact two contrasting restaurants run by the same management, from the same kitchen. One is famous for its roast meats and seafood specialties; the other is a pancake house that serves hearty *pannekochen* (pancakes) on huge plates. *Steenstraat 51, tel. 071/13344. Reservations advised. AE, DC, MC. Closed Sat. lunch and Sun. Moderate–Expensive.*

Jill's. A delightful, bright restaurant run by a cheerful staff and situated off the main square, this spot is ideal for a relaxing meal. A variety of set menus allows you to find something to satisfy almost every palate. Try the fish. *Morsstraat 6. AE, MC. Moderate.*

Dining and Lodging **Nieuw Minerva.** This family-run hotel is a conversion of eight
★ 15th-century buildings. While the original part of the hotel is decorated in Old Dutch style, the newer part is better equipped but has slightly less character. Many of the rooms overlook a quiet tributary of the Rhine. The restaurant caters to most tastes and pockets. The excellent three-course tourist menu offers separate fish, meat, and vegetarian menus. A monthly menu is served with four or six courses of one own's choice. Delicacies are also found on the à la carte menu. *Boommarkt 23, tel. 071/126358. 40 rooms, 30 with bath or shower. Facilities: restaurant. AE, DC, MC, V. Moderate.*

Lodging **Hotel De Doelen.** This small hotel is situated in a characteristic patrician house. The spartan decor is in keeping with the character of the 15th-century house, but the 11 rooms are comfortable and much sought after. *Rapenburg 2, tel. 071/120527. 9 rooms with bath. AE, DC, MC, V. Moderate.*

Utrecht **Het Draeckje.** This typical Dutch restaurant is set in a vaulted
Dining cellar on Utrecht's loveliest canal. It offers a seasonal Dutch menu at reasonable prices. Coffee is accompanied by the local spicy biscuits. *Oudegracht 114–120, tel. 030/321999. Reservations advised on weekends. AE, DC, MC. Closed Sun. Moderate.*

Town Castle Oudaen/"Between Heaven and Earth." In medieval times Utrecht's Oudegracht (Old Canal) was lined with many "town castles" such as this one, and some would say that along with the Dom Tower, this is one of the finest examples of medieval architecture in Utrecht. As a restaurant it is a curious place. You may be confused by the clublike atmosphere as you enter, but you'll find the dining room on the second floor (which may be why it is called "Between Heaven and Earth"). Another unique feature of the Oudaen is that they brew their own beer in the basement and, in addition to serving it on tap, use it as an ingredient in many of their dishes. *Oudegracht 99, tel. 030/*

311864. Reservations accepted. AE, DC, MC, V. Closed lunch (except public house). Moderate.

Lodging **Malie.** The Malie hotel is on a quiet leafy street, a five-minute walk from the old center. This small, friendly hotel has an attractive breakfast room overlooking the garden and terrace. *Maliestraat 2–4, tel. 030/316424. 30 rooms with bath or shower. Facilities: bar, breakfast room. AE, DC, MC, V. Moderate.*

The Hague, Delft, and Rotterdam

Within this itinerary you can visit the Netherlands' most dignified and spacious city—the royal, diplomatic, and governmental seat of Den Haag (in English, better known as The Hague)—and its close neighbor, the leading North Sea beach resort of Scheveningen. Also nearby are Delft, a historic city with many canals and ancient buildings, and the energetic and thoroughly modern international port city of Rotterdam. It is known to the Dutch as "Manhattan on the Maas," both for its office towers and its cultural attractions.

Getting Around

The Hague and Delft are each about 60 kilometers (37½ miles) southwest of Amsterdam and can be reached within less than an hour by fast and frequent trains. The heart of both towns is compact enough to be explored on foot. Scheveningen is reached from The Hague's center by bus or tram. Travelers will find public transportation more convenient than driving because of severe parking problems at the resort. The RET Metro is an easy-to-use option for getting around Rotterdam. There are two lines, blue and red (north–south and east–west), and they cross in the heart of the business district at a major transfer center, which connects one line to the other.

Guided Tours

Boat Trips From The Hague, various boat companies run short day trips and longer candlelight dinner cruises. These can be booked at The Hague VVV or through **Rondvaartbedrijf RVH** (Spui 256, near the central station, tel. 070/3462473). Scheveningen offers fishing-boat tours around the Dutch coast. Contact **Sportsviscentrum Trip** 3 (Scheveningen, tel. 070/3541122). In Delft, the VVV organizes boat tours along the unspoiled canal system.

Depending on the time available (or the time of year) and the extent of your interest, you can cruise the port of Rotterdam on a basic tour of 1¼ hours (year-round) or choose one that lasts as long as 9 hours (midsummer only). **Spido Havenrondvaarten** (Willemsplein, tel. 06/4135400), the main boat company, also operates summer evening music-and-dinner cruises of the inner harbor. The 1¼-hour tour costs Fl. 12. The pier can be reached by taking the Metro blue line toward Spijkenisse to the Leuvehaven station and walking to the end of the boulevard.

Orientation Tours City sightseeing tours of The Hague can be arranged by or through the main VVV office next to the central station. The size and diversity of the city make a bus tour a logical choice.

The Hague, Delft, and Rotterdam

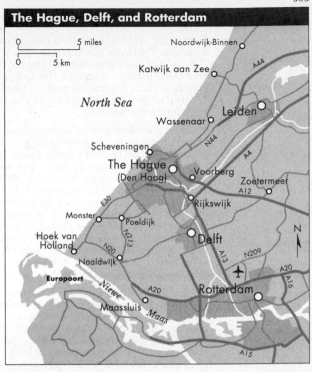

The "Royal Bus Tour" leaves from outside the VVV office at 1:30 every day between April and October. The 3½-hour trip includes background on the royal family and takes passengers past Queen Beatrix's residences. Book in advance at the VVV; cost: Fl. 19.

Scheveningen and Delft are best seen on foot. The Delft VVV office organizes tours, while the Scheveningen VVV will advise on coastal strolls.

In the long summer season (April through September), there are daily one-hour tram tours of Rotterdam conducted by the Rotterdam Tourist Office. The tours, which leave from the central station at 1:15 PM, cost Fl. 12. The same tour, also starting at the central station, followed by a tour of the port, takes 2½ hours and costs Fl. 21.50.

Tourist Information

Delft (Markt 85, tel. 015/126100).
The Hague (Babylon Center, Koningin Julianaplein 30, next to the central station, tel. 070/3546200).
Rotterdam (Coolsingel 67, in Centraal Station, tel. 06/34034065).
Scheveningen (Gevers Deynootweg 126, tel. 070/3546200).

If you're planning to spend a few days in The Hague or Rotterdam, ask for the VVV brochure on city events and entertainment. Tickets for concerts and other entertainment can be reserved in person at the VVV office.

Exploring The Hague, Delft, and Rotterdam

The Hague During the 17th century, when Dutch maritime power was at its zenith, **The Hague** was known as "The Whispering Gallery of Europe" because it was thought to be the secret manipulator of European politics. Although the Golden Age is over, The Hague remains a powerful world diplomatic capital, quietly boastful of its royal connections. It also is the seat of government for the Netherlands.

Its heart is the **Hofvijver** reflecting pool and the complex of gracious **Parliament Buildings** reflected in it. At the center of it all is the **Ridderzaal** (Knight's Hall). Inside are vast beams spanning a width of 18 meters (59 feet), flags, and stained-glass windows. A sense of history pervades the 13th-century great hall. It is now used mainly for ceremonies: Every year the queen's gilded coach brings her here to open Parliament. The two government chambers sit separately in buildings on either side of the Ridderzaal and can be visited by guided tour only when Parliament is not in session. Tours in English are conducted by Stichting Bezoekerscentrum Binnenhof (tel. 070/3646144), located just to the right of the Ridderzaal. Groups should book in advance. *Binnenhof 8a. Open Mon.–Sat. 10–4. Cost: Fl. 4.*

On the far side of the **Binnenhof**, the inner court of the Parliament complex, is a small, well-proportioned Dutch Renaissance building called the **Mauritshuis,** one of the finest small art museums in the world. This diminutive 17th-century palace contains a feast of art from the same period, including six Rembrandts; of these the most powerful is *The Anatomy Lesson of Dr. Tulp*, a theatrical work depicting a gruesome dissection of the lower arm. Also featured are Vermeer's celebrated *Girl Wearing a Turban* and his masterpiece, the glistening *View of Delft*, moodily emerging from a cloudburst. *Korte Vijverberg 8. Admission: Fl. 6.50. Open Tues.–Sat. 10–5, Sun. 11–5.*

Outside the Mauritshuis, follow the Korte Vijverberg past the reflecting pool, which is bordered by patrician houses with revamped 18th- and 19th-century facades, a sign of the area's continuing popularity with the local aristocracy. Only the presence of huge ducks ruffles the surface of this stately lake.

Turn right at Lange Vijverberg and walk a short way until you come to Lange Voorhout, a large L-shaped boulevard. During the last century, horse-drawn trams clattered along its cobbles and deposited dignitaries outside the various palaces. Apart from the trams, not much has changed. Diplomats still eat in the historic Hotel des Indes. For more than 100 years, Hotel des Indes has hosted ambassadors and kings, dancers and spies. Memories of famous guests remain in the form of Emperor Haile Selassie's gold chair and the ballerina Anna Pavlova's silver candlesticks. Pavlova and the spy Mata Hari both have suites named for them. No. 34 once belonged to William I, the first king of the Netherlands, but later it became the royal library; it is now the **Supreme Court.** With its clumsy skewed gable, the headquarters of the Dutch Red Cross at No. 6 seems out of place on this stately avenue. A few doors down, at the corner of Parkstraat, is The Hague's oldest church, the **Kloosterkerk,** built in 1400 and once used by the Black Friars. During the spring, the adjoining square is covered with yellow and purple crocuses; on Thursdays during the summer, it is the scene of a colorful antiques market.

North of Lange Voorhout is the **Panorama Mesdag,** a 122-meter (400-foot) painting-in-the-round that shows the nearby seaside town of Scheveningen as it looked in 1880. Housed in a specially designed building, the painting encircles you. Hendrik Mesdag was a late-19th-century marine painter, and his calming seascape is painted in the typically melancholic colors of The Hague School. Mesdag was assisted by his wife, who painted much of the fishing village, and by a friend, who painted the sky and dunes. *Zeestraat 65b, tel. 070/3642563. Admission: Fl. 4. Open Mon.–Sat. 10–5, Sun. noon–5.*

Just around the corner in Laan van Meerdervoort is the painter's home, now transformed into the **Rijksmuseum H.W. Mesdag.** Paintings by Mesdag and members of The Hague School are hung beside those of Corot, Courbet, and Rousseau. These delicate landscapes represent one of the finest collections of Barbizon School painting outside France. *Laan van Meerdervoort 7f. Admission: Fl. 3.50. Open Tues.–Sat. 10–5, Sun. 1–5.*

The **Vredespaleis** (Peace Palace), near Laan van Meerdervoort, is a monument to world peace through negotiation. Following the first peace conference at The Hague in 1899, the Scottish-American millionaire Andrew Carnegie donated $1.5 million for the construction of a building to house a proposed international court. The Dutch government donated the grounds, and other nations offered furnishings and decorations. Although it still looks like a dull multinational bank, the building has been improved by such gifts as Japanese wall hangings, a Danish fountain, and a grand staircase presented by The Hague. Today the **International Court of Justice,** consisting of 15 jurists, has its seat here. There are guided tours when the court is not in session. *Carnegieplein 2, tel. 070/3469680. Admission: Fl. 3. Open weekdays 10–noon and 2–4.*

The nearby **Haags Gemeentemuseum** (Municipal Art Museum) is the home of the largest collection of Mondrians in the world plus two vast collections of musical instruments—European and non-European. The building itself is also fascinating. It was built in 1935 and is an example of the International Movement in modern architecture. *Stadhouderslaan 41. Admission: Fl. 6. Open Tues.–Sun. 11–5.*

The Hague is a city of parks, the biggest of which is the **Zorgvliet,** separating city from countryside. Opposite the park is the **Omniversum,** described as Europe's first space theater. It is housed in a cylindrical building with a 23-meter (75-foot) dome that acts as a screen for the projection of six–10 daily video presentations of outer space and oceanic voyages. *President Kennedylaan 5, tel. 070/3545454 for reservations and show times. Admission: Fl. 14. Open Tues.–Thurs. 11–4, Fri.–Sun. 11–9.*

Between The Hague and Scheveningen is **Madurodam,** a miniature Holland where the country's important buildings and facilities are duplicated at a scale of 1/52 of what its life-size counterpart would be. None of the details has been forgotten, from the harbor, with its lighthouse and quayside cranes, to the hand-carved furniture in the gabled houses. Son-et-lumière (sound-and-light) shows are planned for the summer months. *Haringkade 17, tel. 070/3553900. Admission: Fl. 11 adults, Fl.*

*6 children. Open late March–May, 9 AM–10:30 PM; June–Aug.,
9 AM–11 PM; Sept., 9 AM–9:30 PM; Oct.–early Jan., 9–6.*

Scheveningen is adjacent to The Hague along the North Sea
coast. A fishing village since the 14th century, it became popular as a beach resort during the last century, when the grand
Kurhaus Hotel was built, which still is a focal point of this beach
community.

The beach itself, protected from tidal erosion by stone jetties,
slopes gently into the North Sea in front of a high promenade
whose function is to protect the boulevard and everything behind it from winter storms. The surface of the beach is fine
sand, and you can bicycle or walk for miles to the north.

At the turn of the century, the **Kurhaus Hotel** stood alone at the
center of the beach as a fashionable and aristocratic resort. After being in decline for a long time, it was restored and reopened, having added a casino among its new attractions.
There is a painted ceiling over the large central court and buffet
restaurant.

Part of the new design around the Kurhaus area includes the
Golfbad, a surf pool complete with artificial waves. **The Pier,**
completed in 1962, stretches 372 meters (1,200 feet) into the
sea. Its four circular end buildings provide a sun terrace and
restaurant, a 43-meter- (141-foot-) high observation tower, an
amusement center with children's play area, and an underwater panorama. At 11 on summer evenings, the Pier is the scene
of dramatic fireworks displays.

Delft   Thirteen kilometers (8 miles) along the A13 from The Hague,
you'll enter **Delft.** There is probably no town in the Netherlands
that is more intimate, more attractive, or more traditional than
this mini-metropolis, whose famous blue-and-white earthenware is popular throughout the world. Compact and easy to explore, despite its web of canals, Delft is best discovered on
foot—although canal boat excursions are available April
through October, as are horse-drawn trams that leave from the
marketplace. Every street is lined with attractive medieval
Gothic and Renaissance houses that bear such names as
Wijnhaus (Wine House) and Boter Brug (Butter Bridge).

In the marketplace, the only lively spot in this tranquil town, is
the **Nieuwe Kerk** (New Church), built during the 14th century,
with its piercing Gothic spire 93 meters (300 feet) high, a magnificent carillon of 48 bells, and the tomb of William the Silent.
Beneath this grotesque black marble sarcophagus is a crypt
containing the remains of members of the Orange-Nassau line,
including all members of the royal family since King William I
ascended the throne during the mid-16th century. *Admission:
Fl. 2. Tower: Fl. 3.25. Open May–Sept., Tues.–Sat. 10–4:30,
also Mon. 10–4:30 in midsummer.*

Walk around the right side of the Nieuwe Kerk, then left at the
back and along the Vrouwenregt canal for a few steps before
taking another left turn into Voldergracht. To the left, the
backs of the houses rise straight from the water as you stroll to
the end of the street, which is marked by the sculptured animal
heads and outdoor stairs of the old **Meat Market** on the right.
Cross the Wijnhaven and turn left along its far side to the
Koornmarkt, a stately canal spanned by a high, arching bridge
that is one of the hallmarks of Delft.

Turn right at the Peperstraat to reach the **Oude Delft canal,** the city's oldest waterway. A few blocks farther along the canal is the **Prinsenhof,** formerly the Convent of St. Agatha, founded in 1400. The chapel inside dates from 1471; its interior is remarkable for the wooden statues under the vaulting ribs. Today the Prinsenhof is a museum that tells the story of the liberation of the Netherlands after 80 years of Spanish occupation (1568–1648). For Dutch royalists, the spot is significant for the assassination of Prince William of Orange in 1584; the bullet holes can still be seen in the wall. *St. Agathaplein 1. Admission: Fl. 3.50. Open Tues.–Sat. 10–5, Sun. 1–5.*

Across the Oude Delft canal is the **Oude Kerk** (Old Church), a vast Gothic monument of the 13th century. Its beautiful tower, surmounted by a brick spire, leans somewhat alarmingly. *Oudegracht. Admission: Fl. 2. Open Apr.–Nov. 10–5.*

Beyond the Prinsenhof on the same side of the Oude Delft canal is the **Lambert van Meerten Museum,** a mansion whose timbered rooms are filled with the country's most complete collection of old Dutch tiles as well as Delft pottery. *Oude Delft 199. Admission: Fl. 3.50. Open Tues.–Sat. 10–5, Sun. 1–5. Also Mon. 1–5 in summer.*

While in Delft, you will want to see the famous local specialty— Delftware. Decorated porcelain was brought to Holland from China on East India Company ships and was so much in demand that Dutch potters felt their livelihood was being threatened. They therefore set about creating pottery to rival Chinese porcelain. There are only two manufacturers that still make hand-painted Delftware: **De Delftse Pauw** and the more famous "Royal" **De Porceleyne Fles.** *De Delftse Pauw: Delftweg 133, tel. 015/124920. Admission free. Open Apr.–mid–Oct., daily 9–4; mid–Oct.–Mar., weekdays 9–4, weekends 11–1. De Porceleyne Fles: Rotterdamsweg 196, tel. 015/560234. Admission free. Open Apr.–Oct., Mon.–Sat. 9–5, Sun. 10–4; Nov.–Mar., weekdays 9–5, Sat. 10–4.*

Rotterdam   Thirteen kilometers (8 miles) farther along A13 is **Rotterdam,** one of the few thoroughly modern cities in the Netherlands and the site of the world's largest and busiest port. Art lovers know Rotterdam for its extensive and outstanding collection of art; philosophers recall it as the city of Erasmus. It is a major stop on the rock 'n' roll concert circuit, and its soccer team is well known. Rotterdam is lively and full of surprises.

The biggest surprise in Rotterdam is the remarkable 30-mile-long **Europoort,** which handles more than 250 million tons of cargo every year and more ships than any other port in the world. It is the delta for three of Europe's most important rivers (the Rhine, the Waal, and the Meuse/Maas) and a seemingly endless corridor of piers, warehouses, tank facilities, and efficiency. You can get to the piers at Willemsplein by tram or Metro (blue line to the Leuvehaven station) from the central station. The 1¼-hour harbor tour (*see* Boat Trips in Guided Tours, *above*) illuminates Rotterdam's vital role in world trade.

As an alternative to the boat tour, you also can survey the harbor from the vantage point of the **Euromast** observation tower. Get there via the Metro red line to Dijkszicht. *Parkhaven 20, tel. 010/4364811. Admission: Fl. 13. Open mid-Mar.–mid-Oct., daily 10–5; mid-Oct.–mid-Mar., daily 10–6. Jan.–Feb., weekends only.*

After the harbor tour, walk down the boulevard past the Metro station into Leuvehaven. On your right as you stroll along the inner harbor is **IMAX Rotterdam,** a gigantic theater in which films are projected onto a screen six stories high. There are earphones for English translation. *Leuvehaven 77, tel. 06/ 4048844. Admission: Fl. 13. Shows Tues.–Sun. 1, 2, 3, 7, 8, and 9. Mon. also during holiday periods.*

Past the theater is a hodgepodge of cranes, barges, steamships, and old shipbuilding machines, even a steam-operated grain elevator. What looks at quick glance to be a sort of maritime junkyard is in fact a work in progress: Volunteers are working daily to restore these vessels and machines. The whole operation is an open-air museum of shipbuilding, shipping, and communications that is part of the **Prins Hendrick Maritime Museum,** housed in a large gray building at the head of the quay. Also moored in this inner harbor adjacent to the museum is the historic 19th-century Royal Dutch Navy warship *De Buffel.* Within the museum are exhibits devoted to the history and activity of the great port outside. *Leuvehaven 1, tel. 06/ 4132680. Open Tues.–Sat. 10–5, Sun. 11–5.*

From the nearby Churchillplein Metro station, take the red line toward Marconiplein to the first stop at Eendrachtsplein, where you will walk along the canal toward the park. As a welcome contrast to the industrial might of the Europoort and Holland's maritime history, the **Boymans–van Beuningen Museum** is an impressive refresher course in Western European art history. The collection includes paintings by many famous master painters, Dutch and otherwise, from the 14th century to the present day. There is an Old Arts section that includes the work of Brueghel, Bosch, and Rembrandt and a renowned print gallery with works by artists as varied as Dürer and Cézanne. Dali and Magritte mix with the Impressionists in the Modern Arts collection. *Mathenesserlaan 18–20, tel. 06/4419400. Admission: Fl. 3. Open Tues.–Sat. 10–5, Sun. 11–5.*

Dining and Lodging

For details and price-category definitions, *see* Dining and Lodging in Staying in Holland.

Delft **Spijshuis De Dis.** At this favorite neighborhood spot, a friendly
Dining staff serves typically Dutch delicacies. Even after a hearty meal of mussels in garlic sauce (a house specialty) or another of the myriad seafood dishes, save room for the chef's pièce de résistance: cinnamon parfait. *Beestenmarket 36, tel. 015/131782. Reservations advised. AE, DC, MC, V.*

Dining and Lodging **Hotel Grand Cafe.** This is the hot spot in central Delft for afternoon coffee or delicious hot chocolate, best enjoyed with one of the splendid desserts. Simple lunches and dinners are available. The hotel is clean, but rooms are modest in size. *Wijnhaven 6–8, tel. 015/1234, fax 015/125164. AE, DC, MC, V.*

Lodging **Hotel De Ark.** This bright, airy hotel in the center of old Delft has recently been restored by a young entrepreneur. Three canal houses have been put together, ensuring that nearly every room has a view of the canal or the large garden in back. Rooms are clean and modern. *Koornmarkt 59–65, tel. 015/157999, fax 015/144997. 22 rooms with bath. AE, DC, MC, V.*
Hotel Leeuwenbrug. This is a traditional Dutch family-style ho-

tel on one of the prettiest canals in Delft. There are two buildings, one more traditional and simpler, with smaller, cheaper
rooms; the annex is more contemporary and businesslike.
Everyone enjoys breakfast overlooking the canal, however, and
rooms on the top floor of the annex overlook the city.
*Koornmarkt 16, tel. 015/147741. 38 rooms with bath. Facilities:
parking. AE, DC, MC, V. Moderate.*

The Hague
Dining

Djawa. Whether or not it is a result of the city's diplomatic heritage is unknown, but The Hague is said to have Holland's highest concentration of Indonesian restaurants. Among them is
this cozy, family-run, neighborhood restaurant located not far
from the center. *Mallemolen 12a, tel. 070/3635763. Reservations accepted. AE, DC, MC, V. Closed lunch. Moderate–Expensive.*

't Goude Hooft. The foundations of the building on the old vegetable market square date from the early 15th century, and town
records show that ever since the 14th century there has been a
tavern of essentially the same name on the very same spot.
When the restaurant's promotions say that The Hague was
built around it, it can be taken as truth. As might be expected,
the ambience is totally Old Dutch; the menu, too, is traditional.
There is a grand terrace café on the square in the summer
months. *Groenmarkt 13, tel. 070/3469713. Reservations accepted. AE, DC, MC, V. Inexpensive–Moderate.*

Dining and Lodging

Corona. Overlooking a charming square in the center of the city
is this pride and joy of the Hague. The restaurant is one of the
best in Holland, and the hotel is first-class, too. For less expensive meals, try the brasserie. *Buitenho 39–42, tel. 070/3637930,
fax 070/3615785, AE, DC, MC, V.*

Rotterdam
Dining

Inn the Picture. This trendy café offers a wide selection of typical Dutch fare. The salads are especially inviting. In summer,
tables offer a view of passing crowds in the shopping district.
Karel Doormanstraat 294, tel. 010/4133204. MC, V.

La Gondola. The hangout of such rock stars as Michael Jackson
and Gloria Estefan—as proved by their photographs on the
wall—this small and spiffy Italian restaurant is on a side street
between Coolsingel boulevard and the Lijnbaan shopping
promenade. The menu is an uncomplicated array of Italian specialties, including pizzas. *Kruiskade 6, tel. 010/4114284. Reservations advised. AE, DC, MC, V. Lunch weekdays only.
Inexpensive.*

Dining and Lodging

Intell. Not the least of the attractions of the Hotel Intell are its
views of Rotterdam harbor—from the rooms, the restaurant,
and even from the fully equipped rooftop health club that includes an 8-by-4-meter swimming pool. This is a busy, cheerful, modern hotel located adjacent to the IMAX super theater
and near both the maritime museum and the Spido harbor tour
pier. Named Le Papillon, the Intell's restaurant is a lively, intimate dining room with the best view in the house! The menu is
traditional Continental, offering such standbys as sole Picasso
and beef stroganoff. Both the Metro and tram stop outside the
door. *Leuvehaven 80, tel. 010/4134139. 150 rooms with bath.
Facilities: parking, bar, restaurant, health club, sauna, pool.
AE, DC, MC, V. Moderate.*

15 Hungary

Hungary sits at the crossroads of Central Europe, having retained its own identity by absorbing countless invasions and foreign occupations. Its industrious, resilient people have a history of brave but unfortunate uprisings: against the Turks in the 17th century, the Habsburgs in 1848, and the Soviet Union in 1956. Each has resulted in a period of readjustment, a return to politics as the art of the possible.

The '60s and '70s saw matters improve politically and materially for the majority of Hungarians. Communist party leader János Kádár remained relatively popular at home and abroad, allowing Hungary to expand and improve trade and relations with the West. The bubble began to burst in the 1980s, however, when the economy stagnated and inflation escalated. The peaceful transition to democracy began when young reformers in the party shunted aside the aging Mr. Kádár in 1988 and began speaking openly about multiparty democracy, a market economy, and cutting ties with Moscow. Events quickly gathered pace, and by spring 1990, as the Iron Curtain fell, Hungarians went to the polls in the first free elections in 40 years. A center-right government led by Prime Minister József Antall took office, sweeping away the Communists and their renamed successor party, the Socialists, who finished fourth.

Two rivers cross the country. The famous Duna (Danube) flows from the west through Budapest on its way to the southern frontier, while the smaller Tisza flows from the northeast across the Nagyalföld (Great Plain). What Hungary lacks in size, it makes up for in beauty and charm. Western Hungary is dominated by the largest lake in Central Europe, Lake Balaton. Although some overdevelopment has blighted its splendor, its shores are still lined with Baroque villages, relaxing spas, magnificent vineyards, and shaded garden restaurants serving the catch of the day. In eastern Hungary, the Nagyalföld offers visitors a chance to explore the folklore and customs of the Magyars (the Hungarians' name for themselves and their language). It is an area of spicy food, strong wine, and the proud *csikós* (horsemen).

However, it is Budapest, a city of more than 2 million people, that draws travelers from all over the world. The hills of Buda rise from the brackish waters of the Danube, which bisects the city; on the flatlands of Pest are an imposing array of hotels, restaurants, and shopping areas. Throughout Hungary, comfortable accommodations can be found for comparatively modest prices, and there's an impressive network of inexpensive guest houses.

Hungarians are known for their hospitality and love talking to foreigners, although their strange language, which has no links to other European tongues, can be a problem. Today, however, everyone seems to be learning English, especially young people. Trying out a few words of German will delight the older generation. But what all Hungarians share is a deep love of music, and the calendar is star-studded with it, from Budapest's famous opera to its annual spring music festival and the serenades of gypsy violinists during evening meals.

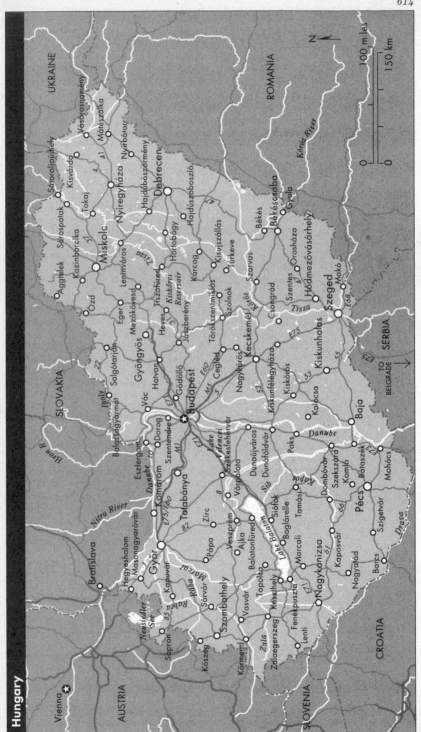

Hungary

American Express offers Travelers Cheques built for two.

American Express® Cheques *for Two*. The first Travelers Cheques that allow either of you to use them because both of you have signed them. And only one of you needs to be present to purchase them.

Cheques *for Two* are accepted anywhere regular American Express Travelers Cheques are, which is just about everywhere. So stop by your bank, AAA* or any American Express Travel Service Office and ask for Cheques *for Two*.

Travelers Cheques

Essential Information

Before You Go

When to Go Many of Hungary's major fairs and festivals take place in the spring and fall. During July and August, Budapest can be hot and the resorts at Lake Balaton crowded, so spring (May) and the end of summer (September) are the ideal times to visit.

Climate The following are average daily maximum and minimum temperatures for Budapest.

Jan.	34F	1C	May	72F	22C	Sept.	73F	23C
	25	- 4		52	11		54	12
Feb.	39F	4C	June	79F	26C	Oct.	61F	16C
	28	- 2		59	15		45	7
Mar.	50F	10C	July	82F	28C	Nov.	46F	8C
	36	2		61	16		37	3
Apr.	63F	17C	Aug.	81F	27C	Dec.	39F	4C
	45	7		61	16		30	- 1

Currency The unit of currency is the forint (Ft.), divided into 100 fillérs (f.). There are bills of 50, 100, 500, 1,000, and 5,000 forints and coins of 1, 2, 5, 10, and 20 forints and 10, 20, and 50 fillérs. The tourist exchange rate was approximately 88 Ft. to the dollar and 130 Ft. to the pound sterling at press time (spring 1993). Note that official exchange rates are adjusted at frequent intervals.

Hungary does not require you to change a certain sum of money for each day of your stay. Exchange money as you need it at banks, hotels, or travel offices, but take care not to change too much, because although in theory you can change back 50% of the original sum when you leave (up to U.S. $100), it may prove difficult in practice—at least until the forint becomes convertible.

Most credit cards are accepted, though don't rely on them in smaller towns or less expensive accommodations and restaurants. Eurocheque holders can cash personal checks in all banks and in most hotels. American Express, which now has a full-service office in Budapest (V Deák Ferenc utca 10, tel. 1/ 1374–394, 1/2510–010, or 1/2515–500; fax 1/2525–220), also dispenses cash to its cardholders.

There is still a black market in hard currency, but changing money on the street is illegal and the bank rate almost always comes close. Stick with official exchange offices.

What It Will Cost Although first-class hotel chains in Budapest charge standard international prices, quality hotels are still modest by Western standards. Even though the introduction of value-added tax (VAT) in 1988 has increased many of the prices in the service industry by up to 25%, and the annual inflation rate is 25%, enjoyable vacations with all the trimmings remain less expensive than in nearby Western cities like Vienna.

Sample Prices Cup of coffee, 60 Ft.; bottle of beer, 100 Ft.–120 Ft.; soft drinks, 20 Ft.–50 Ft.; ham sandwich, 100 Ft.; 1-mile taxi ride, 50 Ft.; museum admission, 30 Ft.–50 Ft.

Visas Only a valid passport is required of U.S., British, and Canadian citizens. For additional information, contact the Hungarian Embassy in the United States (3910 Shoemaker St., NW, Washington, DC 20008, tel. 202/362–6730) or Canada (7 Delaware Ave., Ottawa KP2 OZ2, Ontario, tel. 613/234–8316), or the Hungarian Consulate in London (35b Eaton Pl., London SW1 8BY, tel. 071/235–2664).

Customs
On Arrival Objects for personal use may be imported freely. If you are over 16, you may also bring in 250 grams of tobacco, plus 2 liters of wine, 1 liter of spirits, and 250 grams of perfume. A 30% customs charge is made on gifts valued in Hungary at more than 10,000 Ft.

On Departure Take care when you leave Hungary that you have the right documentation for exporting goods. Keep receipts of any items bought from Konsumtourist, Intertourist, or Képcsarnok Vállalat. A special permit is needed for works of art valued at more than 1,000 Ft.

Language Hungarian (Magyar) tends to look and sound intimidating to everyone at first because it is a non-Indo-European language. However, most people in the tourist trade, from bus drivers to waiters, speak some English or German.

Getting Around

By Car
Documentation To drive in Hungary, U.S. and Canadian visitors need an International Driver's License, and U.K. visitors may use their own domestic license.

Road Conditions There are three classes of roads: highways (designated by the letter M and a single digit), secondary roads (designated by a two-digit number), and minor roads (designated by a three-digit number). Highways and secondary roads are generally excellent. The condition of minor roads varies considerably. There are no toll charges on highways.

Rules of the Road Hungarians drive on the right and observe the usual Continental rules of the road. The speed limit in developed areas is 50 kph (30 mph), on main roads 80 kph (50 mph), and on highways 120 kph (75 mph). Seat belts are compulsory and drinking strictly prohibited—the penalties are very severe.

Gasoline Gas stations are plentiful in and around major cities, and major chains are also opening modern all-service stations on highways in the provinces. A gallon of gasoline *(benzin)* costs about $4. Unleaded gasoline, only slightly more expensive, is usually available at all stations, as is diesel. Interag Shell and Áfor stations at busy traffic centers stay open all night; elsewhere, from 6 AM to 8 PM.

Breakdowns The **Hungarian Automobile Club** runs a 24-hour "Yellow Angels" breakdown service from Budapest XIV (Francia Út 38/A, tel. 1/2528–000). There are repair stations in all the major towns and emergency telephones on the main highways.

By Train Travel by train from Budapest to other large cities or to Lake Balaton is cheap and efficient. Remember to take *gyorsvonat* (express trains) and not *személyvonat* (locals), which are extremely slow. A *helyjegy* (seat reservation), which costs 50 Ft. and is sold up to 60 days in advance, is advisable for all express trains, especially for weekend travel in summer. It is also worth paying a little extra for first-class tickets.

Fares Unlimited-travel tickets for 7 or 10 days are inexpensive—3,280 Ft. and 4,920 Ft., respectively. All students with a valid I.D. receive 50% off; senior citizens get a 20% discount. InterRail cards are available for those under 26, and the Rail Europe Senior Travel Pass entitles senior citizens to a 30% reduction on all trains. Snacks and drinks can be purchased on all express trains, but the supply often runs out quickly, especially in summer, so pack a lunch just in case. For more information about rail travel, contact the **MÁV Passenger Service** (Andrássy út 35, Budapest VI, tel. 1/1228–049 or 1/1228–275).

By Bus Long-distance buses link Budapest with many main cities in Eastern and Western Europe. Services to the eastern part of the country leave from Népstadion station (tel. 1/2524–496). Buses to the west and south leave from the main Volán bus station at Erzsébet tér in the Inner City (tel. 1/1172–966). Although inexpensive, they tend to be crowded, so reserve your seat.

By Boat Hungary is well equipped with nautical transport, and Budapest is situated on a major international waterway—the Danube. Vienna is five hours away by hydrofoil, and many Hungarian resorts are accessible by hydrofoil or boat. For information about excursions or pleasure cruises, contact **MAHART Landing Stage** (Vigadó tér 1, Budapest V, tel. 1/1181–223) or **IBUSZ** (Hungarian Travel Bureau; Károly körút 3/C, Budapest VII, tel. 1/1211–000 or 1/1212–932).

By Bicycle A land of rolling hills and flat plains, Hungary lends itself to bicycling. The larger train stations around Lake Balaton rent bicycles for about 100 Ft. a day. For information about renting in Budapest, contact **Tourinform** (Sütő utca 2, tel. 1/1179–800). **IBUSZ Horse and Hobby Team** provides guided bicycle tours (Retek utca 34, tel. 1/1182–967 or 1/1183–567).

Staying in Hungary

Telephones Pay phones use 5-Ft. coins—the cost of a three-minute local
Local Calls call. Most towns in Hungary can be dialed directly—dial 06 and wait for the buzzing tone, then dial the local number.

International Calls Direct calls to foreign countries can be made from Budapest and all major provincial towns only by using the red push-button telephones, or from hotels and post offices, and by dialing 00 and waiting for the international dialing tone. The phones take 5-, 10-, and 20-Ft. coins. Gray card-operated telephones were recently installed in post offices in Budapest and throughout the Balaton region. The cards—available at post offices—save you from having to continually feed coins into the slot while you're making your call.

Operators International calls can be made through the operator by dialing 09; for operator-assisted calls within Hungary, dial 01. Be patient: The telephone system is antiquated, especially in the countryside.

Information Dial 1/1172–200 for information in English.

Mail The post offices at the Keleti (East) and Nyugati (West) train stations are open 24 hours.

Postal Rates An airmail postcard to the United States, the United Kingdom, and the rest of Western Europe costs 34 Ft., and an airmail letter costs from 44 Ft. Postcards to the United Kingdom and the rest of Western Europe cost 30 Ft., letters 40 Ft.

Receiving Mail A poste restante service, for general delivery, is available in Budapest. The address is Magyar Posta, H-1052 Budapest, Petöfi Sándor utca 17–19.

Opening and Closing Times **Banks** are open weekdays 8–1.

Museums are generally open daily from 10 to 6 and are closed on Mondays.

Shops are open weekdays 10–6, Saturday 9–1. Many shops stay open until 8 on Thursday.

National Holidays January 1; March 15 (Anniversary of 1848 Revolution); April 3 and 4 (Easter and Easter Monday); May 1 (Labor Day); May 22 and 23 (Pentecost); August 20 (St. Stephen's and Constitution Day); October 23 (1956 Revolution Day); December 25 and 26.

Dining There are plenty of good, affordably priced restaurants offering a variety of Hungarian dishes. Meats, rich sauces, and creamy desserts predominate, but the health-conscious will also find salads, even out of season. There are self-service restaurants *(önkiszolgáló étterem)*, snack bars *(bistró* or *étel bár)*, buffets *(büfé)*, cafés *(eszpresszó)*, and bars *(drink-bár)*. The pastry shops *(cukrászda)* are also worth a try.

In almost all restaurants, an inexpensive fixed-price lunch, called a *menü*, is available, usually for as little as 350 Ft. It includes soup or salad, an entrée, and a dessert.

Mealtimes Hungarians eat early—you risk off-hand service and cold food after 9 PM. Lunch, the main meal for many, is served from noon to 2.

Dress At most moderately priced and inexpensive restaurants, casual but neat dress is acceptable.

Ratings Prices are per person and include a first course, main course, and dessert, but no wine or tip. Prices in Budapest tend to be a good 30% higher than elsewhere in Hungary. Best bets are indicated by a star ★.

Category	All Areas
Very Expensive	1,500 Ft.–3,000 Ft.
Expensive	1,000 Ft.–1,500 Ft.
Moderate	600 Ft.–1,000 Ft.
Inexpensive	400 Ft.–600 Ft.

Lodging There are few expensive hotels outside Budapest, but the mod-
Hotels erately priced hotels are generally comfortable and well-run, although single rooms with baths are scarce. Inexpensive establishments—more numerous every year as Hungarians convert unused rooms or second apartments into rental units for tourists—seldom have private baths, but plumbing is adequate almost everywhere.

Rentals Apartments in Budapest and cottages at Lake Balaton are available. Rates and reservations can be obtained from tourist offices in Hungary and abroad. A Budapest apartment might cost 15,000 Ft. a week, while a luxury cottage for two on Lake

Balaton costs around 35,000 Ft. a week. Bookings can be made in Budapest at the **IBUSZ** on Petőfi tér 3 (tel. 1/1185–707), which is open 24 hours a day, or through IBUSZ offices in the United States and Great Britain. (*See* Government Tourist Offices in Chapter 1.)

Guest Houses Also called pensions, these offer simple accommodations—well suited to people on a budget. Some offer simple breakfast facilities. Arrangements can be made through local tourist offices or travel agents abroad.

In the provinces it is safe to accept rooms that you are offered directly: They will almost always be clean and in a relatively good neighborhood, and the prospective landlord will probably not cheat you. *Szoba kiadó* (or the German *Zimmer frei*) means "Room to Rent." The rate per night for a double room in Budapest or at Lake Balaton is around 2,000 Ft., which includes the use of a bathroom but not breakfast. Reservations and referrals can also be made by any tourist office, and if you go that route, you have someone to complain to if things don't work out.

Camping The 140 campsites in Hungary are open from May through September. Rates are 500 Ft.–600 Ft. a day. There's a small charge for hot water and electricity plus an accommodations fee of 25 Ft.–75 Ft. per person per night. Children get a 50% reduction. Camping is forbidden except in appointed areas. Information can be obtained through travel agencies or through the **Hungarian Camping and Caravanning Club** (Budapest IX, Kálvin tér 9, tel. 1/1177–208).

Ratings The following price categories are in forints for a double room with bath and breakfast during the peak season; rates are even lower off-season and in the countryside, sometimes under 1,500 forints for two. For single rooms with bath, count on about 80% of the double-room rate. Best bets are indicated by a star ★.

Category	Budapest	Balaton
Very Expensive	15,000–18,000	9,000–12,000
Expensive	10,000–15,000	7,000– 9,000
Moderate	6,000–10,000	3,500– 7,000
Inexpensive	2,000– 6,000	1,500– 3,500

During the peak season (June through August), full board may be compulsory at the Lake Balaton hotels. During the off-season (in Budapest, September through March; at Lake Balaton, in May and September), rates can be considerably lower than those given above.

Tipping Four decades of socialism didn't alter the Hungarian habit of tipping generously. Cloakroom and gas-pump attendants, hairdressers, waiters, and taxi drivers all expect tips. At least 10% should be added to a restaurant bill or taxi fare. If a gypsy band plays exclusively for your table, you can leave 100 Ft. in the plate discreetly provided for that purpose.

Budapest

Arriving and Departing

By Plane Hungary's international airport, **Ferihegy,** is about 22 kilometers (14 miles) southeast of the city. All **Malév** and **Lufthansa** flights operate from the new Terminal 2 (tel. 1/1578–768 or 1/1577–831); other airlines use Terminal 1 (tel. 1/1572–122). For same-day flight information, call the airport authority (tel. 1/1577–155). The staff takes its time to answer calls, and may not be cordial; be prepared.

Between the Airport and Downtown Buses to and from Erzsébet tér station (Platform 1) in downtown Budapest leave every half hour from 5 AM to 9 PM. The trip takes 30–40 minutes (longer in rush hours) and costs either 100 Ft. or 200 Ft., depending on which terminal you use. The modern minivans of the fast, friendly, and reliable Airport Shuttle service (tel. 1/1578–555) transport you to any destination in Budapest, door to door, for 500 Ft., even less than the least expensive taxi—and most employees speak English. At the airport, buy tickets in the arrivals hall near baggage claim; for your return trip, just call ahead for a pick-up. A taxi ride to the center of Budapest should cost no more than 800 Ft., and take about the same time. Avoid drivers who offer their services before you are out of the arrivals lounge.

By Train There are three main train stations in Budapest: Keleti (East), Nyugati (West), and Déli (South). Trains from Vienna usually operate from the Keleti station, while those to the Balaton depart from the Déli.

By Bus Most buses to Budapest from the western region of Hungary, including those from Vienna, arrive at **Erzsébet tér** station.

By Car The main routes into Budapest are the M1 from Vienna (via Győr) and the M7 from the Balaton.

Getting Around

Budapest is best explored on foot. The maps provided by tourist offices are not very detailed, so arm yourself with one from any of the bookshops in Váci utca or from downtown stationery shops.

By Public Transportation The public transportation system—a metro (subway), buses, streetcars, and trolleybuses—is cheap, efficient, and simple to use but closes down around midnight. However, certain trams and buses run on a limited schedule all night. A day ticket *(napijegy)* costs 150 Ft. and allows unlimited travel on all services within the city limits. You can also buy tickets for single rides for 18 Ft. from metro stations or tobacco shops. You can travel on all trams, buses, and on the subway with this ticket, but you can't change lines.

Bus, streetcar, and trolleybus tickets must be canceled on board—watch how other passengers do it. Don't get caught without a ticket: Spot checks are frequent, and you can be fined several hundred forints.

By Taxi Taxis are plentiful and a good value, but make sure that they have a meter that is working. The initial charge is 20 Ft., plus 20 Ft. per kilometer plus 6 Ft. per minute of waiting time.

There are too many taxis in Budapest, and some drivers try to charge outrageous prices. Stick with **Budataxi** (tel. 1/1294–000), **Citytaxi** (tel. 1/1533–633), **Fötaxi** (tel. 1/1222–222), or **Gabrieltaxi** (tel. 1/1555–000).

By Boat In summer a regular boat service links the north and south of the city, stopping at points on both banks, including Margitsziget (Margaret Island). From May to September boats leave from the quay at Vigadó tér on 1½-hour cruises between the Árpád and Petőfi bridges. The trip, organized by **MAHART**, runs three times a day and costs around 200 Ft. (tel. 1/1181–223).

Important Addresses and Numbers

Tourist Information **Tourinform** (Sütő utca 2 [Metro: Deák Tér], tel. 1/1179–800) is open daily 8–8. **IBUSZ Accommodation Office** (Petőfi tér 3, tel. 1/1185–707) is open 24 hours. **Budapest Tourist** (Roosevelt tér 5, tel. 1/1173–555) is also helpful. *Budapest Week* and *The Budapest Post*, two English-language newspapers that mix politics and culture, carry listings of concerts and foreign-language films.

Embassies U.S. Szabadság tér 12 (Budapest V, tel. 1/1126–450). **Canadian** Budakeszi út 32 (Budapest XII, tel. 1/1767–711). **U.K.** Harmincad utca 6 (Budapest V, tel. 1/1180–907).

Emergencies Police (tel. 07). Ambulance (tel. 04). Doctor: Ask your hotel or embassy for recommendations. U.S. and Canadian visitors are advised to take out full medical insurance. U.K. visitors are covered for emergencies and essential treatment.

English-Language Bookstores **Foreign-Language Book Store** (Budapest V, Váci utca 32), **Central Secondhand Bookshop** (V Múzeum körút 15), **Idegennyelvű Könyvesbolt** (Foreign Bookstore, V Petőfi Sándor utca 1), **Könyvért Téka** (Honvéd utca 5), **Interbright** (XII Tarsay Vilnos utca 13), **Bestsellers** (V Október 6. utca 11), and **Universum** (V Váci utca 31–33). Foreign publications—including those in English—can be bought at the reception desks of major hotels and at newsstands at major traffic centers.

Travel Agencies **American Express** (V Déak Ferenc utca 10, tel. 1/1374–394, 1/2510–010, or 1/2515–500, fax 1/2525–220). **Getz International** (V Falk Miksa utca 5, tel. 1/1120–645, fax 1/1121–014).

Guided Tours

Orientation Tours IBUSZ (*see* Important Addresses and Numbers, *above*) sponsors three-hour bus tours of the city, which operate all year and cost about 1,300 Ft. Starting from Erzsébet tér, they take in parts of both Buda and Pest.

Special-Interest Tours and Excursions IBUSZ and Budapest Tourist organize a number of unusual tours, including trips to the Buda Hills and goulash parties as well as visits to the National Gallery and Parliament and other traditional sights. These tour companies will provide personal guides on request. Several enterprising tour operators now offer oddities such as day trips to former Soviet army bases and historical excursions focusing on Budapest's remaining Communist monuments. Also check at your hotel's Hostess Desk.

Excursions farther afield include day-long trips to the *Puszta* (the Great Plain), the Danube Bend, and Lake Balaton.

Exploring Budapest

Budapest, situated on both banks of the Danube, unites the colorful hills of Buda and the wide boulevards of Pest. Though it was the site of a Roman outpost in the 1st century, the city was not actually created until 1873, when the towns of Obuda, Pest, and Buda were joined. The cultural, political, intellectual, and commercial heart of the nation beats in Budapest; for the 20% of the nation's population who live in the capital, anywhere else is simply "the country."

Much of the charm of a visit to Budapest lies in unexpected glimpses into shadowy courtyards and in long vistas down sunlit cobbled streets. Although some 30,000 buildings were destroyed during World War II and in 1956, the past lingers on in the often crumbling architectural details of the antique structures that remain and in the memories and lifestyles of Budapest's citizens.

The principal sights of the city fall roughly into three areas, each of which can be comfortably covered on foot. The Budapest hills are best explored by public transportation. Note that street names are always being changed to purge all reminders of the Communist regime. If the street you're looking for seems to have disappeared, ask any local—though he or she may well be as bewildered as you are.

Numbers in the margin correspond to points of interest on the Budapest map.

❶ ❷ Take a taxi or bus (No. 16 from **Erzsébet tér**) to **Dísz tér,** at the top of **Várhegy** (Castle Hill), where the painstaking work of reconstruction has been in progress since World War II. Having made their final stand in the Royal Palace itself, the Nazis left behind them a blackened wasteland. Under the rubble, archaeologists discovered the medieval foundations of the palace of King Matthias Corvinus, who, in the 15th century, presided over one of the most splendid courts in Europe.

❸ The **Királyi Palota** (Palace), now a vast museum complex and cultural center, can be reached on foot from Dísz tér—it is one block to the south—or by funicular railway *(Sikló)* from Clark Adám tér. The northern wing of the building is devoted to the **Legújabbkori Történeti Múzeum** (Museum of Contemporary History). The central block houses the **Magyar Nemzeti Galeria** (Hungarian National Gallery), exhibiting a wide range of Hungarian fine art, from medieval paintings to modern sculpture. Names to look for are Munkácsy, a 19th-century Romantic painter, and Csontváry, an early Surrealist whom Picasso much admired. *Dísz tér 17. Museum of Contemporary History: tel. 1/1757–533. Admission: 50 Ft. adults, children free. Hungarian National Gallery: tel. 1/1757–533. Admission: 40 Ft. adults, children free; free on Sat. Open Apr.–Oct., Tues.–Sun. 10–6; Nov.–Mar., Tues.–Sun. 10–4; closed Mon.*

The southern block contains the **Budapesti Történeti Múzeum** (Budapest History Museum). Down in the cellars are the original medieval vaults of the palace, portraits of King Matthias and his second wife, Beatrice of Aragon, and many late-14th-century statues that probably adorned the Renaissance palace. *Buda Castle Palace, Szt. György tér 2, tel. 1/1757–533, ext. 253. Same admission and hours as Hungarian National Gallery (above). Choral concerts Sun. at 11:30 (except July–Aug.).*

❹ The **Mátyás templom** (Matthias Church), northeast of Dísz tér, with its distinctive patterned roof, dates from the 13th century. Built as a mosque by the occupying Turks, it was destroyed and reconstructed in the 19th century, only to be bombed during World War II. Only the south porch is from the original structure. The Habsburg emperors were crowned kings of Hungary here, including Charles IV in 1916. High mass is celebrated every Sunday at 10 AM with an orchestra and choir.

❺ The turn-of-the-century **Halászbástya** (Fishermen's Bastion) is on your left as you leave the church. It was built as a lookout tower to protect what was once a thriving fishing settlement. Its neo-Romanesque columns and arches frame views over the city and river. Near the church, in Hess András tér, are remains of the oldest church on Castle Hill, built by Dominican friars in the 13th century. These have now been tastefully integrated into the modern Hilton hotel.

The town houses lining the streets of the Castle District are largely occupied by offices, restaurants, and diplomatic residences, but the house where Beethoven stayed in 1800 is now
❻ the **Zenetörténeti Múzeum** (Museum of Music History). *Táncsics Mihály utca 7, tel. 1/1759–011. Admission: 40 Ft. Open Wed.–Sun. 10–6, Mon. 4–9.*

❼ The remains of a **medieval synagogue** are also in the neighborhood and open to the public. On display are a number of objects relating to the Jewish community, including religious inscriptions, frescoes, and tombstones dating from the 15th century. *Táncsics Mihály utca 26. Admission: 15 Ft. Open May–Nov., Tues.–Fri. 10–4, weekends 10–6.*

❽ The **Hadtörténeti Múzeum** (Museum of Military History) is at the far end of Castle Hill. The collection includes uniforms and regalia, many belonging to the Hungarian generals who took part in the abortive uprising against Austrian rule in 1848. Other exhibits trace the military history of Hungary from the original Magyar conquest in the 9th century through the period of Ottoman rule and right to the middle of this century. *Tóth Árpád sétány 40, tel. 1/1569–522 or 1/1569–770. Admission: 20 Ft. Open Tues.–Sat. 10–5, Sun. 10–6.*

Nearby stands a monument to Abdurrahman, the last pasha of Buda, commander of the Turkish troops in Hungary, who died, sword in hand, in 1686. For a good view of the Vérmező (Blood Meadow) and the surrounding Buda hills, stroll the length of Tóth Árpád sétány, along the rampart that defended Castle Hill to the west.

The Heart of the City
❾ Cross the **Széchenyi lánchíd** (Chain Bridge) from Clark Adám tér to reach **Roosevelt tér** in Pest, with the 19th-century neoclassical Academy of Sciences on your left. Pest fans out from the **Belváros** (Inner City), which is bounded by the **Kiskörút** (Little Circular Road). The **Nagykörút** (Grand Circular Road) describes a wider semicircle from the Margaret Bridge to Petőfi Bridge. To your right, an elegant promenade, the **Korzó**, runs south along the river.

Time Out The **Bécsi Kávéház** (Vienna Coffeehouse) in the Forum Hotel serves the best coffee and cream pastries in town. *Apáczai Csere János utca 12–14.*

Állami Operaház, **17**

Belvárosi plébánia templom, **12**

Dísz tér, **2**

Erzsébet tér, **1**

Hadtörténeti Múzeum, **8**

Halászbástya, **5**

Királyi Palota, **3**

Március 15 tér, **11**

Mátyás templom, **4**

Medieval Synagogue, **7**

Mezögazdasági Múzeum, **21**

Millenneumi Emlékmü, **18**

Mücsarnok, **20**

Néprajzi Múzeum, **15**

Parlament, **14**

Roosevelt tér, **9**

Szépmüvészeti Múzeum, **19**

Szt. István Bazilika, **16**

Váci utca, **13**

Vigadó tér, **10**

Zenetörténeti Múzeum, **6**

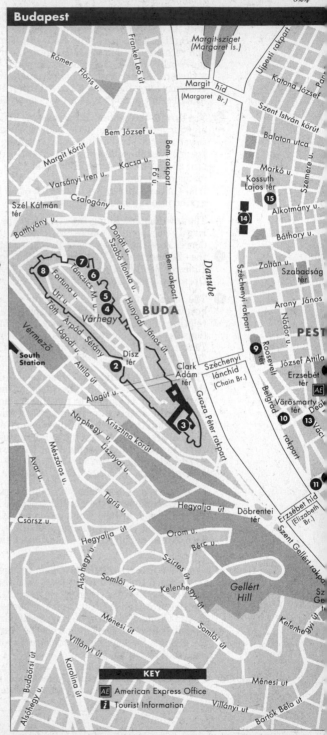

Budapest

Lehel
tér

Rippl-Rónai u.

19

Dózsa György út

18

Hősök
tere

21

20

Városliget

Olof Palme sétány

Ferdinand híd

Váci út

Szegrádi u.

Szinyei Merse u.

Bajza u.

Benczúr u.

Altosi Dürer sor

West
Station

Podmaniczky utca

Nyugati
tér

Teréz körút

Szondi u.

Rózsa u.

Felső erdősor

Városligeti fasor

Dózsa György út

Jókai u.

Aradi u.

Damjanich u.

Dembinszky u.

Nagymező u.

Andrássy (Népköztársaság) útja

Vörösmarty u.

Rottenbiller utca

István út

Lázár u.

17

Paulay Ede u.

Erzsébet körút

Hársfa u.

Thököly út

Verseny u.

East
Station

Király (Majakovszkij) u.

Klauzál u.

Baross
tér

Kerepesi út

Dob u.

Wesselényi u.

Rákóczi út

Fiumei út

Károly körút

Dohány u.

Rákóczi út

Köztársaság
tér

Kerepesi
Temető
Cemetery

ák

Kossuth L.

Múzeum körút

Puskin u.

Szentkirályi u.

József körút

Rökk Szilárd utca

Népszinház u.

Bérkocsis u.

Teleki
László
tér

Luza u.

enciek

Bródy Sándor u.

Déri Miksa u.

Mátyás
tér

Dankó u.

Veres Pálné u.

Múzeum u.

Krúdy u.

József u.

Váci u.

Kálvin
tér

Baross u.

Baross u.

Szigony u.

ndr u.

Vámház körút

Lónyai u.

Üllői út

Nap u.

Práter u.

Diószeghy Sámuel

adság híd
(Liberty Br.)

Fővám tér

Közraktár u.

Ráday u.

Ferenc körút

Tömő u.

Korányi S. u.

N

Danube

Múegyetem rakpart

Boráros
tér

Mester u.

Thaly Kálmán

Üllői út

AIRPORT

Petőfi híd
(Petőfi Br.)

Márton u.

0   440 yards

0   500 meters

⑩ A square called **Vigadó tér** is dominated by the Danube view and Vigadó concert hall, built in a Romantic mix of Byzantine, Moorish, and Romanesque styles, with Hungarian motifs thrown in for good measure. Liszt, Brahms, and Bartók all performed here. Completely destroyed during World War II, it has
⑪ been rebuilt in its original style. Another square, **Március 15 tér,** commemorates the 1848 struggle for independence from the Habsburgs with a statue of the poet Petőfi Sándor, who died later in the uprising. Every March 15, the national holiday commemorating the revolution, the square is packed with patriotic Hungarians. Behind the square is the 12th-century
⑫ **Belvárosi plébánia templom** (Inner City Parish Church), the oldest in Pest. The church has been redone in a variety of western architectural styles; even Turkish influences, such as the Muslim prayer niche, remain. Liszt, who lived only a few yards away, often played the organ here.

Parallel to the Korzó, Pest's riverside promenade, lies Buda-
⑬ pest's most upscale shopping street, **Váci utca. Vörösmarty tér,** a handsome square in the heart of the Inner City, is a good spot to sit and relax. Street musicians and sidewalk cafés make it one of the liveliest places in Budapest.

Time Out Gerbeaud, an elegant pastry shop founded in 1857, retains the old imperial style and has a terrace overlooking the square. A fashionable meeting place, it always seems crowded with tourists and locals devouring the rich chocolate cake known as *dobos torta,* their pleasure undiminished by the surliness of the waitresses. *Vörösmarty tér 7, tel. 1/1181–311.*

North of Roosevelt tér is the riverfront's most striking land-
⑭ mark, the imposing neo-Gothic **Parliament,** now minus the red star on top (open for tours only; call IBUSZ, tel. 1/1185–776, Budapest Tourist, tel. 1/1173–555, or Omnibusz Travel, tel. 1/ 1172–300). To its left sits an expressive statue of József Attila (1905–37), who, in spite of his early death, became known as one of Hungary's greatest poets.

⑮ Across from the Parliament is the **Néprajzi Múzeum** (Museum of Ethnography), with exhibits depicting folk traditions and such social customs as Hungarian costume and folklore. There is a particularly interesting collection from Oceania. *Kossuth Lajos tér 12, tel. 1/1326–340. Admission: 50 Ft. Open Tues.– Sun. 10–6.*

⑯ Dark and massive, the 19th-century **Szt. István Bazilika** (St. Stephen's Basilica) is one of the chief landmarks of Pest. It was planned early in the 19th century as a neoclassical building, but was in the neo-Renaissance style by the time it was completed more than 50 years later. During World War II, the most precious documents from the Municipal Archives were placed in the cellar of the basilica—one of the few available bombproof sites.

Andrássy útja runs 3.2 kilometers (2 miles) from the basilica to
⑰ Hősök tere (Heroes' Square). On the left is the **Állami Operaház** (State Opera House), with its statues of the Muses in the second-floor corner niches. Completed in 1884, it was the crowning achievement of architect Miklós Ybl. It has been restored to its original ornate glory—particularly inside—and has been spared attempts at modernization. There are no performances in summer.

Városliget Park
⑱ In the center of Heroes' Square stands the 36.5-meter (118-foot) **Millenneumi Emlékmű** (Millennium Monument), begun in 1896 to commemorate the 1,000th anniversary of the Magyar Conquest. Statues of Prince Árpád and six other founders of the Magyar nation occupy the base of the monument, while Hungary's greatest rulers and princes are between the columns on either side.

⑲ The **Szépművészeti Múzeum** (Fine Arts Museum) stands on one side of the square. Egyptian, Greek, and Roman artifacts dominate an entire section of the museum, and the collection of ceramics includes many rare pieces. The institution's largely unknown Spanish collection, which includes many works by El Greco and a magnificent painting by Velásquez, is considered the best of its kind outside Spain. *Dózsa György út 41, tel. 1/ 1429-759. Admission: 30 Ft. Open Tues.–Sat. 10–6, Sun. 10–6; closed Jan.–Mar.*

⑳ The **Műcsarnok** (Art Gallery), on the other side of the square, usually houses visiting exhibitions of contemporary Hungarian and international art but is closed for renovation until 1994.

The **Városliget** (City Park) extends beyond the square; on the left as you enter it are the zoo, state circus, amusement park, and outdoor swimming pool of the Széchenyi mineral baths. On
㉑ the right is the **Mezőgazdasági Múzeum** (Agricultural Museum), housed in a number of buildings representing different styles of Hungarian architecture—again a part of the Millennium Exhibition of 1896. *Vajdahunyadvár, Városliget XIV, tel. 1/1420-573. Admission: 30 Ft. Open Tues.–Sat. 10–5, Sun. 10–6.*

On the shores of the artificial lake stands the statue of George Washington, erected in 1906 from donations by Hungarians living in the United States. The **Olaf Palme sétány** (walk) is a pleasant route through the park.

Off the Beaten Track

A *libegő* (chair lift) will take you to the highest point in Budapest, **Jánoshegy** (János Hill), where you can climb a lookout tower for the best view of the city. *Take bus No. 158 from Moszkva tér to last stop, Zugligeti út. Admission: 40 Ft. Open May 15–Sept. 15, daily 9–5.*

For another good view, make the strenuous climb up the staircase that ascends the high cliff overlooking the Danube at the Buda end of the Szabadság Bridge. This will lead you to **Gellért-hegy** (Gellert Hill), named for an 11th-century bishop who was hurled to his death here by some pagan Magyars. During the Middle Ages the hill was associated with witches; nowadays there is a towering memorial to the liberation of Budapest by the Red Army.

Shopping

You'll find plenty of folk art and souvenir shops, foreign-language bookshops, and classical record shops in or around **Váci utca,** but a visit to some of the smaller, more typically Hungarian shops on **Erzsébet** and **Teréz boulevards** and to the modern **Skála-Coop** department store near the Nyugati train station may prove more interesting.

The **central market hall** at IX Vámhaz körút 1–3 is closed for rebuilding, but the **flea market** *(ecseri piac)* some way out on Nagykörösi utca 156 (take bus No. 58 from Boráros tér) stocks antiques, clothes, lamps, and such relics of the former Soviet empire as Red Army caps, Lenin statues, and Gorbachev dolls.

Dining

Private restaurateurs are breathing excitement into the Budapest dining scene. You can choose among Chinese, Mexican, Italian, French, and Czech cuisines—there are even two vegetarian restaurants. Or you can stick to solid, traditional Hungarian fare. Be sure to check out the less expensive spots favored by locals. For price-category definitions, *see* Dining in Staying in Hungary.

Very Expensive **Gundel.** Kings, prime ministers, and Communist party bosses
★ have dined in this turn-of-the-century palazzo since it was founded in 1894, but its elegance and grandeur dissipated under state control. Now relaunched by New York-based restaurateur George Lang, it showcases all that's best in Hungarian cuisine—here prepared with less fat and salt than is usual elsewhere. Waiters in black tie serve traditional favorites such as tender veal in a paprika-and-sour-cream sauce and carp Dorozsma (pan-fried, with mushrooms) to the accompaniment of gypsy music. The cheese and the lively salads come from a special private farm, the strudel is hand-pulled, and the house specialty, Gundel palacsinta is as rich as it sounds: a thin pancake filled with nuts and raisins and topped with a rum-spiked chocolate sauce. The tab for all this is high by Budapest standards, but the bistro menu served in the garden, open as weather permits, offers salads, smoked salmon sandwiches, and cold sliced breast of duck from the same accomplished kitchen at moderate prices. Linger here on balmy summer evenings and listen to the lions roar in the nearby zoo. *XIV Allatkerti ut 2, tel. 1/121–3550, fax 1/142–2917. Reservations required for main dining room but not for garden. Jacket and tie required. AE, DC, MC, V.*

Expensive **Kacsa.** Hungarian and international dishes are done with a light touch and served by candlelight, with quiet piano music in the background, in this restaurant just a few steps from the river. Try the crisp roasted duck. *II Fó utca 75, tel. 1/2019–992. Reservations advised. AE, MC, V.*

Kisbuda Gyöngye. This is the reincarnation of a venerable Budapest favorite that fell victim to foreign buyers. The longtime management, now at a new address, has made their establishment better than ever with art deco furniture and pink tablecloths; a violin-piano duo with a repertoire favoring Mozart set a romantic mood. Try the chicken Cumberland (grilled boneless breasts marinated in basil and spices) or the fresh trout smothered in a cream sauce nutted with mushrooms and capers. *Kenyeres utca 34, tel. 1/1686–402. Reservations advised 2 days ahead. AE.*

Légrádi. The debonair Légrádi brothers look after your every wish here. The scattering of antiques and the lovely Herend china complement the unhurried Old World service. The prices soar to expense-account levels. *V Magyar utca 23, tel. 1/1186–804. Reservations advised. AE. Closed weekends.*

Múzeum. Fans swear that this elegant, candle-lit salon with mirrors, mosaics, and swift-moving waiters has the best dining in Budapest. The salads are generous, the Hungarian wines excellent, and the chef dares to be creative. *VIII Múzeum körút 12, tel. 1/1384–221. Reservations advised. AE.*

Vadrózsa. The name means "wild rose," and there are always fresh ones on the table at this restaurant in an old villa in the exclusive Rozsadomb district. It's elegant to the last detail—even the service is white glove—and the garden is delightful in summer. *II Pentelei Molnár utca 15, tel. 1/1351–118. Reservations advised. AE, DC, V. Dinner only. Closed Mon.*

Moderate ★ **Fórum Grill.** Anyone with a touch of homesickness will enjoy this spot in the Fórum Hotel (*see* Lodging, *below*). The salad bar is fresh and the pizza tasty, and there are even real cheeseburgers and a nonsmoking section. Enjoy the courteous service, and ask about the daily specials. *V Apáczai Csere János utca 12–14, tel. 1/1178–088. AE, DC, MC, V.*

Kispipa. The street outside, a lane full of crumbling old buildings, makes this restaurant's gleaming brass fixtures, stylish art deco chairs, and convivial crowd seem that much more polished. On the extensive menu, the game dishes stand out. *VII Akácfa utca 38, tel. 1/1423–969. Reservations advised. No credit cards. Closed Sun. and holidays.*

Inexpensive **Bohémtanya.** There's always a wait for a table at this lively hangout, but it pays to be patient. The reward: heaping plates of stuffed cabbage, fried pork chops filled with goose liver, and other Hungarian specialties. *VI Paulay Ede utca 6, tel. 1/1221–453. Reservations advised. No credit cards.*

Szerb. Down a sawdust-covered stairway, this lively cellar serves grilled meats on a skewer and other Serbian dishes for a song, along with giant pitchers of beer. *V Nagy Ignác utca 16, tel. 1/1111–858. Reservations advised. No credit cards.*

Lodging

Thirty million tourists came to Hungary last year, and the boom has encouraged hotel building; yet there is sometimes a shortage of rooms, especially in summer.

If you arrive in Budapest without a reservation, go to the IBUSZ travel office at Petöfi tér (tel. 361/1185–707) or to one of the tourist offices at any of the train stations or at the airport. For details and price-category definitions, *see* Lodging in Staying in Hungary.

Very Expensive **Fórum.** This boxy modern riverside hotel consistently wins applause for its gracious appointments, friendly service, and gorgeous views. The central location makes it popular with businesspeople. *V Apáczai Csere János utca 12–14, tel. 1/1178–088, fax 1/1179–808. 408 rooms with bath, 16 suites. Facilities: 2 restaurants, coffee shop, bar, health club. AE, DC, MC, V.*

Expensive **Béke Radisson.** Traditional mixes with modern at this hotel in the heart of the city. While the rooms are modern, the hotel's entrance is presided over by a liveried doorman, and the lobby is full of mosaics and statuary. *VI Teréz körút 43, tel. 1/1323–300, fax 1/1533–380. 238 rooms with bath, 8 suites. Facilities: 2 restaurants, 2 bars, casino, business center, swimming pool, health club. AE, DC, MC, V.*

★ **Gellért.** Nowadays this plump grand old lady of city hotels is shining. The turn-of-the-century architecture is regal, and the thermal bath are wonderfully ornate. (They're like regular swimming pools but more elegant; jets of water come shooting up through the floor at odd moments, and fountains dribble hot water onto the heads of bathers.) *XI Gellért tér 1, tel. 1/1852–200, fax 1/1666–631. 224 rooms with bath, 15 suites. Facilities: thermal pools, terrace restaurant, coffee shop. AE, DC, MC, V.*

Ramada Grand Hotel. This venerable 100-year-old hotel is completely modern, yet retains its period look. It's in a tranquil park, surrounded by gardens on a car-free island in the Danube; the city is closer than it seems. *XIII Margit-sziget, tel. 1/1321–100 or 1/1111–000, fax 1/1533–029. 152 rooms with bath, 10 suites. Facilities: 2 restaurants, coffee shop, bar, thermal baths, beauty shop. AE, DC, MC, V.*

Thermal Hotel Helia. A sleek Scandinavian design and quiet location away from downtown pollution make this new hotel on the Danube a relaxing retreat. Special health packages are available. *XIII Kárpát utca 62–64, tel. 1/1298–650, fax 1/1201–429. 254 rooms with bath, 4 with sauna; 8 suites. Facilities: 2 restaurants (1 with summer terrace), bar, spa. AE, DC, MC, V.*

Victoria. City lights twinkling over the river is the view from rooms at this new establishment that mixes the charm of an inn in the country with ultramodern comforts. The absence of conventions is a plus. *II Bem rakpart 11, tel. 1/2018–644, fax 1/2015–816. 24 rooms with bath, 2 with balcony; 1 suite. Facilities: 24-hr. room service, bar, sauna. AE, DC, MC, V.*

Moderate **Alba Hotel.** Tucked behind an alleyway at the foot of Castle Hill, this new gem of a hotel is a short walk, via the Chain Bridge, from lively business and shopping districts. Swiss management assures efficient service. *I Apor Péter utca 3, tel. 1/1759–244, fax 1/1759–899. 97 rooms with bath. Facilities: nonsmoking rooms, bar, underground parking. AE, DC, MC, V.*

Astoria. Revolutionaries and intellectuals once gathered in the marble-and-gilt Art Deco lobby here. Recent renovations have not obscured its charm, but have meant the addition of other comforts—most notably soundproofing, essential since the Astoria is located at the city's busiest intersection. *V Kossuth Lajos utca 19, tel. 1/1173–411, fax 1/1186–798. 198 rooms with bath or shower. Facilities: nightclub, café, beer hall. AE, DC, MC, V.*

Centrál. Relive history—stay in this hotel, well situated in a leafy diplomatic quarter, as visiting Communist dignitaries once did. The architecture and furnishings are straight out of the 1950s. *VI Munkácsy utca 5–7, tel. 1/1212–000, fax 1/1212–008. 42 rooms with bath. Facilities: restaurant. AE, DC, MC, V.*

Korona. Modern and functional, this Austrian-built hotel is on busy Cálvin tér, near the river and close to the National Museum and other sights. *V Kecskeméti utca 14, tel. 1/1174–111, fax 1/1384–258. 440 rooms with bath. Facilities: pool, restaurant, bar, parking garage. AE, DC, MC, V.*

Liget. It's luxurious, it's postmodern, and with two major museums nearby, it's ideal for art lovers. Városliget, the city park, is a few steps away, and offers respite from traffic and noise. *XIV Dózsa György út 106, tel. 1/1113–200 or 1/1317–159, fax 1/1317–153. 55 rooms with bath. Facilities: coffee shop, bar, sauna. AE, DC, MC, V.*

Nemzeti. The baby-blue Baroque facade stands out in this dingy neighborhood, which turns seedy after dark. The homey atmosphere is the real draw. *VIII József Körút 4, tel. 1/1339–160, fax 1/1140–019. 76 rooms, most with bath. Facilities: restaurant, brasserie. AE, DC, MC, V.*

Inexpensive **Ifjuság.** The modest though attractive hotel was renovated in 1992, and you can't fault the location near Margaret Island. Ask for a room with a view, and you won't be sorry. *II Zivatar utca 3, tel. 1/1154–260, fax 1/1353–989. 100 rooms with bath. Facilities: restaurant. AE, DC, MC, V.*

Kulturinnov. One wing of what looks like a Gothic castle now houses basic budget accommodations. Rooms are clean, and the neighborhood, the luxurious Castle District, is quite pleasant. *I Szentháromság tér 6, tel. 1/1550–122 or 1/1751–651, fax 1/1751–886. 17 rooms, some with 3 or 4 beds, all with shower. Facilities: snack bar, reading room. AE.*

The Arts

Hotels and tourist offices will provide you with a copy of the monthly publication *Programme*, which contains details of all cultural events in the city. The newspaper *Budapest Week* lists upcoming events in English; look for it in hotels and bookshops. Tickets are available from your hotel desk, the **Central Booking Agency** (Vörösmarty tér, tel. 1/1176–222), or from **Budapest Tourist** (Roosevelt tér 5, tel. 1/1173–555).

There are two opera houses, for which dress can be informal. Concerts are given all year at the **Academy of Music** on Liszt F. tér, the **Vigadó** on Vigadó tér and at the **Old Academy of Music** on Vörösmarty utca. Displays of Hungarian folk dancing are held at the **Cultural Center** on Corvin tér.

Arts festivals fill the calendar beginning in early spring. The season's first, the **Spring Art Festival** (Mar.), showcases Hungary's best opera, music, theater, and dance as well as visiting foreign artists. It's followed by the annual **Jazz Festival** (Apr.), and after the opera season ends, by the **Summer Opera Festival** (July–Aug.) at the open-air theater on Margitsziget. Information and tickets are available from the Central Booking Agency, above.

Nightlife

Budapest is a lively city by night. Establishments stay open late and Western European–style *drink-bárs* have sprung up all over the city.

Nightclubs Many of the nightclubs are attached to the luxury hotels. Beware of the inflated prices. Admission starts at 150 Ft. Drinks cost from 200 Ft. to 500 Ft.

Ballantine's Club. The atmosphere is hushed and British; billiards and chess are the games. *VI Andrássy út 19, tel. 1/1227–896. Open 9 AM–11 PM.*

Casanova offers music and dancing in an attractive building where the great lover is said to have spent the night. *I Batthyány tér, tel. 1/2016–819. Open 10 PM–4 AM.*

Pierrot is an elegant café and piano bar well suited for secret rendezvous. *I Fortuna utca 14, tel. 1/1756–971. Open 5 PM–1 AM. No credit cards.*

Cabarets **Horoszkóp,** in the Buda-Penta Hotel, is the favorite among Budapest's younger set. Floor shows begin at 11 PM. *I Krisztina körút 41–43, tel. 1/1566–333. Open 10 PM–4 AM.*
Maxim's, in the Hotel Emke, offers a Parisian-style variety show, complete with leggy chorus girls, at top prices. Shows at 10 PM and midnight. *VII Akácfa utca 3, tel. 1/1420–145. Open 8 PM–3 AM. AE, DC, MC, V.*

Discos The university colleges organize the best discos in town. Try the **ELTE Club** (Eötvös Loránd) in the Inner City, on the corner of Károlyi Mihály utca and Irányi utca. Admission and drink prices are reasonable. Bring some student I.D.

The Danube Bend

About 40 kilometers (25 miles) north of Budapest, the Danube abandons its eastward course and turns abruptly south toward the capital, cutting through the Börzsöny and Visegrád hills. This area is called the Danube Bend and includes the Baroque town of Szentendre, the hilltop castle ruins and town of Visegrád, and the cathedral town of Esztergom. The attractive combination of hillside and river should dispel any notion that Hungary is one vast, boring plain.

Here, in the heartland, are the traces of the country's history—the remains of the Roman Empire's frontiers, the battlefields of the Middle Ages, and the relics of the Hungarian Renaissance. Although the area can be covered by car in a day—the round-trip from Budapest is only 124 kilometers (78 miles)—two days, with a night in Visegrád or Esztergom, would be a better way to savor its charms.

Getting Around

The most pleasant way to get around is by boat or hydrofoil on the Danube. The three main centers—Szentendre, Esztergom, and Visegrád—all have connections with each other and with Budapest. There is also regular bus service connecting all three with each other and with Budapest. Szentendre can also be reached by HÉV commuter rail, departing from the Batthyány tér metro; the fare is 60 Ft.

Guided Tours

IBUSZ organizes day trips from Budapest along the Danube from May through October (4,000 Ft. with lunch) and to Szentendre only on Sundays, May through October. Boat trips run on Wednesdays and Saturdays; buses go on Tuesdays, Fridays, and Saturdays. There is also a special bus trip to Szentendre departing on different days, depending on the season.

Tourist Information

Budapest (Dunatours, VI Bajcsy-Zsilinszky út 17, tel. 1/1314–533 or 1/1115–630, fax 1/1116–827).
Esztergom (IBUSZ Office, Lőrinc utca 1, tel. 33/12–552).
Szentendre (Dunatours, Bacsó part 6, on the quay, tel. 26/11–311).

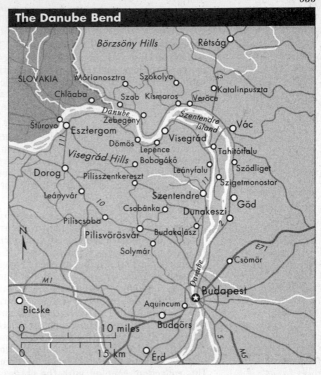

The Danube Bend

Exploring the Danube Bend

Heading north from Budapest toward Szentendre, 19 kilometers (12 miles) by car on Road 11, or by train, on your right look for the reconstructed remains of **Aquincum,** capital of the Roman province of Pannonia. Careful excavations have unearthed a varied selection of artifacts and mosaics, giving a tantalizing inkling of what life was like on the northern fringes of the Roman Empire.

Szentendre, nowadays a flourishing artists' colony with a lively Mediterranean atmosphere, was first settled by Serbs and Greeks fleeing the advancing Turks in the 14th and 17th centuries. There is a Greek Orthodox church in the main square and a Serbian Orthodox cathedral on the hill. The narrow cobbled streets are lined with cheerfully painted houses. Part of the town's artistic reputation can be traced to the life and work of the ceramic artist Margit Kovács, whose work blended Hungarian folk art traditions with motifs from modern art. The **Margit Kovács Pottery Museum,** devoted to her work, is housed in a small 18th-century merchant's house with an attractive courtyard. *Vastag György utca 1, tel. 26/10–244. Admission: 60 Ft. Open Apr.–Oct., daily 10–6; Nov.–Mar., Tues.–Sun. 10–4.*

A short drive up Szabadság Forrás út, or a bus ride from the train station, will take you to the **Szabadtéri Néprajzi Múzeum** (Open-Air Ethnographical Museum), where a collection of buildings has been designed to show Hungarian peasant life and folk architecture in the 19th century. *Szabadság Forrás út,* *tel. 26/12–304. Admission: 60 Ft. Open Apr.–Oct., Tues.–Sun. 10–5.*

Visegrád, 23 kilometers (14 miles) from Szentendre, was the seat of the kings of Hungary in the 14th century. The ruins of the Palace of King Matthias in the main street have been excavated and reconstructed, and there are jousting tournaments here in June. A winding road leads up to a haunting late-medieval fortress, from which you have a fine view of the Danube Bend.

Esztergom, 21 kilometers (13 miles) farther upriver, stands on the site of a Roman fortress. St. Stephen, the first Christian king of Hungary, was crowned here in the year 1000. The kings are long gone, but Esztergom is still the home of the archbishop of Esztergom, the cardinal primate, head of the Catholic church in Hungary.

Thousands of pilgrims visit the imposing **cathedral,** the largest in Hungary, which stands on a hill overlooking the town. It was here, in the center of Hungarian Catholicism, that the famous anti-Communist cleric, Cardinal József Mindszenty, was finally reburied in 1991, ending an era of religious intolerance and prosecution and a sorrowful chapter in Hungarian history. The cathedral also houses a valuable collection of ecclesiastical art. Below it are the streets of Viziváros (Watertown), lined with Baroque buildings. The **Keresztény Múzeum** (Museum of Christian Art) is situated in the Primate's Palace. It is the finest art gallery in Hungary, with a large collection of early Hungarian and Italian paintings. The Italian collection of 14th- and 15th-century works is unusually large for a museum outside Italy. This collection, coupled with the extensive number of early Renaissance paintings from Flanders and the Lower Rhine, provides insights into the transition of European sensibilities from medieval Gothic to the humanistic Renaissance. *Berényi utca 2, tel. 33/13–880. Admission: 50 Ft. Open Tues.–Sun. 10–6.*

To the north of the cathedral, on **Szt. Tamás Hill,** is a small church dedicated to St. Thomas à Becket of Canterbury. From here you can look down on the town and see how the Danube temporarily divides, forming an island that locals use as a base for water skiing and swimming. This part of the Danube forms the frontier with Czechoslovakia.

Dining and Lodging

For details and price-category definitions, *see* Dining and Lodging in Staying in Hungary.

Esztergom
Dining

Primáspince. Arched ceilings and exposed brick walls make a charming setting for refined Hungarian fare at this restaurant just below the cathedral. Try the tournedos Budapest-style, tender beef with sautéed vegetables and paprika, or the thick stuffed pork chops Fiaker-style (stuffed with ham and melted cheese). *Szent István tér 4, tel. 33/13–495. Reservations advised. AE, DC, MC, V. Expensive.*

Fili Falatozó. The hearty German fare is heavy on meat and potatoes. The location on Esztergom's most pleasant old street, just a short stroll from the Danube. *Bajcsy-Zsilinszky utca 51 (no telephone). No reservations or credit cards accepted. Closed Jan.–Feb. Inexpensive.*

Lodging **Fürdő.** This large hotel, built in the 1960s, is starting to look shabby and worn, but for those in need of a good workout, the attached spa and open-air thermal baths make up for the lack of charm. *Bajcsy-Zsilinszky utca 14, tel. 33/11–688, fax 33/11–594. 85 rooms with bath, 3 apartments. Facilities: restaurant, bar. AE, DC, MC, V. Moderate.*

Ria Panzió. In this small, friendly guest house near the cathedral, all rooms face a garden courtyard. *Batthyány utca 11, tel. 33/13–115. 6 rooms. No credit cards. Inexpensive.*

Szentendre **Angyal Borozó.** This wine bar, also a restaurant, serves hefty
Dining portions of Hungarian food. *Alkotmány utca 4, tel. 26/10–160. No reservations or credit cards accepted. Moderate.*

Rab Ráby. Fish soup and fresh grilled trout are the specialties in this popular restaurant with wood beams and equestrian decorations. *Péter Pál utca 1, tel. 26/10–819. Reservations advised in summer. No credit cards. Moderate.*

Lodging **Bükkös Panzió.** Impeccably clean, this stylishly modernized old house is on a small canal just a few minutes' walk from the town center. *Bükkös part 16, tel. 26/12–021, fax 1/1813–967. 16 rooms with bath. Facilities: restaurant. No credit cards. Moderate.*

Visegrád **Silvanus.** Located on a hill, Visegrád hegy, this hotel offers
Lodging spectacular views. It's recommended for motorists and offers a tennis court and linking trails in the forest for the more active. *Fekete-hegy, tel. 27/28–311, fax 26/28–170. 74 rooms, most with bath; 4 suites. Facilities: restaurant, brasserie, terrace café. AE, DC, MC, V. Moderate.*

Vár. Situated at the foot of a steep hill beside the Danube, this is a good choice for those whose priorities include scenery and the great outdoors. There are excellent water-sports facilities nearby, but the level of accommodations is very simple. *Fő utca 9–11, tel. 27/28–264. 15 rooms, all with hot water but no bath. No credit cards. Inexpensive.*

Lake Balaton

Lake Balaton, the largest lake in Central Europe, stretches 80 kilometers (50 miles) across western Hungary. It is within easy reach of Budapest by any means of transportation. Sometimes known as the nation's playground, it goes some way toward making up for Hungary's much-lamented lack of coastline. On its hilly northern shore, ideal for growing grapes, is **Balatonfüred,** the country's oldest and most famous spa town.

The national park on the Tihany Peninsula is just to the south, and regular boat service links Tihany and Balatonfüred with Siófok on the southern shore. This shore is not as attractive as the northern one—being flatter and more crowded with resorts, cottages, and high-rise hotels once used as Communist trade-union retreats. Still, it is worth visiting for its shallower, warmer waters, which make it a better choice for swimming than other locations.

A circular tour taking in Veszprém, Balatonfüred, and Tihany could be managed in a day, but two days, with a night in Tihany or Balatonfüred, would be more relaxed and allow for detours to Herend and its porcelain factory, or to the castle at Nagyvázsony.

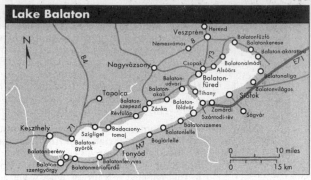

The region is crowded in July and August, so visit at any other time if you can.

Getting Around

Trains from Budapest serve all the resorts on the northern shore; a separate line links the resorts of the southern shore. Road 71 runs along the northern shore; M7 covers the southern. Buses connect most resorts. Regular ferries link the major ones. On summer weekends, traffic can be heavy and driving slow around the lake. Book bus and train tickets in advance then. In winter, note that schedules are curtailed, so check before making plans.

Guided Tours

IBUSZ has several tours to Balaton from Budapest; inquire at the head office in Budapest (*see* Important Addresses and Numbers in Budapest, *above*). Other tours more easily organized from hotels in the Balaton area include boat trips to vineyards, folk music evenings, and overnight trips to local inns.

Tourist Information

Budapest (Balatontourist, VIII Üllői út 52/A, tel. 1/1336–982, fax 1/1339–929).
Balatonfüred (Balatontourist, Blaha L. utca 5, tel. 86/42–822).
Nagyvázsony (Balatontourist, Kinizsi vár, tel. 80/64–318).
Tihany (Balatontourist, Kossuth utca 20, tel. 86/48–512).
Veszprém (Balatontourist, Kossuth Lajos utca 21, tel. 80/26–277).

Exploring Lake Balaton

Hilly **Veszprém** is the center of cultural life in the Balaton region. **Várhegy** (Castle Hill) is the most attractive part of town, north of Szabadság tér. **Hősök Kapuja** (Heroes' Gate), at the entrance to the Castle, houses a small exhibit on Hungary's history. Just past the gate and down a little alley to the left, is the **Tűztorony** (Fire Tower); note that the lower level is medieval while the upper stories are Baroque. There is a good view of the town and surrounding area from the balcony. *Exhibit admission: 10 Ft. Open May–Oct., Tues.–Sun. 10–6.*

Vár utca, the only street in the castle area, leads to a small square in front of the **Bishop's Palace** and **Cathedral;** outdoor concerts are held here in the summer. Vár utca continues past the square up to a terrace erected on the north staircase of the castle. Stand beside the modern statues of St. Stephen and his queen, Gizella, for a far-reaching view of the old quarter of town.

If you are traveling by car, go 5 kilometers (3 miles) west to the village of **Nemesvámos,** where you can slake your thirst or conquer your hunger at **Vámosi Csárda** (Highwayman's Inn). This 18th-century Baroque building takes its name from an infamous 19th-century highwayman who claimed it as one of his bases. Go down to the cellar to see the tables and seats made from tree trunks—a local architectural feature.

Herend, 16 kilometers (10 miles) northwest of Veszprém on Road 8, is the home of Hungary's renowned hand-painted porcelain. The factory, founded in 1839, displays many valuable pieces in its **museum.** *Admission: 30 Ft. Open Tues.–Sun. 10–6.*

From Veszprém, take Road 73 about 20 kilometers (12 miles) south to **Balatonfüred,** a spa and resort with good beaches. It is also one of the finest wine-growing areas of Hungary. Above the main square, where medicinal waters bubble up under a colonnaded pavilion, the hillsides are thick with vines.

A seven-minute boat trip takes you from Balatonfüred to the **Tihany Peninsula,** a national park rich in rare flora and fauna and an ideal place for strolling. From the ferry port, follow green markers to the springs (Oroszkút) or red ones to the top of **Csúcs-hegy,** a hill from which there is a good view of the lake.

The village of **Tihany,** with its famous **abbey,** is on the eastern shore. The abbey building houses a **museum** with exhibits related to the Balaton area. Also worth a look are the pink angels floating on the ceiling of the abbey church, and the abbey organ, on which recitals are given in summer. Consider a special detour to the Rege pastry shop at Batthyány út 38, not far from the abbey. *Batthyány utca 80, tel. 80/48–405. Admission: 20 Ft. Open Tues.–Sun. 10–6.*

The castle of **Nagyvázsony,** about 20 kilometers (12 miles) northwest of Balatonfüred, dates to the early 15th century. The 28-meter-high (92-foot-high) keep is the oldest part, and its upper rooms now house the **Castle Museum.** Try to get to the highest balcony in late afternoon for the best view. The surrounding buildings, preserved in their original style, date from the period when post horses were changed here. *Tel. 80/31–015. Museum admission: 30 Ft. Open Tues.–Sun. 10–6.*

Dining and Lodging

For details and price-category definitions, *see* Dining and Lodging in Staying in Hungary.

Balatonfüred
Dining

Vitorlás. This old villa has a pleasant lake-view terrace where you can watch the yachts and sailboats in the water as you eat good grilled trout and bean soup. *Tagore Sétány 1, tel. 86/43–407. Reservations advised. Dress: casual but neat. AE, DC, MC, V. Moderate.*

Lodging **Annabella.** The cool, spacious guest quarters in this large, Miami-style high-rise are especially pleasant during summer heat. It is surrounded by gardens, away from other hotels but just around the corner from the main square in town. *Deák Ferenc utca 25, tel. 86/42–222, fax 86/43–084. 390 rooms; all double rooms have bath. Facilities: restaurant, indoor/outdoor pool, windsurfing. AE, DC, MC, V. Closed mid-Oct.–mid-Apr. Moderate.*

★ **Arany Csillag.** Once a castle and later the headquarters for the local Soviet garrison, this is now well-worn but atmospheric, and the rooms are spotless; it's a good choice if you've had enough of Hungary's more modern accommodations. At 10 minutes from the beach, it's one of the best buys in Balaton. *Zsigmondi út 1, Balatonfüred 8231, tel. 86/43–466. 80 rooms, none with bath. Facilities: restaurant. No credit cards. Closed Dec.–Mar. Inexpensive.*

Tihany **Halásztanya.** The relaxed atmosphere and gypsy music in the
Dining evening help contribute to the popularity of the Halásztánya, which specializes in fish. *Visszhang utca 11 (no phone). No reservations. Closed Nov.–Mar. Moderate.*

Pál Csárda. Two thatched cottages make up this simple restaurant, where cold fruit soup and fish stew are the specialties. Or you can eat in the garden, which is decorated with gourds and strands of peppers, from which paprika is made. *Visszhang utca 19, no phone. No reservations. Dress: casual. No credit cards. Closed Dec.–Mar. Moderate.*

Lodging **Kolostor.** The cozy, wood-paneled rooms are built into an attic above a restaurant in the heart of Tihany village. *Kossuth út, tel. 86/48–408. 7 rooms with bath. Facilities: breakfast room. No credit cards. Moderate.*

★ **Park.** Lush landscaped gardens surround this stately mansion on the water's edge. Inside, it's all understated elegance; rooms have balconies, views, and crisp sheets embroidered with the names of former communist party bosses. *Fürdötelepi út 1, tel. 86/48–611. 26 rooms with bath. Facilities: restaurant, private beach. AE, DC, MC, V. Summer: Expensive; other seasons: Moderate.*

Veszprém **Diana.** The Diana is just a little southwest of the town center,
Dining but worth the trip if you want to experience the old-fashioned
★ charm of a small provincial Hungarian restaurant. The decor could be called "cozy traditional," and the fish and game specialties are perennial favorites. *József Attila utca 22, tel. 80/21–061. Reservations advised. No credit cards. Moderate.*

Tüztorony Sörklub. At this restaurant on the winding cobblestone street leading to the castle, you can order game specialties such as venison soup and veal stew. Try the cherry strudel for dessert. *Vár utca 1, tel. 80/26–220. No reservations. Dress: casual. No credit cards. Closed Sun. in winter. Inexpensive.*

Lodging **Veszprem.** This modern, comfortable hotel in the center of town now has a fresh paint job and pleasant new furniture. *Budapesti utca 6, tel. 80/24–677, fax 80/24–076. 72 rooms, 4 suites. Facilities: restaurant. No credit cards. Inexpensive.*

16 Iceland

Iceland is anything but icy. Though glaciers cover about 10% of the country, summers in Iceland are relatively warm, and the winter climate is milder than New York's. Coastal farms lie in green, pastoral lowlands, where cows, sheep, and horses graze alongside raging streams. Distant waterfalls plunge from heather-covered mountains with great spiked ridges and snow-capped peaks.

Iceland's name can be blamed on Hrafna-Flóki, a 9th-century Norse settler who failed to plant enough crops to see his live-stock through their first winter. Leaving in a huff, he passed a northern fjord filled with pack ice and cursed the country with a name that's kept tourism in cold storage for 1,100 years.

The second-largest island in Europe, Iceland is in the middle of the North Atlantic, where the warm Gulf Stream from the south meets the cold currents from the north, providing a choice environment for the fish on which the nation depends for over 75% of its export revenue. Beneath some of the country's glaciers are burning fires that become visible during volcanic eruptions—fires that heat the hot springs and geysers that are all over the country. The springs, in turn, provide heat to the country's homes, hospitals, and public swimming pools, keeping the nation's air smokeless and smogless. Except for fish and agricultural products, almost all consumer goods are imported, thus the cost of living is high by any standard.

The first permanent settlers arrived from Norway in 874, though some Irish monks had arrived a century earlier. The country came under foreign rule in 1262 and did not win complete independence until 1944. Today nearly three-fifths of the country's 250,000 people live in Reykjavík and its suburbs.

The biennial Reykjavík Arts Festival, held in the first half of June 1994, promises a splendid feast of visual arts, music, and theater from all corners of the earth, plus the best of Icelandic creative and performing artists. There will also be a lively if unpredictable fringe festival that flourishes in the streets, coffee shops, and unused warehouses of the city.

Essential Information

Before You Go

When to Go The best time to visit is from May through November. The months of June and July are highly recommended, because during that time there is perpetual daylight. In Reykjavík the sun disappears behind the mountains for only a couple of hours, and in the northern part of the island it barely sets at all. The weather is unpredictable: From June through August, sunny days alternate with spells of rain showers and driving winds. Winter weather fluctuates bewilderingly, with temperatures as high as 50°F (10°C) or as low as –50°F (–10°C.). During December the sun shines for only three hours a day, but on a clear and cold evening you can see the Northern Lights dancing among the stars.

Climate Iceland enjoys a temperate ocean climate with cool summers and surprisingly mild winters. In the northern part of the country, the weather is more stable than in the south, with less wind and rain.

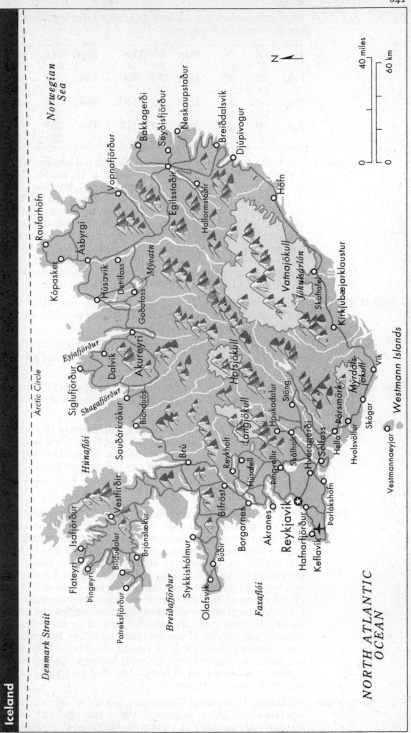

Iceland

Denmark Strait

Norwegian Sea

Arctic Circle

Raufarhöfn
Kópasker
Ásbyrgi
Húsavík
Dettifoss
Goðafoss
Mývatn
Vopnafjörður
Bakkagerði
Seyðisfjörður
Neskaupstaður
Breiðdalsvík
Djúpivogur
Egilsstaðir
Hallormsstaður
Höfn

Eyjafjörður
Siglufjörður
Dalvík
Akureyri
Skagafjörður
Sauðárkrókur
Blönduós
Brú
Reykholt

Vatnajökull
Jökulsárlón
Skaftafell
Kirkjubæjarklaustur

Hofsjökull
Langjökull
Haukadalur
Stöng
Þórsmörk
Mýrdals-jökull
Vík
Skógar

Húnaflói

Vestfirðir
Ísafjörður
Flateyri
Þingeyri
Bíldudalur
Brjánslækur
Patreksfjörður

Bifröst
Húsafell
Þingvellir
Skálholt
Hveragerði
Selfoss
Hella
Hvolsvöllur

Breiðafjörður
Stykkishólmur
Búðir
Ólafsvík
Borgarnes
Akranes

Faxaflói

Reykjavík
Hafnarfjörður
Keflavík
Þorlákshöfn

Westmann Islands
Vestmannaeyjar

NORTH ATLANTIC OCEAN

N

40 miles
60 km

0
0

The following are the average daily maximum and minimum temperatures for Reykjavík.

Jan.	35F	2C	May	50F	10C	Sept.	52F	11C
	28	-2		39	4		43	6
Feb.	37F	3C	June	54F	12C	Oct.	45F	7C
	28	-2		34	7		38	3
Mar.	39F	4C	July	57F	14C	Nov.	39F	4C
	30	-1		48	9		32	0
Apr.	43F	6C	Aug.	56F	14C	Dec.	36F	2C
	33	1		47	8		29	-2

Currency The Icelandic monetary unit is the króna (plural krónur), which is equal to 100 aurar. Coins are the ISK 1, 5, 10, and 50. There are krónur bills in denominations of 100, 500, 1,000, and 5,000. At press time (spring 1993), the rate of exchange was ISK 64 to the dollar and ISK 96 to the pound sterling, but in the generally unstable economic climate, considerable fluctuation occurs. You are not permitted to import or export more than ISK 8,000, but you may bring any amount of foreign currency, which is easily cashed into krónur at the Icelandic banks. Major credit cards, especially MasterCard and Visa, are widely accepted in the capital and by most businesses in the countryside.

What It Will Cost Iceland is expensive. Hotels and restaurants cost about 20% more in Reykjavík than elsewhere in the country. The airport departure tax is about ISK 1,300.

Sample Prices A cup of coffee or soft drink costs about ISK 120; a bottle of beer costs ISK 200; a sandwich or snack about ISK 250; and a 2-mile taxi ride, about ISK 500.

Customs on Arrival Tourists can bring in 1 liter of wine containing up to 21% alcohol or 6 liters of beer, 1 liter of liquor with up to 47% alcohol content, and 200 cigarettes.

Language The official language is Icelandic, a highly inflected North Germanic tongue, brought to the country by early Norse settlers, that has changed little over the centuries. English is widely understood and spoken, particularly by the younger people.

Getting Around

By Car The Ring Road, which encircles the island, still has stretches that are unpaved, although improvements are made every year. Apart from this, there are asphalt roads connecting the major coastal towns and long stretches of paved highway from the capital to Keflavík to Hvolsvöllur in the south and Borgarnes in the west. Except on these highways, driving can be a very bumpy experience, often along lava track or dirt and gravel surfaces. But the superb scenery more than makes up for it. Although service stations and garages are few and far between, the main roads are patrolled, and fellow motorists are friendly and helpful. If you are traveling off the beaten path, you'll need a four-wheel-drive vehicle. An international driver's license is required—you can apply for one at the local police station if you are at least 20 years old and in possession of a valid driver's license from home.

By Plane **Icelandair, Íslandsflug, Norlandair,** and a few other airlines have domestic flights to some 50 towns and villages. Special discounts are available on certain combinations of domestic air routes. Some of these must be arranged when you book your Icelandair flight to Iceland.

By Bus A comprehensive network of buses compensates for the lack of any train network. A good buy, if you want to explore extensively, is the **Omnibus Passport,** which permits you to travel on all scheduled bus routes for one to four weeks. It costs ISK 13,000–ISK 26,000. Another choice is the **Full Circle Passport,** which costs ISK 12,000 and is valid for a circular trip around Iceland on the Ring Road. It will take you to some of the most popular attractions, but if you want to see more, there are scheduled bus tours for which you will have to pay extra. An **Air/Bus Rover Ticket** entitles the bearer to additional discounts on certain Central Highland tours, camping grounds, youth hostels, and ferries. For further information, contact **Reykjavík Central Bus Terminal,** BSI (Vatnsmýrarvegur 10, tel. 91/22300, fax 91/29973).

Staying in Iceland

Telephones Pay phones take ISK 5, ISK 10, and ISK 50 coins and are found
Local Calls in hotels, shops, bus stations, and post offices. There are not many outdoor telephone booths in the towns and villages. Phonecards have recently been introduced, cost ISK 500, and are sold at post offices, hotels, etc.

International Calls You can dial direct to almost anywhere in Europe and the United States. Hotels in Iceland, as elsewhere, add hefty service charges to international calls, so ask about the charges in advance before you place a call from your room.

Operators and For collect calls and assistance with overseas calls, dial 09; for
Information local calls, dial 02; for information, dial 03; for direct international calls, dial 90.

Mail Airmail letters to the United States cost ISK 65; letters to Eu-
Postal Rates rope, ISK 35.

Receiving Mail You can have your mail sent to the post office in any town or village in Iceland. In Reykjavík, have mail sent to the downtown post office (R/O Pósthússtræti, 101 Reykjavík).

Opening and **Banks** are open weekdays 9:15–4. Some branches are also open
Closing Times Thursday 5–6. The bank at Hotel Loftleiðir in Reykjavík is open weekends for foreign exchange only.

Museums are usually open 1–4:30, but some open as early as 10 and others stay open until 7.

Shops are open weekdays 9–6 and Saturdays 9–noon (shopping malls 9–4).

National Holidays January 1; March 31–April 4 (Easter); April 21 (first day of summer); May 1 (Labor Day); May 12 (Ascension Day); May 22–23 (Pentecost); June 17 (National Day); August 1 (public holiday); December 24–26.

Dining Seafood and lamb are the local specialties, and they are recommended. The restaurants are small and varied—East Asian, French, Italian classical, and trendy. A number of them are located in historic, though not always attractive, buildings. Street vendors sell tasty hot dogs with fried onions.

Mealtimes Dinner, served between 6 and 9, is the main meal; a light lunch is usually served between noon and 2. Most restaurants are open from mid-morning until midnight.

Dress Casual dress is acceptable in all but the most formal restaurants, where a jacket and tie are recommended.

Ratings The following ratings are for a three-course meal for one person. Prices include taxes and service charges but not wine or cocktails. Best bets are indicated by a star ★.

Category	Reykjavík	Other Areas
Expensive	over ISK 2,500	over ISK 2,300
Moderate	ISK 1,500– ISK 2,500	ISK 1,200– ISK 2,300
Inexpensive	under ISK 1,500	under ISK 1,200

Lodging There is a wide range of accommodations designed to meet the demands of foreign visitors. The hotels are modern, without luxuries, but they are clean, quiet, and friendly. Reykjavík and most villages have guest houses and private accommodations. Hostels are few and only functional. Lodging in farmhouses is highly recommended: Over 100 participating farms are listed with **Icelandic Farm Holidays** (tel. 91/19200 or 91/623640, fax 91/623644), and many offer fishing, guided tours, and horseback riding. The **Iceland Tourist Board** (tel. 91/27488, fax 91/624749) offers additional information on where to stay.

Ratings Prices are for two people sharing a double room. Best bets are indicated by a star ★.

Category	Reykjavík	Other Areas
Expensive	over ISK 7,000	over ISK 6,000
Moderate	ISK 4,500– ISK 7,000	ISK 3,500– ISK 6,000
Inexpensive	under ISK 4,500	under ISK 3,500

Tipping Tipping is not customary in Iceland.

Reykjavík

Arriving and Departing

By Plane Flights from the United States and Europe arrive at Keflavík Airport, 50 kilometers (30 miles) from Reykjavík. For information on arrivals and departures at Keflavík Airport, call 91/690100.

Between the Airport and Downtown Buses connect with all flights to and from Keflavík. The drive takes 45 minutes and costs ISK 500. Taxis are also available, but they cost no less than ISK 4,500.

By Boat During the summer, the North Atlantic ferry *Norröna* sails from the Faroe Islands, Shetland Islands, Denmark, and Norway to Seyðisfjörður, the magnificent fjords on the east side of Iceland, 720 kilometers (450 miles) from Reykjavík. From Seyðisfjörður, Reykjavík is a 1-hour flight or a 10-hour drive. For information, contact **Smyril Line Passenger Department** (Box 370, 3800 Torshavn, Faroes, or Norræna ferðaskrifstofan, Laugavegur 3, Reykjavík, tel. 91/626362).

Getting Around

Most of the interesting sites are in the city center, within easy walking distance of one another. Sightseeing tours are also a good way to familiarize yourself with the city.

By Bus Buses run from 7 AM to midnight. The flat fare for Reykjavík and suburbs is ISK 100 for adults and ISK 25 for children under 13. Exact change is required. Strips of tickets are available from bus drivers and at bus stations.

By Taxi Rates start at about ISK 300. Because Reykjavík is small, most taxi rides do not exceed ISK 600. The best taxis to call are: **Hreyfill** (tel. 91/685522), **BSR** (tel. 91/611720), and **Bæjarleiðir** (tel. 91/33500).

Important Addresses and Numbers

Tourist Information The tourist information center, Bankastræti 2 (tel. 91/623045, fax 91/624749), is adjacent to the main shopping district. It's open summer, Mon.–Fri. 8:30–6, Sat. 8:30–2, Sun. 10–2; fall–spring, Mon.–Fri. 10–4, Sat. 10–2.

Embassies U.S. (Laufásvegur 21, tel. 91/21900). U.K. (Laufásvegur 49, tel. 91/15883). **Canadian Consulate** (Suðurlandsbraut 10, tel. 91/680820).

Emergencies Police (tel. 11166). Ambulance (tel. 11100). **Doctors and dentists** (weekdays 8 AM–5 PM, tel. 91/696600; weekdays 5 PM–8 AM and weekends, tel. 91/21230). **Pharmacies** operate on a rotating basis during nights and weekends. For information on which pharmacies are open evenings and weekends, call 91/18888.

English-Language Bookstores Eymundsson-Penninn (Austurstræti, tel. 91/27077). **Mál og menning** (Laugavegur 18, tel. 91/24240).

Travel Agencies Iceland Tourist Bureau (Skógarhlid 18, tel. 91/623300, fax 91/625895). Samvinn Travel (Austurstræti 12, tel. 91/27077). Úrval–Útsýn Travel (Álfabakki 16, tel. 91/699300).

Guided Tours

Tour operators use clean, comfortable buses that hold from 16 to 45 people. For information, call the tourist information center (tel. 91/623045).

Orientation Tours Reykjavík Excursions (tel. 91/621011 or 91/688922) offers "Reykjavík City Sightseeing," a daily tour that takes about 2½ hours and includes commercial centers, folk museums, and art centers.

Excursions Reykjavík Excursions (*see above*) has many different types of tours. Perhaps the most interesting are the daily "Gullfoss/ Geysir" tours, an eight-hour visit to volcanic craters, geysers, and waterfalls; a half-day trip that includes a visit to the unique **Blue Lagoon**, where you can bathe in hot mineral-rich springs from the depths of the earth; and three-hour pony-trekking trips. For trout-fishing excursions, contact **Úrval–Útsýn Travel** (tel. 91/699300). For inexpensive, guided excursions lasting from an afternoon to several weeks, try the **Touring Club of Ice-**

land (Mörkin 6, tel. 91/682533) or **Outdoor Life Tours** (Grófin 1, tel. 91/14606).

Exploring Reykjavík

Numbers in the margin correspond to points of interest on the Reykjavík map.

❶ The heart of Reykjavík is **Austurvöllur**, a small square in the center of the city. The 19th-century **Alþingi** (Parliament building), one of the oldest stone buildings in Iceland, faces the square. In the center of the square is a statue of Jón Sigurðsson (1811–79), the national hero who led Iceland's fight for independence, which it achieved fully in 1944.

❷ Next to Alþingi is the **Dómkirkjan** (Lutheran Cathedral), a small, charming stone church. Behind it is **Tjörnin**, a natural pond, where the Reykjavík City Hall opened in 1992. One corner of the pond does not freeze; here thermal springs feed warm water, making it an attraction for birds year-round.

❸ Head back along Lækjargata, beyond Austurvöllur to **Lækjartorg** Square. On the right is the **Bernhöftstorfa** district, a small hill with colorful two-story wooden houses from the mid-19th century. No attempts have been made to modernize the area, and it keeps the spirit of the past. For a century and a half, the biggest building has housed the oldest educational institution
❹ in the country, **Menntaskólinn í Reykjavík,** a college whose graduates have from the early days dominated political and social life in Iceland. On the north side of Lækjartorg is one of the two city bus centers. During the summer this square is lively, with an outdoor market, shops, and cafés.

Time Out **Café Hressó** is one of the oldest coffee shops in Reykjavík. The sweets are delicious, though other places are better for meals. An attractive back garden is open in the summertime. *Austurstræti 20, tel. 91/14353. Moderate.*

❺ Leading west out of the square is Austurstræti, a semi-pedestrian shopping street with the main post office on the right. From here you can take bus No. 10 or 110 from the bus station for a 20-minute ride to the **Arbæjarsafn** (Open-Air Museum). It is actually a "village" of 18th- and 19th-century houses that portray the old way of living. *Tel. 91/84094. Admission: ISK 250 adults, ISK 125 12–18 years, and free for children under 12. Open June–Aug., Tues.–Sat. 10–6; Sept., weekends 10–6; Oct.–May, by appointment.*

❻ You can also take bus No. 4 from the square to the **Ásmundur Sveinsson Gallery.** Sveinsson was a social-realist sculptor who started his career during the 1920s. Some of his originals are in the surrounding garden, which is accessible at all times free of charge. *v/Sigtún, 91/32155. Admission: ISK 200. Open June–Sept., daily 10–4; Oct.–May, Tues., Thurs., and weekends 1–4.*

❼ Most downtown buses pass the **Náttúrufræðistofnun** (Museum of Natural History), located on Hlemmtorg Square along with the city's main bus station. The exhibits here vary from stuffed peacocks to giant sea turtles. *Tel. 91/29822. Admission free. Open Tues. and Thurs.–Sun. 1:30–4:30.*

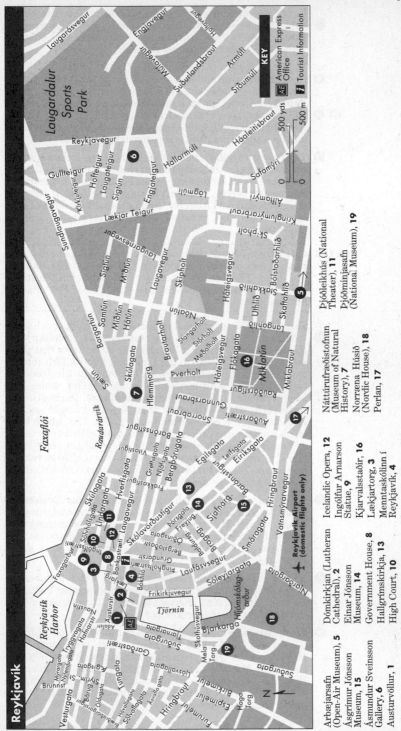

Reykjavík

Arbæjarsafn
(Open-Air Museum), **5**
Ásgrímur Jónsson
Museum, **15**
Ásmundur Sveinsson
Gallery, **6**
Austurvöllur, **1**

Dómkirkjan (Lutheran
Cathedral), **2**
Einar Jónsson
Museum, **14**
Government House, **8**
Hallgrímskirkja, **13**
High Court, **10**

Icelandic Opera, **12**
Ingólfur Arnarson
Statue, **9**
Kjarvalsstaðir, **16**
Lækjartorg, **3**
Menntaskólinn í
Reykjavík, **4**

Náttúrufræðistofnun
(Museum of Natural
History), **7**
Norræna Húsið
(Nordic House), **18**
Perlan, **17**

Þjóðleikhús (National
Theater), **11**
Þjóðminjasafn
(National Museum), **19**

⑧ Leading east out of Lækjartorg square is Bankastræti. On the left-hand side is an 18th-century white building, **Government House.** Initially it was a prison, but it now houses the offices of Iceland's president and prime minister.

Walk left toward Arnarhóll Hill. On top of the hill is the **⑨ Ingólfur Arnarson statue,** named after the first settler in Iceland, a Viking who arrived in 874 and lived in Reykjavík. Nearby is the modern Central Bank. Across the hill is a 19th-century **⑩ ⑪** building that is now the **High Court.** Behind it is the Þjóðleikús (National Theater), built during the 1940s. Most of the other buildings in the area house government ministries.

⑫ Walk along Ingólfsstræti. To the right is the **Icelandic Opera** building, which was Iceland's first cinema and later its first opera house. A bit farther up, across Bankastræti, is the tourist information center. Turn left along Bankastræti. If you walk straight ahead, you'll be able to enjoy the various shops of what used to be the greatest shopping street in Iceland, Laugavegur.

Time Out **Café Laugavegur 22.** This is where the young and innovative pop and rock artists in Reykjavík gather for lunches, dinners, and coffee. The food and prices are reasonable, but the atmosphere can be outrageous. *Tel. 91/13628. Closed Fri. eve. and Sat. Inexpensive.*

⑬ To continue the tour from Bankastræti, turn right onto Skólavörðustígur. At the end of that street towers **Hallgrímskirkja,** a church with a 65-meter (210-foot) gray stone tower that dominates the city's skyline in the same way that its 17th-century namesake, Hallgrímur Pétursson, has dominated Icelandic devotional poetry with his *Hymns of the Passion,* which have been translated into more than 50 languages. During the day the church, which took more than 40 years to build and was completed in the '80s, is open to the public. The **church tower** offers a panoramic view of the compact and colorful city center and its spacious suburbs, which have spread out since World War II in order to accommodate a more than tenfold increase in population. *Tel. 91/10745. Admission to tower: ISK 200 adults, ISK 100 children under 12. Open daily 10–6.*

⑭ Art lovers will want to visit the neighboring **Einar Jónsson Museum,** devoted to the works of Iceland's leading sculptor early in this century. His monumental sculptures have a strong symbolic and mystical content. *v/Skólavörðuholt. Admission: ISK 100. Open weekends, 1:30–4. Sculpture garden open daily, 11–4.*

⑮ Nearby is the **Ásgrímur Jónsson Museum,** which features the works of the popular post-Impressionist painter Ásgrímur Jónsson (1870–1968). *Bergstaðastræti 74. Admission free. Open weekdays 4–10, weekends 2–10.*

⑯ **Kjarvalsstaðir,** a municipal art gallery named in honor of Jóhannes Kjarval (1889–1972), the nation's best-loved painter, is a 10-minute walk away from Hallgrímskirkja. It is nicely situated in the **Miklatún,** one of two spacious parks in Reykjavík. Temporary exhibits show the work of Icelandic and visiting artists. *v/Flókagata, tel. 91/26131. Admission free, except for private exhibitions. Open daily 2–8.*

From the Municipal Art Gallery, cross Miklabraut and head south along any one of the short side streets to the large, glass-domed conservatory, **Perlan,** perched high on a hill. Resting atop five huge hot-water reservoirs that heat the capital area, there's a fine restaurant here as well. *Öskjuhlíð, tel. 91/620200. Admission free. Conservatory: open daily 11:30 AM–10 PM.*

Return to Miklabraut and walk west until you reach the city's other major park, Hljómskàlagarður. On your left is **Norræna Húsið** (Nordic House), a cultural center with exhibitions, lectures, and concerts. *Call for information, tel. 91/17030. Open daily 2–7.*

Northwest of the Nordic House is the campus of the **University of Iceland** (founded 1911). On the campus grounds is the **Þjóðminjasafn** (National Museum), and a visit here is compulsory for anyone interested in Icelandic culture. On display are Viking artifacts, national costumes, weaving, wood carving, and silver works. *Suðurgata 41, tel. 91/28888. Admission free. Open June–Sept., daily 1:30–4; Oct.–May, Tues., Thurs., and weekends 1:30–4.*

From the National Museum, it is a 10-minute walk back to the pond and the city center.

Shopping

The most attractive shops, selling Icelandic woolen goods and arts and crafts, are on Aðalstræti, Hafnarstræti, and Vesturgata streets. Some stores to look for include **Icelandic Handcrafts Center** (Falcon House, Hafnarstræti 3, tel. 91/11784); the **Handknitting Association of Iceland,** (Skólavörð ustígur 19, tel. 91/21890 or 91/21912); and **Rammagerðin** (Hafnarstræti 19, tel. 91/17910 and Kringlan, tel. 91/689960).

Dining

Most Reykjavík restaurants feature excellent seafood dishes, cooked in a wide variety of ways. Many serve European cuisine, as well as local fish and lamb specialties. Reservations are vital on weekends in the better restaurants. Jacket and tie are appreciated but rarely required. Most are open from noon to midnight, and most take major credit cards. Some offer discount lunch or tourist menus. For details and price-category definitions, *see* Dining in Staying in Iceland, *above.*

Expensive **Bumannsklukkan.** One of Reykjavík's newer restaurants, this renovated 19th-century house has an old-style ambience. International cuisine is served, with an emphasis on seafood and traditional Icelandic delicacies. *Amtmannsstígur 1, tel. 91/613303. Reservations advised. AE, DC, MC, V.*

Hótel Holt. First-class service and fare are the trademarks of this fine hotel dining room. The decor is chosen from the owner's unmatched private collection of Icelandic art. *Bergstaðastræti 37, tel. 91/25700. Reservations advised. AE, DC, MC, V.*

★ **Perlan.** Situated atop the Conservatory, you may pay a bit more for the food, but the splendid view, especially at sunset, more than compensates for the price. *Öskjuhlíð, tel. 91/620200. Reservations advised. No lunch. AE, DC, MC, V.*

Viðey. Take a five-minute boat ride from the Sundahöfn harbor in East Reykjavík (for schedule information, call 91/29964 or 91/985–20099) to dine in the restored splendor of the 18th-century Royal Treasurer's residence. French nouvelle cuisine along with excellent game and fish make a memorable end to a visit to this historic island. *Viðey, tel. 91/681045. Reservations advised. No lunch. AE, DC, MC, V.*

★ **Vid Tjörnina.** This restaurant has a homey atmosphere. The chef is a pioneer of Icelandic seafood cuisine; his marinated codcheeks are not to be missed. *Templarasund 3, tel. 91/18555. Reservations advised. AE, MC, V.*

Moderate **Hornid.** Try the Icelandic mountain lamb in this appealing bistro, which has a cosmopolitan flair. *Hafnarstræti 15, tel. 91/20366. Reservations advised. AE, MC, V.*

Potturinn og Pannan. This small restaurant on the edge of the downtown area has service that is brisk and efficient without being impersonal. Lamb and fish dishes and American-style salads are the specialties. *Brautarholt 22, tel. 91/11690. Reservations advised. AE, MC, V.*

Trúbadorinn. This welcoming basement restaurant in the heart of town serves Mexican food, pizza, and other light fare. *Laugavegur 73, tel. 91/622631. Reservations not necessary. AE, DC, MC, V.*

Inexpensive **Café Hressó.** This is the place for a quick snack and some local color; it's as close to a French café as you'll get in Iceland. *Austurstræti 20, tel. 91/14353. Reservations not necessary. MC, V.*

Coffee Wagon. On the waterfront in West Reykjavík, this is the spot where local fishermen typically enjoy their hearty lunches. Try the filling and economical "fish of the day." *Grandagarði 10, tel. 91/15932. Reservations not necessary. No credit cards.*

Lodging

For details and price-category definitions, *see* Lodging in Staying in Iceland, *above.*

Expensive **Holt.** One of Reykjavík's finest hotels, the Holt is in a central
★ residential district. Many of the rooms are furnished with Icelandic works of art. The restaurant (*see* Dining, *above*) is especially good. *Bergstaðastræti 37, tel. 91/25700, fax 91/623025. 50 rooms with bath or shower. Facilities: restaurant and lounge. AE, DC, MC, V.*

Ísland. Reykjavík's newest luxury hotel opened in 1991, in the eastern part of the city, with superb sea and mountain views. *Ármúli 9, tel. 91/688999, fax 91/689957. 119 rooms with bath, 3 suites. Facilities: restaurant, bar, nightclub. AE, DC, MC, V.*

Loftleiðir. The Loftleiðir accommodates both tourists and those attending meetings and conventions. Located near the domestic airport, it's 15 minutes from the center of town. *Reykjavík Airport, tel. 91/22322, fax 91/25320. 218 rooms with bath. Facilities: indoor pool, sauna, solarium, meeting rooms, restaurant, cafeteria, and several lounges. AE, DC, MC, V.*

★ **Saga.** In a class of its own, this hotel is very popular with American businesspeople. All rooms are above the fourth level and have spectacular views of the city and beyond. It's within walking distance of most museums, shops, and restaurants. *Hagatorg, tel. 91/29900, fax 91/623928. 162 rooms with bath. Facilities: meeting rooms, restaurant with live music and dancing, rooftop grill, 6 bars, sauna, in-room video. AE, DC, MC, V.*

Moderate **Höfði.** This recently redecorated hotel is located uptown, beyond the main bus terminal. The Höfði offers simple accommodations, with a breakfast lounge. *Skipholt 27, tel. 91/26210, fax 91/623986. 36 rooms, most with bath. AE, MC, V.*

Lind. Near the Hlemmur city bus station and a 10-minute walk from downtown, it offers few frills but plenty of clean rooms and easy access to the city's best shopping, museums, and galleries. *Rauðarárstígur 18, tel. 91/623350, fax 91/623150. 44 rooms with bath. Facilities: meeting rooms, restaurant, lounge. AE, DC, MC, V.*

Inexpensive **Garður.** This is a student residence, open as a hotel during only the summer when the students are on vacation. It has basic but comfortable rooms, adequate for travelers on a tight budget. It's within easy reach of the National Museum and other attractions. *Hringbraut, tel. 91/15656. 44 rooms without bath. No credit cards. Closed in winter.*

Snorra Guest House. These accommodations are basic but clean, and the rooms are equipped with basins. The main bus station is close by. No breakfast is served. *Snorrabraut 52, tel. 91/16522. 18 rooms. No credit cards.*

The Icelandic Countryside

The real beauty of Iceland is in the countryside: the fjords of the east, the stark mountains of the north, the sands of the south, the rough coastline of the west, and the lava fields of the interior.

Getting Around

There are daily flights to most of the large towns. Although flights are expensive, special family fares and vacation tickets are available. There are car-rental agencies in Reykjavík, as well as in many towns around the country. Scheduled ferries are few and travel mainly to the Westmann Islands, from Þorlákshöfn on the south coast, and to Akranes, from Reykjavík. If you do not have your own car, your best bet is to buy one of the special bus tickets that cover scheduled routes throughout the country (*see* Getting Around in Staying in Iceland, *above*).

Guided Tours

Because of the remoteness of the countryside and the hassles of driving on roads that are often not in good condition, many people prefer a guided bus tour from Reykjavík; both day excursions and longer journeys are available. Such tours are an excellent way to relax and enjoy Iceland's spectacular scenery. Most longer tours operate between June and September and cost from ISK 25,000 to ISK 150,000 per person, including overnight accommodations and three meals a day. On some tours you'll stay in hotels; on others you'll camp out or sleep in tents. Tours typically last from 3 to 19 days and can be booked from abroad through **Icelandair** or travel agencies. For information on tour operators, contact the **Iceland Tourist Board** (Gimli, Lækjargata 3, Reykjavk, tel. 91/29488, fax 91/624749).

Local Tours One-day tours are available in all the major towns in Iceland and can be arranged through agencies in Reykjavík (*see* Important Addresses and Numbers, *above*).

From Akureyri there are several excursions:

Tours to **Lake Mývatn** take about 10 hours and cost about ISK 2,700 per person. On the "Midnight Sun Tour," you'll drive along Eyjafjörður and watch the sun reach its lowest point and then rise again. This is a four-hour tour and costs about ISK 2,500 per person.

From Egilsstaðir there's a tour to Mjóifjörður across the rough mountain passes—a strenuous eight-hour tour costing about ISK 2,200 per person. From Höfn in Hornafjörður you can go by bus on a "Glacier Tour," which lasts 10 hours and costs about ISK 4,500 per person. Boat tours from Stykkishólmur in West Iceland, Isafjörður in the west Fjords, and in the Westmann Islands are excellent and priced reasonably.

Tourist Information

Akureyri (Tourist Center, Hafnarstræti 82, tel. 96/24442).
Egilsstaðir (Kaupvangur 6, tel. 97/12000).
Höfn (Hótel Höfn, Hornafjörður, tel. 97/81240).
Ísafjörður (Tourist Bureau, Aðalstræti 11, tel. 94/3557).
Lake Mývatn (Hótel Reynihlíð, Mývatnssveit, tel. 96/44170).
Ólafsvík (Hótel Nes, Ólafsbraut 19, tel. 93/61300).
Seyðisfjörður (Austfar, Fjarðargata 8, tel. 97/21111).
Snæfellsnes (Hótel Búðir, tel. 93/8111).

Exploring the Iceland Countryside

See the Iceland map for the location of towns on this tour.

The South Iceland is not a crowded place. Between tourist accommodations there can be up to 80 kilometers (50 miles), so you must be prepared for some considerable traveling every day. Start your tour around Iceland from Reykjavík, heading east on the main ring road around the country (Road 1), which you will follow for most of your tour.

In **Hveragerði,** some 40 kilometers (25 miles) away, there are some interesting hot springs and botanic greenhouses where fruits and vegetables are grown. When you have passed **Selfoss,** 8 kilometers (5 miles) farther, you'll be in the heartland of Icelandic farming, and soon you'll cross the longest river in the country, Þjórsá. For an overnight stop in this area, the Edda hotels in **Skógar,** 120 kilometers (75 miles) east of Selfoss, and **Kirkjubæjarklaustur,** 80 kilometers (50 miles) farther east on road 205, are recommended (*see* Dining and Lodging, *below*).

The landscape around Kirkjubæjarklaustur is shaped by 200-year-old lava deposits. When the volcano Laki erupted in 1783, it produced the greatest amount of lava from a single eruption in recorded history.

Traveling the route along the south coast on a clear day, you'll see that the landscape is the area's major tourist attraction. Don't miss the **Skaftafell National Park.** There you can put down your tent for ISK 350 a night. The park is at the root of the glacier Svínafellsjökull, and farther up is the highest mountain in Iceland, Hvannadalshnjúkur, rising to 2,119 meters (6,300 feet). In the park you can walk for an hour or a day through a rare combination of green forest, clear waters, waterfalls, sands, mountains, and glaciers. About 32 kilometers (20 miles) east of the park is the adventure world of **Jökulsárlón,** with its eerie icefloes. Boat tours can be arranged on arrival for ISK 1,000. Information is available at Skaftafell National Park.

One-day downhill skiing and snowmobiling tours to **Vatnajökull** are scheduled from June through September from **Höfn** in Hornafjörður, Road 99. These tours are a once-in-a-lifetime opportunity, as the trip takes you through some great nature spots. Details and general tourist information are available from the Hótel Höfn (tel. 97/81240).

The East   From Höfn the journey continues to Djúpivogur, Road 98, and the east coast, where one fjord lies beside another. From **Breiðdalsvík** there are two alternative routes. The coastal one runs through the fishing villages of **Stöðvarfjörður, Fáskrúðsfjörður,** and **Reyðarfjörður,** which can be reached via Roads 97, 96, and 92, respectively.

From Reyðarfjörður the ring road continues for 32 kilometers (20 miles) to **Egilsstaðir.** If you decide not to follow the coastline from Breiðdalsvík, you'll reach Egilsstaðir across Breiðdalsheiði, which, at approximately 775 meters (2,500 feet), is the highest mountain road in Iceland. The road is excitingly steep and, unfortunately, not the best example of Icelandic highland road engineering. In Egilsstaðir you are about 768 kilometers (480 miles) from Reykjavík, or halfway around the island, so you can either turn back the way you came or continue north. There is a tourist information center where you can get some traveling tips (Kaupvangur 6, tel. 97/11510).

Some 24 kilometers (15 miles) south of Egilsstaðir on Road 931 is **Hallormsstaðarskógur,** the largest forest in Iceland. There you can stop for the night at an Edda hotel, or pitch a tent by the Lögur lagoon. Perhaps you'll spot the Icelandic relative of the Loch Ness monster, which, according to myth, lives in the lagoon. This area is one of the most accessible natural paradises in Iceland, and it is strongly recommended.

From there you can travel around the **Hérað district** and to **Seyðisfjörður,** 48 kilometers (30 miles) from Egilsstaðir on Road 93. Check with the tourist office there for information on such activities as boat trips and pony trekking. Here the Faroese ferry *Norröna* docks weekly on its North Atlantic summer sailing route.

From Egilsstaðir the ring road continues for more than 160 kilometers (100 miles) across remote highlands to **Lake Mývatn.** On this daylong journey through a remote area, you will pass by the highest inhabited farm in the country, Möðruvellir, approximately 418 meters (1,350 feet) above sea level. Lake Mývatn, with its incredibly rich variety of waterfowl, is a mecca for bird lovers and also offers fantastic geological formations. Few people live in the area, but there are two good hotels with restaurants (*see* Dining and Lodging, *below*). Information about bike rentals, fishing, and other activities is available in the Hótel Reynihlíð (tel. 96/44170).

From Lake Mývatn there are two possible routes. One is to go directly along Road 1 to Akureyri, the capital of the north, a journey of 96 kilometers (60 miles). An astonishing attraction on this route is **Goðafoss,** a graceful but forceful waterfall.

The other alternative is to go to **Húsavik** (Road 87) and **Tjörnes** (Road 85) for a day or so, a detour of more than 160 kilometers (100 miles). The major attractions in this area are the thundering waterfall **Dettifoss** (Road 864) and the canyon of **Ásbyrgi,** which legend says is a giant hoofprint left by Sleipnir, an eight-legged horse of the ancient pagan god Odin.

The North and the West The natural surroundings in **Akureyri** are unequaled by any other Icelandic town. Late-19th-century wooden houses give the city center a sense of history, as well as architectural variety. The **Botanic Gardens** (admission free, open daily 8 AM–11 PM) has a fine collection of arctic flora. Akureyri also has the northernmost 18-hole golf course in the world, which hosts the **Midnight Sun Open Golf Tournament** each year around midsummer. For information, call Úrval-Útsýn Travel, tel. 91/699300.

From Akureyri you can go for an evening tour north along the coast of **Eyjafjörður** (Road 82) to see the midnight sun; June and July are the brightest months. Information for traveling in the north of the country is available at the Akureyri tourist center.

Driving from Akureyri to Reykjavík, a journey of 400 kilometers (250 miles) takes an entire day, so if there is time to spare, a stay in **Sauðárkrókur** (Roads 75 and 76), **Blönduós,** or **Borgarnes** can be both pleasant and peaceful. Holders of the Omnibus Passport (*see* Getting Around in Iceland, *above*) should not miss the 320-kilometer (200-mile) detour to **Snæfellsnes,** via Roads 54 and 57, for a couple of days, at least. A night in the presence of the glacier Snæfellsjokull, where Jules Verne's *Journey to the Center of the Earth* begins, is recommended.

From **Ólafsvík,** snowmobile tours to the top of the glacier can be arranged. The trip costs ISK 2,500 per person; information is available from the Hótel Nes (tel. 93/61300).

Another interesting detour, which can take up to a week, is to **Vestfirðir** (the West Fjords) (Roads 68, 69, and 61). From Ísafjörður, trips to the inhabitable parts of Strandarsýsla may be of interest to those who are keen on walking and mountaineering. Information is available at the Vestfirðir Tourist Bureau (Aðalstræti 11, tel. 94/3457).

Dining and Lodging

If you tour Iceland on your own, whether by public transportation or by car, get a list of hotels and guesthouses in the regions from the **Tourist Information Centre** (Bankastræti 2, tel. 91/623045, fax 91/624749). "Farm Holidays in Iceland," lists 42 farms that take visitors. You can also contact **Icelandic Farm Holidays** (91/19200 or 91/623640) for a wide listing of participating farms. In addition, the **Icelandic Touring Club** operates a number of huts for mountaineers and hikers in the remote parts of the country. The huts are clean, warm, and comfortable, but are available during the summer months only on a first-come, first-served basis.

Most restaurants outside Reykjavík are in hotels, and the following list is largely a selection of hotel/restaurants. The cost of lodging in the countryside is less than in Reykjavík, but the meals cost about the same. Most hotels are moderately priced, around ISK 5,500 for a double room with breakfast. Youth hostels and farmhouse lodging are also available around the country, ranging from ISK 1,000 to ISK 2,500 per person. For details and price-category definitions, *see* Dining and Lodging in Staying in Iceland, *above.*

Akureyri
★

Hótel KEA. You'll receive first-class hotel service, and the price is a surprise—real value for the money. There is an excellent kitchen, and moderately priced food is available in the cafeteria. *Hafnarstræti 97, tel. 96/22200, fax 96/21009. 72 rooms with shower. AE, MC, V. Expensive.*

Hótel Norðurland. Newly renovated and well situated in the center of town, this hotel has a restaurant/bar. *Geislagata 7, tel. 96/22600, fax 96/27833. 28 rooms with bath. Facilities: satellite TV, minibars, phones. AE, DC, MC, V. Expensive.*

Hótel Edda. There is good service here and a cafeteria. *Menntaskólinn, tel. 96/24055. 77 rooms without bath. Facilities: swimming pool. AE, MC, V. Moderate.*

Lónsá Youth Hostel. It's lodging only, but there are kitchen facilities available. *Glæsibæjarhreppur, tel. 96/25037. 11 rooms without bath. AE, MC, V. Inexpensive.*

Blönduós
Hótel Blönduós. This small hotel, located in the center of town, has a restaurant. *Aðalgata 6, tel. 95/24126. 18 rooms, 11 with shower. AE, MC, V. Inexpensive.*

Borgarnes
Hótel Borgarnes. One of the biggest and most popular hotels on the west coast, this establishment offers both a cafeteria and an elegant restaurant. *Egilsgata 14–16, tel. 93/71119, fax 93/71443. 36 rooms with shower. AE, DC, MC, V. Expensive.*

Breiðdalsvík
Hótel Bláfell. This is a newly built hotel, but it has no dining facilities. *Sólvellir 14, tel. 97/56770. 15 rooms without bath. AE, MC, V. Inexpensive.*

Búðir
Hótel Búðir. Under the magical glacier Snæfellsjökull and close to a beach of black lava and golden sand, this rustic hotel has an excellent restaurant. *Snæfellsnes, tel. 93/56700. 10 rooms without bath. AE, DC, MC, V. Moderate.*

Djúpivogur
Hótel Framtíð. This small hotel by the harbor has a dining room where home-style food is served in a friendly atmosphere. *Tel. 97/88887. 10 rooms without bath. AE, MC, V. Moderate.*

Berunes Youth Hostel. This small summer hostel offers lodging for 15 people. *Beruneshr., tel. 97/88988. No credit cards. Closed winter. Inexpensive.*

Egilsstaðir
Hótel Valaskjálf. This hotel is large and practical, with a restaurant and a cafeteria. There is dancing on the weekends. *v/ Skógarströnd, tel. 97/11500, fax 97/11501. 66 rooms with shower. AE, MC, V. Moderate.*

Hótel Egilsstaðir. This is a charming farmhouse hotel. *Tel. 97/11114. 10 rooms without bath. No credit cards. Inexpensive.*

Húsey Youth Hostel. A distance from town, this hostel offers lodging only. *Hróarstunga, tel. 97/13010. No credit cards. Inexpensive.*

Hallormsstaður
Hótel Edda. The hotel offers guests little to write home about, but the harmony of forest, lake, and quiet bays more than makes up for its shortcomings. It has a good restaurant. *Hallormsstað, tel. 97/11705. 17 rooms without bath. AE, DC, V. Closed Oct.–Apr. Moderate.*

Hornafjörður
Hótel Höfn. This clean and comfortable hotel has a restaurant with good food and service. Try the excellent almond trout. Fast food is also available at the grill, and there is dancing on

the weekends. *Tel. 97/81240, fax 97/81996. 40 rooms, half with shower. AE, MC, V. Moderate.*

Húsavík   **Hótel Húsavík.** Popular as a ski hotel during winter, this comfortable hotel has both a restaurant and a reasonably priced cafeteria. *Ketilsbraut 22, tel. 96/41220, fax 96/42161. 33 rooms with shower. AE, DC, MC, V. Expensive.*

Hveragerði   **Hótel Örk.** Newly built with a health spa, the Örk has expensive rooms, but meals in the ground-floor restaurant are reasonable. Three- to seven-day "spa cure" retreat packages are available. *Breiðamörk 1, tel. 98/34700. 76 rooms with shower. AE, MC, V. Expensive.*
Ból Youth Hostel. *Hveramörk 14, tel. 98/34198. No dining facilities. No credit cards. Inexpensive.*

Ísafjörður   **Hótel Ísafjörður.** This is a good family hotel. The restaurant offers a great variety of tasty seafood. *Silfurtorg 2, tel. 94/4111, fax 94/4767. 20 rooms with shower. AE, MC, V. Moderate.*

Kirkjubæjarklaustur   **Hótel Edda.** This is an ordinary hotel with a restaurant. *Tel. 98/74799. 55 rooms with shower. Facilities: swimming pool. AE, MC, V. Closed Oct.–Apr. Moderate.*

Mývatn   **Hótel Reynihlíð.** This popular hotel offers a good general information service for tourists and a restaurant. *Mývatnssveit, tel. 96/44170, fax 96/44371. 44 rooms with shower. AE, DC, MC, V. Expensive.*
Hótel Reykjahlíð. This small hotel has an exclusive location by the lake and a restaurant. *Mývatnssveit, tel. 96/44142. 7 rooms without bath. AE, MC, V. Closed Oct.–Apr. Moderate.*

Ólafsvík   **Hótel Nes.** This functional hotel is close to the harbor. Its cafeteria offers good food at moderate prices. *Ólafsbraut 19, tel. 93/61300. 38 rooms without bath. No credit cards. Moderate.*

Saudárkrókur   **Hótel Mælifell.** This attractive hotel has a restaurant and dancing on the weekends. *Aðalgata 7, tel. 95/35265. 6 rooms with shower. AE, MC, V. Moderate.*

Seyðisfjörður   **Hótel Snæfell.** This is a new hotel in an old wooden house. Its
★   glassed-in restaurant, by a picturesque pond, serves good food. *Austurvegur 3, tel. 97/21460. 9 rooms with shower. AE, MC, V. Moderate.*

Skaftafell   **Hótel Freysnes.** This newly built guest house is adjacent to Skaftafell National Park. *Skaftafell, 785 Fagurhólsmýri, tel. 97/81945, fax 97/81946. MC, V. Moderate.*

Skógar   **Hótel Edda.** Close to the waterfall Skógarfoss, this summer hotel is beautifully located with views to the sea and to the mountains and glaciers. It has a restaurant. *Skógar, tel. 98/78870. 36 rooms without bath. AE, MC, V. Closed Oct.–Apr. Moderate.*

17 Ireland

Ireland, one of the westernmost countries in Europe, is a small island on which you are never more than an hour's drive from the sea. It's actually two countries in one. The northeast corner of the island, Northern Ireland, remains a part of the United Kingdom, while the Republic, with a population of only 3½ million, has been independent since 1921.

The Republic of Ireland is virtually free from the "troubles" that dominate the news from Northern Ireland. Over the past few years, millions of pounds have been spent on upgrading tourist facilities, but the attractions of Ireland as a vacation destination remain the same as ever: those of a small, friendly country with a mild climate and a relaxed pace of life, where simple pleasures are to be found in its scenery, its historical heritage, its sporting opportunities, and the informal hospitality of its loquacious inhabitants.

Dublin, the capital, is a thriving modern city. It's a strikingly elegant city, too, a fact of which the Dubliners are well aware. Trinity College, Dublin Castle, and the magnificent public buildings and distinctive Georgian squares of the city have all been restored, allowing the elegance of 18th-century Dublin to emerge again after centuries of neglect.

The Irish way of life is unpretentious and informal. Pubs play an important part in it. The Irish will be found at their most convivial when seated in front of a pint of their famous black beer, Guinness, consumed here in vast quantities. Even if you do not usually frequent bars, a visit to an Irish pub or two will add greatly to the enjoyment of your visit.

The pace of life outside Dublin is even more relaxed. When a local was asked for the Irish-language equivalent of *mañana*, the reply came that there is no word in Irish to convey quite the same sense of urgency. An exaggeration, of course, but the farther you travel from the metropolis, the more you will be inclined to linger. Apart from such sporting attractions as championship golf, horse racing, deep-sea fishing, and angling, the thing to do in Ireland is to take it easy, and look around you.

The lakes of Killarney—a chain of deep-blue lakes—surrounded by romantic, boulder-strewn mountains are justifiably the country's most famous attractions. The Ring of Kerry provides the motorist with a day-long tour through lush coastal vegetation. By contrast, you will have to explore the eerie limestone desert called The Burren, in County Clare, on foot in order to find its rare Alpine and Mediterranean flowers. Likewise, if you want to stand on the summit of the Cliffs of Moher to watch the Atlantic breakers pounding on the rocks 217 meters (700 feet) below you, you'll have to walk a bit first. The blue hills of Connemara remain the inspiration for many paintings. The history buff will delight in the Shannon region, peppered with numerous castles, some of which have been meticulously restored. Throughout the country, there are prehistoric and early Christian remains to be discovered. You can also seek out the places made famous by James Joyce, William Butler Yeats, John Millington Synge, and other well-known writers and gain a new insight into the land and the people who inspired them.

Essential Information

Before You Go

When to Go   The main tourist season runs from June to mid-September.
The attractions of Ireland are not as dependent on the weather
as those in most other northern European countries, and the
scenery is just as attractive in the off-peak times of fall and
spring. Accommodations are more economical in winter, although some of the smaller attractions are closed from October
to March. In all seasons the visitor can expect to encounter
rain.

Climate   Winters are mild though wet; summers can be warm and sunny,
but there's always the risk of a sudden shower. No one ever
went to Ireland for a suntan.

The following are the average daily maximum and minimum
temperatures for Dublin.

Jan.	46F	8C	May	60F	15C	Sept.	63F	17C
	34	1		43	6		48	9
Feb.	47F	8C	June	65F	18C	Oct.	57F	14C
	35	2		48	9		43	6
Mar.	51F	11C	July	67F	19C	Nov.	51F	11C
	37	3		52	11		39	4
Apr.	55F	13C	Aug.	67F	19C	Dec.	47F	8C
	39	4		51	11		37	3

Currency   The unit of currency in Ireland is the pound, or punt (pronounced "poont"), written as IR£ to avoid confusion with the
pound sterling. The currency is divided into the same denominations as in Britain, with IR£1 divided into 100 pence (written
p). There is likely to be some variance in the rates of exchange
between Ireland and the United Kingdom (which includes
Northern Ireland). Change U.K. pounds at a bank when you
get to Ireland (pound coins not accepted); change Irish pounds
before you leave.

U.S. dollars and British currency are accepted only in large hotels and shops licensed as bureaux de change. In general, visitors are expected to use Irish currency. Banks give the best
rate of exchange. The rate of exchange at press time (spring
1993) was IR£59 to the U.S. dollar and IR£90 to the British
pound sterling.

What It Will Cost   Dublin is one of Europe's most expensive cities—an unfortunate state of affairs that manifests itself most obviously in hotel
and restaurant rates. You can generally keep costs lower if you
visit Ireland on a package tour. Alternatively, consider staying
in a guest house or one of the multitude of bed-and-breakfasts;
they provide an economical and atmospheric option (*see* Lodging in Staying in Ireland, *below*). The rest of the country—with
the exception of the better-known hotels and restaurants—is
less expensive than Dublin. That the Irish themselves complain
bitterly about the high cost of living is partly attributable to
the high rate of value-added tax (VAT)—a stinging 21% on
"luxury" goods and 10% on hotel accommodations. Some sample costs make the point. For instance, while a double room in a
moderate Dublin hotel will cost about IR£80, with breakfast
sometimes another IR£7 per person, the current rate for a

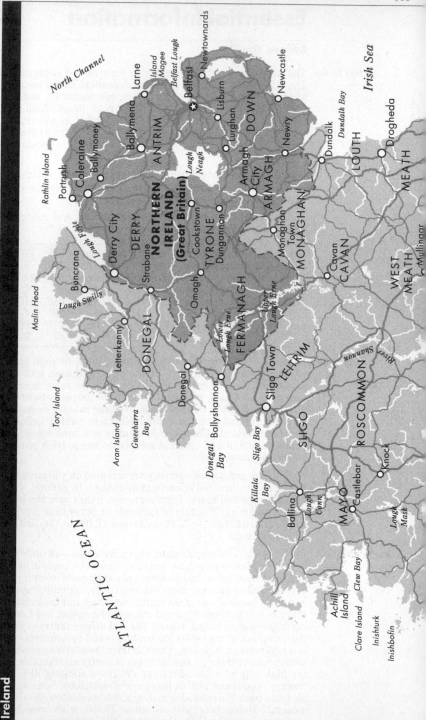

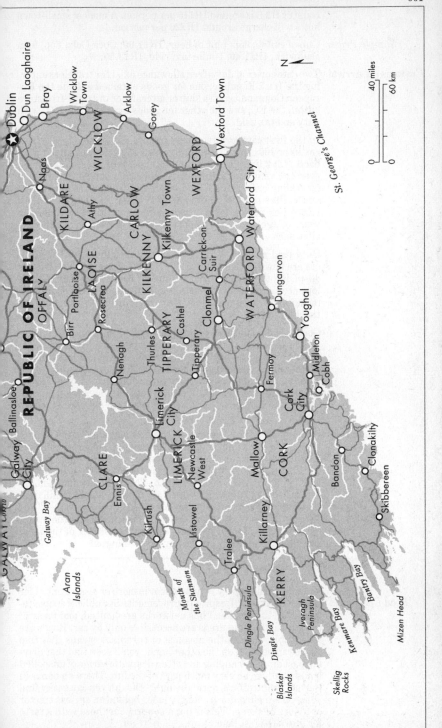

country B&B is around IR£15 per person. A modest small-town hotel will charge around 1R£20 per person.

Sample Prices Cup of coffee, 65p; pint of beer, IR£1.90; Coca-Cola, 85p; ham sandwich, IR£1.40; 1-mile taxi ride, IR£3.50.

Customs on Arrival Two categories of duty-free allowance exist for travelers entering the Irish Republic: one for goods obtained outside the European Community, on a ship or aircraft, or in a duty-free store within the EC; and the other for goods bought in the EC, with duty and tax paid.

In the first category, you may import duty-free: (1) 200 cigarettes or 100 cigarillos or 50 cigars or 250 grams of smoking tobacco; (2) 2 liters of wine, and either 1 liter of alcoholic drink over 22% volume or 2 liters of alcoholic drink under 22% volume (sparkling or fortified wine included); (3) 50 grams of perfume and ¼ liter of toilet water; and (4) other goods to a value of IR£34 per person (IR£17 per person for travelers under 15 years of age); you may import 12 liters of beer as part of this allowance.

Duty paid allowances increased substantially in 1993. Travelers are now entitled to purchase (1) 800 cigarettes, (2) 10 liters of spirits, (3) 45 liters of wine, and (4) 55 liters of beer. The allowances apply only to goods bought in shops in EC countries, including Britain and Northern Ireland, which already have the duty paid.

Goods that cannot be freely imported include firearms, ammunition, explosives, drugs (e.g., narcotics, amphetamines), indecent or obscene books and pictures, oral smokeless tobacco products, meat and meat products, poultry and poultry products, plants and plant products (including shrubs, vegetables, fruit, bulbs, and seeds), domestic cats and dogs from outside the United Kingdom, and live animals from outside Northern Ireland.

Language Officially, the Irish language is the first language of the Republic, but the everyday language of the majority of Irish people is English. Except for the northwest, where many signs are not translated, most signs in the country are written in Irish with an English translation underneath. There is one important exception to this rule, with which all visitors should familiarize themselves: *Fir* and *mná* translate respectively into "men" and "women." The *Gaeltacht*—areas in which Irish *is* the everyday language of most people—comprises only 6% of the land, and all its inhabitants are, in any case, bilingual.

Getting Around

By Car Ireland is one country in which a car is more or less essential for
Road Conditions successful travel. Despite improvements in public transportation, both the train and bus networks are limited, and many of the most intriguing areas are accessible only by car. Roads are reasonable, though the absence of turnpikes means that trip times can be long; on the other hand, you'll soon find that driving past an everchanging and often dramatic series of unspoiled landscapes can be very much part of the fun. There's a bonus in the fact that traffic is normally light, though you can easily find yourself crawling down country lanes behind an ancient tractor or a flock of sheep. This is not a country for those with a taste for life in the fast lane.

All principal roads are designated by the letter N, meaning National Primary Road. Thus, the main highway north from Dublin is N1, the main highway northwest is N2, and so on. Road signs are usually in both Irish and English; in the northwest, most are in Irish only, so make sure you have a good road map. Distances on the new green signposts are in kilometers; the old white signposts give distances in miles.

Rules of the Road Driving is on the left. There is a general speed limit of 96 kph (60 mph) on most roads; in towns, the limit is 48 kph (30 mph). In some areas, the limit is 64 kph (40 mph); this is always clearly posted. At junctions, traffic from the right takes priority.

Seat belts must be worn by the driver and front-seat passengers. Children under 12 must ride in the back. Drunk-driving laws are strict.

Parking Despite the relative lack of traffic, parking in towns is a real problem. Signs with the letter P indicate parking lots, but if there's a stroke through the P, keep away or you'll collect a stiff fine, normally around IR£20. After 6 PM, restrictions are lifted. Give lot attendants about 20p when you leave.

Frontier Posts There are 20 approved routes for crossing the border between the Republic of Ireland and Northern Ireland. If you plan to drive into Northern Ireland in a rented car, be sure the rental company furnishes the necessary papers. Formalities of crossing the border are minimal, though you may find additional checks just north of the border. *Do not* drive on roads near the border marked "Unapproved Road."

By Train **Iarnód Eireann** (Irish Rail) and **Bus Eireann** (Irish Bus) are independent components of the state-owned public transportation company **Coras Iompair Eireann** (CIE). The rail network, although much cut back in the past 25 years, is still extensive, with main routes radiating from Dublin to Cork, Galway, Limerick, Tralee, Killarney, Westport, and Sligo; there is also a line for the north and Belfast. All trains are diesel; cars on principal expresses have air-conditioning. There are two classes on many trains—Super Standard (first class) and Standard (second class). Dining cars are carried on main expresses. There are no sleeping cars.

Speeds are slow in comparison with those of other European trains. Dublin, however, now has a modern commuter train—the DART—running south from the suburb of Howth through the city to Bray on the Wicklow coast, with various stops along the way.

Fares For the strictly independent traveler, the 15-day **Rambler** ticket gives unlimited travel by train and bus and is an excellent value at IR£115. It can be purchased from any city bus terminal or train-station ticket office and is valid for travel on any 15 days in a 30-day period. There is an eight-day **Rambler** ticket (rail and bus) for IR£78, valid for any 8 days in a 15-day period. One- and four-day round-trip train tickets are also available at discounted rates. The **Irish Rover** ticket includes travel in Northern Ireland via rail, bus, and Ulsterbus; it costs IR£115 for 15 days.

By Plane Distances are not great in Ireland, so air travel plays only a small role in internal travel. There are daily flights from Dublin to Shannon, Cork, Waterford, Kerry, Knock, and Galway; all flights take around 30 minutes. There is frequent service to the

Aran Islands, off Galway Bay, from Connemara Airport, Galway. The flight takes 15–25 minutes.

By Bus The provincial bus system operated by Bus Eireann is widespread—more so than the train system—although service can be infrequent in remote areas. But the routes cover the entire country and are often linked to the train services (*see* By Train, *above*) for details of combined train and bus discount tickets.

By Boat Exploring Ireland's lakes, rivers, and canals is a delightful offbeat way to get to know the country. Motor cruisers can be chartered on the Shannon, the longest river in the British Isles. The Irish Tourist Board has details of the wide choice of trips and operators available.

For drifting through the historic Midlands on the Grand Canal and river Barrow, contact **Celtic Canal Cruisers,** Tullamore, County Offaly, tel. 0506/21861.

By Bicycle Biking can be a great way to get around Ireland. Details of bicycle rentals are available from the Irish Tourist Board. Rates average IR£7.50 per day or IR£35 per week. You must pay a IR£30 deposit. Be sure to make reservations, especially in July and August. If you rent a bike in the Republic, you may *not* take it into Northern Ireland; nor may you take a bike rented in Northern Ireland into the Republic.

Staying in Ireland

Telephones There are pay phones in all post offices and most hotels and
Local Calls bars, as well as in street booths. Local calls cost 20p for three minutes, calls within Ireland cost about 50p for three minutes, and calls to Britain cost about IR£1.75 for three minutes. Rates go down by about a third after 6 PM and all day Saturday and Sunday.

International Calls For calls to the United States and Canada, dial 001 followed by the area code. For calls to the United Kingdom, dial 03 followed by the number. Don't make international calls from your hotel room unless absolutely necessary. Most hotels add a 200–300% surcharge to calls.

Mail Airmail rates to the United States, Canada, and the Common-
Postal Rates wealth are 52p for the first 10 grams, air letters 45p, and postcards 38p. Letters to Britain and continental Europe cost 32p, postcards 28p.

Receiving Mail A general delivery service is operated free of charge from Dublin's General Post Office (O'Connell St., Dublin 1, tel. 01/728888).

Shopping Visitors from outside Europe can take advantage of the "cash-
VAT Refunds back" system on value-added tax (VAT) if their purchases total more than IR£50. A cash-back voucher must be filled out by the retailer at the point of sale. The visitor pays the total gross price, including VAT, and receives green and yellow copies of the invoice; both must be retained. These copies are presented to and stamped by customs, as you leave the country. Take the stamped form along to the cashier, and the VAT will be refunded.

Opening and Banks are open weekdays 10–12:30 and 1:30–3, and until 5 on
Closing Times selected days.

Museums are usually open weekdays 10–5, Saturday 10–1, Sunday 2–5. Always make a point of checking, however, as hours can change unexpectedly.

Shops are open Monday–Saturday 9–5:30, closing earlier on Wednesday, Thursday, or Saturday, depending on the locality.

National Holidays January 1; March 17 (St. Patrick's Day); April 1 (Good Friday); April 4 (Easter Monday); June 6 (Whit Monday); August 1 (August Monday); and December 25, 26. If you're planning a visit at Easter, remember that theaters and cinemas are closed for the last three days of the preceding week.

Dining When it comes to food, Ireland has some of the best raw materials in the world: prime beef, locally raised lamb and pork, free-range poultry, game in season, abundant fresh seafood, and locally grown seasonal vegetables. Despite the near-legendary awfulness of much Irish cooking in the recent past, times are definitely changing, and a new generation of chefs is beginning to take greater advantage of this abundance of magnificent produce. In almost all corners of the country, you'll find a substantial choice of restaurants, many in hotels, serving fresh local food that is imaginatively prepared and served.

If your tastes run toward traditional Irish dishes, there are still a few old-fashioned restaurants serving substantial portions of excellent, if plain, home cooking. Look for boiled bacon and cabbage, Irish stew, and *colcannon* (cooked potatoes diced and fried in butter with onions and either cabbage or leeks and covered in thick cream just before serving). The best bet for daytime meals is "pub grub"—a choice of soup and soda bread, two or three hot dishes of the day, salad platters, or sandwiches. Most bars serve food, and a growing number offer coffee and tea as an alternative to alcohol. Guinness, a dark beer, or "stout," brewed with malt, is the Irish national drink. Even if you never go out for a drink at home, you should visit at least one or two pubs in Ireland. The pub is one of the pillars of Irish society, worth visiting as much for entertainment and conversation as for drinking.

Mealtimes Breakfast is served between 8 and 10—earlier by special request only—and is a substantial meal of cereal, bacon, eggs, sausage, and toast. Lunch is eaten between 12:30 and 2. The old tradition of "high tea" taken around 5, followed by a light snack before bed, is still encountered in many Irish homes, including many bed-and-breakfasts. Elsewhere, however, it is generally assumed that you'll be eating between 7 and 9:30 and that this will be your main meal of the day.

Dress A jacket and tie or upscale casual dress are suggested for expensive restaurants. Otherwise casual dress is acceptable.

Ratings Prices are per person and include a first course, a main course, and dessert, but no wine or tip. Sales tax at 10% is included in all Irish restaurant bills. Some places, usually the more expensive establishments, add a 12% or 15% service charge, in which case no tip is necessary; elsewhere a tip of 10% is adequate. Highly recommended restaurants are indicated by a star ★.

Category	Cost
Expensive	over IR£28
Moderate	IR£16–IR£28
Inexpensive	under IR£16

Lodging Accommodations in Ireland range all the way from deluxe castles and renovated stately homes to thatched cottages and farmhouses to humble B&Bs. Standards everywhere are high, and they continue to rise. Pressure on hotel space reaches a peak between June and September, but it's a good idea to make reservations in advance at any time of the year, particularly at the more expensive spots. Rooms can be reserved directly from the United States; ask your travel agent for details. The Irish Tourist Board's Central Reservations Service (14 Upper O'Connell St., Dublin 1, tel. 01/747733, fax 01/743660) can make reservations, as can local tourist board offices.

The Irish Tourist Board (ITB) has an official grading system and publishes a detailed price list of all approved accommodations, including hotels, guest houses, farmhouses, B&Bs, and hostels. No hotel may exceed this price without special authorization from the ITB; prices must also be displayed in every room. Don't hesitate to complain either to the manager or to the ITB, or both, if prices exceed this maximum.

In general, hotels charge per person. In most cases (but not all, especially in more expensive places), the price includes a full breakfast. VAT is included, but some hotels—again, usually the more expensive ones—add a 10–15% service charge. This should be mentioned in their price list. In moderate and inexpensive hotels, be sure to specify whether you want a private bath or shower; the latter is cheaper. Off-season (October–May) prices are reduced by as much as 25%.

Guest Houses Some smaller hotels are graded as guest houses. To qualify, they must have at least five bedrooms. A few may have restaurants; those that do not will often provide evening meals by arrangement. Few will have a bar. Otherwise these rooms can be as comfortable as those of a regular hotel, and in major cities they offer very good value for the money, compared with the inexpensive hotels.

Bed-and-Breakfasts Bed-and-breakfast means just that. The bed can vary from a four-poster in the wing of a castle to a feather bed in a whitewashed farmhouse or the spare bedroom of a modern cottage. Rates are generally around IR£15 per person, though these can vary significantly. Although many larger B&Bs offer rooms with bath or shower, in some you'll have to use the bathroom in the hall and, in many cases, pay 50p–IR£1 extra for the privilege.

Camping There are a variety of beautifully sited campgrounds and trailer parks, but be prepared for wet weather! The ITB publishes a useful booklet "Caravan and Camping Guide" (IR£1).

Ratings Prices are for two people in a double room, based on high season (June–September) rates. Best bets are indicated by a star ★.

Category	Cost
Very Expensive	over IR£150
Expensive	IR£100–IR£150
Moderate	IR£70–IR£100
Inexpensive	under IR£70

Tipping Other than in upscale hotels and restaurants, the Irish are not really used to being tipped. Some hotels and restaurants will add a service charge of about 12% to your bill, so tipping isn't necessary unless you've received particularly good service.

Tip taxi drivers about 10% of the fare if the taxi has been using its meter. For longer journeys, where the fare is agreed in advance, a tip will not be expected unless some kind of commentary (solicited or not) has been provided. In luxury hotels, porters and bellhops will expect IR£1; elsewhere, 50p is adequate. Hairdressers normally expect a tip of about IR£1. You don't tip in pubs, but if there is waiter service in a bar or hotel lounge, leave about 20p.

Dublin

Arriving and Departing

By Plane All flights arrive at Dublin's Collinstown Airport, 10 kilometers (6 miles) north of town. For information on arrival and departure times, call individual airlines.

Between the Airport and Downtown Buses leave every 20 minutes from outside the Arrivals door for the central bus station in downtown Dublin. The ride takes about 30 minutes, depending on the traffic, and the fare is IR£2.50. A taxi ride into town will cost from IR£6 to IR£12, depending on the location of your hotel.

By Train There are three main stations. Heuston Station (at Kingsbridge) is the departure point for the south and southwest; Connolly Station (at Amiens Street), for Belfast, the east coast, and the west; Pearse Station (on Westland Row), for Bray and connections via Dun Laoghaire to the Liverpool/Holyhead ferries. Tel. 01/366222 for information.

By Bus The central bus station, Busaras, is at Store Street near the Custom House. Some buses terminate near Connolly Bridge. Tel. 01/734222 for information on city services (Dublin Bus); tel. 01/366111 for express buses and provincial services (Bus Eireann).

By Car The main access route from the north is N1; from the west, N4; from the south and southwest, N7; from the east coast, N11. On all routes there are clearly marked signs indicating the center of the city: "An Lar."

Getting Around

Dublin is small as capital cities go—the downtown area is positively compact—and the best way to see the city and soak in the full flavor is on foot.

By Train An electric train commuter service, DART (Dublin Area Rapid Transport), serves the suburbs out to Howth, on the north side of the city, and to Bray, County Wicklow, on the south side. Fares are about the same as for buses. Street-direction signs to DART stations read Staisiun/Station. The **Irish Rail** office is at 35 Lower Abbey Street; for rail inquiries, tel. 01/366222.

By Bus Most city buses originate in or pass through the area of O'Connell Street and O'Connell Bridge. If the destination board indicates "An Lar," that means that the bus is going to the city's central area. Timetables (IR£2) are available from the **Dublin Bus** office (59 Upper O'Connell St., tel. 01/720000) and give details of all routes, times of operation, and price codes. The minimum fare is 55p.

By Taxi Taxis do not cruise, but are located beside the central bus station, at train stations, at O'Connell Bridge, at St. Stephen's Green, and near major hotels. They are not of a uniform type or color. Make sure the meter is on. The initial charge is IR£2; the fare is displayed in the cab. A one-mile trip in city traffic costs about IR£3.50.

Important Addresses and Numbers

Tourist Information There is a tourist information office in the entrance hall of the **Irish Tourist Board** headquarters (Baggot Street Bridge, tel. 01/765871); open weekdays 9–5. More conveniently located is the office at 14 Upper O'Connell St. (tel. 01/747733); open weekdays 9–5:30, Saturday 9–1. There is also an office at the airport (tel. 01/376387). From mid-June to September, there is an office at the Ferryport, Dun Laoghaire (tel. 01/280–6984).

Embassies **U.S.** (42 Elgin Rd., Ballsbridge, tel. 01/6888777), **Canadian** (65 St. Stephen's Green, tel. 01/781988), **U.K.** (33 Merrion Rd., tel. 01/269–5211).

Emergencies **Police** (tel. 999), **Ambulance** (tel. 999), **Doctor** (tel. 01/537951 or 01/767273), **Dentist** (tel. 01/679–4311), **Pharmacy** (Hamilton Long, 5 Upper O'Connell St., tel. 01/748456).

Travel Agencies **American Express** (116 Grafton St., tel. 01/772874), **Thomas Cook** (118 Grafton St., tel. 01/771721).

Guided Tours

Orientation Tours Both **Bus Eireann** (tel. 01/366111) and **Gray Line Sightseeing** (tel. 01/619666) offer bus tours of Dublin and its surrounding areas. Both also offer three- and four-hour tours of the main sights in the city center. During the summer **Dublin Bus** (tel. 01/720000, ext. 3028) has a daily three-hour city-center tour using open-top buses in fine weather (£7). From mid-April through September Dublin Bus runs a continuous guided open-top bus tour (IR£5) that allows you to hop on and off the bus as often as you wish and visit some 15 sights along its route.

Special-Interest Tours **Bus Eireann** has a "Traditional Irish Music Night" tour. **Elegant Ireland** (tel. 01/751665) organizes tours for groups interested in architecture and the fine arts; these include visits with the owners of some of Ireland's stately homes and castles.

Walking Tours **Tour Guides Ireland** (tel. 01/679–4291) offers a selection of walking tours, including "Literary Dublin," "Georgian Dublin," and "Pub Tours." The **Irish Tourist Board** has a "Tourist

Trail" walk, which takes in the main sites of central Dublin and can be completed in about three hours.

Excursions **Bus Eireann** (tel. 01/366111) and **Gray Line Sightseeing** (tel. 01/619666) offer day-long tours into the surrounding countryside and longer tours elsewhere; price includes accommodations, breakfast, and admission costs. **CIE Tours International** offers vacations lasting from one to 10 days that include touring by train or bus, accommodations, and main meals. Costs range from around IR£220 (IR£325, including round-trip airfare from London) to IR£352 (IR£390 from London) for an eight-day tour in July and August.

Exploring Dublin

Numbers in the margin correspond to points of interest on the Dublin map.

Dublin is a small city with a population of just over 1 million. For all that, it has a distinctly cosmopolitan air, one that complements happily the individuality of the city and the courtesy and friendliness of its inhabitants. Originally a Viking settlement, Dublin is situated on the banks of the river Liffey. The Liffey divides the city north and south, with the more lively and fashionable spots, such as the Grafton Street shopping area, to be found on the south side. Most of the city's historically interesting buildings date from the 18th century, and, although many of its finer Georgian buildings disappeared in the overenthusiastic redevelopment of the '70s, enough remain, mainly south of the river, to recall the elegant Dublin of the past. The slums romanticized by writers Sean O'Casey and Brendan Behan have virtually been eradicated, but literary Dublin can still be recaptured by those who want to follow the footsteps of Leopold Bloom's progress, as described in James Joyce's *Ulysses*. And Trinity College, alma mater of Oliver Goldsmith, Jonathan Swift, and Samuel Beckett, among others, still provides a haven of tranquillity.

Dubliners are a talkative, self-confident people, eager to have visitors enjoy the pleasures of their city. You can meet a lively cross section of people in the city's numerous bars, probably the best places to sample the famous wit of the only city to have produced three winners of the Nobel Prize for Literature: William Butler Yeats, George Bernard Shaw, and Samuel Beckett.

O'Connell Street ❶ Begin your tour of Dublin at **O'Connell Bridge,** the city's most central landmark. Look closely and you will notice a strange feature: The bridge is wider than it is long. The north side of O'Connell Bridge is dominated by an elaborate memorial to Daniel O'Connell, "The Liberator," erected as a tribute to the great 19th-century orator's achievement in securing Catholic Emancipation in 1829. Today **O'Connell Street** is the city's main shopping area, though it seems decidedly parochial to anyone accustomed to Fifth Avenue or Rodeo Drive. Turn left just before the General Post Office and take a look at Henry Street. This pedestrians-only shopping area leads to the colorful **Moore Street Market,** where street vendors recall their most famous ancestor, Molly Malone, by singing their wares—mainly flowers—in the traditional Dublin style.

❷ The **General Post Office,** known as the GPO, occupies a special place in Irish history. It was from the portico of its handsome

Dublin

KEY

AE American Express Office

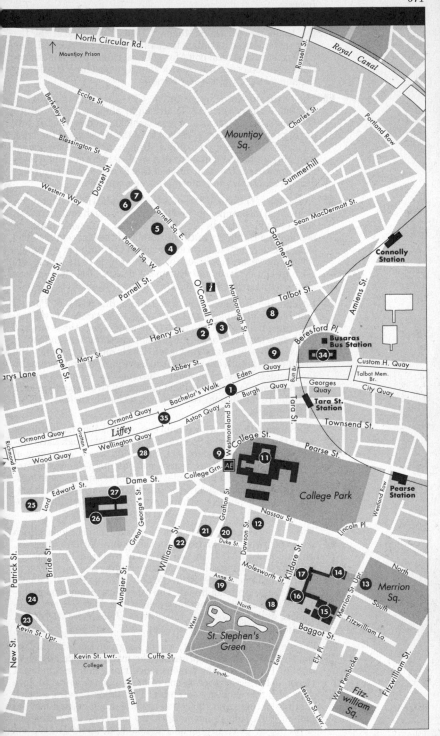

classical facade that Padraig Pearse read the Proclamation of the Republic on Easter Monday, 1916. You can still see the scars of bullets on its pillars from the fighting that ensued. The GPO remains the focal point for political rallies and demonstrations even today and is used as a viewing stand for VIPs during the annual St. Patrick's Day Parade.

❸ **The Gresham Hotel,** opposite the GPO, has played a part in Dublin's history since 1817, although, along with the entire O'Connell Street area, it is less fashionable now than it was during the last century. Just north of the Gresham is the Irish Tourist Board information office; drop in for a free street map, shopping guides, and information on all aspects of Dublin tourism. Opposite is the main office of Bus Eireann, which can supply bus timetables and information on excursions.

❹ At the top of O'Connell Street is the **Rotunda,** the first maternity hospital in Europe, opened in 1755. Not much remains of the once-elegant Rotunda Assembly Rooms, a famous haunt of fashionable Dubliners until the middle of the last century. The **Gate Theater,** housed in an extension of the Rotunda Assembly Rooms, however, continues to attract crowds to its fine repertoire of classic Irish and European drama. The theater was founded by the late Micheál MacLiammoir in 1928.

❺ Beyond the Rotunda, you will have a fine vista of **Parnell Square,** one of Dublin's earliest Georgian squares. You will notice immediately that the first-floor windows of these elegant brick-face buildings are much larger than the others and that it is easy to look in from street level. This is more than simply the result of the architect's desire to achieve perfect proportions on the facades: These rooms were designed as reception rooms, and fashionable hostesses liked passersby to be able to peer in and admire the distinguished guests at their luxurious, candle-lit receptions.

❻ **Charlemont House,** whose impressive Palladian facade dominates the top of Parnell Square, now houses the **Hugh Lane Municipal Gallery of Modern Art.** Sir Hugh Lane, a nephew of Lady Gregory, who was Yeats's curious, high-minded aristocratic patron, was a keen collector of Impressionist paintings. The gallery also contains some interesting works by Irish artists, including Yeats's brother Jack. *Parnell Sq., tel. 01/741903. Admission free. Open Tues.–Sat. 9:30–6, Sun. 11–5.*

❼ The Parnell Square area is rich in literary associations, which are explained and illustrated in the **Dublin Writers Museum,** which opened in 1991 in two carefully restored 18th-century buildings. Paintings, letters, manuscripts, and photographs relating to James Joyce, Sean O'Casey, George Bernard Shaw, W. B. Yeats, Brendan Behan, and others are on permanent display. There are also temporary exhibitions, lectures, and readings, as well as a bookshop. *18–19 Parnell Sq. N, tel. 01/722077. Admission: IR£2. Open Mon.–Sat. 10–5, Sun. 2–6.*

❽ Return to O'Connell Street, where a sign on the left will lead you to **St. Mary's Pro Cathedral,** the main Catholic church of Dublin. Try to catch the famous Palestrina Choir on Sunday at 11 AM. John McCormack is one of many famous voices to have
❾ sung with this exquisite ensemble. The **Abbey Theatre,** a brick building dating from 1966, was given a much-needed new facade in 1991. It has some noteworthy portraits and mementos in the foyer. Seats are usually available at about IR£10, and

with luck you may just have a wonderful evening. The luck element, unfortunately, must be stressed, since the Abbey has had both financial and artistic problems lately.

Time Out On Westmoreland Street is **Bewley's Coffee House** (there's another one nearby on Grafton Street), an institution that has been supplying Dubliners with coffee and buns since 1842. The aroma of coffee is irresistible, and the dark interior, with marble-top tables, original wood fittings, and stained-glass windows, evokes a more leisurely Dublin of the past. *12 Westmoreland St. and 78 Grafton St. Open Mon.–Sat. 9–5:30.*

Trinity and Stephen's Green It is only a short walk across O'Connell Bridge to **Parliament House.** Today this stately early 18th-century building is no more than a branch of the Bank of Ireland; originally, however, it housed the Irish Parliament. The original House of Lords, with its fine coffered ceiling and 1,233-piece Waterford glass chandelier, is open to the public during banking hours (weekdays 10–12:30 and 1:30–3). It's also worth taking a look at the main banking hall, whose judicial character—it was previously the Court of Requests—has been sensitively maintained.

⑪ Across the road is the facade of **Trinity College,** whose memorably atmospheric campus is a must for every visitor. Trinity College, Dublin (familiarly known as TCD) was founded by Elizabeth I in 1591 and offered a free education to Catholics—provided that they accepted the Protestant faith. As a legacy of this condition, right up until 1966, Catholics who wished to study at Trinity had to obtain a dispensation from their bishop or face excommunication. Today more than 70% of Trinity's students are Catholics, a clear indication of how far away those days seem to today's generation.

The facade, built between 1755 and 1759, consists of a magnificent portico with Corinthian columns. The design is repeated on the interior, so the view from outside the gates and from the quadrangle inside is the same. On the sweeping lawn in front of the facade are statues of two of the university's illustrious alumni—statesman Edward Burke and poet Oliver Goldsmith. Other famous students include the philosopher George Berkeley, who gave his name to the San Francisco area campus of the University of California; Jonathan Swift; Thomas Moore; Oscar Wilde; John Millington Synge; Henry Grattan; Wolfe Tone; Robert Emmet; Bram Stoker; Edward Carson; Douglas Hyde; and Samuel Beckett.

The 18th-century building on the left, just inside the entrance, is the chapel. There's an identical building opposite, the Examination Hall. The oldest buildings are the library in the far right-hand corner and a row of redbrick buildings known as the Rubrics, which contain student apartments; both date from 1712.

Ireland's largest collection of books and manuscripts is housed in **Trinity College Library.** There are more than 2½ million volumes gathering dust here; about half a mile of new shelving has to be added every year to keep pace with acquisitions. The library is entered through the library shop. Its principal treasure is the **Book of Kells,** a beautifully illuminated manuscript of the Gospels dating from the 8th century. Because of the beauty and the fame of the Book of Kells, at peak hours you may have to wait in line to enter the library; it's less busy early in the day.

Apart from the many treasures it contains, the aptly named Long Room is impressive in itself, stretching for 65 meters (209 feet). Originally it had a flat plaster ceiling, but the perennial need for more shelving resulted in a decision to raise the level of the roof and add the barrel-vaulted ceiling and the gallery bookcases. *Tel. 01/772941. Admission: IR£1.75. Open weekdays 9:30–4:45, Sat. 9:30–12:45.*

A breath of fresh air will be welcome after the library, so, when you're done admiring the award-winning modern architecture of the New Library and the Arts Building, pass through the gate to the sports grounds—rugby fields on your left, cricket on your right. Leave Trinity by the Lincoln Place Gate—a handy "back door."

⑫ Shoppers will find a detour along Nassau Street in order here. As well as being well endowed with bookstores, it contains the **Kilkenny Design Workshops,** which, besides selling the best in contemporary Irish design for the home, also holds regular exhibits of exciting new work by Irish craftsmen. *Open Mon.– Sat. 9–5.*

Time Out The **Kilkenny Kitchen,** a self-service restaurant on the first floor of the Kilkenny Design Workshops, overlooking the playing fields of Trinity, is an excellent spot for a quick, inexpensive lunch in modern, design-conscious surroundings. The emphasis is on natural fresh foods and home baking. *Nassau St. Open Mon.–Sat. 9–5.*

⑬ Nassau Street will lead you into **Merrion Square,** past a distinctive corner house that was the home of Oscar Wilde's parents. Merrion Square is one of the most pleasant in Dublin. Its flower gardens are well worth a visit in the summer months. Note the brightly colored front doors and the intricate fanlights above them—a distinctive feature of Dublin's domestic architecture.

⑭ The **National Gallery** is the first in a series of important buildings on the west side of the square. It is one of Europe's most agreeable and compact galleries, with more than 2,000 works on view, including a major collection of Irish landscape painting, 17th-century French works, paintings from the Italian and Spanish schools, and a collection of Dutch masters. *Merrion Sq., tel. 01/615133. Admission free. Open Mon.–Wed. 10–6, Thurs. 10–9, Fri.–Sat. 10–6, Sun. 2–5.*

⑮ Next door is **Leinster House,** seat of the Irish Parliament. This imposing 18th-century building has two facades: Its Merrion Square facade is designed in the style of a country house, while the other facade, in Kildare Street, is in the style of a town house. Visitors may be shown the house when the Dail (pronounced "Doyle"), the Irish Parliament, is not in session.

Time Out A half-block detour to your left, between Merrion Square and Stephen's Green, will bring you to the door of **Doheny & Nesbitt's,** an old Victorian-style bar whose traditional "snugs"— individual wood-paneled booths—are popular any time. Usually noisy and smoky, but always friendly, it is one of the few authentic pubs left in the city.

Stephen's Green, as it is always called by Dubliners, suffered more from the planning blight of the philistine '60s than did its neighbor, Merrion Square. An exception is the magnificent

Shelbourne Hotel, which dominates the north side of the green. It is still as fashionable—and as expensive—as ever.

Budget-conscious visitors should put on their finery and try afternoon tea in the elegant splendor of the Shelbourne's **Lord Mayor's Room.** You can experience its old-fashioned luxury for around IR£7.50 (including sandwiches and cakes) per head.

⑯ ⑰ Around the corner on Kildare Street, the town-house facade of Leinster House is flanked by the **National Museum** and the **National Library,** each featuring a massive colonnaded rotunda entrance built in 1890. The museum (Admission: free. Open Tues.–Sat. 10–5, Sun. 2–5) houses a remarkable collection of Irish treasures from 6000 BC to the present, including the Tara Brooch, the Ardagh Chalice, and the Cross of Cong. Every major figure in modern Irish literature, from James Joyce onward, studied in the National Library at some point. In addition to a comprehensive collection of Irish authors, it contains extensive newspaper archives. *Kildare St., tel. 01/618811. Admission free. Open Mon. 10–9, Tues.–Wed. 2–9, Thurs.–Fri. 10–5, Sat. 10–1.*

⑱ The **Genealogical Office**—the starting point for ancestor- tracing—also incorporates the **Heraldic Museum,** which features displays of flags, coins, stamps, silver, and family crests that highlight the uses and development of heraldry in Ireland. *2 Kildare St., tel. 01/618811. Genealogical Office: open weekdays 10–5. Heraldic Museum: admission free. Guided tours Mar.–Oct., cost IR£1. Open weekdays 10–12:30 and 2:30–4.*

⑲ The **Royal Irish Academy,** on Dawson Street, is the country's leading learned society; it has many important manuscripts in its unmodernized 18th-century library (open Mon.–Fri. 9:30–5:15). Just below the academy is **Mansion House,** the official residence of the Lord Mayor of Dublin. Its Round Room was the location of the first assembly of the Dail Eireann—the Irish Parliament—in January 1919. It is now used mainly for exhibitions.

⑳ ㉑ ㉒ **Grafton Street,** which runs between Stephen's Green and Trinity College, is a magnet for shoppers. Check out **Brown Thomas,** Ireland's most elegant and old-fashioned department store; it has an extremely good selection of sporting goods and Waterford crystal—an odd combination. Many of the more stylish boutiques are just off the main pedestrians-only areas, so be sure to poke around likely corners. Don't miss the **Powerscourt Town House,** an imaginative shopping arcade installed in and around the covered courtyard of an impressive 18th-century building. Nearby is the **Civic Museum,** which contains drawings, models, maps of Dublin, and other civic memorabilia. *58 S. William St., tel. 01/679–4260. Admission free. Open Tues.–Sat. 10–6, Sun. 11–4.*

㉓ A short walk from Stephen's Green will bring you to one of the smaller and more unusual gems of old Dublin, **Archbishop Marsh's Library.** It was built in 1701, and access is through a tiny but charming cottage garden. Its interior has been unchanged for more than 300 years and still contains "cages" into which scholars who wanted to peruse rare books were locked. (The cages were to discourage students who, often impecunious, may have been tempted to make the books their own.) *St.*

Patrick's Close, tel. 01/778099. Open Wed.–Fri. 10:30–12:30 and 2–4, Mon. 2–4, Sat. 10:30–12:30.

㉔ Opposite, on Patrick Street, is **St. Patrick's Cathedral.** Legend has it that St. Patrick baptized many converts at a well on the site of the cathedral in the 5th century. The building dates from 1190 and is mainly early English in style. At 93 meters (300 feet), it is the longest church in the country. Its history has not always been happy. In the 17th century, Oliver Cromwell, dour ruler of England and no friend of the Irish, had his troops stable their horses in the cathedral. It wasn't until the 19th century that restoration work to repair the damage was put in hand. St. Patrick's is the national cathedral of the Protestant Church of Ireland and has had many illustrious deans. The most famous was Jonathan Swift, author of *Gulliver's Travels*, who held office from 1713 to 1745. Swift's tomb is in the south aisle, and Dean Swift's corner at the top of the north transept contains his pulpit, his writing table and chair, his portrait, and his death mask. Memorials to many other celebrated figures from Ireland's past line the walls of St. Patrick's. *Patrick St., tel. 01/ 754817. Admission: 80p.*

㉕ St. Patrick's originally stood outside the walls of Dublin. Its close neighbor, **Christ Church Cathedral** (Christ Church Rd.), on the other hand, stood just within the walls and belonged to the See of Dublin. It is for this reason that the city has two cathedrals so close to each other. Christ Church was founded in 1172 by Strongbow, a Norman baron and conqueror of Dublin for the English crown, and it took 50 years to build. Strongbow himself is buried in the cathedral beneath an impressive effigy. The vast and sturdy **crypt** is Dublin's oldest surviving structure and should not be missed.

㉖ Signs in the Christ Church area will lead you to **Dublin Castle.** Guided tours of the lavishly furnished state apartments are offered every half hour and provide one of the most enjoyable sightseeing experiences in town. Only fragments of the original 13th-century building survive; the elegant castle you see today is essentially an 18th-century building. The state apartments were formerly the residence of the English viceroys and are now used by the president of Ireland to entertain visiting heads of state. The state apartments are closed when in official use, so phone first to check. *Off Lord Edward St., tel. 01/777129. Admission: IR£2.50. Open weekdays 10–12:15 and 2–5, weekends 2–5.*

㉗ Step into the **City Hall** on Dame Street to admire the combination of grand classical ornament and understated Georgian simplicity in its circular main hall. It also contains a good example of the kind of gently curving Georgian staircase that is a typical feature of most large town houses in Dublin.

Time Out A mosaic stag's head in the pavement of Dame Street marks the entrance to a narrow alley and a beautiful pub, **The Stag's Head** (1 Dame Court), dating from the early 19th century. Amid tall mirrors, stained-glass skylights, and mounted stags' heads, of course, you can enjoy a typical selection of lunchtime pub grub—smoked salmon sandwiches, hot meat dishes—and a pint of anything.

㉘ Between Dame Street and the river Liffey is a new semipedestrianized area known as **Temple Bar,** which should interest anyone who wants to discover "young Dublin." The area is chock-full of small, imaginative shops; innovative art galleries; and inexpensive restaurants.

29 The **Guinness Brewery,** founded by Arthur Guinness in 1759, dominates the area to the west of Christ Church, covering 60 acres. Guinness is proud of its brewery and invites visitors to attend a 30-minute film shown in a converted hops store next door to the brewery itself. After the film, you can sample the famous black beverage. *Guinness Hop Store, Crane St., tel. 01/536700. Admission: IR£1.50. Open weekdays 10–3.*

Phoenix Park Across the Liffey is **Phoenix Park,** 7,122 square kilometers
and the Liffey (1,760 acres) of green open space. Though the park is open to
30 all, it has only two residents: the president of Ireland and the American ambassador. The park is dominated by a 64 meter-high (205-foot) obelisk, a tribute to the first duke of Wellington. Sunday is the best time to visit: Games of cricket, soccer, polo, baseball, hurling—a combination of lacrosse, baseball, and field hockey—or Irish football will be in progress.

Returning to the city's central area along the north bank of the Liffey, you pass through a fairly run-down section that's scheduled for major redevelopment. A diversion up Church Street to
31 **St. Michan's** will be relished by those with a macabre turn of mind. Open coffins in the vaults beneath the church reveal mummified bodies, some more than 900 years old. The sexton, who can be found at the church gate on weekdays, will guide you around the church and crypt.

32 **Irish Whiskey Corner** is just behind St. Michan's. A 90-year-old warehouse has been converted into a museum to introduce visitors to the pleasures of Irish whiskey. There's an audiovisual show and free tasting. *Bow St., tel. 01/725566. Admission: IR£2. Tours weekdays at 3:30, or by appointment.*

The Liffey has two of Dublin's most famous landmarks, both of them the work of 18th-century architect James Gandon and
33 both among the city's finest buildings. The first is the **Four Courts,** surmounted by a massive copper-covered dome, giving it a distinctive profile. It is the seat of the High Court of Justice of Ireland. The building was completed between 1786 and 1802, then gutted in the Civil War of the '20s; it has since been painstakingly restored. You will recognize the same architect's hand
34 in the **Custom House,** farther down the Liffey. Its graceful dome rises above a central portico, itself linked by arcades to the pavilions at either end. Behind this useful and elegant landmark is an altogether more workaday structure, the central bus station, known as Busaras.

Midway between Gandon's two masterpieces is the Metal
35 Bridge, otherwise known as the **Halfpenny Bridge,** so called because, until early in this century, a toll of a half-penny was charged to cross it. The poet W. B. Yeats was one among many Dubliners who found this too high a price to pay—more a matter of principle than of finance—and so made the detour via O'Connell Bridge. Today no such high-minded concern need prevent you from marching out to the middle of the bridge to admire the view up and down the Liffey as it wends its way through the city.

36 The **Royal Hospital Kilmainham** is a short ride by taxi or bus from the center; it's well worth the trip. The hospital is considered the most important 17th-century building in Ireland and has recently been renovated. It was completed in 1684 as a hospice—the original meaning of the term "hospital"—for veteran soldiers. Note especially the chapel with its magnificent Baroque ceiling. It also houses the **Irish Museum of Modern Art,** which opened in 1991. Parts of the old building, used as a national cultural center, are occasionally closed to the public. *District of Kilmainham, tel. 01/718666. Guided tours: Sun. noon–5 and holidays 2–5; cost IR£2. Exhibitions: open Tues.– Sat. 2–5.*

Devotees of James Joyce may wish to take the DART train south to **Sandycove,** about 8 kilometers (5 miles) out of the city center. It was here, in a Martello tower (a circular fortification built by the British as a defense against possible invasion by Napoleon at the beginning of the 19th century), that the maverick Irish genius lived for some months in 1904. It now houses the **Joyce Museum.** *Sandycove Coast. Admission: IR£1.50 adults, 60p children. Open Apr.–Oct., Mon.–Sat. 10–1 and 2–5, Sun. 2:30–6. Also by appointment, tel. 01/280–8571.*

Off the Beaten Track

It is all too easy for the visitor to forget how close Dublin is to the sea: Take advantage of fine weather and visit the fishing village of **Howth**—it's easily reached on the DART train—and watch the fishermen mending their nets on the pier. Or take the DART in the opposite direction to **Sandycove,** where intrepid all-weather swimmers brave the waves at the men-only **Forty Foot** bathing beach.

Everyone has heard of Waterford glass, but what about Dublin crystal? The **Dublin Crystal Glass Co.** is open year-round, and visitors are welcome to watch skilled crystal cutters at work and to purchase crystal—seconds are available, too—at a discount. Phone for an appointment. *Carysfort Ave., Blackrock, tel. 01/288–7932.*

The **Irish Jewish Museum** was opened in 1985 by Chaim Herzog, the president of Israel and an ex-Dubliner himself, and displays memorabilia of the Irish-Jewish community covering approximately 120 years of history. *3–4 Walworth Rd., tel. 01/283–2703.*

Shopping

Although the rest of the country is well supplied with crafts shops, Dublin is the place to seek out more specialized items— antiques, traditional sportswear, haute couture, designer ceramics, books and prints, silverware and jewelry, and designer handknits.

Shopping Districts The most sophisticated shopping area is around **Grafton Street:** The new **St. Stephen's Green Center** contains 70 stores, large and small, in a vast Moorish-style glass-roof building on the Grafton Street corner. **Molesworth** and **Dawson Streets** are the places to browse for antiques; **Nassau** and **Dawson Streets,** for books; the smaller cross side streets for jewelry, art galleries, and old prints. The pedestrianised **Temple Bar** area, with its young offbeat ambience, has a number of small art galleries, specialty shops (including music and books), and inexpensive

Spend your vacation touring castles. Not train stations.

Vacation Cars. Vacation Prices. Wherever your destination in Europe, there is sure to be one of more than 1,000 Budget locations nearby. Budget offers considerable values on a wide variety of quality cars, and if you book before you leave the U.S., you'll save even more with a special rate package from the Budget World Travel Plan℠. For information and reservations, contact your travel consultant or call Budget in the U.S. at **800-472-3325.** Or, while traveling abroad, call a Budget reservation center.

THE SMART MONEY IS ON BUDGET.®

We feature Ford and other fine cars.   *A system of corporate and licensee owned locations.*

MCI brings Europe and America closer together.

Call the U.S. for less with MCI CALL USA®

It's easy and affordable to call home when you use MCI CALL USA!

- Less expensive than calling through hotel operators
- Available from over 80 countries and locations worldwide
- You're connected to English-speaking MCI® Operators
- Even call 800 numbers in the U.S.†

†Regular MCI CALL USA rates apply to 800 number calls.

Call 1-800-444-3333 in the U.S. to apply for your MCI Card® now!

and adventurous clothes shops. The area is further enlivened by buskers (street musicians) and street artists.

Department Stores The shops north of the river tend to be less expensive and less design-conscious; chain stores and lackluster department stores make up the bulk of them. The **ILAC Shopping Center,** on Henry Street, is worth a look, however. **Switzers** and **Brown Thomas** are Grafton Street's main department stores; the latter is Dublin's most elegantly decorated department store, with many international fashion labels on sale. **Arnotts,** on Henry Street, is Dublin's largest department store and has a good range of cut crystal. Visit **Kilkenny Design Workshops** on Nassau Street for the best selection of Irish designs for the home.

Tweeds and Woolens Ready-made tweeds for men can be found at **Kevin and Howlin,** on Nassau Street, and at **Cleo Ltd.,** on Kildare Street. The **Blarney Woollen Mills,** on Nassau Street, has a good selection of tweed, linen, and woolen sweaters in all price ranges. The **Woolen Mills,** at Halfpenny Bridge, has a good selection of handknits and other woolen sweaters at competitive prices.

Dining

The restaurant scene in Dublin has improved beyond recognition in recent years. Though no one is ever likely to confuse the place with, say, Paris, the days of chewy boiled meats and soggy, tasteless vegetables are long gone. Food still tends to be substantial rather than subtle, but more and more restaurants are at last taking advantage of the magnificent livestock and fish that Ireland has in such abundance. For details and price-category definitions, *see* Dining in Staying in Ireland.

Expensive **Celtic Mews.** This long-established oasis of calm is in a Georgian mews off Baggot Street. A deep wine-colored interior is the backdrop for a collection of fine antiques, and tuxedo-clad waiters provide full silver service at polished or white-clothed tables. Despite the elegance of the setting, the atmosphere is cozy and informal. The chefs have successfully blended classical French and Irish cooking styles. The cuisine ranges from the very rich—Celtic filet mignon, cooked at the table and served in a whiskey and cream sauce—to upscale versions of traditional dishes such as Irish stew made with center loin chops. *109A Lower Baggot St., tel. 01/760796. Reservations advised. AE, DC, MC, V. Closed Sun. and holidays.*

The Commons Restaurant. In the basement of the Georgian showplace, Newman House, you will find this elegantly modern restaurant, where the cream and dark blue walls are hung with specially commissioned Irish art, and French windows open onto a patio used for al fresco lunches. The menu is international with French and Middle-Eastern influences; main courses lean towards fish, but other favorites include lamb cutlets roasted in garlic and thyme. *85–86 St. Stephen's Green, tel. 01/780530. Reservations required. AE, DC, MC, V. No lunch Sat. Closed Sun. and holidays.*

Ernie's. This luxurious place is built around a small floodlit courtyard shaded by an imposing mulberry tree. The rustic interior's granite walls and wood beams are adorned by 135 paintings of Kerry, where, for generations, the late Ernie Evans's family ran the famous Glenbeigh Hotel. The Evans family serves generous portions of the very best seafood—try scallops Mornay or prawns in garlic butter—and steaks. *Mul-*

berry Gardens, Donnybrook, tel. 01/269–3300. Reservations advised. AE, DC, MC, V. Dinner only Sat. Closed Sun., Mon.

★ **King Sitric.** This quayside restaurant in the fishing village-cum-suburb of Howth is a 20-minute ride north of Dublin by DART or cab. It's worth the journey to taste the succulent selection of locally caught seafood; try wild Irish salmon steaks with Hollandaise sauce, or *goujons* of turbot with saffron. You eat in the quietly elegant Georgian dining room of the former harbormaster's house under the supervision of owner-chef Aidan MacManus. *East Pier, Howth, tel. 01/325235. Reservations advised. AE, DC, MC, V. Dinner only. Closed Sun., holidays, Dec. 24–Jan. 1, and the week preceding Easter.*

★ **Le Coq Hardi.** Award-winning owner-chef John Howard is noted for his wine cellar and for such specialties as Coq Hardi smokies—smoked haddock baked in tomato, cream, and cheese—and (in season) roast loin of venison with fresh cranberries and port wine. The seriousness of the cooking is complemented by the polished wood and brass and the gleaming mirrors of the sumptuous interior. *35 Pembroke Rd., Ballsbridge, tel. 01/689070. Reservations required. AE, DC, MC, V. Closed Sun. and holidays.*

Patrick Guilbaud. This is an authentic, rather formal French restaurant with a consistently good reputation, decked out in a refreshing combination of pink, white, and green with hanging plants. The emphasis is firmly on traditional bourgeois cuisine; the Gallic connection is reinforced by the all-French staff. *46 James Pl., tel. 01/764192. Reservations advised. AE, DC, MC, V. Closed Sun. and holidays.*

Moderate **Dobbin's Wine Bistro.** Though Dobbin's aims at a French identity, with its red-and-white gingham tablecloths and sawdust-strewn slate floor, the cooking here is international and imaginative, with an emphasis on fresh Irish produce. Specialties are phyllo pastry with pepper and seafood filling, paupiettes of salmon and sole with spinach and dill sauce, and boned crispy duck with an apple and plum sauce. *Stephen's La., tel. 01/764670. Reservations advised. AE, DC, MC, V. Closed Sun.*

★ **Le Caprice.** This Italian restaurant with busy decor and white linen tablecloths is located right in the city center. The menu includes traditional Continental dishes such as prawn cocktail, deep-fried scampi, and roast duckling a l'orange, as well as an interesting selection of authentic Italian dishes including pasta and veal. This place can develop a real party atmosphere later in the evening if the pianist is in the right mood. *12 St. Andrew's St., tel. 01/679–4050. Reservations accepted. AE, DC, MC, V. Dinner only.*

La Pigalle. This is a charming and unpretentious French restaurant in an old and crooked building that forms part of the archway leading to the Ha'penny Bridge. It is in the heart of, and very much part of, the Temple Bar area scene. The decor is old-fashioned and well-worn, the atmosphere relaxed and the food authentically French, with a menu that changes daily. Typical dishes include fresh asparagus tart, sea trout fillet with sorrel and muscadet, duck breast with apples and calvados. *14 Temple Bar, tel. 01/719262. Reservations advised. MC, V. No dinner weekdays; no lunch Mon.–Sat. Closed Sun.*

Inexpensive **Bad Ass Café.** Definitely one of Dublin's loudest restaurants, this barnlike place, situated in the trendy Temple Bar area, between the Central Bank and the Halfpenny Bridge, is always a fun place to eat. American-style fast food—burgers, chili, and pizzas—and the pounding rock music attract a lively crowd, both the young and the young at heart. Look out for the old-fashioned cash shuttles whizzing around the ceiling! *9–11 Crown Alley, tel. 01/712596. Reservations for large parties recommended. AE, MC, V. Closed Good Friday, and Dec. 25–26.*

Corncucopia Wholefoods. This vegetarian restaurant above a health-food shop provides good value for the money. The seating consists of bar stools at high, narrow glass-top tables. It's popular with student types from nearby Trinity College. The menu includes red lentil soup, avocado quiche, vegetarian spring roll, and vegetarian curry—all of them regular favorites. *19 Wicklow St., tel. 01/777583. No reservations. No credit cards. Closed Sun.*

Da Vicenza. Watching the pizza dough being kneaded, rolled, topped off, and thrust into the brick oven will probably influence your menu choice here. The pizzas are indeed excellent, but the restaurant also offers interesting pasta combinations, and fish and steak. Dark blue blinds and drapery against natural stone and wood are the background for a venue that is popular with all age groups. *133 Upper Leeson St., tel. 01/609906. Reservations advised. AE, DC, MC, V.*

Gallagher's Boxty House. Located behind the Central Bank in the lively Temple Bar area, this highly original Irish eatery has a country cottage ambience, with antique pine furniture complementing the dark green decor. Boxty is a traditional Irish potato bread or cake that is served here as a pancake thin enough to wrap around savory fillings such as bacon and cabbage, chicken with leeks, and smoked fish. Follow these with "brown bread and Bailey's" ice cream or the superb bread-and-butter pudding. *20 Temple Bar, tel. 01/772762. No reservations. V. Closed Christmas and Good Friday.*

Pubs Food All the pubs listed here serve food at lunchtime; some also have food in the early evening. They form an important part of the dining scene in Dublin and make a pleasant and informal alternative to a restaurant meal. In general, a one-course meal should not cost much more than IR£4–IR£5, but a full meal will put you in the lower range of the Moderate category. In general, credit cards are not accepted.

Barry Fitzgerald's. Salads and a freshly cooked house special are available in the upstairs bar at lunch on weekdays. Pre-theater dinners are served in the early evening. *90 Marlboro St., tel. 01/774082.*

Davy Byrne's. James Joyce immortalized Davy Byrne's in his sprawling novel *Ulysses*. Nowadays it's more akin to a cocktail bar than a Dublin pub, but it's good for fresh and smoked salmon, salads, and a hot daily special. Food is available at lunchtime and in the early evening. *21 Duke St., tel. 01/711298.*

Kitty O'Shea's. Kitty O'Shea's cleverly, if a little artificially, recreates the atmosphere of old Dublin. *23–25 Grand Canal St., tel. 01/609965. Reservations accepted for lunch and Sun. brunch.*

Lord Edward Bar. With its Old World ambience, the Lord Edward Bar serves a wide range of salads and a hot dish of the day at lunchtime only. *23 Christ Church Pl., tel. 01/542158.*

Old Stand. Located conveniently close to Grafton Street, the Old Stand offers grilled food, including steaks. *37 Exchequer St., tel. 01/770821.*

Lodging

Although only a few major hotels have opened in Dublin in the past few years, considerable investment in redevelopment, updating of facilities, and refurbishing of some of the older establishments is taking place. As in most major cities, there is a shortage of mid-range accommodations. For value-for-the-money, try one of the registered guest houses; in most respects they are indistinguishable from small hotels. Most economical of all is the bed-and-breakfast. Both guest houses and B&Bs tend to be located in suburban areas—generally a 10-minute bus ride from the center of the city. This is not in itself a great drawback, and savings can be significant.

The Irish Tourist Board (14 Upper O'Connell St.) can usually help if you find yourself without reservations.

There is a VAT of 10% on hotel charges, which should be included in the quoted price. A service charge of 12–15% is also included and listed separately in the bills of top-grade hotels; elsewhere, check to see if the service is included. If it's not, a tip of between 10% and 15% is customary—if you think the service is worth it. For details and price-category definitions, *see* Lodging in Staying in Ireland.

Very Expensive

Berkeley Court. The most quietly elegant of Dublin's large modern hotels, Berkeley Court is located in Ballsbridge—a leafy suburb about a 10-minute cab ride from the center of town. Its new conservatory gives freshness and spaciousness to the atmosphere of the public rooms; among the other new features are five luxury suites, each with its own Jacuzzi. *Lansdowne Rd., Ballsbridge, Dublin 4, tel. 01/601711, fax 01/617238. 207 rooms with bath. Facilities: parking. AE, DC, MC, V.*

Conrad. A subsidiary of Hilton Hotels, the Conrad is firmly aimed at the international business executive. The seven-story redbrick and smoked-glass building is well located just off Stephen's Green. The spacious rooms are decorated in pastel shades of green and brown, the bathrooms fitted in Spanish marble. Alfie Byrne's, the main bar, attempts to re-create the traditional Irish pub atmosphere in spite of its high-powered clientele. *Earlsfort Terrace, tel. 01/765555, fax 01/765076. 190 rooms with bath. Facilities: restaurant, 2 bars, coffee shop, sauna, gym, sporting facilities available by arrangement, parking. AE, DC, MC, V.*

★ **Shelbourne.** The Shelbourne is one of Europe's grand old hotels whose guestbook contains names ranging from the Dalai Lama and Princess Grace to Laurel and Hardy, Richard Burton, and Peter O'Toole. The blazing open fire in its bustling marble lobby, flanked by two huge rose brocade sofas, is proof that the Shelbourne has not lost the sense of grandeur of its past. Between 1986 and 1988, IR£7 million was lavished on major refurbishment, which included restoring many original Georgian features and emphasizing them with luxurious drapes and a prominently displayed collection of fine antiques and heirlooms. A supplement is charged for rooms overlooking the leafy but busy green; the back bedrooms without views are far quieter, however. *27 Stephen's Green, tel. 01/766471, fax 01/616006. 165 rooms with bath. Facilities: 2 bars, restaurant, coffee shop, sporting facilities available by arrangement. AE, DC, MC, V.*

Expensive   **Burlington.** Dublin's largest hotel is popular with American tour groups and Irish and European business travelers. It is about five minutes by car from the city's central area. At night the Burlington's disco and Irish cabaret turn it into a lively spot for overseas visitors. Bedrooms are the usual modern plush in neutral tones. *Upper Leeson St., tel. 01/605222, fax 01/608496. 477 rooms with bath. Facilities: restaurants, bars, disco, and cabaret. AE, DC, MC, V.*

Buswell's. You'll either love or hate Buswell's. The hotel is located just across the street from the Dail, and its bars and conference rooms are dominated by the frantic bustle of politicians and lobbyists. Curiously, Buswell's also has a loyal provincial clientele, who seem blissfully blind to the clashing patterns of carpets, drapes, and wallpaper; the smallness of the bedrooms; and the grim food. The central location (between Stephen's Green and Grafton Street) and charming Georgian facade are a potent attraction for many independent American travelers, too. *Molesworth St., tel. 01/764013, fax 01/762090. 67 rooms with bath. AE, DC, MC, V.*

★ **Gresham.** With a prime central location opposite the historic General Post Office, this place has played a part in Dublin's history since 1817. The interior has a predominantly '30s character, with an emphasis on comfort rather than upscale chic. Bedrooms are reached via long windowless corridors, and the monumentally solid plumbing arrangements give character to the bland modern-repro style of the newly decorated rooms. The hotel feels much bigger than it actually is, and the lobby, decked out with "Gresham (royal) Blue" carpet and gold brocade armchairs, exudes a sense of history. *Higher O'Connell St., tel. 01/746881, fax 01/787175. 200 rooms with bath. AE, DC, MC, V.*

Jury's. This lively and fashionable spot has more atmosphere than most comparable modern hotels. It's a short cab ride from the center of town. Bedrooms are relatively spacious, standard modern plush, and each comes with a picture-window view of town. Exclusive facilities for businesspeople are provided in the 100-room Towers annex. *Ballsbridge, Dublin 4, tel. 01/605000, fax 01/605540. 390 rooms with bath. Facilities: indoor/outdoor pool, Jacuzzi, 2 bars, 3 restaurants, cabaret May–Oct. AE, DC, MC, V.*

Moderate   **Ariel Guest House.** This is Dublin's leading guest house, just a
★ block away from the elegant Berkeley Court and a 10-minute walk from Stephen's Green. The lobby lounge and restaurant of this Victorian villa are furnished with leather and mahogany heirlooms, as are most of their spacious bedrooms, 13 of which were added to the house in 1991. This is a good bet if you're in town for a leisurely, relaxing holiday. *52 Lansdowne Rd., tel. 01/685512, fax 01/685845. 27 rooms with bath. Facilities: restaurant (wine license only), lounge, parking. AE, MC, V. Closed Dec. 21–Jan. 31.*

Ashling. This family-run hotel sits on the edge of the river Liffey, close to Heuston Station. Some may find that the Ashling's relentlessly bright modern decor verges on the garish. It has a faithful following, however, not least because of its proximity to Phoenix Park and its friendly staff. The center of town is a brisk 10–15 minute walk away, taking in many famed landmarks en route. *Parkgate St., Kingsbridge, tel. 01/772324, fax 01/679-3783. 56 rooms with bath. AE, DC, MC, V.*

Longfield's. In 1991 two town houses in the heart of Georgian

Dublin were luxuriously converted into this characterful small hotel. The aim here is to re-create the atmosphere of an elegant private home, making it a good choice for those who like their comfort to come with a bit of local color. The dining room and lounge have open fires in original iron grates, and there is highly polished period furniture in all the public rooms. There are two grades of bedroom, the "superior" ones being noticeably larger. All are well equipped with interesting pieces of Victorian furniture and coordinated drapes and spreads in restful colors, and all have views over the distinctive rooftops and streetscapes of the "Georgian mile." *Fitzwilliam St. Lower, tel. 01/761367, fax 01/761542. 26 rooms with bath. Facilities: restaurant, bar. AE, DC, MC, V.*

Royal Dublin. This new (1991) centrally located Best Western hotel is just within the moderate category if you choose a "standard" room. Its modern facade dominates the top end of busy O'Connell Street. The interior incorporates part of a building that dates from 1752, providing an elegant and relaxing lounge area and restaurant. In contrast, Raffles Bar is a lively spot with a busy local trade. The rooms, decorated in pleasant pastel shades, are exceptionally well appointed by Dublin standards for this price range, and have floor-to-ceiling windows. *40 Upper O'Connell St., tel. 01/733666, fax 01/733120. 120 rooms with bath. AE, DC, MC, V.*

Inexpensive   **Abrae Court Guest House.** This is a typical, large early Victorian house in the highly respectable suburb of Rathgar. It's a 10-minute bus ride to the center of Dublin. There are six bedrooms in the main house; the rest are in a carefully designed period-style annex with ornate stucco ceilings. All are furnished with Irish carpets and handcrafted Irish furniture. The restaurant is open for evening meals. *9 Zion Rd., Rathgar, tel. 01/979944. 14 rooms with bath. Facilities: restaurant (wine license only). MC, V.*

Kilronan House. This guest house, a five-minute walk from St. Stephen's Green, is a favorite with vacationers. The large, late-19th-century terraced house is well converted, and the decor and furnishings are updated each year by the Murray family, who have run the place for the past 30 years. The bedrooms are pleasantly furnished with plush carpeting and pastel colored walls. *70 Adelaide Rd., Dublin 2, tel. 01/755266, fax 01/782841. 10 rooms with bath. Facilities: restaurant (wine license only). MC, V. Closed Dec. 21–Jan. 1.*

★ **Maples House.** According to the ITB's complex grading system, Maples House is a guest house; to the rest of the world, however, it is definitely a small hotel. The lobby of this Edwardian house is decked out with oil paintings, Waterford crystal chandeliers, and a discreetly modern carpet, and is dominated by a vast mirror-topped Victorian rococo sideboard that sets the tone for the ornate decor of the public rooms. The bedrooms are small but adequate, lacking the rococo splendor of the rest of the building. *Iona Rd., Glasnevin, tel. 01/303049, fax 01/303874. 21 rooms with bath. Facilities: grill restaurant and bar. AE, DC, MC, V. Closed Dec. 25, 26.*

Mount Herbert Guest House. Located close to the swank luxury hotels in the tree-lined inner suburb of Ballsbridge, a 10-minute bus ride from Dublin's center of town, the Mount Herbert is popular with budget-minded American visitors in the high season. Bedrooms are small, but all have 10-channel TV and hair dryers. There is no bar on the premises, but there are plenty to choose from nearby. *7 Herbert Rd., Ballsbridge, tel. 01/684321, fax 01/607077. 144 rooms with bath. Facilities: restaurant (wine license only). AE, DC, MC, V.*

The Arts

The fortnightly magazine *In Dublin* contains comprehensive details of upcoming events, including ticket availability. In peak season, consult the free ITB leaflet "Events of the Week."

Theaters Ireland has a rich theatrical tradition. The **Abbey Theatre,** Marlborough Street, is the home of Ireland's national theater company, its name forever associated with J. M. Synge, William Butler Yeats, and Sean O'Casey. The **Peacock Theatre** is the Abbey's more experimental small stage. The **Gate Theatre,** Parnell Square, is an intimate spot for modern drama and plays by Irish writers. The **Gaiety Theatre,** South King Street, features musical comedy, opera, drama, and revues. The **Olympia Theatre,** Dame Street, has seasons of comedy, vaudeville, and ballet. The **Project Arts Centre,** East Essex Street, is an established fringe theater. The new **National Concert Hall,** in Earlsfort Terrace, just off Stephen's Green, is the place to go for classical concerts.

Nightlife

Dublin does not have sophisticated nightclubs in the international sense. Instead, there is a choice of discos (often billed as nightclubs) and cabarets, catering mainly to visitors. There is also a very animated bar-pub scene—some places with live music and folksinging. No visit to this genial city will be complete without spending at least one evening exploring them.

Discos **Annabels** (Mespil Rd., tel. 01/605222) is a popular late-evening spot; so is **The Pink Elephant** (S. Frederick St., tel. 01/775876).

Cabarets The following all offer Irish cabaret, designed to give visitors a taste of Irish entertainment: **Braemor Rooms** (Churchtown, tel. 01/988664); **Burlington Hotel** (Upper Leeson St., tel. 01/605222, open May–Oct.); **Jury's Hotel** (Ballsbridge, tel. 01/605000, open May–mid-Oct.); **Abbey Tavern** (Howth, Co. Dublin, tel. 01/390307).

Pubs Check advertisements in evening papers for "sessions" of folk, ballad, Irish traditional, or jazz music. The **Brazen Head** (20 Lower Bridge St., tel. 01/779549)—Dublin's oldest pub, dating from 1688—and **O'Donoghue's** (15 Merrion Row, tel. 01/614303) feature some form of musical entertainment on most nights. Several of Dublin's centrally located pubs are noted for their character and ambience; they're usually at their liveliest from 5 to 7 PM and again from 10. The **Bailey** (2 Duke St.) is mentioned in *Ulysses* (under its original name, Burton's) and retains something of its Edwardian character, while **William Ryan's** (28 Parkgate St.) is a beautifully preserved Victorian gem. **Henry Grattan** (47–48 Lower Baggot St.) is popular with the business and sporting crowd; **O'Neill's Lounge Bar** (37 Pearse St.) is always busy with students and faculty from nearby Trinity College; and the **Palace Bar** (21 Fleet St.) is a journalists' haunt. You can eavesdrop on Dublin's social elite and their hangers-on at the expensive **Horseshoe Bar** in the Shelbourne Hotel or bask in the theatrical atmosphere of **Neary's** (Chatham St.)

For details on pubs serving food, *see* Dining in Staying in Ireland, *above*.

Dublin to Cork

Ireland can be covered in three itineraries that, taken together, form a clockwise tour of the country, starting and ending in Dublin. Distances in Ireland seem small—the total mileage of the three itineraries combined is less than 960 kilometers (600 miles)—but roads are small and often twisty and hilly, and side attractions are numerous, so you should aim for a daily mileage of no more than 240 kilometers (150 miles). The consistently dazzling scenery, intriguing ruins, and beguiling small villages will lead to many impromptu stops and explorations along the way. (We have tried to provide full addresses for hotels, restaurants, and sights, though many of Ireland's villages and towns are so tiny they barely have street names, much less numbers. If in any doubt, just ask for directions.)

The first tour takes you southwest from Dublin to hilly Cork, the Republic's second-largest city. On the way, you'll see the lush green fields of Ireland's famous stud farms and imposing Cashel, where Ireland built its reputation as the "Land of Saints and Scholars" while most of Europe was slipping into the Dark Ages.

Getting Around

By Train The terminus at Cork is Kent Station. There are direct services from Dublin and Tralee and a suburban line to Cobh (tel. 021/506766 for information).

By Bus The main bus terminus in Cork is at Parnell Place (tel. 021/508188).

By Car All the main car-rental firms have desks at Cork Airport. Be sure to get a map of Cork's complicated one-way system.

By Bicycle Bicycles can be rented from **Kilgrews Cycle Centre** (6 Kyle St., Cork, tel. 021/276255).

Guided Tours

CIE operates a number of trips from Parnell Place in Cork (tel. 021/506066).

Tourist Information

Tourist House (Grand Parade, Cork, tel. 021/273251).

Exploring Dublin to Cork

Leaving Dublin by N7 for **Naas** (pronounced "Nace"), you will pass through the area known as The Pale—that part of Ireland in which English law was formally acknowledged up to Elizabethan times. Beyond Naas, the road takes you to the center of the Irish racing world. **Goff's Kildare Paddocks** at Kill sells more than 50% of all Irish-bred horses. Naas has its own racecourse and lies just 4.8 kilometers (3 miles) from Punchestown, famous for its steeplechases. The **Curragh** begins just after Newbridge and is the biggest area of common land in Ireland,

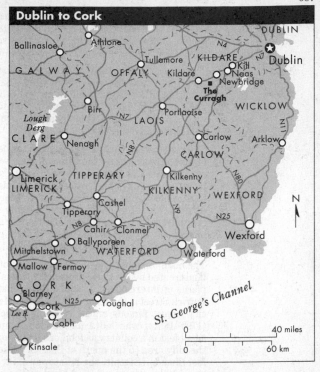

Dublin to Cork

containing about 31 square kilometers (12 square miles). You will see the **Curragh Racecourse,** home of the Irish Derby, on your right-hand side; to the left is the training depot of the Irish army.

If you are interested in horses, **Kildare,** the traditional home of St. Brigid, is not to be missed. The main attraction is the **National Stud and Horse Museum** and its **Japanese Gardens.** *Tel. 045/261617. Open Easter–Oct., weekdays 10:30–5, Sat. 10:30– 5:30, Sun. 2–5:30. Guided tours on request.*

At Portlaoise (pronounced "Portleash")—the location of Ireland's top-security prison—follow N8 to **Cashel.** Your first glimpse of the famous **Rock of Cashel** should be an unforgettably majestic sight: It rises imposingly to a height of 62 meters (200 feet) above the plains and is crowned with a magnificent group of gray stone ruins. The kings of Munster held it as their seat for about seven centuries, and it is here that St. Patrick reputedly plucked a shamrock from the ground, using it as a symbol to explain the mystery of the Trinity, giving Ireland, in the process, its universally recognized symbol. The central building among the ruins is a 13th-century Gothic cathedral; next to it is the Romanesque Cormac's chapel. *Tel. 062/61437. Admission: IR£1 adults, 30p children and senior citizens. Open May–Sept., daily 9–7:30; Oct.–Apr., daily 9:30–4:30.*

Cashel and the next town, **Cahir** (pronounced "Care"), are both popular stopping places to break the Dublin–Cork journey. In the center of Cahir, you will discover a formidable **medieval fortress** with a working portcullis, the gruesome barred gate that was lowered to keep out attackers. An audiovisual display can be seen in the castle complex. *Tel. 052/41011. Admission: IR£1 adults, 40p children and senior citizens. Open June–Sept., daily 10–7:30; Oct.–May, Tues.–Sat. 10–6, Sun. 2–6.*

The road continues through Mitchelstown and Fermoy, both of them busy market towns serving Cork's dairy farmers. A short detour at Mitchelstown will allow you to visit President Reagan's ancestral home, **Ballyporeen,** a pretty little village with wide streets built to accommodate the open-air cattle markets held there until the '60s.

The road to **Cork City** passes through the beautiful wooded glen of Glanmire and along the banks of the river Lee. In the center of Cork, the Lee divides in two, giving the city a profusion of picturesque quays and bridges. The name Cork derives from the Irish *corcaigh,* meaning a marshy place. The city received its first charter in 1185 and grew rapidly in the 17th and 18th centuries with the expansion of its butter trade. It is the major metropolis of the south, and, with a population of about 135,000, the second-largest city in Ireland.

The main business and shopping center of Cork lies on the island created by the two diverging channels of the Lee, and most places of interest are within walking distance of the center. **Patrick Street** is the focal point of Cork. Here, you will find the city's most famous statue, that of **Father Theobald Mathew** (1790–1861), who led a nationwide temperance crusade, no small feat in a country as fond of a drink (or two) as this one. In the hilly area to the north of Patrick Street is the famous 120-foot **Shandon Steeple,** the bell tower of **St. Anne's Church.** It is shaped like a pepper pot and houses the bells immortalized in the song "The Bells of Shandon." Visitors can climb the tower; read the inscriptions on the bells; and, on request, have them rung over Cork. *Admission: IR£1, with bell tower IR£1.50. Open May–Oct., Mon.–Sat. 9:30–5; Nov.–Apr., Mon.–Sat. 10–3:30.*

Patrick Street is the main shopping area of Cork, and here you will find the city's two major department stores, **Roches** and **Cash's.** Cash's has a good selection of Waterford crystal. The liveliest place in town to shop is just off Patrick Street, to the west, near the city center parking lot, in the pedestrians-only **Paul Street** area. The **House of James** stocks the best in modern Irish design, including tableware, ceramics, knitwear, hand-woven tweeds, and high fashion. The **Donegal Shop** next door specializes in made-to-order tweed suits and rain wear. At the top of Paul Street is the **Crawford Art Gallery,** which has an excellent collection of 18th- and 19th-century views of Cork and mounts adventurous exhibitions by modern artists. *Emmet Place, tel. 021/273377. Admission free. Open weekdays 10–5, Sat. 9–1.*

One of Cork's most famous sons was William Penn (1644–1718), founder of the Pennsylvania colony. He is only one of thousands who sailed from Cork's port, the Cove of Cork on Great Island, 24 kilometers (15 miles) down the harbor. **Cobh,** as it is known nowadays, can be reached by train from Kent Station, and the trip provides excellent views of the magnificent harbor. Cobh is an attractive hilly town dominated by its 19th-century **cathedral.** It was the first and last European port of call for transatlantic liners, one of which was the ill-fated *Titanic.* Cobh has other associations with shipwrecks: It was from here that destroyers were sent out in May 1915 to search for survivors of the *Lusitania,* torpedoed by a German submarine with the loss of 1,198 lives. Cobh's maritime past and its links with emigration are documented in a new IR£2 million heritage center known as **The Queenstown Project,** which opened in the town's old railway station in 1993. *Tel. 021/893591. Admission: IR£3.50 adults, IR£2 children and senior citizens. Open Apr.–Sept., weekdays 9:30–7:30, weekends 10–7; Nov.–Jan., daily 10–5. Closed Jan. 9–Apr. 1.*

Fota Island, midway between Cork and Cobh, is a recent and very welcome addition to Cork's tourist attractions. The Royal Zoological Society has created a 238-square-kilometer (70-acre) wildlife park here. *Tel. 021/812678. Admission: IR£2.50 adults, IR£1.25 children and senior citizens. Car park: IR£1.25 per car. Open mid-Mar.–Sept., Tues.–Sat. 11–6, Sun. 1–6.*

Most visitors to Cork want to kiss the famous **Blarney Stone** in the hope of acquiring the "gift of gab." Blarney itself, 8 kilometers (5 miles) from Cork City, should not, however, be taken too seriously as an excursion. All that is left of **Blarney Castle** is its ruined central keep containing the celebrated stone. This is set in the battlements, and to kiss it, you must lie on the walk within the walls, lean your head back, and touch the stone with your lips. Nobody knows how the tradition originated, but Elizabeth I is credited with giving the word *blarney* to the language when, commenting on the unfulfilled promises of Cormac MacCarthy, Lord Blarney of the time, she remarked, "This is all Blarney; what he says, he never means." Adjoining the castle is a first-rate crafts shop, and the outing provides a good opportunity to shop around for traditional Irish goods at competitive prices. *Tel. 021/385252. Admission: IR£2.50 adults, IR£1.50 senior citizens, IR£1 children. Open Mon.–Sat. 9 to sundown, Sun. 9:30–5:30; winter, 9:30–sundown.*

Dining and Lodging

For details and price-category definitions, *see* Dining and Lodging in Staying in Ireland.

Cahir
Lodging
Kilcoran Lodge Hotel. Set in its own grounds on the main road, Kilcoran Lodge Hotel is an ideal place to break the journey with coffee or a plainly cooked lunch. It occupies a bucolic country setting on the southern slope of the Galtees. *Co. Tipperary, just off N8, tel. 052/41288, fax 052/41994. 23 rooms with bath. Facilities: indoor pool, sauna. AE, DC, MC, V. Expensive.*

Cashel
Dining
Chez Hans. Fresh local produce cooked with a French accent is served in this converted chapel at the foot of the famous rock. *Tel. 062/61177. AE, DC, MC, V. Dinner only. Closed Sun., Mon., first 3 weeks Jan. Expensive.*

Lodging
Cashel Palace. This elegant Palladian mansion was once a bishop's palace. It has luxurious rooms and a beautiful garden. *Main St., Co. Tipperary, tel. 062/61411, fax 062/61521. 20 rooms with bath. AE, MC, V. Closed Dec. 25–26. Very Expensive.*

Cork
Dining
★
Arbutus Lodge. One of Ireland's most highly acclaimed restaurants, the Arbutus Lodge is run by the Ryan family and is famous for its excellent wine list. There are 20 rooms as well.

Middle Glanmire Rd., Montenotte, tel. 021/501237. Reservations required. AE, DC, MC, V. Closed Sun. and 1 week at Christmas. Expensive.

★ **Ballymaloe House.** This country-house hotel is half an hour's drive from the city, but it's well worth the effort because the restaurant—run by Myrtle Allen, a world expert on Irish cookery—is outstanding. *Shanagarry, near Ballycotton, tel. 021/652531. Reservations advised. AE, DC, MC, V. Expensive.*

Clifford's. Cork's most fashionable restaurant, just a short walk from Jury's hotel, serves seriously good food in a fun atmosphere. The ground floor of a Georgian house has been strikingly modernized and decorated in black and white. Choose from the owner/chef's small set menu (4 or 5 choices for each course), which includes items such as black sole and prawn in a pepper and lime sauce or medallions of beef in a light port and Chetwynd cheese sauce. *18 Dyke Parade, tel. 021/275333. Reservations advised. AE, DC, MC, V. Sat. dinner only. Closed weekdays 2:30–7. Expensive.*

The Gallery Café. If you can't make it out to Ballymaloe, you can sample their distinctive cooking style at the Crawford Gallery Café—the best inexpensive food in the city, served amid statues and prints from the municipal art collection. *Crawford Gallery, Emmet Pl., tel. 021/274415. Open Mon., Tues., and Sat. 10:30–5:30; Wed.–Fri. 10:30–9:30. Inexpensive.*

Lodging **Jury's.** This modern two-story hotel has a lively bar and occupies a riverside location just five minutes' walk from the downtown area. *Western Rd., tel. 021/276622. 185 rooms with bath. Facilities: 2 restaurants, indoor and outdoor pools, health club, sauna, tennis. AE, DC, MC, V. Closed Dec. 25, 26. Expensive.*

Silver Springs. Situated on its own grounds overlooking the river Lee, five minutes' drive from the town center, this modern low-rise reopened in 1989 after major refurbishment. A popular choice for tour groups, it also has the most up-to-date leisure facilities in town. *Tivoli, tel. 021/507533. 110 rooms with bath. Facilities: indoor pool, sauna, gym, squash, tennis, 2 bars, 2 restaurants, bowling, 9-hole golf. AE, DC, MC, V. Expensive.*

★ **Arbutus Lodge.** This exceptionally comfortable hotel has an outstanding restaurant and panoramic views of the city and the river. *Middle Glanmire Rd., Montenotte, tel. 021/501237. 20 rooms with bath. AE, DC, MC, V. Closed 1 week at Christmas. Moderate.*

Moore's. Good for its central location on a quiet part of the riverbank, the hotel has a fine reputation for friendliness and personal attention. *Morrison's Island, tel. 021/271291. 36 rooms, most with bath. AE, DC, MC, V. Moderate.*

★ **Victoria Lodge.** Originally built in the early 20th century as a Capuchin monastery, this exceptionally well-appointed B&B is located a five-minute drive from the town center; it is also on several bus routes. The rooms are simple but comfortable, with views over the lodge's own grounds. Breakfast is served in the spacious old refectory. *Victoria Cross, tel. 021/542233. 22 rooms with bath. Facilities: restaurant (wine license only), TV lounge. AE, MC. V. Inexpensive.*

Cork to Galway

The trip from Cork to Galway is about 300 kilometers (188 miles) and includes stops in Killarney and Limerick. Killarney and the mysterious regions of the Burren are two very different areas of outstanding natural beauty. The Shannon region around Limerick is littered with castles, both ruined and restored.

Getting Around

By Train Trains run from Cork to Tralee, via Killarney, and from Cork to Limerick, changing at Limerick Junction.

By Bus Buses offer a more flexible service than do trains; details are available from local tourist information offices.

By Car All major rental companies have facilities at Shannon Airport. **Killarney Autos Ltd.** (Park Rd., tel. 064/31355) is the major firm in Killarney. Taxis do not operate on meters; agree on the fare beforehand.

By Bicycle You can rent bicycles from **O'Callaghan Bros.** (College St., Killarney, tel. 064/31465), **D. O'Neill** (Plunkett St., Killarney, tel. 064/315900), and **Limerick Sports Store** (10 William St., Limerick, tel. 061/45647).

Guided Tours

Bus Eireann offers day tours by bus from Killarney and Tralee train stations; check with the tourist office or rail station for details. **Shannon Castle Tours** (tel. 061/61788) and **Gray Line** (tel. 061/32621) also operate tours.

Tourist Information

All tourist information offices are open weekdays 9–6, Sat. 9–1.

Killarney (Town Hall, tel. 064/31633).
Limerick (Arthur's Quay, tel. 061/317522).
Shannon Airport (tel. 061/61664).
Tralee (Godfrey Pl., tel. 066/21288).

Exploring Cork to Galway

Beyond Macroom, the main Cork–Killarney road passes through the west-Cork **Gaelteacht**—a predominantly Irish-speaking region—and begins its climb into the Derrynasaggart Mountains. A detour to the left at Ballyvourney will take you to the lake of **Gougane Barra,** source of the river Lee and now a national park. The 6th-century monk St. Finbar, founder of Cork, had his cell on an island in the lake; this island can now be reached by causeway.

Killarney itself is an undistinguished market town, well developed to handle the tourist trade that flourishes here in the peak season. To find the famous scenery, you must head out of town toward the lakes that lie in a valley running south between the mountains. Part of Killarney's lake district is within **Killarney National Park.** At the heart of the park is the 40,470-square-kilometer (10,000-acre) **Muckross Estate** (open Easter–May and

Cork to Galway

Sept.–Oct., daily 8–7; June–Aug., daily 9–5). Cars are not allowed in the estate, so if you don't want to walk, rent a bicycle in town or take a trip in a jaunting car—a small two-wheeled horse-drawn cart. At the center of the estate is **Muckross House,** a 19th-century manor that contains a folk museum and visitor center. *Tel. 064/31440. Admission: IR£2 adults, IR£1 children. Open Sept.–Oct., daily 9–6; Nov.–mid-Mar., daily 11–5; July and Aug., daily 9–7.*

To get an idea of the splendor of the lakes and streams—of the massive glacial sandstone and limestone rocks and lush vegetation that characterize the Killarney district—take one of the day-long tours of the **Gap of Dunloe, the Upper Lake, Long Range, Middle** and **Lower lakes,** and **Ross Castle.** The central section, the Gap of Dunloe, is not suitable for cars, but horses and jaunting cars are available at **Kate Kearney's Cottage,** which marks the entrance to the gap.

The **Ring of Kerry** will add about 176 kilometers (110 miles) to your trip, but in good weather it provides a pleasant experience. Leave Killarney by the Kenmare road. **Kenmare** is a small market town 34 kilometers (21 miles) from Killarney at the head of Kenmare Bay. Across the water, as you drive out along the Iveragh Peninsula, will be views of the gray-blue mountain ranges of the Beara Peninsula. **Sneem,** on the estuary of the river Ardsheelaun, is one of the prettiest villages in Ireland. Beyond the next village, Caherdaniel, is **Derrynane House,** home of the 19th-century politician and patriot Daniel O'Connell, "The Liberator," and completed by him in 1825. It still contains much of its original furniture. *Tel. 0667/5113. Admission: IR£1* *adults, 30p children and senior citizens. Open mid-June–Sept., daily 10–1 and 2–7; Oct.–mid-June, Tues.–Sat. 10–1, Sun. 2–5.*

The village of **Waterville** is famous as an angling center; it also has a fine sandy beach and a championship golf course. Offshore, protruding in conical shapes from the Atlantic, are the **Skellig Rocks,** which contain the cells of early Christian monks. To learn more about the history and bird life of these islands, visit **The Skellig Experience,** an interpretative center situated where the bridge joins Valentia Island. Landing is prohibited on the Skelligs without a special permit, but the one-and-a-half hour boat cruise offered (weather permitting) at the center is a good substitute. *Tel. 064/31633. Admission: IR£3 adults, IR£1.50 children; with cruise, IR£15 adults, IR£8 children. Open Apr.–June and Sept., daily 9:30–5; July–Aug., daily 9:30–7. Call to confirm cruise times.*

Beyond Cahirciveen, you are on the other side of the Ring, with views across Dingle Bay to the rugged peaks of the Dingle Peninsula. At the head of the bay is **Killorglin,** which has a three-day stint of unbridled merrymaking the first weekend in August, known as Puck Fair.

If time and the weather are on your side, turn off the main Killorglin–Tralee road and make a tour of the **Dingle Peninsula**—one of the wildest and least spoiled regions of Ireland—taking in the **Connor Pass, Mount Brandon, the Gallarus Oratory,** and stopping at **Dunquin** to hear some of Ireland's best traditional musicians. For an adventure off the beaten path, arrange for a boat ride to the **Blasket Islands** and spend a few blissful hours wandering along the cliffs. Dingle town is a handy touring base, with a surprisingly wide choice of good restaurants, open Easter–October.

Tralee is the commercial center of Kerry, but has little to recommend it unless you happen to be visiting in September, when the "Rose of Tralee" is selected from an international lineup of young women of Irish descent. Listowel is similarly transformed during its race week in October. From **Tarbert** (where a ferry provides a handy shortcut directly to County Clare and the Burren), the road skirts the estuary of the river Shannon. **Limerick** is the third-largest city in the Republic, with a population of 60,000; it's also arguably the least attractive city in Ireland. Its Newtown area, however, is dominated by pleasant Georgian buildings.

Bunratty Castle is a famous landmark midway between Limerick and Shannon Airport. It is one of four castles in the area that offer nightly medieval banquets, which, though as fake as they come, at least offer some fairly uninhibited fun. The castle was the stronghold of the princes of Thomond and is the most complete and—despite its ye-olde-world banquets—authentic medieval castle in Ireland, restored in such a way as to give an idea of the 15th- and 16th-century way of life. The **Folk Park** on its grounds has farm buildings and crafts shops typical of the 19th century. *Tel. 061/361511. Admission: IR£3.10 adults, IR£1.60 children. Open daily 9:30–5:30.*

Time Out   Drop in to **Durty Nelly's,** beside Bunratty Castle—it's one of Ireland's most popular old-time bars.

There is an incredible number of castles—almost 900—in the Shannon area, ranging from such fully restored examples as **Knappogue** at Quin, 14 kilometers (9 miles) from Bunratty, to the multitude of crumbling ruins that loom up all over the area.

Beyond Shannon Airport is County Clare and its principal town, **Ennis,** the campaigning base of Eamon de Valera, the New York–born politician whose character and views dominated the Republic during its early years. Just beyond Ennis, a detour to **Corofin** will take you to the **Clare Heritage Center,** which explains the traumatic story of Ireland in the 19th century, a story of famines and untold misery that resulted in the mass emigrations of the Irish to England and the United States. *Tel. 065/27955. Admission: IR£1.50 adults, 50p children. Open Apr.–Oct., daily 10–6; Nov.–Mar., daily 9–7.*

Ennistymon or Lisdoonvarna, both quiet villages with an old-fashioned charm, make excellent bases for touring the Burren. **Lisdoonvarna** has developed something of a reputation over the years as a matchmaking center, with bachelor farmers and single women converging here each year around harvesttime in order to get to know each other better. This strange, rocky, limestone district is a superb nature reserve, with a profusion of unique wildflowers that are at their best in late May. Huge colonies of puffins, kittiwakes, shags, guillemots, and razorbills nest along its coast. The **Burren Display Center** at **Kilfenora** explains the extraordinary geology and wildlife of the area in a simple audiovisual display. *Tel. 065/88030. Admission: IR£1.70 adults, IR£1 children. Open mid-Mar.–Apr.and Sept.–Oct., daily 10–5:45; May–Aug., daily 10–6:45.*

The dramatic **Cliffs of Moher** are a must: They rise vertically out of the sea in a wall that stretches 8 kilometers (5 miles) and varies in height from 217 to 440 meters (700 feet), with **O-'Brien's Tower** at their highest point. This contains a visitor center (open Mar.–Oct., 10–6). On a clear day, the **Aran Islands** are visible from the cliffs, and in the summer there are regular day trips to them from **Doolin,** a small village popular with young travelers and noted for its spontaneous traditional music sessions.

At **Ailwee Cave** near Ballyvaughan, you can take a guided tour into the underworld of the Burren, where 1,041 meters (1,120 yards) of cave, formed millions of years ago, can be explored. *Tel. 065/77036. Admission: IR£2.70 adults, IR£1.40 children. Open mid-Mar.–Sept., Sat. 10–5, Sun. 2–5; Oct.–mid-Mar. weekends and public holidays 10–3.*

The coast road continues into County Galway, through the pretty fishing village of Kinvara. Galway City itself is approached through **Clarinbridge,** the village that hosts Galway's annual Oyster Festival in September, featuring the superlative products of the village's oyster beds.

Dining and Lodging

For details and price-category definitions, *see* Dining and Lodging in Staying in Ireland.

Clarinbridge **Moran's of the Weir.** This waterside traditional thatched cot-
Dining tage is one of Ireland's simplest yet most famous seafood eateries. The specialty here is oysters, but they also serve crab, prawns, mussels, and smoked salmon. *The Weir,*

Kilcolgan, Co. Galway, tel. 091/96113. AE, MC, V. Inexpensive.

Dingle **Beginish.** The best of several small but sophisticated restau-
Dining rants in town, this relaxing place serves local meat and seafood
in a generous version of nouvelle cuisine. *Green St., tel. 066/
51588. AE, DC, MC, V. Closed Mon. and Nov. 1–Mar. Moderate.*

Lodging **Benner's.** This busy town-center hotel has been beautifully restored with country-pine antique furniture in all bedrooms.
*Main St., tel. 066/51638, fax 066/51412. 25 rooms with bath. Fa-
cilities: 2 bars, restaurant. AE, DC, MC, V. Moderate.*

Ennis **The Cloister.** Classic French cuisine is served in this riverside
Dining bar-restaurant. *Abbey St., tel. 065/29521. DC, MC, V. Moderate.*

Lodging **Old Ground.** A gracious, creeper-clad old building, Old Ground
★ has been carefully updated. *O'Connell St., tel. 065/28127, fax
065/28112. 60 rooms with bath. AE, DC, MC, V. Expensive.*
West County. This is a lively modern hotel with adequate rooms
and Irish cabaret nightly in summer. *On N18 Limerick road,
tel. 065/28421, fax 065/28801. 109 rooms with bath. AE, DC,
MC, V. Moderate.*

Ennistymon **Falls Hotel.** A Georgian manor house set in its own grounds just
Lodging outside the village, close to two 18-hole golf courses. *Tel. 065/
★ 71004, fax 065/71367. 22 rooms with bath. AE, DC, MC, V.
Closed Oct. 1–Jan. 1. Inexpensive.*

Kenmare **Park.** A guest feels truly pampered at this antique-laden hotel,
Lodging widely considered to be one of Ireland's best. The French res-
★ taurant is superb. *Tel. 064/41200, fax 064/41200. 48 rooms with
bath. Facilities: tennis, parkland, garden. DC, MC, V. Very
Expensive.*

Killarney **Foley's.** This popular eatery specializes in seafood, steaks, and
Dining Kerry mountain lamb. *23 High St., tel. 064/31217. AE, DC,
★ MC, V. Moderate.*
★ **Gaby's.** For simple and fresh seafood, Gaby's can't be beat. *17
High St., tel. 064/32519. AE, DC, MC, V. Closed Sun. (except
for dinner in July and Aug.), Mon. lunch, and Dec.–mid-Mar.
Moderate.*

Lodging **Cahernane.** This is a manor house-turned-hotel in a pretty setting. *Muckross Rd., tel. 064/31895, fax 064/34340. 52 rooms
with bath. Facilities: 9-hole golf course. AE, DC, MC, V.
Closed Nov.–Easter except Christmas–New Year's Day. Expensive.*
Great Southern. The Great Southern is housed in a vast 19th-
century redbrick building set in large gardens. *Tel. 064/31262,
fax 064/31642. 180 rooms with bath. Facilities: heated indoor
pool. AE, DC, MC, V. Closed Jan.–mid-Mar. Expensive.*
Arbutus. Newly refurbished and centrally located, the Arbutus
benefits from a lively bar and an Old World atmosphere. *College
St., tel. 064/31037, fax 064/34033. 35 rooms with bath. AE, DC,
MC, V. Moderate.*

Limerick **Jury's.** This bright modern hotel is set in its own grounds over-
Lodging looking the Shannon, about a three-minute walk from the town
center. There is good French cuisine in the Copper Room restaurant and live music most nights in the bar. *Ennis Rd., tel.*

061/55366, fax 061/326400. 96 rooms with bath. Facilities: restaurant, bar. AE, DC, MC, V. Moderate.

Glentworth. This is a functional hotel just off Limerick's main street. *Glentworth St., tel. 061/43822, fax 061/413073. 55 rooms, most with bath. AE, DC, MC, V. Inexpensive.*

Lisdoonvarna
Dining

Bruach na Haille. This prettily converted cottage, 2 miles (3 kilometers) from town, serves imaginative, country-style Irish meals. *Roadford, Doolin, tel. 065/74120. V. Moderate.*

Lodging

Hydro. The Hydro is an old-fashioned spa-hotel that has undergone a recent face-lift to make it perfectly adequate for the price. *Tel. 065/74027, fax 065/74406. 70 rooms with bath. V. Closed Nov.–Mar. Inexpensive.*

Sheedy's Spa View. This is a friendly, family-run establishment with open turf fires and an excellent restaurant. *Sulphir Hill, tel. 065/74026, fax 065/74555. 11 rooms with bath. Facilities: restaurant, tennis. AE, DC, MC, V. Closed Oct.–Mar. Inexpensive.*

The Northwest

This route from Galway to Sligo and then back to Dublin, via Kells, takes you through the rugged landscape of Connemara to the fabled Yeats country in the northwest and then skirts the borders of Northern Ireland before returning to Dublin. The entire trip is about 400 kilometers (250 miles) and passes through some of the wildest and loneliest parts of Ireland.

Getting Around

By Train Trains to Galway, Westport, and Sligo operate from Dublin's Heuston or Connolly (Sligo) stations. There is no train service north of Sligo.

By Bus Travel within the area is more flexible by bus; details are available from local tourist information offices.

By Car In Galway, cars can be rented from **Avis** (tel. 091/68901), **Hertz** (tel. 091/66674), or **Murray's** (tel. 091/62222). Taxis do not operate on meters; agree on the fare beforehand.

By Bicycle You can rent bikes from **Cycle Logical** (Galway City, tel. 091/68223), **John Mannion** (Railway View, Clifden, tel. 095/21160), or **Gary's Cycles** (Quay St., Sligo, tel. 071/45418).

Guided Tours

CIE Tours International operates day tours of Connemara out of Galway City and bus tours into the Donegal highlands from Sligo train station; details are available from local tourist offices. **CIE** (tel. 01/302222 Bus Eireann) and **Gray Line** (tel. 01/612325) offer tours of the Boyne Valley and County Meath out of Dublin.

Tourist Information

All are open weekdays 9–6, Sat. 9–1.

Galway (off Eyre Sq., tel. 091/63081).
Sligo (Temple St., tel. 071/61201).
Westport (The Mall, tel. 098/25711).

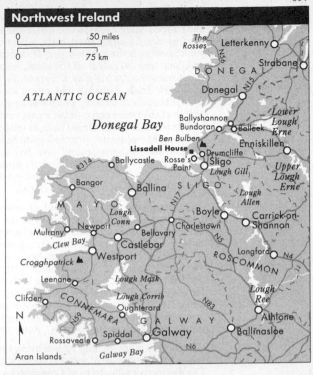

Northwest Ireland

Northwest Ireland map showing: The Rosses, Letterkenny, Strabane, DONEGAL, Donegal, N56, N15, ATLANTIC OCEAN, Lower Lough Erne, Ballyshannon, Bundoran, Belleek, Enniskillen, Donegal Bay, Ben Bulben, Lissadell House, Drumcliffe, Ballycastle, Rosse's Point, Sligo, Upper Lough Erne, R314, Lough Gill, SLIGO, Bangor, Ballina, Lough Allen, N17, Lough Conn, Boyle, Carrick-on-Shannon, MAYO, Newport, Bellavary, Charlestown, N5, Mulrany, Clew Bay, Castlebar, ROSCOMMON, Longford, N4, Croaghpatrick, Westport, Lough Ree, Leenane, Lough Mask, CONNEMARA, Lough Corrib, N83, Clifden, Oughterard, GALWAY, Athlone, N59, Rossaveale, Spiddal, Galway, Ballinasloe, Aran Islands, Galway Bay, N6

Exploring the Northwest

Galway City is the gateway to the ancient province of Connacht, the most westerly seaboard in Europe. Galway City was well established even before the Normans arrived in the 13th century, rebuilding the city walls and turning the little town into a flourishing port. Later its waterfront was frequented by Spanish grandees and traders. The salmon fishing in the river Corrib, which flows through the lower part of the town, is unsurpassed. In early summer, you can stand on the **Weir Bridge** beside the town's cathedral and watch thousands of salmon as they leap and twist through the narrow access to the inner lakes. **Lynch's Castle** in Shop Street, now a bank, is a good example of a 16th-century fortified house—fortified because the neighboring Irish tribes persistently raided Galway City, whose commercial life excluded them. Nowadays the liveliest part of town is around the area between **Eyre Square** (the town's center) and **Spanish Arch.**

Time Out Drop in at **Noctan's** pub on the corner of Abbeygate Street for food at lunchtime and the latest news of what's on in town.

On the west bank of the Corrib estuary, just outside of the Galway town walls, is the **Claddagh,** said to be the oldest fishing village in Ireland. **Salthill Promenade,** with its lively seaside amenities, is the traditional place "to sit and watch the moon rise over Claddagh, and see the sun go down on Galway Bay"— in the words of the city's most famous song.

Connemara is a land of romantic, underpopulated landscapes, and rugged craggy coastlines, where the Irish language is still used by many people. **Rossaveale,** a port on the coast road beyond Spiddal, is the handiest port for a trip to the Aran Islands, 48 kilometers (30 miles) off the coast, where J. M. Synge drew the inspiration for his play *Riders to the Sea.* The islands are still 100% Irish speaking and retain an atmosphere distinct from that of the mainland, which will be appreciated by those in search of the peace and quiet of a past century. **Inishmaan,** the middle island, is considered the most unspoiled of the three and will delight botanists, ornithologists, and walkers. *Sailings daily from Rossaveale and less frequently from Galway; round-trip fare about IR£12. Details from Galway Tourist Information Office. Also accessible by air from Galway City: daily flights, round-trip fare about IR£25.*

Oughterard is an important angling center on Lough Corrib. Boats can be rented for excursions to the lake's many wooded islands. The road to Clifden runs between the Maamturk and the Cloosh Mountains beside a string of small lakes. **Clifden,** the principal town of Connemara, has an almost Alpine setting, nestling on the edge of the Atlantic with a spectacular mountain backdrop. Just beyond Clifden is the **Connemara National Park,** with its many nature trails offering views of sea, mountain, and lake. Its visitor center features an audiovisual presentation and has a collection of farm furniture. *Tel. 095/41054. Admission free. Open Apr.–Oct., daily 10–6.*

Westport is a quiet, mainly 18th-century town overlooking Clew Bay—a wide expanse of water studded with nearly 400 islands. The distinctive silhouette of **Croagpatrick,** a 775-meter mountain, dominates the town. Today some 25,000 pilgrims climb it on the last Sunday in July in honor of St. Patrick, who is believed to have spent 40 days fasting on its summit in AD 441. Whether he did or not, the climb is an exhilarating experience and can be completed in about three hours; it should be attempted only in good weather, however.

County Sligo is noted for its seaside resorts, the famous golf course at Rosse's Point (just outside Sligo Town), and its links with Ireland's most famous 20th-century poet, William Butler Yeats, who is buried just north of **Sligo Town** at Drumcliffe. An important collection of paintings by the poet's brother, Jack B. Yeats, can be seen in the **Sligo Museum** (Stephen St., tel. 071/42212), which also has displays on the folk life of the area. Take a boat from Sligo up to **Lough Gill** and see the **Lake Isle of Innisfree** and other places immortalized in the poetry of W. B. Yeats. His grave is found beneath the slopes of Ben Bulben, just north of the town. Nearby is **Lissadell House,** a substantial mansion dating from 1830 that features prominently in his writings. It was the home of Constance Gore-Booth, later Countess Markeviecz, who took part in the 1916 uprising. *Tel. 071/63150. Admission: IR£2 adults, 50p children. Open May–Sept., Mon.–Sat. 10:30–noon, 2–4:30.*

Bundoran, the southernmost town of Donegal, is one of Ireland's major seaside resorts, with excellent sandy beaches. From **Donegal Town,** you can set off to tour the ever-changing landscape of Donegal's rugged coastline and highlands, visiting the "tweed villages" on the coast at the Rosses, where the famous Donegal tweed is woven.

This route heads back to Dublin through **Belleek,** on the borders of Counties Donegal and Fermanagh, known for its fragile, lustrous china; a factory visit can be arranged (tel. 08/0365–65501). For the remaining towns on this tour, *see* the Ireland country map. Belleek is a frontier post on an approved road that skirts the shores of Lower Lough Erne in Northern Ireland, passing through Enniskillen and reemerging in Belturbet, County Cavan, on the main N3 Dublin road. (Tourists in private cars can cross the border here with a minimum of formality.) The N3 continues across a beautiful patchwork of lakes, the heart of the low-lying lakelands. In **Cavan** you may want to visit the **Crystal Factory,** which runs daily tours of the premises, showing visitors the techniques for blowing and cutting glass. *Dublin Rd., tel. 049/31852. Admission free. Open Mon.–Fri. 9–5; closed first two weeks in Aug.*

The N3 returns you to Dublin by way of **Kells,** in whose 8th-century abbey the Book of Kells was completed; a facsimile can be seen in **St. Columba's Church.** Among the remains of the abbey is a well-preserved round tower and a rare example of a stone-roof church dating from the 9th century. There are five richly sculptured stone crosses in Kells. Just south of **Navan** is the **Hill of Tara,** the religious and cultural capital of Ireland in ancient times. Its importance waned with the arrival of Christianity in the 5th century, and today its crest is, appropriately enough, crowned with a statue of the man who brought Christianity to Ireland—St. Patrick.

Dining and Lodging

For details and price-category definitions, *see* Dining and Lodging in Staying in Ireland.

Cashel Bay
Dining and Lodging

Cashel House. One of Ireland's outstanding country-house hotels, luxurious and secluded, Cashel House attracts an affluent outdoor-loving international clientele. *Cashel Bay, Connemara, Co. Galway, tel. 095/31001, fax 095/31077. 28 rooms with bath. Facilities: bar, restaurant, horseback riding, tennis, private beach, bicycles, fishing. AE, DC, MC, V. Expensive.*

Castlebar
Lodging

Breaffy House. This sturdy castellated stone mansion with a small modern extension is charmingly set in its own parkland. *Located 5 km (3 mi) southeast of town, on the N6, Co. Mayo, tel. and fax 094/22033. 40 rooms with bath. Facilities: 18-hole golf course. AE, DC, MC, V. Moderate.*

Clifden
Lodging

Abbeyglen Castle. This comfortable hotel is quietly set a half-mile west of town, featuring panoramic views over the rolling green hillsides. The secluded garden is a haven for travelweary souls. *Sky Rd., tel. 095/21201, fax 095/21797. 46 rooms with bath. Facilities: heated pool, tennis. AE, DC, MC, V. Closed Jan. Moderate.*

Rock Glen Manor House. Dating from 1815, this converted hunting lodge is 1½ kilometers (1 mile) south of town in exceptionally peaceful surroundings. *Tel. 095/21035, fax 095/21737. 29 rooms with bath. AE, DC, MC, V. Closed Nov.–Feb. Moderate.*

Collooney
Dining and Lodging

Markree Castle. This magnificent 17th-century castle, which also houses the renowned Knockmuldowney Restaurant, is situated on a 1,000-acre estate. The host family offers bed and breakfast, delectable home-cooked French food at dinner, and a traditional Sunday lunch. *11 km (7 mi) south of Sligo Town on N4, Co. Sligo, tel. 071/67800, fax 071/67840. 14 rooms with bath. AE, DC, MC, V. Expensive.*

Cong **Ashford Castle.** This imposing castle is set in its own park on the
Lodging edge of Lough Corrib and has a superb restaurant, the Con-
★ naught Room. President Reagan stayed here in 1984. *Tel. 092/ 46003, fax 092/46260. 82 rooms with bath. Facilities: 9-hole golf course, tennis, fishing, garden. AE, DC, MC, V. Very Expensive.*

Galway City **Malt House.** This is a cheerful, relaxing pub-restaurant hidden
Dining away in a shopping arcade. *Olde Malte Arcade, High St., tel. 091/67866. AE, MC, V. Closed Dec. 24–30. Moderate.*
Noctan's. This excellent, small French restaurant is situated above a popular pub. *17 Cross St., tel. 091/66172. MC, V. Dinner only. Closed Sun.–Mon. Moderate.*

Lodging **Great Southern.** Recently refurbished, this old-style town hotel enjoys a conveniently central location. *Eyre Sq., tel. 091/64041, fax 091/64041. 120 rooms with bath. Facilities: roof-top heated pool, sauna, health complex. AE, DC, MC, V. Expensive.*
Ardilaun House. This hotel is set in pleasant grounds midway between Galway City and the seaside suburb of Salthill. *Taylors Hill, tel. 091/21433, fax 091/21546. 91 rooms with bath. AE, DC, MC, V. Moderate.*

Moycullen **Drimcong House.** The chef-owner prepares his award-winning
Dining meals in a 300-year-old lakeside house, 13 kilometers (8 miles) from Galway City. *1½ km (1 mi) northwest on N59, tel. 091/ 85115. AE, DC, MC, V. Closed Sun. dinner, Mon., and Jan.– Feb. Moderate.*

Sligo Town **Ballincar House.** Just outside of town, this converted country
Lodging house with gardens serves excellent food. *Rosses Point Rd., tel. 071/45361, fax 071/44198. 25 rooms with bath. Facilities: squash, tennis, sauna, solarium. AE, DC, MC, V. Moderate.*
Sligo Park. This is a modern two-story building, set in spacious grounds. *Pearse Rd., tel. 071/60291, fax 071/69556. 60 rooms with bath. AE, DC, MC, V. Moderate.*
Southern. This solid, four-story, 19th-century hotel is set in its own pretty gardens. *Lord Edward St., tel. 071/62101, fax 071/ 60328. 50 rooms, most with bath. AE, DC, MC, V. Inexpensive.*

Westport **Asgard.** The Asgard is a pub with award-winning food in both
Dining its bar and second-floor restaurant. *The Quay, tel. 098/25319. AE, DC, MC, V. Moderate.*

Lodging **Westport Woods.** Woodlands surround this classy modern hotel beside a lake on the edge of town. *Louisburgh Rd., tel. 098/ 25811, fax 098/26212. 56 rooms with bath. Facilities: restaurant (dinner only). AE, DC, MC, V. Expensive.*
Old Railway. A delightful Victorian hotel in the town center, the Old Railway has been fully refurbished with no loss of character. *The Mall, tel. 098/25166, fax 098/25605. 20 rooms with bath. Facilities: 2 restaurants, 2 bars, fishing. AE, DC, MC, V. Moderate.*

18 Italy

Where else in Europe can you find the blend of great art, delicious food and wines, and sheer verve that awaits you in Italy? This Mediterranean country has profoundly contributed to the Western way of life, and has produced some of the world's greatest thinkers, writers, politicians, saints, and artists. Impressive traces of their lives and works can still be seen in the great buildings and lovely countryside.

The whole of Italy is one vast attraction, but the triangle of its most-visited cities—Rome (Roma), Florence (Firenze), and Venice (Venezia)—gives a good idea of the great variety to be found here. In Rome and Florence, especially, you can feel the uninterrupted flow of the ages, from the Classical era of the ancient Romans to the bustle and throb of contemporary life carried on in centuries-old settings. Venice, by contrast, seems suspended in time, the same today as it was when it held sway over the eastern Mediterranean and the Orient. Each of these cities presents a different aspect of the Italian character: the Baroque exuberance of Rome, Florence's serene stylishness, and the dreamy sensuality of Venice.

The uninhibited Italian lifestyle can be entertaining or irritating, depending on how you look at it. Rarely do things run like clockwork here; you are more likely to encounter unexplained delays and incomprehensible complications. Relax: There's usually something you can smile about even in the darkest circumstances.

Trying to soak in Italy's rich artistic heritage is a great challenge to tourists. The country's many museums and churches draw hordes of visitors, all wanting to see the same thing at the same time. From May through September, the Sistine Chapel, Michelangelo's *David*, St. Mark's Square, and other key sights are more often than not swamped by mobs of fellow tourists. Try to see the highlights at off-peak times in the day. If they are open during lunch—and many are not—that is often a good time. Special attractions include the sight of Michelangelo's vibrant original colors on the ceiling of the Sistine Chapel now that it has been cleaned, the scrubbed facades of Rome's glorious Baroque churches, and the restored Gozzoli frescoes in the Palazzo Medici Riccardi in Florence. In Rome, the new archaeological museum near Termini Station should now be open.

Recent regulations barring some automobile traffic from the centers of Rome and Florence have made some areas less noisy, but air pollution remains a serious problem.

Even in the major tourist cities, Italians generally take a friendly interest in their visitors. Only the most blasé waiters and salespeople will be less than courteous and helpful. However, the persistent attention Italian males pay to foreign females can be oppressive and annoying. If you're not interested, the best tactic is to ignore them. It's important to be attentive to matters of personal security in certain parts of the country; always be on guard against pickpockets and purse snatchers in the main tourist cities and in Naples. Especially in Rome, watch out for bands of gypsy children, expert at lifting wallets. Small cities and towns are usually safe.

Making the most of your time in Italy doesn't mean rushing through it. To gain a rich appreciation for Italy, don't try to see everything all at once. Do what you really want to do, and if that means skipping a museum to sit at a pretty café, enjoying the sunshine and a cappuccino, you're getting into the Italian spirit. Art—and life—are to be enjoyed, and the Italians can show you how.

Essential Information

Before You Go

When to Go The main tourist season in Italy runs from mid-April to the end of September. The best months for sightseeing are April, May, June, September, and October, when the weather is generally pleasant and not too hot. Foreign tourists crowd the major cities at Easter, when Italians flock to resorts and the countryside. Avoid traveling in August, when the heat can be oppressive and when vacationing Italians cram roads, trains, and planes, as well as beach and mountain resorts. Especially around the August 15 holiday, such cities as Rome and Milan are deserted, and many restaurants and shops close. Except for such year-round resorts as Taormina and a few on the Italian Riviera, coastal resorts close up tight from October or November to April. The best time for resorts is June and September, when the weather is usually fine and everything is open but not crowded.

The hottest months are July and August, when brief afternoon thunderstorms are common in inland areas. Winters are relatively mild in most places on the tourist circuit, but there are always some rainy spells.

Although low-season rates do not officially apply at hotels in Rome and Florence (in winter) and Milan (in summer) you can usually bargain for discounted rates. You can save on hotel accommodations in Venice and in such resorts as Sorrento and Capri during their low seasons—the winter, early spring, and late-autumn months.

Climate The following are average daily maximum and minimum temperatures for Rome.

Jan.	52F	11C	May	74F	23C	Sept.	79F	26C
	40	5		56	13		62	17
Feb.	55F	13C	June	82F	28C	Oct.	71F	22C
	42	6		63	17		55	13
Mar.	59F	15C	July	87F	30C	Nov.	61F	16C
	45	7		67	20		49	9
Apr.	66F	19C	Aug.	86F	30C	Dec.	55F	13C
	50	10		67	20		44	6

The following are average daily maximum and minimum temperatures for Milan.

Jan.	40F	5C	May	74F	23C	Sept.	75F	24C
	32	0		57	14		61	16
Feb.	46F	8C	June	80F	27C	Oct.	63F	17C
	35	2		63	17		52	11
Mar.	56F	13C	July	84F	29C	Nov.	51F	10C
	43	6		67	20		43	6
Apr.	65F	18C	Aug.	82F	28C	Dec.	43F	6C
	49	9		66	16		35	2

704

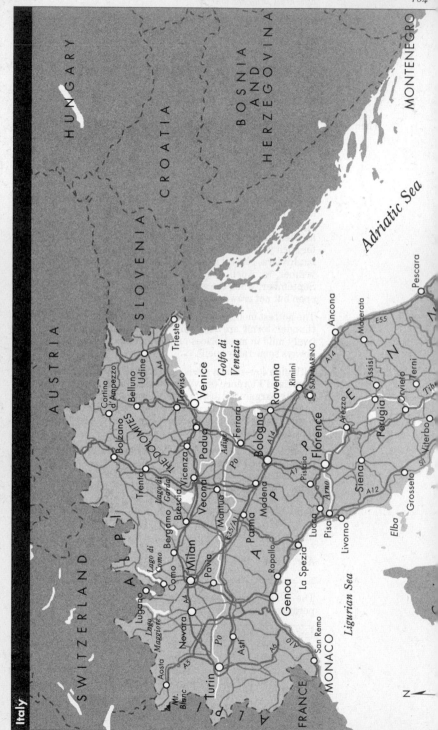

Italy

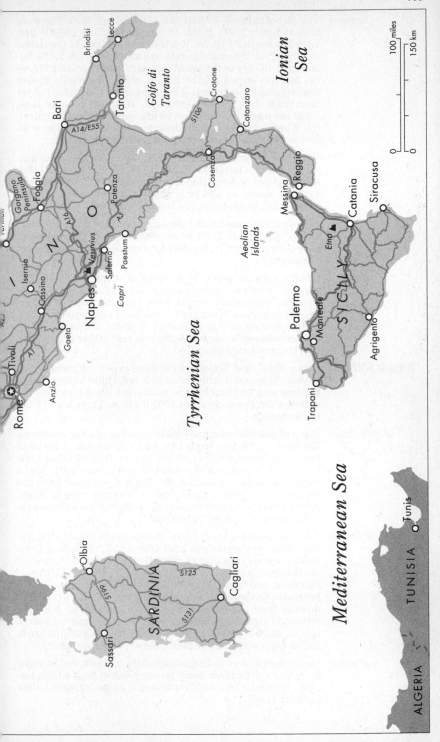

Ionian Sea

100 miles
150 km

Lecce
Brindisi
Taranto
Golfo di Taranto
Crotone
Bari
A14/E55
Catanzaro
S106
Foggia
Gargano Peninsula
Potenza
Cosenza
Reggio
A16
A3
Messina
Isernia
Vesuvius
Salerno
Paestum
Aeolian Islands
Catania
Siracusa
Cassino
Naples
Capri
Etna
SICILY
Gaeta
Palermo
Monreale
Tivoli
Anzio
Agrigento
Rome

Tyrrhenian Sea

Trapani

Olbia
S199
SARDINIA
S125
Sassari
S131
Cagliari

Mediterranean Sea

Tunis
TUNISIA
ALGERIA

Currency The unit of currency in Italy is the lira (plural, lire). There are bills of 1,000, 2,000, 5,000, 10,000, 50,000, and 100,000 lire; coins are worth 10, 20, 50, 100, 200, and 500 lire. At press time (spring 1993), the exchange rate was about 1,200 lire to the dollar and 2,100 lire to the pound sterling. Sooner or later the zeros will be lopped off the lire in order to simplify money dealings and life in general. The long-heralded move has not yet been made, but it seems imminent. If it does come to pass, 5,000 lire would become 5 lire, 50 lire would become 50 centesimi. When it does happen, both old and new values will be in effect until people become accustomed to the new system.

While the present system continues, especially when your purchases run into hundreds of thousands of lire, beware of being shortchanged, a dodge that is practiced at ticket windows and cashiers' desks, as well as in shops and even banks. *Always count your change before you leave the counter.*

Always carry some smaller-denomination bills for sundry purchases; you're less likely to be shortchanged, and you won't have to face the eye-rolling dismay of cashiers chronically short of change.

Credit cards are generally accepted in shops and hotels, but may not be welcome in restaurants, so always look for those little signs in the window or ask when you enter to avoid embarrassing situations. When you wish to leave a tip beyond the 15% service charge (*see* Staying in Italy, Tipping, *below*) that is usually included with your bill, leave it in cash rather than adding it to the credit card slip.

What It Will Cost Rome, Milan, and Venice are the more expensive Italian cities to visit. Taxes are usually included in hotel bills; a cover charge appears as a separate item in restaurant checks, as does the service charge, usually about 15%, if added. There is a 19% tax on car rentals.

Sample Prices A cup of espresso consumed while standing at a bar costs from 800 lire to 1,200 lire, triple that for table service. A bottle of beer costs from 2,000 lire to 3,500 lire, a soft drink about 1,800 lire. A *tramezzino* (small sandwich) costs about 2,000 lire, a more substantial one about 3,000. You will pay about 8,000 lire for a short taxi ride in Rome, less in Florence, more in Milan. Admission to a major museum is about 10,000 lire; a three-hour sightseeing tour, about 36,000 lire.

Customs on Arrival Two still cameras and one movie camera can be brought in duty-free. Travelers arriving in Italy from an EC (European Community) country are allowed, duty-free, a total of 300 cigarettes (*or* 150 cigarillos *or* 75 cigars), 1½ liters of spirits plus 5 liters of still wine, and 75 milliliters of perfume if duty and taxes have been paid on them at the time of purchase. Visitors traveling directly from non-European countries are allowed 400 cigarettes and cigars or tobacco not exceeding 500 grams, 1 liter of spirits, and 2 liters of still wine. Not more than 2 million lire in Italian bank notes may be taken into or out of the country.

Language Italy is accustomed to English-speaking tourists, and in major cities you will find that many people speak at least a little English. In smaller hotels and restaurants, a smattering of Italian comes in handy.

Getting Around

By Car
Road Conditions

The extensive network of *autostrade* (toll superhighways) connecting all major towns is complemented by equally well-maintained but toll-free *superstrade* (express highways), *strade statali* (main roads), and *strade provinciali* (secondary roads).

All are clearly signposted and numbered. The ticket issued on entering an autostrada must be returned on leaving, along with the toll. On some shorter autostrade, mainly connections, the toll is payable on entering.

The Autostrada del Sole (A1, A2, and A3) crosses the country from north to south, connecting Milan to Reggio Calabria. The A4 from west to east connects Turin to Trieste.

Rules of the Road

Driving is on the right. The speed limit on an autostrada is 130 kph (81 mph). On other roads it is 90 kph (56 mph). Other regulations are largely as in the United States except that the police have the power to levy on-the-spot fines—even as high as $500!

Parking

Check with your hotel to determine the best place to park. Parking is greatly restricted in the center of most major Italian cities. Parking in a "Zona Disco" is for limited periods.

Gasoline

Gas costs the equivalent of more than $5 per U.S. gallon, or about 1,500 lire per liter. Vouchers with tourist discounts of about 15%, together with an autostrada credit card and free breakdown service, are available as a package from the AA (Automobile Association) or RAC (Royal Automobile Club). Except on the autostrade, most gas stations are closed Sunday; they also close from 1 to 3 PM and at 7 PM for the night. Self-service pumps can be found in most cities and towns.

Breakdowns

Dial 116 for towing and repairs, also for ambulance and highway police.

By Train

The fastest service on the FS (Ferrovie dello Stato), the state-owned railroad, are the *intercity* trains, for which you pay a supplement and for which seat reservations may be required (and are always advisable). *Espresso* trains usually make more stops and are a little slower. *Diretto* and *locale* are slowest of all. You can buy tickets and make seat reservations at travel agencies displaying the FS symbol up to two months in advance, thereby avoiding long lines at station ticket windows. Tickets within a 100-km (62-mi) range can be purchased at any *tabacchi* (tobacconist's shop). There is a refreshment service on all long-distance trains. Tap water on trains is not drinkable. Carry compact bags for easy overhead storage. Trains are very crowded at holiday times; always reserve.

By Plane

Alitalia and domestic affiliate **ATI,** plus several privately owned companies, provide service throughout Italy. Alitalia offers several discount fares; inquire at travel agencies or at Alitalia agencies in major cities.

By Bus

Regional bus companies provide service over an extensive network of routes throughout Italy. Route information and timetables are usually available at tourist information offices and travel agencies, or at bus company ticket offices. Among the interregional companies providing long-distance service is **SITA** (Viale Cadorna 105, Florence, tel. 055/278611).

By Boat Ferries connect the mainland with all the major islands. Car ferries operate to Sicily, Sardinia, Elba, Ponza, Capri (though cars are not advised), and Ischia, among others. Lake ferries connect the towns on the shores of the Italian lakes: Como, Maggiore, and Garda.

Staying in Italy

Telephones
Local Calls
Pay phones take either 100- or 200-lire coins, a *gettone* (token), or magnetic card. Some older phones take only tokens, which you insert in the slot before picking up the receiver; dial, and when your party answers, push the little knob on the slot to release the token and complete the connection. Tokens can be purchased from the token machine or from the cashier of the store, bar, or other facility where the phone is located. Local calls cost 200 lire for a minimum of 4 minutes. For *teleselezione* (long-distance direct dialing), place several coins in the slot; unused coins are returned when you push the large yellow knob. Buy magnetic cards at tobacconists.

International Calls Since hotels tend to add exorbitant service charges for long-distance and international calls, it's best to go to the "Telefoni" telephone exchange, where the operator assigns you a booth, can help place your call, and will collect payment when you have finished. Telefoni exchanges (usually marked *SIP* or, in Rome, *ASST)* are found in all cities. The cheaper and easier option, however, will be to use your AT&T or MCI calling card. For AT&T dial access number 172–1011 and for MCI dial access number 172–1022. An English-speaking operator will then ask for your calling card number and proceed to connect you with the United States.

Operators and
Information
For Europe and the Mediterranean area, dial 15; for intercontinental service, dial 170.

Mail The Italian mail system is notoriously erratic and often excruciatingly slow. Allow up to 21 days for mail to and from the United States and Canada, almost as much to and from the United Kingdom, and much longer for postcards.

Postal Rates Airmail letters to the United States cost 1,100 lire for up to 20 grams; postcards with a short greeting and signature cost 950 lire, but cost letter rate if the message is lengthy. Airmail letters to the United Kingdom cost 750 lire, postcards 650 lire.

Receiving Mail You can have mail sent to American Express offices or to Italian post offices, marked "Fermo Posta" and addressed to you c/o Palazzo delle Poste, with the name of the city in which you will pick it up. In either case you must show your passport and pay a small fee.

Shopping
Sales-Tax Refunds
Italy's IVA-refund system is complicated and doesn't apply to most purchases. Foreign tourists who have speant more than 930,000 lire (before tax) on a single article can take advantage of it, however. At the time of purchase, with passport or ID in hand, ask the store for an invoice describing the article and price. Non-EC citizens must have the invoice stamped at Customs upon departure from Italy, while EC citizens should have it stamped at Customs in the country to which they are returning. Once back home—and within 90 days of the date of purchase—the buyer must send the stamped invoice back to the store, which should forward the IVA rebate directly to the tourist. If the store participates in the Europe Tax-free Shop-

ping System (those that do display a sign to the effect), things are simpler. The invoice provided is a Tax-free Cheque in the amount of the tax refund, which can be cashed at the Tax-Free Cash Refund window in the transit area of major airports and border crossings.

Bargaining Most shops now have *prezzi fissi* (fixed prices), but you may be able to get a discount on a large purchase. Always bargain with a street vendor or at a market (except for food).

Opening and Closing Times

Banks. Banks are open weekdays 8:30–1:30 and 2:45–3:45.

Churches. Churches are usually open from early morning to noon or 12:30, when they close for about two hours or more, opening again in the afternoon until about 7 PM.

Museums. National museums are usually open until 2 and are often closed on Monday, but there are many exceptions. Non-national museums have entirely different hours, which may vary according to season. Archaeological sites are usually closed on Monday. At all museums and sites, ticket offices close an hour or so before official closing time. Always check with the local tourist office for current hours.

Shops. Shops are open, with individual variations, from 9 to 1 and from 3:30 or 4 to 7 or 7:30. They are open from Monday through Saturday, but close for a half-day during the week; for example, in Rome most shops (except food shops) are closed on Monday morning (Saturday afternoon in July and August). Some tourist-oriented shops are open all day, every day, as in Venice.

National Holidays January 1; January 6 (Epiphany); April 4 (Easter Monday); April 25 (Liberation Day); May 1 (May Day); June 2 (Republic Day); August 15 (the religious feast of the Assumption, known as Ferragosto, when cities are literally deserted and most restaurants and shops are closed); November 1 (All Saints Day); December 8 (Immaculate Conception); December 25 and 26.

Dining Generally speaking, a *ristorante* pays more attention to decor, service, and menu than does a *trattoria*, which is simpler and often family-run. An *osteria* used to be a lowly tavern, though now the term may be used to designate a chic and expensive eatery. A *tavola calda* offers hot dishes and snacks, with seating. A *rosticceria* has the same, to take out.

The menu is always posted in the window or just inside the door of an eating establishment. Check to see what is offered, and note the charges for *coperto* (cover) and *servizio* (service), which will increase your check. A *menu turistico* includes taxes and service, but beverages are extra.

Mealtimes Lunch hour in Rome lasts from 1 to 3, dinner from 8 to 10. Service begins and ends a half-hour earlier in Florence and Venice, later in the south. Practically all restaurants close one day a week; some close for winter or summer vacation.

Precautions Tap water is safe in large cities and almost everywhere else unless noted *Non Potabile*. Bottled mineral water is available everywhere, *gassata* (with bubbles) or *non gassata* (without). If you prefer tap water, ask for *acqua semplice*.

Dress Except for restaurants in the Very Expensive and occasionally in the Expensive categories, where jacket and tie are advisable, casual attire is acceptable.

Ratings Prices are per person and include first course, main course, dessert or fruit, and house wine, where available. Best bets are indicated by a star ★.

Category	Rome, Milan*	Other Areas
Very Expensive	over 120,000 lire	over 80,000 lire
Expensive	65,000–120,000 lire	45,000–80,000 lire
Moderate	40,000–65,000 lire	25,000–45,000 lire
Inexpensive	under 40,000 lire	under 25,000 lire

Note that restaurant prices in Venice are slightly higher than those in Rome and Milan; in small cities prices are usually lower.

Lodging Italy, and especially the main tourist capitals of Rome, Florence, and Venice, offers a good choice of accommodations. Room rates are on a par with other European capitals, although porters, room service, and in-house cleaning and laundering are disappearing in all but the most elegant hotels. Taxes and service are included in the room rate. Breakfast is an extra charge, but you can decline to take breakfast in most hotels (though the desk may not be happy about it); make your preference clear when booking or checking in. Air-conditioning also may be an extra charge. In older hotels, room quality may be uneven; if you don't like the room you're given, ask for another. This applies to noise, too; some front rooms are bigger and have views but get street noise. Specify if you care about having either a bathtub or shower, as not all rooms have both. In Moderate and Inexpensive places, showers may be the drain-in-the-floor type guaranteed to flood the bathroom. Major cities have hotel reservation service booths in the rail stations.

Hotels Italian hotels are officially classified from five-star (deluxe) to one-star (bed-and-breakfasts and small inns). Prices are established officially and a rate card on the back of the door of your room or inside the closet door tells you exactly what you will pay for that particular room. Any variations should be cause for complaint and should be reported to the local tourist office. CIGA, Jolly, Space, Atahotels, and Italhotels are among the reliable chains or groups operating in Italy, with CIGA among the most luxurious. Sheraton hotels are making an impact in Italy in a big way, though most, located in Rome, Florence, Bari, Padua, and Catania, tend to be geared toward convention and business travel. There are a few Relais et Châteaux member hotels that are noted for individual atmosphere, personal service, and luxury; they are also expensive. The AGIP chain is found mostly on main highways. The Family Hotels group, comprised mostly of small Moderate and Inexpensive family-run hotels, offers good value, reliability, and special attention to families.

Standards in one-star hotels are very uneven. At best, rooms are usually spotlessly clean but basic, with shower and toilets down the hall.

Rentals More and more people are discovering the attractions of renting a house, cottage, or apartment in the Italian countryside. These are ideal for families or for groups of up to eight people looking for a bargain—or just independence. Availability is

We can wire money to every major city in Europe almost as fast as you can say, "Zut alors! J'ai perdu mes valises".

How fast? We can send money in 10 minutes or less, to 13,500 locations in over 68 countries worldwide. That's faster than any other international money transfer service. And when you're *sans* luggage, every minute counts.

MoneyGram from American Express® is available throughout Europe. For more information please contact your local American Express Travel Service Office or call: 44-71-839-7541 in England; 33-1-47777000 in France; or 49-69-21050 in Germany. In the U.S. call 1-800-MONEYGRAM.

MoneyGram

INTERNATIONAL MONEY TRANSFERS.

Ten-minute delivery subject to local agent hours of operation. Local send/receive facilities may also vary. ©1993 First Data Corporation.

519 M.P.H.

190 M.P.H.

75 M.P.H.

S:HS 7469

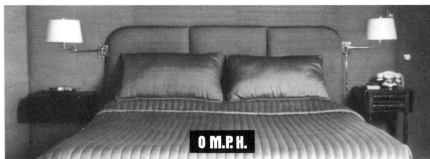

0 M.P.H.

WE LET YOU SEE EUROPE AT YOUR OWN PACE.

Regardless of your personal speed limits, Rail Europe offers everything to get you over, around and through anywhere you want in Europe. For more information, call your travel agent or 1-800-4-EURAIL.

subject to change, so it is best to ask your travel agent or the nearest branch of ENIT, the Italian tourist board, about rentals.

Camping Italy has a wide selection of campgrounds, and the Italians themselves are taking to camping by the thousands, which means that beach or mountain sites will be crammed in July and August. It's best to avoid these peak months and to send for the (necessary) camping license (15,000 lire) from **Federazione Italiana del Campeggio,** Casella Postale 649, 50100 Firenze.

Ratings The following price categories are determined by the cost of two people in a double room. Best bets are indicated by a ★. As with restaurant prices, the cost of hotels in Venice is slightly more than those shown here.

Category	Rome, Milan	Other Areas
Very Expensive	over 450,000 lire	over 350,000 lire
Expensive	300,000–450,000 lire	200,000–350,000 lire
Moderate	195,000–300,000 lire	120,000–200,000 lire
Inexpensive	under 195,000 lire	under 120,000 lire

Tipping Tipping practices vary depending on where you are. Italians tip smaller amounts in small cities and towns, often not at all in cafés and taxis north of Rome. The following guidelines apply in major cities at a Moderate level.

In restaurants, a 15% service charge is usually added to the total, but it doesn't all go to the waiter. In large cities and resorts it is customary to give the waiter a 5% tip in addition to the service charge made on the check.

Charges for service are included in all hotel bills, but smaller tips to staff members are appreciated. In general, chambermaids should be given about 1,000 lire per day, 4,000 lire–5,000 lire per week; bellhops, 1,000 lire–2,000 lire; doormen, about 500 lire. Give the concierge about 15% of his bill for services. Tip a minimum of 1,000 lire for room service and valet service.

Taxi drivers are happy with 5%–10%. Porters at railroad stations and airports charge a fixed rate per suitcase; tip an additional 500 lire per person, more if the porter is very helpful. Service-station attendants are tipped 500 lire–1,000 lire if they are especially helpful. Tip guides about 2,000 lire per person for a half-day tour, more if they are very good.

Rome

Arriving and Departing

By Plane Rome's principal airport is at Fiumicino, 29 kilometers (18 miles) from the city. Though its official name is Leonardo da Vinci Airport, everybody calls it Fiumicino. For flight information, tel. 06/65951. The smaller military airport of Ciampino is on the edge of Rome and is used as an alternative by international and domestic lines, especially for charter flights.

Between the Airport and Downtown The express-train link between Leonardo da Vinci Airport and the Ostiense railway station in downtown Rome offers frequent departures from both ends. The ride takes about 30 minutes. The fare is 6,000 lire. At the Ostiense station you can get a bus or taxi or take the *metro* (subway). Centrally located hotels are a fairly short taxi ride from the Ostiense station. If you need to get to Termini station or thereabouts, the fastest way is to take Metro Line B; follow the signs at the Ostiense station to the Piramide station of the metro.

A taxi to or from the airport at Fiumicino costs about 60,000 lire, including supplements. At a booth inside the terminal you can hire a car with driver for a little more. If you decide to take a taxi, use only yellow or the newer white cabs, which must wait outside the terminal; make sure the meter is running. Gypsy drivers solicit your trade as you come out of customs; they're not reliable, and their rates may be rip-offs.

Ciampino is connected with the Anagnina station of the Metro Line A by bus. A taxi between Ciampino and downtown Rome costs about 35,000 lire.

By Train Termini station is Rome's main train terminal, while Tiburtina and Ostiense stations are used principally by commuters. For train information, try the English-speaking personnel at the Information Office in Termini, or at any travel agency. Tickets and seats can be reserved and purchased at travel agencies bearing the FS (Ferrovie dello Stato) emblem. Short-distance tickets are also sold by tobacconists.

By Bus There is no central bus station in Rome; long-distance and suburban buses terminate either near Termini station or near strategically located metro stops.

By Car The main access routes from the north are the Autostrada del Sole (A1) from Milan and Florence, and the Aurelia highway (SS 1) from Genoa. The principal route to or from points south, such as Naples, is the southern leg of the Autostrada del Sole (A2). All highways connect with the GRA (Grande Raccordo Anulare), a beltway that encircles Rome and funnels traffic into the city. Markings on the GRA are confusing; take time in advance to study which route into the center best suits you.

Getting Around

The best way to see Rome is to choose an area or a sight that you particularly want to see, reach it by bus or Metro (subway), then explore the area on foot, following one of our itineraries or improvising one to suit your mood and interests. Wear comfortable, sturdy shoes, preferably with thick rubber soles to cushion you against the cobblestones. Heed our advice on security, and try to avoid the noise and polluted air of heavily trafficked streets, taking parallel byways wherever possible.

You can buy transportation route maps at newsstands and at ATAC information and ticket booths.

By Metro The subway, or Metro, provides the easiest and fastest way to get around. The Metro opens at 5:30 AM, and the last train leaves each terminal at 11:30 PM. Line A runs from the eastern part of the city to Termini station and past Piazza di Spagna and Piazzale Flaminio to Ottaviano, near St. Peter's and the Vatican Museums. Line B serves Termini, the Colosseum, and the Piramide station (air terminal). The fare is presently 800 lire but may go up to 1,000 lire by 1994. There are change booths and/or ticket machines on station mezzanines; it's best to buy single tickets or books of 5 or 10 ahead of time at newsstands and tobacco shops. A daily tourist ticket known as a BIG is good on buses as well, costs 2,800 lire, and is sold at Metro and ATAC ticket booths.

By Bus Orange ATAC (tel. 06/4695–4444) city buses (and two streetcar lines) run from about 6 AM to midnight, with skeleton *notturno* services on main lines throughout the night. The fare is 800 lire, and tickets are valid on all ATAC lines for 90 minutes; you must buy your ticket before boarding. They are sold singly or in books of five or 10 at tobacco shops and newsstands. Weekly tourist tickets cost 10,000 lire and are sold at ATAC booths. When entering a bus, remember to board at the rear and exit at the middle.

By Taxi Taxis wait at stands and, for a small extra charge, can also be called by telephone. The meter starts at 6,400 lire; there are supplements for service after 10 PM, on Sundays and holidays, and for each piece of baggage. Use yellow or the newer white cabs only, and be very sure to check the meter. To call a cab, tel. 06/3570 or 3875, 4994, 8433.

By Bicycle Bikes provide a pleasant means of getting around when traffic isn't heavy. There are bike-rental shops at Via di Porta Castello 43, near St. Peter's, and at Piazza Navona 69, next to Bar Navona. Rental concessions are at the Piazza di Spagna and Piazza del Popolo Metro stops, and at Largo San Silvestro and Largo Argentina. There are also two in Villa Borghese, at Viale della Pineta and Viale del Bambino on the Pincio.

By Moped You can rent a moped or scooter and mandatory helmet at **Scoot-a-Long** (Via Cavour 302, tel. 06/678–0206) or **St. Peter Moto** (Via di Porta Castello 43, tel. 06/687–5714).

Important Addresses and Numbers

Tourist Information The main **EPT** (Rome Provincial Tourist) office is at Via Parigi 5 (tel. 06/488–3748, open Mon.–Fri. 8:15–7:15, Sat. 8:15–1:15). There are also EPT booths at Termini station and Leonardo da Vinci Airport. A booth on the main floor of the **ENIT** (National Tourist Board) building at Via Marghera 2 (tel. 06/497–1293. Open Mon., Wed., Fri. 9–1 and 4–6; Tues., Thurs. 9–1) can provide information on destinations in Italy outside Rome.

Consulates U.S. (Via Veneto 121, tel. 06/46741). **Canadian** (Via Zara 30, tel. 06/440–3082). **U.K.** (Via Venti Settembre 80a, tel. 06/482–5441).

Emergencies **Police** (tel. 06/4686); **Carabinieri** (tel. 06/112); **Ambulance** (tel. 06/5100 Red Cross). **Doctor:** for a recommendation call your consulate, the private **Salvator Mundi Hospital** (tel. 06/586041), or the **American Hospital** (tel. 06/22551), which has English-speaking staff members. **Pharmacies:** You will find American and British medicines (or their equivalents) and English-speaking personnel at **Farmacia Internazionale Capranica** (Piazza Capranica 96, tel. 06/679–4680), **Farmacia Internazionale Barberini** (Piazza Barberini 49, tel. 06/482–5456), and **Farmacia Doricchi** (Via Venti Settembre 47, tel. 06/487–3880), among others. They are open 8:30–1 and 4–8; some stay open all night.

English-Language Bookstores	You'll find English-language books and magazines at newsstands in the center of Rome, especially on Via Veneto. Also try the **Economy Book and Video Center** (Via Torino 136, tel. 06/474–6877), the **Anglo-American Bookstore** (Via della Vite 57, tel. 06/679–5222), or the **Lion Bookshop** (Via del Babuino 181, tel. 06/322–5837).
Travel Agencies	**American Express** (Piazza di Spagna 38, tel. 06/67641). **CIT** (Piazza Repubblica 64, tel. 06/47941). **Wagons-Lits Travel** (Via Boncompagni 25, tel. 06/481–7655). **Thomas Cook** representative: **World Vision** (Via Paolo Mercuri 6, tel. 06/686–8941).

Guided Tours

Orientation Tours	**American Express** (tel. 06/67641), **CIT** (tel. 06/47941), and **Appian Line** (tel. 06/488–4151) offer three-hour tours in air-conditioned buses with English-speaking guides, covering Rome with four separate itineraries: "Ancient Rome" (including the Roman Forum and Colosseum), "Classic Rome" (including St. Peter's Basilica, Trevi Fountain, and the Janiculum Hill, with its panorama of the city), "Christian Rome" (some major churches and the Catacombs), and the "Vatican Museums and Sistine Chapel." Most tours cost about 36,000 lire, though the Vatican Museums tour is about 46,000 lire. American Express tours depart from Piazza di Spagna, CIT from Piazza della Repubblica, and Appian Line picks sightseers up at their hotels. The least expensive organized bus tour is run by **ATAC**, the municipal bus company. Book tours for about 6,000 lire at the ATAC information booth in front of Termini station.
	American Express can provide a car for up to three persons, limousine for up to seven, and minibus for up to nine, all with English-speaking driver. Guide service is extra. A minibus costs about 400,000 lire for three hours. Almost all operators offer "Rome by Night" tours, with or without dinner and entertainment. Reservations can be made through travel agents.
Special-Interest Tours	You can make your own arrangements (at no cost) to attend a public papal audience in the Vatican or at the Pope's summer residence at Castelgandolfo, or do it through **CIT** (tel. 06/47941), **Appian Line** (tel. 06/488–4151), or **Carrani** (tel. 06/488–0510).
Excursions	Most operators offer half-day excursions to Tivoli to see the Villa d'Este's fountains and gardens; Appian Line's and CIT's half-day tours to Tivoli also include Hadrian's Villa and its impressive ancient ruins. Most operators have all-day excursions to Assisi, to Pompeii and/or Capri, and to Florence.
Personal Guides	Visitors can arrange for a personal guide through **American Express** (tel. 06/67641), **CIT** (47941), or the main **EPT** tourist office (tel. 06/488–3748).

Exploring Rome

Antiquity is taken for granted in Rome, where successive ages have piled the present on top of the past—building, layering, and overlapping their own particular segments of Rome's 2,500 years of history to form a remarkably varied urban complex. Most of the city's major sights are located in a fairly small area known as the *centro*. At its heart lies ancient Rome, where the Forum and Colosseum stand. It was around this core that the other sections of the city grew up through the ages: medieval Rome, which covered the horn of land that pushes the Tiber toward the Vatican and extended across the river into Trastevere; and Renaissance Rome, which was erected upon medieval foundations and extended as far as the Vatican, creating beautiful villas on what was then the outskirts of the city.

The layout of the centro is highly irregular, but several landmarks serve as orientation points to identify the areas that most visitors come to see: the Colosseum, the Pantheon and Piazza Navona, St. Peter's, the Spanish Steps, and Villa Borghese. You'll need a good map to find your way around; newsstands offer a wide choice. Energetic sightseers will walk a lot, a much more pleasant way to see the city now that some traffic has been barred from the centro during the day; others might choose to take taxis, buses, or the Metro. The important thing is to relax and enjoy Rome. Don't try to see everything, but do take time to savor its pleasures. If you are in Rome during a hot spell, do as the Romans do: Start out early in the morning, have a light lunch and a long siesta during the hottest hours, then resume sightseeing in the late afternoon and end your evening with a leisurely meal outdoors, refreshed by cold Frascati wine and the *ponentino*, the cool evening breeze.

Ancient Rome *Numbers in the margin correspond to points of interest on the Rome map.*

❶ Start your first tour at the city's center, in **Piazza Venezia.** Behind the enormous marble monument honoring the first king of
❷ unified Italy, Victor Emmanuel II, stands the **Campidoglio** (Capitol Square) on the Capitoline Hill. The majestic ramp and beautifully proportioned piazza are Michelangelo's handiwork, as are the three palaces. **Palazzo Senatorio** at the center is still the ceremonial seat of Rome's city hall; it was built over the Tabularium, where ancient Rome's state archives were kept.

The palaces flanking the Palazzo Senatorio contain the
❸ **Capitoline Museums.** On the left, the **Museo Capitolino** holds some fine classical sculptures, including the *Dying Gaul*, the *Capitoline Venus*, and a fascinating series of portrait busts of ancient philosophers and emperors. In the courtyard of the
❹ **Palazzo dei Conservatori,** on the right of the piazza, you can use the mammoth fragments of a colossal statue of the emperor Constantine as amusing props for snapshots. Inside you will find splendidly frescoed salons, as well as sculptures and paintings. *Piazza del Campidoglio, tel. 06/671–02071. Admission: 10,000 lire. Open May–Sept., Tues. 9–1:30, 5–8; Wed.–Fri. 9–1:30; Sat. 9–1:30, 7:30–11:30; Sun. 9–1. Oct.–Apr., Tues. and Sat. 9–1:30, 5–8; Wed.–Fri. 9–1:30; Sun. 9–1.*

The Campidoglio is also the site of the very old church of the
❺ **Aracoeli,** which you can reach by way of the stairs on the far side of the Museo Capitolino. Stop in to see the medieval pavement; the Renaissance gilded ceiling that commemorates the victory of Lepanto; some Pinturicchio frescoes; and a much-revered wooden statue of the Holy Child. The Campidoglio gardens offer some good views of the heart of ancient Rome, the Imperial Fora, built when the original Roman Forum became too small for the city's burgeoning needs.

❻ In the valley below the Campidoglio, the **Roman Forum,** once only a marshy hollow, became the political, commercial, and social center of Rome, studded with public meeting halls, shops,

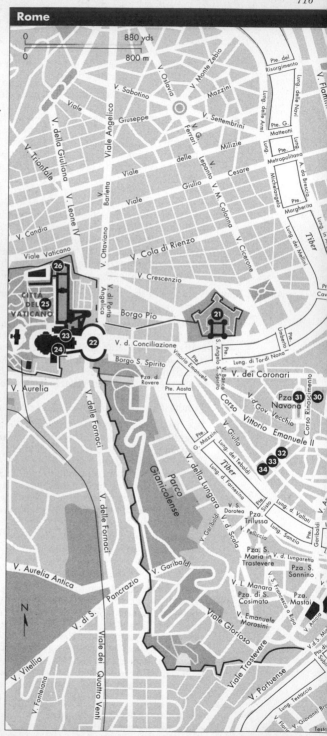

and temples. As Rome declined, these monuments lost their importance and eventually were destroyed by fire or the invasions of barbarians. Rubble accumulated (though much of it was carted off later by medieval home-builders as construction material), and the site reverted to marshy pastureland; sporadic excavations began at the end of the 19th century.

You don't really have to try to make sense of the mass of marble fragments scattered over the area of the Roman Forum. Just consider that 2,000 years ago this was the center of the then-known world. Wander down the Via Sacra and climb the Palatine Hill, where the emperors had their palaces and where 16th-century cardinals strolled in elaborate Italian gardens. From the belvedere you have a good view of the Circus Maximus. *Entrances on Via dei Fori Imperiali, Piazza Santa Maria Nova and Via di San Gregorio, tel. 06/699–0110. Admission: 10,000 lire. Open Apr.–Sept., Mon., Wed.–Sat. 9–6, Tues., Sun. 9–1; Oct.–Mar., Mon., Wed.–Sat. 9–3, Tues., Sun. 9–1.*

❼ Leave the Forum from the exit at Piazza Santa Maria Nova, near the Arch of Titus, and head for the **Colosseum,** inaugurated in AD 80 with a program of games and shows that lasted 100 days. On opening day alone 5,000 wild animals perished in the arena. The Colosseum could hold more than 50,000 spectators; it was faced with marble, decorated with stuccos, and had an ingenious system of awnings to provide shade. Try to see it both in daytime and at night, when yellow floodlights make it a magical sight. The Colosseum, by the way, takes its name from a colossal, 36-meter (115-foot) statue of Nero that stood nearby. You must pay a fee to explore the upper levels, where you can also see a dusty scale model of the arena as it was in its heyday. *Piazza del Colosseo, tel. 06/700–4261. Admission: 6,000 lire to upper levels. Open Mon., Tues., and Thurs.–Sat. 9–one hour before sunset; Sun. and Wed. 9–1.*

Time Out For delicious ice cream try **Ristoro della Salute,** one of Rome's best *gelaterie. Piazza del Colosseo 2a.*

❽ Stroll past the **Arch of Constantine.** The reliefs depict Constantine's victory over Maxentius at the Milvian Bridge. Just before this battle in AD 312, Constantine had a vision of a cross in the heavens and heard the words, "In this sign thou shalt conquer." The victory led not only to the construction of this majestic marble arch but, more important, was a turning point in the history of Christianity: Soon afterward a grateful Constantine decreed that it was a lawful religion and should be tolerated throughout the empire.

❾ A fairly long but pleasant walk takes you to the **Baths of Caracalla,** which numbered among ancient Rome's most beautiful and luxurious, inaugurated by Caracalla in 217 and used until the 6th century. An ancient version of a swanky athletic club, the baths were open to the public; citizens could bathe, socialize, and exercise in huge pools and richly decorated halls and libraries, now towering ruins. An open-air opera performance here can be an exciting experience, especially if the opera is *Aïda,* but dress warmly because the night air is cool and damp. *Via delle Terme di Caracalla. Admission: 6,000 lire. Open Apr.–Sept., Tues.–Sat. 9–6, Sun. and Mon. 9–1; Oct.–Mar., Tues.–Sat. 9–3, Sun.–Mon. 9–1.*

Piazzas and Fountains

⑩

⑪

Piazza del Popolo is one of Rome's most vast and airy squares, but for many years it was just an exceptionally beautiful parking lot with a 3,000-year-old obelisk in the middle. Now most traffic and parking has been barred, and the piazza is open to strollers. The church of **Santa Maria del Popolo** over in the corner of the piazza near the arch stands out more, now that it has been cleaned, and is rich in art, including two stunning Caravaggios in the chapel to the left of the main altar.

Time Out **Rosati** is a café that has never gone out of style, forever a rendezvous of literati, artists, and actors. Its sidewalk tables, tearoom, and upstairs dining room can revive you with an espresso, snack, lunch, or dinner—all with a hefty price tag. *Piazza del Popolo 4. Closed Tues.*

⑫

⑬

If you're interested in antiques, stroll along **Via del Babuino.** If trendy fashions and accessories suit your fancy, take Via del Corso and turn into **Via Condotti,** Rome's most elegant and expensive shopping street. Here you can ogle fabulous jewelry, designer fashions, and accessories in the windows of Buccellati, Ferragamo, Valentino, Gucci, and Bulgari.

Time Out The more-than-200-year-old **Antico Caffè Greco** is the haunt of writers, artists, and well-groomed ladies toting Gucci shopping bags. With its small marble-topped tables and velour settees, it's a nostalgic sort of place—Goethe, Byron, and Liszt were regulars here, and even Buffalo Bill stopped in when his road show came to town. Table service is expensive. *Via Condotti 86. Closed Sun.*

⑭

⑮

Via Condotti gives you a head-on view of the Spanish Steps in **Piazza di Spagna,** and of the church of **Trinità dei Monti.** In the center of the piazza is Bernini's **Fountain of the Barcaccia** (Old Boat), around which Romans and tourists cool themselves on hot summer nights. The 200-year-old **Spanish Steps,** named for the Spanish Embassy to the Holy See, opposite the American Express office, is a popular rendezvous, especially for the young people who throng this area. On weekend afternoons, Via del Corso is packed with wall-to-wall teenagers, and McDonald's, tucked away in a corner of Piazza di Spagna beyond the American Express office, is a mob scene. In contrast, **Babington's Tea Room,** to the left of the Spanish Steps, is a stylish institution that caters to an upscale clientele.

To the right of the Spanish steps is the **Keats and Shelley Memorial House.** Once the home of these romantic poets, it's now a museum. *Piazza di Spagna 26, tel. 06/678–4235. Admission: 4,000 lire. Open June–Sept., weekdays 9–1 and 3–6; Oct.–May, weekdays 9–1 and 2:30–5:30.*

Time Out In a corner of Piazza Mignanelli behind the American Express office is **La Rampa,** one of the best restaurants in this area. It's usually crowded, however, and you may have to wait for a table. *Piazza Mignanelli 18. Closed Sun., Mon. lunch.*

⑯

Head for Via del Tritone and cross this heavily trafficked shopping street into narrow Via della Stamperia, which leads to the **Fountain of Trevi,** a spectacular fantasy of mythical sea creatures and cascades of splashing water. Legend has it that visitors must toss a coin into the fountain to ensure their return to

Rome, but you'll have to force your way past crowds of tourists and aggressive souvenir vendors to do so. The fountain as you see it was completed in the mid-1700s, but there had been a drinking fountain on the site for centuries. Pope Urban VIII almost sparked a revolt when he slapped a tax on wine to cover the expenses of having the fountain repaired.

⑰ At the top of Via del Tritone, **Piazza Barberini** boasts two fountains by Bernini: the jaunty **Triton** in the middle of the square and the **Fountain of the Bees** at the corner of Via Veneto. Decorated with the heraldic Barberini bees, this shell-shaped fountain bears an inscription that was immediately regarded as an unlucky omen by the superstitious Romans, for it erroneously stated that the fountain had been erected in the 22nd year of the reign of Pope Urban VIII, who had commissioned it, while in fact the 21st anniversary of his election was still some weeks away. The wrong numeral was hurriedly erased, but to no avail: Urban died eight days before the beginning of his 22nd year as pontiff.

⑱ A few steps up Via delle Quattro Fontane is **Palazzo Barberini,** Rome's most splendid 17th-century palace, now surrounded by rather unkempt gardens and occupied in part by the **Galleria Nazionale di Arte Antica.** Visit the latter to see Raphael's *Fornarina,* many other good paintings, some lavishly frescoed ceilings, and a charming suite of rooms decorated in 1782 on the occasion of the marriage of a Barberini heiress. *Via delle Quattro Fontane 13, tel. 06/481–4591. Admission: 6,000 lire. Open Tues.–Sat. 9–2, Sun. 9–1.*

⑲ One of Rome's oddest sights is the **crypt** of the **Church of Santa Maria della Concezione** on Via Veneto, just above the Fountain of the Bees. In four chapels under the main church, the skeletons and scattered bones of some 4,000 dead Capuchin monks are arranged in decorative motifs, a macabre practice peculiar to the Baroque age. *Via Veneto 27, tel. 06/462850. Admission free, but a donation is encouraged. Open daily 9–noon and 3–6.*

The lower reaches of Via Veneto are quiet and sedate, but at the intersection with Via Bissolati, otherwise known as "Airline Row," the avenue comes to life. The big white palace on the right is the U.S. Embassy, and the even bigger white palace beyond it is the luxurious **Hotel Excelsior.** Together with Doney's next door and the Café de Paris across the street, the Excelsior was a landmark of La Dolce Vita, that effervescent period during the 1950s when movie stars, playboys, and exiled royalty played hide-and-seek with press agents and *paparazzi,* ducking in and out of nightclubs and hotel rooms along the Via Veneto. The atmosphere of Via Veneto is considerably more sober now, and its cafés cater more to tourists and expensive pickups than to barefoot cinema *contesse.*

Via Veneto ends at **Porta Pinciana,** a gate in the 12-mile stretch of defensive walls built by Emperor Aurelian in the 3rd century; 400 years later, when the Goths got too close for comfort, Belisarius reinforced the gate with two massive towers. Beyond is **Villa Borghese,** most famous of Rome's parks, studded with tall pines that are gradually dying off as pollution and age take their toll. Inside the park, strike off to the right toward
⑳ the **Galleria Borghese,** a pleasure palace created by Cardinal Scipione Borghese in 1613 as a showcase for his fabulous sculp-

ture collection. In the throes of structural repairs for several years, the now-public gallery is, at press time, only partially open to visitors. It's still worth a visit to see the seductive reclining statue of Pauline Borghese by Canova, and some extraordinary works by Bernini, among them the unforgettable *Apollo and Daphne*, in which marble is transformed into flesh and foliage. With restorations dragging on, probably into 1994, a few of the best works, including Caravaggio's, have been moved from the upstairs picture gallery, which is now closed, to the San Michele complex in Trastevere, where they are on view (check locally for hours and admission). *During reconstruction the entrance is on Via Raimondi, reached from Via Pinciana. Via Pinciana (Piazzale Museo Borghese–Villa Borghese), tel. 06/858577. Admission free for the duration of the renovations. Open Mon.–Sat. 9–1:30, Sun. 9–1.*

Castel Sant'Angelo– St. Peter's– Vatican Museums
㉑

Ponte Sant'Angelo, an ancient bridge spanning the Tiber, is decorated with lovely Baroque angels designed by Bernini. From the bridge there are fine views of St. Peter's, in the distance, and of the nearby **Castel Sant'Angelo,** a formidable fortress that was originally built as the tomb of Emperor Hadrian in the 2nd century AD. In its early days, it looked much like the **Augusteo,** or Tomb of Augustus, which still stands more or less in its original form across the river. Hadrian's Tomb was incorporated into the town walls and served as a military stronghold during the barbarian invasions. According to legend it got its present name in the 6th century, when Pope Gregory the Great, passing by in a religious procession, saw an angel with a sword appear above the ramparts to signal the end of the plague that was raging. Enlarged and fortified, the castle became a refuge for the popes, who fled to it along the **Passetto,** an arcaded passageway that links it with the Vatican. Inside the castle you see ancient corridors, medieval cells and Renaissance salons, a museum of antique weapons, courtyards piled with stone cannonballs, and terraces with great views of the city. There's a pleasant bar with outdoor tables on one level. The highest terrace of all, under the newly restored bronze statue of the legendary angel, is the one from which Puccini's heroine, Tosca, threw herself. *Lungotevere Castello 50, tel. 06/687–5036. Admission: 8,000 lire. Open Oct.–Mar., Tues.–Sat. 9–1, Sun. 9–noon, Mon. 2–6:30. From Apr.–Sept. hours vary but are usually Mon.–Sat. 9–7.*

Via della Conciliazione, the broad avenue leading to St. Peter's Basilica, was created by Mussolini's architects by razing blocks of old houses. This opened up a vista of the basilica, giving the eye time to adjust to its mammoth dimensions, and thereby spoiling the effect Bernini sought when he enclosed his vast square (which is really oval) in the embrace of huge quadruple ㉒ colonnades. In **Piazza San Pietro** (St. Peter's Square), which has held up to 400,000 people at one time, look for the stone disks in the pavement halfway between the fountains and the obelisk. From these points the colonnades seem to be formed of a single row of columns all the way around.

When you enter Piazza San Pietro (completed in 1667), you are entering Vatican territory. Since the Lateran Treaty of 1929, **Vatican City** has been an independent and sovereign state, which covers about 44 hectares (108 acres) and is surrounded by thick, high walls. Its gates are watched over by the Swiss Guards, who still wear the colorful dress uniforms designed by

Michelangelo. Sovereign of this little state is John Paul II, 264th Pope of the Roman Catholic Church. At noon on Sunday, ㉓ the Pope appears at his third-floor study window in the **Vatican Palace,** to the right of the basilica, to bless the crowd in the square. (Note: Entry to St. Peter's and the Vatican Museums is barred to those wearing shorts, miniskirts, sleeveless T-shirts, and otherwise revealing clothing. Women should carry scarves to cover bare shoulders and upper arms or wear blouses that come to the elbow. Men should dress modestly, in slacks and shirts.)

㉔ **St. Peter's Basilica** is one of Rome's most impressive sights. It takes a while to absorb the sheer magnificence of it, however, and its rich decoration may not be to everyone's taste. Its size alone is overwhelming, and the basilica is best appreciated when providing the lustrous background for ecclesiastical ceremonies thronged with the faithful. The original basilica was built in the early 4th century AD by the emperor Constantine, over an earlier shrine that supposedly marked the burial place of St. Peter. After more than a thousand years, the old basilica was so decrepit it had to be torn down. The task of building a new, much larger one took almost 200 years and employed the architectural genius of Alberti, Bramante, Raphael, Peruzzi, Antonio Sangallo the Younger, and Michelangelo, who died before the dome he had planned could be completed. Finally, in 1626, St. Peter's Basilica was finished.

The basilica is full of extraordinary works of art. Among the most famous is Michelangelo's *Pietà* (1498), seen in the first chapel on the right just as you enter from the square. Michelangelo has four *Pietàs* to his credit. The earliest and best known can be seen here. Two others are in Florence, and the fourth, the *Rondanini Pietà*, is in Milan.

At the end of the central aisle is the bronze statue of **St. Peter,** its foot worn by centuries of reverent kisses. The bronze throne above the altar in the apse was created by Bernini to contain a simple wood and ivory chair once believed to have belonged to St. Peter. Bernini's bronze *baldacchino* (canopy) over the papal altar was made with metal stripped from the portico of the Pantheon at the order of Pope Urban VIII, one of the powerful Roman Barberini family. His practice of plundering ancient monuments for material to implement his grandiose schemes inspired the famous quip, *"Quod non fecerunt barbari, fecerunt Barberini"* ("What the barbarians didn't do, the Barberini did").

As you stroll up and down the aisles and transepts, observe the fine mosaic copies of famous paintings above the altars, the monumental tombs and statues, and the fine stucco work. Stop at the **Treasury** (Historical Museum), which contains some priceless liturgical objects.

The entrance to the **Crypt of St. Peter's** is in one of the huge piers at the crossing. It's best to leave this visit for last, as the crypt's only exit takes you outside the church. The crypt contains chapels and the tombs of many popes. It occupies the area of the original basilica, over the **grottoes,** where evidence of what may be St. Peter's burial place has been found. You can book special tours of the grottoes. To see the roof and dome of the basilica take the elevator or climb the stairs in the courtyard near the exit of the crypt. From the roof you can climb a short interior staircase to the base of the dome for an overhead view of the interior of the basilica. Only if you are in good shape should you attempt the strenuous climb up the narrow, one-way stairs to the balcony of the lantern atop the dome, where the view embraces the Vatican Gardens as well as all of Rome. *St. Peter's Basilica, tel. 06/698–4466. Open daily 7–7. Treasury (Museo Storico-Artistico): entrance in Sacristy. Admission: 3,000 lire. Open Apr.–Sept., daily 9–6:30; Oct.–Mar., daily 9–5:30. Roof and Dome: entrance in the courtyard to the left as you leave the basilica. Admission: 5,000 lire, including use of elevator to roof, 4,000 lire if you climb the spiral ramp on foot. Open Apr.–Sept., daily 8–6; Oct.–Mar., daily 8–5. Crypt (Tombs of the Popes): entrance alternates among the piers at the crossing. Admission: free. Open Apr.–Sept., daily 7–6; Oct.–Mar., daily 7–5. Grottoes: Apply a few days in advance to Ufficio Scavi, left beyond the Arco delle Campane entrance to the Vatican, or try in the morning for the same day, tel. 06/698–5318. Admission: 8,000 lire for 2-hour guided visit, 5,000 lire with tape cassette. Ufficio Scavi office hours: Mon.–Sat. 9–5; closed Sun. and religious holidays.*

For many visitors, a **papal audience** is the highlight of a trip to Rome. The Pope holds mass audiences on Wednesday morning; during most of the year they take place in a modern audience hall (capacity 7,000) off the left-hand colonnade. In spring and fall they may be held in **St. Peter's Square,** and sometimes at the papal residence at **Castel Gandolfo.** For audience tickets, write well in advance to the Prefettura della Casa Pontificia (00120 Vatican City), indicating the date you prefer, the language you speak, and the hotel in which you will be staying. *You can pick up free tickets from 4–6 PM at the North American College, Via dell 'Umiltà 30 (tel. 06/678–9184), or apply to the Papal Prefecture (Prefettura), which you reach through the Bronze Door in the right-hand colonnade, tel. 06/698–4466. Open Mon. and Tues. 9–1, Wed. 9–shortly before audience commences. Or arrange for tickets through a travel agent: Carrani Tours, Via V.E. Orlando 95, tel. 06/488–0510; Appian Line, Via Barberini 109, tel. 06/488–4151. Admission: about 36,000 lire (including transportation) if booked through an agent or hotel concierge.*

㉕ Guided minibus tours through the **Vatican Gardens** show you some attractive landscaping, a few historical monuments, and the Vatican mosaic school, which produced the mosaics decorating St. Peter's. These tours give you a different perspective on the basilica itself. *Tickets at information office, on the left side of St. Peter's Square, tel. 06/698–4466. Open Mon.–Sat. 8:30–7. Garden tour cost: 16,000 lire. Available Mon., Tues., and Thurs.–Sat.*

From St. Peter's Square information office you can take a shuttle bus (cost: 2,000 lire) direct to the Vatican Museums. This operates every morning, except Wednesday and Sunday, and saves you the 15-minute walk that goes left from the square and continues along the Vatican walls.

㉖ The collections in the **Vatican Museums** cover nearly 8 kilometers (5 miles) of displays. If you have time, allow at least half a day for Castel Sant'Angelo and St. Peter's, and another half-day for the museums. Posters at the museum entrance plot out a choice of four color-coded itineraries; the shortest takes about 90 minutes, the longest more than four hours, depending on your rate of progress.

No matter which tour you take, they all include the famed **Sistine Chapel**. In 1508, Pope Julius II commissioned Michelangelo to fresco the more than 930 square meters (10,000 square feet) of the chapel's ceiling. For four years Michelangelo dedicated himself to painting over fresh plaster, and the result was his masterpiece. The cleaning operations, now completed, have revealed its original and surprisingly brilliant colors.

You can try to avoid the tour groups by going early or late, allowing yourself enough time before the closing hour. In peak season, the crowds definitely detract from your appreciation of this outstanding artistic achievement. Buy an illustrated guide or rent a taped commentary in order to make sense of the figures on the ceiling. A pair of binoculars also helps.

The Vatican collections are so rich that unless you are an expert in art history, you will probably want only to skim the surface, concentrating on pieces that strike your fancy. If you really want to see the museums thoroughly, you will have to come back again and again. Some of the highlights that might be of interest on your first tour include the *Laocoön*, the *Belvedere Torso*, and the *Apollo Belvedere*, which inspired Michelangelo. The Raphael Rooms are decorated with masterful frescoes, and there are more Raphaels in the Picture Gallery *(Pinacoteca)*. At the Quattro Cancelli, near the entrance to the Picture Gallery, a rather spartan cafeteria provides basic nonalcoholic refreshments. *Viale Vaticano, tel. 06/698–3333. Admission: 12,000 lire, free on last Sun. of the month. Open Easter period and July–Sept., weekdays 8:45–5, Sat. 8:45–2; Oct.–June, Mon.–Sat. 9–2. Ticket office closes 1 hour before museums close. Closed Sun., except last Sun. of the month, and on religious holidays: Jan. 1, Jan. 6, Feb. 11, Mar. 19, Easter Sun. and Mon., May 1, Ascension Thurs., Corpus Christi, June 29, Aug. 15–16, Nov. 1, Dec. 8, Dec. 25–26.*

Old Rome ㉗ Take Via del Plebiscito from Piazza Venezia to the huge **Church of the Gesù**. This paragon of Baroque style is the tangible symbol of the power of the Jesuits, who were a major force in the Counter-Reformation in Europe. Encrusted with gold and precious marbles, the Gesù has a fantastically painted ceiling that flows down over the pillars, merging with painted stucco figures to complete the three-dimensional illusion.

㉘ On your way to the Pantheon you will pass **Santa Maria Sopra Minerva**, a Gothic church built over a Roman temple. Inside there are some beautiful frescoes by Filippo Lippi; outside there is a charming elephant by Bernini with an obelisk on its back.

㉙ Originally built in 27 BC by Augustus's general Agrippa and rebuilt by Hadrian in the 2nd century AD, the **Pantheon** is one of Rome's most perfect, best-preserved, and perhaps least appreciated ancient monuments. Romans and tourists alike pay little attention to it, and on summer evenings it serves mainly as a backdrop for all the action in the square in front. It represents a fantastic feat of construction, however. The huge columns of the portico and the original bronze doors form the entrance to a majestic hall covered by the largest dome of its kind ever built, wider even than that of St. Peter's. In ancient times the entire interior was encrusted with rich decorations of gilt bronze and marble, plundered by later emperors and popes. *Piazza della*

Rotonda. Open Oct.–June, Mon.–Sat. 9–5, Sun. 9–1; July–Sept., daily 9–6.

Time Out There are several sidewalk cafés on the square in front of the Pantheon, all of which are good places to nurse a cappuccino while you observe the scene. Serious coffee drinkers also like **Tazza d'Oro** (Via degli Orfani 84), just off Piazza della Rotonda. And for a huge variety of ice cream in natural flavors, **Giolitti** (Via Uffici del Vicario 40; closed Mon.) is generally considered by *gelato* addicts to be the best in Rome. It also has good snacks and a quick-lunch counter.

---

③⓪ On Via della Dogana Vecchia, stop in at the church of **San Luigi dei Francesi** to see the three paintings by Caravaggio in the last chapel on the left; have a few hundred-lire coins handy for the light machine. The clergy of San Luigi considered the artist's roistering and unruly lifestyle scandalous enough, but his realistic treatment of sacred subjects was just too much for them. They rejected his first version of the altarpiece and weren't particularly happy with the other two works either. Thanks to the intercession of Caravaggio's patron, an influential cardinal, they were persuaded to keep them—a lucky thing, since they are now recognized to be among the artist's finest paintings. *Open Fri.–Wed. 7:30–12:30 and 3:30–7, Thurs. 7:30–12:30.*

③① Just beyond San Luigi is **Piazza Navona,** an elongated 17th-century piazza that traces the oval form of the underlying Circus of Diocletian. At the center, Bernini's lively **Fountain of the Four Rivers** is a showpiece. The four statues represent rivers in the four corners of the world: the Nile, with its face covered in allusion to its then unknown source; the Ganges; the Danube; and the River Plate, with its hand raised. And here we have to give the lie to the legend that this was Bernini's mischievous dig at Borromini's design of the facade of the church of **Sant'Agnese in Agone,** from which the statue seems to be shrinking in horror. The fountain was created in 1651; work on the church's facade began some time later. The piazza dozes in the morning, when little groups of pensioners sun themselves on the stone benches and children pedal tricycles around the big fountain. In the late afternoon the sidewalk cafés fill up for the aperitif hour, and in the evening, especially in good weather, the piazza comes to life with a throng of street artists, vendors, tourists, and Romans out for their evening *passeggiata* (promenade).

Time Out The sidewalk tables of the **Tre Scalini** café (Piazza Navona 30; closed Wed.) offer a grandstand view of this gorgeous piazza. Treat yourself to a *tartufo,* the chocolate ice-cream specialty that was invented here. The restaurant is a pleasant place for a moderately priced lunch. For a salad or light lunch, go to **Cul de Sac** (Piazza Pasquino 73, just off Piazza Navona) or to **Insalata Ricca** (Via del Paradiso, next to the church of Sant'Andrea della Valle). Both are informal and inexpensive.

---

③② Across Corso Vittorio is **Campo dei Fiori** (Field of Flowers), the site of a crowded and colorful daily morning market. The hooded bronze figure brooding over the piazza is philosopher Giordano Bruno, who was burned at the stake here for heresy.

③③ The adjacent **Piazza Farnese,** with fountains made of Egyptian granite basins from the Baths of Caracalla, is an airy setting for

③④ **Palazzo Farnese,** now the French Embassy, one of the most beautiful of Rome's many Renaissance palaces. There are several others in the immediate area: **Palazzo Spada,** a Wedgwood kind of palace encrusted with stuccos and statues; **Palazzo della Cancelleria,** a massive building that is now the Papal Chancellery, one of the many Vatican-owned buildings in Rome that enjoy extraterritorial privileges; and the fine old palaces along Via Giulia.

This is a section to wander through, getting the feel of daily life carried on in a centuries-old setting, and looking into the dozens of antiques shops. Stroll along Via Arenula into a rather gloomy part of Rome bounded by Piazza Campitelli and Lungotevere Cenci, the ancient Jewish ghetto. Among the most interesting sights here are the pretty **Fountain of the Tartarughe** (Turtles) on Piazza Mattei, the **Via Portico d'Ottavia,** with medieval inscriptions and friezes on the old buildings, and the **Teatro di Marcello,** a theater built by Julius Caesar to hold 20,000 spectators.

㉟ A pleasant place to end your walk is on **Tiberina Island.** To get
㊱ there, walk across the ancient **Fabricio Bridge,** built in 62 BC, the oldest bridge in the city.

Off the Beaten Track

If the sky promises a gorgeous sunset, head for the **Terrazza del Pincio** above Piazza del Popolo, a vantage point prized by Romans.

For a look at a real patrician palace, see the **Galleria Doria Pamphili,** still the residence of a princely family. You can visit the gallery housing the family's art collection and part of the magnificently furnished private apartments, as well. *Piazza del Collegio Romano 1/a, near Piazza Venezia, tel. 06/679–4365. Admission: 5,000 lire; additional 3,000 lire for guided visit of private rooms. Open Tues., Fri., weekends 10–1; closed Mon., Wed., and Thurs.*

Make an excursion to **Ostia Antica,** the well-preserved Roman port city near the sea, as rewarding as an excursion to Pompeii and much easier to get to from Rome. There's a regular train service from the Ostiense station (Piramide Metro stop). *Via dei Romagnoli, Ostia Antica, tel. 06/565–1405. Admission: 8,000 lire. Open daily 9–1 hour before sunset.*

Delve into the world of the Etruscans, who inhabited Italy even in pre-Roman times and have left fascinating evidence of their relaxed, sensual lifestyle. Visit the **Museo Nazionale di Villa Giulia,** in a gorgeous Renaissance mansion with a full-scale Etruscan temple in the garden. You'll see a smile as enigmatic as that of the Mona Lisa on deities and other figures in terracotta, bronze, and gold. Ask especially to see the **Castellani collection of ancient jewelry** (and copies) hidden away on the upper floor. *Piazza di Villa Giulia 9, tel. 06/320–1951. Admission: 8,000 lire. Open Wed. 9–7, Tues. and Thurs.–Sat. 9–2, Sun. 9–1.*

Shopping

Shopping is part of the fun of being in Rome, no matter what your budget. The best buys are leather goods of all kinds, from gloves to handbags and wallets to jackets; silk goods; and high-quality knitwear. Shops are closed on Sunday and on Monday morning; in July and August, they close on Saturday afternoon as well.

Antiques A well-trained eye will spot some worthy old prints and minor antiques in the city's fascinating little shops. For prints, browse among the stalls at **Piazza Fontanella Borghese;** at **Casali,** Piazza della Rotonda 81a, at the Pantheon; and **Tanca,** Salita de' Crescenzi 10, also near the Pantheon. For minor antiques, **Via dei Coronari** and other streets in the **Piazza Navona** area are good. The most prestigious antiques dealers are situated in **Via del Babuino** and its environs.

Boutiques **Via Condotti,** directly across from the Spanish Steps, and the streets running parallel to Via Condotti, as well as its cross streets, form the most elegant and expensive shopping area in Rome. Lower-price fashions may be found on display at shops on **Via Frattina** and **Via del Corso.**

Shopping Districts In addition to those mentioned, Romans themselves do much of their shopping along **Via Cola di Rienzo** and **Via Nazionale.** Among the huge new shopping malls dotting Rome's outskirts, CinecittàDue is easiest to reach; just take Metro A to the Subaugusta stop. It has 100 shops, as well as snack bars and cafés.

Religious Articles These abound in the shops around St. Peter's, on **Via di Porta Angelica** and **Via della Conciliazione,** and in the souvenir shops tucked away on the roof and at the crypt exit in St. Peter's itself.

Department Stores You'll find a fairly broad selection of women's, men's, and children's fashions and accessories at the **Rinascente** stores on Piazza Colonna and at Piazza Fiume and at the **Coin** department store on Piazzale Appio near San Giovanni Laterano. The **UPIM** and **Standa** chains have shops all over the city that offer medium-quality, low-price goods. The **Croff** chain features housewares.

Food and Flea Markets The open-air markets at **Piazza Vittorio** and **Campo dei Fiori** are colorful sights. The flea market held at **Porta Portese** on Sunday morning is stocked mainly with new or second-hand clothing. If you go, beware of pickpockets and purse snatchers.

Dining

There are plenty of fine restaurants in Rome serving various Italian regional cuisines and international specialties with a flourish of linen and silver, as well as a whopping *conto* (check) at the end. If you want family-style cooking and prices, try a *trattoria,* a usually smallish and unassuming, often family-run place. Fast-food places and Chinese restaurants are proliferating in Rome; very few can be recommended. Fixed-price tourist menus can be scanty and unimaginative. The lunch hour in Rome lasts from about 1 to 3 PM, dinner from 8 or 8:30 to about 10:30, though some restaurants stay open much later. During August many restaurants close for vacation.

For details and price-category definitions, *see* Dining in Staying in Italy.

Very Expensive **El Toulà.** On a little byway off Piazza Nicosia in Old Rome, El ★ Toulà has the warm, welcoming atmosphere of a 19th-century country house, with white walls, antique furniture in dark wood, heavy silver serving dishes, and spectacular arrangements of fruits and flowers. There's a cozy little bar off the entrance where you can sip a *prosecco*, the aperitif best suited to the chef's Venetian specialties, among them the classic *pasta e fagioli* (bean soup), risotto with radicchio, and *fegato alla veneziana* (liver with onions). *Via della Lupa 29/b, tel. 06/687–3750. Reservations required. AE, DC, MC, V. Closed Sat. lunch, Sun., Aug., and Dec. 24–26.*

Le Jardin. Housed in the posh Lord Byron Hotel in the Parioli residential district, Le Jardin is one of Rome's classiest restaurants. Mirrors, fresh flowers, frescoed walls, and soft lights set the mood for dining on selections from an imaginative seasonal menu that might include risotto with seafood or vegetable sauce and *maiale con miele e zenzero* (pork with honey and ginger); everything is beautifully presented, and the service is of a very high standard. *Hotel Lord Byron, Via Giuseppe De Notaris 5, tel. 06/322–0404. Reservations required. Jacket and tie advised. AE, DC, MC, V. Closed Sun.*

★ **Le Restaurant.** The resplendent dining room of the hotel Le Grand is a model of 19th-century opulence, lavish with fine damasks and velvets, crystal chandeliers, and oil paintings. The menu varies with the seasons; there is always a daily recommended menu. Among the specialties are *carpaccio tiepido di pescatrice* (paper-thin slices of raw, marinated monkfish) and *medaglioni di vitello al marsala con tartufo* (veal medallions with marsala wine and truffles). The wine list offers some majestic vintages. *Via Vittorio Emanuele Orlando 3, tel. 06/4709. Reservations advised. AE, DC, MC, V.*

Expensive **Andrea.** Ernest Hemingway and King Farouk used to eat here;
★ FIAT supremo Gianni Agnelli and other Italian power brokers still do. A half-block off Via Veneto, Andrea offers classic Italian cooking in an intimate, clubby ambience in which snowy table linens gleam against a discreet background of dark green paneling. The menu features delicacies such as homemade *tagliolini* (thin noodles) with shrimp and spinach sauce, spaghetti with seafood and truffles, and mouth-watering *carciofi all'Andrea* (artichokes simmered in olive oil). *Via Sardegna 26, tel. 06/482–1891. Reservations advised. AE, DC, MC, V. Closed Sun. and Mon. lunch and most of Aug.*

Coriolano. The only tourists who find their way to this classic restaurant near Porta Pia are likely to be gourmets looking for quintessential Italian food—that means light homemade pastas, choice olive oil, and market-fresh ingredients, especially seafood. Although seafood dishes vary, *tagliolini all'aragosta* (thin noodles with lobster sauce) is usually on the menu, as are *porcini* mushrooms (in season) cooked to a secret recipe. The wine list is predominantly Italian but includes some French and California wines. *Via Ancona 14, tel. 06/855–1122. Reservations advised. AE, DC, MC, V. Closed Sun. and Aug. 1–25.*

Piperno. Located in the old Jewish ghetto next to historic Palazzo Cenci, Piperno has been in business for more than a century. It is *the* place to go for Rome's extraordinary *carciofi alla giudia*, crispy-fried artichokes, Jewish-style. You eat in three small, wood-paneled dining rooms or, in fair weather, at one of a handful of tables outdoors. Try *filetti di baccalà* (very salty fried cod), *pasta e ceci* (a thick soup of pasta tubes and chickpeas), and *fiori di zucca* (stuffed zucchini flowers)—but don't miss the *carciofi. Monte dei Cenci 9, tel. 06/654–2772. Reserva-*

*tions advised. AE, DC, MC, V. Closed Sun. dinner, Mon.,
Christmas, Easter, and Aug.*

★ **Ranieri.** On a quiet street off fashionable Via Condotti near the
Spanish Steps, this historic restaurant was founded by a former chef of Queen Victoria's. It remains a favorite with tourists for its traditional atmosphere and decor, with damask-
covered walls, velvet banquettes, crystal chandeliers, and old
paintings. Among the many specialties on the vast menu are
gnocchi alla parigina (souffléed gnocchi with cheese sauce)
and *mignonettes alla Regina Vittoria* (veal with pâté and an
eight-cheese sauce). *Via Mario de' Fiori 26, tel. 06/679–1592.
Reservations advised. AE, DC, MC, V. Closed Sun.*

Moderate **Colline Emiliane.** Located near Piazza Barberini, the Colline
Emiliane is an unassuming trattoria offering exceptionally
good food. Behind an opaque glass facade, there are a couple of
plain little dining rooms where you are served light homemade
pastas, a very special chicken broth, and meats ranging from
pot roast to *giambonetto di vitella* (roast veal) and *cotoletta alla
bolognese* (veal cutlet with cheese and tomato sauce). *Via degli
Avignonesi 22, tel. 06/481–7538. Reservations advised. No
credit cards. Closed Fri. and Aug.*

La Campana. An inconspicuous trattoria off Via della Scrofa,
this is a place with a long tradition of hospitality; there has been
an inn on this spot since the 15th century. The atmosphere is
now that of a classic Roman eating place, with friendly but
businesslike waiters and a menu that offers Roman specialties
such as *vignarola* (sautéed fava beans, peas, and artichokes),
rigatoni with prosciutto and tomato sauce, and *olivette di
vitello* (tiny veal rolls, served with mashed potatoes). *Vicolo
della Campana 18, tel. 06/686–7820. Dinner reservations advised. AE, MC, V. Closed Mon. and Aug.*

Le Maschere. This cellar restaurant hidden between Largo Argentina and Piazza Campo dei Fiori offers informal ambience
and southern Italian (Calabrian) cuisine. Colored paper garlands and old utensils hang on dark, rustic walls, and you pour
wine from pottery jugs. There is a large antipasto buffet and a
glowing pizza oven; the menu also features pasta with tomato-
and-eggplant sauce, grilled meats, and seafood. *Via Monte
della Farina 29, tel. 06/687–9444. Reservations advised. AE,
DC, MC, V. No lunch. Closed Mon. and mid-Aug.–mid-Sept.*

★ **Mario.** This Tuscan trattoria in the center of Rome's shopping
district has been run by Mario for 30 years. Usually crowded, it
has a friendly, relaxed atmosphere and a faithful clientele, including many journalists from the Foreign Press headquarters
nearby. Hearty Tuscan specialties, such as *pappardelle alla
lepre* (noodles with hare sauce) and *coniglio* (rabbit), are featured on the menu. Try *panzanella* (Tuscan bread salad with
tomatoes) and the house Chianti. *Via della Vite 55, tel. 06/678–
3818. Dinner reservations advised. AE, DC, MC, V. Closed
Sun. and Aug.*

Orso 80. A bustling trattoria located in Old Rome, near Piazza
Navona, it is known for a fabulous antipasto table. The egg pasta is freshly made, and the *bucatini all'amatriciana* (thick spaghetti with a tangy tomato and bacon sauce) is a classic Roman
pasta. There's seafood on the menu, but it can be pricey. For
dessert, try the ricotta cake, a Roman specialty. *Via dell'Orso
33, tel. 06/686–4904. Reservations advised. AE, DC, MC, V.
Closed Mon. and Aug. 10–20.*

Pierluigi. Pierluigi, in the heart of Old Rome, is a longtime favorite. On busy evenings it's almost impossible to find a table, so make sure you reserve well in advance. Seafood predominates—if you fancy a splurge, try the lobster—but traditional Roman dishes are offered, too, such as *orecchiette con broccoli* (disk-shaped pasta with greens) or just simple spaghetti. In warm weather ask for a table in the piazza. *Piazza dei Ricci 144, tel. 06/687–8717. Reservations advised. AE. Closed Mon. and 2 weeks in Aug.*

★ **Romolo.** Generations of Romans have enjoyed the romantic garden courtyard and historic dining room of this charming Trastevere haunt, reputedly once home of Raphael's ladylove, *La Fornarina.* In the evening, a guitarist serenades diners. The cuisine is appropriately Roman; specialties include *mozzarella alla fornarina* (deep-fried mozzarella with ham and anchovies) and *braciolette d'abbacchio scottadito* (grilled baby lamb chops). Alternatively, try one of the new vegetarian pastas featuring carciofi or radicchio. *Via di Porta Settimiana 8, tel. 06/581–8284. Reservations advised. AE, DC, V. Closed Mon. and Aug. 2–23.*

Inexpensive **Abruzzi.** This simple trattoria off Piazza Santi Apostoli near Piazza Venezia specializes in regional cooking of the Abruzzi, a
★ mountainous region southeast of Rome. The straightforward menu and reasonable prices make it a lunchtime favorite for politicians, priests, and both students and professors from the nearby Gregorian papal university. Specialties include *tonnarelli Abruzzi* (square-cut pasta with mushrooms, peas, and ham) and *abbacchio* (roast lamb). *Via del Vaccaro 1, tel. 06/679–3897. Lunch reservations advised. V. Closed Sat and Aug.*

Baffetto. Rome's best-known inexpensive pizza restaurant is plainly decorated and *very* popular; you'll probably have to wait in line outside on the *sampietrini*—the cobblestones. The interior is mostly given over to the ovens, the tiny cash desk, and the simple paper-covered tables. *Bruschetta* (toast) and *crostini* (mozzarella toast) are the only variations on the pizza theme. Expect to share a table. *Via del Governo Vecchio 114, tel. 06/686–1617. No reservations. No credit cards. Closed lunch, Sun., and Aug.*

Fratelli Menghi. A neighborhood trattoria that has been in the same family as long as anyone can remember, Fratelli Menghi consists of several modest dining rooms off the busy kitchen, which produces typical Roman fare for faithful customers, many of whom work nearby. There's usually a thick, hearty soup such as minestrone, *pasta e ceci* (with chick peas), and other Roman standbys including *involtini* (meat roulades). *Via Flaminia 57, tel. 06/320–0803. No reservations. No credit cards. Closed Sun.*

Hostaria Farnese. This is a tiny trattoria between Campo dei Fiori and Piazza Farnese, in the heart of Old Rome. Papa serves, Mamma cooks, and depending on what they've picked up at the Campo dei Fiori market, you may find rigatoni with tuna and basil, spaghetti with vegetable sauce, *spezzatino* (stew), and other homey specialties. *Via dei Baullari 109, tel. 06/654–1595. Reservations advised. AE, V. Closed Thurs.*

Pollarola. Located near Piazza Navona and Campo dei Fiori, this typical Roman trattoria has flowers (artificial) on the tables and an antique Roman column embedded in the rear wall, evidence of its historic site. You can eat outdoors in fair weather. Try a pasta specialty such as *fettuccine al gorgonzola* (noodles with creamy gorgonzola sauce) and a mixed plate from the temptingly fresh array of antipasti. The house wine, white or red, is good. *Piazza della Pollarola 24 (Campo dei Fiori), tel. 06/654-1654. Reservations advised for groups. AE, V. Closed Sun.*

Lodging

The list below covers mostly those hotels that are within walking distance of at least some sights and that are handy to public transportation. Those in the Moderate and Inexpensive categories do not have restaurants but serve Continental breakfast. Rooms facing the street get traffic noise throughout the night, and few hotels in the lower categories have double glazing. Ask for a quiet room, or bring earplugs.

We strongly recommend that you always make reservations in advance. Should you find yourself in the city without reservations, however, contact one of the following EPT offices: at Leonardo da Vinci Airport (tel. 06/601-1255); Termini train station (tel. 06/487-1270); or the main information office at Via Parigi 5 (tel. 06/488-3748), which is near Piazza della Repubblica.

For details and price-category definitions, *see* Lodging in Staying in Italy.

Very Expensive **Cavalieri Hilton.** Though it is outside the main part of Rome and a taxi ride to wherever you are going, this is a large, elegant hotel set in its own park with two excellent restaurants. *Via Cadlolo 101, tel. 06/35091, fax, 06/315-12241. 378 rooms with bath. Facilities: 2 restaurants, pool, terrace. AE, DC, MC, V.*

★ **Hassler-Villa Medici.** Guests can expect a cordial atmosphere and magnificent service at this hotel, just at the top of the Spanish Steps. The public rooms are memorable, especially the first-floor bar (a chic city rendezvous), and the glass-roof lounge, with gold marble walls and hand-painted tile floor. The elegant bedrooms are decorated in a variety of classic styles; some feature frescoed walls. *Piazza Trinità dei Monti 6, tel. 06/678-2651, fax 06/678-9991. 100 rooms with bath. Facilities: garage, bar, garden restaurant, roof restaurant. AE, MC, V.*

Lord Byron. The most elegant hotel in Rome is the Lord Byron. Located in the diplomatic residential section of Rome away from its bustling center, the small villa has neat, fresh, and cheerful bedrooms. Renovations in 1991 included enlarging rooms and adding suites on top floors. The staff offers the best service of any Rome hotel, and its dining room has extremely creative Italian cooking that has earned it two Michelin stars. *Via de Notaris 5, tel. 06/322-0404, fax 06/322-0405. 28 rooms and 9 suites with bath. Facilities: bar, restaurant, garden. AE, DC, MC, V.*

Majestic. In the 19th-century tradition of grand hotels, this prestigious establishment on Via Veneto has been entirely renovated and refurbished in turn-of-the-century style but with up-to-date comforts, including air-conditioning, CNN, and personal safes. Spacious rooms are sumptuously decorated with opulent flower prints, regal stripes, and extravagant drapes, and boast white Carrara marble bathrooms. The restaurant, modeled on a Victorian conservatory, serves excellent Italian cuisine. *Via Veneto 50, tel. 06/48641, fax 06/488-0984. 95 rooms with bath. Facilities: restaurant, bar with terrace, garage. AE, DC, MC, V.*

Expensive **Farnese.** Located near both the Lepanto Metro station and St. Peter's, this 1906 mansion was renovated in 1991 in faithful Art Deco style. Sitting rooms on the main floor and high-ceilinged bedrooms are soberly elegant, with boiseries and rich fabrics. Bathrooms are dazzlingly modern. All rooms have air-conditioning, fridge bar, and color TV. Rates include a lavish buffet breakfast. *Via Alessandro Farnese 30, tel. 06/321–2553, fax 06/321–5129. 25 rooms with bath. Facilities: parking, bar, roof garden. AE, DC, MC, V.*

Forum. A centuries-old palace converted into a fine hotel, the Forum is on a quiet street within hailing distance of the Roman Forum and Piazza Venezia. The wood-paneled lobby and street-level bar are warm and welcoming, as are the smallish, pink-and-beige bedrooms. The view of the Colosseum from the roof-top restaurant is superb: Breakfast here—or a nightcap at the roof bar—can be memorable. *Via Tor dei Conti 25, tel. 06/679–2446, fax 06/678–6479. 76 rooms with bath. Facilities: bar, restaurant. AE, DC, MC, V.*

★ **Victoria.** Oriental rugs, oil paintings, welcoming armchairs, and fresh flowers add charm to the public rooms of this hotel, a favorite of American businesspeople who prize the personalized service and restful atmosphere. Some upper rooms and the roof terrace overlook the Villa Borghese. *Via Campania 41, tel. 06/473931, fax 06/487–1890. 110 rooms with bath. Facilities: bar, restaurant. AE, DC, MC, V.*

Moderate **Carriage.** Few hotels in Rome have this combination of excellent location (near the Spanish Steps), Old World elegance, and reasonable rates. The decor is in soft blue and gold, with subdued Baroque accents added for a touch of luxury. The rooms have antique-reproduction closets and porcelain phones. *Via delle Carrozze 36, tel. 06/699–0124, fax 06/678–8279. 27 rooms with bath. Facilities: bar. AE, DC, MC, V.*

★ **Internazionale.** Within easy walking distance of many downtown sights, this has long been one of Rome's best midsize hotels. Decor throughout is in soothing pastel tones, with some antique pieces, mirrors, and chandeliers heightening the English country-house look. Guests relax in small, homey lounges downstairs and begin the day in the pretty breakfast room. *Via Sistina 79, tel. 06/679–3047, fax 06/678–4764. 40 rooms with bath. AE, DC, MC, V.*

La Residenza. A converted town house near Via Veneto, this hotel offers good value and first-class comfort at reasonable rates. Public areas are spacious and furnished nicely and have a private-home atmosphere. Guest rooms are comfortable and have large closets, TV, fridge bar, and air-conditioning. The color scheme throughout the property is aquamarine and beige. The hotel's clientele is mainly American, and rates include a generous buffet breakfast. *Via Emilia 22, tel. 06/488–0797, fax 06/485721. 27 rooms with bath. Facilities: bar, roof terrace, parking. No credit cards.*

Inexpensive **Margutta.** Centrally located near the Spanish Steps and Piazza ★ del Popolo, this small hotel has an unassuming lobby but bright, attractive bedrooms and modern baths. Three rooms on the top floor are in demand for their views of Rome's rooftops and domes. *Via Laurina 34, tel. 06/322–3674. 24 rooms with bath. AE, DC, MC, V.*

Romae. Strategically located near Termini Station, this midsize hotel has clean, spacious rooms with light-wood furniture and small but bright bathrooms. The cordial, helpful management offers special winter rates and welcomes families. TVs and hair dryers in the rooms plus low rates that include breakfast make this a good value. *Via Palestro 49, tel. 06/446–3554, fax 06/446–3914. 20 rooms with bath. AE, MC, V.*

Suisse. The mood in the Suisse's public rooms may be old-fashioned—the check-in desk is distinctly drab—but the bedrooms, while small, are cheerful enough, with bright bedspreads, framed prints, and some charming old furniture. Some rooms face the (fairly) quiet courtyard. There's an upstairs breakfast room, but no restaurant. *Via Gregoriana 56, tel. 06/678–3649. 28 rooms, half with bath. No credit cards.*

The Arts

Pick up a copy of the *Carnet di Roma* at EPT tourist offices; issued monthly, it's free and has an exhaustive listing of scheduled events and shows. The bi-weekly booklet *Un Ospite a Roma*, free from your hotel concierge, is another source of information, as is *Wanted in Rome*, available at newsstands. If you want to go to the opera, ballet, or to a concert, it's best to ask your concierge to get tickets for you. They are on sale at box offices only, just a few days before performances.

Opera The **Teatro dell'Opera** is on Via del Viminale (tel. 06/6759–5725 for information in English; tel. 06/6759–5721 to book tickets in English); its summer season at the **Baths of Caracalla** from May through August is famous for spectacular performances amid the Roman ruins. Tickets are on sale at the opera box office or at the box office at Caracalla (*see* Exploring Rome, *above*).

Concerts The main concert hall is the **Accademia di Santa Cecilia** (Via della Conciliazione 4, tel. 06/654–1044). The Santa Cecilia Symphony Orchestra has a summer season of concerts.

Film The only English-language movie theater in Rome is the **Pasquino** (Vicolo del Piede, just off Piazza Santa Maria in Trastevere, tel. 06/580–3622). The program is listed in Rome's daily newspapers.

Nightlife

Rome's "in" nightspots change like the flavor of the month, and many fade into oblivion after a brief moment of glory. The best source for an up-to-date list is the weekly entertainment guide, "Trovaroma," published each Thursday in the Italian daily *La Repubblica.*

Bars Jacket and tie are in order in the elegant **Blue Bar** of the Hostaria dell'Orso (Via dei Soldati 25, tel. 06/686–4250), and in **Le Bar** of Le Grand hotel (Via Vittorio Emanuele Orlando 3, tel. 06/4709). **Jeff Blynn's** (Via Zanardelli 12, tel. 06/686–1990), near Piazza Navona, is an upscale watering hole open from 7 PM to 2 AM, with a happy hour from 7 to 10.

Informal wine bars are popular with young Romans. Near the Pantheon is **Spiriti** (Via Sant'Eustachio 5, tel. 06/689–2499); **Trimani Wine Bar** (Via Cernaia 37/b, tel. 06/446–9630), offers light meals. **Birreria Marconi** (Via di Santa Prassede 9c, tel. 06/486636), near Santa Maria Maggiore, is a beer-hall pizzeria. Near the Pantheon, a hub of after-dark activity is **Antico Caffè della Pace** (Via della Pace 3, tel. 06/686–1216). Two popular pubs near Santa Maria Maggiore are **Fiddler's Elbow** (Via dell'Olmata 43, no phone) and **Seaman's Country Pub** (Via G. Lanza 102, tel. 06/489–03145).

Discos and Nightclubs There's deafening disco music for an under-30s crowd at the **Frankie Go** (entrance at Via Luciani 52, tel. 06/322–1251). Special events such as beauty pageants and theme parties are a feature, and there's a restaurant on the premises. **Scarabocchio** (Piazza dei Ponziani 8/c, tel. 06/580–0495) is a disco featuring live music on Wednesday, cabaret on Friday. Sports personalities and other celebrities are attracted to **Veleno** (Via Sardegna 27, tel. 06/482–1838), one of the few places in Rome to offer black dance music, including disco, rap, funk, and soul.

Singles Scene Locals and foreigners of all ages gather at Rome's cafés in **Piazza della Rotonda** in front of the Pantheon, at **Piazza Navona,** and **Piazza Santa Maria in Trastevere.** The cafés on **Via Veneto** and the bars of the big hotels draw tourists mainly and are good places to meet other travelers in the over-30 age group. In fair weather, under-30s will find crowds of contemporaries on the **Spanish Steps,** where it's easy to strike up a conversation.

Florence

Arriving and Departing

By Plane The nearest, medium-size airport is the Galileo Galilei Airport at Pisa (tel. 050/44325), connected with Florence by train direct from the airport to the Santa Maria Novella Station. Service is hourly throughout the day and takes about 60 minutes. Some domestic and a few European flights use Florence's Peretola Airport (tel. 055/373498), connected by bus to the downtown area. Passengers on Alitalia flights through Rome's Leonardo da Vinci airport can take the twice-daily Airport Train from Rome directly to Florence (reserve rail connection when purchasing plane ticket).

By Train The main train station is Santa Maria Novella Station, abbreviated SMN on signs. There is an Azienda Transporti Autolinee Fiorentine (ATAF) city bus information booth across the street from the station (and also at Piazza del Duomo 57/r). Inside the station is an Informazione Turistiche Alberghiere (ITA) hotel association booth, where you can get hotel information and bookings.

By Bus The SITA bus terminal is on Via Santa Caterina di Siena, near Santa Maria Novella train station. The CAP bus terminal is at Via Nazionale 13, also near the station.

By Car The north–south access route to Florence is the Autostrada del Sole (A1) from Milan or Rome. The Florence–Mare autostrada (A11) links Florence with the Tyrrhenian coast, Pisa, and the A12 coastal autostrada.

Getting Around

On Foot You can see most of Florence's major sights on foot, as they are packed into a relatively small area in the city center. It's best not to plan to use a car in Florence; most of the center is off-limits and ATAF buses will take you where you want to go. Wear comfortable shoes and wander to your heart's content. It is easy to find your way around in Florence. There are so many landmarks that you cannot get lost for long. The system of street numbers is unusual, with commercial addresses written with a red "r" and residential addresses in blue (32/r might be next to or even a block away from 32 blue).

By Bus ATAF city buses run from about 5:15 AM to 1 AM. Buy tickets before you board the bus; they are on sale singly or in books of five at many tobacco shops and newsstands. The cost is 1,100 lire for a ticket good for 60 minutes on all lines, 1,500 lire for 120 minutes. An all-day ticket (*turistico*) costs 5,000 lire.

By Taxi Taxis wait at stands. Use only authorized cabs, which are white with a yellow stripe or rectangle on the door. The meter starts at 6,000 lire. To call a taxi, tel. 055/4798 or 055/4390.

By Bicycle You can rent a bicycle at **Alinari** (Via Guelfa 85/r, tel. 055/280500), which has several locations in Florence; **Motorent** (Via San Zanobi 9/r, tel. 055/490113); and at city concessions in several locations, including Piazza della Stazione, Piazza Pitti, and Fortezza da Basso.

By Moped For a moped, go to **Alinari** or **Motorent** (*see* By Bicycle, *above*), or to **Ciao e Basta** (Lungarno Pecori Girardi 1, tel. 055/234–2726).

Important Addresses and Numbers

Tourist Information The municipal tourist office is at Via Cavour 1/r (tel. 055/276–0382; open 8:30–7). The **Azienda Promozione Turistica (APT)** tourist board has its headquarters and an information office at Via Manzoni 16 (tel. 055/234–6284; open Mon.–Sat. 8:30–1:30). There is an information office next to the train station and another near Piazza della Signoria, at Chiasso dei Baroncelli 17/r (tel. 055/230–2124).

Consulates **U.S.** (Lungarno Vespucci 38, tel. 055/239–8276). **U.K.** (Lungarno Corsini 2, tel. 055/284133).

Emergencies **Police** (tel. 113). **Ambulance** (tel. 055/212222). **Doctor:** Call your consulate for recommendations, or call the **Tourist Medical Service** (tel. 055/475411), associated with IAMAT, for English-speaking medical assistance 24 hours a day. **Pharmacies:** There are 24-hour pharmacies at Via Calzaiuoli 7/r (tel. 055/289490); Piazza San Giovanni 20/r (tel. 055/284013); and at the train station (tel. 055/289435).

English-Language Bookstores You'll find English-language magazines and paperbacks on the newsstands in Piazza della Repubblica. **The Paperback Exchange** (Via Fiesolana 31/r, tel. 055/247–8154), in the Santa Croce area, has new and used paperbacks for sale. **The BM Bookshop** (Borgo Ognissanti 4/r, tel. 055/294575) has a good selection of English-language books.

Travel Agencies **American Express** (Via Guicciardini 49/r, tel. 055/288751). **CIT** (Via Cavour 54/r, tel. 055/294306). **Wagons-Lits** (Via del Giglio 27/r, tel. 055/218851).

Guided Tours

Orientation Tours **American Express** (tel. 055/288751), **CIT** (tel. 055/294306), and **SITA** (through hotels and travel agents) offer three-hour tours in air-conditioned buses. Two tours cover most of the important sights: The morning itinerary gives you a look at the outside of the cathedral, baptistry, and bell tower, takes you to the

Accademia to see Michelangelo's *David*, to Piazzale Michelangelo for the view, and perhaps then to the Pitti Palace to visit the Palatine Gallery; the afternoon tour includes Piazza della Signoria, a visit to the Uffizi Gallery and to Santa Croce, and an excursion to Fiesole. The cost is about 45,000 lire for a three-hour tour, including entrance fees, and bookings can be made through travel agents.

Personal Guides **American Express** (tel. 055/288751) can arrange for limousine or minitours and personal guide services. **Europedrive** (Via Bisenzio 35, tel. 055/422–2839) will provide cars with English-speaking drivers.

Special-Interest Tours Inquire at travel agents or at **Agriturist Provinciale** (Piazza San Firenze 3, tel. 055/239–6362) for visits to villa gardens around Florence from April to June, or for visits to farm estates during September and October.

Excursions Operators offer a half-day excursion to Pisa, usually in the afternoon, costing about 38,000 lire, and a full-day excursion to Siena and San Gimignano, costing about 55,000 lire. Pick up a timetable at ATAF information offices near the train station, at Piazza del Duomo 57/r (tel. 055/580528), or at the APT Tourist Office (*see* Tourist Information in Important Addresses and Numbers, *above*).

Both ATAF and tourist information offices offer a free booklet containing information on interesting excursions in the vicinity of Florence, complete with timetables of local bus and train services.

Exploring Florence

Founded by Julius Caesar, Florence has the familiar grid pattern common to all Roman colonies. Except for the major monuments, which are appropriately imposing, the buildings are low and unpretentious. It is a small, compact city of ocher and gray stone and pale plaster; its narrow streets open unexpectedly into spacious squares populated by strollers and pigeons. At its best, it has a gracious and elegant air, though it can at times be a nightmare of mass tourism. Plan, if you can, to visit Florence in late fall, early spring, or even in winter, to avoid the crowds.

A visit to Florence is a visit to the living museum of the Italian Renaissance. The Renaissance began right here in Florence, and the city bears witness to the proud spirit and unparalleled genius of its artists and artisans. In fact, there is so much to see that it is best to savor a small part rather than attempt to absorb it all in a muddled vision.

Numbers in the margin correspond to points of interest on the Florence map.

Piazza del Duomo and Piazza della Signoria ❶ The best place to begin a tour of Florence is **Piazza del Duomo,** where the cathedral, bell tower, and baptistry stand in the rather cramped square. The lofty **cathedral of Santa Maria del Fiore** is one of the longest in the world. Begun by master sculptor and architect Arnolfo di Cambio in 1296, its construction took 140 years to complete. Gothic architecture predominates; the facade was added in the 1870s but is based on Tuscan Gothic models. Inside, the church is cool and austere, a fine example of the architecture of the period. Among the sparse decorations, take a good look at the frescoes of equestrian monuments on the left wall; the one on the right is by Paolo Uccello, the one on the left by Andrea del Castagno. The dome frescoes by Vasari have been hidden by the scaffolding put up some years ago in order to study a plan for restoring the dome itself, Brunelleschi's greatest architectural and technical achievement. It was also the inspiration of such later domes as Michelangelo's dome for St. Peter's in Rome and even the Capitol in Washington. You can climb to the cupola gallery, 463 fatiguing steps up between the two skins of the double dome for a fine view of Florence and the surrounding hills. *Dome entrance is in the left aisle of cathedral. Admission: 5,000 lire. Open Mon.–Sat. 10–5. Cathedral open Mon.–Sat. 10–5, Sun. 2:30–5.*

② Next to the cathedral is Giotto's 14th-century **bell tower,** richly decorated with colored marble and fine sculptures (the originals are in the Museo dell'Opera del Duomo). The 414-step climb to the top is less strenuous than that to the cupola. *Piazza del Duomo. Admission: 5,000 lire. Open Mar.–Oct., daily 9–7; Nov.–Feb., daily 9–4:30.*

③ In front of the cathedral is the **baptistry** (open Mon.–Sat. 1–6, Sun. 9–1), one of the city's oldest and most beloved edifices, where, since the 11th century, Florentines have baptized their children. A gleaming copy of the most famous of the baptistry's three portals has been installed facing the cathedral, where Ghiberti's doors (dubbed "The Gate of Paradise" by Michelan-
④ gelo) stood. The originals have been removed to the **Museo dell'Opera del Duomo** (Cathedral Museum). The museum contains some superb sculptures by Donatello and Luca della Robbia—especially their *cantorie*, or choir decorations—as well as an unfinished *Pietà* by Michelangelo, which was intended for his own tomb. *Piazza del Duomo 9, tel. 055/230–2885. Admission: 5,000 lire. Open Mar.–Oct., Mon.–Sat. 9–7:30; Nov.–Feb., Mon.–Sat. 9–5:30.*

⑤ Stroll down fashionable Via Calzaiuoli to the church of **Orsanmichele,** for centuries an odd combination of first-floor church and second-floor wheat granary. The statues in the niches on the exterior (many are copies) constitute an anthology of the work of eminent Renaissance sculptors, including Donatello, Ghiberti, and Verrocchio, while the tabernacle inside is an extraordinary piece by Andrea Orcagna.

Continuing another two blocks along Via Calzaiuoli you'll come upon **Piazza della Signoria,** the heart of Florence, and the city's largest square. During the long and controversial process of replacing the paving stones over the past few years, well-preserved remnants of Roman and medieval Florence came to light and were thoroughly examined and photographed before being buried again and covered with the new paving. In the center of the square a slab marks the spot where in 1497 Savonarola—the Ayatollah Khomeini of the Middle Ages—induced the Florentines to burn their pictures, books, musical instruments, and other worldly objects—and where a year later he was hanged and then burned at the stake as a heretic. The square, the **Neptune Fountain** by Ammanati, and the surrounding cafés are popular gathering places for Florentines and for tourists who come to admire the massive **Palazzo della Signoria**
⑥ (better known as the **Palazzo Vecchio**), the copy of Michelangelo's *David* on its steps, and the frescoes and artworks in its impressive salons. *Piazza della Signoria, tel. 055/276–*

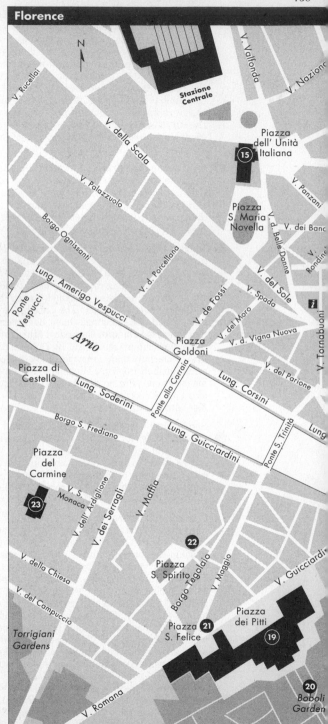

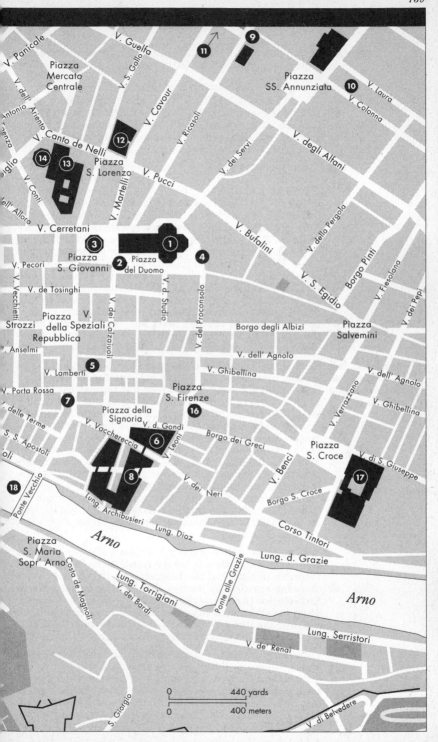

8465. Admission: 8,000 lire; Sun. free. Open weekdays 9–7, Sun. 8–1.

Time Out Stop in at **Rivoire,** a Florentine institution, for some of its delectable ice cream and/or chocolate goodies. *Piazza della Signoria 5/r.*

If you'd like to do a little shopping, make a brief detour off Piazza della Signoria to the **Loggia del Mercato Nuovo** on Via Calimala. It's crammed with souvenirs and straw and leather goods at reasonable prices; bargaining is acceptable here. *Open Mon.–Sat. 8–7 (closed Mon. AM).*

If time is limited, this is your chance to visit the **Uffizi Gallery,** which houses Italy's most important collection of paintings. (Try to see it at a leisurely pace, though—it's too good to rush through!) The Uffizi Palace was built to house the administrative offices of the Medicis, onetime rulers of the city. Later their fabulous art collection was arranged in the Uffizi Gallery on the top floor, which was opened to the public in the 17th century—making this the world's first public gallery of modern times. The emphasis is on Italian art of the Gothic and Renaissance periods. Make sure you see the works by Giotto, and look for the Botticellis in Rooms X–XIV, Michelangelo's *Holy Family* in Room XXV, and the works by Raphael next door. In addition to its art treasures, the gallery offers a magnificent closeup view of Palazzo Vecchio's tower from the little coffee bar at the end of the corridor. *Loggiato Uffizi 6, tel. 055/218341. Admission: 10,000 lire. Open Tues.–Sat. 9–7, Sun. 9–1.*

Accademia, San Marco, San Lorenzo, Santa Maria Novella Start at the **Accademia Gallery,** and try to be first in line at opening time so you can get the full impact of Michelangelo's *David* without having to fight your way through the crowds. Skip the works in the exhibition halls leading to the *David;* they are of minor importance and you'll gain a length on the tour groups. Michelangelo's statue is a tour de force of artistic conception and technical ability, for he was using a piece of stone that had already been worked on by a lesser sculptor. Take time to see the forceful *Slaves,* also by Michelangelo; the roughhewn, unfinished surfaces contrast dramatically with the highly polished, meticulously carved *David.* Michelangelo left the *Slaves* "unfinished" as a symbolic gesture, to accentuate the figures' struggle to escape the bondage of stone. *Via Ricasoli 60, tel. 055/214375. Admission: 10,000 lire. Open Tues.–Sat. 9–2, Sun. 9–1.*

You can make a detour down Via Cesare Battisti to Piazza Santissima Annunziata to see the arcade of the **Ospedale degli Innocenti** (Hospital of the Innocents) by Brunelleschi, with charming roundels by Andrea della Robbia, and the **Museo Archeologico** (Archaeological Museum) on Via della Colonna, under the arch. It has some fine Etruscan and Roman antiquities, and a pretty garden. *Via della Colonna 36, tel. 055/247-8641. Admission: 6,000 lire. Open Tues.–Sat. 9–2, Sun. 9–1.*

Retrace your steps to Piazza San Marco and the **Museo di San Marco,** housed in a 15th-century Dominican monastery. The unfortunate Savonarola meditated on the sins of the Florentines here, and Fra Angelico decorated many of the austere cells and corridors with his brilliantly colored frescoes of religious subjects. (Look for his masterpiece, *The Annunciation.*) Together with many of his paintings arranged on the ground floor, just off the little cloister, they form an interesting collection. *Piazza San Marco 1, tel. 055/210741. Admission: 6,000 lire. Open Tues.–Sat. 9–2, Sun. 9–1.*

⑫ Lined with shops, Via Cavour leads to **Palazzo Medici Riccardi,** a massive Renaissance mansion (*see* Off the Beaten Track, *be-*
⑬ *low*). Turn right here to the elegant **Church of San Lorenzo,** with its Old Sacristy designed by Brunelleschi, and two pulpits by Donatello. Rounding the church, you'll find yourself in the midst of the sprawling **San Lorenzo Market,** dealing in everything and anything, including some interesting leather items. *Piazza San Lorenzo, Via dell'Ariento. Open Tues.–Sat. 8–7.*

Time Out On Via Sant'Antonino near the big covered food market, **Palla d'Oro** is a favorite with market workers for a quick sandwich or plate of pasta, which they usually eat standing at the counter. You can sit at the tables in the back for an extra charge. It's impossibly crowded between 1 and 1:30. *Via Sant'Antonino 45/r. Closed Sun.*

⑭ Enter the **Medici Chapels** from Piazza Madonna degli Aldobrandini, behind San Lorenzo. These remarkable chapels contain the tombs of practically every member of the Medici family, and there were a lot of them, for they guided Florence's destiny from the 15th century to 1737. Cosimo I, a Medici whose acumen made him the richest man in Europe, is buried in the crypt of the Chapel of the Princes, and Donatello's tomb is next to that of his patron. The chapel upstairs is decorated in an eye-dazzling array of colored marble. In Michelangelo's New Sacristy, his tombs of Giuliano and Lorenzo de' Medici bear the justly famed statues of *Dawn* and *Dusk*, and *Night* and *Day*. *Piazza Madonna degli Aldobrandini, tel. 055/213206. Admission: 9,000 lire. Open Tues.–Sat. 9–2, Sun. 9–1.*

Time Out **Baldini** is an unpretentious trattoria, low on atmosphere but offering a good range of antipasti and delicious *fazzoletti*, pasta filled with ricotta and spinach. *Via Panzani 57. Closed Wed.*

You can take either Via Panzani or Via del Melarancio to the
⑮ large square next to the massive church of **Santa Maria Novella,** a handsome building in the Tuscan version of Gothic style. See it from the other end of Piazza Santa Maria Novella for the best view of its facade. Inside are some famous paintings, especially Masaccio's *Trinity*, a Giotto crucifix in the sacristy, and Ghirlandaio's frescoes in the apse. *Piazza Santa Maria Novella, tel. 055/210113. Open Mon.–Sat. 7–11:30 and 3:30–6, Sun. 3:30–6.*

Next door to the church is the entrance to the **cloisters,** worth a visit for their serene atmosphere and the restored Paolo Uccello frescoes. *Piazza Santa Maria Novella 19, tel. 055/282187. Admission: 4,000 lire. Open Mon.–Thurs., Sat. 9–2, Sun. 8–1.*

Only a few blocks behind Piazza della Signoria is the **Bargello,** a fortresslike palace that served as residence of Florence's chief magistrate in medieval times, and later as a prison. Don't be
⑯ put off by its grim look, for it now houses Florence's **Museo Nazionale** (National Museum), a treasure house of Italian Renaissance sculpture. In a historically and visually interesting setting, it displays masterpieces by Donatello, Verrocchio, Michelangelo, and many other major sculptors. This museum is on a par with the Uffizi, so don't shortchange yourself on time. *Via*

del Proconsolo 4, tel. 055/210801. Admission: 6,000 lire. Open Tues.–Sat. 9–2, Sun. 9–1.

Time Out From Piazza San Firenze follow Via degli Anguillara or Borgo dei Greci toward Piazza Santa Croce. Don't miss the chance to taste what's held by many to be the best ice cream in Florence at **Vivoli,** on a little side street, the second left off Via degli Anguillara as you head toward Santa Croce. *Via Isole delle Stinche 7/r. Closed Mon.*

⓱ The mighty church of **Santa Croce** was begun in 1294; inside, Giotto's frescoes brighten two chapels and monumental tombs of Michelangelo, Galileo, Machiavelli, and other Renaissance luminaries line the walls. In the adjacent museum, you can see what remains of a Giotto crucifix, irreparably damaged by a flood in 1966, when water rose to 16 feet in parts of the church. The **Pazzi Chapel** in the cloister is an architectural gem by Brunelleschi. *Piazza Santa Croce, tel. 055/244619. Church open Mon.–Sat. 7–12:30 and 3–6:30, Sun. 3–6. Opera di Santa Croce (Museum and Pazzi Chapel), tel. 055/244619. Admission: 4,000 lire. Open Mar.–Sept., Thurs.–Tues. 10–12:30 and 2:30–6:30; Oct.–Feb., Thurs.–Tues. 10–12:30 and 3–5.*

The monastery of Santa Croce harbors a leather-working school and showroom, with entrances at Via San Giuseppe 5/r and Piazza Santa Croce 16. The entire Santa Croce area is known for its leather factories and inconspicuous shops selling gold and silver jewelry at prices much lower than those of the elegant jewelers near Ponte Vecchio.

Time Out You have several eating options here. For ice cream, the **bar** on Piazza Santa Croce has a tempting selection. If it's a snack you're after, the **Fiaschetteria** (Via dei Neri 17/r) makes sandwiches to order and has a choice of antipasti and a hot dish or two. **Da Marco,** between Santa Croce and the Arno, is a typical trattoria, where you can either eat downstairs or outdoors. (Via dei Benci 13/r. Closed Mon.)

⓲ Now head for the **Ponte Vecchio,** Florence's oldest bridge. It seems to be just another street lined with goldsmiths' shops until you get to the middle and catch a glimpse of the Arno flowing below. Spared during World War II by the retreating Germans (who blew up every other bridge in the city), it also survived the 1966 flood. It leads into the **Oltrarno district,** which has its own charm and still preserves much of the atmosphere of oldtime Florence, full of fascinating craft workshops.

But for the moment you should head straight down Via ⓳ Guicciardini to **Palazzo Pitti,** a 15th-century extravaganza that the Medicis acquired from the Pitti family shortly after the latter had gone deeply into debt to build it. Its long facade on the immense piazza was designed by Brunelleschi: Solid and severe, it looks like a Roman aqueduct turned into a palace. The palace houses several museums: One displays the fabulous Medici collection of objects in silver and gold; another is the **Gallery of Modern Art.** The most famous museum, though, is the **Palatine Gallery,** with an extraordinary collection of paintings, many hung frame-to-frame in a clear case of artistic overkill. Some are high up in dark corners, so try to go on a bright day. *Piazza dei Pitti, tel. 055/210323. Gallery of Modern Art. Admission: 6,000 lire. Palatine Gallery. Admission: 8,000* *lire. Silver Museum. Admission: 6,000 lire (includes admission to the Historical Costume Gallery). All open Tues.–Sat. 9–2, Sun. 9–1.*

⑳ Take time for a refreshing stroll in the **Boboli Gardens** behind Palazzo Pitti, a typical Italian garden laid out in 1550 for Cosimo Medici's wife, Eleanor of Toledo. *Piazza dei Pitti, tel. 055/213440. Admission: 5,000 lire. Open Tues.–Sun. Apr., May, and Sept., 9–6:30; June–Aug., 9–7:30; Oct. and Mar.–Apr., 9–5:30; Nov.–Feb., 9–4:30.*

In the far corner of Piazza dei Pitti, poets Elizabeth Barrett **㉑** and Robert Browning lived in the **Casa Guidi,** facing the smaller Piazza San Felice. *Piazza San Felice 8, tel. 055/284393. Admission free. Open by appointment.*

Time Out From Piazza San Felice it's not far to the **Caffè Notte,** a wine and sandwich shop featuring a different salad every day (corner of Via della Caldaia and Via della Chiesa). For more substantial sustenance, go to the **Cantinone del Gallo Nero,** an atmospheric wine cellar where Chianti is king and locals lunch on soups, pastas, and salads (Via Santo Spirito 6/r. Closed Mon.). A block from the church of Santo Spirito, **Casalinga** (Via dei Michelozzi 9, closed weekends) is a large, popular trattoria, fine for a hearty, inexpensive lunch.

㉒ The church of **Santo Spirito** is important as one of Brunelleschi's finest architectural creations, and it contains some superb paintings, including a Filippino Lippi *Madonna.* Santo Spirito is the hub of a colorful neighborhood of artisans and intellectuals. An **outdoor market** enlivens the square every morning except Sunday; in the afternoon, pigeons, pet owners, and pensioners take over. The area is definitely on an upward trend, with new cafés, restaurants, and upscale shops opening every day.

Walk down Via Sant'Agostino and Via Santa Monaca to the **㉓** church of **Santa Maria del Carmine,** of no architectural interest but of immense significance in the history of Renaissance art. It contains the celebrated frescoes painted by Masaccio in the **Brancacci Chapel,** unveiled not long ago after a lengthy and meticulous restoration. The chapel was a classroom for such artistic giants as Botticelli, Leonardo da Vinci, Michelangelo, and Raphael, since they all came to study Masaccio's realistic use of light and perspective and his creation of space and depth. *Piazza del Carmine, tel. 055/212331. Admission: 6,000 lire. Open Mon. and Wed.–Sat. 10–5, Sun. 1–5.*

Time Out The small trattoria on the square has a friendly atmosphere and is a delightful spot where you can eat outdoors and enjoy the view. *Piazza del Carmine 18/r. Closed Sat. evening and Sun.*

Off the Beaten Track

Few tourists get to see one of Florence's most precious works of art, Benozzo Gozzoli's glorious frescoes in the tiny chapel on the second floor of **Palazzo Medici Riccardi,** representing the Journey of the Magi as a spectacular cavalcade with Lorenzo the Magnificent on a charger. *Via Cavour 1, tel. 055/276–0340.*

Admission: 5,000 lire. Open Mon.–Tues., Thurs.–Sat. 10–6, Sun. 10–noon.

One of Europe's oldest **botanical gardens,** founded in 1545, is a pleasant place for a pause; gardening hobbyists will enjoy the **Botanical Museum** next door. *Via Micheli 3, tel. 055/275–7402. Admission free. Open Mon., Wed., Fri. 9–noon; Sun. in Apr., 1st and 2nd Sun. in May, 9–1.*

The **English Cemetery** is on a cypress-studded knoll in the middle of heavily trafficked Piazza Donatello, not far from the botanical garden. Here you can walk with the shades of Elizabeth Barrett Browning, Algernon Swinburne, and other poets. You will need to ask the custodian to let you into the cemetery. It is kept locked. *Piazza Donatello. Ring bell at entrance for admission.*

Take afternoon tea with the Florentines at **Giacosa,** an elegant café at Via Tornabuoni 83/r, or in the plush salon of the **Hotel Excelsior** on Piazza Ognissanti.

Take the No. 12 or 13 bus from the train station or cathedral up to Piazzale Michelangelo, then walk along Viale dei Colli and climb to **San Miniato al Monte,** a charming green-and-white marble Romanesque church full of artistic riches.

Visit the **synagogue** on Via Farini and the **Jewish Museum** next door, which contains antique scrolls and ritual objects. *Via Farini 4; tel. 055/245252. Call in morning for opening hours.*

Shopping

Florence offers top quality for your money in leather goods, linens and upholstery fabrics, gold and silver jewelry, and cameos. Straw goods, gilded wooden trays and frames, hand-printed paper desk accessories, and ceramic objects make good inexpensive gifts. Many shops offer fine old prints.

Shopping Districts The most fashionable streets in Florence are **Via Tornabuoni** and **Via della Vigna Nuova.** Goldsmiths and jewelry shops can be found on and around the **Ponte Vecchio** and in the **Santa Croce area,** where there is also a high concentration of leather shops.

Antiques Most of Florence's many antiques dealers are located in **Borgo San Jacopo** and **Borgo Ognissanti,** but you'll find plenty of small shops throughout the center of town.

Department Stores **Principe,** in Piazza Strozzi, is a quality apparel store incorporating several designer boutiques. At the other end of the price range, **UPIM,** in Piazza della Repubblica and various other locations, has inexpensive goods of all types.

Markets The big food market at **Piazza del Mercato Centrale** is open in the morning (Mon.–Sat.) and is worth a visit. The **San Lorenzo market** on Piazza San Lorenzo and Via dell'Ariento is a fine place to browse for buys in leather goods and souvenirs (open Tues. and Sat. 8–7; also Sun. in summer). The **Mercato Nuovo,** Via Calimala, which is sometimes called the **Mercato del Porcellino** because of the famous bronze statue of a boar at one side, is packed with stalls selling souvenirs and straw goods (open Tues.–Sat. 8–7; closed Sun. and Mon. mornings in winter). There's a colorful neighborhood market at **Sant'Ambrogio,** Piazza Ghiberti (open Mon.–Sat. mornings), and a permanent flea market at **Piazza Ciompi** (open Mon.–Sat. 9–1 and 4–7, Sun. 9–1 in summer). A huge weekly market takes over Viale Lincoln in the Cascine park every Tuesday morning.

Dining

Mealtimes in Florence are 12:30–noon and 7:30–9 or later. Many Moderate and Inexpensive places are small, and you may have to share a table. Reservations are always advisable; to find a table at inexpensive places, get there early.

For details and price-category definitions, *see* Dining in Staying in Italy.

Very Expensive **Cestello.** The restaurant of the hotel Excelsior has a lovely setting, whether you dine on the rooftop terrace overlooking the Arno in the summer, or in a ritzy salon with coffered ceiling, pink linen tablecloths, and antique paintings in the winter. The menu features such deliciously visual delights as *linguine con rughetta e scampi* (flat spaghetti with chicory and shrimps) and *tagliata di manzo con mosaico di insalatine* (sliced beef on a bed of salad greens arranged in a mosaic pattern). *Piazza Ognissanti 3, tel. 055/264201. Reservations advised in summer. AE, DC, MC, V.*

★ **Enoteca Pinchiorri.** In the beautiful Renaissance palace and its charming garden courtyard that was home to Giovanni da Verrazzano (a 15th-century Florentine navigator), husband-and-wife team Giorgio Pinchiorri and Annie Feolde have created an exceptional restaurant that ranks as one of Italy's best. Guests can enjoy Annie's rediscoveries of traditional Tuscan dishes, or her own brand of imaginatively creative nouvelle cuisine, while Giorgio oversees the extraordinary wine cellar. At upward of 150,000 lire per person, meals here are for real connoisseurs; a fixed menu costs about 95,000 lire. *Via Ghibellina 87, tel. 055/242777. Reservations well in advance are advised at all times. AE, MC, V. Closed Sun., Mon. lunch, Aug. and Dec. 24–28.*

Expensive **Il Verrocchio.** In an elegant 18th-century villa, now a deluxe hotel, this restaurant is about 20 minutes from downtown Florence by car or taxi and well worth the ride. The indoor dining room has a huge fireplace, columns, and a high vaulted ceiling. Outdoors you dine on a terrace overlooking the Arno. The menu changes with the seasons but can be described as creative Tuscan, with such offerings as *agnello con salsa di albicocche* (lamb with apricot sauce) and delicate, fresh pasta dishes. *Villa La Massa, Via La Massa 6, Candeli, tel. 055/666141. Reservations advised. Jacket and tie required. AE, DC, MC, V. Closed Mon. and Tues. lunch Nov.–Mar.*

★ **Terrazza Brunelleschi.** The rooftop restaurant of the hotel Baglioni has the best view in town. The dining room, decorated in pale blue and creamy tones, has big picture windows; the summer-dining terrace is charming, with tables under arbors and turrets for guests to climb to get an even better view. The menu offers such traditional Tuscan dishes as *minestra di fagioli* (bean soup) and other more innovative choices, such as a pâté of peppers and tomato. *Hotel Baglioni, Piazza Unità Italiana 6, tel. 055/215642. Reservations advised, especially in summer. AE, DC, MC, V.*

Moderate **Alle Murate.** Between the Duomo and Santa Croce, this sophisticated but informal restaurant features creative versions of classic Tuscan food, along with specialties of other regions, such as the Calabrian *cavatelli con broccoli* (pasta with broccoli and cheese). In a smaller room called the *vineria*, the menu and service are simpler and prices lower. *Via Ghibellina 52/r, tel. 055/240618. Reservations advised. No credit cards. No lunch. Closed Mon.*

Buca Mario. Visitors can expect to share a table at this characteristically unadorned *buca* (downstairs trattoria), whose menu includes such hearty down-to-earth Tuscan food as homemade *pappardelle* (noodles) and *stracotto* (beef stew with beans). It's near Santa Maria Novella. *Piazza Ottaviani 16/r, tel. 055/214179. Reservations advised in evening. AE, DC, MC, V. Closed Thurs. lunch and Wed. and Aug.*

Cammillo. This is a classic Florentine eating place, with terracotta tiles on the floor and several brick-vaulted rooms where guests enjoy such regional and international specialties as chicken livers with sage and beans or porcini mushrooms *alla parmigiana*, with a touch of truffle. The house wine and olive oil are made by the owners. *Borgo San Jacopo 57/r, tel. 055/212427. Reservations advised; required for dinner. AE, DC, MC, V. Closed Wed., Thurs.; 3 weeks in Aug.; 3 weeks in Dec.*

Cavallini. It makes sense that this restaurant, with its outdoor café, is touristy, particularly since it's situated right on Piazza della Signoria. But it is also consistently good, it's open on Sundays, and it's so handy for collapsing in after a hard day at the Uffizi. The cooking is pure Tuscan, with broad pappardelle noodles, bean soup, and grilled meat on the menu. *Via delle Farina 6/r, tel. 055/215818. Reservations advised, especially for outdoor tables. AE, DC, MC, V. Closed Tues eve., Wed., and Aug. 1–22.*

★ **Il Cibreo.** In an upscale trattoria near the Sant'Ambrogio market, Il Cibreo's young chefs prepare updated versions of traditional Florentine dishes and present them with flair, as in *passato di peperoni gialli* (yellow-pepper soup) and *anatra farcita* (boned duck with a meat, raisin, and pine-nut stuffing). Tables are set outdoors in June and July. *Via dei Macci 118/r, tel. 055/234–1100. Reservations advised for dinner. AE, DC, MC, V. Closed Sun. and Mon. July 25–Sept. 5 and Dec. 31–Jan. 7.*

Il Fagioli. This typical Florentine trattoria near Santa Croce has a simple decor and a menu in which such local dishes as *ribollita* (a sort of minestrone) and involtini predominate. The antipasti are always tempting here, but you're expected to have a two-course meal, besides. *Corso Tintori 47/r, tel. 055/244285. Reservations advised. Dress: informal. No credit cards. Closed Sun. (also Sat., in July and Aug.) and Christmas Day.*

Mario da Ganino. Highly informal, rustic, and cheerful, this trattoria greets you with a taste of mortadella, and offers homemade pastas and *gnudoni* (ravioli without pasta), plus a heavenly cheesecake for dessert. There are plenty of other taste-tempters on the menu. It's tiny, seating only 35, double that in summer at outdoor tables. *Piazza dei Cimatori 4/r, tel. 055/214125. Reservations advised. AE, DC. Closed Sun. and Aug. 15–25.*

Inexpensive **Angiolino.** This bustling little trattoria has a real charcoal grill
★ and an old wood-burning stove to keep its customers warm on nippy days. Glowing with authentic atmosphere, Angiolino offers such Tuscan specialties as *ribollita* (minestrone) and juicy *bistecca alla fiorentina* (T-bone steak basted in olive oil and

black pepper). The bistecca will push the bill up into the Moderate range. *Via Santo Spirito 36/r, tel. 055/239–8976. Reservations advised in the evening. No credit cards. Closed Sun. dinner, Mon., and last 3 weeks in July.*

La Maremmana. A lavish display of produce at the entrance holds promise of what's in store at this typical Florentine trattoria near Santa Croce. The fixed-price menu includes generous servings of local favorites such as *ribollita* (vegetable soup) and *stracotto* (beef stew). There is an à la carte menu, too. *Via dei Macci 77/r, tel. 055/241226. No credit cards. Closed Sun. Reservations advised.*

Za-Za. Near the San Lorenzo market, this is an informal but trendy trattoria with posters of movie stars on the walls and a lively Italian clientele. The food is classic Florentine: ribollita, fagioli served several ways, and good steaks, with everything fresh from the market. *Piazza Mercato Centrale 16/r, tel. 055/215411. Reservations advised. AE, DC, MC, V. Closed Sun. and Aug.*

Lodging

What with mass tourism and trade fairs, rooms are at a premium in Florence for most of the year. Make reservations well in advance. If you arrive without a reservation, the ITA office in the railway station (open 8:20 AM–9 PM) can help you, but there may be a long line. Now that much traffic is banned in the downtown area, many central hotel rooms are quieter. Local traffic and motorcycles can still be bothersome, however, so check the decibel level before you settle in.

For details and price-category definitions, *see* Lodging in Staying in Italy.

Very Expensive **Excelsior.** One of the flagships of the CIGA chain, the Excelsior
★ provides consistently superlative service and is lavishly appointed with old prints, bouquets of flowers, pink marble, and carpets so deep you could lose a shoe in them. The hotel occupies a former patrician palace on the Arno, and many rooms have river views (some with Tuscan antiques scattered around as well). The Cestello restaurant (*see* Dining, *above*) is excellent. *Piazza Ognissanti 3, tel. 055/264201, fax 055/210278. 205 rooms with bath. Facilities: garage. AE, DC, MC, V.*

Regency. One of the Ottaviani family's small, select hotels, the Regency has the intimate and highly refined atmosphere of a private villa, luxuriously furnished with antiques and decorated with great style. Just outside the historic center of the city, it has a charming garden and the pleasant Le Jardin restaurant. *Piazza Massimo d'Azeglio 3, tel. 055/245247, fax 055/234–2937. 31 rooms with bath. Facilities: garage. AE, DC, MC, V.*

Villa Cora. Located in a residential area on a hill overlooking the Oltrarno section of Florence and across the Arno to the Duomo and bell tower, the Villa Cora is a converted private villa. Furnishings are exquisite and the atmosphere is quietly elegant. There are gardens in which to stroll, a pool in which to wallow, and a formal but charming restaurant in which to dine. There is a Mercedes shuttle service between the hotel and the center of Florence. *Viale Machiavelli 18, tel. 055/229–8451, fax 055/229086. 48 rooms with bath. AE, DC, MC, V.*

Expensive **Baglioni.** Spacious, elegant, and very grand, Baglioni has well-
★ proportioned rooms tastefully decorated in antique Florentine
style. Many rooms have leaded glass windows, and some have
views of Santa Maria Novella. The hotel also has a charming
roof terrace, and the splendid Terrazza Brunelleschi restaurant (*see* Dining, *above*), which has the best view in all Florence. *Piazza Unità d'Italia 6, tel. 055/218441, fax 055/215695.
197 rooms with bath. Facilities: garage. AE, DC, MC, V.*

Bernini Palace. The atmosphere here is one of austere yet elegant simplicity. Rooms are not ostentatious but are, rather,
well-furnished in pastel fabrics and mahogany furniture. Entirely air-conditioned and double-glazed, the Bernini has a
quiet, tranquil feel, yet is only a few steps from the frenetically
busy Piazza della Signoria. There is no restaurant, but breakfast is served in a historic salon. *Piazza San Firenze 29, tel.
055/288621, fax 055/268272. 86 rooms with bath. AE, DC, MC,
V.*

★ **Brunelleschi.** This unique hotel in the heart of Florence encompasses a Byzantine tower, a medieval church, and an 18th-cen-
tury palazzo. Architects left sections of ancient stone walls and
brick arches to set off the tasteful contemporary decor in the
public rooms. Bedrooms are decorated with textured, coordinated fabrics in soft colors, and the beige marble bathrooms are
luxurious. The Brunelleschi ranks high for atmosphere and
comfort. *Piazza Sant'Elisabetta (Via dei Calzaioli), tel. 055/
562068, fax 055/219653. 94 rooms with bath. Facilities: restaurant, bar. AE, DC, MC, V.*

★ **Monna Lisa.** This place is the closest you may come to living in
an aristocratic palace in the heart of Florence. American visitors in particular are fond of its smallish but homey bedrooms
and sumptuously comfortable sitting rooms. Ask for a room on
the quiet 17th-century courtyard, especially the one with the
delightful balcony. A lavish buffet breakfast is included in the
price. Make reservations months in advance to be assured of a
room at this very special hotel. *Borgo Pinti 27, tel. 055/247–
9751, fax 055/247–9755. 20 rooms with bath. Facilities: garden,
bar, parking. AE, DC, MC, V.*

Moderate **Loggiato dei Serviti.** You'll find the Loggiato dei Serviti tucked
★ under an arcade in one of the city's quietest and most attractive
squares. Vaulted ceilings and tasteful furnishings (some of
them antiques) go far to make this hotel a real find for those
who want to get the genuine Florentine feel and who will appreciate the 19th-century town house surroundings while enjoying modern creature comforts. There is no restaurant.
*Piazza Santissima Annunziata 3, tel. 055/289592, fax 055/
289595. 29 rooms with bath. AE, DC, MC, V.*

Morandi alla Crocetta. This charming and distinguished residence near Piazza Santissima Annunziata, was once a monastery. It is furnished in the classic style of a gracious Florentine
home, and guests feel like privileged friends of the family. A
new entrance hall and elevator should be added in 1994. Small
and exceptional, it is also a good value and must be booked well
in advance. *Via Laura 50, tel. 055/234–4747, fax 055/248–0954.
9 rooms with bath. AE, DC, MC, V.*

Villa Azalee. In a residential area about five minutes from the
train station, this century-old mansion is set in a large garden.
It has a private-home atmosphere and comfortable living
rooms. Bedrooms are decorated individually and are air-

conditioned. *Viale Fratelli Rosselli 44, tel. 055/214242, fax 055/268264. 24 rooms with bath. AE, DC, MC, V.*

Inexpensive
★
Bellettini. Very centrally located, this small hotel occupies two floors of an old but well-kept building near the Church of San Lorenzo, in an area with plenty of inexpensive eating places. Rooms are ample, with Venetian or Tuscan decor, and bathrooms are modern. The management is friendly and helpful. *Via dei Conti 7, tel. 055/213561, fax 055/283551. 27 rooms, 23 with bath. Facilities: bar, lounge. AE, DC, MC, V.*

Nuova Italia. Near the train station, in a well-kept town house, this hotel is run by a cordial English-speaking family. It's bright with pictures and posters. The clean, ample rooms have a fresh look; many can accommodate extra beds. The low bargain rates include breakfast. *Via Faenza 26, tel. 055/268430, fax 055/210941. 20 rooms with bath. AE, DC, MC, V.*

The Arts

For a list of events, pick up a "Florence Concierge Information" booklet from your hotel desk, or the monthly information bulletin published by the **Comune Aperto** city information office (Via Cavour 1/r). This information is also available at information offices at the station and at Chiasso Baroncelli.

Music and Ballet
Most major musical events are staged at the **Teatro Comunale** (Corso Italia 16, tel. 055/277–9236). The box office (closed Mon.) is open from 9 to 1, and a half-hour before performances. It's best to order your tickets by mail, however, as they're difficult to come by at the last minute. You can also order concert and ballet tickets through **Universalturismo** (Via degli Speziali 7/r, tel. 055/217241). **Amici della Musica** (Friends of Music) puts on a series of concerts at the **Teatro della Pergola** (box office, Via della Pergola 10a/r, tel. 055/247–9651). For program information, contact the Amici della Musica directly at Via Sirtori 49 (tel. 055/608420).

Film
English-language films are shown at the **Cinema Astro,** on Piazza San Simone near Santa Croce. There are two shows every evening, Tuesday through Sunday. It closes in July.

Nightlife

Piano Bars
Many of the top hotels have piano bars; that of the **Plaza Lucchesi** (Lungarno della Zecca Vecchia 38, tel. 055/264141) is particularly spacious and pleasant. The terrace of the hotel **Baglioni** *(see* Lodging, *above)* has no music but has one of the best views in Florence, candlelit tables, and a wonderful atmosphere. **Caffè Pitti** (Piazza dei Pitti 9, tel. 055/239–6241) is a social center for a young international crowd. **Caffè Voltaire** (Via della Scala 9/r, tel. 055/218255) serves Brazilian food and drink and plays Latin music to a lively crowd (closed Mon.).

Nightclubs
The River Club (Lungarno Corsini 8, tel. 055/282465) has winter-garden decor and a large dance floor (closed Sun.). **Capitale** (Via Fosso Macinante 13, tel. 055/356723), in the Cascine park, is open all year.

Discos
Jackie O (Via dell'Erta Canina 24a, tel. 055/234–2442) is a glittering Art Deco disco with lots of mirrors and marble and a trendy clientele (closed Wed.). **Space Electronic** (Via Palazzuolo 37, tel. 055/239–3082) is exactly what its name implies: ul-

tramodern and psychedelic (closed Mon., except from Mar. to Sept., when it's open every night). **Yab Yum** (Via Sassetti 5/r, tel. 055/282018) is another futuristic-style disco popular with the young international set. It's closed Monday.

Tuscany

Tuscany is a blend of rugged hills, fertile valleys, and long stretches of sandy beaches that curve along the west coast of central Italy and fringe the pine-forested coastal plain of the Maremma. The gentle, cypress-studded green hills may seem familiar: Leonardo and Raphael often painted them in the backgrounds of their masterpieces. The cities and towns of Tuscany house the centuries-old heritage of culture and art that produced magnificent medieval cathedrals and the marvels of the Renaissance. Come to Tuscany to enjoy its unchanged and gracious atmosphere of good living, and, above all, its unparalleled artistic treasures, many still in their original settings in tiny old churches and patrician palaces.

Getting Around

By Train The main train network connects Florence with Arezzo and Prato. Another main line runs to Pisa, while a secondary line goes from Prato to the coast via Lucca. Trains also connect Siena with Pisa (via Empoli), a two-hour ride.

By Bus The entire region is crisscrossed by bus lines, good alternatives to trains, especially to Prato from Florence (buses run every 30 min.) and Siena, which is 90 minutes by bus from Florence. Use local buses to tour the many pretty hill towns around Siena, such as San Gimignano, and then take a Tra-In or Lazzi bus from Siena to Arezzo, where you can get back onto the main Rome–Florence train line.

By Car The main autostrade run parallel to the train routes. Roads throughout Tuscany are in good condition, though often narrow.

Guided Tours

American Express (Via Guicciardini 49/r, tel. 055/288751) operates one-day excursions to Siena and San Gimignano out of Florence, and can arrange for cars, drivers, and guides for special-interest tours in Tuscany. **CIT** (Via Cavour 54/r, tel. 055/294306) has a three-day Carosello bus tour from Rome to Florence, Siena, and San Gimignano, as well as a five-day tour that also takes in Venice.

Tourist Information

Arezzo (Piazza Risorgimento 116, tel. 0575/23952).
Cortona (Via Nazionale 72, tel. 0575/630557).
Lucca (Via Vittorio Veneto 40, tel. 0583/493639; Piazza Guidiccione 2, tel.. 0583/491205).
Pisa (Lungarno Mediceo 42, tel. 050/542344; Piazza del Duomo 8, tel. 050/560464).
Pistoia (Piazza del Duomo 4, tel. 0573/21622).
Prato (Via Cairoli 48, tel. 0574/24112).
San Gimignano (Piazza del Duomo, tel. 0577/940008).

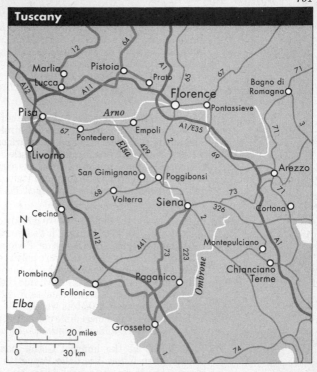

Tuscany

Siena (Via di Città 43, tel. 0577/42209; Piazza del Campo 56, tel. 0577/280551).

Exploring Tuscany

Starting your excursions in Tuscany from Florence, you can go west to Prato and Pistoia, workaday cities with a core of fine medieval buildings, then to the historic cities of Lucca and Pisa. Lucca makes a good base for an excursion to Pisa, which is only about 30 minutes away by car, bus, or train. Heading south from Florence you can explore the Chianti district and make Siena your base for excursions to some unspoiled hill towns: San Gimignano, Montepulciano, and Pienza.

Prato Since the Middle Ages, **Prato,** 21 kilometers (13 miles) north-west of Florence, has been Italy's major textile-producing center: It now supplies the country's knitwear and fashion industries. Ignore the drab industrial outskirts and devote some time to the fine old buildings in the downtown area, crammed with artworks commissioned by Prato's wealthy merchants during the Renaissance. The **Duomo** (cathedral), erected during the Middle Ages, was decorated with paintings and sculptures by some of the most illustrious figures of Tuscan art, among them Fra Filippo Lippi, who took 12 years to complete the frescoes in the apse (perhaps because in the meantime he was being tried for fraud, as well as wooing the nun with whom he then eloped). Look in particular for his passionate portrayals of *Herod's Feast* and *Salome's Dance*. *Piazza del Duomo. Open daily 7–noon and 4–7.*

In the former bishop's palace, now the **Museo dell'Opera del Duomo,** you can see the original reliefs by Donatello for the Pulpit of the Holy Girdle (Mary's belt, supposedly given to Doubting Thomas as evidence of her assumption; the relic is kept in a chapel of the cathedral). *Piazza del Duomo 49, tel. 0574/29339. Admission: 5,000 lire (ticket valid for other Prato museums). Open Mon. and Wed.–Sat. 9:30–12:30 and 3–6:30, Sun. 9:30–12:30.*

Architects and architecture buffs rhapsodize over the church of **Santa Maria delle Carceri,** off Via Cairoli. Built by Giuliano Sangallo in the 1490s, it was a landmark of Renaissance architecture. Next to it, the formidable **castle** built for Frederick II of Hohenstaufen is another impressive sight, the only castle of its type to be seen outside southern Italy. *Piazza Santa Maria delle Carceri. Admission free. Open Tues.–Sat. 9–noon and 3–6, Sun. 9–noon.*

Pistoia **Pistoia** lies about 15 kilometers (9 miles) northwest of Prato. A floricultural capital of Europe, it's surrounded by greenhouses and plant nurseries. Flowers aside, Pistoia's main sights are all in the downtown area, so you can easily see them on the way to Lucca. The Romanesque **Duomo** (cathedral) is flanked by a 13th-century bell tower, while in a side chapel dedicated to San Jacopo (St. James) there's a massive **silver altar** that alone makes the stopover in Pistoia worthwhile. Two hundred years in the making, it's an incredible piece of workmanship, begun in 1287. *Piazza del Duomo. Illumination of altarpiece: 2,000 lire.*

Take a look at the unusual Gothic baptistry opposite the Duomo, then follow Via delle Pappe (to the left behind the Duomo) to admire the superb frieze by Giovanni della Robbia on the Ospedale del Ceppo. Continue on to the church of **Sant'Andrea** (Via Sant'Andrea) to see Pistoia's greatest art treasure, Giovanni Pisano's powerfully sculpted 13th-century **pulpit.** Heading back toward the train station and bus terminal, stop on the way to take in the green-and-white marble church of **San Giovanni Fuorcivitas** (Via Francesco Crispi, off Via Cavour). Highlights here include a *Visitation* by Luca della Robbia, a painting by Taddeo Gaddi, and a holy water font by Giovanni Pisano.

Lucca Your next destination is **Lucca,** Puccini's hometown and a city well-loved by sightseers who appreciate the careful upkeep of its medieval look. Though it hasn't the number of hotels and other tourist trappings that, say, Pisa does, for that very reason it's a pleasant alternative. You can easily make an excursion to Pisa from here—it's only 22 kilometers (14 miles) away. First enjoy the views of the city and countryside from the tree-planted 16th-century ramparts that encircle Lucca. Then explore the city's marvelously elaborate Romanesque churches, fronted with tiers and rows of columns, and looking suspiciously like oversize marble wedding cakes.

From vast **Piazza Napoleone,** a swing around the Old Town will take you past the 11th-century **Duomo** on Piazza San Martino, with its 15th-century tomb of Ilaria del Carretto by Jacopo della Quercia. Don't neglect a ramble through the **Piazza del Mercato,** which preserves the oval form of the Roman amphitheater over which it was built, or the three surrounding streets that are filled with atmosphere: **Via Battisti, Via Fillungo,** and **Via Guinigi.** In addition to the Duomo, Lucca has two other fine churches. **San Frediano** (Piazza San Frediano) is graced with an austere facade ornamented by 13th-century mosaic decoration. Inside, check out the exquisite reliefs by Jacopo della Quercia in the last chapel on the left. **San Michele in Foro** (Piazza San Michele) is an exceptional example of the Pisan Romanesque style and decorative flair peculiar to Lucca: Note its facade, a marriage of arches and columns crowned by a statue of St. Michael.

The **Villa Reale** is 8 kilometers (5 miles) outside town, at Marlia. Gardening buffs, especially, will appreciate this handsome villa, surrounded by attractive parkland and gardens laid out in the 17th century. *Marlia, tel. 0583/30108. Admission: 5,000 lire. Guided visits on the hour, July–Sept., Tues.–Thurs. and Sun. 10, 11, 4, 5, and 6; Oct. and Mar.–June, Tues.–Sun. 10, 11, 3, 4, 5. Closed Nov.–Feb.*

Pisa As you drive southwest, the next Tuscan town of note you'll come to is **Pisa**, a dull, overcommercialized place, though even skeptics have to admit that the **Torre Pendente** (Leaning Tower) really is one of the world's more amazing sights. Theories vary as to whether the now-famous list is due to shifting foundations or to an amazing architectural feat by Bonanno Pisano (the first of three architects to work on the tower). A 294-step staircase spirals its way up the tower, but since the tower was permanently closed to visitors in 1990 because the rate of its tilt was increasing too rapidly, you won't be able to get in. If you want a two-foot marble imitation of the Leaning Tower, perhaps even illuminated from within, this is your chance to grab one at a souvenir stand. *Campo dei Miracoli.*

Pisa has two other fine buildings, and, conveniently enough, they're next to the Leaning Tower. The **baptistery** was begun in 1153 but not completed until 1400, the Pisano family doing most of its decoration. Test out the excellent acoustics (occasionally the guard will slam the great doors shut and then sing a few notes—the resulting echo is very impressive, and costly, too, since he'll expect a tip). *Piazza del Duomo, in the Campo dei Miracoli. Open daily 9–sunset.*

Pisa's **Duomo** is elegantly simple, its facade decorated with geometric and animal shapes. The cavernous interior is supported by a series of 68 columns, while the pulpit is a fine example of Giovanni Pisano's work. Be sure to note the suspended lamp that hangs across from the pulpit; known as Galileo's Lamp, it's said to have inspired his theories on pendular motion. *Piazza del Duomo. Open daily 8–12:45 and 3–sunset.*

Visitors may find it more convenient to take a train back to Florence and get a bus or train there for the 85-minute trip to Siena. For a more leisurely look at the Tuscan countryside, investigate the possibility of taking local trains from Pisa to Siena, changing trains at Empoli and then passing through **Certaldo,** a pretty hill town that's the birthplace of Giovanni Boccaccio, 14th-century author of the *Decameron.*

Siena **Siena** is one of Italy's best-preserved medieval towns, rich both in works of art and in expensive antique shops. The famous **Palio** is held here, a breakneck, 90-second horse race that takes place twice each year in the Piazza del Campo, on July 2 and August 16. Built on three hills, Siena is not an easy town to explore, for everything you'll want to see is either up or down a steep hill or stairway. But it is worth every ounce of effort.

Siena really gives you the chance of seeing and feeling what the Middle Ages must have been like: dark stone palaces that look like fortresses, Gothic church portals, and narrow streets opening out into airy squares.

Siena was a center of learning and art during the Middle Ages, and almost all the public buildings and churches in the town have enough artistic or historical merit to be worth visiting. Unlike most churches, Siena's **Duomo** has a mixture of religious and civic symbols ornamenting both its interior and exterior. The cathedral museum in the unfinished transept contains some fine works of art, notably a celebrated *Maestà* by Duccio di Buoninsegna. The animated frescoes of papal history in the Piccolomini Library (with an entrance off the left aisle of the cathedral) are credited to Pinturicchio and are worth seeking out. *Piazza del Duomo. Cathedral Museum. Admission: 5,000 lire. Open Mar. 14–Sept., daily 9–7:30; Oct.–Nov. 3, daily 9–6:30; Nov. 4–Dec., daily 9–1:30; Jan. 2–Mar. 13, daily 9–1. Library. Admission: 2,000 lire. Open mid-Mar.–Sept., daily 9–7:30; Oct.–Nov. 3, 9–6:30; Nov. 4–Mar. 13, daily 10–1 and 2:30–5.*

Nearby, the fan-shaped **Piazza del Campo** is Siena's main center of activity, with 11 streets leading into it. Farsighted planning has preserved it as a medieval showpiece, containing the 13th-century **Palazzo Pubblico** (City Hall) and the **Torre del Mangia** (Bell Tower). Try to visit both these buildings, the former for Lorenzetti's frescoes on the effects of good and bad government, the latter for the wonderful view (you'll have to climb 503 steps to reach it, however). *Piazza del Campo, tel. 0577/292111. Bell Tower. Admission: 4,000 lire. Open Mar. 15–Nov. 15, daily 10–1 hour before sunset; Nov. 16–Mar. 14, daily 10–1:30. Palazzo Pubblico (Civic Museum). Admission: 6,000 lire. Open Mar. 15–Nov. 15, Mon.–Sat. 9:30–7:30, Sun. 9:30–1:30; Nov.–Mar., daily 9:30–1:30.*

Time Out The **gelateria** at Piazza del Campo 21 makes a good stop for sweet refreshment, but if you need something more substantial, walk east from Piazza del Campo to **Verrocchio** (Logge del Papa 2; closed Wed.), a restaurant serving local fare.

From Siena make an excursion to **San Gimignano,** about a half hour by car and an hour by Tra-In bus (change buses in Poggibonsi). San Gimignano is perhaps the most delightful of the Tuscan medieval hill towns. There were once 79 tall towers here, symbols of power for the wealthy families of the Middle Ages. Thirteen are still standing, giving the town its unique skyline. The bus stops just outside the town gates, from which you can stroll down the main street to the picturesque Piazza della Cisterna.

Just around the corner is the church of the **Collegiata.** Its walls, and those of its chapel dedicated to Santa Fina, are decorated with radiant frescoes (have plenty of 100-lire coins at hand for the light machines). From the steps of the church you can observe the town's countless crows as they circle the tall towers. In the pretty courtyard on the right as you descend the church stairs, there's a shop selling Tuscan and Deruta ceramics, which you'll also find in other shops along the Via San Giovanni. The excellent San Gimignano wine could be another souvenir of your visit; it's sold in gift cartons from just about every shop in town.

If you have a car, you can drive northeast of Siena through the hilly Chianti country on Route 222, or southeast of Siena to the Abbey of Monte Oliveto Maggiore and the hill towns of Montepulciano and Pienza, each worth seeing and much less crowded than San Gimignano. You can also make these excursions (except for the abbey) by bus from Siena, though service is often haphazard.

Arezzo   A local bus takes you from Siena to **Arezzo,** about 48 kilometers (30 miles) east. The route meanders past thickly wooded hills, past vineyards and wheat fields, and through the broad ribbon of the Autostrada del Sole in the fertile Chiana valley, known for its pale beef cattle that provide the classic *bistecca alla fiorentina.* Arezzo is not a particularly beautiful town, though the old, upper town still has a good assortment of medieval and Renaissance buildings. What makes Arezzo worth a visit, however, is its fine array of Tuscan art treasures, including frescoes, stained glass, and ancient Etruscan pottery.

The **Musco Archeologico** (Archaeological Museum) is near the train station, next to what's left of an ancient **Roman amphitheater.** The museum has a rich collection of Etruscan art, artifacts, and pottery, copied by Arezzo's contemporary artisans and sold in the local ceramic shops. *Via Margaritone 10, tel. 0575/20882. Admission: 6,000 lire. Open Tues.–Sat. 9–2, Sun. 9–1.*

Via Guido Monaco, named after the 11th-century originator of the musical scale, leads to the church of **San Francesco,** in which sit some of the town's main attractions, among them the frescoes by Piero della Francesca. Due for restoration after intensive studies of suitable methods, these frescoes may be at least partially hidden for a few years. Though faded, they still rank among the outstanding examples of Italian painting, and art lovers are looking forward to seeing them in renewed splendor. *Push the button on the black box for light. Via Cavour.*

Now you enter the old part of Arezzo, where the poet Petrarch (1304–74), the artist Vasari (1511–74), and the satirical author Pietro Aretino (1492–1556) all lived. Climb Via Cesalpino uphill to the fine Gothic **cathedral** (Piazza del Duomo), then stroll past **Petrarch's House** to **Piazza Grande,** an attractive, sloping square where an extensive open-air fair of antiques and old bric-a-brac is held the first weekend of every month. The shops around the piazza also specialize in antiques, with prices lower than those you will encounter in Florence. The colonnaded apse and bell tower of the Romanesque church of **Santa Maria della Pieve** grace one end of this pleasant piazza.

Cortona   A full day may be enough for you to get the feel of Arezzo, but you may wish to stay overnight, especially during the antiques fair, or if you want to use the town as a base for an excursion to **Cortona,** about 30 kilometers (18 miles) south. This well-preserved, unspoiled medieval hill town is known for its excellent small art gallery and a number of fine antiques shops, as well as for its colony of foreign residents. Cortona has the advantage of being on the main train line, though you will have to take a local bus from the station up into the town, passing the Renaissance church of **Santa Maria del Calcinaio** on the way.

The heart of Cortona is formed by **Piazza della Repubblica** and the adjacent **Piazza Signorelli.** Wander into the courtyard of the picturesque **Palazzo Pretorio,** and, if you want to see a representative collection of Etruscan bronzes, climb its centuries-old stone staircase to the **Museo dell'Accademia Etrusca** (Gallery of Etruscan Art). *Piazza Signorelli 9, tel. 0575/ 630415. Admission: 5,000 lire. Open Apr.–Sept., Tues.–Sun. 10–1 and 4–7; Oct.–Mar., Tues.–Sun. 9–1 and 3–5.*

The nearby **Museo Diocesano** (Diocesan Museum) houses an impressive number of large and splendid paintings by native son Luca Signorelli, as well as a beautiful *Annunciation* by Fra Angelico, a delightful surprise to find in this small, eclectic town. *Piazza del Duomo 1, tel. 0575/62830. Admission: 5,000 lire. Open Apr.–Sept., Tues.–Sun. 9–1 and 3–6:30; Oct.–Mar., Tues.–Sun. 9–1 and 3–5.*

Dining and Lodging

For details and price-category definitions, *see* Dining and Lodging in Staying in Italy.

Arezzo
Dining
★

Buca di San Francesco. Travelers and passing celebrities come to this rustic and historic cellar restaurant for the 13th-century cantina atmosphere, but locals love it for the food, especially ribollita and *sformato di verdure* (vegetable pie). *Piazza San Francesco 1, tel. 0575/23271. Dinner reservations advised. AE, DC, MC, V. Closed Mon. dinner, Tues., and July. Moderate.*

Tastevin. Arezzo's purveyor of creative *nuova cucina* serves traditional Tuscan dishes as well, in two attractive rooms in warm Tuscan provincial style and one in more sophisticated Art Deco. At the cozy bar the talented owner plays and sings Sinatra songs in the evening. Specialties are *risotto Tastevin,* with cream of truffles, and *tagliata Tastevin,* sliced beef with olive oil and rosemary. *Via de' Cenci 9, tel. 0575/28304. Dinner reservations advised. AE, MC, V. Closed Mon., (Sun. in summer), and Aug. Moderate.*

Spiedo d'Oro. Cheery red-and-white tablecloths add a colorful touch to this large, reliable trattoria near the Archaeological Museum. The menu offers such Tuscan home-style specialties as *zuppa di pane* (bread soup), *pappardelle oll'ocio* (noodles with duck sauce), and *ossobuco aretina* (sautéed veal shank). *Via Crispi 12, tel. 0575/22873. Reservations accepted. No credit cards. Closed Thurs. and first 2 weeks in July. Inexpensive.*

Lodging

Continental. The circa-1950 Continental has fairly spacious rooms decorated in white and bright yellow, gleaming bathrooms, and the advantage of a central location within walking distance of all major sights. *Piazza Guido Monaco 7, tel. 0575/ 20251, fax 0575/340485. 74 rooms with bath. Facilities: restaurant. AE, DC, MC, V. Inexpensive.*

Cortona
Dining
★

Tonino. The place to eat in Cortona, it's known for its delicious *antipastissimo* and for succulent steaks of Chiana valley beef. It's best on weekdays, when it's quieter. Both service and food have a touch of class. The dining rooms, on two floors, have large picture windows overlooking the valley. *Piazza Garibaldi, tel. 0575/603100. Weekends reservations advised. AE, DC, MC, V. Closed Mon. dinner and Tues. Moderate.*

Lucca
Dining
★

Buca di Sant'Antonio. A Lucca favorite, located near the church of San Michele, Buca di Sant'Antonio was around more than a century ago, and it still retains something of its rustic look. It specializes in traditional local dishes, some unfamiliar but well worth trying, among them *ravioli di ricotta alle zucchine* (cheese ravioli with zucchini) and kid or lamb roasted with herbs. *Via della Cervia 3, tel. 0583/55881. Dinner reservations advised. AE, DC, MC, V. Closed Sun. dinner, Mon., and July 9–29. Moderate.*

Il Giglio. Off vast Piazza Napoleone, Il Giglio has a quiet, turn-of-the-century charm and a dignified atmosphere. In the summer the tables outdoors have a less formal air. The menu is classic: *crostini* (savory Tuscan chicken liver, anchovy and caper paste on small pieces of toast), *stracotto* (braised beef with mushrooms), and seafood, as well. *Piazza del Giglio 3, tel. 0583/494058. Dinner reservations advised. AE, DC, MC, V. Closed Tues. dinner and Wed. Moderate.*

★ **La Mora.** You'll need a car or a taxi to take you to this charming old way station 10 kilometers (6 miles) outside Lucca, but its authentic local cooking is worth every effort. It is widely considered to be one of the best regional restaurants in Italy. *Via Sesto di Moriano 1748, Ponte a Moriano, tel. 0583/406402. Reservations advised. AE, DC, MC, V. Closed Wed. dinner, Thurs., June 25–July 8, Oct. 10–30. Moderate.*

Lodging
★

Villa La Principessa. This pretty 19th-century country mansion, 3½ kilometers (2 miles) outside Lucca, is an exclusive hotel whose rooms feature original beamed ceilings. All rooms are individually and tastefully decorated. Antique floors, furniture, and portraits set the tone, and the restaurant is known for its fine Tuscan dishes. *Massa Pisana, tel. 0583/370037. 44 rooms with bath. Facilities: park, pool, restaurant. AE, DC, MC, V. Closed Nov. 1–Feb. 18. Expensive.*

Universo. There's plenty of genteel, Old World charm here to please those looking for the atmosphere of times past. In the spacious, high-ceilinged public rooms, the decor is reminiscent of early 1900s style. During a 1989 renovation, rooms were modernized and endowed with TV, fridge-bars, and sparkling new baths. *Piazza del Giglio 1, tel. 0583/49046. 70 rooms, 60 with bath. V. Moderate.*

Ilaria. This small, family-run hotel sits in a pretty location on a minuscule canal within easy walking distance of the main sights. The rooms are smallish but fresh and functional. *Via del Fosso 20, tel. 0583/47558. 17 rooms, 12 with bath or shower. AE, DC, MC, V. Inexpensive.*

Montepulciano
Dining

Cittino. A few plants outside the door mark this plain, family-run trattoria off one of the town's main streets. *Pici* (homemade spaghetti) with meat sauce and local *pecorino* (sheep's milk) cheese are good choices. The house wine is local, too. *Vicolo Via Nuovo 2 (Via Voltaia), tel. 0578/757335. No reservations. No credit cards. Closed Wed. Inexpensive.*

Pievescola
(Casola d'Elsa)
Dining and Lodging

La Suvera. In this Relais hotel in the Tuscan countryside, 27 kilometers (17 miles) from Siena and 56 kilometers (35 miles) from Florence you can savor living in luxury on an aristocratic family estate once owned by Pope Julius II. Rooms and suites are magnificently furnished with antiques and endowed with up-to-the-minute comforts. With salons, a library, Italian garden, swimming pool, and L'Oliviera restaurant (serving estate wines) to enjoy, guests find it hard to tear themselves away.

Pievescola (Casola d'Elsa), off Rte. 541, tel. 0577/960300, fax 0577/960220. 25 rooms with bath, 10 suites. Facilities: restaurant, bar, park, heated swimming pool, sauna, tennis, riding, heliport, conference rooms. AE, DC, MC, V. Closed Nov. 16– Mar. 14. Expensive.

Pisa
Dining

Bruno. A country-inn look, with beamed ceilings and soft lights, makes Bruno a pleasant place to lunch on classic Tuscan dishes, from *zuppa alla pisana* (vegetable soup) to *baccalà con porri* (cod with leeks). It's just outside the old city walls and only a short walk from the bell tower and cathedral. *Via Luigi Bianchi 12, tel. 050/560818. Reservations advised. AE, DC, MC, V. Closed Mon. dinner, Tues., Aug. 1–20. Moderate.*

Spartaco. Centrally located on the station square, Spartaco has the solid look of the well-established trattoria that it is, with contemporary white chairs contrasting with terra-cotta-tiled walls and some fine antique pieces. It's large, and seating doubles in the summer when tables are set out on the square. Specialties include a cocktail of ravioli in different colors and grilled fish, along with the usual Tuscan dishes. *Piazza Vittorio Emanuele 22, tel. 050/23335. Reservations accepted. AE, DC, MC, V. Closed Sun. Moderate.*

Pistoia
Dining

La Casa degli Amici. The name means "the house of friends," and that's the atmosphere that the two industrious ladies who own it succeed in creating in this restaurant, located outside Pistoia's old walls, on the road toward the A11 autostrada exit. They offer homey specialties, such as ribollita, *pasta e fagioli* (pasta and bean soup), and *coniglio alla Vernaccia* (rabbit in white wine). There's a terrace for outdoor dining in the summer. *Via Bonellina 111, tel. 0573/380305. Reservations advised. AE, DC, MC, V. Closed Tues. and Aug. Moderate.*

Il Duomo. This unpretentious trattoria is practically on Piazza del Duomo, and locals as well as tourists enjoy its typical Tuscan ribollita and *carne in umido* (stewed meats) at very reasonable prices. *Via Bracciolini 5, tel. 0573/31948. Reservations accepted. No credit cards. Closed Sun. Inexpensive.*

Prato
Dining

Stefano. At the lower end of the moderate price range, this trattoria is popular with the locals. A simple place, it serves regional dishes such as ribollita, fagioli laced with local olive oil, and grilled meat. *Via Pomeria 23, tel. 0574/34665. No reservations. No credit cards. Closed Sun. Moderate.*

San Gimignano
Dining

Bel Soggiorno. Bel Soggiorno is attached to a small hotel. It has fine views, refectory tables set with linen and candles, and leather-covered chairs. Specialties are *pappardelle alla lepre* (egg noodles with hare sauce) and herbed grilled meat. *Via San Giovanni 89, tel. 0577/940375. Reservations advised. AE, DC, MC, V. Closed Mon. and Jan. 7–Feb. 7. Moderate.*

Dining and Lodging

Pescille. This rambling stone farmhouse, about 3 kilometers (2 miles) outside San Gimignano, with a good view of the town, has been restored as a hotel and furnished in attractive rustic-chic style. The upscale Cinque Gigli restaurant serves Tuscan specialties such as *zuppe* (soup) and *arrosti* (roasted meats). *Località Pescille, tel. 0577/940186, fax 0577/940186. 40 rooms with bath. Facilities: restaurant (closed Wed.), bar, garden, swimming pool, tennis. AE, DC, MC, V. Moderate.*

Siena
Dining
★

Ai Marsili. Located in a medieval palace near the Duomo, Ai Marsili is a spacious, brick-vaulted wine cellar with refectory tables and excellent Tuscan cuisine; it's a place for a leisurely meal accompanied by classic Chianti wines. Specialties include *pici* (homemade spaghetti) with mushroom sauce, and *piccione* (squab). *Via del Castoro 3, tel. 0577/47154. Reservations advised. AE, DC, MC, V. Closed Mon. Moderate.*

Osteria Le Logge. Just off Piazza del Campo, this is a fine choice for an informal but memorable meal. Get there early to claim a table. Among the specialties are *pennette all'Osteria* (creamy pasta) and *tagliata alla rucola* (sliced steak with arugula). *Via del Porrione 33, tel. 0577/48013. Reservations advised. DC, MC, V. Closed Sun., June 10–23 and Nov. 6–24. Moderate.*

Tullio Tre Cristi. To find this historic trattoria, take Via dei Rossi from Via Banchi di Sopra. Even though it was discovered by tourists long ago, it remains true to typical Sienese cooking and atmosphere. Try *spaghetti alle briciole*, a poor-man's pasta with bread crumbs, tomato, and garlic. *Vicolo di Provenzano 1, tel. 0577/280608. Reservations advised. AE, DC, MC, V. Closed Sun. eve., Mon., and Jan. Moderate.*

Le Tre Campane. Boasting a convenient location between Piazza del Campo and the Duomo, this small trattoria displays the colorful banners of Siena's 17 districts. Popular with the locals, it specializes in Tuscan fare and a *trittico* (trio) of pastas. *Piazzetta Bonelli 5, tel. 0577/286091. Reservations advised. No credit cards. Closed Tues. and Jan.–Feb. Inexpensive.*

Lodging **Certosa di Maggiano.** An easy and attractive walk (less than a mile) southeast of Siena takes you to this old Carthusian monastery, which has been converted into a sophisticated oasis furnished in impeccable style. The bedrooms have every comfort, and the atmosphere is that of an aristocratic family villa. *Strada di Certosa 82, tel. 0577/288180, fax 0577/288189. 14 rooms with bath. Facilities: pool, tennis. AE, DC, MC, V. Closed Dec.–Feb. Very Expensive.*

★ **Park Hotel.** Just outside the walls of the old city, Park Hotel is a handsome 15th-century villa on its own grounds. Furnished in classic Tuscan style, with antiques and luxuriant plants in gleaming copper planters on highly polished terra-cotta floors, it has a simple but sophisticated ambience, in which you can pretend you're a house guest of the Medicis. There's a fine restaurant and garden terrace. *Via di Marciano 18, tel. 0577/44803, fax 0577/49020. 69 rooms with bath. Facilities: restaurant, garden terrace, pool, tennis. AE, DC, MC, V. Very Expensive.*

Chiusarelli. A handy location near a parking area and the long-distance bus terminal make this a good choice, and it is only a 10-minute walk from the main sights. In a well-kept neoclassic villa complete with caryatids, Chiusarelli has functional rooms that are airy and reasonably quiet. There is a small garden and a restaurant. *Viale Curtatone 9, tel. 0577/280562, fax 0577/271177. 50 rooms with bath. MC, V. Moderate.*

★ **Santa Caterina.** This Siena hotel opened in 1986 in a totally renovated and air-conditioned town house, a few steps from Porta Romana and a 10-minute walk from the cathedral. It's decorated in classic Tuscan style, with light walls and dark wood furniture. The bedrooms are cheery, with floral prints, and two have the original frescoed ceilings. The hotel has a pretty garden and a small parking area. *Via Piccolomini 7, tel. 0577/221105, fax 0577/271087. 19 rooms with bath. AE, DC, MC, V. Closed mid-Nov.–mid-Mar. Moderate.*

Milan

Arriving and Departing

As Lombardy's capital and the most important financial and commercial center in northern Italy, Milan is well connected with Rome and Florence by fast and frequent rail and air service, though the latter is often delayed in winter by heavy fog.

By Plane Linate Airport, 11 kilometers (7 miles) outside Milan, handles mainly domestic and European flights (tel. 02/7485–2200). Malpensa, 50 kilometers (30 miles) from the city, handles intercontinental flights (tel. 02/7485–2200).

Between the Airport and Downtown Buses connect both airports with Milan, stopping at the central station and at the Porta Garibaldi station. Fare from Linate is 3,000 lire on the special airport bus or 1,100 lire on municipal bus no. 73 (to Piazza San Babila); from Malpensa 10,000 lire. A taxi from Linate to the center of Milan costs about 20,000 lire, from Malpensa about 100,000 lire.

By Train The main train terminal is the central station in Piazzale Duca d'Aosta (tel. 02/67500). Several smaller stations handle commuter trains. There are several fast Intercity trains daily between Rome and Milan, stopping in Florence. A nonstop Intercity leaves from Rome or Milan morning and evening, taking about four hours to go between the two cities.

By Car From Rome and Florence, take the A1 Autostrada. From Venice, take the A4. With bans on parking throughout the center of Milan, it's easier to park on the outskirts and use public transportation.

Getting Around

By Subway Milan's subway network, the Metropolitana, is modern, fast, and easy to use. "MM" signs mark Metropolitana stations. There are at present three lines. The ATM (city transport authority) has an information office on the mezzanine of the Duomo Metro station (tel. 02/875495). Tickets are sold at newsstands at every stop, and in ticket machines *for exact change only*. The fare is 1,100 lire, and the subway runs from 6:20 AM to midnight.

By Bus and Streetcar Buy tickets at newsstands, tobacco shops, and bars. Fare is 1,100 lire. One ticket is valid for 75 minutes on all surface lines, and one subway trip. Daily tickets valid for 24 hours on all public transportation lines are on sale at the Duomo Metro station ATM Information Office, and at Stazione Centrale Metro station.

By Taxi Use yellow cabs only. They wait at stands or can be telephoned in advance (tel. 6767, 8585, or 8388).

Guided Tours

City Tours Three-hour morning or afternoon sightseeing tours depart from Piazzetta Reale, next to the Duomo; the cost is about 50,000 lire and tickets can be purchased at some travel agencies or aboard the bus.

Excursions From April to September the **Autostradale** bus company (Via Pompeo Marchesi 55, tel. 02/4820–3177) and **Autostradale-Viaggi** (Piazza Castello 1, tel. 02/801161) offer an all-day tour of Lake Maggiore, including a boat trip to the Borromean Islands and lunch. The cost is about 105,000 lire.

Personalized Tours Arrange for guide service and interpreters through the **Centro Guide Turistiche** (Via Marconi 1, tel. 02/863210).

Tourist Information

APT information offices (Via Marconi 1, tel. 02/809662; Central Station, tel. 02/669–0432). **Municipal Information Office** (Galleria Vittorio Emanuele at the corner of Piazza della Scala, tel. 02/870545).

Exploring Milan

Numbers in the margin correspond to points of interest on the Milan map.

The center of Milan is the Piazza del Duomo. The massive **Duomo** is one of the largest churches in the world, a mountain of marble fretted with statues, spires, and flying buttresses. The interior is a more solemn Italian Gothic. Take the elevator or walk up 158 steps to the roof, from which—if it's a clear day—you can see over the city to the Lombard plain and the Alps beyond, all through an amazing array of spires and statues. The **Madonnina**, a gleaming gilt statue on the highest spire, is a Milan landmark. *Entrance to elevator and stairway outside the cathedral, to the right. Admission: stairs, 3,000 lire; elevator, 5,000 lire. Open Mar.–Oct., daily 9–5:45; Nov.–Feb. 9–4:15.*

Outside the cathedral to the right is the elegant, glass-roofed **Galleria,** where the Milanese and visitors stroll, window-shop, and sip pricey cappuccinos at trendy cafés. At the other end of the Galleria is **Piazza della Scala,** with Milan's city hall on one side and **Teatro alla Scala,** the world-famous opera house, opposite.

Via Verdi, flanking the opera house, leads to Via Brera, where the **Pinacoteca di Brera** houses one of Italy's great collections of paintings. Most are of a religious nature, confiscated in the 19th century when many religious orders were suppressed and their churches closed. *Via Brera 28, tel. 02/864–63501. Admission: 8,000 lire. Open Tues.–Sat. 9–5:30, Sun. 9–1.*

Time Out A pleasant café with tables outdoors in fair weather is open to Brera visitors, just inside the entrance to the gallery.

After an eyeful of artworks by Mantegna, Raphael, and many other Italian masters, explore the Brera neighborhood, dotted with art galleries, chic little restaurants, and such offbeat cafés as the **Jamaica** (Via Brera 26), once a bohemian hangout. Take Via dei Fiori Chiari in front of the Brera and keep going in the same direction to the moated **Castello Sforzesco,** a somewhat sinister 19th-century reconstruction of the imposing 15th-century fortress built by the Sforzas, who succeeded the Viscontis as lords of Milan in the 15th century. It now houses wide-ranging collections of sculptures, antiques, and ceramics, including Michelangelo's *Rondanini Pietà*, his last work, left

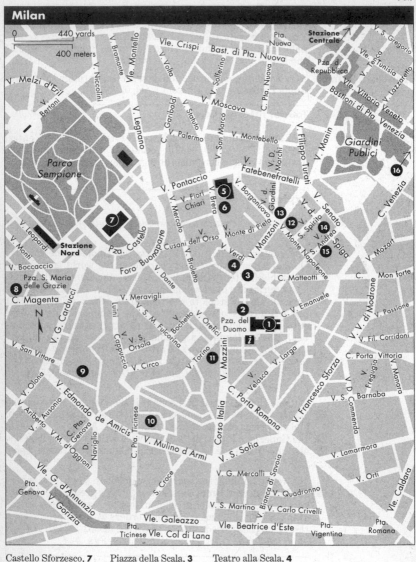

Milan

0 — 440 yards
400 meters

Castello Sforzesco, **7**
Corso Buenos Aires, **16**
Duomo, **1**
Galleria, **2**
Jamaica, **6**

Piazza della Scala, **3**
Pinacoteca di Brera, **5**
San Lorenzo Maggiore, **10**
San Satiro, **11**
Santa Maria delle Grazie, **8**
Sant'Ambrogio, **9**

Teatro alla Scala, **4**
Via Manzoni, **13**
Via Monte Napoleone, **12**
Via Sant'Andrea, **15**
Via della Spiga, **14**

unfinished at his death. *Piazza Castello, tel. 02/6236 ext. 3947. Admission free. Open daily 9:30–5:30; closed last Tues. of month.*

From the vast residence of the Sforzas it's not far to the church
8 of **Santa Maria delle Grazie.** Although portions of the church were designed by Bramante, it plays second fiddle to the **Refectory** next door, where, over a three-year period, Leonardo da Vinci painted his megafamous fresco, *The Last Supper.* The fresco has suffered more than its share of disaster, beginning with the experiments of the artist, who used untested pigments that soon began to deteriorate. *The Last Supper* is now a mere shadow of its former self, despite meticulous restoration that proceeds at a snail's pace. To save what is left, visitors are limited in time and number, and you may have to wait in line to get a glimpse of this world-famous work. *Piazza Santa Maria delle Grazie 2, tel. 02/498–7588. Admission: 6,000 lire. Open Tues.–Sun. 9–1:15. (Hours may vary; check locally.)*

If you are interested in medieval architecture, go to see the
9 medieval church of **Sant'Ambrogio** (Piazza Sant'Ambrogio). Consecrated by St. Ambrose in AD 387, it's the model for all Lombard Romanesque churches, and contains some ancient works of art, including a remarkable 9th-century altar in precious metals and enamels, and some 5th-century mosaics. On December 7, the feast day of St. Ambrose, the streets around the church are the scene of a lively flea market. Another note-
10 worthy church is **San Lorenzo Maggiore** (Corso di Porta Ticinese), with 16 ancient Roman columns in front and some 4th-century mosaics in the Chapel of St. Aquilinus. Closer to
11 Piazza del Duomo on Via Torino, the church of **San Satiro** is another architectural gem in which Bramante's perfect command of proportion and perspective, a characteristic of the Renaissance, made a small interior seem extraordinarily spacious and airy.

Time Out Stop in at the **Peck** shops a few steps from San Satiro. One is a gourmet delicatessen; another has a tempting array of snacks to eat on the premises. *Via Spadari 9; Via Cantù 3.*

12 Now head for Milan's most elegant shopping streets: **Via Monte**
13 14 15 **Napoleone, Via Manzoni, Via della Spiga,** and **Via Sant'Andrea.** The **Café Cova** (Via Monte Napoleone 8) is famous for its pastries; Hemingway loved them. And the **Sant'Ambroeus,** not far away, is the epitome of a genteel tearoom (Corso Matteotti 7). If the chic goods of this area are a shock to your purse, make
16 your way to **Corso Buenos Aires,** near the central station, which has hundreds more shops and accessible prices, too.

Dining

For details and price-category definitions, *see* Dining in Staying in Italy.

Expensive **Biffi Scala.** The elegant Biffi Scala caters mainly to the after-opera crowd that pours in around midnight. Built in 1861, it features a high ceiling and polished wood walls. Specialties include *crespelle alle erbette* (pancakes stuffed with wild mushrooms and other vegetables) and *carpaccio alla Biffi Scala* (thin slices of cured raw beef with a tangy sauce). *Piazza della Scala, tel. 02/866651. Dinner reservations required, especially after the* *opera. AE, DC, MC, V. Closed Sun., Aug. 10–20, and Dec. 24–Jan. 6.*

★ **Boeucc.** Milan's oldest restaurant is situated not far from La Scala and is subtly lighted, with fluted columns, chandeliers, thick carpet, and a garden for warm-weather dining. In addition to the typical Milanese foods, it also serves such exotica as *penne al branzino e zucchine* (pasta with sea bass and zucchini sauce) and *gelato di castagne con zabaglione caldo* (chestnut ice cream with hot zabaglione). *Piazza Belgioioso 2, tel. 02/760–20224. Reservations required. AE. Closed Sat., Sun. lunch, and Aug.*

Don Lisander. This 17th-century chapel has been drastically redecorated, and now features designer lighting, abstract prints, and a modern terra-cotta tile floor, creating an uncompromisingly contemporary effect. Try the *scaloppe di fegato con menta* (calf's-liver scaloppine with fresh mint leaves) or else go for the *branzino al timo* (sea bass with thyme). *Via Manzoni 12A, tel. 02/760–20130. Reservations required. AE, DC, MC, V. Closed Sat. dinner, Sun., 2 weeks in mid-Aug., and 2 weeks at Christmas.*

Giannino. You'll find great character and style at this roomy, old-fashioned restaurant, with oak beams, stained-glass windows, and a huge lobster aquarium. If it's on the menu, be daring and try the *dadolata di capriolo* (venison in cream sauce) or *quaglie con risotto* (quails with rice). *Via A. Sciesa 8, tel. 02/551–95025. Dinner reservations required. AE, DC, MC, V. Closed Sun., Aug.*

Gualtiero Marchesi. Owner Gualtiero Marchesi has written several books on *nuova cucina* (nouvelle cuisine). Your eye, as well as your taste buds, should relish his spaghetti salad with caviar and chives or the *costata di manzo bollita alle piccole verdure* (thinly sliced boiled pork with steamed vegetables). Portions are minuscule. *Via Bonvesin de la Riva 9, tel. 02/741246. Reservations advised. AE, DC, MC, V. Closed Sun., Mon. lunch, Aug., and holidays.*

★ **Savini.** Red carpets and cut-glass chandeliers characterize the classy Savini, a typical, Old World Milanese restaurant whose dining rooms spread over three floors. There's also a "winter garden" from which patrons can people-watch shoppers in the Galleria. The *risotto al salto* (rice cooked as a pancake, tossed in the pan, a Milanese specialty) is excellent here, as is the *costoletta di vitello* (breaded veal cutlets). *Galleria Vittorio Emanuele, tel. 02/720–03433. Dinner reservations advised. AE, DC, MC, V. Closed Sun., 3 weeks in Aug., and 2 weeks at Christmas.*

Moderate **Antica Brasera Meneghina.** A huge fireplace, ornate mirrors,
★ black-and-white tiled floor, and bentwood chairs lend this restaurant a 17th-century air, while the long garden, shaded by a 450-year-old wisteria and containing fig trees, fountains, and frescoes, make it absolutely delightful in the summer. The menu features typical Milanese dishes such as *rustin negàa* (veal cooked in white wine with ham, bacon, sage, and rosemary) and *cassoeula* (casserole of pork, sausage, and cabbage). *Via Circo 10, tel. 02/808108. Winter reservations advised. AE, DC, MC, V. Closed Mon., Aug.*

Antica Trattoria Milanese. In the business district near the Castello Sforzesco, this small, family-run trattoria is crowded with white-collar workers at lunch and regulars at dinner, when lingering is allowed. With a name like this, the cuisine could be nothing but Milanese, with classic risotto and *cotoletta alla Milanese* at the head of the list. *Via Camperio 21, tel. 02/ 864–62333. No reservations. No credit cards. Closed Sun. and Aug.*

★ **Tencitt.** This ultra chic restaurant is decorated in stark black and white, with suffused wall lighting and a striped tent effect on the ceiling. Dishes that sit well with the professional/academic clientele (it's near the university) are the *risotto con zucche e scampi* (rice with squash and shrimp) and the *storione all'erba e cipolline* (sturgeon with herbs and spring onions). *Via Laghetto 2, tel. 02/795560. Reservations required. AE, DC, MC, V. Closed Sat. lunch, Sun., Aug.*

Inexpensive **Al Cantinone.** Operagoers still come to the Cantinone bar for a drink after the final curtain, just as they did a century ago. The decor is basic, the atmosphere lively, the service fast, and the food reliable. The proprietor stocks 240 different wines. Try the *costolette al Cantinone* (veal cutlets with mushrooms, olives, and a cream and tomato sauce). *Via Agnello 19, tel. 02/ 807666. Reservations advised. AE, MC, V. Closed Sat. lunch, Sun., Aug., Christmas, and Easter.*

Birreria-Bistro San Tomaso. A popular lunch spot for trendy Milanese, this place has the informal atmosphere of an old beer hall. At the self-service counter you can have a salad made to order, a cheese platter, or other light fare. It's usually quieter at night, and the kitchen stays open until 1 AM. *Via San Tomaso 5, tel. 02/874510. Reservations advised in evening. No credit cards. Closed Sun.*

La Bruschetta. A winning partnership of Tuscans and Neapolitans runs this tiny, busy, and first-class pizzeria near the Duomo. It features the obligatory wood-burning stove, so you can watch your pizza being cooked, though there are plenty of other dishes to choose from as well—try the *spaghetti alle cozze e vongole* (spaghetti with clams and mussels). *Piazza Beccaria 12, tel. 02/802494. Reservations advised, but service is so fast you don't have to wait long. No credit cards. Closed Mon., 3 weeks in Aug, a few days at Christmas and Easter.*

La Piazzetta. A popular lunch spot in the Brera quarter, it's usually crowded with journalists, actors, and politicians. There's a salad bar, but you'll find hot dishes, too, such as the typically Milanese *ossobuco con risotto* (braised veal shanks with white wine and tomato). *Via Solferino 25, tel. 02/659– 1076. No reservations. No credit cards. Closed Sun., Easter, and Aug.*

Lodging

Make reservations well in advance, particularly when trade fairs are on, which can be most of the year except for August (when many hotels close) and mid-December to mid-January. March and October are months with the highest concentration of fairs, and it's virtually impossible to find a room at this time. Should you arrive without reservations, there's a booking service at Via Palestro 24 (tel. 02/782072).

For details and price-category definitions, *see* Lodging in Staying in Italy.

Very Expensive **Duomo.** Just 20 yards from the cathedral, this hotel's first-, ★ second-, and third-floor rooms all look out onto the church's Gothic gargoyles and pinnacles. The rooms are spacious and snappily furnished in contemporary style. *Via San Raffaele 1, tel. 02/8833, fax 02/864-62027. 160 rooms with bath. Facilities: restaurant, bar. AE, MC, V. Closed Aug.*

Excelsior Gallia. This vast circa-1930 mock-Victorian hotel is located near the central station. In 1992 it emerged from a major renovation that gave it all-new decor and up-to-the-minute comforts. *Piazza Duca d'Aosta 9, tel. 02/6785, fax 02/667-13239. 260 rooms with bath. Facilities: sauna, Turkish bath, health club, restaurant. AE, DC, MC, V.*

Galileo. In spite of its location on busy Corso Europa, this hotel is surprisingly quiet. The rooms have chic designer lighting, tartan carpets, and original modern prints on the walls. The bathrooms are particularly grand, with two basins each. *Corso Europa 9, tel. 02/7743, fax 02/760-20584. 76 rooms with bath. AE, DC, MC, V.*

Pierre. No expense was spared to furnish each room of this luxury hotel in a different style, using the most elegant fabrics and an assortment of modern and antique furniture. Electronic gadgetry is rife: You can open the curtains, turn off the lights, and who knows what else, merely by pressing buttons on a remote-control dial. The Pierre is located near the medieval church of Sant'Ambrogio. *Via De Amicis 32, tel. 02/720-00581, fax 02/805-2157. 47 rooms with bath. Facilities: restaurant, bar. AE, DC, MC, V.*

Principe di Savoia. The most fashionable and glitzy hotel in Milan is the Principe di Savoia. This is where fashion buyers and expense-account businesspeople stay. Dark wood paneling and period furniture, brass lamps, and a stucco lobby are all reminiscent of early 1900s Europe. *Piazza della Repubblica 17, tel. 02/6230, fax 02/659-5838. 287 rooms with bath. Facilities: restaurant, bar. AE, DC, MC, V.*

Expensive   **Carlton-Senato.** Visitors who intend to spend lots of time shopping in nearby high-fashion streets (Via della Spiga, Via Sant'Andrea, and Via Monte Napoleone) will find this place ideally located. The atmosphere is very light and airy, and there are lots of little touches (such as complimentary chocolates and liqueurs in the rooms) to make up for the rather functional room furnishings. *Via Senato 5, tel. 02/760-15535. Fax 02/783-300. 79 rooms with bath. Facilities: restaurant, bar, garage. AE, MC, V. Closed Aug.*

Moderate   **Canada.** This friendly, small hotel is close to Piazza del Duomo on the edge of a district full of shops and restaurants. Recently renovated, it offers good value; all rooms have TV, air-conditioning, and fridge bar. *Via Santa Sofia 16, tel. 02/583-04844, fax 02/583-00282. 35 rooms with bath. AE, DC, MC, V.*

Centro. The fragments of a Roman column and bust in the entrance lead you to expect something more old-fashioned and classier than is the case: The rooms are decorated in 1960s modern, with floral wallpaper and bare wood floors. Avoid rooms on the Via Broletto side—cars rumbling over cobblestones sound like thunder. *Via Broletto 46, tel. 02/875232, fax 02/875578. 54 rooms with bath. Facilities: bar, coffee shop. AE, DC, MC, V.*

Gritti. This bright, clean hotel has a cheerful atmosphere. Rooms are adequate, with picturesque views from the upper floors over the tiled roofs to the gilt Madonnina on top of the Duomo, only a few hundred yards away. *Piazza Santa Maria Beltrade (north end of Via Torino), tel. 02/801056, fax 02/890-10999. 48 rooms with bath. AE, DC, MC, V.*

King. Within easy walking distance of Leonardo's *Last Supper* at Santa Maria delle Grazie, the King has high ceilings and an imposing mock–Louis XV lobby. Built in 1966, it is decorated in pseudo-antique style, with aptly regal red rugs, armchairs, and bedsteads. *Corso Magenta 19, tel. 02/874432, fax 02/890–10798. 48 rooms, 44 with bath. AE, MC, V.*

Inexpensive **London.** Close to the Duomo, the London has clean, good-size, simply furnished rooms and an English-speaking staff. It also has an arrangement with the Opera Prima restaurant in the same building, where guests may take their meals if they wish. *Via Rovello 3, tel. 02/720–20166, fax 02/805–7037. 29 rooms with shower. MC, V. Closed Dec. 25–Jan. 3, Aug.*

San Francisco. In a residential area between the central station and the university, this medium-size pension is handy to subway and bus lines. It also has the advantages of a friendly management, rooms that are bright and clean, and a charming garden. *Viale Lombardia 55, tel. 02/236–1009, fax 02/266–80377. 31 rooms with bath or shower. AE, DC, MC, V.*

The Arts

The most famous spectacle in Milan is the one at **La Scala,** which presents some of the world's most impressive operatic productions. The house is invariably sold out in advance; ask at your hotel whether tickets can be found for you. You can book in advance by mail or fax (0039-2-8879297). You can also book tickets at CIT travel agencies elsewhere in Italy and in foreign countries, but no more than 10 days before the performance. The opera season begins early in December and ends in May. The concert season runs from May to the end of June and from September through November. There is a brief ballet season in September. Programs are available at principal travel agencies and tourist information offices in Italy and abroad. *Box Office, Teatro alla Scala, Piazza della Scala, tel. 02/809126. Open daily noon–7, noon–8:15 on performance days. Closed national holidays and July 28–Aug. 28.*

Venice

Arriving and Departing

By Plane Marco Polo International Airport is situated about 10 kilometers (6 miles) northeast of the city on the mainland. For flight information, tel. 041/661262.

Between the Airport and Downtown Blue ATVO buses make the 25-minute trip in to Piazzale Roma, where the road terminates at Venice; the cost is around 5,000 lire. From Piazzale Roma visitors will most likely have to take a *vaporetto* (water bus) to their hotel (*see* Getting Around, *below*). The Cooperative San Marco motor launch (fare 15,000 lire) can be a more convenient way to reach the city, depending on where your hotel is located. It runs from the airport, via the Lido, dropping passengers across the lagoon at Piazza San Marco. (It works on a limited schedule in winter.) Land taxis are available, running the same route as the buses; the cost is about 45,000 lire. Water taxis (slick high-power motorboats) are very expensive: Negotiate the fare in advance, usually upward of 100,000 lire (the official scale of tariffs is published in the "Guest in Venice" booklet; *see* The Arts, *below*).

By Train Make sure your train goes all the way to Santa Lucia train station in Venice's northwest corner; some trains leave passengers at the Mestre station on the mainland. All trains traveling to and from Santa Lucia stop at Mestre, so to get from Mestre to Santa Lucia, or vice versa, (a journey of about 10 minutes), take the first available train. The APT information booth (tel. 041/719078, open daily 8–8) and the baggage depot in the station are usually festooned with long lines of tourists. If you need a hotel room, go to the AVA hotel association desk (open Apr.–Oct., daily 8 AM–10 PM; Nov.–Mar., daily 8 AM–9:30 PM); there are others at the airport and at the city garage at Piazzale Roma. The deposit (15,000 lire–60,000 lire, depending on the hotel category) is discounted on your hotel bill. Vaporetto landing stages are directly outside the station. *Make sure you know how to get to your hotel before you arrive.* Don't take water taxis, since they are expensive and probably can't take you right to the door of your hotel. By water taxi or vaporetto you'll have to walk some distance anyway. For this reason, try to obtain a map of Venice before you arrive—and take a luggage cart; porters are not always available, and rates are quite high (15,000 lire for one bag and about 5,000 lire for each additional piece of luggage).

By Car If you bring a car to Venice, you will have to pay for a garage or parking space during your stay. Beware of illegal touts who will try to flag you down and offer to arrange parking and hotels. Parking at Piazzale Roma (run by the municipality) costs about 13,000 lire–23,000 lire per day, depending on the size of the car. Parking at the Tronchetto parking area (privately run) costs around 30,000 lire per day under cover, and 18,000 outside. The Venetian Hoteliers Association (AVA) has arranged a discount of around 40% for hotel guests who use the official Tronchetto parking facility. Ask for a voucher on checking into your hotel. Present the voucher at Tronchetto when you pay the parking fee.

There is a vaporetto (presently number 34) from Tronchetto to Piazzale Roma and Piazza San Marco. (In thick fog or when tides are extreme, a bus runs instead to Piazzale Roma, where you can pick up a vaporetto.) Avoid taking private boats—they are a rip-off.

Getting Around

First-time visitors find that getting around Venice presents some unusual problems: the complexity of its layout (the city is made up of more than 100 islands, all linked by bridges); the bewildering unfamiliarity of waterborne transportation; the apparently illogical house numbering system and duplication of street names in its six districts; and the necessity of walking whether you enjoy it or not. It's essential to have a good map showing all street names and water bus routes; buy one at any newsstand.

By Vaporetto ACTV water buses run the length of the Grand Canal and circle the city. There are several lines, some of which connect Venice with the major and minor islands in the lagoon; Line 1 is the Grand Canal local. Timetables are posted on all landing stages where ticket booths are located (open early morning–9 PM). Buy single tickets or books of 10 (the tickets need to be stamped in the automatic machine on the landing stage). The fare is 2,200 lire on most lines, 3,300 lire for the Line 2 express between the train station, Rialto, San Marco, and the Lido. A 24-hour tourist ticket costs 12,000 lire while a three-day ticket costs 18,000 lire; these are not valid on Line 2, but can be especially worthwhile if you are planning to visit the islands (*see* Excursions in Guided Tours, *below*). Vaporetti run every 10–20 minutes during the day; Lines 1 and 2 run more or less every hour between midnight and dawn. Landing stages are clearly marked with name and line number. Check before boarding to make sure the boat is going in your direction.

By Water Taxi Known as *motoscafi*, or *taxi*, these are excessively expensive, and the fare system is as complex as Venice's layout. A minimum fare of about 40,000 lire gets you nowhere, and you'll pay three times as much to get from one end of the Grand Canal to the other. *Always agree on the fare before starting out.* It's probably worth considering taking a water taxi only if you are traveling in a small group.

By Traghetto Few tourists know about the two-man gondolas that ferry people across the Grand Canal at various fixed points. It's the cheapest and shortest gondola ride in Venice, and it can save a lot of walking. The fare is 500 lire, which you hand to one of the gondoliers when you get on. Look for "Traghetto" signs.

By Gondola Don't leave Venice without treating yourself to a gondola ride, preferably in the quiet of the evening when the churning traffic on the canals has died down, the palace windows are illuminated, and the only sounds are the muted splashes of the gondolier's oar. Make sure he understands that you want to see the *rii*, or smaller canals, as well as the Grand Canal. There's supposed to be a fixed minimum rate of about 70,000 lire for 50 minutes. (Official tariffs are quoted in the "Guest in Venice" booklet; *see* The Arts, *below*.) Come to terms with your gondolier *before* stepping into his boat.

On Foot This is the only way to reach many parts of Venice, so wear comfortable shoes. Invest in a good map that names all the streets, and count on getting lost more than once.

Important Addresses and Numbers

Tourist Information The main Venice **APT Tourist Office** (tel. 041/522–6356) is at Calle dell'Ascensione 71C, just off Piazza San Marco, under the arcade in the far left corner opposite the basilica. Open Mon.– Sat., Nov.–Mar., 8:30–1:30; Apr.–Oct., 8:30–7:30. There are APT information booths at the Santa Lucia station (tel. 041/719078) and on the Lido (Gran Viale S.M. Elisabetta 6A, tel. 041/526–5721, fax 041/529–8720).

Consulates U.K. (Campo Santa Maria della Carità 1051, Dorsoduro, tel. 041/522–7207). U.S. (The nearest U.S. Consulate is in Milan, at Largo Donegani 1, tel. 02/652841).

Emergencies Police (tel. 113). **Ambulance** (tel. 041/523–0000). **Doctor:** Try the emergency room at Venice's hospital (tel. 041/523–0000), or call the British Consulate (*see above*) and ask for recommendations. **Pharmacies: Farmacia Italo-Inglese** (Calle della Mandola, tel. 041/522–4837); **Farmacia Internazionale** (Calle Larga XXII Marzo, tel. 041/522–2311). Pharmacies are open weekdays 9–12:30 and 4–7:45; Saturday 9–12:45; Sunday and night service by turns, with details posted outside every chemist, or available by dialing tel. 192.

Travel Agencies **American Express** (San Moisè 1471, tel. 041/520–0844). **Wagons-Lits Travel** (Piazzetta dei Leoncini 289, tel. 041/522–3405).

Guided Tours

Orientation Tours **American Express** and other operators offer two-hour walking tours of the San Marco area, taking in the basilica and the Doge's Palace. The cost is about 30,000 lire. American Express also has an afternoon walking tour from April to October that ends with a gondola ride. The cost is about 35,000 lire.

Special-Interest Tours Some tour operators offer group gondola rides with serenade. The cost is about 35,000 lire. During the summer free guided tours of the Basilica di San Marco are offered by the Patriarchate of Venice; information is available at a desk in the atrium of the church (tel. 041/520–0333). There are several tours daily, except Sunday, and some tours are in English, including one at 11 AM.

Excursions Don't take organized tours to the islands of Murano, Burano, and/or Torcello. These tours are annoyingly commercial and emphasize glass factory showrooms, pressuring you to buy. You can easily do these islands on your own. Boats depart from the landing stages at Fondamente Nuove on the north side of Venice; if you are starting out from the other side of the city, you can take a Murano-bound Line 5, or a Line 5 to the Fondamente Nuove and change. **American Express** offers a bus trip to the Venetian Villas and Padua. The cost is about 75,000 lire, and they run from April to October on Tuesday, Thursday, and weekends.

Personal Guides **American Express** can provide guides for walking or gondola tours of Venice, or cars with driver and guide for excursions on the mainland. Pick up a list of licensed guides and their rates from the **APT** Information Office in Piazza San Marco (tel. 041/522–6356).

Exploring Venice

Venice—La Serenissima, the Most Serene—is disorienting in its complexity, an extraordinary labyrinth of narrow streets and waterways, opening now and again onto some airy square or broad canal. The majority of its magnificent palazzi are slowly crumbling; though this sounds like a recipe for a down-at-the-heels slum, somehow in Venice the shabby, derelict effect is magically transformed into one of supreme beauty and charm, rather than horrible urban decay. The place is romantic, especially at night when the lights from the vaporetti and the stars overhead pick out the gargoyles and arches of the centuries-old facades. For hundreds of years Venice was the unrivaled mistress of trade between Europe and the Orient, and the staunch bulwark of Christendom against the tide of Turkish expansion. Though the power and glory of its days as a wealthy city-republic are gone, the art and exotic aura remain.

To enjoy the city, you will have to come to terms with the crowds of day trippers, who take over the center around San Marco, from May through September. Hot and sultry in the summer, Venice is much more welcoming in early spring and late fall. Romantics like it in the winter when prices are much lower, the streets are often deserted, and the sea mists impart a haunting melancholy to the *campi* (squares) and canals. Piazza San Marco (St. Mark's Square) is the pulse of Venice, but after joining with the crowds to visit the Basilica di San Marco and the Doge's Palace, strike out on your own and just follow where your feet take you—you won't be disappointed.

Numbers in the margin correspond to points of interest on the Venice map.

Piazza San Marco and the Accademia

❶ Even the pigeons have to fight for space on **Piazza San Marco,** the most famous piazza in Venice, and pedestrian traffic jams clog the surrounding byways. Despite the crowds, San Marco is the logical starting place of each of our various itineraries. Pick up pamphlets at the **APT Information Office** in the far left corner of Piazza San Marco, opposite the basilica. The information office is in the wing built by order of Napoleon to complete the much earlier palaces on either side of the square, enclosing it to form what he called "the most beautiful drawing room in all of ❷ Europe." Upstairs is the **Museo Correr,** with eclectic collections of historical objects and a picture gallery of fine 13th–17th-century paintings. *Piazza San Marco, Ala Napoleonica, tel. 041/522–5625. Admission: 5,000 lire. Open Apr.–Oct., Wed.–Mon. 9–7; Nov.–Mar., Wed.–Mon. 9–4.*

❸ The **Basilica di San Marco** (St. Mark's Basilica) was begun in the 11th century to hold the relics of St. Mark the Evangelist, the city's patron saint, and its richly decorated facade is surmounted by copies of the four famous gilded bronze horses (the originals are in the basilica's upstairs museum). Inside, golden mosaics sheathe walls and domes, lending an extraordinarily exotic aura, half Christian church, half Middle Eastern mosque. Be sure to see the **Pala d'Oro,** an eye-filling 10th-century altarpiece in gold and silver, studded with precious gems and enamels. From the atrium, climb the steep stairway to the museum: The bronze horses alone are worth the effort. *The Basilica is open from early morning, but tourist visits are allowed Mon.–Sat. 9:30–5:30, Sun. 2:30–5:30. No admission to those wearing shorts or other revealing clothing. Pala d'Oro and Treasury. Admission: 2,000 lire. Open Mon.–Sat. 10–4, Sun. 1:45–4. Gallery and Museum. Admission: 2,000 lire. Open Apr.–Sept., daily 9:30–5:30; Oct.–Mar., daily 10–4.*

❹ Next to St. Mark's is the **Palazzo Ducale** (Doge's Palace), which, during Venice's prime, was the epicenter of the Serene Republic's great empire. More than just a palace, it was a combination White House, Senate, Supreme Court, torture chamber, and prison. The building's exterior is striking; the lower stories consist of two rows of fragile-seeming arches, while above rests a massive pink-and-white marble wall whose solidity is barely interrupted by its six great Gothic windows. The interior is a maze of vast halls, monumental staircases, secret corridors, state apartments, and the sinister prison cells and torture chamber. The palace is filled with frescoes, paintings, carvings, and a few examples of statuary by some of the Renaissance's greatest artists. Don't miss the famous view from the balcony, overlooking the piazza and St. Mark's Basin and the church of San Giorgio Maggiore across the lagoon. *Piazzetta San Marco, tel. 041/522–4951. Admission: 8,000 lire. Open Apr.–Oct., daily 9–7; Nov.–Mar., daily 9–4.*

❺ For a pigeon's-eye view of Venice take the elevator up to the top of the **Campanile di San Marco** (St. Mark's bell tower) in Piazza San Marco, a reconstruction of the 1,000-year-old tower that

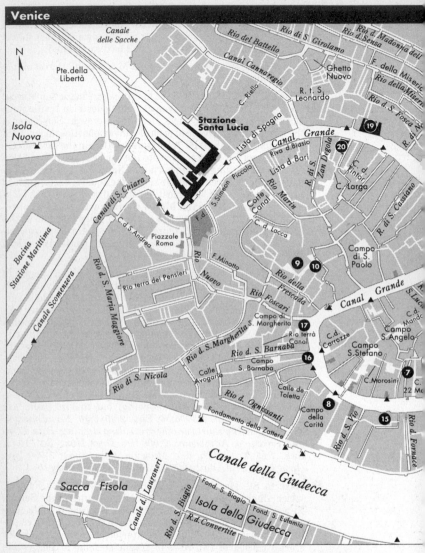

Venice

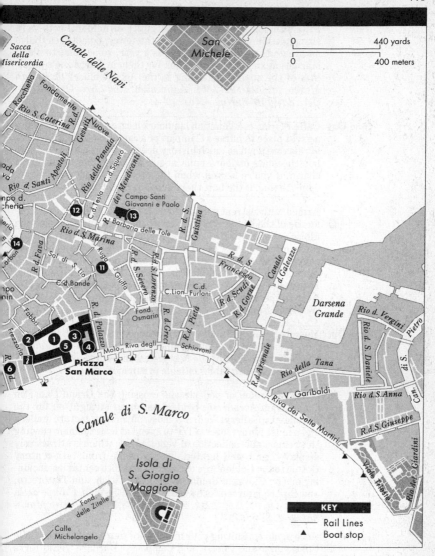

Sacca della Misericordia

Canale delle Navi

San Michele

0   440 yards
0   400 meters

Rocchetta
Fondamente d.
Rio S. Caterina
Gesuiti Nuove

Rio d. Santi Apostoli
Strada
ya
mpo d.
cheria

Rio della Panada
C. d. Squero
C. d. Isla
R. dei Mendicanti

Campo Santi
Giovanni e Paolo

12
13

Rio d. S. Marina
R. Barbaria delle Tole
R. d. S.
Giustina

14
Rio d. Fava
Sal. di S. Lio
R. d.
Ruga
Giuffa
R. d. S. Severo
R. d. S. Lorenzo
C. d. Bande
11
R. d. S.
Francesco
R. d. S.

mpo
nin
Fabbri
R. d. Palazzo
Fond.
Osmarin
R. d. Greci
C. Lion
C. d.
Furlani
R. d. Pietà
R. d. Scudi
R. d. Corna
Canale
d. Galeazze

Darsena
Grande

Rio d. Vergini
Rio d. S. Daniele
Pietro
di S.

2 **1** **3**
5 **4**
Frezzaria
i
6 R. d.
Molo
Riva degli
Schiavoni
R. d. Arsenale
Rio della Tana

Piazza San Marco

V. Garibaldi
Riva dei Sette Martiri
Rio d. S. Anna
R. d. S. Giuseppe
Can.
Rio dei Giardini

Canale di S. Marco

Isola di
S. Giorgio
Maggiore

Fond. delle Zitelle
Calle Michelangelo

Viale Trieste

KEY	
——	Rail Lines
▲	Boat stop

collapsed one morning in 1912, practically without warning. Fifteenth-century clerics found guilty of immoral acts were suspended in wooden cages from the tower, sometimes to live on bread and water for as long as a year, sometimes to die of starvation and exposure. (Look for them in Carpaccio's paintings of the square that hang in the Accademia.) *Piazza San Marco, tel. 041/522–4064. Admission: 4,000 lire. Open Apr.–Oct., daily 10–8; Nov.–Mar. 10–4.*

Time Out   **Caffè Florian** is a Venetian landmark located on the square. It's a great place to nurse a Campari or a cappuccino. The pleasure of relaxing amid so much history does not come cheap. A pot of hot chocolate indoors runs about $6—and there's an extra charge if you're served when the orchestra is playing. If you drink sitting at the bar, there is no service charge.

Armed with a street map, head west out of San Marco (with the facade of the basilica to your back), making your way past **San Moisè**'s elaborate Baroque facade and by the American Express office, on to Calle Larga 22 Marzo. Continue on to the church of **Santa Maria del Giglio**, behind the **Gritti Palace** hotel. Across the bridge behind the church, **Piazzesi** on Campiello Feltrina is famous for its handprinted paper and desk accessories. In the next little square, **Norelene** (Campo San Maurizio 2606) has stunning handprinted fabrics.

Time Out   You must cross yet another bridge to get to Campo Santo Stefano, also known as Campo Morosini, where you can indulge yourself with some of the best ice cream you've ever eaten, at **Paolin**, a bar with tables outside in summer.

Join the stream of pedestrians crossing the Grand Canal on the wooden **Accademia Bridge,** and head straight on for the **Accademia Gallery**, Venice's most important picture gallery and a must for art lovers. Try to spend at least an hour viewing this remarkable collection of Venetian art, which is attractively displayed and well lighted. Works range from 14th-century Gothic to the Golden Age of the 15th and 16th centuries, including oils by Giovanni Bellini, Giorgione, Titian, and Tintoretto, and superb later works by Veronese and Tiepolo. *Campo della Carità, tel. 041/522–2247. Admission: 8,000 lire. Open Mon.–Sat. 9–2, Sun. 9–1.*

Once again consulting your map, make your way through Calle Contarini, Calle Toletta, and Campo San Barnaba to Rio Terra Canal, where **Mondonovo** ranks as one of the city's most interesting mask shops (Venetians, who originated Italy's most splendid carnival, love masks of all kinds, from gilded lions to painted sun faces and sinister death's heads). Just around the corner is Campo Santa Margherita, which has a homey feel.

Continue past Campo San Pantalon to Campo San Rocco, just beside the immense church of the Frari. In the 1500s, Tintoretto embellished the **Scuola di San Rocco** with more than 50 canvases; they are an impressive sight, dark paintings aglow with figures hurtling dramatically through space amid flashes of light and color. *The Crucifixion* in the Albergo (the room just off the great hall) is held to be his masterpiece. *Campo di San Rocco, tel. 041/523–4864. Admission: 6,000 lire. Open weekdays 10–1, weekends 10–4.*

⑩ The church of Santa Maria Gloriosa dei Frari (known simply as the **Frari**) is one of Venice's most important churches, a vast soaring Gothic building of brick. Since it is the principal church of the Franciscans, its design is suitably austere to reflect that order's vows of poverty, though paradoxically it contains a number of the most sumptuous pictures in any Venetian church. Chief among them are the magnificent Titian altarpiece, the immense *Assumption of the Virgin* over the main altar. Titian was buried here at the ripe old age of 88, the only one of 70,000 plague victims to be given a personal church burial. *Campo dei Frari. Admission: 1,000 lire. Open Apr.–Oct., Mon.–Sat. 9–noon and 2:30–6, Sun. 3–6; Nov.–Mar., Mon.–Sat. 9:30–noon and 3–5:30, Sun. 3–5:30.*

San Zanipolo and the Rialto Backtracking once again to Piazza San Marco, go to the arch under the Torre dell'Orologio (Clock Tower) and head northeast into the **Merceria,** one of Venice's busiest streets and, with the **Frezzeria** and **Calle dei Fabbri,** part of the shopping area that extends across the Grand Canal into the **Rialto district.** At Campo San Zulian, turn right into Calle della Guerra and Calle **⑪** delle Bande to the graceful white marble church of **Santa Maria Formosa;** it's situated right on a lively square (of the same name) with a few sidewalk cafés and a small vegetable market on weekday mornings.

Use your map to follow Calle Borgoloco into Campo San Marina, where you turn right, cross the little canal, and take Calle **⑫** Castelli to **Santa Maria dei Miracoli** (Campo dei Miracoli). Perfectly proportioned and sheathed in marble, this late-15th-century building embodies all the classical serenity of the early Renaissance. The interior is decorated with marble reliefs by the church's architect, Pietro Lombardo, and his son Tullio.

Retrace your steps along Calle Castelli and cross the bridge into Calle delle Erbe, following signs for "SS. Giovanni e Paolo." The massive Dominican church of Santi Giovanni e **⑬** Paolo—**San Zanipolo,** as it's known in the slurred Venetian dialect—is the twin (and rival) of the Franciscan Frari. The church is a kind of pantheon of the doges (25 are buried here), and contains a wealth of artworks. Outside in the campo stands Verrocchio's equestrian statue of Colleoni, who fought for the Venetian cause in the mid-1400s.

Cross the canal in front of the church, and continue along Calle Larga Giacinto Gallina, crossing a pair of bridges to Campiello Santa Maria Nova. Take Salizzada San Canciano to Salizzada San Giovanni Crisostomo to find yourself once again in the **⑭** mainstream of pedestrians winding their way to the **Rialto Bridge.** Street stalls hung with scarves and gondolier's hats signal that you are entering the heart of Venice's shopping district. Cross over the bridge, and you'll find yourself on the edge of the famous market. Try to visit the Rialto market when it's in full swing (Tues.–Sat. mornings; Mondays are quiet because the fish market is closed), with fruit and vegetable vendors hawking their wares in a colorful and noisy jumble of sights and sounds. Not far beyond is the fish market, where you'll probably find sea creatures you've never seen before (and possibly won't want to see again). A left turn into Ruga San Giovanni and Ruga del Ravano will bring you face to face with scores of shops: At **La Scialuppa** (Calle Saoneri 2695) you'll find hand-carved wooden models of gondolas and their graceful oar locks known as *forcole*.

The Grand Canal Just off Piazzetta di San Marco (the square in front of the Doge's Palace) you can catch Vaporetto Line 1 at either the San Marco or San Zaccaria landing stages (on Riva degli Schiavoni), to set off on a boat tour along the **Grand Canal.** Serving as Venice's main thoroughfare, the canal winds in the shape of an "S" for more than 3½ kilometers (2 miles) through the heart of the city, past some 200 Gothic-Renaissance palaces. Although restrictions have been introduced to diminish the erosive effect of wash on buildings, this is still the route taken by vaporetti, gondolas, water taxis, mail boats, police boats, fire boats, ambulance boats, barges carrying provisions and building materials, bridal boats, and funeral boats. Your vaporetto tour will give you an idea of the opulent beauty of its palaces and a peek into the side streets and tiny canals where the Venetians go about their daily business. *Vaporetto Line 1. Cost: 2,200 lire.*

Here are some of the key buildings that this tour passes, departing from the San Marco landing: The **Accademia Gallery,** with its fine collection of 14th- to 18th-century Venetian paint-
⑮ ings, that were visited earlier. The **Peggy Guggenheim Museum,** housed in the incomplete Palazzo Venier dei Leoni, has an exceptional modern art collection (*see* Off the Beaten Track, *be-*
⑯ *low*). The **Ca'Rezzonico** was built between the mid-17th and 18th centuries and is now a museum of 18th-century Venetian
⑰ paintings and furniture. **Ca'Foscari** is a 15th-century Gothic building that was once the home of Doge Foscari, who was unwillingly deposed and died the following day! Today it's the
⑱ headquarters of Venice's university. **Ca'd'Oro** is the most flowery palace on the canal; it now houses the Galleria Franchetti.
⑲ The **Palazzo Vendramin Calergi** is a Renaissance building where Wagner died in 1883. It's also the winter home of the mu-
⑳ nicipal casino. The **Fondaco dei Turchi** was an original Byzantine "house-warehouse" of a rich Venetian merchant, but the building suffered some fanciful remodeling during the 19th century. It is now the Natural History Museum.

Off the Beaten Track

Explore the **Ghetto,** where Venice's Jewish community lived in cramped quarters for many centuries, and visit the **Museo Ebraico** (Jewish Museum, Campo del Ghetto Nuovo, tel. 041/715359; admission 4,000 lire, with tour 10,000 lire; open June–Sept., Sun.–Fri. 10–7, Oct.–May, Sun.–Fri. 10–4.) and the Ghetto's several synagogues. In the same area, go to view the Tintorettos in the Gothic church of the **Madonna dell'Orto** (off Fondamenta Madonna dell' Orto).

Visit late heiress Peggy Guggenheim's house and collection of modern art at the **Palazzo Venier dei Leoni** on the Grand Canal. *Entrance: Calle San Cristoforo, Dorsoduro, tel. 041/520–6288. Admission: 7,000 lire, free 6–9 PM on Sat. Open Apr.–Oct., Sun., Mon., Wed.–Fri. 11–6, Sat. 11–9 PM.*

Have an ice cream at one of the cafés on the Zattere and watch the big ships steam slowly down the Giudecca Canal.

Explore the island of San Pietro di Castello, at the end of Via Garibaldi. The Renaissance church of **San Pietro** and its tipsy bell tower stand on a grassy square surrounded by workaday canals and boatyards. San Pietro was Venice's cathedral for centuries (San Marco was officially the Doges' private chapel).

Take Vaporetto Line 20 from Riva degli Schiavoni to visit the Armenian monastery on the island of San Lazzaro degli Armeni, near the Lido. *Tel. 041/526-0104. Donation welcome. Open daily 3-5.*

Shopping

Glass Venetian glass is as famous as the city's gondolas, and almost every shop window displays it. There's a lot of cheap glass for sale; if you want something better, among the top showrooms are **Venini** (Piazzetta dei Leoncini 314), **Pauly** (Calle dell' Ascensione 72, opposite the APT information office), **Salviati** (Piazza San Marco 78 and 110), **Cenedese** (Piazza San Marco 139), and **Isola** (Campo San Moisè and Merceria San Zulian 723). On the island of Murano, where prices are generally no lower than in Venice, **Domus** (Fondamenta dei Vetrai) has a good selection.

Shopping District The main shopping area extends from Piazza San Marco through the Mercerie and Calle dei Fabbri toward the Rialto.

Department Stores The **Coin** store (off Campo San Bartolomeo) specializes in fashion and accessories. **Standa** has stores on Campo San Luca and Strada Nuova, where you can pick up medium-price goods of all kinds.

Dining

Venetians love seafood, which figures prominently on most restaurant menus, sometimes to the exclusion of any meat dishes. However, fish is generally expensive, and you should bear this in mind when ordering: The price given on menus for fish as a main course is often per 100 grams, not the total cost of what you are served, which could be two or three times that amount. This is not sharp practice, but a conventional way of pricing fish in Italy. Venice is not a particularly cheap place to eat, but there are good restaurants huddled along Venice's squares and seemingly endless canals. City specialties include *pasta e fagioli;* (pasta-and-bean soup); risotto and all kinds of seafood; and the delicious *fegato alla veneziana*, thin strips of liver cooked with onions, served with grilled *polenta* (cornmeal cakes).

For details and price-category definitions, *see* Dining in Staying in Italy.

Very Expensive **Grand Canal.** The Hotel Monaco's restaurant is a favorite with Venetians, who enjoy eating on the lovely canal-side terrace in summer, looking across the mouth of the Grand Canal to the island of San Giorgio Maggiore, and in the cozy dining room in winter. All the pasta is made fresh daily on the premises, and the smoked and marinaded salmon are also produced in the restaurant's kitchen. The traditional Venetian dishes are very well prepared; the chef, Angelo Maiocco, also offers delicious meat and fish dishes, such as *Scampi alla Ca'd'Oro* (scampi in cognac sauce, served with rice). *Calle Vallaresso 1325, San Marco, tel. 041/520-0211. Reseverations advised. Jacket advised at dinner. AE, DC, MC, V.*
La Caravella. La Caravella is decorated like the dining saloon of an old Venetian sailing ship, with lots of authentic touches. The menu is long and slightly intimidating, though the highly competent mâitre d' will advise you well. The *granseola* (crab) is

marvelous in any of several versions. (The same kitchen also serves the slightly less expensive **Cortile** restaurant next door, which has a pretty garden court for summer and wood-paneled salons for winter.) *Calle Larga XXII Marzo 2397, San Marco, tel. 041/520–8901. Reservations required. AE, DC, MC, V. Closed Wed. Nov.–Apr.*

Da Fiore. Long a favorite with Venetians, Da Fiore has been discovered by tourists, so reservations are imperative. It's known for its excellent seafood dinners, which might include such specialties as *pasticcio di pesce* (fish pie) and *seppioline* (little cuttlefish). Not easy to find, it's just off Campo San Polo. *Calle dello Scaleter 2202, San Polo, tel. 041/721308. Reservations required. AE, DC, MC, V. Closed Sun., Mon., Aug. 10–early Sept., and Dec. 25–Jan. 15.*

Expensive **Da Arturo.** The tiny Da Arturo is a refreshing change from the numerous seafood restaurants of which Venetians are so fond. The cordial proprietor prefers, instead, to offer antipasti with seasonal vegetables and such meat dishes as the excellent *braciolona di maiale* (pork chop in vinegar). *Calle degli Assassini 3656, San Marco, tel. 041/528–6974. Reservations required. No credit cards. Closed Sun., Aug., and Dec. 20–31.*

Fiaschetteria Toscana. This is one of the city's best restaurants, which is why you'll see so many Venetians in the pleasant upstairs dining room or under the arbor in the square out front. Courteous, cheerful waiters serve such specialties as *rombo* (turbot) with capers and an exceptionally good *pasta alla buranella* (pasta with shrimp, au gratin). *Campo San Giovanni Crisostomo 5719, Cannaregio, tel. 041/528–5281. Reservations advised. AE, DC, MC, V. Closed Tues. and first 2 weeks in July.*

Moderate **Al Mondo Novo.** This excellent fish restaurant is owned by a fish wholesaler in the Rialto market, so you can be sure that everything is absolutely fresh. Specialties prepared by Signora Trevisan, the owner's wife, include *cape sante* (pilgrim scallops) and *cape longhe* (razor clams), risottos and pasta dishes, and charcoal-grilled fish. Meat dishes are also available. The manager, Pino Calliandro, offers set menus on request to suit your taste and pocket, and service continues till midnight or later if there's a demand for it. *Salizzada San Lio 5409, Castello, tel. 041/520–0698. Reservations advised. AE, MC, V. Closed Sun. dinner and Mon. Feb.–Mar.*

Da Gigio. An attractive, friendly, family-run trattoria on the quayside of a canal just off the Strada Nuova. Da Gigio is popular with Venetians and visiting Italians, who appreciate the affable service and excellently cooked, homemade pasta, fish and meat dishes, and high-quality draft wine. Its barroom makes a pleasant, informal setting for simple lunches. *Fondamenta de la Chiesa 3628A, Cannaregio, tel. 041/528–5140. Reservations advised for dinner. AE, DC, MC, V. Closed Sun. dinner, Mon., 2 weeks in mid-Jan., and 2 weeks in Aug.*

Da Ignazio. A smiling waiter will welcome you to this attractive little trattoria in the San Polo district, where you'll find a tempting display of fruits and vegetables fresh from the Rialto market. Specialties include pasta e fagioli and *seppie* (cuttlefish). *Calle dei Saoneri, near San Polo, tel. 041/523–4852. Dinner reservations advised. AE, DC, MC, V. Closed Sat.*

Inexpensive **L'Incontro.** This trattoria has a faithful clientele of Venetians and visitors, attracted by generous meat dishes, friendly waiters, and reasonable prices. Menu choices include juicy steaks, wild duck, boar, and (with advance notice) roast suckling pig. L'Incontro is between San Barnaba and Campo Santa Margherita. *Rio Terra Canal 3062A, Dorsoduro, tel. 041/522–2404. Reservations advised. MC, V. Closed Mon.*

Metropole Buffet. Here at the Hotel Metropole's buffet, in a charming, comfortable room overlooking the waterfront by the Pietà Church, you can eat a substantial and tasty lunch or dinner, helping yourself from a varied selection of starters, soup, pastas, hot and cold fish and meat dishes, and desserts, all for around 40,000 lire. The price even includes a highly drinkable Bianco di Custoza (a light white wine from the Veneto region) on draft. *Riva degli Schiavoni 4149, Castello, tel. 041/520–5044. Reservations advised. AE, DC, MC, V.*

Vino Vino. This is an informal annex of the upscale Antico Martini around the corner, and it's one of the few places where you can eat lightly at almost any time of the day (it's open 10 AM–1 AM). The place has a 1920s look: cream-colored walls covered with small prints and ceramic plates, marble tables, and café chairs. Venetians stop in for snacks and a glass of wine from an impressive assortment. *Calle delle Veste 2007/a (off Campo San Fantin), San Marco, tel. 041/523-7027. No reservations. AE, DC, MC, V. Closed Tues.*

Lodging

Venice is made up almost entirely of time-worn buildings, so it stands to reason that the majority of hotels are in renovated palaces. However, space is at a premium in this city, and even in the best hotels, rooms can be small and with little natural light. Conservation restrictions on buildings often preclude the installation of such amenities as elevators, air-conditioning systems, and satellite dishes (if any of these facilities is of paramount importance to you, check on their availability before booking). So don't come to Venice expecting to find the standard modern hotel room—you will almost certainly be disappointed. On the other hand, Venice's luxury hotels can offer rooms of fabulous opulence and elegance, and even in the more modest hotels you can find comfortable rooms of great charm and character, sometimes with stunning views.

Venice attracts visitors all year round, although the winter months are generally much quieter, and most hotels offer lower rates during this period. It is always worth booking in advance, but if you haven't, the AVA (Venetian Hoteliers Association) desk at the railway station (tel. 041/715016 and 041/715288; open Apr.–Oct., daily 8 AM–10 PM, Nov.–Mar., daily 8 AM–9:30 PM), at the airport (open Apr.–Oct., daily 10–9; Nov.–Mar., daily 10:30–6:30), and at the municipal parking garage at Piazzale Roma (open Apr.–Oct., daily 9 AM–10 PM; Nov.–Mar., daily 9–9) will help you find a room after your arrival in the city.

For details and price-category definitions, *see* Lodging in Staying in Italy.

Very Expensive   **Cipriani.** A sybaritic oasis of stunningly decorated rooms and suites with marble baths and Jacuzzis, the Cipriani is located across St. Mark's Basin on the island of Giudecca (pronounced Joo-DEK-ka), offering a panorama of romantic views of the entire lagoon. The hotel launch whisks guests back and forth to Piazza San Marco at any hour of the day or night. Cooking courses and fitness programs are offered as special programs to occupy the guests. Some rooms have pretty garden patios. The newly restored Palazzo Vendramin annex of the Cipriani (with 7 suites and 3 double rooms) is open all year. *Giudecca 10, tel. 041/520–7744, fax 041/520–3930. 98 rooms with bath. Facilities: pool, gardens, tennis, health club. AE, DC, MC, V. Closed Nov.–mid-Mar.*

Danieli. Parts of this rather large hotel are built around a 15th-century palazzo bathed in sumptuous Venetian colors, though the Danieli also has several modern annexes that some find bland and impersonal, and the lower-price rooms can be exceedingly drab. Still, it's a favorite with celebrities and English-speaking visitors, and the dining terrace does have a fantastic view of St. Mark's Basin. *Riva degli Schiavoni 4196, Castello, tel. 041/522–6480, fax 041/520–0208. 230 rooms with bath. AE, DC, MC, V.*

★ **Gritti Palace.** The atmosphere of an aristocratic private home is what the management is after here, and they succeed beautifully. Fresh flowers, fine antiques, sumptuous appointments, and Old World service make this a terrific choice for anyone who wants to be totally pampered. The dining terrace overlooking the Grand Canal is best in the evening when boat traffic dies down. *Campo Santa Maria del Giglio 2467, San Marco, tel. 041/794611, fax 041/520–0942. 98 rooms with bath. AE, DC, MC, V.*

Expensive **Londra Palace.** You get the obligatory view of San Giorgio and St. Mark's Basin at this distinguished hotel whose rooms are decorated in dark paisley prints, with such sumptuous touches as canopied beds. French chefs preside over Les Deux Lions restaurant, now a haven of *cuisine française*, and the piano bar is open late. The hotel offers a complimentary Mercedes for one-day excursions and free entrance to the casino. *Riva degli Schiavoni 4171, Castello, tel. 041/520–0533, fax 041/522–5032. 69 rooms with bath. Facilities: terrace, solarium. AE, DC, MC, V.*

★ **Metropole.** Guests can step from their water taxi or gondola into the lobby of this small, very well-run hotel, rich in precious antiques, just five minutes from Piazza San Marco. Many rooms have a view of the lagoon, others overlook the garden at the back, but all are furnished with style. *Riva degli Schiavoni 4149, Castello, tel. 041/520–5044, fax 041/522–3679. 72 rooms with bath. Facilities: buffet restaurant (see* Dining, *above), bar. AE, DC, MC, V.*

Moderate **Accademia.** There's plenty of atmosphere and a touch of the ro-
★ mantic in this delightful hotel in a 17th-century villa. Rooms are comfortable and brightly furnished, as are the sitting rooms on the ground floor. Many rooms overlook the gardens, where you can sit in warm weather. *Fondamenta Bollani 1058, Dorsoduro, tel. 041/523–7846, fax 041/523–9152. 27 rooms, most with bath. Facilities: gardens, bar. AE, DC, MC, V.*

Alboretti. Redecorated in 1988, this small hotel is simply but attractively furnished. Despite its size and central location, the Alboretti has a little garden courtyard off the breakfast room and a lounge upstairs from the tiny lobby and bar area. There is no elevator. Together with its moderately priced restaurant, the Alboretti is a good value. *Rio Terra Sant'Agnese 882, Dorsoduro, tel. 041/523–0058, fax 041/521–0158. 19 rooms with bath. Facilities: restaurant. AE, MC, V.*

La Residenza. A Gothic palace makes a delightful setting for this charming hotel, conveniently close to both San Marco and the San Zaccaria landing stage. Breakfast is served in a real antique-furnished Venetian salon. Make reservations well in advance. *Campo Bandiera e Moro 3608, Castello, tel. 041/528–5315, fax 041/523–8859. 19 rooms, some with bath. AE, DC, MC, V. Closed 2nd week Jan.–mid-Feb., mid-Nov.–2nd week Dec.*

Paganelli. This charming, small hotel, located on the waterfront near Piazza San Marco and with an annex on the quiet square of Campo San Zaccaria, is tastefully decorated in the Venetian style. Three rooms overlook the lagoon, and six have good views over the square. *Riva degli Schiavoni 4182, Castello, tel. 041/522–4324, fax 041/523–9267. 22 rooms, 19 with bath or shower. AE, DC, MC, V.*

Inexpensive **Bucintoro.** This friendly, family-run hotel on the waterfront by the Arsenal, slightly off the tourist track, is the only hotel in Venice where every room has a view over the lagoon. The rooms are clean and simple, and the price unbeatable for such a spectacular position. *Riva San Biagio 2135, Castello, tel. 041/522–3240, fax 041/523–5224. 28 rooms, 18 with bath. No credit cards. Closed Jan.–mid-Feb.*

Locanda Fiorita. This welcoming, newly refurbished hotel is tucked away in a sunny little square (where breakfast is served in the summer), just off Campo Santo Stefano, near the Accademia Bridge, and is very central for sightseeing. The rooms have beamed ceilings and are simply furnished. *Campiello Novo 3457, San Marco, tel. 041/523–4754. 10 rooms, 7 with shower. AE, MC, V. Closed 2 weeks Nov.–Dec.*

Riva. This small hotel close to San Marco stands in a picturesque spot at the junction of three canals, much used by all manner of Venetian watercraft—endlessly fascinating to watch but a little noisy early in the morning. It has recently been well refurbished by its enthusiastic new owner. *Ponte dell'Angelo 5310, Castello, tel. 041/522–7034. 12 rooms, 10 with bath. No credit cards. Closed mid-Nov.–Feb. 1, except for 2 weeks at Christmas.*

The Arts

For a program of events, pick up the free "Guest in Venice" booklet, available from the Assessorato al Turismo (Ca 'Giustinian, 2nd floor, Calle del Ridotto), near Piazza San Marco, or at most hotel desks. Your hotel may also be able to get you tickets for some events.

Concerts There are regular concerts at the Pietà Church, with an emphasis on Vivaldi, and at San Stae—though prices tend to be high and the quality of performance uneven. Concerts, sometimes free, are also held by visiting choirs and musicians in other churches. For information on these often short-notice events, ask at the APT office, and look for posters on walls and in restaurants and shops. The **Kele e Teo Agency** (Piazza San Marco 4930, tel. 041/520–8722) supplies tickets for many of the city's musical events.

Opera The season at **Teatro La Fenice** (Campo San Fantin, tel. 041/521–0161, fax 041/522–1768) runs all year, except for August, with an opera in performance most months. The box office is open September to July, Monday–Saturday 9:30–12:30 and 4–6, except when there's a performance on Sunday, in which case the box office is open Sunday and remains closed the following Monday.

Nightlife

The **Martini Scala Club** (Calle delle Veste, near Teatro La Fenice, tel. 041/522–4121) is an elegant piano bar with late-night restaurant. The bars of the top hotels stay open as long as their customers keep on drinking. Dedicated nighthawks should get a copy of *Notturno Veneziano (Venetian Nightlife)*, a guide to live music venues, discos, and late bars in and around Venice, published by the Assessorato alla Gioventù, the Municipality's Youth Department (Corte Contarini 1529, 4th floor, near Piazza San Marco). It's available free at APT information offices, at present only in Italian, but with useful maps and easy-to-follow notes. Night spots popular with young people are **Ai Canottieri** (Fondamenta San Giobbe 690, Cannaregio, tel. 041/71548, live music Tues., closed Sun.) and **Paradiso Perduto** (Fondamenta Misericordia 2540, Cannaregio, tel. 041/720581, live music Sun., closed Wed.).

Campania

Campania (the region of Naples, the Amalfi coast, and other sights) is where most people's preconceived ideas of Italy become a reality. You'll find lots of sun, good food that relies heavily on tomatoes and mozzarella, acres of classical ruins, and gorgeous scenery. The exuberance of the locals doesn't leave much room for efficient organization, however, and you may have to revise your concept of real time; here minutes dilate into hours at the drop of a hat.

Once a city that rivaled Paris as a brilliant and refined cultural capital, Napoli (Naples) is afflicted by acute urban decay and chronic delinquency. You need patience, stamina, and a healthy dose of caution to visit Naples on your own, but it's worth it for those who have a sense of adventure and the capacity to discern the enormous riches the city has accumulated in its 2,000-year existence.

On the other hand, if you want the fun without the hassle, head for Sorrento, Capri, and the Amalfi coast, legendary haunts of the sirens who tried to lure Odysseus off course. Sorrento is touristy but has some fine old hotels and beautiful views; it's a good base for a leisurely excursion to Pompeii. Capri is a pint-size paradise, though sometimes too crowded for comfort, while the Amalfi coast has some enchanting towns and spectacular scenery.

Getting Around

By Plane There are several daily flights between Rome and Naples's Capodichino Airport (tel. 081/780–5763), 7 kilometers (4 miles) north of the downtown area. During the summer months there's a direct helicopter service between Capodichino, Capri, and Ischia; for information, tel. 081/789–6273 or 081/584–1481.

By Train A great number of trains run between Rome and Naples every day; Intercity trains make the journey in less than two hours. There are several stations in Naples, and a network of suburban trains connects the city with several points of interest in

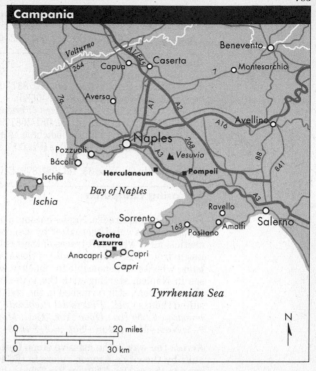

Campania

Volturno
264
Capua
Caserta
Benevento
Montesarchio
7
Aversa
79
A1
A2
A16
Avellino
Naples
268
Vesuvio
A3
Pozzuoli
Bácoli
Ischia
Herculaneum
Pompeii
88
841
Bay of Naples
Ischia
Ravello
Sorrento
163
Positano
Amalfi
A3
Salerno
Grotta Azzurra
Anacapri
Capri
Capri

Tyrrhenian Sea

N

| 0 | 20 miles |
| 0 | 30 km |

Campania. The central station is at Piazza Garibaldi. For train information, tel. 081/553–4188. Naples has a Metropolitana (subway); though it's old and trains are infrequent, it beats the traffic. The fare is 1,000 lire.

By Bus For bus information, call **SITA** (tel. 081/552–2176) or the Naples Transport Board (tel. 081/553–4188).

By Car The Naples–Pompeii–Salerno toll road has exits at Ercolano (Herculaneum) and Pompeii, and connects with the tortuous coastal road to Sorrento and the Amalfi coast at the Castellamare exit. Driving within Naples is not recommended: Window smashing and robbery are not uncommon.

By Boat Boats and hydrofoils for the islands, the Sorrento peninsula, and the Amalfi coast leave from the Molo Beverello, near Naples's Piazza Municipio. **Caremar** (tel. 081/551–3882), **Navigazione Libera del Golfo** (tel. 081/552–7209), and **Lauro** (tel. 081/551–3236) operate a frequent passenger and car ferry service, while hydrofoils of the Caremar, Navigazione Libera del Golfo, and **Alilauro** (tel. 081/761–1004) lines leave from both Molo Beverello and the hydrofoil station at Mergellina pier, from which **SNAV** (tel. 081/761–2348) also operates.

Guided Tours

Aside from the one-, two-, or three-day guided tours of the area departing from Rome, offered by **American Express** (tel. 06/67641), **CIT** (tel. 06/47941), **Appian Line** (tel. 06/488–4151) and other operators, **CIT** in Naples (Piazza Municipio 72, tel. 081/

552–5426) has a wide range of half-day and all-day tours on the mainland and to the islands. Similar tours are offered by **Tourcar** (Piazza Matteotti 1, tel. 081/552–0429).

Tourist Information

Capri (Marina Grande pier, tel. 081/837–0634; and Piazza Umberto I, Capri town, tel. 081/837–0686).
Naples. EPT Information Offices (Piazza dei Martiri 58, tel. 081/405311; central station, tel. 081/268779; Mergellina station, tel. 081/761–2102; and Capodichino Airport, tel. 081/780–5761). AAST Information Office (Piazza del Gesù, tel. 081/552–3328).
Sorrento (Via De Maio 35, tel. 081/878–2104).

Exploring Campania

Naples   Founded by the Greeks, **Naples** became a playground of the Romans and was ruled thereafter by a succession of foreign dynasties, all of which left traces of their cultures in the city and its environs. The most splendid of these rulers were the Bourbons, who were responsible for much of what you will want to see in Naples, starting with the 17th-century **Palazzo Reale** (Royal Palace), still furnished in the lavish Baroque style that suited them so well. *Piazza del Plebiscito, tel. 081/413888. Admission: 6,000 lire. Open Apr.–Oct., Mon–Sat. 9–7:30, Sun. 9–1; Nov.–Mar., Mon.–Sat. 9–2, Sun. 9–1.*

Across the way is the massive stone **Castel Nuovo,** which was built by the city's Aragon rulers in the 13th century; it's not open to the public. Walk up Via Toledo, keeping an eye on the antics of the Neapolitans, whose daily lives are fraught with theatrical gestures and fiery speeches. They all seem to be actors in their own human comedy.

Time Out   Stop in at **Caflisch,** a historic café that has recently added a good fast-food counter, and try a *sfogliatella*, a delicious, clamshaped Neapolitan pastry. *Via Toledo 253.*

Continue along Via Toledo, also known as Via Roma, and make a detour to the right to see the oddly faceted stone facade and elaborate Baroque interior of the church of the **Gesù** (Via Benedetto Croce) and, directly opposite, the church of **Santa Chiara,** built in the early 1300s in Provençal Gothic style. A favorite Neapolitan song celebrates the quiet beauty of its cloister, decorated in delicate floral tiles.

Time Out   For an authentic Neapolitan pizza in a genuine pizzeria, stop in at **Lombardi,** where you can have a classic pizza made in a wood-fired brick oven or a full meal in a tiny, crowded setting with no frills and lots of atmosphere. *Via Benedetto Croce 59.*

Another detour off Via Toledo, to the left this time, takes you from **Piazza Dante** to the Montesanto funicular, which ascends to the Vomero hill, where you can see the bastions of **Castel Sant'Elmo** and visit the museum in the **Certosa di San Martino,** a Carthusian monastery restored in the 17th century. It contains an eclectic collection of Neapolitan landscape paintings, royal carriages, and *presepi* (Christmas crèches). Check out the view from the balcony off room No. 25. *Certosa di San*

Martino, tel. 081/578–1769. Admission: 6,000 lire. Open Tues.–Sat. 9–2, Sun. 9–1.

Return to Piazza Dante and follow Via Pessina (an extension of Via Toledo) to the **Museo Archeologico Nazionale.** Dusty and unkempt, the museum undergoes perpetual renovations, but it holds one of the world's great collections of antiquities. Greek and Roman sculptures, vividly colored mosaics, countless objects from Pompeii and Herculaneum, and an equestrian statue of the Roman emperor Nerva are all worth seeing. *Piazza Museo, tel. 081/440166. Admission: 8,000 lire. Open May–Sept., Mon.–Sat. 9–7:30, Sun. 9–1; Oct.–Apr., Mon.–Sat. 9–2, Sun. 9–1.*

About a mile north on the same road (take a bus or a taxi), you'll come to the **Museo di Capodimonte,** housed in an 18th-century palace built by Bourbon king Charles III, and surrounded by a vast park that must have been lovely when it was better cared for. In the picture gallery are some fine Renaissance paintings; climb the stairs to the terrace for a magnificent view of Naples and the bay. Downstairs you can visit the State Apartments and see the extensive collection of porcelain, much of it produced in the Bourbons' own factory right here on the grounds. *Parco di Capodimonte, tel. 081/744–1307. Admission: 8,000 lire. Tues.–Sat. 9–2, Sun. 9–1.*

Herculaneum **Herculaneum** (Ercolano) lies 14 kilometers (9 miles) southeast of Naples. Reputed to have been founded by the legendary Hercules, the elite Roman resort was devastated by the same volcanic eruption that buried Pompeii in AD 79. Recent excavations have revealed that many died on the shore in an attempt to escape, as a slow-moving mud slide embalmed the entire town by covering it with an 11-meter-deep (35-foot-deep) blanket of volcanic ash and ooze. While that may have been unfortunate for Herculaneum's residents, it has helped preserve the site in pristine detail for nearly two millenia. *Corso Ercolano, tel. 081/ 739–0963. Admission: 8,000 lire. Open daily 9–one hour before sunset.*

Pompeii **Pompeii,** a larger community 8 kilometers (5 miles) farther to the east, lost even more residents. An estimated 2,000 of them perished on that fateful August day. The ancient city of Pompeii was much larger than Herculaneum, and excavations have progressed to a much greater extent (though the remains are not as well preserved, due to some 18th-century scavenging for museum-quality artworks, most of which you are able to see at Naples's Museo Archeologico Nazionale; *see above*). This prosperous Roman city had an extensive forum, lavish baths and temples, and patrician villas richly decorated with frescoes. It's worth buying a detailed guide of the site in order to give meaning and understanding to the ruins and their importance. Be sure to see the **Villa dei Misteri,** whose frescoes are in mint condition. Perhaps that is a slight exaggeration, but the paintings are so rich with detail and depth of color that one finds it difficult to believe that they are 1,900 years old. Have lots of small change handy to tip the guards at the more important houses so they will unlock the gates for you. *Pompeii Scavi, tel. 081/861–1051. Admission: 10,000 lire. Open daily 9–one hour before sunset.*

Sorrento Another 28 kilometers (18 miles) southwest is **Sorrento,** in the not-too-distant past a small, genteel resort for a fashionable elite. Now the town has spread out along the crest of its fabled cliffs. Once this was an area full of secret haunts for the few tourists who came for the beauty of this coastline. Now, it has been "discovered" and the secret haunts are the playground for package tours. In Sorrento's case, however, the change is not as grim as it sounds, since nothing can dim the delights of the marvelous climate and view of the Bay of Naples. For the best views go to the **Villa Comunale,** near the old church of **San Francesco** (in itself worth a visit), or to the terrace behind the **Museo Correale.** The museum, an attractive 18th-century villa, houses an interesting collection of decorative arts (furniture, china, and so on) and paintings of the Neapolitan school. *Via Capasso. Admission: 5,000 lire; gardens only, 2,000 lire. Open Apr.–Sept., Mon. and Wed.–Sat. 9–12:30 and 5–7, Sun. 9–12:30; Oct.–Mar., Mon. and Wed.–Sat. 9–12:30 and 3–5, Sun. 9–12:30.*

Capri Sorrento makes a convenient jumping-off spot for a boat trip to **Capri.** No matter how many day-trippers crowd onto the island, no matter how touristy certain sections have become, Capri remains one of Italy's loveliest places. Incoming visitors disembark at Marina Grande, from where you can take some time out for an excursion to the **Grotta Azzurra** (Blue Grotto). Be warned that this must rank as one of the country's all-time great rip-offs: Motorboat, rowboat, and grotto admissions are charged separately, and if there's a line of boats waiting, you'll have little time to enjoy the grotto's marvelous colors. At Marina Grande you can also embark on a boat excursion around the island.

A cog railway or bus service takes you up to the town of Capri, where you can stroll through the **Piazzetta,** a choice place from which to watch the action and window-shop expensive boutiques on your way to the **Gardens of Augustus,** which have gorgeous views. The town of Capri is deliberately commercial and self-consciously picturesque. To get away from the crowds, hike to **Villa Jovis,** one of the many villas that Roman emperor Tiberius built on the island, at the end of a lane that climbs steeply uphill. The walk takes about 45 minutes, with pretty views all the way and a final spectacular vista of the entire Bay of Naples and part of the Gulf of Salerno. *Via Tiberio. Admission: 4,000 lire. Open daily 9–one hour before sunset.*

Or take the bus or a jaunty open taxi to **Anacapri** and look for the little church of **San Michele,** off Via Orlandi, where a magnificent handpainted majolica tile floor shows you an 18th-century vision of the Garden of Eden. *Admission: 2,000 lire. Open Easter–Nov., Mon.–Sat. 10–6, Sun. 10–2.*

From Piazza della Vittoria, picturesque Via Capodimonte leads to **Villa San Michele,** charming former home of Swedish scientist-author Axel Munthe. *Via Axel Munthe. Admission: 5,000 lire. Open Apr.–Sept., daily 9–6; Oct.–Mar., daily 10:30–3:30.*

Amalfi and From Sorrento, the coastal drive down to the resort town of
Positano Amalfi provides some of the most dramatic and beautiful scenery you'll find in all of Italy. **Positano**'s jumble of pastel houses, topped by whitewashed cupolas, cling to the mountainside above the sea. The town—the prettiest along this stretch of coast—attracts a sophisticated group of visitors and summer residents who find that its relaxed and friendly atmosphere

more than compensates for the sheer effort of moving about this exhaustingly vertical town, most of whose streets are stairways. This former fishing village has now opted for the more regular and lucrative rewards of tourism and commercialized fashion. Practically every other shop is a boutique displaying locally made casual wear. The beach is the town's main focal point, with a little promenade and a multitude of café-restaurants.

Amalfi itself is a charming maze of covered alleys and narrow byways straggling up the steep mountainside. The piazza just below the cathedral forms the town's heart—a colorful assortment of pottery stalls, cafés, and postcard shops grouped around a venerable old fountain. The cathedral's exterior is its most impressive feature, so there's no need to climb all those stairs unless you really want to.

Ravello   Do not miss **Ravello,** 16 kilometers (10 miles) north of Amalfi. Ravello is not actually on the coast, but on a high mountain bluff overlooking the sea. The road up to the village is a series of switchbacks, and the village itself clings precariously on the mountain spur. The village flourished during the 13th century and then fell into a tranquillity that has remained unchanged for the past six centuries. The center of the town is **Piazza Duomo,** with its cathedral, founded in 1087 and recently restored. Note its fine bronze 12th-century door, and, just inside on the left, the pulpit with mosaics telling the story of Jonah and the whale. Look to the right as well and you will see another pulpit with fantastic carved animals.

To the right of the cathedral is the entrance to the 11th-century **Villa Rufolo.** The composer Richard Wagner once stayed in Ravello, and there is a Wagner festival every summer on the villa's garden terrace. There is a moorish cloister with interlacing pointed arches, beautiful gardens, an 11th-century tower, and a belvedere with a fine view of the coast.

Across the square from the cathedral is a lovely walk leading to the Villa Cimbrone. At the entrance to the villa complex is a small cloister that looks medieval but was actually built in 1917, with two bas-reliefs: one representing nine Norman warriors, the other illustrating the seven deadly sins. Then, the long avenue leads through peaceful gardens scattered with grottoes, small temples, and statues emphasizing a contemplative silence to a belvedere and terrace where, on a clear day, the view stretches out over the Mediterranean Sea.

Dining and Lodging

For details and price-category definitions, *see* Dining and Lodging in Staying in Italy.

Amalfi   **La Caravella.** Tucked away under some arches lining the coast
Dining   road, the Caravella has a nondescript entrance but pleasant interior decorated in a medley of colors and paintings of old Amalfi. It's small and intimate, and proprietor Antonio describes the cuisine as *"sfiziosa"* (taste-tempting). Specialties include *scialatelli* (homemade pasta with shellfish sauce) and *pesce al limone* (fresh fish with lemon sauce). *Via M. Camera 12, tel. 089/871029. Reservations advised. AE, MC, V. Closed Tues. and Nov. 10–30. Moderate.*

Lodging
★ **Santa Caterina.** A large mansion perched above terraced and flowered hillsides on the coast road just outside Amalfi proper, the Santa Caterina is one of the best hotels on the entire coast. The rooms are tastefully decorated, and most have small terraces or balconies with great views. There are lounges and terraces for relaxing, and an elevator whisks guests down to the seaside saltwater pool, bar, and swimming area. Amid lemon and orange groves, there are two romantic villa annexes. Some rooms and suites are in the Very Expensive category. *Strada Amalfitana 9, tel. 089/871012, fax 089/871351. 54 rooms with bath. Facilities: restaurant, bar, pool, beach bar, parking. AE, DC, MC, V. Expensive.*

Capri **Al Grottino.** This small family-run restaurant, with a handy lo-
Dining cation near the Piazzetta, sports autographed photographs of
★ celebrity customers. House specialties are gnocchi with mozzarella and *linguine con gamberini* (pasta with shrimp sauce). *Via Longano 27, tel. 081/837-0584. Dinner reservations advised. AE, DC, MC, V. Closed Tues. and Nov. 3–Mar. 20. Moderate.*

Da Gemma. One of Capri's favorite places for a homey atmosphere and a good meal, Da Gemma features *pappardelle all'aragosta* (egg noodles with lobster sauce) and fritto misto. If you're budgeting, don't order fish that you pay for by weight; it's always expensive. You can have pizza as a starter in the evening. *Via Madre Serafina 6, tel. 081/837-7113. Reservations advised. AE, DC, MC, V. Closed Mon. and Nov. Moderate.*

La Capannina. Only a few steps away from Capri's social center, the Piazzetta, La Capannina has a delightful vine-hung courtyard for summer dining and a reputation as one of the island's best eating places. Antipasto features fried ravioli and eggplant stuffed with ricotta, and house specialties include chicken, scaloppine and a refreshing, homemade lemon liqueur. *Via Botteghe 14, tel. 081/837-0732. Reservations advised. AE, MC, V. Closed Wed. (except during Aug.) and Nov.–mid-Mar. Moderate.*

Lodging **Quisisana.** One of Italy's poshest hotels is sited right in the center of the town of Capri. The rooms are spacious, and many have arcaded balconies with views of the sea; the decor is traditional or contemporary, with some antique accents. From the small terrace at the entrance you can watch all Capri go by, but the enclosed garden and pool in the back are perfect for getting away from it all. The bar and restaurant are casual in a terribly elegant way. *Via Camerelle 2, tel. 081/837-0788, fax 081/837-6080. 143 rooms with bath. Facilities: restaurant, pool, tennis. AE, DC, MC, V. Closed Dec.–mid-Mar. Very Expensive.*

★ **Villa Brunella.** The glassed-in bar of this family-run hotel is on the lane leading to Punta Tragara and the Faraglioni. From that level you descend to the restaurant, with the rooms and the swimming pool all on lower levels. Furnishings are tastefully casual and comfortable, and the views from all levels are wonderful. Be prepared to climb stairs; there's no elevator. *Via Tragara 24, tel. 081/837-0122, fax 081/837-0430. 18 rooms with bath. Facilities: restaurant, bar, pool. No credit cards. Closed Nov.–Mar. Expensive.*

Villa Sarah. Just a 10-minute walk from the Piazzetta, the Sarah is a whitewashed Mediterranean villa with bright, simply furnished rooms. There's a garden and small bar, but no restaurant. *Via Tiberio 3/A, tel. 081/837-7817. 20 rooms with bath. AE. Closed Nov.–Mar. Moderate.*

Naples **La Sacrestia.** This lovely restaurant is in an elevated position,
Dining above Mergellina, with a fine view and a delightful summer terrace. The menu offers traditional Neapolitan cuisine; among
the specialties are *linguine con salsetta segreta* (pasta with
finely chopped garden vegetables) and *spigola* (sea bass), either steamed or baked. *Via Orazio 116, tel. 081/761–1051. Reservations required. AE, DC, MC, V. Closed Mon. (Sept.–
June), Sun. (in July), and Aug. Expensive.*

★ **Ciro a Santa Brigida.** Centrally located off Via Toledo near the
Castel Nuovo, this no-frills restaurant is a favorite with businesspeople, artists, and journalists. Tables are arranged on
two levels, and the decor is classic trattoria. This is the place to
try traditional Neapolitan *sartù di riso* (a rich rice dish with
meat and peas) and *melanzane alla parmigiana* or *scaloppe
alla Ciro*, eggplant with prosciutto and mozzarella. There's
pizza, too. *Via Santa Brigida 71, tel. 081/552–4072. Reservations advised. AE, DC, MC, V. Closed Sun. and Aug. Moderate.*

La Bersagliera. This restaurant has been making tourists happy for years, with a great location on the Santa Lucia waterfront, cheerful waiters, mandolin music, and good spaghetti
alla disgraziata (with tomatoes, capers, and black olives) and
mozzarella in carrozza (cheese fried in batter). *Borgo Mar-
inaro 10, tel. 081/764–6016. Reservations advised. AE, DC,
MC, V. Closed Tues. Moderate.*

Lodging **Excelsior.** Splendidly located on the shore drive, the Excelsior
has views of the bay from its front rooms. The spacious bedrooms are well furnished in informal floral prints or more formal Empire style; all have a comfortable, traditional air. The
salons are formal, with chandeliers and wall paintings, and the
excellent Casanova restaurant is elegant. *Via Partenope 48,
tel. 081/764–0111, fax 081/764–9743. 138 rooms with bath. Facilities: restaurant, bar, sauna, garage. AE, DC, MC, V. Very
Expensive.*

★ **Jolly Ambassador.** This hotel occupies the top 14 floors of a
downtown skyscraper, and its rooms and roof restaurant have
wonderful views of Naples and the bay. It's furnished in dark
brown, beige, and white in the functional, modern style typical
of this reliable chain, which promises comfort and efficiency in
a city where these are scarce commodities. *Via Medina 70, tel.
081/416000, fax 081/551–8010. 251 rooms with bath. Facilities:
restaurant. AE, DC, MC, V. Expensive.*

Rex. This hotel occupies a fairly quiet location near the Santa
Lucia waterfront. It is situated on the first two floors of an Art
Nouveau building and lacks an elevator. The decor ranges from
1950s modern to fake period pieces and even some folk art, hap-
hazardly combined. Although it has no restaurant, there are
many in the area. *Via Palepoli 12, tel. 081/764–9389, fax 081/
764–9227. 40 rooms, 37 with bath or shower. Facilities: bar, garage. AE, DC, MC, V. Moderate.*

Positano **Capurale.** Among all the popular restaurants on the beach
Dining promenade, Capurale (just around the corner) has the best food
and lowest prices. Tables are set under vines on a breezy sidewalk in the summer, upstairs and indoors in winter. Spaghetti
con melanzane and *crêpes al formaggio* (cheese-filled crepes)
are good choices here. *Via Marina, tel. 089/875374. Reservations advised for outdoor tables. No credit cards. Closed Nov.
3–Mar. Moderate.*

Lodging **Il San Pietro di Positano.** Situated on the side of a cliff, this is quite possibly one of the world's most attractive hotels because of its magnificent views of the sea and the Amalfi coast. The decor of the hotel is eclectic, with unusual antiques and, everywhere, hanging bougainvillea. The furnishings are perfectly arranged to give a sense of openness and create a feeling of opulence. The guest rooms are decorated with an eye to detail, but their views steal the show. Verdant with plants, the light, open dining room offers fine Italian cuisine. An elevator takes guests to the hotel's small beach area. *Via Laurito 2, tel. 089/875455, fax 081/811449. 55 rooms with bath. Facilities: restaurant, beach, pool, tennis. AE, DC, MC, V. Closed Nov.–Mar. Very Expensive.*

Le Sirenuse. The most fashionable hotel in Positano is this converted 18th-century villa that has been in the same family for eight generations. The hotel is set into the hillside about 200 feet above Positano's harbor. Most of the bedrooms face the sea—these are the best. Because of the hotel's location, the dining room is like a long, closed-in terrace overlooking the village of Positano—a magnificent view. The cuisine varies from acceptable to excellent. *Via C. Colombo 30, tel. 089/875066, fax 081/811798. 62 rooms with bath. Facilities: restaurant, pool, sauna. AE, DC, MC, V. Very Expensive.*

Palazzo Murat. The location is perfect, in the heart of town, near the beachside promenade, but set within a walled garden. The old wing is a historic palazzo, with tall windows and wrought-iron balconies; the newer wing is a whitewashed Mediterranean building with arches and terraces. Guests can relax in antique-strewn lounges or on the charming vine-draped patio. *Via dei Mulini 23, tel. 089/875177, fax 089/811419. 28 rooms with bath. Facilities: bar, garden. AE, DC, MC, V. Closed Nov. 5–Mar. Moderate.*

Ravello **Hotel Palumbo.** Of all the hotels on the Amalfi coast, the Hotel
Lodging Palumbo is the most genteel—a refined 12th-century retreat. Some of the bedrooms do tend to be small, but they are beautifully furnished and full of character. Also, the rooms facing the sea are the choice ones—and the more expensive. The lounge area is filled with the owner's antiques and, with the greatest of ease, guests quickly come to view the Hotel Palumbo as their private palazzo. *Via Toro 28, tel. 089/857244, fax 089/858133. 13 rooms with bath. Facilities: restaurant, bar, garden. AE, DC, MC, V. Very Expensive.*

Sorrento **Antica Trattoria.** This is a homey, hospitable place with a gar-
Dining den for summer dining. The specialties of the house are a classic *pennette al profumo di bosco* (pasta with a creamy mushroom and ham sauce), fish (which can be expensive), and *melanzane alla parmigiana*. *Via Giuliani 33, tel. 081/807–1082. Dinner reservations advised. No credit cards. Closed Mon., Jan. 10–Feb. 10. Moderate.*

La Belle Époque. Occupying a 19th-century villa perched on the edge of the vine-covered gorge of the Mulini, this is an elegant veranda restaurant. Try the *scialatelli Belle Époque* (homemade pasta with mozzarella and eggplant). *Via Fuorimura 7, tel. 081/878–1216. Reservations advised. AE, DC, MC, V. Closed Mon. Moderate.*

★ **Parrucchiano.** One of the town's best and oldest, Parrucchiano features greenhouse-type dining rooms dripping with vines and dotted with plants. Among the antipasti, try the *panzarotti* (pastry crust filled with mozzarella and tomato), and for a main course, the *scalloppe alla sorrentina*, again with mozzarella and tomato. *Corso Italia 71, tel. 081/878–1321. Reservations advised. MC, V. Closed Wed. Nov.–May. Moderate.*

Lodging **Cocumella.** In a lovely cliffside garden in a quiet residential area just outside Sorrento, this historic old villa (it features a 17th-century chapel) has been totally renovated for comfort. Furnishings are a tasteful blend of antique and modern; there are vaulted ceilings and archways, a dining veranda, and stunning tiled floors. Cocumella has an exclusive, elegant atmosphere without being stuffy. *Via Cocumella 7, tel. 081/878–2933, fax 081/878–3712. 60 rooms with bath. Facilities: restaurant, garden, parking, pool, tennis. AE, DC, MC, V. Very Expensive.*

★ **Bellevue Syrene.** A palatial villa in a garden overlooking the sea, the Syrene features solid, old-fashioned comforts, along with plenty of charm and antique paintings. *Piazza della Vittoria 5, tel. 081/878–1024, fax 081/878–3963. 50 rooms with bath. Facilities: restaurant, bar, garden, private beach, parking, conference rooms. AE, DC, MC, V. Expensive–Very Expensive.*

Excelsior Vittoria. In the heart of Sorrento, but removed from the main square by an arbored walk, the Excelsior Vittoria is right on the cliff and has old-fashioned, Art Nouveau furnishings, some very grand, though faded. Tenor Enrico Caruso's bedroom is preserved as a relic; guest bedrooms are spacious and elegant in a turn-of-the-century way. It overlooks the bay and is recommended for those who like a lot of atmosphere with their views. *Piazza Tasso 34, tel. 081/807–1044, fax 081/877–1206. 106 rooms with bath. Facilities: restaurant, pool, garden, parking. AE, DC, MC, V. Expensive.*

Eden. Eden occupies a fairly quiet but central location, with a garden. The bedrooms are bright but undistinguished; the lounge and lobby have more character. It's an unpretentious but friendly hotel, although it can get crowded in high season. *Via Correale 25, tel. 081/878–1909, fax 081/807–2016. 60 rooms with bath. Facilities: restaurant, bar, parking, pool. AE, MC, V. Closed Nov.–Feb. Moderate.*

19 Luxembourg

Luxembourg, one of the smallest countries in the United Nations, measures only 2,587 square kilometers (999 square miles), less than the size of Rhode Island. It is dwarfed by its neighbors—Germany, Belgium, and France–yet from its history of invasion, occupation, and siege, you might think those square miles were built over solid gold. In fact, it was Luxembourg's very defenses against centuries of attack that rendered it all the more desirable: From AD 963, when Siegfried built a castle on the high promontory of the Bock, the once-grander duchy encased itself in layer upon layer of fortifications until by the mid-19th century its very invulnerability was considered a threat to those not commanding its thick stone walls. After successive invasions—by the Burgundians, the Hapsburgs, the French, the Spanish, the Dutch, and the Austrians—Luxembourg was ultimately dismantled in the name of peace, its neutrality guaranteed by the 1867 Treaty of London, and its function reduced to that of a buffer zone. What remains of its walls, while impressive, is only a reminder of what was one of the strongholds of Europe—the "Gibraltar of the North."

Luxembourg is besieged again, this time by bankers and Eurocrats. Its Boulevard Royal bristles with international banks—enough to rival Switzerland—and just outside the old city, a new colony has been populated by *fonctionnaires* for the European Community, the heir to the Common Market. Fiercely protecting its share of the expanding bureaucracy from competitive co-capitals Strasbourg and Brussels, Luxembourg digs its heels in once again, vying not only for political autonomy but for its newfound prosperity and clout. Thus the national motto takes on new meaning: *Mir wëlle bleiwe wat mir sin,* or "We want to stay what we are"—nowadays, a viable Grand Duchy in the heart of modern Europe.

Visitors will find evidence of Luxembourg's military past scattered around the Grand Duchy's luxurious countryside: There are castles by the dozen, set in the densely wooded hills of La Petite Suisse (Little Switzerland) to the east, in the crests and valleys of the Ardennes to the north, and along the riverbanks of the Our and the Moselle, the latter renowned for its crisp white wines.

Essential Information

Before You Go

When to Go The main tourist season in Luxembourg is the same as in Belgium—early May to late September. But temperatures in Luxembourg tend to be cooler than those in Belgium, particularly in the hilly north, where there is frequently snow in winter.

Climate In general, temperatures in Luxembourg are moderate. It does drizzle frequently, however, so be sure to bring a raincoat.

The following are the average daily maximum and minimum temperatures for Luxembourg.

Luxembourg

Jan.	37F	3C	May	65F	18C	Sept.	66F	19C
	29	– 1		46	8		50	10
Feb.	40F	4C	June	70F	21C	Oct.	56F	13C
	31	– 1		52	11		43	6
Mar.	49F	10C	July	73F	23C	Nov.	44F	7C
	35	1		55	13		37	3
Apr.	57F	14C	Aug.	71F	22C	Dec.	39F	4C
	40	4		54	12		32	0

Currency   In Luxembourg, as in Belgium, the unit of currency is the franc. Luxembourg issues its own currency in bills of 100, 500, and 1,000 francs and coins of 1, 5, 20, and 50 francs. Belgian currency can be used freely in Luxembourg, and the two currencies have exactly the same value. However, Luxembourg currency is not valid in Belgium. At press time (spring 1993), the exchange rate was 32.6 fr.L. to the U.S. dollar, 39 fr. L. to the Canadian dollar, and 50 fr.L. to the pound sterling.

What It Will Cost   Luxembourg is a developed and sophisticated country with a high standard and cost of living. Luxembourg City is an international banking center, and a number of European institutions are based there, a fact that tends to push prices slightly higher in the capital than in the countryside.

Sample Prices   Cup of coffee, 50 fr.L.; glass of beer, 40–60 fr.L.; movie ticket, 200 fr.L.; 3-mile taxi ride, 600 fr.L.

Customs on Arrival   For information on customs regulations, *see* Customs on Arrival in Belgium.

Language Native Luxembourgers speak three languages fluently: Luxembourgish (best described as a dialect of German), German, and French. Many also speak English.

Staying in Luxembourg

Telephones You can find public phones both on the street and in city post offices. A local call costs about 10 fr.L. (slightly more from restaurants and gas stations). The cheapest way to make an international call is to dial direct from a public phone; in a post office, you may be required to make a deposit before the call. Post offices also sell a *Telekaart* in units of 50 and 150, which can be used in nearly half the booths in the Grand Duchy. For operator-assisted calls, dial 0010.

Mail Airmail postcards and letters weighing less than 20 grams cost
Postal Rates 22 fr.L. to the United States. Letters and postcards to the United Kingdom cost 14 fr.L.

Receiving Mail If you are uncertain where you'll be staying, have your mail sent in care of American Express (6/8 rue Origer, 2269 Luxembourg).

Shopping Purchases of goods for export may qualify for a sales tax (TVA)
Sales Tax Refunds refund of 12%. Ask the shop to fill out a refund form. You must then have the form stamped by customs officers on leaving either Luxembourg, Belgium, or Holland.

Opening and **Banks** generally are open weekdays 8:30–noon and 1:30–4:30,
Closing Times though more and more remain open through the lunch hour.

Museums. Opening hours vary, so check individual listings. Many close on Monday, and most also close for lunch between noon and 2.

Shops. Large city department stores and shops are generally open weekdays, except Monday morning, and Saturday 9–noon and 2–6. A few small family businesses are open Sunday morning from 8 to noon.

National Holidays January 1; February 14–15 (Carnival); April 3 (Easter Monday); May 1 (May Day); May 12 (Ascension); May 22 (Pentecost Monday); June 23 (National Day); August 15 (Assumption); November 1 (All Saints' Day); November 2 (All Souls Day); December 25, 26.

Dining Restaurants in Luxembourg offer their best deals at lunch, when you can find a *plat du jour* (one-course special) or *menu* (two or three courses included in price) at bargain rates. Pizzerias offer an excellent and popular source of cheap food, with pasta, risotti, and wood-oven pizzas making a full meal. Light lunches—easy on the stomach if not always the wallet—can be found in chic pastry shops, where you point to the dishes in the display case (a slice of *pâté en croute*, an egg salad, a few small casseroles to be heated), then take your number upstairs to the *salon de consommation*, where your drink order will be taken and your meal served.

Mealtimes Most hotels serve breakfast until 10. Lunch hours are noon–2, sometimes extending until 3. Long accustomed to the Continental style of dining heavily at midday, business-conscious Luxembourgers now eat their main meal in the evening between 7 and 10.

Lodging

Hotels Most hotels in the capital are relatively modern and vary from the international style, mainly near the airport, to family-run establishments in town. Outside Luxembourg City, many hotels are housed in more picturesque buildings, often in beautiful countryside settings. Prices vary considerably between town and country, but as Luxembourg City is an important business center, many of its hotels offer reduced rates on weekends, particularly out of season.

Youth Hostels Inexpensive youth hostels are plentiful in Luxembourg. They are often set in ancient fortresses and castles. For information, contact **Centrale des Auberges de Jeunesse** (18 pl. d'Armes, L-1136, Luxembourg, tel. 25588).

Camping The Grand Duchy is probably the best-organized country in Europe for camping. It offers some 120 sites, all with full amenities and most with scenic views. Listings are published annually by the National Tourist Office.

Tipping In Luxembourg hotels and restaurants, taxes and service charges are included in the overall bill and it is not necessary to leave more. If you wish to, round off the sum to the nearest 50 fr.L. or 100 fr.L. Bellhops and doormen should receive between 50 fr.L. and 100 fr.L., depending on the grade of the hotel. At the movies, tip the usher 20 fr.L. if you are seated personally. In theaters, tip about 20 fr.L. for checking your coat, and the same to the program seller. In public washrooms the attendant will usually expect between 5 fr.L. and 10 fr.L. Taxi drivers expect a tip; add about 15% to the amount on the meter.

Luxembourg City

Arriving and Departing

By Plane All international flights arrive at Luxembourg's Findel Airport, 6 kilometers (4 miles) from the city.

Between the Airport and Downtown Bus No. 9 leaves the airport at regular intervals for Luxembourg's main bus depot, located just beside the train station. Bus No. 4 (and, less directly, Nos. 11 and 12) goes to the city center. Individual tickets cost 30 fr.L. A taxi will cost you about 600 fr.L. If you are driving, follow the signs for the Centre Ville (city center).

Getting Around

One of the best transportation options in Luxembourg is the **Oeko-Carnet,** a block of five one-day tickets good for unlimited transportation on trains and buses throughout the country. Cards are on sale, for 460 fr.L., at Gare Centrale (the main train station) in Luxembourg City, or at Aldringen Center, located underground in front of the central post office.

By Bus Luxembourg City has a highly efficient bus service. The blue-and-yellow buses outside the city train station will take you all around the city and also to some of the outlying areas. Get details about services at the information counter in the station arrivals hall. Fares are low, but the best bet is to buy a 10-ride ticket (230 fr.L.), available from banks or from the bus station in the Aldringen Center. Other buses, connecting Luxembourg

City with towns throughout the country, leave from Gare Centrale.

By Train Luxembourg is served by frequent direct trains from Paris and Brussels. From Paris, travel time is about four hours; from Brussels, just under three hours. From Amsterdam, the journey is via Brussels and takes about six hours. There are connections from most German cities via Koblenz. Outside Luxembourg City, three major train routes extend north, south, and east into the Moselle Valley. For all train information, phone 492424. All service is from Gare Centrale in place de la Gare.

By Car A car is a liability in this small, walkable city. You can easily see the rest of the country in a day or two, and you might want to rent a car for this purpose. Major highways and smaller roads are excellent and fairly uncrowded. Speed limits have recently dropped to 120 kph (70 mph) on highways, 90 kph (55 mph) on major roads, and 50 kph (30 mph) in built-up areas.

Street parking in Luxembourg City is difficult. Make use of one of the underground parking lots, or park at the sizable Parking Glacis next to the Municipal Theater, five minutes' walk from the city center.

By Bicycle Bicycling is a popular sport in Luxembourg, and it is an excellent way to see the city and outlying regions. A new brochure, "Cycling Tracks," is available from the Luxembourg National Tourist Office, Box 1001, L-1010 Luxembourg. Bikes can be rented in Luxembourg City at **Luxembourg DELTA** (8 Bisserwee, tel. 4796–2383), from March 30 through October 31; in Reisdorf, Diekirch, and Echternach, rent bikes at the tourist office (**Syndicat d'Initiative**). Maps are available from the tourist office.

By Taxi There are taxi stands near Gare Centrale and the main post office; it is almost impossible to stop one in the streets. To call a taxi, phone 480058 or 482233.

Important Addresses and Numbers

Tourist Information The main **Office Nationale du Tourisme (ONT)** in Luxembourg City (Aerogare [Air Terminal] bus depot, place de la Gare, tel. 481199) is open daily (except Sun. Nov.–Mar.) 9–noon and 2–6:30 (July–mid-Sept., 9–7:30). The Luxembourg City tourist office (place d'Armes, tel. 222809) is open mid-Sept.–mid-June, Mon.–Sat. 9–1 and 2–6; mid-June–mid-Sept., weekdays 9–7, Sat. 9–1 and 2–7, Sun. 10–noon and 2–6.

Embassies U.S. (22 blvd. Emmanuel Servais, tel. 460123). U.K. (14 blvd. F. D. Roosevelt, tel. 229864). Canada: The Brussels embassy (ave. de Tervuren 2, 1040 Brussels, tel. 00322/7356040) covers Luxembourg.

Emergencies Police, Ambulance, Doctor, Dentist (tel. 012). Pharmacies in Luxembourg stay open nights on a rotation system. Signs listing late-night facilities are posted outside each pharmacy.

English-Language Bookstores For books and magazines in English, try **Magasin Anglais** (13 allée Scheffer, tel. 224925).

Travel Agencies American Express (6/8 rue Origer, tel. 496041). C.I.T. (pl. de la Gare, tel. 485102). Keiser Tours (34 rue Philippe II, tel. 472717). Wagons Lits (Thomas Cook) (99 Grand-rue, tel.

460315). **Emile Weitzel** (15 rue Notre-Dame, tel. 22931). **Sotour** (including youth travel) (15 pl. du Theatre, tel. 461514).

Guided Tours

Orientation Tours   **Sales-Lentz** offers tours of the city every morning during the peak tourist season (Apr. 1–Oct. 31). The tours leave from the bus station, next to the railway station, platform 5, or from place de la Constitution, under the Gelle Fra, visiting the historic sights of the center, the new European area, and some of the villas on the city outskirts, together with the military cemeteries: General Patton is buried in the American one. Tours cost 290 fr.L. Another tour of the city and countryside takes visitors to the monuments of Luxembourg City, the cemeteries, and the restored castle of Bourglinster. (Apr., May, and Oct., weekends 2:30–5:45; June–Sept., Tues., Thurs., Sat., and Sun. 2:30–5:45. Cost: 320 fr. L.) Other more complete tours of the Grand Duchy are available to groups of 10 or more. For information and bookings, contact Sales-Lentz (26 rue du Curé, L-1368, tel. 461818). From April to October, minitrain tours of the Old Town and the Petrusse Valley start from the place de la Constitution (tel. 461617; 220 fr. L adults, 160 fr. L. children under 17).

Walking Tours   A self-guided city tour with headphones and cassette can be rented at the bus booth on the place de la Constitution for 100 fr. L–120 fr. L, depending on length of tape. Information on weekend walking tours can be obtained from the tourist office or from the **Fédération Luxembourgeoise des Marches Populaires** (Boite Postale 794, L-2018 Luxembourg). Also consult the *Agenda Touristique,* published by the National Tourist Office.

Excursions   Pick up the booklet "Circuits Auto-Pedestres," available at newsstands, bookstores, and the central tourist office (895 fr.L.), for information on combination driving-walking tours outside the city.

Exploring Luxembourg City

Numbers in the margin correspond to points of interest on the Luxembourg City map.

This walk takes you through Luxembourg City's maze of ancient military fortifications, now transformed into peaceful paths. Begin at Gare Centrale, in the southern section of the city. As you head right from the station toward the city center along avenue de la Gare, you will pass through a bustling shopping district.

❶ Take the **Passerelle Viaduct,** a 19th-century road bridge that links the station with the valley of the Petrusse. The Petrusse is more of a brook than a river and is now contained by concrete, but the valley has become a singularly beautiful park. From here you'll see the rocky ledges—partly natural, partly man-made—on which the city was founded.

❷ At the cathedral end of the Passerelle, on the right, take the steps and curving sidewalk up to **Monument de la Solidarité Nationale** (National Monument to Luxembourg Unity), and admire its perpetual flame. It was erected in 1971 to commemo-

Luxembourg City

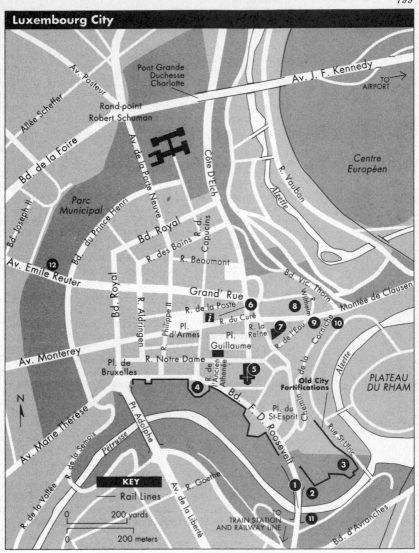

Bock, **10**

Cathédrale
Notre-Dame, **5**

Chapelle de
St-Quirin, **11**

Citadelle du
St-Esprit, **3**

Grand Ducal Palace, **7**

Maquette, **6**

Monument de la
Solidarité Nationale, **2**

Musée National, **8**

Passerelle, **1**

Place de la
Constitution, **4**

St-Michel, **9**

Villa Vauban, **12**

rate Luxembourg's sacrifices and intact survival following World War II.

❸ To the right of the monument, follow the road along the remains of the old city fortifications, known as the **Citadelle du St-Esprit** (Citadel of the Holy Spirit). This 17th-century citadel was built by Vauban, the French military engineer, in the typical style of thrusting wedges. From the end you can see the three spires of the cathedral, the curve of the Alzette, and the incongruous white tower of the European parliament.

❹ Retrace your steps along the old city fortifications, cross boulevard F. D. Roosevelt, and continue on to the **place de la Constitution,** marked by the war memorial, a striking gilt *Gëlle Fra* or Golden Woman. Here you'll find the entrance to the ancient **Petrusse casemates,** military tunnels carved into the bedrock. During the many phases of the fortress's construction, the rock itself was hollowed out to form a honeycomb of passages running for nearly 24 kilometers (15 miles) below the town. These were used both for storage and as a place of refuge when the city was under attack. Two sections of the passages are open to the public. These sections contain former barracks, cavernous abattoirs, bakeries, and a deep well. *Admission: 50 fr.L. adults, 30 fr.L. children. Open July–Sept.*

❺ Take rue de l'ancien Athénée alongside the former Jesuit college, now the National Library. In rue Notre-Dame to your right is the main entrance to the **Cathédrale Notre-Dame,** with its Baroque organ gallery and crypt containing the tomb of John the Blind, the 14th-century king of Bohemia and count of Luxembourg. The valley side of the church was rebuilt in 1935; the roof of the main tower was rebuilt after a fire in 1985. *Open daily 7:30–noon and 2–7; crypt open only by request.*

Opposite the cathedral lies the place Guillaume, known locally as the Knuedler, a name derived from the girdle worn by Franciscan monks who once had a monastery on the site. On market days (Wednesday and Saturday mornings) the square is noisy and colorful.

Time Out The place Guillaume is an excellent spot to sit in an outdoor café and enjoy the passing scene. You might also walk one block north along rue Chimay to the smaller place d'Armes and have lunch at the fashionable **Le Rabelais** (4 pl. d'Armes, tel. 222202) or the traditional and reasonably priced **l'Académie** (11 pl. d'Armes, tel. 227131).

❻ The lively place d'Armes, with its cafés and restaurants, lies just beyond the place Guillaume. Open-air concerts are held every evening in summer. The town tourist office is located on the square, and on rue du Curé there is a small museum that houses the **Maquette,** a model of the fortress at various stages of its construction: It provides a fascinating glimpse of the historical city. *Admission: 40 fr.L. adults, 20 fr.L. children. Open July–Aug. only, 10–12:30 and 2–6.*

❼ From place Guillaume, rue de la Reine leads to the **Grand Ducal Palace,** currently closed for renovations (the duke works and resides temporarily in the Villa Vauban, in the municipal park).

Behind the palace is the oldest part of town, the Marché-aux-Poissons, site of the old fish market and originally the crossing point of two Roman roads. Now a quiet square, it comes alive on

Easter Monday with the quaint, if obscure, Emais'chen Festival in which lovers exchange terra-cotta bird whistles and everyone indulges in *thüringer* (the standard local sausage) and the ubiquitous *gromperekichelcher* (fried potato patties).

8 On the left is the **Musée National** (National Museum), set in an attractive row of 16th-century houses. The museum contains an eclectic collection of exhibits from the Stone Age to the Space Age, encompassing humble village crafts and fine arts. The Gallo-Roman collection features a fascinating assortment of small treasures—toga buckles, miniature deities—unearthed along the ancient routes that crisscrossed Luxembourg in the first centuries AD. Dramatic views over the ramparts compensate for the slightly confusing museum route. The museum now houses the spectacular Bentinck-Thyssen collection of 15th- to 19th-century art, including works by Breughel, Rembrandt, Canaletto, and other masters. *Admission free. Open Tues.- Fri. 10–4:45, Sat. 2–5:45, Sun. 10–11:45 and 2–5:45.*

Time Out In the rue Wiltheim, which runs alongside the Musée de l'Etat, is the **Welle Man,** the quintessentially Luxembourgish museum bar. Sit on the tiny terrace and enjoy the magnificent view along the Alzette Valley or admire the massive carved furniture inside. Sip a glass of Elbling or Rivaner, local white wines, or try a kir, made from black-currant liqueur and white wine. Open until 7 PM. *rue Wiltheim 12. No credit cards. Closed Mon. Inexpensive.*

9 At the bottom of rue Wiltheim is the gate of **St.-Michel** and its Trois Tours (Three Towers), the oldest of which was built around 1050. During the French Revolution, the guillotine was set up in these towers. From here you can clearly see the source of Luxembourg's strength as a fortress.

10 Facing the valley, to your right is the **Bock** promontory, the site of the earliest castle (AD 963) and always the duchy's most fortified point. From the Bock, steep cliffs plunge downward to the Alzette Valley. The Bock also has a series of passages similar to the Petrusse Casemates. *Admission: 50 fr.L. adults, 30 fr.L. children. Open Mar.–Oct., daily 10–5.*

The scenic ramparts of the Bock's **Corniche** provide a view over the lower town, known as the Grund. Many of the houses on the right were refuges, used in times of danger by nobles and churchmen from the surrounding area. The massive towers on the far side of the valley date to the Wenceslas fortifications, which, in 1390, extended the protected area, and the block-like *casernes* (barracks) were built in the 17th century by the French.

At the ruined fortifications of the Citadelle du St-Ésprit, take the elevator down to the Grund, and turn right on leaving the tunnel. As you follow the valley below the cliffs, you'll see two signs marking the high-water points of two devastating floods; that's why the rivers have been tamed with locks and concrete today. Turn right into the green Petrusse Valley park. On the **11** left, the little **chapel of St-Quirin** is built into the rock near the Passerelle Viaduct. The cave it surrounds is said to have been carved by the Celts; it is known to have housed a chapel since at least the 4th century. The relics of St-Quirin, transferred in 1050 from Avignon to Deutz-on-Rhine, spent a night in the chapel. At Pont Adolphe, walk back up to city level and you are suddenly face-to-face with the 20th century. The boulevard Royal, once the main moat of the fortress, is now Luxembourg's Wall Street, packed with the famous names of the international banking scene.

From here you can either take avenue de la Liberté, an important shopping street, toward the station or head back into town, perhaps to the Grand Rue shopping area. Or if you want to extend your tour, take avenue Emile Reuter to the municipal park and **Villa Vauban,** the Duke's temporary lodging during palace renovations. Portions of its permanent collection of Dutch and Flemish paintings may be seen at the Musée de l'Etat.

Off the Beaten Track

Walk up boulevard Royal to rond-point Robert Schuman, named for one of the founders of the European Common Market, and cross the Pont Grande Duchesse Charlotte (with stunning views of the valley) to **Plateau Kirchberg,** a moonscape of modern architecture housing the European Court of Justice and various branches of the European Community. The most prominent structure—at 23 stories, Luxembourg's only skyscraper—is home to the secretariat of the European Parliament.

Shopping

Luxembourg City has two main shopping areas: the **Grand-Rue** and the **avenue de la Gare.** Jewelry and designer fashions are particularly well represented in the Grand-Rue. There are a few small department stores near the train station, but most of the stores in this area are specialty shops. Luxembourg chocolates, called *knippercher*, are popular purchases, available from the best pastry shops. Luxembourg's most famous product is Villeroy and Boch porcelain, available in most gift shops here. Feast your eyes at the glossy main shop, located at rue du Fossé 2, then buy at the excellent second-quality factory outlet (rue Rollingergrund 330).

Excursions from Luxembourg City

It would be a shame to leave Luxembourg without having explored some of the areas around the capital. To see the Ardennes, take Route N7 to **Diekirch,** where there is a church dating from the 7th century with Frankish tombs in the crypt. There are traces here of even older civilizations: the **Devil's Altar,** a Celtic dolmen, and some 4th-century Roman mosaics from nearby villas.

Another rewarding drive is northeast on Route E29 to **Echternach,** where St. Willibrord, a 7th-century English missionary, founded a Benedictine abbey. Many of the abbey buildings are now schools, but each year on the Tuesday after Pentecost, 15,000 pilgrims flock to the basilica, which is built on the site of the original chapel. In the crypt are frescoes dating to the 11th century.

To take in some of Luxembourg's best castles, allow a full day to take E27 northeast toward Junglinster, then cut north to **Bourglinster,** fully restored and complete with café;

Larochette, its castle still inhabited, although the owners allow visitors to wander the older ruins out back; and **Beaufort,** a dramatic mix of ruins and restored chambers. Then follow the German border north to **Vianden,** perhaps the most spectacular of all, and still in the possession of the grand-duke's family.

Dining

"French quality, German quantity"—that's an apt and common description of Luxembourg cuisine. Yet this tiny country has its own earthy specialties, fresh off the farm: *judd mat gardebohn'en* (salted pork with fava beans); *Eslecker ham* or *jambon d'Ardennes* (pearly-pink raw-smoked ham served cold with pickled onions); *choucroute* (sauerkraut); *treipen* (blood pudding); and batter-fried *merlan* (whiting). A few restaurants still feature them, though nowadays you're as likely to find Chinese, Thai, Japanese, Indian, and—leading the ethnic selection by several laps—Italian. And there are more star-studded *"gastronomique"* restaurants in Luxembourg per capita than in any other European country. Many restaurants—including some of these world-class venues—offer an accessibly priced menu at lunch. Crisp, fruity white wines from the banks of the Moselle range from the humble Elbling and Rivaner to fine Pinot Gris and Riesling.

Dress　Stylish, casual dress is generally acceptable in most restaurants, but when in doubt, err on the formal side. In expensive French restaurants, formal dress is taken for granted.

Ratings　Prices quoted here are per person and include a first course, main course, and dessert, but not wine. Best bets are indicated by a star ★.

Category	All Areas
Very Expensive	over 2,500 fr.L.
Expensive	1,200–2,500 fr.L.
Moderate	600–1,200 fr.L.
Inexpensive	under 600 fr.L.

Very Expensive　**Clairefontaine.** Located next to the foreign ministry, this lavish but dignified gastronomic dining spot attracts luminaries and heads of state (including François Mitterrand and the pope), who are pampered by chef Tony Tintinger. His inspirations include a showcase of foie gras specialties, innovative fish dishes (soufflé of langoustines perfumed with star anise), and game novelties (tournedos of doe larded with wild mushrooms). There's a business lunch, a three-course prix-fixe, and a thorough menu dégustation, all complemented by an extensive wine cellar. It's less expensive, if less romantic, than St-Michel (*see below*). *9 pl. de Clairefontaine, tel. 462211. Reservations required. AE, DC, MC, V. Closed Sat. dinner, Sun.*

St-Michel. Located in a 16th-century building behind the ducal palace, warmly lit, intimate, and filled with antiques (but not stuffy), this is one of the finest restaurants in the region. A five-course *menu dégustation* (tasting menu) and a three-course *menu découverte* (discovery) showcase Breton-born chef Pierrick Guillou's extraordinary skills. Specialties include *cotriade croisicaise*, a traditional Breton fish stew. The wine list is exhaustive. *32 rue de l'Eau, tel. 223215. Reservations required. AE, DC, MC, V. Closed Sat.–Sun.*

Expensive **La Lorraine.** Strategically placed on the place d'Armes, with terrace tables under its awnings, this seafood restaurant caters to tourists passing by but also serves serious meals upstairs in a formal dining room. A retail shop around the corner shows off the coast-fresh quality of their wares: Heaps of briny oysters, glistening turbot and sole, wriggling crabs. Once prepared, they live up to their promise: Baked skate in hazelnut butter with capers, puff-pastry with sole, and morel are good bets. *pl. d'Armes 7, tel. 474620. Reservations advised. Jacket advised indoors. AE, DC, MC, V. Closed Sat. lunch, Sun.*

Speltz. In a chic, restored 17th-century home in the middle of the pedestrian shopping area, this stylish restaurant caters to a young business crowd, serving a reasonable prix-fixe lunch that may include Vosges quail in Armagnac gelée, or venison stew with herbed *spätzle* (small dumplings). *8 rue Chimay, tel. 474950. Reservations advised. Jacket and tie advised. AE, DC, MC, V. Closed Sat., Sun.*

Moderate **Ancre d'Or.** This tidy, friendly brasserie, just off the place
★ Guillaume, serves a wide variety of old-time Luxembourgish specialties as well as good *cuisine bourgeoise.* Try their *judd mat gardebohn'en, kuddelfleck* (breaded tripe), or *treipen* (rich blood sausages served with red cabbage and apple sauce). The apple tart (Luxembourgish style, with custard base) is homemade. Portions are generous, service friendly, and the clientele local. *23 rue du Fossé, tel. 472973. Reservations advised at lunch. MC, V. Closed Sun.*

Kamakura. If heavy Western cuisine palls, take the elevator from the Citadelle du St-Esprit to the up-and-coming Grund and try this chic Japanese restaurant. A number of fixed-price menus offer a variety of delicate, nouvelle-accented dishes, artfully presented and graciously served. A la carte specialties, considerably more expensive, include impeccably fresh sashimi (raw fish) and light tempura vegetables. *2–4 rue Munster, tel. 470604. Reservations accepted. AE, DC, MC, V. Closed Sun.*

★ **La Trattoria dei Quattro.** Despite an undesirable location—on one of the sleazier back streets around the avenue de la Gare shopping area–this restaurant merits the trip off the beaten track. It's set in a 150-year-old town house with an impressive carved wooden ceiling and fireplace. Excellent homemade pastas include *maccheroni alla Sarda* (sauced with tomato, onion, tuna, and fennel seeds) and *bucatini alla melanzani e funghi* (with eggplant and mushrooms). *64 rue Fort-neipperg, tel. 490039. Reservations accepted. AE, DC, MC, V. Closed Sun.*

★ **Mousel's Cantine.** Directly adjoining the great Mousel brewery (there are beer taps that feed from tanks within), this fresh, comfortable café serves up heaping platters of local specialties—braised and grilled ham, sausage, *gardebohn'en* (fava beans), sauerkraut, and fried potatoes—to be washed down with crockery steins of creamy *Gezwickelte Béier* (unfiltered beer). The front café is brighter, with sanded tabletops, but the tiny fluorescent-lit dining room has windows into the brewery. *46 montée de Clausen, tel. 470198. Reservations advised. MV, V. Closed Sun.*

Inexpensive **Ems.** Directly across the street from the train station, this lively diner-equivalent (vinyl booths, posted specials) draws a loyal clientele for its vast portions of *moules* (mussels) in a rich wine-and-garlic broth, accompanied by *frites* (french fries) and a bottle of sharp, cold Auxerrois or Rivaner. For dessert, try one of the huge ice-cream specialties. Food is served until 1 AM. *30 pl. de la Gare, tel. 487799. Reservations not necessary. AE, DC, MC, V.*

Taverne Bit. With sanded tabletops and dark-wood banquettes, this is a cozy and very local pub, where you can drink a *clensch* (stein) of draft Bitburger beer (from just across the German border) and have a plate of sausage with good potato salad, a plate of cold ham, or *kachkes*, the pungent local cheese spread, served with baked potatoes. It's just off the Parking Glacis. *43 allée Scheffer, tel. 460751. Reservations not necessary. No credit cards. Closed Sat. PM, Sun.*

Lodging

Hotels in Luxembourg City are located in three main areas: the town center, the station area, and the area close to the airport. By far the largest number are around the station. Most hotels are modern, but a warm welcome and high standards compensate for the relative lack of character.

Ratings   Price categories are determined by the cost of a double room (Continental breakfast is sometimes included in the room price). Best bets are indicated by a star ★.

Category	Cost
Very Expensive	over 5,000 fr.L.
Expensive	3,500–5,000 fr.L.
Moderate	2,500–3,500 fr.L.
Inexpensive	under 2,500 fr.L.

Very Expensive
★ **Le Royal.** Located in the city center, on the Wall Street of Luxembourg and within steps of parks, shopping, and the old town, this is the best choice for luxury. It's solid, modern (opened 1984), and sleek, with a great deal of lacquer, marble, and glass. Opt for a back room toward the park if possible; those facing the boulevard Royal have traffic noise leaking through the double-glazed windows. The piano bar is popular, as is the brasserie Le Jardin, especially when the fountain terrace is open. *12 blvd. Royal, tel. 41616; fax 225948. 180 rooms with bath. Facilities: 2 restaurants, piano bar, exercise equipment, pool, hairdresser; sauna and tennis for a fee. AE, DC, MC, V.*

Expensive **Arcotel.** Opened in 1985 on the busy shopping street between the old town and the train station, this airtight, modernized hotel provides a quiet getaway from the city outside. Decorated in warm shades of beige and rose, with polished wood and brass, it offers solid baths and extra comforts—hair dryers in the bathroom, drinks in the Bokhara-lined lounge—to make up for typically small rooms. *43 av. de la Gare, tel. 494001; fax 405624. 30 rooms with bath. Facilities: breakfast room (no restaurant). AE, DC, MC, V.*

★ **Cravat.** This charming Luxembourg relic—moderately grand, modestly glamorous—continues to hold forth at the best location in town, straddling the valley and the old town. Built in several phases since the turn of the century, it features a mix of solid old architectural details; and though corridors have a dated, institutional air, the rooms are fresh and welcoming in a variety of tastefully retro styles. The Deco coffee shop still draws fur-hatted ladies of a certain age to tea. *29 blvd. F. D. Roosevelt, tel. 221975; fax 226711. 60 rooms with bath. Facilities: restaurant, coffee shop, bar. AE, DC, MC, V.*

Moderate **Auberge du Coin.** At the edge of a quiet, dignified residential
★ area but within easy reach of the station and the old town, this pleasant hotel was completely renovated in 1989 in pure "new Luxembourg" style—stone and terra-cotta floors, wood-framed double windows, polished oak, Persian rugs, and tropical plants. Rooms are freshly furnished in bright knotty pine with new tile baths. There's a lovely French restaurant and a comfortable oak-and-stone bar as well. Prices are at the high end of this category; the nine-room matching annex down the street, which has no elevator, costs slightly less. *2 blvd. de la Petrusse, tel. 402101; fax 403666. 23 rooms with bath. Facilities: restaurant, bar. AE, DC, MC, V.*

Empire. Slick, freshly decorated, simple, and aimed at single businesspeople (there are only three double rooms), this station hotel offers all comforts and a few bargain no-bath rooms (though all have toilets). Both a pizzeria and a French restaurant adjoin. *34 pl. de la Gare, tel. 485252; fax 491937. 31 rooms with bath. Facilities: restaurant, pizzeria, bar. AE, DC, MC, V.*

★ **Italia.** This is a valuable and remarkably inexpensive find in the *gare* area: a former private apartment converted into hotel rooms, some with plaster details and cabinetry left behind. Rooms are solid and freshly furnished, all with private tiled bathrooms. The somewhat pricey restaurant downstairs is one of the city's better Italian eateries. *15–17 rue d'Anvers, tel. 486626; fax 480807. 20 rooms with bath. Facilities: restaurant, bar, garden. AE, DC, MC, V.*

Nobilis. Built new in 1980 on the busy avenue de la Gare and decorated in heavy wood and earth tones, this is a welcoming, relatively quiet property with business-class comforts. Despite double-glazed windows in front, back rooms (over the parking area) are considerably quieter, and cost only slightly more. *47 av. de la Gare, tel. 494971; fax 403101. 44 rooms with bath. Facilities: restaurant, coffee shop, bar. AE, DC, MC, V.*

Inexpensive **Bristol.** Though on a street near the train station that is lined with strip joints and flophouses (as well as legitimate shops and restaurants), this modest hotel offers comfortable, secure lodging and fresh decor. The lobby/bar is warm and familial, and baths are newly refurbished. A few bathless rooms on the first and fourth floors go for bargain rates. *11 rue de Strasbourg, tel. 485830; fax 486480. 30 rooms, 22 with shower/toilet. Facilities: bar for guests only. AE, DC, MC, V.*

★ **Carlton.** In this vast 1918 hotel, buffered from the rue de Strasbourg scene by a rank of stores and opening onto a quiet inner court, budget travelers will find roomy, quiet quarters. The beveled glass, oak parquet, and terrazzo floors are original—but so are the toilets, all located down the hall. Each room has antique beds, floral-print comforters, and a sink; wood floors, despite creaks, are white-glove clean. *9 rue de Strasbourg, tel. 484802; fax 486480. 50 rooms without toilet. Facilities: breakfast room, bar. No credit cards.*

20 Malta

The Mediterranean island of Malta, and its two sister islands, Gozo and Comino, enjoy a mild, sunny climate and attractive bays and beaches—a felicitous setting for such a festive and hospitable people.

For those interested in history and archaeology, tiny Malta—with only 28 kilometers (17 miles) between its two farthest points—displays the remains of a long and eventful history. Among the most fascinating ruins are Neolithic temples and stone megaliths left by prehistoric inhabitants. In AD 60, St. Paul, shipwrecked here, converted the people to Christianity. Other, less welcome visitors, attracted by Malta's strategic position, conquered and ruled. These included the Phoenicians, Carthaginians, and Romans.

The Knights of the Order of St. John of Jerusalem arrived here in 1530 after they had been driven from their stronghold on the island of Rhodes by the Ottoman emperor Suleiman the Magnificent. In 1565, with only a handful of men, the Knights held Malta against the Ottoman Turks in a dramatic and bloody siege. They ruled the islands until Napoleon arrived in 1798 and left massive fortifications, rich architecture, and the city of Valletta, Malta's capital.

The British drove the French out in 1800 and gave the island the distinctive British feel that it still retains. In 1942, during World War II, King George VI awarded the Maltese people the George Cross for their courage in withstanding repeated German and Italian attacks, especially from the air. Malta gained independence from Britain in 1964 and was declared a republic within the Commonwealth in 1974. On December 2–3, 1989, the island hosted the first Bush-Gorbachev summit, marking the beginning of improved relations between the two superpowers.

Essential Information

Before You Go

When to Go The archipelago is a year-round delight, but May through October is the time of the main tourist season. April and May are the months for spring freshness; the summer months can be very hot, though sometimes tempered by sea breezes. August is just too hot for touring. If you visit in the winter, you'll find the climate pleasant and mild, but you may encounter sudden rainstorms.

Climate The following are the average daily maximum and minimum temperatures for Valletta.

Jan.	58F	14C	May	71F	22C	Sept.	81F	27C
	50	10		61	16		71	22
Feb.	59F	15C	June	79F	26C	Oct.	75F	24C
	51	10		67	19		66	19
Mar.	61F	16C	July	84F	29C	Nov.	67F	20C
	52	11		72	22		60	16
Apr.	65F	18C	Aug.	85F	29C	Dec.	61F	16C
	56	13		73	23		54	12

Currency The unit of currency is the Maltese lira (Lm), also sometimes referred to as the pound. It's divided into 100 cents, and the

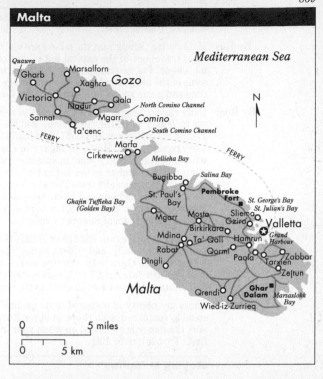

Malta

Mediterranean Sea

Quawra

Gharb • Marsalforn

Xaghra *Gozo*

Victoria

Nadur   Qala   *North Comino Channel*

Sannat   Mgarr   *Comino*

Ta'cenc   *South Comino Channel*

FERRY   Marfa

Cirkewwa   *Mellieha Bay*

FERRY

Bugibba   *Salina Bay*

St. Paul's   **Pembroke**
Bay   **Fort**   St. George's Bay

Ghajin Tuffieha Bay   St. Julian's Bay
(Golden Bay)   Mgarr   Mosta   Sliema

Gzira   *Valletta*

Birkirkara   Hamrun   *Grand
Harbour*

Mdina   Ta' Qali

Rabat   Qormi   Zabbar

Dingli   Paola   Tarxien

Zejtun

Malta   Qrendi   **Ghar
Dalam**   *Marsaxlokk
Bay*

Wied-iz-Zurrieq

0 _____ 5 miles

0 _____ 5 km

cents are divided into 10 mils; but in recent years the mils have dropped out of circulation. There are Lm 20, Lm 10, Lm 5, and Lm 2 bills; coins—1¢, 2¢, 5¢, 10¢, 25¢, 50¢, and Lm 1—are bronze and silver. At press time (spring 1993), the exchange rate was Lm .36 to the dollar and Lm .57 to the pound sterling.

What It Will Cost   Malta is one of the cheapest holiday destinations in Europe, though with the rapid tourist development, prices are inevitably rising. Prices tend to be uniform across the island, except in Valletta, the capital, where they are slightly higher.

Sample Prices   Cup of coffee, 25¢ (Maltese); bottle of beer, 25¢; Coca-Cola, 15¢.

Customs on Arrival   You may bring into Malta, duty-free, 200 cigarettes, one bottle of liquor, one bottle of wine, and one bottle of perfume. You may bring in up to Lm 50 in currency.

Language   The spelling of many Maltese words can be bewildering. Fortunately, both Maltese and English are the official languages on the island, so you shouldn't experience any problems. Italian is widely spoken, too.

Getting Around

By Car   The roads around Valletta are busy most mornings, but a new road network has made it easier to reach Sliema–St. Julian's from the airport. Road conditions are generally good, and driving around the island is pleasant. Driving is on the left-hand side of the road. Speed limits are 40 kph (25 mph) in towns, 65 kph (40 mph) elsewhere. International and British driving licenses are acceptable.

By Bus Most routes throughout the island are via Valletta, which facilitates travel out of the capital but makes cross-country trips a bit longer. Public transportation is very inexpensive. Though some of the old green buses show their age, they are usually on time and plans are in hand to renew the fleet.

By Boat Daily car/passenger ferries operate year-round from Cirkewwa to Mġarr on Gozo. Telephone 243964 in Malta; 580435 or 571884 in Cirkewwa; and 556114 or 556743 in Gozo for details. The crossing from Marfa to Mġarr in Gozo lasts 25 minutes, with departures every hour in summer and every two hours in winter. The round-trip fare is Lm 1 adults, 50¢ children. There is also one service daily from Pietà to Gozo, leaving in the morning and taking an hour and 15 minutes each way. The fare from Mġarr (passenger plus car) is Lm 3.50. A ferry service links the tourist resort town of Sliema to Valletta.

By Helicopter **Malta Air Charter** (tel. 882916 or 882920) flies to and from Gozo several times daily and offers helicopter sightseeing tours. Flight time to Gozo is 10 minutes and costs Lm 17 round-trip (open return date) and Lm 15 (same-day return). Twenty- and 40-minute tours cost Lm 12 and Lm 20, respectively.

By Taxi There are plenty of metered taxis available and fares are reasonable compared with those in other European countries. Be sure the meter is switched on when your trip starts, or bargain first. Tip the driver 10%.

Staying in Malta

Telephones There is direct dialing to most parts of the world from Malta. The best place to make calls is either from your hotel or from the Overseas Telephone Division of Telemalta at St. George's, Qawra, St. Paul's Bay, Sliema, Valletta, and Luqa International Airport. The international dialing access code is 00. Overseas telephone operator (tel. 194), time check (tel. 194), flight inquiries (tel. 249600).

Mail Airmail letters to the United States cost 14¢; postcards cost 12¢. Airmail letters to the United Kingdom cost 10¢; postcards 10¢.

Opening and Closing Times Banks are open weekdays 8:30–12:30, Saturday 8:30–noon. Summer hours are weekdays 8–noon, Saturday 8–11:30. Banks in tourist areas are also open in the afternoon.

Museums run by the Museums Department are generally open mid-June through September, daily 8–2; October through mid-June, daily 8:30–5; closed holidays. Other museums' hours may vary slightly, so check locally.

Shops are open Monday–Saturday 9–1 and 4–7.

National Holidays January 1; February 10 (St. Paul's shipwreck); March 19 (St. Joseph's Day); March 31 (Freedom Day); April 1 (Good Friday); May 1 (Workers' Day); June 7 (Sette Giugno); June 29 (Sts. Peter and Paul); August 15 (Assumption, or Santa Marija); September 8 (Our Lady of Victories); September 21 (Independence Day); December 8 (Immaculate Conception); December 13 (Republic Day); December 25.

Dining There is a good choice of restaurants, ranging from expensive hotel restaurants to fast-food hamburger joints. Local specialties include *torta tal-lampuki* (dorado fish pie), *dentici* (sea bream), and tuna. *Minestra* is the local variant of minestrone soup, and the *timpana* (baked macaroni and meat) is filling. Rabbit, stewed or fried, is a national dish. Accompany your meal with the locally produced wine: *Marsovin* comes in red, white, or rosé; *Lachryma Vitis*, in red or white—try sampling the house wines, too. Maltese beers are excellent; highly popular are Cisk Lager and Hop Leaf. Lowenbrau recently began brewing in Malta, too.

Precautions The water in Malta is safe to drink, with the only drawback being its salty taste: Many prefer bottled mineral water.

Dress A jacket and tie are suggested for higher-priced restaurants. Otherwise, casual dress is acceptable.

Ratings Prices are for a three-course meal, not including wine, sales tax, and tip. Best bets are indicated by a star ★.

Category	Cost*
Expensive	over Lm 9
Moderate	Lm 6–Lm 9
Inexpensive	under Lm 6

10% sales tax is charged on meals eaten in all but the most informal restaurants.

Lodging Malta has a variety of lodgings, from deluxe modern hotels to modest guest houses. There are also self-contained complexes geared mainly to package tours.

Ratings Prices are for two people sharing a double room and exclude the 5% room tax.

Category	Cost
Very Expensive	over Lm 35
Expensive	Lm 22–Lm 35
Moderate	Lm 12–Lm 22
Inexpensive	under Lm 12

Tipping A tip of 10% is expected when a service charge is not included.

Valletta

Arriving and Departing

By Plane There are no direct flights from the United States, but several airlines, including **Air Malta,** fly from London, Paris, Frankfurt, Athens, and Rome to Luqa Airport, 6 kilometers (4 miles) south of Valletta.

Between the Airport and Downtown There is a local bus service that passes through the town of Luqa on its way to Valletta, with a stop in front of the airport. It operates every 10 or 15 minutes from 6 AM to 11 PM; the trip takes about 30 minutes, and the fare is about 10¢.

Taxis are also available and prices are posted on a board at the taxi stand.

By Boat The **Gozo Channel Co.** (tel. 243964) operates weekly car and passenger ferries from Catania, Sicily, during the summer. The **Tirrenia Line** (Malta agents: **SMS,** 311 Republic St., Valletta, tel. 232211 or U.K. agents: **Serena Holidays,** 40–42 Kenway Rd., London SW5 ORA, tel. 071/370–6293) operates ferries year-round, three times a week (Tuesday, Friday, Sunday) from Syracuse, Catania, and Reggio Calabria, and a weekly (Thursday) ferry service from Naples.

Virtu (tel. 318854) runs an express ferry service during the summer from Catania (Tuesday, Friday, Saturday, Sunday); Pozzallo (Monday, Wednesday, Thursday, Friday, Sunday); and Licata (Wednesday, Sunday); and in winter, from Catania (Saturday) and Pozzallo (Thursday).

Important Addresses and Numbers

Tourist Information **Gozo** (Mġarr Harbor, tel. 553343).
St. Julian's Bay (Balluta Bay, tel. 342671 or 342672).
Sliema (Bisazza St., tel. 313409).
Valletta (1 City Gate Arcade, tel. 237747; Luqa Airport, tel. 249600; or 280 Republic St., tel. 224444 or 228282).

Embassies **U.S. Development House** (St. Anne St., Floriana, tel. 243653). **British High Commission** (7 St. Anne St., Floriana, tel. 233134).

Emergencies **Hospital:** St. Luke's (Gwardamangia, tel. 241251) or Craig Hospital (Gozo, tel. 561600). **Police** (tel. 191). **Ambulance** (tel. 196). **Fire Brigade** (tel. 199).

Travel Agencies **Thomas Cook** (Il-Pjazzetta, Tower Road, Sliema, tel. 344225). **American Express** (representative) (Brockdorff, 14 Zachary St., Valletta, tel. 232141).

Guided Tours

Orientation Sightseeing tours are arranged by local travel agents and the large hotels. There are half-day, full-day, and "Malta by Night" taxi tours; rates vary according to the sights covered and whether or not meals are included. Contact the tourist offices above for details.

One-hour boat tours of the harbor of Valletta leave regularly from Sliema jetty. Prices vary; buy tickets at most travel agencies.

Personal Guides Licensed guides can be hired through the tourist information office at the City Gate Arcade in Valletta.

Exploring Valletta

The minicity of Valletta, with ornate palaces and museums, protected by massive honey-colored fortifications, was built by the Knights of the Order of St. John who occupied the island from 1530 to 1798.

The main entrance to the city is through the arched **City Gate** (where all bus routes end), which leads onto Republic Street, the spine of the city and the main shopping street. From Republic Street, other streets are laid out on a grid pattern. Some streets are stepped. Houses along the narrow streets have overhanging wooden balconies, which foreign artists visiting the island love to paint.

Valletta's small size makes it ideal to explore on foot. Before setting out along Republic Street, stop at the tourist information office for maps, brochures, and a copy of *What's On*. On your left is the Auberge de Provence (the hostel of the knights from Provence), which now houses the **National Museum of Archaeology.** Its collection includes finds from Malta's many prehistoric sites—Tarxien, Hagar Qim, and the Hypogeum at Paola. You'll see pottery, statuettes, temple carvings, and, on the upper floor, finds from Punic and Roman tombs. *Republic St., tel. 225577. Admission: Lm 1. Open mid-June–Sept., daily 8–2; Oct.–mid-June, daily 8:30–5; closed holidays.*

From Republic Street, turn right at the Inter-Flora kiosk and head to St. John's Square. Dominating the square (where an open-air market is held) is **St. John's co-Cathedral.** This was the Order of St. John's own church, completed in 1578. It is by far Malta's most important treasure. A side chapel was given to each national group of knights, who decorated it in their own distinctive way. The cathedral **museum** includes the oratory in which hangs *The Beheading of St. John*, the masterpiece painted by Caravaggio when he was staying on Malta in 1608. In the museum, you'll find a rich collection of Flemish tapestries based on drawings by Poussin and Rubens, antique embroidered vestments, and illuminated manuscripts. Keep your ticket, since you can use it to get into the cathedral at Mdina. *St. John's Sq. Museum admission: 50¢. Open weekdays 9:30–noon and 3–5:30.*

While in St. John's Square, visit the **Government Craft Center,** which has a wide range of traditional, handmade goods. *Open weekdays 9–7, Sat. 9–1 and 4–7.*

Continue along Republic Street to the **Grand Master's Palace,** where Malta's parliament sits. You can walk through the shady courtyards. Inside, friezes in the sumptuously decorated state apartments depict scenes from the history of the Knights. There is also a gallery with Gobelin tapestries. At the back of the building is the **Armoury of the Knights,** with displays of arms and armor down through the ages. *Republic St. Admission: Lm 1. Open mid-June–Sept., daily 8–2; Oct.–mid-June, 8:30–5; closed holidays.*

Also on Republic Street, spend some time at Casa Rocca Piccola, a traditional 16th-century Maltese house. Continue to Fort St. Elmo and the War Museum. **Fort St. Elmo** was built by the Knights to defend the harbor. Though completely destroyed during the siege of 1565, it was rebuilt by succeeding military leaders. Today part of the fort houses the **War Museum,** with its collection of armaments largely related to Malta's role in World War II. Here you can see an Italian E-boat and the Gladiator *Faith*, one of three Gloster Gladiator biplanes that defended the island. The other two, *Hope* and *Charity*, were shot down in the air battles of 1942–44. *St. Elmo. Admission: Lm 1. Open mid-June–Sept., daily 8–2; Oct.–mid-June, daily 8:30–5; closed holidays.*

Continue along the seawall to the **Hospital of the Order** at the end of Merchants Street. This gracious building has been converted into the Mediterranean Conference Center. For an excellent introduction to the island, see the "Malta Experience," a multimedia presentation on the history of Malta that is given here six times a day. *Admission: Lm 2.*

Continue along the seawall and climb up to the **Upper Barrakka Gardens.** Once part of the city's defenses, they're now a pleasant area from which to watch the comings and goings in the Grand Harbour.

Then walk down to Merchants Street, which is dominated by an open-air market. Here, the hagglers among you can snap up some terrific bargains. Next, cut along South Street, across Republic Street, to the **National Museum of Fine Art.** The former 18th-century palace has paintings from the 16th century to the present day, including works by Tintoretto, Preti, and Tiepolo, as well as local artists. *South St., tel. 225769. Admission: Lm 1. Open mid-June–Sept., daily 8–2; Oct.–mid-June, daily 8:30–5; closed holidays.*

Dining

For details and price-category definitions, *see* Dining in Staying in Malta.

Expensive **Giannini.** Atop Valletta's mighty bastions, this is one of the city's most elegant restaurants. Leading local politicos and the fashionable set dine here on Maltese-Italian cuisine, especially seafood, while enjoying the marvelous view. *23 Windmill St., tel. 237121 or 236575. Reservations required. AE, DC, MC, V.*

Moderate **Pappagallo.** This restaurant in Valletta is popular with locals
★ and visitors alike. Traditional Maltese food is featured, and the bustling atmosphere is warm and friendly. *Melita St., tel. 236195. Reservations advised. AE, DC, MC, V. Closed Mar.*
Scalini. An attractive cellar restaurant with walls of Malta's golden limestone, it features seafood and Italian-style pastas. The fixed-price menu is a good value. *32 South St., tel. 246221. Dress: casual. Reservations advised. AE, DC, MC, V.*

Inexpensive **The Lantern.** This friendly spot is run by two brothers who thrive on pampering clients. The unattractive 18th-century town-house location may not win any design awards, but the food is delicious and served in a traditional Maltese atmosphere. *20 Sapper St., Valletta, tel. 227521. Reservations advised.*
Pizzeria Bologna. A street-level annex of the good restaurant upstairs, and beside the Grand Master's Palace, it serves delicious pizzas with an interesting choice of ingredients. *59 Republic St., tel. 238014. Open until 9 in the evening.*

Lodging

For details and price-category definitions, *see* Lodging in Staying in Malta.

Very Expensive **Holiday Inn Crowne Plaza.** This large resort hotel is in Sliema, close to the sea and the major shopping area. It offers a full range of resort activities from swimming and windsurfing to dining and dancing. *Tigne St., Sliema, tel. 341173, fax 311292. 180 rooms with bath. Facilities: restaurant, bar, pool, tennis, gym, sauna. AE, DC, MC, V.*

Expensive **Fortina Hotel.** At Sliema seafront, the Fortina has excellent views of Valletta's dramatic fortifications, which are floodlit magnificently at night. The atmosphere here is relaxed and informal; the service, attentive. It's also close to the departure points for Valletta harbor cruises. *Tigne Seafront, tel. 343380 or 342976, fax 339388. 134 rooms with bath. Facilities: game room, waterfront lido with pool and snack bar, sunroof. AE, DC, MC, V.*

Grand Hotel des Lapins. A modern building on the banks of the Ta' Xbiex seafront, this hotel has contemporary decor, and it overlooks Malta's newest yacht marina. It's popular with businesspeople, but offers resort facilities, too. *Ta' Xbiex Seafront, tel. 342551, fax 319392. 150 rooms with bath. Facilities: restaurant, bar, pool, tennis. AE, DC, MC, V.*

Moderate **Castille.** For a touch of old Malta, stay at the Castille in what used to be a 16th-century palazzo. This is a gracious, comfortable, Old World hotel with a friendly, relaxed ambience. It has an ideal central location, close to the museums and the bus terminus. There's a good rooftop restaurant with an excellent fixed-price menu offering several choices. A pianist plays most evenings during dinner, and the views across the harbor are stunning. *St. Paul St., tel. 243677 or 243678, fax 243679. 35 rooms with bath. Facilities: coffee shop-bar, sun terrace. AE.*

Osborne. Centrally located in Valletta, it has spacious rooms and undistinguished decor. Spend a few minutes in the rooftop lounge and enjoy the view. *South St., tel. 232128, fax 232120. 50 rooms with bath. Facilities: restaurant. AE, DC, MC, V.*

Medina Motel. This is a good value close to the island's old capital, Mdina. It is not luxurious but is quite comfortable nonetheless, with a full fitness center and an indoor heated swimming pool. *Labour Ave., Rabat, tel. 453230. 45 rooms with bath. MC, V.*

Beyond Valletta

It is impractical to attempt a tour of Malta and Gozo in one day. Allow at least two days for the main island—three to include Valletta—and one full day for Gozo.

The rest of Malta has much to offer, ranging from strange prehistoric sites to richly decorated churches.

Leaving Valletta, head first for the **Hypogeum** at **Paola,** 6 kilometers (3½ miles) south of the capital. This massive area of underground chambers was used for burials more than 4,000 years ago. Built on three levels, the chambers descend to 40 feet beneath the ground, and there are examples of fine carving to be seen. *Admission: Lm 1. Open mid-June–Sept., daily 8–2; Oct.–mid-June, daily 8:30–5; closed holidays.*

Nearby is **Tarxien,** an ordinary suburban town with extraordinary megalithic monuments. The **Tarxien Temples** are three interconnecting temples with curious carvings, oracular chambers, and altars, all dating from about 2000 BC. *Admission: Lm 1. Open mid-June–Sept., daily 8–2; Oct.–mid-June, daily 8:30–5; closed holidays.*

Now make your way south to **Ghar Dalam.** A cave here, dating from the late Stone Age, was found to contain the semifossilized remains of long-extinct species of dwarf elephants and hippopotamuses that roamed the island. You can visit the cave and see the fossils on display in the small museum. *Admission: Lm 1. Open mid-June–Sept., daily 8–2; Oct.–mid-June, daily 8:30–5; closed holidays.*

Follow the coast northwest to the **Blue Grotto,** near Wied iz-Zurrieq. This is part of a group of water-filled caves made vivid by the phosphorescent marine life that colors the water a distinctive and magical blue. You can reach the grotto only by sea. Boatmen will take you there for about Lm 2.

Take the northwest route to Rabat and Mdina, visiting **Buskett,** a very old and colorful garden, along the way. This trip is best in the spring when the orange and lemon trees are in blossom. In **Rabat,** visit the beautiful **St. Paul's Church,** built next to a grotto where St. Paul is said to have taken refuge when he was shipwrecked on Malta in AD 60. Also of interest are the 4th-century **catacombs** of St. Paul and St. Agatha, unusual for their rock agape tables where mourners held celebratory meals for the dead. *Admission: Lm 1. Open mid-June–Sept., daily 8–2; Oct.–mid-June, daily 8:30–5; closed holidays.*

The Crafts Village at Ta' Qali is geared mainly toward tourists. Browse through the shops, but be cautious when buying. Here, in this converted World War II aerodrome, you can see filigree silver, gold jewelry, and hand-blown Mdina glass being made by age-old methods. There are also leather workshops and pottery shops selling gaily colored items. Some of the seconds in the glass workshops are good buys; the faults are often noticeable only to those with a trained eye.

Adjoining Rabat is **Mdina,** Malta's ancient walled capital. The Maltese have a special love for what is often called the Silent City. It certainly lives up to its sobriquet: There's no traffic here, and the noise of the busy world outside somehow doesn't penetrate the thick, golden walls. Wandering through the peaceful streets is like entering an earlier age. Visit the serene baroque cathedral of **St. Peter and St. Paul** for a look at Preti's 17th-century fresco *The Shipwreck of St. Paul* and the new **Mdina Dungeons** for a feel of the old Malta. In the museum (you can use the ticket from the cathedral museum of St. John's in Valletta), see the Dürer woodcuts and illuminated manuscripts. *Admission: 50¢. Open Mon.–Sat. 9–1 and 2–5.*

You have two choices. The first is to make your way back to Valletta by way of **Mosta** to see the **Church of St. Mary.** The Rotunda, as it is also known, has the third-largest unsupported dome in Europe, after the Pantheon and St. Peter's, both in Rome. You can also see the bomb (now rendered harmless) that crashed through the dome during a service in 1942 and fell to the ground without exploding—a miraculous escape for those in the crowded church.

The second—and better—choice is to head for the northwest tip of the island and take a ferry from Cirkewwa to **Gozo,** Malta's lusher, quieter sister island. The capital, Victoria, is a charming old town with attractive cafés and bars around the main square. In it lies the hilltop citadel of **Gran Castello,** with an impressive Baroque cathedral. The museum here offers displays of ceremonial silver and manuscripts. *Admission: Lm 1. Open mid-June–Sept., daily 8–2; Oct.–mid-June, daily 8:30–5; closed holidays.*

The town also has a recent **Folklore Museum** (Milite Bernardo St.) and an impressive archaeological collection in the **Gozo Museum** (Cathedral Square). *Admission to each: Lm 1. Open mid-June–Sept., daily 8–2; Oct.–mid-June, daily 8:30–5; closed holidays.*

On Xaghra plateau stands the extraordinary pair of **Ggantija Prehistoric Temples.** *Admission: Lm 1. Open mid-June–Sept., daily 8–2; Oct.–mid-June, daily 8:30–5; closed holidays.*

In the town of **Xaghra** itself, there are two underground alabaster caves with delicately colored stalagmites and stalactites. In the cliffs nearby is the cave where the sea nymph Calypso, mentioned in Homer's *Odyssey,* is said to have lived; with such stunning views, it's easy to imagine that the myth might be true.

Dining and Lodging

For details and price-category definitions, *see* Dining and Lodging in Staying in Malta.

Gozo   **Ta' Ċenċ.** Surprisingly, the little island of Gozo harbors one of
Lodging   the best hotels in this part of the Mediterranean. The Ta' Ċenċ is a luxurious paradise, and its location on the coast about 4 miles out of Victoria ensures guests' privacy and accommodates a full range of water sports. For this reason it's favored for top-level conventions, though it's small enough to be exclusive. *Ta' Ċenċ, near Sannat, tel. 561522 or 561525, fax 558199. 50 rooms with bath. Facilities: restaurant, bar, pools, tennis, disco. AE, DC, MC, V. Very Expensive.*
Calypso. This modern hotel has so many services and facilities that it's almost like a small town in itself. The choice of dining spots includes a Chinese restaurant. The rooms are comfortably furnished and have balconies, most with sea views. *Marsalforn, tel. 562000; fax 562012. 92 rooms with bath. Facilities: restaurants, nightclub, rooftop splash pool, boutique, bank. AE, DC, MC, V. Moderate.*
Cornucopia. For pleasant, personal service and a restful vacation, try this lovingly restored farmhouse near the village of Xaghra—it's an ideal base for exploring the island, and the sea is just a short drive away. There's a good restaurant and barbecues in the summer. *10 Gnien Imrik St., Xaghra, tel. 556486 or 553866; fax 552910. 40 rooms with bath. Facilities: restaurant, pool. AE, DC, MC, V. Moderate.*

St. Julian's   **San Giuliano.** St. Julian's and Sliema are Malta's smartest sea-
Dining   side resorts and main entertainment districts as well as the site of many restaurants and discos, especially in nearby Paceville. The San Giuliano is a fashionable restaurant in a rustic, fishermen's-wharf setting. San Giuliano offers terrace dining directly on St. Julian's small fishing harbor. The menu features Maltese-Italian dishes. *Spinola Bay, tel. 332000. Reservations required. AE, DC, MC, V. Expensive.*
Barracuda. This characterful old house perched precariously on columns—thus commanding a superb view of St. Julian's Bay—is now one of Malta's most delightful and efficiently run restaurants. Seafood, not surprisingly, is the drawing card here. *194/5 Main St., St. Julian's, tel. and fax 337370. AE, DC, MC, V. Moderate.*

21 Norway

Norway has some of the most remote and dramatic scenery in Europe. Along the west coast, deep fjords knife into steep mountain ranges. Inland, cross-country ski trails follow frozen trout streams and downhill trails career through forests whose floors teem with wildflowers and berries during the summer. In older villages, wooden houses spill down toward docks where Viking ships—and later, whaling vessels—once were moored. Today the maritime horizon is dominated by tankers and derricks, for oil is now Norway's economic lifeblood. Fishing and timber, however, still provide many Norwegians with a staple income.

Inhabited since 1700 BC, Norway is today considered a peaceful nation. This was hardly so during the Viking period (the 9th and 10th centuries AD), when, apart from vicious infighting at home, the Vikings were marauding as far afield as Seville and Iceland. This fierce fighting spirit remained, despite Norway's subsequent centuries of subjugation by the Danes and Swedes. Independence came early this century but was put to the test during World War II, when the Germans occupied the country. Norwegian Resistance fighters rose to the challenge, eventually squashing Nazi efforts to develop atomic weapons.

The foundations for modern Norwegian culture were laid in the 19th century, during the period of union with Sweden, which lasted until 1905. Oslo blossomed at this time, and Norway produced its three greatest men of arts and letters: composer Edvard Grieg (1843–1907), dramatist Henrik Ibsen (1828–1906), and painter Edvard Munch (1863–1944). The polar explorers Roald Amundsen and Fridtjof Nansen also lived during this period.

All other facts aside, Norway is most famous for its fjords, which were formed during an ice age a million years ago. The ice cap burrowed deep into existing mountain-bound riverbeds, creating enormous pressure. There was less pressure along the coast, so the entrances to most fjords are shallow, about 155 meters (508 feet), while inland depths reach 1,240 meters (4,067 feet). Although Norway's entire coastline is riddled with fjords, the most breathtaking sights are on the west coast between Stavanger and Trondheim.

Oil-prosperous or fisherman-poor, friendly or taciturn, Norwegians remain outdoor fanatics, firmly in the grip of their own country's natural beauty. Norway's high prices and its vastness (it is over 3,200 difficult road-kilometers [2,000 miles] long) are the only reasons the country isn't overrun with tourists. Norway doesn't seem quite as expensive as it did a few years ago because low inflation and increased competition in the tourist industry have kept prices stable. There are discount schemes and travel strategies that can lower the cost of traveling here even more (*see* What It Will Cost in Before You Go, *below*).

Essential Information

Before You Go

When to Go Cross-country skiing was born in Norway, and the country remains an important winter sports center. While much of the terrain is dark and impassable through the winter, you can

cross-country or downhill ski within Oslo's city limits. January, February, and early March are good skiing months, and hotel rooms are plentiful then. Avoid late March and April, when sleet, rain, and countless thaws and refreezings may ruin the good skiing snow and leave the roads—and spirits—in bad shape. Bear in mind that the country virtually closes down for the five-day Easter holidays, when Norwegians make their annual migration to the mountains. If you plan to visit at this time, reserve well in advance. Hotels are more crowded and expensive during this period, but some offer discounts during the two weeks before Easter—which is a good time for skiing.

Summers are generally mild. Then there's the famous midnight sun: Even in the "southern" city of Oslo, night seems more like twilight around midnight, and dawn comes by 2 AM. The weather can be fickle, however, and rain gear and sturdy waterproof shoes are recommended even during the summer. The best times to avoid crowds in museums and on ferries are May and September; Norwegians themselves are on vacation in July and the first part of August.

Climate The following are the average daily maximum and minimum temperatures for Oslo.

Jan.	28F	– 2C	May	61F	16C	Sept.	60F	16C
	19	– 7		43	6		46	8
Feb.	30F	– 1C	June	68F	20C	Oct.	48F	9C
	19	– 7		50	10		38	3
Mar.	39F	4C	July	72F	22C	Nov.	38F	3C
	25	– 4		55	13		31	– 1
Apr.	50F	10C	Aug.	70F	21C	Dec.	32F	0C
	34	1		53	12		25	– 4

Currency The unit of currency in Norway is the krone, written as Kr. on price tags but officially written as NOK. It is divided into 100 øre. Bills of NOK 50, 100, 500, and 1,000 are in general use. Coins are 50 øre and 1, 5, and 10 kroner. Credit cards are accepted in most hotels, stores, restaurants, and many gas stations and garages, but generally not in smaller shops and inns in rural areas. The exchange rate at press time (spring 1993) was NOK 6.80 to the dollar and NOK 10.5 to the pound sterling.

What It Will Cost Norway has a high standard—and cost—of living, but there are ways of saving money by taking advantage of some special offers for accommodations and travel during the tourist season and on weekends throughout the year.

The **Oslo Card**—valid for one, two, or three days—entitles you to free admission to museums and galleries and unlimited travel on the Oslo Transport system and the Norwegian Railways commuter trains within the city limits, free parking, free admission to the Tusenfryd amusement park, public swimming pools, and racetracks, and discounts at various stores, cinemas, and sports centers. You can get the card at Oslo's tourist information offices and hotels (*see* Important Addresses and Numbers in Oslo, *below*). A one-day card costs NOK 95 adults, NOK 45 children; two days NOK 140 adults, NOK 65 children; three days NOK 170 adults, NOK 80 children.

Hotels in larger towns have special weekend and summer rates from late June to early August, and some chains have their own discount schemes—see Norway's annual accommodation guide. Discounts in rural hotels are offered to guests staying several days; meals are then included in the rate. Meals are generally expensive, so take hotel breakfast when it's offered. Alcohol is very expensive and is sold only during strictly regulated hours.

Sample Prices Cup of coffee, NOK 12–NOK 18; bottle of beer, NOK 40–NOK 45; soft drink, NOK 20–NOK 25; ham sandwich, NOK 40; 1-mile taxi ride, NOK 40 (for night rates, add 15%).

Customs on Arrival Residents of non-European countries who are over 16 may import duty-free into Norway 400 cigarettes or 500 grams of other tobacco goods, souvenirs, and gifts to the value of NOK 3,500. Residents of European countries who are over 16 may import 200 cigarettes or 250 grams of tobacco or cigars, a small amount of perfume or eau de cologne, and goods to the value of NOK 1,200. Anyone over 20 may bring in 1 liter of wine and 1 liter of liquor or 2 liters of wine and beer.

Language In larger cities, on public transportation, and in most commercial establishments, people speak English. Younger Norwegians generally speak it well; English is the main foreign language taught in schools, and movies and cable TV reinforce its popularity.

There are two official forms of the Norwegian language plus many dialects, so don't be disappointed if you've studied it but find that you can't understand everyone. Typical of Scandinavian languages, Norwegian's additional vowels—æ, ø, and å—come at the end of the alphabet.

Getting Around

By Car
Road Conditions Away from the major routes, roads are narrow and winding, so don't expect to cover more than 240 kilometers (150 miles) in a day, especially in fjord country. The climate plays havoc with the roads: Even the best roads suffer from frost, and the mountain passes may be closed in winter. Snow tires (preferably studded) are compulsory in winter; if you're planning to rent, choose a smaller model with front-wheel drive.

Rules of the Road Driving is on the right. The speed limit is 90 kph (56 mph) on highways, 80 kph (50 mph) on main roads, 50 kph (31 mph) in towns, and 30–40 kph (19–25 mph) in residential areas. Throughout the year, low-beam headlights are mandatory. For assistance contact **Norges Automobil Forbund (NAF)**—the Norwegian Automobile Association (Storgaten 2, 0155 Oslo, tel. 22341400). It is important to remember to yield to the vehicle approaching from the right. Passing areas on narrow roads are marked with a white M (for *Møteplass*) on a blue background.

Parking Street parking in cities and towns is clearly marked. There are also municipal parking lots. You cannot park on main roads or on bends. Details can be found in the leaflet "Parking in Oslo," available free from tourist offices and gas stations.

Gasoline Gas costs about NOK 7.50 per liter.

Breakdowns The Norwegian Automobile Association (NAF) patrols main roads and has emergency telephones on mountain roads. For NAF 24-hour service, dial 22341600.

By Train Trains are punctual and comfortable, and most routes are scenic. They fan out from Oslo and leave the coasts (except in the south) to buses and ferries. Reservations are required on all express (*ekspresstog*) services. The Oslo–Bergen route is superbly scenic, while the Oslo–Trondheim–Bodø route takes you within the Arctic Circle. The trains leave Oslo from Sentralstasjonen (Oslo S or Central Station) on Jernbanetorget (at the beginning of Karl Johans gate).

Fares   Apart from the Europe-wide passes (EurailPass and Inter-Rail), two kinds of Scandinavian passes are available: Nordturist and ScanRail. **Nordturist** allows unlimited travel in Norway, Sweden, Denmark, and Finland for 21 days. The cost is NOK 1,980 (second class) or NOK 2,640 (first class). Travelers from 12–25 years of age pay NOK 1,470 and 1,980. Tickets are available through **NSB Travel**, the Norwegian State Railway (21–24 Cockspur St., London SW1Y 5DA, tel. 071/930-6666). In the U.S., contact ScanAm, 933 Highway 23, Pompton Plains, NJ 07444, tel. 201/835-7070 or 800/545-2204. **ScanRail's** range of flexible rail passes offers a set number of travel days within a period of time throughout the four Scandinavian countries. They are available through **Rail Europe** in New York (tel. 914/682-2999) and **NSB Travel** in London. Credit-card payments are accepted. Minifares during off-peak times (green routes) are also available.

By Plane   The remoteness of so much of Norway means that air travel is a necessity for many inhabitants. The main Scandinavian airline, **SAS**, operates a network, along with **Braathens SAFE** and **Widerøe**. Fares are high, but the time saved makes it attractive if you are in a hurry. For longer distances, flying can be cheaper than driving a rented car and paying for gas and incidentals. Inquire about "Visit Norway" passes, which give you relatively cheap domestic-flight coupons (usually good only for summer travel). Norwegian airlines can be contacted at the following addresses: **SAS** (Oslo City, Stenersgate 1A, 0184 Oslo, tel. 22596050 or 22170020); **Braathens SAFE AS** (Haakon VII's gate 2, 0161 Oslo, tel. 67597000 or 22834470); **Norsk Air** (Torp Airport, Sandefjord, tel. 33469000); and **Widerøes Flyveselskap AS** (Mustads vei 1, 0283 Oslo, tel. 22736500).

By Bus   The Norwegian bus network makes up for some of the limitations of the country's train system, and several of the routes are particularly scenic. For example, the north Norway bus service, starting at Fauske (on the train line to Bodø), goes right up to Kirkenes on the Russian-Norwegian border, covering the 1,000 kilometers (625 miles) within four days. Long-distance bus routes also connect Norway with all its Scandinavian neighbors. Most buses leave from Bussterminalen (Galleri Oslo, Schweigaardsgate 10, tel. 22170166), close to Oslo Central Station.

By Ferry   Norway's long, fjord-indented coastline is served by an intricate and essential network of ferries and passenger ships. A wide choice of services is available, from simple hops across fjords (saving many miles of traveling) and excursions among the thousands of islands to luxury cruises and long journeys up the coast. Most ferries carry cars. Reservations are required on journeys of more than one day but are not needed for simple fjord crossings. Many ferries are small and have limited space, so book ahead if possible; this will allow you to drive onto the ferry ahead of the cars that are waiting in line. Fares and exact times of departures depend on the season and availability of ships. Contact the main Norwegian travel office, Nortra (*see* *below*), or contact the Norway Information Center (*see* Important Addresses and Numbers, *below*) for details.

One of the world's great sea voyages is aboard the mail-and-passenger ship called Hurtigruten, which runs up the Norwegian coast from Bergen to Kirkenes, well above the Arctic Circle. Contact the Bergen Line, 505 Fifth Avenue, New York, NY 10017, tel. 212/986–2711, or the Tromsø Main Office, tel. 77686088.

Nortra (Norwegian Travel Association), Postboks 499, Sentrum, 0105 Oslo, tel. 22427044, fax 22336998, will answer your queries about long-distance travel.

Staying in Norway

Telephones Norway's phone system is one of the world's most expensive, so try to make calls when rates are reduced (5 PM–8 AM weekdays and all day on weekends). Also, avoid using room phones in hotels. In public booths, place coins in the phone before dialing. The largest coins accepted are NOK 10, with most older phones taking only NOK 1 or NOK 5 coins, so make sure you have enough small change. The minimum deposit is NOK 3.

Local Calls The cost of calls within Norway varies according to distance: Within Oslo, the cost goes up according to the amount of time used after the three-minute flat fee. Check the Oslo phone book for dialing information. In 1993, telephone numbers throughout Norway changed from six digits to eight digits; area codes were eliminated.

International Calls To call North America, dial 095–1, then the area code and number. For the United Kingdom, dial 095–44, then the area code (minus the first 0) and number. Beginning in January 1995, you will need to dial 00 for an international connection.

Operators and Information For local information, dial 180. For international information, dial 181.

Mail
Postal Rates Letters and postcards to the United States cost NOK 5.50 for the first 20 grams. For the United Kingdom, the rate is NOK 4.50 for the first 20 grams.

Receiving Mail Have letters marked "poste restante" after the name of the town, with the last name underlined. The service is free, and letters are directed to the nearest main post office. American Express offices will also hold mail (nonmembers pay a small charge on collection).

Shopping
VAT Refunds Much of the 18.03% Norwegian value-added tax (VAT) will be refunded to visitors who spend more than NOK 300 in any single store. Ask for a special tax-free check and show your passport to confirm that you are not a resident. All purchases must be sealed and presented together with the tax-free check at the tax-free counter at ports, on ferries destined for abroad, and at airports and border posts. The VAT will be refunded, minus a service charge. General information about the tax-free system is available by calling tel. 67149901.

Opening and Closing Times **Banks** are open weekdays 8:15–3:30; summer hours are 8:15–3. (All post offices change money.)

Museums are usually open Tuesday to Sunday 10–3 or 4. Many, but not all, are closed on Monday.

Shops, though times vary, are usually open weekdays 9 or 10–5 (Thursday until 7) and Saturday 9–1 or 2. Shopping malls are often open until 8 on weeknights.

National Holidays January 1; April 1–4 (Easter); May 1 (Labor Day); May 17 (Constitution Day); May 12 (Ascension); May 22–23 (Pentecost); December 25–26.

Dining The Norwegian diet emphasizes protein and carbohydrates. Breakfast is usually a large buffet of smoked fish, cheeses, sausage, cold meats, and whole-grain breads accompanied by tea, good coffee, or milk. Lunch is often similar to breakfast, or the famous, but not very filling, *smørbrød* open sandwich. Restaurant and hotel dinners are usually three-course meals, often starting with soup and ending with fresh fruit and berries. The main course may be salmon, trout, or other fish; alternatives can include lamb or pork, reindeer, or even ptarmigan. Remember that the most expensive part of eating is drinking (*see* What It Will Cost in Before You Go, *above*) and that alcohol is not served on Sunday in most areas except Oslo and a handful of other regions. One consolation is the quality of the water, which is still among the purest in the world despite the growing problem of acid rain.

Mealtimes Lunch is from noon to 3 at restaurants featuring a *koldtbord*, the famous Scandinavian buffet. Few Scandinavians ever partake of this, except when dining at mountain resorts. Dinner has traditionally been early, but in hotels and major restaurants it is now more often from 6 to 11. Some rural places still serve dinner from 4 to 7, however.

Dress Jacket and tie or high-fashion casual wear are recommended for restaurants in the Very Expensive and Expensive categories, although during the summer, neat casual dress is acceptable in most places.

Ratings Prices are per person and include a first course, main course, and dessert, without wine or tip. Outside the major cities, prices are considerably less. Service is always included (*see* Tipping, *below*). Best bets are indicated by a star ★.

Category	Oslo
Very Expensive	over NOK 450
Expensive	NOK 300–NOK 450
Moderate	NOK 125–NOK 300
Inexpensive	under NOK 125

Lodging Accommodations in Norway are usually spotless, and smaller
Hotels establishments are often family-run. Service is thoughtful and considerate, right down to blackout curtains to block out the midnight sun. Passes are available for discounts in hotels. The **Scandinavia Bonus Pass,** costing approximately $23 and also valid in Denmark, Sweden, and Finland, gives up to 50% discounts in 250 hotels during summer (May 15–Oct. 1). In addition, children under 15 stay in their parents' room at no extra charge. Contact **Inter Nor Hotels** (Dronningensgate 40, 0154 Oslo, tel. 22334200). Or consult Norway's accommodations guide, free from any tourist office. **Nordturist** passes (*see* Get-

ting Around by Train, *above*) also offer discounts of about 40% in nearly 110 top hotels in the Reso chain.

Camping Camping is a popular way of keeping down costs. There are more than 1,400 authorized campsites in the country, many set in spectacular surroundings. Prices vary according to the facilities provided: A family with a car and tent can expect to pay about NOK 100 per night. Some campsites have log cabins available from about NOK 250 per night. *Camping Norway* is available from tourist offices and **NAF** (the Norwegian Automobile Association), Storgaten 2, 0155 Oslo, tel. 22341400.

Youth Hostels There are about 90 youth hostels in Norway; some are schools or farms doing extra summer duty. You must be a member of the Youth Hostel Association (YHA) to stay in the hostels, but there are no age restrictions. Contact **Norske Vandrerhjem (NoVa)** (Dronningensgate 26, 0154 Oslo, tel. 22421410).

International YHA guides are available to members in the United Kingdom and North America. (There are no age restrictions for membership.) In the United States, contact **American Youth Hostels Inc.** (733 15th St. NW, Suite 840, Washington, DC 20005, tel. 202/783–6161, fax 202/783–6171). In Canada, contact **Canadian Hostelling Association** (1600 James Naismith Dr., Suite 608, Gloucester, Ont. K1B 5N4, tel. 613/748–5638).

Rentals Norwegians escape to mountain cabins whenever they have a chance. Stay in one for a week or two and you'll see why—magnificent scenery; pure air; edible wild berries; and the chance to hike, fish, or cross-country ski. For information on renting cabins, farms, or private homes, write to Den Norske Hytteformidling A.S, Box 3404, Bjølsen, 0406 Oslo, tel. 22356710. Or get the brochure *Norsk Hytteferie* from tourist offices. An unusual alternative is to rent a *rorbu* (fisherman's dwelling) in the northerly Lofoten Islands. Contact Destination Lofoten, Box 210, N–8301 Svolvær, tel. 76073000.

Ratings Prices are summer rates and are for two people in a double room with bath and include breakfast, service, and all taxes. Best bets are indicated by a star ★.

Category	Oslo	Other Areas
Very Expensive	over NOK 1,300	over NOK 1,000
Expensive	NOK 1,000–NOK 1,300	NOK 850–NOK 1,000
Moderate	NOK 800–NOK 1,000	NOK 650–NOK 850
Inexpensive	under NOK 800	under NOK 650

Tipping A 10%–12% service charge is added to most bills at hotels and restaurants. If you have had exceptional service, then give an additional 5% tip. It is not the custom to tip taxi drivers unless they help with luggage; porters at airports have set fees per bag, but the carts are free. If a doorman hails a taxi for you, you can give NOK 5. On sightseeing tours, tip the guide NOK 10–NOK 15 if you are satisfied. Tip with local currency only.

Oslo

Arriving and Departing

By Plane Oslo Fornebu Airport on the edge of the fjord, about 20 minutes west of Oslo, has international and domestic services. Charter flights go to Gardermoen Airport, about 50 minutes north.

Between the Buses from Bussterminalen (Galleri Oslo) to Fornebu leave ev-
Airport and ery 15 minutes (starting at 6 AM) and run every half hour on
Downtown weekends; the fare is NOK 30. Alternatively, take bus No. 31 from Jernbanetorget, marked "Snarøya." The fare is NOK 20; the bus makes a round-trip once hourly. Buses meet flights to Gardermoen and take passengers to the Central Station; the fare is NOK 60. Taxis between Fornebu and downtown cost NOK 120.

By Train Trains on international or domestic long-distance and express routes arrive at Oslo Central Station. Suburban trains depart from Oslo Central Station, Stortinget, and National Theater Station.

Getting Around

By Public It's best to get around Oslo by using the **Oslo Card** (*see* What It
Transportation Will Cost, *above*), which offers unlimited travel for one, two, or three days on all of Oslo's public transportation systems—bus, T-bane (the subway), streetcar, and local ferries. Buy the Oslo Card at Oslo tourist offices, from hotels, travel agents in Oslo, and larger stores (*see* Important Addresses and Numbers, *below*).

If using public transportation only occasionally, you can get tickets (adults NOK 15, children NOK 7.50) at bus and subway stops. For NOK 35, the **Tourist Ticket** gives 24 hours' unlimited travel on any means of public transportation, including the summer ferries to Bygdøy. The **Flexikort** gives you 10 subway, bus, or streetcar rides for NOK 130, including transfers.

By Taxi A taxi is available if the roof light is on. There are taxi stands at Oslo Central Station and usually alongside Narvesen news-stands, or call 22388090; during peak hours, though, you may have to wait.

Important Addresses and Numbers

Tourist The **Oslo Tourist Information Office** (tel. 22830050) is at the
Information **Norway Information Center,** Vestbaneplassen 1, tel. 22839100. Open Oct.–Apr., weekdays 9–4; May, daily 9–6; June–Aug., daily 9–8; Sept., weekdays 9–4, weekends 9–4. **Oslo Central Station,** tel. 22171124. Open 8 AM–11 PM. **Trafikanten,** Oslo Central Station, tel. 22177030. Open daily 7 AM–8 PM.

Embassies U.S. (Drammensvn. 18, tel. 22448550). **Canadian** (Oscarsgate 20, tel. 22466955). **U.K.** (Thos. Heftyesgate 8, tel. 22552400).

Emergencies **Police** (Grønlandsleiret 44, tel. 22669050, 24-hour service). **Ambulance:** 24-hour service (tel. 22117070). **Dentist** (Oslo Kommunale Tannlegevakt, Tøyen Center, Kolstadsgate 18, Oslo 6, tel. 22673000). Emergencies, weekdays 8 PM–11 PM, weekends and holidays 11 AM–2 PM. **Pharmacy: Jernbanetorgets Apotek** (Jernbanetorget 4B, tel. 22412482. Open 24 hours).

Post Office The main post office, located at Dronningensgate 15, is open Monday–Friday 8–8, Saturday 9–3. The **Telegraph Office** is at Kongensgate 21.

English-Language Bookstores Tanum (Karl Johans gate 43, tel. 22429310). **Qvist** (Drammensvn. 16, tel. 22445269, beside the U.S. Embassy).

Travel Agencies Winge (agent for American Express): Karl Johans gate 33/35, tel. 22412030; **Bennett:** Pilestredet 35, tel. 22943600 **Berg-Hansen** (agent for Thomas Cook): 3 Arbiensgate, tel. 22551901. **NSB Travel Agency:** Stortingsgate 28, tel. 22838850.

Guided Tours

Orientation Tours H. M. K. provides three three-hour tours and one full-day tour departing from the Rådhuset (harbor side). Tickets are available on the bus or from Oslo Tourist Information Office (*see* Important Addresses and Numbers, *above*). The "Oslo Highlights" morning tour goes to the Vigeland Sculpture Park, Holmenkollen Ski Jump, the Viking Ship Museum, and the *Kon-Tiki.* The "Art and History tour" includes Akershus Castle and Church, Gamle Aker Church, National Gallery, Stavechurch at Norwegian Folk Museum, and Holmenkollen Ski Jump. *Each tour costs NOK 160 adults, NOK 80 children. Open Apr.–Sept., daily at 10 AM.*

The "Afternoon Tour" goes to the Holmenkollen Ski Jump, Vigeland Sculpture Park, the Viking Ships, and the polar ship *Fram* at Bygdøy. Each tour costs NOK 160 adults, NOK 80 children. Open Apr.–Oct., daily at 1:30.

The "Full Day Sightseeing Tour" lasts from 10 to 4 and includes most of what Oslo has to offer. *Tour: NOK 300 adults, NOK 150 children under 12.*

Båtservice Sightseeing has seven different boat and/or bus tours departing from Rådhusbrygge 3—from a 50-minute minicruise (NOK 50 adults, NOK 25 children) departing every hour all summer to an all-day grand tour of Oslo by boat and bus (NOK 250 adults, NOK 125 children). Book at 22200715.

Walking Tours The "Oslo Guide" brochure (free from the tourist office) has several walking tours on its map. Some go farther afield and link up with public transportation.

Personal Guides Taxis give sightseeing tours in English for NOK 250 per hour. Call 22388070 for reservations.

Exploring Oslo

Oslo is a small capital city, with a population of just less than half a million. The downtown area is compact, but the geographic limits of Oslo spread out to include forests, fjords, and mountains, which give the city a pristine airiness that complements its urban amenities. Oslo has an excellent public transportation network. Explore downtown on foot, enjoying its jazz clubs and museums, then venture beyond via bus, streetcar, or train.

Numbers in the margin correspond to points of interest on the Oslo map.

Oslo's main street, **Karl Johans gate,** runs right through the center of town, from Oslo Central Station uphill to the Royal

Palace. Half its length is closed to traffic, and it is in this section that you will find many of the city's shops and outdoor cafés.

❶ Start at the **Slottet** (Royal Palace), the king's residence (not open to the public). The palace was built during the early 19th-century neoclassical style and is as sober, sturdy, and unpretentious as the Norwegian character. The surrounding park is open to the public. Time your visit to coincide with the changing of the guard (daily at 1:30). When the king is in residence (signaled by a red flag), the Royal Guard strikes up the band.

❷ Walk down Karl Johans gate to the old **Universitet** (University), which is made up of the three big buildings on your left. The main hall of the university is decorated with murals by Edvard Munch (1863–1944), Norway's most famous artist. The hall (*aula*) is open only during July. The Nobel Peace Prize is presented there each year on December 10. *Admission to hall free. Open July, weekdays noon–2.*

❸ Behind the University is the **Nasjonalgalleriet** (National Gallery), Norway's largest public gallery. It has a small but high-quality selection of paintings by European artists, but of particular interest is the collection of works by Norwegian artists. Edvard Munch is represented here, but most of his work is in the Munch Museum (*see below*), east of the center. *Universitetgaten 13. Admission free. Open Mon., Wed., Fri. 10–4, Thurs. 10–8, Sat. and Sun. 11–3.*

❹ The **Historisk Museum** (Historical Museum) is in back of the National Gallery. It features displays of daily life and art from the Viking period, including treasures recovered from Viking ships. The Ethnographic Section houses a collection related to the great polar explorer Roald Amundsen, the first man to reach the South Pole. *Frederiksgate 2. Admission free. Open summer, Tues.–Sun. 11–3; winter, Tues.–Sun. noon–3.*

❺ Return to Karl Johans gate and cross over for a closer look at the **Nationaltheatret,** watched over by the statues of Bjørnstjerne Bjørnson and Henrik Ibsen. Bjørnson was the nationalist poet who wrote Norway's anthem. Internationally lauded playwright Ibsen wrote *Peer Gynt* (he personally requested Edvard Grieg's musical accompaniment), *A Doll's House,* and *Hedda Gabler,* among others. He worried that his plays, packed with allegory, myth, and sociological and emotional angst, might not have appeal outside Norway. Instead, they were universally recognized and changed the face of modern theater.

Time Out Stop for a snack or a drink at one of the cafés surrounding **Studenterlunden** pond, which is the setting for band concerts and other special events.

❻ At the far (eastern) end of the pond is the **Storting** (Parliament), a bow-fronted yellow-brick building stretched across the block. It is open to visitors by request when Parliament is not in session: A guided tour takes visitors around the frescoed interior and into the debating chamber. *Karl Johans gate 22, tel. 22313050. Admission free.*

❼ Karl Johans gate is closed to traffic near the staid **Domkirken** (Cathedral), with its bronze door. The much-renovated cathedral, consecrated in 1697, is modest by the standards of some other European capital cities, but the interior is rich with

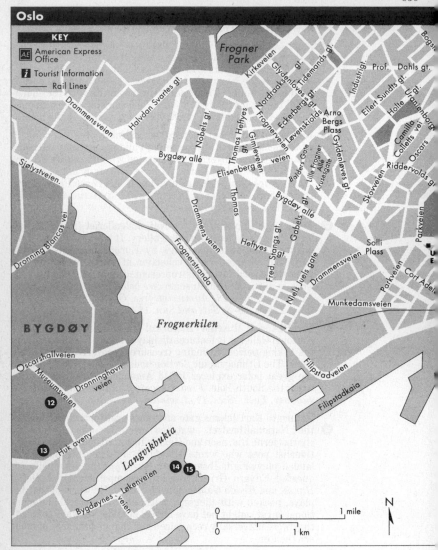

Oslo

KEY

AE American Express Office

i Tourist Information

—— Rail Lines

Frogner Park

BYGDØY

Frognerkilen

Langvikbukta

0   1 mile

0   1 km

N

Aker Brygge and harbor, **10**

Akershus Slott, **8**

Domkirken, **7**

Framhuset, **15**

Historisk Museum, **4**

Kon-Tiki Museum, **14**

Munch-Museet, **16**

Museet for Samtidskunst, **9**

Nasjonalgalleriet, **3**

Nationaltheatret, **5**

Norsk Folkemuseum, **12**

Rådhuset, **11**

Slottet, **1**

Storting, **6**

Universitet, **2**

Vikingskiphuset, **13**

Seilduksgt.

Helgesens gt.

Grüners gt.

Helgesens gt.

Colletts gt.

Waldemar Thranes gt.

Akersbakken

Maridalsveien

Akerselva

Sofienberggt.

Møllerveien   Nordregt.

Parkveien

Pilestredet

Ullevålsveien

Akersveien

Trondheimsveien

Jens Bjelkes gt.

Holbergs gate

Wessels gt.

Nordahl Bruns gt.

St. Olavsgt.

Hausmanns gt.

Frederiks Gate

1

Universitetsgt.

Henrik Ibsens gt.

Møllergt.

Torgt.

Urtegt.

16

4 **3**

2

Karl

Rosenkrantz' gt.

Grubbe

Youngs-torget

Storgt.

Norbygt.

Tøyengt.

mmensveien

AE

Akersgata

5

Johans

Grensen

nkedamsveien

6

Gate

Stortorvet

Brugt.

Grønlandsleiret

Stortingsgt.

Nedre Vollgt.

Stortorvet

Storgt.

Løkkegata

7

Oslo
Spektrum

Olav Vsgt.

11

Slottsgt.

Prinsens gt.

Oslo City

Rådhusgt.

Nedre Slottsgt.

Tollbugata

Kirkegata

Dronningens gt.

Skippergt.

Fred Olsens gt.

Strandgt.

■ **Central
Station**

Nylandsveien

Schweigaards gt.

okkveien

10

Akershusstranda

Mynt gt.

9

Bispegt.

Pipervika

8

Kongens Gate

Skippergt.

Bjørvika

Akerselva

Bispevika

SØRENGA

Oslo gt.

Oslofjorden

Mosseveien

Ekebergsletta

treasures, such as the Baroque carved wooden altarpiece and pulpit. The ceiling frescoes by Hugo Lous Mohr were done after World War II. Behind the cathedral is an area of arcades, small restaurants, and street musicians. *Stortorvet 1. Admission free. Open weekdays 10–3.*

Facing the cathedral, turn right at Kirkegata. Three blocks down, turn right onto Rådhusgate and then almost immediately left onto Kongens gate. This takes you to **Akershus Castle** on the harbor. The castle was built during the Middle Ages but restored in 1527 by Christian IV of Denmark—Denmark then ruled Norway—after it was damaged by fire; he then laid out the present city of Oslo (naming it Christiania after himself) around his new residence. Oslo's street plan still follows his design. Some rooms are open for guided tours, and the grounds form a park around the castle. The grounds also house the **Forsvarsmuseet** and **Hjemmefrontmuseum** (Norwegian Defense and Resistance museums). Both give you a feel for the Norwegian fighting spirit throughout history and especially during the German occupation, when the Nazis set up headquarters on this site and had a number of patriots executed here. *Akershus Castle and Museums. Entrance from Festningsplassen, tel. 02/412521. Admission: NOK 15 adults, NOK 5 children. Guided tours of the castle, May–Sept., Mon.–Sat. 11, 1, and 3, Sun. 1 and 3. Museums open weekdays 10–4, Sun. 12:30–4.*

Just behind Akershus Castle, in the direction of Oslo Central Station, is the **Contemporary Art Museum,** housed in the Bank of Norway's old building. *Bankplassen 4, tel. 22335820. Admission free. Open Tues.–Fri. 11–7, Sat.–Sun. 11–4.*

Continue along the waterfront toward the central **harbor**—the heart of Oslo and head of the fjord. Shops and cafés stay open late at **Aker Brygge,** the new quayside shopping and cultural center, with a theater, cinemas, and galleries among the shops, restaurants, and cafés. You don't have to buy anything—just sit amid the fountains and statues and watch the activities.

The large redbrick **Rådhuset** (City Hall) is on the waterfront, too: Note the friezes in the courtyard, depicting scenes from Norwegian folklore, then go inside and see murals depicting daily life in Norway, historical events, and Resistance activities. You can set your watch by the astronomical clock in the inner courtyard. *Admission: NOK 15 adults, NOK 5 children. Open Mon.–Sat. 9:15–3:30, Thurs. 9–7. Tours daily.*

The **Norway Information Center** is on the right side across the street when facing the harbor. From nearby Pipervika Bay, you can board a ferry in the summertime for the seven-minute crossing of the fjord to the **Bygdøy** peninsula, where there is a complex of seafaring museums. *Ferries run Apr.–Sept., at 15 past and 15 to each hour.*

The first ferry stop is Dronningen. From here, walk up a well-marked road to the **Norsk Folkemuseum** (Open Air Museum), a large park where historic farmhouses, some of them centuries old, have been collected from all over the country and reassembled. A whole section of 19th-century Oslo was moved here, as was a 12th-century wooden stave church. There are displays of weaving and sheepshearing on Sunday, and throughout the park there are guides in period costume. *Museumsveien 10. Admission: NOK 35. Open daily 10–4.*

Around the corner (signs will lead you) is the second museum.

⑬ The **Vikingskiphuset** (Viking Ship Museum) contains 9th-century ships recovered from the fjord, where they had been ritually sunk while carrying the mortal remains of Viking kings and queens to the next world. Also on display are the treasures and jewelry that accompanied the royal bodies on their last voyage. The ornate craftsmanship evident in the ships and jewelry dispels any notion that the Vikings were skilled only in looting and pillaging. *Huk aveny. Admission: NOK 20 adults, NOK 10 children. Open Nov.–Mar., daily 11–3; Apr. and Oct., daily 11–4; May–Aug., daily 9–6; Sept., daily 11–5.*

Reboard the ferry or follow signs for the 20-minute walk to the

⑭ **Kon-Tiki Museum,** where the *Kon-Tiki* raft and the reed boat *RA II* are on view. Thor Heyerdahl made no concessions to the modern world when he crossed the Pacific *(Kon-Tiki)* and the Atlantic *(RA II)* in these boats. *Admission: NOK 20 adults, NOK 10 children. Open Oct.–Mar., daily 10:30–4; Apr.–May 17 and Sept., daily 10:30–5; May 18–Aug. 31, daily 9–6.*

Directly across from the Kon-Tiki Museum is a large triangular

⑮ building, the **Framhuset.** This museum is devoted to the polar ship *Fram,* the sturdy wooden vessel that belonged to bipolar explorer Fridtjof Nansen. (It was also used by Amundsen.) In 1893 Nansen led an expedition that reached latitude 86°14′N, the most northerly latitude to have been reached at that time. The book *Farthest North* tells his story. (Active in Russian famine-relief work, Nansen received a Nobel Peace Prize in 1922.) You can board the ship and imagine yourself in one of the tiny berths, while outside a force-nine gale is blowing and the temperature is dozens of degrees below freezing. *Admission: NOK 15 adults, NOK 8 children. Open Apr., daily 11–2:45; May 1–15, daily 10–4:45; May 16–Sept., daily 9–5:45; Oct., daily 10–2:45; Nov., weekends 11–2:45.*

Time Out Before catching the ferry back to the center of Oslo, consider a meal or snack at **Lanternen Kro.** In summer you can sit on the terrace, which commands a view of the entire harbor. Or you can stop at **Rodeløkken Kafé** for homemade waffles and coffee. It's just a short walk from the Folk Museum, right near the king's farm.

Back at City Hall, board bus No. 29 to **Tøyen,** the area north-

⑯ east of Oslo, where you'll find the **Munch-Museet** (Munch Museum). In 1940, four years before his death, Munch bequeathed much of his work to the city of Oslo; the museum opened in 1963, the centennial of his birth. Although only a fraction of its 22,000 items—books, paintings, drawings, prints, sculptures, and letters—are on display, you can still get a sense of the tortured expressionism that was to have such an effect on European painting. *Tøyengaten 53. Admission: NOK 30 adults, NOK 10 children. Open June–Sept. 15, Tues.–Sat. 10–6, Sun. noon–6; Sept. 16–May, Tues.–Sat. 10–4, Sun. noon–6.*

Off the Beaten Track

The jury is still out on the question of the artistic merit of Gustav Vigeland's *Wheel of Life and Monolith,* but few would deny the perseverance involved in its creation. Over 15 meters (50 feet) high and covered with more than 100 linked human forms, this sculpture is the focal point of **Frogner Park,** in northwest Oslo. Open-air restaurants, tennis courts, and swimming pools provide additional diversions. To get there, take streetcar No. 2 or T-banc train Nos. 13, 14, 15, or 16 and get off at Majorstua. *Free. Park open 24 hours.*

Walk down Frognerveien to Krusesgate and turn left for a view of what Oslo looked like 100 years ago. The decorative gingerbread houses are on the historic preservation list.

The **Holmenkollen ski jump,** at 62 meters (203 feet) above ground level, is one of the world's highest and the site of an international contest each March. At the base is a ski museum carved into the rock. To get there, board any Frognerseter/Holmenkollen suburban train from National-theatret; get off at Holmenkollen. The half-hour ride sweeps from down underground up to 403 meters (1,322 feet) above sea level.

The forests within Oslo's vast city limits include 11 sports chalets, geared to exercise and the outdoor life. The areas around **Skullerudstua** and **Skistua** are recommended for their walking and skiing trails. Contact Oslo Kommune (Forestry Services, Skogvesenet, tel. 22381870). Or, for winter or summer "safaris" through the forest by Land-Rover, contact the main tourist office (*see* Important Addresses and Numbers, *above*).

Head east on streetcar No. 9 (from Nationaltheatret or Jernbanetorget) to the Sjømannsskolen stop to see 5,000-year-old carvings on the runic stones near **Ekebergseletta park.** They are across the road from the park on Karlsborgveien and marked by a sign reading *Fortidsminne.* Walk through the park and take Oslogate and then Bispegata to the **Oslo Ladegård,** which has scale models of old Oslo on the site of the 13th-century Bispegard (Bishop's Palace). *Admission: NOK 20 adults, NOK 10 children. Open May–Sept.; guided tours on Wed. at 6 and Sun. at 1.*

Beyond Oslo, trips include a visit to **Lillehammer,** designated as the site of the 1994 Winter Olympics, and home of **Maihaugen De Sandvigske Samlinger,** one of the largest open-air museums in northern Europe (tel. 61250135). Lillehammer is at the top of the long finger of **Lake Mjøsa** and is reached by train from Oslo Central Station in about two hours. A paddle steamer, **D/S** *Skibladner,* travels the length of the lake (six hours each way) in summer, making several stops. At the southern tip of the lake is **Eidsvoll,** where the Norwegians announced their new constitution in 1814, marking the end to centuries of domination by Denmark. There are limitless possibilities for outdoor activities in the region, all within reach of Oslo.

Shopping

Gift Ideas Since prices here are controlled, Oslo is the obvious place to do your shopping. In addition, the selection is widest here: Pewter, silver, enamelware, crystal, sheepskin, leather, and knitwear are all appealing samples of Norwegian craftsmanship.

Shopping Districts Many of the larger stores are in the area between the Storting and the cathedral; much of this area is for pedestrians only. The **Basarhallene,** at the back of the cathedral, is an art and handicrafts boutique center. Oslo's newest shopping area is **Aker Brygge** (once a shipbuilding wharf). Located right on the waterfront, it is a complex of stalls, offices, and garden cafés.

Check out Bogstadveien/Hegdehaugsveien, which runs from Majorstua to Parkveien. This street offers a good selection of stores and has plenty of places to rest your tired feet and quench your thirst. Shops stay open until 5 PM (Thursday to 7 PM).

Department Stores and Malls Oslo's department stores, **Steen & Strøm** and **Christiania Glasmagasin,** are both in the shopping district near the cathedral. **Paléet** on Karl Johans gate is a new, elegant addition to Oslo's main street, with 40 shops and 10 restaurants.

Food and Flea Markets Every Saturday during spring, summer, and fall, there is a flea market at Vestkanttorget, two blocks away from Frogner Park. Check the papers for local flea markets.

Dining

For details and price-category definitions, *see* Dining in Staying in Norway. Best bets are indicated by a star ★.

Very Expensive
★ **Bagatelle.** Bagatelle was the first restaurant with a Norwegian chef serving Norwegian food to merit a Michelin star. Choose the five- or seven-course menus for the full range of Chef Hellstrøm's talents. The wine list is extensive, chairs are comfortable, service is impeccable, and the best of Norwegian contemporary art adorns the walls. *Bygdøy alle 3, tel. 22446397. Reservations recommended. AE, DC, MC, V. Open Mon.–Sat. 6 PM–11 PM.*

★ **D'Artagnan.** Among gourmands, D'Artagnan is a favorite. Stellar food and excellent service make this a place to remember. Try chef Freddie Nielsen's Grand Menu with an appropriate wine from the well-stocked cellar. *Øvre Slottsgate 16, tel. 22415062. Reservations required. AE, DC, MC, V.*

Expensive **Babette's Gjestehus.** This warm and intimate restaurant has an international menu with a French accent. *Rådhuspassasjen, tel. 22416464. Reservations required. AE, DC, MC, V. No weekday lunch. Closed Sun.*

★ **De Fem Stuer.** Chef Bent Stiansen, gold medalist in the Bocuse d'Or World Championships for Chefs in 1993, prepares food that is even better than the view. Enjoy modern versions of Norwegian specialties, with the accent on fish and game. *Holmenkollen Park Hotel, Kongeveien 26, tel. 22922000, fax 22146192. Reservations recommended. AE, DC, MC, V.*

Feinschmecker. Located in a fashionable residential area only minutes from the center of town, this restaurant specializes in modern Scandinavian cuisine. The desserts are especially good. Lars Erik Underthun, the silver medal winner at the 1991 Bocuse d'Or World Championships for Chefs, is in charge here. *Balchens gate 5, tel. 22441777. Reservations required for dinner. AE, DC, MC, V. Closed Sun.*

★ **Theatercafeen.** This Oslo institution is the last Viennese-style café in northern Europe and is a favorite with the literary and entertainment crowd. The daily menu is a good value. Save room for dessert, which the pastry chef also makes for Norway's royal family. *Hotel Continental, Stortingsgata 24/26, tel. 22419060. Reservations required. AE, DC, MC, V.*

Moderate **D/S Louise.** This casual restaurant in a maritime setting is part of the Aker Brygge shopping/entertainment complex. *Stranden 3, tel. 22830060. Reservations accepted. AE, DC, MC, V.*

Frognerseteren. Located just above the Holmenkollen Ski Jump, this restaurant looks down on the entire city. Take the Holmenkollbanen to the end station and then walk downhill to the restaurant. Follow the signs. The newly renovated upstairs room has the same view as the more expensive panorama veranda. There is also an outdoor café. *Voksenkollen, tel. 22143736. Reservations accepted. AE, DC, MC, V.*

Gamle Raadhus. The "old city hall," Oslo's oldest restaurant, is located in a building dating from 1641. Specialties include mussels and fresh shrimp. *Nedre Slottsgate 1, tel. 22420107. Reservations advised. AE, DC, MC, V. Closed Sun.*

Kastanjen. The short menu at this neighborhood restaurant changes often and features all seasonal ingredients. The three-course fixed-price dinner is an excellent value. *Bygdøy alle 18, tel. 22434467. Reservations recommended. AE, DC, MC, V. Closed Sun.*

Lofotstua. This rustic fish restaurant has a cozy atmosphere and personal service. Good, moderately priced food is served—typical specialties include fresh cod and seafood from Lofoten. *Kirkeveien 40, tel. 22469396. Reservations advised. AE, DC, MC, V. Closed Sat.*

A Touch of France. The bouillabaisse at this intimate, French brasserie is out of this world. *Øvre Slottsgate 16, tel. 22425697. Reservations advised. AE, DC, MC, V.*

Inexpensive **Albin Upp.** This cozy wine and snack bar in a farmer's renovated
★ cottage is about a 10-minute streetcar ride from town—catch the No. 1. Contemporary art is on display downstairs. *Briskebyveien 42, tel. 22557192. No reservations. No credit cards. Lunch only. Closed weekends.*

★ **Nye Kaffistova.** This cafeteria serves Norwegian "country-style" cooking at reasonable prices. *Rosenkrantz' gate 8, tel. 22429974. No reservations. AE, DC, MC, V.*

Vegeta. Next to the Nationaltheatret bus and streetcar station, this is a popular spot for hot and cold vegetarian meals and salads. It is a nonsmoking restaurant. The all-you-can-eat specials offer top value. *Munkedamsvn. 3B, tel. 22834232. No reservations. No credit cards.*

Lodging

The tourist office's accommodations bureaus (open daily 8 AM–11 PM) in Oslo Central Station can help you find rooms in hotels, pensions, and private homes. You must apply in person and pay a fee of NOK 20 (NOK 10 children) plus 10% of the room rate, which will be refunded when you check in. For details and price-category definitions, *see* Lodging in Staying in Norway. Best bets are indicated by a star ★.

Very Expensive **Grand.** It's hard to beat the Grand's location on Oslo's main
★ street, opposite the Parliament and Studenterlunden. The hotel has comforts and history to match its name: Ibsen had a permanent table in Grand Café, a famous Oslo rendezvous. The Palmen, just off the lobby, is where Oslo matrons drink their afternoon tea. *Karl Johans gate 31, tel. 22429390, fax 22421225. 215 rooms with bath and shower, 60 suites. Facilities: 3 restaurants, 2 bars, indoor pool, sauna, solarium, parking facilities. AE, DC, MC, V.*

★ **Holmenkollen Park Rica.** Near the ski jump, this hotel is an imposing building in the old romantic folkloric style with a luxurious annex. The rooms are bright, and most have balconies with excellent views of the city and the fjord below. The hotel runs a shuttle bus for its guests, since it's a 20-minute drive from downtown. It's probably the best place for anyone hoping to do some skiing. *Kongeveien 26, tel. 22922000, fax 22141692. 192 rooms with bath. Facilities: 2 restaurants, bar, nightclub, whirlpool, sauna, indoor pool, ski trails. AE, DC, MC, V.*

SAS Scandinavia Hotel. The SAS is a comfortable business hotel with impeccable service. The airport bus stops right outside. Summit 21 is the rooftop lunch bar, with commanding views of the entire city. Downstairs you'll find a shopping center and the city air terminal. *Holbergs gate 30, tel. 22113000, fax 22113017. 491 rooms with bath. Facilities: 2 restaurants, 2 bars, nightclub, indoor pool, disco. AE, DC, MC, V.*

Expensive **Ambassadeur.** Located just behind the Royal Palace, this hotel has 42 individually designed rooms and personalized service. The Ambassadeur restaurant serves modern Scandinavian food. *Camilla Colletts vei 15, tel. 22441835, fax 22444791. 42 rooms with bath or shower. Facilities: restaurant, bar, sauna. AE, DC, MC, V.*

Frogner House Hotel. This charming new hotel, located in the heart of the business and residential area of Frogner, looks modest from the outside but offers all the elegance and comfort of a patrician home. *Skovveien 8, tel. 22560056, fax 22560500. 44 rooms with bath. Facilities: no-smoking and allergen-free rooms, breakfast, room service. AE, DC, MC, V.*

Gabelshus Hotel. Only five minutes from the center of town, the Gabelshus is a moderate-size hotel on an attractive side street. The rooms are spacious and airy, and the hotel has the feel of a large country house. *Gabels gate 16, tel. 22552260, fax 22442730. 45 rooms with bath. Facilities: restaurant. AE, DC, MC, V.*

SAS Park Royal Hotel. Ten minutes from Oslo, this hotel is clean, efficient, and convenient to Fornebu Airport. The rooms are American motel-style, and the top-class facilities are well suited for business stays. *Fornebuparken, Lysaker, tel. 67120220, fax 67120011. 254 rooms and 14 suites with bath. Facilities: restaurant, sauna, fitness room, tennis courts, direct airport check-in, executive office space. AE, DC, MC, V.*

Moderate **Bondeheimen.** Oslo's most Norwegian hotel has modern, comfortable rooms and a staff that wears national costumes. *Rosenkrantz' gate 8, tel. 22429530, fax 22419437. 76 rooms with shower. Facilities: café, shop, sauna, solarium. AE, DC, MC, V.*

Cecil Hotel. Built in 1989, just off Stortingsgata right in the heart of town, this bed-and-breakfast–only hotel is a good value for the money. *Stortingsgata 8, tel. 22427000, fax 22422670. 112 rooms with bath. AE, DC, MC, V.*

Europa. This centrally located modern bed-and-breakfast is a moderately priced alternative to its next-door neighbor, the SAS Scandinavia Hotel. The rooms are comfortable (all have color TV), and there are special reductions for children. *St. Olavs gate 31, tel. 22209990, fax 22112727. 158 rooms with bath. AE, DC, MC, V.*

Stefan. The service is cheerful and accommodating in this hotel in the center of Oslo. One of its main attractions is the popular restaurant on the top floor, with Oslo's best buffet lunch, featuring traditional Norwegian dishes. *Rosenkrantz' gate 1, tel. 22429250, fax 22337022. 130 rooms with bath or shower. Facilities: restaurant. AE, DC, MC, V.*

Inexpensive **Gyldenløve.** Centrally located at Bogstadveien, this bed-and-breakfast hotel—renovated in 1992—offers quality at a reasonable price and 160 well-equipped rooms with all conveniences. *Bogstadveien 20, tel. 22601090, fax 22603390. 160 rooms with bath or shower. AE, DC, MC, V.*

Munch Hotel. This bed-and-breakfast hotel, renovated in 1993, has large but rather basic rooms. It's a 10-minute walk from downtown. *Munchs gate 5, tel. 22424275, fax 22206469. 180 rooms with shower. AE, DC, MC, V.*

Ritz. A little less grand than some of the others that share its name, this Ritz is about seven minutes from downtown by streetcar. *Fr. Stangs gate, tel. 22443960, fax 22446713. 42 rooms with bath or shower. AE, DC, MC, V.*

The Arts

Considering the size of the city, Oslo has a surprisingly good artistic life. Consult the "Oslo Guide" or "Oslo This Week" for details. Winter is *the* cultural season, with the **Nationaltheatret** featuring modern plays (all in Norwegian), classics, and a good sampling of Ibsen. **Det Norske Teatret** (Kristian IVs gate 8), one of Europe's most modern theater complexes, features musicals and plays.

Oslo's modern **Konserthuset** (Concert Hall), at Munkedamsveien 14, is the home of the Oslo Philharmonic, famous for its recordings of Tchaikovsky's symphonies. A smaller hall in the same building is the setting for performances of chamber music and—in summer only—folk dancing, held Monday and Thursday at 9 in July and August. In addition to the **Museum of Contemporary Art,** there's a good modern collection at the **Henie-Onstad Kunstsenter** (tel. 67543050) at Høvikodden. This center specializes in 20th-century art and was a gift from the Norwegian Olympic skater Sonja Henie and her husband, shipowner Niels Onstad. Open Tue.–Fri. 9–7, Sat.–Mon. 11–5.

Nightlife

Oslo used to be a place where the sidewalks rolled up at 8. Now Karl Johansgate is a lively place into the wee hours. There are loads of music cafés and clubs, as well as more conventional night spots. A few good ones are **Barock** (Universitetsgate 26, tel. 22334216), **Cruise Kafé** (Aker Brygge 1, tel. 22836430), **Rockefeller** (Torggata 16—entrance from Mariboes gate, tel. 22203232), **Smuget** (Rosenkrantzgt. 22, tel. 22425262), and **LIPP** (Olav Vs gate 2, tel. 22414400). Why not go to a movie? All films are screened in the original language with Norwegian subtitles. Tickets cost NOK 45.

The Coast Road to Stavanger

This tour follows the Sørland coast south of Oslo toward the busy port Kristiansand and then west to Stavanger. It is an area where whaling has given way to canneries, lumber, paper production, and petrochemicals. Yet the beauty of this 608-kilometer (380-mile) route has not been greatly marred, and you'll find seaside towns, rocky headlands, and stretches of forest

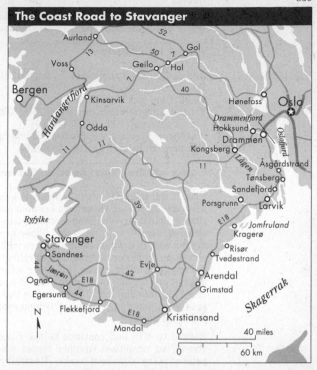

The Coast Road to Stavanger

(fjord country does not begin until north of Stavanger). The route outlined here follows the coast, but it is also possible to reach Stavanger via an inland route through the Telemark region.

Getting Around

By Car Driving is recommended because it gives visitors the chance to stop at coastal villages that are either not served by trains or have only sporadic service. The route is simple: E18 as far as Flekkefjord, then Route 44 to Stavanger.

By Train The best train service is the Sørland line, which leaves Oslo Central Station and goes all the way to Stavanger. The Oslo–Drammen stretch is an engineering feat and features Norway's longest tunnel, an 11-kilometer (7-mile) construction through sheer rock.

By Bus Local buses cover the entire route, but they take much longer than the train. For details on fares and schedules, check with the tourist offices listed below or the main one in Oslo (*see* Important Addresses and Numbers in Oslo, *above*).

Guided Tours

During the summer there is a daily boat excursion from Oslo to the coastal resorts of Kragerø, Jomfruland, and Risør southwest of the capital in the direction of Stavanger. Sightseers return the same day, and refreshments are served on board. The excursion is organized by the Norway Information Center (*see* Important Addresses and Numbers, *above*).

Tourist Information

Arendal (Nedre Tyholmsvei 7b, tel. 37122193).
Drammen (Rådhuset, tel. 32806210).
Flekkefjord (tel. 38324254).
Kristiansand (Dronningens gate 2, tel. 38226065).
Larvik (Storgaten 20, tel. 33410100).
Stavanger (Stavanger Kulturhus, Sølvberget, tel. 51535100).
Tønsberg (Storgaten 55, tel. 33310220).

Exploring the Coast Road to Stavanger

From Oslo, take E18 west for about 40 kilometers (25 miles) to the bustling port of **Drammen**. Located at the mouth of a large timber-floating river, Drammen operates as a processing and shipping center for lumber and paper products. Take a short detour west of town on Route 11, turn right on Kongsgate, and climb the mile-long series of spiraling tunnels leading to **Spiraltoppen** at **Bragernes Hill**. During the '50s, locals decided against any further quarrying of building stone and turned instead to tunneling for it. The result is this scenic and dramatic road with panoramic views of **Drammensfjord** and the larger **Oslofjord** beyond.

Return to E18 and continue to the coastal town of **Åsgård-strand**, an unspoiled summer resort where Edvard Munch painted many of his best works. His small yellow frame house is open to visitors during the summer (admission: NOK 10). Farther along is **Tønsberg**, which inhabitants claim is Norway's oldest town, founded in AD 870. The steep hill, Slottsfjellet, beside the train station leads to the ruins of **Tønsberghus**, an extensive fortress and abbey. The outlook tower, built in 1870 to commemorate the town's millennium, has a good view of the coast. The rise of Oslo as Norway's capital led to the decline of Tønsberg, although it thrived as a whaling port in the 1700s.

Attractive **Sandefjord**, 15 kilometers (9 miles) down E18, is a port that served as the base for the Norwegian whaling fleet until after World War II, when large-scale competition from the Soviet Union and Japan made the operation uneconomical. The port remains busy as a depot for timber shipping.

Just beyond Sandefjord, E18 crosses the important lumbering river Lågen and then follows it to the port of **Larvik**, which is the terminus for ferries to Frederikshavn in Denmark. Like Tønsberg and Sandefjord, Larvik once looked to whaling for its livelihood, but it, too, has turned to lumber and ferrying for employment.

The **Maritime Museum** is located in the former customs house and chronicles Larvik's seafaring history. It emphasizes Thor Heyerdahl's voyages, with models of *Kon-Tiki* and *RA II*. *Admission charges and opening times vary; check with the tourist office.*

After Larvik, progress is faster, as E18 cuts across some of the narrower peninsulas on its way south. Side roads offer the chance to explore the smaller coastal village of **Kragerø**, where Edvard Munch spent many summers painting. Next is **Risør**, with picturesque, white-painted, patrician 19th-century harbor-front homes; and **Tvedestrand,** with charming old sections of town. They are all very popular summer resorts.

Arendal, 120 kilometers (75 miles) beyond Larvik, was once called the Venice of Scandinavia, but the canals have now been turned into wide streets. The atmosphere of bygone whaling prosperity in this and other Sørland ports is like that of Nantucket, with tidy cottages and grandiose captains' houses all within shouting distance of the docks. Explore Arendal's **Tyholmen quarter** for a glimpse into this 19th-century world.

Kristiansand is another 50 kilometers (31 miles) along the coast from Arendal. It is the largest town at Sørlandet and has important air, sea, road, and rail links. It was laid out during the 17th century in a grid pattern, with the imposing **Christiansholm Fort** guarding the eastern harbor approach. (Exhibitions are sometimes held inside the fort during the summer.) Just to the northeast of Kristiansand is the open-air **West Agder County Museum,** with 30 old buildings and farms rebuilt in the local style of the 18th and 19th centuries. There are also displays of folklore and costumes. *Admission: NOK 10 adults, NOK 5 children. Open Mon.–Sat. 10–6, Sun. noon–6.*

A must for children is a visit to the nearby **Kardemomme By** (Cardamom Town) (tel. 38046200) and the zoo and leisure park. *Admission: NOK 130 adults, NOK 110 children. Open summer, daily 9–7; off-season, daily 10–3.*

Continue along E18 for another 30 kilometers (19 miles) to **Mandal,** Norway's most southerly town, famous for its beach, salmon, and 18th- and 19th-century houses. For the next 30 kilometers (19 miles), the road climbs and weaves its way through steep, wooded valleys and then descends to the fishing port of **Flekkefjord,** with its charming **Hollenderbyen,** or Dutch Quarter.

E18 heads inland here to Stavanger, but it is more rewarding to follow the coast road (Route 44) past the fishing port of **Egersund,** 40 kilometers (25 miles) ahead, and a little farther to **Ogna,** with its sandy beach. For the last hour or so before Stavanger, you will be in the region known as the **Jæren.** Flat and stony, it is the largest expanse of level terrain in this mountainous country. The mild climate and the absence of good harbors mean that the population here turned to agriculture, and the miles of stone walls are a testament to their labor.

Stavanger, at the end of the tour, is a former trading town that has become a champion (some environmentalists say victim) of the oil boom. It is now the fourth largest city in Norway. Drilling platforms and oil tankers take the place of fishing boats in the harbor. In sharp contrast to the new high-rise complexes, there is an old quarter with narrow cobbled lanes and clapboard houses at odd angles. The town is believed to date from the 8th century; its Anglo-Norman **St. Svithuns Cathedral,** next to the central market, was established in 1125 by the bishop of Winchester in England. (Trading and ecclesiastical links between Norway and England were strong throughout the Middle Ages.)

Ledaal is a fine patrician mansion where the king resides when he's visiting Stavanger and that is part of the **Stavanger Museum.** It houses relics from the area and a special maritime display. An ultramodern concert hall and arts center opened in Stavanger during the mid-'80s. Also of interest is **Viste Cave** outside the city. It is said to be 6,000 years old. Nearby **Ullandhaug** is a reconstructed Iron Age farm. The **Canning Museum** is a reconstructed sardine factory dating from 1890 to 1920; here you'll get a lesson in the production of sardines and fish conserves.

The **Norwegian Emigration Center** specializes in genealogy and family research, helping to bridge the gap between Norway and the families of Norwegians who emigrated to America. *Bergjelandsgate 30, tel. 51501267. Open weekdays 9–3.*

The **Ryfylke fjords** north and east of Stavanger form the southern end of the fjord country. The city is a good base for exploring this region, with the "white fleet" of low-slung seabuses making daily excursions into even the most distant fjords of Ryfylke. The Lysefjord excursion is superb.

Dining and Lodging

For details and price-category definitions, *see* Dining and Lodging in Staying in Norway. Best bets are indicated by a star ★.

Arendal
Dining

Madam Reiersen. This authentic restaurant on the waterfront serves good food in an informal atmosphere. *Nedre Tyholmsveien 3, tel. 37021900. No reservations. AE, DC, MC, V. Moderate.*

Lodging

Inter Nor Tyholmen. This new maritime hotel is located at Tyholmen, with the sea at close quarters and a splendid view of the fjord. It also boasts an open-air restaurant, Bryggekanten. *Teaterplassen 2, tel. 37026800, fax 37026801. 60 rooms with bath. Facilities: restaurant, bar. AE, DC, MC, V. Moderate.*

Drammen
Dining

Spiraltoppen Café. Located at the top of Bragernes Hill, this café offers excellent views as well as good food. *Bragernesåsen, tel. 32837815. No reservations. AE, DC, MC, V. Moderate.*

Lodging

Rica Park. This comfortable and centrally located hotel has well-equipped rooms and two good restaurants, a bar, and a nightclub. *Gamle Kirkeplass 3, tel. 32838280, fax 32893207. 103 rooms with bath or shower. Facilities: 2 restaurants, bar, nightclub. AE, DC, MC, V. Moderate.*

Kristiansand
Dining

Restaurant Sjøhuset. Seafood and fish are best bets in this rustic waterfront restaurant. *Østre Strandgate 12a, tel. 38026260. No reservations. AE, DC, MC, V. Moderate.*

Lodging

Rica Fregatten. You're right in the center of town in this medium-size hotel, a stone's throw from the Town Hall and Cathedral. The comfortable and well-appointed rooms were renovated in 1992, and there is a good restaurant, the Captain's Table. *Dronningens gate 66, tel. 38021500, fax 38021019. 47 rooms with bath. Facilities: restaurant, bar. AE, DC, MC, V. Moderate.*

Larvik
Lodging

Grand. The rooms are spotless and service is attentive in this large hotel overlooking the fjord. There is a choice of restaurants in which to sample the local fish soup and smoked meat platters, particularly good at lunchtime. *Storgaten 38–40, tel. 33187800, fax 33187045. 97 rooms with bath. Facilities: restaurants. AE, DC, MC, V. Moderate.*

Sandefjord
Dining
★

Edgar Ludl's Gourmet. Enjoy fish specialties prepared by Master Chef Ludl in the best restaurant outside Oslo. The seven-course menu is an excellent choice. *Rådhusgate 7, tel. 33462741, fax 33462741. Reservations advised. AE, DC, MC, V. Closed Sun. Moderate.*

Lodging
★

Park. Overlooking Sandefjord's attractive harbor, the imposing Park is one of the best hotels in Norway. The rooms are large and comfortable, with excellent views over the water. The service is flawless. *Strandpromenaden 9, tel. 33465550, fax 33467900. 174 rooms with bath or shower. Facilities: restaurants, bar, pool, saunas. AE, DC, MC, V. Expensive.*

Stavanger
Dining

Sjøhuset Skagen. This restored 17th-century wharf house specializes in seafood plus lots of atmosphere. *Skagenkaien, tel. 51526190, fax 51521472. Reservations advised. AE, DC, MC, V. Moderate.*

Straen. This famous fish restaurant, located in the oldest part of town, offers a wide selection of delicious fresh seafood. There is a night club, a rock café, and a pub on the premises. *Nedre Strandgate 15, tel. 51526100, fax 51567798. AE, DC, MC, V. Closed Sun. Moderate.*

Lodging

SAS Royal. Like its counterpart in Oslo (SAS Scandinavia Hotel), the Royal is modern, elegant, and efficient but still has a pleasant, informal atmosphere. The rooms are large and comfortable, and the hotel is capable of catering to your every need, whether you are there on business or vacation. *Løkkevn. 26, tel. 51567000, fax 51567460. 196 rooms with bath. Facilities: 2 restaurants, pool, sauna, airline check-in, business service center. AE, DC, MC, V. Expensive.*

Commandør. The Commandør is much smaller and considerably more basic than the Royal, but it offers clean and comfortable accommodations. *Valberg gate 9, tel. 51895300, fax 51895301. 40 rooms with bath. AE, DC, MC, V. Moderate.*

Through Telemark to Bergen

Bergen is Norway's second-largest city. To get there, you pass through the Telemark area, midway between Oslo and Bergen. This region is characterized by steep valleys, pine forests, lakes, and fast-flowing rivers that are full of trout. Here is Morgedal, the cradle of skiing. Then you'll go on to Hardangervidda, a wild mountain area and national park that was the stronghold of Norway's Resistance fighters during World War II, and then down to the beautiful Hardangerfjord. Few places on earth match western Norway for spectacular scenic beauty, for this is the fabled land of the fjords.

Fjord transportation is good, since crossing fjords is a necessary as well as a scenic way to travel in Norway. Hardangerfjord, Sognefjord, and Nordfjord are three of the deepest and most popular fjords. Local tourist offices will be able to recommend excursions and travel routes.

Guided Tours

Bergen is the gateway to the fjords, and excursions cover most of the last half of this tour as well as the fjords farther north.

Through Telemark to Bergen

Contact the tourist information offices (*see below*) for details of these constantly changing tours.

Tourist Information

Bergen (Slottsgate 1, tel. 55313860; Bryggen 7, tel. 55321480).
Drammen (Rådhuset, tel. 32806210).
Kinsarvik (tel. 53663112).
Kongsberg (Schwabesgate 1, tel. 32731526).
Røldal (tel. 53647245).

Exploring Through Telemark to Bergen

Take E18 west from Oslo to nearby **Drammen** (*see* Exploring the Coast Road to Stavanger, *above*). Follow Route 11 through Drammen and continue west for about 40 kilometers (25 miles) to **Kongsberg,** by the fast-flowing Lågen River. Kongsberg was founded in 1624 as a silver-mining town. Although there is no more mining, the old mines at Saggrenda are open for guided tours. **Norske Bergverksmuseum** includes the Silver Mines Collection, the Ski Museum, and the Royal Mint Museum. In the center of town is an 18th-century Rococo church, which reflects the town's former source of wealth—silver.

Kongsberg is one of the gateways to Telemark, which is just beyond Meheia on the county border. Forests give way to rocky peaks and desolate spaces farther into the plateau. **Heddal** is the first stop in Telemark. Norway's largest stave church is here. Stave churches, built with wooden planks staked vertically into the ground or base, date from the medieval period and are found almost exclusively in southern Norway. The Heddal church is typical of stave churches in that it has richly carved ornamentation on the doors and around the aisle.

Route 11 climbs from Heddal and skirts the large Telemark plateau. You'll see the **Lifjell** area's highest peak, Røydalsnuten, 1,291 meters (4,234 feet), on the left before descending toward **Seljord,** on the lake of the same name. The countryside by the lake is richer than that on the plateau; meadows and pastureland run down to the lakefront. The attractive village of Seljord has ornamented wooden houses and a medieval church.

Continue south from Seljord, making sure to stay right (on Route 11) at the Brunkeberg crossroads, while the other road continues south to Kristiansand. You are now entering the steep valley of **Morgedal**. It was here in the last century that Sondre Nordheim developed the slalom method of skiing—*sla lom* means "make turns." You can get the full story on the development of skiing at the **Olav Bjåland's Museum**, named for the south polar explorer and ski hero. *Admission NOK 15. Open June 15–Aug. 15, daily 10–5.*

Turn left at Høydalsmo for a scenic diversion to mountainbound **Dalen**. At Dalen is **Tokke I,** one of Europe's largest hydroelectric power stations. From here it's an 8-kilometer (5-mile) drive to **Eidsborg,** where there is a stave church and a dramatic view of the Dalen Valley.

From Dalen you can also drive up to one of Telemark's wonders, the **Ravnejuvet ravine,** a 310-meter (1,016-foot) sheer drop into the Tokke Valley. Throw paper into the ravine and a peculiar updraft returns it to you.

Take Route 38 from Dalen along the Tokke Valley to **Åmot**. The 93-meter (305-foot) Hyllandfoss Falls were destroyed by the hydroelectric project, but the drive is still spectacular.

Rejoin Route 11 at Åmot. At the next crossroads (**Haukeligrend**), Route 11 really begins to climb, and you'll see why the Norwegians are so proud of keeping this route open all year. Before you leave Telemark, you'll pass through the 6-kilometer (4-mile) Haukeli Tunnel and then begin a long descent to **Røldal,** another lakefront village with a hydroelectric plant.

Turn north on Route 13 a few miles after Røldal, and drive to the **Sørfjord** at Odda. Continue along the fjord to the attractive village of **Kinsarvik**. For the best view of the junction of the Sørfjord and the mighty Hardangerfjord, take the ferry across the Sørfjord to Utne. On the dramatic 30-minute ferry crossing from Utne to Kvanndal, you will know why this area was such a rich source of inspiration for Romantic composer Edvard Grieg.

At Kvanndal, turn left on Route 7. The road follows the fjord west, then veers right to **Norheimsund**. After climbing another coastal mountain spur, it winds through the wild **Tokagjel Gorge** and across the mountains of **Kvamskogen,** then descends tortuously into Bergen, capital of the fjords.

Bergen is Norway's second-largest city, with a population of 217,000. Before oil brought an influx of foreigners to Stavanger, it was the most international of the country's cities, having been an important trading and military center when Oslo was an obscure village. Bergen was a member of the medieval Hanseatic League and offered an ice-free harbor and convenient trading location on the west coast. Natives of Bergen still think of Oslo as a dour provincial town.

Despite numerous fires in its past, much of medieval Bergen has remained. Seven surrounding mountains set off the weathered wooden houses, cobbled streets, and Hanseatic-era warehouses of the **Bryggen** (harbor area). Founded in 1070, the town was first called Bjørgvin.

The best way to get a feel for Bergen's medieval trading heyday is to visit the **Hanseatic Museum** on the Bryggen. One of the oldest and best-preserved of Bergen's wooden buildings, it is furnished in 16th-century style. The guided tour is excellent. *Admission: NOK 15 adults, NOK 8 children. Open June–Aug.,* *daily 9–5; May, Sept., daily 11–2; Oct.–Apr., Mon., Wed., Fri., Sun. 11–2.*

On the western end of the Vågen is the **Rosenkrantz Tower,** part of the **Bergenhus,** the 13th-century fortress guarding the harbor entrance. The tower and fortress were destroyed during World War II, but were meticulously restored during the '60s and are now rich with furnishings and household items from the 16th century. *Admission: NOK 10 adults, NOK 5 children. Open mid-May–mid-Sept., daily 10–4; mid-Sept.–mid-May, Sun. 12–3, or upon request.*

Across the Vågen is the **Nordnes peninsula,** where you can look back toward the city and the mountainous backdrop. Save time to meander through the winding back streets, intersected by broad *almenninger* (wide avenues built as protection against fires). For the best view of Bergen and its surroundings, take the funicular from the corner of Lille Øvregate and Vetrlidsalmenning. It climbs 310 meters (1,016 feet) to the top of **Fløyen,** one of the seven mountains guarding this ancient port.

Troldhaugen manor on Nordås Lake, once home to Edvard Grieg, is now a museum and includes a new chamber music hall. Recitals are held each Wednesday and Sunday at 7:30 PM from late June through early August. *Troldhaugsveien, Hop, Bergen, tel. 55911791. Admission: NOK 15 adults, NOK 8 children. Open May–Sept., daily 9:30–5:30.*

Dining and Lodging

For details and price-category definitions, *see* Dining and Lodging in Staying in Norway. Best bets are indicated by a star ★.

Bergen   **Bellevue.** It's hard to imagine a more imposing or dramatic set-
Dining   ting for a restaurant than the Bellevue's, high up on a hillside
  ★   looking down on Bergen. The restaurant itself is a 17th-century manor house. Fine crystal and silverware accompany the excellent food. *Bellevuebakken 9, tel. 55310240. Reservations required. AE, DC, V. Expensive.*

  ★   **Lucullus.** This French-inspired seafood restaurant is, appropriately enough, in the Hotel Neptun. It has an excellent wine cellar, with special emphasis on white wines to go with the fish. *Walckendorffsgate 8, tel. 55901000, fax 55233202. Reservations recommended. AE, DC, V. Closed weekends. Expensive.*

Enhjørningen (Unicorn). One of Bergen's most popular seafood restaurants, Unicorn is located in an old Hanseatic warehouse. *Bryggen, tel. 55327919. Reservations required. AE, DC, MC, V. Moderate.*

Lodging   **SAS Royal.** Located right at the harbor, the SAS Royal was opened in 1982 on the site of old warehouses. Ravaged since 1170 by a series of nine fires, the warehouses were rebuilt each time in the same style, which SAS has incorporated into this well-equipped hotel. *Bryggen, tel. 55543000, fax 55324808. 267 rooms with bath. Facilities: 2 restaurants, pub, bar, discothèque, pool, sauna, Hanseatic exhibition. AE, DC, MC, V. Very Expensive.*

Augustin. This small but excellent hotel in the center of town has been recently restored to its original late–Art Nouveau character, complete with period furniture in the lobby. *C.*

Sundtsgate 24, tel. 55230025, fax 55233130. 38 rooms with bath. AE, DC, MC, V. Moderate.

Bryggen Orion. Facing the harbor in the center of town, the recently renovated (1991) hotel is surrounded by Bergen's most famous sights. *Bradbenken 3, tel. 55318080; fax 55329414. 229 rooms with bath. Facilities: restaurant, bar, nightclub. AE, DC, MC, V. Moderate.*

Kinsarvik **Kinsarvik Fjord Hotel.** This handsome hotel near the busy ferry
Lodging port offers good views of Hardangerfjord and the glacier. The rooms are bright and spacious. *Kinsarvik, tel. 53663100, fax 53663374. 62 rooms with bath or shower. AE, MC, V. Moderate.*

Kongsberg **Gamle Kongsberg Kro.** Located by the waterfall at Nybro-
Dining fossen, with a mini-golf course nearby, this newly restored café offers hearty Norwegian dishes at moderate prices. *Thornesveien 4, tel. 03/731633. No reservations. AE, DC, MC, V. Moderate.*

Utne **Utne Hotel.** The white frame house dates from 1722, and the ho-
Dining and Lodging tel, the oldest in Norway, has been run by the same family since 1787. The Utne has all the cared-for atmosphere of an old home. The dining room is wood paneled and hand painted, decorated with copper pans, old china, and paintings. The rooms, many of which have good views of the ferry port and Hardangerfjord, are filled with period furniture. The Utne makes a good base for hiking or cycling. *Utne, tel. 5366983. 24 rooms with bath or shower. AE, DC, MC, V. Moderate.*

Above Bergen: The Far North

The fjords continue northward from Bergen all the way to Kirkenes, at Norway's border with the Republic of Russia. Norway's north is for anyone eager to hike, climb, fish, birdwatch (seabirds), see Lapland, or experience—in June and July—the unending days of the midnight sun. The Lofoten Islands present the grand face of the "Lofoten Wall"—a rocky, 96-kilometer-long (60-mile-long) massif surrounded by the sea and broken into six pieces. Svolvær, the most populated island, has a thriving summer artists' colony. It's also known for winter cod fishing.

Getting Around

By Ship One of the best ways to travel in northern Norway is the **Hurtigrute,** or coastal steamer, which begins in Bergen and turns around 2,000 nautical kilometers (1,250 miles) later at Kirkenes. Many steamers run this route, so you can put in at any of the ports for any length of time and pick up the next one coming through: Major tourist offices have schedules and reservations are essential (*see* Important Addresses and Numbers in Oslo, *above*, and Getting Around by Ferry, *above*).

By Car E6 and its feeder roads are the only route available north of Trondheim, where the country narrows dramatically.

By Train Major train routes are Oslo–Bergen and Oslo–Trondheim–Bodø (the Trondheim–Bodø leg takes one day). From Bodø there are tours to the Lofoten and Vesterålen Islands and to the

Væren Islands, two tiny, remote islands at the tail of the Lofoten chain. You can get to Svolvær, the Lofotens' main port, via ferry from Skutvik.

To get all the way to Nordkapp (the North Cape, the northernmost mainland point in Norway and Europe) and the Land of the Midnight Sun, you must continue your trip by bus from Fauske.

Guided Tours

The major towns north of Bergen are Ålesund, Trondheim, Bodø, Narvik, Tromsø, Hammerfest, and Kirkenes. The area covered is enormous, so use the local tourist offices (*see below*) for tour information, area maps, and tours. Special tours are included below in Exploring, where each town is individually described. Cheaper accommodations are the rule in the north, whether you stay in a cabin, campsite, guest house, or *rorbu*—fishermen's huts in the islands that are available for rent outside the January to April fishing season. These days, many *rorbuer* are built to be motels.

Tourist Information

Ålesund (Rådhuset [City Hall], tel. 70121202).
Bodø (Sjøgata 21, tel. 75526000).
Hammerfest (tel. 78412185).
Kirkenes (off the E6 in a wooden hut behind Rica Hotel [on Pasvikveien], tel. 78992544).
Narvik (Kongensgate 66, tel. 76943309).
Tromsø (Storgata 61, tel. 77610000).
Trondheim (Munkegata 19, tel. 73929394).

Exploring the Far North

See the Norway country map for the location of towns on this tour.

The steamer is probably the best route from Ålesund to Trondheim because no main road connects them directly. **Ålesund,** a much-overlooked coastal city flanked by fjords, is perhaps the only example you'll find of true architectural eccentricity in Norway. After a fire here during the early 1900s, anyone who had any aspirations to architecture designed his or her own new home, and the result is a rich, playful mixture of styles ranging from austere to Art Nouveau. There are excellent tours of the Romsdal, Geiranger, and Hjørund fjords. Pick up the free "Ålesund Guide" and "On Foot in Ålesund" from the tourist office (*see* Tourist Information, *above*).

Trondheim sits at the southern end of Norway's widest fjord, Trondheimfjord. This waterbound city is the third largest in the country and is the traditional coronation place of Norwegian royalty. Scandinavia's largest medieval building, **Nidaros Cathedral,** started in 1320 but not completed until about 70 years ago, is here. For centuries it served as a goal for religious pilgrims. There is a historic fish market that is worth seeing. Scandinavia's two largest wooden buildings are in Trondheim. One is the rococo **Stiftsgården,** a royal palace built in 1774, and the other is a student dormitory.

After Trondheim, the country thins into a vertebral cord of land hugging the border with Sweden and hunching over the top of Finland. **Bodø** is the first major town above the Polar Circle. As the northern terminus of the Nordland railway, Bodø is bathed in midnight sun from early June to mid-July. For those who want boat excursions to **coastal bird colonies** (the Væren Islands), Bodø is the best base. The city was bombed by the Germans in 1940. The stunning, contemporary **Bodø Cathedral**, its spire separated from the main building, was built after the war. Inside are rich, modern tapestries; outside is a war memorial. The **Nordland County Museum** depicts the life of the Lapps *(Same)*, as well as regional history. *Prinsengate 116, tel. 75526128. Admission: NOK 10 adults, NOK 2 children. Open weekdays 9–3, weekends noon–3.*

If you've never seen a real **maelstrom**—a furious natural whirlpool—inquire at the tourist office (*see* Tourist Information, *above*) about **Saltstraumen.** Bodø is considered a gateway to the Lofoten and Vesterålen islands; the tourist office will make the necessary arrangements.

Time Out   Alongside the maelstrom is **Saltstraumen Hotel.** Try the poached halibut—delicious!

Narvik is a rebuilt city, an "ice-free" seaport, and a major shipping center for iron ore. An excellent railway connects it to the mines across the Swedish border. Its old outline was erased by war damage. The **Krigsminne War Museum** has gripping displays on wartime intrigues and suffering. *Kongensgate, near the main square. Admission: NOK 20. Open Mar.–Sept., daily 10–2; Jun.–Aug., daily 10–10.*

Tours of the busy **Narvik docks** start from the LKAB building. For panoramic views, hop the *gondolbaner* (cable car) up **Fagernesfjellet's** 682-meter (2,237-foot) cliffs (fare: NOK 60). Hiking it takes at least two hours. Also try to see the **Brennholtet rock carvings.** Note that the tourist office (*see* Tourist Information, *above*) rents rooms in private homes as well as hotels. Narvik is a good base for mountain excursions.

Tromsø dubs itself "the Paris of the North" for the nightlife inspired by the midnight sun. Looming over this remote arctic university town are 1,860-meter (6,100-foot) peaks with permanent snowcaps. Tromsø trails off into the islands: Half the town lives offshore. Its population is about 50,000. Be sure to see the spectacular **Arctic Church,** with its eastern wall made entirely of stained glass, across the long stretch of **Tromsø bridge.** Coated in aluminum, its triangular peaks make a bizarre mirror for the midnight sun.

Be sure to walk around old Tromsø (along the waterfront) and to visit the **Tromsø Museum,** which concentrates on science, the Lapp people, and northern churches. *Lars Thøringsvei 10, Folkeparken; take Bus 27 or 22. Admission: NOK 10 adults, NOK 5 children. Open Sept.–May, weekdays 8:30–3:30, Sat. noon–3, Sun. 11–4; June–Aug., daily 9–7.*

Hammerfest is the world's northernmost town. It is surrounded by Lapp settlements and is home to the **Royal and Ancient Polar Bear Society.** Don't visit the society if you don't like real stuffed bears. *Town Hall basement. Admission free. Open in summer, daily 7:30 AM–9 PM.*

Hammerfest is an elegant, festive-looking port town despite having been razed twice in its history. During the late 19th century the town was leveled by fire. Years later, defeated German troops destroyed the town as they retreated to avoid leaving anything to the Russians.

Dining and Lodging

For details and price-category definitions, *see* Dining and Lodging in Staying in Norway.

Ålesund   **Fjellstua.** This mountaintop restaurant has tremendous views
Dining   over the surrounding peaks, islands, and fjords. There are several different eating facilities here, but the main restaurant serves a variety of dishes and homemade desserts. *Fjellstua, tel. 70126582. Reservations not necessary. AE, DC, V. Closed Dec.–Easter. Moderate.*

Sjøbua. Located at Brunholmen on an old wharf, Sjøbua offers an excellent seafood selection. You can even pick your own dinner from a saltwater aquarium. *Brunholmgata 1, tel. 70127100. Reservations recommended. AE, DC, V. Moderate.*

Lodging   **Rica Parken.** Renovated in 1990, this is the largest and best-equipped hotel in Ålesund. *Storgata 16, tel. 70125050, fax 70122164. 138 rooms with bath. Facilities: restaurants, bar, disco, sauna, gym. AE, DC, MC, V. Expensive.*

Bryggen Home. This dockside warehouse was converted into a hotel in 1990. There are splendid views over the water. *Apotekergate 1–3, tel. 70126400, fax 70121180. 82 rooms with bath or shower. Facilities: sauna, solarium. AE, DC, MC, V. Moderate.*

Atlantica. Its exterior is austere, but once inside you'll get unspoiled views of the mountains and fjords. This clean, ultramodern hotel is centrally located. *Rasmus Rønneberg gate 4, tel. 70129100, fax 70126252. 45 rooms with bath or shower. Facilities: unlicensed café. AE, DC, MC, V. Inexpensive–Moderate.*

Bodø   **Marlene Restaurant.** Set within the SAS Royal hotel, the
Dining   Marlene offers a superb seafood buffet throughout the summer. Be sure to try one of the salmon dishes. *Storgata 2, tel. 75524100, fax 75527493. Reservations advised. AE, DC, MC, V. Moderate–Expensive.*

Turisthytta. This mountaintop lodge (accessible by taxi) is a fine place to eat if you want to bask in the midnight sun. There is a good range of dishes, from snacks and open-faced sandwiches to fresh fish. *Turisthytta, tel. 75583300. Reservations advised. No credit cards. Moderate.*

Lodging   **SAS Royal.** This grandiose hotel is throbbing with life, with enough amenities to keep you entertained virtually around the clock. *Storgata 2, tel. 75524100, fax 75527493. 190 rooms with bath. Facilities: restaurant, wine bar, nightclub, health club, sauna. AE, DC, MC, V. Expensive.*

Norrøna. This bed-and-breakfast–style establishment is comfortable, with the location just as grand as that of the SAS Royal next door. *Storgata 4, tel. 75525550, fax 75523388. 150 rooms with bath or shower. AE, DC, V. Moderate.*

Hammerfest   **Hammerfest Hotel.** On the pleasant Rådhusplassen, this guest
Dining and Lodging   house has handsome, harborview rooms for tolerable prices in a town where hotels are expensive. *Strandgata 2–4, tel.*

78411622, fax 78412127. 54 rooms with bath or shower. Facilities: restaurant, cafeteria. AE, DC, MC, V. Expensive.

Narvik
Dining and Lodging

Grand Royal Hotel. This is a classy, handsome hotel, enhanced by a staff that is eager to please. The location, right by the train station, is a plus, and there are many chances to try the skiing and fishing nearby. The Grand Royal was renovated in 1987 and the rooms are well equipped. *Kongensgate 64, tel. 76941500, fax 76945531. 108 rooms with bath. Facilities: 2 restaurants, gym, sauna, nightclub. AE, DC, MC, V. Expensive.*

Tromsø
Dining and Lodging

SAS Royal. Each room in this beautifully set hotel gives splendid views over Tromsø's shoreline, although the location is in the heart of town. *Sjøgata 7, tel. 77656000, fax 77685474. 200 rooms with bath. Facilities: restaurant, bar. AE, DC, MC, V. Expensive.*

Saga. Situated on a pretty town square, the Saga combines its central location with the staff's expertise. Its restaurant has affordable, hearty meals, and the rooms—although somewhat basic—are quiet and comfortable. *Richard Withs Plass 2, tel. 77681180, fax 77682380. 52 rooms with bath. Facilities: restaurant, cafeteria. AE, DC, MC, V. Moderate.*

Trondheim
Dining

Bryggen. This popular restaurant, set near the Gamle Bybro (Old Town Bridge), serves a feast of Norwegian gourmet specialties with a Gallic flourish. With a choice of creperie, wine and cheese room, and bistro serving French cuisine, you can't go wrong. *Ø Bakklandet 66, tel. 73520230. Reservations advised. AE, DC, MC, V. Expensive (lunch Moderate).*

Palmehaven. Situated in the Hotel Britannia, this famous restaurant has traditions dating back to 1918. It is the place to celebrate special occasions. *Dronningensgate 5, tel. 73535353, fax 73512900. Reservations required. AE, DC, MC, V. Expensive.*

Tavern på Sverresborg. Outside the city, at the open-air Folk Museum, this restaurant serves Norwegian specialties. *Sverresborg, tel. 73520932. No reservations. No credit cards. Moderate.*

Lodging

Royal Garden Hotel. Trondheim's finest hotel has excellent facilities for sports and fitness, as well as many features to help handicapped guests. *Kjøpmannsgate 73, tel. 73521100, fax 73531766. 297 rooms with bath. Facilities: 3 restaurants, bar, sauna, indoor pool, gymnasium. AE, DC, MC, V. Expensive.*

Ambassadeur. Take in the panoramic view from the roof terrace of this first-rate modern hotel, about 93 meters (101 yards) from the market square. The deep blue waters of the Trondheimsfjord reflect the dramatic and irregular coastline. Most rooms in the Ambassadeur have fireplaces, and some have balconies. *Elvegate 18, tel. 73527050, fax 73527052. 34 rooms with bath. Facilities: restaurant, bar. AE, DC, MC, V. Moderate.*

Singsaker Sommerhotell. This dormitory becomes a comfortable hotel every summer. *Singsaker, tel. 73520092, fax 73520635. 104 rooms with bath. Facilities: restaurant, sauna. AE, MC, V. Inexpensive.*

22 Poland

Poland is a land rich in natural beauty and contrasts. Its landscape varies from rolling plains with slow-moving rivers, broad fields, and scattered villages to lakes, forests, and marshes in the north and jagged mountains in the south. This makes possible a wide variety of outdoor activities, from hunting to hiking, sailing, and skiing.

Every one of the major cities, with the exception of Kraków and Łódź, had to be rebuilt after the destruction of World War II. Particularly fine restoration work has been done on Warsaw's Old Town and in Gdańsk on the Baltic coast.

Poland's geographic position between Germany and Russia has determined its history of almost continual war and struggle for independence since the late 18th century. After "liberation" by the Red Army in 1945, a Communist government was imposed. Although the country recovered economically and experienced rapid industrialization, more than 40 years of Communist rule left Poland in prolonged economic crisis. The hopes and aspirations of the postwar generations remained unfulfilled.

Social discontent erupted in 1980 with strikes and the formation of Solidarity, the first free trade union in the Communist bloc. After a year, martial law was imposed and Solidarity was banned. Though martial law was lifted in 1983, and Poland now has a non-Communist government, life for the average Pole remains hard, and no one has simple answers to the country's complicated political and economic problems. In spite of all this, the Polish people continue to be resilient, resourceful, and hopeful.

Poles openly welcome visitors; their uninhibited sense of hospitality makes them eager to please their guests. It is easy to make friends here and to exchange views with strangers on trains and buses. Poles have a passionate interest in all things Western, from current affairs to the arts, clothes, and music.

Essential Information

Before You Go

When to Go The official tourist season runs from May through September. The best times for sightseeing are late spring and early fall. Major cultural events usually take place in the cities during the fall. The early spring is often wet and windy.

Below are the average daily maximum and minimum temperatures for Warsaw.

Jan.	32F	0C	May	67F	20C	Sept.	66F	19C
	22	6		48	9		49	10
Feb.	32F	0C	June	73F	23C	Oct.	55F	13C
	21	- 6		54	12		41	5
Mar.	42F	6C	July	75F	24C	Nov.	42F	6C
	28	- 2		58	16		33	1
Apr.	53F	12C	Aug.	73F	23C	Dec.	35F	2C
	37	3		56	14		28	- 3

Currency The monetary unit in Poland is the złoty (zł). There are notes of 10, 20, 50, 100, 200, 500, 1,000, 2,000, 5,000, 10,000 20,000, 50,000, 100,000, 200,000, 500,000, and 1,000,000 złotys, and

coins of 1, 2, 5, 10, 20, 50, and 100 złotys (rarely seen). At press time (spring 1993), the bank exchange rate was about zł 15,250 to the U.S. dollar and zł 23,600 to the pound sterling. Since spring 1989, the złoty has been legally exchangeable at a free market rate in banks (*Bank Narodowy* and *Pekao* are the largest) and private exchange bureaus (*Kantor wymiany walut*), which sometimes offer slightly better rates than do the banks. If you run out of złotys, you will find that Polish taxi drivers, waiters, and porters will usually accept dollars or any other Western currency.

Credit Cards American Express, Diners Club, MasterCard, and Visa are accepted in all Orbis hotels, in the better restaurants and nightclubs, and for other Orbis services. In small cafés and shops, credit cards may not be accepted.

What It Will Cost At press time (spring 1993), it was still illegal to import or export złotys. This may change if the new Polish government goes through with plans to make the złoty fully convertible on the international market. Still, don't buy more złotys than you need, or you will have to go to the trouble of changing them back at the end of your trip.

Poland is now one of the more expensive countries of Eastern Europe, and inflation is still high by Western standards, despite the reforms of 1990. Prices are highest in the big cities, especially in Warsaw. The more you stray off the tourist track, the cheaper your vacation will be.

Sample Prices A cup of coffee, zł 6,000–25,000; a bottle of beer, zł 10,000–30,000; a soft drink, zł 5,000–25,000; a ham sandwich, zł 10,000–30,000; 1-mile taxi ride, zł 15,000.

Museums Admission fees to museums and other attractions are also rising in line with inflation, and seem ever-changing. At press time (spring 1993), fees ranged from zł 4,000 to zł 35,000.

Visas U.S. and British citizens are no longer required to obtain visas for entry to Poland; Canadian citizens and citizens of other countries that have not yet abolished visas for Poles, must pay the equivalent of $35 (more for multiple-entry visas). Apply at any Orbis office (the official Polish tourist agency), an affiliated travel agent, or from the Polish Consulate General in any country. Each visitor must complete three visa application forms and provide two photographs. Allow about two weeks for processing. Visas are issued for 90 days but can be extended in Poland, if necessary, either through the local county police headquarters or through Orbis.

You can contact the **Polish Consulate General** at the following addresses: **In the United States:** 233 Madison Ave., New York, NY 10016 (tel. 212/391–0844); 1530 North Lake Shore Dr., Chicago, IL 60610 (tel. 312/337–8166); 2224 Wyoming Ave., Washington DC 20008 (tel. 202/234–2501). **In Canada:** 1500 Pine Ave., Montreal, Quebec H3G (tel. 514/937–9481); 2603 Lakeshore Blvd. W., Toronto, Ont. M8V 1G5 (tel. 416/252–5471). **In the United Kingdom:** 73 New Cavendish St., London W1 (tel. 071/636–4533).

Customs on Arrival Persons over 17 may bring in duty-free: personal belongings, including musical instruments, typewriter, radio, 2 cameras with 24 rolls of film; up to 250 cigarettes or 50 cigars and 1 liter each of wine and spirits; and goods to the value of $200. Any amount of foreign currency may be brought in but must be declared on arrival.

Language Polish is a Slavic language that uses the Roman alphabet but has several additional characters and diacritics. Because it has a much higher incidence of consonant clusters than English, most English speakers find it's a difficult language to decipher, much less pronounce. Most older Poles know German; the younger generation usually knows some English. In the big cities you will find people who speak English, especially in hotels, but you may have difficulty in the provinces and countryside.

Getting Around

By Car
Road Conditions Despite the extensive road network, driving conditions, even on main roads, have deteriorated in the past few years. Minor roads tend to be narrow and cluttered with horse-drawn carts and farm animals. Drivers in a hurry should stick to roads marked E or T.

Rules of the Road Driving is on the right, as in the United States. The speed limit on highways is 110 kph (68 mph) and on roads in built-up areas, 60 kph (37 mph). A built-up area is marked by a white rectangular sign with the name of the town on it.

Gasoline The price of gas is between $5.50 and $6.50 for 10 liters of high octane. Filling stations are located every 30 kilometers (20 miles) or so and are usually open 6 AM–10 PM; there are some 24-hour stations.

Breakdowns Poland's **Motoring Association** (PZMot) offers breakdown, repair, and towing services to members of various international insurance organizations. For names of affiliated organizations, check with Orbis before you leave home. Carry a spare-parts kit. For emergency road help, call 981 or 954.

Car Rentals You can rent cars from Avis or Hertz at international airports or through Orbis offices. Rates vary according to season, car model, and mileage. Fly/drive vacations are also available through Orbis.

By Train Poland's PKP railway network is extensive and inexpensive. Most trains have first- and second-class accommodations, but Western visitors usually prefer to travel first-class. You should arrive at the station well before departure time. The fastest trains are intercity and express trains, which require reservations. Some Orbis offices furnish information, reservations, and tickets. Overnight trains have first- and second-class sleeping cars and second-class couchettes. Most long-distance trains carry buffets, but the quality of the food is unpredictable and you may want to bring your own.

Fares Polish trains run at three speeds—*ekspresowy* (express), *pośpieszny* (fast), and *osobowy* (slow)—and fares vary according to the speed of the train. You pay more for intercity and express; return tickets cost exactly twice the single fare.

By Plane **LOT,** Poland's national airline, operates daily flights linking five main cities: **Warsaw, Kraków, Gdańsk, Wrocław,** and **Rzeszów.** Fares begin at about $60 round-trip and can be paid for in złotys. Tickets and information are available from LOT or Orbis offices. All flights booked through Orbis in the United Kingdom carry a discount, but it is cheaper to pay in local currency in Poland. Be sure to book well in advance, especially for the summer season.

By Bus **PKS,** the national bus company, offers long-distance service to most cities. Express buses, on which you can reserve seats, are somewhat more expensive than trains but often—except in the case of a few major intercity routes—get to their destination more quickly. For really out-of-the-way destinations, the bus is often the only means of transportation. PKS bus stations are usually located near railway stations. Tickets and information are best obtained from Orbis. Warsaw's central bus terminal is at aleje Jerozolimskie 144.

Staying in Poland

Telephones
Local Calls Public phone booths take tokens *(żetony)*: zł 600 for local calls and zł 4,000 or 6,000 for long-distance calls, which must be made from special booths, usually situated in post offices. Place a token in the groove on the side or top of the phone, lift the receiver, and dial the number. Many phones automatically absorb the token; in others you must push it into the machine when the call is answered. Card phones were recently introduced at the international airport and some hotels and can be used for both local and long-distance calls. Cards (zł 35,000) are available at post offices and some newspaper kiosks.

International Calls Post offices and first-class hotels have assigned booths, at which you pay after the completion of your call. To place an international call, dial 901; for domestic long-distance calls, dial 900. There's a heavy surcharge on calls made from hotel rooms.

Information For general information (including international codes), tel. 913.

Mail
Postal Rates Airmail letters to the United States cost zł 4,000; postcards, zł 3,500. Letters to the United Kingdom or Europe cost zł 3,500; postcards, zł 3,000. Post offices are open 8 AM–8 PM (except weekends). At least one post office is open 24 hours in every major city. In Warsaw the post office is located at ulica Świętokrzyska 31.

Opening and Closing Times Banks are open weekdays 8 or 9 AM–3 PM or 6 PM.

Museum opening hours vary greatly, but they are generally open Tuesday–Sunday 9–5.

Shops. Food shops are open weekdays 7 AM–7 PM, Saturday 7 AM–1 PM; some are now open on Sunday. Other stores are open weekdays 11 AM–7 PM and Saturday 9 AM–1 PM.

National Holidays January 1; April 3 (Easter); May 1 (Labor Day); May 3 (Constitution Day); June 2 (Corpus Christi); August 15 (Assumption); November 1 (Remembrance); November 11 (rebirth of Polish state, 1918); December 25, 26.

Dining Polish food and drink are basically Slavic with Baltic overtones. There is a heavy emphasis on soups and meat (especially pork) as well as freshwater fish. Much use is made of cream, and pastries are rich and often delectable.

The most popular soup is *barszcz* (known to many Americans as borscht), a clear beet soup often served with such Polish favorites as sausage, cabbage, potatoes, sour cream, coarse rye bread, and beer. Other dishes include *pierogi* (a kind of ravioli), which may be stuffed with savory or sweet fillings; *gołąbki*, cabbage leaves stuffed with minced meat; *bigos*, sauerkraut with meat and mushrooms; and *flaki*, a select dish of tripe, served boiled or fried. Polish beer is good; vodka is a specialty and is often downed before, with, and after meals.

Zajazdy (roadside inns), which are less expensive than regular restaurants, serve more traditional food. As elsewhere in Central Europe, cafés are a way of life in Poland and are often stocked with delicious pastries and ice creams.

Mealtimes At home, Poles eat late lunches (their main meal) and late suppers. Many restaurants, however, close around 9 PM. Most hotel restaurants serve the evening meal until 10:30.

Precautions Tap water is unsafe, so ask for mineral water. Beware of meat dishes served in cheap snack bars. Avoid the food on trains.

Dress In Warsaw and Kraków, formal dress is customary at Very Expensive and Expensive restaurants. Casual dress is appropriate elsewhere.

Ratings Prices are for one person and include three courses and service but no drinks. Best bets are indicated by a star ★.

Category	Warsaw	Other Areas
Very Expensive	over zł 500,000	over zł 400,000
Expensive	zł 300,000–500,000	zł 200,000–400,000
Moderate	zł 150,000–300,000	zł 100,000–200,000
Inexpensive	under zł 150,000	under zł 100,000

Lodging
Hotels The government rates hotel accommodations on the basis of one to five stars. Orbis hotels, owned by the state tourist office and currently undergoing privatization, have almost all been accorded four or five stars and guarantee a reasonable standard of cleanliness and service. They range in price from Moderate to Very Expensive and include a number of foreign-built luxury hotels, such as the InterContinental. In recent years Orbis hotels have faced competition from a growing number of privately owned lodgings, often part of international chains and mostly at the top end of the price range.

Municipal Hotels and Dom Turysty hotels are run by local authorities or the Polish Tourist Association. They are often rather old and limited in bath and shower facilities. Prices are Inexpensive.

Roadside Inns A number of roadside inns, often very attractive, offer inexpensive food and a few guest rooms at moderate rates.

Private
Accommodations Rooms can be arranged either in advance through Orbis or on the spot at the local tourist information office. Villas, lodges, rooms, or houses are available, and the prices are often negotiable. Rates vary from about $6 for a room to more than $150 for a villa.

Ratings The following chart is based on a rate for two people in a double room, with bath or shower and breakfast. These prices are in U.S. dollars. Best bets are indicated by a star ★.

Category	Cost
Very Expensive	over $200
Expensive	$90–$200
Moderate	$50–$90
Inexpensive	under $50

Tipping Waiters get a standard 10% of the bill. Hotel porters and doormen should get about zł 10,000. In Warsaw and other big towns frequented by foreign tourists, waiters also often expect a tip to help find you a table. If you choose to tip in foreign currency (readily accepted), remember that $1 is about an hour's wage.

Warsaw

Arriving and Departing

By Plane   All international flights arrive at Warsaw's Okęcie Airport (Port Lotniczy) just southwest of the city. Terminal 1 serves international flights from the West; Terminal 2 serves domestic and East European flights. For flight information, contact the airlines, or call the airport at tel. 022/46–96–70 or 022/46–11–43.

Between the Airport   LOT operates a regular bus service into Warsaw. Orbis cars
and Downtown   and minivans also transport visitors to their hotels. Warsaw city transport bus 175, which runs past almost all major downtown hotels, leaves Okęcie every 10 minutes during peak hours, and every 14 minutes at other times. The trip takes about 15 minutes and the fare is zł 4,000; after 11 PM, it is raised to zł 8,000.

By Train   Trains to and from Western Europe arrive at Dworzec Centralny on aleje Jerozolimskie in the center of town. For tickets and information, contact Orbis.

By Car   There are seven main access routes to Warsaw, all leading to the center of the city. Drivers heading to or from the West will use the E8 or E12 highways.

Getting Around

By Tram and Bus   These are often crowded, but they are the cheapest way of getting around. Trams and buses (including express buses) cost zł 4,000. The bus fare goes up to zł 8,000 between 11 PM and 5:30 AM. Tickets must be bought in advance from **Ruch** newsstands or street vendors. You must cancel your own ticket in a machine on the tram or bus when you get on; watch others do it.

By Taxi   Taxis are a relatively cheap ride—about zł 15,000 per mile (1.6 kilometers)—and you can either hail them or line up at a stand. Taxis are readily available at stands downtown; the Marriott and Victoria hotels have their own monogrammed fleets. There is an efficient radio taxi service, tel. 919.

By Buggy   Horse-drawn carriages can be rented at a negotiated price from the Old Town Market Square.

Important Addresses and Numbers

Tourist   The **Center for Tourist Information** is open 24 hours; it is located
Information   at plac Zamkowy 1, tel. 022/27–00–00. **Orbis** offices in Warsaw include: ulica Bracka 16, tel. 022/26–02–71; and ulica Marszałkowska 142, tel. 022/27–80–31 or 022/27–36–73.

Embassies   U.S. (al. Ujazdowskie 29–31, tel. 02/628–30–41). **Canadian** (ul. Matejki 1/5, tel. 022/29–80–51). **U.K.** (al. Róż 1, tel. 02/628–10–01). **U.K. Consulate** (ul. Wawelska 14, tel. 022/25–30–31).

Emergencies   **Police** (tel. 997). **Ambulance** (tel. 998). **Doctor** (tel. 998 or call your embassy).

Travel Agencies   **American Express** (ul. Bagińskiego 1, tel. 022/635–20–02). **Thomas Cook** (ul. Nowy Świat 64, tel. 022/26–47–29). **Travelines** (ul. Bracka 7, tel. 022/21–66–96). **Polish Motoring Association** (PZMot, al. Jerozolimskie 63, tel. 022/29–45–50).

Guided Tours

Bus tours of the city depart in the morning and afternoon from the major hotels. **Orbis** also has half-day excursions into the surrounding countryside. These usually include a meal and some form of traditional entertainment. Check for details with your hotel, the Orbis office, or tourist information office.

Exploring Warsaw

At the end of World War II, Warsaw lay in ruins, a victim of systematic Nazi destruction. Only one-third of its prewar population survived the horrors of German occupation. The experience has left its mark on the city and is visible everywhere in the memorial plaques describing mass executions of civilians and in the bullet holes on the facades of buildings. Against all the odds, Warsaw's survivors have rebuilt their historic city. The old districts have been painstakingly reconstructed according to old prints and paintings, including those of Belotto and Canaletto from the 18th century. The result, a city of warm pastel colors, is remarkable.

Surrounding the old districts, however, is the modern Warsaw, built since the war in utilitarian Socialist-Realist style. Whether you like it or not is your business, but it is worth noting as a testimony to one approach to urban life. The sights of Warsaw are all relatively close to each other, making most attractions accessible by foot.

Numbers in the margin correspond to points of interest on the Warsaw map.

The Old Town
❶ A walking tour of the old historic district takes about two hours. Begin in the heart of the city at **plac Zamkowy** (Castle Square), where you will see a slender column supporting the **statue of Zygmunt (Sigismund) III Wasa,** the king who made Warsaw his capital in the early 17th century. It is the city's oldest monument and, symbolically, the first to be rebuilt after
❷ the wartime devastation. Dominating the square is the **Zamek Królewski** (Royal Castle). Restoring the interior was a herculean task, requiring workers to relearn traditional skills, match ancient woods and fabrics, and even reopen abandoned quarries to find just the right kind of stone. *Plac Zamkowy 4, tel. 022/635-39-95. Admission: zł 30,000 adults, zł 15,000 children. Tours start hourly from the side entrance. Open Tues.-Sat. 10-2:30, Sun. 9-2:30.*

Enter the narrow streets of the **Stare Miasto** (Old Town), with its colorful medieval houses, cobblestone alleys, uneven roofs, and wrought-iron grillwork. On your right as you proceed
❸ along ulica Świętojańska is the **Bazylika świętego Jana** (Cathedral Church of St. John), the oldest church in Warsaw, dating back to the 14th century. Several Polish kings were crowned
❹ here. Soon you will reach the **Rynek Starego Miasta** (Old Market Square), the charming and intimate center of the old town. The old town hall, which once stood in the middle, was pulled down in the 19th century. It was not replaced, and today the square is full of open-air cafés, tubs of flowering plants, and the inevitable artists displaying their talents for the tourists. At night the brightly lighted Rynek (marketplace) is the place to go for good food and atmosphere.

⑤ Continue along ulica Nowomiejska until you get to the pinnacled red-brick **Barbakan,** a fine example of a 16th-century defensive fortification. From here you can see the partially restored town wall that was built to enclose the Old Town, and enjoy a splendid view of the Vistula River, with the district of Praga on its east bank.

Follow the street called ulica Freta to Warsaw's **Nowe Miasto** (New Town), which was founded at the turn of the 15th century. Rebuilt after the war in 18th-century style, this district has a more elegant and spacious feeling about it. Of interest here is
⑥ the **Muzeum Marii Skłodowskiej-Curie,** where the woman who discovered radium and polonium was born. *Ul. Freta 16, tel. 022/31–80–92. Admission: zł 4,000. Open Tues.–Sat. 10–4:30, Sun. 10–2:30.*

Time Out The **U Pana Michała** tearooms (ul. Freta 4–6) offer a variety of teas—as well as coffee—for nonsmokers.

The Royal Route All towns with kings had their Royal Routes; the one in Warsaw stretched south from Castle Square down Krakowskie Przedmieście, curving through Nowy Świat and on along aleje
⑦ Ujazdowskie to the **Pałac Belweder** (Belvedere Palace) and Łazienki Park. Some of Warsaw's finest churches and palaces are found along this route, as well as the names of famous Poles. A few blocks south of plac Zamkowy on Krakowskie
⑧ Przedmieście, you'll come to the **University of Warsaw** on your
⑨ left. Farther down, on your right, the **Kościoł świętego Krzyża** (Holy Cross Church) contains a pillar in which the heart of the great Polish composer Frédéric Chopin is entombed. As you pass the statue of Nicolaus Copernicus, Poland's most famous astronomer, you enter the busy Nowy Świat thoroughfare. Crossing aleje Jerozolimskie, on your left is the **former headquarters of the Polish Communist party,** a large solid gray building typical of the Socialist-Realist architectural style, which now houses banks and Poland's new stock exchange.

Aleje Ujazdowskie is considered by many locals to be Warsaw's finest street. It is lined with magnificent buildings and has something of a French flavor to it. Down at its southern end, before the name inexplicably changes to Belwederska, the French-style landscaped **Park Łazienkowski** (Łazienki Park), with pavilions and a royal palace, stands in refreshing contrast
⑩ to the bustling streets. The **Pałac Łazienkowski** (Łazienki Palace), a gem of Polish neoclassicism, was the private residence of Stanisław August Poniatowski, last king of Poland. It overlooks a lake stocked with huge carp. At the impressionistic Chopin monument nearby, you can stop for a well-deserved rest and, on summer Sundays, listen to an open-air concert. *Tel. 022/21–62–41. Admission: zł 14,000 adults, zł 8,000 children. Open Tues.–Sat. 9:30–3.*

The Royal Route extends along ulica Belwederska, ulica Jana
⑪ Sobieskiego, and aleja Wilanowska to **Wilanów,** 10 kilometers (6 miles) from the town center. This charming Baroque palace was the summer residence of King Jan III Sobieski, who, in 1683, stopped the Ottoman advance on Europe at the Battle of Vienna. The palace interior is open and houses antique furniture and a fine poster museum. *Ul. Wiertnicza l, tel. 022/42–07–95. Admission: zł 20,000 adults, zł 10,000 children. Open Wed.–Mon. 10–2:30.*

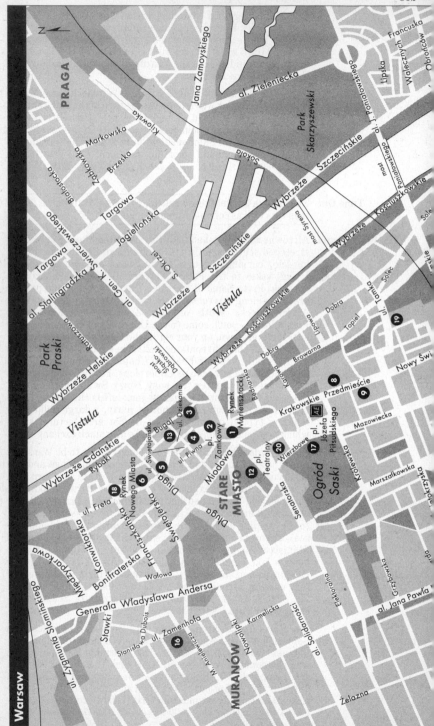

Warsaw

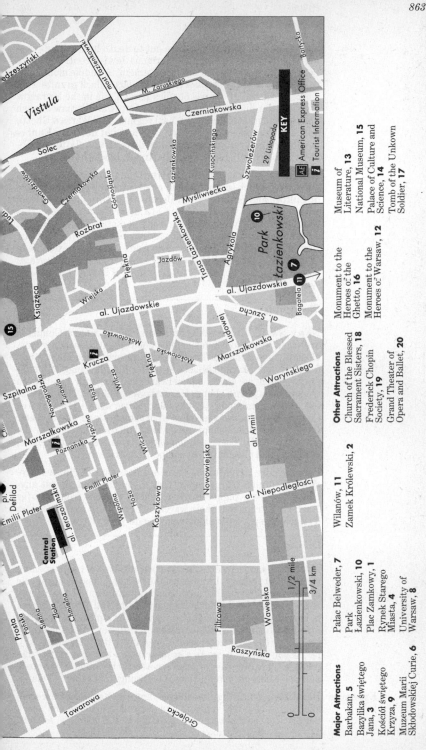

Major Attractions
Barbakan, **5**
Bazylika świętego Jana, **3**
Kościół świętego Krzyża, **9**
Muzeum Marii Skłodowskiej Curie, **6**

Pałac Belweder, **7**
Park Łazienkowski, **10**
Plac Zamkowy, **1**
Rynek Starego Miasta, **4**
University of Warsaw, **8**

Wilanów, **11**
Zamek Królewski, **2**

Other Attractions
Church of the Blessed Sacrament Sisters, **18**
Frederick Chopin Society, **19**
Grand Theater of Opera and Ballet, **20**

Monument to the Heroes of the Ghetto, **16**
Monument to the Heroes of Warsaw, **12**

Museum of Literature, **13**
National Museum, **15**
Palace of Culture and Science, **14**
Tomb of the Unkown Soldier, **17**

KEY
AE American Express Office
i Tourist Information

Off the Beaten Track

Some 3 million Polish Jews were put to death by the Nazis during World War II ending the enormous Jewish contribution to Polish culture, tradition, and achievement. A simple monument to the **Heroes of the Warsaw Ghetto,** a slab of dark granite with a bronze bas relief, stands on ulica Zamenhofa in the Muranów district, the historic heart of the old prewar Warsaw Jewish district and ghetto under the Nazi regime. The Warsaw Ghetto uprising that broke out in April 1943 was put down with unbelievable ferocity, and the Muranów district was flattened. Today there are only bleak gray apartment blocks here.

With ironic humor, Warsaw locals tell you that the best vantage point from which to admire their city is atop the 37-story **Palace of Culture and Science.** Why? Because it is the only point from which you can't see the Palace of Culture and Science. This wedding-cake-style skyscraper was a personal gift from Stalin. Although it is disliked by Poles as a symbol of Soviet domination, it does afford a panoramic view and is the best example in Warsaw of 1950s "Socialist Gothic" architecture. *Plac Defilad, tel. 022/20–02–11 ext. 2777. Admission: zł 20,000. Open daily 9–5.*

Shopping

Nowy Świat, Krakowskie Przedmieście, and ulica Chmielna are lined with boutiques selling good-quality leather goods, clothing, and trinkets. Try the **Cepelia** stores (plac Konstytucji 5 and Rynek Starego Miasta 8–10) for a wide range of handicrafts, such as glass, enamelware, amber, and handwoven woolen rugs. **Orno** shops (Marszałkowska 83 and Nowy Świat 52) offer handmade jewelry and silverware. **Desa** stores (Marszałkowska 34) specialize in ornaments and objets d'art. **Pewex** and **Baltona** shops can be found all over the city (try the Victoria hotel). These sell imported items, especially spirits, clothing, and chocolates, at competitive prices.

For the more adventurous there is a flea market, **Bazar Różyckiego,** on ulica Targowa 55, where you can find almost anything. An even bigger market, where visitors from all over Eastern Europe sell their wares, is open daily at the **Stadion Tysiąclecia** sports stadium, near Rondo Waszyngtona.

Dining

More and more interesting restaurants have been opening throughout the city, but some of the best and most atmospheric dining rooms are still to be found on and around the Rynek Starego Miasta (Old Market Square) in the Old Town. The area is brightly lighted at night and makes for a pleasant walk before or after dinner. Reservations for dinner can be made by telephone (by your hotel receptionist if you don't speak Polish), but if you decide to go to a restaurant on the spur of the moment, a table (for Westerners) can usually be found. For details and price-category definitions, *see* Dining in Staying in Poland.

Expensive   **Bazyliszek.** Dimly lighted and elegant, the Bazyliszek excels in such game as boar, venison, and duck. A good café and snack bar are located downstairs. *Rynek Starego Miasta 7/9, tel. 022/ 31–18–41. Reservations advised. AE, DC, MC, V.*

★ **Canaletto.** Located in the Victoria InterContinental hotel, this is probably the best restaurant in town; it serves Polish specialties with a good selection of European wines. The two paintings of old Warsaw on the walls are by Canaletto himself. *Plac Piłsudskiego, tel. 022/27-92-91. Reservations advised. AE, DC, MC, V.*

Forum. Another good hotel restaurant, the Forum's menu offers traditional Polish mixed with conventional Central European meat dishes. Like Canaletto, it is frequented by Western businesspeople and tourists. *Ul. Nowogrodzka 24, tel. 022/21-01-19. Reservations advised. AE, DC, MC, V.*

Moderate **Flik.** A new restaurant in Mokotów, Flik is light and spacious
★ and boasts a lantern-lit terrace overlooking the Morskie Oko park. The proprietors are interested in good food and tend toward nouvelle cuisine. Try the fresh salmon to start. *Ul. Puławska 43, tel. 022/49-43-34. Reservations advised. AE, DC, MC, V.*

Kamienne Schodki. This intimate, candlelit restaurant is located in one of the Market Square's medieval houses. Its main specialty is duck; also try the pastries. *Rynek Starego Miasta 26, tel. 022/31-08-22. Reservations advised. No credit cards.*

Pod Samsonem. This small restaurant, decorated in wood, has a smoke-filled Warsaw atmosphere and friendly waitresses. The fish and pierogi are good when available. *Ul. Freta 3/5, tel. 022/31-17-88. Reservations accepted. No credit cards.*

Lodging

Orbis hotels are recommended for convenience and high standards. The rooms are comfortable though standardized, with functional, nondescript carpeting and furniture. Some rooms are beginning to show signs of wear. Private accommodations are cheap and hospitable, and are available through Orbis or through the Center for Tourist Information. There is no off-season for tourism. For details and price-category definitions, *see* Lodging in Staying in Poland.

Very Expensive **Bristol.** Warsaw's most famous hotel was reopened in December 1992 after more than a decade of renovation and modernization. Once owned by Ignacy Paderewski, the concert pianist who served as Poland's prime minister in 1919–1920, the Bristol was always at the center of Warsaw's social life. Distinguished guests have included Charles de Gaulle and Marlene Dietrich. *Krakowskie Przedmieście 42-44, tel. 02/625-25-25, fax 02/625-25-77. 163 rooms with bath, 43 suites. Facilities: 2 restaurants, 2 bars, café, satellite TV in suites, sauna, solarium, pool. AE, DC, MC, V.*

Holiday Inn. This five-story hotel in the center of the city opened in 1989. All rooms are equipped with color TV offering four satellite programs. One floor is reserved for nonsmokers. *Ul. Złota 2, tel. 022/20-03-41, fax 022/30-05-69. 338 rooms with bath. Facilities: restaurants, bars, business center, health club, sauna. AE, DC, MC, V.*

★ **Marriott.** The Warsaw Marriott was completed in late 1989, and at 40 stories (20 make up the hotel; the rest are set aside for office and retail shopping space), it is also the city's tallest building. Luxuries include 11 restaurants, 24-hour room service, and color TV in every room. *Al. Jerozolimskie 65, tel. 022/30-63-06, fax 022/21-12-90. 525 rooms with bath. Facilities:*

restaurants and bars, casino, health club, swimming pool, sauna, shopping arcade. AE, DC, MC, V.

Expensive **Hotel Europejski.** This fine old Warsaw hotel is located in the
★ heart of the city. It was built in the 19th century in neo-Renaissance style, and its decor is elegant and refined. The rooms
are spacious and attractive; some have hosted kings, presi-
dents, and diplomats. The hotel takes pride in its restaurant.
*Krakowskie Przedmieście 13, tel. 022/26–50–51, fax 022/26–
11–11. 279 rooms, most with bath or shower. Facilities: restaurant. AE, DC, MC, V.*

Hotel Forum. The Swedes built this InterContinental chain hotel in the '70s. Frequented by businesspeople and the Arab
community, it has a good restaurant. A room higher up will
give you a view of the city. *Ul. Nowogrodzka 24, tel. 022/21–02–
71, fax 022/25–81–57. 750 rooms, some with bath or shower. Facilities: restaurant, nightclub, hairdresser. AE, DC, MC, V.*

Victoria InterContinental. Frequented by Western businesspeople, this is a large 1970s hotel in an ideal location in the center of town. It has a variety of facilities, including a fine
restaurant and nightclub. Try to get a room facing Victory
Square. *Ul. Królewska 11, tel. 022/27–92–71, fax 022/27–98–
56. 370 rooms, most with bath or shower. Facilities: restaurant,
nightclub, casino, sauna, indoor pool. AE, DC, MC, V.*

Moderate **Hotel Solec.** This comfortable, modest, '70s hotel is down by the
river in a residential area of the central town. Food and service
are good, but the hotel tends to be inundated with tour groups.
*Ul. Zagórna 1, tel. 022/25–92–41, fax 022/21–64–42. 150 rooms
with bath. AE, DC, MC, V.*

Novotel. This small member of the French Novotel chain is ideal
for visitors with a car and is well situated near Warsaw's airport (fortunately, *not* under any flight paths). *Ul. 1 Sierpnia 1,
tel. 022/46–40–51, fax 022/46–36–86. 150 rooms with bath. Facilities: restaurant, café, outdoor pool. AE, DC, MC, V.*

Orbis Grand. Conveniently located in the center of the city, this
large hotel was built in the 1950s and is a prime example of the
Socialist-Realist architecture of the period. It has a rooftop
restaurant-café and offers live jazz, dancing, or cabaret in the
evening. *Ul. Krucza 28, tel. 022/29–40–51, fax 022/21–97–24.
415 rooms, some with shower. Facilities: restaurant, nightclub, indoor pool, hairdresser, Pewex shop. AE, DC, MC, V.*

★ **Zajazd Napoleoński.** This small, privately owned inn has an excellent restaurant and deluxe facilities. Napoleon reputedly
stayed here when his Grand Army passed through Warsaw on
its way to Russia. It is situated about 12.8 kilometers (8 miles)
outside of town. Book well in advance. *Ul. Płowiecka 83, tel.
022/15–30–68. 22 rooms with bath, 3 suites. Facilities: restaurant. AE, DC, MC, V.*

The Arts

For information, buy the newspaper *Życie Warszawy* or *Gazeta
Wyborcza* at Ruch newsstands. Tickets can be ordered by your
Orbis hotel receptionist, through the tourist information center (pl. Zamkowy 1, tel. 022/27–00–00), or at the ticket office on
ulica Marszałkowska 104.

Theaters There are 17 theaters in Warsaw, attesting to the popularity of
this art form, but none offers English performances. **Teatr
Narodowy,** opened in 1764 and the oldest in Poland, is on plac

Teatralny; at press time it was closed for repairs after a major fire, but it may be reopened during 1994. **Teatr Polski Kameralny** (Foksal 16) has a small stage. **Współczesny** (Mokotowska 13) shows contemporary works.

Concerts **The National Philharmonic** puts on the best concerts. The hall is on ulica Sienkiewicza 12. An excellent new concert hall, opened in 1992, is the **Studio Concertowe Polskiego Radia** (Woronicza 17). In the summer, free Chopin concerts take place both at the Chopin monument in **Łazienki Park** and each Sunday at **Żelazowa Wola,** the composer's birthplace, 58 kilometers (36 miles) outside Warsaw.

Opera **Teatr Wielki** (plac Teatralny) hosts the Grand Theater of Opera and Ballet. It has a superb operatic stage—one of the largest in Europe.

Nightlife

Cabaret The Victoria, Forum, Grand, Europejski, and Marriott hotels all have nightclubs that are popular with Westerners. The acts vary, so check listings in the press. These clubs also present striptease and jazz.

Bars **Gwiazdeczka** (Piwna 42) is a noisy, hip, upscale joint, popular with chic young Warsovians. **The Irish Pub** (Koszykowa 1) is a fashionable recent addition to Warsaw's night spots. **Harenda** (Krakowskie Przedmieście 4–6), with an outdoor terrace in summer, is open all night.

Jazz Clubs **Akwarium** (Emilii Platter) and **Wanda Warska's Modern Music Club** (Stare Miasto) are popular jazz clubs. A new jazz club that is winning a major following is **Jazz Club 77** (Marszałkowska 77–79).

Discos Apart from the hotels, the most popular discos are **Hybrydy** (Złota 7) and **Stodoła** (Batorego 10).

Cafés Warsaw is filled with cafés *(kawiarnie)*, which move outdoors in the summer. They are popular meeting places and usually serve delicious coffee and pastries in the best Central European style.

Ambassador is an elegant and brightly lit café with a tree-lined terrace for summer visitors. *Ul. Matejki 4.*
Bonbonierka was recently reopened as a vegetarian café-cum-restaurant, with cane furniture and a resident harpist. *Rynek Nowego Miasta 13–15.*
Le Petit Trianon is a tiny, intimate 18th-century French-style restaurant and café. It is difficult to find a seat, but worth it once you do. *Ul. Piwna 40.*
Telimena is a small corner café with an art gallery on the ground floor. *Krakowskie Przedmieście 27.*
Wilanowska has definitely seen better days, but its crumbling elegance has a certain appeal. *Plac Trzech Krzyży 3.*

Kraków and Environs

Kraków (Cracow), seat of Poland's oldest university and once the capital of the country (before losing the honor to Warsaw in 1611), is one of the few Polish cities that escaped devastation during World War II. Today Kraków's fine ramparts, towers, facades, and churches, illustrating seven centuries of Polish architecture, make it a major attraction for visitors. Its location—about 270 kilometers (160 miles) south of Warsaw—also makes it a good base for hiking and skiing trips in the mountains of southern Poland.

Also within exploring range from Kraków are the famous Polish shrine to the Virgin Mary at Częstochowa, and, at Auschwitz (Oświęcim), the grim reminder of man's capacity for inhumanity.

Getting Around

Kraków is reached by major highways—E7 direct from Warsaw and E82 from Częstochowa. Trains link Kraków with most major destinations in Poland; the station is in the city center near the Old Town, on ulica Pawia. The bus station is nearby.

Guided Tours

Bus or walking tours of Kraków and its environs are provided by **Orbis**. Horse-drawn carriages can be rented at the main market square for a negotiated price.

Tourist Information

Częstochowa (al. najświętszej Marii Panny 37/39, tel. 833/467–55).
Kraków (ul. Pawia 8, tel. 012/22–95–10).

Exploring Kraków

Numbers in the margin correspond to points of interest on the Kraków map.

Kraków's old city is ringed by a park called the **Planty**. The park replaced the old walls of the town, which were torn down in the mid-19th century. Begin your tour at **Brama Floriańska** (St. Florian's Gate), which leads to the old town. The gate is guarded by an imposing 15th-century fortress called the **Barbakan**. Enter the city, passing along ulica Floriańska, the beginning of the Royal Route through the town.

Time Out Don't pass up the chance to stop for refreshments at Kraków's most famous café, **Jama Michalikowa** (ul. Floriańska 45), which now has a nonsmoking area. It serves good coffee and excellent ice cream.

Ulica Floriańska leads to the **Rynek Główny** (main market), one of the largest and finest Renaissance squares in Europe. The calm of this spacious square, with its pigeons and flower stalls, is interrupted every hour by four short bugle calls drifting down from the spire of the Church of the Virgin Mary. The plaintive notes recall a centuries-old tradition in memory of a trumpeter whose throat was pierced by a well-aimed enemy arrow as he was warning his fellow citizens of an impending Tartar attack. The square Gothic **Kościół Mariacki** (Church of the Virgin Mary) contains a 15th-century wooden altarpiece—the largest in the world—carved by Wit Stwosz. The faces of the saints are reputedly those of Cracovian burghers. In the center of the square stands a covered market called **Sukiennice** (Cloth Hall), built in the 14th century but remodeled during the Ren-

Kraków

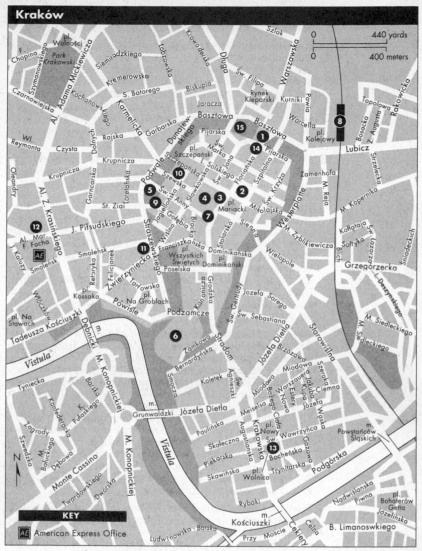

KEY

AE American Express Office

Major Attractions

Brama Floriańska, **1**

Jagiellonian
University, **5**

Kosciół Mariacki, **3**

Rynek Główny, **2**

Sukiennice, **4**

Wawel Castle and
Cathedral, **6**

Other Attractions

Barbakan, **14**

Central Station, **8**

Czartoryski
Museum, **15**

Ethnographic
Museum, **13**

Helena Modrzejewska
Stary Theater, **10**

Jagiellonian
University Museum, **9**

K. Szymanowski State
Philharmonic Hall, **11**

National Museum, **12**

St. Adalbert
Romanesque
Church, **7**

aissance. The ground floor is still in business, selling trinkets and folk art souvenirs. *Open Mon.–Sat. 10–6, Sun. 10–5.*

From the Main Market, turn down ulica świętej Anny to No. 8, ⑤ the **Collegium Maius**, the oldest building of the famous **Jagiellonian University** (founded 1364). Its pride is the Italian-style arcaded courtyard. Inside is a museum where you can see the Copernicus globe, the first on which the American continents were shown, as well as astronomy instruments belonging to Kraków's most famous graduate. *Admission free. Courtyard open Mon.–Sat. 8–6. Museum shown by appointment only, 10–noon.*

⑥ Backtracking on ulica Grodzka will lead you to the **Wawel Castle and Cathedral.** This impressive complex of Gothic and Renaissance buildings stands on fortifications dating as far back as the 8th century. Inside the castle is a museum with an exotic collection of Oriental tents that were captured from the Turks at the battle of Vienna in 1683 and rare 16th-century Flemish tapestries. Wawel Cathedral is where, until the 18th century, Polish kings were crowned and buried. Until 1978, the cathedral was the principal church of the see of Archbishop Karol Wojtyła, now known as Pope John Paul II. *Ul. Grodzka, tel. 012/22–51–55. Castle. Admission: zł 30,000 adults, zł 15,000 children. Open Tues., Thurs., Sat., Sun. 10–3, Wed. and Fri. noon–6. Cathedral Museum. Admission: zł 10,000. Open Tues.–Sun. 10–3.*

About 50 kilometers (30 miles) west of Kraków is Oświęcim, better known by its German name, **Auschwitz.** Here 4 million victims, mostly Jews, were executed by the Nazis in the Auschwitz and Birkenau concentration camps. Auschwitz is now a museum, with restored crematoria and barracks housing dramatic displays of Nazi atrocities. The buildings at Birkenau, a 15-minute walk away, have been left just as they were found in 1945 by the Soviet Army. Oświęcim itself is an industrial town with good connections from Kraków; buses and trains leave Kraków approximately every hour, and signs in Oświęcim direct visitors to the camp. *Auschwitz: admission free. Open Mar. and Nov., Tues.–Sun. 8–4; Apr. and Oct., Tues.–Sun. 8–5; May and Sept., daily 8–6; June–Aug., daily 8–7; Dec.–Feb., Tues.–Sun. 8–3. Birkenau: open all times.*

Wieliczka, about 8 kilometers (5 miles) southeast of Kraków, is the oldest salt mine in Europe, in operation since the end of the 13th century. It is famous for its magnificent underground chapel hewn in crystal rock, the **Chapel of the Blessed Kinga.** The mines are likely to be closed to visitors throughout 1994.

Częstochowa, 120 kilometers (70 miles) from Kraków and reached by regular trains and buses, is the home of the holiest shrine in a country that is more than 90% Catholic. Inside the 14th-century **Pauline monastery** on Jasna Góra (Light Hill) is the famous *Black Madonna*, a painting of Our Lady of Częstochowa attributed by legend to St. Luke. It was here that an invading Swedish army was halted in 1655 and finally driven out of the country. About 25 miles southwest of Kraków is the little town of **Wadowice,** birthplace of Pope John Paul II. *Wadowice Museum. Admission: zł 20,000 adults, zł 10,000 children. Open Tues.–Sat. 10–3, Sun. 10–5.*

Dining and Lodging

For details and price-category definitions, *see* Dining and Lodging in Staying in Poland.

Częstochowa
Lodging

Polonia. The Polonia makes a good base for exploring the Pauline monastery, and since most of the other guests are pilgrims, the atmosphere is an interesting mixture of piety and good fun. *Ul. Piłsudskiego 9, tel. 833/440–67, fax 833/65–11–05. 62 rooms, most with bath or shower. No credit cards. Inexpensive.*

Kraków
Dining

Staropolska. Traditional Polish cuisine is served in a medieval setting. Try the pork, duck, or veal. *Ul. Sienna 4, tel. 012/22–58–21. Reservations advised. Expensive.*

★ **Wierzynek.** One of the best restaurants in the country, Wierzynek serves traditional Polish specialties and excels in soups and game. It was here, after a historic meeting in 1364, that the king of Poland wined and dined the Holy Roman Emperor Charles IV, five kings, and a score of princes. *Rynek Główny 15, tel. 012/22–14–04. Reservations advised. AE, DC, MC, V. Expensive.*

Dining and Lodging

Francuski. This small hotel is just inside the old town's walls, within walking distance of all the main sites. Built at the turn of the century, it offers an intimate atmosphere and friendly service. The rooms are elegant in a homey, East European way. The excellent restaurant is tranquil and plush and has a café with dancing. The hotel reopened in late 1991 after extensive renovations. *Ul. Pijarska 13, tel. 012/22–51–22, fax 012/22–52–70. 42 rooms, most with bath or shower. Facilities: restaurant, café. AE, DC, MC, V. Expensive.*

★ **Cracovia.** This large, Orbis-run, five-story hotel boasts one of the best restaurants in town. There is also a lively nightclub where Western tourists like to meet. *Al. marszałka F. Focha 1, tel. 012/22–86–66, fax 012/21–95–86. 427 rooms with bath. Facilities: restaurant, nightclub. AE, DC, MC, V. Moderate.*

Holiday Inn. This was the first Holiday Inn in Eastern Europe. Rather bland but comfortable with a fine restaurant, this highrise establishment is pleasantly located near Cracow's Green Meadows. *Ul. Koniewa 7, tel. 012/37–50–44, fax 012/37–59–38. 310 rooms with bath. Facilities: restaurant, solarium, sauna, indoor pool. AE, DC, MC, V. Moderate.*

Lodging

Forum. Opened in 1988, this Orbis hotel stands on the south bank of the Vistula, commanding a fine view of the Wawel castle. *Ul. Marii Konopnickiej 28, tel. 012/66–95–00, fax 012/66–58–27. 280 rooms with bath. Facilities: restaurant, sauna, indoor pool, tennis courts, beauty salon. AE, DC, MC, V. Expensive.*

★ **Grand.** Reopened in 1990 after a 12-year renovation, this late-19th-century hotel in the heart of the Old Town is elegant and comfortable. It has reproduction period furniture but modern bathrooms and facilities. *Ul. Sławkowska 5–7, tel. 012/21–72–55, fax 012/21–83–60. 50 rooms with bath. Facilities: restaurant, café, exercise room. AE, DC, MC, V. Expensive.*

Europejski. This small, older hotel overlooking the Planty park has now been renovated, and most of the rooms have shower or bath. *Ul. Lubicz 5, tel. 012/22–09–11, fax 012/22–89–25. 55 rooms, some with bath. No credit cards. Inexpensive.*

Gdańsk and the North

In contrast to Kraków and the south, Poland north of Warsaw is the land of medieval castles and châteaus, dense forests and lakes, and fishing villages and beaches. If you don't have a car, consider going straight to Gdańsk and making excursions from there.

Getting Around

Gdańsk is a major transportation hub, with an airport just outside town (and good bus connections to downtown) and major road and rail connections with the rest of the country.

Guided Tours

Orbis arranges an eight-day tour of Warsaw, Toruń, Gdańsk, and Poznań. It also handles group and individual tours of Toruń, Gdańsk, and the surrounding areas.

Tourist Information

Elbląg (ul. 3 Maja 1, tel. 850/247–76; Orbis, ul. Hetmańska 23, tel. 850/223–64).
Gdańsk (ul. Heweliusza 8, tel. 058/31–03–38; Orbis, pl. Górskiego 1, tel. 058/31–49–44).
Ostróda (Orbis, ul. Czarnieckiego 10, tel. 889–82/35–57).
Płock (ul. Tuńska 4, tel. 824/226–00; Orbis, al. Jachowa 47, tel. 824/229–89).
Toruń (ul. Kopernika 27, tel. 856/272–99; Orbis, ul. Żeglarska 31, tel. 856/261–30).

Exploring Gdańsk and the North

From Warsaw, follow routes E81 and 107 through **Płock**. Once you get through Płock's industrial area, you'll find a lovely medieval city that was, for a short time, capital of Poland. Worth seeing are the 12th-century cathedral, where two Polish kings are buried, and the dramatic 14th-century Teutonic castle. Continue through Włocławek to Toruń, where an overnight stay is recommended.

Toruń, birthplace of Nicolaus Copernicus, is an interesting medieval city that grew wealthy due to its location on the north-south trading route along the Vistula. Its old town district is a remarkably successful blend of Gothic buildings—churches, town hall, and burghers' homes—with Renaissance and Baroque patricians' houses. The Town Hall's Tower (1274) is the oldest town hall building in Poland. Don't leave without trying some of Toruń's famous gingerbread and honey cakes.

The route leading north from Toruń to Gdańsk passes through some of the oldest towns in Poland. Along the way are many medieval castles, châteaus, and churches that testify to the wealth and strategic importance of the area. Two short detours are a must: one is to **Kwidzyń** to see the original 14th-century castle and cathedral complex, which is free and open to the public. The other is to **Malbork**. This huge castle, 58 kilometers (36 miles) from Gdańsk, was one of the most powerful strongholds in medieval Europe. From 1308 to 1457, it was the residence of

Gdańsk and the North

the Grand Masters of the Teutonic Order. The Teutonic Knights were a thorn in Poland's side until their defeat at the battle of Grunwald in 1410. Inside Malbork castle is a museum with beautiful examples of amber—including lumps as large as melons and pieces containing perfect specimens of prehistoric insects. *tel. 850/06–33–64. Open Tues.–Sat. 10–3, Sun. 10–5. Admission: zł 20,000 adults, zł 10,000 children.*

Gdańsk, once the free city of Danzig, is another of Poland's beautifully restored towns, displaying a rich heritage of Gothic, Renaissance, and Mannerist architecture. This is where the first shots of World War II were fired and where the free trade union Solidarity was born after strikes in 1980. The city's old town has a wonderful collection of historic town houses and narrow streets. The splendid Długa and Długi Targ streets (best for shopping) form the axis of the city and are good starting points for walks into other districts. The evocative **Solidarity Monument** stands outside the Lenin shipyards—erected in honor of workers killed by the regime during strikes in 1970. The nearby town of **Sopot** is Poland's most popular seaside resort.

For a different route back to Warsaw, follow highway E81 southeast through Poland's scenic forest and lake district. The area is rich in nature and wildlife attractions, as well as places of historical interest. Recommended is a diversion (or night stop) 42 kilometers (26 miles) east of Ostróda to the medieval town of **Olsztyn.** The old town was once administered and fortified by Copernicus.

About 30 kilometers (19 miles) farther south on E81 is **Olsztynek,** where the **Museum of Folk Buildings** has a collection of timber buildings from different parts of the country. They include a small Mazurian thatch-roofed church, an inn, a mill, a forge, old windmills, and thatched cottages, some of which have been furnished period-style. *Tel. 889/19–24–64. Admission: zł 25,000 adults, zł 10,000 children. Open May–Sept., Tues.–Sun. 9–4; closed Mon.*

Time Out Located on E81, 5 kilometers (3 miles) north of Olsztynek, the **Mazurski** is a good place to stop for a meal. The food varies, but is generally tasty. *Moderate.*

Another diversion, 17 kilometers (10½ miles) west of Olsztynek, is the **site of the battle of Grunwald,** possibly the greatest battle of the Middle Ages. Here on July 15, 1410, Władysław Jagiełło and his Polish Lithuanian army annihilated the Grand Master of the Teutonic Order, Ulrich von Jungingen, and thousands of his knights. A small museum on the site (open summer only, 10–10) graphically explains the course of the battle.

Dining and Lodging

For details and price-category definitions, *see* Dining and Lodging in Staying in Poland.

Elbląg **Karczma Słupska.** This is the best restaurant in town. It's usu-
Dining ally crowded and specializes in fresh fish. *Ul. Krótka 1. No reservations. No credit cards. Moderate.*

Gdańsk **Pod Łososiem.** The name of this restaurant refers to salmon,
Dining which, if available on the day you visit, is highly recommended. *Ul. Szeroka 51, tel. 058/31–76–52. Reservations advised. AE, DC, MC, V. Expensive.*
Pod Wieżą. This restaurant has a reputation for good meat dishes and generous portions. If they're on the menu when you visit, try the *zupa rybna* (fish soup), veal steak with mushroom sauce, or roast duck with apples and brown rice. *Piwna 51, tel. 058/31–39–24. Reservations advised. AE, DC, MC, V. Expensive.*
★ **Kaszubska.** The specialties here come from Kashubia. Smoked fish dishes are highly recommended. *Ul. Kartuska 76, tel. 058/32–06–02. Reservations advised. AE, DC, MC, V. Moderate.*

Lodging **Tawerna.** This well-established restaurant overlooking the riv-
★ er serves traditional Polish and Germanic dishes such as pork cutlets and seafood. Yes, it's touristy, but the food is delicious. *Ul. Powroźnicza 19–20, off Długi Targ, tel. 58/31–92–48. Reservations advised. Dress: casual. No credit cards. Moderate.*
Hewelius. This large, modern, high-rise hotel is within walking distance of the old town. The rooms are spacious, and blandly furnished, with all the modern conveniences. *Ul. Heweliusza 22, tel. 058/31–56–31, fax 31 058/31–19–22. 250 rooms, most with bath. Facilities: restaurant, nightclub. AE, DC, MC, V. Moderate.*
★ **Marina.** Built in 1982, this large high rise, popular with Western businesspeople, is one of the newer hotels in Poland and probably the best in town. Upper floors have splendid views. *Ul. Jelitkowska 20, tel. 058/53–20–79, fax 058/53–04–60. 193 rooms with bath or shower. Facilities: restaurant, nightclub,*

indoor pool, tennis courts, bowling alley. AE, DC, MC, V. Moderate.

Olsztyn
Lodging

Orbis Novotel. This standard 1970s hotel is typical of the kind found in Poland. It is, however, the most comfortable lodging in the area and is located in beautiful surroundings on the shores of lake Ukiel. *Ul. Sielska 4A, tel. 889/27–40–81, fax 889/27–54–03. 98 rooms with bath. Facilities: restaurant, pool. Moderate.*

Ostróda
Lodging

This town is not visited by many foreign tourists and is lacking in good-quality facilities. The undistinguished **Panorama Hotel** is the best, unless Orbis can locate private lodging for you. *Ul. Krasickiego 23, tel. 889/82–22–27. Inexpensive.*

Toruń
Dining
★

Pod Kurantem. Regional cuisine is featured in this attractive old wine cellar. Slow service is the penalty for popularity. *Rynek Staromiejski 28. No telephone. No reservations. No credit cards. Expensive.*

Zajazd Staropolski. This restaurant features excellent meat dishes and soups in a restored 17th-century interior. *Ul. Żeglarska 10/14, tel. 856/260–60. Reservations advised. Moderate.*

Wodnik. This large café along the banks of the Vistula is very popular with locals. *Blwd. Filadelfijski, tel. 856/287–55. No credit cards. Inexpensive.*

Lodging

Helios. This friendly, medium-size hotel is situated in the city center and offers a good restaurant (albeit with slow service). *Ul. Kraszewskiego 1, tel. 856/250–33, fax 856/235–65. 140 rooms, most with bath or shower. Facilities: restaurant, sauna, nightclub, beauty parlor. AE, DC, MC, V. Moderate.*

Kosmos. A functional 1960s hotel, Kosmos is beginning to show signs of wear and tear. It is situated near the river, in the city center. *Ul. Portowa 2, tel. 856/270–85. 180 rooms, most with bath or shower. AE, DC, MC, V. Inexpensive.*

23 Portugal

Given its long Atlantic coastline, it isn't surprising that Portugal has been a maritime nation for most of its history. The valor of its seamen is well known; from the charting of the Azores archipelago in 1427 to the discovery of Japan in 1542, Portuguese explorers unlocked the major sea routes to southern Africa, India, the Far East, and the Americas. To commemorate this great era of exploration, a period that reached its height in the 15th century under the influence of Prince Henry the Navigator, the years 1988 to 2000 have been set aside for various celebrations throughout the country.

Despite its sailors' worldly adventures, Portugal itself has remained relatively undiscovered. Although it shares the Iberian Peninsula with Spain, it attracts far fewer visitors—a strange fact, because Portugal has much to recommend it to tourists: fine beaches, beautiful castles, charming fishing villages, well-maintained hotels and *pousadas* (government-owned inns), excellent restaurants, and colorful folk traditions.

About the size of Indiana, Portugal is so small that its main attractions can be seen during a short visit; at the country's widest point the distance between the Atlantic and Spain is a mere 240 kilometers (150 miles). Short distances don't mean monotony, however, for this narrow coastal strip of land has more geographic and climatic variations than virtually any other nation in Western Europe.

Although Portugal has seen numerous divisions in modern times, the country has traditionally been divided into six historic provinces. Most visitors head for the low-lying plains of the southern Algarve or the region around the Lisbon/Estoril coast, but as traditional tourist destinations become more crowded, adventurous travelers are venturing in other directions. The northern and central provinces—Minho, Beiras, and Trás-os-Montes—are largely unspoiled, full of tiny villages and splendid scenery. The major drawbacks here are the lack of first-class accommodations and poor secondary roads. With the recent infusion of substantial EC funds, however, this condition has been improving rapidly. The main highways from Lisbon to the North and the frontier are now in good shape. In the south the once fearsome EN125, which spans the Algarve from east to west, has been widened and largely tamed, and a high-speed trans-Algarve expressway is under construction. Defensive driving is the name of the game: The Portuguese are ranked among the world's most reckless drivers.

Observant visitors are likely to notice differences between Portugal's northern and southern regions and people. The northern character is decidedly more Celtic, while in the south, Moorish ancestry is apparent. But throughout the country, the Portuguese people are welcoming wherever you meet them.

We have concentrated our Exploring sections on the southern part of the country—the section most frequented by foreign visitors—including Lisbon—Portugal's sophisticated capital—and the Algarve.

Essential Information

Before You Go

When to Go The tourist season runs from spring through autumn, but some parts of the country—especially the Algarve, which boasts 3,000 hours of sunshine annually—are balmy even in winter. Hotel prices are greatly reduced between November and February, except in Lisbon where business visitors keep prices uniformly high throughout the year.

Climate Since Portugal's entire coast is on the Atlantic Ocean, the country's climate is temperate year-round. Portugal rarely suffers the extremes of heat that Mediterranean countries do. Even in August, the hottest month, the Algarve and the Alentejo are the only regions where the midday heat may be uncomfortable, but most travelers go to the beaches there to swim and soak up the sun. What rain there is falls from November to March; December and January can be chilly outside the Algarve, and very wet to the north, but there is no snow except in the mountains of the Serra da Estrela in the northeast. The almond blossoms and vivid wildflowers that cover the countryside start to bloom early in February. The dry months, June–September, can turn much of the landscape the tawny color of a lion's hide, but there is always a breeze in the evening in Lisbon, as well as along the Estoril coast west of the capital.

The following are the average daily maximum and minimum temperatures for Lisbon.

Jan.	57F	14C	May	71F	21C	Sept.	79F	26C
	46	8		55	13		62	17
Feb.	59F	15C	June	77F	25C	Oct.	72F	22C
	47	8		60	15		58	14
Mar.	63F	17C	July	81F	27C	Nov.	63F	17C
	50	10		63	17		52	11
Apr.	67F	20C	Aug.	82F	28C	Dec.	58F	15C
	53	12		63	17		47	9

Currency The unit of currency in Portugal is the *escudo*, which can be divided into 100 centavos. Escudos come in bills of 500$00, 1,000$00, 2,000$00, 5,000$00, and 10,000$00. (In Portugal the dollar sign stands between the escudo and the centavo.) Coins come in 1$00, 2$50, 5$00, 10$00, 20$00, 50$00, 100$00, and 200$00. Newly minted 1$00, 5$00, and 10$00 yellow-colored coins can be confused for older coins still in circulation, so make sure you know exactly what you're spending.

At press time (spring 1993), the exchange rate was 154$00 to the U.S. dollar and 234$00 to the pound sterling. Owing to the complications of dealing in millions of escudos, 1,000$00 is always called a *conto*, so 10,000$00 is referred to as 10 contos. Credit cards are accepted in all the larger shops and restaurants, as well as in hotels; however, better exchange rates are obtained in banks and *cambios* (exchange offices). Short-changing is rare, but, as in every country, restaurant bills should be checked. Change in post offices and railway booking offices should also be counted. Shopkeepers are usually honest.

What It Will Cost While the cost of hotels and restaurants in Portugal is still reasonable, inflation is pushing prices up to levels approaching those found in the more affluent countries in northern Europe. Some of Portugal's best food bargains are to be enjoyed in its many simple seaside restaurants. The most expensive areas are Lisbon, the Algarve, and the tourist resort areas along the Tagus estuary. The least expensive areas are country towns, which all have reasonably priced hotels and *pensões*, or pensions, as well as numerous café-type restaurants. A sales, or value-added, tax (called IVA) of 16% is imposed on hotel and restaurant bills and on car rentals and such services as car repairs.

Sample Prices Cup of coffee, 100$00; bottle of beer, 125$00; soft drink, 175$00; bottle of house wine, 750$00; ham sandwich, 225$00; 1-mile taxi ride, 400$00; city bus ride, 135$00; museum entrance, 250$00.

Customs on Arrival Non–European-Community (EC) visitors over age 17 are allowed to bring the following items into Portugal duty-free: 200 cigarettes or 250 grams of tobacco, 1 liter of liquor (over 22% volume) or 2 liters (under 22% volume), 2 liters of wine, 100 ml of perfume, and a reasonable amount of personal effects (camera, binoculars, etc). There is no limit on money brought into the country. However, no more than 100,000$00 in Portuguese currency or the equivalent of 500,000$00 in foreign currency may be taken out without proof that an equal amount or more was brought into Portugal. Computerized customs services make random and often thorough checks on arrival.

Language Portuguese is easy to read by anyone with even slight knowledge of a Latin language, but it is difficult to pronounce and understand (most people speak quickly and elliptically). However, you will find that in the larger cities and major resorts many people, especially the young, speak English and, occasionally, French.

Getting Around

By Car The few turnpikes (moderate tolls) and the major highways be-
Road Conditions tween Lisbon and the Algarve, Oporto, and Guincho beyond Cascais alongside the river Tagus are in good shape. For the most part, road conditions in Portugal have greatly improved, but minor roads are often poor and winding with unpredictable surfaces.

Thanks to a series of newly constructed highways that bypass towns and villages, the once grueling drive between the Algarve and Lisbon is now a pleasure. EN 125, the principal east-west Algarve highway, has been widened and resurfaced. New bridges have eliminated the formerly horrendous bottlenecks at Portimão and replaced the ferry across the Guadiana River from Vila Real de Santo António to Spain.

There are no superhighways from Lisbon direct to the nearest frontier post with Spain at Caia, outside Elvas, but the route over the Tagus bridge through Setúbal (turnpike from Lisbon), to Montemoro-Novo, Arraiolos, and Estremoz, is good and fast.

Rules of the Road Driving is on the right. At the junction of two roads of equal size, traffic coming from the right has priority. Vehicles already in a traffic circle have priority over those entering it from any point. Traffic in the country is light, but local people are apt to walk in the road and occasional horse- or donkey-drawn carts may hold things up. After dark watch out for motorbikes and donkey carts without lights. Seat belts are obligatory. Horns should not be used in built-up areas, and a reflective red warning triangle, for use in a breakdown, must be carried. The speed limit on turnpikes is 120 kph (72 mph); on other roads it is 90 kph (54 mph), and in built-up areas, 50–60 kph (30–36 mph).

Parking   Lisbon and Oporto are experimenting with parking meters, although these are still rare. Parking lots and underground garages abound in major cities, but those in Lisbon and Oporto are no longer cheap. Parking on side streets is usually chaotic, and in Lisbon and Oporto it's often very difficult to find a parking space near city-center hotels.

Gasoline   Gas prices are among the highest in Europe: 146$00 per liter for super and 136$00 for regular. Unleaded gas is now available for 130$00. Many gas stations around the country are self-service. Credit cards are widely accepted.

Breakdowns   All large garages in and around towns have breakdown services. Special orange emergency (SOS) telephones are located at intervals on turnpikes and highways. Motorists in Portugal are very helpful; if your car breaks down, aid from a passing driver is usually forthcoming within a short time. The national automobile organization, **Automóvel Clube de Portugal** (Rua Rosa Araújo 24/26, 1200 Lisbon, tel. 01/356–3931) provides reciprocal membership with other European automobile associations, provided the membership is up-to-date.

By Train   The Portuguese railway system is surprisingly extensive for such a small country. Trains are clean and leave on time, but there are few express runs except between Lisbon and Oporto. These take just over three hours for the 210-mile journey. Several of the Oporto–Lisbon trains take cars, as does one train a day between Lisbon, Castelo Branco, and Guarda and some Lisbon–Algarve trains. Cars must be at the station an hour before departure; prices are reasonable, and tickets can be bought then or in advance. Most trains have first- and second-class compartments; suburban lines around Lisbon have a single class. Tickets should be bought, and seats reserved if desired, at the stations or through travel agents, two or three days in advance. Advance reservations are essential on Lisbon–Oporto express trains. Timetables are mostly the same on Saturday and Sunday as on weekdays, except on suburban lines. **Wasteels–Expresso** (Ave. António Augusto Aguiar 88, 1000 Lisbon, tel. 01/57965) is reliable for all local and international train tickets and reservations.

Special **tourist passes** can be obtained through travel agents or at main train stations. These are valid for periods of 7, 14, or 21 days for first- and second-class travel on any domestic train service; mileage is unlimited. At press time (spring 1992), the cost was 15,200$00 for 7 days; 24,200$00 for 14 days; and 34,600$00 for 21 days. Child passes cost exactly half those amounts.

International trains to Madrid, Paris, and other parts of Europe depart from the Santa Apolonia Station in Lisbon and Campanhã in Oporto.

By Plane   The internal air services of **TAP Air Portugal** are good. Lisbon is linked at least four times daily with Oporto and Faro; daily with Funchal (Madeira), more at peak periods; weekly with Porto Santo, an island some way off Madeira; and several times a week with the archipelago of the Azores. Flights to Viseu, Vila Real, and Bragança are all run by TAP (Praça Marques Pombal 3, 1200 Lisbon, tel. 01/386–1020). **LAR Transregional Airlines** (Rua C, Edificio 70, Aeroporto de Lisboa, tel. 01/8487119) provides the most extensive domestic air service along with flights to Seville, Bordeaux, and Santiago de Compostela.

By Bus The nationalized bus company, **Rodoviaria Nacional,** has passenger terminals in Lisbon (Ave. Casal Ribeiro 18, tel. 01/545439), with regular bus services throughout Portugal. Several private companies offer luxury service between major cities. For information and reservations in Lisbon, contact the main tourist office (*see* Important Addresses and Numbers *in Lisbon, below*) or **Mundial Turismo** (Ave. António Augusto de Aguiar 90–A, tel. 01/356–3521). Most long-distance buses have toilet facilities, and the fares are often cheaper than for trains.

By Boat Ferries across the river Tagus leave from Praça do Comércio, Cais do Sodré, and Belém. From June to September, a two-hour boat excursion leaves the ferry station at Praça do Comércio in Lisbon daily at 2:30 PM. The price is 3,000$00. There are also cruises to Cascais; details from **Transtejo** (Terreiro do Paço, tel. 01/886–4100).

Boat trips on the river Douro (Oporto) are organized from May to October by **Porto Ferreira** (Rua da Cavalhosa, 19, Vila Nova de Gaia, Oporto). They leave every day on the hour, except Saturday afternoon and Sunday. Overnight cruises are also available. Contact **Endouro** (Rua da Reboleira, 49 4000 Porto, tel. 02/324236, fax 02/317260).

By Bicycle **Tip Tours** (Ave. Costa Pinto 91-A, 2750 Cascais, tel. 01/486–2150) rents out bicycles by the day or half day. **Cycling through the Centuries** (Box 877, San Antonio, FL 33576–0877, tel. 800/245–4226, fax 904/588–4158 or, in Portugal, tel. 01/486–2044, fax 01/486–1409) offers bicycle tours throughout the country with accommodations in first-class hotels and romantic country inns. Each tour is accompanied by a guide, a mechanic, and a van for luggage.

Staying in Portugal

Telephones Pay phones take 10$00, 20$00, and 50$00 coins; 10$00 is the minimum payment for short local calls (some pay phones may not accept the newly minted yellow-colored coins). Pay phones marked *credifone* will accept plastic phone cards, which can be purchased at post offices and most tobacconist shops. Long-distance calls cost less from 8 PM to 7 AM. All telephone calls are more expensive when made from a hotel, so it is wise to make international calls from a post office, where you will be assigned a private booth. Collect calls can also be made from post offices, and some telephone booths accept international calls.

Mail Postal rates, both domestic and foreign, increase twice a year. Country post offices close for lunch and at 6 PM on weekdays; they are not open on weekends. Main post offices in towns are open weekdays 8:30 to 6. In Lisbon, the post office in the Praça dos Restauradores is open daily until 10 PM.

Receiving Mail Mail can be sent in care of American Express Star (Ave. Sidonio Pais 4, 1000 Lisbon, tel. 01/355–9871); there is no service charge. Main post offices also accept poste restante letters.

Shopping Bargaining is not common in city stores or shops, but it is sometimes possible in flea markets, antiques shops, and outdoor markets that sell fruit, vegetables, and household goods. The **Centro de Turismo Artesanato** (Rua Castilho 61, 1200 Lisbon) will ship goods abroad even if they were not bought in Portugal. By air to the United States, parcels take about three weeks; by sea, two months.

IVA Refunds IVA is included in the price of goods, but the tax on items over a certain value can be reclaimed, although the methods are time-consuming. For Americans and other non-EC residents, the tax paid on individual items costing more than 10,000$00 can be reclaimed in cash on presentation of receipts and a special *Tax-free Shopping Cheque* to special departments in airports (in Lisbon, near Gate 23). You can also have the check stamped at any border crossing and receive the refund by mail or credit card. Shops specializing in IVA-refund purchases are clearly marked throughout the country, and shop assistants can help with the forms. For details in Lisbon call 01/418–8703.

Opening and Closing Times Banks are open weekdays 8:30 to 3 PM; they do not close for lunch. There are automatic currency-exchange machines in Lisbon in the Praça dos Restauradores and in major cities.

Museums are usually open 10–12:30 and 2–5. Most close on Sunday afternoon, and they are all closed on Monday. Most palaces close on Tuesday.

Shops are open weekdays 9–1 and 3–7, Saturdays 9–1. Shopping malls and supermarkets in Lisbon and other cities remain open until 10 PM or midnight and are often open on Sunday.

National Holidays January 1; February 15 (Carnival, Shrove Tuesday); April 1 (Good Friday); April 25 (Anniversary of the Revolution); May 1 (Labor Day); June 2 (Corpus Christi); June 10 (National Day); August 15 (Assumption); October 5 (Day of the Republic); November 1 (All Saints Day); December 1 (Independence Day); December 8 (Immaculate Conception); December 25.

Dining Eating is taken quite seriously in Portugal, and, not surprisingly, seafood is a staple. Freshly caught lobster, crab, shrimp, tuna, sole, and squid are prepared in innumerable ways, but if you want to sample a little bit of everything, try *caldeirada*, a piquant stew made with whatever is freshest from the sea. In the Algarve, *cataplana* is a must: It's a mouth-watering mixture of clams, ham, tomatoes, onions, garlic, and herbs, named for the dish in which it is cooked. There are some excellent local wines, and in modest restaurants even the *vinho da casa* (house wine) is usually very good. Water is generally safe, but visitors may want to drink bottled water—*sem gas* for still, *com gas* for fizzy—from one of the many excellent Portuguese spas.

Mealtimes Lunch usually begins around 1 PM; dinner is served at about 8 PM.

Dress and Reservations Jacket and tie are advised for most restaurants in the Expensive category, but otherwise casual dress is acceptable. Unless noted, reservations are not necessary.

Ratings Prices are per person, without alcohol. Taxes and service are usually included, but a tip of 5%–10% is always appreciated. Best bets are indicated by a star ★.

Category	All Areas
Expensive	over 5,000$00
Moderate	2,500$00–5,000$00
Inexpensive	under 2,500$00

Lodging Visitors have a wide choice of lodging in Portugal, which offers some of the lowest rates in Europe for accommodations. Hotels are graded from one up to five stars, as are the smaller inns called *estalagems*, which usually provide breakfast only. Pensões go up to four stars and often include meals. The state-subsidized *pousadas*, most of which are situated in castles, old monasteries, or have been built where there is a particularly fine view, are five-star luxury properties. *Residencials* (between a pensão and a hotel) are located in most towns and larger villages; most rooms have private baths or showers, and breakfast is usually included in the charge. They are extremely good value, around 4,000$00–6,000$00, but usually they have only a few rooms from which to choose. Therefore, we don't review many residencials under Lodging, below.

A recent innovation is *Turismo no Espaço Rural* (Tourism in the Country), in which private homeowners all over the country offer visitors a room and breakfast (and sometimes provide dinner on request). This is an excellent way to experience life on a country estate or in a small village. Details are available from several agencies, including **P.I.T.** (Alto da Pampilheira, Torre D2–8°A, 2750 Cascais, tel. 01/486–7958, fax 01/284–2901) and **Privetur** (Rua João Penha, 10, 1200 Lisbon, tel. 01/690549, fax 01/388–8115).

Tourist offices can help visitors with hotel or other reservations and will provide lists of the local hostelries without charge (except in Lisbon). Few international chains have hotels in Portugal.

Aparthotels, with double rooms, bath, and kitchenette, are to be found in the main resorts and are good value. Villas can be rented by the week or longer in the Algarve from various agents. Among the better-run complexes are the Luz Bay Club and Luz Ocean Club, at Luz near Lagos, where all the well-designed villas have daily maid service.

Camping Camping has become increasingly popular in Portugal in recent years, and there are now more than 150 campsites throughout the country offering a wide range of facilities. The best equipped have markets, swimming pools, and tennis courts. For additional information, contact **Federação Portuguesa de Campismo** (Ave. 5 Outubro 15-3, 1000 Lisbon, tel. 01/315–2715).

Ratings Prices are for two people in a double room, based on high-season rates. Highly recommended lodgings are indicated by a star ★.

Category	All Areas
Very Expensive	over 35,000$00
Expensive	20,000$00–35,000$00

Moderate	13,000$00–20,000$00
Inexpensive	under 13,000$00

Tipping In Portugal, modest tips are usually expected by those who render services. Service is included in bills at hotels and most restaurants. In luxury hotels, give the porter who carries your luggage 200$00; in less expensive establishments, 100$00. If the maid brings your breakfast, give her 100$00 a day or 500$00 for a stay of a week. If you regularly dine in the hotel, give between 500$00 and 1,000$00 to your waiter at the end of your stay, somewhat less to the wine waiter if you order wine with every meal. Otherwise tip 5%–10% on restaurant bills, except at inexpensive establishments, where you may just leave any coins given in change. Taxi drivers get 10%; cinema and theater ushers who seat you, 20$00 to 50$00; train and airport porters, 100$00 per bag; service-station attendants, 10$00–20$00 for gas, 20$00–50$00 for checking tires and cleaning windshields; hairdressers, around 10%.

Lisbon

Arriving and Departing

By Plane Lisbon's Portela Airport is only about 20 minutes from the city by car or taxi. The airport is small, but has been recently modernized; for information, tel. 01/802060.

Between the Airport and Downtown There is a special bus service from the airport into the city center called the *Linha Verde* (Green Line), but taxis here are so much cheaper than in other European capitals that visitors would be wise to take a taxi straight to their destination. The cost into Lisbon is about 900$00, and to Estoril or Sintra, 6,000$00. There are no trains or subways between the airport and the city.

By Train International trains from Paris and Madrid arrive at Santa Apolonia Station (tel. 01/888–4025), in the center of the city. There is a tourist office at the station and plenty of taxis and porters, but car-rental firms do not have offices there.

Getting Around

Lisbon is a hilly city, and the sidewalks are paved with cobblestones, so walking can be tiring, even when you're wearing comfortable shoes. Fortunately, Lisbon's tram service is one of the best in Europe and buses go all over the city. A **Tourist Pass** for unlimited rides on the tram or bus costs 320$00 for 24 hours, 1,550$00 for a week, or 1,100$00 for four days; it can be purchased at the Cais do Sodré Station and other terminals. Books of 20 discount tickets are also available.

By Tram and Bus Buses and trams operate from 6 AM to 1 AM. Try tram routes 13, 24, 28, 29, and 30 for an inexpensive tour of the city; buses nos. 52 and 53 cross the Tagus bridge. Many of the buses are double-deckers, affording an exceptional view of the city's architecture, which includes a remarkable number of Art Nouveau buildings. There's a flat fare of 135$00 per journey.

By Subway The subway, called the Metropolitano, operates from 6:30 AM to 1 AM; it is modern and efficient but covers a limited route.

You're unlikely to use it, but if you do—watch out for pickpockets during rush hour.

By Taxi Taxis can be easily recognized by a lighted sign on green roofs. There are ranks in the main squares, and you can hail a cruising vehicle, though this can be difficult late at night. Taxis take up to four passengers at no extra charge. Rates start at 200$00.

Important Addresses and Numbers

Tourist Information The main Lisbon tourist office (tel. 01/3463643) is located in the Palacio Foz, Praça dos Restauradores, at the Baixa end of the Avenida da Liberdade, the main artery of the city; open Mon.–Sat. 9–8, Sun. 10–6. The tourist office at Lisbon airport (tel. 01/849–3689) is open daily 9–midnight, and the office at the Santa Apolónia station (tel. 01/886–7848) is open daily 8–1:30.

Embassies U.S. (Av. Forças Armadas, tel. 01/726–6600); **Canadian** (Av. da Liberdade 144-3, tel. 01/3474892); **U.K.** (Rua S. Domingos à Lapa 37, tel. 01/3961191).

Emergencies SOS Emergencies (tel. 115). **Police** (tel. 01/3466141). **Ambulance** (tel. 01/301–7777). **Fire Brigade** (tel. 01/606060). **Doctor:** British Hospital (Rua Saraiva de Carvalho 49, tel. 01/395–5067. At night you can contact English-speaking doctors at tel. 01/808424. **Pharmacies:** open weekdays 9–1, 3–7, Saturday 9–1; consult notice on door for nearest one open on weekends or after hours, or call tel. 118 for additional listings.

Travel Agencies American Express Star (Av. Sidonio Pais 4, tel. 01/355–9871). **Wagons-Lits** (Av. da Liberdade 103, tel. 01/346–5344). **Viagens Rawes** (Travessa do Corpo Santo 15, tel. 01/347–4089).

Guided Tours

Orientation Tours and Excursions Various companies organize half-day tours of Lisbon and environs and also full-day trips to more distant places of interest. Those listed below are reliable and offer similar trips and prices. Reservations can be made through any travel agent or hotel. A half-day tour of Lisbon will cost about 4,500$00. A full-day trip north to Obidos, Nazaré, and Fatima will run about 12,000$00. A full day east on the "Roman Route" to Evora and Monsaraz will cost about 10,000$00. Companies are **RN Gray Line Tours** (Av. Sidónio Pais, 2–3°, tel. 01/577523); **Capristanos** (Av. Duque de Loulé 47, tel. 01/543580); **Citirama** (Av. Praia da Vitoria, 12–b, tel. 01/355–8569); and **Tip Tours** (Av. Costa Pinto 91–A, 2750 Cascais, tel. 01/483–3821).

Personal Guides You can arrange to have the services of a personal guide by contacting the main Lisbon tourist office (*see* Important Addresses and Numbers, *above*). Beware of unauthorized guides who will approach you at some of the most popular attractions. These people will usually try to "guide" you to a particular shop or restaurant.

Exploring Lisbon

North of the river Tagus estuary, spread out over a string of hills, Portugal's capital presents unending treats for the eye. Its wide boulevards are bordered by black-and-white mosaic sidewalks made up of tiny cobblestones called *calçada*. Modern, pastel-colored apartment blocks vie for attention with Art

Nouveau houses faced with decorative tiles. Winding, hilly streets provide scores of *miradouros*, natural vantage points that offer spectacular views of the bay.

Lisbon is not a city that is easily explored on foot. The steep inclines of many streets present a tough challenge to the casual tourist, and visitors are often surprised to find that, because of the hills, places that appear to be close to one another on a map are actually on different levels. Yet the effort is worthwhile—judicious use of trams, a funicular railway, and the majestic city-center elevator make walking tours enjoyable even on the hottest summer day.

With a population of around a million, Lisbon is a small capital by European standards. Its center stretches north from the spacious Praça do Comércio, one of the largest riverside squares in Europe, to the Rossio, a smaller square lined by shops and sidewalk cafés. This district is known as the Baixa (Low District), and it is one of the earliest examples of town planning on a large scale. The grid of parallel streets between the two squares was built after an earthquake and tidal wave destroyed much of the city in 1755.

The Alfama, the old Moorish quarter that survived the earthquake, lies just to the east of the Baixa, while Belém, where many of the royal palaces and museums are situated, is about 3.2 kilometers (2 miles) to the west.

Numbers in the margin correspond to points of interest on the Lisbon map.

Castelo de São Jorge and the Alfama The Moors, who imposed their rule on most of the southern Iberian Peninsula during the 8th century, left their mark on Lisbon in many ways. The most visible examples are undoubtedly the imposing castle, set on one of the city's highest hills; and the Alfama, a district of narrow, twisting streets that wind their way up toward the castle. The best way to tour this area of Lisbon is to take a taxi—they're plentiful and cheap—to the castle and walk down; otherwise you'll have little energy left for sightseeing.

1 Although the **Castelo de São Jorge** (St. George's Castle) is Moorish in construction, it stands on the site of a fortification used by the Visigoths in the 5th century. Today its idyllic atmosphere is shattered only by the shrieks of the many peacocks that strut through the grounds, a well-tended area that is also home to swans, turkeys, ducks, ravens, and other birds. The castle walls enclose an Arabian palace that formed the residence of the kings of Portugal until the 16th century; there is also a small village lived in by artists and craftspeople. Panoramic views of Lisbon can be seen from the castle walls, but visitors should take care, since the uneven, slippery surfaces have barely been touched for centuries. *Admission free. Open Apr.–Nov., daily 10–8; Dec.–Mar., daily 10–6.*

2 After leaving the castle by its impressive gate, wander down through the warren of streets that make up the **Alfama.** This jumble of whitewashed houses, with their flower-laden balconies and red-tile roofs, managed to survive devastating earthquakes because it rests on foundations of dense bedrock. The Alfama district is a notorious place for getting lost in, but it's relatively compact and you'll keep coming upon the same main squares and streets. Find your way to the Largo Rodrigues de

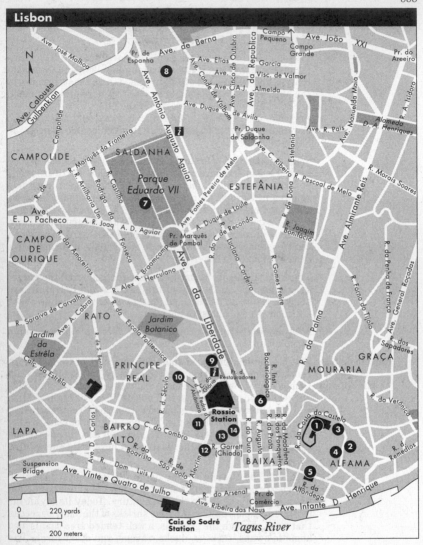

Lisbon

Alfama, **2**

Castelo de São
Jorge, **1**

Elevador da Glória, **9**

Elevador de Santa
Justa, **14**

Gulbenkian
Foundation, **8**

Igreja do Carmo, **13**

Igreja de São
Roque, **11**

Instituto do Vinho do
Porto, **10**

Largo do Chiado, **12**

Museu de Artes
Decorativas, **4**

Museu da Marioneta, **3**

Parque
Eduardo VII, **7**

Rossio, **6**

Sé, **5**

Freitas, a street to the east of the castle, then take a look at the
❸ **Museu da Marioneta** (Puppet Museum) at No. 19A (Admission:
200$00. Open Tues.–Sun. 11–1 and 3–6). From there head
south along the Rua de São Tome to the Largo das Portas do
❹ Sol, where you'll find the **Museu de Artes Decorativas** (Museum
of Decorative Arts) in the Fundaçaõ Ricardo Espirito Santo
(Admission: 500$00. Open Tues.–Sat. 10–1 and 2:30–5). More
than 20 workshops teach rare handicrafts—bookbinding, or-
mulu, carving, and cabinetmaking.

Head southwest past the Largo de Santa Luzia along the Rua
do Limoeiro, which eventually becomes the Rua Augusto Rosa.
❺ This route takes you past the Sé (cathedral), which is also worth
a visit. Built in the 12th century, the Sé has an austere Romanesque interior; its extremely thick walls bear witness to the
fact that it also served as a fortress. *Largo da Sé. Admission
free. Open daily 8:30–noon and 2–6*.

Continue northwest from the cathedral along the Rua de Santo
António da Sé, turn left along the Rua da Conceiçao, then right
and north up the Rua Augusta. A 10-minute stroll along this
street takes you through the **Baixa**, which is also one of
Lisbon's main shopping and banking districts. Semipedestrianized, this old-fashioned area boasts a small crafts market,
some of the best shoe shops in Europe, and a host of delicatessens selling anything from game birds to *queijo da serra*—a delicious mountain cheese from the Serra da Estrela range north
of Lisbon.

Avenida da   Rua Augusta leads into the **Rossio**, Lisbon's principal square,
Liberdade   which in turn opens on its northwestern end into the Praça dos
❻ Restauradores. This can be considered the beginning of mod-
ern Lisbon, for here the broad, tree-lined **Avenida da Liberdade**
(sometimes known as the Portuguese Champs-Élysées) begins
its northwesterly ascent, and ends just over 1.6 kilometers
❼ (1 mile) away at the **Parque Eduardo VII** (Edward VII Park).

A leisurely stroll from the Praça dos Restauradores to the park
takes about 45 minutes. As you make your way up the Liberdade, you'll find several cafés at its southern end serving coffee
and cool drinks. Most notable is the open-air *esplanada* (café),
which faces the main post office on the right. You'll also pass
through a pleasant mixture of ornate 19th-century architecture and Art Deco buildings from the '30s. Rare flowers, trees,
and shrubs thrive in the *estufa fria* (cold greenhouse) and the
estufa quente (hot greenhouse). *Parque Eduardo VII. Admission: 70$00. Open winter, daily 9–5; summer, daily 9–6*.

Turn right from the park and head north along the Avenida António Augusto de Aguiar. A 15-minute walk will bring you to
the busy Praça de Espanha, to the right of which, in the Parque
❽ de Palhava, is the renowned **Fundaçaõ Calouste Gulbenkian**, a
cultural trust. The foundation's art center houses treasures
that were collected by Armenian oil magnate Calouste
Gulbenkian (1869–1955) and donated to the people of Portugal.
The collection includes superb examples of Greek and Roman
coins, Persian carpets, Chinese porcelain, and paintings by
such Old Masters as Rembrandt and Rubens. *Ave. de Berna 45
tel. 01/795–0236. Admission: 200$00, free Sun. Open June–
Sept., Tues., Thurs., Fri., and Sun. 10–5, Wed. and Sat.
2–7:30; Oct.–May, Tues.–Sun. 10–5; closed Mon. year-round.*

The complex also houses a good modern art museum (same times and price as the main museum) and two concert halls where music and ballet festivals are held during the winter and spring. Modestly priced tickets are available at the box office (tel. 01/774167).

Bairro Alto Lisbon's **Bairro Alto** (High District) is largely made up of 18th- and 19th-century buildings that house an intriguing mixture of restaurants, theaters, nightclubs, churches, bars, and antiques shops. The best way to start a tour of this area is via the ➒ **Elevador da Glória** (funicular railway), located on the western side of Avenida da Liberdade by the Praça dos Restauradores. The trip takes about a minute and drops passengers at the São Pedro de Alcântara miradouro, a viewpoint that looks toward the castle and the Alfama (Cost: 135$00. Open 5 AM–midnight).

➓ Across the street from the miradouro is the **Solar do Vinho do Porto** (Port Wine Institute), where, in its cozy, clublike lounge, visitors can sample from more than 100 brands of Portugal's most famous beverage—from the extra-dry white varieties to the older, ruby-red vintages. *Rua S. Pedro de Alcântara 45, tel. 01/347–5707. Admission free. Prices of tastings vary, starting at 100$00. Open Mon.–Sat. 10–10.*

From the institute, turn right and walk down Rua da Misericórdia. On your left is the Largo Trindade Coelho, site of the ⑪ highly decorative **Igreja de São Roque** (Church of São Roque). The church is best known for the flamboyant 18th-century **Capela de São João Baptista** (Chapel of St. John the Baptist), but it is nonetheless a showpiece in its own right. Adjoining the church is the **Museu de Arte Sacra** (Museum of Sacred Art). *Admission: 250$00. Open Tues.–Sun. 10–5.*

Continue south down Rua da Misericórdia until you reach the ⑫ **Largo do Chiado** on your left. The Chiado, once Lisbon's chic shopping district, was badly damaged by a fire in August 1988, but it still houses some of the city's most fashionable department stores. An ambitious building program is restoring the area's former glory.

Time Out The Chiado's wood-paneled coffee shops attract tourists and local bohemian-types alike; the most popular of these is the **Brasileira,** which features a life-size statue of Fernando Pessoa, Portugal's national poet, at one of the sidewalk tables. *Rua Garrett 120, tel. 01/3469541. Closed Sun. Inexpensive.*

North of the Chiado, on the Largo do Carmo, lies the partially ⑬ ruined **Igreja do Carmo** (Carmo Church), one of the few older structures in the area to have survived the 1755 earthquake. Today its sacristy houses an **archaeological museum.** *Museu Arqueologico. Largo do Carmo. Admission: 300$00. Open Mon.–Sat. 10–1 and 2–5.*

Return directly to the Praça dos Restauradores via the nearby ⑭ **Elevador de Santa Justa** (the Santa Justa elevator), which is enclosed in a Gothic tower created by Raul Mesnier, the Portuguese protégé of Gustave Eiffel. *Cost: 135$00. Open 5 AM–midnight.*

Numbers in the margin correspond to points of interest on the Belém map.

Belém   To see the best examples of that uniquely Portuguese, late-Gothic architecture known as Manueline, head for Belém, at the far southwestern edge of Lisbon. If you are traveling in a group of three or four, taxis are the cheapest means of transportation; otherwise take a No. 15, 16, or 17 tram from the Praça do Comércio for a more scenic, if bumpier, journey.

⓯   Trams Nos. 15 and 16 stop directly outside the **Mosteiro dos Jerónimos,** Belém's Hieronymite monastery, located in the Praça do Império. This impressive structure was conceived and planned by King Manuel I at the beginning of the 16th century to honor the discoveries of such great explorers as Vasco da Gama, who is buried here. Construction of the monastery began in 1502, and was largely financed by treasures brought back from the so-called *descobrimentos*—the "discoveries" made by the Portuguese in Africa, Asia, and South America. Don't miss the stunning double cloister with its arches and pillars heavily sculpted with marine motifs. *Admission to church free. Closed noon–2. Admission to cloisters: 400$00. Open Oct.–Apr., daily 10–5; May–Sept., daily 10–6:30.*

⓰   The **Museu de Marinha** (Maritime Museum) is located at the other end of the monastery. Its huge collection reflects Portugal's long seafaring tradition, and exhibitions range from early maps and navigational instruments to entire ships, including the sleek caravels that took Portuguese explorers and traders around the globe. *Admission: 250$00, free Sun. 10–noon. Open Tues.–Sun. 10–5.*

Time Out   There are a number of small restaurants and inexpensive cafés close to the monastery on Rua de Belém. Stop for coffee at the **Fabrica dos Pasteis de Belém** (the Belém Pastry Factory) to sample the delicious custard pastries served hot with cinammon and powdered sugar. *Rua de Belém 86–88.*

⓱   Across from the monastery at the water's edge stands the **Monumento dos Descobrimentos** (Monument to the Discoveries). Built in 1960, this modern tribute to the seafaring explorers stands on what was the departure point of many of their voyages. An interesting mosaic, surrounded by an intricate wave pattern composed of black-and-white cobblestones, lies at the foot of the monument. *Admission for elevator: 225$00. Open Tues.–Sun. 10–5.*

⓲   A 15-minute walk west of the monument brings you to the **Torre de Belém** (the Belém Tower), another fine example of Manueline architecture with openwork balconies, loggia, and domed turrets. Although it was built in the early 16th century on an island in the middle of the river Tagus, today the tower stands near the north bank—the river's course has changed over the centuries. *Av. da Torre de Belém and Av. de India. Admission: 400$00 June–Sept.; free Oct.–May, Sun. 10–2. Open Tues.–Sun., 10–6:30 summer, 10–5 winter.*

⓳   Away from the Tagus and southeast of the monastery, on the Praça Afonso de Albuquerque, is the **Museu Nacional do Coches** (National Coach Museum), which houses one of the largest collections of coaches in the world. The oldest vehicle on display was made for Philip II of Spain in the late 16th century, but the most stunning exhibits are three golden Baroque coaches, created in Rome for King John V in 1716. *Admission: summer 400$00, winter 250$00; free Sun. Open summer,*

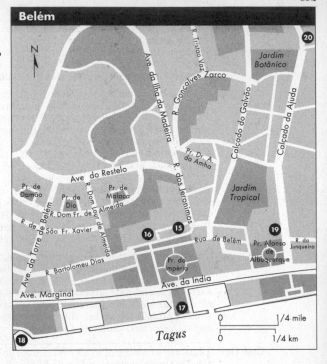

Tues.–Sun. 10–1 and 2:30–6:30; winter, Tues.–Sun. 10–1 and 2:30–5:30.

Head north of the coach museum on Calçada da Ajuda to the **Palácio da Ajuda** (Ajuda Palace). Once a royal residence, this impressive building now contains a collection of 18th- and 19th-century paintings, furniture, and tapestries. *Largo da Ajuda. Admission: 200$00; free Sun. 10–2. Guided tours arranged on request. Open Thurs.–Tues. 10–5. Closed Wed.*

Off the Beaten Track

North of the city in the suburb of São Domingos de Benfica is one of the most beautiful private houses in the capital. The **Palácio da Fronteira** was built in the late 17th century and contains splendid reception rooms with 18th-century figurative tiles, contemporary furniture, and paintings, but it is the gardens that are unique. A long rectangular water tank is backed by 17th-century tiled panels of heroic-size knights on prancing horses. Stone steps at either side lead to a terraced walk above, between pyramid pavilions roofed with copper-colored tiles. This beautiful conceit is surrounded by a topiary garden, statuary, fountains, and terraces. *Largo de S. Domingos de Benfica 1. Admission to gardens: 300$00; to palace and gardens: 1,000$00. Open Mon.–Sat. for 1-hr. tour, but visitors must arrive between 10:45 and 11 AM.*

Portuguese **bullfighting** is a treat on a summer evening—particularly since the bull is not killed in the ring (although it is killed when the event has finished) but is wrestled to the ground by a group of *forcados* in their traditional red-and-green costumes. The bull, its horns padded, is also fought from horseback in what is a first-class display of the remarkable Portuguese riding skills. The ornate Campo Pequeno (Avenida da República) hosts weekly bullfights from Easter to September, on Sunday afternoons and Thursday evenings. Prices range from 2,500$00 to 9,000$00, depending on the seat.

Shopping

Shopping Districts Fire destroyed much of Lisbon's choicest shopping street in 1988; however, an extensive reconstruction project is well under way. Another important shopping area is in the **Baixa** quarter (between the Rossio and the river Tagus). The blue-and-pink towers of the **Amoreiras,** a huge modern shopping center (open daily 9 AM–11 PM) located on Avenida Engeneiro Duarte Pacheco, dominate the Lisbon skyline.

Flea Markets A **Feira da Ladra** (flea market) is held on Tuesday and Saturday in the Largo de Santa Clara behind the Church of São Vicente, near the Alfama district.

Gift Ideas Fine leather handbags and luggage are sold at **Galeão** (Rua
Leather Goods Augusto 190) and at **Casa Canada** (Rua Augusta 232). Shoe stores abound in Lisbon, but they may have a limited selection of large sizes (the Portuguese have relatively small feet); however, the better shops can make shoes to order, on short notice. Leather gloves can be purchased at a variety of specialty shops on Rua do Carmo and Rua Aurea.

Handicrafts **Viúva Lamego** (Largo do Intendente 25) has the largest selection of tiles and pottery, while **Fabrica Sant'Ana** (Rua do Alecrim 95), in the Chiado, sells wonderful handpainted ceramics and tiles. For embroidered goods and baskets, try **Casa Regional da Ilha Verde** (Rua Paiva de Andrade 4) or **Tito Cunha** (Rua Aurea 286). **Casa Quintão** (Rua Ivens 30), probably has the largest selection of *arraiolos* rugs, the traditional, hand-embroidered Portuguese carpets, in town. For fine porcelain, visit **Vista Alegre** (Largo do Chiado 18).

Jewelry and **Antonio da Silva** (Praça Luis de Camoes 40) at the top of the
Antiques Chiado, specializes in antique silver and jewelry, as does **Barreto e Goncalves** (Rua das Portas De Santo Antão 17). Most of the antique shops are along the Rua Escola Politecnica, the Rua de São Bento and the Rua de Santa Marta. Look for characteristic Portuguese gold- and silver-filigree work at **Sarmento** (Rua do Ouro 251).

Dining

For details and price-category definitions, *see* Dining in Staying in Portugal.

Expensive **António Clara.** Housed in an attractive Art Nouveau building, this restaurant serves French and international dishes with a flourish in an elegant room with a decorated ceiling, heavy draperies, and huge chandelier. *Av. República 38, tel. 01/796–6380. Reservations advised. AE, DC, MC, V. Closed Sun.*

★ **Aviz.** One of the best and classiest restaurants in Lisbon, Aviz has a Belle Époque decor—even the rest rooms are impressive—and an excellent French and international menu. *Rua*

Serpa Pinto 12, tel. 01/342–8391. Reservations required. AE, DC, MC, V. Closed Sat. lunch and Sun.

Casa da Comida. Imaginative French and Portuguese fare is served in a former private house surrounding a flower-filled patio. *Travessa das Amoreiras 1, tel. 01/659386. Reservations advised. AE, DC, MC, V. Closed Sat. lunch and Sun.*

Gambrinus. One of Lisbon's older restaurants, Gambrinus is noted for its fish and shellfish. Enter through an inconspicuous door on a busy street to one of the restaurant's numerous small dining rooms. *Rua Portas S. Antão 23–25, tel. 01/346–8974. Reservations advised. AE, MC, V.*

Michel's. Innovative French cooking and an intimate atmosphere can be found in this attractive restaurant in the village within the walls of St. George's Castle. *Largo S. Cruz do Castelo 5, tel. 01/886–4338. AE, DC, MC, V. Closed Sat. lunch and Sun.*

O Terraço. On the top of the Tivoli hotel, The Terrace offers a panoramic view of Lisbon. The food is excellent, especially the dishes cooked on the grill, and the service is quietly attentive. *Av. da Liberdade 185, tel. 01/530181. AE, DC, MC, V.*

★ **Tavares.** Superb food, an excellent wine list, and a handsome Edwardian dining room have made this one of Lisbon's most famous restaurants. *Rua Misericórdia 37, tel. 01/342–1112. Reservations advised. AE, DC, MC, V. Closed Sat. and Sun. lunch.*

Moderate
★ **Alcântara.** Ranked among the trendier, newer restaurants, this one is smartly decorated with a glorious modernistic design. The menu features traditional Portuguese specialties and a good wine list. *Rua Maria Luisa Holstein 15, tel. 363–7176. Reservations necessary. AE, DC, MC, V. Open until 2 AM for dinner only.*

Comida de Santo. The Brazilian-style food is excellent, and is served in an attractive, bohemian atmosphere. Lively Brazilian music ensures that this restaurant is packed during later hours. *Rua Engenheiro Miguel Pais 39, tel. 01/396–3339. AE, DC, MC, V.*

O Paco. Good steaks, regional food, and folkloric decor attract a literary crowd to this restaurant opposite the Gulbenkian Foundation. *Av. Berna 44, tel. 01/797–0642. AE, DC, MC, V. Closed Mon.*

Pap' Açorda. This very popular restaurant in the Bairro Alto is housed in a converted bakery. It offers good food and service in a pleasant garden atmosphere. *Rua da Atalaia 57–59, tel. 01/346–4811. Reservations advised. AE, DC, MC, V. Closed Sat. lunch and Sun.*

Solmar. Located near the Rossio, Lisbon's main square, this large restaurant is best known for its seafood and shellfish, but try the wild boar or venison in season. *Rua Portas de S. Antão 108, tel. 01/346–0010. AE, DC, MC, V.*

Inexpensive
A Quinta. A menu of Portuguese, Russian, and Hungarian dishes is available at this country-style restaurant that overlooks the Baixa and the Tagus from next to the top of the Santa Justa elevator. *Passarela do Elevador de Santa Justa, at Largo do Carmo, tel. 01/346–5588. AE, DC, MC, V. Closed Sun.*

Bonjardim. Known as *Rei dos Frangos* (the King of Chickens), the Bonjardim specializes in the spit-roasted variety. Just off the Restauradores, it gets very crowded at peak hours. *Travesssa S. Antão 11, tel. 01/342–7424. AE, DC, MC, V.*

Chimarrão. A lively, attractive restaurant near the Roma metro stop, Chimarrão features authentic Brazilian dishes, an extensive salad bar, and a large selection of grilled meats. *Avenida Roma 90 D, tel. 01/800784. MC, V.*

Lodging

Lisbon has a good array of accommodations in all price categories, ranging from major international chain hotels to charming little family-run establishments. During peak season reservations should be made well in advance. For details and price-category definitions, *see* Lodging in Staying in Portugal.

Very Expensive **Lisboa Sheraton.** This is a typical Sheraton hotel with a huge newly refurbished reception area and medium-size rooms. The deluxe units in the Towers section, which has a separate reception desk in the lobby and a private lounge, are about the same size but are more luxuriously appointed. The hotel is centrally located and is just across the street from a large shopping center. Parking is difficult. *Rua Latino Coelho 1, tel. 01/575757, fax 01/547164. 386 rooms with bath. Facilities: pool, health club and sauna. AE, DC, MC, V.*

Meridien Lisboa. The rooms in Lisbon's newest luxury hotel are a bit on the small side, but they are soundproofed and attractively decorated; the front ones overlook the park. *Rua Castilho 149, tel. 01/690400, fax 01/693231. 331 rooms with bath. Facilities: health club with sauna, shops, garage. AE, DC, MC, V.*

★ **Ritz Lisboa.** One of the finest hotels in Europe, this Interconti-nental is renowned for its excellent service. The large, hand-somely decorated guest rooms all have terraces, and the elegantly appointed public rooms feature tapestries, antique reproductions, and fine paintings. The best rooms are in the front overlooking Parque Eduardo VII. There's convenient dining at the outstanding restaurant and grill. *Rua Rodrigo da Fonseca 88, tel. 01/692020, fax 01/691783. 304 rooms with bath. Facilities: shops, garage. AE, DC, MC, V.*

Expensive **Lisboa Penta.** The city's largest hotel, the Penta is located about midway between the airport and the city center, next to the U.S. Embassy and close to the Gulbenkian Foundation (shuttle-bus service to the center of the city is available). The rooms are rather small, but each one has a terrace. *Av. dos Combatantes, tel. 01/726-4554, fax 01/726-4281. 592 rooms with bath. Facilities: outdoor pool, health club and solarium, squash courts, shops, garage. AE, DC, MC, V.*

★ **Tivoli Lisboa.** Located on Lisbon's main avenue, this comfort-able, well-run establishment has a large public area furnished with inviting armchairs and sofas. The guest rooms are all pleasant, but the ones in the rear are quieter. There's also a good restaurant, and the grill on the top floor has wonderful views of the city and the Tagus. *Av. da Liberdade 185, tel. 01/530181, fax 01/579461. 326 rooms with bath. Facilities: outdoor pool, tennis courts, shops, garage. AE, DC, MC, V.*

Moderate **Albergaria Senhora do Monte.** The rooms in this unpretentious
★ little hotel, located in the oldest part of town near St. George's Castle, have terraces that offer some of the loveliest views of Lisbon, especially at night when the castle and Carmo ruins in the middle distance are softly illuminated. The top-floor grill has a picture window. *Calçada do Monte 39, tel. 01/886-6002,*

fax 01/877783. 28 rooms with bath. Facilities: restaurant, bar, grill. AE, DC, MC, V.

Fenix. Located at the top of Avenida da Liberdade, this recently remodeled hotel has largish guest rooms and a pleasant first-floor lounge. Its restaurant serves good Portuguese food. *Praça Marquês de Pombal 8, tel. 01/386–2121, fax 01/386–0131. 113 rooms with bath. Facilities: restaurant. AE, DC, MC, V.*

Florida. This centrally located hotel has a pleasant atmosphere and is popular with Americans. *Rua Duque de Palmela 32, tel. 01/576145, fax 01/543584. 112 rooms with bath. Facilities: bar. AE, DC, MC, V.*

★ **Hotel Pullman.** Tasteful modern architecture and a convenient location make this new hotel a favorite with the international business community. Moderately sized guest rooms are comfortably furnished in pleasing colors. The small elegant lobby is bordered by an intimate piano bar. *Av. da Liberdade 123–125, tel. 01/342–9202, fax 01/342–9222. 170 rooms with bath. Facilities: restaurant, bar, garage. AE, DC, MC, V.*

★ **Novotel Lisboa.** There's an attentive staff and a quiet, welcoming atmosphere at this pleasant, modern hotel near the U.S. Embassy. The public rooms are spacious and the guest rooms attractive. *Av. Jose Malhoa, tel. 01/726–6022, fax 01/726–6496. 246 rooms with bath. Facilities: pool, garage. AE, MC, V.*

York House. A former 17th-century convent, this residencia is set in a shady garden, up a long flight of steps, near the Museu de Arte Antiga (Museum of Ancient Art). It has a good restaurant, and full or half board is available. Book well in advance: This atmospheric place is small and has a loyal following. *Rua das Janelas Verdes 32, tel. 01/396–2435, fax 01/397–2793. 54 rooms with bath. Facilities: restaurant, bar, garden. AE, DC, MC, V.*

Inexpensive **Eduardo VII.** An elegant old hotel, the Eduardo is well situated
★ in the center of the city. The best rooms are in the front, but the ones in the rear are quieter. The top-floor restaurant has a marvelous view of the city and the Tagus. *Av. Fontes Pereira de Melo 5, tel. 01/530141, fax 01/5333879. 121 rooms with bath. Facilities: restaurant. AE, DC, MC, V.*

Flamingo. Another good value choice near the top of the Avenida da Liberdade, this hotel has a friendly staff and pleasant guest rooms, though the ones in the front tend to be noisy. There's a pay parking lot right next door, which is a bonus in this busy area. *Rua Castilho 41, tel. 01/386–2191, fax 01/386–2195. 39 rooms with bath. Facilities: restaurant, bar, shops. AE, DC, MC, V.*

The Arts

Two local newspaper supplements provide listings of music, theater, ballet, film, and other entertainment in Lisbon: *Sete*, published on Wednesdays, and *Sabado*, published on Fridays.

Plays are performed in Portuguese at the **Teatro Nacional de D. Maria II** (Praça Dom Pedro IV, tel. 01/342–2210) year-round except in July, and there are revues at small theaters in the Parque Mayer. Classical music, opera, and ballet are presented in the beautiful **Teatro Nacional de Opera de São Carlos** (Rua Serpa Pinto 9, tel. 01/3465914). Classical music and ballet are also staged from autumn to summer by the **Fundação Calouste Gulbenkian** (Ave. Berna 45, tel. 01/7935139). Of particular interest is the annual Early Music and Baroque Festival held in churches and museums around Lisbon every spring; for details *see* the Gulbenkian Foundation in Exploring Lisbon, *above*. The **Nova Filarmonica,** a recently established national orchestra, performs concerts around the country throughout the year; consult local papers for details.

Nightlife

The most popular night spots in Lisbon are the *adegas típicas* (wine cellars), where customers dine on Portuguese specialties, drink wine, and listen to *fado* (traditional Portuguese folk music), those haunting melodies unique to Portugal. Most of these establishments are scattered throughout the Alfama and Bairro Alto districts. Try the **Senhor Vinho** (Rua Meio a Lapa 18, tel. 01/397556. Closed Sun.), **Lisboa à Noite** (Rua das Gaveas 69, tel. 01/3468557. Closed Sun.), or the **Machado** (Rua do Norte 91, tel. 01/346-0095. Closed Mon.). The singing starts at 10 PM, and reservations are advised. Lisbon's top spot for live jazz is **The Hot Clube** (Praça da Alegria 39, tel. 01/346-7369. Closed Sun.-Mon.), where sessions don't usually begin until 11 PM.

Discos New discos open and close frequently in Lisbon, and many have high cover charges. Among the more respectable ones are **Xafarix** (Av. Dom Carlos I, tel. 01/669487), **Banana Power** (Rua Cascais 51, tel. 01/3631815), **Trump's** (Rua Imprensa Nacional, 104–B, tel. 01/397-1059), and **Alcântara-Mar** (Rua da Cozinha Económica 11, tel. 01/363-6432). The current sensation is **Kremlin** (Rua Escadinhas da Praia 5, tel. 01/608768).

The Portuguese Riviera

Just 32 kilometers (20 miles) west of Lisbon lies a stretch of coastline known as the Portuguese Riviera. Over the years, the casino at Estoril and the beaches, both there and in Cascais, have provided playgrounds for the wealthy, as well as homes for expatriates and exiled European royalty. To the north of these towns lie the lush, green mountains of Sintra and to the northeast, the historic town of Queluz, dominated by its 18th-century rococo palace and formal gardens.

The villas, châteaus, and luxury *quintas* (country properties) of Sintra contrast notably with Cascais and Estoril, where life revolves around the sea. Beaches here differ both in quality and cleanliness. Some display the blue Council of Europe flag, which signals a high standard of unpolluted water and sands, but others leave much to be desired—be guided by your nose. The waters off Cascais and Estoril are calmer, though sullied as a result of their proximity to the meeting of the sea and Lisbon's Tagus estuary. To the north, around Guincho's rocky promontory and the Praia de Maças coast, the Atlantic Ocean is often windswept and rough but provides good surfing, windsurfing, and scuba diving. The entire region offers comprehensive sports facilities: golf courses, horseback riding, fishing, tennis, squash, swimming, water sports, grand prix racing, mountain climbing, and country walking.

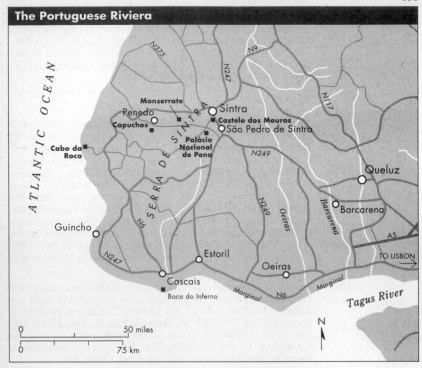

The Portuguese Riviera

Getting Around

The area is served by three main roads—the often congested four-lane coastal road (the Marginal), the N117 to Sintra, and the A5 expressway, which links Lisbon with Cascais. A commuter train leaves every quarter of an hour from Cais do Sodré Station in Lisbon for the trip to Estoril and then to Cascais, four stops farther. The 30-minute-total journey affords splendid sea views as it hugs the shore. A one-way ticket costs 160$00. Trains from Lisbon's Rossio station run every quarter of an hour to Queluz, taking 20 minutes, and on to Sintra, which takes 40 minutes.

Guided Tours

Catur (Largo da Academia Nacional de Belas Artes 12, 1200 Lisbon, tel. 01/3467974) offers a nine-hour excursion that takes in principal sites; it costs 11,000$00 and includes lunch. **Citirama Viagens e Turismo SA** (Av. Praia de Vitória 12-B, 1000 Lisbon, tel. 01/355–8569) offers a similar tour at a lower price. Both tours have daily departures.

Tourist Information

Cascais (Viscount Luz 14–r/c, tel. 01/486–8204).
Estoril (Arcadas do Parque, tel. 01/486–0113 or 01/486–7044).
Sintra (Praça da Republica 3, tel. 01/9231157 or 01/9233919).

Exploring the Portuguese Riviera

Leave Lisbon by car via the Marginal highway (following signs for Cascais/Estoril) and take the curving coastal route to Estoril. Both Estoril and Cascais are favored residential areas; thanks to their special microclimate, they boast milder winters than does nearby Lisbon.

Estoril   **Estoril** is filled with grand homes and gardens, and many of its large mansions date from the last century when the resort was a favorite with the European aristocracy. Portugal's jet-set resort is expensive, with little in the way of sights. People-watching is always a satisfying pastime, and one of the best places for it is on the **Tamariz esplanade,** especially from an alfresco restaurant. A palm-studded coastline, plush accommodations, sports facilities, and restaurants are among Estoril's other attractions, but it is perhaps best known for its **casino,** an excellent gambling hall and night spot that includes a restaurant, bar, theater, and art gallery. A major open-air handicrafts and ceramics fair is held each summer (July–September), and many of the Costa do Sol summer music festival concerts and ballets are staged here (a schedule is available at the tourist office).

Time Out   The luxurious **Hotel Palácio** (*see* Dining and Lodging, *below*), in Parque do Estoril, is worth a visit simply to take tea in one of its ample salons. During World War II, it was an espionage center where the Germans and Allies kept watch on each other in neutral Portugal, and where exiled European courts waited out the war.

Cascais   **Cascais** lies less than 3.2 kilometers (2 miles) west of Estoril. A pretty but heavily developed tourist resort, it is packed with shopping centers, restaurants, cinemas, and hotels. The three beaches are small and crowded, and in summer, parking is a real headache. Even so, there are still some sights worth seeing, including the **Igreja de Nossa Senhora da Assunção** (Church of Our Lady of the Assumption), which contains paintings by Portuguese artist Josefa de Óbidos. *Largo de Igreja. Admission free. Open daily 9–1 and 5–8.*

Less than 2 kilometers (about 1¼ miles) out of the town center, in the direction of Guincho beach, lies the notorious **Boca do Inferno,** or Hell's Mouth. This rugged section of coastline is made up of numerous grottoes; visitors are able to see the full impact of the sea as it pounds into the walkways and viewing platforms. A path leads down to a secluded beach.

Not far from the grottoes, back toward Cascais, is the **Museu Conde de Castro Guimarães** (Museum of the Count of Castro Guimarães), a large, stately home set in spacious grounds. It houses some good paintings, ceramics, furniture, and other items. *Estrada da Boca do Inferno. Admission: 150$00, free Sun. Open Tues.–Sun. 11–12:30 and 2–5.*

The **Parque do Marachel Carmona,** which contains a lake and a modest zoo, is adjacent to the museum. Enter alongside the Cascais football stadium, where a jazz festival takes place every summer. *Open daily 9–6.*

Towering above central Cascais is a large pink tourist complex called the **Parque do Gandarinha** (Gandarinha Park). Close by, you'll find the new **Museu do Mar** (Museum of the Sea), which opened in 1988. *Admission: 120$00; free Sun. Open Tues.–Sun. 10–4:45.*

From Cascais, take the scenic drive along the Guincho coast road toward Sintra, a fairy-tale region with centuries-old ties to a host of eccentric and famous Englishmen, among them the poet Lord Byron. Pass the rocky surfing beach at **Guincho** and follow the curving cliffs until you come to **Cabo da Roca** (Cape of the Rocks). Stop here at the lighthouse for a look at continental Europe's westernmost landfall.

Back on the main road, turn into the hills at the end of Praia do Guincho. This is the beginning of the **Serra de Sintra** (Sintra Mountains), and here, at **Capuchos,** you can visit the tiny friary, built in 1560 by Franciscan monks. The 12 diminutive cells, hacked out of solid rock, are lined with cork for warmth and insulation—hence the nickname the "Cork Convent." *Admission 50$00. Open Tues.–Sun. 10–12:30 and 2:30–5.*

Return to the main road and follow its winding course through the village of **Penedo,** which offers terrific views of the sea and the surrounding mountains, until you reach the world-renowned gardens of **Monserrate,** 5½ kilometers (3 miles) from the superb Palácio de Seteais hotel (*see below*). This botanical wonderland was laid out by Scottish gardeners in the mid-1800s and is the site of an exotic and architecturally extravagant domed Moorish palace (closed to visitors). In addition to a dazzling array of tree and plant species, the gardens house one of the largest collections of fern varieties in the world. *Admission: 55$00. Open daily 9–5.*

Time Out   Follow the signs to Seteais and stop for a meal at the **Palácio de Seteais** (Seteais Palace), built by a Dutchman in the 18th century. Now a luxury hotel (*see* Dining and Lodging, *below*), the Seteais has an excellent but expensive restaurant, and its stately rooms are decorated with delicate wall and roof frescoes. *Tel. 01/9233200. AE, DC, MC, V.*

From here, the main road gently winds down toward **Sintra.** One of Portugal's oldest towns, Sintra. is full of art, history, and architecture. At the center of the **Old Town** near the Hotel Tivoli Sintra stands the 14th- century **Palácio Nacional de Sintra** (Sintra Palace). This twin-chimneyed building, a combination of Moorish and Gothic architectural styles, was once the summer residence of the House of Avis, Portugal's royal lineage. Today it's a museum that houses some fine examples of mozarabic *azulejos* (handpainted tiles). *Admission: summer 400$00, winter 200$00, free Sun. morning. Open Mon., Tue., and Thurs.–Sun. 10–1 and 2–5.*

If you stand on the steps of the palace and look up toward the Sintra Mountains, you can spot the 8th-century ruins of the **Castelo dos Mouros** (Moors' Castle), which defied hundreds of invaders until it was finally conquered by Dom Afonso Henriques in 1147. For a closer look, follow the steep, partially cobbled road that leads up to the ruins; or, if you're a romantic, rent one of the horse and carriages outside the palace for the trip. From the castle's serrated walls, you can see why its Moorish architects chose the site: The panoramic views falling away on all sides are breathtaking. *Estrada da Pena, tel. 01/9230137. Admission free. Open daily 10–5.*

Farther up the same road you'll reach the **Palácio Nacional de Pena** (the Pena Palace), a Wagnerian-style extravaganza built by the King Consort Ferdinand Saxe-Coburg in 1840. It is a cauldron of clashing styles, from Arabian to Victorian, and was home to the final kings of Portugal, the last of whom went into exile in 1910 after a republican revolt. The nucleus of the palace is a convent commissioned by Dom Fernando, consort to Queen Dona Maria II. The palace is surrounded by a splendid park filled with a lush variety of trees and flowers brought from every corner of the Portuguese empire by Dom Fernando in the 1840s. *Admission for guided tour: summer 400$00, winter 200$00, free Sun. 10–2. Open Tues.–Sun. 10–5.*

Back in downtown Sintra, the **Museu do Brinquedo** (Toy Museum) houses an enjoyable collection of dolls and traditional toys from this region of Portugal. *Largo Latino Coelho 9, tel. 01/ 9232875, ext. 280. Admission: 200$00. Open Tues.–Sun. 10– 12:30 and 2:30–5.*

If you're in the area on the second or fourth Sunday of each month, visit the **Feira de Sintra** (Sintra Fair) in the nearby village of **São Pedro de Sintra,** 2 kilometers (about 1¼ miles) to the south. This is one of the best-known fairs in the country.

From the fairgrounds, drive past a gas station to the traffic circle and take N249 back toward Lisbon, keeping an eye out for the left turnoff to **Queluz.** As soon as you swing off the main road, you'll be confronted by the magnificent **Palácio Nacional de Queluz** (Queluz Palace). Partially inspired by Versailles, this salmon-pink rococo palace was begun by Dom Pedro III in 1747 and took 40 years to complete. The formal landscaping and waterways that surround it are the work of the French designer Jean-Baptiste Robillon. Restored after a disastrous fire in 1934, the palace is used today for formal banquets, music festivals, and as accommodations for visiting heads of state. Visitors may walk through the elegant state rooms, including the Music Salon, the Hall of the Ambassadors, and the mirrored Throne Room with its crystal chandeliers and gilt trimmings. The 14-kilometer (8½-mile) drive back to Lisbon takes about 15 minutes. *Admission: summer 400$00, winter 200$00. Open Mon. and Wed.–Sun. 10–1 and 2–5.*

Dining and Lodging

For details and price-category definitions, *see* Dining and Lodging in Staying in Portugal.

Cascais
Dining

João Padeiro. This restaurant, located in the town center, serves the best sole in the region—and other seafood as well— amid cheerful surroundings. *Rua Visconde da Luz 12, tel. 01/ 4830232. AE, DC, MC, V. Closed Tues. Expensive.*
Beira Mar. This well-established restaurant located behind the fish market, has a wide variety of fish and meat dishes. The atmosphere is comfortable and unpretentious. *Rua das Flores 6, tel. 01/483–0152. AE, DC, MC, V. Closed Thurs. Moderate.*

Dining and Lodging

Hotel Albatroz. Situated on a rocky outcrop, this attractive old house, converted from an aristocrat's summer residence, is the most luxurious of Cascais's hotels. Though it's been extended and modernized, it has retained its character, with charming bedrooms and a pleasant terrace bar. The restaurant boasts superior views of the sea and over the coast toward Lisbon; it specializes in fish dishes. *Rua Frederico Arouca 100, tel. 01/ 483–2821, fax 01/484–4827. 40 rooms with bath. Facilities: bar, restaurant, pool, garage. Restaurant reservations required. AE, DC, MC, V. Very Expensive (hotel), Expensive (restaurant).*

★ **Restaurante/Estalagem Muchaxo.** The sound of the sea accompanies your meal at this restaurant nestled on the rocks overlooking Guincho beach. It is one of Cascais's oldest and best-known eating places, and the Portuguese and fish specialties here are beautifully cooked and presented. There are also 24 rooms available for guests. *Praia do Guincho, tel. 01/487– 0221. Restaurant reservations advised. AE, DC, MC, V. Moderate (inn), Expensive (restaurant).*

Estoril
Dining

A Choupana. Just outside town, toward Lisbon, this restaurant overlooks the beach. You can sample high-quality fresh fish, seafood, and other local dishes and dance to a live band until 2 AM. *Estrada Marginal, São João de Estoril, tel. 01/468–3099. Reservations advised. AE, DC, MC, V. Expensive.*

The English Bar. This mock-Tudor-style establishment serves good international cuisine in friendly, comfortable surroundings. There are good views over the beach to Cascais. *Av. Marginal, Monte Estoril, tel. 01/468–0413. Reservations advised. AE, DC, MC, V. Closed Sun. Moderate.*

Restaurante Frolic. The Frolic is a friendly restaurant/bar next to Hotel Palácio. Try the delectable cakes. *Av. Clotilde, tel. 01/ 468–1219. AE, DC, MC, V. Closed Sun. Inexpensive.*

Dining and Lodging
★

Hotel Palácio. During World War II, exiled European courts came to this luxurious hotel to wait out the war. The pastel rooms are decorated in Regency style and the hotel contains one of Portugal's most famous restaurants, the elegant Restaurant Grill Four Seasons, which serves buffets around the garden pool in summer. It's a two-minute walk from the beach, and golfers can use the hotel's membership to tee-off at the Estoril golf course. *Parque do Estoril, tel. 01/468–0400, fax 01/468– 4867. 162 rooms with bath. Facilities: outdoor pool, restaurant. Restaurant reservations advised. AE, DC, MC, V. Very Expensive.*

Lodging

Hotel Estoril Eden. This is a comfortable, apartment hotel with tastefully decorated rooms and superb views over the sweeping Estoril coast. It is one minute off the beach via an underpass. *Av. Saboia 209, tel. 01/467–0573, fax 01/467–0848. 162 units, some rooms with bath and cooking facilities. Facilities: pool, gym, restaurant. AE, DC, MC, V. Expensive.*

Queluz
Dining

Restaurante de Cozinha Velha. This restaurant was formerly the great kitchens of the adjoining Queluz Palace and is magnificently decorated with an open fireplace that dominates the room. There are some fine wines in the cellar to go with the traditional Portuguese cooking. *Palácio Nacional de Queluz, tel. 01/435–0232. Reservations advised. AE, DC, MC, V. Expensive.*

Sintra
Dining

Tacho Real. The Tacho Real serves high-quality local and international food in a luxurious setting. *Rua do Ferraria 4, tel. 01/ 923–5277. Reservations advised. AE, DC, MC, V. Closed Wed. Expensive.*

Solar São Pedro. Highly recommended by its habitués, this restaurant specializes in French cooking. Its English-speaking host adds to the warm and friendly atmosphere. *Largo da Feira*

12, São Pedro de Sintra, tel. 01/923–1860. Reservations advised. AE, DC, MC, V. Closed Wed. Moderate.

Lodging **Palácio de Seteais.** This luxurious former palace set in its own grounds (see Exploring the Portuguese Riviera, above) houses a splendid restaurant. *Rua Barbosa do Bocage 8, tel. 01/ 9233200, fax 01/923–4277, 30 rooms with bath. Facilities: restaurant, pool, tennis courts, horseback riding. AE, DC, MC, V. Very Expensive.*

Tivoli Sintra. Right in the center of Sintra, the Tivoli has excellent views over the valleys and its own welcoming restaurant, the Monserrate. Prices are lower in the winter. *Praça da República, tel. 01/923–3505, fax 01/923–1572. 75 rooms with bath. Facilities: restaurant, bar, garage. AE, DC, MC, V. Expensive.*

The Algarve

The Algarve, Portugal's southernmost holiday resort, encompasses some 240 kilometers (150 miles) of sun-drenched coast below the Serra de Monchique and the Serra do Caldeirão. It is the top destination for foreign visitors to Portugal. During the past two decades, this area, indelibly marked by centuries of Arab occupation, has been heavily developed in an effort to create a playground for international sun worshipers. Well known by Europeans as a holiday center of clean, sandy beaches; championship golf courses; and local color, this section of Portugal is only now being discovered by Americans. Although some parts of the coastline have been seriously overbuilt, there are still plenty of picturesque fishing villages and secluded beaches to leaven the concentration of hotels, casinos, disco nightclubs, and sports facilities.

Getting Around

Faro, the capital of the Algarve, is only 45 minutes from Lisbon by air. **TAP Air Portugal** has daily service from Lisbon, and there are frequent international flights to Faro from London, Frankfurt, and Brussels. There is also daily bus and rail service between Lisbon and several towns in the Algarve; trips take 4–6 hours, depending on your destination. The highway from Lisbon to Faro or Portimão takes about 3–3½ hours.

The main east-west highway in the Algarve is the two-lane N125, which extends 165 kilometers (100 miles) from Vila Real de Santo António, on the Spanish border, to a point above Cabo de São Vicente. This road does not run right along the coast, but turnoffs to beachside destinations mentioned here are posted along the route. A few kilometers inland a trans-Algarve expressway is under construction. Local rail and bus services link most of the villages and towns in the Algarve, and organized guided bus tours of some of the more noteworthy villages and towns depart from Faro, Quarteira, Vilamoura, Albufeira, Portimão, and Lagos.

Tourist Information

Local tourist offices can be found in the following towns:

Albufeira (Rua 5 de Outubro, tel. 089/512144).
Armação de Pêra (Ave. Marginal, tel. 082/312145).

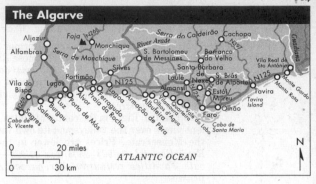

The Algarve

ATLANTIC OCEAN

0   20 miles

0   30 km

N

Faro (Airport, tel. 089/818582; Rua da Misericorida 8/12, tel. 089/803604; Rua Ataide de Oliveira 100, tel. 089/803667).
Lagos (Largo Marquês de Pombal, tel. 082/763031).
Loulé (Edifico do Castelo, tel. 089/63900).
Olhão (Largo da Lagoa, tel. 089/713936).
Portimão (Largo 1° de Dezembro, tel. 082/22065 or 082/23695).
Praia da Rocha (Ave. Tomás Cabreira, tel. 082/22290).
Quarteira (Ave. Infante de Sagres, tel. 082/312217).
Sagres (Promontório de Sagres, tel. 082/64125).
Silves (Rua 25 de Abril, tel. 082/442255).
Tavira (Praça da República, tel. 081/22511).
Vila Real de Santo António (Praça Marquês de Pombal, tel. 081/44495; Frontier Tourist Post, tel. 081/43272).

Exploring the Algarve

To reach the Algarve from Lisbon, cross the Tagus bridge and take the A2 toll road to Setúbal. Turn off at the signs for Alcácer-do-Sal, and Grandola/Ourique. Turn right at the intersection with EN125, the Algarve's main east–west thoroughfare, for Portimão, Lagos, and the western part of the province. Go straight for Albufeira and left for Faro and the eastern end. The road is now a highway and is the fastest route to the Algarve; the trip takes about 3½ hours.

Visitors coming to the Algarve from Spain by car can now drive from Ayamonte, the Spanish frontier town, across a new suspension bridge over the River Guadiana to **Vila Real de Santo António.** This showcase of 18th-century Portuguese town planning is set out on a grid pattern, similar to the Baixa section of Lisbon, though there isn't really much to see here. A few miles west of this border town, pine woods and orchards break up the flat landscape around **Monte Gordo,** a town of brightly colored houses and extensive tourist facilities, including hotels, a casino, nightclubs, and discos. The long, flat stretch of beach here is steeply sloped, and swimmers quickly find themselves in deep water.

Tavira Continuing west past the excellent **Manta Rota** beach, you come to **Tavira,** which many people call the prettiest town in the Algarve. Situated at the mouth of the River Gilão, it is famous for its figs, arcaded streets, a seven-arched Roman bridge, old Moorish defense walls, and interesting churches. There are good sand beaches on nearby **Tavira Island,** which is reached by ferry (summer only) from the town beach, a 10-minute drive from the town center. Another 22 kilometers (14 miles) west lies the fishing port and market town of **Olhão.** Founded in the 18th century, Olhão is notable for its North African–style architecture—cube-shaped whitewashed buildings—and the best food markets in the Algarve.

Faro   From Olhão it's just 9 kilometers (6 miles) to **Faro,** the provincial capital of the Algarve, located roughly at the center of the coast. When this city was finally taken by Afonso III in 1249, it ended the Arab domination of Portugal, and remnants of the medieval walls and gates that surrounded the city then can still be seen in the older district, the **Cidade Velha.** One of the gates, the **Arco da Vila,** with a white marble statue of St. Thomas Aquinas in a niche at the top, leads to the grand Largo de Sé. The **Gothic cathedral** here has a stunning interior decorated with 17th-century tiles (Admission free. Open weekdays 10–noon, Sat. 5 for service, Sun. 8–1). There are also several fascinating museums in Faro, notably the **Museu do Etnografia Regional** (Algarve Ethnographic Museum) on Rua do Pé da Cruz, with good historical and folkloric displays (Admission: 100$00. Open Tues.–Sun. 10–1 and 4–7); and the **Museu Marítimo** (Maritime Museum) on Rua Comunidade Lusiada near the yacht basin, next to the Hotel Eva (Admission: 100$00. Open Mon.–Sat. 10–11 and 2:30–4:30). The **Museu Municipal** (Municipal Museum) on Largo Afonso III has a section dedicated to the Roman remains found at Milreu (Admission: 120$00. Open Mon.–Sat. 9–noon and 2–5). There's a large sand beach on Faro Island, the **Praia de Faro,** which is connected to land by road or reached by ferry from the jetty below the old town.

About 9 kilometers (6 miles) north of Faro, a road branches east from N2 to the village of **Estói,** where you'll find the 18th-century **Palácio do Visconde de Estói.** The palace itself is closed to the public, but the caretaker will let passing visitors in to stroll around the gardens (a tip of 200$00 or more is always welcome). Close by are the extensive 1st-century **Roman ruins** at **Milreu** (Admission free. Open Tues.–Sun. 9–noon and 2–5). Another worthwhile excursion from Faro is to **Loulé,** about 17 kilometers (10 miles) northwest of Faro; take N125–4 northwest from N125. This little market town in the hills was once a Moorish stronghold and is now best known for its crafts—you can usually see coppersmiths and leather craftsmen toiling in their workshops along the narrow streets—and the highly decorative white chimney stacks on its houses.

You can also visit the restored ruins of a medieval Saracen **castle** (within which is the town's museum) and the recently restored 13th-century parish church nearby, which is decorated with handsome tiles and wood carvings and features an unusual wrought-iron pulpit. *Castle and museum at Largo D. Pedro I: Admission free. Open daily 9–12:30 and 2:30–5. Church at Largo Pr. C. da Silva: Admission free. Open Mon.–Sat. 9–12 and 2–5:30.*

Back on N125, in the town of **Almansil,** stop at the 18th-century Baroque chapel of **São Lourenço,** with its blue-and-white tile panels and intricate gilt work. The cottages next to the church have been transformed into a lovely art gallery. As you continue west, look for turnoffs to the south for the beach resort areas of Vale do Lobo, Quarteira, and Vilamoura. The tennis center at **Vale do Lobo,** one of the Algarve's earliest resort developments, is among the best in Europe. **Quarteira,** once a quiet fishing village, is now a bustling high-rise resort, with golf courses and tennis courts, as well as an excellent beach. **Vilamoura** is one of the most highly developed resort centers in the Algarve: There's a large yacht marina, several golf courses, a major tennis center, one of Europe's largest shooting centers, and other sports facilities, as well as modern luxury hotels and a casino.

Albufeira   If you continue on N125, you'll soon arrive at the **Albufeira** turnoff. At one time an attractive fishing village, the town has long since mushroomed into the Algarve's largest and busiest resort, too brash for many. Even the dried-up riverbed has been turned into a parking lot. But with its steep, narrow streets and hundreds of whitewashed houses snuggled on the slopes of nearby hills, Albufeira still has a distinctly Moorish flavor. Its attractions include the lively fish market (held daily); interesting rock formations, caves, and grottoes along the beach; and plenty of night life. Just about 14 kilometers (8 miles) west of the town is the erstwhile fishing village of **Armação de Pêra**, now a bustling resort that has the largest beach in the Algarve. From here you can hop aboard one of the local boats that take sightseers on cruises to the caves and grottoes along the shore.

At **Lagoa**, a market town known for its wine, turn north to **Silves**, 7 kilometers (4 miles) up the N124-1. Once the Moorish capital of the Algarve, Silves lost its importance after it was almost completely destroyed by the 1755 earthquake. The 12th-century sandstone **fortress**, together with its impressive parapets, was restored in 1835 and still dominates the town. Below the fortress stands the 12th–13th-century **Santa Maria da Sé** (Cathedral of Saint Mary), which was built upon the site of a Moorish mosque. (Admission free. Fortress and church open daily 9–5:30.) The excellent **Museu Arqueologia** features artifacts from prehistoric times through the 17th century. (Admission: 250$00. Open Mon.–Sat. 10–1 and 2–5). The **Cruz de Portugal**, a 16th-century limestone cross, stands on the road to Messines.

Portimão   Return to N125 and continue to **Portimão**, the most important fishing port in the Algarve. There was a settlement here at the mouth of the river Arade even before the Romans arrived. This is a cheerful, busy town and a good center for shopping. Although the colorful fishing boats now unload their catch at a modern terminal across the river, the open-air restaurants along the quay are a pleasant place to sample the local specialty: charcoal-grilled sardines with chewy fresh bread and red wine. Across the bridge, in the fishing hamlet of **Ferragudo**, are the ruins of a 16th-century castle, and 3 kilometers (about 2 miles) south of Portimão is **Praia da Rocha**. Now dominated by high-rise apartments and hotels, this was the first resort in the Algarve to be developed; it can still boast of an excellent beach, made all the more interesting by a series of huge, colored rocks that have been worn by sea and wind into strange shapes.

For an entirely different aspect of the Algarve, you can drive north from Portimão on routes N124 and 266 about 24 kilometers (15 miles) into the hills of the Serra de Monchique to the spa town of **Monchique**. Besides its attractive 19th-century buildings, in a shady wood, there's a theraputic spa that dates from Roman times.

Return to N125 to continue your route west through **Lagos,** a busy fishing port with an attractive harbor and some startling cove beaches in the vicinity that attract a bustling holiday crowd. The 18th-century Baroque **Igreja de Santo António** (Church of Santo António), off Rua General Alberto Silveira, is renowned for its gilt, carved wood, and exuberant decoration. An amusing regional museum is alongside. (Admission 200$00. Open Tues–Sat. 9:30–12:30 and 2–5.) Lagos is the western terminus of the coastal railway that runs from Vila Real de Santo António, connecting with the Lisbon line at Tunes.

Sagres After Lagos, the terrain becomes more rugged as you approach the windy headland at **Sagres,** where Prince Henry established his famous school of navigation in the 15th century. Take N268 south from N125 at Vila do Bispo to the promontory hundreds of feet above the sea. From here, a small road leads through the tunnel-like entrance to the **Forteleza de Sagres** (Sagres Fortress), which was rebuilt in the 17th century. The **Compass Rose,** made of stone and earth, in the courtyard was uncovered in this century, but is believed to have been used by Prince Henry in his calculations. The **Graça Chapel** is also located inside the fortress (which is always open), as are Henry's house and his school of navigation—the first of its kind. Both are now used as a youth hostel.

There are spectacular views from here and from **Cabo de São Vicente** (Cape São Vicente) 6 kilometers (4 miles) to the west. This point, the most southwesterly tip of the European continent, where the landmass juts into the rough waters of the Atlantic, is sometimes called *O Fim do Mundo,* "the end of the world." Admiral Nelson defeated the Spanish off this cape in 1797. The lighthouse at Cape São Vicente is said to have the strongest reflectors in Europe, casting a beam 96 kilometers (60 miles) out to sea; it is open to the public. From this breathtaking spot, where Christopher Columbus, Vasco da Gama, Ferdinand Magellan, and other great explorers learned their craft 500 years ago, you can return to the sybaritic diversions of the modern Algarve along N125.

Dining and Lodging

For details and price-category definitions, *see* Dining and Lodging in Staying in Portugal.

Albufeira **Estalagem Vila Joya.** One of the most luxurious restaurants and
Dining elegant inns in the Algarve has 13 Moorish-style rooms and
★ three suites if you'd like to stay the night. *Praia da Galé, tel. 089/591839, fax 089/591201. Reservations needed. AE, DC, MC. Very Expensive.*
A Ruina. A rustic restaurant on the beach, built on several levels, this is the place for good views and charcoal-grilled seafood. *Praia dos Pescadores, tel. 089/512094. DC, MC. Moderate.*
Cabaz da Praia. This long-established restaurant has a spectacular view of the main beach, as well as a cliffside terrace. Try the soufflé omelets (served at lunchtime only). *Praça Miguel Bombarda 7, tel. 089/512137. Reservations recommended. No credit cards. Closed Thur. Inexpensive.*

Lodging **Sheraton Algarve.** This is a new luxury hotel in a spectacular cliff-top location overlooking the sea and with access to some of the Algarve's finest beaches. The architecture and decor blend traditional Moorish features with modern elements. *Praia da Falésia, 8200 Albufeira, tel. 089/501999, fax 089/501950. 215 rooms with bath. Facilities: restaurant, bar, 9-hole golf course, indoor and outdoor pools, gym, sauna, tennis. AE, DC, MC, V. Very Expensive.*

Hotel da Aldeia. Adjacent to Ouro Beach, 2 kilometers (1¼ miles) east of Albufeira, this hotel within a large tourist complex is built in the traditional Algarvian style. Most rooms have terraces overlooking the pool and gardens. *Av. Dr. Francisco Sá Carneiro, Areias de São João, tel. 089/ 588861-2, fax 089/ 588864. 133 rooms with bath. Facilities: restaurant, 2 pools, tennis court, minigolf, health club. AE, MC, V. Moderate.*

Alvor
Lodging
★

Golfe da Penina. This impressive golf hotel, on 360 well-maintained, secluded acres off the main road between Portimão and Lagos, has spacious, elegant public rooms, pleasant guest rooms, and offers attentive service. Most of the guest rooms have balconies; those in the back of the hotel face the Serra de Monchique and have the best views. The excellent golf courses were designed by Henry Cotton, and golf greens fees are waived for hotel guests. There's a special bus to the beach. *Montes de Alvor, tel. 082/415415, fax 082/415000. 192 rooms with bath. Facilities: 18-hole championship golf course plus two 9-hole courses, tennis, Olympic-sized pool, private beach, small private airport, sauna, billiards room, shops. AE, DC, MC, V. Very Expensive.*

Aparthotel Torralta. This large complex, offering good-size rooms, fully equipped kitchens, and daily maid service, is a very good value and has exceptionally low winter rates. *Praia de Alvor, tel. 082/459211, fax 082/459171. 655 units. Facilities: pools, horseback riding, restaurants, discos, tennis, shop. AE, DC, MC, V. Moderate.*

Armação de Pêra
Dining

A Santola. This well-established, delightful restaurant overlooking the beach is probably the best in town. There is a varied menu, but the seafood is especially good. Try the excellent cataplana. *Largo da Fortaleza, tel. 082/312332. Reservations advised. AE, MC, V. Moderate.*

Lodging

Hotel Viking. About half a mile west of town, the Viking stands near the coast, with its swimming pools, tennis courts, and bars situated between the main building and the cliff top. The hotel isn't far from the beach, where you can bargain with the local fishermen for a sail around the grottoes. *Praia da Senhora da Rocha, tel. 082/314876, -7, -8, -9, fax 082/314852. 184 rooms with bath. Facilities: bars, pools, tennis courts, disco. AE, DC, MC, V. Expensive.*

Faro
Dining

Cidade Velha. Located in an 18th-century house within the walls of the Old City, this small, intimate restaurant serves excellent international cuisine. *Rua Domingos Guieiro 19, tel. 089/27145. Reservations advised. MC, V. Expensive.*

Restaurante Adega Nova. Traditional Portuguese dishes are served at massive wooden tables at this restaurant that has plenty of atmosphere. *Rua Francisco Barreto 24, tel. 089/ 813433. No credit cards. Moderate.*

Lodging

Hotel Eva. This well-appointed modern hotel block is located on the main square overlooking the yacht basin. The best rooms overlook the sea, and there's a courtesy bus to the beach. *Av. da República, tel. 089/803354, fax 089/802304. 150 rooms with* *bath. Facilities: pool, restaurant, disco. AE, DC, MC, V. Moderate.*

Casa de Lumena. This 150-year-old Faro mansion has been tastefully converted into a small hotel. Each room has its own individual ambience. *Praça Alexandre Herculano 27, tel. 089/801990, fax 089/804019. 12 rooms with bath. Facilities: restaurant, courtyard bar. AE, DC, MC, V. Inexpensive.*

Lagos **Alpendre.** This is one of the oldest and best restaurants in the
Dining Algarve. The service is leisurely and the food excellent: French-influenced dishes complement the local fish and shellfish. *Rua António Barbosa Viana 17, tel. 082/762705. Reservations advised. AE, MC, V. Expensive.*

★ **Dom Sebastião.** Portuguese cooking and charcoal-grilled specials and fish are the main attractions at this cheerful restaurant. It has a wide range of Portuguese aged wines. *Rua 25 de Abril 20, tel. 082/762795. Reservations advised. AE, DC, MC, V. Closed Sun. in winter. Moderate–Expensive.*

Lodging **Hotel de Lagos.** This modern hotel is attractively laid out at the eastern edge of the old town and is within easy walking distance of all the sights and restaurants. The rooms are large and the restaurant is good. There is a regular courtesy bus to the beach, where the hotel has outstanding club facilities. *Rua Nova da Aldeia, tel. 082/769967, fax 082/769920. 317 rooms with bath. Facilities: health club, pool, volleyball, windsurfing, tennis, billiards, garage. AE, DC, MC, V. Expensive.*

Luz **Luz Bay Club.** You can rent well-appointed, self-service villas
Lodging (with daily maid service) here for short or long stays. One of the better villa complexes in the Algarve, the Luz Bay Club is located near the beach between Lagos and Sagres. *Rua Direita, 101, Praia da Luz, tel. 082/789640, fax 082/789641. Facilities: 3 pools, tennis courts, windsurfing, 3 restaurants, various sports. AE, DC, MC, V. Expensive.*

Monchique **Restaurant Teresinha.** Simply decorated, this modest restau-
Dining rant serves good country cooking: Try the local ham or one of
★ the chicken recipes. Desserts are outstanding. The terrace overlooks a lovely valley and the coastline. *Estrada da Foia, tel. 082/92392. MC, V. Closed Mon. Inexpensive.*

Dining and Lodging **Estalagem Abrigo da Montanha.** This pleasant inn, noted for its garden of magnolias and camelias, serves excellent regional dishes. It also has 6 bedrooms. *Estrada da Foia, tel. 082/92131, fax 082/93660. 6 rooms with bath. AE, DC, MC, V. Moderate (restaurant), Inexpensive (inn).*

Monte Gordo **Mota.** The Mota is a lively, unpretentious restaurant located
Dining right on the sand. Noted for its seafood and regional cuisine, it has live music in the evenings. *On the beach at Monte Gordo, tel. 081/42650. Reservations not necessary. No credit cards. Inexpensive.*

Lodging **Alcazar.** This is one of the most attractive hotels in town, with unusual architecture and interior design. *Rua de Ceuta, tel. 081/512184, fax 081/512242. 95 rooms with bath. Facilities: pool. AE, DC, MC, V. Moderate.*

Vasco da Gama. This long, relatively low-lying hotel occupies a choice position on the extensive, sandy beach. The staff is friendly and helpful. *Av. Infante Dom Henrique, tel. 081/44321, fax 081/42322. 165 rooms with bath. Facilities: restau-*

rant, pool, tennis, bowling, disco, water sports. *AE*, *DC*, *MC*, *V*. *Moderate*.

Olhos d' Agua **La Cigale.** Located near Albufeira, this restaurant—one of the
Dining best known in the Algarve—combines French and native Portuguese cuisine. *On the beach, tel. 089/501637. Reservations advised. DC, MC, V. Closed Dec., Jan., Feb. Expensive.*

Portimão **A Lanterna.** This well-run restaurant is located just over the
Dining bridge at Parchal, on the Ferragudo side. Its specialty is duck, but try the exceptional fish soup or smoked fish. *Tel. 082/23948. Reservations advised. MC, V. Closed Sun. Moderate.*
A Vela. A pleasant restaurant decorated in Moorish fashion, A Vela has a spacious open kitchen that produces a varied selection of tasty Portuguese and international specialties. *Rua Dr., Manuel de Almeida 97, tel. 082/414016. Reservations advised in summer. AE, DC, MC, V. Closed Sun. Moderate.*

Praia da Rocha **Safari.** This lively Portuguese seafront restaurant has a dis-
Dining tinctly African flavor. Seafood and delicious Angolan recipes are the specialties. *Rua António Feu, tel. 082/23540. Reservations advised. AE, DC, MC, V. Moderate.*

Lodging **Algarve.** This modern, luxurious hotel is perched on a cliff top. Decorated in Moorish style, it has good-size rooms and a large, attentive staff. There is an exciting disco set into the cliffs, with windows looking out between the rocks. *Av. Tomás Cabreira, tel. 082/415001, fax 082/415999. 220 rooms with bath. Facilities: pool, disco, tennis courts, health center, bar. AE, DC, MC, V. Very Expensive.*
Hotel Bela Vista. A small, tastefully decorated beachfront hotel with magnificent traditional tiles, Hotel Bela Vista is one of the most delightful accommodations on the Algarve. *Av. Marginal, tel. 082/24055, fax 082/415369. 14 rooms with bath. Early reservations essential. AE, DC, MC, V. Expensive.*

Sagres **Pousada do Infante.** Housed in a sprawling, traditional-style,
Dining and Lodging red-tile-roof building, this pousada affords spectacular views of
★ the sea and craggy rock cliffs. The moderate-size rooms are well appointed and have small balconies. *8650 Sagres, tel. 082/64222, fax 082/64225. 39 rooms with bath. Facilities: restaurant, bar, tennis, pool. AE, DC, MC, V. Expensive.*

Santa Barbara **Hotel Apartamento La Reserve.** This intimate luxury hotel in
de Nexe the hills, 10 kilometers (6 miles) inland from Faro and set with-
Dining and Lodging in a 6–acre park, offers high-class, air-conditioned suites, all with kitchenette. However, don't fail to eat in the restaurant, which serves elegant cuisine with a French accent. Specialties include duck vendome and quail Don Quixote. *Santa Barbara de Nexe, 8000 Faro, tel. 089/90234, fax 089/90402. 20 suites with terraces. Facilities: restaurant, bar, pool, tennis. No credit cards. Dinner only; reservations required. Closed Tues. Expensive (restaurant and hotel).*

Vale do Lobo **Dona Filipa.** One of the best hotels in the Algarve, the Dona
Lodging Filipa has a lavish and striking interior, pleasant rooms, and first-rate service. Set in extensive, beautifully landscaped grounds near the beach, the hotel houses a chic restaurant that offers an excellent international menu. Greens fees for the nearby 18-hole golf course are included in room rates. *Vale do Lobo/Almansil, tel. 089/394141, fax 089/394288. 147 rooms with bath. Facilities: golf, pool, restaurant, tennis center. AE, DC, MC, V. Very Expensive.*

Vilamoura
Lodging

Hotel Dom Pedro. Situated in the heart of this highly successful vacation complex, the Dom Pedro is close to the casino and not far from the beach. Each room is attractively furnished and has its own balcony. *Tel. 089/389650, fax 089/389669. 261 rooms with bath. AE, DC, MC, V. Moderate.*

Vila Real de Santo António
Dining

Caves do Guadiana. Located in a large, old-fashioned building facing the fishing docks, this restaurant is well known for its seafood and Portuguese specialties. *Av. República 90, tel. 081/44498. No reservations. DC, MC. Closed Thurs. Inexpensive.*

24 Romania

Romania is not an easy place to visit as a tourist, but it is perhaps the most beautiful country in Eastern Europe. Its natural tourist attractions are varied, from the summer resorts on the Black Sea coast to the winter ski resorts in the rugged Carpathian Mountains; but perhaps even more surprising are the numerous medieval towns and traditional rural villages that are among the most unspoiled and unchanged in Europe.

The overthrow of the Ceauşescu regime in December 1989 started a continuing process of reform toward a Western-style democracy and market economy. Shortages are easing, and the range of available goods and services is increasing, although rising prices have hit many Romanians hard. But the many problems and inefficiencies remaining from Ceauşescu's time are often outweighed by the traditional hospitality that the Romanian people are free to express since the 1989 revolution.

Comparable in size to the state of Oregon, Romania is made up of the provinces of Walachia, Moldavia, and Transylvania and borders the former Soviet republics of Ukraine and Moldavia, Bulgaria, the former Yugoslavia, and Hungary. With a population of 23 million, Romania is a "Latin Island" in a sea of Slavs and Magyars. Her people are the descendants of the Dacian tribe and of the Roman soldiers who garrisoned this easternmost province of the Roman Empire. Barbaric invasions, struggles against the Turks, the Austro-Hungarian domination of Transylvania, and a strong French cultural influence have endowed them with a rich heritage to add to a folk culture that survives to this day.

Bucharest, with its wide, tree-lined avenues, Arcul de Triumf, and lively café life, was once known as the Paris of the East. Transylvania, a region wrapped in myth, is home to a sizable minority of Hungarians and a small minority of Germans with their own folk traditions and distinctive building styles. This area has long been a favorite with tourists because of the real and fictional sites associated with Dracula. Many enchanting Orthodox monasteries, including some of medieval origin that sport colorful frescoes on their outside walls, characterize the remote and mountainous region of Moldavia.

To the northeast of Bucharest lies the Danube Delta, a watery wilderness populated by fishermen (many of Ukrainian origin) and visited by hundreds of rare bird species. The Carpathian mountain ranges, which form a crown in the center of the country, offer the double pleasure of skiing during the winter and hiking during the summer. The unattractive effects of industrialization are generally confined to the cities, with life in the countryside remaining picturesquely simple. Horse and cart is a popular means of transportation, horse-drawn plows a common sight, and folk costume everyday wear in the northern regions of Maramures and Bukovina.

Romania is a bargain for package tourists. Prepaid package holidays to ski, spa, and seaside resorts offer the best available standards at a very reasonable cost. Independent travelers, however, often pay much more overall for their visit and find wide variations in quality. The country is now in the throes of privatization of its state monopolies, including its tourism industry. Much chaos has resulted from restructuring, and visitors may experience continual changes in prices, amenities, and quality of services. Nevertheless, conditions for visitors

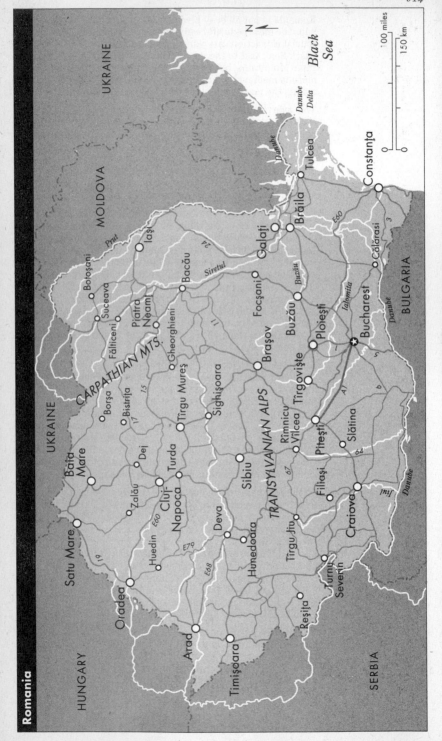

Romania

are improving all the time. More and better restaurants, refreshment facilities, and new shops are opening in many of the larger towns.

If you are traveling independently, you may wish to take some food supplies with you. Vegetarians are warned that there is a limited range of produce available, especially in winter. However, most towns now have private markets where local farmers sell produce at very reasonable prices. Bread is usually available in Bucharest (shop early!), but it is often hard to find in the smaller towns. Dairy products remain in short supply, though cheese can usually be found at peasant markets.

Visitors should use water purification tablets or boil their tap water, since hepatitis is a danger in Romania. Alternatively, drinking-water fountains in most towns provide natural spring water, and bottled mineral water is available in many restaurants. All visitors should bring an emergency supply of toilet paper, a full first-aid kit, a flashlight for poorly lit streets and corridors, and, in summer, insect repellent. Since medical facilities do not meet Western standards, it is best to take along your own vitamins and medication (including needles and syringes for injections).

Romania enjoyed a period of comparative prosperity during the 1970s, but it is currently the poorest country in Europe after Albania. Petty theft is a widespread problem, although the streets are fairly safe at night. Romanians still have limited experience in dealing with foreigners, and are sometimes envious of Westerners' wealth. Their efforts on your behalf may charm you, but they could also be cheating you. Tips, gifts, and even bribes are often expected, but use discretion or you may be regarded as patronizing.

Tourists nowadays may roam much as they wish, and many enjoy "discovering" old churches and buildings, museums, and craft workshops, or wandering through the beautiful countryside.

Romania is likely to remain underexplored until its serious economic difficulties are resolved, but, in the meantime, the package tourist is still assured a good price, while the intrepid independent traveler will experience a part of Europe rich in tradition, one that has largely avoided the pressures and complexities of modern times.

Essential Information

Before You Go

When to Go Bucharest, like Paris, is at its best during the spring. The Black Sea resorts open in mid- to late May and close at the end of September. Winter ski resorts in the Carpathians are now well developed and increasingly popular, while the best time for touring the interior is late spring to fall.

Climate The Romanian climate is temperate and generally free of extremes, but snow as late as April is not unknown, and the lowlands can be very hot in midsummer.

The following are the average daily maximum and minimum temperatures for Bucharest.

Jan.	34F	1C	May	74F	23C	Sept.	78F	25C
	19	– 7		51	10		52	11
Feb.	38F	4C	June	81F	27C	Oct.	65F	18C
	23	– 5		57	14		43	6
Mar.	50F	10C	July	86F	30C	Nov.	49F	10C
	30	– 1		60	16		35	2
Apr.	64F	18C	Aug.	85F	30C	Dec.	39F	4C
	41	5		59	15		26	– 3

Currency The unit of currency is the *leu* (plural *lei*). There are coins of 1, 3, 5, 10, 20, 50, and 100 lei. Banknotes come in denominations of 100, 200, 500, 1000, and 5,000 lei. The Romanian currency is expected to continue to drop sharply in value, causing frequent price rises; costs are therefore best calculated in hard currency. At press time (spring 1993), the official exchange rate was approximately 480 lei to the dollar and 740 to the pound sterling. The price of a pack of Western cigarettes rose from 200 lei to 450 lei in 1992, but because of exchange-rate inflation, the "real" cost only rose from 77¢ to 93¢. Prices of basic items, artificially low from Communism, are gradually being increased.

Because of high inflation, check on your arrival that low-denomination notes and coins are still in use. There is no longer an obligatory currency exchange, and an increasing number of licensed exchange offices (*casă de schimb*) have been competing to offer rates far higher than official rates, and almost equal to those available on the illegal and risky black market. Retain your exchange receipts, as you may need to prove your money was changed legally. Except for air tickets, by law foreigners must pay in lei, though hard currency is widely accepted. The financial police (*garda financiară*) are useful if you experience difficulty. You may not import or export lei.

Credit Cards Major credit cards are welcome in a number of major hotels and their restaurants, but are not accepted in most shops and independent restaurants.

What It Will Cost Prices of hotels and restaurants can be as expensive as those in Western Europe as far as the independent traveler is concerned. Those with prepaid arrangements, however, may enjoy reductions of up to 30% and more.

Sample Prices Museum admission usually costs less than 20¢, a bottle of imported beer in a restaurant around $1; a bottle of good local wine in a top restaurant around $6. A one-mile taxi ride will cost around 35¢.

Visas All visitors to Romania must have a visa, obtainable from Romanian embassies abroad or at border stations (for those with prepaid arrangements, the cost of the visa is often included). Send the visa fee ($31), a stamped, self-addressed envelope, and your passport to the relevant office: in the **United States,** Embassy of Romania, 1607 23rd Street, NW, Washington DC 20008, tel. 202/387–6902, fax 202/232–4748; in **Canada,** Romanian Consulate, 111 Peter Street, Suite 530, Toronto, Ontario M5V 2H1, tel. 416/585–5802, fax 416/585–4798; Romanian Consulate, 1111 Street Urbain, Suite M-09, Montreal, Quebec H2Z 146, tel. 514/876–1793; Embassy of Romania, 655 Rideau St., Ottawa, Ontario, tel. 613/789–3709; in the **United Kingdom,** Consular Section of the Romanian Embassy, 4 Palace Green, London W8, tel. 071/937–9667, fax 071/937–8069.

Customs You may bring in 2 cameras, 20 rolls of film, 1 small movie camera, 2 rolls of movie film, a typewriter, binoculars, a radio/tape recorder, 200 cigarettes, 2 liters of liquor and 4 of wine or beer. Gifts are permitted, though you may be charged duty for some electronic goods. Camping and sports equipment may be imported freely. Declare video cameras, personal computers, and expensive jewelry on arrival.

Souvenirs and gifts may be taken out of Romania, provided their value does not exceed 50% of the currency you have changed legally—so keep your receipts. In addition, you may export five paintings from the Plastic Artists' Union. You'll need an export license to take antiques.

Language Romanian sounds appealingly familiar to anyone who speaks a smattering of French, Italian, or Spanish. French is widely spoken and understood in Romanian cities. Romanians involved with the tourist industry, in all hotels and major resorts, usually speak English.

Getting Around

By Car
Road Conditions A good network of main roads covers the country, though the great majority are still a single lane wide in each direction. Some roads are badly potholed, and a few roads have not been paved. Progress may be impeded by convoys of farm machinery or slow-moving trucks, by horses and carts, or herds of animals. Night driving can be dangerous: Roads and vehicles are lighted either poorly or not at all.

Rules of the Road Driving is on the right, as in the United States. Speed limits are 60 kph (37 mph) in built-up areas and 80 kph–90 kph (50 mph–55 mph) on all other roads. Driving after drinking any alcohol whatsoever is prohibited. Police are empowered to levy on-the-spot fines. Vehicle spot checks are frequent, but police are generally courteous to foreigners. Road signs are the same as in Western Europe.

Gasoline Gas stations are scarce and usually found on main roads at the edge of towns. They sell *regular* (90-octane), *premium* (98-octane), and *motorina* (diesel), but rarely unleaded. Gas prices remain well below those in Western Europe, but shortages sometimes cause waits of several hours. Gas coupons for foreigners—and the privilege of jumping to the front of the line—have been phased out. The Automobil Clubul Roman (*see* Breakdowns, *below*) and tourist offices can provide visitors with a useful Tourist and Motor Car Map that pinpoints the location of each gas station.

Breakdowns **Automobil Clubul Roman** (ACR, Strada Cihoski 2, Bucharest 1, tel. 1/6110408) offers mechanical assistance in case of breakdowns and medical and legal assistance at fixed rates in case of accidents. For breakdowns, dial tel. 927 in Bucharest and tel. 12345 elsewhere. Spare parts are scarce, so carry extras. Thefts of parts from vehicles under repair are frequent.

By Train Romanian Railways (CFR) operates *expres, accelerat, rapide,* and *personal* trains; if possible, avoid the *personal* trains because they are very slow. Trains are inexpensive but are often crowded, with carriages in poor repair. First class is worth the extra cost. A *vagon de dormit* (sleeper) or cheap *cușeta*, with bunk beds, is available on longer journeys. It is always advisable to buy a seat reservation in advance, but you cannot buy the ticket itself at a train station more than one hour before departure. If your reserved seat is already occupied, it may have been sold twice. If you're in Bucharest, go to the Advance Reserve Office, Strada Brezoianu 10, tel. 1/6132642/3/4. For international reservations, go to CFR International (B-dul I.C., Bratianu 44, tel. 1/6134008). You will be charged a small commission fee, but it is a less time-consuming process than buying your ticket at the railway station.

By Plane **Tarom** operates daily flights to major Romanian cities from Bucharest's Baneasa Airport. During the summer, additional flights link Constanța with major cities, including Cluj and Iași. Be prepared for delays and cancellations. Prices average $42 round-trip. External flights can be booked at the central reservations office, Strada Brezoianu 10, and at some major hotels. For domestic flights go to Strada Buzesti 61, tel. 01/6594125.

By Bus Bus stations, or *autogara*, are usually located near train stations. Buses are generally crowded and far from luxurious. Tickets are sold at the stations up to two hours before departure.

By Boat Regular passenger services operate on various sections of the Danube; tickets are available at the ports.

Staying in Romania

Telephones All large Romanian towns can be dialed directly, and international direct dialing is slowly being introduced in Bucharest. The system is stretched, and you may have to order and wait a long time for nonlocal calls. It is less expensive to telephone from the post office than from hotels. Post offices have a waiting system whereby you order your call and pay at the counter. When your call is ready, the name of the town or country you are phoning is announced, together with the number of the cabin you should proceed to for your call. Private business services are opening in large towns, offering phone, fax, and telex facilities. Coin-operated telephones at roadsides, airports, and train stations may work only for local calls.

Telephone numbers in Bucharest, and area codes throughout Romania, changed in late 1992. The area code for Bucharest is now 01, and telephone numbers in the city now have 3, 6, or 7 as a prefix, followed by a seven-digit number. Long distance calls should now be prefixed with a 0 followed by the former area code. For information dial the relevant area code, then 11515; in Bucharest it is 931 (A–L) and 932 (M–Z). Your hotel's front desk or a phone book will be much more helpful.

Mail The central post office in Bucharest is at Calea Victoriei 37 and is open Monday–Thursday 7:30 AM–7 PM, Friday–Saturday 8 AM–2 PM. The telephone section is open 24 hours a day.

Postal Rates Rates are increasing regularly in line with inflation, so check before you post.

Opening and Closing Times **Banks** are open weekdays 9 to 12:30 or 1. Licensed exchange (schimb) bureaus are open weekday afternoons and Saturday mornings.

Museums are usually open from 10 to 6, but it's best to check with local tourist offices. Most museums are closed on Monday, and some are also closed on Tuesday.

Shops are generally open Monday–Friday from 9 or 10 AM to 6 or 8 PM and shut between 1 and 3, though some food shops open earlier. Many shops are closed on Saturday afternoons.

National Holidays January 1; January 2; April 4 (Easter Monday); May 1; December 25.

Dining Shortages have eased and poor standards have now improved sufficiently for the better hotels and restaurants to offer reasonable cuisine and menu choices. Elsewhere, expect poorly cooked dishes based around pork or beef. Vegetables and salads may be canned or pickled. Traditional Romanian main courses are not usually offered, but you might try *gustare*, a platter of hot or cold mixed hors d'oeuvres, or *ciorbă*, a soup stock, slightly spicy and sour. Overcharging is a hazard outside the bigger restaurants with printed menus. You can insist on seeing the prices, but small establishments may genuinely not have a menu prepared for just one or two dishes.

Mealtimes Outside Bucharest and the Black Sea and Carpathian resorts, many restaurants will have stopped serving by 9 PM, although an increasing number have begun staying open until 11 PM or later. Restaurants usually open at midday.

Precautions The far less expensive *bufet expres, lacto vegetarian* snack bars, and *autoservire* cannot be recommended, but creamy cakes are available at the better *cofetarie* (coffee shops). Romanian coffee is served with grounds; instant coffee is called *nes*. You may want to bring your own coffee whitener, as milk is in short supply.

Dress There are no dress rules as such, but Romanians themselves usually wear smart, informal clothes for an expensive evening out. Casual dress is appropriate elsewhere.

Ratings Prices are per person and include first course, main course, and dessert, plus wine and tip. Because high inflation means local prices frequently change, ratings are given in dollars, which remain reasonably constant. But your bill will be in lei. Best bets are indicated by a star ★.

Category	Cost
Very Expensive	over $12
Expensive	$9–$12
Moderate	$5–$9
Inexpensive	under $5

Lodging Prepaid arrangements through travel agencies abroad often benefit from discounted prices. Some schemes, such as fly-drive holidays, give bed-and-breakfast accommodation vouchers (these cannot be bought in Romania). Most places take vouchers; in deluxe hotels, you have to pay a little extra. Otherwise, book accommodations directly with hotels, or through tourism agencies. Some agencies deal only with their local areas; those spawned from the formerly monolithic national tourism office (ONT)—the *agenția de turism*—and from the former youth tourism bureau, now known as the *Compania de Turism pentru Tineret* (CTT), offer nationwide services. Visitors on very tight budgets may want to avoid the cheap, but often cheerless, hotels used by many Romanians. Rooms in private homes can be booked through many of the ONT offices—this is a good alternative to hotels. Private citizens come to railway stations and offer spare rooms in their homes, but use discretion and be prepared to bargain. Inexpensive accommodations such as pensions or hostels are almost nonexistent, and student hostels are not available to foreigners.

Hotels The star system of hotel classification is only just being introduced in Romania. Instead, you will encounter Deluxe categories A and B, First-class categories A and B, and so on. Deluxe A is equivalent to five-star or Very Expensive, Deluxe B to four-star or Expensive, first-class A to three-star or Moderate, and first-class B to two-star or Inexpensive. Standards of facilities, including plumbing and hot water, may not be good even in the top hotels, and decline rapidly through the categories. Ask at the front desk when hot water will be available. In principle, at least, all hotels leave a certain quota of rooms unoccupied until 8 PM for unexpected foreign visitors.

Rentals A few delightfully rustic cottages may be rented at such ski resorts as Sinaia and Predeal. Details are available from Romanian tourist offices abroad (*see* Important Addresses and Numbers in Bucharest, *below*).

Camping There are more than 100 campsites in Romania; they provide an inexpensive way of exploring the country, but standards vary. The best ones are at Braşov, Cluj, Sibiu, and Suceava, which also offer reasonable bungalow accommodations. They all have showers with hot water at least some of the time. The worst ones—Hunedoară, Iaşi, Moldoviţa—have no running water apart from a natural spring and very unpleasant toilets. Rates vary. Usually campsites are clean and comfortable but are only for use during the summer. Details are available from Romanian tourist offices abroad.

Ratings The following hotel price categories are for two people in a double room. Guests staying in single rooms are charged a supplement. Prices are estimates for high season. Because of inflation, ratings are given according to hard-currency equivalents—but you must pay in lei. (Note that hotels may insist on your buying lei from them to pay your bill, unless you can produce an exchange receipt to prove you changed your money legally.) Best bets are indicated by a star ★.

Category	Bucharest	Black Sea Coast
Very Expensive	over $100	over $80
Expensive	$60–$100	$50–$80
Moderate	$35–$60	$30–$50
Inexpensive	under $35	under $30

Tipping A 12% service charge is added to meals at most restaurants. Elsewhere, a 10% tip is welcomed, and is expected by taxi drivers and porters.

Bucharest

Arriving and Departing

By Plane All international flights to Romania land at Bucharest's Otopeni Airport (tel. 01/6333137), 16 kilometers (9 miles) north of the city.

Between the Airport and Downtown Bus no. 783 leaves the airport every 30 minutes between 4 AM and midnight, stopping in the main squares before terminating in Piata Unirii. The journey takes an hour and costs 15¢. Your hotel can arrange transport by car from the airport. Taxi drivers at the airport seek business aggressively and charge outrageously in dollars. Note that the "official" fare is in lei, and the equivalent of about $5 with tip, so bargain.

By Train There are five main stations in Bucharest, though international lines operate from Gara de Nord (tel. 01/952). For tickets and information, go to the Advance Booking Office (Str. Brezoianu 10, tel. 01/6132642). For international trains, go to CFR International (B-dul I.C. Brátianu 44, tel. 01/6134008).

By Car There are three main access routes into the city—E70 west from the Hungarian border, E60 north via Braşov, and E70/E85 south to Bulgaria. Bucharest has poor signposting and many tortuous one-way systems: *Unde este centrul* (**oon**-day **yes**-tay **tchen**-trul)? or "Where is the town center?" is essential vocabulary.

Getting Around

Bucharest is spacious and sprawling. Though the old heart of the city and the two main arteries running the length of it are best explored on foot, long, wide avenues and vast squares make some form of transportation necessary. New tourist maps are being printed and may be available at tourism agencies and hotels. It is generally safe on the streets at night, but watch out for vehicles and hidden potholes.

By Subway Four lines of the subway system are now in operation. Change is available from kiosks inside stations, and you may travel any distance. The system closes at 1 AM.

By Tram, Bus, and Trolley Bus These are uncomfortable, crowded, and infrequent, but service is extensive. A ticket valid for two trips of any length can be purchased from kiosks near bus stops or from tobacconists; validate your ticket when you board. There are also day and week passes *(abonaments)*, but more expensive *maxi taxis* (minibuses that stop on request) and express buses take fares on board. The system shuts down at midnight.

By Taxi Hail in the street, or phone 01/953—they speak English. The price should be around 28¢ a kilometer, charged in lei.

Important Addresses and Numbers

Tourist Information The main **Romanian National Tourist Office (ONT)** is located at 7 Boulevard General Magheru (tel. 01/6144058) and deals with all inquiries related to tourism (open weekdays 8–8 and weekends 8–2). There are ONT offices at Otopeni Airport, open 24 hours, and at the Gara de Nord, open 8–8 Monday–Saturday. ONT is currently being broken up and privatized, so its office signs in most Romanian towns now read *Agenţia de Turism*. The **Compania de Turism pentru Tineret (CTT)** at B-dul Nicolae Balcescu 21 (tel. 01/6133841) also has branches nationwide.

For information before your trip, write or call **in the United States** (573 Third Avenue, New York, NY 10016, tel. 212/697–6971); **in the United Kingdom** (17 Nottingham Street, London W1M 3RD, tel. 071/224–3692).

Guided Tours

A wide variety of tours is promised for 1994 from the growing number of competing tourism agencies, many of which maintain desks in the larger hotels. Tours range from sightseeing in the city—by car with your own driver, if you prefer—to weekend excursions to the Danube Delta or the monasteries of Bukovina.

Exploring Bucharest

The old story goes that a simple peasant named Bucur settled on the site upon which the city now stands. True or not, the name Bucureşti was first officially used only in 1459, by none other than Vlad Ţepeş, the real-life Dracula (sometimes known as Vlad the Impaler for his bloodthirsty habit of impaling unfortunate victims on wooden stakes). Two centuries later, this citadel on the Dimboviţa (the river that flows through Bucharest) became the capital of Walachia, and after another 200 years, it was named the capital of Romania. The city gradually developed into a place of bustling trade and gracious living, with ornate and varied architecture, landscaped parks, busy, winding streets, and wide boulevards. It became known before the Second World War as the Paris of the Balkans; like Paris, Bucharest is still at its best in the spring, but its past glory is now only hinted at. The high-rise Intercontinental Hotel now dominates the main crossroads at Piaţa Universităţii; northwards, up the main shopping streets of Bulevardul Nicolae Bălcescu, Bulevardul General Magheru, and Bulevardul Ana Ipătescu, only the occasional older building survives. However, along Calea Victoriei, a flavor of Bucharest's grander past can be savored, especially at the former royal palace opposite the Romanian senate (formerly Communist Party headquarters) in Piaţa Revoluţiei. Here, one also sees reminders of the December 1989 revolution, including the slow restoration of the domed National Library, gutted by fire, and bullet holes on walls nearby. Modest, touching monuments to the more than 1,000 people killed in the revolution can be found here, and Piaţa Universităţii has a wall still festooned with protest posters.

South along Calea Victoriei is the busy Lipscani trading district, a remnant of the old city that used to sprawl farther southward before it was bulldozed in Nicolae Ceauşescu's megalomaniacal drive to redevelop the capital. Piaţa Unirii is the hub of his enormously expensive and impractical vision, which involved the forced displacement of thousands of people and the demolition of many houses, churches, and synagogues. Cranes now stand eerily idle above unfinished tower blocks with colonnaded, white marble frontages. They flank a lengthy boulevard leading to the enormous, empty, and unfinished Palace of the People, second in size only to the Pentagon. With such a massive diversion of resources, it is not surprising that Bucharest is potholed and faded, and suffers shortages and erratic services. But happily, the city continues to offer many places of historic interest, as well as cinemas, theaters, concert halls, and an opera house.

Numbers in the margin correspond to points of interest on the Bucharest map.

Historic Bucharest ❶ A tour of this city should start at its core, the **Curtea Veche** (old Princely Court) and the Lipscani District. The Princely Court now houses **Muzeul Curtea Veche-Palatul Voievodal,** a museum exhibiting the remains of the palace built by Vlad Țepeș during the 15th century. One section of the cellar wall presents the palace's history from the 15th century onward. You can see the rounded river stones used in the early construction, later alternating with red brick, and later still in plain brick. Prisoners were once kept in these cellars, which extend far into the surrounding city; a pair of ancient skulls belonging to two young *boyars* (aristocrats), decapitated at the end of the 17th century, will interest some. *Str. Iuliu Maniu 31. Admission charged. Open Tues.–Sun. 10–6.*

❷ The **Biserica din Curtea Veche** (Curtea Veche Church), beside the Princely Court, was founded during the 16th century and remains an important center of worship in the city. Nearby, ❸ **Hanul lui Manuc** (Manuc's Inn), a renovated 19th-century inn arranged in the traditional Romanian fashion around a courtyard, now houses a hotel and restaurant. Manuc was a wealthy Armenian merchant who died in Russia by poisoning—at the hand of a famous French fortune-teller who, having forecast Manuc's death on a certain day, could not risk ruining her reputation. The 1812 Russian-Turkish Peace Treaty was signed here.

Nearby, **Lipscani** is a bustling area of narrow streets, open stalls, and small artisans' shops that combine to create the atmosphere of a bazaar. At Strada Selari 11–13, you'll find glassblowers hard at work; glassware is sold next door. On ❹ Strada Stavreopolos, a small but exquisite **Biserica Ortodoxă** (Orthodox church) combines late-Renaissance and Byzantine styles with elements of the Romanian folk-art style. Go inside to look at the superb wood and stone carving and a richly ornate iconostasis, the painted screen that partitions off the altar. Boxes on either side of the entrance contain votive candles—for the living on the left, for the "sleeping" on the right.

Time Out Down the road, at Strada Stavreopolos 3, is the **Carul cu Bere,** serving half-liter tankards of beer, appetizers, and Turkish coffee.

❺ At the end of the street is the **Muzeul Național de Istorie** (Romanian History Museum), which contains a vast collection of exhibits from neolithic to modern times. The Treasury, which can be visited and paid for separately, has a startling collection of objects in gold and precious stones—royal crowns, weapons, plates, and jewelry—dating from the 4th millennium BC through the 20th century. Opposite the Treasury is a full-size ❻ replica of **Columna Traiană** (Trajan's Column; the original is in Rome), commemorating a Roman victory over Dacia in AD 2. *Calea Victoriei 12. Admission charged. Treasury open Tues.–Sun. 10–5, last ticket at 4 PM. Museum open Wed.–Sun. 10–4.*

Bucharest

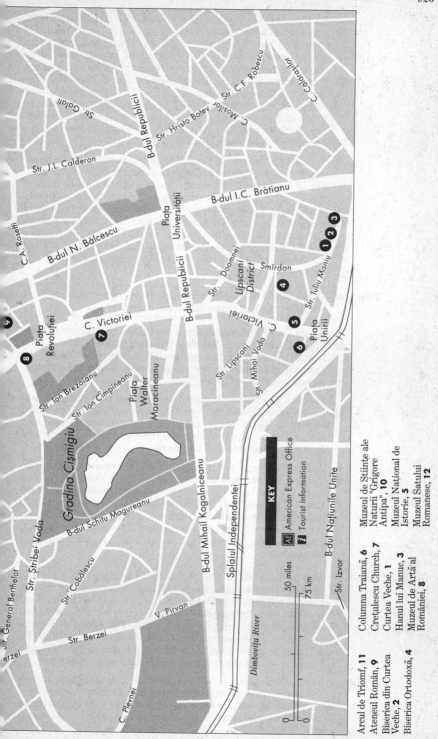

KEY

AE American Express Office

i Tourist Information

Arcul de Triomf, **11**
Ateneul Român, **9**
Biserica din Curtea Veche, **2**
Biserica Ortodoxă, **4**

Columna Traiană, **6**
Crețulescu Church, **7**
Curtea Veche, **1**
Hanul lui Manuc, **3**
Muzeul de Artă al României, **8**

Muzeul de Științe ale Naturii "Grigore Antipa", **10**
Muzeul Național de Istorie, **5**
Muzeul Satului Romanesc, **12**

0 ——— 50 miles
0 ——— 75 km

⑦ Turning north along the Calea Victoriei, you'll pass a military club and academy before reaching the pretty little **Creţulescu Church** on your left. Built in 1722, the church and some of its original frescoes were restored during the 1930s. Immediately north is a massive building, once the royal palace and now the **⑧** Palace of the Republic. The **Muzeul de Artă al României** (National Art Museum) is housed here, with its fine collection of Romanian art, including works by the world-famous sculptor Brâncuşi. The foreign section has a wonderful Brueghel collection and is well worth a visit. *Str. Stribei Voda 1. Museum admission charged. Open Wed.–Sun. 10–6.*

Opposite the palace, in Piaţa Revoluţiei, was the former headquarters of the Romanian Communist party. Before the revolution in December 1989, no one was allowed to walk in front of this building. During the uprising the square was a major site of the fighting that destroyed the National Library, parts of **⑨** the Palace, and the Cina restaurant next to the **Ateneul Român** (Romanian Athenaeum Concert Hall). The Ateneul, dating from 1888, with its Baroque dome and Greek columns, survived the upheavals and still houses the George Enescu Philharmonic Orchestra.

Time Out The cafeteria of the **Athenée Palace Hotel,** opposite the concert hall, has excellent cream cakes and a terrace.

⑩ Follow Calea Victoriei as far as the Piaţa Victoriei. Opposite is the **Muzeul de Ştiinţe Naturale "Grigore Antipa"** (Natural History Museum), with its exceptional butterfly collection and the skeleton of *Dinotherium gigantissimum. Şoseaua Kiseleff 1. Admission charged. Open Tues.–Sun. 10–5.*

⑪ Şoseaua Kiseleff, a pleasant tree-lined avenue, brings you to the **Arcul de Triumf,** built in 1922 to commemorate the Allied victory in World War I. Originally constructed of wood and stucco, it was rebuilt during the 1930s and carved by some of Romania's most talented sculptors.

⑫ Still farther north lies Herăstrău Park, accommodating the fascinating **Muzeul Satului Romanesc** (Village Museum), as well as Herăstrău Lake. The museum is outstanding, with more than 300 authentic, fully furnished peasants' houses, with folk styles taken from all over Romania. *Şoseaua Kiseleff 28. Admission charged. Open winter, daily 8–4; summer, daily 10–7.*

Shopping

Gifts and Souvenirs New private shops are beginning to bring extra style and choice to Bucharest, but note the astonishing customs restrictions (*see* Customs in Before You Go, *above*) that prohibit exporting even bric-a-brac. Keep receipts of all purchases, regardless of their legal export status. The **Apollo** gallery, in the National Theater building next to the Intercontinental Hotel, and the galleries in the fascinating **Hanul cu Tei** off Strada Lipscani sell art that you may legally take home with you.

Market The main food market is in Piaţa Amzei, open seven days a week and best visited during the morning. It sells a limited variety of cheese, fruit, and flowers. If you decide to visit outlying flea markets such as Piaţa Obor, take a guide to avoid being hassled and ripped off.

Dining

The restaurants of the Continental, Bucureşti, and Intercontinental hotels are all recommended for a reasonable meal in
pleasant surroundings. Some, like the **Balada**, at the top of the
Intercontinental, offer a folklore show or live music. Although
prices are not unreasonable, it is possible to rack up quite a total: Many restaurants have no menu, and waiters' recommendations can be expensive. Also note that most places will serve
wine only by the bottle and not by the glass. For details and
price-category definitions, *see* Dining in Staying in Romania.

Very Expensive **Hotel Bucureşti.** The restaurant in this modern hotel sometimes has a loud band playing in the evenings, but the air-conditioning makes it comfortable, and it is one of the few places
where you can enjoy good, genuine Romanian cuisine. *Calea
Victoriei 63–81, tel. 01/155850 or 154640. Reservations not necessary. AE, DC, MC, V.*
Rapsodia. Located on the ground floor of the modern Hotel Intercontinental, this is a quiet, elegant restaurant with a pianist
in the evenings. There is a wide choice of authentic Romanian
and international dishes. *B-dul Nicolae Bălcescu 4–6. Reservations not necessary. AE, DC, MC, V.*

Expensive **Capşa.** Elegant in the Belle Epoque style, the Capşa was
★ founded in 1842 and has a tradition of haute cuisine that it is
struggling to maintain. Recommendations from the headwait-
er are useful, but if you can't decide, try the tasty *musaka*. The
restaurant also has some excellent vintage wines, and the desserts are delicious. *Calea Victoriei 34, tel. 01/134482. No credit
cards.*
La Premiera. One of Bucharest's most popular restaurants is
conveniently located at the back of the National Theatre. The
good selection of Romanian and French cuisine includes excellent salads, even in winter. In summer, you can enjoy La
Premiera's terrace. *Str. Arghezi 9, tel. 01/312. Reservations
advised. AE, DC, V.*

Moderate **Dong Hai.** One of many new Chinese restaurants springing up
★ in Bucharest, this large, well-decorated restaurant in the
Lipscani district serves authentic Chinese cuisine. *Str.
Blánari 14, tel. 01/6156494. Reservations not necessary. No
credit cards.*
Select Restaurant. Located in the pleasant primavera district,
this restaurant offers good Romanian food in a friendly atmosphere at reasonable prices. Fish lovers will enjoy the locally
caught sturgeon; the *mici* (small, spicy sausages) is also worthwhile. *Aleea Alexandru 18, tel. 01/6792177. Reservations advised. No credit cards.*

Lodging

Hotels in Bucharest are often heavily booked during the tourist season. If you don't have reservations, the ONT office will
be of help in suggesting available alternatives. For details and
price-category definitions, *see* Lodging in Staying in Romania.

Very Expensive **Bucureşti.** The city's largest hotel has an excellent central location and spacious, pleasantly furnished rooms. Its modern am-
bience is complemented by the vast range of facilities. *Calea
Victoriei 63–81, tel. 01/6155850, fax 01/3120927. 402 rooms*

with bath. Facilities: 2 pools, health club, sauna, cafeteria, restaurant. AE, DC, MC, V.

★ **Continental.** This small, turn-of-the-century hotel recalls Bucharest's more gracious past. Furnishings are traditional, but rooms have air-conditioning. It is excellently located in the Lipscani district. *Calea Victoriei 56, tel. 01/6145348, fax 01/3120134. 53 rooms with bath. Facilities: restaurant, coffee shop, bar. AE, DC, MC, V.*

Flora. The modern Flora, situated on the outskirts of the city near Herăstrău Park, offers its cosmopolitan clientele top facilities for geriatric (antiaging) treatment. The sun terraces are havens of relaxation. Most guests stay in this quiet, restful hotel for at least two weeks. *B-dul Poligrafiei 1, tel. 01/6184640, fax 01/3128344. 155 rooms with bath. Facilities: pool, spa-care unit, health club, sauna, restaurant. AE, DC, MC, V.*

★ **Intercontinental.** Designed principally for business clients, the Intercontinental offers American-style accommodation in the city's tallest building. Every room is air-conditioned and has a balcony. *B-dul N. Bălcescu 4–6, tel. 01/6140400, fax 01/3120486. 423 rooms with bath. Facilities: fitness center, sun terrace, pool, nightclub, minicasino, 7 bars and restaurants. AE, DC, MC, V.*

Expensive **Ambassador.** The 13-story Ambassador was built in 1937 and enjoys a fine central location. Although a little shabby, its rooms are comfortably furnished. The restaurant is not recommended, but there is a good café. *B-dul General Magheru 6–8, tel. 01/6159080, fax 01/3121239. 233 rooms with bath. Facilities: restaurant, café. AE, DC, MC, V.*

Bulevard. This old-style hotel is conveniently situated near the main tourist attractions. Small and intimate, though a bit shabby, this hotel has an Old-World feel and benefits from attractive *fin de siècle* furnishings. Category B rooms are less expensive, since their windows don't look out onto the busy Bulevardul Mihail Kogălniceanu (this means they can be quieter, however). *B-dul Mihail Kogălniceanu 1, tel. 01/6130310, fax 01/3123923. 89 rooms with bath. AE, DC, MC, V.*

Parc. Located near Herăstrău Park and the Flora Hotel, the Parc is modern and within easy reach of the airport; many guests stay here before moving on to the Black Sea resorts. There's a good restaurant that provides music every evening. *B-dul Poligrafiei 3, tel. 01/6180950, fax 01/3128419. 314 rooms with bath. Facilities: restaurant, pool, sauna, tennis. AE, DC, MC, V.*

Moderate **Capitol.** The circa 1900 Capitol is situated in a lively part of town near the Cişmigiu Gardens. In days gone by, it was the stomping ground of Bucharest's mainstream artists and writers. Today the Capitol is modernized and offers comfortable rooms—though the literati have long since moved on. *Calea Victoriei 29, tel. 01/6139440. 70 rooms with bath. Facilities: restaurant. No credit cards.*

★ **Triumf.** This comfortable hotel is set on its own grounds slightly outside the city center near the Arcul de Triumf. Formerly the President, it used to serve only the Communist elite. The more expensive rooms are miniapartments. *Şoseaua Kiseleff 12, tel. 01/6184110, fax 01/3128411. 98 rooms, 49 with bath. Facilities: restaurant, bar, tennis court. AE, DC, V.*

The Arts

You can enjoy Bucharest's lively theater and music life at prices way below those in the West. Tickets can be obtained directly from the theater or hall or from your hotel (for a commission fee). Performances usually begin at 7 PM (6 in winter). **Opera Română** (The Opera House, B-dul Mihail Kogălniceanu 70) has some good productions, but don't expect to find the same quality as you would in Prague or Budapest. The **Teatrul de Operetă** (Operetta House) is now located at the **Teatrul National** (National Theater, B-dul N. Bălcescu 2), which also offers serious drama. For lighter entertainment, try the **Teatrul de Comedie** (Comedy Theater, Str. Mandinesti); despite the language barrier, there is often enough spectacle to ensure a very good evening's entertainment. **Teatrul Tăndărică** (The Tandarica Puppet Theater, Calea Victoriei 50), has an international reputation, and the **Teatrul Evreesc de Stat** (State Jewish Theater, Str. Barasch 15), stages Yiddish-language performances. Don't miss the fine folkloric show at the **Rapsodia Română Artistic Ensemble** (Str. Lipscani 53). The **Cinematica Romana** (Str. Eforie 5) runs a daily program of old, undubbed American and English films.

Nightlife

Increasing numbers of bars and restaurants stay open late. Coffee shops, however, are usually closed after 8 PM.

Nightclubs The **Athenée Palace** and **Intercontinental** hotels have nightclubs with floor shows, and many others are popping up as well. **Vox Maris,** opposite the Bulevard hotel, and **Club A,** on Str. Blánar, are among several late-night discos. **Şarpele Roşu** (Str. Icoanei Piaţa Galaţi), or "Red Snake," has a pleasant, bohemian atmosphere, with Gypsy bands playing until 3 AM.

Cafés Cafés with outdoor terraces remain a feature of the city. Try the **Athenée** Palace or, in winter, the excellent indoor **Ana Café** (Str. Aviator Radu Beller 6), just north of Piaţa Dorobanţi.

The Black Sea Coast and Danube Delta

The southeastern Dobrogea region, only 45 minutes by air from Bucharest, 210 kilometers (130 miles) by road, is one of the major focal points of Romania's rich history. Within a clearly defined area are the historic port of Constanţa; the Romanian Riviera pleasure coast; the renowned Murfatlar vineyards; Roman, Greek, and earlier ruins; and the Danube Delta, one of Europe's leading wildlife sanctuaries. The rapid development of the Black Sea resorts and increasing interest in the delta region mean that tourist amenities (such as hotels and restaurants) and train, bus, and plane connections are good.

Getting Around

By Bus Bus trips from the Black Sea resorts and Constanta to the Danube Delta, the Murfatlar vineyards, Istria, and the sunken city of Adamclisi are arranged by an increasing number of tourism agencies.

The Black Sea Coast

By Car Rental cars, with or without drivers, are available through Societatea Comercială Litoral (formerly ONT) offices, hotels, and specialized agencies.

By Boat Regular passenger and sightseeing boats operate along the middle and southern arms of the Danube Delta. Motorboats are available for hire, or rent one of the more restful fishermen's boats.

Guided Tours

Tours always involve some hours on the road, so it is better to go for more than one day. The **Societatea Comercială Litoral** has the most tour experience. Try trips to the Bukovina monasteries, the Prahova Mountains, or, especially, the Danube Delta.

Tourist Information

Constanța. Societatea Comercială Litoral (B-dul Tomis 69, tel. 0/916/17181). **CTT** (Hotel Tineretului, B-dul Tomis 20–26, tel. 091/613590, fax 091/611290).
Mamaia. Societatea Comercială Mamaia (Hotel București, tel. 0918/31025).
Tulcea. Societatea Comercială Deltarom (Hotel Delta, Str. Isaccei 2, tel. 0915/14720, fax 0915/16260). **CTT** (Str. Babadag Bloc B1, tel. 0915/12496, fax 0915/16842).

Exploring the Black Sea Coast and Danube Delta

Tulcea, the main town of the Danube Delta, is the gateway to the splendors of the region. Built on seven hills, this former Oriental-style market town is now an important sea and river port, as well as the center of the Romanian fish industry. The **Muzeul Deltei Dunării** (Danube Delta Museum) provides a good introduction to the flora, fauna, and way of life of the communities in the area. *Str. Progresului 32. Admission charged. Open daily 10–6.*

The **Delta Dunării** (Danube Delta) is Europe's largest wetlands reserve, covering 2,681 square kilometers (1,676 square miles), with a sprawling, watery wilderness that stretches from the Ukrainian border to a series of lakes north of the Black Sea resorts. It is Europe's youngest land; more than 43.7 square meters (47 square yards) are added each year by normal silting action. As it approaches the delta, the great Danube divides into three. The northernmost branch forms the border with the Ukraine, the middle arm leads to the busy port of Sulina, and the southernmost arm meanders gently toward the little port of Sfîntu Ghcorghe. From these channels, countless canals widen into tree-fringed lakes, reed islands, and pools covered with water lilies; there are sand dunes and pockets of lush forest.

More than 80% of the delta area is water. Over 300 bird species visit the area; 70 of them come from as far away as China and India. The delta is a natural stopover for migratory birds, but the most characteristic bird is the common pelican, the featured star of this bird-watchers' paradise. Fishing provides most of the area's inhabitants, many of whom are of Ukrainian origin, with a livelihood. Common sights are the long lines of fishing boats strung together to be towed by motorboats to remote fishing grounds. Smaller communities, such as Independenţa on the southern arm and Crişan on the middle arm, rent out the services of a fisherman and his boat to foreigners. The waters here are particularly rich in catfish, perch, carp, and caviar-bearing sturgeon.

There are good roads to the Black Sea resorts from Tulcea that take you to **Babadag** via the strange, eroded Măcin hills. It was here, according to local legend, that Jason and his Argonauts cast anchor in their search for the mythical golden fleece. Farther south is **Istria,** an impressive archaeological site, founded in 6 BC by Greek merchants from Miletus. There are traces of early Christian churches and baths and even residential, commercial, and industrial districts. A useful English-language booklet, available on the spot, will help make sense of the remains of several cultures.

Istria lies only 60 kilometers (37 miles) from **Mamaia,** the largest of the Black Sea resorts. Mamaia is situated on a strip of land bordered by the Black Sea and fine beaches on one side and the fresh waters of the Mamaia Lake on the other. All the resorts along this stretch of the coast have high-rise modern apartments, villas, restaurants, nightclubs, and discos. There are cruises down the coast to Mangalia and along the new channel linking the Danube with the Black Sea near Constanţa. Sea-fishing expeditions can also be arranged for early risers, with all equipment provided. These resorts offer everything necessary for a complete vacation by the sea.

Constanţa is Romania's second-largest city and only a short ride by trolley bus from Mamaia. With a polyglot flavor characteristic of so many seaports, Constanţa is steeped in history. The famous Roman poet Ovid was exiled here from Rome in AD 8, probably for his part in court scandals and for the amorality of his poem *Ars amandi (The Art of Making Love)*. A city square has been named in his honor and provides a fine backdrop for a statue of him by the sculptor Ettore Ferrari. Behind the statue, in the former town hall, is one of the best museums in Europe, the **Muzuel Naţional de Istorie şi Arheologie** (National History and Archaeological Museum). Of special interest here are the statuettes of *The Thinker* and *The Seated Woman*, from the neolithic Hamangian culture (4000 to 3000 BC). Collections from the Greek, Roman, and Daco-Roman cultures are generally outstanding. *Piaţa Ovidiu 12. Admission charged. Open Tues.–Sun. 10–6.*

Near the museum is **Edificiu Roman cu Mozaic,** a Roman complex of warehouses and shops from the 4th century AD, including a magnificent mosaic floor measuring over 6,510 square meters (21,000 square feet) (Piaţa Ovidiu 1). Not far away are the remains of the Roman baths from the same period. The **Parcul Arheologic** (Archaeology Park) on Boulevard Republicii contains items dating from the 3rd and 4th centuries AD and from a 6th-century tower. Modern-day attractions include an **Acvariul,** or aquarium (Str. Februarie 16), and **Delfinariul,** the dolphinarium (B-dul Mamaia 265), which offers aquatic displays by trained dolphins.

A string of seaside resorts lies just south of Constanţa. **Eforie Nord** is an up-to-date thermal treatment center. A series of resorts built during the 1960s are named for the coast's Greco-Roman past—**Neptun, Jupiter, Venus,** and **Saturn.** Not in any way typically Romanian, these resorts offer good amenities for relaxed, seaside vacations. The old port of **Mangalia** is the southernmost resort.

Most of the old Greek city of **Callatis** lies underwater now, but a section of the walls and the remains of a Roman villa are still visible.

There are regular excursions from the seaside resorts to the **Columna Traiană** (replica of Trajan's Column), the **Podgoriile Murfatlar** (Murfatlar vineyards) for wine tastings, and the ruins of the Roman town at **Tropaeum Trajani.**

Dining and Lodging

For details and price-category definitions, *see* Dining and Lodging in Staying in Romania. Travelers are advised not to rely on credit cards in this region since many resorts are not yet equipped to accept them.

Constanţa
Dining
Cazinou. A turn-of-the-century former casino situated close to the aquarium, the Cazinou is decorated in an ornate 20th-century style; there's an adjoining bar by the sea. Seafood dishes are the house specialties. *Str. Februarie 16, tel. 091/617416. Reservations advised. No credit cards. Very Expensive.*

Lodging
Palace. Located near the city's historic center, the large and gracious old Palace has recently been renovated. It has a good restaurant and a terrace overlooking the sea and the tourist

port of Tomis. *Str. Remus Opreanu 5–7, tel. 091/614696. 132 rooms with bath. Facilities: restaurant. Expensive.*

Continental. Older, slightly less luxurious, but larger than the Palace, the Continental is conveniently situated near the open-air archaeological museum in the downtown area. *B-dul Republicii 20, tel. 091/615660. 140 rooms with bath. AE. Moderate.*

Crişan
Lodging

Lebăda. This is a comfortable hotel from which to make fishing trips into the more remote parts of the delta. *Sulina Canal, mile 14.5, tel. 0915/14720. 74 rooms with bath. Facilities: restaurant, currency exchange. Moderate.*

Mamaia
Dining

Satul de Vacanţa. This holiday village is an attractive complex of traditional Romanian buildings, built in styles from all over Romania and featuring many small restaurants that serve local specialties. *Inexpensive–Expensive.*

Insula lui Ovidiu. This is a reed-thatched complex of rustic-style buildings with lively music every evening. A relaxed, informal atmosphere provides a good setting for delicious seafood dishes. *Lake Siurghiol. No telephone. Reservations not necessary. Moderate.*

Lodging

Rex. One of King Carol's former residences, this is the largest and grandest of all the hotels in Mamaia. An outdoor swimming pool, an excellent restaurant, a bar, and a cafeteria are among its facilities. *Tel. 0918/31595 or 0918/31520, fax 0918/31515. 102 rooms with bath. Very Expensive.*

Ambasador, Lido, and **Savoy.** Among the many modern hotels, these three are all newly built and moderately priced. They are grouped in a horseshoe around open-air pools near the beach at the north end of the resort. *Moderate.*

Tulcea
Lodging

Delta. A large, modern hotel on the banks of the Danube, the Delta currently has a mixed reputation. Amenities include a restaurant, bar, and cafeteria. *Str. Isaacei 2, tel. 0915/14720, fax 0915/16260. 117 rooms with bath. Moderate.*

25 Slovakia

Even if it had not developed separately for nearly a millennium under Hungarian and Habsburg rule, the newly independent Slovak Republic (Slovensko) would be different from its Bohemian neighbor (*see* Chapter 7) in a great many respects. The mountains are higher here; the veneer less sophisticated. The people seem more carefree, and the folk culture is particularly rich.

Although they speak a language closely related to Czech, the Slovaks have a strong sense of national identity, and indeed the two Slavic groups developed quite separately. Although united in the 9th century as part of the Great Moravian Empire, the Slovaks were conquered a century later by the Magyars and remained under Hungarian domination until 1918. After the Tartar invasions of the 13th century, many Saxons were invited to resettle the land, exploit the rich mineral resources, and thereby develop the economy. In the 15th and 16th centuries, Romanian shepherds migrated from Wallachia through the Carpathians into Slovakia, and the merging of these varied groups with the resident Slavs bequeathed to the region a rich folk culture and some unique forms of architecture, especially in the east.

Bratislava, the capital of Hungary for nearly 300 years until 1784, and now the capital of the new republic, is a disappointment to many visitors. The 40 years of Communist rule left a clear mark on the city, hiding its ancient beauty with hulking, and now dilapidated, futurist structures. Take time, however, to walk the picturesque streets of the Old Town, now undergoing frenzied revitalization. The city is filled with good concert halls, restaurants, and wine bars.

Most visitors head for the great peaks of the High Tatras. The smallest Alpine range in the world, the Tatras rise magnificently from the foothills of northern Slovakia. The tourist infrastructure here is very good, catering especially to hikers and skiers. Visitors who come to admire the peaks, however, often overlook the exquisite medieval towns of the Spiš in the plains and valleys below the Tatras and the beautiful 18th-century wood churches farther east.

Essential Information

Before You Go

When to Go Organized sightseeing tours run from April or May through October. Some monuments, especially castles, either close entirely or open for shorter hours during the winter. Hotel rates drop during the off-season except during festivals. The High Tatra mountains come into their own in winter (Dec.–Feb.), when skiers from all over Eastern Europe crowd the slopes and resorts. If you're not into skiing, try visiting the mountains in late spring (May or June) or fall, when the colors are dazzling and you'll have the hotels and restaurants pretty much to yourself.

Climate The following are the average daily maximum and minimum temperatures for Bratislava.

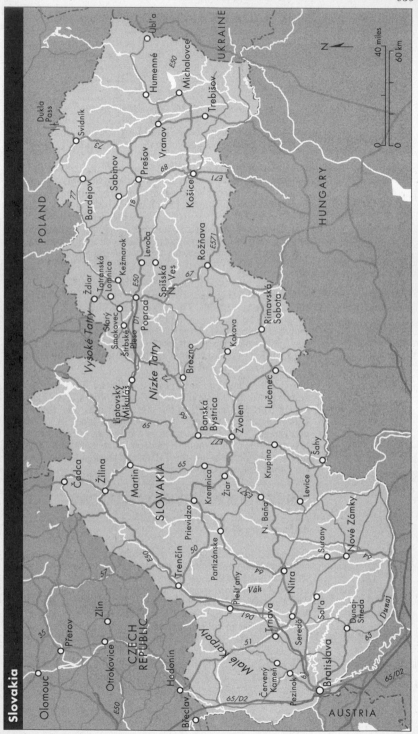

Jan.	36F	2C	May	70F	21C	Sept.	72F	22C
	27	– 3		52	11		54	12
Feb.	39F	4C	June	75F	24C	Oct.	59F	15C
	28	– 2		57	14		45	7
Mar.	48F	9C	July	79F	26C	Nov.	46F	8C
	34	1		61	16		37	3
Apr.	61F	16C	Aug.	79F	26C	Dec.	39F	4C
	43	6		61	16		32	0

Currency The unit of currency in Slovakia is the crown, or koruna, written as Sk, and divided into 100 halér. There are bills of 10, 20, 50, 100, 500, and 1,000 Sk and coins of 5, 10, 20, and 50 halér and 1, 2, and 5 Sk.

At press time (spring 1993), the koruna was trading at around 28.2 Sk to the dollar and 43.8 Sk to the pound.

Credit cards are widely accepted in establishments used by foreign tourists.

What It Will Cost Costs are highest in Bratislava and only slightly less in the High Tatra resorts and main spas, although even in those places you can now find bargain private accommodations. The prices at tourist resorts in the outlying areas and off the beaten track are incredibly low. The least expensive areas are central and eastern Slovakia.

Sample Prices Cup of coffee, 10 Sk; beer (½ liter), 10 Sk–15 Sk; Coca-Cola, 10 Sk–15 Sk; ham sandwich, 15 Sk; 1-mile taxi ride, 100 Sk.

Museums Admission to museums, galleries, and castles ranges from 5 Sk to 50 Sk.

Visas U.S. and British citizens do not need visas to enter Slovakia. Visa requirements have been temporarily reintroduced for Canadian citizens; check whether this is still the case with the consulate. Apply to the Consulate of the Slovak Federal Republic, 50 Rideau Terrace, Ottawa, Ontario K1M 2A1, tel. 316/749–4442.

Customs Valuable items should be entered on your customs declaration.
On Arrival You can bring in 250 cigarettes (or their equivalent in tobacco), 2 liters of wine, 1 liter of spirits, ½ liter of eau de cologne, and gifts to the value of 1,000 Sk.

On Departure Crystal not purchased with hard currency may be subject to a tax of 100% of its retail price. To be on the safe side, hang on to all receipts. Only antiques bought at specially designated shops may be exported.

Language English is spoken fairly widely among both the young and those associated with the tourist industry. You will come across English speakers elsewhere, though not frequently. German is widely understood throughout the country.

Getting Around

By Car Main roads are usually good, if sometimes narrow, and traffic is
Road Conditions light, especially away from main centers. **Bratislava** is not a good city for drivers, and finding a parking space can be a problem. Hence, for touring the capital, walking is the best option. It's very useful to have a car when exploring central and eastern Slovakia, however, where many of the interesting sights

are outside the larger towns and are difficult to reach with mass transit.

Rules of the Road Drive on the right. Speed limits are 60 kph (37 mph) in built-up areas, 90 kph (55 mph) on open roads, and 110 kph (68 mph) on expressways. Seat belts are compulsory outside built-up areas; drinking and driving is strictly prohibited.

Gasoline Gasoline is expensive, averaging $3 a gallon. Service stations are usually located along main roads on the outskirts of towns and cities. Finding a station in Bratislava is difficult. Fill up on the freeway as you approach the city to avoid frustration. Lead-free gasoline, known as "Natural," is still available only at select stations, so tank up when you see it.

Breakdowns For accidents, call the emergency number (tel. 155). In case of an auto breakdown, in Bratislava contact the 24-hour service (tel. 07/363711). The *Auto Atlas ČSFR* (available at any bookstore) has a list of emergency road-repair numbers in various towns.

By Train Train service is erratic to all but the largest cities—**Poprad, Prešov, Košice,** and **Banská Bystrica.** Good, if slow, electric rail service, however, connects Poprad with the resorts of the **High Tatras.** If you're going just to the Tatras, you won't need any other kind of transportation.

By Bus Bus service in Bratislava is very cheap and reasonably frequent, and you can use it with confidence to reach any of the places in the tours below. You may have trouble reading the detailed information on the timetable, so try to ask if you're not sure where a particular bus is headed.

The **CSAD** bus network in Slovakia is dense, linking all of the towns on the tours given here. Leave a couple of extra days, however, to compensate for the infrequent service to the smaller towns.

Staying in Slovakia

Telephones These cost 1 Sk from a pay phone. Lift the receiver, place the *Local Calls* coin in the holder, dial, and insert the coin when your party picks up. Public phones are located in metro stations and on street corners; unfortunately, they're often out of order. Try asking in a hotel if you're stuck.

International Calls You'll pay an enormous surcharge if you make calls from your hotel. There's automatic dialing to many countries, including North America and the United Kingdom. For international inquiries, dial 0132 for the United States, Canada, or the United Kingdom. ATT's USADirect number for Slovakia is 004200010.

Mail Airmail letters to the United States and Canada cost 11 Sk up *Postal Rates* to 10 grams, postcards 6 Sk. Airmail letters to the United Kingdom cost 8 Sk up to 20 grams, postcards 5 Sk.

Receiving Mail Mail can be sent to Poste Restante at any main post office; there's no charge to claim it.

Opening and **Banks** are open weekdays 8–3. **Museums** are usually open **Closing Times** Tues.–Sun. 10–5. **Shops** are generally open weekdays 9–6 (Thurs. 9–8); some close between noon and 2. Many are also open Sat. 9–noon (department stores, 9–4).

National Holidays January 1; April 4 (Easter Monday); May 9 (Liberation Day); July 5; December 25, 26.

Dining If you prepay your hotel through the **Czech and Slovak Travel Bureau and Tourist Office (Čedok)**, try to avoid being stuck with meal vouchers. With few Čedok-run hotels left, these are only a frustration. For meals not limited by vouchers, you can choose among restaurants, wine cellars, the more down-to-earth beer taverns, cafeterias, and a growing number of coffee shops and snack bars. Most restaurants are remarkably reasonable, but privatization is beginning to push up prices in a few places.

The most typical main dish is roast pork (or duck or goose) with sauerkraut. Dumplings in various forms, generally with a rich gravy, accompany many dishes. Peppers are frequently used as well to spice up bland entrées. Look for *haluški*, a tasty Slovak noodle dish, usually served with sheep cheese. Fresh green vegetables and salads are still rare, but there are plenty of the pickled variety.

Mealtimes Lunch is usually from 11:30 to 2 or 3; dinner from 6 to 9:30 or 10. Some places are open all day, and in Bratislava you might find it easier to find a table during off hours.

Ratings Prices are reasonable by American standards, even in the more expensive restaurants. The following prices are for meals made up of a first course, main course, and dessert (excluding wine and tip). Best bets are indicated by a star ★.

Category	Cost
Very Expensive	over 600 Sk
Expensive	400 Sk–600 Sk
Moderate	200 Sk–400 Sk
Inexpensive	under 200 Sk

Lodging Travelers to Slovakia can choose from among hotels, motels, private accommodations, and campsites. Many older properties are gradually being renovated, and the best have great character and style. There is still an acute shortage of hotel rooms during the peak season, so make reservations well in advance. Many private room agencies are now in operation, and as long as you arrive before 9 PM, you should be able to get a room. The standards of facilities and services hardly match those in the West, so don't be surprised by faulty plumbing or indifferent reception clerks.

Hotels These are officially graded with from one to five stars. Many hotels used by foreign visitors—Interhotels—belong to Čedok and are mainly in the three- to five-star categories. These will have all or some rooms with bath or shower. Čedok can also handle reservations for some non-Čedok hotels, such as those run by Balnea (the spa treatment organization); CKM (the Youth Travel Bureau); and municipal organizations, some of which are excellent.

Hotel bills can be paid in crowns, though some hotels try to insist on hard currency.

Private Accommodations Čedok can help you find a private room in Bratislava and other larger cities. These accommodations are invariably cheaper (around $20) and often more comfortable than hotels, though you may have to sacrifice something in privacy. You can also wander the main roads looking for signs declaring "Room Free," or more frequently, in German, "Zimmer Frei" or "Privatzimmer."

Rates Prices are for double rooms, generally not including breakfast. Prices at the lower end of the scale apply to low season. At certain periods, such as Easter or during festivals, there may be an increase of 15%–25%. Best bets are indicated by a star ★.

Category	Cost
Very Expensive	over $100
Expensive	$50–$100
Moderate	$15–$50
Inexpensive	under $15

Tipping Small sums of hard currency will certainly be most welcome. To reward good service in a restaurant, round up the bill to the nearest multiple of 10; 10% is considered appropriate on very large tabs. Tip porters who bring bags to your rooms 20 Sk. For room service, a 20 Sk tip is enough. In taxis, round up the bill by 10%. Give tour guides and helpful concierges between 20 Sk and 30 Sk for services rendered.

Bratislava

Arriving and Departing

By Plane The most convenient international airport for Bratislava is in Vienna, approximately 50 kilometers (30 miles) away. Four buses a day stop at Schwechat en route to Bratislava, or you could even take a taxi; the journey takes just over an hour, depending on the border crossing. From Prague's Ruzyně Airport you can take a ČSA domestic flight to Bratislava for less than 1,000 Sk; the flight takes about an hour.

If time is a factor during your stay in Slovakia, flying may be an option to consider for reaching the relatively far-flung Tatras and eastern Slovakia. ČSA has reasonably priced daily flights from Prague to Poprad (the regional airport for the Tatras) and flies twice daily from Prague to Košice via Bratislava. For further information, contact the ČSA offices in Prague (tel. 02/2146), Poprad (tel. 092/24190), or Košice (tel. 095/22578).

By Train Reasonably efficient train service connects Prague and Bratislava. Trains leave from Prague's main station (Hlavní nádraží, and the journey takes five hours. There are four trains a day to and from Vienna, with the journey lasting just over an hour.

By Bus There are numerous buses from Prague to Bratislava; the journey costs less than 200 Sk and takes about five hours. From Vienna, there are four buses a day from Autobusbahnhof Wien Mitte. The journey takes between 1½ and two hours. The **Autobus Stanica** in Bratislava is just outside the center; you can take trolleybus No. 217 to Mierové námestie or bus No. 107 to the Castle (Hrad).

By Car There are good freeways from Prague to Bratislava via Brno (D1 and D2); the 315-kilometer (203-mile) journey takes about 3½ hours. From Vienna, take the A4 and then Route 8 to Bratislava. The 60-kilometer (37-mile) trip will take about 1½ hours.

Getting Around

By Car Bratislava is not a good city for drivers, and finding a parking space can be a problem; hence, for touring the republic's capital, walking is the best option. If you do need to rent a car, you can do so either at Čedok or at the Hotel Forum.

By Bus Bus service in Bratislava is very cheap and reasonably frequent, and you can use it with confidence to reach any of the main sights.

Important Addresses and Numbers

Tourist Information Bratislava has its own tourist information service, **Bratislavská informačná a propagačná služba (BIPS)** (Laurinska ul. 1, 81101, tel. 07/33715 or 07/334370). The office is in a corner building a few steps down from Hlavné námestie 4, in the direction of the river. It's open weekdays 8–4:30 (8–6 in summer) and Saturday 8–1. The **Čedok** office (Jesenského 5, tel. 07/52002; open weekdays 9–6, Sat. 9–noon) can help with accommodations and provide information on Bratislava and surrounding areas.

Emergencies **Police:** tel. 158. **Ambulance:** tel. 155.

Late-night Pharmacies Pharmacies *(lekárna)* take turns staying open late or on Sunday. Look for the list posted on the front door of each pharmacy. For after-hours service, ring the bell; you will be served through a little hatch-door.

Guided Tours

The best tours of Bratislava are offered by **BIPS** (*see* Tourist Information, *above*), although out of the summer season they are given only in German and only on weekends. These tours start at 2 PM at the National Theater; they last two hours and cost 270 Sk per person. Čedok offers tours from May through September on Wednesday and Saturday, starting at 1:45 from the Devin Hotel (Riečna ul. 4, tel. 07/330851). You can combine these with an afternoon tour of the Small Carpathians (departing at 4:45 PM, also from the Devin), which includes dinner at the Zochová Chata. Čedok can also arrange an individual guide at a cost of around 150 Sk.

Exploring Bratislava

Many visitors are disappointed by **Bratislava.** Expecting a Slovak version of Prague, they discover instead a rather shabby city that seems to embody more the previous regime's blind faith in modernity than the stormy history of this once Hungarian and now Slovak capital. Originally settled by a variety of Celts and Romans, the city became part of the Great Moravian Empire under Prince Břetislav. After a short period under the Bohemian Přemysl princes, Bratislava was brought into the

Hungarian kingdom by Stephan I at the end of the 10th century. The Hungarians called it Pozsony; the German settlers, Pressburg; and the original Slovaks called it Bratislava after Prince Břetislav.

Numbers in the margin correspond to points of interest on the Bratislava map.

❶ Begin your tour of the city at the modern square **Námestie SNP.** An abbreviation for *Slovenské Národné Povstanie* (Slovak National Uprising), these three letters appear on streets, squares, bridges, and posters throughout Slovakia. This anti-Nazi resistance movement involved partisan fighting, organized partly but not exclusively by the Communists, in Slovakia's mountainous areas during the final years of the war. In 1992 this was the center for demonstrations in support of Slovak independence, and you will often see the Slovak flag (red, blue, and white with a double cross) flying from the partisan's gun.

❷ From here walk up toward **Hurbanovo námestie.** Across the road, unobtrusively located between a large shoe store and a bookshop, is the enchanting entrance to the old town. A small bridge, decorated with wrought-iron railings and statues of St. John Nepomuk and St. Michael, takes you over the old mote, now blossoming with trees and fountains, into the intricate barbican, a set of gates and houses that made up the medieval fortifications. After going through the first archway, you come **❸** to the narrow **Michalská ulica;** in front of you is the **Michalská brána** (Michael's Gate), the last remaining of the original three city gates.

❹ A little farther down Michalská ulica on the right is the **Palác Uhorskej kráľ'ovskej komory** (Hungarian Royal Chamber), a Baroque palace that housed the Hungarian nobles' parliament from 1802 until 1848; it is now used as the University Library. Go through the arched passageway at the back of this building, and you'll emerge in a tiny square dominated by the **Church and Convent of the Poor Clares.**

Follow Farská ulica up to the corner, and turn left on **Kapitulská ulica,** noticing the ground stone depicting two kissing lizards. At the bottom of the street is the side wall of the **❺** **Dóm svätého Martina** (St. Martin's Cathedral). Construction of this massive plain Gothic church, with its 280-foot steeple twinkling with gold trim, began in the 14th century. Between the 16th and 19th centuries, the Cathedral saw the coronation of 17 Hungarian royals. You can enter the church through a door on this side (Kapitulská ulica). The peace is disturbed by the noise of traffic zooming by on the elevated freeway built in the 1970s across the front entrance, reducing the church to an irrelevant religious relic.

❻ As you leave the church and walk around to the front, the freeway leading to the futuristic spaceship bridge, **Most SNP,** is the first thing you see. Follow the steps under the passageway and up the other side in the direction of the Castle.

Time Out At the top of the wood stairs, you come to the **Arkadia** restaurant and café, one of Bratislava's better private establishments, situated in a beautiful old house. Here you can get good coffee and desserts or a full meal before the ascent to the castle.

Dóm Sv. Martina, **5**
Hrad, **7**
Hurbanovo
námestie, **2**
Jezuitský Kostol, **9**
Michalská Brána, **3**
Most SNP, **6**
Námestie SNP, **1**
Palác Uhorskej
Kráľovskej Komory, **4**
Primaciálny Palác, **11**
Stará Radnica, **10**
Židovská Ulica, **8**

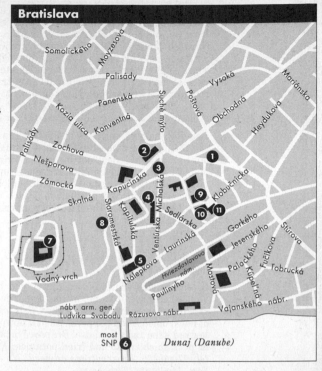

Bratislava

Continue up the steps, through a Gothic arched gateway built in 1480, until you reach the **Hrad** (castle) area. The original fortifications date from the 9th century. The Hungarian kings expanded the castle into a large royal residence, and the Habsburgs turned it into a very successful defense against the Turks. Its current design, square with four corner towers, stems from the 17th century, although the existing castle had to be completely rebuilt after a disastrous fire in 1811. In the castle, you'll find the **Slovenské národné múzeum** (Slovak National Museum). The exhibits cover glassmaking, medieval warfare, and coinmaking. *Zámocká ul., tel. 07/311444. Admission: 40 Sk. adults, 10 Sk. children and students. Open Tues.– Sun., 10–5.*

Leave the castle by the same route, but instead of climbing the last stairs by the Arkadia restaurant, continue down the old-world Beblaveho ulica. Continue along **Židovská ulica.** The name, Jews' Street, marks this area as the former Jewish ghetto. Walk up Židovská until you come to a thin concrete bridge that connects with the reconstructed city walls across the freeway.

Across the road you'll find steps leading down into the Old Town. Go through the Františkánske námestie into the adjoining square, **Hlavné námestie,** which is lined with old houses and palaces representing the spectrum of architectural styles from Gothic (No. 2), through Baroque (No. 4) and Rococo (No. 7), to a wonderfully decorative example of Art Nouveau at No. 10. To your immediate left as you come into the square is the richly decorated **Jezuitský kostol** (Jesuit Church). Next door is the

colorful agglomeration of old bits and pieces that makes up the
⑩ **Stará radnica** (Old Town Hall). The imaginative roofing stems
from the end of the 15th century, and the wall paintings from
the 16th century. Walk through the arched passageway, still
with early Gothic ribbing, into a wonderfully cheery Renaissance courtyard with romantic arcades and gables. Toward the
back of the courtyard, you'll find the entrance to the **Mestské
múzeum** (City Museum), which documents Bratislava's varied
past. *Primaciálne nám., tel. 07/334690. Admission: 4 Sk.
adults, 1 Sk. children and students. Open Tues.–Sun. 10–5.*

Leaving the back entrance of the Old Town Hall, you come to
the **Primaciálne námestie** (Primates' Square), with the glori-
⑪ ous pale pink, classical elegance of the **Primaciálny palác** (Primates' Palace). If the building is open, go up to the dazzling hall
of mirrors. In this room, Napoleon and Habsburg Emperor
Franz I signed the Bratislava Peace of 1805, following
Napoleon's victory at the Battle of Austerlitz.

Dining

For details and price-category definitions, *see* Dining in Staying in Slovakia, *above*.

★ **Klaštorná vináreň.** Old-town dining can be a delight in the
vaulted cellars of this old monastery. The spiciness of Slovak
cooking comes alive in dishes like *Čikós tokáň,* a fiery mixture
of pork, onions, and peppers. Wash it down with a glass of mellow red wine and a fire hose. *Bravcové ražníci* is milder, a tender pork shish kebab and fried potatoes. *Františkanská ul. 1,
tel. 07/330430. Reservations advised. No credit cards. Closed
Sun. Moderate–Expensive.*
Rybársky cech. The name means "Fishermen's Guild," and this
restaurant, which has Bratislava's smartest interior, is in the
guild house on the river embankment below the castle. It's really two restaurants in one: freshwater fish is served upstairs;
pricier saltwater varieties are offered on the ground floor.
*Žižkova ul. 1, tel. 07/313049. Reservations advised. No credit
cards. Closed Sat. Moderate–Expensive.*
Modrá Hviezda. The first of a new breed of small, privately
owned wine cellars, the "Blue Star" eschews the international
standards in favor of regional Slovak fare. Be sure to try the
bryndza (baked sheep-cheese) pie and the tasty goulash.
*Beblavého 14, tel. 07/332747. Reservations advised. No credit
cards. Moderate.*
Michalská. This light, airy luncheon restaurant, with an adjacent stand-up buffet, is situated in a convenient spot in the
heart of the old town. Soup, *halušky* (noodles with sheep
cheese), and salad make a meal fit for a king. *Michalská ul. 1,
tel. 07/332389. Reservations not necessary. No credit cards.
Inexpensive.*
Stará Sladovňa. This mammoth beer hall in known lovingly, and
fittingly, as "Mamut" to Bratislavans. Locals come here for the
Bohemian beer on tap and for inexpensive, filling meals. The
place seats almost 2,000, so don't worry about reservations.
Cintorínska ul. 32, tel. 07/51101. No credit cards. Inexpensive.

Lodging

For details and price-category definitions, *see* Lodging in Staying in Slovakia, *above*.

Forum Bratislava. The Forum opened in 1989 in downtown Bratislava, offering top facilities. It houses a French as well as a Slovak restaurant and several cafés and bars. *Mierove námestie 2, tel. 07/348111, fax 07/314645. 219 rooms with bath. Facilities: nightclub, saunas, pool, solarium, health club. AE, DC, MC, V. Very Expensive.*

★ **Danube.** Opened in 1992 to rival the Forum in atmosphere and services. The latter may retain an overall edge, but the Danube, at approximately two-thirds the price, is the better value for the money. The Danube also wins hands down on location—alongside the river, with a stunning view of the castle out the front door. *Rybné námestie 1, tel. 07/55355, fax 07/50218. 280 rooms with bath. Facilities: restaurants, nightclub, health club, pool, sauna, solarium. AE, DC, MC, V. Expensive.*

Devin (Interhotel). This modern hotel has a good location by the Danube and provides a view of the castle. Its café and various restaurants are pleasant, but the rooms are a disappointment. *Riečna ul. 4, tel. 07/330852 or 07/330854. 93 rooms, 87 with bath. Facilities: 3 restaurants, nightclub. AE, DC, MC, V. Expensive.*

Highlights of Slovakia

Most visitors head for the great peaks of the High Tatras, with their excellent tourist facilities; and this is where most tours will take you. The mountains *are* spectacular, but also worth seeing are the exquisite medieval towns of Spiš in the plains and valleys below the High Tatras and the beautiful 18th-century country churches farther east. Away from main centers, these areas are short on tourist amenities, so if creature comforts are important to you, stick to the Tatras.

Getting Around

By Plane ČSA's 40-minute flights from Bratislava to Poprad connect with services from Prague once or twice daily and are very reasonable.

By Train Train service is erratic to all but the largest cities—**Poprad, Prešov, Košice,** and **Banská Bystrica.** (Bratislava to Poprad by express train takes four hours.) Good, if slow, electric rail service, however, connects Poprad with the resorts of the **High Tatras.** If you're going just to the Tatras, you won't need any other kind of transportation.

By Bus The ČSAD bus network is dense, linking all of the towns mentioned Exploring Slovakia, *below.* Leave a couple of extra days, however, to compensate for infrequent service to smaller towns. Consult local timetables or the ČSAD office in Bratislava for specific information.

Guided Tours

Čedok's seven-day **Grand Tour of Slovakia,** which leaves from Bratislava every other Saturday from June through September, stops in the High Tatras, Kežmarok, Košice, and Banská Bystrica. The tour includes all meals and accommodations. For more information, contact the Čedok office in Bratislava (tel. 07/55280).

The Tatras and Eastern Slovakia

Slovair offers a novel biplane flight over the Tatras from Poprad airport. Contact the Čedok office in Poprad (tel. 092/23651). The Čedok office in Starý Smokovec (tel. 0969/2417) is also help-ful in arranging tours of the Tatras and the surrounding area.

Tourist Information

Bardejov (Nám. Osloboditeľov 46, tel. 0935/2134).
Bratislava (Štúrova 13, tel. 07/55280).
Prešov (Hlavná ul. 1, tel. 091/24040).
Smokovec (Starý Smokovec V/22, tel. 0969/24174).
Žilina (Hodžova ul. 9, tel. 089/23347).

Exploring Slovakia

Despite its charms, there's no denying that Bratislava is in-tensely industrial. If you're not going on to the mountains and fresh air of the High Tatras (*see below*), a good one- or two-day natural respite can be had less than an hour north of the city, in the **Malé Karpaty** (Small Carpathian) mountains. Drive or take the bus to the dusty wine-making town of **Modra,** and from there, follow the signs to **Zochová Chata,** some 8 kilometers (5 miles) away in the hills. The *chata* is really a cozy mountain cha-let, with big rooms, plenty of period furniture, and a romantic *koliba* (tavern) that serves the best roast chicken in Slovakia. Trails fan out in all directions from the chata. For a full day's walk, follow the yellow-marked path about three hours to the Renaissance castle **Červený Kameň** ("red rock"). The blue-marked path will take you back to Zochová Chata.

Whether you travel by car, bus, or train, your route will follow the Vah Valley for most of the way to **Poprad,** a transit point for Slovakia's most magnificent natural treasure, the High Tatras. While Poprad itself is a dreary place, its suburb of **Spišská Sobota,** reached by bus Nos. 2, 3, or 4, is, however, a little gem. It was one of 24 small Gothic towns in a medieval region known as **Spiš.** Steep shingled roofs, high timberframed gables, and brick-arched doorways are the main features of the rich merchants' dwelling, usually grouped around a main square dominated by a Gothic church, often with a separate Renaissance bell tower. Keep in mind the name Pavol of Levoča, one of the great woodcarvers of the 16th century. The main altar in **Sv. Juraj** (the Church of St. George) is his work. The **museum** is worth a visit. *Admission: 4 Sk. Open Mon.–Sat. 9–4.*

Both an electric train network and a winding highway link Poprad with the resorts spread about on the lower slopes of the High Tatras. **Štrbské Pleso** is the highest of the towns and the best launching point for mountain excursions. A rewarding two-hour trek of moderate difficulty leads from here to **Popradské Pleso,** one of dozens of tiny, isolated Alpine lakes that dot the Tatras. **Smokovec** is really three resorts in one (Starý, Nový, and Horný) and has the most varied amenities. For the most effortless high-level trip, though, go to **Tatranská Lomnica,** from which a two-stage cable car will take you via Skalnaté Pleso to Lomnický štít, which at 8,635 feet high is the second-highest peak in the range. From Skalnaté Pleso, you can take the red-marked Magistrale trail down to **Hrebienok,** where you can board a funicular and ride down to Stary Smokovec. The **Museum of the Tatra National Park** at Tatranská Lomnica offers an excellent introduction to the area's natural and human history. *Admission: 6 Sk, 2 Sk for children. Open weekdays 8:30–noon and 1–5, weekends 8–noon.*

Leave Poprad on Highway 18 east. Restoration work on **Levoča,** the most famous of the Spiš towns, is well under way, and the overlays of Renaissance on Gothic are extremely satisfying to the eye (note especially Nos. 43, 45, 47, and 49 on the main square). Pavol of Levoča's work on the main altar of **Sv. Jakub** (the Church of St. James) on the main square is both monumental in size and exquisite in its detail.

The surrounding countryside is dotted with more medieval towns. About 16 kilometers (10 miles) to the east, the massive, partly restored ruins of **Spiš Castle,** above Spišské Podhradie, dominate the surrounding pastures and orchards. Some of **Prešov's** fortifications survive, and its spindle-shaped main square is lined with buildings in the Gothic, Renaissance, and Baroque styles. You have now left Spiš and entered **Šariš,** a region whose proximity to the Orthodox east has left a unique legacy of both Orthodox and Greek Catholic (Uniate) churches. The Uniates are particularly interesting because, though they acknowledge the pope's supremacy, they have retained their own litergy and their clergy are permitted to marry.

Bardejov is a splendid walled town and makes the best center from which to set out on a journey of exploration, as long as you're prepared to get lost along some rough minor roads while seeking out the 17th- and 18th-century wooden churches of **Bodružal, Ladomirová, Mirola,** and **Šemetkovce**—and the right person to open them up for you. You'll find these churches east

and northeast of **Svidník,** near the border with Poland (follow
the road to the Dukla Pass). These churches jostle for attention
with the dramatic collection of Nazi and Soviet tanks and
planes dotted around this area to commemorate the fighting
that took place in 1944. Easier to find is the 15th-century
church of **Hvervartov** (Roman Catholic), 10 kilometers (6 miles)
southwest of Bardejov—a fascinating example of timber Gothic
with some famous 17th-century frescoes.

Dining and Lodging

For details and price-category definitions, *see* Dining and
Lodging in Staying in Slovakia, *above.*

Bardejov   **Minerál.** This rather sterile modern hotel lies in a quiet location
Lodging   in the spa town of Bardejovské kúpele, 3½ miles from Bardejov
proper. *Bardejovské kúpele, tel. 0935/4122. 60 rooms with
shower. Facilities: tennis courts. No credit cards. Moderate.*

Smokovec   **Tatranská kúria.** The Tatranská's rustic decor and Slovak spe-
Dining   cialties will provide some insight into local life. Dishes include
rezeň kúria (pork cutlets with a cheese and ham filling in a
cheese pastry) and *bryndzové pirohy* (cheese-filled pastry
served with cream and bacon). *Starý Smokovec, tel. 0969/2806.
Reservations not necessary. No credit cards. Closes early.
Moderate.*

Lodging   **Bellevue.** This modern high rise with well-appointed rooms lies
about 200 yards from the resort center. Rates include breakfast and dinner. *Horný Smokovec, tel. 0969/2941. 103 rooms, 63
with bath. Facilities: saunas, pool. AE, DC, MC, V. Expensive.*
Grand Hotel. The town's oldest hotel has a wonderful air of
faded fin-de-siècle elegance. It's right in the resort center,
with a reasonable restaurant. Rooms without bath are Moderate. *Starý Smokovec, tel. 0969/2154. 83 rooms, some with bath.
Facilities: restaurant, nightclub, pool, sauna. AE, DC, MC,
V. Expensive.*
Villa Dr. Szontagh. Away from the action in Nový Smokovec,
this steepled chalet, formerly known as the Tokájík, offers
mostly peace and quiet. The darkly furnished rooms and public
areas are well maintained, and the courtly staff goes out of its
way to please. *Nový Smokovec, tel. 0969/2061. 11 rooms with
bath. Facilities: restaurant, wine cellar. Breakfast not included. No credit cards. Moderate.*

Tatranská   **Zboujnícka koliba.** This tavern offers a small range of Slovak
Lomnica   specialties prepared over an open fire, amid rustic decor and
Dining   accompanied by folk music. *Near Grandhotel Praha, tel. 0969/
967630. Reservations not necessary. No credit cards. Dinner
only. Closed Sun. Moderate.*

Lodging   **Grandhotel Praha.** A renovated turn-of-the-century building,
the Grandhotel has large, comfortable rooms decorated with a
traditional touch. The restaurant has an air of elegance that is
unusual in Slovakia. *Tel. 0969/967941. 92 rooms with bath. Facilities: restaurant, nightclub. AE, DC, MC, V. Expensive.*

26 Spain

Spain has long had a rather schizophrenic reputation as a vacation destination among English-speaking tourists. On the one hand, as Europe's premier package-vacation destination, the country is almost instinctively associated in many minds with the worst excesses of the cheap-holiday-in-the-sun, an image conjured up by the vast numbers of faceless hotels along the Mediterranean coasts. The other half of the equation is infinitely more appealing. For Spain is also the land of the fountain-singing courtyards of Moorish Granada and Córdoba, of dusty plains where Don Quixote fought imaginary enemies, and of timeless hilltop towns. Spain also acquired a new gloss on the international scene in 1992, when it played host to two major events of world stature: the Olympic Games in Barcelona, and the International Exposition in Seville. Both events brought with them major face-lifts to the cities and regions hosting them, as well as quite dramatic improvements to their infrastructures.

Still, if it's beaches you're after, there is the jet-set Costa del Sol in the south, or San Sebastián in the Basque country, formerly the summer capital of Spain. Farther west is the resort city of Santander and La Coruña, a long-standing favorite of British visitors. In the east is the Costa Brava, while to the south, around Alicante, is the Costa Blanca, with its most popular tourist center at Benidorm. When you tire of roasting in the sun, rent a car and head for one of the thousands of castles, ruins, or museums. Perhaps the number-one tourist attraction is the Alhambra, in Granada. Following close behind it come the Mosque of Córdoba, and the Alcázar and cathedral of Seville. Ávila is a historic walled town and Segovia boasts a Roman aqueduct and proud Alcázar. Madrid, the capital, contains some of the greatest art collections in the world, while Toledo, home of El Greco and boasting a cathedral, synagogues, and startling views, is one of Spain's greatest treasures. Finally, Barcelona, capital of Catalonia, has a charm and vitality quite its own.

Essential Information

Before You Go

When to Go The tourist season runs from Easter to mid-October. The best months for sightseeing are May, June, September, and early October, when the weather is usually pleasant and sunny without being unbearably hot. During July and August try to avoid Madrid or the inland cities of Andalusia, where the heat can be stifling and many places close down at 1 PM. If you visit Spain in high summer, the best bet is to head for the coastal resorts or to mountain regions such as the Pyrenees or Picos de Europa. The one exception to Spain's high summer temperatures is the north coast, where the climate is similar to that of northern Europe.

Visitors should be aware of the seasonal events that can clog parts of the country, reserving in advance if traveling during peak periods. Easter is always a busy time, especially in Madrid, Barcelona, and the main Andalusian cities of Seville, Córdoba, Granada, Málaga, and the Costa del Sol resorts. July and August, when most Spaniards and other Europeans take their annual vacations, see the heaviest crowds, particularly in coastal resorts. Holiday weekends are naturally busy, and major fiestas, such as

Pamplona's bull runnings, make advance booking essential and cause prices to soar. Off-season travel offers fewer crowds and lower rates in many hotels.

Climate The following are the average daily maximum and minimum temperatures for Madrid.

Jan.	47F	9C	May	70F	21C	Sept.	77F	25C
	35	2		50	10		57	14
Feb.	52F	11C	June	80F	27C	Oct.	65F	18C
	36	2		58	15		49	10
Mar.	59F	15C	July	87F	31C	Nov.	55F	13C
	41	5		63	17		42	5
Apr.	65F	18C	Aug.	85F	30C	Dec.	48F	9C
	45	7		63	17		36	2

Currency The unit of currency in Spain is the peseta. There are bills of 500, 1,000, 2,000, 5,000, and 10,000 ptas. Coins are 1 pta., 5, 25, 50, 100, 200, and 500 ptas. The 2- and 10-pta. coins and the old 100-pta. bills are rare but still legal tender. Note that pay phones in Spain won't accept the new, smaller 5- and 25-pta. coins first minted in 1991. Following the recent European currency shakeup, which resulted in several devaluations of the peseta, most foreigners find that their currency now goes farther in Spain than it had in recent years. At press time (spring 1993), the exchange rate was about 124. 8 ptas. to the U.S. dollar and 189. 7 ptas. to the pound sterling.

Credit Cards Most hotels, restaurants, and stores (though not gas stations) accept payment by credit card. Visa is the most widely accepted piece of plastic, followed by MasterCard (called Euro-Card in Spain). More expensive establishments may also take American Express and Diners Club.

Changing Money The word to look for is "Cambio" (exchange). Most Spanish banks take a 1½% commission, though some less scrupulous places charge more; always check, as rates can vary greatly. To change money in a bank, you need your passport and a lot of patience, because filling out the forms takes time. Hotels offer rates lower than banks, but they rarely make a commission, so you may well break even. Restaurants and stores, with the exception of those catering to the tour bus trade, do not usually accept payment by dollars or traveler's checks. If you have a credit card with a Personal Identification Number (PIN), you'll be able to make withdrawals or get cash advances at most cash machines at Spanish banks.

Currency Regulations Visitors may take any amount of foreign currency in bills or traveler's checks into Spain as well as any amount of pesetas. When leaving Spain, you may take out only 100,000 ptas. per person in Spanish bank notes and foreign currency up to the equivalent of 500,000 ptas, unless you can prove you declared the excess at customs on entering the country.

What It Will Cost Prices rose fast during the first decade of Spain's democracy, and Spain's inflation rate was one of the highest in Europe. By the 1990s, however, inflation had been curbed; in 1993, it was just a little over 5%. Generally speaking, the cost of living in Spain is now on a par with that of most other European countries, and the days when Spain was the bargain basement of Europe are truly over, although the weakness of the peseta has somewhat improved the buying power of visitors from North

Spain

El Ferrol
La Coruña
Villalba
Ribadeo
Luarca
Gijón
Ribadesella
Santander
Bay of Biscay
Santiago de Compostela
Lugo
Oviedo
Mieres
Cangas de Onis
PICOS DE EUROPA
Bilbao
Muros
Pontevedra
Orense
CANTABRIAN MTS.
Ponferrada
Astorga
León
Burgos
Lo
Vigo
Tui/Túy
Benavente
Palencia
Valladolid
Duero
Zamora
Tordesillas
Salamanca
Adanero
Segovia
SIERRA DE GUADARR
Ciudad Rodrigo
Avila
El Escorial
SIERRA DE GUADARP
Guadala
MADRID
PORTUGAL
Plasencia
SIERRA DE GREDOS
Toledo
Talavera de la Reina
Aranjuez
T
Tajo
Guadalupe
Alcázar de San Juan
Cáceres
Trujillo
Mérida
Guadiana
Abenójar
Ciudad Real
Valdepeñas
Badajoz
Almadén
Zafra
Jerez de los Caballeros
Fregenal de la Sierra
SIERRA MORENA
Córdoba
Bailén
Linares
Ub
Aroche
Baeza
Jaén
Seville
Guadalquivir
Ecija
Baena
Guadix
Carmona
Lucena
Granada
SIERRA
Huelva
Antequera
Loja
Gulf of Cadiz
Sanlúcar de Barrameda
Ronda
Nerja
COSTA DE LA LUZ
Cádiz
Jerez de la Frontera
Torremolinos
Málaga
Motril
ATLANTIC OCEAN
Estepona
Fuengirola
Marbella
COSTA DEL SOL
TO CANARY ISLANDS
Algeciras
Gibraltar
Strait of Gibraltar

America and the U.K. The 1992 completion of the country's integration into the European Community (EC) and the euphoria accompanying the Olympic games and Seville's Expo '92 were, unfortunately, accompanied by sometimes shocking price increases. These have been reversed to a certain extent, though Seville and Barcelona are still quite expensive. In general, the cost of lodging is roughly comparable to that in France and Great Britain. You can still eat fairly cheaply in Spain, but if you go to quality restaurants, it will cost you dearly; in general, the cost of eating out rose about 5% in 1993. Snacks in cafés and bars are expensive by American or British standards, and alcohol is generally reasonable, except for cocktails in hotel bars. Trains and long-distance buses are relatively inexpensive, and car-rental rates are lower than in some European countries. City buses and subways are a good value, and cab fares are bargains compared with rates in the United States.

Taxes A value-added tax known as IVA was introduced in 1986 when Spain joined the European Community (EC). IVA is levied at 6% on most goods and services, but a luxury rate of 15% applies to four- and five-star hotels and to car rental. IVA is always included in the purchase price of goods in stores, but for hotels and car rentals, the tax will be added to your bill. Many restaurants include IVA in their menu prices, but plenty—usually the more expensive ones—do not. Large stores, such as the Corte Inglés and Galerías Preciados, operate a tax refund plan for foreign visitors who are not EC nationals; but to qualify for this refund, you need to spend at least 48,000 ptas. in any one store and, in theory, on any one item. There is no airport tax in Spain.

Sample Prices A cup of coffee will cost around 100 ptas., a Coca-Cola 130 ptas., bottled beer 120–150 ptas., a small draught beer 100 ptas., a glass of wine in a bar 80 ptas., an American-style cocktail 350 ptas., a ham sandwich 250 ptas., an ice-cream cone about 100 ptas., a local bus or subway ride 100 ptas.–125 ptas., and a one-mile taxi ride about 400 ptas.

Language In major cities and coastal resorts you should have no trouble finding people who speak English. In such places, reception staff in hotels of three or more stars are required to speak English. Don't expect the man in the street or the bus driver to speak English, although you may be pleasantly surprised.

Getting Around

By Car Roads marked A *(autopista)* are toll roads. N stands for national or main roads, and C for country roads. A huge road improvement scheme has been largely completed, but many N roads are still single-lane and the going can be slow. Tolls vary but are high; for example, Bilbao–Zaragoza 2,930 ptas., Salou–Valencia 2,065 ptas., Seville–Jerez 585 ptas.

Road Conditions

Rules of the Road Driving is on the right, and horns and high-beam headlights may not be used in cities. Front seat belts are compulsory on the highway but not in cities (except the M30 Madrid ring road). Children may not ride in front seats. At traffic circles, give way to traffic coming from the right unless your road has priority. Your home driving license is essential and must be carried with you at all times, along with your car insurance and vehicle registration document. You will also need an International Driving License and a Green Card if you are bringing your own car into Spain. Speed limits are 120 kph (74 mph) on autopistas, 100 kph (62 mph) on N roads, 90 kph (56 mph) on C roads, and 60 kph (37 mph) in cities unless otherwise signed.

Parking Parking restrictions should be checked locally. In many cities, a blue line on the street indicates residents-only parking; other cars are towed promptly. In other places, curbside signs inform you of legal parking times. Never leave *anything* on view inside a parked car. Thefts are common, and it is safer to leave your car in one of the many paying parking lots; charges are reasonable.

Gasoline At press time, gas cost 99 ptas. a liter for super and 97 ptas. a liter for regular. Unleaded gas *(sin plomo)* is now available at a steadily increasing number of pumps. There is attendant service at most pumps, but there's no need to tip for just a fill-up. Few gas stations accept payment by credit card.

By Train The Spanish railroad system, known usually by its initials RENFE, has greatly improved in recent years. Air-conditioned trains are now widespread but by no means universal. Most overnight trains have first- and second-class sleeping cars and second-class *literas* (couchettes). Dining, buffet, and refreshment services are available on most long-distance trains. There are various types of trains—*talgo*, ELT (electric unit expresses), TER (diesel rail cars), and ordinary *expresos* and *rápidos*. Fares are determined by the kind of train you travel on and not just by the distance traveled. Talgos are by far the quickest, most comfortable, and the most expensive train; *expresos* and *rápidos* are the slowest and cheapest of the long-distance services. In spring 1992, a high-speed train known as the AVE (Alto Velocidad Español) began service between Madrid and Seville, reducing travel time between these cities from six to two and a half hours (fares vary, but the AVE can cost almost as much as flying). A few lines, such as the narrow-gauge FEVE routes along the north coast from San Sebastián to El Ferrol and on the Costa Blanca around Alicante, do not belong to the national RENFE network, and international rail passes are not valid on these lines.

Ticket Purchase and Seat Reservation Tickets can be bought from any station (whether or not it is your point of departure), and from downtown RENFE offices and travel agents displaying the blue and yellow RENFE sign. The latter are often best in the busy holiday season. At stations, buy your advance tickets from the window marked "Largo Recorrido, Venta Anticipada" (Long Distance, Advance Sales). Seat reservation can be made up to 60 days in advance and is obligatory on all the better long-distance services.

Fare Savers The **RENFE Tourist Card** is an unlimited-kilometers pass, valid for 8, 15, or 22 days' travel, and can be bought by anyone who lives outside Spain. It is available for first- or second-class travel and can be purchased from RENFE's General Representative in Europe (3 Ave. Marceau, 75116 Paris, France, tel. 14/723–52–00); from selected travel agencies and main railroad stations abroad; and within Spain, at RENFE travel offices and the stations of Madrid, Barcelona, Port Bou, and Irún. At press time (spring 1993) the second-class pass cost 11,500 ptas. for 8 days, 18,500 ptas. for 15 days, and 24,000 ptas. for 22 days. RENFE has no representative in the United States.

Blue Days *(Días Azules)* leaflets are available from RENFE offices and stations and show those days of the year (approximately 270) when you can travel at reduced rates. Be warned, though, that some of these bargains may apply only to Spaniards or to foreigners officially resident in Spain.

By Plane **Iberia** and its subsidiary **Aviaco** operate a wide network of domestic flights, linking all the main cities and the Balearic Islands. Distances are great and internal airfares still are low by European standards, so plane travel around Spain is well worth considering. Flights from the mainland to the Balearics are heavily booked in summer, and the Madrid–Málaga route is frequently overbooked at Easter and in high season. A frequent shuttle service operates between Madrid and Barcelona. Iberia has its own offices in most major Spanish cities and acts as agent for Aviaco. In Madrid, Iberia headquarters are at Velázquez 130 (tel. 91/585–8585, or call Inforiberia for flight information, tel. 91/411–2545). Flights can also be booked at most travel agencies. For information on other airlines' flights to and within Spain, call the airline itself, or call the airport (tel. 91/205–8343) and ask for your airline.

By Bus Spain has an excellent bus network, but there is no national or nationwide bus company. The network simply consists of numerous private regional bus companies *(empresas)* and there are therefore no comprehensive bus passes. Some of the buses on major routes are now quite luxurious, although this is not always the case in some of the more rural areas. Buses tend to be more frequent than trains, are sometimes cheaper, and often allow you to see more of the countryside. On major routes and at holiday times it is advisable to buy your ticket a day or two in advance. Some cities have central bus stations but in many, including Madrid and Barcelona, buses leave from various boarding points. Always check with the local tourist office. Bus stations, unlike train stations, usually provide luggage storage facilities.

Staying in Spain

Telephones Pay phones are supposed to work with coins of 25 and either 50
Local Calls or 100 ptas. (smaller 5- and 25-ptas. coins do not work in the machines). Twenty-five ptas. is the minimum for short local calls. In the older gray phones, place several coins in the slot, or in the groove on top of the phone, lift the receiver, and dial the number. Coins then fall into the machine as needed. In the newer green phones, place several coins in the slot, watch the display unit and feed as needed. These phones take 100-pta. coins. Area codes always begin with a 9 and are different for each province. In Madrid province, the code is 91; in Cantabria, it's 942. If you're dialing from outside the country, drop the 9.

International Calls Calling abroad can be done from any pay phone marked "Teléfono Internacional." Though usable for short European calls, pay phones are feasible only for brief transatlantic calls. Use 50-pta. (or 100-pta. if the phone takes them) coins initially, then coins of any denomination to prolong your call. Dial 07 for international, wait for the tone to change, then 1 for the United States, or 44 for England, followed by the area code and number. For calls to England, omit the initial 0 from the area code. For lengthy international calls, go to the *telefónica*, a telephone office found in all sizable towns, where an operator assigns you a private booth and collects payment at the end of the call; this is the least expensive and by far the easiest way of phoning abroad. The cost of calls made from your hotel room includes a hefty service charge, even for collect calls.

Operators and Information For the operator and information for the city you are in, dial 003; for information for the rest of Spain, just ask the 003 information operator. If you're in Madrid, dial 008 to make collect calls to countries in Europe; 005 for the rest of the world. From most other places in Spain, dial 9198 for Europe and 9191 for the rest of the world. In the Catalan provinces, dial 9398 for Europe and 9391 for the rest of the world. U.S. long-distance companies now have special access numbers: ATT (tel. 900/99–00–11), MCI (tel. 900/99–00–14), Sprint (tel. 900/99–00–13).

Mail
Postal Rates To the United States, airmail letters up to 15 grams and postcards each cost 83 ptas. (These were the rates at press time [spring 1993]; they were expected to climb in late 1993). To the United Kingdom and other EC countries, letters up to 20 grams and postcards each cost 45 ptas. To non–EC European countries, letters and postcards up to 20 grams cost 60 ptas. If you wish to expedite your overseas mail, send it *Urgente* for 160 ptas. over the regular airmail cost. Within Spain, letters and postcards each cost 27 ptas.; within a city in Spain, letters and postcards cost 17 ptas. Mailboxes are yellow with red stripes, and the slot marked "Extranjero" is the one for mail going abroad. Buy your stamps *(sellos)* at a post office *(correos)* or in a tobacco shop *(estanco)*.

Receiving Mail If you're uncertain where you'll be staying, have mail sent to American Express or to the Poste Restante *(Lista de Correos)* of the local post office. To claim your mail, you'll need to show your passport. American Express has a $2 service charge per letter for non-cardholders. The Spanish mail is notoriously slow and not always very efficient.

Shopping
Sales Tax Refunds If you purchase goods up to a value of 48,000 ptas. or more in any one store (and in theory this should be on only *one* item), you are entitled to a refund of the IVA tax paid (usually 6% but more in the case of certain luxury goods), provided you leave Spain within three months. You will be given two copies of the sales invoice, which you must present at customs together with the goods as you leave Spain. Once the invoice has been stamped by customs, mail the blue copy back to the store, which will then mail your tax refund to you. If you are leaving via the airports of Madrid, Barcelona, Málaga or Palma de Mallorca, you can get your tax refund immediately from the Banco Exterior de España in the airport. The above does not apply to residents of EC countries, who must claim their IVA refund through customs in their own country. The Corte Inglés and Galerías Preciados department stores operate the above system, but don't be surprised if other stores are unfamiliar with the tax-refund procedure and do not have the necessary forms.

Bargaining Prices in city stores and produce markets are fixed; bargaining is possible only in flea markets, some antiques stores, and with gypsy vendors, with whom it is *essential*, though you'd do best to turn them down flat as their goods are almost always fake and grossly overpriced.

Opening and Closing Times Banks are open Monday through Saturday 9–2 from October to June; during the summer months they are closed on Saturdays.

Museums and churches. Opening times vary. Most are open in the morning, and most museums close one day a week, often Monday.

Post offices are usually open weekdays 9–2, but this can vary; check locally.

Stores are open weekdays from 9 or 10 until 1:30 or 2, then again in the afternoon from around 4 to 7 in winter, and 5 to 8 in summer. In some cities, especially in summer, stores close on Saturday afternoon. The Corte Inglés and Galerías Preciados department stores in major cities are open continuously from 10 to 8, and some stores in tourist resorts also stay open through the siesta.

National Holidays January 1; January 6 (Epiphany); March 19 (St. Joseph); March 31 (Holy Thursday); April 1 (Good Friday); May 1 (May Day); June 2 (Corpus Christi); July 25 (St. James); August 15 (Assumption); October 12 (National Day); November 1 (All Saints' Day); December 6 (Constitution); December 8 (Immaculate Conception); December 25. Other holidays include May 2 (in the province of Madrid) and June 24 (St. John). These holidays are not celebrated in every region; always check locally.

Dining Visitors have a choice of restaurants, tapas bars, and cafés. Restaurants are strictly for lunch and dinner; they do not serve breakfast. Tapas bars are ideal for a glass of wine or beer accompanied by an array of savory tidbits *(tapas)*. Cafés, called *cafeterías*, are basically coffee houses serving snacks, light meals, tapas, pastries, and coffee, tea, and alcoholic drinks. They also serve breakfast and are perfect for afternoon tea.

Mealtimes Mealtimes in Spain are much later than in any other European country. Lunch begins between 1 and 2:30, with 2 being the usual time, and 3 more normal on Sunday. Dinner is usually available from 8:30 onward, but 10 PM is the usual time in the larger cities and resorts. An important point to remember is that lunch is the main meal, not dinner. Tapas bars are busiest between noon and 2 and from 8 PM on. Cafés are usually open from around 8 AM to midnight.

Precautions Tap water is said to be safe to drink in all but the remotest villages (in Madrid, tap water, from the surrounding Guadarrama Mountains, is excellent; in Barcelona, it's safe but tastes terrible). However, most Spaniards drink bottled mineral water; ask for either *agua sin gas* (without bubbles) or *agua con gas* (with). A good paella should be served only at lunchtime and should be prepared to order (usually 30 minutes); beware the all-too-cheap version.

Typical Dishes Paella—a mixture of saffron-flavored rice with seafood, chicken, and vegetables—is Spain's national dish. Gazpacho, a cold soup usually made of crushed garlic, tomatoes, and olive oil and garnished with diced vegetables, is a traditional Andalusian dish and is served mainly in summer. The Basque Country and Galicia are the gourmet regions of Spain, and both serve outstanding fish and seafood. Asturias is famous for its *fabadas* (bean stews), cider, and dairy products; Extremadura for its hams and sausages; and Castile for its roasts, especially *cochinillo* (suckling pig), *cordero asado* (roast lamb), and *perdiz* (partridge). The best wines are those from the Rioja and Penedés regions. Valdepeñas is a pleasant table wine, and most places serve a perfectly acceptable house wine called *vino de la* *casa.* Sherries from Jerez de la Frontera make fine aperitifs; ask for a *fino* or a *manzanilla;* both are dry. In summer you can try *horchata,* a sweet white drink made from ground nuts, or *granizados de limón* or *de café,* lemon juice or coffee served over crushed ice. *Un café solo* is a small, black, strong coffee, and *café con leche* is coffee with cream, cappuccino-style; weak black American-style coffee is hard to come by.

Dress In Very Expensive and Expensive restaurants, jacket and tie are the norm. Elsewhere, casual dress is appropriate.

Ratings Spanish restaurants are officially classified from five forks down to one fork, with most places falling into the two- or three-fork category. In our rating system, prices are per person and include a first course, main course, and dessert, but not wine or tip. Sales tax (IVA) is usually included in the menu price; check the menu for *IVA incluído* or *IVA no incluído.* When it's not included, an additional 6% (15% in the fancier restaurants) will be added to your bill. Most restaurants offer a fixed-price menu called a *menú del día;* however, this is often offered only at lunch, and at dinner tends to be merely a re-heated midday offering. This is usually the cheapest way of eating; *à la carte* dining is more expensive. Service charges are never added to your bill; leave around 10%, less in inexpensive restaurants and bars. Major centers such as Madrid, Barcelona, Marbella, and Seville tend to be a bit more expensive. Best bets are indicated by a star ★.

Category	All Areas
Very Expensive	over 9,000 ptas.
Expensive	6,000 ptas.–9,000 ptas.
Moderate	3,000 ptas.–6,000 ptas.
Inexpensive	under 3,000 ptas.

Lodging Spain has a wide range of accommodations, including luxury palaces, medieval monasteries, converted 19th-century houses, modern hotels, high rises on the coasts, and inexpensive hostels in family homes. All hotels and hostels are listed with their rates in the annual *Guía de Hoteles* available from bookstores and kiosks for around 650 ptas., or you can see a copy in local tourist offices. Rates are always quoted per room, and not per person. Single occupancy of a double room costs 80% of the normal price. Breakfast is rarely included in the quoted room rate; always check. The quality of rooms, particularly in older properties, can be uneven; always ask to see your room *before* you sign the acceptance slip. If you want a private bathroom in a less expensive hotel, state your preference for shower or bathtub; the latter usually costs more though many hotels have both.

Hotels and Hostels Hotels are officially classified from five stars (the highest) to one star, hostels from three stars to one star. Hostels—not the youth hostels associated with the English word—are usually a family home converted to provide accommodations that often occupy only part of a building. If an R appears on the blue hotel or hostel plaque, the hotel is classified as a *residencia,* and full dining services are not provided, though breakfast and cafeteria facilities may be available. A three-star hostel usually equates with a two-star hotel; two- and one-star hostels offer simple, basic accommodations. The main hotel chains are Husa, Iberotel Melia, Sol, and Tryp, and the state-run *paradores* (tourist hotels). Holiday Inn, InterContinental, and Trusthouse Forte also own some of the best hotels in Madrid, Barcelona, and Seville; only these and the paradores have any special character. The others mostly provide clean, comfortable accommodation in the two- to four-star range.

In many hotels rates vary fairly dramatically according to the time of year. The hotel year is divided into *estación alta*, *media*, and *baja* (high, mid, and low season); high season usually covers the summer and Easter and Christmas periods, plus the major fiestas. IVA is rarely included in the quoted room rates, so be prepared for an additional 6%, or, in the case of luxury four- and five-star hotels, 13%, to be added to your bill. Service charges are never included.

Paradors There are 86 state-owned-and-run paradors, many of which are located in magnificent medieval castles or convents or in places of great natural beauty. Most of these fall into the four-star category and are priced accordingly. Most have restaurants that specialize in local regional cuisine and serve a full breakfast. The most popular paradors (Granada's San Francisco parador, for example) are booked far in advance, and many close for a month or two in winter (January or February) for renovations. For more information or to make reservations, contact **Paradores** (Velazquez 18, Spain, tel. 91/435–9700, 91/435–9744, or 91/435–9768), **Keytel International** (402 Edgware Rd., London, W2 1ED, UK, tel. 081/402–8182) or **Marketing Ahead Inc.**, 433 5th Ave., New York, NY 10016, USA, tel. 212/686–9213.

Villas Villas are plentiful all along the Mediterranean coast, and cottages in Cantabria and Asturias on the north coast are available from a few agencies. Several agencies in both the United States and United Kingdom specialize in renting property; check with the Spanish National Tourist Office.

Camping There are approximately 530 campsites in Spain, with the highest concentration along the Mediterranean coast. The season runs from April to October, though some sites are open year-round. Sites are listed in the annual publication *Guía de Campings* available from bookstores or local tourist offices, and further details are available from the Spanish National Tourist Office. Reservations for the most popular seaside sites can be made either directly with the site or through camping reservations at: Federación Española de Campings (Príncipe de Vergara 85, 2°-dcha, 28006 Madrid, tel. 91/562–9994).

Ratings Prices are for two people in a double room and do not include breakfast. Best bets are indicated by a star ★.

Category	Major City	Other Areas
Very Expensive	over 22,000 ptas.	over 18,000 ptas.
Expensive	15,000–22,000 ptas.	12,000–18,000 ptas.
Moderate	9,000–15,000 ptas.	7,000–12,000 ptas.
Inexpensive	under 9,000 ptas.	under 7,000 ptas.

Tipping Spaniards appreciate being tipped, though the practice is becoming less widespread. Restaurants and hotels are by law not allowed to add a service charge to your bill, though confusingly your bill for both will most likely say *servicios e impuestos incluídos* (service and tax included). Ignore this unhelpful piece of advice, and leave 10% in most restaurants where you have had a full meal; in humbler eating places, bars, and cafés, 5%–10% is enough, or you can round out the bill to the nearest 100 ptas. A cocktail waiter in a hotel will expect at least 30 ptas. a drink, maybe 50 ptas. in a luxury establishment. Tip taxi drivers about 10% when they use the meter, otherwise *nothing*—they'll have seen to it themselves. Gas-station attendants get no tip for pumping gas, but they get about 50 ptas. for checking tires and oil and cleaning windshields. Train and airport porters usually operate on a fixed rate of about 60 ptas.– 100 ptas. a bag. Coat-check attendants get 25 ptas.–50 ptas., and rest-room attendants get 10 ptas.–25 ptas. In top hotels doormen get 100 ptas.–150 ptas. for carrying bags to the check-in counter or for hailing taxis, and bellhops get 100 ptas. for room service or for each bag they carry to your room. In moderate hotels about 50 ptas. is adequate for the same services. Leave your chambermaid about 300 ptas. for a week's stay. There's no need to tip for just a couple of nights. The waiter in your hotel dining room will appreciate 500 ptas. a week.

Madrid

Arriving and Departing

By Plane All international and domestic flights arrive at Madrid's Barajas Airport (tel. 91/205–8343), 16 kilometers (10 miles) northeast of town just off the N-II Barcelona highway. For information on arrival and departure times, call **Inforiberia** (tel. 91/411–2545) or the airline concerned.

Between the Buses leave the national and international terminals every 15
Airport and minutes from 5:40 AM to 2 AM for the downtown terminal at Plaza
Downtown de Colón just off the Paseo de la Castellana. The ride takes about 20 minutes and the fare at press time was 275 ptas. Most city hotels are then only a short taxi ride away. The fastest and most expensive route into town (usually about 1,500 ptas., but up to 2,000 ptas. plus tip in traffic) is by taxi. Pay what is on the meter plus 300 ptas. surcharge and 50 ptas. for each suitcase. By car, take the N-II, which becomes Avenida de América, into town, then head straight into Calle María de Molina and left on either Calle Serrano or the Castellana.

By Train Madrid has three railroad stations. Chamartín, in the northern suburbs beyond the Plaza de Castilla, is the main station, with trains to France, the north, and the northeast (including Barcelona). Most trains to Valencia, Alicante, and Andalusia now leave from here, too, but stop at Atocha station, at the southern end of Paseo del Prado on the Glorieta del Emperador Carlos V. Also departing from Atocha, where a new station was built in 1989, are trains to Toledo, Granada, Extremadura, and Lisbon. In 1992, a convenient new metro stop (Atocha RENFE) was opened in Atocha station, connecting it to the city subway system. The old Atocha station, designed by Eiffel and refurbished in 1990–91, was reopened in 1992 as the Madrid terminus for a new high-speed rail service to Seville.

Norte (or Príncipe Pío), on Paseo de la Florida, in the west of town below the Plaza de España, is the departure point for Ávila, Segovia, El Escorial, Salamanca, Santiago, La Coruña, and all destinations in Galicia.

For all train information, call RENFE (tel. 91/530–0202, in Spanish only), or go to its offices at Alcalá 4, or on the second floor of Torre de Madrid in the Plaza de España, right above the main tourist office (open weekdays 9–3 and 5–7, Sat. 9–3). There's another RENFE office at Barajas Airport in the International Arrivals Hall, or you can purchase tickets at any of the three main stations, or from travel agents displaying the blue and yellow RENFE sign.

By Bus Madrid has no central bus station. The two main bus stations are the Estación del Sur (Canarias 17, tel. 91/468–4200), nearest metro Palos de la Frontera, for buses to Toledo, La Mancha, Alicante, and Andalusia; and Auto-Rés (Plaza Conde de Casal 6, tel. 91/551–7200), nearest metro Conde de Casal, for buses to Extremadura, Cuenca, Salamanca, Valladolid, Valencia, and Zamora. Auto-Rés has a central ticket and information office at Salud 19 near the Hotel Arosa, just off Gran Vía. Buses to other destinations leave from various points, so check with the tourist office. The Basque country and most of north central Spain is served by Auto Continental (Alenza 20, nearest metro Ríos Rosas, tel. 91/533–0400). For Ávila, Segovia, and La Granja, Empresa La Sepulvedana (tel. 91/533–4800) leaves from Paseo de la Florida 11, next to the Norte station, a few steps from the Norte metro stop. Empresa Herranz (tel. 91/543–3645 or 91/543–8167), serving San Lorenzo de El Escorial and the Valley of the Fallen, departs from the base of Calle Fernandez de los Ríos, a few yards from the Moncloa metro stop. La Veloz (Avda. Mediterraneo 49, tel. 91/409–7602) serves Chinchón.

By Car The main roads are north–south, the Paseo de la Castellana and Paseo del Prado; and east–west, Calle de Alcalá, Gran Vía, and Calle de la Princesa. The M30 ring road circles Madrid to the east and south. For Burgos and France, drive north up the Castellana and follow the signs for the N-I. For Barcelona, head up the Castellana to Plaza Dr. Marañón, then right onto María de Molina and the N-II; for Andalusia and Toledo, head south down Paseo del Prado, then follow the signs to the N-IV and N401, respectively. For Segovia, Ávila, and El Escorial, head west along Princesa to Avenida Puerta de Hierro and onto the N-VI La Coruña road.

Getting Around

Madrid is a fairly compact city and most of the main sights can be visited on foot. But if you're staying in one of the modern hotels in the north of town off the Castellana, you may well need to use the bus or subway (metro). As a rough guide, the walk from the Prado to the Royal Palace at a comfortable sightseeing pace but without stopping takes around 30 minutes; from Plaza del Callao on Gran Vía to the Plaza Mayor, it takes about 15 minutes.

By Metro The subway offers the simplest and quickest means of transport and is open from 6 AM to 1:30 AM. Metro maps are available from ticket offices, hotels, and tourist offices. Fares at press time were 125 ptas. a ride. Savings can be made by buying a *taco* of 10 tickets for 490 ptas., or a tourist card called **Metrotour** that is good for unlimited travel for three or five days. Keep some change (5, 25, 50, and 100 ptas.) handy for the ticket machines, especially after 10 PM; the machines give change and are handy for beating often long lines for tickets.

By Bus City buses are red and run from 6 AM to midnight (though check, as some stop earlier). Again there is a flat-fare system, with each ride costing 125 ptas. The smaller, yellow microbuses also cost 125 ptas. and are slightly faster. Route plans are displayed at bus stops *(paradas)*, and a map of the entire system is available from EMT (Empresa Municipal de Transportes) booths on Plaza de la Cibeles, Callao, or Puerta del Sol. Savings can be made by buying a **Bonobus** (490 ptas.), good for 10 rides, from EMT booths or any branch of the Caja de Ahorros de Madrid.

By Taxi Madrid has more than 18,000 taxis, and fares are low by New York or London standards. The meter starts at 140 ptas. and each additional kilometer costs 65 ptas. The average city ride costs about 500 ptas., and there is a surcharge of 150 ptas. between 11 PM and 6 AM and on holidays from 6 AM to 11 PM. A supplemental fare of 150 ptas. applies to trips to the bullring or soccer matches, and there is a charge of 50 ptas. per suitcase. The airport surcharge is 300 ptas. Cabs available for hire display a "Libre" sign during the day and a green light at night. They hold four passengers. Make sure the driver puts his meter on when you start your ride, and tip up to about 10% of the fare.

Important Addresses and Numbers

Tourist Information The main Madrid tourist office (tel. 91/541–2325) is on the ground floor of the Torre de Madrid in Plaza de España, near the beginning of Calle de la Princesa, and is open weekdays 9–7, Saturdays 9:30–1:30. Another Madrid Provincial Tourist Office (Duque de Medinacelli 2, tel. 91/429–4951) is conveniently located on a small street across from the Palace Hotel. The much less useful municipal tourist office is at Plaza Mayor 3 (tel. 91/266–5477) and is open weekdays 10–1:30 and 4–7, Saturdays 10–1:30. A third office is in the International Arrivals Hall of Barajas Airport (tel. 91/305–8656) and is open weekdays 8–8, Saturdays 8–1.

Embassies U.S. (Serrano 75, tel. 91/577–4000), **Canadian** (Núñez de Balboa 35, tel. 91/431–4300), **U.K.** (Fernando el Santo 16, tel. 91/308–0459).

Emergencies Police: (National Police, tel. 091; Municipal Police, tel. 092; Main Police [Policía Nacional] Station, Puerta del Sol 7, tel. 91/522–0435). To report lost passports, go to Los Madrazos 9 just off the top of Paseo del Prado (tel. 91/521–9350). **Ambulance:** tel. 91/522–2222 or 91/588–4400. **Doctor:** Your hotel reception will contact the nearest doctor for you. Emergency clinics: **Hospital 12 de Octubre** (Avda. Córdoba, tel. 91/390–8000) and **La Paz Ciudad Sanitaria** (Paseo de la Castellana 261, tel. 91/734–3200). English-speaking doctors are available at Conde de Aranda 7 (tel. 91/435–1595). **Pharmacies:** A list of pharmacies open 24 hours *(farmacias de guardia)* is published daily in *El País*. Hotel receptions usually have a copy. **Company** (Puerta del Sol 14) has English-speaking pharmacists. It does not stock American medicines but will recognize many American brand names.

English-Language Bookstores	**Booksellers S.A.** (José Abascal 48, tel. 91/442–8104) and **Turner's English Bookshop** (Génova 3, tel. 91/310–4359).
Travel Agencies	**American Express** (Plaza de las Cortes 2, tel. 91/322–5500), **Marsans** (Gran Vía 59, tel. 91/247–7300), **Wagons-Lits** (Alcalá 23, tel. 91/522–4334).
Airlines	**Iberia** (Goya 29, tel. 91/581–8155; for flight information, call Inforiberia, tel. 91/411–2545), **British Airways** (Serrano 60, 5th floor, tel. 91/431–7575), and **TWA** (Plaza de Colón 2, tel. 91/410–6007 or 91/410–6012).

Guided Tours

Orientation Tours City sightseeing tours are run by **Juliá Tours** (Gran Vía 68, tel. 91/571–2558), **Pullmantur** (Plaza de Oriente 8, tel. 91/541–1807), and **Trapsatur** (San Bernardo 23, tel. 91/542–6666). All three run the same tours, mostly in 48-seat buses and conducted in Spanish and English. Book tours directly with the offices above, through any travel agent, or through your hotel. Departure points are from the addresses above, though in many cases you can be picked up at your hotel. "Madrid Artístico" is a morning tour of the city with visits to the Royal Palace and Prado Museum, entrance fees included. The "Madrid Panorámico" tour includes the University City, Casa del Campo park, and the northern reaches of the Castellana. This is a half-day tour, usually in the afternoon, and makes an ideal orientation for the first-time visitor. Also offered are "Madrid de Noche," a night tour combining a drive round the illuminations, dinner in a restaurant, flamenco show, and cabaret at La Scala nightclub; and "Panorámico y Toros," on bullfight days only (usually Sunday), a panoramic drive and visit to a bullfight.

Walking and Special-Interest Tours Spanish-speaking people can take advantage of a hugely popular selection of tours recently launched by the **Ayuntamiento** (city hall) under the title "Conozcamos Madrid." Walking tours are held most mornings and afternoons in spring and summer, and visit many of the capital's hidden corners, as well as the major sights. Special-interest tours include "Madrid's Railroads," "Medicine in Madrid," "Goya's Madrid," and "Commerce and Finance in Madrid." Some tours are by bus, others on foot. Schedules are listed in the "Conozcamos Madrid" leaflet available from the municipal tourist office.

Excursions **Juliá Tours, Pullmantur,** and **Trapsatur** run full- or half-day trips to El Escorial, Ávila, Segovia, Toledo, and Aranjuez, and in summer to Cuenca and Salamanca; for additional details, *see* Madrid Environs, *below.* The "Tren de la Fresa" (Strawberry Train) is a popular excursion on summer weekends; a 19th-century train carries passengers from the old Delicias Station to Aranjuez and back. Tickets can be obtained from RENFE offices, travel agents, and the Delicias Station (Paseo de las Delicias 61). Other one- or two-day excursions by train to such places as Ávila, Cuenca, or Salamanca are available on weekends in summer. Contact RENFE for details.

Exploring Madrid

Numbers in the margin correspond to points of interest on the Madrid map.

You can walk the following route in a day, or even half a day if you stop only to visit the Prado and Royal Palace. Two days should give you time for browsing. Begin in the Plaza Atocha, more properly known as the Glorieta del Emperador Carlos V, at the bottom of the Paseo del Prado, and check out what's ❶ showing in the **Centro de Arte Reina Sofía** (Reina Sofía Arts Center) opened by Queen Sofía in 1986. This converted hospital, home of art and sculpture exhibitions and symbol of Madrid's new cultural pride, is fast becoming one of Europe's most dynamic venues—a Madrileño rival to Paris's Pompidou Center. It also recently became home to Picasso's *Guernica*, the horrific painting depicting the April 1937 carpet bombing of the Basque Country's traditional capital by Nazi warplanes aiding Franco during the Spanish Civil War (1936–39). The main entrance is on Calle de Santa Isabel 52. *Tel. 91/467–5062. Admission: 500 ptas. Open Mon., Wed.–Sat. 10–9; Sun. 10–2.*

Walk up Paseo del Prado to Madrid's number-one sight, the fa- ❷ mous **Museo del Prado** (Prado Museum), one of the world's most important art galleries. Plan on spending at least 1½ days here, though it will take at least two full days to view its treasures properly. Brace yourself for the crowds. The greatest treasures—the Velázquez, Murillo, Zurbarán, El Greco, and Goya galleries—are all on the upstairs floor. Two of the best works are Velázquez's *Surrender of Breda* and his most famous work, *Las Meninas*, which occupies a privileged position in a room of its own. The Goya galleries contain the artist's none-too-flattering royal portraits—Goya believed in painting the truth—his exquisitely beautiful *Marquesa de Santa Cruz*, and his famous *Naked Maja* and *Clothed Maja*, for which the 13th duchess of Alba was said to have posed. Goya's most moving works, the *Second of May* and the *Fusillade of Moncloa* or *Third of May*, vividly depict the sufferings of Madrid patriots at the hands of Napoleon's invading troops in 1808. Before you leave, feast your eyes on the fantastic flights of fancy of Hieronymus Bosch's *Garden of Earthly Delights* and his triptych *The Hay Wagon*, both downstairs on the ground floor. *Paseo del Prado s/n, tel. 91/420–2836. Admission: 475 ptas., Open Tues.–Sat. 9–7, Sun. 9–2.*

❸ Across the street is the **Ritz,** the grand old lady of Madrid's hotels, built in 1910 by Alfonso XIII when he realized that his capital had no hotels elegant enough to accommodate the guests at his wedding in 1906. The Ritz garden is a delightfully aristocratic place to lunch in summer—men always need ties.

❹ The **Parque del Retiro** (Retiro Park) once a royal retreat, is today Madrid's prettiest park. Visit the beautiful rose garden, **La Rosaleda,** and enjoy the many statues and fountains. You can hire a carriage, row a boat on **El Estanque,** gaze up at the monumental **statue to Alfonso XII,** one of Spain's least notable kings though you wouldn't think so to judge by its size, or wonder at the **Monument to the Fallen Angel**—Madrid claims the dubious privilege of being the only capital to have a statue dedicated to the Devil. The **Palacio de Velázquez** and the beautiful steel-and-glass **Palacio de Cristal,** built as a tropical plant house in the 19th century, now host art exhibits.

Leaving the Retiro via its northwest corner, you come to the ❺ Plaza de la Independencia, dominated by the **Puerta de Alcalá,** a grandiose gateway built in 1779 for Charles III. A customs post once stood beside the gate, as did the old bullring until it

Major Attractions

Centro de Arte Reina Sofia, 1

Cibeles Fountain, 6

Convento de las Descalzas Reales, 9

Museo del Prado, 2

Palacio Real, 12

Parque del Retiro, 4

Plaza de la Villa, 11

Plaza Mayor, 10

Puerta de Alcalá, 5

Puerta del Sol, 8

Real Academia de Bellas Artes, 7

Ritz, 3

Royal Carriage Museum, 13

Other Attractions

Biblioteca Nacional, 18

Municipal Museum, 15

Museo Arqueológico, 19

Museo de Artes Decorativas, 20

Museo de Cera (Wax Museum), 17

Museo Romántico, 16

Torre de Madrid, 14

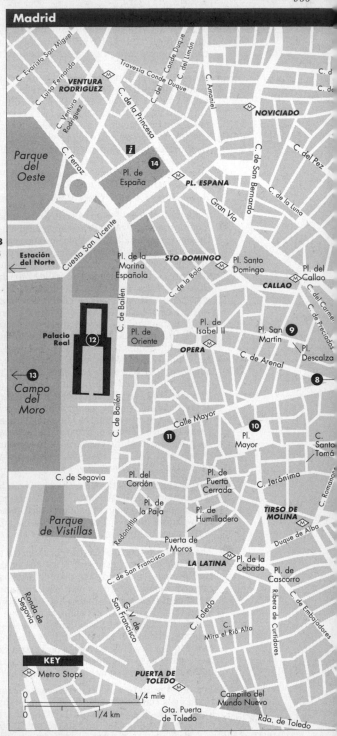

Madrid

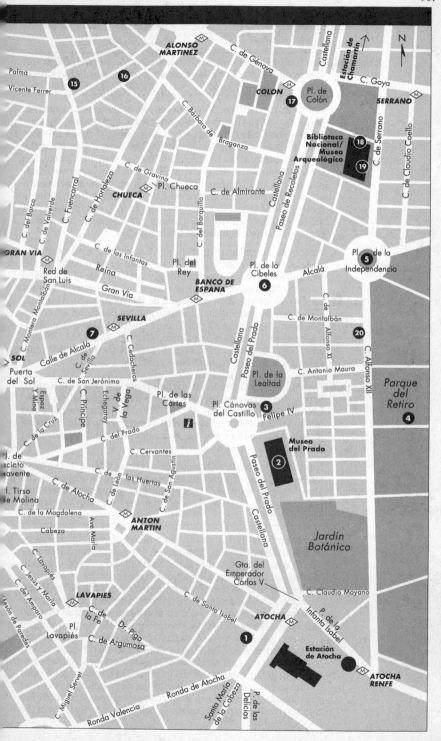

Palma

Vicente Ferrer

15

16

ALONSO MARTINEZ

C. de Génova

COLON

17 Pl. de Colón

Estación de Chamartín

C. Goya

SERRANO

18 C. de Serrano

Biblioteca Nacional/ Museo Arqueológico

19

C. de Claudio Coello

C. de Bárbara de Braganza

C. de Gravina

Pl. Chueca

CHUECA

C. de Almirante

C. del Barquillo

Castellana

Paseo de Recoletos

C. del Barco

C. de Valverde

C. Fuencarral

C. de Hortaleza

C. de las Infantas

Pl. del Rey

Pl. de la Cibeles

6

Alcalá

Pl. de la Independencia

5

GRAN VIA

Red de San Luis

Reina

Gran Via

BANCO DE ESPAÑA

C. de Montalbán

C. de

Alfonso XI

20

C. Alfonso XII

C. Montera

C. Montalbán

SEVILLA

7

Calle de Alcalá

C. de Sevilla

C. Cedaceros

Castellana

Paseo del Prado

Pl. de la Lealtad

C. Antonio Maura

SOL

Puerta del Sol

C. de San Jerónimo

Echegaray

C. V. de la Vega

Pl. de las Cortes

Pl. Cánovas del Castillo

3

Felipe IV

Parque del Retiro

4

Espoz Y Mina

C. Príncipe

C. del Prado

i

Pl. de acinto avente

C. de la Cruz

C. Cervantes

Museo del Prado

2

l. Tirso e Molina

C. de Atocha

C. de León

las Huertas

C. de San Agustín

C. de la Magdalena

Cabeza

Ave María

ANTON MARTIN

Jardín Botánico

C. Lavapiés

C. Jesús y María

C. del Amparo

LAVAPIES

Pl. Lavapiés

C. de la Fe

Dr. Piga

C. de Argumosa

Gta. del Emperador Carlos V

C. Claudio Moyano

Mesón de Paredes

C. de Santa Isabel

ATOCHA

1

P. de la Infanta Isabel

C. Miguel Servet

Ronda de Atocha

Ronda Valencia

Santa María de la Cabeza

Estación de Atocha

P. de las Delicias

ATOCHA RENFE

N

was moved to its present site at Ventas in the 1920s. At the turn of the century, the Puerta de Alcalá more or less marked the eastern limits of Madrid.

Time Out The **Café León** (Alcalá 57), with its marble-topped tables and charming Old World air, is an ideal place for some light refreshment.

Continue to the **Plaza de la Cibeles,** one of the great landmarks of the city, at the intersection of its two main arteries, the Castellana and Calle de Alcalá. If you can see it through the roar and fumes of the thundering traffic, the square's center is the **6** **Cibeles Fountain,** the unofficial emblem of Madrid. Cybele, the Greek goddess of fertility, languidly rides her lion-drawn chariot, overlooked by the mighty **Palacio de Comunicaciónes,** a splendidly pompous cathedral-like building often jokingly dubbed Our Lady of Communications. In fact, it's the main post office, erected in 1918. The famous goddess looks her best at night when she's illuminated by floodlights.

Now head down the long and busy Calle de Alcalá toward the Puerta del Sol, resisting the temptation to turn right up the Gran Vía, which beckons temptingly with its mile of stores and cafés. Before you reach the Puerta del Sol, art lovers may want **7** to step inside the **Real Academia de Bellas Artes** at Alcalá 13. This recently refurbished fine arts gallery boasts an art collection second only to the Prado's and features all the great Spanish masters: Velázquez, El Greco, Murillo, Zurbarán, Ribera, and Goya. *Alcalá 13, tel. 91/532-1546. Admission: 300 ptas. Open Tues.-Fri. 9-7, Sat., Sun., and Mon. 9-3.*

Time Out A small detour down Sevilla, then right down San Jerónimo, brings you to two atmospheric places for a drink or light lunch. **Lhardy** (San Jerónimo 8, tel. 91/521-3385) is a veritable Old Madrid institution that opened as a pastry shop in 1839. Today it combines the roles of expensive restaurant and delicatessen. *Closed Sun. evening and in Aug.*

Next door, at No. 6, on the corner of Espoz y Mina, is the more moderately priced **Museo de Jamón,** a relative newcomer on the Madrid scene, with hundreds of hams hanging from its ceilings. It's ideal for a beer or glass of wine and a generous plate of cheese or ham.

8 The **Puerta del Sol** is at the very heart of Madrid. Its name means Gate of the Sun, though the old gate disappeared long ago. It's easy to feel you're at the heart of things here—indeed, of all of Spain—for the kilometer distances for the whole nation are measured from the zero marker in front of the Police Headquarters. The square was expertly revamped in 1986 and now accommodates both a copy of **La Mariblanca** (a statue that 250 years ago adorned a fountain here) and, at the bottom of Calle Carmen, the much-loved statue of the **bear and *madroño*** (strawberry tree). The Puerta del Sol is inextricably linked with the history of Madrid and of the nation. Here, half a century ago, a generation of literati gathered in the long-gone cafés to thrash out the burning issues of the day; and if you can cast your thoughts back almost 200 years, you can conjure up the heroic deeds of the patriots' uprising immortalized by Goya in the *Second of May.*

This is a good place to break the tour if you've had enough sight-seeing for one day. Head north up Preciados or Montera for some of the busiest and best shopping streets in the city or southeast toward Plaza Santa Ana for tavern-hopping in Old Madrid.

Time Out If it's teatime (6–7 PM), don't miss **La Mallorquina** (Calle Mayor 2, tel. 91/521–1201), an old pastry shop between Calle Mayor and Arenal. Delicious pastries are sold at the downstairs counter; the old-fashioned upstairs tea salon offers an age-old tea ritual and unbeatable views over the Puerta del Sol.

❾ Art lovers will want to make a detour to the **Convento de las Descalzas Reales** on Plaza Descalzas Reales just above Arenal. It was founded by Juana de Austria, daughter of Charles V, and is still inhabited by nuns. Over the centuries the nuns, daughters of the royal and noble, endowed the convent with an enormous wealth of jewels, religious ornaments, superb Flemish tapestries, and the works of such great masters as Titian and Rubens. A bit off the main tourist track, it's one of Madrid's better-kept secrets. Your ticket includes admission to the nearby, but less interesting, **Convento de la Encarnación.** *Plaza de las Descalzas Reales, tel. 91/248-7404. Admission: 350 ptas. Guided tours only. Open Tues.–Thurs., Sat. 10–1 and 4–5:30; Fri. and Sun. 10–1.*

❿ Walk up **Calle Mayor,** the Main Street of Old Madrid, past the shops full of religious statues and satins for bishops' robes, to the **Plaza Mayor,** the capital's greatest architectural showpiece. It was built in 1617–19 for Philip III—that's Philip on the horse in the middle. The plaza has witnessed the canonization of saints, burning of heretics, fireworks and bullfights, and is still one of the great gathering places of Madrid.

Time Out In summer you can relax over a drink in any of the delightful sidewalk cafés that adorn the square; in winter, head for the **Mesón del Corregidor** (tel. 91/266–5056) at No. 8, near the Cuchilleros arch. This colorful tavern restaurant has typical dishes and tapas.

⓫ If you're here in the morning, take a look inside the 19th-century steel-and-glass San Miguel market, a colorful provisions market, before continuing down Calle Mayor to the **Plaza de la Villa.** The square's notable cluster of buildings includes some of the oldest houses in Madrid. The **Casa de la Villa,** the Madrid city hall, was built in 1644 and has also served as the city prison and the mayor's home. Its sumptuous salons are occasionally open to the public; ask about guided tours, which are sometimes offered in English. An archway joins the Casa de la Villa to the **Casa Cisneros,** a palace built in 1537 for the nephew of Cardinal Cisneros, primate of Spain and infamous inquisitor general. Across the square, the **Torre de Lujanes** is one of the oldest buildings in Madrid. It once imprisoned Francis I of France, archenemy of the Emperor Charles V.

Time Out If it's lunchtime, close by is a moderately priced restaurant that is a long-standing Madrid tradition: **Casa Ciriaco** on Calle Mayor 80 (tel. 91/559–5066).

The last stop on the tour, but Madrid's second most important
⑫ sight, is the **Palacio Real** (Royal Palace). This magnificent
granite and limestone residence was begun by Philip V, the
first Bourbon king of Spain, who was always homesick for his
beloved Versailles, the opulence and splendor of which he did
his best to emulate. His efforts were successful, to judge by the
2,800 rooms with their lavish Rococo decorations, precious carpets, porcelain, time pieces, mirrors, and chandeliers. From
1764, when Charles III first moved in, till the coming of the
Second Republic and the abdication of Alfonso XIII in 1931, the
Royal Palace proved a very stylish abode for Spanish monarchs.
Today King Juan Carlos, who lives in the far less ostentatious
Zarzuela Palace outside Madrid, uses it only for official state
functions. The Palace can be visited only on guided tours,
sometimes available in English. Allow 1½–2 hours for a visit. A
visita completa (full visit), including the Royal Carriage Museum (*see below*), Royal Pharmacy, and other outbuildings, costs
500 ptas.; many visitors opt for the *Salones Oficiales* (State
Rooms) ticket at 325 ptas. *Bailén s/n, tel. 91/559–7404. Admission: 500 ptas. for entire complex, 325 ptas. for palace only.
Open Mon.–Sat. 9:30–5:15, Sun. 9–2:15. Closed during frequent official functions.*

⑬ The **Royal Carriage Museum,** which belongs to the palace (and
has the same hours) but has a separate entrance on Paseo
Vírgen del Puerto, can be visited only on an all-inclusive ticket.
One of its highlights is the wedding carriage of Alfonso XIII
and his English bride, Victoria Eugenia, granddaughter of
Queen Victoria, which was damaged by a bomb thrown at it in
the Calle Mayor during their wedding procession in 1906; another is the chair that carried the gout-stricken old Emperor
Charles V to his retirement at the remote monastery of Yuste.

Off the Beaten Track

Stroll around the narrow streets of the **Chueca** between
Hortaleza and Paseo de Recoletos. Look for the architectural
features of the old houses; the dark, atmospheric bars and restaurants well known to discerning Madrileños; and the small
stores with their wooden counters and brass fittings, many of
which have been run by the same family for generations. Calle
de las Infantas has some real gems: the **Bolsa de los Licores** at
No. 13, selling wines and liqueurs from every corner of Europe;
the splendid silver shop at No. 25; the Old World grocery store
Casa Jerez at No. 32. And don't miss the **Tienda de Vinos** restaurant in Augusto Figueroa, affectionately nicknamed "El
Comunista" and long famed for its rock-bottom prices. The
whole quarter seems to come straight from the pages of a 19th-
century novel.

For a dramatic view of the northwest quadrant of the city and
the adjoining Casa de Campo park, take the Metro to the
Moncloa stop and climb the Faro de Moncloa, a recently opened
285-foot observatory. *Admission: 200 ptas. Open daily 10–2
and 4–8.*

The old **Lavapiés** quarter, between Calle Atocha and Embaja-
dores, is another area with plenty of atmosphere. Traditionally
one of the poorest parts of Old Madrid, it is now the home of
artists and actors, writers and musicians. Health-food restaurants—a novelty in Spain generally—have flourished. You

can get a good cheap lunch at **La Biotika,** Amor de Diós 3 (tel. 91/429–0780), or **El Granero de Lavapiés,** Argumosa 10. In summer you can eat in the courtyard of the old tenement building **La Corrala,** Mesón de Paredes 32, and watch a *zarzuela* performance on its ancient balconies.

Casa Mingo (Paseo de la Florida 2, tel. 91/547–7918) is an Asturian tavern behind Norte Station. A real Madrid institution, it has long been famous for its Asturian cider, goat cheese, and succulent chicken at amazingly low prices.

Shopping

Gift Ideas There are no special regional crafts associated with Madrid itself, but traditional Spanish goods are on sale in many stores. The **Corte Inglés** and **Galerías Preciados** department stores both stock good displays of Lladró porcelain, as do several specialist shops on the Gran Vía and behind the Plaza hotel on Plaza de España. Department stores stock good displays of fans, but for really superb examples, try the long-established **Casa Diego** in Puerta del Sol. Two stores opposite the Prado on Plaza Cánovas del Castillo, **Artesanía Toledana** and **El Escudo de Toledo,** have a wide selection of souvenirs, especially Toledo swords, inlaid marquetry ware, and pottery. Carefully selected handicrafts from all over Spain—ceramics, furniture, glassware, rugs, embroidery, and more—are sold at **Artespaña** (Plaza de las Cortes 3, Gran Vía 32, and Hermosilla 14), a government-run crafts store.

Antiques The main areas to see are the Plaza de las Cortes, the Carrera San Jerónimo, and the Rastro flea market, along the Ribera de Curtidores and the courtyards just off it.

Boutiques Calle Serrano has the largest collection of smart boutiques and designer fashions. Another up-and-coming area is around Calle Argensola, just south of Calle Génova. **Loewe,** Spain's most prestigious leather store, has boutiques on Serrano 26 and Gran Vía 8. **Adolfo Domínguez,** one of Spain's top designers, has several boutiques in Salamanca, and another on Calle Orense in the north of town.

Shopping Districts The main shopping area in the heart of Madrid is around the pedestrian streets of **Preciados** and **Montera,** between Puerta del Sol and Plaza Callao on Gran Vía. The smartest and most expensive district is the **Barrio de Salamanca** northeast of Cibeles, centered around Serrano, Velázquez, and Goya. **Calle Mayor** and the streets to the east of **Plaza Mayor** are lined with fascinating old-fashioned stores straight out of the 19th century.

Department Stores El Corte Inglés is the biggest, brightest, and most successful Spanish chain store. Its main branch is on Preciados, just off the Puerta del Sol. **Galerías Preciados** is its main rival, with branches on Plaza Callao right off Gran Vía, Calle Arapiles, Goya corner of Conde de Peñalver, Serrano and Ortega y Gasset, and its newest branch at La Vaguada. Both stores are open Monday–Saturday 10–8, and neither closes for the siesta.

Food and The Rastro, Madrid's most famous flea market, operates on
Flea Markets Sundays from 9 to 2 around the Plaza del Cascorro and the Ribera de Curtidores. A **stamp and coin** market is held on Sunday mornings in the Plaza Mayor, and there's a **secondhand book**

market most days on the Cuesta Claudio Moyano near Atocha Station.

Bullfighting

The Madrid bullfighting season runs from March to October. Fights are held on Sunday, and sometimes also on Thursday; starting times vary between 4:30 and 7 PM. The pinnacle of the spectacle may be seen during the three weeks of daily bullfights held during the San Isidro festivals in May. The bullring is at Las Ventas (formally known as the Plaza de Toros Monumental), Alcalá 237 (metro Ventas). You can buy your ticket there shortly before the fight, or, with a 20% surcharge, at the agencies that line Calle Victoria, just off Carrera San Jerónimo and Puerta del Sol.

Dining

For details and price-category definitions, *see* Dining in Staying in Spain.

Very Expensive
★ **Irízar Jatetxea.** Owned by the famous Basque restaurateur Luis Irízar, this is one of Madrid's most luxurious and renowned restaurants. It's opposite the Teatro Zarzuela (next to Armstrong's) and the cuisine is Basque, but much influenced by nouvelle cuisine from France and Navarre. Definitely a place for a treat. *Jovellanos 3, tel. 91/531–4593. Reservations advised. AE, DC, V. Closed Sat. lunch, Sun.*

Zalacaín. The ambience in this modern building attempts to duplicate that of a private villa, with plush decor and alcove-separated rooms. Located just off the Castellana and María de Molina, it is one of only two Spanish restaurants to be awarded three Michelin stars. *Alvarez de Baena 4, tel. 91/561–5935. Reservations required. AE, DC, MC, V. Closed Sat. lunch, Sun., Holy Week, Aug.*

Expensive
★ **El Cenador del Prado.** This elegant and stylish restaurant just off Plaza Santa Ana offers beautiful decor and an imaginative menu with more than a hint of nouvelle cuisine. The chef learned his trade in New York, and specialties include *caracoles con setas en hojaldre* (snails and mushrooms en croute) and *salmón marinado a la pimienta verde* (salmon marinated in green peppers). *Calle del Prado 4, tel. 91/429–1561 and 429–1549. Reservations advised. AE, DC, MC, V. Closed Sat. lunch, Sun., 2 weeks in Aug.*

La Dorada. One of Madrid's most outstanding fish restaurants, the seafood here is flown in daily in the owner's private plane from the Costa del Sol. Its sister restaurants in Barcelona and Seville are equally esteemed. It's located in the modern north of town, near the Azca Center and Holiday Inn. *Orense 64, tel. 91/570–2002. Reservations required. AE, DC, MC, V. Closed Sun., Aug.*

La Gamella. American-born Dick Stephens, a former ballet dancer and choreographer, has made a name for himself in Madrid with his very nouveau dishes, some of them wonderfully creative. Right off Retiro Park and the Puerta de Alcalá, the rust-red dining room is dark and attractive. Try the fillet of duck with raspberry sauce or sausage wrapped in pastry with sweet red peppers, a house specialty; for dessert, the bittersweet chocolate cake's downright sinful. *Calle Alfonso XII 4,* *tel. 91/532–4509. Reservations advised. AE, DC, MC, V. Closed Sat. lunch and Sun.*

Solchaga. Here you can choose between several dining rooms, each with its own distinctive character. Pot-bellied stoves and ornate gilt mirrors help convey the atmosphere of an old-fashioned private house rather than a restaurant; a charming find. *Plaza de Alonso Martínez 2, tel. 91/447–1496. Reservations advised. AE, DC, MC, V. Closed Sat. lunch, Sun.*

Moderate **La Barraca.** A Valencian restaurant with cheerful blue-and-white decor, colorful windowboxes, and ceramic tiles, this is the place to go for a wonderful choice of paellas. Located just off Gran Vía (Alcalá end), behind Loewe, it's popular with businesspeople and foreign visitors. Try the *paella reina* or the *paella de mariscos. Reina 29, tel. 91/532–7154. Reservations advised. AE, DC, MC, V.*

Botín. Madrid's oldest and most famous restaurant, just off the Plaza Mayor, has been catering to diners since 1725. Its decor and food are traditionally Castilian. *Cochinillo* (suckling pig) and *cordero asado* (roast lamb) are its specialties. It was a favorite with Hemingway; today it's very touristy and a bit overrated, but fun. Insist on the *cueva* or upstairs dining room. *Cuchilleros 17, tel. 91/266–3026. Reservations advised, especially at night. AE, DC, MC. V.*

Carmencita. Dating to 1850, this charming restaurant is small and intimate, with ceramic wall tiles, brass hat racks, and photos of bullfighters. The menu recounts the famous who have dined here and their life stories. The cuisine is part traditional, part nouvelle with an emphasis on *pasteles* (a kind of mousse) both savory and sweet. *Libertad 16, on the corner of San Marcos in the Chueca area above Gran Vía; tel. 91/531–6612. Reservations advised. AE, DC, MC, V. Closed Sat. lunch and Sun.*

Casa Ciriaco. In this atmospheric old standby only a few paces from the Plaza Mayor and city hall, the Madrid of 50 years ago lives on. You won't find many foreigners here—just businesspeople and locals enjoying traditional Spanish cooking and delicious *fresones* (strawberries) for dessert. *Mayor 84, tel. 91/559–5066. Reservations accepted. No credit cards. Closed Wed., and Aug.*

★ **Fuente Real.** Dining here is like eating in a turn-of-the-century home. Tucked away between Mayor and Arenal, it's brimming with personal mementos such as antique dolls, Indian figures, and Mexican Christmas decorations. The cuisine is French and Spanish with an emphasis on high-quality meats and crêpes. Try the *pastel de espinacas* (spinach mousse) or *crêpes de puerros* (leeks). *Fuentes 1, tel. 91/559–6613. Reservations not necessary. AE, MC, V. Closed Sun. PM and Mon.*

Inexpensive **El Cuchi.** "Hemingway *never* ate here" is the sign that will lure
★ you inside this colorful tavern at the bottom of the Cuchilleros steps off the Plaza Mayor. A fun-packed experience awaits. The ceilings are plastered with photos of Mexican revolutionaries, huge blackboards announce the menu and list the calories in the irresistible desserts, and home-baked rolls are lowered in baskets from the ceiling to your table. Salads are on the house. El Cuchi stays open all afternoon, which is unusual in Spain. *Cuchilleros 3, tel. 91/266–4424. Reservations advised. AE, DC, MC, V.*

El Luarqués. One of many budget restaurants on this street, El Luarqués is decorated with photos of the port of Luarca on Spain's north coast, and it's always packed with Madrileños who recognize its good value. *Fabada asturiana* (bean and meat stew) and *arroz con leche* (rice pudding) are two of its Asturian specialties. *Ventura de la Vega 16, tel. 91/429–6174. No reservations. No credit cards. Closed Sun. evening, Mon., and Aug.*

Lodging

Hotels around the center in the midst of all the sights and shops are mostly located in old 19th-century houses. Most of the newer hotels that conform to American standards of comfort are located in the northern part of town on either side of the Castellana and are a short metro or bus ride from the center. There are hotel reservation desks in the national and international terminals of the airport, and at Chamartín station (tel. 91/315–7894). Or you can contact **La Brújula** (tel. 91/248–9705) on the sixth floor of the Torre de Madrid in Plaza de España, which is open 9–9. It has English-speaking staff and can book hotels all over Spain for a fee of 200 ptas.

For details and price-category definitions, *see* Lodging in Staying in Spain.

Very Expensive **Fénix.** Located just off the Castellana near the Plaza Colón and convenient for the Salamanca shopping district, this is fast becoming Madrid's leading four-star hotel. It's a favorite with influential businesspeople and conveys a feeling of style and luxury. Its bar and cafeteria are popular meeting places. *Hermosilla 2, tel. 91/431–6700, fax 91/576–0661. 204 rooms. AE, DC, MC, V.*

Palace. This dignified turn-of-the-century hotel opposite parliament and the Prado is a slightly less dazzling step-sister of the nearby Ritz but is full of charm and style. Long a favorite of politicians and journalists, its Belle Epoque decor—especially the glass dome over the lounge—is superb. *Plaza de las Cortes 7, tel. 91/429–7551, fax 91/420–2547. 480 rooms, 20 suites. AE, DC, MC, V.*

★ **Ritz.** Spain's most exclusive hotel is elegant and aristocratic with beautiful rooms, spacious suites, and sumptuous public salons furnished with antiques and handwoven carpets. Its palatial restaurant is justly famous, and its garden terrace is the perfect setting for summer dining. Features are brunches with harp music on weekends and tea or supper chamber concerts from February through May. Close to the Retiro Park and overlooking the famous Prado Museum, it offers pure unadulterated luxury. It is substantially more expensive than most other hotels in this category. *Plaza Lealtad 5, tel. 91/521–2857, fax 91/532–8776. 158 rooms. AE, DC, MC, V.*

Villamagna. Second in luxury only to the Ritz, the Villamagna's modern facade belies a palatial interior exquisitely furnished with 18th-century antiques. Set in a delightful garden, it offers all the facilities one would expect in a hotel of international repute. It is substantially more expensive than most other hotels in this category. *Paseo de la Castellana 22, tel. 576–7500, fax 91/575–9504. 164 rooms. AE, DC, MC, V.*

Expensive **Alcalá.** Close to the Retiro Park and Goya shopping area, this
★ comfortable hotel has long been recognized for high standards. Bedrooms are well furnished, and the cafeteria serves a good lunch menu for around 1,200 ptas. The hotel restaurant, Le Basque (closed Sun. and Mon. lunch), is owned by Luis Irízar of

the famous Irízar Jatetxea restaurant, and its Basque culinary delights are well known to Madrileños. *Alcalá 66, tel. 91/435–1060, fax 91/435–1105. 153 rooms. AE, DC, MC, V.*

Emperador. This older hotel on the corner of San Bernardo has been renovated throughout, and storm windows now help to shut out the roar of Gran Vía traffic. All the rooms have TV and VCR, and a special feature is the rooftop pool and terrace with superb views. *Gran Vía 53, tel. 91/247–2800, fax 91/247–2817. 231 rooms. AE, DC, MC, V.*

Plaza. This elegant hotel at the bottom of Gran Vía has long been a favorite with American visitors. New storm windows cut down the traffic noise, security safes have been installed in each room, and the mattresses have all been replaced with firmer ones more suited to American tastes. The view from its legendary rooftop pool is a favorite with Spanish and foreign photographers. *Plaza de España, tel. 91/247–1200, fax 91/248–2389. 306 rooms. AE, DC, MC, V.*

Sanvy. Backing onto the Fénix, the Sanvy, located just off the Plaza Colón on the edge of the Salamanca district, is a comfortable, well-renovated hotel with a swimming pool on the top floor. Its Belagua Restaurant is gaining prestige. *Goya 3, tel. 91/576–0800, fax 91/575–2443. 141 rooms. AE, DC, MC, V.*

Moderate **Capitol.** If you like being right in the center of things, then this hotel on the Plaza Callao is for you. It's an older hotel, but four floors have been renovated; the rooms on these floors are more comfortable indeed, but also 30% more expensive. There's a well-decorated reception area and a pleasant cafeteria for breakfast. *Gran Vía 41, tel. 91/521–8391, fax 91/247–1238. 145 rooms. AE, DC, V.*

Mayorazgo. This is an older hotel that has yet to be renovated, but it's comfortable as long as you're not seeking all the conveniences of home. Advantages include its friendly, old-fashioned service and its prime location right in the heart of town, tucked away in a quiet back street off Gran Vía that leads down to Plaza de España. *Flor Baja 3, tel. 91/247–2600, fax 91/541–2485. 200 rooms. AE, DC, MC, V.*

Paris. Overlooking the Puerta del Sol, the Paris is a stylish hotel full of old-fashioned appeal. It has an impressive turn-of-the-century lobby and a restaurant where you can dine for around 1,500 ptas. Recently refurbished, the hotel has managed to retain its character while adding modern amenities. *Alcalá 2, tel. 91/521–6496. 114 rooms. MC, V.*

Rex. This is a sister hotel to the Capitol next door, and both belong to the Tryp chain. It's located on the corner of Silva just down from Callao, and the lobby, bar, restaurant, and two floors have so far been completely refurbished. The unrenovated rooms are considerably cheaper, but you'll be much more comfortable in one of the newer ones. *Gran Vía 43, tel. 91/247–4800, fax 91/247–1238. 147 rooms. AE, DC, V.*

Inexpensive **Cliper.** This simple hotel offers good value for the cost-conscious traveler. It's tucked away in a side street off the central part of Gran Vía between Callao and Red San Luis. *Chinchilla 6, tel. 91/531–1700. 52 rooms. AE, MC, V.*

★ **Inglés.** The exterior may seem shabby but don't be deterred. The Inglés is a long-standing budget favorite. Its rooms are comfortable, with good facilities, and the location is a real bonus: You're a short walk from the Puerta del Sol one way, and from the Prado the other; inexpensive restaurants and atmospheric bars are right at hand. *Echegaray 10, tel. 91/429–6551, fax 91/420–2423. 58 rooms. AE, DC, MC, V.*

Bars and Cafés

Bars **The Mesones.** The most traditional and colorful taverns are on Cuchilleros and Cava San Miguel just west of Plaza Mayor, where you'll find a whole array of mesones with names like **Tortilla, Champiñón,** and **Huevo.**

Old Madrid. Wander the narrow streets between Puerta del Sol and Plaza Santa Ana, which are packed with traditional tapas bars. Favorites here are the **Cervecería Alemana,** Plaza Santa Ana 6, a beer hall founded more than 100 years ago by Germans and patronized, inevitably, by Hemingway; **Los Gabrieles,** Echegaray 17, with magnificent ceramic decor; **La Trucha,** Manuel Fernández y González 3, with loads of atmosphere; and **Viva Madrid,** Fernández y González 7, a lovely old bar.

Calle Huertas. Fashionable wine bars with turn-of-the-century decor and chamber or guitar music, often live, line this street. **La Fídula** at No. 57 and **El Hecho** at No. 56 are two of the best.

Plaza Santa Barbara. This area just off Alonso Martínez is packed with fashionable bars and beer halls. Stroll along Santa Teresa, Orellana, Campoamor, or Fernando VI and take your pick. The **Cervecería Santa Barbara** in the plaza itself is one of the most colorful, a popular beer hall with a good range of tapas.

Cafés If you like cafés with an old-fashioned atmosphere, dark wooden counters, brass pumps, and marble-topped tables, try any of the following: **Café Comercial,** Glorieta de Bilbao 7; **Café Gijón,** Paseo de Recoletos 21, a former literary hangout and the most famous of the cafés of old, now one of the many café-terraces that line the Castellana; **Café León,** Alcalá 57, just up from Cibeles; **Café Roma** on Serrano; and **El Espejo,** Paseo de Recoletos 31, with art-nouveau decor and an outdoor terrace in summer. And don't forget **La Mallorquina** tearooms on Puerta del Sol (*see* Exploring, *above*).

The Arts

Details of all cultural events are listed in the daily newspaper *El País* or in the weekly *Guía del Ocio*.

Concerts and Opera The main concert hall is the new **Auditorio Nacional de Madrid** (tel. 91/337–0100), Príncipe de Vergara 146 (metro, Cruz del Royo), which opened at the end of 1988. The old **Teatro Real** (tel. 91/248–1405) on the Plaza de Oriente opposite the Royal Palace is being converted into Madrid's long-needed opera house and may reopen in 1994; inquire at the tourist office.

Zarzuela and Dance Zarzuela, a combination of light opera and dance ideal for non-Spanish speakers, is held at the **Teatro Nacional Lírico de la Zarzuela,** Jovellanos 4, tel. 91/429–8216. The season runs from October to July.

Theater If language is no problem, check out the fringe theaters in Lavapiés (*see* Off the Beaten Track, *above*) and the **Centro Cultural de la Villa** (tel. 91/575–6080) beneath the Plaza Colón, and the open-air events in the Retiro Park. Other leading theaters—you'll also need reasonable Spanish—include the **Círculo**

de Bellas Artes, Marqués de Casa Riera 2, just off Alcalá 42 (tel. 91/531–7700); the **Teatro Español,** Príncipe 25 on Plaza Santa Ana (tel. 91/429–6297) for Spanish classics; and the **Teatro María Guerrero,** Tamayo y Baus 4 (tel. 91/319–4769), home of the Centro Dramático Nacional, for plays by García Lorca. Most theaters have two curtains, at 7 and 10:30 PM, and close on Mondays. Tickets are inexpensive and often easy to come by on the night of performance.

Films Foreign films are mostly dubbed into Spanish, but movies in English are listed in *El País* or *Guía del Ocio* under "V.O.," meaning *versión original.* A dozen or so theaters now show films in English; some of the best bets are **Alphaville** and **Cines Renoir,** both in Mártin de los Heros, just off Plaza España, and the **Filmoteca Español** (Santa Isabel 3), a city-run institution where first-rate V.O. films change daily.

Nightlife

Cabaret **Florida Park** (tel. 91/573–7805), in the Retiro Park, offers dinner and a show that often features ballet, Spanish dance, or flamenco and is open Monday to Saturday from 9:30 PM with shows at 10:45 PM. **Berlin** (Costanilla de San Pedro 11, tel. 91/266–2034) opens at 9:30 PM for a dinner that is good by most cabaret standards, followed by a show and dancing until 4 AM. **La Scala** (Rosario Pino 7, tel. 91/571–4411), in the Meliá Castilla hotel, is Madrid's top nightclub, with dinner, dancing, cabaret at 8:30, and a second, less expensive show around midnight. This is the one visited by most night tours.

Flamenco Madrid offers the widest choice of flamenco shows in Spain; some are good, but many are aimed at the tourist trade. Dinner tends to be mediocre and overpriced, but it ensures the best seats; otherwise, opt for the show and a drink *(consumición)* only, usually starting around 11 PM and costing around 3,000 ptas.–3,500 ptas. **Arco de Cuchilleros** (Cuchilleros 7, tel. 91/266–5867), behind the Plaza Mayor, is one of the better, cheaper ones. **Café de Chinitas** (Torija 7, tel. 91/248–5135) and **Corral de la Morería** (Morería 17, tel. 91/265–8446 and 265–1137) are two of the more authentic places where well-known troupes perform. Another choice is **Corral de la Pacheca** (Juan Ramón Jiménez 26, tel. 91/458–1113). **Zambra** (Velázquez 8, tel. 91/435–5164), in the Hotel Wellington, is one of the smartest (jacket and tie essential), with a good show and dinner served into the small hours.

Jazz The leading club of the moment is **Café Central** (Plaza de Angel 10), followed by **Clamores** (Albuquerque 14). Others include **Café Jazz Populart** (Huertas 22) and **El Despertar** (Torrecilla del Leal 18). Excellent jazz frequently comes to Madrid as part of city-hosted seasonal festivals; check the local press for listings and venues.

Casino **Madrid's Casino** (tel. 91/859–0312) is 28 kilometers (17 miles) out at Torrelodones on the N-VI road to La Coruña. *Open 5 PM–4 AM. Free transportation service from Plaza de España 6.*

Madrid Environs

The beauty of the historic cities surrounding Madrid and the role they have played in their country's history rank them among Spain's most worthwhile sights. Ancient Toledo, the former capital, the great palace-monastery of El Escorial, the sturdy medieval walls of Ávila, Segovia's Roman aqueduct and fairy-tale Alcázar, and the magnificent Plaza Mayor of the old university town of Salamanca all lie within an hour or so from the capital.

All the towns below, with the possible exception of Salamanca, can easily be visited on day-trips from Madrid. But if you've had your fill of the hustle and bustle of Spain's booming capital, you'll find it far more rewarding to tour from one place to another, spending a day or two in one or more of these fascinating locales. Then, long after the day-trippers have gone home, you can enjoy the real charm of these small provincial towns and wander at leisure through their medieval streets.

Getting There from Madrid

Trains to Toledo leave from Madrid's Atocha Station; to Salamanca, from Norte Station; and to Ávila and Segovia from either Atocha or Chamartín Cercanías. Trains to El Escorial leave from the Norte, Atocha, and Chamartín Cercanías stations.

Getting Around

There's a direct train line between El Escorial, Ávila, and Salamanca; otherwise, train connections are poor and you'll do better to go by bus. All places are linked by bus services and the local tourist offices will advise on schedules. Toledo's bus station is on the Ronda de Castilla la Mancha (tel. 925/215850) just off the road from Madrid. Ávila's bus station is on Avenida de Madrid (tel. 918/220154); Segovia's is on Paseo Ezequiel González (tel. 911/427725); and Salamanca's is on Filiberto Villalobos 73 (tel. 923/236717). The N403 from Toledo to Ávila passes through spectacular scenery in the Sierra de Gredos mountains, as does the C505 Ávila–El Escorial route. From El Escorial to Segovia, both the Puerto de León and Puerto de Navacerrada mountain passes offer magnificent views. The N501 from Ávila to Salamanca will take you across the tawny plain of Castile.

Tourist Information

Ávila (Plaza de la Catedral 4, tel. 918/211387); open weekdays 8–3 and 4–6 (5–7 in summer), Saturday 9–1:30 only.
El Escorial (Floridablanca 10, tel. 91/8901554); open weekdays 9–2 and 3–5, Saturday 9–1:45.
Salamanca (Gran Vía 41, tel. 923/268571); open weekdays 9:30–2 and 4:30–8, Saturday 10–2. There's also an information booth on the Plaza Mayor (market side).
Segovia (Plaza Mayor 10, tel. 911/430328); open Monday–Saturday 9–2; also weekdays 4–6 in summer only.
Toledo (Puerta Nueva de Bisagra tel. 925/220843); open weekdays 9–2 and 4–6, Saturday 9:30–1:30.

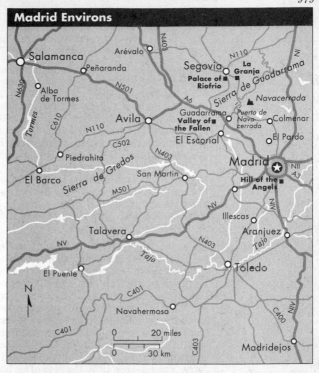

Madrid Environs

Exploring the Madrid Environs

The following tour goes from Toledo to El Escorial, the Valley of the Fallen, La Granja, Segovia, Riofrio, Ávila, Alba de Tormes, and Salamanca.

Head south from Madrid on the road to Toledo. About 20 minutes from the capital look left for a prominent rounded hill topped by a statue of Christ. This is the **Hill of the Angels,** which marks the geographical center of the Iberian Peninsula. After 90 minutes of drab, industrial scenery, the unforgettable silhouette of **Toledo** suddenly rises before you, the imposing bulk of the Alcazar and the slender spire of the cathedral dominating the skyline. This former capital, where Moors, Jews, and Christians once lived in harmony, is now a living national monument, depicting all the elements of Spanish civilization in hand-carved, sun-mellowed stone. For a stunning view and to capture the beauty of Toledo as El Greco knew it, begin with a panoramic drive around the Carretera de Circunvalación, crossing over the Alcántara bridge and returning by way of the bridge of San Martín. As you gaze at the city rising like an island in its own bend of the Tagus, reflect how little the city skyline has changed in the four centuries since El Greco painted *Storm Over Toledo.*

Toledo is a small city steeped in history and full of magnificent buildings. It was the capital of Spain under both Moors and Christians until some whim caused Philip II to move his capital to Madrid in 1561. Begin your visit with a drink in one of the many terrace cafés on the central **Plaza Zocodover,** study a map, and try to get your bearings, for a veritable labyrinth confronts you as you try to find your way to Toledo's great treasures. While here, search the square's pastry shops for the typical marzipan candies *(mazapanes)* of Toledo.

Begin your tour with a visit to the 13th-century **Cathedral,** seat of the Cardinal Primate of Spain, and one of the great cathedrals of Spain. Somber but elaborate, it blazes with jeweled chalices, gorgeous ecclesiastical vestments, historic tapestries, some 750 stained-glass windows, and paintings by Tintoretto, Titian, Murillo, El Greco, Velázquez, and Goya. The cathedral has two surprises: a **Mozarabic chapel,** where Mass is still celebrated on Sundays according to an ancient Mozarabic rite handed down from the days of the Visigoths (AD 419–711); and its unique **Transparente,** an extravagent Baroque roof that gives a theatrical glimpse into heaven as the sunlight pours down through a mass of figures and clouds. *Admission: 350 ptas. Open Tues.–Sat. 10:30–1 and 3:30–6 (7 in summer), Sun. 10:30–1:30 and 4–6.*

En route to the real jewel of Toledo, the **Chapel of Santo Tomé,** you'll pass a host of souvenir shops on Calle Santo Tomé, bursting with damascene knives and swords, blue-and-yellow pottery from nearby Talavera, and El Greco reproductions. In the tiny chapel that houses El Greco's masterpiece, *The Burial of the Count of Orgaz,* you can capture the true spirit of the Greek painter who adopted Spain, and in particular Toledo, as his home. Do you recognize the sixth man from the left among the painting's earthly contingent? Or the young boy in the left-hand corner? The first is El Greco himself, the second his son Jorge Manuel—see 1578, the year of his birth, embroidered on his handkerchief. *Admission: 100 ptas. Open daily 10–1:45 and 3:30–5:45 (6:45 in summer).*

Not far away is **El Greco's House,** a replica containing copies of his works. *Tel. 925/224046. Admission: 200 ptas. Open Tues.–Sat. 10–2 and 4–6, Sun. 10–2.*

The splendid **Sinagoga del Tránsito** stands on the corner of Samuel Levi and Reyes Católicos. Commissioned in 1366 by Samuel Levi, chancellor to Pedro the Cruel, the synagogue shows Christian and Moorish as well as Jewish influences in its architecture and decoration—look at the stars of David interspersed with the arms of Castile and León. There's also a small **Sephardic Museum** chronicling the life of Toledo's former Jewish community. *Admission: 200 ptas. Open Tues.–Sat. 10–2 and 4–6, Sun. 10–2.*

Another synagogue, the incongruously named **Santa María la Blanca** (it was given as a church to the Knights of Calatrava in 1405), is just along the street. Its history may have been Jewish and Christian, but its architecture is definitely Moorish, for it resembles a mosque with five naves, horseshoe arches, and capitals decorated with texts from the Koran. *Admission: 100 ptas. Open daily 10–2 and 3:30–6 (until 7 in summer).*

Across the road is **San Juan de los Reyes,** a beautiful Gothic church begun by Ferdinand and Isabella in 1476. Wander around its fine cloisters and don't miss the iron manacles on the outer walls; they were placed there by Christians freed by the Moors. The Catholic Kings originally intended to be buried here, but then their great triumph at Granada in 1492 changed their plans. *Admission: 100 ptas. Open daily 10–1:45 and 3:30–6 (7 in summer).*

Walk down the hill through the ancient **Cambrón Gate** and your visit to Toledo is over. Should you have more time, however, head for the **Museum of Santa Cruz,** just off the Zocodover, with its splendid El Grecos. *Tel. 925/221036. Admission: 200 ptas. Open Mon. 10–2, 4:30–6:30, Tues.–Sat. 10–6:30, Sun. 10–2.*

Also consider a visit to the **Hospital de Tavera,** outside the walls, where you can see Ribera's amazing *Bearded Woman. Tel. 925/220451. Admission: 300 ptas. Open daily 10–1:30 and 3:30–6.*

In the foothills of the Guadarrama Mountains, 50 kilometers (31 miles) to the northwest of Madrid, and 120 kilometers (74 miles) from Toledo, lies **San Lorenzo del Escorial,** burial place of Spanish kings and queens. The **Monastery,** built by the religious fanatic Philip II as a memorial to his father, Charles V, is a vast rectangular edifice, conceived and executed with a monotonous magnificence worthy of the Spanish royal necropolis. It was designed by Juan de Herrera, Spain's greatest Renaissance architect. The **Royal Pantheon** contains the tombs of monarchs from Charles V to Alfonso XIII, grandfather of Juan Carlos, and those of their consorts. Only two kings are missing, Philip V, who chose to be buried in his beloved La Granja, and Ferdinand VI, buried in Madrid. In the **Pantheon of the Infantes** rest the 60 royal children who died in infancy, and those queens who bore no heirs. The lavishly bejeweled tomb here belongs to Don Juan, bastard son of Charles V and half brother of Philip II, dashing hero and victor of the Battle of Lepanto. The monastery's other highlights are the magnificent **Library of Philip II,** with 40,000 rare volumes and 2,700 illuminated manuscripts, including the diary of Santa Teresa, and the **Royal Apartments.** Contrast the spartan private apartment of Philip II and the simple bedroom in which he died in 1598 with the beautiful carpets, porcelain, and tapestries with which his less austere successors embellished the rest of his somber monastery-palace. *Tel. 91/890–5905. Admission: 500 ptas. for whole complex, including Casita del Príncipe. Open Tues.–Sun. 10–6 (7 in summer). Last entry is 45 mins. before closing time.*

Eight kilometers (5 miles) along the road to Segovia, the mighty cross of the **Valley of the Fallen** looms up on your left. This vast basilica hewn out of sheer granite was built by General Franco between 1940 and 1959 as a monument to the dead of Spain's Civil War of 1936–39. Buried here are 43,000 war dead, José Antonio Primo de Rivera, founder of the Falangists and early martyr of the war, and Franco himself, who died in 1975. A funicular to the top of the monument costs 200 ptas. *Tel. 91/890–5611. Admission: 400 ptas. Open Tues.–Sat. 10–7 (6 in winter).*

A spectacular drive lies ahead for those who use the local road rather than the autoroute, from the resort of Navacerrada up through the Guadarrama Mountains by way of the **Navacerrada pass** at 1,860 meters (6,000 feet). The steep descent through fragrant pine forests via the hairpin bends of the Siete Revueltas (Seven Curves) brings you straight into La Granja.

The **Palace of La Granja,** with its splendid formal gardens and fountains, was built between 1719 and 1739 by the homesick

Philip V, first Bourbon king of Spain and grandson of France's Louis XIV, to remind him of his beloved Versailles. The whole place is like an exquisite piece of France in a Spanish wood, and it's small wonder that Philip chose to be buried here in the splendor of his own creation rather than in the austerity of El Escorial. The splendid gardens are open until dusk and you can stroll around them for free except when the fountains are playing. *Tel. 911/470020. Palace admission: 400 ptas. Palace open Tues.–Sun. 10–6; winter, Tues.–Sat. 10–1:30 and 3–5, Sun. 10–2.*

From La Granja, a 10-minute drive will bring you to the golden-stone market town of **Segovia.** In front of you rises the majestic Roman aqueduct, its huge granite blocks held together without mortar. At its foot is a small bronze statue of Romulus and the wolf, presented by Rome in 1974 to commemorate the 2,000-year history of Spain's most complete Roman monument.

Drive around the base of the rock on which Segovia stands. The Ronda de Santa Lucía leads to the most romantic view of the Alcázar, perched high on its rock like the prow of a mighty ship. Return via the Carretera de los Hoyos for yet another magical view, this time of the venerable cathedral rising from the ramparts. Next, fend off the pestering gypsies around the aqueduct and make for the **Calle Real,** the main shopping street. As you climb, you'll pass the Romanesque church of **San Martín,** with its porticoed outer gallery. Continue to the picturesque **Plaza Mayor** with its colorful ceramic stalls (good bargains) and pleasant cafés set against the backdrop of ancient arcaded houses and one of the loveliest, externally, at least, Gothic cathedrals in Spain.

Segovia **cathedral** was the last Gothic cathedral to be built in Spain (the one in Ávila was the first). Begun in 1525 by order of Charles V, its interior is sadly disappointing, as many of its treasures were carried off by Napoleon's troops in the Peninsular War of the early 1800s. Its museum has the first book printed in Spain (1472). You should also seek out the tomb of Don Pedro, two-year-old son of Henry IV who slipped from his nurse's arms and tumbled to his death over the battlements of the Alcázar (his distraught nurse cast herself over after him). *Admission: 200 ptas. Open daily in summer, 9–5; in winter, Mon.–Sat. 9:30–1 and 3–6, Sun. 9:30–6.*

The turreted **Alcázar** with its *esgrafiado* facade—an architectural peculiarity of Segovia whereby houses were embellished with small pieces of coke—is largely a fanciful re-creation of the 1880s, the original 13th-century castle having been destroyed by fire in 1862. The view from its ramparts—and, even better, from its tower if you can manage the 156 steps—is breathtaking. The Alcázar served as a major residence of the Catholic Kings. Here Isabella met Ferdinand, and from here she set out to be crowned Queen of Castile. The interior successfully re-creates the era of this dual monarchy that established Spain's Golden Age. *Tel. 911/430176. Admission: 200 ptas. Open daily 10–6 in winter, 10–7 in summer.*

The **Palace of Riofrio,** 8 kilometers (5 miles) south of Segovia, off the road to San Rafael, was bought by Isabel Farnese, widow of Philip V, with the idea of turning it into a splendid dwelling along the lines of Madrid's Royal Palace. Her dream was never fulfilled, and the palace, which houses a small **Hunting**

Museum, is now of minor importance. Far more attractive is its surrounding **parkland,** where deer will come right up to your car. *Admission: 300 ptas. Palace open Tues.–Sat. 10–1:30 and 3–5, Sun. 10–2.*

Ávila, almost 1,240 meters (4,000 feet) above sea level, is the highest provincial capital in Spain. Alfonso VI and his son-in-law, Count Raimundo de Borgoña, rebuilt the town and walls in 1090, bringing it permanently under Christian control. It is these walls, the most complete military installations of their kind in Spain, that give Ávila its special medieval quality. Thick and solid, with 88 towers tufted with numerous untidy storks' nests, they stretch for 2½ kilometers (1½ miles) around the entire city and make an ideal focus for the start of your visit. For a superb overall view and photo spot, drive out to the **Cuatro Postes,** three-quarters of a kilometer (half a mile) out on the road to Salamanca.

The personality of Santa Teresa the Mystic, to whom the city is dedicated, lives today as vividly as it did in the 16th century. Several religious institutions associated with the life of the saint are open to visitors, the most popular of which is the **Convent of Santa Teresa,** which stands on the site of her birthplace. There's an ornate Baroque chapel, a small gift shop, and a museum with some of her relics: her rosary, books, walking stick, a sole of her sandal, and her finger wearing her wedding ring. *Admission free. Located at Plaza de la Santa, just inside the southern gate. Open daily 9:30–1:30 and 3:30–9.*

Ávila's other ecclesiastical monuments are far older and more rewarding than those that commemorate the saint. The impregnable hulk of the **cathedral** is in many ways more akin to a fortress than a house of God. Though of Romanesque origin— the Romanesque sections are recognizable by their red and white brickwork—it is usually claimed as Spain's first Gothic cathedral. Inside, the ornate alabaster tomb of Cardinal Alonso de Madrigal, a 15th-century bishop whose swarthy complexion earned him the nickname of "El Tostado" (the toasted one) is thought to be the work of Domenico Fancelli, who also sculpted the tomb of Prince Juan in Santo Tomás and the sepulchers of the Catholic Kings in Granada's Royal Chapel. *Tel. 918/211641. Admission free. Cathedral open daily 8–1:30 and 3–7 (5:30 in winter). Cathedral Museum open daily 10–1:30 and 3–7 (5:30 in winter). Admission: 100 ptas.*

The **Basilica of San Vicente,** just outside the walls, is one of Ávila's finest Romanesque churches, standing on the spot where St. Vincent and his sisters Sabina and Cristeta were martyred in AD 306. Here, too, Santa Teresa is said to have experienced the vision that told her to reform the Carmelite order. *Admission: 50 ptas. Open Tues.–Sun. 10–1 and 4–6 (7 in summer).*

Before continuing to the **Monastery of Santo Tomás,** you can relax in the pleasant **Plaza de Santa Teresa** with its outdoor cafés and statue of the saint erected for Pope John Paul's visit in 1982. Built between 1482 and 1493 by Ferdinand and Isabella, who used it as a summer palace, it houses the tomb of their only son, Prince Juan—who died at the age of 19 while a student at Salamanca—as well as the tomb of that far less lovable character, the notorious Inquisitor General Tomás de Torquemada.

Admission: monastery free, cloisters 50 ptas., Museum of Eastern Art 50 ptas. Open daily 10–1 and 4–7.

From Ávila it's straight sailing all the way to Salamanca unless you're a devotee of Santa Teresa and choose to take a small detour to the old ducal town of **Alba de Tormes** to visit the **Carmelite Convent** (open daily 9–2 and 4–8), where the saint is buried.

Salamanca is an ancient city, and your first glimpse of it is bound to be unforgettable. Beside the road flows the Tormes River and beyond it rise the old houses of the city and the golden walls, turrets, and domes of the Plateresque cathedrals. "Plateresque" comes from *plata* (silver) and implies that the stone is chiseled and engraved as intricately as that delicate metal. A superb example of this style is the facade of the Dominican **Monastery of San Esteban** (150 ptas.; open daily 9–1 and 4–7, 5–8 in summer), which you'll pass on your way to the cathedrals. The **old cathedral** far outshines its younger sister, the **new cathedral,** in beauty. (The new cathedral's funds ran out during construction—1513–1733—leaving a rather bare interior.) Inside the sturdy Romanesque walls of the old cathedral, built between 1102 and 1160, your attention will be drawn to Nicolás Florentino's stunning altarpiece with 53 brightly painted panels. Don't miss the splendid **cloisters,** which now house a worthwhile collection of religious art, and the **Degree Chapel,** where anxious students sought inspiration on the night before their final exams. *New cathedral free; old cathedral and cloisters 200 ptas. Open daily 10–1:30 and 4–5:30 (9:30–2 and 3:30–7 in summer).*

Founded by Alfonso IX in 1218, **Salamanca University** is to Spain what Oxford University is to England. On its famous **doorway** in the Patio de las Escuelas, a profusion of Plateresque carving surrounds the medallions of Ferdinand and Isabella. See if you can find the famous frog and skull, said to bring good luck to students in their examinations. Inside, the **lecture room** of Fray Luis de León has remained untouched since the days of the great scholar, and the prestigious **Library** boasts some 50,000 parchment and leather-bound volumes. *Tel. 923/294400, ext. 1150. Library admission: 150 ptas. Open Mon.–Sat. 9:30–1:30 and 4:30–6:30, Sun. 10–1.*

Now make for Salamanca's greatest jewel, the elegant 18th-century **Plaza Mayor.** Here you can browse in stores offering typical *charro* jewelry (silver and black flowerheads), head down the steps to the market in search of colorful tapas bars, or simply relax in an outdoor café. In this, the city's crowning glory, and the most exquisite square in Spain, you've found the perfect place to end your tour of Salamanca and Castile.

Dining and Lodging

For details and price-category definitions, *see* Dining and Lodging in Staying in Spain.

Ávila
Dining

El Fogón de Santa Teresa. Traditional Castilian roasts, lamb chops, and trout feature on the menu of this attractive restaurant in the vaults of the Palacio de Valderrábanos. *Alemania 3, tel. 918/211023. AE, DC, MC, V. Moderate.*

★ **El Rastro.** This ancient inn tucked into the city walls is Ávila's most atmospheric place to dine. Local specialties include Ávila's famous veal *(ternera)* and *yemas de Santa Teresa,* a dessert made from candied egg yolks. *Plaza del Rastro 1, tel. 918/211218. AE, DC, MC, V. Moderate.*

El Torreón. Castilian specialties are served in this typical mesón situated in the basement of the old Velada Palace, opposite the cathedral. *Tostado 1, tel. 918/213171. AE, MC, V. Moderate.*

Lodging **Palacio de Valderrábanos.** Ávila's best hotel is located in a 15th-century mansion opposite the cathedral. It was once the residence of the first bishop of Ávila. *Plaza Catedral 9, tel. 918/211023. 73 rooms. AE, DC, MC, V. Expensive.*

★ **Parador Raimundo de Borgoña.** The location of this parador in a 15th-century palace just inside the northern walls of the city is superb. The rooms are decorated in traditional Castilian style and have spacious, well-equipped bathrooms. Some rooms also have four-poster beds and a view of the city walls. Its dining room is atmospheric and serves local Ávilan dishes, including the inevitable yemas, and the parador garden offers the only access to the walls. *Marqués de Canales y Chozas 16, tel. 918/211340. 62 rooms. AE, DC, MC, V. Expensive.*

Don Carmelo. This functional, modern, and comfortable hotel, close to the station, is Ávila's best moderate bet. *Paseo Don Carmelo 30, tel. 918/228050. 60 rooms. V. Moderate.*

El Escorial **Charolés.** This elegant restaurant has a terrace above the
Dining street for summer dining. Its meat dishes are famous through-
★ out the region. Try the *charolés a la pimienta* (pepper steak). Fresh fish is brought in daily from Spain's north coast. *Floridablanca 24, tel. 91/890–5975. Reservations required most weekends. AE, DC, MC, V. Expensive.*

Mesón de la Cueva. Founded in 1768, this atmospheric mesón has several small, rustic dining rooms. This inn is a must for ambience, and the food is good, too. *San Antón 4, tel. 91/890–1516. Reservations advised on weekends. AE, DC, MC, V. Moderate–Expensive.*

El Candil. One of the best of the many middle-range restaurants in El Escorial, El Candil is situated above a bar on the corner of Plaza San Lorenzo on the village's main street. In summer you can dine outdoors in the square, a delightful spot. *Reina Victoria 12, tel. 91/890–4103. AE, DC, MC, V. Moderate.*

Lodging **Victoria Palace.** The rooms at the back of this grand old-world hotel close to the monastery have balconies and a splendid view toward Madrid; there's a garden and pool, too. *Juan de Toledo 4, tel. 91/890–1511. 89 rooms. AE, DC, MC, V. Expensive.*

Miranda Suizo. Rooms are comfortable in this charming old hotel on the main street, and the hotel café, with its dark wood fittings and marble tables, is right out of the 19th century. *Floridablanca 20, tel. 91/890–4711. 47 rooms. AE, DC, MC, V. Moderate.*

Salamanca **Chapeau.** This chic spot carefully offers both meat and fish
Dining carefully roasted in its wood-fired ovens. Try their *pimientos*
★ *rellenos* (stuffed peppers) and orange mousse for dessert. *Gran Vía 20, tel. 923/271833. Reservations advised. AE, DC, MC, V. Closed Sun. in summer. Expensive.*

Chez Victor. Chez Victor attracts a regular clientele with its French-inspired cuisine. *Espoz y Mina 26, tel. 923/213123. Reservations advised. AE, DC, MC, V. Closed Sun. evening, Mon., and Aug. Expensive.*

El Mesón. There's plenty of colorful atmosphere and good traditional Castilian food in this typical mesón just off the Plaza Mayor, beside the Gran Hotel. *Plaza Poeta Iglesias 10; tel. 923/ 217222. AE, MC, V. Closed Jan. Moderate.*

Río de la Plata. This small, atmospheric restaurant close to El Mesón and the Gran Hotel, serves superb *farinato* sausage; it's a great find. *Plaza del Peso 1, tel. 923/219005. AE, MC, V. Closed Mon., July. Moderate.*

Lodging **Parador.** One of Spain's newest—and ugliest—paradors stands across the river, with superb views of the city's skyline. Its rooms are spacious and comfortable and there's a pool, but it's a bit far from the center. *Teso de la Feria 2, tel. 923/268700, fax 923/215438. 108 rooms. AE, DC, MC, V. Expensive.*

Castellano III. Overlooking the Alamedilla Park just a few minutes' walk from the center, this comfortable, modern hotel is considered the best medium-price hotel in town. *San Francisco Javier 2, tel. 923/261611, fax 923/266741. 73 rooms. AE, MC, V. Moderate.*

Condal. A functional but comfortable hotel in a central location just off Calle Azafranal, two minutes from the Plaza Mayor. *Santa Eulalia 2, tel. 923/218400. 70 rooms. AE, DC, MC, V. Inexpensive.*

Segovia **Casa Duque.** Located at the end of the main shopping street,
Dining this restaurant has several floors of beautifully decorated traditional dining rooms and is the main rival to the famous Cándido. There's plenty of local atmosphere, and the food is pure Castilian—try the *ponche segoviano* for dessert. *Cervantes 12, tel. 911/430537. Reservations advised on weekends. AE, DC, MC, V. Moderate–Expensive.*

★ **Mesón de Cándido.** Segovia's most prestigious restaurant has seven dining rooms pulsating with atmosphere and decorated with bullfighting memorabilia and photos of the dignitaries who have dined here over the years. Specialties are *cochinillo* (suckling pig) and *cordero asado* (roast lamb). *Plaza Azoguejo 5, tel. 911/425911. Reservations required for Sun. lunch. AE, DC, MC, V. Moderate–Expensive.*

La Oficina. Traditional Castilian dishes are served in two delightful dining rooms that date back to 1893. It's just off Plaza Mayor. *Cronista Lecea 10, tel. 911/431643. AE, DC, MC, V. Moderate.*

Lodging **Los Linajes.** The advantages of this pleasant, modern hotel, built in Castilian style, are its central location and its superb views. *Dr. Velasco 9, tel. 911/431201, fax 911/431501. 53 rooms. AE, DC, MC, V. Expensive.*

★ **Parador.** To the north of town is this modern parador offering comfortable, spacious rooms and a pool. The views of the city, especially when illuminated, are magnificent. The restaurant offers superior parador cooking. *Off the N601 toward Valladolid, tel. 911/443737, fax 911/437362. 103 rooms. AE, DC, MC, V. Expensive.*

Acueducto. Ask for a room at the front in this comfortable older hotel with balconies overlooking the famous aqueduct. Well renovated, it's Segovia's best medium-range bet. *Padre Claret 10, tel. 911/424800, fax 911/428446. 78 rooms. MC, V. Moderate.*

Toledo **Asador Adolfo.** This restaurant is situated near the cathedral
Dining and is well known for its good food (try the superb roast meat and the *pimentos del piquillo rellenos de pescado*) and service.

Calle de la Granada 6, tel. 925/227321. AE, DC, MC, V. Closed Sun. evening. Expensive.

★ **Hostal del Cardenal.** Toledo's best restaurant is set in the 17th-century palace of Cardinal Lorenzana, up against the city ramparts, and boasts five dining rooms and a delightful garden for summer dining. The first choice of every tourist, both food and service are excellent (try the roast suckling pig). *Paseo Recaredo 24, tel. 925/220862. Reservations required in high season. AE, MC, V. Expensive.*

Casa Aurelio. There are two branches of this popular restaurant, both around the corner from the cathedral. Try the partridge or quail. *Sinagoga 6, tel. 925/221392, and Sinagoga 1, tel. 925/221392. AE, DC, MC, V. Closed Wed. Moderate.*

Los Cuatro Tiempos. The picturesque downstairs bar, decorated with ceramic tiles, is an ideal place for a *fino* and tapas before you head upstairs for a traditional Toledo meal. *Sixto Ramón Parro 7, tel. 925/223782. MC, V. Inexpensive–Moderate.*

Los Arcos. Located off Toledo de Ohio, this attractive modern restaurant offers good-value *menus del día* as well as inexpensive main courses such as roast partridge, and is fast gaining in popularity. *Cordonerías 11, tel. 925/210051. AE, DC, MC, V. Inexpensive.*

Lodging **Parador Conde de Orgaz.** This is one of Spain's most popular
★ paradores, and the best and most expensive hotel in Toledo (a 15-minute drive from city center). It's a modern parador built in traditional Toledo style and stands on a hill across the river, commanding magnificent views of the city. Book far ahead. *Paseo de los Cigarrales, tel. 925/221850, fax 925/225166. 77 rooms. AE, DC, MC, V. Expensive.*

Alfonso VI. This pleasant modern hotel has Castilian-style decor and is conveniently located in the center of town by the lcázar. *Gen. Moscardó 2, tel. 925/222600, fax 925/214458. 80 rooms. AE, DC, MC, V. Moderate.*

María Cristina. You'll pass this comfortable new hotel on your way from Madrid. Located beside the bullring, it opened in 1986 and provides excellent facilities. Its El Abside restaurant is fast gaining in prestige. *Marqués de Mendigorría 1, tel. 925/213202. 65 rooms. AE, V. Moderate.*

Maravilla. This simple but very central old-world hotel just off Plaza Zocodover has a good, old-fashioned restaurant. *Barrio Rey 7, tel. 925/223304. 18 rooms. AE, DC, MC, V. Inexpensive.*

Barcelona

Arriving and Departing

By Plane All international and domestic flights arrive at El Prat de Llobregat airport, 14 kilometers (8½ miles) south of Barcelona just off the main highway to Castelldefels and Sitges. For information on arrival and departure times, call the airport (tel. 93/478–5000 or 478–5032) or Iberia information (tel. 93/301–3993).

Between the The airport–city train leaves every 30 minutes between 6:30 AM
Airport and and 11 PM and reaches the Barcelona Central (Sants) Station in 15
Downtown minutes; a new extension now carries you to the Plaça de Catalunya, at the head of the Ramblas, in the heart of the old city. Taxis will then take you to your hotel. The Aerobus service con-

nects the airport with Plaza Catalunya every 15 minutes between 6:25 AM and 11 PM; pay the driver the fare of 375 ptas. RENFE provides a bus service to the Central Station during the night hours. A cab from the airport to your hotel, including airport and luggage surcharges, will cost about 2,000 ptas.

By Train The old Terminal (or França) Station on Avenida Marquès de l'Argentera reopened in 1992 after major renovations and now serves as the main terminal for trains to France and some express trains to points in Spain. The Central (Sants) station, which had been the main station, serves suburban destinations as well as most cities in Spain. Inquire at the tourist office to find out which station you need. Many trains also stop at the Passeig de Gràcia underground station at the junction of Aragó. This station is closer to the Plaça de Catalunya and Ramblas area than Central (Sants), but though tickets and information are available here, luggage carts and taxi ranks are not. Check with tourist offices for current travel information and phone numbers. For RENFE information, call 93/490–0202 (24 hours).

By Bus Barcelona has no central bus station, but many buses operate from the old Estació Vilanova (or Norte) at the end of Avenida Vilanova. **Juliá,** Ronda Universitat 5, runs buses to Zaragoza and Montserrat; and **Alsina Graëlls,** Ronda Universitat 4, to Lérida and Andorra.

Getting Around

Modern Barcelona above the Plaça de Catalunya is mostly built on a grid system, though there's no helpful numbering system as in the United States. The Old Town from the Plaça de Catalunya to the port is a warren of narrow streets, however, and you'll need a good street map to get around. Most sightseeing can be done on foot—you won't have any other choice in the Gothic Quarter—but you'll need to use the metro or buses to link sightseeing areas.

By Metro The subway is the fastest way of getting around, as well as the easiest to use. You pay a flat fare of 90 ptas. no matter how far you travel, or purchase a **targeta multiviatge,** good for 10 rides (460 ptas.). Plans of the system are available from main metro stations or from branches of the Caixa savings bank.

By Bus City buses run from about 5:30 or 6 AM to 10:30 PM, though some stop earlier. Again, there's a flat-fare system (90 ptas.). Plans of the routes followed are displayed at bus stops. A reduced-rate targeta multiviatge, good for 10 rides, can be purchased at the transport kiosk on Plaça de Catalunya (460 ptas.).

By Taxi Taxis are black and yellow, and when available for hire show a "Libre" sign in the daytime and a green light at night. The meter starts at 250 ptas., and there are small supplements for luggage (100 ptas. per case), Sundays and fiestas, rides from a station or the port (varies according to zone), and for going to or from the bullring or a soccer match. The supplement to the airport is 300 ptas. There are cab stands all over town; cabs may also be flagged down on the street. Make sure the driver puts on his meter.

By Cable Car and Funicular Montjuïc Funicular is a cog railroad that runs from the junction of Avenida Parallel and Nou de la Rambla to the Miramar Amusement Park on Montjuïc. It runs only when the amusement park is open (11–8:15 in winter, noon–2:45 and 4:30–9:25 in summer). A cable car (*teleferic*) then runs from the amusement park up to Montjuïc Castle (noon–8 daily in summer; winter, weekends only, 11–7:30).

A **Transbordador Aeri Harbor Cable Car** runs from Miramar on Montjuïc across the harbor to the Torre de Jaume I on Barcelona *moll* (jetty), and on to the Torre de Sant Sebastià at the end of Passeig Nacional in Barceloneta. You can board at either stage. The cable car runs from 11:30 AM to 6 PM in winter, 11 AM to 10 PM in summer.

To reach Tibidabo summit, take either bus No. 58 or the Ferrocarrils de la Generalitat train from Plaça de Catalunya to Avenida Tibidabo, then the *tramvía blau* (blue tram) to Peu del Funicular, and the Tibidabo Funicular from there to the Tibidabo Fairground. The funicular runs every half hour from 7:15 AM to 9:45 PM.

By Boat **Golondrinas** harbor boats operate short harbor trips from the Portal de la Pau near the Columbus Monument between 10 AM and 1:30 PM weekends only in winter, daily in summer between 10 AM and 8 PM.

Important Addresses and Numbers

Tourist Information The city's three main tourist offices are at the **Central** (Sants) train station (tel. 93/491–4431; open daily 8–8), the **Francia** train station (tel. 93/319–5758; open daily 8–8), and at the **airport** (tel. 93/478–4704; open Mon.–Sat. 9:30–8).

Information on the province and city can be found at the useful office at Gran Vía 658 (tel. 93/301–7443; open weekdays 9–7, Sat. 9–2).

During special events and conferences, a tourist office is open at the **Palacio de Congresos** (Avda. Maria Cristina, tel. 93/423–3101, ext. 8356); a small office with some pamphlets and maps is at the **Ajuntament** (Plaça Sant Jaume, tel. 93/402–7000, ext. 433; open summer, daily 9–8; and cultural information is available during the summer at the **Palau de la Virreina** (Ramblas 99, tel. 93/301–7775; open daily 9:30–9).

American Visitors' Bureau (Gran Vía 591 between Rambla de Catalunya and Balmes, 3rd floor, tel. 93/301–0150 or 301–0032).

Consulates **U.S.** (Paseo Reina Elisenda de Moncada 23, tel. 93/280–2227), **Canadian** (Vía Augusta 125, tel. 93/209–0634), **U.K.** (Diagonal 477, tel. 93/419–9044).

Emergencies **Police** (National Police, tel. 091; Municipal Police, tel. 092; Main Police [Policía Nacional] Station, Vía Laietana 43, tel. 93/301–6666). **Ambulance** (tel. 93/329–7766). **Doctor: Hospital Clínico** (Casanova 143, tel. 93/323–1414); **Hospital Evangélico** (Alegre de Dalt 87, tel. 93/219–7100).

English-Language Bookstores Several bookstalls on the Ramblas sell English guidebooks and novels. Also try **Librería Laie** (Pau Claris 85) or **Librería Francesca** (Passeig de Gràcia 91).

Travel Agencies **American Express** (Passeig de Gràcia 101, tel. 93/217–0070), **Wagons-Lits** (Gran Vía de las Corts Catalanes 670, tel. 93/318–7975), **Viajes Iberia** (Rambla de los Estudios 130, tel. 93/317–9320).

Guided Tours

Orientation Tours City sightseeing tours are run by **Juliá Tours** (Ronda Universitat 5, tel. 93/317–6454) and **Pullmantur** (Gran Vía Corts Catalanes 635, tel. 93/317–1297). Tours leave from the above terminals, though it may be possible to be picked up at your hotel. The content and price of tours are the same with both agencies. A morning sightseeing tour visits the Gothic Quarter and Montjuïc; an afternoon tour concentrates on Gaudí and the Picasso Museum. "Panorámica y Toros" (usually on Sundays only) takes in a bullfight and city drive; and various night tours include a flamenco show, dinner in a restaurant, and cabaret at La Scala.

Excursions These are run by **Juliá Tours** and **Pullmantur** and are booked as above. Principal trips are a half-day tour to **Montserrat** to visit the monastery and shrine of the famous Black Virgin; a full-day trip to the **Costa Brava** resorts, including a boat cruise to Lloret de Mar; and a full-day trip to **Andorra** for tax-free shopping.

Exploring Barcelona

Numbers in the margin correspond to points of interest on the Barcelona map.

Barcelona, capital of Catalonia and Spain's second-largest city, thrives on its business acumen and industrial muscle. Its hardworking citizens are almost militant in their use of their own language—with street names, museum exhibits, newspapers, radio programs, and movies all in Catalan. Their latest cause for rejoicing was the realization of their long-cherished goal to host the Olympic Games, held in Barcelona in summer 1992 after a massive building program. The Games' legacy to the city includes a vastly improved ring road and several other highways; four new beaches and an entire new neighborhood in what used to be the rundown industrial district of Barceloneta; an adjoining marina; and a new sports stadium and pools on the hill of Montjuïc. This thriving metropolis also has a rich history and an abundance of sights. Few places can rival the narrow alleys of its Gothic Quarter for medieval atmosphere, the elegance and distinction of its Modernista Eixample area, or the fantasies of Gaudí's whimsical imagination.

It should take you two full days of sightseeing to complete the following tour. The first part covers the Gothic Quarter, the Picasso Museum, and the Ramblas. The second part takes you to Passeig de Gràcia, the Sagrada Familia, and Montjuïc.

Start on Plaça de la Seu, where on Sunday morning the citizens of Barcelona gather to dance the *Sardana*, a symbol of Catalan **1** pride. Step inside the magnificent Gothic **catedral** (cathedral) built between 1298 and 1450, though the spire and Gothic facade were not added until 1892. Highlights are the beautifully carved **choir stalls,** Santa Eulalia's tomb in the crypt, the battle-scarred crucifix from Don Juan's galley in the **Lepanto Chapel,** and the cloisters. *Tel. 93/315–1554. Admission free. Open daily 7:45–1:30 and 4–7:45.*

2 Around the corner is the **Museu Frederic Marès** (Frederic MarèsMuseum), where you can browse for hours among the miscellany of sculptor-collector Frederic Marès. Displayed here is everything from polychrome crucifixes to hat pins, pipes, and walking sticks. *Plaça Sant Iu 5, tel. 93/310–5800. Admission: 250 ptas. Open Tues.–Sat. 10–5, Sun. 10–2.*

❸ The neighboring **Plaça del Rei** embodies the very essence of the Gothic Quarter. Legend has it that after Columbus's first voyage to America, the Catholic Kings received him in the **Saló de Tinell,** a magnificent banqueting hall built in 1362. Other ancient buildings around the square are the **Lieutenant's Palace;** the 14th-century **Chapel of St. Agatha,** built right into the Roman city wall; and the **Padellás Palace,** which houses the City History Museum.

Cross Vía Laietana, walk down Princesa, and turn right into Montcada, where you come to one of Barcelona's most popular ❹ attractions, the **Museu Picasso** (Picasso Museum). Two 15th-century palaces provide a striking setting for the collections donated in 1963 and 1970, first by Picasso's secretary, then by the artist himself. The collection ranges from early childhood sketches done in Málaga to exhibition posters done in Paris shortly before his death. Of particular interest are his Blue Period pictures and his variations on Velázquez's *Las Meninas. Tel. 93/319–6310. Admission: 50 ptas. Open Tues.–Sat. 10–8, Sun. 10–3.*

Time Out At the bottom of Montcada, on the left, is **La Pizza Nostra** (Arc de Sant Vicens 2, tel. 93/319–9058), an ideal spot for a cup of coffee, a slice of cheesecake, or a pizza and a glass of wine.

❺ **Santa María del Mar** is one of the loveliest Gothic churches in Barcelona. It was built between 1329 and 1383 in fulfillment of a vow made a century earlier by Jaume I to build a church for the Virgin of the Sailors. Its simple beauty is enhanced by a stunning rose window and magnificent soaring columns. *Open daily 8–1 and 4–7:30.*

Continue up Carrer Argentería, cross Vía Laietana, and walk ❻ along Jaume I till you come to **Plaça Sant Jaume,** an impressive square built in the 1840s in the heart of the Gothic Quarter. The two imposing buildings facing each other across the square are very much older. The 15th-century **Ajuntament,** or City Hall, has an impressive black and gold mural (1928) by Josep María Sert (who also painted the murals for New York's Waldorf Astoria) and the famous **Saló de Cent,** from which the Council of One Hundred ruled the city from 1372 to 1714. The **Palau de la Generalitat,** seat of the Catalan Regional Government, is a 15th-century palace open to the public on Sunday mornings only.

Time Out Among the best lunch spots in this area are **Agut d'Avignon** and **La Cuineta** (*see* Dining, *below*), and **Tinell** (Frenería 8, tel. 93/315–4604).

Continue along the Carrer Ferrán, with its attractive 19th-❼ century shops and numerous Modernista touches, to the **Plaça Reial.** Here in this splendid, if rather dilapidated, 19th-century square, arcaded houses overlook the wrought-iron **Fountain of the Three Graces,** and lampposts designed by a young Gaudí in 1879. Watch out for drug pushers here; the safest and most colorful time to come is on a Sunday morning when crowds gather at the stamp and coin stalls and listen to soap-box orators.

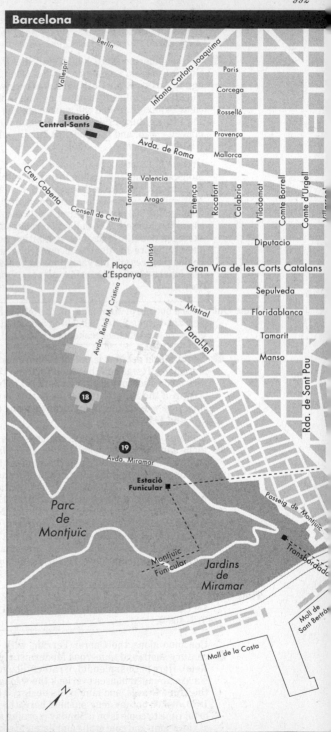

Barcelona

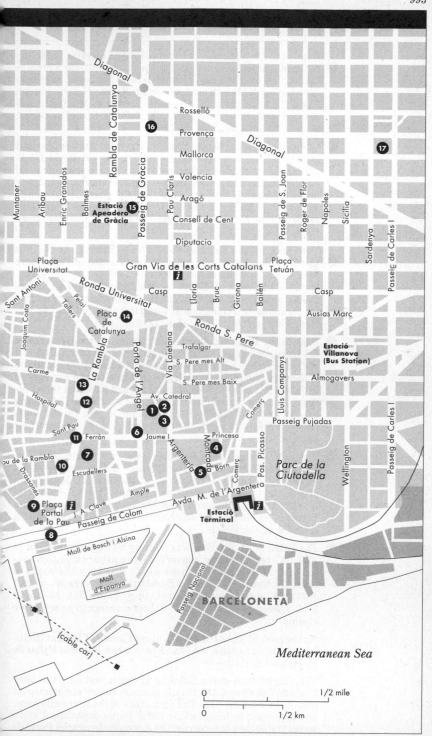

Time Out   Nearby are two atmospheric restaurants, **Los Caracoles** and **Can Culleretes.**

⑧ Head to the bottom of Ramblas and take an elevator to the top of the **Monument a Colon** (Columbus Monument) for a breathtaking view over the city. Columbus faces out to sea, overlooking a replica of his own boat, the *Santa María.* (Nearby you can board the cable car that crosses the harbor to Montjuïc.) *Admission: 200 ptas. adults, 100 ptas. children. Open Tues.–Sat. 10–2 and 3:30–6:30, Sun. 10–7.*

⑨ Our next stop is the **Museu Marítim** (Maritime Museum) housed in the 13th-century Atarazanas Reales, the old Royal Dockyards. The museum is packed with ships, figureheads, nautical paraphernalia, and several early navigation charts, including a map by Amerigo Vespucci, and the 1439 chart of Gabriel de Valseca from Mallorca, the oldest chart in Europe. *Plaça Portal de la Pau 1, tel. 93/318–3245. Admission: 150 ptas. Open Tues.–Sat. 10–2 and 4–7, Sun. 10–2.*

⑩ Turn back up the Ramblas to Nou de la Rambla. At No. 3 is Gaudí's **Palau Güell,** which houses the **Museum of Performing Arts.** Gaudí built this mansion between 1885 and 1890 for his patron, Count Eusebi de Güell, and it's the only one of his houses that is readily open to the public. It makes an intriguing setting for the museum's collection of theatrical memorabilia. *Admission: 100 ptas. Open Tues.–Sat. 11–2 and 5–8.*

⑪ Back to the Ramblas and our next landmark, the **Gran Teatre del Liceu,** on the corner of Sant Pau. Built between 1845 and 1847, the Liceu claims to be the world's oldest opera house and is the only one in Spain. A fairly mundane facade conceals an exquisite interior with ornamental gilt and plush red velvet fittings. Anna Pavlova danced here in 1930, and Maria Callas sang here in 1959. *Tel. 93/318–9122. Admission: free. Guided tours (some in English) weekdays 11:30 and 12:15; tel. reservations advised.*

⑫ This next stretch of the **Ramblas** is the most fascinating. The colorful paving stones on the Plaça de la Boquería were designed by Joan Miró. Glance up at the swirling Modernista dragon and the Art Nouveau street lamps. Then take a look inside the bustling **Boquería Food Market** and the **Casa Antigua Figueras,** an old grocery store on the corner of Petxina, with a splendid mosaic facade.

⑬ The **Palau de la Virreina** was built by a viceroy from Peru in 1778. It's recently been converted into a major exhibition center, and you should check to see what's showing while you're in town. *Corner of Carme and Rambla de las Flores 99, tel. 93/301–7775. Admission: 300 ptas. Open Tues.–Sat. 10–2 and 4:30–9, Sun. 10–2, Mon. 4:30–9. Last entrance 30 mins. before closing.*

On the next block is the 18th-century **Church of Betlem** (Bethlehem) and, opposite, the handsome ocher Baroque **Palau de Moja,** built in 1702.

⑭ The final stretch of the Ramblas brings us out onto the busy **Plaça de Catalunya,** the frantic business center and transport hub of the modern city. The first stage of the tour ends here. You may want to head for the Corte Inglés department store across the square or for any of the stores on the nearby **Porta de** l'Angel. Alternatively, you can relax on the terrace of the ancient **Café Zurich** on the corner of Pelai, or stop at the colorful beer hall, the **Cervecería,** opposite the Hostal Continental.

Above the Plaça de Catalunya you come into modern Barcelona and an elegant area known as the **Eixample,** which was laid out in the late 19th century as part of the city's expansion scheme. Much of the building here was done at the height of the **Modernista** movement, a Spanish and mainly Barcelonian offshoot of Art Nouveau, whose leading exponents were the architects Antoní Gaudí, Domènech i Montaner, and Puig i Cadafalch. The principal thoroughfares of the Eixample are the Rambla de Catalunya and the Passeig de Gràcia, where some of the city's most elegant shops and cafés are found. Modernista houses are one of Barcelona's special drawing cards, so walk up **Passeig de**
⓯ **Gràcia** until you come to the **Manzana de la Discordía,** or Block of Discord, between Consell de Cent and Aragó. Its name is a pun on the word *manzana,* which means both "block" and "apple." The houses here are quite fantastic: The floral **Casa Lleó Morera** at No. 35 is by Domènech i Montaner. The pseudo-Gothic **Casa Amatller** at No. 41 is by Puig i Cadafalch. At No. 43 is Gaudí's **Casa Batlló.** Farther along the street on the right, on
⓰ the corner of Provença, is Gaudí's **Casa Milà** (Passeig de Gràcia 92), more often known as **La Pedrera** (which, along with Casa Batlló, was dramatically spruced up in conjunction with the 1992 Olympics). Its remarkable curving stone facade with ornamental balconies actually ripples its way around the corner of the block.

Time Out You can ponder the vagaries of Gaudí's work over a drink in **Amarcord,** a terrace café in the Pedrera building. If you're feeling a bit homesick, sip a cocktail or munch a deep-pan pizza in the **Chicago Pizza Pie Factory** at Provença 300. For a more sedate, old-world tearoom, head for the **Salón de Té Mauri** on the corner of Rambla de Catalunya and Provença.

Now take the metro at Diagonal directly to Barcelona's most
⓱ eccentric landmark, Gaudí's **Temple Expiatori de la Sagrada Família** (Expiatory Church of the Holy Family). Far from finished at his untimely death in 1926—the absentminded Gaudí was run over by a tram and died in a pauper's hospital—this striking creation will cause consternation or wonder, shrieks of protest or cries of rapture. In 1936 during the Civil War the citizens of Barcelona loved their crazy temple enough to spare it from the flames that engulfed all their other churches except the cathedral. An elevator takes visitors to the top of one of the towers for a magnificent view of the city. Gaudí is buried in the crypt. *Tel. 93/255–0247. Admission: 400 ptas. Open Sept.–June., daily 9–7; July–Aug., daily 9–9.*

Way across town to the south, the hill of **Montjuïc** was named for the Jewish community that once lived on its slopes. Montjuïc is home to a castle, an amusement park, several delightful gardens, a model Spanish village, an illuminated fountain, the recently rebuilt Mies van der Rohe Pavilion, and a cluster of museums—all of which could keep you busy for a day or more. This was the principal venue for the 1992 Olympics.

⓲ One of the leading attractions here is the **Museu d'Art de Catalunya** (Museum of Catalan Art) in the Palau Nacional atop a long flight of steps. The collection of Romanesque and Gothic art treasures—medieval frescoes and altarpieces, mostly from small churches and chapels in the Pyrenees—is simply staggering. Just three rooms were open at press time, but the entire museum was expected to open by 1994 after extensive renovations; ask at the tourist office for current information.

⑲ Nearby is the **Fundació Miró** (Miró Foundation), a gift from the artist Joan Miró to his native city. One of Barcelona's most exciting contemporary galleries, it has several exhibition areas, many of them devoted to Miró's works. Miró himself now rests in the cemetery on the southern slopes of Montjuïc. *Admission: 400 ptas. Open Tues.–Sat. 11–7 (9:30 on Thurs.), Sun. 10:30–2:30.*

Off the Beaten Track

If you're hooked on **Modernista** architecture, you can follow a walking trail around the **Dreta de l'Eixample,** the area to the right of Rambla de Catalunya. Ask at a tourist office for a Gaudí or Modernismo trail brochure for the Eixample. Attend a concert at Domènech i Montaner's fantastic **Palau de la Música.** Make a trip to the **Parc Güell,** Gaudí's magical but uncompleted attempt at creating a garden city. *Open May–Aug., daily 10–9; Sept.–Apr., daily 10–7. Metro: Lesseps. Bus: 24.*

Explore the **Major de Gràcia** area, above the Diagonal. It's a small, almost independent village within a large city, a warren of narrow streets, changing name at every corner, and filled with tiny shops where you'll find everything from old-fashioned tin lanterns to feather dusters.

Take a stroll around **Barceloneta,** the old fishermen's quarter built in 1755 below Terminal Station and the Ciutadela Park. Along its narrow streets are atmospheric taverns (try C. Maquinista). There are no-frills fish restaurants on the Passeig Nacional and beach restaurants along the Passeig Marítim that are well known to locals and worth experiencing. This area, particularly the buildings fronting the water, underwent a major transformation from faded industrial to elegant when the government built the Olympic Village to house athletes nearby.

Hunt out the tiny **Shoe Museum** in Plaça Sant Felip Neri, in a hidden corner of the Gothic Quarter, between the cathedral and Bishop's Palace. The collection includes clowns' shoes and a pair worn by Pablo Casals. *Admission: 100 ptas. Open Tues.–Sun. 11–2.*

Shopping

Gift Ideas There are no special handicrafts associated with Barcelona, but you'll have no trouble finding typical Spanish goods anywhere in town. If you're into fashion and jewelry, then you've come to the right place, as Barcelona makes all the headlines on Spain's booming fashion front. **Xavier Roca i Coll,** Sant Pere mes Baix 24, just off Laietana, specializes in silver models of Barcelona's buildings.

Antiques Carrer de la Palla and Banys Nous in the Gothic Quarter are lined with antiques shops where you'll find old maps, books, paintings, and furniture. An **antiques market** is held every Thursday morning in Plaça Nova in front of the cathedral. The

Centre d'Antiquaris, Passeig de Gràcia 57, has some 75 antiques stores. **Gothsland,** Consell de Cent 331, specializes in Modernista designs.

Boutiques The most fashionable boutiques are in the **Galerías** on Passeig de Gràcia and Rambla de Catalunya. Others are on Gran Vía between Balmes and Pau Claris; and on the Diagonal between Ganduxer and Passeig de Gràcia. **Adolfo Domínguez,** Spain's top designer, is at Passeig de Gràcia 89 and Valencia 245; **Loewe,** Spain's top leather store, is at Passeig de Gràcia 35 and Diagonal 570; **Joaquín Berao,** a top jewelry designer, is at Rosselló 277.

Shopping Districts Elegant shopping districts are the Passeig de Gràcia, Rambla de Catalunya, and the Diagonal. For more affordable, more old-fashioned, and typically Spanish-style shops, explore the area between Ramblas and Vía Laietana, especially around C. Ferran. The area around Plaça del Pi from Boquería to Portaferrisa and Canuda is recommended for young fashion stores and imaginative gift shops.

Department Stores **El Corte Inglés** is on the Plaça de Catalunya 14 (tel. 93/302–1212) and at Diagonal 617 (tel. 93/419–2828) near María Cristina metro. **Galerías Preciados** is at Porta de l'Angel 19 just off the Plaça de Catalunya; Diagonal 471 on the Plaça Francesc Macià; and Avenida Meridiana 352. All are open Monday to Saturday 10–8.

Food and Flea Markets The **Boquería** or **Sant Josep Market** on the Ramblas between Carme and Hospital is a superb, colorful food market, held every day except Sunday. **Els Encants,** Barcelona's fascinating Flea Market, is held every Monday, Wednesday, Friday, and Saturday at the end of Dos de Maig on the Plaça Glòries Catalanes. **Sant Antoní Market,** at the end of Ronda Sant Antoní, is an old-fashioned food and clothes market, best on Sundays when there's a secondhand **book market** with old postcards, press cuttings, lithographs, and prints. There's a **stamp and coin market** in the Plaça Reial on Sunday mornings, and an **artists' market** in the Placeta del Pi just off Ramblas and Boquería on Saturday mornings.

Bullfighting

Barcelona has two bullrings, the **Arènes Monumental** on Gran Vía and Carles I, and the smaller, rarely used, **Arènes les Arenes** on the Plaça d'Espanya. Bullfights are held on Sundays between March and October; check the newspaper for details. The official ticket office, where there is no markup on tickets, is at Muntaner 24 (tel. 93/453–3821) near Gran Vía. There's a **Bullfighting Museum** at the Monumental ring, open March–October, daily 10–1 and 5:30–7.

Bars and Cafés

Cafés and Tearooms **Zurich** (Plaça de Catalunya 35), on the corner of Pelai, is one of the oldest and most traditional cafés, perfect for watching the world go by. **The Croissant Show** (Santa Anna 10 just off Ramblas), is a small coffee and pastry shop, ideal for a quick mid-morning or afternoon break. **Salón de Té Mauri,** on the corner of Rambla de Catalunya and Provença, and **Salón de Té Libre i Serra** (Ronda Sant Pere 3), are both traditional tearooms with a good selection of pastries.

Tapas Bars You'll find these all over town, but two of the most colorful are **Alt Heidelberg** (Ronda Universitat 5), with German beer on tap and German sausages, and the **Cervecería** at the top of Ramblas, opposite the Hostal Continental.

Cocktail Bars These places are both popular and plentiful everywhere, but the two best areas are the **Passeig del Born,** which is near the Picasso Museum and very fashionable with the affluent young, and the **Eixample,** near Passeig de Gràcia. A bar called **Dry Martini** (Aribau 162), has more than 80 different gins; **Ideal Cocktail Bar,** at Aribau 89, has some good malt whiskeys. **El Paraigua,** on Plaça Sant Miquel, in the Gothic Quarter behind the city hall, serves cocktails in a stylish setting with classical music. **Boadas** (Tallers 1), on the corner of Ramblas, has been going strong for over 50 years.

Champagne Bars *Xampanyerías,* serving sparkling Catalan *cava,* are popular all over town and are something of a Barcelona specialty. Try **Brut** (Trompetas 3), in the Picasso Museum area; **La Cava del Palau** (Verdaguer i Callis 10), near the Palau de la Música; **La Folie** (Bailén 169), one of the best; or **La Xampanyería** (Provença 236), on the corner of Enric Granados.

Special Cafés **Els Quatre Gats** (Montsió 5, off Porta de l'Angel) is a reconstruction of the original café that opened in 1897, and a real Barcelona institution. Literary discussions, jazz, and classical music recitals take place in this café where Picasso held his first show, Albéniz and Granados played their piano compositions, and Ramón Casas painted two of its original murals. **Café de l'Opera** (Ramblas 74), right opposite the Liceu, is a long-standing Barcelona tradition, ideal for a coffee or drink at any time of day.

Dining

For details and price-category definitions, *see* Dining in Staying in Spain.

Very Expensive **Eldorado Petit.** Luis Cruañas moved to Barcelona from the Costa Brava in 1984 and opened this restaurant, which rapidly became known as the best in Barcelona and one of the top restaurants in Spain. The setting—a private villa with a delightful garden for summer dining—is simply beautiful, and so is the cuisine. *Dolors Monserdá 51, tel. 93/204-5153. Reservations required. AE, MC, V. Closed Sun. and 2 weeks in Aug.*

★

Expensive **Agut d'Avignon.** This venerable Barcelona institution takes a bit of finding; it's near the junction of Ferran and Avinyó in the Gothic Quarter. The ambience is rustic and it's a favorite with businesspeople and politicians from over the road in the Generalitat. The cuisine is traditional Catalan and game specialties are recommended in season. *Trinidad 3, tel. 93/302–6034. Reservations required. AE, DC, MC, V. Closed Holy Week.*

★ **Azulete.** This is one of Barcelona's most beautiful restaurants—its dining room is an old conservatory filled with flowers and plants. The highly imaginative cuisine is a mixture of Catalan, French, and Italian with an interesting blend of traditional and new dishes. *Vía Augusta 281, tel. 93/203–5943. Reservations required. AE, DC, MC, V. Closed Sat. lunch, Sun., and first 2 weeks of Aug.*

La Cuineta. This small intimate restaurant in a 17th-century house just off Plaça Sant Jaume specializes in Catalan nouvelle cuisine. The decor is smart but charming, the service professional; and it's popular with businesspeople at lunchtime. *Paradis 4, tel. 93/315–0812. Reservations accepted. AE, DC, MC, V. Closed Mon.*

Quo Vadis. Located just off the Ramblas, near the Boquería Market and Betlem Church, is an unimpressive facade camouflaging one of Barcelona's most respected restaurants. Its much-praised cuisine includes delicacies like *pot pourri de setas* (mushrooms), *lubina al hinojo* (sea bass in fennel), and *hígado de ganso con ciruelas* (goose liver with cherries). *Carmen 7, tel. 93/317–7447. Reservations advised. AE, DC, MC, V. Closed Sun.*

Moderate **Can Culleretes.** This picturesque old restaurant began life as a pastry shop in 1786, and it is one of the most atmospheric and reasonable finds in Barcelona. Located on an alleyway between Ferran and Boquería, its three dining rooms are decorated with photos of visiting celebrities. It serves real Catalan cooking and is very much a family concern; don't be put off by the prostitutes outside! *Quintana 5, tel. 93/317–3022. Reservations accepted. AE, MC, V. Closed Sun. evening and Mon.*

Los Caracoles. Just below the Plaça Reial is Barcelona's most famous restaurant, which caters to tourists but has real atmosphere. Its walls are hung thick with photos of bullfighters and visiting celebrities; its specialties are mussels, paella and, of course, snails (*caracoles*). Don't miss it; it's fun. *Escudellers 14, tel. 93/309–3185. Reservations accepted. AE, DC, MC, V.*

★ **Sete Portes.** With plenty of old-world charm, this delightful restaurant near the waterfront has been going strong since 1836. The cooking is Catalan, the portions enormous, and specialties are *paella de pescado* and *zarzuela sete portes* (seafood casserole). *Passeig Isabel II 14, tel. 93/315–3910. Reservations advised on weekends. AE, DC, MC, V. Open 1 PM–1 AM.*

★ **Sopeta Una.** Dining in this delightful small restaurant with old-fashioned decor and intimate atmosphere is more like eating in a private home. The menu is in Catalan, all the dishes are Catalan, and the atmosphere is very genteel and middle class. For dessert, try the traditional Catalan *música*—a plate of raisins, almonds, and dried fruit served with a glass of muscatel. It's near the Palau de la Música; don't be put off by the narrow street. *Verdaguer i Callis 6, tel. 93/319–6131. Reservations accepted. V. Closed Sun., and Mon. AM.*

Inexpensive ★ **Agut.** Simple, hearty Catalan fare awaits you in this unpretentious restaurant in the lower reaches of the Gothic Quarter. Founded in 1924, its popularity has never waned. There's plenty of wine to wash down the traditional home cooking, but you won't find frills like coffee or liqueurs. *Gignàs 16, tel. 93/319–3315. Reservations not necessary. No credit cards. Closed Sun. evening, Mon., and July.*

★ **Egipte.** This small, friendly restaurant hidden away in a very convenient location behind the Boquería Market—though it's far better known to locals than to visitors—is a real find. Its traditional Catalan home cooking, huge desserts, and swift personable service all contribute to its popularity and good value. *Jerusalem 12, tel. 93/301–6208. No reservations. No credit cards.*

Lodging

For a city of its size and importance, Barcelona has long been underendowed with hotels. The 1992 Olympic Games, however, brought with them some new hotels—generally of the featureless modern variety—and also spurred the renovation and cleaning up of most of the older ones. Prices rose dramatically for the Games, but have fallen back to more reasonable levels now. Hotels in the Ramblas and Gothic Quarter have plenty of old-world charm, but are less strong on creature comforts; those in the Eixample are mostly '50s or '60s buildings, often recently renovated; and the newest hotels are found out along the Diagonal or beyond, in the residential district of Sarriá. There are hotel reservation desks at the airport and Sants Central Station.

For details and price-category definitions, *see* Lodging in Staying in Spain.

Very Expensive **Avenida Palace.** Right in the center of town, between the Rambla de Catalunya and Passeig de Gràcia, this hotel dates from 1952 but conveys a feeling of elegance and Old World style. Some rooms are rather plain, but most have been recently renovated and there's a superbly ornate lobby. *Gran Vía 605, tel. 93/301–9600, fax 93/318–1234. 211 rooms. AE, DC, MC, V.*

Meliá Barcelona. This is a bit far out off the Diagonal, but if you like modern, luxurious hotels, this is the one for you. It's been dramatically refurbished with a spectacular waterfall and special executive floor ideal for businesspeople. *Avda Sarriá 50, tel. 93/410–6060, fax 93/321–5179. 314 rooms. AE, DC, MC, V.*

★ **Ritz.** Founded in 1919 by Caesar Ritz, this is still the grand old lady of Barcelona hotels. Extensive refurbishment has now restored it to its former splendor. The entrance lobby is aweinspiring, the rooms spacious, and the service impeccable. *Gran Vía 668, tel. 93/318–5200, fax 93/318–0148. 161 rooms. AE, DC, MC, V.*

Expensive ★ **Colón.** This cozy, older hotel has a unique charm and intimacy reminiscent of an English country hotel, though some refurbishing would be very welcome. It's in an ideal location right in the heart of the Gothic Quarter, and the rooms on the front overlook the cathedral and square. It was a great favorite of Joan Miró. *Avda. Catedral 7, tel. 93/301–1404, fax 93/317–2915. 155 rooms. AE, DC, MC, V.*

★ **Condes de Barcelona.** As this is one of Barcelona's most popular hotels, rooms need to be booked well in advance. The decor is stunning, with marble floors and columns, an impressive staircase, and an outstanding bar area, but no restaurant. Guest rooms are on the small side. *Passeig de Gràcia 75, tel. 93/487–3737; for reservations, 93/215–7931, fax 93/216–0835. 100 rooms. AE, DC, MC, V.*

Regente. This smallish hotel on the corner of Valencia has a rooftop pool, plenty of style and charm, and a wonderful Modernista lobby. *Rambla de Catalunya 76, tel. 93/215–2570, fax 93/487–3227. 78 rooms. AE, DC, MC, V.*

Rialto. In the heart of the Gothic Quarter, just two paces down from the Plaça Sant Jaume, this old 19th-century house has been renovated to high standards of comfort while preserving its charm. Here you're surrounded by sights, shops, and some of Barcelona's best restaurants. *Ferran 40, tel. 93/318–5212, fax 93/315–3819. 128 rooms. AE, DC, MC, V.*

Moderate   **Gran Vía.** Architectural features are the special charm of this
19th-century mansion, close to the main tourist office. The
original chapel has been preserved, and you can have breakfast
in a hall of mirrors, climb its Modernista staircase, and call
from elaborate Belle Epoque phone booths. *Gran Vía 642, tel.
93/318-1900, fax 93/318-9997. 48 rooms. AE, DC, MC, V.*

★ **Oriente.** Barcelona's oldest hotel opened in 1843. Its public
rooms are a delight—the ballroom and dining rooms have lost
none of their 19th-century magnificence—though the bedrooms have undergone rather featureless renovation. It's located just below the Liceu and its terrace café is the perfect
place for a drink. *Ramblas 45, tel. 93/302-2558. 142 rooms.
AE, DC, MC, V.*

Inexpensive   **Continental.** Something of a legend among cost-conscious travelers, this comfortable hostel with canopied balconies stands at
the top of Ramblas, just below Plaça Catalunya. The rooms are
homey and comfortable, the staff is friendly, and the location's
ideal. Buffet breakfasts are a plus. *Ramblas 136, tel. 93/301-
2570, fax 93/302-7360. 34 rooms. V.*

España. The Domenechi Montaner–designed Modernista interior renders this hotel an amazing bargain for those who put
architectural style before comfort. The high-ceilinged downstairs features a breakfast room decorated with mermaids,
elaborate woodwork, and an Art Nouveau chimney in the cafeteria. The rooms themselves, however, are very basic, and the
neighborhood can be a bit daunting for women walking alone.
San Pau 9, tel. 93/318-1758. 75 rooms. AE, DC, MC, V.

The Arts

To find out what's on in town, look in the daily papers or in the
weekly *Guía del Ocio*, available from newsstands all over town.
Actes a la Ciutat is a weekly list of cultural events published by
the Ajuntament and available from its information office on
Plaça Sant Jaume.

Concerts   Catalans are great music lovers, and their main concert hall is
Palau de la Música (Amadeo Vives 1, tel. 93/317-9982). The
ticket office is open weekdays 11–1 and 5–8 and Saturday 5–8
only. Its Sunday morning concerts are a popular tradition.
Tickets are reasonable and can usually be purchased just before the concert.

Opera   The **Gran Teatre del Liceu** is one of the world's finest opera
houses, considered by some second only to Milan's La Scala.
The box office for advance bookings is on Sant Pau 1 (tel. 93/
318-9122), open weekdays 8–3, Saturday 9–1. Tickets for
same-day performances are on sale in the Ramblas entrance
11–1:30 and 4 PM onward. Tickets are inexpensive by New York
or London standards.

Dance   You can watch the traditional Catalan Sardana danced in front
of the cathedral on Sunday mornings and often on Wednesday
evenings, too.

Theater   Most theater performances are in Catalan but look out for mime
shows, especially if Els Joglars or La Claca, two famous Catalan troupes, are appearing.

Film   Most foreign movies are dubbed into Spanish. Try the
Filmoteca on Travessera de Gràcia 63, on the corner of Tusset,
for original English-language films.

Nightlife

Cabaret   **Belle Epoque** (Muntaner 246, tel. 93/209–7385) is a beautifully decorated music hall with the most sophisticated shows. **El Mediévolo** (Gran Vía 459, tel. 93/243–1566) has medieval feasts and entertainment; it's all geared to tourists but fun.

Jazz Clubs   Try **Abraxas Jazz Auditorium** (Gelabert 26); **La Cova del Drac** (Tuset 30, just off the Diagonal); and **Zeleste** (Almogávares 122).

Rock   Check out **Zeleste** (Almogávares 122). Major concerts are usually held in sports stadiums; keep an eye out for posters.

Flamenco   The best place is **El Patio Andaluz** (Aribau 242, tel. 93/209–3378). **El Cordobés** (Ramblas 35, tel. 93/317–6853) is aimed at tour groups but can be fun.

Casino   The **Gran Casino de Barcelona** (tel. 93/893–3866), 42 kilometers (26 miles) south in Sant Pere de Ribes, near Sitges, also has a dance hall and some excellent international shows in a 19th-century atmosphere. Jacket and tie essential.

Moorish Spain

Stretching from the dark mountains of the Sierra Morena in the north, west to the plains of the Guadalquivir valley, and south to the mighty snowcapped Sierra Nevada, Andalusia rings with echoes of the Moors. In the kingdom they called Al-Andalus, these Muslim invaders from North Africa dwelt for almost 800 years, from their first conquest of Spanish soil (Gibraltar) in 711 to their expulsion from Granada in 1492. And to this day the cities and landscapes of Andalusia are rich in their legacy. The great Mosque of Córdoba, the magical Alhambra Palace in Granada, and the Giralda tower, landmark of Seville, were the inspired creations of Moorish architects and craftsmen working at the behest of Al-Andalus's Arab emirs. The brilliant white villages with narrow streets and sturdy-walled houses clustered round cool inner patios, the whitewashed facades with heavily grilled windows, and the deep wailing song of Andalusia's flamenco, so reminiscent of the muezzin's call to prayer, all stem from centuries of Moorish occupation.

Getting There from Madrid

Seville, Córdoba, and Granada all lie on direct train routes from Madrid. Service is frequent from both Chamartín and Atocha stations in Madrid, and includes overnight trains (to Seville and Granada), slower day trains, and express talgos. In addition, the high-speed AVE train connecting Seville and Atocha Station began service in 1992 on entirely new track; it's very expensive but has cut traveling time on that route from 5½–6 hours to about 2½ hours. Most bus service from Madrid to Moorish Spain operates out of the Estación del Sur (*see* Arriving and Departing in Madrid, *above*). If you drive, follow the N-IV, which takes you through the scorched orange plains of La Mancha to Córdoba, then along the Guadalquivir River to Seville. The N323 road, which splits from the N-IV at Bailén, takes you past lovely olive groves and rolling hills to Granada.

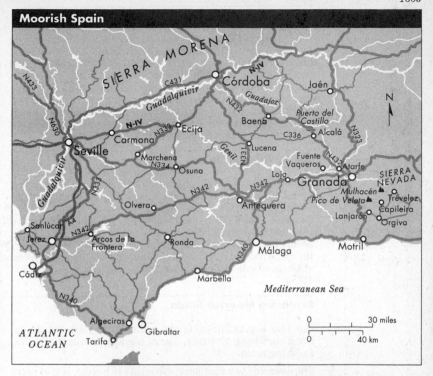

Moorish Spain

Getting Around

Seville and Córdoba are linked by direct train service. Buses are a better choice between Seville and Granada, and between Córdoba and Granada, as trains are relatively slow and infrequent and often involve a time-consuming change. **Seville's** older bus station (tel. 95/441–7111) is between José María Osborne and Manuel Vazquez Sagastizabal; a new bus station is closer to downtown (Arjona, next to the Cachorro Bridge, tel. 95/490–8040). Check with the tourist office to determine which one you'll need. The city also has a spanking new train station, Santa Justa (at José Laquillo and Avda. Kansas City, tel. 95/441–4111), built in conjunction with the 1992 International Exposition. In **Granada,** the main bus station is Alsina Gräells (Camino de Ronda 97, tel. 958/251358). The train station is at the end of Avenida Andaluces; the RENFE office is located at Reyes Católicos 63, tel. 958/223119. **Córdoba** has no central bus depot, so check at the tourist office for the appropriate company. The long-distance train station is on the Avenida de America (RENFE office: Ronda de los Tejares 10, tel. 957/475884).

Driving in Moorish Spain, long an anathema to travelers, has been largely transformed by improvements made for the 1992 festivities. If you like winding roads and gorgeous landscapes, consider driving.

Guided Tours

Guided tours of Seville, Córdoba, Granada, and Ronda are run by **Juliá Tours, Pullmantur,** and **Trapsatur,** both from Madrid and resorts of the Costa del Sol; check with travel agents. Local excursions may be available from Seville to the sherry bodegas and equestrian museum of Jerez de la Frontera. From Granada, there's a weekly day trip to the villages of the Alpujarras; check details with tourist offices. In Córdoba, **Viajes Vincit** (Alonso de Burgos 1, tel. 957/472316) runs daily sightseeing tours of the city that include a visit to the Mosque.

Tourist Information

Córdoba (Plaza de Judá Leví, tel. 957/472000, and the much less useful office at Palacio de Congresos y Exposiciones, Torrijos 10, tel. 957/471235).
Granada (Plaza Mariana Pineda 10, tel. 958/226688, and Libreros 2, tel. 958/225990).
Seville (Av. Constitución 21B, tel. 95/422–1404, not far from the cathedral and Archives of the Indies, and the smaller office at Costurero de la Reina, Paseo de las Delícias 9, tel. 95/423–4465).

Exploring Moorish Spain

Our tour begins in Seville and continues to Carmona, Ecija, Córdoba, Baena, Granada, Sierra Nevada, Lanjarón, Orgiva, and Alpujarras.

The downside to a visit here, especially to Seville, is that petty crime, much of it directed against tourists, is rife. Purse snatching and thefts from cars, frequently when drivers are in them, are depressingly familiar. *Always* keep your car doors *and* trunk locked. *Never* leave any valuables in your car. Leave your passport, traveler's checks, and credit cards in your hotel's safe, *never* in your room. Don't carry expensive cameras or wear jewelry. Take only the minimum amount of cash with you. There comes a point, however—if your windshield is smashed or your bag is snatched, for example—when all the precautions in the world will prove inadequate. If you're unlucky, it's an equally depressing fact that the police, again especially in Seville, have adopted a distinctly casual attitude to such thefts, and often combine indifference to beleaguered tourists with rudeness in about equal measure. Frankly, there's little you can do except remain calm.

Numbers in the margin correspond to points of interest on the Seville map.

Seville Lying on the banks of the Guadalquivir, **Seville**—Spain's fourth-largest city and capital of Andalusia—is one of the most beautiful and romantic cities in Europe. Here in this city of the sensuous Carmen and the amorous Don Juan, famed for the spectacle of its Holy Week processions and April Fair, you'll come close to the spiritual heart of Moorish Andalusia. You'll also find some dramatic improvements, courtesy of the International Exposition hosted by the city in 1992. They include the development of La Cartuja Island, where the fairgrounds were built; seven new bridges and a refurbished riverfront esplanade; the new Maestranza opera house built on the river; improved roads in the city and throughout the region; and new railroad and bus stations. Begin your visit in the **catedral** (cathedral), begun in 1402, a century and a half after St. Ferdinand delivered Seville from the Moors. This great Gothic edifice, which took just over a century to build, is traditionally described in superlatives. It's the biggest and highest cathedral in Spain, the largest Gothic building in the world, and the world's third-largest church after St. Peter's in Rome and St. Paul's in London. And it boasts the world's largest carved wooden altarpiece. Despite such impressive statistics, the inside can be dark and gloomy with too many overly ornate Baroque trappings. But seek out the beautiful Virgins by Murillo and Zurbarán, and reflect on the history enshrined in these walls. In a silver urn before the high altar rest the precious relics of Seville's liberator, St. Ferdinand, said to have died from excessive fasting, and down in the crypt are the tombs of his descendants Pedro the Cruel, founder of the Alcázar, and his mistress María de Padilla. But above all, you'll want to pay your respects to Christopher Columbus, whose mortal vestiges are enshrined in a flamboyant mausoleum in the south aisle. Borne aloft by statues representing the four medieval kingdoms of Spain, it's to be hoped the great voyager has found peace at last after the transatlantic quarrels that carried his body from Valladolid to Santo Domingo and from Havana to Seville. *Admission: 300 ptas. Open Mon.–Sat. 10–5, Sun. 2–4. Cathedral also open for Mass.*

Every day the bell that summons the faithful to prayer rings out from a Moorish minaret, relic of the Arab mosque whose admirable tower of Abu Yakoub the Sevillians could not bring themselves to destroy. Topped in 1565–68 by a bell tower and weather vane and called the **Giralda,** this splendid example of Moorish art is one of the marvels of Seville. In place of steps, a gently sloping ramp climbs to the viewing platform 71 meters (230 feet) above Seville's rooftops. St. Ferdinand is said to have ridden his horse to the top to admire the view of the city he had conquered. Seven centuries later your view of the Golden Tower and shimmering Guadalquivir will be equally breathtaking. Try, too, to see the Giralda at night when the floodlights cast a new magic on this gem of Islamic art. *Open same hours as Cathedral and visited on same ticket. Admission to Giralda only: 200 ptas.*

The high fortified walls of the **Alcázar** belie the exquisite delicacy of the palace's interior. It was built by Pedro the Cruel—so known because he murdered his stepmother and four of his half-brothers—who lived here with his mistress María de Padilla from 1350 to 1369. Don't mistake this for a genuine Moorish palace as it was built more than 100 years after the reconquest of Seville; rather, its style is Mudéjar—built by Moorish craftsmen working under orders of a Christian king. The Catholic Kings (Ferdinand and Isabella), whose only son, Prince Juan, was born in the Alcázar in 1478, added a wing to serve as administration center for their New World empire, and Charles V enlarged it further for his marriage celebrations in 1526. Pedro's Mudéjar palace centers around the beautiful **Patio de las Doncellas** (Court of the Damsels) whose name pays tribute to the annual gift of 100 virgins to the Moorish sultans whose palace once stood on the site. Resplendent with the most delicate of lacelike stucco and gleaming azulejo decorations, it is immediately reminiscent of Granada's Alhambra, and is in

Seville

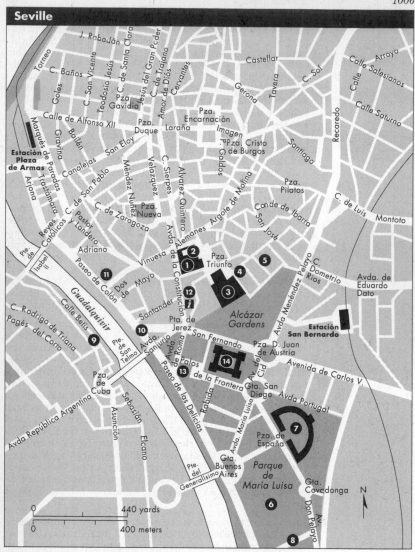

0 ————— 440 yards
0 ————— 400 meters

N

Major Attractions

Alcázar, **3**

Barrio de
Santa Cruz, **5**

Calle Betis, **9**

Catedral, **1**

Giralda, **2**

Maestranza
Bullring, **11**

Parque de
María Luisa, **6**

Patio de las
Banderas, **4**

Plaza de America, **8**

Plaza de España, **7**

Torre de Oro, **10**

Other Attractions

Museo Arte
Comtemporaneo, **12**

San Telmo Palace, **13**

Tobacco Factory
(University), **14**

fact the work of Granada craftsmen. Opening off this are the apartments of María de Padilla, whose hold over her lover, and seemingly her courtiers, too, was so great that they apparently vied with one another to drink her bath water!

The **Alcázar Gardens** are fragrant with jasmine and myrtle, an orange tree said to have been planted by Pedro the Cruel, and a lily pond well stocked with fat, contented goldfish. The end of your visit brings you to the **Patio de las Banderas** for an unrivaled view of the Giralda. *Palace and gardens admission: 600 ptas. Open daily 9:30–7.*

The **Barrio de Santa Cruz,** with its twisting alleyways, cobbled squares, and whitewashed houses, is a perfect setting for an operetta. Once the home of Seville's Jews, it was much favored by 17th-century noblemen and today boasts some of the most expensive properties in Seville. All the romantic images you've ever had of Spain will come to life here: Every house gleams white or deep ocher yellow; wrought-iron grilles adorn the windows, and every balcony and patio is bedecked with geraniums and petunias. You'll find the most beautiful patio at Callejón del Agua 12. Ancient bars nestle side by side with antiques shops. Don't miss the famous **Casa Román** bar in Plaza de los Venerables Sacerdotes with its ceilings hung thick with some of the best hams in Seville, or the **Hostería del Laurel** next door, where in summer you can dine in one of the loveliest squares in the city. Souvenir and excellent ceramic shops surround the **Plaza Doña Elvira,** where the young of Seville gather to play guitars around the fountain and azulejo benches. And in the **Plaza Alianza,** with its well-stocked antiques shops and **John Fulton gallery** (Fulton is the only American ever to qualify as a full-fledged bullfighter), stop a moment and admire the simplicity of the crucifix on the wall, framed in a profusion of bougainvillea.

Take a cab, or better still, hire a horse carriage from the Plaza Virgen de los Reyes, below the Giralda, and visit **Parque de María Luisa** (María Luisa Park), whose gardens are a delightful blend of formal design and wild vegetation, shady walkways and sequestered nooks. In the 1920s the park was redesigned to form the site of the 1929 Hispanic-American exhibition, and the impressive villas you see here today are the fair's remaining pavilions. Visit the monumental **Plaza de España,** whose grandiose pavilion of Spain was the centerpiece of the exhibition. At the opposite end of the park you can feed the hundreds of white doves that gather round the fountains of the lovely **Plaza de América;** it's a magical spot to while away the sleepy hours of the siesta.

An early evening stroll along the **Calle Betis** on the far side of the Guadalquivir is a delight few foreigners know about. Between the San Telmo and Isabel II bridges, the vista of the sparkling water, the palm-lined banks, and the silhouette of the **Torre de Oro** (Tower of Gold) (built 1220; admission: 100 ptas., open Tues.–Fri. 10–2, weekends 10–1) and the **Maestranza Bullring** (built 1760–63), one of Spain's oldest, is simply stunning. *Admission for plaza tours and bullfighting museum: 200 ptas. Open Mon.–Sat. 10–1:30).*

Thirty kilometers (19 miles) from Seville, the N-IV brings you to **Carmona.** This unspoiled Andalusian town of Roman and Moorish origin is worth a visit, either to stay at the parador or to enjoy its wealth of Mudéjar and Renaissance churches, and its streets of whitewashed houses of clear Moorish influence. Most worthwhile is the **Church of San Pedro** begun in 1466, whose extraordinary interior is an unbroken mass of sculptures and gilded surfaces, and whose tower, erected in 1704, is an unabashed imitation of Seville's famous Giralda. Carmona's most moving monument is its splendid **Roman Necropolis,** where in huge underground chambers some 900 family tombs dating from the 2nd to the 4th century AD have been chiseled out of the rock. *Admission: 250 ptas. Open Tues.–Fri. 10–2 and 4–6, weekends 10–1.*

A little farther along the N-IV brings you to **Ecija,** a dazzling white cluster reputed to be the hottest town in Spain–its nickname is *sarten de Andalucía,* "Andalusia's frying pan." With its history going back to Greek and Roman times, you'll find plenty of Renaissance and Baroque palaces here and a bewildering array of churches whose towers and turrets rise before you as you approach along the main road.

Numbers in the margin correspond to points of interest on the Córdoba map.

Córdoba   Ancient **Córdoba,** city of the caliphs, is one of Spain's oldest cities and the greatest embodiment of Moorish heritage in all Andalusia. From the 8th to the 11th centuries, the Moorish emirs and Caliphs of the West held court here and it became one of the Western world's greatest centers of art, culture, and learning. Moors, Christians, and Jews lived together in harmony within its walls. Two of Córdoba's most famous native sons were Averröes, the great Arab scientist, and Maimónides, the notable Jewish doctor and philosopher. But above all it is for its famous **❶ Mezquita** (mosque), one of the finest built by the Moors, that Córdoba is known first and foremost. Its founder was Abd ar-Rahman I (756–788), and it was completed by Al Mansur (976–1002) around the year 987. As you step inside you'll come face to face with a forest of gleaming pillars of precious marble, jasper, and onyx, rising to a roof of red-and-white horseshoe arches, one of the most characteristic traits of Moorish architecture. Not even the heavy Baroque cathedral that Charles V so mistakenly built in its midst—and later regretted—can detract from the overpowering impact and mystery wrought by the art of these Moorish craftsmen. It was indeed a fitting setting for the original copy of the Koran and a bone from the arm of the Prophet Mohammed, holy relics once housed in the Mezquita that were responsible for bringing thousands of pilgrims to its doors in the great years before St. Ferdinand reconquered Córdoba for the Christians in 1236. The mosque opens onto the **Patio de los Naranjos** (Orange Tree Courtyard), perfumed in springtime by orange blossoms, and the bell tower, which served as the mosque's minaret. It's well worth climbing the uneven steps to the top for the view of the Guadalquivir river and the tiled rooftops of the old city. *Tel. 957–470512. Admission: 500 ptas. Open daily May–Sept., 10:30–1:30 and 4–6; Oct.–Apr., 10:30–1:30 and 3:30–5:30.*

Near the mosque, the streets of Torrijos, Cardenal Herrero, and Deanes are lined with tempting souvenir shops specializing in local handicrafts, especially the filigree silver and embossed leather for which Córdoba is famous. In her niche on **❷** Cardenal Herrero, the **Virgen de los Faroles** (Virgin of the Lanterns) stands demurely behind a lantern-hung grille, rather

Córdoba

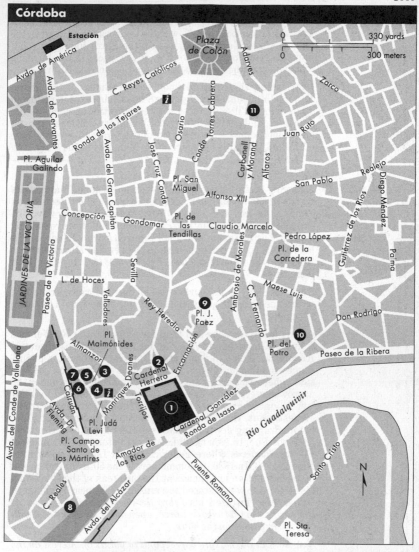

Estación

Plaza de Colón

Avda. de América

Avda. de Cervantes

Avda. de Cervantes

Pl. Aguilar Galindo

JARDINES DE LA VICTORIA

Paseo de la Victoria

Ronda de los Tejares

C. Reyes Católicos

Avda. del Gran Capitán

José Cruz Conde

Osario

Conde Torres Cabrera

Adarves

Zarco

Juan Ruto

Realejo

Diego Méndez

Concepción

Gondomar

Pl. San Miguel

Alfonso XIII

Pl. de las Tendillas

Claudio Marcelo

Carbonell y Morand

Alfaros

San Pablo

Gutiérrez de los Ríos

Parma

L. de Hoces

Sevilla

Valladares

Rey Heredia

Pl. J. Paez

Ambrosio de Morales

Pedro López

Pl. de la Corredera

Maese Luis

C.S. Fernando

Don Rodrigo

Pl. Maimónides

Almanzor

Manríquez Deanes

Torrijos

Encarnación

Pl. del Potro

Paseo de la Ribera

Cardenal Herrero

Cardenal González

Ronda de Isasa

Río Guadalquivir

Santo Cristo

Avda. del Conde de Vallellano

Cairuán

Avda. Dr. Fleming

Pl. Judá Levi

Pl. Campo Santo de los Mártires

Amador de los Ríos

Puente Romano

C. Reales

Avda. del Alcázar

Pl. Sta. Teresa

N

0   330 yards
0   300 meters

Major Attractions
Judería, **3**
Maimónides Statue, **6**
Mezquita, **1**
Museo Taurino, **5**
Plaza Judá Levi, **4**

Synagogue, **7**
Virgen de los
Faroles, **2**

Other Attractions
Alcázar, **8**
Cristo de los
Faroles, **11**
Museo Arqueológico, **9**
Museo de
Bellas Artes, **10**

like a lovely lady awaiting a serenade. In a narrow alleyway off to your left is the **Callejón de las Flores,** its houses decked with hanging flower baskets. Now make your way westward to the

❸ ❹ old **Judería,** or Jewish quarter. On the **Plaza Judá Leví** you'll find the municipal tourist office. A few paces down, on Calle Manríquez, is another outstanding patio open to visitors.

❺ Overlooking the Plaza Maimónides (or Bulas) is the **Museo Taurino** (Museum of Bullfighting), housed in two delightful old mansions. You'll see a well-displayed collection of memorabilia, paintings, and posters by early 20th-century Córdoban artists, and rooms dedicated to great Córdoban *toreros*—even the hide of the bull that killed the legendary Manolete in 1947. *Tel. 957/ 472000, ext. 211. Admission: 200 ptas. Open Tues.–Sat. 9:30– 1:30 and 5–8 (4–7 in winter).*

❻ A moving statue of the great Jewish philosopher **Maimónides** stands in the Plaza Tiberiades. A few paces along Judíos, you

❼ come to the only **synagogue** in Andalusia to have survived the expulsion of the Jews in 1492. It's one of only three remaining synagogues in Spain—the other two you saw in Toledo—built before 1492 and it boasts some fine Hebrew and Mudéjar stucco tracery and a women's gallery. *Tel. 957/298133. Admission: 75 ptas. Open Tues.–Sat. 10–2 and 3:30–5:30, Sun. 10–1:30.*

Across the way is the courtyard of El Zoco, a former Arab souk, with some pleasant shops and stalls, and sometimes a bar open in summer.

As you leave Córdoba and head for Granada, the N432 climbs from the Guadalquivir valley up into the mountains of central Andalusia. It is 63 kilometers (39 miles) to **Baena,** a picturesque Andalusian town of white houses clustered on the hillside, where you may want to stop for a drink and wander the narrow streets and squares as yet largely untouched by tourism. Mountain views line the route as the road twists toward its highest point, the 931-meter (3,000-foot) Puerto del Castillo, before dropping down onto the *vega* (fertile plain) of Granada. At Pinos Puente, you can take a short detour to the village of **Fuente Vaqueros** where Federico García Lorca was born on June 5, 1898. In 1986, to commemorate the 50th anniversary of his assassination in Granada at the outbreak of the Civil War, his birthplace was restored as a museum. The nearby village of Valderrubio inspired his *Libro de Poemas* and *La Casa de Bernarda Alba. Museo de Lorca, open daily 10–1 and 6–8 with tours every hour on the hour.*

Numbers in the margin correspond to points of interest on the Granada map.

Granada   The city of **Granada** rises majestically on three hills dwarfed by the mighty snowcapped peaks of the Sierra Nevada, which boasts the highest roads in Europe. Atop one of these hills the pink-gold palace of the Alhambra, at once splendidly imposing yet infinitely delicate, gazes out across the rooftops and gypsy caves of the Sacromonte to the fertile *vega* rich in orchards, tobacco fields, and poplar groves. Granada, the last stronghold of the Moors and the most treasured of all their cities, fell finally to the Catholic Kings in January 1492. For Ferdinand and Isabella their conquest of Granada was the fulfillment of a long-cherished dream to rid Spain of the Infidel, and here they built

❶ the flamboyant **Capilla Real** (Royal Chapel) where they have lain side by side since 1521, later joined by their daughter

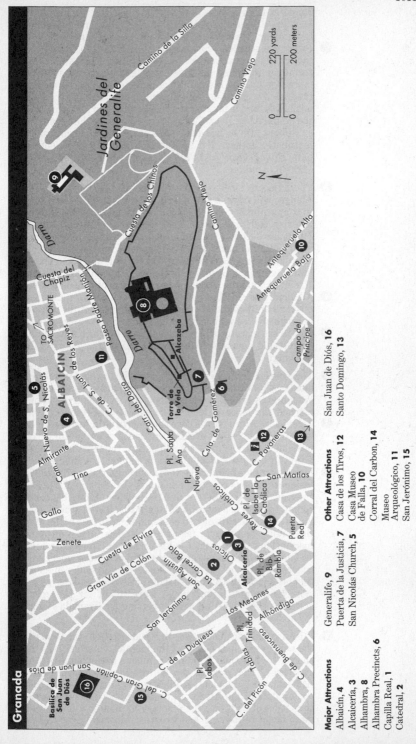

Granada

Major Attractions
Albaicín, **4**
Alcaicería, **3**
Alhambra, **8**
Alhambra Precincts, **6**
Capilla Real, **1**
Catedral, **2**

Generalife, **9**
Puerta de la Justicia, **7**
San Nicolás Church, **5**

Other Attractions
Casa de los Tiros, **12**
Casa Museo
de Falla, **10**
Corral del Carbon, **14**
Museo
Arqueológico, **11**
San Jerónimo, **15**

San Juan de Diós, **16**
Santo Domingo, **13**

Juana la Loca. Begin your tour in the nearby Plaza de Bib-Rambla, a pleasant square with flower stalls and outdoor cafés in summer, then pay a quick visit to the huge Renaissance ❷ **catedral** (cathedral) commissioned in 1521 by Charles V who thought the Royal Chapel "too small for so much glory" and determined to house his illustrious grandparents somewhere more worthy. But his ambitions came to little, for Granada Cathedral is a grandiose and gloomy monument, not completed until 1714, and is far surpassed in beauty and historic value by the neighboring Royal Chapel, which, despite the great emperor's plans, still houses the tombs of his grandparents and less fortunate mother. *Tel. 958/229239. Admission to both: 150 ptas. Royal chapel and Cathedral open daily 10:30–1 and 4–7 (3:30–6 in winter).*

❸ The adjacent streets of the **Alcaicería,** the old Arab silk exchange, will prove a haven for souvenir hunters. Here you can find any number of local handicrafts inspired by Granada's Moorish heritage: brass and copperware, green and blue Fajalauza pottery, wooden boxes, tables and chess sets inlaid with mother of pearl, and woven goods from the villages of the Alpujarras in which the colors green, red, and black predominate. Across the Gran Vía de Colón, Granada's main shopping street, the narrow streets begin to wind up the slopes of the ❹ **Albaicín,** the old Moorish quarter, which is now a fascinating mixture of dilapidated white houses and beautiful *cármenes,* luxurious villas with fragrant gardens. Few visitors find their ❺ way to the balcony of **San Nicolás Church,** which affords an unforgettable view of the Alhambra, particularly when it is floodlit at night.

❻ The Cuesta de Gomérez climbs steeply to the **Alhambra precincts,** where the Duke of Wellington planted shady elms and Washington Irving tarried among the gypsies from whom he learned the Moorish legends so evocatively recounted in his ❼ *Tales of the Alhambra.* Above the **Puerta de la Justicia** the hand of Fatima, her fingers evoking the five laws of the Koran, beckons you inside the mystical Alhambra, the most imposing and infinitely beautiful of all Andalusia's Moorish monuments. The ❽ history of the **Alhambra** is woven through the centuries. Once inside its famous courts the legends of the Patio of the Lions, the Hall of the Two Sisters, and the murder of the Abencerrajes spring to life in a profusion of lacy walls, frothy stucco, gleaming tiles, and ornate domed ceilings. Here in this realm of myrtles and fountains, festooned arches and mysterious inscriptions, every corner holds its secret. Here the emirs installed their harems, accorded their favorites the most lavish of courts, and bathed in marble baths. In the midst of so much that is delicate the Baroque palace of Charles V seems an intrusion, heavy and incongruous, were it not for the splendid acoustics that make it a perfect setting for Granada's summer music festival.

❾ Wisteria, jasmine, and roses line your route to the **Generalife,** the nearby summer palace of the caliphs, where crystal drops shower from slender fountains against a background of stately cypresses. The view of the white, clustered houses of the Albaicín, the Sacromonte riddled with gypsy caves, and the imposing bulk of the Alhambra towering above the tiled roofs of the city will etch on your memory an indelible image of this most beautiful setting and greatest Moorish legacy. *Admis-*

sion to Alhambra and Generalife, 525 ptas. Free Sun. after 3. Open Nov.–Feb., daily 9–6, Mar.–Oct., daily 9–8. Floodlit visits daily 10 PM–midnight (8–10 PM in winter). Ticket office closes 45 mins. before closing times above.

If you have a day to spare, you can drive to the mountains of the nearby **Sierra Nevada.** The ski resort itself, where you can ski from December to May, is truly unmemorable, but the surrounding scenery viewed from the highest mountain route in Europe makes for a memorable day out. A bus leaves Granada daily at 9 AM and returns at around 6 PM; ask at the tourist office for details. Above the resort the road climbs to the Pico de Veleta, Spain's second-highest mountain at 3,100 meters (10,000 feet), and the view across the Alpujarra range to the sea at Motril is simply stunning. Away to the left rises the mighty Mulhacén, at 3,558 meters (11,477 feet), Spain's highest peak.

If you opt instead for a trip to the villages of the high **Alpujarras,** leave Granada on the N323 toward Motril, then branch east to **Lanjarón,** a delightful old spa town with an air of faded gentility. From Orgiva, the main town of the Alpujarras, the highest road in Europe ascends to picturesque villages like **Bubión, Capileira** beneath the summit of the Veleta, and **Trevélez,** Europe's highest village, on the slopes of Mulhacén. These ancient villages, only recently brushed by modern tourism, became the final refuge of the Moors as they fled the Conquest of Granada, and here they remained until their expulsion from Spain in 1609. With their squat, square houses and flat roofs so reminiscent of the land across the Straits of Gibraltar, they are the last vestige of Andalusia's great Moorish past.

Dining and Lodging

For details and price-category definitions, *see* Dining and Lodging in Staying in Spain.

Carmona
Lodging
★
Parador Alcázar del Rey Don Pedro. The beauty of this modern parador is its splendid, peaceful setting in the ruins of the old Moorish alcázar on top of the hill above Carmona, and its magnificent views across the vast fertile plain below. *Tel. 95/414–1010, fax 95/414–1712. 59 rooms. Facilities: pool. AE, DC, MC, V. Expensive.*

Córdoba
Dining
★
El Caballo Rojo. The Red Horse, located close to the mosque, is Córdoba's most outstanding restaurant, famous throughout Andalusia and all of Spain. The decor resembles a cool Andalusian patio, and the menu features traditional specialties such as *rabo de toro* (bull's tail); *salmorejo,* a local version of gazpacho with chunks of ham and egg; and other exotic creations inspired by Córdoba's Moorish heritage. *Cardenal Herrero 28, tel. 957/ 475375. Reservations advised. AE, DC, MC, V. Expensive.*

El Blasón. Under the same management as El Caballo Rojo, this charming restaurant is fast gaining a name for fine food and unbeatable ambience. Located in an old inn with a pleasant tapas patio and a whole array of restaurants upstairs, its specialties include *salmón con naranjas* (salmon in oranges) and *ternera con salsa de alcaparrones* (roast veal in caper sauce). *José Zorrilla 11, tel. 957/480625. AE, DC, MC, V. Moderate.*

El Cardenal. Close to the mosque, beside the Marisa hotel, this restaurant in the heart of Córdoba's tourist center offers a stylish setting for lunch or dinner. A marble staircase with Oriental carpets leads up to the second-floor dining room. Good food and professional service complement the cool, agreeable atmosphere. *Cardenal Herrero 14, tel. 957/480346. AE, DC, MC, V. Closed Sun. evening and Mon. in winter. Moderate.*

★ **El Churrasco.** Ranking second only to El Caballo Rojo, this atmospheric restaurant with a patio is famous for its grilled meat dishes. Specialties are, of course, *churrasco*, a pork dish in pepper sauce, and an excellent salmorejo. *Romero 16, tel. 957/290819. AE, DC, MC, V. Closed Aug. Moderate.*

La Almudaina. This attractive restaurant is located in a 15th-century house and former school that overlooks the Alcázar at the entrance to the Judería. It has an Andalusian patio, and the decor and cooking are both typical of Córdoba. *Campo Santo de los Mártires 1, tel. 957/474342. AE, DC, MC, V. Closed Sun. evening. Moderate.*

Lodging **Adarve.** This delightful contemporary hotel on the east side of
★ the mosque is built in Andalusian Moorish style with a charming patio and ceramic decor. The hotel itself has no restaurant, but guests can dine in the attractive Mesón del Bandolero in Calle Torrijos on the opposite side of the mosque. *Magistral González Francés 15, tel. 957/481102, fax 957/475079. 103 rooms. Facilities: pool, garage parking. AE, DC, MC, V. Expensive–Very Expensive.*

Maimónides. Its location is convenient, right beside the mosque, with restaurants and souvenir shops outside the door. The lobby is impressive, the staff is friendly and helpful, and rooms are functional but comfortable. *Torrijos 4, tel. 957/471500, fax 957/475079. 83 rooms. AE, DC, MC, V. Expensive.*

El Califa. This is a small, modern hotel in a reasonably quiet, central location in the heart of the old city. It accepts no tour groups, only individual guests, and is a comfortable place to stay, with the sights and shops close at hand. *Lope de Hoces 14, tel. 957/299400. 65 rooms. MC, V. Moderate–Expensive.*

Marisa. A charming old Andalusian house whose location in the heart of the old town overlooking the mosque's Patio de los Naranjos is its prime virtue. You'll find the decor quaint and charming, and the rates reasonable. *Cardenal Herrero 6, tel. 957/473142. 28 rooms. MC, V. Moderate.*

Granada **Baroca.** Located one block above the Camino de Ronda, the lo-
Dining cals consider this Granada's best restaurant. The menu favors
★ international cuisine; desserts are especially good. Service is professional and the ambience agreeable. *Pedro Antonio de Alarcón 34, tel. 958/265061. Reservations advised. AE, DC, MC, V. Closed Sun. and Aug. Expensive.*

Carmen de San Miguel. This is a restaurant to visit for its superb setting in a villa with an outdoor terrace and magnificent views over Granada. Located on the Alhambra hill beside the Alhambra Palace hotel, the setting is unbeatable, the food is average Continental-style cuisine. *Paseo Torres Bermejas 3, tel. 958/226723. AE, DC, MC, V. Closed Sun. evening. Expensive.*

Cunini. Located in the center of town, close to the cathedral, Cunini has long been famous for the quality of its seafood. *Pescadería 9 or Capuchina 14, tel. 958/250777. Reservations advised. AE, DC, MC, V. Closed Mon. Expensive.*

Sevilla. This is a very atmospheric, colorful restaurant located in the Alcaicería beside the cathedral. There's a superb tapas bar at the entrance, and the dining room is picturesque but rather small and crowded. The menu can be rather tourist-oriented, but try their *sopa Sevillana* (fish soup). *Oficios 12, tel. 958/221223. AE, DC, MC, V. Closed Sun. evening. Moderate.*

Los Manueles. This old inn is one of Granada's long-standing traditions. The walls are decorated with ceramic tiles, and the ceiling is hung with hams. There's lots of atmosphere, good old-fashioned service, and plenty of traditional Granada cooking. *Zaragoza 2, tel. 958/223415. AE, DC, MC, V. Inexpensive.*

Lodging **Parador de San Francisco.** Magnificently located in an old convent right within the Alhambra precincts, the parador was where Queen Isabella was entombed before the completion of the Royal Chapel. It's one of Spain's most popular hotels, and you need to book at least four months in advance. *Alhambra, tel. 958/221443, fax 958/222264. 39 rooms. AE, DC, MC, V. Very Expensive.*

★ **Alhambra Palace.** This flamboyant ocher-red Moorish-style palace was built about 1910 and sits halfway up the hill to the Alhambra. The mood is more harried than at the more isolated parador. Though recently renovated, it remains a conversation piece with rich carpets, tapestries, and Moorish tiles. Rooms overlooking the town are preferable. The terrace is the perfect place for an early evening drink as the sun sets over the Sierra Nevada. *Peña Partida 2, tel. 958/221468, fax 958/226404. 121 rooms. AE, DC, MC, V. Expensive–Very Expensive.*

América. A simple but charming hotel within the Alhambra precincts. It's very popular so you'll need to reserve a room months ahead. The location is magnificent, and guests can linger over breakfast on a delightful patio. *Real de la Alhambra 53, tel. 958/227471. 14 rooms. No credit cards. Open Mar.–Oct. only. Moderate.*

Juan Miguel. This comfortable, modern hotel right in the center of town opened in 1987. The rooms are well equipped, service is professional, and there's a good restaurant. *Acera del Darro 24, tel. 958/258912. 66 rooms. AE, DC, MC, V. Moderate.*

Inglaterra. Set in a period house just two blocks above the Gran Vía de Colón in the heart of town, this is a hotel that will appeal to those who prefer Old World charm to creature comforts, though accommodations are perfectly adequate for the reasonable rates. *Cetti Meriem 6, tel. 958/221559, fax 958/221586. 36 rooms. AE, DC, MC, V. Inexpensive.*

Seville **Egaña Oriza.** This is currently one of Seville's most fashionable
Dining restaurants. Basque specialties include *merluza con almejas*
★ *en salsa verde* (white fish in clam sauce) and *solomillo con foie en salsa de trufas* (steak with goose liver pâté in truffle sauce). It's opposite the old tobacco factory, now Seville University. *San Fernando 41, tel. 95/422–7211. Reservations required. AE, DC, MC, V. Closed Sat. lunch, Sun., and Aug. Expensive.*

La Albahaca. Set in an attractive old house in the heart of the Barrio Santa Cruz, the Albahaca offers plenty of style and atmosphere and original, imaginative cuisine. Specialties of the chef, who was formerly in the Hotel Alfonso XIII, are *ajo blanco con pasas de Corinto* (garlic with raisins) and *filetitos de ciervo con ciruelas* (venison and cherries). *Plaza Santa Cruz 12, tel. 95/422–0714. Reservations advised. AE, DC, MC, V. Closed Sun. Expensive.*

La Isla. Located in the center of town between the cathedral and the Convent of La Caridad, La Isla has long been famous for its superb seafood and paella. *Arfe 25, tel. 95/421–5376. AE, DC, MC, V. Closed Mon. and Aug. Expensive.*

San Marco. The brothers Ramacciotti serve Italian-influenced cuisine in an 18th-century mansion with a classic Andalusian patio—a wonderful spot for a summer meal. Try the *ravioli rellenos de lubina en salsa de almejas* (ravioli stuffed with sea bass in a clam sauce), *cordero relleno de espinacas y setas* (lamb stuffed with spinach and forest mushrooms), or any of a delectable array of desserts. *Cuna 6, tel. 95/421–2440. Reservations advised. AE, DC, V. Closed Sun., Mon. lunch, and Aug. Expensive.*

El Bacalao. This popular fish restaurant, opposite the church of Santa Catalina, is in an Andalusian house decorated with ceramic tiles. As its name suggests, the house specialty is *bacalao* (cod); try the *bacalao con arroz* or the *bacalao al pilpil*. *Plaza Ponce de León 15, tel. 95/421–6670. Reservations advised. AE, DC, MC, V. Closed Sun. and Aug. Moderate.*

★ **La Judería.** This bright, modern restaurant near the Hotel Fernando III is fast gaining recognition for the quality of its Andalusian and international cuisine and reasonable prices. Fish dishes from the north of Spain and meat from Ávila are specialties. Try *cordero lechal* (roast baby lamb) or *urta a la roteña* (a fish dish unique to Rota). *Cano y Cueto 13, tel. 95/441–2052. Reservations required. AE, DC, MC, V. Closed Tues. and first 2 weeks in Aug. Moderate.*

★ **Mesón Don Raimundo.** Located in an old convent close to the cathedral, the atmosphere and decor are deliberately Sevillian. Its bar is the perfect place to sample a *fino* and some splendid tapas, and the restaurant, when not catering to tour groups, is one of Seville's most delightful. *Argote de Molina 26, tel. 95/422–3355. Reservations advised. AE, DC, MC, V. Closed Sun. evening. Moderate.*

Mesón Castellano. This recently refurbished old house opposite the church of San José is an ideal place for lunch after a morning's shopping on Calle Sierpes. Specialties are Castilian meat dishes. *Jovellanos 6, tel. 95/421–4028. Open for lunch only. AE, DC, MC, V. Closed Sun. Inexpensive.*

Lodging **Alfonso XIII.** This ornate Mudéjar-style palace was built for Alfonso XIII's visit to the 1929 exhibition. It is worth a visit for its splendid Moorish decor, despite the fact that parts of the hotel are faded and fall short of five-star expectations. Rooms are overpriced and desperately need to be redecorated. The restaurant is elegant but falls short of expectations also. *San Fernando 2, tel. 95/422–2850, fax 95/421–6033. 128 rooms and 21 suites. Facilities: restaurant, pool. AE, DC, MC, V. Very Expensive.*

Colón. This classic Seville hotel reopened at the end of 1988 after several years of renovation. The rooms and suites have been modernized to a high degree of comfort while retaining much of their style. It's located right in the heart of town, close to the main shopping center. You can dine in the elegant El Burladero restaurant or in the more typical La Tasca. *Canalejas 1, tel. 95/422–2900, fax 95/422–0938. 204 rooms and 14 suites. AE, DC, MC, V. Very Expensive.*

★ **Doña María.** Close to the cathedral, this is one of Seville's most charming hotels. Some rooms are small and plain; others are tastefully furnished with antiques. Room 310 has a four-poster double bed, and 305 two single four-posters; both have spacious bathrooms. There's no restaurant, but there's a rooftop pool with a good view of the Giralda. *Don Remondo 19, tel. 95/422–4990, fax 95/421–9546. 61 rooms. AE, DC, MC, V. Expensive.*

Bécquer. This functional, modern hotel with attentive service is convenient for the shopping center and offers comfortable if unexciting accommodations. It's one of the best moderate bets, with a parking garage but no restaurant. *Reyes Católicos 4, tel. 95/422–8900, fax 95/421–4400. Telex 72884. 126 rooms. AE, DC, MC, V. Moderate.*

Giralda. Recently modernized and extensively renovated, this is a comfortable, functional hotel with spacious, light rooms decorated in typical Castilian style. Located in a cul-de-sac off Avenida Menéndez Pelayo, it lies on the edge of the old city; rooms on the fifth floor are best. *Sierra Nevada 3, tel. 95/441–6661, fax 95/441–9352. 107 rooms, garage. AE, DC, MC, V. Moderate.*

Girarda. One of several very basic family-run hotels in the Barrio Santa Cruz, the Girarda is in an old, Moorish-style building with a colorful interior patio that also serves as a restaurant. Antonia Miranda runs the place in the absence of her bullfighter husband, Pedro Sanchez Martínez. *Justin de Neve 8, tel. 95/421–5113. 5 rooms. No credit cards. Inexpensive.*

Internacional. Well maintained and charming, this Old World hotel lies in the narrow streets of the old town near Casa Pilatos. *Aguilas 17, tel. 95/421–3207. 26 rooms. Inexpensive.*

Murillo. This picturesque hotel in the heart of the Barrio Santa Cruz was redecorated in 1987. The rooms are simple and small, but the setting is a virtue. You can't reach the hotel by car, but porters with trolleys will fetch your luggage from your taxi. *Lope de Rueda 7, tel. 95/421–6095, fax 95/421–9616. 61 rooms, 30 with bath, 31 with shower. AE, DC, MC, V. Inexpensive.*

The Arts and Nightlife

Granada
Flamenco

There are several "impromptu" flamenco shows in the caves of the Sacromonte, but these can be dismally bad and little more than tourist rip-offs. Go only if accompanied by a Spanish friend who knows his way around. There are also two regular flamenco clubs that cater largely to tourists and tour groups: **Jardines Neptuno** (tel. 958/252050) and **Reina Mora** (tel. 958/278228). Both can be booked through your hotel.

Seville
Flamenco

Regular flamenco clubs cater largely to tourists, but their shows are colorful and offer a good introduction for the uninitiated. Try any of the following: **El Arenal** (Rodo 7, tel. 95/421–6492); **Los Gallos** (Plaza Santa Cruz 11, tel. 95/421–6981), a small intimate club in the heart of the Barrio Santa Cruz offering fairly pure flamenco; and **El Patio Sevillano** (Paseo de Colón, tel. 95/421–4120), which caters largely to tour groups.

Bullfights

Corridas take place at the Maestranza bullring on Paseo de Colón, usually on Sunday from Easter to October. The best are during the April Fair. Tickets can be bought in advance from the windows at the ring (one of the oldest and most picturesque in Spain) or from the kiosks in Calle Sierpes (these charge a commission). The ring and a bullfighting museum may be visited year-round. *Tel. 95/422–3506. Admission: 200 ptas. Open Mon.–Sat. 10–1:30.*

Costa del Sol

What were impoverished fishing villages in the 1950s are now retirement villages and package-tour meccas for northern Europeans and Americans. Despite the abuses of this naturally lovely area during the boom years of the 1960s and '70s, and the continuing brashness of the resorts that cater to the package-tour trade, the Costa del Sol has managed to preserve at least some semblance of charm. Behind the hideous concrete monsters—some of which are now being demolished—you'll come across old cottages and villas set in gardens that blossom with jasmine and bougainvillea. The sun still sets over miles of beaches and the lights of small fishing craft still twinkle in the distance. Most of your time should be devoted to indolence—sunbathing and swimming (though not in the polluted Mediterranean; all hotels have pools for this reason). When you need something to do, you can head inland to the historic town of Ronda and the perched white villages of Andalusia. You can also make a day trip to Gibraltar or Tangier.

Getting There

Daily flights on Iberia and Aviaco connect Málaga with Madrid and Barcelona. Iberia (tel. 95/213–6126), British Airways, and charter airlines such as Dan Air offer frequent service from London; most other major European cities also have direct air links. You'll have to make connections in Madrid for all flights from the United States. Málaga Airport (tel. 95/224–0000) is 12 kilometers (7 miles) west of the city. City buses run from the airport to the city every 20 minutes (fare: 100 ptas., 6:20 AM–10:40 PM); the Portillo bus company (tel. 95/236–0091) has frequent service from the airport to Torremolinos. A suburban train serving Málaga, Torremolinos, and Fuegirola also stops at the airport every half hour. From Madrid, Málaga is easily reached by a half-dozen rapid trains a day.

Getting Around

Buses are the best means of transport on the Costa del Sol (as well as from Seville or Granada). Málaga's long-distance station is on the Paseo de los Tilos (tel. 95/235–0061); nearby, on Muelle de Heredía, a smaller station serves suburban destinations. The main bus company serving the Costa del Sol is **Portillo** (Cordoba 7, tel. 95/236–0091), which also has stations in Torremolinos, Fuengirola, and Marbella. **Alsina Gräells** (Plaza de Toros Vieja, 95/231–8295) has service to Granada, Córdoba, Seville, and Nerja. The train station in Málaga (Explanada de la Estación, tel. 95/236–0202) is a 15-minute walk from the city center, across the river. The **RENFE** office (Stracham 2, tel. 95/221–4127) is more convenient for tickets and information.

Guided Tours

Organized one- and two-day excursions to places such as Seville, Granada, Córdoba, Ronda, Gibraltar, and Tangier are run by **Juliá Tours, Pullmantur,** and numerous smaller companies from all the Costa del Sol resorts and can be booked through your hotel desk or any travel agent.

Costa del Sol

Tourist Information

The most helpful tourist offices, by far, are in Málaga and Marbella. The Málaga office covers the entire province.

Estepona (Paseo Marítimo Pedro Manrique, tel. 95/280–0913).
Fuengirola (Av. Jesús Santos Rein 6, tel. 95/246–7457).
Gibraltar (On Cathedral Square, the Piazza, and John Mackintosh Square, tel. 9567/76400).
Málaga (Pasaje de Chinitas 4, tel. 95/221–3445, and at the airport in both national and international terminals).
Marbella (Miguel Cano 1, tel. 95/277–1442).
Nerja (Puerta del Mar 2, tel. 95/252–1531).
Ronda (Plaza de España 1, tel. 95/287–1272).
Torremolinos (Plaza Pablo Ruiz Picasso, tel. 95/237–1159).

Exploring the Costa del Sol

Our tour of the Costa del Sol begins in Nerja, some 50 kilometers (30 miles) to the east of Málaga, and takes us along the coast as far as Gibraltar, with a detour inland to the picturesque town of Ronda set high in the mountains.

Nerja is a small but expanding resort that so far has escaped the worst excesses of the property developers. Its growth to date has been largely confined to villages such as El Capistrano, one of the showpieces of the Costa del Sol. There's pleasant bathing here, though the sand is gray and gritty. The **Balcón de Europa** is a fantastic lookout, high above the sea. The famous **Cuevas de Nerja** (a series of stalactite caves) are off the road to Almuñecar and Almería. A kind of vast underground cathedral, they contain the world's largest known stalactite (62 meters [203 feet] long). *Tel. 95/252–0076. Admission: 325 ptas. Open daily summer 10:30–6, winter 10:30–2 and 3:30–6.*

Málaga is a busy port city with ancient streets and lovely villas set among exotic foliage, but it has little to recommend it to the overnight visitor. The central Plaza de la Marina, overlooking the port, is a pleasant place for a drink. The main shops are along the Calle Marqués de Larios.

The **Alcazaba** is a fortress begun in the 8th century when Málaga was the most important port of the Moorish kingdom. The ruins of the Roman amphitheater at its entrance were uncovered when the fort was restored. The inner palace dates from the 11th century when, for a short period after the breakup of the Caliphate of the West in Córdoba, it became the residence of the Moorish emirs. Today you'll find the **Archaeological Museum** here and a good collection of Moorish art. *Tel. 95/221–6005. Admission: 20 ptas. Open Mon.–Sat. 11–2 and 5–8, Sun. 10–2 (4–7 in winter).*

Energetic souls can climb through the Alcazaba gardens to the summit of **Gibralfaro.** Others can drive by way of Calle Victoria or take the parador minibus that leaves roughly every 1½ hours from near the cathedral on Molina Lario. The Gibralfaro fortifications were built for Yusuf I in the 14th century. The Moors called it Jebelfaro, which means "rock of the lighthouse," after the beacon that stood here to guide ships into the harbor and warn of invasions by pirates. Today the beacon has gone, but there's a small parador that makes a delightful place for a drink or a meal and has some stunning views.

As you approach **Torremolinos** through an ocean of concrete blocks, it's hard to grasp that as recently as the early 1960s this was an inconsequential fishing village. Today, this grossly overdeveloped resort is a prime example of 20th-century tourism run riot. The town center, with its brash Nogalera Plaza, is full of overpriced bars and restaurants. Much more attractive is the district of La Carihuela, farther west, below the Avenida Carlota Alexandra. You'll find some old fishermen's cottages here, a few excellent seafood restaurants, and a traffic-free esplanade for an enjoyable stroll on a summer evening.

Head west from Torremolinos, toward the similar but more staid resorts of **Benalmádena** and **Fuengirola,** both retirement havens for British and American senior citizens. A short drive from Fuengirola up into the mountains takes you to the picturesque—and over-photographed—village of **Mijas.** Though the vast tourist-oriented main square may seem like an extension of the Costa's tawdry bazaar, there are hillside streets of whitewashed houses where you'll discover an authentic village atmosphere that has changed little since the days before the tourist boom of the 1960s. Visit the bullring, the nearby church, and the chapel of Mijas's patroness, the Virgen de la Peña (to the side of the main square), and enjoy shopping for quality gifts and souvenirs.

Marbella is the most fashionable and sedate resort area along the coast. It does have a certain Florida land boom feel to it, but development has been controlled, and Marbella will, let's hope, never turn into another Torremolinos. The town's charming old Moorish quarter may be crowded with up-market boutiques and a modern, T-shirt-and-fudge section along the main drag; but when people speak of Marbella they refer both to the town and to the resorts—some more exclusive than others—stretching 16 kilometers (10 miles) or so on either side of town, between the highway and the beach. If you're vacationing in southern Spain, this is the place to stay. There's championship golf and tennis, fashionable waterfront cafés, and trendy shopping arcades.

A short drive up into the hills behind Marbella brings you to the village of **Ojén.** Its typical streets are a far cry from the promenades of the coastal resorts. Look out for the traditional pottery sold here and for the picturesque cemetery, with its rows of burial-urn chambers.

Back on the coastal highway, Marbella's Golden Mile, with its mosque, Arab banks, and residence of King Fahd of Saudi Arabia, proclaims the ever-growing influence of wealthy Arabs in this playground of the rich. In **Puerto Banús,** Marbella's plush marina, with its flashy yachts, fashionable people, and expensive restaurants, the glittering parade outshines even St. Tropez in ritzy glamour.

Ronda is reached via a spectacular mountain road from San Pedro de Alcántara. One of the oldest towns in Spain, and last stronghold of the legendary Andalusian bandits, Ronda's most dramatic feature is its ravine, known as **El Tajo,** which is 279 meters (900 feet) across and divides the old Moorish town from the "new town" of El Mercadillo. Spanning the gorge is the **Puente Nuevo,** an amazing architectural feat built between 1755 and 1793, whose parapet offers dizzying views of the River Guadalevin way below. Countless people have plunged to their death from this bridge, including its own architect, who accidentally fell over while inspecting his work, and numerous victims of the Civil War of 1936–39 who were hurled into the ravine—an episode recounted in Hemingway's *For Whom the Bell Tolls.* Ronda is visited more for its setting, breathtaking views, and ancient houses than for any particular monument. Stroll the old streets of **La Ciudad;** drop in at the historic **Reina Victoria** hotel, built by the English from Gibraltar as a fashionable resting place on their Algeciras to Bobadilla railroad line; and visit the **bullring,** one of the earliest and most beautiful rings in Spain. Here Ronda's most famous native son, Pedro Romero (1754–1839), father of modern bullfighting, is said to have killed 5,600 bulls during his 30-year career; and in the **Bullfighting Museum** you can see posters dating back to the very first fights held in the ring in May 1785. The ring is privately owned now, but 3–4 fights a year are still held in the summer months. Tickets are exceedingly difficult to come by (tel. 95/287-7977, admission to ring and museum: 200 ptas., open daily 10–6). Above all, don't miss the cliff-top walk and the gardens of the **Alameda del Tajo,** where you can contemplate one of the most dramatic views in all of Andalusia.

Returning to the coast road, the next town is **Estepona,** which until recently marked the end of the urban sprawl of the Costa del Sol. Estepona lacks the hideous high rises of Torremolinos and Fuengirola, and set back from the main highway, it's not hard to make out the old fishing village this once was. Wander the streets of the Moorish village, around the central food market and the **Church of San Francisco,** and you'll find a pleasant contrast to the excesses higher up the coast.

Nineteen kilometers (11¾ miles) northwest of Estepona, the mountain village of **Casares** lies high in the Sierra Bermeja. Streets of ancient white houses perch on the slopes beneath a ruined Moorish castle. Admire the view of the Mediterranean and check out the village's thriving ceramics industry.

Between Estepona and Gibraltar, the highway is flanked by prosperous vacation developments known as *urbanizaciones*. These have mushroomed since the border between Spain and Gibraltar was reopened in 1985. The architecture here is much more in keeping with traditional Andalusian style than the concrete blocks of earlier developments. The new **Puerto de Sotogrande** near Manilva is one of the showpieces of the area.

Gibraltar

To enter **Gibraltar,** simply walk or drive across the border at La Línea and show your passport. In theory car drivers need an International Driver's License, insurance certificate, and registration book; in practice, these regulations are usually waived. It is also possible to fly into Gibraltar on daily flights from London but, as yet, there are no flights from Spanish airports. There are, however, plenty of bus tours from Spain. **Juliá Tours, Pullmantur,** and many smaller agencies, run daily tours (not Sunday) to Gibraltar from most Costa del Sol resorts. Alternatively, you can take the regular **Portillo** bus to La Línea and walk across the border. In summer, **Portillo** runs an inexpensive daily tour to Gibraltar from Torremolinos bus station. Once you reach Gibraltar the official language is English and the currency is the British pound sterling, though pesetas are also accepted.

The Rock of Gibraltar acquired its name in AD 711 when it was captured by the Moorish chieftain Tarik at the start of the Arab invasion of Spain. It became known as Jebel Tarik (Rock of Tarik), later corrupted to Gibraltar. After successive periods of Moorish and Spanish domination, Gibraltar was captured by an Anglo-Dutch fleet in 1704 and ceded to the British by the Treaty of Utrecht in 1713. This tiny British colony, whose impressive silhouette dominates the straits between Spain and Morocco, is a rock just 5⅔ kilometers (3⅜ miles) long, three-quarter kilometers (half a mile) wide, and 425 meters (1,369 feet) high.

On entering Gibraltar by road you have to cross the airport runway on the narrow strip of land that links the Rock with La Línea in Spain. Here you have a choice. You can either plunge straight into exploring Gibraltar town, or opt for a tour around the Rock. Several minibus tours are readily available at this point of entry.

Numbers in the margin correspond to points of interest on the Gibraltar map.

The tour around the Rock is best begun on the eastern side. As you enter Gibraltar, turn left down Devil's Tower Road, and

❶ drive as far as **Catalan Bay,** a small fishing village founded by Genoese settlers in the 18th century, and now one of the Rock's most picturesque resorts. The road continues on beneath water catchments that supply the colony's drinking water, to another

❷ resort, **Sandy Bay,** and then plunges through the Dudley Ward

❸ Tunnel to bring you out at the Rock's most southerly tip, **Punta**

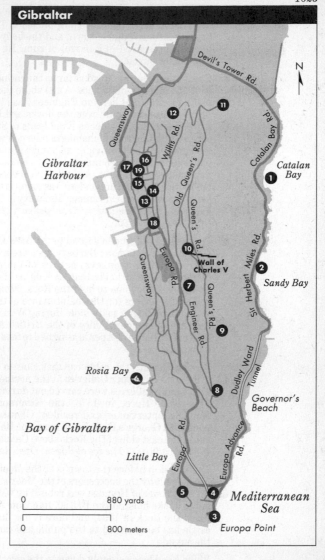

Grande de Europa (Europa Point). Stop here to admire the view across the Straits to the coast of Morocco, 22½ kilometers (14 miles) away. You are standing on what in ancient times was called one of the two Pillars of Hercules. Across the water in Morocco, a mountain between the cities of Ceuta and Tangier formed the second pillar. The Europa Point lighthouse has stood above the meeting point of the Atlantic and the Mediterranean since 1841. Plaques explain the history of the gun installations here, and, nearby on Europa Flats, you can see the **Nun's Well,** an ancient Moorish cistern, and the **Shrine of Our Lady of Europe,** venerated by sailors since 1462.

Europa Road winds its way high on the western slopes above **Rosia Bay,** to which Nelson's flagship, HMS *Victory,* was towed after the Battle of Trafalgar in 1805. Aboard were the dead of the battle, who are now buried in Trafalgar Cemetery on the southern edge of town, and the body of Admiral Nelson himself, preserved in a barrel of rum. He was then taken to London for burial.

7 Continue on Europa Road as far as the **casino** (Europa Rd., tel. 9567/76666, open daily 9 PM–4 AM) above the Alameda Gardens.

8 Make a sharp right here up Engineer Road to **Jews Gate,** an unbeatable lookout point over the docks and Bay of Gibraltar to

9 Algeciras in Spain. Queens Road leads to **St. Michael's Cave,** a series of underground chambers adorned with stalactites and stalagmites, which provides an admirable setting for concerts, ballet, and drama. Sound-and-light shows are held here most days at 11 AM and 4 PM. A skull of Neanderthal Woman (now in the British Museum in London) was found in the caves some eight years *before* the world-famous discovery in Germany's Neander Valley in 1856. *Admission: £1.50 per car, plus £3 per occupant. Open daily 10–5:30.*

10 Drive down Old Queen's Road to the **Apes' Den** near the **Wall of Charles V.** The famous Barbary apes are a breed of cinnamon-colored, tailless monkeys, natives of the Atlas Mountains in Morocco. Legend holds that as long as the apes remain, the British will continue to hold the Rock. Winston Churchill himself issued orders for the maintenance of the ape colony when its numbers began to dwindle during World War II. Today the apes are the responsibility of the British Army, and a special Officer in Charge of Apes is assigned to feed them twice daily at 8 AM and 4 PM.

Passing beneath the cable car that runs to the Rock's summit,
11 drive up to the **Upper Galleries** at the northern end of the Rock. These huge galleries were carved out during the Great Siege of 1779–1783. Here, in 1878, the Governor, Lord Napier of Magdala, entertained ex-President Ulysses S. Grant at a banquet in **St. George's Hall.** From here, the **Holyland Tunnel** leads out to the east side of the Rock above Catalan Bay. *Admission: 70 pence adults, 40 pence children. Open daily 10–6.*

The last stop before the town is at the **Moorish Castle** on Willis Road. Built by the successors of the Moorish invader Tarik, the
12 present **Tower of Homage** was rebuilt by the Moors in 1333. Admiral Rooke hoisted the British flag from its top when he captured the Rock in 1704, and here it has flown ever since. The castle has been closed to the public and can be seen only from the outside.

Willis Road leads steeply down to the colorful, congested town of Gibraltar where the dignified Regency architecture of Britain blends with the shutters, balconies, and patios of southern Spain. Apart from the attraction of shops, restaurants, and pubs on Main Street, you'll want to visit some of the following:
13 the **Governor's Residence,** where the ceremonial Changing of the Guard once took place weekly (it now occurs 4–5 times a
14 year; ask at the tourist office); the **Law Courts,** where the famous case of the *Mary Celeste* sailing ship was heard in 1872;
15 the Anglican **Cathedral of the Holy Trinity;** the Catholic
16 17 **Cathedral of St. Mary the Crowned;** and the **Gibraltar Museum,** whose exhibits recall the history of the Rock throughout the ages. *Gibraltar Museum, Bomb House La., tel. 9567–74289.*

Admission: £1.50 adults, £1 children. Open Mon.–Fri. 10–6, Sat. 10–2.

⑱ Finally, the **Nefusot Yehudada Synagogue** on Line Wall Road is worth a look for its inspired architecture, and, if you're inter-
⑲ ested in guns, the **Koehler Gun** in **Casemates Square** at the northern end of Main Street is an impressive example of the type of gun developed during the Great Siege.

Dining and Lodging

For details and price-category definitions, *see* Dining and Lodging in Staying in Spain.

Estepona **Alcaría de Ramos.** José Ramos, winner of the National Gastron-
Dining omy Prize, opened this restaurant outside town in 1990, and it has quickly garnered a large and loyal following. Try the *ensalada de lentejas con salmón ahumado* (lentil salad with smoked salmon), followed by *cordero asado* (roast lamb) and the chef's justly famous fried ice cream. *Rte. N340, km. 167, tel. 95/288–6178. Reservations advised. V. Closed for lunch, Sun., and June 15–July 15. Moderate–Expensive.*

★ **Antonio.** Head for the patio of this prize-winning restaurant, if you can beat the crowds of locals who flock to the place. Try the *ensalada de pimientos asados* (roast pepper salad) or the *fritura malaguena* (fried fish Malaga style). *Puerto Deportivo, tel. 95/280–1142. Reservations advised. DC, MC, V. Moderate.*

Lodging **Santa Marta.** This is a small, quiet hotel with just 37 rooms in chalet bungalows set in a large, peaceful garden. Some rooms are a little faded after 30 years, but the tranquil setting is a plus. Good lunches are served by the pool. *Rte. N340, km. 173, tel. 95/288–8180. 37 rooms with bath. AE, MC, V. Open Apr.– Sept. only. Moderate.*

Gibraltar **La Bayuca.** This is one of the Rock's longest-established res-
Dining taurants. Prince Charles and Prince Andrew have dined here when on naval service. It is especially renowned for its onion soup and Mediterranean dishes. *21 Turnbull's La., tel. 9567/ 75119. Reservations advised. AE, DC, MC, V. Closed Tues. and Sun. lunch. Expensive.*

Country Cottage. Opposite the Catholic cathedral, this is the place to go for a taste of Old England. Enjoy steak and kidney pie, Angus steak, and roast beef, by candlelight. *13 Giro's Passage, tel. 9567/70084. Reservations advised. AE, MC, V. Closed Sun. Moderate–Expensive.*

Lodging **Rock.** The Rock has undergone a massive refurbishment pro-
★ gram with the aim of bolstering its reputation as Gibraltar's su- preme luxury hotel. You'll find a comfortable, old-fashioned English atmosphere, along with a pool, sun terrace, and gar- dens. Located on Gibraltar's western slopes, the hotel over- looks the town and harbor. *3 Europa Rd., tel. 9567/73000. 143 rooms with bath. AE, DC. Expensive.*

Bristol. This colonial-style hotel is just off Gibraltar's main street, right in the heart of town. Rooms are large and comfort- able, and the tropical garden is a real haven for those guests who want to relax in peaceful isolation. *10 Cathedral Sq., tel. 9567/76800. 60 rooms with bath. AE, DC, MC, V. Moderate.*

Málaga **Café de Paris.** The owner of this stylish restaurant in the Paseo
Dining Marítimo area is a former chef of Maxim's in Paris, and La Haci- enda in Marbella. The *menú degustación* lets you try a little of

everything. Specialties include *rodaballo con espinacas* (sea bass and spinach). *Vélez Málaga 8, tel. 95/222–5043. Reservations advised. AE, DC, MC, V. Closed Sun. Expensive.*

Antonio Martín. This is another old Málaga standby, with a splendid terrace overlooking the ocean, at the beginning of the Paseo Marítimo. It's long been famous for its fresh seafood and paella. Try the local *fritura malagueña. Paseo Marítimo 4, tel. 95/222–2113. Reservations advised. AE, DC, MC, V. Closed Sun. evening. Moderate.*

Casa Pedro. It's crowded and noisy, but Malgueños have been flosking to this no-frills fish restaurant for more than 50 years. Located in the seaside suburb of El Palo, the restaurant has a huge, bare dining room that overlooks the ocean. Try joining the hordes of local families who come here for lunch on Sundays. It's quieter at other times. *Quitapenas 121, El Paso beach (bus No. 11), tel. 95/229–0003. Reservations advised Sun. AE, DC, MC, V. Closed Mon. dinner and Nov. Moderate.*

Rincon de Mata. This is one of the best of the many restaurants in the pedestrian shopping streets between Calle Larios and Calle Nueva. Its menu is more original than most. In summer, there are tables outside on the sidewalk. *Esparteros 8, tel. 95/222–3135. Reservations not necessary. V. Moderate.*

La Cancela. This is a colorful restaurant in the center of town, just off Calle Granada. Dine indoors or alfresco. *Denís Belgrano 3, tel. 95/222–3125. Reservations not necessary. AE, DC, MC, V. Closed Wed. Inexpensive.*

Lodging **Los Naranjos.** This small hotel owned by the Luz chain is situated on a pleasant avenue in a residential district a little to the east of the city center. There's a small garden in front, but rooms overlooking the street can be noisy. *Paseo de Sancha 35, tel. 95/222–4317. 41 rooms. AE, DC, V. Expensive.*

★ **Parador de Gibralfaro.** Located in a small wood on top of Gibralfaro mountain 3½ kilometers (2 miles) above the city, this tiny parador has recently been renovated and offers spectacular views over the city and bay. Its accommodations are the best in Málaga, and it's a good place to dine even if you're not staying here. A bus service runs between the parador and cathedral. *Gibralfaro, tel. 95/222–1902. 12 rooms. Reservations essential, long in advance. AE, DC, MC, V. Expensive.*

Las Vegas. In a pleasant part of town, just east of the center, this recently renovated hotel has a dining room overlooking the Paseo Marítimo, an outdoor pool, and a large leafy garden. Rooms at the back enjoy a good view of the ocean. *Paseo de Sancha 22, tel. 95/221–7712. 100 rooms. AE, DC, MC, V. Moderate.*

Victoria. This small, recently renovated hostel in an old house just off Calle Larios offers excellent budget accommodations in a convenient central location. *Sancha de Lara 3, tel. 95/222–4223. 13 rooms. AE, V. Inexpensive.*

Marbella **La Hacienda.** This restaurant, owned by Belgian chef-proprietor Paul Schiff, belongs to the Relais Gourmand group and *Dining* is one of the highest rated in Spain. The menu reflects the influ-
★ ence of both Paul Schiff's native Belgium and his adopted Andalusia. The *menú degustación* at around 5,500 ptas. will enable you to sample the very best creations of this famous European chef. *Las Chapas, Rte. N340, km. 193, 12 km (7 mi) east on the road to Málaga; tel. 95/283–1267. Reservations required. AE, DC, MC, V. Closed Mon., Tues., and mid-Nov.–mid-Dec. Very Expensive.*

La Meridiana. Another of Marbella's most outstanding restaurants and a favorite with the local jet set, La Meridiana is located just west of town, toward Puerto Banús, and is famous for its original Bauhaus-type architecture and the superb quality and freshness of the ingredients. *Camino de la Cruz, tel. 95/ 277–6190. Reservations required. AE, DC, MC, V. Closed Mon., Tues. lunch, and lunch in summer. Very Expensive.*

La Dorada. Fresh fish and shellfish top the menu in this two-story building with an outdoor dining area on each floor. Specialties of the house include *fritura malaguena* (fried fish Malaga style) served sizzling and fresh from the pan, and excellent *mariscos* (shellfish), such as *coquinas* (small cockles), *cigalos* (small crayfish), and *bogavantes* (similar to crayfish). *Ctra. Cadiz-Malaga (N340), km. 176, tel. 95/282–1034. AE, DC, V. Closed Aug. Expensive.*

★ **La Fonda.** In a beautiful 18th-century house with antique furniture and located in one of the loveliest old squares in Marbella, La Fonda is owned by one of Madrid's leading restaurateurs. Its cuisine combines the best of Spanish, French, and Austrian influences, and it has been awarded the National Gastronomy Prize. A delightful patio filled with potted plants makes a perfect setting for summer dining. *Plaza del Santo Cristo 9, tel. 95/277–2512. Reservations advised. AE, DC, V. Open for dinner only, 8 PM–midnight. Closed Sun. Expensive.*

Mesón del Pollo. This small, charming "house of chicken" illustrates how Marbella, despite tourism, remains truly Spanish. Porcelain lampshades, azulejo tiles, a dozen tables, and the scent of roasting chicken fill this popular lunch spot. Try the *pollo a la sevillana* dinner (roast chicken with squid, fried potatoes, salad, and cider) or *fritura malagueña*, or sample tapas of octopus or meatballs. *Antonio Martín, across from the El Fuerte Hotel, no tel. No reservations. No credit cards. Inexpensive.*

Lodging The only reason to stay in town is if you're on a tight budget and have no car. Students can stay in small, family-run hotels in the old quarter of Marbella for as little as $15–$20 a night. There are a few reasonably priced, package-tour-type high-rise hotels only a block from the busy town beach. For most visitors, air-conditioning in summer is a must. The ocean is uninviting at times, thanks to improper pollution controls, so a hotel pool is a plus. Most visitors prefer to stay at one of the sparkling white resorts strung along the beach on either side of town. Finding the right one is critical.

★ **Los Monteros.** Situated 2½ kilometers (1½ miles) east of Marbella, on the road to Málaga, this deluxe hotel offers all the facilities of a top hotel, including an 18-hole golf course, seven tennis courts, three pools, horseback riding, and gourmet dining in its famous El Corzo Grill restaurant. This is the third most expensive hotel in Spain, after the Ritz and Villa Magna in Madrid. Eighty percent of the guests are British, which may explain the somewhat starched formality of the rooms. *Urb. Los Monteros, tel. 95/277–1700. 171 rooms. AE, DC, MC, V. Very Expensive.*

Marbella Club. The grande dame of Marbella tends to attract an older clientele. The bungalow-style rooms run from cramped to spacious, and the decor varies considerably; specify the type you prefer, but ask for a room that's been recently renovated. The grounds are exquisite. Breakfast is served on a patio where songbirds flit through the vegetation. *Rte. N340, km.*

178, tel. 95/277–1300. 100 rooms with bath. Facilities: restaurant, bar, gym, sauna, nightclub, hairdresser, tennis. AE, DC, MC, V. Very Expensive.

Puente Romano. A spectacular, modern hotel and apartment complex of low, white-stucco buildings located 2 miles west of Marbella on the road to Puerto Banús. The "village" has a Roman bridge in its beautifully landscaped grounds as well as two pools, a tennis club, and a disco run by Régine. *Rte. N340, km. 184, tel. 95/277–0100. 220 rooms. AE, DC, V. Very Expensive.*

El Fuerte. This is the best of the few hotels in the center of Marbella, with simple, adequate rooms. It's located in a 1950s-type building in the midst of a large garden with an outdoor pool. *Avda. El Fuerte, tel. 95/277–1500. 146 rooms. AE, DC, V. Moderate.*

★ **Pilar.** This may be the best find in Marbella: a cheerful, relatively large, and charming hotel in a central location—and very fairly priced to boot. It was taken over in 1992 by Scotsman Michael Wright, a former butler and master of guest houses in Edinburgh. It's clean and intimate, and includes such delightful surprises as a log fire in winter. *Mesoncillo 4, tel. 95/282–9936. 16 rooms. Facilities: bar serving breakfast. No credit cards. Inexpensive.*

Mijas
Dining

Valparaíso. *Pato a la naranja* (duck in an orange sauce) is one of the specialties served in a pleasant villa with garden and terrace on the road from Fuengirola to Mijas. *Tel. 95/248–5996. AE, DC, MC, V. Dinner only. Closed Sun. Expensive.*

La Reja. This charming restaurant has two dining rooms overlooking the main square of Plaza Virgen de la Peña. There's an atmospheric bar and an inexpensive pizzeria, too. *Caños 9, tel. 95/248–5068. Reservations accepted. AE, DC, MC, V. Closed Mon. Moderate.*

Mirlo Blanco. Here you can sample Basque specialties such as *txangurro* (crab) and *merluza a la vasca* (hake with asparagus, eggs, and clam sauce). *Plaza Constitución 13, tel. 95/248–5700. Reservations accepted. AE, DC, V. Moderate.*

Lodging

★ **Byblos Andaluz.** In this new luxury hotel set in a huge garden of palms, cypresses, and fountains, you'll find every comfort. Facilities include pools, saunas, tennis, and an 18-hole golf course. Its Le Nailhac restaurant is famous for its French cuisine; special low-calorie meals are also available. *Urbano Mijas-Golf, tel. 95/247–3050, fax 95/247–6783. 144 rooms. AE, DC, MC, V. Very Expensive.*

★ **Mijas.** You'll find this hotel at the entrance to Mijas village. The hotel is modern and peaceful, with a delightful rose garden, terrace, and afternoon tea. *Urbano Tamisa, tel. 95/248–5800, fax 95/248–5825. 106 rooms. AE, DC, MC, V. Expensive.*

Nerja
Dining

Casa Luque. This is one of the most authentically Spanish of Nerja's restaurants, located in a charming old Andalusian house behind the Balcón de Europa church. *Plaza Cavana 2, tel. 95/252–1004. Reservations accepted. AE, V. Closed Mon. and Feb. Moderate.*

Cortijo. This is a small, family-run restaurant in a 200-year-old house. Andalusian dishes share the menu with international favorites. *Barrio 26, no phone. DC, MC, V. Inexpensive.*

Lodging

Monica. Nerja's newest beach hotel opened in 1986. It's spacious and luxurious, with Moorish-style architecture. Facilities include tennis, pool, nightclub, and disco. *Playa*

Torrecilla, tel. 95/252–1100. 234 rooms. AE, DC, MC, V. Expensive.

★ **Parador.** All the rooms in this small parador a little to the east of the center of Nerja have balconies overlooking the sea. There's a pleasant leafy garden and outdoor pool, and an elevator takes you down to the beach. *El Tablazo, tel. 95/252–0050, fax 95/252–1997. 73 rooms. AE, DC, MC, V. Expensive.*

Ronda **Don Miguel.** Located by the bridge over the Tajo gorge, the
Dining restaurant's terrace offers spectacular views of the ravine. Lamb is a specialty; try *pierna de cordero lechal Don Miguel* (leg of baby lamb). *Villanueva 4, tel. 95/287–1090. Reservations advised. AE, DC, MC, V. Closed Tues. evening and all day Sun. June–Sept.; closed Tues. evening and all day Wed. Oct.–May. Expensive.*
Pedro Romero. Located opposite the bullring, this restaurant is, not surprisingly, packed with colorful taurine decor. Among the traditional regional recipes worth trying is the *sopa de mesón*—the soup of the house. *Virgen de la Paz 18, tel. 95/287–1110. AE, DC, MC, V. Moderate.*

Lodging **Reina Victoria.** A spectacularly situated Old-World hotel with a distinctly British air, the Reina Victoria sits atop the very rim of the gorge. Its views and style are tops, but its facilities are often overwhelmed by tour groups. *Jerez 25, tel. 95/287–1240, fax 95/287–1075. 89 rooms. AE, DC, MC, V. Moderate-Expensive.*
Polo. A cozy, old-fashioned hotel in the center of town, Polo sports a reasonably priced restaurant. The staff is friendly and the rooms simple but comfortable. *Mariano Soubiron 8, tel. 95/287–2447. 33 rooms. AE, DC, V. Moderate.*

Torremolinos **Casa Guaquin.** Casa Guaquin is widely known as the best sea-
Dining food restaurant in the region. Changing daily catches are served on a seaside patio alongside such menu stalwarts as *coquillas al ajillo* (sea cockles in garlic sauce). *Paseo Marítimo 63, tel. 95/238–4530. AE, V. Closed Thurs. Moderate.*
El Atrio. This small, stylish restaurant is located in the Pueblo Blanco. Its cuisine is predominantly French. In summer, you can dine on the terrace. *Casablanca 9, tel. 95/238–8850. AE, V. Open 8 PM–midnight. Closed Sun. and Dec. Moderate.*
El Roqueo. Owned by a former fisherman, this is one of the locals' favorite Carihuela fish restaurants. Ingredients are always fresh and the prices are very reasonable. *Carmen 35, tel. 95/238–4946. AE, V. Closed Tues. and Nov. Moderate.*
Juan. This is a good place to enjoy seafood in summer, with a sunny outdoor patio facing the sea. The specialties include the great Costa del Sol standbys: *sopa de mariscos* (shellfish soup), *dorada al horno* (oven-roasted giltheads), and *fritura malagueña. Paseo Marítimo 29, La Carihuela, tel. 95/238–5656. AE, DC, MC, V. Moderate.*

Lodging **Cervantes.** This busy cosmopolitan hotel in the heart of town has comfortable rooms, good service, and a well-known dining room on its top floor. *Las Mercedes, tel. 95/238–4033, fax 95/238–4857. 393 rooms. Facilities: pool, sauna, nightclub. AE, DC, MC, V. Expensive.*
Meliá Torremolinos. Torremolinos's only five-star hotel is located west of town. It overlooks the sea and offers all the facilities of a luxury hotel, but standards are not always up to par. *Avda. Carlota Alessandri 109, tel. 95/238–0500, fax 95/238–0538. 282 rooms. Facilities: pool. AE, DC, MC, V. Expensive.*

Tropicana. Located on the beach at the far end of the Carihuela is a comfortable, relaxing resort hotel with several good restaurants nearby. *Trópico 6, tel. 95/238-6600, fax 95/238-0568. 86 rooms. Facilities: pool. AE, DC, MC, V. Moderate.*

★ **Miami.** Set in an old Andalusian villa in a shady garden to the west of the Carihuela, this is something of a find amid the ocean of concrete blocks. *Aladino 14, tel. 95/238-5255. 26 rooms. No credit cards. Inexpensive.*

BOO.

Sprint's WorldTraveler FŌNCARD. The easy way to call from around the world.

Imagine trying to place a call in another country: You have to deal with foreign currency. Alien operators. And phones that look like they're from another planet.

Talk about frightening.

Now imagine making the same call with a Sprint WorldTraveler FŌNCARD™:

To begin with, you'll reach an English-speaking operator just by dialing one easy, toll-free access code. An access code, by the way, that's right on your calling card.

Not only that, you won't have any trouble remembering your card number. Because it's based on your home phone number.

Now what could be easier than that? So call today and find out how you can get a WorldTraveler FŌNCARD.

Because we may not be able to do anything about the phones you'll have to call from. But at least it won't be a ghastly experience.

1·800·347·8989

There's only one airline that offers as many travel choices as Scandinavia itself.

Scandinavia is fjords, archipelagoes, rolling countryside, ancient castles, and quaint inns. It's lively capitals, gourmet restaurants, museums, first class hotels, opera and ballet. A region of wonderful contrasts and friendly, English-speaking people.

And SAS the airline with the most nonstop flights to Scandinavia, offers the most ways for you to enjoy your visit. Select from a full range of escorted tours as well as independent fly/drive and fly/cruise packages.

There's only one place like it. Scandinavia.

For information and reservations, contact your travel agent or call SAS at 800-221-2350.

Scandinavia

DENMARK · FINLAND · ICELAND · NORWAY · SWEDEN

27 Sweden

Sweden's 450,707 square kilometers (173,349 square miles) contain only 8.5 million people, so its population density ranks among Europe's lowest, and its vast open spaces and good, uncrowded roads make it a country where you can easily escape the frantic pace of modern life. But the long, narrow shape of the country means that on a typical visit it is possible to explore only a relatively small area, and it is unwise to be overly ambitious when planning your trip. The distances are considerable, especially by European standards—almost 1,600 kilometers (1,000 miles) as the crow flies, from north to south. The 2,128-kilometer (1,330-mile) train journey from Trelleborg, in the far south, through endless birch forests to Riksgränsen, in the Arctic north, is said to be the world's longest stretch of continuously electrified railroad.

The recently formed Swedish Travel and Tourist Council, which replaced the government-run Swedish Tourist Board in August 1992, would be the first to admit that it faces something of an uphill task in marketing the country to the overseas visitor, not only because it does not have the long-established tourist industry of neighboring Norway nor of traditional favorites France, Italy, and Switzerland, but because of recent price increases that have made it one of the most expensive countries in Europe. However, those who can afford to visit Sweden usually return home raving about its high standards of lodging and dining. Even the most modest establishment is always spotlessly clean, and you will be given a warm welcome (almost certainly in excellent English, too).

Sweden's scenic attractions may not be as spectacular as the Norwegian fjords across the border, but the country offers a varied landscape, with more than 96,000 lakes and a jagged coastline with countless archipelagoes, forests, mountains, and rushing rivers. While Sweden is very much a modern country, it zealously guards its rural heritage. Most city dwellers have access to second homes in the country to which they retreat as often as possible. Traditional arts and crafts are also highly prized.

The cities, too, make the most of their natural settings and are carefully planned, with an emphasis on light and open spaces. Stockholm, one of the most beautiful of European capitals, is the major attraction, though Gothenburg, on the west coast, and Malmö, just across the sound from Denmark, are worthy of short visits as well.

Essential Information

Before You Go

When to Go The main tourist season runs from June through August, but Sweden needs to extend the season to encourage visitors from abroad. It's disappointing to note how many visitor attractions do not start operating until mid-June and then suddenly restrict their opening times or close down altogether in mid-August, when the Swedes' own vacation season ends and the children return to school. The weather can also be magnificent in the spring and fall, and there are plenty of tourists who prefer sightseeing when fewer people are around.

Sweden

Norwegian
Sea

NORWAY

FINLAND

Gulf
of
Bothnia

Gulf of Finland

ESTONIA

Baltic
Sea

Gulf of
Riga

LATVIA

LITHUANIA

DENMARK

Kiruna

Gällivare
Jokkmokk

Luleälven

Arjeplog
Tärnaby
Arvidsjaur
Töre
Törneå
Sorsele
E79
Kalix
Piteå
Luleå
Storuman
95
Lycksele
Skellefteå
342
Åsele
Umeälven
92
Umeå
Strömsund
90
Åre
Östersund
E75
Tännäs
Ljungan
Sundsvall
84
Idre
Hudiksvall
70
Bollnäs
Mora
Söderhamn
62
Falun
Gävle
80
Borlänge
Avesta
Fagersta
E4
Karlstad
Uppsala
E18
Mellerud
Västerås
Stockholm
Strömstad
Örebro
Mälaren
Vänern
Gotska
Uddevalla
Norrköping
Sandön
Trollhättan
Vättern
Göteborg
Linköping
40
Jönköping
Visby
Borås
Nässjö
E4
Falkenberg
Värnamo
Gotland
E6
Oskarshamn
Halmstad
23
Växjö
Öland
Helsingborg
Kalmar
Malmö
Karlskrona
Kristianstad
Trelleborg
Ystad

N

0   50 miles
0   75 km

Kluralven

400

Sweden virtually shuts up shop for the entire month of July. The concentrated nature of the Swedes' own vacation period can sometimes make it difficult to get hotel reservations during July and early August. On the other hand, the big city hotels, which cater mainly to business travelers, reduce their rates drastically in the summer, when their ordinary clients are on vacation. (If you're traveling in winter, the high season for business travel, be forewarned that prices are very high.) Ask your travel agent about special discount schemes offered by the major hotel groups, or contact the recently established tourist information center, **Next Stop Sweden** (Box 10134, 121 28 Stockholm, tel. 08/725–5500, fax 08/649–8882). Once you're in Sweden, you might also pay a visit to **Upptack Sverige Butiken** (Discover Sweden Boutique, Stureplan 8, tel. 08/611–7430) for well-priced seasonal package tours throughout Sweden.

Climate As in the rest of northern Europe, Sweden's summer weather is unpredictable, but, as a general rule, it is more likely to be rainy on the west coast than on the east. When the sun shines, the climate is usually agreeable; it is rarely unbearably hot. In Stockholm it never really gets dark in midsummer, while in the far north, above the Arctic Circle, the sun doesn't set between the end of May and the middle of July.

The following are the average daily maximum and minimum temperatures for Stockholm.

Jan.	30F	– 1C	**May**	58F	14C	**Sept.**	60F	15C
	23	– 5		43	6		49	9
Feb.	30F	– 1C	**June**	67F	19C	**Oct.**	49F	9C
	22	– 5		51	11		41	5
Mar.	37F	3C	**July**	71F	22C	**Nov.**	40F	5C
	26	– 4		57	14		34	1
Apr.	47F	8C	**Aug.**	68F	20C	**Dec.**	35F	3C
	34F	1C		55F	13C		28F	– 2C

Currency The unit of currency in Sweden is the krona (plural kronor), which is divided into 100 öre and is written as SEK or kr. Coins come in values of 50 öre and 1, 5, or 10 kronor, while bills come in denominations of 20, 50, 100, 500, and 1,000 SEK. Traveler's checks and foreign currency can be exchanged at banks all over Sweden and at post offices bearing the NB Exchange sign. At press time (spring 1993), the exchange rate was 7.2 kronor to the dollar and 10.6 kronor to the pound sterling.

What It Will Cost Sweden is an expensive country. Hotel prices are above the European average, but, as in most countries, the most expensive hotels are found in major cities. Restaurant prices are generally high, but there are bargains to be had: Look for the *dagens rätt* (dish of the day) in many city restaurants. This costs about SEK 50–SEK 65 and can include a main dish, salad, soft drink, bread and butter, and coffee.

Many hotels have special low summer rates and cut costs during weekends in winter. But because of heavy taxes and excise duties, liquor prices are among the highest in Europe. It pays to take in your maximum duty-free allowance. Value-added tax (known as *Moms* in Swedish) is imposed on most goods and services at a rate of 25%, with the exception of a 21% Moms on food, hotels, restaurants, and transportation. You can avoid most of the tax on goods if you take advantage of the tax-free shopping service offered at more than 13,000 stores throughout the country (*see* Shopping in Staying in Sweden, *below*).

Sample Prices Cup of coffee, SEK 10–SEK 15; bottle of beer, SEK 30–SEK 40; Coca-Cola, SEK 12–SEK 15; ham sandwich, SEK 25–SEK 35; 1-mile taxi ride, SEK 70 (depending on the taxi company).

Customs on Arrival You may bring duty-free into Sweden 400 cigarettes or 200 cigarillos or 100 cigars or 500 grams of tobacco. You may also import 1 liter of spirits and 1 liter of wine *or* 2 liters of beer, plus a reasonable amount of perfume and other goods to the value of SEK 600. Residents over the age of 15 of other European countries may bring duty-free into Sweden 200 cigarettes or 100 cigarillos, or 50 cigars or 250 grams of tobacco; visitors aged 20 or more may import 1 liter of spirits, 1 liter of wine, and 2 liters of beer, plus a reasonable amount of perfume, and other goods to the value of SEK 600. There are no limits on the amount of foreign currency that can be imported or exported.

Language Virtually all Swedes you are likely to meet will speak English, for it is a mandatory subject in all schools and is the main foreign language that Swedish children learn. Some of the older people you meet in the rural areas may not be quite so familiar with English, but you'll soon find someone who can help out.

Getting Around

By Car
Road Conditions Sweden has an excellent highway network of more than 80,000 kilometers (50,000 miles). The fastest routes are those with numbers prefixed with an E (for "European"), some of which are the equivalent of American superhighways or British motorways—for part of the way, at least. Road E4, for instance, covers the entire distance from Malmö, in the south, to Stockholm, and on to Sundsvall and Umeå, in the north, finishing at Haparanda, on the frontier with Finland. All main and secondary roads are well surfaced, but some minor roads, particularly in the north, are graveled.

Rules of the Road You drive on the right and, no matter where you sit in a car, you must wear a seat belt. You must also have low-beam headlights on at all times. Signs indicate five basic speed limits, ranging from 30 kph (19 mph) in school or playground areas to 110 kph (69 mph) on long stretches of E roads.

Parking Park on the right-hand side of the road, but if you want to park overnight, particularly in suburban areas, be sure not to do so on the night the street is being cleaned; signs should indicate when this occurs. Parking meters and, increasingly, timed ticket machines, are available for use in larger towns, usually between 8 AM and 6 PM. The fee varies from about SEK 8 to SEK 20 per hour. A circular sign with a red cross on a blue background with a red border means parking is prohibited. A yellow plate with a red border below it means restricted parking. The fees for parking tickets are extraordinarily high in Sweden.

Gasoline Sweden has some of the highest gasoline rates in Europe, about SEK 7.80 per liter, depending on the grade. Lead-free gasoline is readily available. Most gas stations are self-service places, indicated by the sign Tanka Själv. Many have automatic pumps, which accept SEK 50 or SEK 100 bills, and where you can fill up at any time, night or day. Some take credit cards.

Breakdowns The **Larmtjänst** organization, run by a confederation of Swedish insurance companies, provides a 24-hour breakdown service. Its phone numbers are listed in all telephone books. A toll-free emergency number, tel. 020/910040, is also available.

By Train Sweden's rail network, mostly electrified, is highly efficient, and trains operate frequently, particularly on the main routes linking Stockholm with Gothenburg and Malmö, on which there is frequent service. First- and second-class cars are provided on all main routes, and sleeping cars are available in both classes on overnight trains. On long-distance trains, there is usually a buffet or dining car. Seat reservations are advisable, and on some trains—indicated with R or IC on the timetable—they are compulsory. Reservations can be made right up to departure time at a cost of SEK 20 per seat (tel. 020/757575). In addition, the Swedish rail network operates four daily high-speed trains called the X2000 between Stockholm and Gothenburg (the trip takes less than three hours).

Fares On "Low price" or "Red" departures, fares are reduced by 50%, so careful planning is necessary to take advantage of the lower prices. Passengers paying low fares cannot make stopovers and the tickets are valid for only 36 hours.

By Plane Sweden's domestic air network is highly developed. Most major cities are served by **SAS** (tel. 020/727–555) or its domestic partner **Linjeflyg** (tel. 020/727–000). From Stockholm, there are services to about 30 points around the country. SAS and Linjeflyg offer cut-rate round-trip "minifares" every day of the week on selected flights, and these fares are available on most services during the peak tourist season, from late June to mid-August. Some even more favorable offers on domestic flights are frequently available from the end of June through early August and during the Christmas and Easter seasons.

By Bus Sweden has an excellent network of express bus services that provides an inexpensive and relatively speedy way of getting around the country. **Swebus,** tel. 031/103285 (Gothenburg) or 08/237190 (Stockholm), offers daily bus services from most major Swedish cities to various parts of Sweden. A number of other private companies operate weekend-only services on additional routes. In the far north of Sweden, post buses delivering mail to remote areas also carry passengers, and provide an offbeat and inexpensive way of seeing the countryside.

By Boat The classic boat trip in Sweden is the four-day journey along the Göta Canal between Gothenburg and Stockholm, operated by **Göta Kanal,** Gothenburg, tel. 031/806315.

By Bicycle Cycling is a popular activity in Sweden, and the country's uncongested roads make it ideal for extended bike tours. Bicycles can be rented throughout the country; inquire at the local tourist information office. Rental costs average around SEK 80 per day or SEK 400 per week. The **Swedish Touring Club** (STF) in Stockholm (tel. 08/790–3100) can give you information about cycling packages that include bike rental, overnight accommodations, and meals. **Cykelfrämjandet** (tel. 08/321680) has an English-language guide to cycling trips.

Staying in Sweden

Telephones Sweden has plenty of pay phones, although they are not found
Local Calls (as in many other European countries) in post offices. There

are, however, special offices marked Tele or Telebutik from which you can make calls. To make calls from a pay phone, you should have SEK 1, SEK 5, or SEK 10 coins available. You can also purchase a *telefonkort* (telephone card) from a Telebutik, pressbyrå, or hospital for SEK 45 or SEK 80, which can be cheaper if you make numerous domestic calls. For a local call, you need two SEK 1 coins.

International Calls These can be made from any pay phone. For calls to the United States and Canada, dial 009, then 1 (the country code), then wait for a second dial tone before dialing the area code and number. When dialing the United Kingdom, omit the initial zero on area codes (for Central London you would dial 009 followed by 44, wait for the second tone, then dial 71 and the local number). Making calls from your hotel room is convenient but can be expensive, so check with the front desk about rates first. You pay the normal rate at Telebutik offices.

Operators and The international exchange number is 0018. Dial 07975 for di-
Information rectory assistance in Sweden, 0013 for the Nordic Area, and 0019 for foreign inquiries.

Mail Airmail letters and postcards to the United States and Canada
Postal Rates weighing less than 20 grams cost SEK 6.00. Postcards and letters within Europe cost SEK 5.00.

Receiving Mail If you're uncertain where you will be staying, have your mail sent to Poste Restante, S-101 10 Stockholm. The address for collection is Vasagatan 28–32. A Poste Restante service is also offered by American Express (*see* Important Addresses and Numbers in Stockholm, *below*).

Shopping Swedish goods have earned an international reputation for elegance and quality, and any visitor to the country should spend some time exploring the many impressive shops and department stores. The midsummer tourist season is as good a time as any to go shopping, for that is when many stores have their annual sales. The best buys are to be found in glassware, stainless steel, pottery and ceramics, leather goods, and textiles. You will find a wide selection of goods available in such major stores as **NK, Åhléns, PUB,** and **Domus,** which have branches all over the country.

High-quality furniture is a Swedish specialty, and it is worthwhile visiting one of the many branches of **IKEA,** a shop usually located on the outskirts of major towns. IKEA's prices are extremely competitive, and the company also operates an export service. For glassware at bargain prices, head for the "Kingdom of Glass" (*see* The West Coast and the Glass Country, *below*). All the major glassworks, including **Orrefors** and **Kosta Boda,** have large factory outlets where you can pick up "seconds" (normally indistinguishable from the perfect product) at only a fraction of the normal retail price. For clothing, the best center is Borås, not far from Gothenburg. Here you can find bargains from the leading mail-order companies. In country areas, look for the local **Hemslöjd** craft centers, featuring high-quality clothing and needlework items.

VAT Refunds About 13,000 Swedish shops—1,000 in Stockholm alone—participate in the tax-free shopping service for visitors, enabling you to claim a refund on most of the value-added tax (Moms) that you have paid. Shops taking part in the scheme display a distinctive black, blue, and yellow sticker in the window. (Some stores offer the service only on purchases worth more than SEK 200.) Whenever you make a purchase in a participating store, you are given a "tax-free shopping check" equivalent to the tax paid, less a handling charge. This check can be cashed when you leave Sweden, either at the airport or aboard ferries. You should have your passport with you when you make your purchase and when you claim your refund.

Opening and Closing Times **Banks** are open weekdays 9:30–3, but some stay open until 5:30 in some larger cities. Banks at Stockholm's Arlanda Airport and Gothenburg's Landvetter Airport open every day, with extended hours. "Forex" currency-exchange offices operate in downtown Stockholm, Gothenburg, and Malmö, also with extended hours.

Hours vary widely, but **museums** are typically open weekdays 10–4 or 10–5. Many are also open on weekends but may close on Monday.

Shops are generally open weekdays 9 or 9:30–6 and Saturday 9–1 or 9–4. Some department stores remain open until 8 or 10 on certain evenings, and some are also open Sunday noon–4 in major cities. Many supermarkets open on Sunday.

National Holidays January 1; January 6 (Epiphany); April 1 (Good Friday); April 4 (Easter Monday); May 1 (Labor Day); May 12 (Ascension); May 22, 23 (Pentecost); June 25 (Midsummer's Eve); June 26 (Midsummer's Day); November 6 (All Saints' Day); December 25, 26.

Dining Swedish cuisine used to be considered somewhat uninteresting, but lately it has become much more cosmopolitan. The inevitable fast-food outlets, such as McDonald's and Burger King, have come on the scene, as well as Clock, the homegrown version. But there is also a good range of more conventional restaurants, from the usual top-class establishments to less expensive places where you can pick up a somewhat cheaper lunch or snack. Snacks can also be enjoyed in a *Konditori*, which offers inexpensive sandwiches, pastries, and pies with coffee, tea, or soft drinks. A cross between a café and a coffee shop, the Konditori can be found in every city and town.

Many restaurants all over the country specialize in *Husmanskost*—literally "home cooking"—which is based on traditional Swedish recipes.

Sweden is best known for its *smörgåsbord*, a word whose correct pronunciation defeats non-Swedes. It consists of a tempting buffet of hot and cold dishes, usually with a strong emphasis on seafood, notably herring, prepared in a wide variety of ways. Authentic smörgåsbord can be enjoyed all over the country, but the best is found in the many inns in Skåne, where you can eat as much as you want for about SEK 200. Many Swedish hotels serve a lavish smörgåsbord-style breakfast, often included in the room price. Do justice to your breakfast and you'll probably want to skip lunch!

Mealtimes Swedes eat early. Restaurants start serving lunch at about 11 AM, and outside the main cities you may find that they close quite early in the evening (often by 9) or may not even open at all for dinner. Don't wait too long to look for someplace to have a meal.

Dress Except for the most formal restaurants, where a jacket and tie are preferable, casual—or casual chic—attire is perfectly acceptable for restaurants in all price categories.

Ratings Prices are per person and include a first course, and main course (Swedes tend to skip desserts), but no drinks. Service charges and Moms are included in the meal, so there is no need to tip. Best bets are indicated by a star ★.

Category	Cost
Very Expensive	over SEK 350
Expensive	SEK 250–SEK 350
Moderate	SEK 120–SEK 250
Inexpensive	under SEK 120

Lodging Sweden offers a wide range of accommodations, from simple village rooms and campsites to top-class hotels of the highest international standard. Except at the major hotels in the larger cities that cater mainly to business clientele, rates are fairly reasonable. Prices are normally on a per-room basis and include all taxes and service and usually breakfast. Apart from the more modest inns and the cheapest budget establishments, private baths and showers are now standard features, although it is just as well to double-check when making your reservation. Whatever their size, virtually all Swedish hotels provide scrupulously clean accommodations and courteous service. In Stockholm, there is a hotel reservation office—**Hotellcentralen**—at the central train station and at the Stockholm Tourist Center in the Sweden House. In other areas, local tourist offices will help you with hotel reservations.

Hotels You can get a good idea of the facilities and prices at a particular hotel by consulting the official annual guide, "Hotels in Sweden," obtainable free of charge from the Swedish Travel and Tourist Council. There is a good selection of hotels in all price categories in every town and city, though major international chains such as Sheraton have made only small inroads in Sweden thus far. The main homegrown chains are Scandic and RESO. The Sweden Hotels group has about 100 independently owned hotels and offers a central reservation office. The group also has its own classification scheme—A, B, or C—based on the facilities available at each establishment. CountrySide Sweden is a group of 35 handpicked resort hotels, some of them restored historic manor houses or centuries-old inns. Most have been family-run for generations.

House-Rental Vacations In Sweden, these are popular among other Europeans, particularly the British and Germans. There are about 250 chalet villages with amenities, such as grocery stores, restaurants, saunas, and tennis courts. You can often arrange such accommodations on the spot at local tourist information offices. An alternative is a package, such as the one offered by **Scandinavian Seaways**, that combines a ferry trip from Britain across the North Sea with a stay in a chalet village. Scandinavian Seaways is based in the United Kingdom at Parkeston Quay, Harwich, Essex (tel. 0255/240240). Their number in Gothenburg is 031/650600.

Camping   Camping is also popular in Sweden. There are about 750 officially approved sites throughout the country, most located next to the sea or a lake and offering such activities as windsurfing, riding, and tennis. They are generally open between June 1 and September 1, though some are available year round. The National Swedish Camping Association publishes, in English, an abbreviated list of sites.

Ratings   Prices are for two people in a double room, based on summer season rates. Best bets are indicated by a star ★.

Category	Cost
Very Expensive	over SEK 1,200
Expensive	SEK 970–SEK 1,200
Moderate	SEK 725–SEK 970
Inexpensive	under SEK 725

Tipping   Swedes seldom expect tips. In hotels, tip the porter about SEK 5 per item). Taxi drivers do not expect a tip. The fee for leaving a coat in the checkroom is between SEK 6 and SEK 15. This is a consistent but irritating feature of the Swedish restaurant scene because you must always dispose of your coat or sports jacket, whether you want to or not.

Stockholm

Arriving and Departing

By Plane   All international flights arrive at Arlanda Airport, 40 kilometers (25 miles) north of the city. The airport is linked to Stockholm by a fast freeway. For information on arrival and departure times, call the individual airlines.

Between the Airport and Downtown   Buses leave both the international and domestic terminals every 10–15 minutes, from 7:10 AM to 10:30 PM, and run to the city terminal at Klarabergsviadukten next to the central train station. The bus costs SEK 50 per person. A taxi from the airport will cost at least SEK 250 (be sure to ask the driver if he offers the standard SEK 250 airport-to-city rate before you get into the taxi), but a possible alternative if you are not traveling alone is the SAS limousine service to any point in Greater Stockholm. It operates as a shared taxi at SEK 300 plus Moms. If two or three people travel together in a limousine to the same address, only one pays the full rate; all others pay SEK 75 plus Moms.

By Train   Major domestic and international services arrive at Stockholm Central Station on Vasagatan, in the heart of the city. This is also the terminus for local commuter services. For 24-hour train information, tel. 020/757575. At the station there is a ticket and information office, where you can make seat or sleeping-car reservations. An automatic ticket-issuing machine is also available. Seat reservations on the regular train cost SEK 20, couchettes SEK 80, and beds SEK 160. Seat reservations on the X2000, the high-speed train between Stockholm and Gothenburg, costs SEK 265. Add SEK 743 for the first-class fare and SEK 425 for the second-class fare.

By Bus Long-distance buses, from such places as Härnösand and Sundsvall, arrive at Norra Bantorget, a few blocks north of the central train station, and all others at Klarabergsviadukten, just beside it. Bus tickets can also be bought at the railroad reservations office.

By Car There are two main access routes from the west and south: the E20 main highway from Gothenburg and E4 from Malmö, which continues as the main route to Sundsvall, the far north, and Finland. All routes to the city center are well marked.

Getting Around

The most cost-effective way of getting around Stockholm is to use a **Stockholmskortet** (Key to Stockholm) card. Besides giving unlimited transportation on city subway, bus, and rail services, it offers free admission to 50 museums and several sightseeing trips. The card costs SEK 150 for 24 hours, SEK 300 for two days, and SEK 450 for three days. It is available from the tourist center at Sweden House, at Kungsträdgården, and the Hotellcentralen accommodations bureau at the central train station.

Maps and timetables for all city transportation networks are available from the Stockholm Transit Authority (SL) information desks at Norrmalmstorg or Sergels Torg. You can also obtain information by phone (tel. 08/6001000).

By Bus and Subway The Stockholm Transit Authority (SL) operates both the bus and subway systems. Tickets for the two networks are interchangeable.

The subway system, known as T-banan (the *T* stands for tunnel), is the easiest and fastest way of getting around the city. Some of the stations offer permanent art exhibitions. Station entrances are marked with a blue T on a white background. The T-banan has about 100 stations and covers more than 60 route-miles. Trains run frequently between 5 AM and 2 AM.

Tickets are available at ticket counters, but it is cheaper to buy a special discount coupon that gives a significant savings compared with buying separate tickets each time you travel. The coupons are available at Pressbyrån newsstands. A one-day ticket for the city center alone, valid on both bus and subway, costs SEK 30. A ticket covering the entire Greater Stockholm area costs SEK 55 for 24 hours or SEK 105 for 72 hours. People under 18 or over 65 pay half price. Also available from the Pressbyrån newsstands are SEK 80 T-banan coupons, good for 20 subway rides.

The Stockholm bus network is one of the world's largest. Services run not only within the central area but also to out-of-town points of interest, such as Waxholm, with its historic fortress, and Gustavsberg, with its well-known porcelain factory. Within Greater Stockholm, buses run throughout the night.

By Train SL operates conventional train services from Stockholm Central Station to a number of nearby points, including Nynäshamn, a departure point for ferries to the island of Gotland. Trains also run from the Slussen station to the fashionable seaside resort of Saltsjöbaden.

By Taxi Taxis are expensive and sometimes difficult to find on the street (although you may find one at a designated taxi stand). Typically, a trip of 10 kilometers (6 miles) will cost SEK 103 between 6 AM and 7 PM on weekdays and SEK 113 on weekday nights; weekend prices are SEK 127, including Moms. Major taxi companies are Taxi Stockholm (tel. 08/150000), Taxi 1 (tel. 08/670–0000), and Taxikurir (tel. 08/300000).

Important Addresses and Numbers

Tourist Information The main tourist center is at **Sweden House** (Kungsträdgården, tel. 08/789–2490), which was undergoing extensive renovation at press time. During the peak tourist season (mid-June to mid-August), it is open weekdays 8:30–6; weekends 8–5. The current off-season hours are 9–5 and 9–2, respectively. Besides providing information, it is the main ticket center for sightseeing excursions. There are also information centers at the central train station, in the City Hall (summer only), and in the Kaknäs TV Tower. When planning to visit any of the tourist attractions in Stockholm, be sure to call ahead as opening times and prices are subject to change.

Embassies U.S. (Strandvägen 101, tel. 08/783–5300). **Canadian** (Tegelbacken 4, tel. 08/613–9900). **U.K.** (Skarpögatan 6–8, tel. 08/667–0140).

Emergencies **Police** (tel. 08/769–3000; emergencies only: 90000); **Ambulance** (tel. 90000); **Doctor** (Medical Care Information, tel. 08/644–9200)—tourists can get hospital attention in the district where they are staying or can contact the private clinic, **City Akuten** (tel. 08/117102); **Dentist** (tel. 08/654–1117); **Pharmacy: C. W. Scheele** (tel. 08/248280) (all are indicated by the sign Apotek).

English-Language Bookstores Most bookstores have a good selection of English books. **Akademibokhandeln** (Mäster Samuelsgatan 32, tel. 08/214890), which belongs to a chain of bookstores, has the widest selection of paperbacks, dictionaries, and maps in many languages.

Travel Agencies **American Express** (Birger Jarlsgatan 1, tel. 08/235330). **Thomas Cook** (Ulvsundavägan 178B, Bromma, tel. 88/764–5555).

Guided Tours

Orientation Tours Some 30 different tours—by foot, boat, bus, or a combination of these—are available during the summer. Some last only 30 minutes, others an entire day. A popular three-hour bus tour, costing SEK 200, runs daily at 9:45 AM and 1:45 PM. The tour includes City Hall, Storkyrkan in Gamla Stan, the Wasa Ship, and the Royal Palace, among other stops. Tickets can be purchased from the Excursion Shop at Sweden House. A convenient budget-price tour by boat and/or bus is SL's "Tourist Route" (Turistlinjen). The tour departs every 15 minutes during peak vacation periods and every half hour at other times; you can get on and off at any one of the 14 stops. This tour is free for holders of the Key to Stockholm card but is conducted in Swedish only.

Boat Tours You'll find a bewildering variety of tours available at Stockholm's quaysides. The **Waxholm Steamship Company** (tel. 08/679–5830) operates scheduled services to many islands in the archipelago on its famous white steamers. Trips range from one to three hours each way. Popular one-day excursions include Waxholm, Utö, Sandhamn, and Möja. Conventional sightseeing tours include a one-hour circular city tour run by the **Strömma Canal Company** (tel. 08/233375). It leaves from the Nybroplan quay every hour between 10 and 5 in summer.

Special-Interest Tours A range of special-interest tours is available in the Stockholm area, especially in summer. These include a weekend at a chalet in the archipelago, rental of a small fishing boat, or the chance to buy porcelain at the Gustavsberg porcelain factory, just outside Stockholm. Several outstanding 17th-century villas and estates within an hour or two of Stockholm have been converted into quaint, high-quality hotels, such as the stately Ulvhälls Herrgård in Strängnäs on Lake Mälaren. Contact the tourist center at the Sweden House for details.

Excursions Don't miss the boat trip to the Palace of Drottningholm, the 17th-century private residence of the Swedish Royal Family and a smaller version of Versailles. Departures are every half hour between 10 and 4:30 during the summer from the City Hall Bridge (Stadshusbron). Another popular trip goes from Stadshusbron to the ancient towns of Sigtuna and Skokloster. By changing boats you can continue to Uppsala to catch the train back to Stockholm. Information is available from the **Strömma Canal Company** (tel. 08/233375) or the tourist center at Sweden House.

Personal Guides Contact the **Guide Center** at **Stockholm Information Service** (tel. 08/789–2426).

Exploring Stockholm

Numbers in the margin correspond to points of interest on the Stockholm map.

Because Stockholm's main attractions are concentrated in a relatively small area, the city itself can be explored in several days. But if you want to take advantage of some of the full-day excursions offered, it is worthwhile to devote a full week to your visit.

The city of Stockholm, built on 14 small islands among open bays and narrow channels, has been dubbed the "Venice of the North." It is a handsome, civilized city, full of parks, squares, and airy boulevards, yet it is also a bustling, modern metropolis. Glass-and-steel skyscrapers abound, but in the center you are never more than five minutes' walk from twisting, medieval streets and waterside walks.

The first written mention of Stockholm dates from 1252, when a powerful regent named Birger Jarl is said to have built a fortified castle here. And it must have been this strategic position, where the calm, fresh waters of Lake Mälaren meet the salty Baltic Sea, that prompted King Gustav Vasa to take over the city in 1523, and King Gustavus Adolphus to make it the heart of an empire a century later.

During the Thirty Years' War (1618–48), Sweden gained importance as a Baltic trading state, and Stockholm grew commensurately. But by the beginning of the 18th century, Swedish influence had begun to wane, and Stockholm's development had slowed. It did not revive until the Industrial Revolution, when the hub of the city moved north from the Old Town area.

City Hall and the Old Town Anyone in Stockholm with limited time should give priority to a tour of **Gamla Stan** (the Old Town), a labyrinth of narrow, medieval streets, alleys, and quiet squares just south of the city center. Ideally, you should devote an entire day to this district. But before crossing the bridge, pay a visit to the modern-day

❶ **City Hall,** constructed in 1923 and now one of the symbols of Stockholm. You'll need an early start, since there is only one guided tour per day, at 10 AM (also at noon on Saturday and Sunday). Lavish mosaics grace the walls of the **Golden Hall,** and the **Prince's Gallery** features a collection of large murals by Prince Eugene, brother of King Gustav V. Take the elevator to the top of the 106-meter (348-foot) tower for a magnificent view of the city. *Tel. 08/785–9074. Admission: SEK 25. Tower admission: SEK 10. Tower open May–Sept., daily 10–3.*

❷ Crossing into the Old Town, the first thing you'll see is the magnificent **Riddarholm Church,** where a host of Swedish kings are buried. *Tel. 08/789–8500. Admission: SEK 10. Open Mon.–Sat. 10–3, Sun. noon–3.*

❸ From there proceed to the **Royal Palace,** preferably by noon, when you can see the colorful changing-of-the-guard ceremony. The smartly dressed guards seem superfluous, since tourists wander at will into the castle courtyard and around the grounds. Several separate attractions are open to the public. Be sure to visit the **Royal Armory,** with its outstanding collection of weaponry and royal regalia. The **Treasury** houses the Swedish crown jewels, including the regalia used for the coronation of King Erik XIV in 1561. You can also visit the **State Apartments,** where the king swears in each successive government. *Tel. 08/789–8500. Admission: SEK 30 for Armory and Treasury; SEK 30 for State Apartments. Call ahead for opening hours, as they are subject to change.*

❹ From the palace, stroll down **Västerlånggatan,** one of two main shopping streets in the Old Town. This is a popular shopping area, brimming with boutiques and antiques shops. Walk down to the Skeppsbron waterfront, then head back toward the center over the Ström bridge, where anglers cast for salmon. If you feel like a rest, stop off at **Kungsträdgården** and watch the world go by. Originally built as a royal kitchen garden, the property was turned into a public park in 1562. During the summer, entertainment and activities abound, and you can catch a glimpse of local people playing open-air chess with giant chessmen.

Djurgården Be sure to spend at least a day visiting the many attractions on the large island of **Djurgården.** Although it's only a short walk from the city center, the most pleasant way to approach it is by ferry from Skeppsbron, in the Old Town. The ferries drop you off near two of Stockholm's best-known attractions, the Vasa Museum and Gröna Lund Tivoli. (Or you might want to take the reinstated streetcar, which runs along refurbished tracks from Norrmalmstorg, near the city center, to **Prince Eugene's Waldemarsudde,** [tel. 08/662–2800], an art museum in the former summer residence of a Swedish prince, on a peninsula in Djurgården.) The *Vasa,* a restored 17th-century warship, is one of the oldest preserved war vessels in the world and has become Sweden's most popular tourist sight. She sank ignominiously in Stockholm Harbor on her maiden voyage in 1628, reportedly because she was not carrying sufficient ballast. Recovered in 1961, she has been restored to her original appearance and has now been moved into a spectacular new museum, **❺** the **Vasamuseet,** which opened in 1990. It features guided tours, films, and displays. *Galarvarvet, tel. 08/666–4800. Admission: SEK 40 adults, SEK 10 students. Open daily 9:30–7.*

6 **Gröna Lund Tivoli,** Stockholm's version of the famous Copenhagen amusement park, is a favorite family attraction, featuring hair-raising roller coasters as well as tamer delights. *Tel. 08/ 665-7000. Open late Apr.–early Sept. Call ahead for prices and hours, as they are subject to change.*

7 Just across the road is **Skansen,** a large, open-air folk museum consisting of 150 reconstructed traditional buildings from Sweden's different regions. Here you can see a variety of handicraft displays and demonstrations. There is also an attractive open-air zoo—with many native Scandinavian species, such as lynxes, wolves, and brown bears—as well as an excellent aquarium. *Tel. 08/663-0500. Call ahead for prices and times, as they are subject to change.*

Time Out For a mediocre snack and a great view, try the **Solliden Restaurant** at Skansen. Skansen also offers a selection of open-air snack bars and cafés; Gröna Lund has four different restaurants.

8 From the zoo, head back toward the city center. Just before the Djurgård bridge, you come to the **Nordic Museum,** which, like Skansen, provides an insight into the way Swedish people have lived over the past 500 years. The collection includes displays of peasant costumes, folk art, and Lapp culture. *Tel. 08/666-4600. Admission: SEK 30–SEK 50 adults. Call ahead for prices and hours.*

9 Once you're back on the "mainland," drop into the **Museum of National Antiquities.** Though its name is uninspiring, it houses some remarkable Viking gold and silver treasures. **The Royal Cabinet of Coin,** located in the same building, boasts the world's largest coin. *Tel. 08/783-9400. Narvavägen 13–17. Admission free.*

Stockholm Environs

The region surrounding Stockholm offers many attractions that can easily be seen on day trips out of the capital.

One "must" is the trip to the majestic 16th-century **Gripsholm Castle,** at Mariefred, on the southern side of Lake Mälaren and about 64 kilometers (40 miles) from Stockholm. Gripsholm, with its drawbridge and four massive round towers, is one of Sweden's most romantic castles. There had been a castle on the site as early as the 1380s, but it was destroyed, and King Gustav Vasa had the present building erected in 1577. Today the castle is best known for housing the Swedish state collection of portraits and is one of the largest portrait galleries in the world, with some 3,400 paintings.

The most pleasant way of traveling to Gripsholm from Stockholm is on the vintage steamer *Mariefred*, the last coal-fired ship on Lake Mälaren. Departures, between mid-June and late August, are from the city hall, daily except Monday at 10 AM, returning from Mariefred at 4:30. The journey takes 3½ hours each way, and there is a restaurant on board. *Tel. 08/669-8850. Round-trip fare: SEK 140. Castle tel. 0159/10194. Admission to castle: SEK 30.*

Another popular boat trip goes to **Skokloster Palace,** about 70 kilometers (44 miles) from Stockholm. Departures are from the

Stockholm

Major Attractions
City Hall, **1**
Gröna Lund Tivoli, **6**
Kungsträdgården, **4**
Museum of National Antiquities, **9**
Nordic Museum, **8**
Riddarholm Church, **2**
Royal Palace, **3**
Skansen, **7**
Vasamuseet, **5**

Other Attractions
Cathedral, **22**
Concert Hall, **12**
House of Nobles, **20**
Kaknäs TV Tower, **15**
Kulturhuset, **23**
Museum of Far Eastern Antiquities, **18**
Museum of Modern Art, **14**
National Museum, **16**

NK, **24**
Parliament, **21**
Prince Eugene's Waldemarsudde, **25**
Royal Dramatic Theater, **11**
Royal Library, **13**
Royal Opera House, **17**
Stock Exchange, **10**
Supreme Court, **19**

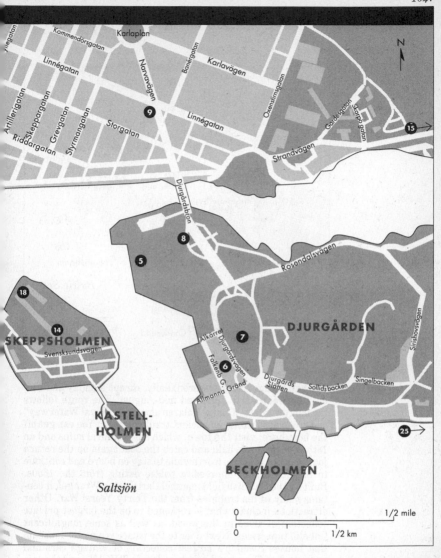

Stockholm Environs

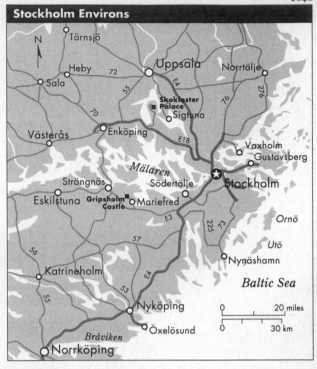

city hall bridge (Stadshusbron) daily, except Monday and Friday, between early June and mid-August. The route follows the narrow inlets of Lake Mälaren along the "Royal Waterway" and stops at **Sigtuna**, an ancient trading center. You can get off the boat here; visit the town, which has medieval ruins and an 18th-century town hall; and catch the boat again on the return journey. But it is also worthwhile to stay on board and continue to Skokloster, an impressive palace dating from the 1650s. Built by the Swedish field marshal Carl Gustav Wrangel, it contains many of his trophies from the Thirty Years' War. Other attractions include what is reckoned to be the largest private collection of arms in the world, as well as some magnificent Gobelin tapestries. Next door to the palace is a motor museum that houses Sweden's largest collection of vintage cars and motorcycles. The round-trip boat fare is SEK 135, and there is a restaurant and cafeteria on board. *Palace tel. 018/386–077. Admission to Skokloster Palace: SEK 50 (free with Key to Stockholm card). Admission to motor museum: SEK 25 (free with Key to Stockholm card). Open daily noon–4.*

Lovers of the sea could easily spend an entire week cruising among the 24,000 islands in the **Stockholm archipelago.** The **Båtluffarkortet** (Inter-Skerries Card), available from early June to mid-August, gives you 16 days' unlimited travel on the Waxholm Steamship Company boats, which operate scheduled services throughout the archipelago. The card is on sale in the Excursion Shop at the Sweden House Tourist Center and at the Waxholm Steamship Company terminal at Strömkajen. It costs around SEK 250.

Off the Beaten Track

Just over 155 meters (508 feet) tall, the **Kaknäs TV Tower** at Djurgården is the highest structure in Scandinavia. From the top you can catch a magnificent view of the city and surrounding archipelago. Facilities include a cafeteria, restaurant, and gift shop. *Djurgården, tel. 08/667–8083. Admission: SEK 20.*

You can see the world's largest variety of water lilies at the **Bergianska Botanical Garden,** just north of the city center. The lily's leaves are more than 2.17 meters (7 feet) in diameter. *Frescati, tel. 08/153912.*

Fjäderholmarna (the Feather Islets), the collective name for a group of four secluded islands in the Stockholm archipelago, have been open to the public only since the early '80s, after 50 years as a military zone. There is a museum depicting life in the archipelago, as well as the largest aquarium in Scandinavia, housing many species of Baltic marine life. Boats leave from Slussen, Strömkajen, and Nybroplan in downtown Stockholm. *Fjäderholmarna, tel. 08/718–0100.*

Shopping

Gift Ideas   Stockholm is an ideal place to find items that reflect the best in Swedish design and elegance, particularly glass, porcelain, furs, handicrafts, home furnishings, and leather goods. The quality is uniformly high, and you can take advantage of the tax-free shopping service in most stores (*see* Shopping in Staying in Sweden, *above*).

Department Stores   The largest is **NK,** on Hamngatan, where you can find just about anything. Other major stores are **PUB,** on Hötorget, and **Åhléns City,** on Klarabergsgatan. All three are open Sundays. A new shopping complex is **Sturegallerian,** a covered gallery built on the site of the former public baths at Stureplan. There are about 50 shops, plus a number of restaurants.

Shopping Districts   The center of Stockholm's shopping activity has shifted from Kungsgatan to Hamngatan, a wide boulevard along which a huge, covered shopping complex called **Gallerian** has been built. The **Old Town** area is best for handicrafts, antiquarian bookshops, and art shops.

Food and Flea Markets   One of the biggest flea markets in northern Europe is located in **Skärholmen** shopping center, a 20-minute subway ride from the downtown area. Market hours are weekdays 11–6, Saturday 9–3, Sunday 10–3. Superior food markets selling such Swedish specialties as marinated salmon and reindeer can be found on **Ostermalmstorg** and **Hötorget.**

Glassware   For the best buys, try **Nordiska Kristall,** on Kungsgatan, or **Rosenthal Studio-Haus,** on Birger Jarlsgatan. The latter operates its own shipping service. **Arioso,** on Västerlånggatan in the Old Town, is good for modern crystal and ceramics, and **Önske-butiken,** on the corner of Kungsgatan and Sveavägen, specializes in crystal as well as porcelain.

Handicrafts   A good center for all kinds of Swedish handicrafts in wood and metal is **Svensk Hemslöjd,** on Sveavägen. It also sells embroidery kits and many types of weaving and knitting yarn. **Stockholms Läns Hemslöjdsförening,** on Drottninggatan, has a wide selection of Swedish folk costumes and handicraft souvenirs from different parts of Sweden.

Dining

Prices quoted here are per person and include a first course, main course, tax, and service, but not wine. For details and price-category descriptions, *see* Dining in Staying in Sweden. Best bets are indicated by a star ★.

Very Expensive **Operakällaren.** Located in part of the elegant Opera House building, this is one of Stockholm's best-known traditional restaurants, featuring both Scandinavian and Continental cuisine. It is famed for its smörgåsbord, particularly during the pre-Christmas period. The restaurant faces Kungsträdgården, the waterfront, and the Royal Palace. *Operahuset, tel. 08/ 111125. Reservations advised. AE, DC, MC, V.*

Paul and Norbert. A very cozy, 32-seat restaurant on Stockholm's most elegant avenue, Paul and Norbert is noted for its French-style cuisine, using indigenous wild game such as reindeer, elk, partridge, and grouse, as well as fish. The decor is rustic but refined. *Strandvägen 9, tel. 08/663–8183. Reservations required. AE, DC, MC, V. Closed weekends. Call for yearly closing dates.*

Ulriksdals Värdshus. This is a beautifully located country inn built in 1868 and set in a castle park on the outskirts of town. It offers both Swedish and international cuisines, but is particularly noted for its lunchtime smörgåsbord. *Ulriksdals Slottspark, tel. 08/850815. Reservations advised. AE, DC, MC, V. Closed Sun. dinner and Christmas.*

Expensive ★ **Clas på Hörnet.** Located just outside the city center, Clas på Hörnet is a small, intimate establishment occupying the ground floor of a restored 200-year-old town house, now a hotel (*see* Lodging, *below*). It offers a choice of international or Swedish cuisine. *Surbrunnsgatan 20, tel. 08/165136. Reservations advised. AE, DC, MC, V. Closed Christmas.*

★ **Den Gyldene Freden.** Once a favorite haunt of Stockholm's artists and composers, the 272-year-old Den Gyldene Freden has Old Town ambience. The cuisine is a tasteful combination of French and Swedish. Every Thursday, the Swedish Academy, whose members choose the winner of the Nobel Prize in literature, meets for lunch on the second floor. *Österlånggatan 51, tel. 08/249760. Reservations advised. AE, DC, MC, V. Closed Sun. and Christmas.*

Nils Emil. Frequented by members of the Swedish royal family, this unpretentious yet elegant restaurant is noted for its delicious Swedish cuisine and generous helpings. Walls are decorated with paintings of the archipelago, birthplace of chef/ owner Nils Emil. The personable chef likes to visit his patrons' tables to keep tabs on the quality of the meals and service. *Folkungagatan 122, tel. 08/407209. Reservations required. AE, DC, MC, V.*

★ **Stallmästaregården.** A historic old inn with an attractive courtyard and garden, Stallmästaregården is in the Haga Park, some distance from the city center. But the fine French and Swedish cuisine is well worth the journey. In the summer meals are served in the courtyard overlooking Brunnsviken Lake. A lower, fixed-price menu is available. *Norrtull, near Haga, tel. 08/610–1301. Reservations advised. AE, DC, MC, V.*

Wedholms Fisk. Serving only fresh fish and shellfish, this open and high-ceilinged restaurant is located across a small bay from the Royal Dramatic Theater. The tartar of salmon and grilled sole are noteworthy. Portions are generous. The artwork featuring Scandinavian artists is part of the personal collection of the owner. *Nybrokajen 17, tel. 08/611–7874. Reservations advised. AE, DC, MC, V. Closed Sun. and July.*

Moderate
★ **Bakfickan.** The name means "hip pocket" and is appropriate because this restaurant is tucked around the back of the Opera House complex. It's a budget-price alternative to the nearby Operakällaren and is particularly popular at lunchtime, offering Swedish home cooking and a range of daily dishes. Counter and table service are available. *Operahuset, tel. 08/207745. No reservations. AE, DC, MC, V. Closed Sun.*

Eriks Backficka. An extremely popular dining spot among local residents, this unpretentious eatery serves a wide variety of Swedish dishes. The bustling 120-seat restaurant is located a block from the elegant waterside street Strandvägen, a flight down from street level. The same owner operates Eriks Gamla Stan, one of Stockholm's most exclusive restaurants. *Frederikshovsgatan 4, tel. 08/660–1599. Reservations advised. AE, DC, MC, V. Closed Christmas and weekends in July.*

Gondolen. Suspended under the gangway of the *Katarina* elevator at Slussen, Gondolen offers a magnificent view over the harbor, Lake Mälaren, and the Baltic Sea. The cuisine is international, and a range of fixed-price menus is available. *Slussen, tel. 08/640–2021. Reservations advised. AE, DC, MC, V. Closed Christmas and New Year's Day.*

Martini. This centrally located, popular Italian restaurant is a great people-watching hangout. People line up to get a seat during the summer, when the terrace is open. The main restaurant is below street level, but the decor is light and the atmosphere bustling. *Norrmalmstorg 4, tel. 08/679–8220. Reservations advised. AE, DC, MC, V.*

Sturehof. Centrally located, with an unpretentious, nautical ambience, Sturehof's specialty is its seafood. It also boasts an English-style pub. *Stureplan 2, tel. 08/679–8750. Reservations advised. AE, DC, MC, V. Closed Sat. lunch, Sun., Christmas, New Year's Day, and June 25.*

Inexpensive
Cassi. This centrally located restaurant specializes in French cuisine at reasonable prices. *Narvavägen 30, tel. 08/661–7461. Reservations not necessary. MC, V. Closed Sat.*

★ **Open Gate.** Located near the Slussen locks, on the south side of Stockholm Harbor, this is a popular, trendy Art Deco Italian-style trattoria. Pasta dishes are the house specialty. *Högbergsgatan 40, tel. 08/643–9776. No reservations. AE, DC, MC, V.*

Örtagården. This all-vegetarian, no-smoking restaurant is one floor up from the Östermalmshallen market hall. It offers an attractive buffet, with soups, salads, and hot dishes, served in a turn-of-the-century atmosphere. *Nybrogatan 31, tel. 08/662–1728. MC, V. Closed Christmas and New Year's Day.*

Lodging

Stockholm has plenty of hotels in most price brackets, although relatively few in the Inexpensive category. Many hotels cut their rates in the summer season, however, when business travelers are on vacation, so that during this time even a hotel classified as Very Expensive can become affordable. The major hotel chains also have a number of bargain schemes available on weekends throughout the year and daily during the summer.

Almost 50 hotels offer the "Stockholm Package," providing accommodations for one night, costing between SEK 305 and SEK 655 per person, including breakfast and a Stockholmskortet (Key to Stockholm) card (*see* Getting Around, *above*). Get details of the package from the **Stockholm Information Service,** Excursion Shop, Box 7542, S-103 93 Stockholm (tel. 08/789–2000 or 08/789–2490). Also, you can call **The Hotel Center** (tel. 08/240880) or reserve the package through travel agents.

If you arrive in Stockholm without a hotel reservation, the **Hotellcentralen** in the central train station will arrange accommodations for you. The office is open daily 8 AM–9 PM, June–September; weekdays 8:30–5 the rest of the year, except for December 20–January 2, when it is open 10–5. There is a reservations office in the Sweden House (*see* Important Addresses and Numbers, *above*) as well. There's a small fee for each reservation. Or phone one of the central reservations offices run by the major hotel groups: RESO (tel. 08/720–8100 or 08/720–8830), Scandic (tel. 08/610–5050), Sweden Hotels (tel. 08/204311), or Best Western (tel. 08/300420).

Prices quoted here are for two people in a double room. For details and price-category definitions, *see* Lodging in Staying in Sweden. Best bets are indicated by a star ★.

Very Expensive **Amaranten.** Only five minutes' walk from the central train station, Amaranten is a large, modern hotel, built in 1969 and refurbished in 1988. The "executive tower" offers a roof garden and 52 rooms. Guests enjoy a gourmet restaurant and brasserie, and piano bar. *Kungsholmsgatan 31, tel. 08/654–1060, fax 08/652–6248. 410 rooms with bath. Facilities: sauna, pool, restaurants, piano bar, solarium. AE, DC, MC, V.*

★ **Continental.** Located in the city center across from the central train station, the Continental is popular with American guests. It was first opened about 26 years ago and was renovated just a few years ago. It offers three restaurants in different price brackets. *Klara Vattugränd 4, tel. 08/244020, fax 08/113695. 250 rooms with bath. Facilities: 3 restaurants. AE, DC, MC, V.*

★ **Diplomat.** This is an elegant hotel located within easy walking distance of Djurgården Park and Skansen and offering magnificent views over Stockholm Harbor. The building itself is a turn-of-the-century town house that was converted into a hotel in 1966. The teahouse is a popular spot for light meals. *Strandvägen 7C, tel. 08/663–5800, fax 08/783–6634. 130 rooms with bath. Facilities: teahouse. AE, DC, MC, V. Closed Christmas and New Year's Day.*

Grand. Located on the waterfront in the center of town, the Grand is a large, gracious, Old World–style hotel dating back to 1874. It faces the Royal Palace. The two restaurants—French and Swedish—offer harbor views. The bar serves light snacks. *S. Blasieholmshamnen 8, tel. 08/221020, fax 08/611–8686. 319 rooms with bath, most with waterfront views. Facilities: sauna, 2 restaurants, beauty salon. AE, DC, MC, V.*

★ **Lady Hamilton.** Considered one of Stockholm's most desirable hotels, the Lady Hamilton, in the Old Town, was built as a private home in 1470 and has been a hotel only since 1980. It houses an extensive collection of antiques, including one of George Romney's portraits of Lady Hamilton. *Storkyrkobrinken 5, tel. 08/234680, fax 08/111148. 34 rooms with bath.*

Facilities: sauna, pool, cafeteria. AE, DC, MC, V. Closed Christmas.

Reisen. The building dates from 1819, although it was refurbished several years ago. It's situated in a waterfront sector of the Old Town and offers a fine restaurant, a grill, and what is reputed to be the best piano bar in town. The swimming pool is built under medieval arches. *Skeppsbron 12–14, tel. 08/223260, fax 08/201559. 113 rooms with bath. Facilities: restaurants, piano bar, sauna, pool, library. AE, DC, MC, V. Closed Christmas and New Year's Day.*

SAS Royal Viking. This is a large modern hotel adjoining the central train station and the airport bus terminal. Some rooms are on the small side. The restaurant was modernized in 1990, and another amenity is the Sky bar on the top floor. There is an SAS check-in counter in the lobby. *Vasagatan 1, tel. 08/141000, fax 08/108180. 319 rooms with bath. Facilities: restaurant, bar, sauna, pool, rooms for disabled guests. AE, DC, MC, V. Closed Christmas.*

SAS Strand. Acquired in 1986 by the SAS group, this is a gracious, Old World hotel. It was built in 1912 but was recently modernized. No two rooms are the same; many are furnished with antiques. An SAS check-in counter adjoins the main reception area. The Piazza is an indoor restaurant with an outdoor feel to it. Its specialty is Italian cuisine, and there is a superb wine list. *Nybrokajen 9, tel. 08/678–7800, fax 08/611–2436. 138 rooms with bath. Facilities: restaurant, sauna, function rooms. AE, DC, MC, V.*

Scandic Crown. A modern hotel with a panoramic view of the Old Town and City Hall, the Scandic Crown is on Stockholm's increasingly trendy south side. Noteworthy is the Couronne d'Or, a French eatery, and a wine cellar with wines dating to 1650. *Guldgränd 8, tel. 08/702–2500, fax 08/642–8358. 264 rooms with bath. Facilities: 2 restaurants, bar, indoor pool, solarium, sauna. AE, DC, MC, V. Closed Christmas.*

Expensive **Clas på Hörnet.** An 18th-century inn converted into a small ho-
★ tel in 1982, Clas på Hörnet is just outside the city center. Its rooms, furnished with antiques of the period, go quickly. If you can't manage to reserve one, at least have a meal in the gourmet restaurant (*see* Dining, *above*). *Surbrunnsgatan 20, tel. 08/165130, fax 08/612–5315. 10 rooms with bath. Facilities: restaurant. AE, DC, MC, V.*

Hotel Stockholm. You can't get much closer to the center of Stockholm than this modern hotel, which occupies the sixth and seventh floors of an office building on one of the city's main squares. Hotel Stockholm is a clean, efficient hotel intended for those who want to spend their waking hours shopping, sightseeing, or on business. Breakfast is included in the room rates. *Norrmalmstorg 1, tel. 08/678–1320, fax 08/611–2103. 92 rooms with shower or bath. Facilities: 30-seat conference room. AE, DC, MC, V. Closed Christmas–New Year's Day.*

Karelia. A turn-of-the-century building on one of the main shopping streets, Karelia has a Finnish atmosphere. There is a Finnish restaurant for dining and dancing plus a separate restaurant specializing in Russian cuisine, the only such one in Stockholm. *Birger Jarlsgatan 35, tel. 08/247660, fax 08/241511. 87 rooms with bath or shower. Facilities: 2 restaurants. AE, DC, MC, V. Closed Christmas.*

Lord Nelson. This companion hotel to the Lady Hamilton was built in much the same style. Its location on a busy pedestrian street in the Old Town makes it rather noisy at night. The atmosphere throughout is distinctly nautical—even down to the cabin-size rooms. The café is open until 8 PM daily. *Västerlånggatan 22, tel. 08/232390, fax 08/101089. 31 rooms with bath. Facilities: café. AE, DC, MC, V. Closed Christmas and New Year's Day.*

Moderate **Birger Jarl.** A short subway ride from the city center, Birger Jarl is a modern, characteristically Scandinavian hotel that opened in 1974. There is no full-service restaurant. *Tulegatan 8, tel. 08/151020, fax 08/693-7366. 252 rooms with bath. Facilities: sauna, pool, coffee shop. AE, DC, MC, V. Closed Christmas and New Year's Day.*

City. A large, modern-style hotel built in the 1940s but modernized in 1982–83, City is located near the city center and the Hötorget market. It is owned by the Salvation Army, so alcohol is not served. Breakfast is served in the atrium Winter Garden. *Slöjdgatan 7, tel. 08/222240, fax 08/208224. 300 rooms with bath. Facilities: restaurant, café, sauna, rooms for disabled guests. AE, DC, MC, V.*

Gamla Stan. A quiet, cozy hotel in the Old Town, the Gamla Stan was recently renovated, and each room is uniquely decorated. Breakfast is included. *Lilla Nygatan 25, tel. 08/244450, fax 08/216483. 51 rooms with shower. AE, DC, MC, V. Closed between Christmas and New Year's Day.*

Stockholm. This hotel has an unusual location—the upper floors of a downtown office building. The mainly modern decor is offset by traditional Swedish furnishings that help create a family atmosphere. Only breakfast is served. *Norrmalmstorg 1, tel. 08/678-1320, fax 08/611-2103. 92 rooms with bath. AE, DC, MC, V. Closed Christmas and New Year's Day.*

Inexpensive **Alexandra.** Although it is in the Södermalm area, to the south of the Old Town, the Alexandra is only five minutes by subway from the city center. It is a small, modern hotel, opened 20 years ago and renovated in 1988. Only breakfast is served. *Magnus Ladulåsgatan 42, tel. 08/840320, fax 08/720-5353. 79 rooms with bath. Facilities: sauna, solarium. AE, DC, MC, V. Closed Christmas and New Year's Day.*

Gustav af Klint. A "hotel ship" moored at Stadsgården quay, near Slussen subway station, the Gustav af Klint is divided into two sections—a hotel and a hostel. There is a cafeteria and restaurant, and you can dine on deck in summer. *Stadsgårdskajen 153, tel. 08/640-4077, fax 08/640-6416. 14 cabins with showers. 80 hostel beds. Facilities: restaurant, cafeteria. AE, MC, V. Closed Christmas and New Year's Day.*

Långholmen. This former prison, built in 1724, was converted into a combined hotel and hostel in 1989. It is located on the island of Långholmen, which has popular bathing beaches. The Inn, next door, serves Swedish home cooking, and the wine cellar offers light snacks. *Långholmen, tel. 08/668-0500, fax 08/841096. 101 rooms with shower. Facilities: mini-golf course and boule court. AE, DC, MC, V.*

The Arts

Stockholm's main theater and concert season runs from September through May or June, so there are not many major performances during the height of the tourist season. But for a list of events, pick up the free booklet "Stockholm This Week," available from hotels and tourist information offices. You can get last-minute tickets to theaters and shows at the cut-price ticket booth on Norrmalmstorg Square. Tickets sold here are priced 25% below box office rates. The booth is open Monday to Friday 11–6 and Saturday 11–4. There is also a **central reservation office** for regular-price tickets (tel. 08/108800).

Concerts The city's main concert hall is the **Concert House** (Konserthuset) at Hötorget 8, home of the Stockholm Philharmonic Orchestra. The main season runs from mid-September to mid-May. In addition to full-scale evening concerts, there are "coffee break" or lunchtime concerts some days (tel. 08/221800). During the summer, free concerts are given in many city parks. For information, phone 08/785–8182.

Opera The season at the **Royal Opera House,** just across the bridge from the Royal Palace, runs from mid-August to early June and offers performances at top-class international standards (tel. 08/248240). And from early June to early September, there are performances of opera, ballet, and orchestral music at the exquisite **Drottningholm Court Theater,** which was the setting for Ingmar Bergman's film *The Magic Flute.* The original 18th-century stage machinery is still used in these productions. You can get to Drottningholm by subway and bus or by special theater-bus (leaving from the Grand hotel or Vasagatan, opposite the central train station). For tickets, call 08/660–8225.

Theater Stockholm has about 20 top-rank theaters, but dramatic productions are unlikely to interest those who don't understand Swedish. A better option is to go to a musical; several city theaters hold regular performances. Plays in English are featured at the **Regina Theater** (Drottninggatan 71A, tel. 08/207000).

Film English and American films predominate, and they are screened with the original soundtrack and Swedish subtitles. Programs are listed in the local evening newspapers, though titles are usually in Swedish. Movie buffs should visit **Filmstaden** (Film City), Mäster Samuelsgatan 25 (tel. 08/840500), where 15 cinemas under one roof show a variety of films from noon until midnight.

Nightlife

Cabaret Stockholm's biggest nightclub, **Börsen** (Jakobsgatan 6, tel. 08/787–8500), offers high-quality Swedish and international cabaret shows. Another popular spot is the **Cabaret Club** (Barnhusgatan 12, tel. 08/110608). Although it can accommodate 450 guests, reservations are advised.

Bars and Nightclubs **Café Opera** (tel. 08/110026) is a popular meeting place for young and old alike. It has the longest bar in town, plus dining and roulette, and dancing after midnight. Piano bars are also an important part of the Stockholm scene. **Riche** (tel. 08/611–8450) is another popular watering hole in the city center. Try the **Anglais Bar** at the Hotel Anglais (tel. 08/614–1600) or the **Clipper Club** at the Hotel Reisen, Skeppsbron (tel. 08/223260). Not to be forgotten is the recently renovated restaurant/bar **Berns Salon** (Berzelii Park 9, tel. 08/614–0500). Worth a visit is the Red Room, a private dining room on the second floor, where playwright August Strindberg once held court.

Irish pubs have recently become very popular among the happy-hour crowds, with **Limerick** (Tegnergatan 10, tel. 08/673–4398), **Dubliner** (Birger Jarlspassagen, tel. 08/697–7707), and

Bagpiper's Inn (Rörstrandsgatan 21, tel. 08/311855) currently leading the pack.

Jazz Clubs **Fasching** (Kungsgatan 63, tel. 08/216267) is Stockholm's largest, but another popular spot is **Stampen** (Stora Nygatan 5, tel. 08/205793). Get here in good time if you want a seat, and phone first to be sure the establishment hasn't been reserved for a private party.

Discos **Galaxy** (Strömsborg, tel. 08/215400) is one of the most popular night spots, catering to a variety of musical tastes. There is an outdoor bar and dining area in summer. Others are **Downtown** (Norrlandsgatan 5A, tel. 08/119488) and **Karlsson** (Kungsgatan 65, tel. 08/119298).

Uppsala and the Folklore District

The area of Sweden referred to as the "Folklore District"—essentially the provinces of Dalarna and Värmland—has the merit of being both easily accessible from Stockholm and the best region in which to see something of the country's enduring folk traditions. This itinerary takes you to Dalarna through the ancient city of Uppsala and returns to Stockholm through the Bergslagen region, the heart of the centuries-old Swedish iron industry.

Getting Around

The route can be covered entirely by train. The ride from Stockholm to Uppsala takes only 45 minutes, and the service is fairly frequent. A car, however, will give you the flexibility to explore some of the attractions that are not easily accessible by public transportation.

Guided Tours

While Uppsala is compact enough to explore on foot, guided sightseeing tours are available. As scheduled tours are no longer offered, you can book a guided tour in advance by calling the Guide Service, tel. 018/274818.

Tourist Information

Falun (Stora Torget, tel. 023/83637).
Ludvika (Sporthallen, tel. 0240/86050).
Mora (Ångbåtskajen, tel. 0250/26550).
Örebro (Drottninggatan 9, tel. 019/211080).
Rättvik (Torget, tel. 0248/10910).
Uppsala (Fyris Torg, tel. 018/117500 and 018/274800 and at Uppsala Castle in summer).

Exploring Uppsala and the Folklore District

Uppsala is really the cradle of Swedish civilization, so it is well worth spending a day or two exploring it. If you opt for a guided tour, you should first stop by **Gamla Uppsala** (Old Uppsala), which is dominated by three huge burial mounds. During the 5th century AD, Aun, Egil, and Adils, the first Swedish kings,

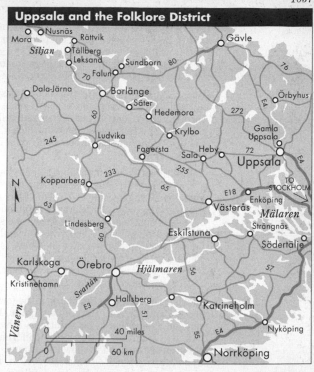

Uppsala and the Folklore District

were buried here. Adjoining the burial mounds are a church, the seat of Sweden's first archbishop, built on the site of a former pagan temple, and the Odinsborg restaurant, where you can sample local mead, brewed from a 14th-century recipe. Check all prices and times listed below with the local tourist office, as they are subject to change unless otherwise stated.

Back in **Uppsala** itself, your first stop should be the enormous **cathedral**, with its twin towers dominating the city skyline. The cathedral has been the seat of the archbishop of the Swedish church for 700 years, although its present appearance owes much to major restoration work completed during the late 19th century. Make a point of visiting the **Cathedral Museum** in the north tower, which boasts one of Europe's finest collections of ecclesiastical textiles. *Admission free. Open June–Aug., daily 8–8; Sept.–May, daily 8–6.*

Nearby, in a strategic position atop a hill, is **Uppsala Castle.** This prepossessing structure was built during the 1540s by King Gustav Vasa. Having broken his ties with the Vatican, the king was eager to show who was actually running the country. He arranged to have the cannons aimed directly at the archbishop's palace. *Open mid-Apr.–Sept.*

Uppsala is the site of Scandinavia's oldest university, founded in 1477. Be sure to visit one of its most venerable buildings, the **Gustavianum,** located near the cathedral. Just below the cupola is the anatomical theater, where public dissections of executed convicts were a popular 17th-century tourist attraction.

One of Uppsala's most famous sons was Carl von Linné, known as Linnaeus. A professor of botany at the university during the 1740s, he developed a system of plant and animal classification that is still used today. You can visit the **gardens** he designed, as well as his former residence, now a **museum**. *Admission to garden: free. Admission to museum: SEK 10.*

From Uppsala, the route heads northwest through a pleasant agricultural landscape into the province of Dalarna, passing through **Säter,** one of the best-preserved wooden villages in Sweden. This is a pleasant spot in which to just wander around. For an overnight stop it is best to head for Falun, Dalarna's provincial capital.

Falun is best known for a huge hole in the ground, referred to as the **"Great Pit."** The hole has been there since 1687, when an abandoned copper mine collapsed. Other mines on the site are still working today. You can take a guided tour down into some of the old shafts and hear the gruesome story of 17th-century miner Fat Mats, whose body was perfectly preserved in brine for 40 years following a cave-in. There is also a museum that tells the story of the local mining industry. *Admission: SEK 50. Open May 1–Aug. 31, daily 10–4:30; Sept. 1–Nov. 15 and Mar. 1–Apr. 30, weekends only 12:30–4:30.*

Just outside Falun, at **Sundborn,** is the former home of Swedish artist Carl Larsson. Here, in an idyllic, lakeside setting, you can see a selection of his paintings, which owe much to local folk-art traditions. His grandchildren and great-grandchildren are on hand to show you around. *Admission: SEK 50. Open May–Sept., Mon.–Sat. 10–5, Sun. 1–5.*

The real center of Dalarna folklore is the area around **Lake Siljan,** by far the largest of the 6,000 lakes in the province. Begin your tour at the attractive lakeside village of **Tällberg,** or at **Mora,** toward the north end of the lake. In the neighboring village of **Rättvik,** hundreds of people wearing traditional costumes arrive in longboats to attend Midsummer church services. Mora itself is best known as the home of the artist Anders Zorn. His house and a museum featuring his paintings are open to the public. *Admission to museum: SEK 20. Admission to home: SEK 25. Check with Mora tourist information for opening hours.*

Near Mora is the village of **Nusnäs.** This is the village where the famous, brightly colored **Dalarna wooden horses** are produced. You can visit either of the two workshops where they are made.

Heading south again you'll come to **Ludvika,** an important center of the old Bergslagen mining region. This region stretches from the forests of Värmland in the west to the coastal forges in the east. Ludvika has a notable open-air mining museum, **Gammelgården.** *Check times and prices with the Ludvika Tourist Office.* There is also a **Railway Engine Museum** that features three steam turbine–driven iron-ore engines, the only ones of their kind in the world. *Admission: SEK 20. Open June 1–Aug. 31, daily 10–6.*

Another local attraction is **Luosa Cottage.** The poet Dan Andersson lived here in the early part of the century so he could experience for himself the rigorous life of the local charcoal burners. An annual music and poetry festival is held at the cottage and in nearby towns in Andersson's memory, late July–

early August. *Admission to cottage: SEK 20. Open Tues.–Sun. 11–5.*

Continuing south from Ludvika, you'll come to **Örebro,** a sizable town at the western edge of **Lake Hjälmaren,** which is connected to Lake Mälaren and the sea by the Hjälmare Canal. Örebro received its charter in the 13th century and developed as a trading center for the farmers and miners of the Bergslagen region. Rising from a small island in the Svartån River, right in the center of town, is an imposing **castle,** parts of which date to the 13th century. The castle is now the residence of the regional governor. Guided tours run from mid-June to the end of August. Check with the Örebro tourist office for further information. An added attraction is the excellent restaurant in the castle.

To get a feel for the Örebro of bygone days, wander around the **Wadköping** district, where a number of old houses and craftsmen's workshops have been painstakingly preserved. At the north end of town is **Svampen** (The Mushroom), a water tower rising 59 meters (193 feet) into the air. If you take the elevator to the top, you'll get a magnificent view of the surrounding countryside. There is also a cafeteria and tourist office. *The tower is open Apr. 15–Sept. 15, daily 9–9.*

Direct train service from Örebro back to Stockholm operates at two-hour intervals, and the journey takes just under three hours. You can also take the hourly train to Hallsberg and change there to the frequent Gothenburg–Stockholm service.

Dining and Lodging

For details and price-category definitions, *see* Dining and Lodging in Staying in Sweden. Best bets are indicated by a star ★.

Falun
Lodging

Bergmästaren. In the town center, Bergmästaren is a small, cozy hotel built in traditional Dalarna style and filled with antique furnishings. *Bergskolegränd 7, tel. 023/63600, fax 023/22524. 89 rooms, most with bath. Facilities: sauna, solarium, restaurant. AE, DC, MC, V. Closed Christmas. Expensive.*

Hotel Falun. Located in the center of the city, Hotel Falun is a medium-size hotel built in the 1950s. Breakfast is included. *Centrumhuset, Trotzgatan 16, tel. 023/29180, fax 023/13006. 25 rooms, most with showers. AE, DC, MC, V. Moderate.*

Ludvika
Lodging

Grand. A medium-size, modern-style hotel, the Grand is located in the town center. *Eriksgatan 6, tel. 0240/18220, fax 0240/11018. 102 rooms with bath. Facilities: sauna, disco, 2 restaurants. AE, DC, MC, V. Expensive.*

Rex. The Rex is a fairly basic but modern hotel conveniently located near the city center. It was built in 1960. Its restaurant serves breakfast only. *Engelbrektsgatan 9, tel. 0240/13690. 28 rooms, 15 with shower. AE, DC, MC, V. Closed Christmas and 1 week in summer. Inexpensive.*

Mora
Lodging
★

Siljan. Taking its name from the nearby lake, the largest in Dalarna, the Siljan is a popular, small, but modern-style hotel. *Moragatan 6, tel. 0250/13000, fax 0250/13098. 46 rooms, most with bath. Facilities: sauna, disco, restaurant. AE, DC, MC, V. Moderate.*

Örebro
Dining and Lodging

RESO Grand. Located in the heart of town, the Grand is the city's largest hotel. It was built in 1985 and offers all the modern comforts. *Fabriksgatan 23, tel. 019/150200, fax 019/185814. 221 rooms with bath. Facilities: sauna, Jacuzzi, à la carte restaurant, VIP rooms. AE, DC, MC, V. Expensive.*

City. Also built in 1985, City is a modern, centrally located hotel. It offers special facilities for disabled guests and those suffering from allergies. The restaurant serves "home cooking" at lunchtime and more elaborate, à la carte fare in the evening. *Kungsgatan 24, tel. 019/100200, fax 019/137446. 113 rooms with bath or shower. Facilities: restaurant. AE, DC, MC, V. Moderate.*

Tällberg
Lodging
★

Åkerblads. Located near the shores of Lake Siljan, Åkerblads is a real rural Swedish experience. The hotel occupies a typical Dalarna farmstead, parts of which date to the 16th century. It is run by the 14th and 15th generations of the Åkerblad family. A hotel since 1910, it was modernized in 1987. The restaurant serves table d'hôte meals only. *793 03 Tällberg, tel. 0247/50800, fax 0247/50652. 64 rooms, some with bath. Facilities: sauna, Jacuzzi, restaurant, pub-style bar. AE, DC, MC, V. Moderate.*

Uppsala
Dining
★

Domtrappkällaren. One of the city's most popular restaurants, Domtrappkällaren is located in a 14th-century cellar near the cathedral. The cuisine is a mixture of French and Swedish. *St. Eriksgränd 5, tel. 018/130955, fax 018/153380. Reservations required. Facilities: restaurant. AE, DC, MC, V. Expensive.*

Lodging

Sara Gillet. A centrally located, medium-size hotel, the Sara Gillet was opened 18 years ago and has been recently modernized. *Dragarbrunnsgatan 23, tel. 018/155360. 169 rooms with bath. AE, DC, MC, V. Closed Christmas. Expensive.*

Grand Hotel Hörnan. An Old World, medium-size hotel, the Grand Hotel Hörnan is in the city center near the train station. Opened in 1906, it has been refurbished during the past several years. *Bangårdsgatan 1, tel. 018/139380, fax 018/120311. 37 rooms with shower. AE, MC, V. Closed July. Moderate.*

The West Coast and the Glass Country

For many visitors traveling to Sweden by ferry, Gothenburg (or Göteborg) is the port of arrival. But those who arrive in Stockholm should not miss making a side trip to this great shipping city and Sweden's scenic western coast. This itinerary combines a western trip with a route through the Glass Country to the medieval fortress town of Kalmar, on the east coast.

Getting Around

As with the previous itinerary, the route can be followed by both train and car. Regular trains for Gothenburg depart from Stockholm's central train station about every hour, and normal travel time is about four hours. There are also four daily high-speed trains (the X2000), which take less than three hours between the two cities, but these require a supplementary fare of SEK 265 in first class (this includes breakfast on morning trains and sandwich snacks the rest of the day) or SEK 137 in second class. Seat reservations are compulsory on most trains to Goth-

The West Coast and the Glass Country

Uddevalla — Falköping — Norrköping
Trollhättan — Lake Vättern — Linköping
Gothenburg
Borås — Jönköping — Huskvarna
Nässjö — Västervik
Riddersberg
Varberg — Värnamo — Oskarshamn
Falkenberg — Alvesta
Halmstad — Växjö — Nybro — Kalmar
Laholm — Öland
Helsingborg — Karlshamn — Karlskrona
Hässelholm — Ronneby
DEN. — Landskrona — Kristianstad
Malmö — Baltic Sea — N
Trelleborg — Ystad
0 — 40 miles
0 — 60 km
Kattegat

enburg. There are also hourly flights to Gothenburg from Stockholm's Arlanda Airport between 7 AM and 10 PM on weekdays, slightly less frequently on weekends. The trip by air takes 55 minutes.

For getting around the city of Gothenburg itself, the best transportation option for the visitor is the **Göteborgskortet** (Key to Gothenburg) card, similar to the Key to Stockholm card. This entitles the user to free travel on all public transportation, free parking, and free admission to the Liseberg amusement park and all city museums. Prices for the card are SEK 120 for one day, SEK 200 for two days, and SEK 250 for three days. Cards for children under 18 are SEK 60 for one day, SEK 100 for two days, and SEK 140 for three days.

Guided Tours

In the summer, sightseeing tours of Gothenburg leave regularly from Kungsportsplatsen, just beside the city tourist office. They must be reserved at the office in advance.

Tourist Information

Gothenburg (Kungsportsplatsen 2, tel. 031/100740).
Jönköping (Djurläkartorget, tel. 036/105050).
Kalmar (Larmgatan 6, tel. 0480/15350).
Växjö (Kronobergsgatan 8, tel. 0470/41410).

Exploring the West Coast and the Glass Country

Visitors arriving in **Gothenburg** by car often drive straight through the city in their haste to reach their coastal vacation spots, but it is well worth spending a day or two exploring this attractive harbor city. A quayside jungle of cranes and warehouses attests to the city's industrial might, yet within 10 minutes' walk of the waterfront is an elegant, modern city of broad avenues, green parks, and gardens. It is an easy city to explore. Most of the major attractions are within walking distance of each other, and there is an excellent streetcar network. In the summer, you can even take a sightseeing trip on a vintage open-air streetcar.

Gothenburg's development was pioneered mainly by British merchants in the 19th century, when it acquired the nickname "Little London." But a more accurate name would have been "Little Amsterdam," for the city was designed during the 17th century by Dutch architects, who gave it its extensive network of straight streets divided by canals. There is only one major canal today, but you can explore it on one of the popular "Paddan" sightseeing boats. The boats got their nickname, Swedish for toad, because of their short, squat shape, necessary for negotiating the city's 20 low bridges. You embark at the **Paddan terminal** at Kungsportsplatsen. *Fare: SEK 55. Departures: early May–mid-Sept., daily 10–5; late June–early Aug., daily 10–9. Check with Gothenburg tourist information for specific dates.*

The hub of Gothenburg is **Kungsportsavenyn,** better known as "The Avenue." It is a broad, tree-lined boulevard flanked with elegant shops, restaurants, and sidewalk cafés. In summer it has a distinctively Parisian air. The avenue ends at **Götaplatsen Square,** home of the municipal theater, concert hall, and library (where there's an excellent selection of English-language newspapers). Just off the avenue is **Trädgårdsföreningen,** a newly constructed Butterfly House featuring 40 different species and an attractive park with a magnificent Palm House that was built in 1878 and recently restored. *Admission to park: SEK 10. Admission to Palm House: SEK 10. Open May–Aug., daily 7 AM–9 PM; Sept.–Apr., daily 7–6. Admission to Butterfly House: SEK 20. Open June–Aug., Tues.–Sat. 10–5, Sun. 11–5; hours vary during rest of year; check with Butterfly House (tel. 031/611911) or tourist information.*

If you're interested in shopping, the best place to go is **Nordstan,** a covered complex of shops near the central train station. Many of its businesses participate in the tax-free shopping service. In the harbor near the Nordstan shopping complex, you will find the new **Maritime Center.** The center houses a historic collection of ships, including a destroyer, a lightship, a trawler, and tugboats. *Admission: SEK 35. Open May–Aug., daily 11–5; late Feb.–late Nov., weekends 11–5.*

To reach **Jönköping,** the next stop on the journey, take the train from Gothenburg's central train station and change at Falköping. Jönköping is an attractive town on the southern shores of **Lake Vättern,** Sweden's second-largest lake.

Jönköping, which celebrated its 700th anniversary in 1984, is known as the "matchstick town." For it was here, during the 19th century, that the match-manufacturing industry got its start. The **Matchstick Museum,** built on the site of the first factory, has an exhibition on the development and manufacture of matches. *Open throughout the year. Check opening times with the Jönköping Tourist Office.*

A few miles from Jönköping is **Riddersberg,** former home of the famous wood sculptor Calle Örnemark, which can be reached by local bus from the Jönköping train station. The house has now been transformed into an arts center featuring exhibitions by various Swedish artists as well as some remarkable sculptures by Örnemark. Check opening times and prices with the Jönköping Tourist Office.

To the southeast of Jönköping lies **Växjö,** Kronoberg County's main town and the best center for exploring Sweden's Glass Country. It is also an important sightseeing destination for some 10,000 American visitors each year, for it was from this area that their Swedish ancestors set sail during the 19th century. The **Emigrants' House,** located in the town center, tells the story of the migration, during which close to 1 million Swedes—one-quarter of the entire population—departed for the promised land. The museum exhibits provide a vivid sense of the rigorous journey, and an archive room and research center allow American visitors to trace their ancestry. On the second Sunday in August, Växjö celebrates "Minnesota Day." Swedes and Swedish-Americans come together to commemorate their common heritage with American-style square dancing and other festivities.

Many of Sweden's most famous glassworks are within easy reach of Växjö, and it is usually possible to take an organized sightseeing tour of the facilities. Inquire at the tourist office for information. The manufacture of Swedish glass dates to 1556, when Venetian glassblowers were first invited to the Swedish court. But it was another 200 years before glass manufacturing became a real Swedish industry. The area between Växjö and Kalmar was chosen for its dense forest, which offered limitless wood supplies for heating the furnaces. All the major Swedish glass companies, including **Orrefors** and **Kosta Boda,** still have their works in this area, and all of them are open to the public. They also have shops where you can pick up near-perfect seconds at bargain prices. *Open weekdays 9–6, Sat. 9–3, Sun. noon–4 (no glass manufacturing on Sat. and Sun. in winter).*

An attractive coastal town, **Kalmar** is dominated by its imposing seaside castle. The town was once known as the "lock and key" of Sweden, for it is situated on the southern frontier of the kingdom, and thus open to constant enemy invasion. The castle's history goes back 800 years, although the present building dates only from the 16th century, when it was rebuilt by King Gustav Vasa. *Admission: SEK 20. Open daily. Tel. 0480/56500 for hours. Closed major holidays.*

To return to Stockholm from Kalmar, catch the train to Alvesta (the service runs every two hours) and change there for the Stockholm service. Two trains—one day service and one night service—run direct to Stockholm each day. The journey takes about 6½ hours. **Linjeflyg** operates several flights a day to Stockholm from the Kalmar airport, located 5 kilometers (3 miles) from the town center. The trip takes about 45 minutes. For information, phone 0480/58800 or 0480/58811.

Dining and Lodging

For details and price-category definitions, *see* Dining and Lodging in Staying in Sweden. Best bets are indicated by a star ★.

Gothenburg **Räkan.** An informal and popular restaurant, Räkan makes the
Dining most of an unusual gimmick. The tables are arranged around a
★ long tank, and if you order shrimp, the house specialty, they arrive at your table in radio-controlled boats you navigate yourself. *Lorensbergsgatan 16, tel. 031/169839. Reservations required. AE, DC, MC, V. Closed lunchtime on weekends, Christmas, New Year's Day. Expensive (with moderate fixed-price menus also available).*

★ **Sjömagasinet.** Situated in a 200-year-old renovated shipping warehouse, this waterfront restaurant, with its view of the harbor and the suspended bridge, specializes in fish. During the summer, an outdoor terrace is open. *Klippanskulturreservat, tel. 031/246510. Reservations required. AE, DC, MC, V. Expensive (with moderate fixed-price menu also available in the winter).*

Weise. A centrally located restaurant with a German-beercellar atmosphere, Weise was once a haunt of local painters and intellectuals and still retains something of that ambience. The tables and chairs date from 1892. It specializes in traditional Swedish home cooking, serving such dishes as pork and brown beans. *Drottninggatan 23, tel. 031/131402. Reservations advised. AE, DC, MC, V. Moderate.*

Åtta Glas. A casual, lively restaurant in what was formerly a barge, Åtta Glas offers excellent views of the river and of Kungsportsbron, a bridge spanning the center of town. The second floor boasts a bar especially popular with the younger crowd on weekends. The two standard specials—ox fillet or grilled salmon—are the best deals at SEK 59, and a children's menu, which includes ice cream, is popular with families. *Kungsportsbrön, tel. 031/136015. Reservations advised. AE, DC, MC, V. Inexpensive.*

Lodging **Sheraton Hotel and Towers.** Opened in 1986, the Sheraton Hotel
★ and Towers is Gothenburg's most modern and spectacular international-style hotel. It features an atrium lobby and several restaurants with varying prices. *Södra Hamngatan 59–65, tel. 031/806000, fax 031/159888. 343 rooms with bath. Facilities: restaurants, health club, nightclub, 16 rooms especially equipped for disabled guests. AE, DC, MC, V. Closed Christmas. Very Expensive.*

★ **Eggers.** Dating to 1859, Eggers probably has more Old World character than any other hotel in the city. It is located near the train station and was most likely the last port of call in Sweden for many emigrants to the United States. The rooms feature antique furnishings. *Drottningtorget, tel. 031/806070, fax 031/154243. 77 rooms with bath. AE, DC, MC, V. Closed Christmas. Expensive.*

Liseberg Heden. Not far from the famous Liseberg amusement park, Liseberg Heden is a popular, modern family hotel. It offers a sauna and gourmet restaurant. *Sten Sturegatan, tel. 031/200280, fax 031/165283. 160 rooms with bath. Facilities: restaurant, sauna. AE, DC, MC, V. Closed Christmas and New Year's Day. Moderate.*

Hotel Klang. This popular, family-run hotel is 10 minutes' walk from the central train station. The rooms are simple and clean.

Only breakfast is served. *Stora Badhusetgatan 28, tel. 031/ 174050, fax 031/174058. 50 rooms with shower or bath. AE, DC, MC, V. Closed Christmas and New Year's Day. Inexpensive.*

Jönköping **Mäster Gudmunds Källare.** Nestled in cozy, 16th-century cellar
Dining vaults and only two minutes from the train station is this par-
★ ticularly inviting restaurant. The cuisine is international. *Kapellgatan 2, tel. 036/112633. Reservations advised. AE, DC, MC, V. Closed Christmas, New Year's Day, Midsummer. Moderate.*

Lodging **Stora Hotellet.** Stora Hotellet is an old-fashioned establishment opened in 1861 but recently modernized. Its restaurant serves international cuisine. *Hotellplan, tel. 036/119300, fax 036/ 119320. 110 rooms with shower. Facilities: restaurant, bar, sauna, tennis courts. AE, DC, MC, V. Expensive.*
John Bauer Hotel (Best Western). Located in the center of town, this modern, family-run hotel overlooks Lake Munksjön and was named after a local artist famous for his fairy-tale illustrations of trolls, forests, and mystical landscapes. *Södra Strandgatan 15, tel. 036/100500, fax 038/112788. 100 rooms with shower or bath. Facilities: bar, terrace, steam room, sauna, solarium, games room. AE, DC, MC, V. Closed Christmas and New Year's Day. Moderate.*

Kalmar **Slottshotellet.** Situated in a gracious old town house on a quiet
Lodging street, Slottshotellet bears no resemblance to a hotel from the outside. Inside, however, you'll find a host of modern facilities. Only breakfast is served. *Slottsvägen 7, tel. 0480/88260, fax 0480/11993. 36 rooms with shower. Facilities: sauna, solarium. AE, DC, MC, V. Expensive.*
Stadshotellet. Located in the city center, Stadshotellet is a large, Old World hotel. The main building dates from the 19th century. *Storgatan 14, tel. 0480/15180, fax 0480/15840. 138 rooms with bath or shower. Facilities: restaurant, Jacuzzi, disco. AE, DC, MC, V. Closed Christmas. Expensive.*
Continental. The Continental is a fairly basic but comfortable family hotel. Only breakfast is served. *Larmgatan 10, tel. 0480/ 15140, fax 0480/13755. 39 rooms, most with bath or shower. AE, DC, MC, V. Inexpensive.*

Växjö **Sara Statt.** A conveniently located, traditional hotel, Sara Statt
Lodging is popular with tour groups. The building dates from the early 19th century, but the rooms themselves are modern, and the hotel has a resident piano bar and à la carte restaurant. *Kungsgatan 6, tel. 0470/13400, fax 0470/44837. 130 rooms with bath or shower. Facilities: restaurant, piano bar. AE, DC, MC, V. Closed Christmas Eve. Expensive.*
Esplanad. Centrally located, Esplanad is a small, family hotel offering basic amenities; it has been recently renovated. Only breakfast is served. *Norra Esplanaden 21A, tel. 0470/22580, fax 0470/26226. 27 rooms, most with shower. MC, V. Closed Christmas and New Year's Day. Inexpensive.*

28 Switzerland

In Switzerland they keep their coziness under strict control: An electric eye beams open a sliding glass door into a room lined with carved wood, copper, and old-fashioned rafters. That is the paradox of the Swiss, whose two primary aesthetics pitch high-tech urban efficiency against rustic Alpine comfort. Fiercely devout, rigorously clean, prompt as their world-renowned watches, the Swiss are a people who drink their eau de vie in firelit *stübli* (cozy little pubs)—but rarely on Sunday. Liquors here are measured with scientific precision into glasses marked for one or two centiliters, and the local wines come in sized carafes that are reminiscent of laboratory beakers. And as for passion—well, the "double" beds have separate mattresses and sheets that tuck firmly down the middle. (Foreigners with more lusty Latin tastes may request a French—that is, a standard double—bed.) Switzerland is a country of contrasts: While cowbells tinkle on the slopes of Klewenalp, the hum of commerce in Zürich isn't far away. As befurred and bejeweled socialites shop in Geneva, across the country in Appenzell women stand beside their husbands on the Landsgemeinde-Platz to raise their hands in the local vote—a right they didn't win until 1990.

But the trains run on time. In fact, all Swiss public transportation is chillingly precise: Step up to a tram stop, check the posted arrival time, and watch your second hand sweep toward the 12 as the streetcar pulls into view. Sleek, swift national trains may be the best in the world, while the roads and autoroutes are direct, scenic, and pothole-free.

Switzerland comprises most of the attractions of its larger European neighbors—Alpine grandeur, urban sophistication, ancient villages, scintillating ski slopes, and all-around artistic excellence. It's the heart of the Reformation, the homeland of William Tell; its cities are full of historic landmarks, its countryside strewn with castles. The varied cuisine reflects an ethnic mix, with three distinct cultures dominating: French in the southwest, Italian in the southeast, and German—a 70% majority—in the north and east.

All these assets have combined to create a major center of tourism, and the Swiss are happy to pave the way. A welcoming if reserved people, many of them well versed in English, they have earned their age-old reputation as fine hosts. Their hotels and inns are famous for cleanliness and efficiency, and the notorious high prices are justified, for the most part, by standards unrivaled in the world.

Essential Information

Before You Go

When to Go Switzerland functions as a year-round tourist attraction. Winter sports begin around Christmas and usually last until mid-April, depending on the state of the snow. The countryside is a delight in spring when the wild flowers are in bloom, and the fall colors rival those in New England. In the Ticino (the Italian-speaking area) and around Lake Geneva (Lac Léman), summer stays late: There is often sparkling weather in September and October, and the popular resorts are less crowded then. After that, though, beware: Throughout Switzerland, resorts

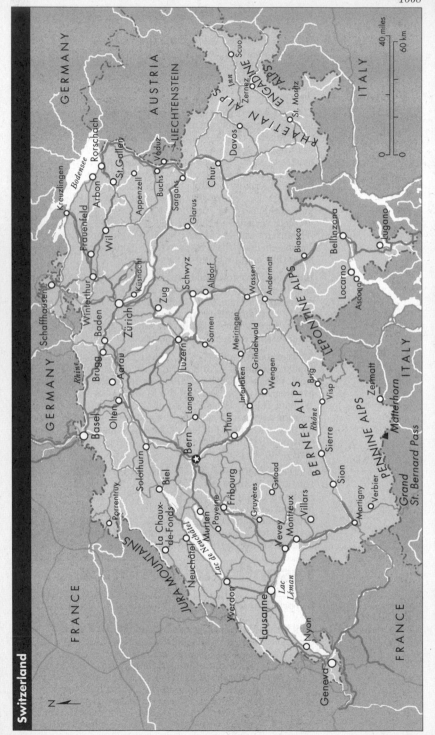

Switzerland

1068

may close up altogether in November and May. Always check with the local tourist office.

Climate Summer in Switzerland is generally warm and sunny, though the higher you go, of course, the cooler it gets, especially at night. Winter is cold everywhere: In low-lying areas the weather is frequently damp and overcast, while in the Alps there are often brilliantly clear days, but it is guaranteed to be cold and snowy—especially above 1,400 meters (4,600 feet).

Summer or winter, some areas of Switzerland are prone to an Alpine wind that blows from the south and is known as the *Föhn*. This gives rise to clear but rather oppressive weather, which the Swiss claim causes headaches. The only exception to the general weather patterns is the Ticino. Here, protected by the Alps, the weather is positively Mediterranean; even in winter, it is significantly warmer than elsewhere.

The following are the average daily maximum and minimum temperatures for Zürich.

Jan.	36F	2C	May	67F	19C	Sept.	69F	20C
	26	− 3		47	8		51	11
Feb.	41F	5C	June	73F	23C	Oct.	57F	14C
	28	− 2		53	12		43	6
Mar.	51F	11C	July	76F	25C	Nov.	45F	7C
	34	1		56	14		35	2
Apr.	59F	15C	Aug.	75F	24C	Dec.	37F	3C
	40	− 4		56	14		29	− 2

Currency The unit of currency is the Swiss franc (Fr.), divided into 100 rappen (known as centimes in French-speaking areas). There are coins of 5, 10, 20, and 50 rappen and of 1, 2, and 5 francs. The bills are of 10, 20, 50, 100, 500, and 1,000 francs.

At press time (spring 1993), the Swiss franc stood at 1.53 to the dollar and 2.18 to the pound sterling.

All banks will change your money, though many impose a minimum and a slight fee. Traveler's checks get a better exchange rate, as do cash advances on major credit cards. Main airports and train stations have exchange offices (bureaux de change) that are open longer hours than banks and often offer equally good rates of exchange. Most hotels and some restaurants will change money but usually at a far less favorable rate. Most major credit cards are generally, though not universally, accepted at hotels, restaurants, and shops.

What It Will Cost High standards of living mean that Switzerland is generally expensive: If it's luxury you're after, you'll pay more for it here than in almost any other European country. You'll find plenty of reasonably priced hotels and restaurants, however, if you look for them. Those who have visited Switzerland before will be surprised at how little prices have changed recently: Inflation has been less than 2% for years.

As in any other European country, the cities are more expensive than are the smaller towns. Zürich and Geneva are the priciest; Basel, Bern, and Lugano are also quite expensive. Holiday resorts—especially the better-known Alpine ski centers—rival cities for high prices. Elsewhere, prices drop appreciably, particularly off the beaten track and in the northeast.

Sample Prices Cup of coffee, 2.50 Fr.; bottle of beer, 2.50–3 Fr.; Coca-Cola, 2.50 Fr.; ham sandwich, 7 Fr.; a 1-mile taxi ride, 10 Fr. (except in Geneva, Lugano, or Zürich).

Customs on Arrival There are two levels of duty-free allowance for visitors to Switzerland. Residents of non-European countries may import 400 cigarettes or 100 cigars or 500 grams of tobacco, plus 2 liters of alcoholic beverage below 15% and 1 liter of alcoholic beverage in excess of 15%. Residents of European countries may import 200 cigarettes or 50 cigars or 250 grams of tobacco, plus 2 liters of alcoholic beverage below 15% and 1 liter of alcoholic beverage in excess of 15%. These allowances apply only to those age 17 and above.

There are no restrictions on the import or export of any currency.

Language French is spoken in the southwest, around Lake Geneva, and in the cantons of Fribourg, Neuchâtel, Jura, Vaud, and the western portion of Valais; Italian is spoken in the Ticino, and lilting dialects of German are spoken everywhere else—in more than 70% of the country, in fact. The Romance language called Romansch has regained a firm foothold throughout the Upper and Lower Engadine regions of the canton Graubünden, where it takes the form of five different dialects. English, however, is spoken widely. Many public signs are in English, as well as in the regional language, and all hotels, restaurants, tourist offices, train stations, banks, and shops will have someone who can speak English comfortably.

Getting Around

By Plane **Swissair** connects the cities of Zürich, Basel, and Geneva. The airline offers flexible packages (Box 845, New York, NY 10102, tel. 800/688–7947) from April through October for the independent traveler who flies at least one way between North America and Europe on Swissair or Delta. "The Swiss Travel Invention" allows visitors to tailor-fit their Swiss holiday to include hotels, car rentals, rail vacations, and guided tours at great savings. Swissair also offers personalized ski packages consisting of round-trip flights, surface travel by rail or bus, and a choice of hotels at ski resorts. **Crossair** is Switzerland's domestic airline, flying between local airports and bringing in visitors from various Continental cities as well, including London, Rome, Barcelona, Berlin, and Amsterdam.

By Car Swiss roads are usually well surfaced but wind about consider-
Road Conditions ably—especially in the mountains. Don't plan on achieving high average speeds. When estimating likely travel times, look carefully at the map: There may be only 32.3 kilometers (20 miles) between one point and another, but there could also be a mountain pass along the way. There is a well-developed highway network, though some notable gaps still exist in the south along an east–west line, roughly between Lugano and Sion. Under some mountain passes, there are tunnels through which cars can be transported by train while passengers remain in the cars—an experience not unlike riding through the world's longest car wash.

A combination of steep or winding routes and hazardous weather conditions may close some roads during the winter. Dial 120 or 163 for bulletins and advance information on road conditions.

Rules of the Road Driving is on the right. In built-up areas, the speed limit is 50 kph (30 mph), and on main highways, it's 120 kph (75 mph). On other roads outside built-up areas, the limit is 80 kph (50 mph). Strongly contested efforts are being made to raise these limits.

Children under 12 are not permitted to sit in the front seat. Driving with parking lights is prohibited, and lights are mandatory in heavy rain and under other conditions of poor visibility; you *must* use headlights in road tunnels.

To use the main highways, you must display a disk or *vignette*, which you can buy from the Swiss National Tourist Office before you leave or at the border stations when you enter the country. It costs 30 Fr. (unless a threatened election raises it to 35 Fr.) and is valid until the end of the year. Cars rented within Switzerland already have these disks.

Traffic going up a mountain has priority except for postal buses coming down. A sign with a yellow posthorn on a blue background means that postal buses have priority.

During the winter, snow chains are advisable—sometimes mandatory. They can be rented in all areas, and snow-chain service stations have signs marked "Service de Chaînes à Neige," or "Schneekettendienst."

Parking Parking areas are clearly marked. Parking in public lots normally costs between .5 Fr. and 1 Fr. per hour.

Gasoline Lead-free (*sans plomb* or *bleifrei*) gas costs .98 Fr. per liter, and leaded premium costs 1.06 per liter (again subject to an impending vote: It could be raised 20%). Leaded regular is no longer available.

Breakdowns Assistance is available through the telephone exchange: Ask for "Autohilfe." The Touring Club Suisse has a 24-hour breakdown service. Useful organizations are the **Automobile Club de Suisse** (ACS, Wasserwerkegasse 39, Bern) and the **Touring Club Suisse** (TCS, 9 rue Pierre Fatio, Geneva), both of which have branches throughout Switzerland.

By Train Switzerland's trains are among Europe's finest. Generally, they are swift (except through the mountains), immaculate, and unnervingly punctual. Don't linger between international connections: The Swiss don't wait for languorous travelers. If you plan to use the trains extensively, get a timetable (*Offizieles Kursbuch* or *Horaire*), which costs 14 Fr., or a portable, pocket version called "Fribo" for 10.80 Fr. A useful booklet called "Switzerland by Rail," available from the Swiss National Tourist Office (SNTO), describes 20 excursions that can be made by public transportation, as well as including timetables for the best train connections to Zürich and Geneva airports.

Trains described as Inter-City or Express are the fastest, stopping only at principal towns. *Regionalzug* means a local train, often affording the most spectacular views. Meals, snacks, and drinks are provided on most main services. Seat reservations are useful during rush hours and high season, especially on international trains.

Fares There are numerous concessions for visitors. The **Swiss Pass** is the best value, offering unlimited travel on Swiss Federal Railways, postal buses, lake steamers, and the local bus and tram service of 30 cities. It also gives reductions on many privately owned railways, cable cars, and mountain railways. It's available from the Swiss National Tourist Office and from travel agents outside Switzerland. The card is valid for eight days (250 Fr. 2nd-class, 360 Fr. 1st-class), 15 days (290 Fr. 2nd-class, 420 Fr. 1st-class), or one month (400 Fr. 2nd-class, 580 Fr. 1st-class). There is also a new 3-day **Flexi Pass** (180 Fr.), which offers the same unlimited travel options of a regular Swiss Pass for any 3 days within a 15-day period. Prices are for second-class travel; first-class travel costs about 40% more.

Within some popular tourist areas, **Regional Holiday Season Tickets,** issued for 15 days, give 5 days of free travel by train, postal buses, steamers, and mountain railways, with half fare for the rest of the validity of the card. Central Switzerland offers a similar pass for 7 days, with 2 days of free travel. Prices vary widely, depending upon the region and period of validity, but if you like to cover a lot of ground, they do assure you of savings over full fare. Increasingly popular with tourists is a **Swiss Half-Fare Travel Card,** which allows half-fare travel for 30 days (85 Fr.) or one year (150 Fr.).

The new **Swiss Card,** which can be purchased in the United States through RailEurope (226–230 Westchester Ave., White Plains, NY 10604, tel. 914/682–5172 or 800/345–1990) and at train stations at the Zürich and Geneva airports and in Basel, is valid for 30 days and grants full round-trip travel from your arrival point to any destination in the country, plus a half-price reduction on any further excursions during your stay (160 Fr. first class, 130 Fr. second class). For more information about train travel in Switzerland, get the free "Swiss Travel System" or "Discover Switzerland" brochures from the SNTO.

For 20 Fr. per bag round-trip, travelers holding tickets or passes on Swiss Federal Railways can forward their luggage to their final destination, allowing passengers to make stops on the way unencumbered.

By Bus Switzerland's famous yellow postal buses link main cities with villages off the beaten track. Both postal and city buses follow posted schedules to the minute: You can set your watch by them. Free timetables can be picked up at any post office.

The Swiss Pass (*see above*) gives unlimited travel on the postal buses. The **Postal Coach Weekly Card** gives unlimited travel within certain regions where train travel is limited and can be bought at local post offices.

The postal buses pay special attention to hikers. You can get a free booklet, "The Best River and Lakeside Walks," from the SNTO. The booklet describes 28 walks you can enjoy by hopping on and off postal buses. Most walks take around three hours.

By Boat Drifting across a Swiss lake and stopping off here and there at picturesque villages nestling by the water makes a relaxing day's excursion, especially if you are lucky enough to catch one of the elegant old paddle steamers. Trips are scheduled on most of the lakes, with increased service in summer. Unlimited travel is free to holders of the **Swiss Pass** (*see above*). For those not traveling by train, there is also a **Swiss Boat Pass,** which allows half-fare travel on all lake steamers for the entire year (35 Fr., Jan. 1–Dec. 31).

By Bicycle Bikes can be rented at all train stations and returned to any station. Rates are 19 Fr. per day or 76 Fr. per week for a conventional bike, 31 Fr. per day and 124 Fr. per week for a mountain bike. Families can rent two adult bikes and bikes for the children for 48 Fr. per day, 208 Fr. per week. Groups get reductions according to the number of bikes involved. Reservations are necessary by 6 PM the day before use by individuals and a week ahead for groups. **Touring Club Suisse** (9 rue Pierre Fatio, CH-1211 Geneva 3, tel. 022/7371212) also rents bikes from its local offices at prices ranging from 14 Fr. to 24 Fr. per day.

Staying in Switzerland

Telephones There is direct dialing to every location in Switzerland. For lo-
Local Calls cal and international codes, consult the pink pages at the front of the telephone book.

International Calls You can dial most international numbers direct from Switzerland, adding a 00 before the country's code. If you want a number that cannot be reached directly, dial 114 for a connection. Dial 191 for international numbers and information. It's cheapest to use the booths in train stations and post offices; calls made from your hotel cost a great deal more. The PTT phone card, available in 10 Fr. and 20 Fr. units, allows you to call from any adapted public phone. You can buy cards at the post office or train station. Rates are lower between 5 PM and 7 PM, after 9 PM, and on weekends. Calls to the United States cost 2 Fr. per minute, to the United Kingdom 1.40 Fr. per minute.

Operators and All telephone operators speak English, and instructions are
Information printed in English in all telephone booths.

Mail Mail rates are divided into first class (air mail) and second class
Postal Rates (surface). Letters and postcards to the United States up to 20 grams cost 1.80 Fr. first class, .90 Fr. second class; to the United Kingdom, 1 Fr. first class, .80 Fr. second class.

Receiving Mail If you're uncertain where you'll be staying, you can have your mail, marked Poste Restante or Postlagernd, sent to any post office in Switzerland. The sender's name and address must be on the back, and you'll need proof of identity to collect it. You can also have your mail sent to American Express for a small fee, payable when you collect it.

Shopping A 6.2% value-added tax (VAT) on all goods is included in the
VAT Refunds price. Nonresidents who have spent at least 500 Fr. at one time at a particular store may claim a VAT refund at the time of purchase, or the shop will send the refund to your home. In order to qualify for a refund, you *must* sign a form at the time of purchase and present it to Swiss customs on departure.

Bargaining Don't try bargaining: Except at the humblest flea market, it just doesn't work. As with everything in Switzerland, prices are efficiently controlled.

Opening and **Banks** are open weekdays 8:30–4:30 or 5.
Closing Times
Museums times vary considerably, though many close on Monday. Check locally.

Shops are generally open 8–noon and 1:30–6:30. Some close at 4 on Saturday, and some are closed Monday morning. In cities, many large stores do not close for lunch. In train stations, some shops remain open until 9 PM, and in Geneva and Zürich airports, shops remain open on Sunday.

National Holidays January 1, 2; April 1 (Good Friday); April 3, 4 (Easter); May 12 (Ascension); May 22 (Pentecost Sunday); December 25, 26. May 1 (Labor Day) and August 1 (National Day) are also celebrated, though not throughout the country.

Dining Options range from luxury establishments to modest cafés, *stübli* (cozy little pubs), and restaurants specializing in local cuisine.

Because the Swiss are so good at preparing everyone else's cuisine, it is sometimes said that they have none of their own, but there definitely is a distinct and characteristic Swiss cuisine. Switzerland is the home of great cheeses—Gruyère, Emmentaler, Appenzeller, and Vacherin—which form the basis of many dishes. *Raclette* is cheese melted over a fire and served with potatoes and pickles, *Rösti* are hash brown potatoes, and *fondue* is a bubbling pot of melted cheeses flavored with garlic and kirsch, into which you dip chunks of bread. Other Swiss specialties to look for are *Geschnetzeltes Kalbfleisch* (veal bits in cream sauce), *polenta* (cornmeal mush) in the Italian region, and fine game in autumn. A wide variety of Swiss sausages make both filling and inexpensive meals, and in every region the breads are varied and superb.

Mealtimes At home, the main Swiss meal of the day is lunch, with a snack in the evening. Restaurants, however, are open at midday and during the evening; often limited menus are offered all day. Watch for *Tagesteller* or *menus* (fixed-price lunch platters or menus), which enable you to experience the best restaurants without paying high à la carte rates.

Dress Jacket and tie are suggested for restaurants in the Very Expensive and Expensive categories; casual dress is acceptable elsewhere.

Ratings Prices are per person, without wine or coffee, but including tip and taxes. Best bets are indicated by a star ★.

Category	Zürich/Geneva	Other Areas
Very Expensive	over 90 Fr.	over 70 Fr.
Expensive	50 Fr.–90 Fr.	40 Fr.–70 Fr.
Moderate	30 Fr.–50 Fr.	20 Fr.–40 Fr.
Inexpensive	under 30 Fr.	under 20 Fr.

Lodging Switzerland's accommodations cover a broad range, from the most luxurious hotels to the more economical rooms in private homes. Pick up the *Schweizer Hotelführer (Swiss Hotel Guide)* from the SNTO before you leave home. The guide is free and lists all the members of the Swiss Hotel Association (comprising nearly 90% of the nation's accommodations); it tells you everything you'll want to know.

Most hotel rooms today have private bath and shower; those that don't are usually considerably cheaper. Single rooms are generally about two-thirds the price of doubles, but this can vary considerably. Remember that the no-nonsense Swiss sleep in separate beds or, at best, a double with separate bedding. If you prefer more sociable arrangements, ask for the rare "matrimonial" or "French" bed. Service charges and taxes are included in the price quoted and the bill you pay. Breakfast is included unless there is a clear notice to the contrary. In resorts especially, half pension (choice of a noon or evening meal) may be included in the room price. If you choose to eat à la carte or elsewhere, the management will generally reduce your price. Give them plenty of notice, however.

All major towns and train stations have hotel-finding services, which sometimes charge a small fee. Local tourist offices will also help.

Hotels   Hotels are graded from one star (the lowest) to five stars. Always confirm what you are paying before you register, and check the posted price when you get to your room. Major credit cards are generally accepted, but make sure beforehand.

Two important hotel chains are the Romantik Hotels and Restaurants and Relais et Châteaux, with premises that are generally either in historic houses or houses that have some special character. Another chain that has a good reputation is Best Western, affiliated with the familiar American chain. Relais du Silence hotels are usually isolated in a peaceful, natural setting—or urban oasis—with first-class comforts. The Check-In E and G Hotels are small hotels, boardinghouses, and mountain lodges that offer accommodations at reasonable prices. Details are available from the SNTO, which also offers pamphlets recommending family hotels and a list of hotels and restaurants that cater specifically to Jewish travelers.

Rentals   Switzerland has literally thousands of furnished chalets. Off-season, per-day prices are around 50 Fr. per person for four sharing a chalet. In peak season, prices would be at least twice that. Deluxe chalets cost much more. For more information, pick up an illustrated brochure from the **Swiss Touring Club** (9 rue Pierre Fatio, CH-1211 Geneva 3) or from **Uto-Ring AG** (Beethovenstr. 24, CH-8002 Zürich). In the United States, write to **Interhome** (36 Carlos Dr., Fairfield, NJ 07006). In Britain, contact **Interhome** (383 Richmond Rd., Twickenham, Middlesex TW1 2EF). You may save considerably if you write directly to the village or resort you wish to rent in, specifying your projected dates and number of beds needed: Prices start at around 20 Fr. per person without an agency's commission.

Ratings   Prices are for two people in a double room with bath or shower, including taxes, service charges, and breakfast. Best bets are indicated by a star ★.

Category	Zürich/Geneva	Other Areas
Very Expensive	over 450 Fr.	over 250 Fr.
Expensive	250 Fr.–450 Fr.	180 Fr.–250 Fr.
Moderate	140 Fr.–250 Fr.	120 Fr.–180 Fr.
Inexpensive	under 140 Fr.	under 120 Fr.

Tipping   Although restaurants include service charges of 15% with the taxes in your hotel and restaurant bill, you will be expected to leave a small additional tip: 1 Fr. or 2 Fr. per person for a modest meal, 5 Fr. for a first-class meal, and 10 Fr. at one of the exclusive gastronomic restaurants in the Very Expensive range. When possible, tip in cash. Elsewhere, give bathroom attendants 1 Fr. and hotel maids 2 Fr. Theater and opera-house ushers get 2 Fr. Hotel porters and doormen should get about 1 Fr. per bag.

Zürich

Arriving and Departing

By Plane Kloten (tel. 01/8121212) is Switzerland's most important airport and is among the most sophisticated in the world. Several airlines fly directly to Zürich from major cities in the United States, Canada, and the United Kingdom.

Swissair flies nonstop from New York, Chicago, Toronto, Montreal, Atlanta, Los Angeles, and Boston. "Fly Rail Baggage" allows Swissair passengers departing Switzerland to check their bags at any of 120 rail or postal bus stations throughout the country; luggage is automatically transferred to the airplane. At eight Swiss railway stations, passengers may complete all check-in procedures for Swissair flights, including boarding-pass issuance and baggage forwarding.

Between the Airport and Downtown Beneath the air terminals, there's a train station with an efficient, direct service into the Hauptbahnhof (main station) in the center of Zürich. Fast trains run every 20 minutes, and the trip takes about 10 minutes. The fare is 4.50 Fr., and the ticket office is in the airport. There are express trains to most Swiss cities at least every hour. Trains run from 6 AM to midnight.

Taxis are very expensive: about 40 Fr. into town. Some hotels provide their own bus service. Cars can be rented at the airport.

By Bus All bus services to Zürich will drop you at the Hauptbahnhof.

By Train Zürich is the northern crossroads of Switzerland, with swift and timely trains arriving from Basel, Geneva, Bern, and Lugano. All routes lead to the Hauptbahnhof in the city center.

By Car There are direct highways from the border crossings with France, Germany, and Italy. Germany is the nearest.

Getting Around

Although Zürich is Switzerland's largest city, it has a population of only 362,000 and is not large by European standards. That's one of its nicest features: You can explore it comfortably on foot.

By Bus and Streetcar The city's transportation network is excellent. **VBZ Züri-Line** (Zürich Public Transport) buses run from 5:30 AM to midnight, every six minutes on all routes at peak hours, and about every 12 minutes at other times. Before you board the bus, you must buy your ticket from the automatic vending machines found at every stop. A ticket for all travel for 24 hours is a good buy at 6 Fr. Free route plans are available from VBZ offices.

By Taxi Taxis are very expensive, with a 8 Fr. minimum, and should be avoided unless you have no other means of getting around.

Important Addresses and Numbers

Tourist Information The tourist office is located at Bahnhofplatz 15 (Main Station), tel. 01/2114000. Open Apr.–Oct., weekdays 8:30–9:30, weekends 8:30 AM–8:30 PM; Nov.–Mar., Mon.–Fri. 8:30–7:30, weekends 8:30–6:30.

Consulates U.S. (Zollikerstr. 141, tel. 01/4222566). U.K. (Dufourstr. 56, tel. 01/2611520).

Emergencies Police (tel. 117). Ambulance (tel. 144). Doctor/Dentist Referral (tel. 01/2614700). Pharmacy: Bellevue (Theaterstr. 14, tel. 01/2525600) offers an all-night service.

English-Language Bookstores For books and magazines, try Payot (Bahnhofstr. 9). Travel Book Shop (Rindermarkt 20).

Travel Agencies American Express (Bahnhofstr. 20, tel. 01/2118370). Kuoni (Bahnhofplatz 7, tel. 01/2213411).

Guided Tours

Orientation Tours There are four bus tours available. The daily "Sights of Zürich" tour (22 Fr. adults, 11 Fr. children) gives a good general idea of the city in two hours. "In and Around Zürich" goes farther and includes an aerial cableway trip to Felsenegg. This is also a daily tour that takes 2½ hours; it costs 30 Fr. adults, 15 Fr. children. The May-to-October tour, "Zürich by Night," takes in everything from folklore to striptease in 3½ hours (69 Fr.). The "Old-timer" circuit tours the city by old-fashioned tram (16 Fr. adults, 8 Fr. children 6–12). All tours start from the main station. Contact the tourist office for reservations.

Walking Tours From June to October, conducted walking tours (16 Fr. adults, 6 Fr. children 6–12) start from the tourist office and take roughly two hours.

Excursions There are many bus excursions to other areas, such as the Bernese Oberland, St. Gotthard, the Ticino, Lucerne, and Geneva. Since these depend on the season and weather, it's best to book them after you arrive and can check with the tourist office.

Exploring Zürich

Zürich is not at all what you'd expect. Stroll around on a fine spring day and you'll ask yourself if this can really be one of the great business centers of the world: The lake glistening and blue in the sun, the sidewalk cafés, the swans gliding in to land on the river, the hushed and haunted old squares of medieval guildhouses, the elegant shops. There's not a gnome (a mocking nickname for a Swiss banker) in sight. The point is that for all its economic importance, Zürich is a place where people enjoy life. Hardworking when need be, the Swiss love the good things in life and have the money to enjoy them.

Zürich started in 15 BC as a Roman customs post on the Lindenhof overlooking the river Limmat, but its growth really began around the 10th century AD. It became a free imperial city in 1336, a center of the Reformation in 1519, and then gradually assumed commercial importance during the 1800s. Today there is peace as well as prosperity here, and since Zürich is so compact, you can take it in in a morning's stroll.

Numbers in the margin correspond to points of interest on the Zürich map.

Collect your map (it's essential) from the tourist office (Bahnhofplatz 15), then start your walk from the nearby ❶ **Bahnhofstrasse,** famous for its shops and cafés and as the center of the banking network, though you'd be unlikely to guess it. Take Rennweg on your left, and then turn left again into the Fortunagasse, a quaint medieval street leading to the ❷ **Lindenhof,** a square where there are remains of Zürich's Roman origins. The fountain commemorates the ingenuity of the Zürich women who, when the city was besieged by the Habsburgs in 1292, donned armor and marched around the walls. The invaders thought they were reinforcements and beat a hasty retreat.

An alley on the right leads to a picturesque square dating from ❸ the Middle Ages, with the **Peterskirche,** Zürich's oldest parish church (13th century), which also happens to have the largest clockface in Europe. Walk down to the river and follow it to the ❹ 13th century **Fraumünster** (church), which has modern stained-glass windows by Chagall. There are two handsome guildhalls nearby: the **Zunfthaus zur Waag** hall of the linen weavers (Münsterhof 8), built in 1637, and the **Zunfthaus zur Meise** (Münsterhof 20), built during the 18th century for the wine merchants.

Time Out Head away from the river to the Bahnhofstrasse, then to Paradelplatz to visit **Sprüngli,** the famous café-sweets shop where glossy Zürichers gather to see and be seen. The chocolate truffles are sinfully rich.

Continue along Bahnhofstrasse to Bürkliplatz and cross the **Quai Bridge** to take in the impressive views of the lake and town. Art lovers might want to first continue up Rämistrasse to ❺ the **Kunsthaus** (Art Gallery), with its varied high-quality collection of medieval paintings, Dutch and Italian Baroque, and Impressionist works, as well as an excellent representation of Swiss artists, including nearly 100 works by Hodler. There also are representative works of the Dadaist movement, which was conceived in Zürich by French exile Hans Arp. *Heimpl. 1, tel. 01/2516755. Admission: 4 Fr. Open Tues.–Thurs. 10–9, Fri.–Sun. 10–5.*

❻ Now head left to the **Wasserkirche** (Water Church), dating from the 15th century and a lovely example of late-Gothic architecture. It is attached to the **Helmhaus,** originally an 18th-century cloth market.

❼ Now turn right toward the **Grossmünster** church, which dates from the 11th century. During the 3rd century AD, St. Felix and his sister Regula were martyred by the Romans. Legend maintains that having been beheaded, they then walked up the hill carrying their heads and collapsed on the spot where the Grossmünster now stands. On the south tower you can see a statue of Charlemagne (768–814), emperor of the West, who founded the church when his horse stumbled on the same site. During the 16th century, the Zürich reformer Huldrych Zwingli preached sermons here that were so threatening in their promise of fire and brimstone that Martin Luther himself was frightened.

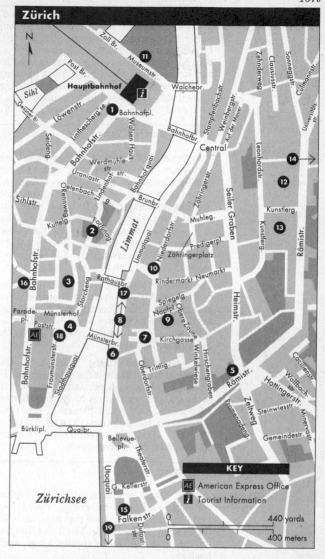

Zürich

Main Attractions
Bahnhofstrasse, 1
Fraumünster, 4
Grossmünster, 7
Kunsthaus, 5
Limmatquai, 8
Lindenhof, 2
Niederdorf, 10
Old Town, 9
Peterskirche, 3
Schweizerisches
Landesmuseum, 11
Wasserkirche, 6

Other Attractions
Centre Le
Corbusier, 19
Federal Institute of
Technology, 12
Opernhaus, 15
Rathaus, 17
Stadthaus, 18
University of
Zürich, 13
Wohnmuseum, 16
Zoo, 14

KEY

AE American Express Office

i Tourist Information

0   440 yards

0   400 meters

8   Back at the river on the **Limmatquai** are some of Zürich's most enchanting old buildings. Today most of them are restaurants. In the **Haus zum Ruden,** a 13th-century noblemen's hall, you will eat under a 300-year-old wooden ceiling. Other notable buildings here are the **Zunfthaus zur Saffran** (built in 1723 for haberdashers) and the **Zunfthaus zur Zimmerleuten** (built in 1708 for carpenters). The 17th-century Baroque **Rathaus** (Town Hall) is nearby.

9   Turn right into the **Altstadt** (old town), and you will enter a maze of fascinating medieval streets where time seems to have stood still. The Rindermarkt, Napfplatz, and Kirchgasse all have their charming old houses.

⑩ Head back to the river through **Niederdorf** (Zürich's nightlife district) and cross the bridge to the Hauptbahnhof. On the ⑪ northern edge of the Hauptbahnhof, go to the **Schweizerisches Landesmuseum**, housed in a curious 19th-century building, for a look at Swiss history. There are fascinating pre-Romanesque and Romanesque church art, glass paintings from the 15th to the 17th century, splendid ceramic stoves, gold and silver from Celtic times, and weapons from many ages. *Museumstr. 2, tel. 01/2186565. Admission free. Open Tues.–Sun. 10–5.*

Off the Beaten Track

Wealthy Zürich spends its money when the occasion calls for it, and as a result its citizens and visitors benefit from a surfeit of excellent museums and galleries—many of them rarely mentioned outside Zürich itself. One of the most outstanding is the **Stiftung Sammlung E.G. Bührle** (Collection of the E.G. Bührle Foundation), a once-private collection of European art housed in a suburban mansion. Especially noteworthy are its French Impressionist and early modern paintings. *Zollikerstr. 172, tel. 01/4220086. Admission: 6.60 Fr. adults, 3 Fr. children. Open Tues. and Fri. 2–5 and Wed. 5–8.*

The **Museum Rietberg** is a wonderful gathering of art from India, China, Africa, Japan, and Southeast Asia, contained in the neoclassical Villa Wesendonck, where Richard Wagner once lived (as in *Wesendonck Songs*). *Gablerstr. 15, tel. 01/2024528. Admission: 3 Fr. adults, children 1 Fr. Open Tues., Thurs.–Sun. 10–5, Wed. 10–9.*

The **Graphiksammlung** (Graphics Collection) of the Eidgenössische Technische Hochschule (Federal Institute of Technology) displays portions of its vast library of woodcuts, etchings, and engravings by European masters such as Dürer, Rembrandt, Goya, and Picasso. From time to time there are good thematic exhibitions drawn from the collection. *Rämistr. 101, tel. 01/2564046. Admission free. Open Mon., Tues., Thurs., Fri. 10–5; Wed. 10–8.*

Shopping

Gift Ideas Typical Swiss products, all of the highest quality, include watches in all price categories, clocks, jewelry, music boxes, embroidered goods, wood carvings, and the famous multiblade Swiss army pocket knife. You'll also find fine household linens, delicate cotton or woolen underthings, and Zürich-made Fogal hosiery.

Shopping Districts The **Bahnhofstrasse** is one of the most bountiful shopping streets in Switzerland. Here you'll find **Jelmoli** (Seidengasse 1), Switzerland's largest department store, carrying a wide range of tasteful Swiss goods. **Heimatwerk** (Bahnhofstr. 2) specializes in handmade Swiss crafts, all of excellent quality. For high fashion, go to **Trois Pommes** (Storchengasse 6/7) and **Grieder** (Bahnhofstrasse 30), and for the finest porcelain, glass, and silverware, visit **Sequin-Dormann** (Bahnhofstr. 69a). If you have a sweet tooth, stock up on truffles at **Sprüngli** (Paradeplatz).

In the **Old Town** and off the **Limmatquai,** you'll find boutiques, antiques shops, bookstores, and galleries in picturesque byways. The **Löwenstrasse** has a diversity of upscale shops; the

Langstrasse is another good shopping area and often has slightly lower prices. Under the central train station, **Shopville** offers a variety of middle-class stores and snack bars.

Food and Flea Markets In many parts of town, there are lively markets where fruit, vegetables, and flowers are competitively priced. The best are at **Bürkliplatz, Helvetiaplatz,** and **Milkbuckstrasse** (open Tues. and Fri. 6 AM–11 AM).

At Bürkliplatz, at the lake end of the Bahnhofstrasse, there's a flea market that's open May through October, and a curio market is held at **Rosenhof** every Thursday and Saturday between April and Christmas.

Dining

You're likely to be served seconds in Zürich's generous restaurants, where the rest of your *Rösti* (hash brown potatoes) and *Geschnetzeltes Kalbfleisch nach Zürcher Art* (veal bits in cream sauce, "Zürich style") simmer in copper pans by your table while you relish the hefty first portion. This is a Germanic city, after all, though its status as a minor world capital means that most international cuisines are represented as well. But brace yourself: The cash register rings portentously when the waiter places your order. Watch for posted *Tagesteller* specials, a good source of savings. For details and price-category definitions, *see* Dining in Staying in Switzerland.

Very Expensive **Königstuhl.** ★ This trendy, tongue-in-cheek take on Zürich's *Zunfthäuser* (guildhalls) has caught on with a vengeance. Itself the Zunfthaus zur Schneidern (Cutters' Guildhall), with a relatively traditional meeting hall on the top floor, this complex consisting of bar, bistro, and first-class restaurant functions more as an anti-zunfthaus: It's been entirely redone in cool gray graphite and glass, with halogen lighting and broad, droll allusions to Zürich's heavy Teutonic taste. The cuisine is equally irreverent, with light, moderately priced suppers (appetizers, pastas) downstairs in the bistro and superb international experiments in the soigné restaurant upstairs. There's a lovely courtyard terrace for summer dining. *Stüssihofstatt 3, tel. 01/ 2617618. Bistro: reservations advised, jacket advised. Restaurant: reservations required, jacket and tie advised. AE, DC, MC, V.*

La Rotonde. Even when it's not illuminated by candlelight, the Dolder Grand Hotel's haute cuisine restaurant is one of the most romantic spots in Zürich. Housed in a great arc of a room, La Rotonde provides sweeping park views that attract the lunchtime business crowd. Main courses may include grilled salmon with finely diced lobster, scallops, and shrimp in a hazelnut oil sauce, and sweetbreads on a bed of *gnocchi* with asparagus and truffles. The 70 Fr. prix-fixe dinner is a particularly good value. For those who love hors d'oeuvres, there's a Sunday afternoon buffet of nothing but starters. *Dolder Grand Hotel, Kurhausstr. 65, tel. 01/2516231. Reservations advised. Jacket and tie advised. AE, DC, MC, V.*

★ **Petermann's Kunststuben.** This is one of Switzerland's gastronomic meccas, and while it's south of the city center, in Küssnacht on the lake's eastern shore, it's more than worth the 8-kilometer (5-mile) pilgrimage. The ever-evolving menu may include lobster with artichoke and almond oil; grilled turbot with lemon sauce and capers; and a ragout of oxtail with Barolo.

Seestr. 160, Küssnacht, tel. 01/9100715. Reservations required. Jacket and tie advised. AE, DC, MC, V. Closed Sun. and Mon.

Tübli. Tucked on a back alley in the more venturesome Niederdorf neighborhood, this intimate little Züricher secret continues to draw insiders for some of the best—and most innovative—cuisine in the city center. Eschewing à la carte standbys for ever-changing weekly seven-course menus, chef Martin Surbeck experiments with almost indiscriminate pleasure with literally far-fetched ingredients: Portuguese *chocolat* for his fish carpaccio, Norwegian reindeer with mulberry-flower mousseline, or passion-fruit soufflé. *Schneggengasse 8, tel. 01/2512471. Reservations advised. Jacket advised. AE, DC, MC, V. Closed weekends.*

Expensive **Blaue Ente.** Part of a shopping gallery in a converted mill south
★ of the city center, this modern, upmarket restaurant and bar draw well-dressed crowds from advertising and the arts. In a setting of whitewashed brick and glass, with jazz filtering through from the adjoining bar, guests sample a pot-au-feu of clams, prawns, and saffron, or lamb with potato pancakes and eggplant. Take the No. 2 tram toward Tiefenbrunnen. *Mühle Tiefenbrunnen, tel. 01/4227706. Reservations required. Jacket advised. AE, DC, MC, V.*

★ **Kronenhalle.** From Stravinsky, Brecht, and Joyce to Nureyev, Deneuve, and St-Laurent, this beloved landmark has always drawn a stellar crowd for its genial atmosphere, hearty cooking, and astonishing collection of 20th-century art. Try the herring in double cream, tournedos with truffle sauce, or duck à l'orange with red cabbage and *Spätzli* (tiny dumplings). And be sure to have a cocktail in the adjoining bar: *Le tout* Zürich drinks here. *Rämistr. 4, tel. 01/2516669. Reservations advised. Jacket and tie advised. AE, DC, MC, V.*

Veltliner Keller. Though its rich, carved-wood decor borrows from Graubündner Alpine culture, this ancient and atmospheric dining spot is no tourist trap: The house, built in 1325 and functioning as a restaurant since 1551, has always stored Italian-Swiss Valtellina wines, which were carried over the Alps and imported to Zürich. The traditional kitchen favors heavy meat standards, but is flexible and reasonably deft with seafood as well. *Schlüsselgasse 8, tel. 01/2213228. Reservations advised. Jacket and tie advised. AE, DC, MC, V.*

Moderate **Oepfelchammer.** This was once the haunt of Zürich's beloved
★ writer Gottfried Keller, and, recently restored, it still draws unpretentious literati. One room's dark and graffiti-scribbled bar, with sagging timbers and slanting floors; the other's a welcoming little dining room, with carved oak paneling, a coffered ceiling, and pink damask linens. The traditional meats—calf's liver, veal, tripe in white wine sauce—come in generous portions; salads are fresh and seasonal. It's always packed, and service can be slow, so stake out a table and spend the evening. *Rindermarkt 12, tel. 01/2512336. Reservations advised. Dress: casual. MC, V. Closed Sun.*

Zunfthaus zur Schmiden. The sense of history and the magnificent mix of Gothic wood, leaded glass, and tile stoves justify a visit to this popular landmark, the guildhouse of blacksmiths and barbers since 1412. All the classics are served in enormous portions, and there's a considerable selection of alternatives, fish among them. The guild's own house wine is fine.

Marktgasse 20, tel. 01/2515287. Reservations advised. Dress: casual but neat. AE, DC, MC, V.

Inexpensive **Bierhalle Kropf.** Under the giant boar's head and century-old
★ murals that have been recently restored, businesspeople, workers, and shoppers crowd shared tables to feast on generous hot dishes and a great selection of sausages. The *Leberknödli* (liver dumplings) are tasty, *Apfelköchli* (fried apple slices) tender and sweet, and the bread chewy and delicious—though you pay for every chunk you eat. *In Gassen 16, tel. 01/2211805. Reservations advised. Dress: casual. AE, DC, MC, V.*

Rheinfelder Bierhaus. Dark and smoky, with every wooden table squeezing in mixed parties of workers, bikers, shoppers, and tourists, this is a solid old institution in the Niederdorf area. There's rich *Rindpfeffer* (preserved beef stew) with homemade *Spätzli*, tender liver with *Rösti*, sausage dishes, and once a month, the chef's pride: an incongruous but freshly homemade paella. *Marktgasse 19, tel. 01/2512991. Reservations not necessary. Dress: casual. No credit cards.*

Zeughauskeller. Built as an arsenal in 1487, this enormous stone and beam hall offers hearty meat platters and a variety of beers and wines amid comfortable and friendly chaos. Waitresses are harried and brisk, especially at lunchtime, when crowds are thick. They're not unaccustomed to tourists, but locals consider this their home away from home. *Bahnhofstr. 28 (at Paradeplatz), tel. 01/2112690. Reservations advised at lunch. Dress: casual. No credit cards.*

Lodging

Zürich has an enormous range of hotels, from some of the most chic and prestigious in the country to modest guest houses. Prices tend to be higher than anywhere else in Europe, but you can be sure that you will get what you pay for: Quality and good service are guaranteed. For details and price-category definitions, *see* Lodging in Staying in Switzerland.

Very Expensive **Baur au Lac.** This is the hoary, highbrow patrician of Swiss hotels, with luxury facilities but none of the glitz associated with
★ the flashier upstarts among prestige resorts. Its broad back is turned to the commercial center, and its front rooms overlook the lake, canal, and manicured lawns of the hotel's private park. Decor is posh, discreet, and firmly fixed in the Age of Reason. In summer, meals are served in the glassed park Pavilion along the canal; in winter, in the glowing Restaurant Français. The Grillroom is a business tradition. *Talstr. 1, CH–8022, tel. 01/2211650, fax 01/2118139. 156 rooms with bath. Facilities: 3 restaurants, bar, disco, beauty shop, Rolls-Royce limousine service, parking. AE, DC, MC, V.*

★ **Dolder Grand.** A cross between Camp David and Maria Theresa's summer palace, this sprawling Victorian fantasy-palace sits high on a wooded hill over Zürich, quickly reached from Römerhof by funicular railway (free for guests) and offering splendid views and complete self-sufficiency. It was opened in 1899 as a summer resort, a picturesque hodgepodge of turrets, cupolas, half-timbers, and mansards; the uncompromisingly modern wing was added in 1964, but from inside the connection is seamless. The garden and forest views behind nearly match those of the golf course, park, and city itself. Restaurant la Rotonde excels in traditional French cuisine (*see* Dining, *above). Kurhausstr. 65, CH-8032, tel. 01/2516231, fax 01/ 2518829. 207 rooms with bath. Facilities: French restaurant, terrace cafe, bar, hairdresser, underground parking, swimming pool with wave machine, 9-hole golf course, tennis courts, ice-skating rink. AE, DC, MC, V.*

★ **Savoy Baur en Ville.** The oldest hotel in Zürich, built in 1838, this luxurious downtown landmark was gutted in 1975 and reconstructed as an airtight urban gem. It's directly on the Paradeplatz and at the hub of the banking, shopping, and sightseeing districts. The rooms have a warm, postmodern decor, with pearwood cabinetry, brass, and chintz, and there are two fine restaurants—one French, the other Italian—as well as a city-slick café. *Paradeplatz, CH-8022, tel. 01/2115360, fax 01/ 2111467. 112 rooms with bath. Facilities: 2 restaurants, café. AE, DC, MC, V.*

Expensive **Neues Schloss.** Headed by Bernard Seiler, an heir to the Zer-
★ matt hotel dynasty, this small, discreet hotel in the business district (southeast of Paradeplatz) shows its bloodlines, offering a cordial welcome, good service, and the warmth of a tastefully furnished private home. Its restaurant, Le Jardin, is airy and floral, and popular at lunch. *Stockerstr. 17, CH-8022, tel. 01/2016550, fax 01/2016418. 59 rooms with bath. Facilities: restaurant. AE, DC, MC, V.*

Splügenschloss. Constructed at the turn of the century as luxury apartments, this Relais et Châteaux property maintains an ornate and historic decor, with antiques in rooms as well as throughout public spaces. Some rooms have been paneled completely in Alpine-style pine, others in fussy florals. Its location southeast of the Neues Schloss may be a little out of the way for tourists, but atmosphere buffs will find it worth the effort. *Splügenstr. 2, CH-8002, tel. 01/2010800, fax 01/2014286. 55 rooms. Facilities: restaurant, bar. AE, DC, MC, V.*

★ **Zum Storchen.** In a stunning central location, tucked between Fraumünster and St. Peter on the gull-studded banks of the Limmat, this airy 600-year-old structure houses an impeccable modern hotel. It has warmly appointed rooms, some with French windows that open over the water, and a lovely terrace restaurant as well as a cozy, guildhouselike dining room. *Weinplatz 2, CH-8001, tel. 01/2115510, fax 01/2116451. 77 rooms with bath. Facilities: restaurant, terrace café, snack bar, bar. AE, DC, MC, V.*

Moderate **City.** Near the Bahnhofstrasse, train station, and Löwen-
strasse shopping district, this is a hotel in miniature, with small furnishings and baths and a high proportion of single rooms. It's recently been renewed to chic pastel polish, and some rooms fall in the Expensive category. *Löwenstr. 34, CH-8021, tel. 01/2112055, fax 01/2120036. 83 rooms. AE, DC, MC, V.*

★ **Rössli.** Young, trendy, and completely high-tech, this hip new spot in Oberdorf, near the Grossmünster, offers a refreshing antidote to Zürich's medievalism. Decor is white-on-white, with metallic-tiled baths, vivid lithographs, and splashy fabrics; hair dryers, robes, and fax connections keep services above average, especially for the price. The adjoining bar is very popular with young locals. *Rössligasse 7, CH-8001, tel. 01/ 2522121, fax 01/252213. 12 rooms with bath. Facilities: bar. AE, DC, MC, V.*

★ **Sonnenberg.** If you're traveling by car and want to avoid the urban rush, escape to this hillside refuge east of town. There are breathtaking views of the city, lake, and mountains, and land-scaped grounds with a lovely terrace restaurant. The wood, stone, and beam decor reinforces the resort atmosphere. It's run by the friendly Wismer family. Take tram No. 3 or No. 8 to Klusplatz, then walk 10 minutes uphill. *Aurorastr. 98, CH-8030, tel. 01/2620062, fax 01/2620633. 35 rooms with bath. Facilities: restaurant, terrace cáfe. AE, DC, MC, V.*

Wellenberg. Another effort at high style but not as effective as the Rössli, this new, central hotel sports a postmodern retro look, with burled wood, black lacquer, Art Deco travel posters, and Hollywood photos. Rooms are relatively roomy, if occasionally garish, and the location—on Niederdorf's Hirschen-platz—is superb. *Niederdorfstr. 10, CH-8001, tel. 01/2624300, fax 01/2513130. 46 rooms with bath. AE, DC, MC, V.*

Inexpensive
★ **Italia.** Far west of the river, in a barren but perfectly safe neighborhood, this cozy, Old World family hotel spills over with doilies, overstuffed chairs, and mismatched antiques. Rooms—at rock-bottom prices—have sinks only, with a big, homey bathroom on each floor. The Papagni family runs the leather-and-wood restaurant downstairs, and serves crowds under the chestnut pollards in the popular summer garden. Take bus No. 31 from the train station to Kanonengasse. *Zeughausstr. 61, CH-8004, tel. 01/2410555. 36 rooms without bath. Facilities: restaurant. No credit cards.*

Linde Oberstrasse. Near the university in a sterile residential area, this small hotel, built as a guildhouse in 1628, offers a handful of modest but agreeable rooms. The decor has been comfortably modernized, and though baths are down the hall, there is a sink, TV, and minibar in each room to compensate. The restaurant is comfortable and, though renovated to dated-modern style, maintains its traditional atmosphere and solid menu. *Universitätstr. 91, CH-8033, tel. 01/3622109. 10 rooms without bath. Facilities: restaurant. AE, DC, MC, V.*

Vorderer Sternen. On the edge of the Old Town and near the lake, this plain but adequate establishment takes in the bustle (and noise) of the city. It's steps from the opera house, theaters, art galleries, cinemas, and a shopping area; it's also close to the Bellevueplatz tram junction. There's a dependable and popular restaurant downstairs with moderate standards. *Theaterstr. 22, CH-8001 tel. 01/2514949, fax 01/2529063. 15 rooms without bath. AE, DC, MC, V.*

The Arts

Pick up *Zürich News*, published each week by the tourist of-fice, to check what's on. Ticket reservations can be made through the **Billetzentrale** (Werdmühleplatz, tel. 01/2212283; open weekdays 10–6:30, Sat. 10–2). **Musik Hug** (Limmatquai 26, tel. 01/2212540) and **Jecklin** (Rämistr. 30, tel. 01/2617733) are good ticket sources as well.

The **Zürich Tonhalle Orchestra** (Claridenstr. 7, tel. 01/2063434) ranks among Europe's best. The **Opernhaus** (Falkenstr., tel. 01/2620909) is renowned for its adventurous opera, operetta, and ballet productions. The **Schauspielhaus** (Rämistr. 34, tel. 01/2655858) is one of the finest German-speaking theaters in the world. Zürich has 40 movie theaters, with English-lan-guage films appearing regularly.

Nightlife

Zürich has a lively nightlife scene, largely centered in the Niederdorf, parallel to the Limmat, across from the Hauptbahnhof. Many spots are short-lived, so check in advance. Informal dress is acceptable in most places, but again, check to make sure. The hotel porter is a good source of information.

Bars and Lounges The narrow bar at the **Kronenhalle** (Rämistr. 4, tel. 01/2511597) draws mobs of well-heeled locals and internationals for its prize-winning cocktails. The **Jules Verne Panorama Bar** (Uraniahaus, tel. 01/2111155) offers cocktails with a wraparound view of downtown Zürich. **Champagnertreff** in the Hotel Central (Central 1, tel. 01/2515555) is a popular Deco-look piano bar with several champagnes available by the glass. **Odeon** (Am Bellevue, tel. 01/2511650) serves a young, arty set until 4 AM. Some beer halls, including **Bierhalle Kropf** (In Gassen 16, tel. 01/2211805) and **Zeughauskeller** (Bahnhofstr. 28, tel. 01/2112690), serve a variety of draft beers in an old-Zürich atmosphere.

Cabaret/Nightclubs There's a variety show (dancers, magicians) at **Polygon** (Marktgasse 17, tel. 01/2521110). There are strip shows all over town, as well as the traditional nightclub atmosphere at **Le Privé** (Stauffacherstr. 106, tel. 01/2416487), **Moulin Rouge** (Mühlegasse 14, tel. 01/2620730), and the slightly more sophisticated **Terrace** (Limmatquai 3, tel. 01/2511074).

Discos **Mascotte** (Theaterstr. 10, tel. 01/2524481) is, at the moment, popular with all ages on weeknights, but caters to young crowds on weekends. **Nautic Club** (Wythenquai 61, tel. 01/2026676) opens onto the lakefront on summer nights. **Le Petit Prince** (Bleicherweg 21, tel. 01/2011739) attracts an upscale crowd. Even more exclusive is **Diagonal,** at the Hotel Baur au Lac (Talstr. 1, tel. 01/2117396), where you must be a hotel guest—or the guest of one.

Jazz **Casa Bar** (Münstergasse 30, tel. 01/2612002) is the exclusive domain of jazz, with music until 2 AM.

Excursion from Zürich: Liechtenstein

For an international day trip out of Zürich, dip a toe into tiny Liechtenstein: There isn't room for much more. Just 80 kilometers (50 miles) southeast on the Austrian border, this miniature principality covers a scant 158 square kilometers (61 square miles). An independent nation since 1719, Liechtenstein has a customs union with Switzerland, which means they share trains, currency, and diplomats—but not stamps, which is why collectors prize the local releases. It's easiest to get there by car, since Liechtenstein is so small that Swiss trains pass through without stopping. If you're using a train pass, ride to Sargans or Buchs and take a postbus across the border to Liechtenstein's capital, Vaduz.

Tourist Information The principal tourist office in Liechtenstein is at Städtle 37, Box 139, FL 9490, Vaduz, tel. 075/2321443. It's open weekdays 8–noon and 1:30–5.

Exploring Liechtenstein Green and mountainous, its Rhineshores lined with vineyards, greater Liechtenstein is best seen by car. But if you're on foot, you won't be stuck: The postbuses are prompt and take you everywhere at a scenic snail's pace.

In fairy-tale **Vaduz**, Prince Johannes Adam Pius still lives in **Vaduz Castle**, a massive 16th-century fortress perched high on the cliff over the city. Only honored guests of the prince tour the interior, but its exterior and the views from the grounds are worth the climb. In the modern center of town, head for the tourist information office to have your passport stamped with the Liechtenstein crown. Upstairs, the **Prince's Art Gallery and the State Art Collection** display Flemish masters. *Städtle 37, tel. 075/2322341. Admission: 3 Fr. adults, 1.5 Fr. children. Open Apr.–Oct., daily 10–noon and 1:30–5:30; Nov.–Mar., daily 10–noon and 1:30–5.*

On the same floor, the **Postage Stamp Museum** attracts philatelists from all over the world to see the 300 frames of beautifully designed—and relatively rare—stamps. Place subscriptions here for future first-day covers. *Städtle 37, tel. 075/2366109. Admission free. Open Apr.–Oct., daily 10–noon and 1:30–5:30; Nov.–Mar., 10–noon and 1:30–5.*

Next, move on to the **Liechtenstein National Museum,** which houses historical artifacts, church carvings, ancient coins, and arms from the prince's collection. *Städtle 43, tel. 075/22310. Admission: 2 Fr. Open May–Sept., daily 10–noon and 1:30–5:30; Oct.–Apr., Tues.–Sun. 2–5:30; may be closed into 1994 for renovations.*

★ In **Schaan,** just north of Vaduz, visit the Roman excavations and the parish church built on the foundations of a Roman fort. Or drive up to the chalets of picturesque **Triesenberg** for spectacular views of the Rhine Valley. Higher still, **Malbun** is a sundrenched ski bowl with comfortable slopes and a low-key family ambience.

Dining For details and price-category definitions, *see* Dining in Staying in Switzerland.

★ **Real.** Surrounded by slick, new decor, you'll find rich, old-style Austrian-French cuisine in all its buttery glory, prepared these days by Martin Real, son of the unpretentious former chef, Felix Real. The menu offers game, seafood, soufflés, and an extraordinary wine list. Downstairs is a more casual stübli. There are a handful of small but fresh decked rooms upstairs, with new tile baths. *Städtle 21, Vaduz, tel. 075/2322222. Reservations advised. Jacket and tie advised upstairs. AE, DC, MC, V. Very Expensive.*

★ **Wirthschaft zum Löwen.** Though there's plenty of French, Swiss, and Austrian influence, Liechtenstein has a cuisine of its own, and this is the place to try it. In a wood-shingled farmhouse on the Austrian border, the friendly Biedermann family serves tender homemade *Schwartenmagen* (the pressed porkmold known unfortunately as headcheese in English), pungent *Sauerkäse* (sour cheese), and *Käseknöpfli* (cheese dumplings), plus lovely meats and the local crusty, chewy bread. *Schellenberg, tel. 075/3731162. Reservations advised. V. Inexpensive.*

Lodging For details and price-category definitions, *see* Lodging in Staying in Switzerland.

Park-Hotel Sonnenhof. A garden oasis commanding a superb view over the valley and mountains beyond, this hillside retreat offers discreet luxury minutes from downtown Vaduz. Some rooms open directly onto the lawns; others have balconies. It has an excellent restaurant exclusive to guests. *Mareestr. 29, tel. 075/2321192, fax 075/2320053. 29 rooms with bath. Facilities: indoor pool, sauna. AE, DC, MC, V. Very Expensive.*

Engel. Directly on the main tourist street, its café bulging with bus-tour crowds, this simple hotel/restaurant manages to maintain a local, comfortable ambience. The Huber family oversees the easygoing pub downstairs; the restaurant upstairs serves Chinese food. The rooms were renovated in winter 1991. *Städtle 13, tel. 075/2320313, fax 075/2331159. 17 rooms with bath. Facilities: restaurant, café, terrace. AE, DC, MC, V. Moderate.*

Alpenhotel. Well above the mists of the Rhine in sunny Malbun, this 82-year-old chalet has been remodeled and a modern wing added. The old rooms are small and cozy; the higher-priced new rooms are modern and spare. The Vögeli family's welcoming smiles and good food have made it a local institution. *Tel. 075/2631181, fax 075/2639646. 25 rooms with bath. Facilities: restaurant, café, indoor pool. AE, DC, MC, V. Inexpensive.*

Geneva

Arriving and Departing

By Plane Cointrin (tel. 022/7993111), Geneva's airport, is served by several airlines that fly directly to the city from New York, Toronto, or London. Swissair also has flights from Chicago and Los Angeles. Check with individual airlines for their schedules.

Swissair ticketholders departing from Cointrin can check their luggage through to the airplane from 120 rail and postal bus stations, and also get their boarding passes at eight train stations.

Between the Airport and Downtown Cointrin has a direct rail link with Cornavin (tel. 022/7316450), the city's main train station, which is located in the center of town. Trains run about every 10 minutes from 5:30 AM to midnight. The trip takes about six minutes, and the fare is 4.40 Fr. for second class.

There is regular city bus service from the airport to the center of Geneva. The bus takes about 20 minutes, and the fare is 2 Fr. Some hotels have their own bus service.

Taxis, though plentiful, are very expensive, charging at least 25 Fr. to the city center.

By Train All services—domestic and international—use Cornavin Station in the center of the city. For information, dial 022/7316450.

By Bus Buses generally arrive at and depart from the bus station at place Dorcière, behind the English church in the city center.

By Car Since Geneva sits on France's doorstep, entry from France, just a few minutes away, is very convenient. Or enter from the north via Lausanne.

Getting Around

By Bus and Streetcar There are scheduled services by local buses and trains every few minutes on all routes. Before you board, you must buy your ticket (2 Fr.) from the machines at the stops (they have English instructions). Save money and buy a ticket covering unlimited travel all day within the city center for 5 Fr. If you have a **Swiss Pass,** you can travel free (*see* Getting Around Switzerland by Train, *above*).

By Taxi Taxis are extremely expensive; use them only if there's no alternative. There is a 5 Fr. minimum charge per passenger just to get into the cab plus a charge of 2 Fr. per kilometer.

Guided Tours

Orientation Tours Bus tours around Geneva are operated by **Key Tours** (tel. 022/7314140). They leave from the bus station in place Dorcière, behind the English church, at 10 and 2. These tours, which involve some walking in the Old Town, last about two hours and cost 24 Fr.

Special-Interest Tours The United Nations organizes tours around the Palais des Nations. Take bus No. 8 or F past Nations to the Appia stop. Enter by the Pregny Gate in the avenue de la Paix. Tours, lasting about an hour, are given regularly from January to March and November to mid-December, weekdays 10–noon and 2–4; April to June, September, and October, daily 10–noon and 2–4; July and August, daily 9–noon and 2–6. They cost 8 Fr. for adults, 3.50 Fr. for children 6–18.

The tourist office will provide you with an audio-guided tour (in English) of the Old Town that covers 26 points of interest, complete with map, cassette, and player; rental is 10 Fr. A refundable deposit of 50 Fr. is required.

Excursions There are bus excursions from Geneva to Lausanne, Montreux, the Mont Blanc area, the Jura, and the Bernese Oberland. They vary considerably according to the weather and time of year, so inquire locally.

Boat excursions vary for the same reasons. When the weather is good, take one of the delightful daylong trips that stop at some of the waterside villages on the vineyard-fringed lake; some trips also pass by or stop at the 13th-century Château de Chillon, the inspiration for Byron's *The Prisoner of Chillon*. Full details are available from **Mouettes Genevoises** (tel. 022/7322944), **Swissboat** (tel. 022/7367935), **Compagnie de Navigation** (tel. 022/3112521), or from the tourist office.

Tourist Information

The **Office du Tourisme de Genève** (Cornavin Station, Case Postale 440, CH-1211, tel. 022/7385200; open July–Sept., daily 8AM–10PM; Oct.–June, Mon.–Sat. 9–6, Sun. 4–8). **Thomas Cook** (64 rue de Lausanne, tel. 022/7324555).

Exploring Geneva

Draped at the foot of the Juras and the Alps on the westernmost tip of Lake Geneva (or Lac Léman, as the natives know it), Geneva is the most cosmopolitan and graceful of Swiss cities and the stronghold of the French-speaking territory. Just a stone's throw from the French border and 160 kilometers (100 miles) or so from Lyon, its grand mansarded mansions stand guard beside the river Rhône, where yachts bob, gulls dive, and Rolls-

Royces purr beside manicured promenades. The combination of Swiss efficiency and French savoir faire gives the city a chic polish, and the infusion of international blood from the United Nations adds a heterogeneity that is rare in cities with a population of only 160,000.

Headquarters of the World Health Organization and the International Red Cross, Geneva has always been a city of humanity and enlightenment, offering refuge to writers Voltaire, Hugo, Dumas, Balzac, and Stendhal, as well as to religious reformers Calvin and Knox. Byron, Shelley, Wagner, and Liszt all fled from scandals to Geneva's sheltering arms.

A Roman seat for 500 years (from 120 BC), then home to early Burgundians, Geneva flourished under bishop-princess into the 11th century, fending off the greedy dukes of Savoy in conflicts that lasted into the 17th century. Under the guiding fervor of Calvin, Geneva rejected Catholicism and became a stronghold of Protestant reforms. In 1798 it fell to the French, but joined the Swiss Confederation as a canton in 1815, shortly after Napoleon's defeat. The French accent remains nonetheless.

Numbers in the margin correspond to points of interest on the Geneva map.

Start your walk from Gare de Cornavin (Cornavin Station) and

❶ head down the rue du Mont-Blanc to the **Pont du Mont-Blanc,** which spans the westernmost point of Lac Léman as it squeezes back into the Rhône. From the middle of the bridge (if it's clear) you can see the snowy peak of Mont Blanc itself, and from March to October you'll have a fine view of the **Jet d'Eau,** Europe's highest fountain, gushing 145 meters (475 feet) into the air.

Back at the foot of the bridge, turn right onto quai du Mont-

❷ Blanc to reach the **Monument Brunswick,** the high-Victorian tomb of a duke of Brunswick who left his fortune to Geneva in 1873. Just north are the city's grandest hotels, overlooking a manicured garden walk and the embarkation points for excursion boats. If you continue north a considerable distance through elegant parks and turn inland on the avenue de la Paix,

❸ you'll reach the enormous **International Complex,** where the **Palais des Nations** houses the European seat of the United Nations. (You can also reach it by taking bus No. 8 or F from the train station. For guided tour information, *see* Special-Interest Tours, *above*.)

Or turn left from the Pont du Mont-Blanc and walk down the

❹ elegant quai des Bergues. In the center of the Rhône is the **Ile Rousseau** (Rousseau Island), with a statue of the Swiss-born

❺ philosopher. Turn left onto the **Pont de l'Ile,** where the tall Tour de l'Ile, once a medieval prison, houses the tourist office. Turn left again and cross the place Bel-Air, the center of the business and banking district, and follow the rue de la Corraterie to the

❻ **place Neuve.** Here you'll see the **Grand Théâtre,** which hosts opera, ballet, and sometimes the Orchestre de la Suisse Romande (it also performs at nearby Victoria Hall), and the **Conservatoire de Musique.** Also at this address is the **Musée Rath,** with top-notch temporary exhibitions. *Tel. 022/3105270. Admission and hours vary with exhibition; check local listings.*

Above the ancient ramparts on your left are some of the wealthiest old homes in Geneva. Enter the gated park before you, the promenade des Bastions, site of the university, and keep left ❼ until you see the famous **Monument de la Réformation,** which pays homage to such Protestant pioneers as Bèze, Calvin, Farel, and Knox. Passing the uphill ramp and continuing to the farther rear gate, take the park exit just beyond the monument and turn left on the rue St-Leger, passing through the ivy-covered arch and winding into the **Vieille Ville,** or Old Town.

When you reach the ancient place du Bourg-de-Four, once a Roman forum, turn right on rue des Chaudronniers and head for ❽ the **Musée d'Art et Histoire,** with its fine collection of paintings, sculpture, and archaeological relics. *2 rue Charles-Galland, tel. 022/3114340. Admission free. Open Tues.–Sun. 10–5.*

❾ Just beyond are the spiraling cupolas of the **Eglise Russe** (Rus-❿ sian Church) and the **Collection Baur** of Oriental arts. *8 rue Munier-Romilly, tel. 022/3461729. Admission: 5 Fr. Open Tues.–Sun. 2–6.*

Alternatively, from the place du Bourg-de-Four, head left up ⓫ any number of narrow streets and stairs toward the **Cathédrale St-Pierre,** with its schizophrenic mix of Classical and Gothic styles. Under its nave (entrance outside) is concealed one of the biggest **archaeological digs** in Europe, a massive excavation of the cathedral's early Christian predecessors, now restored as a stunning maze of backlit walkways over mosaics, baptisteries, and ancient foundations. *Tel. 022/7385650. Admission to site: 5 Fr. Open Tues.–Sun. 10–1 and 2–6.*

⓬ Calvin worshiped in the cathedral; he made the **Temple de l'Auditoire,** a small Gothic church just south of the cathedral toward place du Bourg-de-Four, into his lecture hall, where he taught missionaries his doctrines of reform. *Place de la Taconnerie, tel. 022/738–5650. Open Oct.–May, weekdays 9–noon and 2–5, Sat. 9:30–12:30 and 2–5, Sun. 2–5; June–Sept., weekdays 9–noon and 2–6, Sat. 9:30–12:30 and 2–6, Sun. 2–6. English-speaking hostess available Sun. and Mon.*

Behind the Temple de l'Auditoire, on the rue de l'Hôtel de ⓭ Ville, is the 16th-century **Hôtel de Ville,** where in 1864, in the Alabama Hall, the Geneva Convention was signed by 16 countries, laying the foundations for the International Red Cross. *Individual visits by request. Guided group tours by advance arrangement, tel. 022/3272202.*

The winding, cobbled streets leading from the cathedral down to the modern city are lined with antiques shops, galleries, and unique but often expensive boutiques. The medieval Grand' Rue is the oldest in Geneva, the rue de l'Hôtel de Ville features lovely 17th-century homes, and the rue Calvin has noble mansions of the 18th century (No. 11 is on the site of Jean Calvin's house). No. 6 on the rue du Puits-St-Pierre is the ⓮ **Maison Tavel,** the oldest building in town and home of an intimate re-creation of daily life and urban history. *Tel. 022/3102900. Admission free. Open Tues.–Sun. 10–5.*

Down the hill, plunge back into the new city and one of the most luxurious shopping districts in Europe, which stretches temptingly between the quai Général-Guisan, rue du Rhône, rue de la Croix d'Or, and rue du Marché. It's tough enough to resist top name *prêt-à-porter* (ready-to-wear clothing), dazzling jewelry

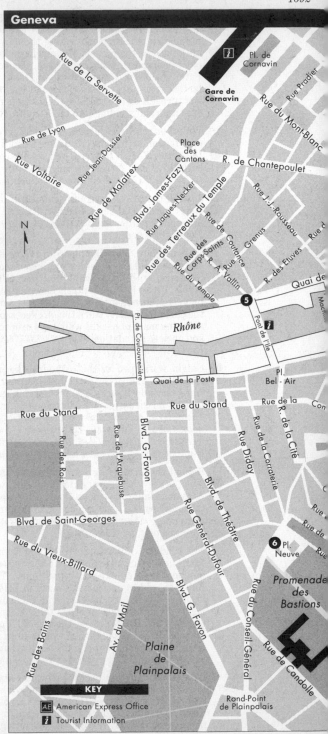

Geneva

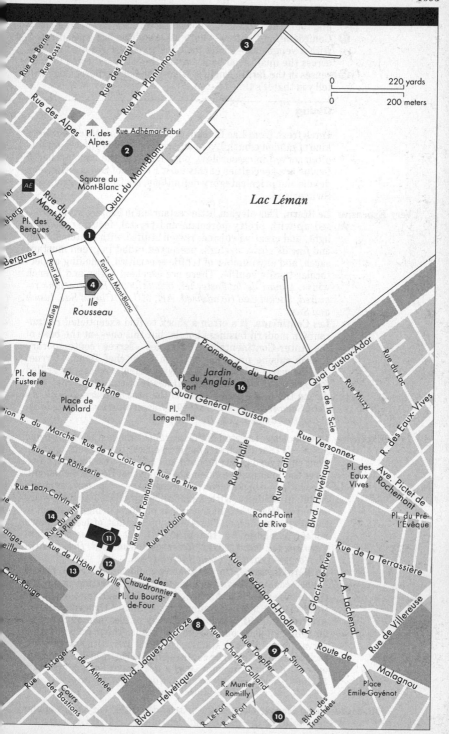

Lac Léman

0   220 yards
0   200 meters

Rue de Berne
Rue Rossi
Rue des Pâquis
Rue Ph. Plantamour
Rue des Alpes
Pl. des Alpes
Rue Adhémar-Fabri
Quai du Mont-Blanc
Square du Mont-Blanc
Rue du Mont-Blanc
AE
Pl. des Bergues
Bergues
Pont des Bergues
Pont du Mont-Blanc
Ile Rousseau
Pl. de la Fusterie
Rue du Rhône
Place de Molard
R. du Marché
Rue de la Rôtisserie
Rue de la Croix d'Or
Rue de Rive
Rue Jean-Calvin
Rue du Puits-St-Pierre
Rue de la Fontaine
Rue Verdaine
Rue de l'Hôtel-de-Ville
Rue des Chaudronniers
Pl. du Bourg-de-Four
Croix-Rouge
St-Léger
R. de l'Athénée
Blvd. Jaques-Dalcroze
Blvd. Helvétique
Rue Charles-Galland
R. Munier-Romilly
R. Le-Fort
R. Le-Fort
Cours des Bastions
Rue du Port
Jardin Anglais
Quai Général - Guisan
Pl. Longemalle
Promenade du Lac
Quai Gustav-Ador
Rue du Lac
Rue Muzy
R. de la Scie
R. des Eaux-Vives
Rue Versonnex
Rue d'Italie
Rue P.-Fatio
Blvd. Helvétique
Pl. des Eaux Vives
Ave. Pictet de Rochemont
Pl. du Pré-l'Évêque
Rond-Point de Rive
Rue de la Terrassière
R. A. Lachenal
Rue Ferdinand-Hodler
R. d. Glacis-de-Rive
Rue de Villereuse
Rue Toepffer
R. Sturm
Route de
Malagnou
Place Emile-Gayénot
Blvd. des Tranchées

1
2
3
4
8
9
10
11
12
13
14
16

and watches, luscious chocolates, and luxurious furs and leathers, but the glittering boutiques of the new three-story ⑮ **Confédération-Centre**—where all the above are concentrated with a vengeance—could melt the strongest resolve. Escape across the quai, head back toward the lake, and come to your ⑯ senses in the **Jardin Anglais,** where the famous floral clock will tell you that it's time to stop.

Dining

Perch fresh from Lac Léman, cream-sauced *omble chevalier* (a kind of salmon trout), Lyonnaise *cardon* (a celerylike vegetable often served in casseroles), pigs' feet, and the famous cheese fondue are specialties of this most French of Swiss cities. For details and price-category definitions, *see* Dining in Staying in Switzerland.

Very Expensive **Le Béarn.** This elegant little restaurant in Empire style, dressed up with pretty porcelain and crystal, features modern, ★ light, and creative cuisine: ravioli stuffed with Scotch salmon and *fine de claire* oysters, preserved rabbit in green mustard sauce, and any number of truffle specialties, including a spectacular truffle soufflé. There are excellent Swiss and French wines. *4 quai de la Poste, tel. 022/3210028. Reservations required. Jacket and tie advised. AE, MC, V. Closed Sat. lunch and Sun.*

Les Continents. It's often a shock to find exceptional restaurants in modern business hotels, but this one—at the base of the Inter-Continental's 18 stories—serves contemporary French cuisine prepared by Irish super-chef Tommy Byrne. Try the warm salad of scallops with Oriental spices, or grilled foie gras. All the international heads of state have met here during the peace conferences of the past 25 years. *7–9 ch. du Petit-Saconnex, tel. 022/7346091. Reservations required. Jacket and tie advised. AE, DC, MC, V.*

Expensive **La Cassolette.** Located in the heart of Carouge, the picturesque ★ *cité sarde* (Sardinian city) of old houses, tiny streets, and ancient courtyards, this modern and colorful upscale bistro features the imaginative cuisine of young chef Réné Fracheboud. Specialties—chicken livers in orange sauce on pastry, or boned rabbit in Madeira with sweet-and-sour glazed turnips—are served on Miami-bright triangular platters, in high contrast to the very pink decor. There's an unusual list of lesser-known wines, available by the glass. *31 rue Jacques Dalphin, Carouge, tel. 022/3420318. Reservations advised. Dress: casual. No credit cards. Closed Sat. and Sun.*

La Mère Royaume. Only in Geneva could you find good, classic French cooking served in a pseudo-historic setting under the careful direction of a charming Italian couple. Even the name is Genevois: La Mère Royaume was a kind of Genevois Joan of Arc, who in 1691 repulsed the army of the duke of Savoy by dumping hot soup on the soldiers' heads. The main restaurant serves formal French standards—duck liver with raspberries, rack of lamb with garlic confit—but the rustic bistro offers inexpensive plats du jour. *9 rue des Corps-Saints, tel. 022/7327008. Reservations advised. Jacket and tie advised. AE, DC, MC, V. Closed Sat. lunch and Sun.*

Moderate **Boeuf Rouge.** Despite its kitschy decor this cozy and popular ★ spot delivers the real thing: rich, unadulterated Lyon cuisine, from the bacon, egg, and greens *salade Lyonnaise* to the homemade *boudin blanc*, a delicate, pistachio-studded white sausage in morel cream sauce. There's sausage with lentils, too, and duck pâté served with a crock of *cornichons*, and authentic *tarte tatin*. *17 rue Alfred-Vincent, tel. 022/7327537. Reservations advised. Dress: casual. V. Closed weekends.*

★ **La Favola.** Run by a young Ticinese couple from Locarno, this quirky little restaurant may be the most picturesque in town. The tiny dining room, at the top of a vertiginous spiral staircase, strikes a delicate balance between rustic and fussy, with its lace window panels, embroidered cloths, polished parquet, and rough-beamed ceiling sponge-painted in Roman shades of ochre and rust. The food finds the same delicate balance between country simple and city chic: carpaccio with olive paste or white truffles, ravioli of duck à l'orange. *15 rue Jean Calvin, tel. 022/3117437. Reservations advised. Dress: casual. No credit cards. Closed weekends.*

Le Pied-de-Cochon. While visiting antiques shops and art galleries in the Vielle Ville, stop for lunch or supper in this old bistro, which retains its original beams and zinc-top bar. Crowded, noisy, smoky, lively, it faces the Palais de Justice and shelters famous lawyers who plead celebrated causes; there are artists and workers as well. The good, simple fare includes *pieds de cochon* (pigs' feet), of course, either grilled, with mushrooms, with lentils, or *dessossés* (boned), as well as simple Lyonnais dishes, including *petit salé* (pork belly), ham, grilled *andouillettes* (little pork sausages), tripe, and salads. *4 place du Bourg-de-Four, tel. 022/3104797. Reservations advised. Dress: casual. AE, DC, MC, V. Closed weekends.*

Inexpensive
★ **Les Armures.** In the picturesque and historic hotel at the summit of the Old Town (*see Lodging, below*) and two steps from the Cathédrale St-Pierre, this atmospheric restaurant offers several dining halls, all decorated with authentic arms from the Middle Ages. The broad menu of Swiss specialties ranges from fondue to *choucroute* to *Rösti*, but some of the dishes are pure Genevois. There also are inexpensive pizzas and a good selection of salads. Everyone comes here, from workers to politicians—Jimmy Carter adored the place on his last visit. *1 rue du Puits-St-Pierre, tel. 022/3103442. Reservations advised. Dress: casual. AE, DC, MC, V.*

★ **Taverne de la Madeleine.** Tucked into the commercial maze between the Rue de la Croix d'Or and the Old Town, by l'Eglise de la Madeleine, this casual, alcohol-free café claims to be the oldest eatery in Geneva. It's run by the city's temperance league, and thus loses the business clientele that insist on a pitcher of Fendant with their meals: All the more room for you to relax over homemade *choucroute*, perch, or fresh-baked fruit tarts in the charming Victorian upstairs dining room. There are big, fresh salads, vegetable plates, and a variety of loose-leaf teas. *20 rue Toutes-âmes, tel. 022/3106070. Reservations advised. Dress: casual. No credit cards.*

Lodging

For details and price-category definitions, *see* Lodging in Staying in Switzerland.

Very Expensive **Beau-Rivage.** Hushed and genteel, this grand old Victorian palace has been largely restored to its 1865 splendor: It's all velvet, parquet, and frescoes, and there's a marble fountain in the lobby. Front rooms take in magnificent Right Bank views, as does the terrace restaurant on the first floor, over the prestigious French restaurant Le Chat Botté. In 1898, Empress Elizabeth of Austria died here after being shot only 100 meters away. *13 quai du Mont-Blanc, CH-1201, tel. 022/7310221, fax 022/7389847. 115 rooms with bath. Facilities: two restaurants, terrace café, bar, video. AE, DC, MC, V.*

★ **Le Richemond.** Under the management of the Armleder family since 1875, this Right Bank landmark maintains its Victorian presence without looking like a museum. Nor does it feel like one: This is a lively, thriving, contemporary inn, proud of recent guests (Michael Jackson) as well as past ones (Colette, Miró, Chagall). Only the restaurant Le Gentilhomme indulges in museumlike conservatism: Amid pompous red velvet, crystal, and gilt, you can indulge in a meal Escoffier would have relished. There's classic but showy French cuisine, old wines, brandy, cigars, and your share of the 8 kilos of caviar they serve a day. *Jardin Brunswick, CH-1211, tel. 022/7311400, fax 022/7316709. 98 rooms with bath. Facilities: two restaurants, bar, terrace café, hairdresser. AE, DC, MC, V.*

Expensive **Les Armures.** In the heart of the Vielle Ville, this archaeological treasure has been restored to 17th-century splendor, and its charming original stonework, frescoes, and stenciled beams accompany impeccable modern comforts. Its few rooms are intimate, combining appropriate Old World furnishings with slick marble baths. Its casual restaurant is an Old Town must (*see* Dining, *above*). Approach by car can be difficult. *1 rue du Puits-St-Pierre, tel. 022/3109172, fax 022/3109846. 28 rooms with bath. Facilities: restaurant, bar, VCR. AE, DC, MC, V.*

★ **Metropole.** Built in 1855, lent to the city of Geneva to house Red Cross archives for prisoners of war and now lovingly restored by its management of 27 years, the Metropole has as much riverside splendor as its Right Bank sisters—at a lower price. There's a relaxed, unfussy ambience despite the grand scale, with leather and hunting prints mixed in with discreet pastels. Riverside rooms are noisier, over traffic, but the view compensates; ask for the quieter third or fourth floors. It's seconds from the best shopping and minutes from the Old Town. *34 quai Général-Guisan, tel. 022/2111344, fax 022/3111350. 140 rooms with bath. Facilities: two restaurants, terrace café, bar. AE, DC, MC, V.*

Moderate **Strasbourg-Univers.** A stylish oasis in the slightly sleazy train-station neighborhood, this just-renovated spot offers sleek decor, convenience, and four-star quality at a three-star price. The new look is marble and faux exotic wood; a few older, less flashy rooms, redone eight years ago, still don't show the wear. *10 rue Pradier, tel. 022/7322562, fax 022/7384208. 58 rooms with bath or shower. AE, DC, MC, V.*

★ **Touring-Balance.** The lower floors are tired but gracious, with French doors and a chic new paint job; ask to stay in the slick, solid high-tech rooms on the higher floors. There are gallery-quality lithos in every room. *13 pl. Longemalle, tel. 022/287122, fax 022/3104045. 64 rooms with bath. Facilities: restaurant, café. AE, DC, MC, V.*

Inexpensive **De la Cloche.** This once luxurious walk-up flat has tidy, tasteful
★ new decor that hasn't altered its period details, and the courtyard setting is so quiet you can hear birds in the garden. Good-size rooms with high ceilings share baths down the hall. The

prices are still the lowest in town. *6 rue de la Cloche, tel. 022/ 7329481. 8 rooms without shower.*

Des Tourelles. Once worthy of a czar, now host to the backpacking crowd, this fading Victorian offers enormous bay-windowed corner rooms, many with marble fireplaces, French doors, and views over the Rhône. The furnishings are sparse and strictly functional, but the staff is young and friendly. Bring earplugs: The location is extremely noisy, over roaring bridge traffic. *2 blvd. James-Fazy, tel. 022/7324423, fax 022/ 7327620. 25 rooms, some with shower. AE, DC, MC, V.*

Luzern

Arriving and Departing

By Plane   The nearest international airport is **Kloten** in **Zürich,** approximately 54 kilometers (33 miles) from Luzern. **Swissair** flies in most often from the United States and the United Kingdom. Easy rail connections, departing hourly, whisk you on to Luzern within 50 minutes.

By Car   It's easy to reach Luzern from Zürich by road, approaching from national expressway N3 south, connecting to N4 via the secondary E41, in the direction of Zug, and continuing on N4 to the city. Approaching from the southern, St. Gotthard Pass route, or after cutting through the Furka Pass by rail ferry, you descend below Andermatt to Altdorf, where a view-stifling tunnel sweeps you through to the shores of the lake and on to the city. Arriving from Basel in the northwest, it's a clean sweep by N2 into Luzern.

By Train   Luzern functions as a rail crossroads, with express trains connecting hourly from Zürich and every two hours from Geneva, the latter with a change at Bern. For rail information, call the station (tel. 041/213111).

Getting Around

Luzern's modest scale allows you to explore most of the city easily on foot, but you will want to resort to mass transit to visit far-flung attractions like the Verkehrshaus (Transit Museum) and nearby Alpine viewpoints.

By Bus   The city bus system offers easy access throughout the urban area. If you're staying in a Luzern hotel, you will be eligible for a special **Guest-Ticket,** offering unlimited rides for two days for a minimal fee of 5 Fr.

By Taxi   Given the small scale of the old town and the narrowness of most of its streets, taxis can prove a pricey encumbrance.

By Boat   It's a crime to see this city and the surrounding mountainous region only from the shore; some of its most impressive landscapes can be seen from the decks of one of the cruise ships that ply the Vierwaldstättersee (Lake Lucerne). The boats of the Schiffahrtsgesellschaft des Vierwaldstättersee (tel. 041/ 404540) operate on a standardized, mass-transit-style schedule, criss-crossing the lake and stopping at scenic resorts and historic sites. Rides are included in a Swiss Pass or Swiss Boat Pass.

Important Addresses and Numbers

Tourist Information
The city tourist office, near the Bahnhof (Frankenstrasse 1, tel. 041/517171), offers information April–October, weekdays 8:30–6, Saturday 9–5, Sunday 9–1; and November–March, weekdays 8:30–noon and 2–6, Saturday 9–1. There is also an accommodations service.

Emergencies
Police (tel. 117). **Medical, dental, and pharmacy referral** (tel. 111). **Auto breakdown:** Tourist Club of Switzerland (tel. 140), **Swiss Automobile Club** (tel. 041/231000).

Guided Tours

Orientation Tours
The Luzern tourist office offers a two-hour guided walking tour of Luzern, departing from the office daily at 10; from May through September, there are 4 PM tours as well. The 12 Fr. price includes a drink.

Excursions
You may want to take a high-altitude day trip to **Mount Pilatus, Mount Rigi,** or—if you're bound for the highest—the **Titlis,** above Engelberg. All can be accomplished by combination train and cograil travel, though to mount the Titlis you must complete the journey by a series of cablecar rides. For information, check at the Central Switzerland regional tourist office (Vehkehrsverband Zentralschweiz, Alpenstr. 1, Luzern, tel. 041/511891) or at the city tourist office. Boat and bus trips to William Tell country—**Altdorf** and **Bürglen**—make the most of both scenery and local legend.

Exploring Luzern

Where the River Reuss flows out of the Vierwaldstättersee, Luzern's old town straddles the narrowed waters with the greater concentration of city life lying on the river's right bank. To get a feel for this riverfront center, start at the right-bank end of the prominent **Kapellbrücke,** with its flanking water tower. Stay on this side for the moment and head down the **Rathausquai,** lined with hotels and cafés on the right, a sloping reinforced bank on the left. Facing the end of a modern bridge (the Rathaus-Steg) stands the **Altes Rathaus** (Old Town Hall), built between 1599 and 1606 in the late-Renaissance style.

Numbers in the margin correspond to points of interest on the Luzern map.

1 Just to the right of the Rathaus, the **Am Rhyn-Haus** (Am Rhyn House) contains an impressive collection of late paintings by Picasso. *Furrengasse, tel. 041/511773. Admission: 5 Fr. adults, 3 Fr. students. Open daily 11–1 and 2–4.*

Turn right and climb the stairs past the ornately frescoed **Zunfthaus zu Pfistern,** a guild hall dating from the late 15th and early 16th century, to the Kornmarkt, former site of the local grain market. Cross the square and cut left into the **Weinmarkt,** the loveliest of Luzern's several squares. Its Gothic central fountain depicts St. Mauritius, patron saint of warriors, and its surrounding buildings are flamboyantly frescoed in 16th-century style.

2 Leave the square from its west end, turn right on Kramgasse, and cross the Mühlenplatz to the **Spreuerbrücke,** a narrow, weathered all-wood covered bridge dating from 1408. Its inte-

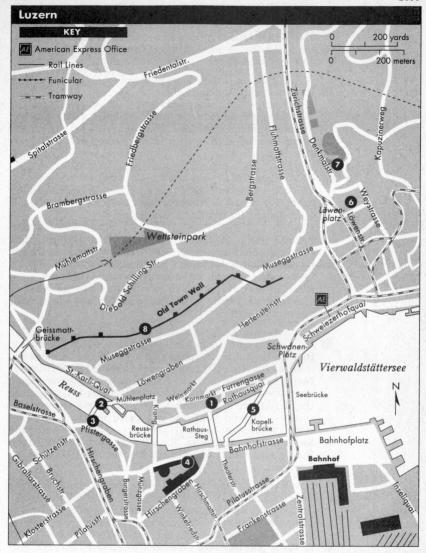

Luzern

KEY

- **AE** American Express Office
- —— Rail Lines
- •••• Funicular
- —=— Tramway

Friedentalstr.

Spitalstrasse

Friedbergstrasse

Brambergstrasse

Mühlemattstr.

Wettsteinpark

Diebold Schilling-Str.

Bergstrasse

Fluhmattstrasse

Zürichstrasse

Denkmalstr.

Kapuzinerweg

7

6 *Löwen-platz*

Weystrasse

Löwenstr.

Museggstrasse

Old Town Wall

Geissmatt-brücke

8

Museggstrasse

St.-Karli-Quai

Reuss

Baselstrasse

2

Mühlenplatz

3

Pfistergasse

Reuss-brücke

Kramg.

Löwengraben

Weinmarkt

Kornmarkt

Furrengasse

1

Rathausquai

Rathaus-Steg

Hertensteinstr.

AE

Schweizerhofquai

Schwanen-Platz

Vierwaldstättersee

5

Kapell-brücke

Seebrücke

N

Schützenstr.

Gibraltarstrasse

Bruchstr.

Hirschengraben

Burgerstrasse

Münzgasse

4

Hirschengraben

Hirschmattstr.

Theaterstr.

Bahnhofstrasse

Pilatusstrasse

Zentralstrasse

Bahnhofplatz

Bahnhof

Inseliquai

Klosterstrasse

Pilatusstr.

Winkelriedstr.

Frankenstrasse

Am Rhyn-Haus, **1**
Bourbaki-Panorama, **6**
Historisches
Museum, **3**
Jesuitenkirche, **4**
Kapellbrücke, **5**

Löwendenkmal, **7**
Spreuerbrücke, **2**
Zytturm, **8**

rior gables frame a series of eerie, well-preserved paintings (by Kaspar Meglinger) of the Dance of Death; they date from the 17th century, though their style and inspiration—tracing to the plague that devastated Luzern and all of Europe in the 14th century—is medieval.

At the other end of the bridge, on the left bank, stands the stylish **Historisches Museum** (Historical Museum). Its exhibitions of city sculptures, Swiss arms and flags, and reconstructed rooms depict rural and urban life. The late-Gothic building was an armory, dating from 1567. *Pfistergasse 24, tel. 041/245424. Admission: 4 Fr. Open Tues.–Fri. 10–noon and 2–5, weekends 10–5.*

Time Out   Follow Baselstrasse west to a funicular that carries you up (3 Fr.) to the **Château Gütsch,** where you can have a drink on the panoramic terrace and take in a bird's-eye view of the old town, the river, and the fortification walls.

From the end of the Spreuerbrücke, cut back upstream along Pfistergasse and turn left onto Bahnhofstrasse to reach the Baroque **Jesuitenkirche** (Jesuit Church), constructed 1667–78. Its symmetrical entrance is flanked by two onion-domed towers, added in 1893. Do not fail to go inside: Its vast interior, restored to mint condition, is a rococo explosion of gilt, marble, and epic frescoes.

Continue past the Rathaus-Steg bridge, but before you enter the **Kapellbrücke** (Chapel Bridge), take a look at its exterior from the right. It snakes diagonally across the water and, when it was built in the early 14th century, served as the division between the lake and the river. Its shingled roof and grand stone water tower (now housing a souvenir stand) are to Luzern what the Matterhorn is to Zermatt. Walk the length of this dark, creaky landmark; you'll see 112 gable panels, painted by Heinrich Wägmann in the 17th century, depicting Luzern and Swiss history, stories of St. Leodegar and St. Mauritius, Luzern's patron saints, and coats of arms from local patrician families.

Now break away from the old town and work through thick pedestrian and bus traffic at Schwanenplatz to Haldenstrasse. Turn left on Zürichstrasse or Löwenstrasse and continue to **Löwenplatz,** which is dominated by an enormous conical wooden structure, like a remnant of a Victorian world's fair. That's its spirit: The **Bourbaki-Panorama** was created between 1876 and 1878 as a genuine, step-right-up tourist attraction: The conical roof covers a sweeping, wraparound epic painting of the French Army of the East retreating into Switzerland at Verrières—a famous episode in the Franco-Prussian War. *Löwenpl., tel. 041/529942. Admission: 3 Fr. Open May–Sept., daily 9–6; Mar.–Apr. and Oct., daily 9–5.*

Just beyond lies yet another 19th-century wonder, a Luzern landmark that is certainly one of the world's most evocative public sculptures: the **Löwendenkmal** (Lion Monument). Designed by Danish sculptor Berthel Thorwaldsen and carved out of a sheer sandstone face by Lucas Ahorn of Konstanz, it's a simple image of a dying lion, his chin sagging on his shield, a broken stump of spear in his side. It commemorates the 760 Swiss guards and their officers who died defending Louis XVI of France at the Tuileries in Paris in 1792. The Latin inscription translates: "To the bravery and fidelity of the Swiss."

Return down Löwenstrasse and, at Löwenplatz, turn right on Museggstrasse. This long street cuts through an original city gate and runs parallel to the **watchtowers** and **crenellated walls** of old Luzern, constructed around 1400. The clock in the **Zytturm,** the fourth of the towers, was made in Basel in 1385 and still keeps time.

❽

Off the Beaten Track

Not easily included in a walking tour of central Luzern but one of the city's (if not Switzerland's) greater attractions, the **Verkehrshaus** (Swiss Transport Museum) can be reached by steamer, car, or city bus. It's almost a world's fair in itself, with a complex of buildings and exhibitions both indoors and out, including dioramas, live demonstrations, and a "Swissorama" (360-degree screen) film about Switzerland. Every mode of transit is discussed, from stagecoaches and bicycles to jumbo jets and space capsules. *Lidostr. 5, tel. 041/314444. Admission: 15 Fr. adults, 8 Fr. children under 16. Open Mar.–Oct., daily 9–6; Nov.–Feb., weekdays 10–4, Sun. 10–5.*

Shopping

Luzern offers a good concentration of general Swiss goods: At **Sturzenegger** (Schwanenpl. 7, tel. 041/511958), you'll find fine St.-Gallen-made linens and embroidered niceties; at **Mühlebach & Birrer** (Kapellpl., tel. 041/516673) there's a selection of Alpen-style (although Austrian-made) Geiger clothing (boiled-wool jackets, edelweiss-embroidered sweaters) as well as Swiss-made handkerchiefs. **Schmid-Linder** (Denkmalstr. 9, tel. 041/514346) sells a comprehensive line of Swiss kitsch: cuckoo clocks, cowbells, embroidery, and a large stock of wood carvings from Brienz, in the Berner Oberland. **Innerschweizer Heimatwerk** (Franziskanerpl. 14, tel. 041/236944) sells nothing but goods—most of them contemporary rather than traditional—made in the region by independent craftspeople, from handweaving to ceramics and wooden toys. Watch dealers are unusually competitive, and the two enormous patriarchs of the business—**Gübelin** (Schweizerhofquai, tel. 041/515142) and **Bucherer** (Schwanenpl., tel. 041/437700) advertise heavily and offer inexpensive souvenirs to lure shoppers into their luxurious showrooms. Gübelin is the exclusive source for Audemars Piguet, Patek Philippe, and its own house brand; Bucherer represents Piaget and Rolex. An abundance of small shops carry Tissot, Rado, Corum, and others—but prices are controlled by the manufacturer, and discounts are rare. Watch for closeouts on out-of-date models.

Dining

Rooted in the German territory of Switzerland and the surrounding farmlands, Central Switzerland's native cuisine is down-home and hearty. Luzern takes pride in its *Kügelipaschtetli,* puffed pastry nests filled with tiny veal meatballs, mushrooms, cream sauce, occasionally raisins, and bits of chicken, pork, or sweetbreads. Watch for lake fish such as *Egli* (perch), *Hecht* (pike), *Forellen* (trout), and *Felchen* (whitefish).

Though most often served baked or fried, a Luzern tradition offers them sautéed and sauced with tomatoes, mushrooms, and capers. After your meal here, have a steaming mug of coffee laced with *Träsch*, a harsh schnapps blended from the dregs of other eaux-de-vie; the locals leave their spoon in the cup as they drink.

Moderate–
Very Expensive
★

La Vague (Hotel des Balances). This chic restaurant/bistro offers a combination as desirable as it is rare: soigné decor, a shimmering riverside view, and adventurous, worldly, cuisine that features local fish. A standing fixed-price "menu de poissons du lac" may offer crayfish soup, grilled omble chevalier (a kind of salmon-trout) in vegetable vinaigrette, and steamed perch in chive butter. A house specialty is light, fresh fish fondue for two. *Weinmarkt, tel. 041/511851. Reservations advised. Dress: casual in bistro, jacket advised in restaurant. AE, DC, MC, V. Restaurant: Very Expensive. Bistro: Moderate.*

Expensive
★

Wilden Mann. You may choose the ancient original tavern, all dark beams and family crests, its origins as a rest-stop for St. Gotthard travelers traced back to 1517; or you may opt for the more formal adjoining Liedertafel restaurant, with wainscoting, vaulting, and candlelight. On either side, the menu and prices are the same—and the cooking is outstanding. *Bahnhofstr. 30, tel. 041/231666. Reservations advised. Dress: casual in Burgerstube, jacket and tie advised in Liedertafel. AE, DC, MC, V.*

Moderate
★

Galliker. Step past the ancient façade into an all-wood room roaring with local action, where Luzerners drink, smoke, and bask in their culinary roots. Brisk, motherly waitresses serve the dishes Mutti used to make: Fresh *Kutteln* (tripe) in rich white wine sauce with cumin seeds; real *Kalbskopf* (chopped fresh veal head) served with heaps of green onions and warm vinaigrette; authentic Luzerner *Kügelipastetli;* and their famous simmered-beef, pot-au-feu, served only on Tuesday, Wednesday, and Saturday. *Schützenstr. 1, tel. 041/221002. Reservations advised. Dress: casual. AE, MC, V. Closed Sun. and Mon., mid-July–mid-Aug.*

Rebstock/Hofstube. At the opposite end of the culinary spectrum from Galliker, this up-to-date kitchen offers modern, international fare, including rabbit, lamb, oriental, and vegetarian specialties. The lively bentwood brasserie hums with locals lunching by the bar, while the more formal, old-style restaurant glows with wood and brass under a low-beamed herringbone ceiling. *St.-Leodegarstr. 3, tel. 041/513581. Reservations advised. Dress: casual. AE, DC, MC, V.*

Inexpensive

Zur Pfistern. One of the architectural focal points of the old town waterfront, this floridly decorated old guildhouse—its origins trace back to 1341—offers a good selection of moderate meals in addition to higher-priced standards. Lake fish and *pastetli* (meat pies made with puffed pastry) are good local options. In summer the small first-floor balcony may provide the best seat in town for a postcard waterfront view. *Kornmarkt 4, tel. 041/513650. Reservations not necessary. Dress: casual. AE, DC, MC, V.*

Lodging

Luzern provides a convenient home base for excursions around the Vierwaldstättersee and all over the region. Unlike most Swiss cities, Luzern has high and low seasons, and drops prices considerably in winter.

Very Expensive **National.** Founded in 1870 and once home base to gastronomic kings Cesar Ritz and August Escoffier, the hotel dominates the lakeside promenade—its mansarded facade stretches the length of two city blocks. The service matches the scale. Rooms are French provincial with brass beds, the domed bar is decked with mahogany and crystal, and the marble-columned breakfast hall is splendid. *Haldenstr. 4, tel. 041/501111, fax 041/515539. 130 rooms. Facilities: restaurant, indoor pool, sauna, fitness center, solarium. AE, DC, MC, V.*

Palace. Brilliantly refurbished and subtly modernized to take in broader lake views, the Palace sports a classic look with a touch of postmodern. Built in 1906 to share the waterfront with the National, it's lighter, airier, and altogether sleek. *Haldenstr. 10, tel. 041/502222, fax 041/516976. 296 rooms. Facilities: restaurant, bar, terrace, 2 saunas, steam bath, solarium, fitness center, parking. AE, DC, MC, V.*

Expensive **Chateau Gütsch.** Any antiquity in this "castle" built as a hotel in 1888 is strictly contrived, but honeymooners, groups, and determined romantics seeking out storybook Europe enjoy the Disneyland-like experience: the turrets and towers worthy of Mad Ludwig of Bavaria, the cellars, crypts, and corridors lined with a hodgepodge of relics, not to mention the magnificent hilltop site above Luzern, once a lookout point. Rooms are decked out for romance as well, with different themes and schemes, and several four-poster canopy beds. *Kanonenstr., tel. 041/220272, fax 041/220252. 120 rooms. Facilities: restaurant, terrace, outdoor pool, private forest. AE, DC, MC, V.*

★ **Des Balances.** Restored and renewed, outside and in, this riverfront property built in the 19th century on the site of an ancient guildhouse gleams with style. State-of-the-art tile baths, up-to-date pastel decor, and one of the best sites in town make this the slickest in its price class. Nearly every window frames a period scene outdoors. *Metzgerrainle 7, tel. 041/511851, fax 041/516451. 100 rooms. Facilities: 2 restaurants, piano bar, riverfront balcony. AE, DC, MC, V.*

★ **Wilden Mann.** Living up to its reputation, the city's best-known hotel offers its guests a gracious and authentic experience of Old Luzern. Joining several old houses that once were part of the town wall, the structure has been renewed to maintain its Reformation ambience, with stone, beams, brass, hand-painted tiles, and burnished wood everywhere. Standard rooms have a prim 19th-century look. *Bahnhofstr. 30, tel. 041/231666, fax 041/231629. 80 rooms. Facilities: 2 restaurants. AE, DC, MC, V.*

Moderate **Des Alpes.** With a terrific riverfront location in the bustling heart of the old town, this historic hotel has been completely renovated inside to look like a laminate-and-vinyl chain motel. Rooms are generously proportioned, tidy, and sleek; front doubles, several with balconies, overlook the water and promenade. Cheaper back rooms face the old town. *Rathausquai 5, tel. 041/515825, fax 041/517451. 80 rooms. Facilities: restaurant, terrace café. AE, DC, MC, V.*

★ **Zum Weissen Kreuz.** Now renovated and upgraded, this former bargain hotel on the waterfront is slick, bright, and airtight, with tile, stucco, oak, and pine to soften the modern edges. Some rooms face the lake, others the old town. *Furrengasse 19, tel. 041/514040, fax 041/514060. 51 rooms. AE, DC, MC, V.*

Inexpensive **Schlüssel.** On the Franziskanerplatz, with several rooms overlooking the Franciscan church and fountain, this spare, no-nonsense little lodging attracts young bargain hunters. It's a pleasant combination of tidy new touches (quarry tile, white paint) and antiquity: You can have breakfast in a low, crossvaulted "crypt" and admire the fine old lobby beams. *Franziskanerpl. 12, tel. 041/231061. 20 rooms. Facilities: breakfast room. MC, V.*

★ **SSR Touristen.** Despite its friendly collegiate atmosphere, this cheery dormlike spot is anything but a backpackers' flophouse. It has a terrific setting on the Reuss, around the corner from the old town. Rooms are available with or without bath. *St. Karliquai, tel. 041/512474, fax 041/528414. 100 beds. AE, DC, MC, V.*

The Arts

Luzern hosts the **International Music Festival** for three weeks in August every year. Performances take place at the **Kunsthaus** (Frohburgstr. 6, tel. 041/233880). For more information, contact International Musikfestwochen (Postfach, CH-6002, Luzern, tel. 041/235272). The **Allgemeine Musikgesellschaft Luzern** (AML), the local orchestra in residence, offers a season of concerts from October through June, also in the Kunsthaus.

Nightlife

Bars and Lounges **Des Balances** hotel has a hip, upscale piano bar (Metzgerrainle 7, tel. 041/511851), and **Château Gütsch** *(Kanonenstrasse)* draws a sedate dinner-and-dancing crowd. **Mr. Pickwick** (Rathausquai 6, tel. 041/515927) is a Swiss version of an English pub.

Casinos The most sophisticated nightlife in Luzern is found in the **Casino** (Haldenstr. 6, tel. 041/512751), on the northern shore by the grand hotels. You can play boule in the Gambling Room (5 Fr. federally-imposed betting limit), dance in the **Babilonia** club, watch a strip show in the **Red Rose,** or have a Swiss meal in **Le Chalet** while watching a folklore display.

Discos **Flora Club** (Seidenhofstr. 5, tel. 041/244444) mixes dancing with folklore shows.

Lugano

Arriving and Departing

By Plane There are short connecting flights by **Crossair**—the Swiss domestic network—to Lugano Airport (tel. 091/505001) from Zürich, Geneva, Basel, and Bern, as well as from Paris, Nice, Rome, Florence, and Venice. The nearest intercontinental airport is at Milan, Italy, about 56 kilometers (35 miles) away.

Between the Airport and Downtown There is no longer a regular bus service between the local airport and central Lugano, 7 kilometers (4 miles) away; taxis, costing about 25 Fr. to the center, are the only option.

By Train There's a train from Zürich seven minutes past every hour, and the trip takes about three hours. If you're coming from Geneva, you can catch the Milan express at various times, changing at Domodossola and Bellinzona. Daytimes, there's a train 30 minutes past every hour from Milan's Centrale Station; the trip takes about 1½ hours. Always keep passports handy and confirm times with the SNTO. For train information in Lugano, tel. 091/226502.

By Car There are fast, direct highways from Milan and from Zürich. If you are planning to come from Geneva, check the weather conditions with the automobile associations beforehand.

Getting Around

By Bus Well-integrated services run regularly on all local routes. You must buy your ticket from the machine at the stop before you board.

By Train With or without a Swiss Pass, get a **Regional Holiday Season Ticket** for Lugano from the tourist office. One of these gives unlimited free travel for seven consecutive days on most rail and steamer routes and a 50% or 25% discount on longer trips. It costs 78 Fr. for adults (68 Fr. for holders of a Swiss Pass) and 39 Fr. for children 6–16. The newest version offers any three out of seven days free on most routes, with 50% or 25% reductions on the remaining four days. Its price is 60 Fr. for adults, 50 Fr. for Swiss Pass holders, and 30 Fr. for children.

By Taxi Though less expensive than in Zürich or Geneva, taxis are still not cheap, with a 10 Fr. minimum. In a pinch, call 091/512121 or 091/519191.

By Boat The **Navigation Company of Lake Lugano** (tel. 091/515223) offers cruise-boat excursions around the bay to the romantic fishing village of Gandria and toward the Villa Favorita. Use it like public transit, following a schedule and paying according to distance, or look into special tickets: Seven consecutive days' unlimited travel cost 50 Fr., 3 days within a week cost 44 Fr.; an all-day pass costs 30 Fr.

Guided Tours

The tourist office is the best source of information about hiking tours into the mountains surrounding Lugano; it offers several topographical maps and suggested itineraries. There are bus trips to Locarno, Ascona, Lake Como, Lake Maggiore, Milan, Venice, St. Moritz, Florence, the Alpine passes, and the Italian market in Como. A free guided walking tour of Lugano leaves the tourist office every Tuesday at 9:30 AM.

Tourist Information

Ente Turistico Lugano (riva Albertolli 5, CH-6901, tel. 091/214664; open Oct.–June, weekdays 9–6; July–Sept., weekdays 9–6:30; Apr.–Oct., Sat. 9–5).

Exploring Lugano

Its sparkling bay, with dark, conical mountains rising from the beautiful Lago di Lugano, has earned Lugano the nickname "Rio of the Old World." The largest city in the Ticino—the Italian-speaking corner of Switzerland—Lugano has not escaped some of the inevitable overdevelopment of a successful resort town. There's thick traffic, right up to the waterfront, much of it manic Italian-style, and it has more than its share of concrete waterfront high-rise hotels, with balconies skewed to claim rooms with a view no matter what the aesthetic cost.

But the view from the waterfront is unforgettable, the boulevards are fashionable, and the old quarter is still reminiscent of sleepy old towns in Italy. And the sacred *passeggiata*—the afternoon stroll to see and be seen that winds down every Italian day—asserts the city's true personality as a graceful, sophisticated Old World resort—not Swiss, not Italian . . . just Lugano.

Numbers in the margin correspond to points of interest on the Lugano map.

Start your walk under the broad porticoes of the tourist office and cross over to the tree-lined promenade, where you can stroll along the waterfront and take in stunning mountain views. Head left along the waterfront and into the **Parco Civico,** with its cacti, exotic shrubs, and more than 1,000 varieties of roses. There's an aviary, a tiny "deer zoo," and a fine view of the bay from its peninsula. The **Villa Ciani,** temporarily closed for renovations, contains paintings and sculpture from Tintoretto to Giacometti.

There's also the canton's **Museuo Cantonale di Storia Naturale** (Museum of Natural History), which contains exhibits on animals, plants, and mushrooms. *Viale Cattaneo 4, tel. 091/237827. Admission free. Open Tues.–Sat. 9–noon and 2–5.*

If you continue left along the waterfront, you'll find the **Lido,** with a stretch of sandy beach, several swimming pools, and a restaurant. *Admission: 5 Fr. adults, 2 Fr. children 2–14.*

Or follow the promenade right until you reach the **Imbarcadero Centrale,** where steamers launch into the bay, and turn inland to the **Piazza della Riforma,** the scene of Lugano's vigorous Italian life, where the modish locals socialize in outdoor cafés. From here, enter the **Old Town** and follow the steep, narrow streets lined with chic Italian clothing shops and small markets offering pungent local cheeses and porcini mushrooms. Swiss culture asserts itself only at lunch stands, where *panini* (small sandwiches) are made not only of prosciutto, tuna, or mozzarella but of sauerkraut and sausage as well.

On the street of the same name, you'll find the **Cathedral San Lorenzo,** with its graceful Renaissance facade and noteworthy frescoes inside. Then shop your way down the Via Nassa until you reach the **Church of Santa Maria degli Angioli** in Piazza Luini, started in 1455. Within, you'll find a splendid fresco of the *Passion and Crucifixion* by Bernardino Luini (1475–1532).

Across the street, the waterfront **Giardino Belvedere** (Belvedere Gardens) frame 12 modern sculptures with palms, camelias, oleanders, and magnolias. At the far end, to your

Lugano

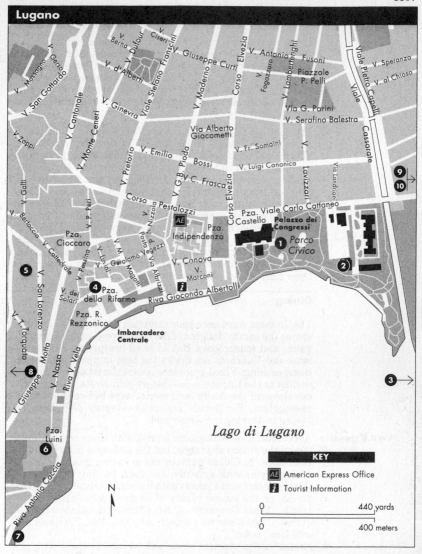

Lago di Lugano

KEY

AE American Express Office

i Tourist Information

0 ————— 440 yards

0 ————— 400 meters

Cathedral San
Lorenzo, **5**

Church of Santa Maria
degli Angioli, **6**

Giardino Belvedere, **7**

Lido, **3**

Museo Cantonale di
Storia Naturale, **2**

Parco Civico, **1**

Parco Tassino, **8**

Parco degli Ulivi, **9**

Piazza della Riforma, **4**

Villa Favorita, **10**

right, there's **public bathing** on the Riva Caccia. *Admission (bathing): 3 Fr., 2 Fr. children. Open mid-May–mid-Sept.*

If you want to see more of Lugano's luxurious parklands, take the funicular from the Old Town to the train station: Behind the

⑧ station, deer greet you as you enter the floral **Parco Tassino.** Or take bus No. 2 east to the San Domenico stop in Castagnola to

⑨ reach the **Parco degli Ulivi** (Olive Park), where you can climb the olive-lined slopes of Monte Brè for views of the surrounding mountains.

⑩ The dust has finally settled at the **Villa Favorita,** owned by art baron and *real* Baron Heinrich von Thyssen, and you'll find the villa not only completely renovated but also with a portion of its magnificent art collection back on the walls. In a controversial bidding war, much of the collection was transferred to Madrid—at least temporarily—but a significant display of 19th- and 20th-century paintings and watercolors from Europe and America remains, shown to better advantage than ever in the renewed space. Artists represented include Thomas Hart Benton, Giorgio de Chirico, Frederic Church, Lucien Freud, Edward Hopper, Franz Marc, Jackson Pollock, and Andrew Wyeth. *Strada Castagnola, tel. 091/516152. Admission: 12 Fr. Open Easter–Oct., Tues.–Sun. 10–5.*

Dining

The Ticinese were once poor mountain people, so their cuisine shares the earthy delights of the Piemontese: polenta, gnocchi, game, and mushrooms. But as in all prosperous resorts, the mink-and-Vuarnets set draws the best in upmarket international cooking. Fixed-price lunches are almost always cheaper, so dine as the Luganese do—before your siesta. That way you can sleep off the fruity local merlot wine before the requisite passeggiata. For details and price-category definitions, *see* Dining in Staying in Switzerland.

Very Expensive **Al Portone.** The settings are formal, with silver and lace dress-
★ ing up the stucco and stone, but the ambience is strictly easy. Chef Roberto Galizzi pursues *nuova cucina* (nouvelle cuisine, Italian-style) with ambition and flair, putting local spins on classics: roast veal kidneys with balsamic vinegar, seafood carpaccio, or the simple luxury of creamed potatoes with white truffle. *Viale Cassarate 3, tel. 091/235995. Reservations required. Jacket and tie advised. AE, DC, MC, V. Closed Sun. and Mon. noon.*

★ **Santabbondio.** Ancient stone and terracotta blend with pristine pastels in this upgraded grotto, where superb and imaginative new Franco-Italian dishes are served in intimate little dining rooms and on a flower-filled terrace. Watch for lobster risotto or scallops in orange-basil sauce to confirm what locals assert. It's a cab ride from town, toward the airport, but worth the trip. *Via ai Grotti di Gentilino, Lugano/Sorengo, tel. 091/ 548535. Reservations advised. Jacket advised. AE, DC, MC, V. Closed Sat. lunch, Sun. night, and Mon.*

Expensive **Galleria.** Though the setting aspires to formal hauteur, with contemporary appointments and modern art, family warmth and vigor peek through the chinks in the facade, and in the end this is a comfortable source of good middle-class Italian cooking. *Via Vegezzi, tel. 091/236288. Reservations advised. Jacket advised. AE, DC, MC, V. Closed Sun.*

★ **Locanda del Boschetto.** The grill is the first thing you see in this no-nonsense restaurant, a specialist in simple but sensational seafood *alla griglia* (grilled). Crisp linens contrast with rustic wood touches, and the low-key service is helpful and down-to-earth. *Via Boschetto 8, tel. 091/542493. Reservations advised. AE, DC, MC, V. Closed Mon.*

Moderate
★ **Al Barilotto.** Despite its generic pizzeria decor and American-style salad bar, this restaurant draws local crowds for grilled meats, homemade pasta, and wood-oven pizza. Take bus No. 10 from the center. *Hôtel de la Paix, Via Cattori 18, tel. 091/542331. Reservations advised. AE, DC, MC, V.*

Inexpensive
★ **La Tinera.** This tiny taverna crowds loyal locals, tourists, and families onto wooden benches for authentic regional specialties, hearty meats, and pastas. Regional wine is served in traditional ceramic bowls. It's tucked down an alley off Via Pessina in the Old Town. *Via dei Gorini 2, tel. 091/235219. Reservations advised. AE, DC, MC, V.*

Sayonara. There's nothing Japanese about it: This is a modern urban pizzeria with several rooms that are crowded at lunchtime with a mix of tourists and shoppers. The old copper polenta pot stirs automatically year-round, with polenta offered in several combinations, one of them with mountain hare. *Via F. Soave 10, tel. 091/220170. Reservations not necessary. AE, DC, MC, V.*

Lodging

There are few Inexpensive hotels in the downtown area, but a brief drive into the surrounding countryside increases your options. Since this is a summer resort, many hotels close for the winter, so call ahead. For details and price-category definitions, *see* Lodging in Staying in Switzerland.

Very Expensive
★ **Splendide Royale.** You can choose between the sleek modern (1983) wing and the more florid period rooms in the original 1887 villa: Either will give you the pampered Old-World-resort feeling the name implies. It's just across from the lake, with a pretty s-shaped pool and a glamorous, if stuffy, dining hall. *Riva Caccia, tel. 091/542001, fax 091/548931. 186 rooms. Facilities: restaurant, bar, terrace, indoor pool, sauna, massage. AE, DC, MC, V.*

★ **Ticino.** In this warmly appointed, 16th-century house in the heart of the Old Town, shuttered windows look out from every room onto a glassed-in garden and courtyard, and there are vaulted halls lined with art and antiques. This member of the Romantik Hotels is steps away from the funicular to the station. *Piazza Cioccaro 1, tel. 091/227772, fax 091/236278. 23 rooms with bath. Facilities: restaurant, garden courtyard, parking. AE, DC, MC, V.*

★ **Villa Principe Leopoldo.** In a price range all its own, but with Old World service and splendor to match, this sumptuously appointed garden mansion sits on a hillside high over the lake. There is free transportation to the airport and town. *Via Montalbano 5, tel. 091/558855, fax 091/558825. 24 suites with bath. Facilities: restaurant, bar, pool, indoor golf, hydromassage, solarium, tennis courts, covered parking, sauna, whirlpool, fitness center. AE, DC, MC, V.*

Expensive
Du Lac-Seehof. This discreet and simple hotel offers you more lakefront luxury for your money than the glossier Grand Eden

down the same beach. All rooms face the lake, but the sixth floor is the quietest. *Riva Paradiso 3, tel. 091/541921, fax 091/546173. 53 rooms with bath. Facilities: restaurant, terrace bar, pool, private swimming area on lake, sauna, solarium, massage room. AE, DC, MC, V.*

Moderate **Alba.** This solid little hotel, surrounded by landscaped grounds
★ and an interior that is lavish in the extreme, is ideal for lovers with a sense of camp or honeymooners looking for romantic privacy. Mirrors, gilt, plush, and crystal fill the public areas, and the beds are all ruffles and swags. *Via delle Scuole 11, tel. 091/543731, fax 091/544523. 25 rooms with bath. Facilities: restaurant, bar, garden. AE, DC, MC, V.*

★ **Flora.** Though it's one of the cheapest hotels in town, this 70-year-old lodging has been reasonably well maintained. The room decor is minimal, a holdover of the '60s (red-orange prints, wood-grain Formica), and the once-elegant dining hall has seen better days. But some rooms have balconies, and there's a sheltered garden terrace for balmy nights. *Via Geretta 16, tel. 091/541671, fax 091/542738. 33 rooms with bath. Facilities: restaurant, bar, terrace, small outdoor pool. AE, DC, MC, V.*

International au Lac. This is a big, old-fashioned, friendly city hotel, half a block from the lake, with many lake-view rooms. It's next to Santa Maria degli Angioli, on the edge of the shopping district and the Old Town. *Via Nassa 68, tel. 091/227541, fax 091/227544. 86 rooms with bath. Facilities: restaurant, garden. AE, DC, MC, V.*

★ **Park-Hotel Nizza.** This former villa (modernized in 1974) affords panoramic views from its spot on the lower slopes of San Salvatore, well above the lake, and thus is an uphill hike from town. The mostly small rooms are decorated with antique reproductions; there is no extra charge for lake views. An ultramodern bar overlooks the lake, and a good restaurant serves vegetables (and even wine) from its own garden. There's a shuttle service to Paradiso. *Via Guidino 14, tel. 091/541771, fax 091/541773. 30 rooms with bath. Facilities: restaurant, bar, outdoor pool, garden. AE, DC, MC, V.*

San Carlo. The San Carlo offers one of the better deals in a high-priced town: It's small, clean, freshly furnished, and right on the main shopping street, a block from the waterfront. There are no frills, but the friendly atmosphere. *Via Nassa 28, tel. 091/227107, fax 091/228022. 22 rooms with bath. Facilities: breakfast only. AE, DC, MC, V.*

Bern

Arriving and Departing

By Plane **Belp** (tel. 031/9613411) is a small airport, 9 kilometers (6 miles) south of the city, with flights from London, Paris, Nice, Venice, and Lugano. A bus from the airport to the train station costs 12 Fr., a taxi about 35 Fr.

By Train Bern is a major link between Geneva, Zürich, and Basel, with fast connections running usually every hour from the enormous central station. The high-speed French TGV gets to Paris in 4½ hours.

By Car The Geneva-Zürich expressway runs by Bern, with crossroads leading to Basel and Lugano as well.

Getting Around

By Bus and Tram Bern is a small, concentrated city, and it's easy to get around on foot. There are 6½ kilometers (4 miles) of covered shopping arcades in the center. Bus and tram service is excellent, however, if you don't feel like walking. Fares range from 1.30 Fr. to 1.90 Fr. Buy individual tickets from the dispenser at the tram or bus stop; the posted map will tell you the cost. Tourist cards for unlimited rides are available at 4 Fr. for one day, 6 Fr. for two, and 9 Fr. for three. Buy them at the bahnhof tourist office or from the public-transportation ticket office in the subway leading down to the main station (take the escalator in front of Loeb's department store and turn right through the Christoffel Tower). A **Swiss Pass** will allow you to travel free.

By Taxi This cumbersome alternative to walking costs between 6 Fr. and 15 Fr. across town.

Important Addresses and Numbers

Tourist Information The tourist office is located at Bahnhofplatz (main station, tel. 031/3116611); it's open May–June, daily 9–8:30; Oct.–May, Mon.–Sat. 9–6:30 and Sun. 10–5.

Embassies **U.S.** (Jubiläumsstr. 93, tel. 031/3526381). **Canadian** (88 Kirchenfeldstr., tel. 031/3526381). **U.K.** (Thunstr. 50, tel. 031/3525021).

Emergencies **Police** (tel. 117). **Ambulance** (tel. 144). **Doctor/Dentist** (tel. 3119211). **All-night pharmacy** (tel. 3119211).

Guided Tours

Walking Tours A two-hour tour around the Old Town, covering all the principal sights, is offered daily by the tourist office.

Excursions Bern prides itself on its central location, and offers easy access to Zürich and Geneva as well as to the remote farmlands of the Bernese Mittelland, where you can visit the Emmental Valley. The most popular (though expensive) outing is to the Jungfrau in the Alpine Bernese Oberland. The train passes through Interlaken, Lauterbrunne, Wengen, and Kleine Scheidegg to the Jungfraujoch, which, at 3,513 meters (11,333 feet), has the highest rail station in Europe. Contact the tourist office.

Exploring Bern

No cosmopolitan nonsense here: The local specialties are fatback and sauerkraut, the annual fair features the humble onion, and the president takes the tram to work. Walking down broad, medieval streets past squares teeming with farmers' markets and cafés full of shirt-sleeved politicos, you might forget that Bern is the federal capital—indeed, the geographic and political hub—of a sophisticated and prosperous nation.

It earned its pivotal position through a history of power and influence that dates to the 12th century, when Berchtold V of the Holy Roman Empire established a fortress on this gooseneck in the river Aare. By the 15th century the Bernese had overcome the Burgundians to expand their territories west to Geneva. Napoleon held them briefly—from 1798 until his defeat in 1815—but by 1848 Bern was back in charge, as the capital of the Swiss Confederation.

Today it's not the massive Bundeshaus (capitol building) that dominates the city, but the perfectly preserved arcades, the fountains, and the thick, sturdy towers of the Middle Ages. They're the reason UNESCO granted Bern World Landmark status, ranking it with the Pyramids and the Taj Mahal.

Numbers in the margin correspond to points of interest on the Bern map.

❶ Start on the busy **Bahnhofplatz** in front of the grand old Schweizerhof hotel, facing the station. To your left is the ❷ **Heiliggeistkirche** (Church of the Holy Spirit), finished in 1729 and at odds with both the modern and the medieval in Bern. Head right up Bollwerk and turn right into Kleeplatz and ❸ Hodlerstrasse, where you'll come to the **Kunstmuseum Bern** on your left. Originally dedicated to collecting Swiss art, it houses an exceptional group of works by Ferdinand Hodler, including some enormous, striking allegories; there are landscapes and portraits as well. But the concentration is no longer entirely Swiss, and early Bern masters mingle with Fra Angelico, and Böcklin and Anker share space with artists of the caliber of Cézanne, Rouault, and Picasso. The museum's pride—and its justified claim to fame—is its collection of more than 2,000 works by Paul Klee, who lived in Bern. *Hodlerstrasse 8–12, tel. 031/ 3110944. Admission: 4 Fr. Open Tues. 10–9; Wed.–Sun. 10–5.*

Walk down Spitalgasse outside the arcades to see some of the city's stunning architecture; inside the sheltered walkways, you'll be seduced by modern shops and cafés.

❹ Head for the **Pfeiferbrunnen** (Bagpiper Fountain), the first of the city's many signature fountains erected between 1539 and ❺ 1546, and the **Käfigturm** (Prison Tower), which dates from the 13th and 14th centuries. There's a small museum of economic and cultural life inside. *Tel. 031/3112306. Admission free. Open Tues.–Sun. 10–1 and 2–6, also Thurs. 6–9.*

❻ ❼ Continue down Marktgasse past the **Anna Seiler** and **Marksman** ❽ **fountains** to the **Zytgloggeturm** (clock tower), built as a city gate in 1191 but transformed by the addition of an astronomical clock in 1530. To your right is the Theaterplatz, to your left the ❾ **Kindlifresserbrunnen** (Ogre Fountain) and the Kornhausplatz, ❿ where you will see the imposing 18th-century **Kornhaus** (granary), its magnificent vaulted cellar a popular beer hall today. Now walk past the clock tower and observe the clock from the east side. At four minutes before every hour, you can see the famous mechanical puppet bears perform their ancient dance.

Continue down Kramgasse, past fine 18th-century houses and ⓫ ⓬ the **Zähringer** and **Samson fountains.** Turn left at the next small ⓭ intersection and head for Rathausplatz, with its **Vennerbrun-** ⓮ **nen** (Ensign Fountain), and the late-Gothic **Rathaus** (city hall), where the city and cantonal government meet.

Head back to the main route, here named Gerechtigkeitsgasse, ⓯ and continue past the **Gerechtigkeitsbrunnen** (Justice Fountain) and lovely patrician houses. Artisan shops, galleries, and antiquaries line this leg of the endless arcades. Turn left at the bottom and head down the steep Nydegg Stalden through one

1113

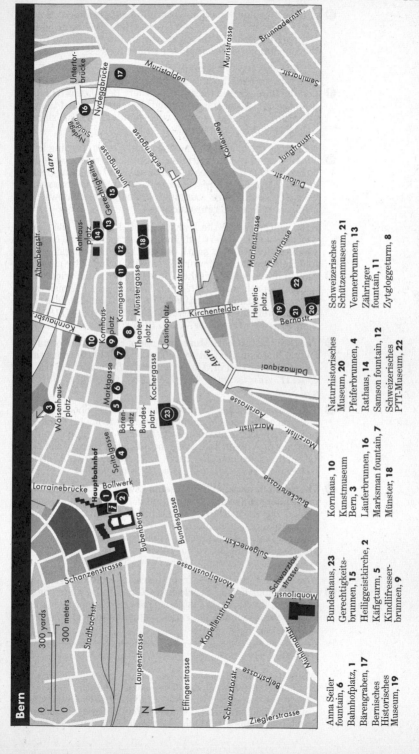

Bern

Anna Seiler
fountain, **6**
Bahnhofplatz, **1**
Bärengraben, **17**
Bernisches
Historisches
Museum, **19**

Bundeshaus, **23**
Gerechtigkeits-
brunnen, **15**
Heiliggeistkirche, **2**
Käfigturm, **5**
Kindlifresser-
brunnen, **9**

Kornhaus, **10**
Kunstmuseum
Bern, **3**
Läuferbrunnen, **16**
Marksman fountain, **7**
Münster, **18**

Naturhistorisches
Museum, **20**
Pfeiferbrunnen, **4**
Rathaus, **14**
Samson fountain, **12**
Schweizerisches
PTT-Museum, **22**

Schweizerisches
Schützenmuseum, **21**
Vennerbrunnen, **13**
Zähringer
fountain, **11**
Zytgloggeturm, **8**

⑯ of the city's oldest sections, past the **Läuferbrunnen** (Messenger Fountain), to the river Aare. Here the **Nydeggkirche** (Nydegg Church), on the right, was built from 1341 to 1571 on the foundations of Berchtold V's ruined fortress.

Cross the river by the **Untertorbrücke** (Bridge under the Gate), then turn right and climb up to the **Nydeggbrücke.** Here you'll ⑰ find the **Bärengraben** (Bear Pits), where Bern keeps its famous live mascots. According to legend, Berchtold named the town after the first animal he killed while hunting—a bear, since the woods were thick with them.

Now cross the bridge and head back into town, turning left up ⑱ Junkerngasse to the magnificent Gothic **Münster** (cathedral), begun in 1421. It features a fine portal (1490) depicting the *Last Judgment*, recently restored and repainted in extravagant hues. There also are stunning stained-glass windows, both originals and period reproductions.

Arty boutiques line the Münstergasse, leading to the **Casino,** which houses a concert hall and restaurants, but no casino. If you head even farther south (across the river yet again), you'll find Helvetiaplatz, a historic square surrounded by museums. ⑲ The **Bernisches Historisches Museum** (Bern Historical Museum) has a prehistoric collection, 15th-century Flemish tapestries, and Bernese sculptures. Its fine Islamic holdings are imaginatively displayed. *Helvetiaplatz 5, tel. 031/3511811. Admission: 3 Fr. Open Tues.–Sun. 10–5.*

⑳ The **Naturhistorisches Museum** is one of Europe's major natural history museums. It features enormous wildlife dioramas and a splendid collection of Alpine minerals. *Bernastr. 15, tel. 031/ 3507111. Admission: 3 Fr. Open Mon. 2–5, Tues.–Sat. 9–5, and Sun. 10–5.*

㉑ The **Schweizerisches Schützenmuseum** (Swiss Shooting Museum) traces the development of firearms from 1817 and celebrates Swiss marksmanship beyond the apple-splitting accuracy of William Tell. It's in between the History and Natural History museums. *Bernastr. 5, tel. 031/3510127. Admission free. Open Tues.–Sat. 2–4, Sun. 10–noon and 2–4.*

㉒ The **Schweizerisches PTT-Museum** (Swiss Postal and Telecommunications Museum), now housed in its striking new building behind the Bernisches Historisches Museum, offers detailed documents, art, and artifacts of early technology to trace the history of the mail system in Switzerland, from Roman messengers to telegraph and radio. *Helvetiastr. 16, tel. 031/3387777. Admission: 2 Fr. adults. Open Tues.–Sun. 10–5.*

Alternatively, head back from the casino on Kochergasse past ㉓ the enormous domed **Bundeshaus** (Capitol). By night, be sure to stick to Kochergasse instead of the riverview promenade behind the capitol building; some visitors have been annoyed by obvious drug traffic.

Dining

While Bern teeters between two cultures politically, Teutonic conquers Gallic when it comes to cuisine. Dining in Bern is usually a down-to-earth affair, with Italian home cooking running a close second to the local standard fare of meat and potatoes. Specialties include the famous *Bernerplatte* (sauerkraut with boiled beef, fatty pork, sausages, ham, and tongue), *Buurehamme* (hot smoked ham), and *Ratsherrentopf* (rösti with roast veal, beef, liver, and sausage). Coffee and *Kuchen* (pastry) are the four-o'clock norm.

For details and price-category definitions, *see* Dining in Staying in Switzerland.

Very Expensive **Bellevue-Grill.** When Parliament is in town, this haute-cuisine
★ landmark is transformed from a local gourmet mecca to a political clubhouse where the movers-and-shakers put their heads together over healthy portions of updated classics—such as veal liver *Geschnetzeltes* with raspberries. *Kochergasse 3–5, tel. 031/3224545. Reservations advised. Jacket and tie advised. AE, DC, MC, V.*

★ **Schultheissenstube.** The intimate, rustic dining room, with a clublike bar in the center and an adjoining all-wood stübli, looks less like a gastronomic haven than a country pub, and the folksy music piped in furthers the delusion. Yet the cooking is sophisticated, international, and imaginative—duck liver in vanilla vinegar, oyster-and-champagne risotto, seafood lasagne with saffron, Cornish hen with goose liver sauce. *Hotel Schweizerhof, Bahnhofplatz 11, tel. 031/3114501. Reservations advised. Jacket and tie advised. AE, DC, MC, V.*

Expensive **Jack's Brasserie.** In the Hotel Schweizerhof, this street-level restaurant, with high ceilings, wainscoting, and roomy banquettes, is airy and bustling, frequented by shoppers, Parliament members, and businesspeople who enjoy its urbane atmosphere. You can enjoy a drink here by day or settle in at mealtime for a smartly served menu of French classics with a light touch. *Hotel Schweizerhof, Bahnhofplatz 11, tel. 031/3114501. Reservations advised. Jacket and tie advised. AE, DC, MC, V.*

★ **Zum Rathaus.** Across from the Rathaus in the Old Town, this atmospheric, all-wood landmark has been a restaurant since 1863, though the row house dates from the 17th century. Downstairs, the setting is casual and comfortable, while the upstairs "Marcuard-Stübli" is considerably more formal; during the summer, opt for the outdoor café on the Rathausplatz. The cooking ranges from local meat standards to game, salmon, and hearty pastries. *Rathausplatz 5, tel. 031/3116183. Reservations advised upstairs. Dress: casual downstairs, jacket suggested upstairs. AE, DC, MC, V.*

Moderate **Della Casa.** You can stay downstairs in the steamy, rowdy
★ stübli, where necktied businessmen roll up their sleeves and play cards, or you can head up to the restaurant, where they leave their jackets on. It's an unofficial parliament headquarters, with generous local and Italian specialties. *Schauplatzgasse 16, tel. 031/3112142. Reservations advised. Jacket advised. DC, MC, V. No credit cards downstairs.*

★ **Lorenzini.** In a town where the cozy or stuffy holds sway, this hip, bright spot stands apart. Delicious homemade pasta and changing menus featuring the specialties of different Italian regions are served with authentic, contemporary flair. The clientele is a mix of voguish yuppies; the café-bar downstairs draws the young and even more seriously chic. *Marktgass-Passage 3, tel. 031/3117850. Reservations advised. Dress: casual but neat. DC, MC, V.*

Zunft zu Webern. Founded as a weavers' guildhouse and built in 1704, this classic building has been renovated on the ground floor in a slick but traditional style, with gleaming new wood and bright lighting. The cuisine reflects the sophisticated decor, with generous portions of such upgraded standards as lamb stew with saffron. *Gerechtigkeitsgasse 68, tel. 031/3114258. Reservations not necessary. Dress: casual. MC, V.*

Inexpensive **Brasserie zum Bärengraben.** Directly across from the bear pits,
★ this popular, easygoing little local institution, with the thinnest veneer of a French accent, serves inexpensive lunches to shoppers, tourists, businesspeople, and retirees, who settle in with a newspaper and a *dezi* (deciliter) of wine. The menu offers many old-style basics—*Kalbskopf am Vinaigrette* (chopped veal in vinaigrette), pig's feet, stuffed cabbage—and wonderful pastries. *Muristalden 1, tel. 031/3314218. Reservations advised. Dress: casual. No credit cards.*

Harmonie. Run by the same family since 1900, this leaded-glass and old-wood café-restaurant serves inexpensive basics: sausage-and-rösti, *Käseschnitte* (cheese toast), *bauern* omelets (farm-style, with bacon, potatoes, onions, and herbs), and fondue. It's lively and a little dingy, very friendly, and welcoming to foreigners. *Hotelgasse 3, tel. 031/3113840. Reservations not necessary. Dress: casual. No credit cards.*

★ **Klötzlikeller.** A cozy muraled wine cellar, this is much more intimate than the famous Kornhauskeller and just as lovely. There's a good, if limited, menu of meat specialties. *Gerechtigkeitsgasse 62, tel. 031/3117456. Reservations not necessary. Dress: casual. AE, MC, V.*

Kornhauskeller. This spectacular vaulted old wine cellar, under the Kornhaus granary, is now a popular beer hall with live music on weekends. Decent hot food is served as an afterthought. *Kornhausplatz 18, tel. 031/3111133. Reservations not necessary. Dress: casual. AE, DC, MC, V.*

Lodging

For details and price-category definitions, *see* Lodging in Staying in Switzerland.

Very Expensive **Bellevue Palace.** This is a palace indeed, with a view that gives
★ it an advantage over its friendly rival in luxury, the Schweizerhof. It is 75 years old, with Art Nouveau details that include a sweeping staircase and a spectacular stained-glass ceiling in the lobby. Decor in the rooms varies greatly, but each is deluxe. *Kochergasse 3–5, tel. 031/3204545, fax 031/3114743. 155 rooms with bath. Facilities: 2 restaurants, grill, bar, summer terrace café. AE, DC, MC, V.*

★ **Schweizerhof.** The quarters are roomy and luxuriously appointed (most double rooms are the size of junior suites and, at 320 Fr., a great value); halls are decorated with antiques from the collection of the Gauer family, the hotel's owners; and this grand, graceful landmark by the Bahnhof offers excellent service. *Bahnhofplatz 11, tel. 031/3114501, fax 031/3122179. 94 rooms with bath. Facilities: 3 restaurants, café, gourmet deli, bar, nightclub, conference rooms. AE, DC, MC, V.*

Expensive **Bären/Bristol.** These neighboring properties have been twinned as dependable business-class hotels, with modern interiors and first-class comforts. The restaurant, Bärenbar, where bears figure heavily in the decor, serves drinks and snacks. *Schauplatzgasse 4–10, tel. 031/3113367, fax 031/3116983 (Bären); tel. 031/3110101, fax 031/3119479 (Bristol).*

149 rooms, 91 with bath. Facilities: bar, café, video, sauna. AE, DC, MC, V.

★ **Belle Epoque.** This relatively new hotel with period furnishings is more suggestive of fin de siècle Paris than you might expect in Germanic Bern: Every inch of the arcaded row house is filled with authentic Art Nouveau and Jugendstil antiques. Despite the historic look, amenities, including white-tile baths and electric blinds, are state-of-the-art. *Gerechtigkeitsgasse 18, tel. 031/3114336, fax 031/3113936. 33 rooms with bath. Facilities: piano bar, gallery. Breakfast only. AE, DC, MC, V.*

Bern. Behind a spare and imposing neoclassical facade, this former theater and formerly modest hotel has been transformed into a sleek, modern gem, with an airshaft garden "courtyard" lighting the better rooms. *Zeughausgasse 9, tel. 031/3121021, fax 031/3121147. 96 rooms with bath. Facilities: 2 restaurants, rooftop terrace café, piano bar. AE, DC, MC, V.*

Innere Enge. Opened in December 1992, this renovated early 18th-century inn has been transformed into a slick deluxe business hotel. Spacious, light, and airy thanks to generous windows that take in views toward the Bernese Alps, it's located outside the city center. Marian's Jazzroom, in the Louis Armstrong Bar, features top jazz acts. Take Bus No. 21 ("Bremgarten") from the train station. *Engestr. 54, tel. 031/3096111, fax 031/3096112. 26 rooms with bath. Facilities: restaurant, café, jazz bar. AE, DC, MC, V. Expensive.*

Moderate
★ **Goldener Adler.** The exterior of this 1764 building is a magnificent patrician town house, but its interior is modern and modest, with linoleum baths and severe Formica furniture. The ambience is comfortable and familial nonetheless: The same family has run it for more than 100 years. *Gerechtigkeitsgasse 7, tel. 031/3111725, fax 031/3113761. 40 rooms with bath. Facilities: restaurant, terrace café. AE, DC, MC, V.*

★ **Krebs.** A classic, small, Swiss hotel, Krebs is impeccable and solid, managed with an eye on every detail. The spare decor is warmed with wood and made comfortable by the personal, friendly service of the Buri family. A handful of inexpensive rooms without bath offer excellent value. *Genfergasse 8, tel. 031/3114942, fax 031/3111035. 44 rooms, 41 with shower. Facilities: restaurant. AE, DC, MC, V.*

Inexpensive
Glocke. Though it's very plain and occasionally shabby, there's a young, friendly management here and two lively restaurants, one a "Swiss Chalet," with dancing and folklore shows, the other Italian. The rooms have a fresh paint job, tile baths, and homey, unmatched towels. A few rooms without baths cost less. *Rathausgasse 75, tel. 031/3113771, fax 031/3111008. 20 rooms, some with bath. Facilities: 2 restaurants, entertainment. AE, DC, MC, V.*

Goldener Schlüssel. This is a bright, tidy spot with wood, crisp linens, and tiled baths. It's in the heart of the Old Town, so the rooms are quieter in the back. There are two good restaurants serving Swiss and international specialties. *Rathausgasse 72, tel. 031/3110216, fax 031/3115688. 29 rooms, some with shower. Facilities: 2 restaurants. DC, MC, V.*

★ **Hospiz zur Heimat.** The elegant 18th-century exterior belies the dormitory gloom inside, but the baths are new and the rooms are immaculate. It's in an excellent Old Town location. *Gerechtigkeitsgasse 50, tel. 031/3110436, fax 031/3123386. 40 rooms, some with bath. AE, DC, MC, V.*

Jardin. In a commercial neighborhood far above the Old Town, this is a solid, roomy middle-class hotel, with fresh decor and baths in every room. It's easily reached by tram No. 9 to Breitenrainplatz. *Militärstrasse 38, tel. 031/3330117, fax 031/ 3330943. 17 rooms with bath. Facilities: AE, DC, MC, V.*

Marthahaus. Take bus No. 20 over the Kornhaus Bridge to this spare, old-style pension in a residential neighborhood north of the Old Town, where rates are low and the service is friendly. *Wyttenbachstrasse 22a, tel. 031/3324135. 40 rooms without bath. Breakfast only. No credit cards.*

Zermatt

Lying at an altitude of 1,616 meters (5,300 feet), Zermatt offers the ultimate Swiss-Alpine experience: spectacular mountains, a roaring stream, state-of-the-art transport facilities, and a broad range of high-quality accommodations, some of them radiating rustic atmosphere, plus 230 kilometers (143 miles) of downhill runs and 7 kilometers (4 miles) of cross-country trails. But its greatest claim to fame remains the **Matterhorn** (4,477 meters, 14,690 feet), which attracts swarms of package-tour sightseers pushing shoulder to shoulder to get yet another shot of this genuine wonder of the Western world.

Arriving and Departing

Zermatt is a car-free resort isolated at the end of the Mattertal, a rugged valley at the eastern end of the Alpine canton of Valais. A good mountain highway and the Brig-Visp-Zermatt Railway cut south through the valley from Visp, the crossroads of the main Valais east–west routes. The airports of Zürich and Geneva are roughly equidistant from Brig, but by approaching from Geneva you can avoid crossing mountain passes.

By Train The Brig-Visp-Zermatt Railway, a private narrow-gauge rail system, runs from Brig to Visp, connecting on to Zermatt. All major rail routes connect through Brig, whether you approach from Geneva or Lausanne in the west, from the Lötschberg line that tunnels through from Kandersteg and the Bernese Oberland, or from the Simplon Pass that connects from Italy.

By Car You may drive up the Mattertal as far as Täsch, where you must abandon your car in a large parking lot and catch the train as it completes its climb into Zermatt.

Getting Around

Because Zermatt permits no private cars, your only means of transit are electric taxis that shuttle arriving guests to their hotels and back. The village is relatively small and easily covered on foot.

By Cable Car and Mountain Rail Hiking as well as skiing are Zermatt's raison d'être, but you may want to get a head start into the heights by riding part of the sophisticated network of cable cars, lifts, cogwheel rails, and even an underground metro that carry you above the village center into the wilderness. Excursions to the Klein, Matterhorn, and Gornergrat are particularly spectacular.

Important Addresses and Numbers

Tourist   The main tourist office, the **Verkehrsbüro Zermatt,** is located
Information   across from the train station (Bahnhofplatz, CH-3920 Zermatt,
tel. 028/661181).

Emergencies   **Police** (tel. 028/673822). **Ambulance** (tel. 028/672000).

Exploring Zermatt

Zermatt lies in a hollow of meadows and trees ringed by mountains—among them the broad **Monte Rosa** (4,554 meters/
14,940 feet) and its tallest peak, the **Dufourspitze** (at 4,634 me-
ters/15,200 feet, the highest point in Switzerland)—of which
visitors hear relatively little, so all-consuming is the cult of the
Matterhorn. But the Matterhorn deserves the idolatry:
Though it has become an almost self-parodying icon, like the
Eiffel Tower or the Statue of Liberty, this distinctive snaggle-
toothed pyramid, isolated on all sides from surrounding peaks,
is larger than life as it rears up over the village.

Despite its celebrity mountain, Zermatt remains a resort with
its feet on the ground, protecting its regional quirks along with
its wildlife and its tumbledown *mazots* (little grain-storage
sheds raised on mushroomlike stone bases to keep the mice
away), which crowd between glass-and-concrete chalets like
old tenements between skyscrapers. Streets twist past weathered wood walls, flower boxes, and haphazard stone roofs until
they break into open country that inevitably slopes uphill.

In 1891, the cog railway between Visp and Zermatt took its
first summer run and began disgorging tourists with profitable
regularity—though it didn't plow through in wintertime until
1927. But what really drew the first tourists and made Zermatt
a household word was Edward Whymper's spectacular—and
catastrophic—conquering of the Matterhorn in 1865.
Whymper and his band of six made the successful trek to the
mountain's summit before tragedy struck. During the treacherous descent, four of the men slid against one another and fell
4,000 feet to their death. The body of one was never recovered,
but the others lie in the grim little cemetery behind the Zermatt church in the village center.

If you want to gain the broader perspective of high altitudes
without risking life or limb, take the trip up the Gornergrat—
the train is used for excursions as well as ski transport. Part of
the rail system completed in 1898 and the highest open-air rail
system in Europe (the tracks to the Jungfraujoch, though higher, bore through the face of the Eiger), it connects out of the
main Zermatt train station and climbs slowly up the valley to
the **Riffelberg,** which at 2,582 meters (8,469 feet) offers wide-
open views of the Matterhorn. From **Rotenboden,** at 2,819 meters (9,246 feet), a short downhill walk leads to the **Riffelsee,**
which obligingly provides photographers with a postcard-per-
fect reflection of the famous peak. At the end of the 9-kilometer
(14½-mile) line, the train stops at the summit station of
Gornergrat (3,130 meters/10,266 feet), and passengers pour
onto the observation terraces to take in the majestic views of
the Matterhorn, Monte Rosa, Gorner glacier, and scores of other peaks and glaciers. There's a departure every 24 minutes between 8 AM and 7 PM. The round-trip fare is 50 Fr. Bring warm
clothes, sunglasses, and sturdy shoes.

Dining

Located at the German end of the mostly French canton of Valais, Zermatt offers a variety of French and German cooking, from veal and rösti to raclette and fondue. Specialties often feature pungent mountain cheese: *Käseschnitte*, for instance, are substantial little casseroles of bread, cheese, and often ham, baked until the whey saturates the crusty bread and the cheese browns to gold. Air-dried beef is another Valais treat: The meat is pressed into a dense brick and dried in mountain breezes. It is served in thin, translucent slices, with gherkins and crisp pickled onions. For price-category definitions, *see* Dining in Staying in Switzerland.

Moderate **Enzo's Hitte.** Whether for long lunches between sessions on the
★ slopes or for the traditional wind-down après-ski, this mountain restaurant in tiny Findeln, between the Sunnegga and Blauherd ski areas, is still de rigueur, especially with the hip young English and Americans. The Matterhorn views are astonishing, the decor stylish, the staff chic—and the food surprisingly fine. Traditional hot dishes and nontraditional pastas share billing with good homemade desserts. *Findeln, tel. 028/ 672588. Dress: casual. No credit cards. Closed May–mid-June, Oct.–Nov.*

★ **Zum See.** Beyond Findeln in a tiny village by the same name, Zum See has become something of an institution, serving light meals of a quality and level of invention that would merit acclaim even if the restaurant weren't in the middle of nowhere at 1,766 meters (5,792 feet). During the summer its shaded picnic tables draw hikers who reward themselves at the finish of a day's climb; during the winter its low, cozy log dining room gives skiers a glow with a fine assortment of brandies. *Tel. 028/ 672045. Reservations suggested in the evening. Dress: casual. No credit cards. Closed May–June, Oct.–mid-Nov.*

Inexpensive **Elsie Bar.** Directly across from the church, this popular après-ski haunt looks like a log cabin inside, and draws an international crowd into its barroom for cocktails, American-style. Light meals include cheese specialties and snails. *Tel. 028/672431. Dress: casual. AE, DC, MC, V.*

Lodging

At high season—Christmas and New Year's, Easter, and late summer—Zermatt's high prices rival those of Zürich and Geneva. But read the fine print carefully when you plan your visit: Most hotels include half-pension in their price, offering breakfast and your choice of a noon or evening meal. Hotels that call themselves "garni" do not offer pension dining plans. For price-category definitions, *see* Lodging in Staying in Switzerland.

Very Expensive **Mont Cervin.** One of the flagships of the Seiler dynasty, this is a
★ sleek, luxurious, and urbane mountain hotel. First built in 1852, it's unusually low-slung for a grand hotel, with dark beams and classic decor; a few rooms are full of rustic stucco and carved blond wood. Jacket and tie are required in the guests' dining hall, and for the Friday gala buffet, it's black tie only. *Tel. 028/661122, fax 028/672878. 105 rooms with bath. Facilities: restaurant, grill, dancing, sports center, sauna, solarium, indoor pool. AE, DC, MC, V.*

Zermatterhof. The Cervin's rival for five-star luxury, this 19th-century hotel has recently undergone major renovations to better emphasize its rustic beginnings. Both restaurants, including the elegant new one opened last year, are for guests only, with half-pension included in the price. *Tel. 028/661100, fax 028/674842. 93 rooms with bath. Facilities: 2 restaurants, sauna, fitness center, indoor pool. AE, DC, MC, V.*

Expensive
★ **Monte Rosa.** Behind its graceful shuttered façade you will find flagstone floors, brass, stained and beveled glass, pine, fireplaces, and an overdecorated Victorian dining hall, fully restored. The bar is an après-ski must. *Tel. 028/661131, fax 028/671160. 51 rooms. Facilities: restaurant, access to Mont Cervin pool, sauna, sun terrace. AE, DC, MC, V.*

Pollux. Constructed in 1978 and renovated in 1989, this simple but chic modern hotel is directly on the main pedestrian shopping street. A French restaurant serves seafood specialties, and an appealing old-fashioned stübli draws locals for its low-price lunches, snacks, and Valais cheese specialties; the terrace café sits directly on the busy street. *Tel. 028/671946, fax 028/675426. 32 rooms with bath. Facilities: restaurant, stübli, terrace, dancing, sauna, solarium, garden. AE, DC, MC, V.*

Moderate
★ **Julen.** Its 1937 chalet-style construction, knotty-pine decor, and impeccable 1981 renovation qualify this lodge for membership in the Romantik chain, which assures guests of authentic regional comforts. The main restaurant offers French cooking, and the welcoming stübli serves lamb specialties from locally raised flocks. *Tel. 028/672481, fax 028/671481. 37 rooms with bath. Facilities: restaurant, café, terrace, sauna, solarium. AE, DC, MC, V.*

Romantica. Among the scores of anonymous modern hotels around Zermatt, this modest structure offers an exceptional location directly above the town center. Its tidy gardens and flower boxes, game trophies, and old-style stove soften the cookie-cutter look, and its plain rooms benefit from big windows and balconies. Views take in the mountains (though not the Matterhorn) over a graceful clutter of stone roofs. *Tel. 028/671505, fax 028/675815. 14 rooms with bath. Facilities: bar. AE, MC, V.*

Inexpensive
Alphubel. Although it is surrounded by other hotels and is steps from the main street, this modest, comfortable pension feels off the beaten track—and it offers large sunny balconies in its south-side rooms. The interior reflects the 1954 construction—a little institutional—but there's a sauna in the basement guests can use for a slight surcharge. *Tel. 028/673003, fax 028/676684. 32 rooms, 16 with bath. Facilities: restaurant, sauna. AE, MC, V.*

★ **Mischabel.** This proud old budget pension—run by the same family for 40 years—provides comfort, atmosphere, and a central location few places can match at twice the price, with balconies on the south side framing a perfect Matterhorn view. Creaky, homey, and covered with knotty pine aged to the color of toffee, its rooms have sinks only, though you'll find linoleum-lined showers on every floor. *Tel. 028/671131. 28 rooms with bath. Facilities: restaurant. No credit cards.*

★ **Touring.** Its reassuringly traditional architecture and snug, sunny all-pine rooms, combined with an elevated location outside town and excellent Matterhorn views, make this an appealing choice for travelers who wish to avoid the chic "downtown" scene. Built in 1958 and tastefully updated in 1989, it's family-run, and rooms with Matterhorn views cost only 2 Fr. extra. *Tel. 028/671177, fax 028/674601. 24 rooms, 10 with bath. Facilities: restaurant, stübli. MC, V.*

29 Turkey

Turkey is one place to which the term "East meets West" really applies, both literally and figuratively. It is in Turkey's largest city, Istanbul, that the continents of Europe and Asia meet, separated only by the Bosporus, which flows 29 kilometers (18 miles) from the Black Sea to the Sea of Marmara.

Although most of Turkey's landmass is in Asia, Turkey has faced West politically since 1923, when Mustapha Kemal, better known as Atatürk, founded the modern republic. He transformed the remnants of the shattered Ottoman Empire into a secular state with a Western outlook. So thorough was this changeover—culturally, politically, and economically—that in 1987, 49 years after Atatürk's death, Turkey applied to the European Community (EC) for full membership. It has been a member of the North Atlantic Treaty Organization (NATO) since 1952.

For 16 centuries Istanbul, originally known as Byzantium, played a major part in world politics, first as the capital of the Eastern Roman Empire, when it was known as Constantinople, then, as capital of the Ottoman Empire, the most powerful Islamic empire in the world, when it was renamed Istanbul. Atatürk moved the capital to Ankara at the inception of the Turkish Republic.

The legacy of the Greeks, Romans, Ottomans, and numerous other civilizations has made the country a vast outdoor museum. The most spectacular of the reconstructed classical sites are along the western Aegean coast and the southwest Mediterranean coast, which are lined with magnificent sandy beaches and sleepy little fishing villages, as well as busy holiday spots with sophisticated tourism facilities.

For those with more time, an extra five to seven days, an excursion inland to central Anatolia and the eroded lunar valleys of the Cappadocia area will show some of the enormous diversity of the landscapes and people of Turkey.

Essential Information

Before You Go

When to Go   The height of the tourist season runs from April through October. July and August are the busiest and warmest months. April through June and September and October are the best months to visit archaeological sites or Istanbul and the Marmara area because the days are cooler and the crowds are smaller.

Climate   The Mediterranean and Aegean coasts have mild winters and hot summers. You can swim in the sea from late April through October. The Black Sea coast is mild and damp, with a rainfall of 228 centimeters (90 inches) a year.

The following are the average daily maximum and minimum temperatures for Istanbul.

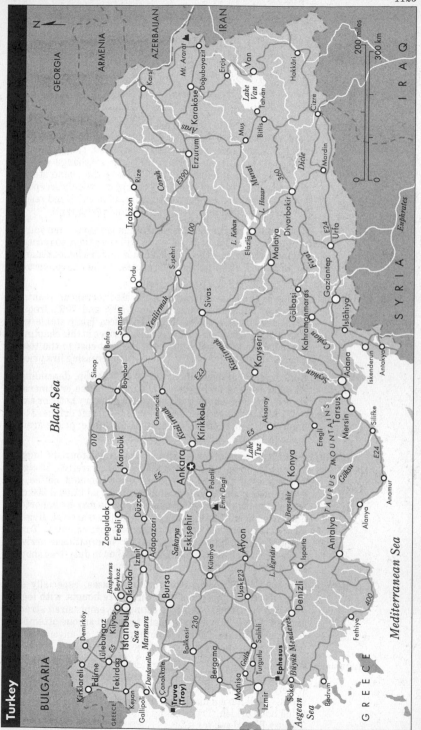

Turkey

Jan.	46F	8C	May	69F	21C	Sept.	76F	24C
	37	3		53	12		61	16
Feb.	47F	9C	June	77F	25C	Oct.	68F	20C
	36	2		60	16		55	13
Mar.	51F	11C	July	82F	28C	Nov.	59F	15C
	38	3		65	18		48	9
Apr.	60F	16C	Aug.	82F	28C	Dec.	51F	11C
	45	7		66	19		41	5

Currency The monetary unit is the Turkish lira (TL), which comes in bank notes of 1,000, 5,000, 10,000, 20,000, 50,000, 100,000, and 250,000. Coins come in denominations of 500, 1,000, 2,500, and 5,000. At press time (spring 1993), the exchange rate was 10,500 TL to the dollar and 15,500 TL to the pound sterling. Major credit cards and traveler's checks are widely accepted in hotels, shops, and expensive restaurants in cities and resorts, but rarely in villages and small shops and restaurants.

Be certain to retain your original exchange slips when you convert money into Turkish lira—you will need them to reconvert the money. Because the Turkish lira is worth a lot less than the dollar or most other foreign currencies, it's best to convert only what you plan to spend.

What It Will Cost Turkey is the least expensive of the Mediterranean countries. Although inflation hovers between 50% and 70%, frequent small devaluations of the lira keep prices fairly stable when measured against foreign currencies. Prices in this chapter are quoted in dollars, which indicate the real cost to the tourist more accurately than do the constantly increasing lira prices.

Sample Prices Coffee can range from about 30¢ to $2.50 a cup, depending on whether it's the less expensive Turkish coffee or American-style coffee and whether it's served in a luxury hotel or a café; tea, 20¢ to $2.50 a glass; local beer, $1–$3; soft drinks, $1–$4; lamb shish kebab, $1.50–$7; taxi, $1 for 1 mile; prices are 50% higher between midnight and 6 AM.

Customs
On Arrival Turkish customs officials rarely look through tourists' luggage on arrival. You are allowed to take in 400 cigarettes, 50 cigars, 200 grams of tobacco, 1.5 kilograms of instant coffee, 500 grams of tea, and 2.5 liters of alcohol. An additional 600 cigarettes, 100 cigars, or 500 grams of tobacco may be imported if purchased at the Turkish duty-free shops on arrival. Register all valuable personal items in your passport on entry. Turkey has duty-free shops in airports for international arrivals. Items are usually less expensive here than in duty-free shops in European airports or in in-flight offerings.

On Departure You must keep receipts of your purchases, especially such items as carpets, as proof that they were bought with legally exchanged currency. Also, it cannot be emphasized strongly enough that Turkey is extremely tough on anyone attempting to export antiques without authorization or anyone caught with illegal drugs, regardless of the amount.

Language Atatürk launched language reforms that replaced Arabic script with the Latin-based alphabet. English and German are widely spoken in cities and resorts. In the villages or in remote areas, you'll have a hard time finding anyone who speaks anything but Turkish. Try learning a few basic Turkish words; the Turks will love you for it.

Getting Around

By Car
Road Conditions
Turkey has excellent roads—25,000 miles of well-maintained, paved highways—but signposts are few, lighting is scarce, and city traffic is chaotic. City streets and highways are jammed with vehicles operated by high-speed lunatics and drivers who constantly blast their horns. In Istanbul, it's safer and faster to drive on the modern highways. Avoid the many small one-way streets, since you never know when someone is going to barrel down one of them in the wrong direction. Better yet, leave your car in a garage and use public transportation or take taxis. Parking is a big problem in the cities and larger towns. Archaeological and historical sites are indicated by yellow signposts.

Rules of the Road
The best way to see Turkey is by car, but be warned that it has one of the highest accident rates in Europe. In general, Turkish driving conforms to Mediterranean customs, with driving on the right and passing on the left. But watch out for drivers passing on a curve or on the top of a hill. Other hazards are peasant carts, which are unlit at night, and motorcycles weaving in and out of traffic.

Gasoline
Throughout the country Mobil, Shell, and British Petroleum, as well as two Turkish oil companies, have gas stations that are open 24 hours on the main highways. Others are open from 6 AM to 10 PM.

Breakdowns
Before you start out, check with your hotel or a tourist information office about how, in case of an emergency, to contact one of the road rescue services available on some highways. Turkish mechanics in the villages will usually manage to get you going again, at least until you reach a city for full repairs. In the cities, entire streets are given over to car-repair shops. Prices are not high, but it's good to give a small tip to the person who does the actual repair work. If you're not in the shop during the repairs, take all the car documents with you. **The Touring and Automobile Club (TTOK)** (Sisli Halaskargazi Cad. 364, tel. 1/231–4631) gives information about driving in Turkey and offers a repair service.

By Train
Although there are express trains in Turkey, the term is usually a misnomer. These trains ply several long-distance routes, but they tend to be slow. The best trains are Fatih Expres, Anadolu, and Mavi. Dining cars on some trains have waiter service and serve surprisingly good and inexpensive food. Overnight expresses have sleeping cars and bunk beds.

Fares
Train fares tend to be less expensive than bus fares. Seats on the best trains, as well as those with sleeping berths, should be booked in advance. Round-trip fares are cheaper than two one-way fares. There are 10% student discounts (30% Dec.–May) and 30% discounts for groups of 24 or more. In railroad stations, buy tickets at windows marked "Bilgisayar Giseleri."

By Bus
Buses, which are run by private companies, are much faster than trains and provide excellent, inexpensive service. Buses are available, virtually around the clock, between all cities and towns. They are fairly comfortable and many are air-conditioned. Companies have their own fixed fares for different routes. Istanbul to Ankara, for instance, varies from $8 to $13; Istanbul to Izmir varies from $11 to $16. *Su* (bottled water) is included in the fare. You can purchase tickets at stands in a town's *otogar* (central bus terminal) or at branch offices in city

centers. All seats are reserved. Fares vary among competing companies, but most buses between major cities are double-deckers and have toilets. Companies such as Varan, Ulusoy, and Pamukkale offer no-smoking seating. For very short trips, or getting around within a city, take minibuses or a *dolmuş* (shared taxi). Both are inexpensive and comfortable.

By Plane **Turkish Airlines (THY)** operates an extensive domestic network. There are at least nine flights daily on weekdays between Istanbul and Ankara. During the summer, many flights between the cities and coastal resorts are added. Try to arrive at the airport at least 45 minutes before your flight because security checks, which are rigidly enforced without exception, can be time-consuming. Checked luggage is placed on trolleys on the tarmac and must be identified by boarding passengers before it is put on the plane. Unidentified luggage is left behind and checked for bombs or firearms.

THY offers several discounts on domestic flights: 10% for family members, including spouses; 50% for children under 13; 90% for children under two; and 50% for sports groups of seven or more. The THY sales office is at Taksim Square (tel. 1/252–1106; reservations by phone, tel. 1/574–8200).

By Boat **Turkish Maritime Lines** operates car ferry and cruise services from Istanbul. Cruises are in great demand, so make your reservations well in advance, either through the head office in Istanbul (Rihtim Cad. 1, Karaköy, tel. 1/244–0207) or through **Sunquest Holidays Ltd.** in London (Aldine House, Aldine St., London W128AW, tel. 081/800–5455).

The **Black Sea Ferry** sails from May through September from Istanbul to Samsun and Trabzon and back, from Karaköy Dock in Istanbul. One-way fares to Trabzon are about $30 for a reclining seat, $38 to $94 for cabins, and $50 for cars. The Istanbul to Izmir car ferry departs three days a week. The price of a one-way ticket with no meals included varies between $38 and $122, and $40 for a car.

Staying in Turkey

Telephones Most pay phones are yellow, push-button models, although a few older, operator-controlled telephones are still in use. Multilingual directions are posted in phone booths.

Local Calls Public phones use *jetons* (tokens), which can be purchased for 400 TL at post offices and street booths. For a local call, deposit the token, wait until the light at the top of the phone goes off, then dial the number. If you need operator assistance for long-distance calls within Turkey, dial 131. For intercity automatic calls, dial 9, wait for a buzzing sound, then dial the city code and the number. Jetons are available for 1,000 TL and 3,000 TL for long-distance calls. Telephone cards are also available for intercity and international calls.

International Calls For all international calls dial 9, wait for the buzz, dial 9 again, then dial the country code, area or city code, and the number. You can use the higher-price jetons for this, or reach an international operator by dialing 132.

If you must make a call abroad, you're better off calling from a phone booth and using jetons or a telephone credit card; hotels in Turkey, as elsewhere, have hefty service charges for international calls.

Mail Post offices are painted bright yellow and have PTT (Post, Telegraph, and Telephone) signs on the front. The major ones are open Monday–Saturday from 8 AM to 9 PM, Sundays from 9 to 7. Smaller branches open Monday–Saturday 8:30–5.

Receiving Mail If you're uncertain where you'll be staying, have mail sent to Post Restante, Merkez Postanesi (central post office) in the town of your choice.

Shopping The best part of shopping in Turkey is visiting the *bedestans*
Bargaining (bazaars), all brimming with copper and brassware items, hand-painted ceramics, alabaster and onyx goods, fabrics, and richly colored carpets. The key word for shopping in the bazaars is "bargain." You must be willing to bargain, and bargain hard. It's great fun once you get the hang of it. As a rule of thumb, offer 50% less after you're given the initial price and be prepared to go up by about 25% to 30% of the first asking price. It's both bad manners and bad business to underbid grossly or to start bargaining if you're not serious about buying. Outside the bazaars prices are usually fixed, although in resort areas some shopkeepers may be willing to bargain if you ask for a "better price." Part of the fun of roaming through the bazaars is having a free glass of *çay* (tea), which vendors will offer you whether you're a serious shopper or just browsing. Beware of antiques: Chances are you will end up with an expensive fake, but even if you do find the genuine article, it's illegal to export antiques of any type.

VAT Refunds Value-added tax (VAT) is nearly always included in the price. You can claim back the VAT if you buy articles from authorized shops. The net total value of articles subject to VAT on your invoice must be over $22 (50,000 TL), and these articles must be exported within three months of purchase. The invoice must be stamped by customs. If the VAT to be refunded is less than 50,000 TL, you can obtain it from a bank outside customs boundaries where the dealer has an account. Otherwise, mail the stamped invoice back to the dealer within one month of departure and the dealer will send back a check.

Opening and **Banks** are open weekdays, 8:30–noon and 1:30–5.
Closing Times
Mosques are usually open to the public, except during *namaz* (prayer hours), which are observed five times a day. These times are based on the position of the sun, so they vary throughout the seasons between the following hours: sunrise (5–7), lunchtime (noon–1, when the sun is directly overhead), afternoon (3–4), sunset (5–7), bedtime (9–10). Prayers last 30–40 minutes.

Museums are generally open Tuesday–Sunday, 9:30–4:30, and closed Monday. Palaces, open the same hours, are closed Thursday instead of Monday.

Shops are closed daily from 1 PM to 2 PM and all day Sunday. Generally they're open Monday–Saturday, 9:30–1 and 2–7. There are some exceptions in the resort areas, where shops stay open until 9 PM and are often open on Sunday.

National Holidays January 1; March 13 (sunset) to March 15 (sunset): *Seker Bayrami* (sugar feast), three-day feast marking the end of Ramadan, a month-long Islamic observance that includes daytime fasting and is based on the Muhammadan lunar calendar, varying yearly; April 23 (National Independence and Children's Day); May 19 (Atatürk's Commemoration, Youth and Sports Day); May 21 (sunset) to May 24 (sunset): *Kurban Bayrami* (sacrificial feast), Turkey's most important religious holiday, celebrating Abraham's willingness to sacrifice his son to God, varying yearly according to the lunar calendar; August 30 (Victory Day); October 28 (half-day) and 29 (Republic Day).

Dining Turkish cuisine is one of the best in the world. The old cliché about it being hard to find a bad meal in Paris more aptly describes Istanbul, where the tiniest little hole-in-the-wall serves delicious food. It's also extremely healthy, full of fresh vegetables, yogurt, legumes, and grains, not to mention fresh seafood, roast lamb, and kebabs made of lamb, beef, or chicken. Because Turkey is predominantly Muslim, pork is not readily available. But there's plenty of alcohol, including local beer and wine, which are excellent and inexpensive. Particularly good wines are Villa Doluca and Kavaklidere, available in *beyaz* (white) and *kirmizi* (red). The most popular local beer is Efes Pilsen. The national alcoholic drink, *raki*, is made from grapes and aniseed. Turks mix it with water or ice and sip it throughout their meal or serve it as an aperitif.

Hotel restaurants have English-language menus and usually serve a bland version of Continental cuisine. Far more adventurous and tasty are meals in *restorans* and in *lokantas* (Turkish restaurants). Most lokantas do not have menus because they serve only what's fresh and in season, which varies daily. At lokantas, you simply sit back and let the waiter bring food to your table, beginning with a tray of *mezes* (appetizers). You point to the dishes that look inviting and take as many as you want. Then you select your main course from fresh meat or fish—displayed in glass-covered refrigerated units—which is then cooked to order or from a steam table laden with casseroles and stews. For lighter meals there are *kebabcis*, tiny restaurants specializing in kebabs served with salad and yogurt, and *pidecis*, selling *pides*, a pizzalike snack on flat bread, topped with butter, cheese, egg, or ground lamb, and baked in a wood-fired oven.

Mealtimes Lunch is generally served from noon to 3 and dinner from 7 to 10. In the cities you can find restaurants or cafés open virtually anytime of day or night, but in the villages, finding a restaurant open at odd hours can be a problem.

Dress Except for Very Expensive restaurants, where formal dress is appropriate, informal dress is acceptable at restaurants in all price categories.

Precautions Tap water is heavily chlorinated and supposedly safe to drink in cities and resorts. It's best to play it safe, however, and drink *maden suyu* (bottled mineral water) or *şişe suyu* (bottled water), which is better tasting and inexpensive.

Ratings Prices are per person and include an appetizer, main course, and dessert. Wine and gratuities are not included. Best bets are indicated by a star ★.

Category	Major Cities	Other Areas
Very Expensive	over $40	over $30
Expensive	$25–$40	$20–$30
Moderate	$12–$25	$10–$20
Inexpensive	under $12	under $10

Lodging Hotels are officially classified in Turkey as HL (luxury), H1 to H5 (first- to fifth-class); motels, M1 to M2 (first- to second-class); and P, *pansiyons* (guest houses). The classification is misleading because the lack of a restaurant or a lounge automatically relegates the establishment to the bottom of the ratings. A lower-grade hotel may actually be far more charming and comfortable than one with a higher rating. There are also many local establishments that are licensed but not included in the official ratings list. You can obtain their names from local tourist offices.

Accommodations range from international luxury chains in Istanbul, Ankara, and Izmir to comfortable, family-run pansiyons. Plan ahead for the peak summer season, when resort hotels are often booked solid by tour companies. Turkey does not have central hotel reservations offices.

Rates vary from $10 to more than $200 a night for a double room. In the less expensive hotels, the plumbing and furnishings will probably leave much to be desired. You can find very acceptable, clean double rooms with bath for between $30 and $70, with breakfast included. Room rates are displayed in the reception area. It is accepted practice in Turkey to ask to see the room in advance.

Ratings Prices are for two people in a double room, including 20% VAT and a 10–15% service charge. Best bets are indicated by a star ★.

Category	Major Cities	Other Areas
Very Expensive	over $200	over $150
Expensive	$100–$200	$100–$150
Moderate	$60–$100	$50–$100
Inexpensive	under $60	under $50

Tipping Except at inexpensive restaurants, a 10% to 15% charge is added to the bill. Since the money does not necessarily find its way to the waiter, leave an additional 10% on the table or hand it to the waiter. In the top restaurants, waiters expect tips of between 10% and 15%. Hotel porters expect between $2 and $5, and the chambermaid, about $2 a day. Taxi drivers don't expect tips, although they are becoming accustomed to foreigners giving them something. Round off the fare to the nearest 500 TL. At Turkish baths, the staff that attends you expects to share a tip of 30% to 35% of the bill. Don't worry about missing them—they'll be lined up expectantly on your departure.

Istanbul

Arriving and Departing

By Plane   All international and domestic flights arrive at Istanbul's Atatürk Airport. For arrival and departure information, call the individual airline or the airport's information desk (tel. 1/573–2920).

Between the Airport and Downtown   Shuttle buses run between the airport's international and domestic terminals to the Turkish Airlines (THY) terminal in downtown Istanbul, at Meşrutiyet Caddesi, near the Galata Tower. Buses depart for the airport at the same address every hour from 6 AM to 11 PM. After that, departure time depends on the number of passengers. Allow at least 45 minutes for the bus ride. Plan to be at the airport two hours before your international flight because of the lengthy security and check-in procedures. The ride from the airport into town takes from 30 to 40 minutes, depending on traffic. Taxis charge about $15 to Taksim Square and $11 to Sultanahmet.

By Train   Trains from the west arrive at Sirkeci station (tel. 1/527–0050 or 0051) in Old Istanbul. Eastbound trains to Anatolia depart from Haydarpasa station (tel. 1/348–8020) on the Asian side.

By Bus   Buses arrive at Topkapi terminal (not to be confused with the area around the Topkapi Palace) just outside the city at the Cannon Gate. The smaller Trakya Otogari terminal is used for buses serving cities and villages on the European side of Turkey. The Anadolu Otogari serves Anatolian Turkey and European destinations. A few buses from Anatolia arrive at Harem terminal, on the eastern shore of the Bosphorus. Some bus companies have *servis arabasi* (minibus services) to the hotel areas of Taksim Square and Aksaray. There are local buses (Nos. 83, 71, 72, 73, and 76 to Taksim and Nos. 84, 89, 92, 93, and 94 to Eminönü from Topkapi terminal), as well as *dolmuşlar* (shared taxis). If you arrive with baggage, it is much easier to take a taxi, which will cost about $8 to Taksim from the bus terminals and about $5 to Old Istanbul.

By Car   If you drive in from the west, take the busy E5 highway, also called Londra Asfalti, which leads from Edirne to Atatürk Airport and on through the city walls at Cannon Gate (Topkapi). E5 heading out of Istanbul leads into central Anatolia and on to Iran and Syria. An alternative to E5, when leaving the city, is to take one of the numerous car ferries that ply the Sea of Marmara and the Dardanelles from Kabataş Dock, or try the overnight ferry to İzmir, which leaves from Sarayburnu.

Getting Around

The best way to get around all the magnificent monuments in Sultanahmet in Old Istanbul is to walk. They're all within easy distance of each other, along streets filled with peddlers, shoeshine boys, children playing, and craftsmen working. To get to other areas, you can take a bus or one of the many ferries that steam between the Asian and European continents. Dolmuş vehicles and taxis are plentiful, inexpensive, and more comfortable than city buses. There's no subway system, but there is the Tünel, a tiny underground train that's handy for getting up the steep hill from Karaköy to the bottom of Istiklal Caddesi. It runs every 10 minutes and costs about 25¢.

By Bus Buy a ticket before boarding a bus. You can buy tickets, individually or in books of 10, at ticket stands around the city. Shoeshine boys or men on the street will also sell them to you for a few cents more. Fares are about 25¢ per ride.

By Dolmuş These are shared taxis that stop at one of the blue and white dolmuş signs. The destination is shown either on a roof sign or a card in the front window. Many of them are classic American cars from the '50s.

By Taxi Taxis are inexpensive. Since most drivers do not speak English and may not know the street names, write down the street you want, the nearby main streets, and the name of the area. Taxis are metered. Although tipping is not expected, you should round off the fare to the nearest 500 TL.

By Boat For a fun and inexpensive ride, take the *Anadolu Kavaği* boat along the Bosporus to its mouth at the Black Sea. The boat leaves year-round from the Eminönü Docks, next to the Galata Bridge on the Old Istanbul side, at 10:30 AM and 1:30 PM, with two extra trips on weekdays and four extra trips on Sundays from April to September. The fare is $6 (round-trip). The trip takes one hour and 45 minutes one way. You can disembark at any of the stops and return by land if you wish. Regular ferries depart from Kabataş Dock, near Dolmabahçe Palace on the European side, to Üsküdar on the Asian side; and also from Eminönü Docks 1 and 2, near Sirkeci station.

Important Addresses and Numbers

Tourist Information Official tourist information offices are at **Atatürk Airport** (tel. 1/573–7399 or 1/573–4136); the **Hilton Hotel** (tel. 1/233–0592); **Karaköy Yolcu Salonu,** International Maritime Passenger Terminal (tel. 1/149–5776); and in a pavilion in the **Sultanamet** district of Old Istanbul (Divan Yolu Cad. 3, tel. 1/522–4903).

Consulates U.S. (Meşrutiyet Caddesi 147, Tepebaşi, Beyoğlu, tel. 1/251–3602). **Canada** (Büyükdere Caddesi 107/3, Bengün Han, tel. 1/272–5174). **U.K.** (Meşrutiyet Caddesi 34, Tepebaşi, Beyoğlu, tel. 1/244–7540).

Emergencies **Tourism Police** (tel. 1/528–5369 or 1/527–4503). **Ambulance** (tel. 177). **Doctors:** For an English-speaking doctor, call the American Hospital (Güzelbahçe Sok. 20, Nişantaşi, tel. 1/231–4050/69) or Beyoğlu Hospital (Kulédibi, Karaköy, tel. 1/251–5900). **Pharmacies:** There is one on duty 24 hours in every neighborhood; tel. 111 for details. Consult the notice in the window of any pharmacy for the name and address of the nearest all-night shop. One that's centrally located is **Taksim** in the Taksim district (Istiklal Cad. 17, tel. 1/149–2252).

English-Language Bookstores The most complete is **Redhouse,** near the Grand Bazaar (Riza Paşa Yokuşu 50, Sultanahmet, tel. 1/527–8100). Others include **Haşet Bookshop** (Istiklal Cad. 469, tel. 1/249–1006), with several branches, including one in the Hilton and the Sheraton hotels, and **Net,** publishers of tourism guides (Yerebatan Cad. 15/3, Sultanahmet, tel. 1/520–8406).

Travel Agencies Most are concentrated along Cumhuriyet Caddesi, off Taksim Square, in the hotel area. They include **American Express** (Hilton Hotel, Cumhuriyet Cad., Harbiye, tel. 1/241–0248 or 1/

241–0249); **Intra** (Halaskargazi Cad. 111/2, Harbiye, tel. 1/247–8174 or 1/240–3891); **Orion Tur** (Halaskargazi Cad. 287/1, Osmanbey, tel. 1/248–8014 or 248–8437); **Setur** (Cumhuriyet Cad. 107, Harbiye, tel. 1/230–0336); and **Vitur** (Cumhuriyet Cad. 269/4, Harbiye, tel. 1/230–0895).

Guided Tours

Tours are arranged through travel agencies (*see* Travel Agencies, above). Choices include the "Classical Tour," either half- or full-day. The half-day tour costs $25 and includes Sancta Sophia, the Museum of Turkish and Islamic Arts, the Hippodrome, Yerebatan Sarayi, and the Blue Mosque; the full-day tour costs $50, and, in addition to the above sights, includes Topkapi Palace, the Süleymaniye Mosque, the Covered or Egyptian Bazaar, and lunch. The "Bosporus Tour" costs $25 for a half day or $50 for a full day, and includes lunch at Sariyer and visits to the Dolmabahçe and Beylerbeyi palaces. The "Night Tour" costs $50 and includes dinner and drinks at Kervansaray or Galata, where there is a show. The full-day guided "Classical Tour" by private car costs between $60 and $90 per person.

Exploring Istanbul

Istanbul is a noisy, chaotic, and exciting city, where Asia meets Europe and spires and domes of mosques and medieval palaces dominate the skyline. At dawn, when the call to the muezzin's prayer rebounds from ancient minarets, many people are making their way home from the nightclubs and bars, while others are kneeling on their prayer rugs, facing Mecca.

Day and night, Istanbul has a schizophrenic air to it. Women in jeans, business suits, or elegant designer outfits pass women wearing the long skirts and head coverings that village women have worn for generations. Donkey-drawn carts vie with old Chevrolets and Pontiacs for dominance of the noisy, narrow streets, and the world's most fascinating Oriental bazaar competes with Western boutiques for the time and attention of both tourists and locals.

Ironically, Istanbul's Asian side is filled with Western-style sprawling suburbs, while its European side contains Old Istanbul—an Oriental wonderland of mosques, opulent palaces, and crowded bazaars. The Golden Horn, an inlet 6½ kilometers (4 miles) long, flows off the Bosporus on the European side, separating Old Istanbul from New Town. The center of New Town is Beyoğlu, a modern district filled with hotels, banks, and shops grouped around Taksim Square. There are three bridges spanning the Golden Horn: the Atatürk, the Galata, and the Haliç. The historic Galata Bridge, which has been replaced by a modern drawbridge, is a central landmark and a good place to get your bearings. From here, you can see the city's layout and its seven hills. The bridge will also give you a taste of Istanbul's frenetic street life. It's filled with peddlers selling everything from pistachio nuts and spices to curly-toed slippers fancy enough for a sultan; fishermen grill their catch on coal braziers and sell them to passersby. None of this sits well with motorists, who blast their horns constantly, usually to no avail. If you want to orient yourself in a quieter way, take a boat trip from the docks on the Eminönü side of the Galata Bridge up the Bosporus.

Numbers in the margin correspond to points of interest on the Istanbul map.

Old Istanbul (Sultanahmet) ❶ The number-one attraction in Istanbul is **Topkapi Palace** (Topkapi Saray), located on Seraglio Point in Old Istanbul, known as Sultanahmet. The palace, which dates from the 15th century, was the residence of a number of sultans and their harems until the mid-19th century. In order to avoid the crowds, try to get there by 9 AM, when the gates open. If you're arriving by taxi, tell the driver you want the Topkapi *Saray* (palace) in Sultanahmet, or you could end up at the Topkapi bus terminal on the outskirts of town.

Sultan Mehmet II built the first palace during the 1450s, shortly after the Ottoman conquest of Constantinople. Over the centuries, sultan after sultan added ever more elaborate architectural fantasies, until the palace eventually ended up with more than four courtyards and some 5,000 residents, many of them concubines and eunuchs. Topkapi was the residence and center of bloodshed and drama for the Ottoman rulers until the 1850s, when Sultan Abdül Mecit moved with his harem to the European-style Dolmabahçe Palace farther up the Bosphorus coast.

❷ In Topkapi's outer courtyard are the **Church of St. Irene** (Aya Irini), open only during festival days for concerts, and the ❸ **Court of the Janissaries** (Merasim Avlusu), members of the sultan's elite guard.

Adjacent to the ticket office is the **Bab-i-Selam** (Gate of Salutation), built in 1524 by Süleyman the Magnificent, who was the only person allowed to pass through it. From the towers on either side, prisoners were kept until they were executed beside the fountain outside the gate in the first courtyard. In the second courtyard, amid the rose gardens, is the **Divan-i-Humayun,** the assembly room of the council of state, once presided over by the grand vizir (prime minister). The sultan would sit behind a latticed window, hidden by a curtain so no one would know when he was listening, although occasionally he would pull the curtain aside to comment.

One of the most popular tours in Topkapi is the **Harem,** a maze of nearly 400 halls, terraces, rooms, wings, and apartments grouped around the sultan's private quarters on the west side of the second courtyard. Forty rooms have been meticulously restored and are open to the public. Next to the entrance are the quarters of the eunuchs and about 200 of the lesser concubines, who were lodged in tiny cubicles, as cramped and uncomfortable as the main rooms of the Harem are large and opulent. Tours begin about every half hour. *Admission: $1.*

In the third courtyard is the **Treasury** (Hazine Dairesi), four rooms filled with jewels, including two uncut emeralds, each weighing 3½ kilograms (7.7 pounds), that once hung from the ceiling. Here, too, you will be dazzled by the emerald dagger used in the movie *Topkapi* and the 84-carat "Spoonmaker" diamond that, according to legend, was found by a pauper and traded for three wooden spoons.

Time Out Just past the Treasury, on the right side of the courtyard, are steps leading to a 19th-century Rococo Mecidiye pavilion, now the **Konyali Restaurant** (tel. 1/513–9696), which serves excellent Turkish food and has a magnificent view of the *seraglio*

Archaeological
Museum, **4**

Blue Mosque, **6**

Church of St. Irene, **2**

Cistern Basilica, **9**

Court of the
Janissaries, **3**

Dolmabahçe
Mosque, **16**

Dolmabahçe Palace, **17**

Egyptian Bazaar, **13**

Flower Market, **15**

Galata Tower, **14**

Grand Bazaar, **10**

Hippodrome, **7**

Istanbul
University, **11**

Museum of Turkish
and Islamic Arts, **8**

Sancta Sophia, **5**

Süleymaniye
Mosque, **12**

Topkapi Palace, **1**

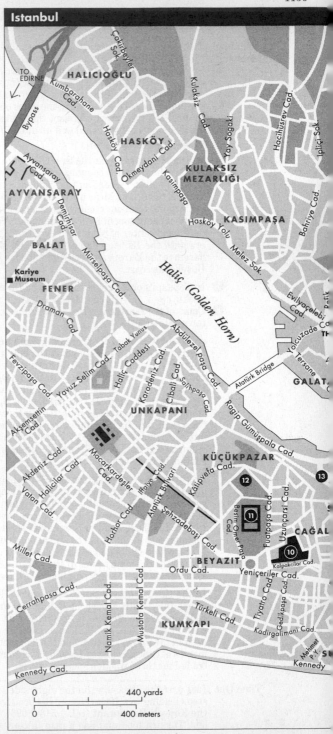

Istanbul

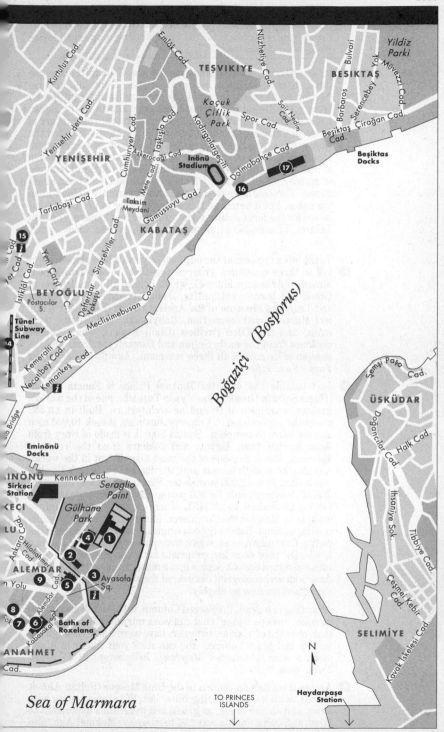

TEŞVIKIYE

BEŞIKTAŞ

Yildiz Parki

Nüzhetiye Cad.

Kutulus Cad.

Emlák Cad.

Bulvari

Müvezzi Cad.

Koçuk Çiftlik Park

Spor Cad.

Sait Nadim Cad.

Barbaros

Serencebey

Çirağan Cad.

Beşiktaş Cad.

Beşiktas Docks

YENIŞEHIR

Yenisehir dere Cad.

Cumhuriyet Cad.

Taşkişla Cad.

Askerocaği Cad.

Kadirgalargeçil

Mete Cad.

Inönü Stadium

Dolmabahçe Cad.

17

16

Tarlabaşi Cad.

Taksim Meydani

Gümüssuyu Cad.

KABATAŞ

15
i

Cad.

er Cad.

Yeni Çarşi

Istiklál Cad.

BEYOĞLU

Postacilar S.

Defterdar Yokuşu

Sira-selviler Cad.

Meclisimebusan Cad.

Boğaziçi (Bosporus)

Şemşi Paşa Cad.

Tünel Subway Line

4

Kemeralti Cad.

Necatibey Cad.

Kemankeş Cad.

i

ÜSKÜDAR

Doğancilar Cad.

Halk Cad.

a Bridge

Eminönü Docks

İNÖNÜ

Sirkeci Station

Kennedy Cad.

Seraglio Point

Gülhane Park

KECI

LU

Ankara Cad.

Hilaliahmer Cad.

4

1

2

ALEMDAR

9

5

3

Ayasofa Sq.

i

Ihsaniye Sok.

Tibbiye Cad.

n Yolu

Alemdar Cad.

8

7

6

Kabasakal Sok.

Baths of Roxelana

ANAHMET

Cad.

Çeşmei Kebir Cad.

SELIMIYE

N

Sea of Marmara

Kavak Iskelesi Cad.

TO PRINCES ISLANDS

Haydarpaşa Station

(sultan's household, including the harem) and the Golden Horn. On a terrace below is an outdoor café with an even better view. Go early or reserve a table to beat the tour-group crush. *Open Wed.–Mon. Lunch only.*

In the fourth and last courtyard of the Topkapi Palace are small, elegant summer houses, mosques, fountains, and reflecting pools scattered amid the gardens on different levels. Here you will find the **Erivan Kiosk,** also known as the Revan Kiosk, built by Murat IV in 1636 to commemorate his capture of Rivan in Caucasus. In another kiosk in the gardens, called the **Golden Cage** (Iftariye), the closest relatives of the reigning sultan lived in strict confinement under what amounted to house arrest. The custom began during the 1800s after the old custom of murdering all possible rivals to the throne had been abandoned. The confinement of the heirs apparently helped keep the peace, but it deprived them of any chance to prepare themselves for the formidable task of ruling a great empire. *Topkapi Palace. Admission: $4.25, harem $1. Open Wed.–Mon. 9:30–5:30.*

4 To the left as you enter the outer courtyard, a lane slopes downhill to three museums grouped together: the **Archaeological Museum** (Arkeoloji Müzesi), which houses a fine collection of Greek and Roman antiquities, including finds from Ephesus and Troy; the **Museum of the Ancient Orient** (Eski Şark Eserleri Müzesi), with Sumerian, Babylonian, and Hittite treasures; and the **Tiled Pavilion** (Çinili Köşkü), which houses ceramics from the early Seljuk and Osmanli empires. The admission price covers all three museums. *Admission: $2. Open Tues.–Sun. 9:30–5.*

5 Just outside the walls of Topkapi Palace is **Sancta Sophia** (Hagia Sofia in Greek, Ayasofya in Turkish), one of the world's greatest examples of Byzantine architecture. Built in AD 532 under the supervision of Emperor Justinian, it took 10,000 men and six years to complete. Sancta Sophia is made of ivory from Asia, marble from Egypt, and columns from the ruins of Ephesus. The dome, one of the most magnificent in the world, was also the world's largest until the dome at St. Peter's Basilica was built in Rome 1,000 years later. Sancta Sophia was the cathedral of Constantinople for 900 years, surviving earthquakes and looting Crusaders until 1453, when it was converted into a mosque by Mehmet the Conqueror. Minarets were added by succeeding sultans. Sancta Sophia originally had many mosaics depicting Christian scenes, which were plastered over by Süleyman I, who felt they were inappropriate for a mosque. In 1935, Atatürk converted Sancta Sophia into a museum. Shortly after that, American archaeologists discovered the mosaics, which were restored and are now on display.

According to legend, the **Sacred Column,** in the north aisle of the mosque, "weeps water" that can work miracles. It's so popular that, over the centuries, believers have worn a hole through the marble and brass column. You can stick your finger in it and make a wish. *Ayasofya Meydani. Admission: $4.25. Open Tues.–Sun. 9:30–5.*

6 Across from Sancta Sophia is the **Blue Mosque** (Sultan Ahmet Camii), with its shimmering blue tiles, 260 stained-glass windows, and six minarets, as grand and beautiful a monument to Islam as Sancta Sophia was to Christianity. Mehmet Aga, also known as Sedefkar (Worker of Mother of Pearl) built the mosque during the reign of Sultan Ahmet I in eight years, beginning in 1609, nearly 1,100 years after the completion of Sancta Sophia. His goal was to surpass Justinian's masterpiece, and many in the world believe he succeeded.

Press through the throng of touts and enter the mosque at the side entrance that faces Sancta Sophia. You must remove your shoes and leave them at the entrance. Immodest clothing is not allowed, but an attendant at the door will lend you a robe if he feels you are not dressed appropriately. *Admission free. Open daily 9–5.*

The **Carpet and Kilim museums** (Hünkar Kasri) are in the mosque's stone-vaulted cellars and upstairs at the end of a stone ramp, where the sultans rested before and after their prayers. *Admission: $1.50 adults, 25¢ students. Open Tues.–Sat. 8:30–5.*

7 The **Hippodrome** is a long park directly in front of the Blue Mosque. As a Roman stadium with 100,000 seats, it was once the focal point for public entertainment, including chariot races and circuses. It was also the site of many riots and public executions. What remain today are an **Egyptian Obelisk** (Dikilitas), the **Column of Constantinos** (Örme Sütun), and the **Serpentine Column** (Yilanli Sütun) taken from the Temple of Apollo at Delphi in Greece. You'll also encounter thousands of peddlers selling postcards, nuts, and trinkets.

On the western side of the Hippodrome is **Ibrahim Paşa Palace,** the grandiose residence of the son-in-law and grand vizir of Süleyman the Magnificent. Ibrahim Paşa was executed when he became too powerful for Süleyman's liking. The palace now
8 houses the **Museum of Turkish and Islamic Arts,** which gives a superb insight into the lifestyles of Turks of every level of society, from the 8th century to the present. *Şifahane Sok, across from the Blue Mosque, in line with the Serpentine Column. Admission: $2.50. Open Tues.–Sun. 9:30–5.*

Walk back along the length of the Hippodrome and cross the busy main road, Divanyolu. Turn left onto Hilaliahmer
9 Caddesi. On your left is the **Cistern Basilica** (Yerebatan Sarayi). This is an underground network of waterways first excavated by Emperor Constantine in the 3rd century and then by Emperor Justinian in the 6th century. It has 336 marble columns rising 8 meters (26 feet) to support Byzantine arches and domes. The cistern was always kept full as a precaution against long sieges. *Yerebatan Cad. Admission: $2. Open Wed.–Mon. 9–5.*

Time Out If you need some time out and want a real treat, spend an hour in a Turkish bath. One of the best is Cağaloğlu **Hamami,** near Sancta Sophia in a magnificent 18th-century building. *Ismail Gürkan Cad. 34, tel. 1/522–2424. Admission: $8 for self-service bath, $15 for full service, $24 for deluxe Ottoman massage. Open daily 8–8 for women; 7 AM–10 PM for men.*

10 The next grand attraction is the **Grand Bazaar** (Kapali Carsişi) about a quarter-mile northwest of the Hippodrome (a 15-minute walk or 5-minute taxi ride). The Grand Bazaar, also called the Covered Bazaar, is a maze of 65 winding, covered streets, with 4,000 shops, tiny cafés, and restaurants. Originally built by Mehmet the Conqueror in the 1450s, it was ravaged by two modern-day fires, one in 1954 that virtually destroyed it, and a smaller one in 1974. In both cases, the bazaar was quickly rebuilt. It's a shopper's paradise, filled with thousands of different items, including carpets, fabrics, clothing, brassware, furniture, and gold jewelry. *Yeniçeriler Cad. and Fuatpaşa Cad. Admission free. Open Apr.–Oct., Mon.–Sat. 8:30–7; Nov.–Mar., Mon.–Sat. 8:30–6:30.*

⓫ When you leave the bazaar, cross Fuatpaşa Caddesi and walk around the grounds of **Istanbul University,** which has a magnificent gateway facing Beyazit Square. Follow Besim Ömer Paşa Caddesi, the western border of the university, to the right to ⓬ the 16th-century **Süleymaniye Mosque.** The mosque was designed by Sinan, the architectural genius who masterminded more than 350 buildings and monuments under the direction of Süleyman the Magnificent. This is Sinan's grandest and most famous monument, and the burial site of both himself and his patron, Süleyman. *Admission free. Open daily outside prayer hours.*

⓭ The Grand Bazaar isn't the only bazaar in Istanbul. Another one worth visiting is the **Egyptian Bazaar** (Misir Carsişi). You reach it by walking down Çarşi Caddesi to Çakmakçilar Yokuşu and Firincilar Sokak, and then into Sabunchani Sokak, where you will see the back of the bazaar. It was built in the 17th century as a means of rental income for the upkeep of the Yeni Mosque. The bazaar was once a vast pharmacy, filled with burlap bags overflowing with herbs and spices for folk remedies. Today, you're more likely to see bags full of fruit, nuts, Royal Jelly from the beehives of the Aegean coast, and white sacks spilling over with culinary spices. It's a lively, colorful scene. Nearby are the fruit and fish markets, which are equally colorful. *Next to Yeni Cami. Open Mon.–Sat. 8–7.*

Time Out **Pandeli.** Excellent food is served in this frenetic turn-of-the-century restaurant, with its domed alcoves. It can be reached up two flights of stairs over the arched gateway to the Egyptian Bazaar. *Misir Carsişi, Eminönü, tel. 1/527–3909. AE, DC, MC, V. Lunch only. Closed Sun. Moderate.*

New Town New Town is the area on the northern shore of the Golden Horn, the waterway that cuts through Istanbul and divides Europe from Asia. The area's most prominent landmark is the ⓮ **Galata Tower,** built by the Genoese in 1349 as part of their fortifications. In this century, it served as a fire lookout until 1960. Today it houses a restaurant and nightclub (*see* Nightlife, *below*), and a daytime viewing tower. *Büyük Hendek Cad. Admission: $1. Open daily 9–8.*

⓯ North of the tower is the **Flower Market** (Çiçek Pasaji), off Istiklâl Caddesi, a lively blend of flower stalls, tiny restaurants, bars, and street musicians.

⓰ Next head for **Dolmabahçe Mosque** and **Dolmabahçe Palace,** which are reached by following Istiklâl Caddesi to Taksim Square and then taking Gümüssuyu Caddesi around the square to a junction. You will see the Dolmabahçe Mosque on your right and the clock tower and gateway to Dolmabahçe Palace on your left. The mosque is a separate building from the palace. It was founded by Valide Sultan Bezmialem, mother of Abdül

Mecit I, and was completed in 1853. *Admission free. Open daily outside prayer hours.*

❶ The **Dolmabahçe Palace** was also built in 1853 and, until the declaration of the modern republic in 1923, was the residence of the last sultans of the Ottoman Empire. It was also the residence of Atatürk, who died here in 1938. The palace, floodlit at night, is an extraordinary mixture of Hindu, Turkish, and European styles of architecture and interior design. Queen Victoria's contribution to the lavishness was a chandelier weighing 4½ tons. Guided tours of the palace take about 80 minutes. *Gümüssuyu Cad. Admission: $4.80. Open Apr.–Oct. 9–4; Nov.–Mar. 9–3. Closed Mon. and Thurs.*

Shopping

Gift Ideas The **Grand Bazaar** *(see* Exploring Istanbul, *above)* is a treasure trove of all things Turkish—carpets, brass, copper, jewelry, textiles, and leather goods.

Stores Stores and boutiques are located in New Town on such streets as **Istiklâl Caddesi,** which runs off Taksim Square, and **Rumeli, Halaskargazi,** and **Valikonagi Caddeleri,** north of the Hilton Hotel. Two streets in the Kadiköy area that offer good shopping are **Bağdat and Bahariye Caddeleri. Ataköy Shopping and Tourism Center** is a large shopping and leisure mall near the airport. It's a good place for children, too.

Markets **Balikpazari** (fish market) is in Beyoğlu Caddesi, off Istiklâl Caddesi. Despite its name, you will find anything connected with food at this market. A **flea market** is held in Beyazit Square, near the Grand Bazaar, every Sunday. A crafts market, with street entertainment, is open on Sundays along the Bosporus at Ortaköy. A weekend crafts market is also held on Bekar Sokak, off Istiklal Caddesi.

Dining

Istanbul has a wide range of eating establishments, with prices to match. Most of the major hotels have dining rooms serving rather bland international cuisine. It's far more rewarding to eat in Turkish restaurants. For details and price-category definitions, *see* Dining in Staying in Turkey.

Very Expensive **Bebek Ambassadeurs.** Here you can dine on French and international cuisines while enjoying the views over the Bosporus from the terrace. *Cevdet Paşa Cad. 113, Bebek, tel. 1/263–3002. Reservations advised. AE, DC, MC, V.*

Club 29. This popular restaurant serves French and Turkish cuisines. After midnight a discotheque upstairs is open until 4 AM. *Nispetiye Cad. 29, Etiler, tel. 1/263–5411. Reservations required. AE, DC, MC, V. No lunch.*

Körfez. The restaurant boat ferries guests across the Bosphorus from Rumeli Hisari. *Kanlica, tel. 1/332–0108. Reservations advised. AE, DC, MC, V. Closed Mon.*

Expensive **Abdullah Efendi.** Here you'll find a great selection of Istanbul fish and other dishes served in a garden overlooking the Bosporus. *Koru Caddesi 11, Emirgan, tel. 1/277–5721. Reservations advised. AE, DC, MC, V.*

Divan. You'll enjoy gourmet Turkish and international cuisine, elegant surroundings, and excellent service at this restaurant, located in the Divan hotel. *Cumhuriyet Cad. 2, Elmadağ, tel. 1/231–4100. Reservations advised. AE, DC, MC, V.*

Gelik. This restaurant, located in a two-story 19th-century villa, is usually packed, often with people who want to savor its specialty: all types of meat cooked in deep wells. *Sahil Yolu, Ataköy, tel. 1/560–7284. Reservations advised. AE, DC, MC, V.*

Moderate   **Borsa Lokantasi.** This unpretentious restaurant serves some of the best food in Turkey. The baked lamb in eggplant purée and the stuffed artichokes are not to be missed. *Yaliköskü Cad. Yaliköskü Han 60–62, Eminönü, tel. 1/522–4173. Reservations not necessary. No credit cards. Lunch only. Closed Sun. Another branch at Halaskargazi Cad. 90/1, Osmanbey, tel. 1/232–4200. AE, DC, MC, V.*

Dört Mevsim. Located in a large Victorian building, Dört Mevsim is noted for its blend of Turkish and French cuisine and for its owners, Gay and Musa, an Anglo-Turkish couple who opened it in 1965. On any given day, you'll find them in the kitchen overseeing such delights as shrimp in cognac sauce and baked marinated lamb. *Istiklâl Cad. 509, Beyoğlu, tel. 1/245–8941. Reservations advised. AE, DC, MC, V. Closed Sun.*

Hanedan. The emphasis is on kebabs, all kinds, all excellent; better-than-average mezes as starters, too. The setting is lively, by the Besiktas ferry terminal. *Çiğdem Sok. 27, Besiktas, tel. 1/260–4854. Reservations advised. AE, MC, V.*

Inexpensive   **Hacibaba.** This is a large, cheerful-looking place, with a terrace overlooking a churchyard. Fish, meat, and a wide variety of vegetable dishes are on display for your selection. Before you choose your main course, you'll be offered a tray of appetizers that can be a meal in themselves. *Istiklal Cad. 49, Taksim, tel. 1/244–1886. Reservations advised. AE, DC, MC, V.*

★ **Haci Salih.** A tiny, family-run restaurant, Haci Salih has only 10 tables, so you may have to line up and wait—but it's worth it. Traditional Turkish food is the fare here, with special emphasis on vegetable dishes and lamb. Alcohol is not served, but you can bring your own. *Anadolu Han 201, off Istiklal Cad., tel. 1/243–4528. Reservations sometimes accepted. No credit cards. Lunch only. Closed Sun.*

Kaptan. An animated, crowded fish restaurant near the Bosphorus. It's worth taking a taxi here. *Birinçi Cad. 53, Arnavutköy, tel. 1/265–8487. Reservations advised. V.*

Rejans. Founded by three Russian dancing girls fleeing the Revolution, this restaurant offers traditional East European decor and excellent Russian food and vodka, served by eccentric old waiters. *Istiklâl Cad., Olivo Geçidi 15, Galatasaray, tel. 1/244–1610. Reservations required. DC, MC, V. Closed Sun.*

Lodging

The top hotels are located mainly around Taksim Square in New Town. Hotels generally include the 15% VAT and a service charge of 10–15% in the rate. Modern, middle-range hotels usually have a friendly staff, which compensates for the generally bland architecture and interiors. In Old Istanbul, the Aksaray, Laleli, Sultanahmet, and Beyazit areas have many conveniently located, inexpensive small hotels and family-run pansiyons. Istanbul has a chronic shortage of beds, so plan ahead. For details and price-category definitions, *see* Lodging in Staying in Turkey.

Very Expensive ★ **Çirağan Palace.** This 19th-century Ottoman palace is the city's most luxurious—and expensive—hotel. The setting is exceptional, right on the Bosporus and adjacent to lush Yildiz Park. *Cad. 84, Besiktas, tel. 1/258–3377, fax 1/259–6687. 340 rooms with bath. Facilities: Turkish bath, health spa, pool, bar, 4 restaurants, casino, shops. AE, DC, MC, V.*

The Hilton. Lavishly decorated with Turkish rugs and large brass urns, this is one of the best Hiltons in the chain. Ask for a room with a view of the Bosporus. *Cumhuriyet Cad., Harbiye, tel. 1/231–4646, fax 1/240–4165. 510 rooms with bath. Facilities: Turkish baths, beauty and health spa, pool, rooftop bar and restaurant, tennis, squash, shopping arcade, casino, conference facilities. AE, DC, MC, V.*

★ **Pera Palace.** A grand hotel with a genuinely Turkish feel, the Pera Palace was built in 1892 to accommodate guests arriving on the *Orient Express.* Although it has been modernized, the hotel has lost none of its original Victorian opulence. Ask to see the room where Atatürk used to stay—it's been maintained with some of his personal belongings. *Meşrutiyet Cad. 98, Tepebaşi, tel. 1/251–4560, fax 1/251–4089. 145 rooms with bath. Facilities: bar. AE, DC, MC, V.*

The Sheraton. Taksim Park provides a splendid setting for this hotel. All rooms have views of the Bosporus or the square. For a night's spree, try the rooftop restaurant and nightclub. *Taksim Park, Taksim, tel. 1/231–2121, fax 1/231–2180. 437 rooms with bath. Facilities: restaurant, bar, nightclub, pool, health and beauty spa. AE, DC, MC, V.*

Expensive **Ayasofia Pansiyons.** These guest houses are part of an imaginative project undertaken by the Touring and Automobile Club to restore a little street of historic wooden houses along the outer wall of Topkapi Palace. One of the houses has been converted into a library and two into pansiyons, furnished in late Osmanli style, with excellent dining rooms. During the summer, tea and refreshments are served in the gardens to guests and non-guests alike. *Soğukçesme Sokak, Sultanahmet, tel. 1/513–3660, fax 1/512–3669. 63 rooms with bath. AE, MC, V.*

Divan. This is a quiet modern hotel with an excellent restaurant, located very close to Taksim Square. *Cumhuriyet Cad. 2, Şisli, tel. 1/231–4100. 180 rooms with bath. Facilities: restaurant, bar, tea shop, beauty salon. AE, DC, MC.*

★ **Yeşil Ev (Green House).** Practically next door to the Blue Mosque, this 19th-century building is decorated in old-fashioned Ottoman style with lace curtains and latticed shutters. Its high-walled garden restaurant is a verdant and peaceful oasis in the midst of frenetic Istanbul. *Kabasakal Sok. 5, Sultanahmet, tel. 1/517–6785, fax 1/517–6780. 20 rooms with bath. Facilities: restaurant and garden. AE, MC, V.*

Moderate **Barin.** Modern, clean, and comfortable, with good, friendly service, the Barin caters to business travelers as well as tourists. *Fevziye Cad. 7, Sehzadebaşi, tel. 1/513–9100, fax 1/526–4440. 65 rooms with bath. AE, DC, MC, V.*

★ **Barut's Guesthouse.** Quiet and secluded and in the heart of Old Istanbul, Barut's has a roof terrace overlooking the Sea of Marmara. A friendly, pleasant establishment, the hotel has a modern art gallery in its foyer. *Ishakpaşa Cad. 8, Sultanahmet, tel. 1/516–0357, fax 1/516–2944. 23 rooms with bath. MC, V.*

Büyük Londra. This is another Victorian hotel, similar to the Pera Palace, but not as grand, that has grown old gracefully. *Meşrutiyet Cad. 117, Tepebaşi, tel. 1/245–0670, fax 1/245–0671. 54 rooms with bath. AE, MC, V.*

Inexpensive **Berk Guest House.** Clean and exceptionally comfortable, this is run by an English-speaking couple, Güngör and Nevin Evrensel. Two rooms have balconies overlooking a garden. The guest house is expected to be expanded. *Kutlugün Sok. 27, Cankurtaran, Sultanahmet, tel. 1/516–9671, fax 1/517–7715. 7 rooms with bath. No credit cards.*

Plaza. This is an older, well-run hotel overlooking the Bosphorus. *Siraselviler Cad. Arslanyataği Sok. 19, Taksim, tel. 1/245–3273. 18 rooms with bath. No credit cards.*

The Arts

Entertainment in Istanbul ranges from the **Istanbul International Festival**—held late June through mid-July and attracting internationally renowned artists and performers—to local folklore and theatrical groups, some amateur, some professional. Because there is no central ticket agency, ask your hotel to help you. You can also pick up tickets at the box office or through a local tourist office.

For tickets to the Istanbul International Festival, apply to the **Istanbul Foundation for Culture and Arts** (Kültür ve Sanat Vakfi, Yildiz, Besiktaş, tel. 1/261–3294 and 1/260–9072). Performances, which include modern and classical music, ballet, opera, and theater, are given throughout the city in historic buildings, such as St. Irene Church and Rumeli Castle. The highlight of the festival is the performance of Mozart's opera *Abduction from the Seraglio*, at Topkapi Palace, the site that inspired the opera.

Concerts Tickets for performances at the main concert hall, **Atatürk Kültür Merkezi,** are available from the box office at Taksim Square (tel. 1/251–5600). From October through May, the **Istanbul State Symphony** gives performances here. It's also the location for ballet and dance companies. The Touring and Automobile Association organizes chamber music performances at **Beyaz Kösk** and **Hidiv Kasri,** two 19th-century minipalaces. For information, contact the **Touring and Automobile Association** (Halaskargazi Cad. 364, Şişli, tel. 1/231–4631).

Nightlife

Bars and **Kulis** (Cumhuriyet Cad. 117, tel. 1/246–9345), an all-night
Nightclubs hangout for actors and writers, offers good piano music. Open daily 10 PM–5 AM. Local young professionals patronize **Zihni** (Bronz Sok. 1A, Macka, tel. 1/246–9043) for lunch or evening cocktails. Open daily noon–3 and 6–10.

Bebek Bar (Bebek Ambassadeurs Hotel, Cevdet Paşa Cad. 113, Bebek, tel. 1/263–3000) has views over the Bosporus. Open daily until 1 AM.

Orient Express Bar (Pera Palace Hotel, Meşrutiyet Cad. 98, Tepebaşi, tel. 1/251–4560) distills the atmosphere of old Istanbul with the lingering presence of the rich, powerful, and famous (from Atatürk to Italian king Victor Emmanuel to Josephine Baker) who once played here.

İpekyolu (Lamartin Cad. 26/1, Taksim, tel. 1/135-6642) draws a smart, young, and wealthy Turkish crowd for traditional Turkish music, minutes from the modern high-rise hotels.

A well-established nightclub is **Kervansaray** (Cumhuriyet Cad. 30, Elmadağ, tel. 1/247-1630), where you can dine, dance, and watch belly-dancing shows. Open daily 8 PM-midnight. Two other good places for floor shows are **Balim** (Kemerhatun Mah. Hamalbaşi Cad. 8, Beyoğlu, tel. 1/249-5608) and **Olimpia** (Acar Sok. Tomtom Mah., off İstiklal Cad., tel. 1/244-9456). **Galata Tower** (Kuledibi, tel. 1/245-1160) offers dinner between 8:30 and 10, with a Turkish show and dancing from 10 PM to 1 AM.

Jazz   **Hayal Kahvesi** (Büyük Parmakkapi Sok. 19, Beyoğlu, tel. 1/244-2558) is a bohemian side-street bar with wood furniture and lace curtains. Local groups perform jazz, blues, and rock; Tuesday and Friday are jazz nights.

Discos   A chic disco with space-age decor and hip atmosphere is **Juliana's,** which also offers live music (Swissotel The Bosporus, Macka, tel. 1/259-0940), open nightly 8 PM-4 AM. **Discorium** (Esentepe, tel. 1/274-8410) is highly recommended. Men are admitted only if accompanied by a woman. **Çubuklu 29** (Bahçeburun, Çubuklu, tel. 1/331-2829), situated by the Bosporus on the Asian side, is open from mid-June through September. **Regine** (Cumhuriyet Cad. 16, Elmadağ, tel. 1/246-7449) is an upscale disco-nightclub, open from 10 PM to 4 AM.

The Aegean Coast

Some of the finest reconstructed Greek and Roman cities, including the fabled Pergamum, Ephesus, Aphrodisias, and Troy, are to be found in this region of Turkey. Bright yellow road signs pointing to historical sites or to those currently undergoing excavation are everywhere here. There are so many Greek and Roman ruins, in fact, that some haven't yet been excavated and others are going to seed.

Grand or small, all the sites are steeped in atmosphere and are best explored early in the morning or late in the afternoon, when there are fewer crowds. You can escape the heat of the day on one of the sandy beaches that line the coast.

Getting Around

The E24 from Çanakkale follows the coast until it turns inland at Kuşadasi to meet the Mediterranean again at Antalya. All the towns on the itinerary are served by direct bus routes, and there are connecting services to the ancient sites.

Guided Tours

The travel agencies in all the major towns offer tours of the historical sites. **Troy-Anzac Tours** (tel. 196/75849 or 196/75847), in central Çanakkale, has guided tours of the battlefields at Gallipoli. The tour takes about four hours and costs about $11 per person, including breakfast. Travel agencies along Teyyare Caddesi in Kuşadasi offer escorted tours to Ephesus; Priene, Miletus, and Didyma; and Aphrodisias and Pamukkale.

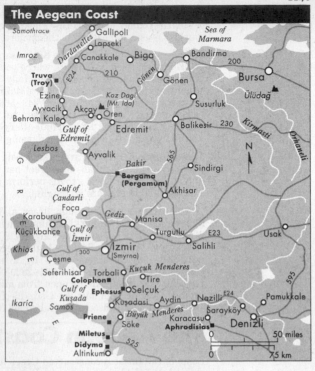

The Aegean Coast

Tourist Information

Contact the tourist office in each town for names of travel agencies and licensed tour guides.

Ayvalik (Yat Limani Karşisi, tel. 663/22122).
Bergama (Zafer Mah. Izmir Cad. 54, tel. 541/31862).
Bursa (Ulu Cami Parki, Atatürk Cad. 1, tel. 24/212359).
Çanakkale (Iskele Meyd. 67, tel. 196/71187).
Çeşme (Iskele Meyd. 8, tel. 549/26653).
İzmir (Atatürk Cad. 418, Alsancak, tel. 51/220207; Gaziosmanpasa Bul. 1/C, tel. 51/842147).
Kuşadasi (Iskele Meyd. tel. 636/41103).

Exploring the Aegean Coast

Bursa **Bursa,** the first capital of the Ottoman Empire, is known as Yeşil (Green) Bursa, not only because of its many trees and parks but also because of its **Yeşil Cami** (Green Mosque) and **Yeşil Turbe** (Green Mausoleum). Both the mosque and mausoleum derive their names from the green tiles that line the interior of the buildings. They are located opposite each other on Yeşil Caddesi (Green Avenue). *Admission free. Open daily outside prayer hours.*

Bursa is also the site of **Uludağ** (the Great Mountain), Turkey's most popular ski resort. To fully appreciate why the town is called Green Bursa, take a ride on the *teleferik* (cable car) from Namazgah Caddesi up the mountain for a panoramic view.

The town square is called **Heykel,** which means "statue," and is named for its statue of Atatürk. Off Heykel, along Atatürk Caddesi, is the **Ulu Cami** (Great Mosque) with its distinctive silhouette of 20 domes. *Admission free. Open daily outside prayer hours.*

Troy Long thought to be simply an imaginary city from Homer's *Iliad,* Troy was excavated in the 1870s by Heinrich Schliemann, a German amateur archaeologist who also found the remains of nine successive civilizations, one on top of the other, dating back 5,000 years. Considering Troy's fame, the site is surprisingly small. It's best to take a guided tour to appreciate fully the significance of this discovery and the unwavering passion of the man who proved that Troy was not just another ancient myth. *Admission: $2.50. Open daily 8–7.*

The E24 highway leads around the **Gulf of Edremit,** a glorious area of olive groves, pine forests, and small seaside resorts. **Ayvalik,** 5 kilometers (3 miles) off the main bus route, between Çanakkale and Izmir, is an ideal place to stay while visiting the ruins of ancient Pergamum, 40 kilometers (24 miles) away. From Ayvalik you can take boats to **Ali Bey Adasi,** a tiny island with pleasant waterfront restaurants, and to the Greek island of Lesbos.

Pergamum **Pergamum** is reached by driving southeast along E24 following the signs toward Bergama, the modern-day name of the ancient Greek-Roman site. If you're traveling by bus, be certain it is going all the way to Bergama, or you'll find yourself dropped off at the turn-in, 8 kilometers (5 miles) from the site.

Because the ruins of Pergamum are spread out over several miles, it's best to take a taxi from one site to the next. The most noteworthy places are the Asklepieion, the Ethnological Museum, the Red Hall, and the **Acropolis.** *Admission: $2.50. Open Apr.–Oct., daily 8:30–6:30; Nov.–Mar., daily 8:30–5:30*

Pergamum's glory peaked during the Greek Attalid dynasty (241–133 BC), when it was one of the world's most magnificent architectural and artistic centers—especially so under the rule of Eumenes II, who lavished his great wealth on the city. Greek rule continued until 133 BC, when the mad Attalus III died, bequeathing the entire kingdom to Rome.

The most famous building at the acropolis is the **library,** which once contained a collection of 200,000 books, all on papyrus. The library's collection was second only to the one in Alexandria, Egypt. When the troops of Julius Caesar burned down the library in Alexandria, Mark Antony consoled Cleopatra by shipping the entire collection of books from Pergamum to Alexandria. These, too, went up in flames 400 years later, in wars between Muslims and Christians.

Izmir The coastal area between Bergama and Izmir, 104 kilometers (64 miles), was once thick with ancient Greek settlements. Today only Izmir remains. Called Smyrna by the Greeks, it was a vital trading port that was often ravaged by wars and earthquakes. Izmir was completely destroyed by a fire in 1922 following Turkey's War of Independence against Greece. The war was a bloody battle to win back the Aegean coast, which had been given to the Greeks in the 1920 Treaty of Sèvres. Atatürk was in Izmir helping to celebrate the victory when celebrations soon turned to horror as the fire engulfed the city.

The city was quickly rebuilt, and it then became known by its Turkish name, İzmir. It's a lively, modern city filled with wide boulevards and apartment houses and office buildings. The center of the city is **Kültürpark,** a large green park that is the site of İzmir's industrial fair from late August to late September, a time when most hotels are full.

On top of İzmir's highest hill is the **Kadifekale** (Velvet Fortress), built in the 3rd century BC by Lysimachos. It is easily reached by dolmuş and is one of the few ancient ruins that was not destroyed in the fire. At the foot of the hill is the restored **Agora,** the market of ancient Smyrna. The modern-day marketplace is in **Konak Square,** a maze of tiny streets filled with shops and covered stalls. *Open 8–8. Closed Sun.*

Kuşadasi **Kuşadasi,** about 80 kilometers (50 miles) south of İzmir on Route 300, has grown since the late 1970s from a fishing village into a sprawling, hyperactive town geared to serving thousands of tourists who visit the nearby ruins and beaches. Although it's packed with curio shops, Kuşadasi has managed to retain a pleasant atmosphere.

Ephesus The major attraction near Kuşadasi is **Ephesus,** a city created by the Ionians in the 11th century BC and now one of the grandest reconstructed ancient sites in the world. It is the showpiece of Aegean archaeology. Ephesus was a powerful trading port and the sacred center for the cult of Artemis, Greek goddess of chastity, the moon, and hunting. The Ionians built a temple in her honor, one of the Seven Wonders of the Ancient World. During the Roman period, it became a shrine for the Roman goddess Diana. Today waterlogged foundations are all that remain of the temple.

Allow yourself one full day to tour Ephesus. The city is especially appealing out of season, when it can seem like a ghost town with its shimmering, long, white marble road grooved by chariot wheels.

Some of the splendors you can see here include the two-story **Library of Celsus;** houses of noblemen, with their terraces and courtyards; a 25,000-seat **amphitheater,** still used today during the Selçuk Ephesus Festival of Culture and Art; remains of the municipal baths; and a brothel. *Admission: $5.50. Admission to the houses on the slopes: $1.20. Open daily 8:30–6 (summer), 8:30–5 (winter).*

Selçuk On Ayasoluk Hill in **Selçuk,** 4 kilometers (2½ miles) from Ephesus, is the restored **Basilica of St. John** (St. Jean Aniti), containing the tomb of the apostle. Near the entrance to the basilica is the **Ephesus Museum,** with two statues of Artemis. The museum also has marvelous frescoes and mosaics among its treasures. *Admission: $2.50. Basilica and museum open Tues.–Sun. 8:30–6.*

St. Paul and St. John preached in both Ephesus and Selçuk and changed the cult of Artemis into the cult of the Virgin Mary. **Meryemana,** 5 kilometers (3 miles) from Ephesus, has the **House of Mary,** thought to have been the place where St. John took the mother of Jesus after the crucifixion and where some believe she ascended to heaven. *Admission $1.20. Open daily 7:30–sunset.*

Priene and Miletus Priene and Miletus, 40 kilometers (25 miles) from Kuşadasi, are sister cities, also founded by the Ionians in 11 BC. Nearby is

Didyma, a holy sanctuary dedicated to Apollo. **Priene,** on top of a steep hill, was an artistic and cultural center. Its main attraction is the **Temple of Athena,** a spectacular sight, with its five fluted columns and its backdrop of mountains and the fertile plains of the Meander River. You can also see the city's small amphitheater, gymnasium, council chambers, marketplace, and stadium. *Admission: $1.20. Open daily 8:30–6.*

Nearby, **Miletus,** once a prosperous port, was the first Greek city to use coins for money. It also became an Ionian intellectual center and home to such philosophers as Thales, Anaximander, and Anaximenes, all of whom made contributions to mathematics and the natural sciences.

The city's most magnificent building is the **Great Theater,** a remarkably intact 25,000-seat amphitheater built by the Ionians and kept up by the Romans. Climb to the highest seats in the amphitheater for a view across the city to the bay. *Admission: ruins $1.20, museum $1.20. Open Tues.–Sun. 8:30–6.* The temple of **Didyma** is reached by a 32-kilometer (20-mile) road called the **Sacred Way,** starting from Miletus at the bay. The temple's oracles were as revered as those of Delphi. Under the courtyard is a network of corridors whose walls would throw the oracle's voice into deep and ghostly echoes. The messages would then be interpreted by the priests. Fragments of bas-relief include a gigantic head of Medusa and a small statue of Poseidon and his wife, Amphitrite. *Admission: $1.20. Open daily 8:30–6.*

Pamukkale   East of Kuşadasi, 215 kilometers (133 miles) away, is **Pamukkale,** which first appears as an enormous chalky white cliff rising some 102 meters (330 feet) from the plains. Mineral-rich volcanic spring water cascades over basins and natural terraces, crystallizing into white stalactites, curtains of solidified water seemingly suspended in air. The hot springs in the area were popular with the ancient Romans, who believed they had curative powers. You can see the remains of Roman baths among the ruins of nearby **Hierapolis.** The village of Pamukkale has many small hotels surrounding the hot springs, which are used today by people who still believe that they can cure a variety of problems, including rheumatism. Farther down in the village are inexpensive pansiyons, some also with hot springs. It's best to stay in Pamukkale overnight before heading on to the ruins of **Aphrodisias,** a city of 60,000 dedicated to Aphrodite, the Greek goddess of love and fertility. It thrived from 100 BC to AD 500. Aphrodisias is reached via **Karacasu,** a good place to stop for lunch; fresh trout is the local specialty. Aphrodisias is filled with marble baths, temples, and theaters, all overrun with wild blackberries and pomegranates. Across a field sprinkled with poppies and sunflowers is a well-preserved **stadium,** which was built for 30,000 spectators.

Dining and Lodging

For details and price-category definitions, *see* Dining and Lodging in Staying in Turkey.

Ayvalik   **Büyük Berk.** This is a modern hotel on Ayvalik's best beach,
Lodging   about 3½ kilometers (2 miles) from the center of town. *Sarimsakli Mev., tel. 663/41045, fax 663/41194. 180 rooms with bath. Facilities: outdoor pool, restaurant, disco. AE, DC, MC, V. Moderate.*

Ankara Oteli. Located on Sarimsakli beach, just a few feet from the surf, the Ankara Oteli gives excellent value for the money. *Sarimsakli Mev., tel. 663/41195 or 663/41048, fax 663/40022. 57 rooms with bath. Facilities: café, bar, game room. No credit cards. Inexpensive.*

Bergama **Tusan Bergama Moteli.** On the main road leading into Berga-
Lodging ma, the Tusan has a pool fed by hot springs. The rooms are simple and clean. *İzmir Yolu, Çati Mev., tel. 541/31173, fax 663/26284. 42 rooms with bath. No credit cards. Moderate.*

Bursa **Cumurcul.** This old house converted into a restaurant is a local
Dining favorite. Grilled meats and fish are both attentively prepared. *Çekirge Cad. tel. 24/353–707. Reservations advised. V. Moderate.*

Özkent. Located in Kültür Park, the Özkent serves excellent Turkish food in a quiet setting. *Kültür Park, tel. 24/167666. Reservations advised. AE, DC, MC, V. Moderate.*

Lodging **Celik Palace.** The main attraction of this luxurious five-star ho-
★ tel is a domed, Roman-style pool fed by hot springs. *Çekirge Cad. 79, tel. 24/353500, fax 24/361910. 173 rooms with bath. Facilities: restaurant, bar, pool, nightclub, disco. AE, DC, MC, V. Expensive.*

Ada Palas. Located near Kültür Park, this hotel has an inviting thermal pool. *Murat Cad. 21, tel. 24/361600, fax 24/364656. 39 rooms with bath. V. Moderate.*

Çanakkale, Troy, **Akol.** This modern, new hotel is on the waterfront in Çanak-
and Gallipoli kale; ask for a room with a terrace overlooking the Dardenelles.
Lodging *Kordonboyu, tel. 196/79456, fax 196/72897. 138 rooms with bath. Facilities: bar, restaurant, outdoor pool, disco. AE, MC, V. Moderate.*

Büyük Truva. Near the center of Çanakkale, the Truva is an excellent base for sightseeing. *Kordonboyu, tel. 196/71024, fax 196/0903. 66 rooms with bath. No credit cards. Moderate.*

Tusan. Surrounded by a pine forest on a beach at Güzelyali, north of Troy, the Tusan is one of the most popular hotels in the area. Be certain to reserve well in advance. *Güzelyali, tel. 1973/8210 and 1973/8204, fax 1973/8226. 64 rooms with bath. MC, V. Closed Oct.–Feb. Inexpensive.*

Çeşme **Kanuni Kervansaray.** Built in 1528 during the reign of Sül-
Lodging leyman the Magnificent, the Kervansaray is decorated in traditional Turkish style. It has an excellent restaurant, with outdoor dining in an ancient courtyard. Adjacent to the hotel is a medieval castle. *Çarşi Cad., tel. 549/27177 or 26492, fax 26496. 32 rooms with bath. AE, DC, MC, V. Expensive.*

İzmir **Büyük Efes.** Elegant but showing its age, this hotel is distin-
Lodging guished by a beautiful and relaxing enclosed garden. *Cumhuriyet Mey., tel. 51/844300, fax 51/415695. 446 rooms with bath. Facilities: restaurant, 2 outdoor pools, disco, auditorium, casino. AE, DC, MC, V. Very Expensive.*

Kismet. Tastefully decorated, the Kismet is a quiet, comfortable hotel with friendly service. *1377 Sok. 9, tel. 51/633853, fax 51/214856. 68 rooms with bath. Facilities: restaurant, bar, sauna. AE, MC, V. Moderate.*

Kuşadasi **Sultan Han.** Full of atmosphere, with excellent food to boot,
Dining Sultan Han is an old house built around a courtyard, where the
★ focal point is a gigantic tree. You can dine in the courtyard or upstairs in small rooms. One of the specialties is fresh seafood,

which you select from platters piled high with fish and shellfish of every possible variety. Ask to have your after-dinner coffee served upstairs, where you can sit on cushions at low brass tables. *Bahar Sok. 8, tel. 636/43849. Reservations required. No credit cards. Expensive.*

★ **İbrahim Ustanin Yeri.** Hands down, this spot is the best restaurant in Kuşadasi. The barbecued shrimp and chicken are great, and the fish is always the day's catch. It's also one of the few restaurants around with no blaring TV. *Türkmen Mah. 50, Yıl Caddesi 3, tel. 636/48063. Reservations suggested. AE, DC, MC, V. Moderate.*

Lodging **Club Kervansaray.** A refurbished, 300-year-old caravansary, this hotel is decorated in the Ottoman style and loaded with charm and atmosphere. It's in the center of town and features a restaurant with a floor show. There's dancing after dinner in the courtyard, where the camels were once kept. *Atatürk Bul. 1, tel. 636/44115, fax 636/42423. 40 rooms with bath. Facilities: restaurant, café, nightclub, bar. AE, DC, MC, V. Expensive.*

★ **Kismet.** Although it's a small hotel, Kismet is run on a grand scale, surrounded by beautifully maintained gardens on a promontory overlooking the marina on one side and the Aegean on the other. Ask for rooms in the garden annex. Its popularity makes reservations a must. *Akyar Mev., tel. 636/42005, fax 636/44914. 98 rooms with bath. Facilities: private beach, restaurant. AE, MC, V. Closed Nov.–Mar. Expensive.*

Aran. Although it's quite a climb up the steep hill to this hotel, it's worth it for the view from the roof terrace. *Kaya Aldogan Cad. 4, tel. 636/11076. 22 rooms with bath. No credit cards. Inexpensive.*

Pammukale **Tusan.** The best feature of the Tusan is its pool, one of the most
Lodging inviting in the area. The rooms are basic and comfortable. The one-story building is at the top of a steep hill. *Tel. 6218/2010, fax 6218/2059. 47 rooms with bath. Facilities: restaurant, outdoor pool. AE, DC, MC, V. Moderate.*

Selçuk **Hulya.** This is a pleasant, family-run pansiyon, where one of
Lodging the family members is a fisherman who brings in some of his daily catch. You can enjoy a delicious fish meal cooked to order. *Atatürk Cad., Ozgur Sok. 15, tel. 5451/2120. No credit cards. Inexpensive.*

Kale Han. Located in a refurbished stone inn, Kale Han is another pansiyon run by a warm, welcoming family. *Atatürk Cad. 49, tel. 5451/6154, fax 5451/2169. 50 rooms with shower. MC, V. Inexpensive.*

The Mediterranean Coast

Until the mid-1970s, Turkey's southwest coast was inaccessible to all but the most determined travelers—those intrepid souls in four-wheel-drive vehicles or on the backs of donkeys. Today well-maintained highways wind through the area and jets full of tourists arrive at the new Dalaman Airport.

Thanks to strict developmental control, the area has maintained its Turkish flavor, with low, whitewashed buildings and tiled roofs. The beaches are clean, and you can swim and snorkel in turquoise waters so clear that it is possible to see fish 6 meters (20 feet) below. There are excellent outdoor cafés and

seafood restaurants in which to dine, and you won't find a shortage of bars, discos, and nightclubs.

Getting Around

By Car   Although the highways between towns are well maintained, the smaller roads are usually unpaved and very rough.

By Boat   There are lots of coves and picnic areas accessible only by boat. For a small fee, local fishermen will take you to and from the coves; also, you can take one of the many water taxis. Or charter a small yacht, with or without skipper, at the marinas of Bodrum and Marmaris. Many people charter boats and join small flotillas that leave the marinas daily for sightseeing in the summer. One of the most enjoyable ways to see the coast is to take a one- or two-week **Blue Voyage** cruise on a *gulet*, a wooden craft with a full crew. There are also three-night mini Blue Voyage trips for scuba divers and snorkelers. For information, contact the following Blue Voyage agencies: in the United States, **Club Voyages,** Box 7648, Shrewsbury, NJ 07702, tel. 908/291–8228; in the United Kingdom, **Explore,** 1 Frederick Street, Aldershot, Hants GU11 1LQ, tel. 02/523–19448; **Simply Turkey,** 8 Chiswick Terrace, Acton Lane, London W4, tel. 081/747–1011; **Falcon Sailing,** 13 Hillgate Street, London W8, tel. 071/727–0232.

Guided Tours and Tourist Information

Local tourist offices list all the guided tours for the area and will also arrange for local guides.

Bodrum (Iskele Meyd. 12, tel. 614/61091).
Dalaman (Dalaman Airport, tel. 6119/1220).
Datça (Iskele Mah. Hükümet Binasi, tel. 6145/3163 or 3546).
Kaş (Cumhuriyet Meyd. 5, tel. 322/61238).
Marmaris (Iskele Meyd. 39, tel. 612/211035).

Exploring the Mediterranean Coast

Bodrum Bodrum, which sits between two crescent-shaped bays, has for years been the favorite haunt of the Turkish upper classes. Today the elite are joined by thousands of foreign visitors, and the area is rapidly filling with hotels and guest houses, cafés, restaurants, and discos. Many compare it to St. Tropez on the French Riviera. Fortunately, it is still beautiful and unspoiled, with gleaming whitewashed buildings covered with bougainvillea and magnificent unobstructed vistas of the bays. People flock to Bodrum not for its beach, which is a disappointment, but for its fine dining and nightlife. You'll find beautiful beaches in the outlying villages on the peninsula—**Torba, Türkbükü, Yalikavak, Turgutreis, Akyarlar, Ortakent, Bitez,** and **Gümbet.** Easy to reach by minibus or dolmuş, these villages are about an hour's drive away and have clean hotels and plenty of outdoor restaurants. One of the outstanding sights in Bodrum is **Bodrum Castle,** known as the **Castle of St. Peter.** Located between the two bays, the castle was built by crusaders in the 11th century. It has beautiful gardens and a **Museum of Underwater Archaeology.** *Castle and museum admission: $2.50. Open Tues.–Sun. 8:30–noon and 1–5.*

The peninsula is downright littered with ancient Greek and Roman ruins, although getting to some of them involves driving over rough dirt roads. Five kilometers (3 miles) from Bodrum is **Halikarnas,** a well-preserved 10,000-seat Greek amphitheater built in the 1st century BC and still used for town festivals. *Admission free. Open daily 8:30–sunset.*

Marmaris Another beach resort situated in the middle of two bays is **Marmaris,** which has some of the best sailing on the Mediterranean. It is 178 kilometers (111 miles) along Route 400 from Bodrum via Muğla. You'll climb steep, winding mountain passes, with cliffs that drop straight into the sea. The final 30 kilometers (19 miles) into Marmaris is a broad boulevard lined with eucalyptus trees. Marmaris, like Bodrum, is a sophisticated resort with boutiques, elegant restaurants, and plenty of nightlife. Nearby are quiet villages that are easy to reach by boat or taxi. One of these is **Knidos,** where you can see the ruins of Aphrodite's circular temple and an ancient theater. By road, Knidos is a very rough 108 kilometers (67 miles) from Marmaris. It's easier and quicker to take a boat. Another town is **Turunç,** worth a day's visit, especially for its beaches.

Freshwater **Lake Köyceğiz** can be reached by boat through the reed beds of the **Dalyan delta.** This entire area is a wildlife preserve, filled with such birds as kingfishers, kestrels, egrets, and cranes. Köyceğiz and **Dalyan** villages, both 20 minutes' drive from Dalaman Airport, are good stopping-off places for exploring the area. It costs about $20 to rent a boat with a boatsman to sail from Dalyan to the ruins and beach.

Ölü Deniz One of Turkey's greatest natural wonders is **Ölü Deniz,** an azure lagoon flanked by long, white beaches. The area is about 145 kilometers (90 miles) from Bodrum. There are a few wooden chalets in camping grounds and one beachfront hotel. Opposite the beach, you'll find small restaurants with rooftop bars, many with live music that goes on all night.

Southeast of Fethiye, near Route 400, are several ancient sites, including the ruins of **Pinara,** one of the most important cities of the former Roman province of Lycia. Near Pinara, up a steep and strenuous dirt road, you'll find nearly 200 Roman tombs cut honeycomb-fashion into the face of the cliffs. *Admission: $1.20. Open daily 8:30–sunset.*

Xanthos Return to Route 400 and head 18 kilometers (11 miles) south toward the village of Kinik. At Kinik leave the main highway and take a mile-long bumpy road to **Xanthos,** another major city of ancient Lycia. It was excavated in 1838; much of what was found here is now in the British Museum in London. What's left is still well worth the bumpy ride: the acropolis, the Tomb of Harpies, some plastercast reliefs, and ruins of some Byzantine buildings. *Admission: $1.20. Open daily 8:30–sunset.*

Patara and Kalkan Ten minutes from Xanthos is **Patara,** once the city's port. Here you'll find ruins scattered around the marshes and sand dunes. The area's long, wide beaches remain beautiful and unspoiled, despite the fact that they attract hundreds of Turkish families and tourists. The nearest place to stay is **Kalkan,** a fishing village 20 minutes away by minibus.

Kaş **Kaş,** 30 kilometers (18 miles) from Kalkan, is another fishing village that has become a popular resort, and is also developing into a major yachting center. Although luxury hotels have replaced many of the tiny houses on the hills, there are still plenty of old-fashioned pansiyons for those on a budget. One of the attractions here is a day trip by boat to the underwater city of **Kekova,** where you can look overboard and see ancient Roman and Greek columns that were once part of a thriving city before the area was flooded. Kekova is especially popular with scuba divers and snorkelers, but to scuba-dive or fish in this area, a permit must be obtained from the directorate of the harbor and from the directorate of the ministry of tourism. Motorboats leave daily at 9:30 and cost about $15.

For romantic ruins, it would be hard to beat **Phaselis.** The Roman agora, theater, aqueduct, and a necropolis with fine sarcophagi are scattered throughout the pine woods that surround the Temple of Athena. Overgrown streets descend to the translucent water, which is ideal for swimming.

Kemer is the center of intensive touristic development, with hotels and restaurants, a well-equipped marina, and club-style holiday villages that make you forget you're in Turkey. The remaining 35 kilometers (26 miles) are increasingly occupied by villas and motels along the smooth pebbles of Konyalti Beach, which stretches to the outskirts of Antalya.

Antalya The resort of **Antalya,** on the Mediterranean, is a good base for several worthwhile excursions. The city is on a beautifully restored harbor and is filled with narrow streets lined with small houses, restaurants, and pansiyons. On the hilltop are tea gardens where you can enjoy tea made in an old-fashioned samovar and look across the bay to the Taurus Mountains, which parallel the coast. To the right of the port is the 13th-century **Fluted Minaret** (Yivli Minare). The Hisar Café, Tophane tea garden, and Mermerli tea garden all overlook Antalya's harbor.

Dining and Lodging

For details and price-category definitions, *see* Dining and Lodging in Staying in Turkey.

Antalya **Talya.** This is a luxurious resort hotel with its own beach that
Lodging you reach by taking an elevator down the side of the cliff. From
★ every angle there's a view of the sea. It has a five-star rating and gets booked up quickly in high season. *Fevzi Çakmak Cad., tel. 31/486800, fax 31/415400. 204 rooms with bath. Facilities: disco, restaurant, pool, game room, fitness room, Turkish hamam, spa. AE, DC, MC, V. Very Expensive.*
Turban Adalya. Built in 1869 as a bank, the Turban Adalya has been imaginatively transformed into a luxurious hotel overlooking the colorful fishing port. *Kaleiçi Yat Limani, tel. 31/418066, fax 31/423679. 28 rooms with bath. Facilities: restaurant. AE, DC, MC, V. Expensive.*
Altun Pansiyon. The recently renovated pansiyon is located near the Fluted Minaret and minutes from the seaport. It has a well-stocked bar and a pleasant courtyard, and the staff is extremely helpful. *Kaleiçi Mev. 10, tel. 31/416624, fax 31/414010. 10 rooms with shower. No credit cards. Inexpensive.*

Bodrum **Club Pirinç.** This restaurant has a pleasant bar, nine guest
Dining rooms, a swimming pool, and offers Turkish-French cuisine. *Akçabuk Mev., Kumbahçe, tel. 6141/2902. No credit cards. Expensive.*
Restaurant No. 7. Octopus casseroles are a specialty. *Eski Banka Sok. 7. Expensive.*
Balik Restaurant. Specialties include fish, meat, and chicken kebabs. *Yeniçarşi 28, tel. 6141/1454. No credit cards. Moderate.*
Korfez Restaurant. This is a seaside fish restaurant. *Cumhuriyet Cad. 18, tel. 6141/1169. No credit cards. Moderate.*

Lodging **Manzara Aparhotel.** On a hill looking across the bay toward Bodrum Castle, the Manzara is a group of 20 small apartments, each with living room, kitchen, and terrace. At peak times, you may have to pay half-board. *Kumbahçe Mah. Meteoroloji Yani, tel. 614/61719, fax 614/61720. Facilities: restaurant, outdoor pool, bar. AE, V. Expensive.*
Merhaba Pansiyon. Here, on the waterfront, you'll find a beautiful roof terrace and simply furnished but clean rooms. *Akasya Sok. 5, tel. 614/62115. No credit cards. Inexpensive.*

Dalyan **Yali Restaurant.** This is a waterside eatery reached by a short
Dining boatride from Dalyan. It's also a good stopping-off point if you're planning a walk to the Kaunus ruins. *Tel. 6116/1150. No credit cards. Inexpensive.*

Lodging **Hotel Turtle.** This is a quiet 10-room hotel tucked away in a bay of orchards on the lakeside. The hotel boat picks up guests from Dalyan. Vefa Ülkü, the owner, cooks excellent dishes served under a big plane tree. *Küçük Karaağaç, Sultaniye Köyü, Köyceğiz, tel. 6114/1487. No credit cards. Moderate.*
Kaunos Hotel. Overlooking the river, some of the rooms have

views. The hotel has a good outdoor restaurant. *Posta Kodu 48810, Dalyan, tel. 6116/1057. Inexpensive.*

Kalkan **Kalkan Han.** A rambling old house in the back part of the vil-
Lodging lage, the Kalkan Han has a special treat for visitors: a roof terrace with sweeping views of the bay, a perfect place to enjoy
breakfast. *Koyici Mev., tel. 3215/1151. 16 rooms with bath. No
credit cards. Closed Nov.–Apr. Moderate.*
Balikci Han. This delightful pansiyon is in a converted 19th-
century inn, directly on the waterfront. *Tel. 3215/1075. 7 rooms
with bath. No credit cards. Inexpensive.*

Kaş **Mercan.** On the eastern side of the harbor, the Mercan serves
Dining good, basic Turkish food in an attractive open-air setting. The
water is so close you can actually hear fish jumping. *Hukumet
Cad. No credit cards. Moderate.*

Lodging **Kaş Oteli.** This hotel has wonderful views of the Greek island of
Kastellorizo. There's good swimming off the rocks in front of
the hotel, or you can laze in the sun with drinks and snacks from
the bar or restaurant. *Hastana Cad. 15, tel. 3226/1271. Facilities: bar, restaurant. No credit cards. Closed Nov.–Apr. Moderate.*
Mimosa. This hotel is conveniently located on a hill near the bus
station, with plain but perfectly adequate rooms, all with balconies and views. *Elmali Cad., tel. 3226/1272. 22 rooms with
bath. Facilities: swimming pool. No credit cards. Moderate.*
Çan Otel. Turkish carpets and antiques grace this village house
that's been lovingly restored and turned into a pansiyon. It's on
a tiny side street near the harbor. *Off Hukumet Cad., tel. 3226/
1441. No credit cards. Inexpensive.*

Köyceğiz **Hotel Özay.** This lakeside hotel is quiet, modern, and efficiently
Lodging run. *Kordon Boyu 11, Köyceğiz, tel. 6114/1300. 22 rooms with
bath. Facilities: restaurant, bar, swimming pool. AE, DC,
MC, V. Expensive.*
Hotel Deniz Feneri. The owner is an artist whose wood carvings
hang in Golbasi Restaurant. The hotel is located in a picturesque square; the rooms are basic. *Atatürk Square, Köyceğiz,
tel. 6114/1777. No credit cards. Inexpensive.*

Ölü Deniz **Beyaz Yunus.** Wicker chairs and wooden floors fill this domed
Dining restaurant, whose name means "white dolphin." The most ele-
★ gant restaurant in the area, it's situated on a promontory near
Padirali and serves Continental and Turkish cuisines imaginatively prepared and presented. *No telephone. Reservations not
necessary. No credit cards. Expensive.*
Kebapici Salonu. You can grill meat at your table in this outdoor
restaurant, where tables and chairs are clustered around trees
in a field. Meals are served with meze, salad, and wine. *Behind
Han Camp, no telephone. Reservations not necessary. No
credit cards. Inexpensive.*

Lodging **Meri Oteli.** Located on a steep incline above the lagoon, this is a
series of bungalows, with rooms a bit down-at-the-heel but
clean. These are the only accommodations at the lagoon. *Tel.
6151/1482. 75 rooms with bath. Facilities: restaurant. AE, DC,
MC, V. Moderate.*

Central Anatolia and Cappadocia

Cappadocia, an area filled with ruins of ancient civilizations, is in the eastern part of Anatolia. Cappadocia has changed little over the centuries. People travel between their farms and villages in horse-drawn carts, women drape their houses with strings of apricots and paprika for drying in the sun, and nomads pitch their black tents beside sunflower fields and cook on tiny fires that send smoke billowing through the tops of the tents. And in the distance, a minaret pierces the sky.

Getting Around

By Car There are good roads between Istanbul and the main cities of Anatolia—Ankara (the capital of Turkey), Konya, and Kayseri. The highways are generally well maintained and lead to all the major sites. Minor roads are full of potholes and are very rough. On narrow, winding roads, look out for oncoming trucks, whose drivers apparently don't believe in staying on their side of the road.

By Bus There is a good interlinking bus network between most towns and cities, and fares are reasonable.

By Train Though there are frequent trains between the main cities, they are almost nonexistent between small towns. It's much quicker to take a bus.

By Taxi Drivers are usually willing to take you to historical sites out of town for reasonable fares.

Guided Tours

Since the Cappadocia area is so vast, you'll need at least two days to see the main sights. If you are driving, consider hiring a guide for about $15–$30 a day. Local tourist offices and hotels will be able to recommend guides and excursions.

Tourist Information

Check with local tourist offices for names of travel agencies and English-speaking guides.

Ankara (Gazi Mustafa Kemal Bul. 121, Demirtepe, tel. 4/229–2631).
Aksaray (Ankara Cad. Dinçer Apt. 2/2, tel. 481/32474).
Kayseri (Kagni Pazari 61, tel. 35/319295).
Konya (Mevlana Cad. 21, tel. 33/511074).
Nevşehir (Atatürk Cad. Hastane Yani, tel. 485/31137).
Ürgüp (Kayseri Cad. 37, tel. 4868/4059).

Exploring Central Anatolia and Cappadocia

An hour's drive, 30 kilometers (19 miles), to the northwest of Antalya is **Termessos,** which has an almost complete Roman amphitheater built on a mountainside, and the unexcavated remains of a Roman city on the other side of the mountain. There are organized tours to Termessos from Antalya. *Admission free. Open daily 9–5:30.*

Central Anatolia and Cappadocia

NORTHERN PORTION OF CYPRUS
OCCUPIED BY TURKEY

0   50 miles

0   75 km

Perge, 19 kilometers (11 miles) east of Antalya, has many Roman ruins to explore. You can climb up a 22,000-seat amphitheater, walk down a restored colonnaded street, visit well-preserved thermal baths and a Roman basilica, and see the spot where St. Paul preached his first sermon in AD 45. *Admission: $2.50. Open daily 9–5:30.*

Nearby is **Aspendos,** 44 kilometers (23 miles) to the east of Antalya, which contains Turkey's best-preserved amphitheater. The acoustics are so fine that modern-day performers don't need microphones or amplifiers. *Admission: $2.50. Open daily 9–5:30.*

Konya, home of the Whirling Dervishes, is reached by driving 427 kilometers (267 miles) northeast of Antalya past **Lake Beyşehir.** There is also a longer and more difficult road via **Lake Eğridir.** The Whirling Dervishes belong to a religious order founded in the 13th century by Melvana, a Muslim mystic, who said, "There are many ways of knowing God. I choose the dance and music." You can see the dervishes whirl to the sounds of a flute at the annual commemorative rites held in Konya in early December. Tickets are available from travel agencies or from the Konya tourist information office (*see above*).

Sultan Han, 95 kilometers (59 miles) northeast of Konya, is Anatolia's largest and best-preserved caravansary, once a place of rest and shelter for travelers and their camels plying the ancient trade routes.

Cappadocia roughly forms the triangular area between **Kayseri, Nevşehir**, and **Niğde**. Most of the main sights are within an even smaller triangular area linked by Ürgüp, Göreme, and Avanos. **Ürgürp** is the center from which to explore the villages and the best place to shop, as well as to arrange tours.

The softness of the rock in this area was ideal for hollowing out cave dwellings and forming defenses from invading armies. The Cappadocians carved out about 40 underground cities, with some structures as deep as 20 stories underground. The largest of these cities housed 20,000 people. Each had dormitories, dining halls, sewage disposal systems, ventilation chimneys, a cemetery, and a prison. Large millstones sealed off the entrances from enemies. Two of these cities are open to the public, one at **Derinkuyu**, 21 kilometers (13 miles) south of Nevşehir, and the other at **Kaymakli**, 30 kilometers (9 miles) south of Nevşehir. *Admission: $2.50. Open daily 8–sunset.*

The Christians also hid in these underground cities when the Islamic forces swept through Cappadocia in the 7th century. Some of the earliest relics of Christianity are to be found in the **Göreme Valley**, a few miles east of Nevşehir. There are dozens of old churches and monasteries covered by frescoes. For a history of the area, visit the **Göreme Open-Air Museum**, 1 kilometer (.62 miles) outside of Göreme village on the Ürgüp road. *Admission free. Open daily 8:30–5:30.*

Dining and Lodging

For details and price-category definitions, *see* Dining and Lodging in Staying in Turkey.

Avanos **Zelve.** This is a small modern hotel in the center of town.
Lodging *Hükümet Meydani, tel. 4861/4524, fax 4861/4687. 29 rooms with bath. AE, DC, MC, V. Moderate.*

Göreme **Ataman.** Run by tourist guide Abbas and his wife Şermin, this
Dining restaurant is built into the face of a rock. *Tel. 4857/2310. Reservations not necessary. DC, MC, V. Inexpensive.*

Konya **Ali Baba Kebapçisi.** This restaurant serves good kebabs and is
Dining famous for its Firin kebab, cooked over an open charcoal fire. *Eski Avukatlar Sokak 11/A, tel. 33/510307. Reservations not necessary. No credit cards. Inexpensive.*
Bolu Restaurant. You can eat dishes here for which Konya is reknowned: *etli ekmek* (flat bread with ground lamb) and *tereyağli borek* (buttered pastries). *Pürküklü Mah. 31/c, tel. 33/524533. Reservations not necessary. Inexpensive.*

Lodging **Başak Palas.** An older but charming small hotel, Başak Palas is also comfortable. *Hukumet Alani 3, tel. 33/111338. 40 rooms, most with bath. No credit cards. Inexpensive.*

Ürgüp **Hanedan.** In the cellar of an old Greek house, the Hanedan is on
Dining a hill a short distance from town. You can sit on the terrace and watch the sunset across the plains toward the mountains. The food is very good and is presented with flair. *Nevşehir Yolu Üzeri, tel. 4868/4266. Reservations required for groups. DC, MC, V. Moderate.*

Lodging **Büyük.** In the center of town, this is a friendly hotel that features folk dancing in the evenings—you're encouraged to join in but can just sit back and watch if you prefer. *Kayseri Cad., tel. 4868/1060. 49 rooms with bath. No credit cards. Moderate.*

Hitit. The family-run Hitit is a comfortable, small hotel with a restaurant serving basic but enjoyable food. *Dumlupinar Cad. 54, tel. 4868/1481. 15 rooms without bath. No credit cards. Inexpensive.*

Index

Personal Itinerary

Departure   *Date*

           Time

Transportation

Arrival   *Date*   *Time*

Departure   *Date*   *Time*

Transportation

Accommodations

Arrival   *Date*   *Time*

Departure   *Date*   *Time*

Transportation

Accommodations

Arrival   *Date*   *Time*

Departure   *Date*   *Time*

Transportation

Accommodations

Escape to ancient cities and exotic

islands  *with CNN Travel Guide, a*

wealth of valuable advice. Host Valerie Voss will take you

to all of your favorite destinations,

including those off the beaten path.

Tune into your passport to the world.

CNN TRAVEL GUIDE
SATURDAY 10:00 PMᴘᴛ   SUNDAY 8:30 AMᴇᴛ

Fodor's Travel Guides

Available at bookstores everywhere, or call 1–800–533–6478, 24 hours a day.

U.S. Guides

Alaska

Arizona

Boston

California

Cape Cod, Martha's Vineyard, Nantucket

The Carolinas & the Georgia Coast

Chicago

Colorado

Florida

Hawaii

Las Vegas, Reno, Tahoe

Los Angeles

Maine, Vermont, New Hampshire

Maui

Miami & the Keys

New England

New Orleans

New York City

Pacific North Coast

Philadelphia & the Pennsylvania Dutch Country

The Rockies

San Diego

San Francisco

Santa Fe, Taos, Albuquerque

Seattle & Vancouver

The South

The U.S. & British Virgin Islands

The Upper Great Lakes Region

USA

Vacations in New York State

Vacations on the Jersey Shore

Virginia & Maryland

Waikiki

Walt Disney World and the Orlando Area

Washington, D.C.

Foreign Guides

Acapulco, Ixtapa, Zihuatanejo

Australia & New Zealand

Austria

The Bahamas

Baja & Mexico's Pacific Coast Resorts

Barbados

Berlin

Bermuda

Brazil

Brittany & Normandy

Budapest

Canada

Cancun, Cozumel, Yucatan Peninsula

Caribbean

China

Costa Rica, Belize, Guatemala

The Czech Republic & Slovakia

Eastern Europe

Egypt

Euro Disney

Europe

Europe's Great Cities

Florence & Tuscany

France

Germany

Great Britain

Greece

The Himalayan Countries

Hong Kong

India

Ireland

Israel

Italy

Japan

Kenya & Tanzania

Korea

London

Madrid & Barcelona

Mexico

Montreal & Quebec City

Morocco

Moscow & St. Petersburg

The Netherlands, Belgium & Luxembourg

New Zealand

Norway

Nova Scotia, Prince Edward Island & New Brunswick

Paris

Portugal

Provence & the Riviera

Rome

Russia & the Baltic Countries

Scandinavia

Scotland

Singapore

South America

Southeast Asia

Spain

Sweden

Switzerland

Thailand

Tokyo

Toronto

Turkey

Vienna & the Danube Valley

Yugoslavia

Special Series

Fodor's Affordables

Caribbean

Europe

Florida

France

Germany

Great Britain

London

Italy

Paris

Fodor's Bed & Breakfast and Country Inns Guides

Canada's Great Country Inns

California

Cottages, B&Bs and Country Inns of England and Wales

Mid-Atlantic Region

New England

The Pacific Northwest

The South

The Southwest

The Upper Great Lakes Region

The West Coast

The Berkeley Guides

California

Central America

Eastern Europe

France

Germany

Great Britain & Ireland

Mexico

Pacific Northwest & Alaska

San Francisco

Fodor's Exploring Guides

Australia

Britain

California

The Caribbean

Florida

France

Germany

Ireland

Italy

London

New York City

Paris

Rome

Singapore & Malaysia

Spain

Thailand

Fodor's Flashmaps

New York

Washington, D.C.

Fodor's Pocket Guides

Bahamas

Barbados

Jamaica

London

New York City

Paris

Puerto Rico

San Francisco

Washington, D.C.

Fodor's Sports

Cycling

Hiking

Running

Sailing

The Insider's Guide to the Best Canadian Skiing

Skiing in the USA & Canada

Fodor's Three-In-Ones (guidebook, language cassette, and phrase book)

France

Germany

Italy

Mexico

Spain

Fodor's Special-Interest Guides

Accessible USA

Cruises and Ports of Call

Euro Disney

Halliday's New England Food Explorer

Healthy Escapes

London Companion

Shadow Traffic's New York Shortcuts and Traffic Tips

Sunday in New York

Walt Disney World and the Orlando Area

Walt Disney World for Adults

Fodor's Touring Guides

Touring Europe

Touring USA: Eastern Edition

Fodor's Vacation Planners

Great American Vacations

National Parks of the East

National Parks of the West

The Wall Street Journal Guides to Business Travel

Europe

International Cities

Pacific Rim

USA & Canada

WHEREVER
YOU TRAVEL,
*H*ELP IS NEVER
FAR AWAY.

From planning your trip to providing travel assistance along the way, American Express® Travel Service Offices* are always there to help.

Amsterdam	*Geneva*	*Munich*
Athens	*Helsinki*	*Oslo*
Barcelona	*Istanbul*	*Paris*
Berlin	*Lisbon*	*Prague*
Brussels	*Ljubljana*	*Rome*
Budapest	*London*	*Stockholm*
Copenhagen	*Madrid*	*Venice*
Dublin	*Marbella*	*Vienna*
Dubrovnik	*Milan*	*Warsaw*
Edinburgh	*Monte Carlo*	*Zagreb*
Florence	*Moscow*	*Zurich*

American Express Travel Service Offices are found in central locations throughout Europe.

INTRODUCING

At last, your own personalized list of what's going on in the cities you're visiting.

Keyed to the days when you're there, customized for your interests, and sent to you before you leave home.

Exclusive for purchasers of Fodor's Guides...

Introducing a revolutionary way to get customized, time-sensitive travel information just before your trip.

Now you can obtain detailed information about what's going on in each city you'll be visiting <u>before</u> you leave home—up-to-the-minute, objective information about the events and activities that interest you most.

Your Itinerary:
Customized reports available for 160 destinations

This is a special offer for purchasers of Fodor's guides – a customized Travel Update to fit your specific interests and your itinerary.

Travel Updates contain the kind of time-sensitive insider information you can get only from local contacts – or from city magazines and newspapers once you arrive. But now you can have the same information before you leave for your trip.

The choice is yours: current art exhibits, theater, music festivals and special concerts, sporting events, antiques and flower shows, shopping, fitness, and more.

The information comes from hundreds of correspondents and thousands of sources worldwide. Updated continuously, it's like having your own personal concierge or friend in the city.

You specify the cities and when you'll be there. We'll do the rest — personalizing the information for you the way no guidebook can.

It's the perfect extension to your Fodor's guide and the best way to make the most of your valuable travel time.

Reg
The
in this
domain
tion as J
worthwhile
the performa
Tickets are us
venue. Altern
mances are cance
given. For more in
Open-Air Theatre, In
NW1 4NP Open Air
Tel: 935-5756. Ends: 9-1.
International Air Tattoo
Held biennially, the world
military air display :
demostra-
tions, mili-
band-

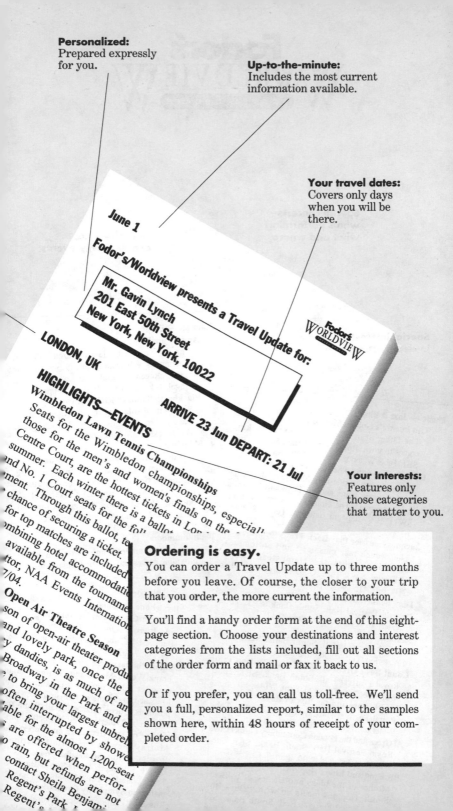

Personalized:
Prepared expressly
for you.

Up-to-the-minute:
Includes the most current
information available.

Your travel dates:
Covers only days
when you will be
there.

June 1

Fodor's/Worldview presents a Travel Update for:

Mr. Gavin Lynch
201 East 50th Street
New York, New York, 10022

Fodor's
WORLDVIEW

LONDON, UK

ARRIVE 23 Jun DEPART: 21 Jul

Your Interests:
Features only
those categories
that matter to you.

HIGHLIGHTS—EVENTS

Wimbledon Lawn Tennis Championships

Seats for the Wimbledon championships, especiall...
those for the men's and women's finals on the ...
Centre Court, are the hottest tickets in Lon...
summer. Each winter there is a ballot...
and No. 1 Court seats for the fol...
ment. Through this ballot, te...
chance of securing a ticket. ...
for top matches are included ...
mbining hotel accommodati...
available from the tournam...
tor, NAA Events Internation...
7/04.

Open Air Theatre Season

son of open-air theater produ...
and lovely park, once the e...
y dandies, is as much of an...
Broadway in the Park and e...
to bring your largest unbrel...
often interrupted by showe...
able for the almost 1,200-seat...
are offered when perfor-...
o rain, but refunds are not...
contact Sheila Benjami...
Regent's Park ...
Regent'...

Special concerts—
who's performing
what and where

One-of-a-kind,
one-time-only events

Special interest,
in-depth listings

Children — Events
Angel Canal Festival
The festivities include a children's funfair, entertainers, a boat rally and displays on the water. Regent's Canal. Islington. N1. Tube: Angel. Tel: 267 9100. 11:30am-5:30pm. 7/04.

Blackheath Summer Kite Festival
Stunt kite displays with parachuting teddy bears and trade stands. Free admission. SE3. BR: Blackheath. 10am. 6/27.

Megabugs
Children will delight in this infestation of giant robotic insects, including a praying mantic 60 times life size. Mon-Sat 10am-6pm; Sun 11am-6pm. Admission 4.50 pounds. Natural History Museum, Cromwell Road. SW7. Tube: South Kensington. Tel: 938 9123. Ends 10/01.

Childminders
This establishment employs only women, providing nurses and qualified nannies to

Music — Jazz & Blues
Tito Puente's Golden Men of Latin Jazz
The father of mambo and Cuban rumba king comes to town. Royal Festival Hall. South Bank. SE1. Tube: Waterloo. Tel: 928 8800. 8pm. 7/15.

Georgie Fame and The New York Band
Riding a popular tide with his latest album, the smoky-voiced Fame and his keyboard are on a tour yet again. The Grand. Clapham Junction. SW11. BR: Clapham Junction. Tel: 738 9000. 7:30pm. 7/07.

Jacques Loussier Play Bach Trio
The French jazz classicist and colleagues. Kenwood Lakeside. Hampstead Lane. Kenwood. NW3. Tube: Golders Green, then bus 210. Tel: 413 1443. 7pm. 7/10.

Tony Bennett and Ronnie Scott
Royal Festival Hall. South Bank. SE1. Tube: Waterloo. Tel: 928 8800. 8pm. 7/11.

Santana
Royal Festival Hall. South Bank. SE1. Tube: Waterloo. Tel: 928 8800. 8pm. 7/12.

Count Basie Orchestra and Nancy Wilson Trio
Royal Festival Hall. South Bank. SE1. Tube: Waterloo. Tel: 928 8800. 8pm. 7/14.

King Pleasure and the Biscuit Boys
Royal Festival Hall. South Bank. SE1. Tube: Waterloo. Tel: 928 8800. 6:30 and 9pm. 7/16.

Al Green and the London Community Gospel Choir
Royal Festival Hall. South Bank. SE1. Tube: Waterloo. Tel: 928 8800. 8pm. 7/13.

BB King and Linda Hopkins
Mother of the blues and successor to Bessi Smith, Hopkins meets up with "Blues Boy Royal Festival Hall. South Bank. SE

Music — Classical
Marylebone Sinfonia
Kenneth Gowen conducts music by Pucci and Rossini. Queen Elizabeth Hall. Sou Bank. SE1. Tube: Waterloo. Tel: 928 880 7:45pm. 7/16.

London Philharmonic
Franz Welser-Moest and George Benjam conduct selections by Alexander Goe Messiaen, and some of Benjamin's own co positions. Queen Elizabeth Hall. South Ba SE1. Tube: Waterloo. Tel: 928 8800. 8pm.

London Pro Arte Orchestra and Forest Cho
Murray Stewart conducts selections Rossini, Haydn and Jonathan Willcocks. Queen Elizabeth Hall. South Bank. S Tube: Waterloo. Tel: 928 8800. 7:45pm. 7/

Kensington Symphony Orchestra
Russell Keable conducts Dvorak's Dr

Here's what you get . . .

Detailed information about what's going on — precisely when you'll be there.

Show openings
during your visit

Reviews by
local critics

Exhibitions & Shows—Antique & Flower
Westminster Antiques Fair
Over 50 stands with pre-1830 furniture and other Victorian and earlier items. Thu-Fri 11am-8pm; Sat-Sun 11am-6pm. Admission 4 pounds, children free. Old Royal Horticultural Hall. Vincent Square. SW1. Tel: 0444/48 25 14. 6-24 thru 6/27.

Royal Horticultural Society Flower Show
The show includes displays of carnations, summer fruit and vegetables. Tue 11am-7pm; Wed 10am-5pm. Admission Tue 4 pounds, Wed 2 pounds. Royal Horticultural Halls. Greycoat Street and Vincent Square. SW1. Tube: Victoria. 7/20 thru 7/21.

mpton Court Palace International Flower Show
Major international garden and flower show king place in conjunction with the British

eater — Musical
Sunset Boulevard
In June, the four Andrew Lloyd Webber musicals which dominated London's stages in the 1980s (Cats, Starlight Express, Phantom of the Opera and Aspects of Love) are joined by the composer's latest work, a show rumored to have his best music to date. The 1950 Billy Wilder film about a helpless young writer who is drawn into the world of a possessive, aging silent screen star offers rich opportunities for Webber's evolving style. Soaring, aching melodies, lush technical effects and psychological thrills are all expected. Patti Lupone stars. Mon-Sat at 8pm; matinee Thu-Sat at 3pm. In-person sales only at the box office; credit card bookings, Tel: 344 0055. Admission 15-32.50 pounds. Adelphi Theatre. The Strand. WC2. Tube: Charing Cross. Tel: 836 7611. Starts: 6/21

Leonardo A Portrait of Love
A new musical about the great Renaissance arti and inventor comes in for a London premier tested by a brief run at Oxford's Old Fire Stati ntumn. The work explores the relations Vinci and the woman '

Spectator Sports — Other Sports
Greyhound Racing: Wembley Stadium
This dog track offers good views of greyhound racing held on Mon, Wed and Fri. No credit cards. Stadium Way. Wembley. HA9. Tube: Wembley Park. Tel: 902 8833.

Benson & Hedges Cricket Cup Final
Lord's Cricket Ground. St. John's Wood Road. NW8. Tube: St. John's Wood. Tel: 289 1611. 11am. 7/10.

siness-Fax & Overnight Mail
Post Office, Trafalgar Square Branch
Offers a network of fax services, the Intelpost system, throughout the country and abroad. Mon-Sat 8am-8pm, Sun 9am-5pm. William IV Street. WC2. Tube: Charing Cross. Tel: 02

Alberquerque • Atlanta • Atlantic City • N
Baltimore • Boston • Chicago • Cincinnati
Cleveland • Dallas/Ft.Worth • Denver • De
• Houston • Kansas City • Las Vegas • Los
Angeles • Memphis • Miami • Milwaukee •
New Orleans • New York City • Milwaukee •
Springs • Philadelphia • Phoenix • Orlando •
Portland • Salt Lake • San Antonio • Pittsburg
San Franc • San Di
Oslo • Wash St Louis • Tamp
Hawaii • Kauai • Maui • Abacos • Bimini
Express • lu • Island
Ber Countryside • Hamilton Islar
Antigua & B vis • Torto

Fodor's
WORLDVIEW
TRAVEL UPDATE

a Gorda • Barbados • Dominica • Grer
cia • St. Vincent • Trinidad &Tobago •
ymans • Puerto Plata • Santo Doming
Aruba • Bonaire • Curacao • St. Ma
ec City • Montreal • Ottawa • Toror
Vancouver • Guadeloupe • Martiniqu
helemy • St. Martin • Kingston • Ixta
o Bay • Negril • Ocho Rios • Ponce
n • Grand Turk • Providenciales • S
St. John • St. Thomas • Acapulco •
& Isla Mujeres • Cozumel • Guadal
a • Los Cabos • Manzinillo • Mazatl
City • Monterrey • Oaxaca • Puerto
do • Puerto Vallarta • Veracruz • Ix
dam • Athens • Barcel

Interest Categories

For your personalized Travel Update, choose the categories you're most interested in from this list. Every Travel Update automatically provides you with *Event Highlights* – the best of what's happening during the dates of your trip.

1.	**Business Services**	Fax & Overnight Mail, Computer Rentals, Photocopying, Secretarial , Messenger, Translation Services

Dining

2.	**All Day Dining**	Breakfast & Brunch, Cafes & Tea Rooms, Late-Night Dining
3.	**Local Cuisine**	In Every Price Range—from Budget Restaurants to the Special Splurge
4.	**European Cuisine**	Continental, French, Italian
5.	**Asian Cuisine**	Chinese, Far Eastern, Japanese, Indian
6.	**Americas Cuisine**	American, Mexican & Latin
7.	**Nightlife**	Bars, Dance Clubs, Comedy Clubs, Pubs & Beer Halls
8.	**Entertainment**	Theater—Drama, Musicals, Dance, Ticket Agencies
9.	**Music**	Classical, Traditional & Ethnic, Jazz & Blues, Pop, Rock
10.	**Children's Activities**	Events, Attractions
11.	**Tours**	Local Tours, Day Trips, Overnight Excursions, Cruises
12.	**Exhibitions, Festivals & Shows**	Antiques & Flower, History & Cultural, Art Exhibitions, Fairs & Craft Shows, Music & Art Festivals
13.	**Shopping**	Districts & Malls, Markets, Regional Specialities
14.	**Fitness**	Bicycling, Health Clubs, Hiking, Jogging
15.	**Recreational Sports**	Boating/Sailing, Fishing, Ice Skating, Skiing, Snorkeling/Scuba, Swimming
16.	**Spectator Sports**	Auto Racing, Baseball, Basketball, Football, Horse Racing, Ice Hockey, Soccer

Please note that interest category content will vary by season, destination, and length of stay.

Destinations

The Fodor's/Worldview Travel Update covers more than 160 destinations worldwide. Choose the destinations that match your itinerary from this list. (Choose bulleted destinations only.)

United States (Mainland)
- Albuquerque
- Atlanta
- Atlantic City
- Baltimore
- Boston
- Chicago
- Cincinnati
- Cleveland
- Dallas/Ft. Worth
- Denver
- Detroit
- Houston
- Kansas City
- Las Vegas
- Los Angeles
- Memphis
- Miami
- Milwaukee
- Minneapolis/ St. Paul
- New Orleans
- New York City
- Orlando
- Palm Springs
- Philadelphia
- Phoenix
- Pittsburgh
- Portland
- St. Louis
- Salt Lake City
- San Antonio
- San Diego
- San Francisco
- Seattle
- Tampa
- Washington, DC

Alaska
- Anchorage/Fairbanks/Juneau

Hawaii
- Honolulu
- Island of Hawaii
- Kauai
- Maui

Canada
- Quebec City
- Montreal
- Ottawa
- Toronto
- Vancouver

Bahamas
- Abacos
- Eleuthera/ Harbour Island
- Exumas
- Freeport
- Nassau & Paradise Island

Bermuda
- Bermuda Countryside
- Hamilton

British Leeward Islands
- Anguilla
- Antigua & Barbuda
- Montserrat
- St. Kitts & Nevis

British Virgin Islands
- Tortola & Virgin Gorda

British Windward Islands
- Barbados
- Dominica
- Grenada
- St. Lucia
- St. Vincent
- Trinidad & Tobago

Cayman Islands
- The Caymans

Dominican Republic
- Puerto Plata
- Santo Domingo

Dutch Leeward Islands
- Aruba
- Bonaire
- Curacao

Dutch Windward Islands
- St. Maarten

French West Indies
- Guadeloupe
- Martinique
- St. Barthelemy
- St. Martin

Jamaica
- Kingston
- Montego Bay
- Negril
- Ocho Rios

Puerto Rico
- Ponce
- San Juan

Turks & Caicos
- Grand Turk
- Providenciales

U.S. Virgin Islands
- St. Croix
- St. John
- St. Thomas

Mexico
- Acapulco
- Cancun & Isla Mujeres
- Cozumel
- Guadalajara
- Ixtapa & Zihuatanejo
- Los Cabos
- Manzanillo
- Mazatlan
- Mexico City
- Monterrey
- Oaxaca
- Puerto Escondido
- Puerto Vallarta
- Veracruz

Europe
- Amsterdam
- Athens
- Barcelona
- Berlin
- Brussels
- Budapest
- Copenhagen
- Dublin
- Edinburgh
- Florence
- Frankfurt
- French Riviera
- Geneva
- Glasgow
- Interlaken
- Istanbul
- Lausanne
- Lisbon
- London
- Madrid
- Milan
- Moscow
- Munich
- Oslo
- Paris
- Prague
- Provence
- Rome
- Salzburg
- St. Petersburg
- Stockholm
- Venice
- Vienna
- Zurich

Pacific Rim Australia & New Zealand
- Auckland
- Melbourne
- Sydney

China
- Beijing
- Guangzhou
- Shanghai

Japan
- Kyoto
- Nagoya
- Osaka
- Tokyo
- Yokohama

Other
- Bangkok
- Hong Kong & Macau
- Manila
- Seoul
- Singapore
- Taipei

Fodor's
WORLDVIEW Order Form

THIS TRAVEL UPDATE IS FOR (Please print):

Name

Address

City	State	ZIP
Country	Tel # ( ) -	

Title of this Fodor's guide:

Store and location where guide was purchased:

INDICATE YOUR DESTINATIONS/DATES: Write in below the destinations you want to order. Then fill in your arrival and departure dates for each destination.

		Month Day		Month Day
(Sample) LONDON	From:	6 / 21	To:	6 / 30
1	From:	/	To:	/
2	From:	/	To:	/
3	From:	/	To:	/

You can order up to three destinations per Travel Update. Only destinations listed on the previous page are applicable. Maximum amount of time covered by a Travel Update cannot exceed 30 days.

CHOOSE YOUR INTERESTS: Select up to eight categories from the list of interest categories shown on the previous page and circle the numbers below:

1 2 3 4 5 6 7 8 9 10 11 12 13 14 15 16

CHOOSE HOW YOU WANT YOUR TRAVEL UPDATE DELIVERED (Check one):

❑ Please mail my Travel Update to the address above **OR**

❑ Fax it to me at **Fax #** ( ) -

DELIVERY CHARGE (Check one)

	Within U.S. & Canada	Outside U.S. & Canada
First Class Mail	❑ $2.50	❑ $5.00
Fax	❑ $5.00	❑ $10.00
Priority Delivery	❑ $15.00	❑ $27.00

All orders will be sent within 48 hours of receipt of a completed order form.

ADD UP YOUR ORDER HERE. *SPECIAL OFFER FOR FODOR'S PURCHASERS ONLY!*

	Suggested Retail Price	Your Price	This Order
First destination ordered	$13.95	$ 7.95	$ 7.95
Second destination (if applicable)	$ 9.95	$ 4.95	+
Third destination (if applicable)	$ 9.95	$ 4.95	+
Plus delivery charge from above			+
		TOTAL:	$

METHOD OF PAYMENT (Check one): ❑ AmEx ❑ MC ❑ Visa ❑ Discover
❑ Personal Check ❑ Money Order

Make check or money order payable to: Fodor's Worldview Travel Update

Credit Card #   **Expiration Date:**

Authorized Signature

SEND THIS COMPLETED FORM TO:
Fodor's Worldview Travel Update, 114 Sansome Street, Suite 700, San Francisco, CA 94104

OR CALL OR FAX US 24-HOURS A DAY
Telephone **1-800-799-9609** • Fax **1-800-799-9619** (From within the U.S. & Canada)
(Outside the U.S. & Canada: Telephone 415-616-9988 • Fax 415-616-9989)

(Please have this guide in front of you when you call so we can verify purchase.)

Offer valid until 12/31/94.